Our online Companion Website presents a complete and tested application in C++ that uses OpenGL to draw the 'Sierpinski Gasket,' similar to that seen on the inside front cover and described in Chapter 2.

In this version of the Sierpinski Gasket, the user clicks the mouse at three points on the screen to make the image appear in full color. Upon the first click the screen is erased but the point clicked is seen as a tiny dot. The user then clicks twice more and another Sierpinski Gasket is drawn. The colors depend upon the positions of the points clicked.

Computer Graphics
Using OpenGL
Third Edition

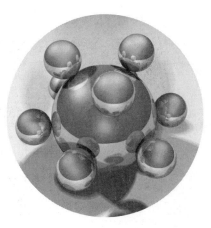

F. S. Hill, Jr. and Stephen M. Kelley, Jr.

Department of Electrical and Computer Engineering
University of Massachusetts

PEARSON

Prentice
Hall

Upper Saddle River, NJ 07458

Library of Congress Cataloging-in-Publication Data

Hill, Francis S.

  Computer graphics : using OpenGL / F. S. Hill, Jr. and Stephen M. Kelley.

  --3rd ed.

    p. cm.

  ISBN 0-13-149670-0

  1. Computer graphics.   2. OpenGL   I. Kelley, Stephen M.   II. Title.

  T385.H549   2006

  006.6--dc22   2006037202

Vice President and Editorial Director, ECS: *Marcia J. Horton*
Executive Editor: *Tracy Dunkelberger*
Associate Editor: *Carole Snyder*
Editorial Assistant: *Christianna Lee*
Executive Managing Editor: *Vince O'Brien*
Managing Editor: *Camille Trentacoste*
Production Editor: *Patty Donovan*
Director of Creative Services: *Paul Belfanti*
Creative Director: *Juan Lopez*
Art Director: *Heather Scott*
Cover Designer: *Tamara Newnam*
Cover Art: *Sven Maerivoet*
Managing Editor, AV Management and Production: *Patricia Burns*
Art Editor: *Xiaohong Zhu*
Manufacturing Manager, ESM: *Alexis Heydt-Long*
Manufacturing Buyer: *Lisa McDowell*
Executive Marketing Manager: *Robin O'Brien*
Marketing Assistant: *Mack Patterson*

© 2007, 2001, 1990 Pearson Education, Inc.
Pearson Prentice Hall
Pearson Education, Inc.
Upper Saddle River, NJ 07458

Printed in the United States of America

10 9 8 7 6 5 4 3 2 1

ISBN: 0-13-149670-0

Pearson Education Ltd., *London*
Pearson Education Australia Pty. Ltd., *Sydney*
Pearson Education Singapore, Pte. Ltd.
Pearson Education North Asia Ltd., *Hong Kong*
Pearson Education Canada, Inc., *Toronto*
Pearson Educación de Mexico, S.A. de C.V.
Pearson Education—Japan, *Tokyo*
Pearson Education Malaysia, Pte. Ltd.
Pearson Education, Inc., Upper Saddle River, New Jersey

Preface

This book provides an introduction to computer graphics for students who wish to learn the basic principles and techniques of the field and who also want to write substantial graphics applications themselves. The field of computer graphics continues to enjoy tremendous vitality and growth. Feature-length animated movies have generated heady excitement about what graphics can do, and ready access to graphics through computer games and the internet is stimulating people to learn how to do it themselves.

Graphics systems are getting better, faster, and cheaper at a bewildering rate, and many new techniques are emerging each year from researchers and practitioners around the world. The underlying principles and approaches, however, comprise a stable and coherent body of knowledge, much of which can be acquired through a single course in graphics. This book organizes the ideas and methods to bring readers who begin with modest programming skills to the point where they can design and produce significant graphics programs.

INTENDED AUDIENCE

This book is designed as a text for either a one- or two-semester course at the senior undergraduate or first-year graduate level. It can also be used for self-study. It is intended principally for students majoring in computer science or engineering but will also suit students in other fields, such as physics and mathematics.

Mathematical Background Required

The reader should have the equivalent of one year of college mathematics; knowledge of elementary algebra, geometry, trigonometry, and elementary calculus is assumed. Some exposure to vectors and matrices is useful but not essential; vector and matrix techniques are introduced in the context of graphics as they are needed, and an appendix summarizes the key ideas.

Computer graphics tends to use a lot of mathematics to express the underlying geometric relationships between lines, surfaces, and the viewing "eye". Although no single mathematical notion is difficult in itself, the number of tools required can be daunting. The book places particular emphasis on the reasons for using this or that technique, and on how the objects of interest in a graphics program are properly described by the mathematical objects we use.

Computer Programming Background Required

In general, the reader should have at least one semester of experience writing computer programs in C, C++, or Java™. A lot of the programming in graphics involves the direct translation of geometric relationships into code, and so uses straightforward variables, functions, arrays, looping, and testing, which are similar from language to language. C++ is used throughout the book, but much of the material will be familiar to someone with a background only in C.

It is helpful for the reader to have experience as well in manipulating structs in C or classes in C++. These are used to capture the rather complicated structure of some graphical objects that reside in a scene, where the object (say, a castle or an airplane) consists of many parts, and these parts themselves consist of complex subparts. Some experience with elementary linked data structures such as linked lists or trees is also desirable but not essential.

A reader with knowledge of C but not C++ will need to pick up the basics of object-oriented programming. We define a number of useful classes (such as the Mesh, Scene, Camera, and Texture classes) and show why they are so convenient and usable. Some of the hallmarks of object-oriented programming, such as inheritance and polymorphism, are used in a few contexts to make the programmer's job easier, but we don't place inordinate emphasis on a pure object-oriented approach.

Philosophy

The book has been completely reorganized and rewritten from the first two editions, but the basic philosophy remains: Computer graphics is learned by doing it. One must write and test real programs to comprehend fully what is going on. A principal goal of the book is to show readers how to translate a particular design "task" into its underlying geometric components, to find a suitable mathematical representation for the objects involved, and finally to translate this representation into suitable algorithms and program code. Readers first learn how to develop simple routines to produce pictures. Then methods for producing drawings of ever more complex objects are presented in a step-by-step fashion.

Exercises and Problems

More than 350 practice exercises appear throughout the book. Most of these are of the "stop-and-think" variety that require no programming and allow readers to self-test their grasp of the material. Some urge the student to implement some of the new ideas in program code.

In addition, over 50 **Case Studies** appear at the end of chapters. Normally they are programming projects suitable for homework assignments, and they range from the simple to the challenging. These Case Studies expand on the material within their chapter and often extend ideas in new directions. Whether or not they are actually carried out by students, the Case Studies should be studied as an integral part of the chapter.

A suggested "Level of Effort" is associated with each Case Study to indicate the approximate amount of time a student may need to invest to accomplish the task. Programming is an unpredictable business and students' abilities vary, but the rough guide is as follows:

Level of Effort:

I: A simple project that can be implemented in an evening, suitable to be made due at the next class meeting.

II: A more extensive project that might be assigned due in a week, so that a student has thinking time for designing the program, and adequate time for the iterative (and sometimes frustrating) testing and debugging cycle that projects always seem to require.

III: A major project that might require three weeks for design and implementation. Such a project requires substantial design effort and careful program layout, and the student will (correctly) view it as a major accomplishment.

The Use of OpenGL

A frequent stumbling block as one first brushes up against computer graphics is getting started making pictures. It's often easy enough to write a program, but there must be an underlying tool that ultimately draws the lines and curves on the screen. It's a boon that such a tool exists and is readily available. OpenGL emerged from

Silicon Graphics Inc., in 1992, and has become a **widely adopted graphics application programming interface** (API). It provides the actual drawing tools through a collection of functions that are called within an application. As described in Appendix 1, it is available (usually through free downloads over the Internet) for all types of computer systems encountered in colleges, universities, and industry. It is easy to install and learn, and its longevity as a standard API is being nurtured and overseen by the OpenGL Architecture Review Board (ARB), an industry consortium responsible for guiding its evolution.

One aspect of OpenGL that suits it so well for use in a computer graphics course is its "device independence" or portability. Many university computer laboratories contain a variety of different computer types. A student can develop and run a program on any available computer. The *same* program can then be run on a different computer, for testing or grading purposes perhaps, and the graphics will be the *same* on the two machines.

OpenGL offers a rich and highly usable API for 2D graphics and image manipulation, but its real power emerges with 3D graphics. Using OpenGL students can progress rapidly and produce stunning animations in only a single-semester course.

The History and Evolution of OpenGL and Its Extensions

OpenGL has remained a successful cross-platform graphics API since its specification (version 1.0) was finalized in 1992. This version was largely compatible with a proprietary API called IrisGL that was designed and supported by Silicon Graphics, Inc., to establish an industry standard. Silicon Graphics collaborated with several other graphics hardware companies to create an open standard, which they named "OpenGL". It is not surprising that, during the subsequent decade, people worked hard to make OpenGL better and more powerful. Graphics hardware has also developed rapidly during this time in the form of increasingly capable (faster) accelerators (graphics cards), making application programmers ever hungrier for an API that does what OpenGL should do best. OpenGL provides a collection of functions that allow the programmer use of new hardware functionality as it becomes available.

Whenever a powerful software system evolves, the problem of standards emerges. Silicon Graphics formed an organization to oversee the evolution of OpenGL and called this body the OpenGL Architecture Review Board, or ARB. The primary task of the ARB is to guide OpenGL by controlling the specification and conformance tests. An OpenGL specification is a thorough description of what each OpenGL function and token is used for. The ARB currently has as members 3DlLabs, Apple, IBM, Intel, NVIDIA, ATI, SGI, and Sun Microsystems, among others.

The functions defined in the specification are implemented in graphics drivers by graphics hardware manufacturers. This takes time and money, so there is usually a delay between the specification and the release of supporting drivers. The OpenGL 2.0 specification was released in September 2004 and incorporates the powerful OpenGL Shading language, which we shall describe in Chapter 8. The previous release was of OpenGL 1.5, whose specification was released in 2003.

Computer graphics is such a rapidly developing field that application programmers would become impatient waiting for "official" releases of OpenGL versions. There must be a mechanism whereby smaller increments in OpenGL functionality can be developed and tested on the latest graphics hardware. To answer this need the ARB offers a well-defined **Extension** mechanism. A list of the extensions is available at the OpenGL Extension Registry (http://oss.sgi.com/projects/ogl-sample/registry/), which defines naming conventions, guidelines for new extensions, and other relevant extension discussions. Accessing extensions is a platform-specific task, and the available extensions will depend on the installed graphics hardware. Libraries such as GLEW and GLEE exist to simplify the process of using extensions in applications.

Extensions allow OpenGL to be extended in small increments to embrace functionality of new hardware at a reasonable cost; these extensions only need the approval of the extension registry and therefore can take place fairly rapidly. When it feels that an extension can add "core" functionality to OpenGL, the ARB can decide to include the extension as part of the core of OpenGL, in turn increasing OpenGL's version number. Chapter 8 continues this discussion.

The Use of C++ as the Programming Language

C++, through a first programming course, is now familiar enough to most students in engineering and computer science that it is the natural choice as the programming language to use. It offers several advantages over C, such as passing parameters to functions by reference, which reduces the need for explicit pointers and simplifies reading the code. File I/O is also greatly simplified through streams, and in general the syntax for all kinds of I/O is clearer in C++ than in C. To keep things simple in this book, no emphasis is placed on implementing operators in C++.

Furthermore, it is easy to develop handy utility classes in C++, such as those for 2D or 3D points, a line, a window, or a color, which make code simpler and more robust. Students see the benefit of hiding the details of a geometric object within the object itself, and of imbuing the object with the ability to do things like draw itself, or test whether it intersects another object.

The Emphasis on 3D Computer Graphics

Because playing games on PCs has become so popular, and so many dazzling animations are appearing in movies, students are particularly interested in developing 3D interactive graphics applications. Several chapters from the first and second editions of this book have been rewritten and rearranged in order to get to topics in 3D graphics as quickly as possible. In a number of situations concepts are presented for the 2D case and the 3D case together, which helps to clarify the similarities and differences between the two.

Describing 3D Scenes Using the Scene Design Language

It can be very awkward and time consuming to design a scene of many 3D objects using "raw" OpenGL commands (for example, describing a cube by its six faces each time it is used can become tedious). So a simple Scene Design Language (SDL) is introduced in Chapter 5 (and fully defined in an appendix). Using this language, students can describe scenes with familiar terms like "cube," "sphere," and "rotate," and build files of such instructions that can be read into their program at runtime. Code for an interpreter is provided in an appendix (and on the book's web site) that can read SDL files and build a list of objects described in the file. It is then a simple matter to use OpenGL to draw the scene from the object list.

This same language and interpreter are put to fine use in Chapter 12 on ray tracing, where the student develops code for ray tracing a scene described using SDL. This permits students to design and ray trace much more elaborate and interesting scenes than they could otherwise.

ORGANIZATION OF THE BOOK AND COURSE PLANS

This book includes much more than can be covered in a one-semester course, or even in a two-semester course (which was also the case for the first two editions). The book has been arranged so the instructor can select different groups of chapters for close study, depending on the length of a course and the interests and backgrounds of the class. Several such paths through the book are suggested here, after the principal topics in each chapter are described.

Brief Overview of Each Chapter

Chapter 1

This chapter gives an overview of the computer graphics field, with examples of how various fields are using graphics. The different kinds of available graphics display systems are described, along with the types of primitives (polygons, text, images, etc.) that a graphic system displays. The chapter also describes some of the many kinds of input devices (mouse, tablet, data glove, etc.) in common use.

Chapter 2

This chapter gets students started with writing graphics applications. Programming using OpenGL is described and several complete line-drawing applications are developed (including the popular Sierpinski gasket). Techniques are discussed for using OpenGL to draw various primitives, such as polylines and polygons, and for using the mouse and keyboard in an interactive graphics application. Case Studies at the end of the chapter provide interesting programming projects, which help students get a clear initial sense of how a graphics application is implemented. One Case Study focuses on building a class for which the application programmer can properly initialize and open an OpenGL window for drawing.

Chapter 3

This chapter develops the central notion of the window-to-viewport mapping, for sizing and positioning pictures on the display. Do-it-yourself management of windows and viewports is discussed, as is using OpenGL to handle the details. Zooming and panning to achieve interesting visual effects are described, as is simple animation of figures. The drawing of complex polygon-based figures, circles, and arcs is discussed. The parametric form for representing curves is discussed for both 2D and 3D curves.

Chapter 4

This chapter reviews vectors and their basic operations, showing the great benefits to be gained by using vector tools in graphics. Students familiar with vectors can read this chapter quickly, focusing on how vectors describe relations between the geometric objects they are manipulating in their programs. One useful property of vectors is that many vector operations may be treated without regard for the dimensionality of the space in question. The use of the cross product, on the other hand, is restricted to three-dimensional vectors.

The notion of a coordinate frame is introduced, and it is shown how this makes it natural to work with homogeneous coordinates. Affine combinations of points are discussed to clarify the difference between vectors and points (to help avoid a common pitfall when writing graphics applications). Several applications involving interpolation, elementary Bezier curves, and line intersections are developed. The fundamental algorithm to clip a line against a convex polygon is developed in detail. (An interesting project for 2D ray tracing is suggested in a Case Study.)

Chapter 5

Transformations are of central importance in computer graphics, and students sometimes have difficulty developing intuition about them—particularly about 3D transformations. This chapter develops the underlying theory of transforming figures and coordinate systems using affine transformations in both the 2D and 3D cases. Homogeneous coordinates are used from the start for describing transformations. Special care is given to rotations in 3D, which are notoriously difficult to visualize.

An overview of the OpenGL viewing pipeline is then developed, and the roles of the modelview, projection, and viewport transformations are described. Drawing of 3D objects using OpenGL's tools is developed. The use of the Scene Description Language (SDL) is introduced, and it is shown how to use the SDL interpreter to read in a description of a 3D scene from a file, and to draw the objects.

Chapter 6

This chapter develops tools for modeling and drawing complicated mesh objects. Example meshes are developed, including polyhedra such as the dodecahedron and Buckyball, and more complex shapes such as domes, tubes that undulate through space, and surfaces of revolution. Techniques are developed for rendering these objects with either flat or smooth shading.

Chapter 7

This chapter develops tools for flexible viewing of 3D scenes. The synthetic camera that forms perspective views is defined and its relationship to the low-level viewing tools OpenGL provides is discussed. A convenient Camera class is built that encapsulates the details of manipulating the camera and makes it easy to fly the camera through a scene in an animation.

The mathematics of perspective projections is then developed in detail along with a discussion of how OpenGL produces perspective views through matrix manipulations. The clipping algorithm that operates in homogeneous coordinate space (which OpenGL also uses) is developed in detail. Methods for producing stereo views are also introduced.

Chapter 8

This chapter tackles ways to make pictures of 3D scenes more realistic. Shading models (also called illumination models) are developed that compute the various light components (ambient, diffuse, and specular) that reflect off objects that are bathed in light. Methods for using OpenGL to set up light sources and alter the surface material properties of objects are described. The depth-buffer method of hidden surface removal that OpenGL uses is described in detail. Techniques for painting texture onto the surface of an object to make it more realistic are developed, for both procedural and image textures. Methods for adding simple shadows to pictures are developed.

Chapter 9

Chapter 9 discusses powerful graphics methods for manipulating images formed on a raster display. The basic pixmap is revisited as a fundamental object for storing and manipulating images, and a number of operations for pixmaps are developed. The classical Bresenham's algorithm for line drawing is described in detail. Particular attention is given to filling a polygonal region. The phenomenon of aliasing (also known as "jaggies") that plagues graphics programmers is discussed and some techniques for reducing aliasing are developed. The techniques of error diffusion, which produce the effect of more colors than a device can display, are also described.

Chapter 10

This chapter is devoted to the design and drawing of smooth curves and surfaces. The theory of Bezier and B-spline curves is described, along with that for rational B-splines that leads to NURBS curves. Interactive curve design is discussed, wherein a designer specifies a set of control points with a mouse and uses a curve generation algorithm to preview the curve. The curve may either interpolate the points or merely be attracted to them.

Complex surface design using Bezier, B-spline, and NURBS patches is also developed, and the issue of joining two patches together seamlessly is addressed.

Chapter 11

This chapter discusses some intricacies of the human color vision system and addresses the problem of representing colors numerically. The CIE standard chromaticity diagram is described, along with various ways to use it in color calculations. Color gamuts of various devices are also discussed, as are different color spaces and conversions of colors between them.

Chapter 12

Chapter 12 introduces the powerful ray tracing approach to rendering scenes with high realism. Working through this chapter, the student can develop first a primitive but simple ray tracer, and then add on capabilities to produce ultimately a full ray tracer that can produce dazzling images. Methods to intersect rays with various shapes are first described, followed by ways to render the objects using different shading models. Techniques for painting texture onto ray traced surfaces, both 3D textures such as marble and image-based textures, are described in detail. Methods to speed up ray tracing using bounding boxes (extents) and bsp trees are also developed.

Some great advantages of ray tracing are that it automatically performs hidden surface removal, and it easily creates exact shadows of objects. In addition, it allows one to simulate the reflection of light from shiny surfaces as well as the refraction of light through a transparent object. Methods to accomplish each of these are described. The chapter ends with a discussion of ray tracing complex objects formed using Constructive Solid Geometry (CSG).

Suggested Paths Through the Book

All suggested paths include Chapters 1 through 5 as fundamental, although Chapter 4 can be perused independently by students familiar with vectors.

Possible Course Plans

- For a *one-semester undergraduate course* where interest is highest in **3D graphics**: Chapters 1 through 5, with parts of Chapters 6 and 7.
- If *extending to a two-semester course* add the rest of Chapter 7 and parts of Chapters 8, 9, and 10.
- For a *one-semester undergraduate course* where interest is highest in **2D and raster graphics**: Chapters 1 through 3, with parts of Chapters 4 and 5.
- If extending to a *two-semester course* add parts of Chapters 7 and 8, and include Chapters 9 and 10 and parts of Chapter 11.
- For a *one-semester graduate course* where interest is highest in **3D graphics**: Chapters 1 through 7, with parts of Chapters 8.
- If *extending to a two-semester graduate course* add the rest of Chapter 8, and include parts of Chapters 9 and all of Chapters 10 through 12.

- For a *one-semester graduate course* where interest is highest in **2D and raster graphics**: Chapters 1 through 3, with parts of Chapters 4 through 9.
- If *extending to a two-semester course* add Chapter 9 and parts of Chapters 10 through 12.

Book Appendices:

- Appendix 1: Obtaining and Installing OpenGL and GLUT
- Appendix 2: Mathematics for Computer Graphics
- Appendix 3: Useful Classes and Scene Description Language (SDL)
- Appendix 4: Fractals and the Mandelbrot Set
- Appendix 5: Relative Drawing and Turtle Graphics

Supplements

Materials are available through the book's site on the Internet. www.fshilljr.com; The source code in the book comes in a variety of fashions; some are simple functions and others are complete working programs. Those with a caption "Complete Working Application" have been compiled and tested thoroughly. Many code samples and utility libraries are available here, as well as images and textures. All may be used freely.

ACKNOWLEDGMENTS

The first and second editions of this text grew out of notes used in courses that I [Hill] have been teaching at the University of Massachusetts for the last 25 years. During this time a large number of students have helped to develop demonstrations and make suggestions for improving the courses. They have also produced many exquisite graphical samples, some of which appear here. Some students and colleagues who were particularly helpful in the first and second editions are Tarik Abou-Raya, Earl Billingsley, Dennis Chen, Daniel Dee, Brett Diamond, John Greco, Tom Kopec, Adam Lavine, Russell Turner, Bill Verts, Shel Walker, Noel Llopis, Russell Swan, Chandrashekhara A., Emmanuel Agu, Tom Laramee, Chang Su, Xiongzi Li, Jung-Yao Huang, Andrew Slater, Anjul Srivastava, and Steve Morin. I apologize for any inadvertent omissions.

Several colleagues have provided inspiration and guidance during the germination of the three editions. I am particularly grateful to Professor Charles Hutchinson (Dartmouth College) for his support in starting the graphics effort at the university, to Professor Michael Wozny (RPI) for his enthusiasm and encouragement in its development, and to Charlie Rupp for the many creative ideas in graphics he passed on to me. I would especially like to thank Daniel Bergeron (UNH), who made substantial contributions to the coherence and readability of the first edition.

I would like to thank the following individuals, and many others who are not mentioned by name, for their advice and help: Edward Hammerand, Arkansas State University, Deborah Walters, SUNY at Buffalo, Suzanne M. Lea, University of North Carolina at Greensboro, John Neitzke, Northeast Missouri State University, Norman Hosay, University of New Haven, David F. McAllister, North Carolina State University, John DeCatrel, Florida State University, Steve Cunningham, California State University, Stanislaus, Paul Heckbert, Carnegie Mellon University, Angelo Yfantis, University of Nevada, Lee H. Tichenor, Western Illinois University, Norman Wittels, Worcester Polytechnic Institute, Matthew Ward, Worcester Polytechnic Institute, Richard E. Neapolitan, Northeastern Illinois University, Jack E.

Bresenham, Winthrop University, Michael Goss, Colorado State University, Bikash Sabata, Wayne State University, Mike Purapura, Alcoa, Norton Starr, Amherst College, and Paul T. Barham, North Carolina State University. Special thanks are due to Edward Angel at the University of New Mexico, who so rightly aimed me at OpenGL as the standard API to use for the second edition of this book, without his guidance the second edition would have been a far less successful project. A portion of the programming examples have been contributed by Rob Hall, University of Massachusetts, Amherst. Sven Maerivoet contributed welcome support and many suggestions based on our second edition.

Portions of the book were written while on sabbatical working with Dr. Hermann Maurer (http://www.iicm.edu/maurer) at the Institute for Information Processing and Computer Supported Media, Technical University Graz in Graz, Austria, and portions were written while on a Fulbright grant at the Indian Institute of Science in Bangalore. I am grateful for the stimulation and support I received during these visits.

This book would not have been possible without my gifted partner Stephen Kelley, of Intangible Inc. www.intangibleinc.com. He and I met and joined forces in August of 2000 in connection with a National Science Foundation grant to teach the fundamentals of computer graphics. Stephen developed all of the visuals and demonstrations for the course and he was also responsible for the video production and post editing.

While working on this book, Stephen was always helpful and enthusiastic, and it was a joy to work with him. He also provided strong technical help to me through his deep knowledge of operating systems as well as his artistic sense, necessary to teach people about computer graphics. Some people are indeed fortunate in the partner they choose for an immense project such as this and I was particularly fortunate to have Stephen work with me. Stephen would like to thank his family and friends for their support on all his endeavors.

Finally, thanks to my parents, to my wife Merilee, and to my children Greta, Jessie, and Rosy, for all their patience and support while this third edition slowly took shape. My daughter Jessie welcomed her own daughter, Lily, on 8/22/05, and while I can't say Lily has shown great patience and support during the preparation of this book, I know she would have, had she been here then, and anyway she is so beautiful that the world now has a special glow because she is in it.

Note to the Reader: How to View the Stereo Pictures

Several stereoscopic figures appear in the book to clarify discussions of 3D objects. They appear as a pair of nearly identical figures placed side by side. To gain the full value of these stereo pictures, coerce your left eye to look at the left-hand one and your right eye to look at the right-hand one; this may be facilitated by holding the figures at arm's length. This may take some practice: some people catch on quickly; others, after many bleary-eyed attempts; some people, never. Of course the figures still help to clarify the discussion, even without the stereo effect.

One way to practice is to hold the index fingers of each hand upright in front of you, about 2 inches apart, and to stare through them at a blank wall in the distance. Each eye sees two fingers, of course, but two of the fingers seem to overlap in the middle. This overlap is precisely what is desired when looking at stereo figures: Each eye sees two figures, but the middle ones are brought into perfect overlap. When the middle ones fuse together like this, the brain constructs out of them a single 3D image. Some people find it helpful to place a piece of white cardboard between the two figures and to rest their nose on it. The cardboard barrier prevents each eye from seeing the image intended for the other eye.

Contents

7   Three-Dimensional Viewing   327

8   Rendering Faces for Visual Realism   376

11 Color Theory   580

12 *Introduction to Ray Tracing*   611

Chapter 1

Introduction to Computer Graphics

"Begin at the beginning," the King said gravely, "and go on till you come to the end; then stop."

Alice in Wonderland
Lewis Carroll,
(1832–1898)

GOALS OF THE CHAPTER

○ To provide an overview of the computer graphics field.

○ To describe the important input and output graphics devices.

Preview

Section 1.1 introduces the area of computer graphics, and Section 1.2 gives a number of examples of how computer graphics are used today. Section 1.3 looks at the primitive ingredients that make a computer generated picture. In particular, Section 1.3.4 introduces the notion of a raster image that is used throughout the book. In Section 1.4 we describe a number of graphics display devices that are in common use today, and Section 1.5 surveys various input devices that are used in interactive graphics applications.

1.1 WHAT IS COMPUTER GRAPHICS?

Good question. People use the term "computer graphics" to mean different things in different contexts. Most simply, computer graphics are **pictures** that are generated by a computer. Everywhere you look today you can find examples, especially in magazines and on television. This book was typeset using a computer: every character (even this **G**) was drawn from a library of character shapes stored in computer memory. Books and magazines abound with pictures created on a computer. Some images look so natural you can't distinguish them from photographs of a real scene. Others have an artificial or surreal look, intended to achieve some visual effect. For example movies today show scenes that never existed, but were carefully crafted by computer, mixing the real and the imagined.

Computer graphics also refers to the **tools** used to make such pictures (a color image is available as Plate 1). This book describes what the tools are and how to write programs that use them. Figure 1.1 shows some spectacular results of the techniques discussed throughout this book. We teach the reader how to generate images such as this.

There are both hardware and software tools. Hardware tools include video monitors, graphics cards, and printers that display graphics, as well as input devices, such

1

FIGURE 1.1 A ray-traced image including reflections and shadows. (Courtesy of Sven Maerivoet)

as a mouse, data glove, and trackball, that let users point to items and draw figures. The computer itself, of course, is a hardware tool, augmented by special circuitry to facilitate graphical display or image capture.

As for software tools, you are already familiar with the usual ones: the operating system, editor (or text processor), compiler, and debugger that are found in any programming environment. For graphics there must also be a collection of graphics routines that produce the pictures themselves. For example, all graphics libraries have functions to draw a simple line or circle (or characters such as **G**). Some—like OpenGL—go well beyond this, containing functions to draw and manage windows with pull-down menus as well as input and dialog boxes. Some graphics libraries (again including OpenGL) offer very sophisticated 3D functions. They allow the programmer to set up a camera in a 3D coordinate system and to take snapshots of objects.

In this book we show how to write programs that utilize graphics libraries, and how to add functionality to them. Not too long ago, programmers were compelled to use highly device-dependent libraries, designed for use on one specific computer system with one specific display device type. This made it very difficult to *port* a program to another system or to use it with another device when the need arises, as it always does. In most cases the programmer had to make substantial changes to the program to get it working, and the process was time consuming and highly error prone. Happily the situation is far better today. *Device-independent graphics* libraries are available that allow the programmer to use a common set of functions within an application and to run the *same* application on a variety of systems and displays. OpenGL is such a library, and it serves as the main tool we shall use in this book. The OpenGL way of creating graphics is used widely in both academia and industry. We begin a detailed discussion of OpenGL in Chapter 2.

Finally, computer graphics often means the whole **field of study** that involves these tools and the pictures they produce. (So it's used in the singular form: computer graphics is . . .). The field is often acknowledged to have started in the early 1960s with Ivan Sutherland's pioneering doctoral thesis at MIT on "Sketchpad: A Man-Machine Graphical Communications System." Interest in graphics grew quickly, in both academia and industry, and there were rapid advances in display technology and in the algorithms used to manage pictorial information. The graphics special interest group, SIGGRAPH,[1] was formed in 1969 and is very active today around the world. (The must-not-miss annual SIGGRAPH meeting now attracts 30,000 participants a year.) More can be found at http://www.siggraph.org. Today hundreds of companies around the world have some aspect of computer graphics as their main source of revenue, and the subject of computer graphics is taught in most computer science or engineering departments.

---

[1]   SIGGRAPH is a special interest group in the ACM: the Association for Computing Machinery.

Computer graphics is a very appealing field of study. You learn to write programs that create pictures, rather than streams of text or numbers. Humans respond readily to pictorial information and are able to absorb much more information from pictures than from a collection of numbers. Our eye–brain system is highly attuned to recognizing visual patterns. Reading text is, of course, a form of pattern recognition: we instantly recognize character shapes, form them into words, and interpret their meaning. But we are even more acute when glancing at a picture. What might be an inscrutable blather of numbers when presented as text becomes an instantly recognizable shape or pattern when presented graphically. The amount of information in a picture can be enormous. We not only recognize what is in the picture but also glean a world of information from its subtle details and texture.

People study computer graphics for many reasons. Some just want a better set of tools for plotting curves and presenting the data they encounter in their other studies or work. Some want to write computer-animated games, while others are looking for a new medium for artistic expression. Most people want to be more productive and to communicate ideas better, and computer graphics can be a great help.

Who Is This User? Normally, the user is the person who watches the graphics of interest being displayed on the screen as the application proceeds. There are several ways in which the graphics generated by the program can be delivered:

- **Frame-by-frame:** A single frame can be drawn while the user waits (very boring).
- **Frame-by-frame under control of the user:** A sequence of frames can be drawn, as in a corporate PowerPoint® presentation; the user presses a key to move on to the next slide, but otherwise has no way of interacting with the slides (much less boring).
- **Animation:** A sequence of frames proceeds at a particular rate while the user watches with delight (exciting, as in such animated movies as *The Incredibles*® and *Shrek*®).
- **Interactive program:** An interactive graphics presentation is watched, where the user controls the flow from one frame to another using an input device such as a mouse or keyboard, in a manner that was unpredictable at the time the program was written. This can delight the eye. A computer game is a familiar case of an interactive graphics presentation.

In this book we will sometimes use the word "user" and sometimes the word "viewer" for the person described above. In some situations, such as playing computer games, we may use the word "player."

There is also the input side. A program generates output—pictures or otherwise—from a combination of the algorithms executed in the program and the data the user inputs to the program. Some programs accept input crudely but easily through characters and numbers typed at the keyboard. Graphics programs, on the other hand, emphasize more natural types of input: the movement of a mouse on a desktop, the strokes of a pen on a drawing tablet, or the motion of the user's head and hands. In this book we examine many techniques of interactive computer graphics; that is, we combine the techniques of natural user input with those that produce graphical output.

1.2 WHERE COMPUTER-GENERATED PICTURES ARE USED

> Any sufficiently advanced technology is indistinguishable from magic.
>
> *Arthur C. Clarke*
> *(1917–)*

Computer graphics can draw pictures of actual objects with dazzling realism. But computer graphics can also draw things that could never be viewed in reality (such as the view inside a volcano, on the surface of Jupiter, or inside the head of a hospital patient). The programmer describes an object of interest through some algorithm in a program, and the program generates a picture from this model.

In this section we look briefly at some applications that use computer graphics to demonstrate a range of situations that can benefit from graphics. This list is far from complete: it is merely suggestive. Later we shall describe several of these applications in detail as Case Studies.

1.2.1 Art, Entertainment, and Publishing

Computer graphics is widely used in the production of movies, television programs, books, games, and magazines. The cost of graphics systems has decreased dramatically in recent years, and powerful software and hardware tools have been developed to utilize their increased performance. Talented designers can now routinely use computers to create special effects, animations, and high-quality publications. Figure 1.2 shows an example of a computer game in action. A color version is available in Plate 2.

FIGURE 1.2 A screen shot from a 3D computer-based game. (Courtesy of High Moon Studios, Inc.)

Development of Computer Games

Many readers study computer graphics because of an underlying interest in learning how to write game programs. Techniques to do this will be presented as we progress. Here we give a capsule summary of the development of games over the last few decades. This is a nontechnical summary. It provides perspective on how rapidly the field of computer graphics has evolved (and continues to evolve) and on some of the issues in making a computer game successful and attractive.

In 1952 A. S. Douglas wrote his Ph.D. dissertation at the University of Cambridge on human–computer interaction. Douglas developed one of the earliest graphical computer games, a version of tic-tac-toe. Another pioneering video game was created by William Higinbotham in 1958. His game, called "Tennis for Two" (a lot like Pong), was created and played on a Brookhaven National Laboratory oscilloscope (Figure 1.3).

In 1962 Steve Russell invented "Spacewar!" which later led to the creation of the first coin-operated arcade game by Nolan Bushnell along with Ted Dabney in 1971. In 1967 Ralph Baer wrote the first video game, "Chase," using a television set as a display. Nolan Bushnell and Ted Dabney formed Atari Computers in 1972, and in 1980 Atari's "Asteroids" and "Lunar Lander" became the first two computer games

FIGURE 1.3 The piece of equipment used to develop the game "Tennis for Two." (Courtesy of Brookhaven National Laboratory)

to be registered in the copyright office. The Atari system led to the familiar Nintendo, SEGA, and PlayStation (and so on) gaming systems.

As this is just a brief survey, we will defer till later a discussion of how such games might by written. In particular we shall address issues of modeling the scenes in a game, how programs can control the interaction between the main player and the characters in the game, and the production of texture, which is so important in making the scenes realistic. Each of these goals requires ever-faster transfer of data from the CPU to the monitor, and ever-increasing power in the video card. One genre of games for which advanced graphics cards have become essential is *first-person* shooter games. Wolfenstein 3D$^{©}$ (Figure 1.4), developed in 1992, was the first of its kind, and it quickly led to other popular games such as the Doom$^{©}$ and Quake$^{©}$ series.

FIGURE 1.4 A screen shot of Wolfenstein 3D$^{©}$. (Courtesy of iD Software)

These first-person shooter games immerse the player in a scene from the main player's perspective. This makes vivid how real the environment appears (how ugly the enemies are), the effects of being shot at, and the barriers that pop up and prevent the player from moving and ducking. Wolfenstein 3D$^{©}$, in connection, with ray casting, is discussed in Chapter 12.

Computer Games

Figures 1.2 and 1.4 show images from two different computer games. The player moves joysticks, pushes buttons, and pulls triggers, and the computer-generated image must respond instantly. Special hardware is often used to speed up the generation of successive images. Arcade games provide some of the greatest challenges to graphics programmers, as the action must be realistic and at the same time very fast.

Movie Production, Animation, and Special Effects

Computer-animated commercials are seen regularly on television, and some very impressive animations are being integrated into feature movies. Animations are created by writing a sequence of images onto film or videotape, each image only slightly different from the one before. When the film or videotape is played back at 20 to 30 frames a second, the human eye blends the images and sees smooth motion.

Browsing on the World Wide Web

We live in a networked world, and it seems everyone surfs on the World Wide Web. The user moves the mouse to a spot on the screen and clicks to choose the next web site to visit, and a page of information is sent over the internet. The browser must rapidly interpret the data on the page and draw it on the screen as high-quality text and graphics. Figure 1.5 shows a screenshot from the World Wide Web.

FIGURE 1.5 Screenshot of a page from the World Wide Web. (Courtesy of Intangible Inc.)

Slide, Book, and Magazine Design

Computer graphics are commonly used in **page layout** programs to design the final look of each page of a book or magazine. The user can interactively move text and graphics around to find the most pleasing arrangement.

Another form of publishing is sometimes called presentation graphics. In a business or educational setting high-quality slides are designed to be shown to a large variety of audiences. Figure 1.6 shows an example. Slides often contain bar charts or pie charts that summarize complex information in a readily digestible form. They must be of high quality and have visual appeal in order to make a particular point.

A **paint system** is another tool for the creation of computer-generated images. A common example is *Adobe Photoshop*,[2] acting as both a photo manipulation program and a paint system. The user fashions the image by sketching—often using a

---

[2]   Abode Photoshop is a trademark of Adobe Systems, Inc.

FIGURE 1.6 Example slide for an educational presentation.

mouse or a tablet—and by selecting colors and patterns to create the desired effects. Figure 1.7 shows a screenshot of such a system. (Plate 3 shows a color version.) The system provides an assortment of tools: previously rendered images can be retrieved from mass storage and merged with new images; palettes of different colors can be accessed and displayed; and many different textures can be created by means of simple commands. These systems are often used to create pages you encounter on the World Wide Web.

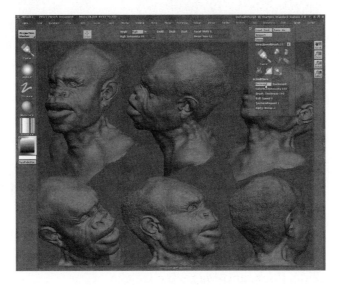

FIGURE 1.7 Screenshot of a paint system. Courtesy of zBrush.

1.2.2 Computer Graphics, Perception, and Image Processing

The fields of computer graphics and image processing are blending together more each year: it's getting harder (and less important) to know where the boundary between them lies. In this book we focus on computer graphics, but we also describe a number of techniques that historically would have been confined to the image-processing field.

The main task in computer graphics is to create pictures and images, synthesizing them based on some description, or model, in a computer. The main task in image processing, on the other hand, is to improve or alter images that were created elsewhere, perhaps digitized from photographs or captured by a video recorder. Processing can remove specks of noise from an image, enhance its contrast, sharpen its edges, and fix its colors. Software routines can be used to search for certain features in an image and highlight them to make them more noticeable or understandable.

Figure 1.8, part a, shows an image obtained by digitally scanning a photograph. Part b shows the image after its contrast has been enhanced, specks of noise have been removed, and edges sharpened.

FIGURE 1.8 Enhancing a scanned image: a) original, b) enhanced.

a)   b)

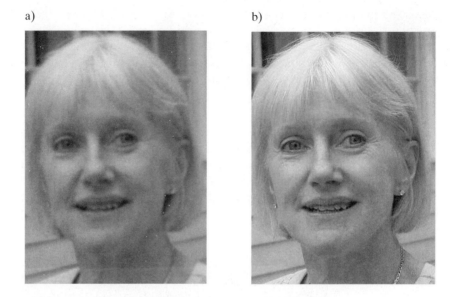

The movie industry has recently capitalized on the marriage of computer graphics and image processing in dramatic ways. Envision a scene from a classic movie—say, *Finding Nemo* or *Who Framed Roger Rabbit?*—composed by mixing computer-generated imagery and digitized images.

1.2.3 Monitoring a Process

Highly complex systems like factories, power plants, and air traffic control systems must be carefully monitored; often there must be a human in the loop to watch out for impending trouble. A status display must give the operator up-to-the-moment information to be interpreted instantly. Measurements are made of the system every second or as needed, and the data are transmitted to the monitoring station, converted to graphical information, and presented to the operator.

An air traffic control system consists of monitors that display where nearby planes are situated. The user sees a schematic representation that gives the whole picture at a glance. Various icons can flash or change color to alert the user to changes that need attention.

1.2.4 Displaying Simulations

Some systems, like those for air traffic control, actually exist and can be measured in real time. Others have never been built, possibly could never be built, and exist only as equations and algorithms in a computer. But they can still be tested and run through their paces as if they existed, and valuable simulated information can be obtained. This information is often made available to people by representing it graphically.

A variety of systems can be profitably simulated: the movement of a robot as it shuttles down the slope of an active volcano; the response of the human body to the introduction of a dangerous foreign substance; or the effect of global warming due to an increase of hydrocarbons. The classic example is a **flight simulator**. The system is an airplane with a certain shape and flying characteristics, along with a world consisting of a landing field, mountains, other planes, and of course air, all modeled appropriately.

The dynamics of the airplane's motion are modeled on a computer. During simulated flight, as the pilot moves the controls, the program calculates new positions and speeds for the simulated plane. The pilot sees a simulated view outside the cockpit. Flight simulator programs are among the most demanding and difficult graphics applications to write, because they must respond so rapidly. Figure 1.9 shows an actual control panel of an airplane's cockpit.

FIGURE 1.9 Simulation of the control panel of an actual airplane. (Courtesy of Gergely Óhegyi)

These examples illustrate an important aspect of computer graphics:

*Computer graphics has the ability to display objects as if they already physically exist, when in actuality they are only models inside a compute*r. For example, Plate 4 shows a simulated view of the surface of Mars.

1.2.5 Computer-Aided Design: CAD

A number of disciplines make heavy use of interactive computer graphics to facilitate the design of some system or product—for example, the casing of an electric drill. The computer holds in memory a model of the device in question, and a picture based on the model is displayed for the user to examine. The designer can rotate the object and zoom in for a closer look, perhaps using a trackball or data glove to carry out the manipulation. To speed up the rendering a **wireframe** drawing is used, whereby the shape of the object is suggested by a grid of connected lines.

The designer scrutinizes the current model of the drill and then indicates certain changes to its shape, whereupon the model is updated and rendered again. When the shape seems proper, the user requests a more realistic view. This might take longer to render. As we discuss in depth later, the algorithms that produce full-color renderings with shadows, glossy highlights, and fine detail can be complex.

Analysis and simulation can be used here, too. The shape of the drill might have the right visual appeal, but the casing might be too weak or too heavy, or perhaps uncomfortable to grip. Algorithms can be applied to the model of the drill to analyze its weight and heft and to test whether the inner workings will fit properly inside the casing. Further algorithms can test whether the particular shape is too expensive to produce in steel or aluminum, and even whether the internal parts can be assembled conveniently in the final manufacturing process. The computer can be a powerful ally throughout design and manufacturing. Our focus in this book is on producing images of an object that provide the designer with the right information.

Computer-aided Architectural Design (CAAD)

Computer graphics can also help architects design and model buildings. A model might be the floor plan to a house, school, or hospital, as in Figure 1.10. An architect can adjust the digital floor plans, moving a wall here or adjusting a window there with the mouse. CAAD programs also produce a fully rendered version, showing how the structure would appear in three dimensions. Computer graphics allows an architect to move locations of windows and doors and to display different textures such as brick or stucco. Using interactive controls, the architect can even do a walk-through, showing a client how the house will be experienced when it has been built.

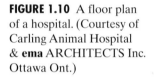

FIGURE 1.10 A floor plan of a hospital. (Courtesy of Carling Animal Hospital & **ema** ARCHITECTS Inc. Ottawa Ont.)

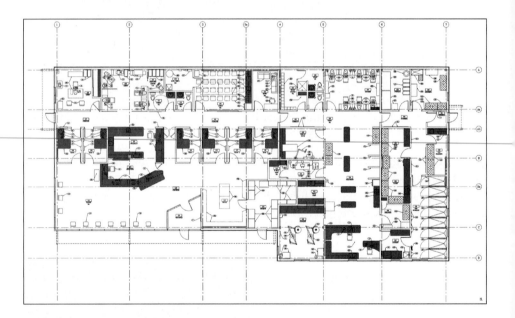

1.2.6 Scientific Analysis and Volume Visualization

Scientific data are often complex, and relationships among the variables of an experiment can be difficult to visualize. Graphics provides a superb tool for presenting scientific information in a way that can be easily grasped. Seeing data displayed in the right way, you often have new insights into the underlying process you are investigating. By displaying data properly, you can also communicate ideas better to colleagues.

Figure 1.11 shows an example. A surface is seen to undulate in a fashion the eye can grasp immediately. The surface height represents one quantity (such as temperature or the viscosity), which is displayed against two other quantities to produce a three-dimensional plot. By contrast, if these data were presented as just a table of numbers, one would have to study the table laboriously in order to obtain the same information.

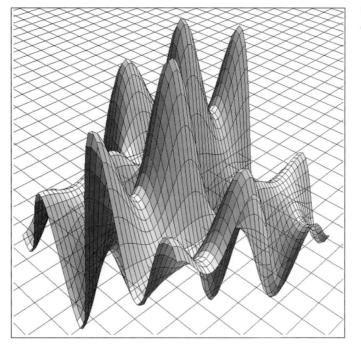

FIGURE 1.11 Display of complex scientific data.

Volume Visualization

A complex problem which is made simpler by image processing is the scanning of the human head (Figure 1.12). Areas of different colors immediately inform a physician about the health of each part of the brain. An image of a three-dimensional object such as the brain can be constructed by creating a number of slices and superimposing them to form the final image.

This approach has given rise to a special field of study within computer graphics called **volume visualization**. Graphics presents an opportunity to display huge

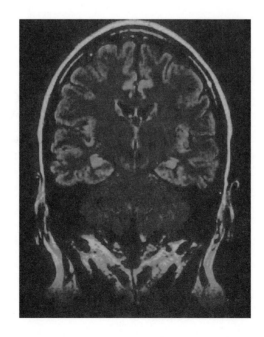

FIGURE 1.12 View of the human brain using volume visualization. (Courtesy of Dr. Richard Rubin, UMASS-Amherst).

amounts of data. For example, a variety of programs can assist in readily recognizing and analyzing data for weather patterns which might indicate inclement weather.

Besides helping humans understand measured data, computer graphics is well suited for providing insight into complex mathematical ideas. Several powerful programs (*Mathematica*©, MathLab©, MathCad©, etc.) have been developed recently that allow a user to enter equations and rules about various quantities and then to see the resulting objects displayed in some fashion. For instance, Figure 1.13a shows a surface generated by a mathematical formula. It is displayed using *Mathematica* by typing the single instruction:

```
ParametricPlot3D[{t,u,Sin[t u]},{t,0,3},{u,0,3}]
```

The intricacies of the formula are nicely revealed at a glance, and the user can adjust some parameters in order to view this surface from different viewpoints. Figure 1.13b also uses *Mathematica* to draw a complex three-dimensional object (a stellated icosahedron) to assist the user in studying its structure.

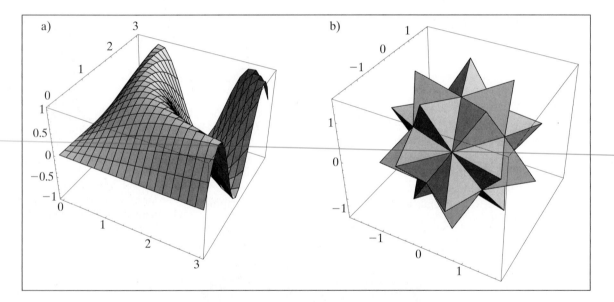

FIGURE 1.13 Displays by *Mathematica* of a) a complex mathematical surface, and b) a mathematically defined solid object.

1.3 ELEMENTS OF PICTURES CREATED IN COMPUTER GRAPHICS

> This is like deja vu all over again.
>
> *Yogi Berra*
> *(1925–)*

What makes up a computer-drawn picture? The basic objects of which such pictures are composed are called **output primitives**. One useful categorization is:

- points
- lines
- polylines
- text
- filled regions
- raster images

We will see that these types overlap somewhat, but this terminology provides a good starting point. We describe each type of primitive in turn, and hint at typical software routines such as those in OpenGL that are used to draw them. More detail on these tools is given in later chapters, of course. We also discuss the various attributes of each output primitive. The **attributes** of a graphic primitive are the characteristics that affect how it appears, such as color and thickness.

1.3.1 Polylines

A polyline is a connected sequence of straight lines. Each example in Figure 1.14 contains several polylines: a) one polyline extends from the nose of the dinosaur to its tail; b) the plot of the mathematical function is a single polyline, and c) the wireframe picture of a chess pawn contains many polylines that outline its shape.

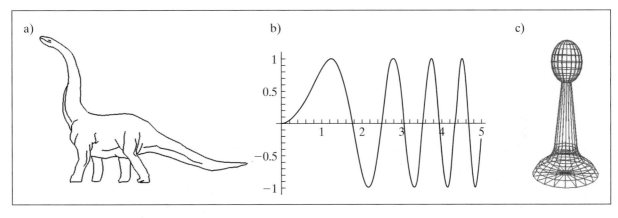

FIGURE 1.14 a) A polyline drawing of a dinosaur, b) a plot of a mathematical function, c) a wireframe rendering of a 3D object.

Note that a polyline can appear as a smooth curve. Figure 1.15 shows a magnification of a curve revealing its underlying short line segments. The eye blends them into an apparently smooth curve.

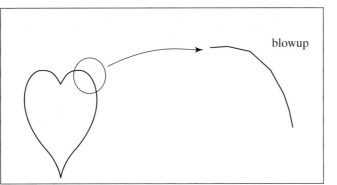

blowup

FIGURE 1.15 A curved line made up of straight line segments.

Pictures made up of polylines are sometimes called **line drawings**. Some devices, like a pen plotter, are specifically designed to produce line drawings.

The simplest polyline is a single straight line segment. A line segment is specified by its two endpoints, say (x_1, y_1) and (x_2, y_2). A drawing routine for a line might look like

```
drawLine(x1, y1, x2, y2);
```

It draws a line between the two endpoints. We develop such a tool later and show many examples of its use. At that point we get specific about how coordinates like x_1 are represented (by integers or by real numbers), and how colors can be represented in a program.

A special case arises when a line segment shrinks to a single point and is drawn as a dot. Even the lowly dot has important uses in computer graphics, as we see later. A dot might be programmed using the routine

```
drawDot(x1, y1);
```

Although, as we shall see, OpenGL does it somewhat differently.

When there are several lines in a polyline, each is called an **edge**, and two adjacent lines meet at a **vertex**. The edges of a polyline can cross one another, as seen in the figures. Polylines are specified as a list of vertices, each given by a coordinate pair:

$$(x_0, y_0), (x_1, y_1), (x_2, y_2), \ldots, (x_n\ y_n) \tag{1.1}$$

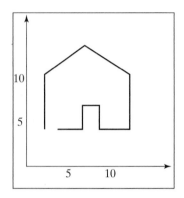

FIGURE 1.16 An example polyline.

For instance, the polyline shown in Figure 1.16 is given by the sequence $(2, 4)$, $(2, 11), (6, 14), (12, 11), (12, 4) \ldots$ (What are the remaining vertices in this polyline?)

To draw polylines we will need a tool, as in the following line of code:

```
drawPolyline(poly);
```

where the variable poly is a list containing all the endpoints (x_i, y_i) in some fashion. There are various ways to capture a list in a program, each having its advantages and disadvantages.

A polyline need not form a closed figure, but if the first and last points are connected by an edge, the polyline is a **polygon**. If, in addition, no two edges cross, the polygon is called **simple**. Figure 1.17 shows some interesting polygons; only a) and d) are simple. Polygons are fundamental in computer graphics, partly because they are so easy to define. Many drawing (rendering) algorithms have been finely tuned to operate optimally with polygons. Polygons are described in depth in Chapter 3.

FIGURE 1.17 Examples of polygons.

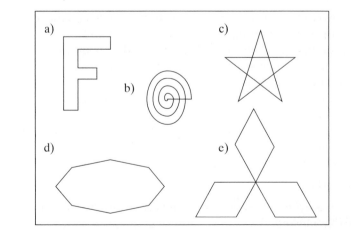

Attributes of Lines and Polylines

Important attributes of a polyline are the color and thickness of its edges, the manner in which the edges are dashed, and the manner in which thick edges blend together at their endpoints. Typically all of the edges of a polyline are given the same attributes.

The first two polylines in Figure 1.18 are distinguished by the line thickness attribute. The third polyline is drawn using dashed segments.

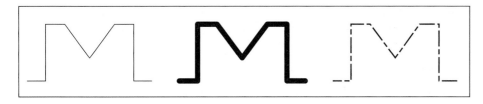

FIGURE 1.18 Polylines with different attributes.

When a line is thick, its ends have shapes, and a user must decide how two adjacent edges join. Figure 1.19 shows various possibilities. Part a shows "butt-end" lines that leave an unseemly "crack" at the joint. Part b shows rounded ends on the lines, so that they join smoothly. Part c shows a mitered joint, and part d shows a trimmed mitered joint. Software tools are available in some packages to allow the user to choose the type of joining.

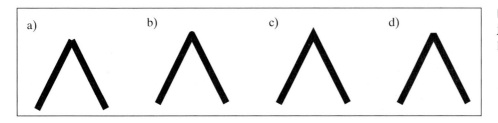

FIGURE 1.19 Some ways of joining two thick lines in a polyline.

The attributes of a polyline are sometimes set by calling routines such as

```
setDash(dash7) or setLineThickness(thickness).
```

1.3.2 Text

Some graphics devices have two distinct display modes, a **text mode** and a **graphics mode**. The text mode is used for simple input/output of characters to control the operating system or edit the code in a program. Text displayed in this mode uses a built-in character generator. The character generator is capable of drawing alphabetic, numeric, and punctuation characters, and some selection of special symbols such as ♥, δ and ⊕ . Usually these characters can't be placed arbitrarily on the display but only in some row and column of a built-in grid.

A graphics mode offers a richer set of character shapes and characters can be placed arbitrarily. Figure 1.20 shows some examples of text drawn graphically.

A tool to draw a character string might look like:

```
drawString(x, y, string);
```

It places the starting point of the string at position (x, y) and draws the sequence of characters stored in the variable string.

FIGURE 1.20 Some examples of text drawn graphically.

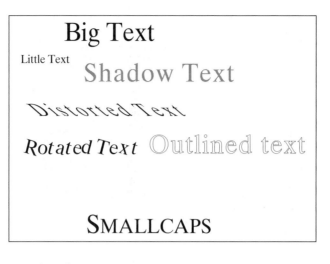

Text Attributes

There are many text attributes, the most important of which are typeface, color, size, spacing, and orientation.

Font. A font is a specific set of character shapes (a **typeface**) in a particular style and size. Figure 1.21 shows various character fonts.

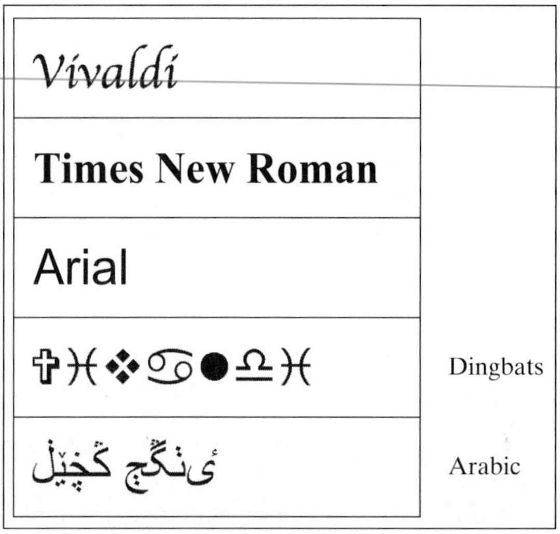

FIGURE 1.21 Some examples of fonts.

The shape of each character can be defined by a polyline (or by more complicated curves such as Bezier curves—see Chapter 11), as shown in Figure 1.22a, or by an arrangement of dots, as shown in part b. Graphics packages come with a set of predefined fonts, and additional fonts can be purchased from companies that specialize in designing them.

Orientation of characters and strings. Characters may also be drawn tilted along some direction. Tilted strings are often used to annotate parts of a graph.

The graphic presentation of high-quality text is a complex subject. Barely perceptible differences in detail can change pleasing text into ugly text. Indeed, we see so much printed material in our daily lives that we subliminally expect characters to be displayed with certain shapes, spacing, and subtle balances.

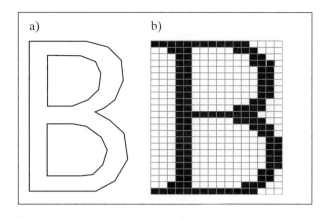

FIGURE 1.22 A character shape defined by a) a polyline and by b) a pattern of dots.

1.3.3 Filled Regions

The **filled region** (sometimes called *fill area*) primitive is a shape filled with some color or pattern. The boundary of a filled region is often a polygon (although more complex regions are considered in Chapter 4). Figure 1.23 shows several filled polygons. Polygon *A* is filled with its edges visible, whereas *B* is filled with its border left undrawn. Polygons *C* and *D* are nonsimple. Polygon *D* even contains polygonal holes. Such shapes can still be filled, but one must specify exactly what is meant by a polygon's interior, since filling algorithms differ depending on the definition. Algorithms for performing the filling action are discussed in Chapter 10.

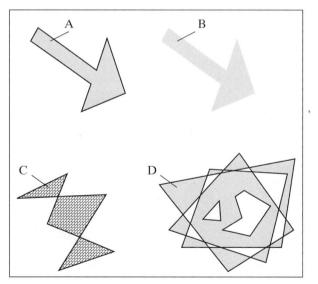

FIGURE 1.23 Examples of filled polygons.

To draw a filled polygon one would use a routine like:

```
fillPolygon(poly, pattern);
```

where the variable `poly` holds the data for the polygon—the same kind of list as for a polyline—and the variable `pattern` is some description of the pattern to be used for filling. We discuss details in Chapter 4.

Figure 1.24 shows the use of filled regions to shade the different faces of a 3D object. Each polygonal face of the object is filled with a certain shade of gray that corresponds to the amount of light that would reflect off that face. This makes the object appear to be bathed in light from a certain direction. Shading of 3D objects is discussed in Chapter 8.

FIGURE 1.24 Filling polygonal faces of 3D objects to suggest proper shading.

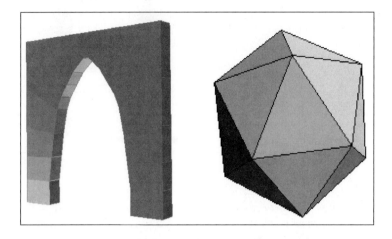

The attributes of a filled region include the attributes of the enclosing border, as well as the pattern and color of the filling.

1.3.4 Raster Images

Figure 1.25a shows a **raster image** of a chess piece. It is made up of many small cells, in different shades of gray, as revealed in the magnified version, Figure 1.25b. The individual cells are often called **pixels** (short for "picture elements"). Normally your eye can't see the individual cells; it blends them together and synthesizes an overall picture.

a)   b)

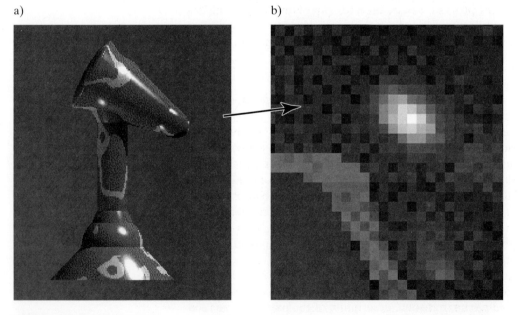

FIGURE 1.25 a) A raster image of a chess piece, b) a magnification of the image. (Courtesy of Andrew Slater)

A raster image is stored in a computer as an array of numerical values. This array is thought of as being rectangular, with a certain number of rows and a certain number of columns. Each numerical value represents the value of the pixel stored there. The array as a whole is often called a **pixel map**. The term **bitmap** is also used (although some people think this term should be reserved for pixel maps wherein each pixel is represented by a single bit, having the value 0 or 1).

Figure 1.26 shows a simple example where a figure is represented by a 18-by-19 array (18 rows by 19 columns) of cells in three shades of gray. Suppose the three gray levels are encoded as the values 1, 2, and 7, where higher numbers are taken to be darker shades of gray. Figure 1.26b shows the numerical values of the pixel map for the upper left 6-by-8 portion of the image.

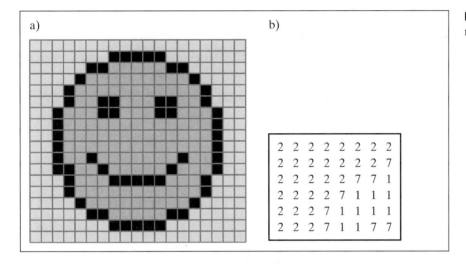

FIGURE 1.26 A simple figure represented as a bitmap.

How are raster images created? Three principal sources are:

1. **Hand-designed images.**

    A designer determines what values are needed for each cell, and types them into memory. Sometimes a paint program can be used to help automate this: the designer can draw and manipulate various graphical shapes, viewing what has been made so far. When satisfied, the designer stores the result in a file. The icon in Figure 1.26 was created this way.

2. **Computed images.**

    An algorithm is used to render a scene, which might be modeled abstractly in computer memory. As a simple example, a scene might consist of a single yellow smooth sphere illuminated by a light source that emanates orange light. The model describes the size and position of the sphere, the placement of the light source, and the hypothetical camera that is to take the picture. The raster image plays the role of the film in the camera. In order to create the raster image, an algorithm must calculate the color of light that falls on each pixel of the image in the camera. This is the way in which ray traced images such as the chess piece in Figure 1.25 are created.

    Raster images also frequently contain images of straight lines. A line is created in an image by setting the proper pixels to the line's color. But it can require quite a bit of computation to determine the sequence of pixels that best fit the ideal line between two given endpoints. Bresenham's algorithm (see Chapter 9) provides a very efficient approach to determining these pixels.

    Figure 1.27a shows a raster image featuring several straight lines, a circular arc, and some text characters. Figure 1.27b shows a close-up of the raster image in order to expose the individual pixels on the lines. For a horizontal or vertical line the black square pixels line up nicely, forming a sharp line. But for the other lines and the arc the best collection of pixels produces only an approximation to the curve desired. In addition, the result shows the dread **jaggies** that have a relentless presence in raster images. This view is so close up that individual pixels are visible and the image is described as a **pixilated** version of Figure 1.27a.

FIGURE 1.27 a) A collection of lines and text, b) magnification of part a, having jaggies c) individual pixels visible in an extreme close up.

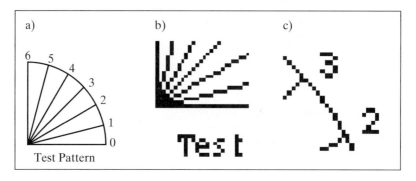

3. Scanned images.

   A photograph or television image can be digitized. In effect a grid is placed over the original image, and at each grid point the device reads into memory the closest color that it can display. The bitmap is then stored in a file for later use. The image of the kitten in Figure 1.28 was formed this way.

FIGURE 1.28 A scanned image.

Because raster images are simply arrays of numbers, they can be subsequently processed to good effect by a computer. For instance, Figure 1.29 shows three successive enlargements of the kitten image. These are formed by pixel replication (discussed in detail in Chapter 9). (Notice the high degree of *pixilation*.) Each pixel has been replicated three times in each direction in part a; six times in part b, and twelve times in part c.

a) b) c)

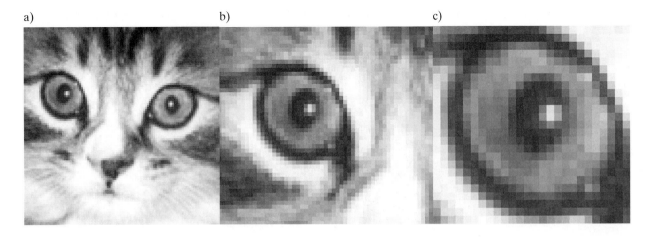

FIGURE 1.29 Three successive blow-ups of the kitten image: a) three times enlargement, b) six times enlargement, c) twelve times enlargement.

As another example, one often needs to clean up, or enhance, a scanned image— for instance, to remove specks of noise or to reveal important details. Figure 1.30a shows the kitten image with gray levels altered to increase the contrast and make details more evident, and Figure 1.30b shows the effect of edge sharpening, achieved by a form of filtering the image.

a) b)

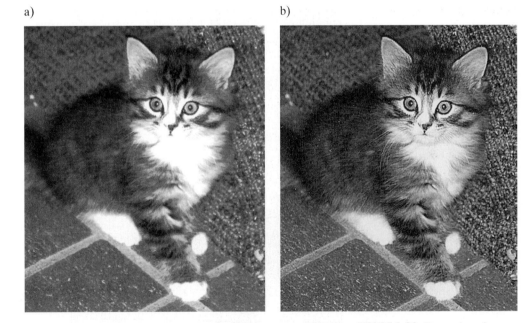

FIGURE 1.30 Examples of image enhancement.

Figure 1.31 shows two examples of editing an image to accomplish some visual effect. Part a shows the kitten image embossed, and part b shows it distorted geometrically.

1.3.5 Representation of Gray Shades and Color for Raster Images

An important aspect of a raster image is the manner in which the various colors or shades of gray are represented in the bitmap. We briefly survey the most common methods here.

a)   b)

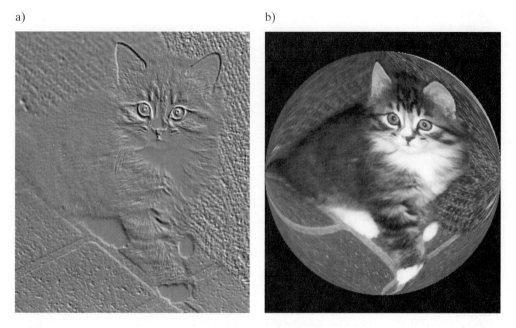

FIGURE 1.31 a) The embossed image, b) geometrically distorted image.

Grayscale Raster Images

If a raster image has only two pixel values, it is called **bilevel**. Figure 1.32a shows a simple bilevel image, representing a familiar arrow-shaped cursor frequently seen on a computer screen. Its raster consists of 16 rows of 8 pixels each. Figure 1.32b shows the bitmap of this image as an array of 1's and 0's. The image shown at the left associates black with a 1 and white with a 0, but this association might just as easily be reversed. Since one bit of information is sufficient to distinguish two values, a bilevel image is often referred to as a **1-bit-per-pixel** image.

FIGURE 1.32 a) A bilevel image of a cursor, and b) its bitmap.

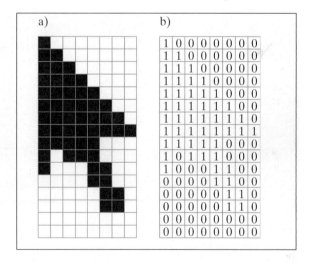

When the pixels in a grayscale image take on more than two values, each pixel requires more than a single bit to represent it in memory. Grayscale images are often classified in terms of their **pixel depth**, the number of bits needed to represent their gray levels. Since an n-bit quantity has 2^n possible values, there can be 2^n gray levels in an image with pixel depth n. The most common values of n:

- 2 bits/pixel produce 4 gray levels
- 4 bits/pixel produce 16 gray levels
- 8 bits/pixel produce 256 gray levels

Figure 1.33 shows 16 gray levels ranging from black to white. Each of the sixteen possible pixel values is associated with a binary **4-tuple** such as 0110 or 1110. Here 0000 represents black, 1111 denotes white, and the other 14 values represent gray levels in between.

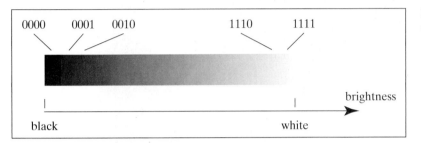

FIGURE 1.33 Sixteen levels of gray.

Many grayscale images[3] employ 256 gray levels, since this usually gives a scanned image acceptable quality. Each pixel is represented by some 8-bit values such as 01101110. The pixel value usually represents brightness, where black is represented by 00000000, white by 11111111, and a medium gray by 10000000.

Effect of Pixel Depth: Grayscale Quantization

Sometimes an image that initially uses 8 bits per pixel is altered so that fewer bits per pixel are used. This might occur if a particular display device is incapable of displaying so many levels, or if the full image takes up too much memory. Figures 1.34 and 1.35 show the effect on the kitten image if pixel values are simply truncated to fewer bits. The loss in fidelity is hardly noticeable for the images in Figure 1.34, which use 6 and 3 bits/pixel (providing 64 and 8 different shades of gray, respectively).

a) b)

FIGURE 1.34 The image reduced to 6 bits/pixel and 3 bits/pixel.

---

[3] Thousands are available on the Internet, frequently as GIF, JPEG, or TIFF images.

a)   b)

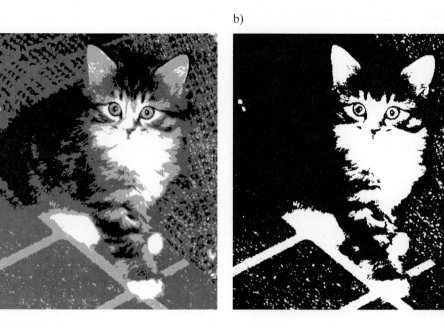

FIGURE 1.35 The image reduced to a) 2 bits/pixel and b) 1 bit/pixel.

Note that some areas of the figure that show gradations of gray in the original now show a lake of uniform gray. This is often called **banding**, since areas that should show a gradual shift in the gray level in the original instead show a sequence of uniform gray bands.

Figure 1.35 shows the cases of 2 and 1 bits/pixel. In part a the four levels are clearly visible, and there is a great deal of banding. In part b there is only black and white, and much of the original image information has been lost. In Chapter 9 we show techniques such as dithering for improving the quality of an image when too few bits are used for each pixel.

Color Raster Images

Color images are desirable because they match our daily experience more closely than do grayscale images. Color raster images have become more common in recent years, as the cost of high-quality color displays is low. The cost of scanners that digitize color photos is also now very reasonable.

Each pixel in a color image has a color value, a numerical value that somehow represents a color. There are a number of ways to associate numbers and colors, but one of the most common is to describe a color as a combination of amounts of red, green, and blue light. Each pixel value is a **3-tuple**, such as (23, 14, 51), that prescribes the intensities of the red, green, and blue light components in that order.

Color Value	Displayed
0, 0, 0	Black
0, 0, 1	Blue
0, 1, 0	Green
0, 1, 1	Cyan
1, 0, 0	Red
1, 0, 1	Magenta
1, 1, 0	Yellow
1, 1, 1	White

FIGURE 1.36 A common correspondence between color value and perceived color.

The number of bits used to represent the color of each pixel is often called its **color depth**. The colors red, green, and blue are called **primaries**, as discussed in Chapter 10. Each value in the (red, green, blue) 3-tuple has a certain number of bits, and the color depth is the sum of these values. A color depth of three allows one bit for each component. For instance, the pixel value (0, 1, 1) means that the red component is off, but both green and blue are on. In most displays the contributions from each component are added together, so (0, 1, 1) would represent the addition of green and blue light, which is perceived as cyan. Since each component can be on or off, there are eight possible colors, as tabulated in Figure 1.36. As expected, equal amounts of red, green, and blue, (1, 1, 1), produce white.

A color depth of three rarely offers enough precision for specifying the value of each component, so larger color depths are used. Because a byte is such a natural quantity to manipulate on a computer, many images have a color depth of twenty-four, or 8 bits per primary. Each pixel then can have 2^{24} or over 2 billion colors. Such images are known as **true color** images and have as good color reproduction as the eye can preceive. But such images require a great deal of memory: one byte for every pixel. A high quality image of 1280 by 1024 pixels requires over one million bytes!

1.4 GRAPHICS DISPLAY DEVICES

> *The artist is nothing without the gift, but the gift is nothing without work.*
>
> *Emile Zola*
> *(1896–1962)*

We present an overview of some hardware devices that are used to display computer graphics. The devices include video monitors, plotters, and printers. A rich variety of graphics displays have been developed over the last thirty years, and new ones are appearing all the time. The quest is to display pictures of ever higher quality that recreate more faithfully what is in the artist's or engineer's mind. In this section we look over the types of pictures that are being produced today, how they are being used, and the kinds of devices used to display them. We look at ways to measure the quality of an image, and we see how different kinds of display devices compare.

1.4.1 Line Drawing Displays

Some devices are naturally line drawers. Because of the technology of the time, most early computer graphics were generated by line-drawing devices. The classic example is the **pen plotter**. A pen plotter moves a pen over a piece of paper to some spot that is specified by the computer, leaving a trail of ink of some color. Some plotters have a carousel that holds several pens, which the program can exchange automatically in order to draw in different colors. Usually the choice of available colors is very limited: a separate pen is used for each color. The quality of a line drawing is related to the precision with which the pen is positioned and the sharpness of the lines drawn.

There are various kinds of pen plotters. **Flatbed plotters** move the pen in two dimensions over a stationary sheet of paper. **Drum plotters** move the paper back and forth on a drum to provide one direction of motion, while the pen moves back and forth at the top of the drum to provide the other direction.

There are also video displays, called "vector," "random-scan," or "calligraphic" displays, that produce line drawings. They have internal circuitry specially designed to sweep an electronic beam from point to point across the face of a CRT or LCD display, leaving a glowing trail.

Vector displays, however, cannot show smoothly shaded regions or scanned images. Region filling is usually simulated by **cross hatching** with different line patterns, as suggested in Figure 1.37. Today raster displays have largely replaced vector displays except in very specialized applications.

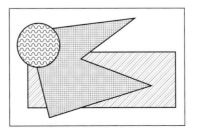

FIGURE 1.37 Cross hatching to simulate filling a region.

1.4.2 Raster Displays

Most displays used today for computer graphics are raster displays. The most familiar is the **video monitor** connected to a personal computer or workstation (see Figure 1.38). Other common examples produce **hard** copy (usually on paper) of an image: the **laser printer, dot matrix printer, inkjet plotter**, and **film recorder**. We describe the most important of these below.

a)

b)

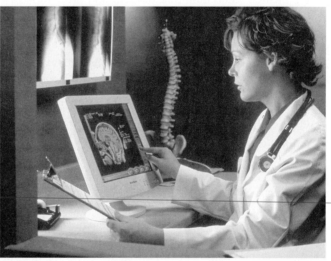

FIGURE 1.38 a) A video monitor on a PC, b) flat screen displaying x-rays.

Raster devices have a **display surface** on which the image is presented. The surface is organized as a certain #, say 480, of rows and a certain #, say 640, of columns. This display surface can show $480 \times 640 \approx 307{,}200$ pixels simultaneously. Such displays have a built-in coordinate system that associates a given pixel in an image with a given physical position on the display surface. Figure 1.39 shows an example. Here the horizontal coordinate sx increases from left to right, and the vertical coordinate sy increases from top to bottom. This upside-down coordinate system is common in raster devices.

FIGURE 1.39 The built-in coordinate system for the surface of a raster display.

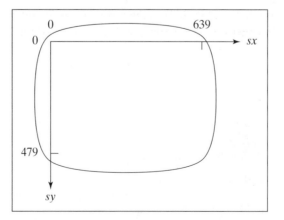

Raster displays are always connected one way or another to a **frame buffer**, a region of memory sufficiently large to hold all of the pixel values for the display (i.e., to hold the bitmap). The frame buffer may be physical memory on-board the display, or it may reside in the host computer. Alternatively, a graphics card installed in a personal computer might house the memory required for the frame buffer.

Figure 1.40 suggests how an image is created and displayed. The graphics program is stored in system memory and is executed instruction by instruction by the central processing unit (CPU). The program computes an appropriate value for each pixel and loads it into the frame buffer. (This is the part we focus on later when it comes to programming the application: computing correct pixel values and writing them into the frame buffer.)

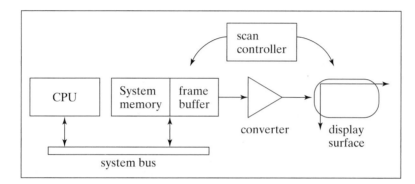

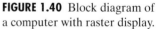

FIGURE 1.40 Block diagram of a computer with raster display.

A **scan controller** takes care of the actual display process. It runs autonomously (rather than under program control) and does the same thing pixel after pixel. It causes the frame buffer to send each pixel through a converter to the appropriate physical locations on the display surface. The converter takes a pixel value such as 01001011 and converts it to the corresponding color-value quantity that produces a spot of color on the display.

The Scanning Process

Figure 1.41 provides more detail on the scanning process. The main issue is how each pixel value in the frame buffer is sent to the correct physical location on the display surface. Each pixel in the frame buffer is, of course, stored at some memory location and corresponds to some position on the display. Suppose we say that the pixel value that corresponds to the (x, y) location $(136, 252)$ on the screen is stored at frame buffer location mem[136][252].

When the scan controller sends this address $(136, 252)$ to the frame buffer, it emits the value mem[136][252]. The controller also simultaneously addresses position $(136, 252)$ on the display surface.

The value mem[136][252] is converted to a corresponding color in the conversion circuit, and the color is sent to the proper position $(136, 252)$ on the display surface.

To scan out the image in the entire frame buffer, every pixel value is visited once, and its corresponding spot on the display surface is excited with the proper intensity or color.

In some devices this scanning must be repeated many times per second, in order to refresh the picture on the monitor. The video monitor to be described next does much of the work.

With these generalities laid down, we look briefly at some specific raster devices and see the different types that arise.

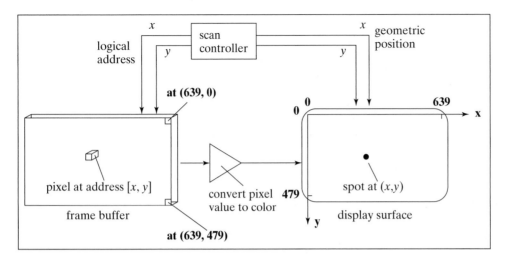

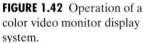

FIGURE 1.41 Scanning out an image from the frame buffer to the display surface.

Video Monitors

Many video monitors are based on a **CRT**, or cathode-ray tube, similar to the display in a television set. Figure 1.42 adds some details to the preceding general description for a system using a video monitor as the display device. In particular, the conversion process from pixel value to spot of light is illustrated. The system shown has a color depth of 6 bits; the frame buffer is shown as having 6 bit planes. Each pixel uses 1 bit from each of the planes.

FIGURE 1.42 Operation of a color video monitor display system.

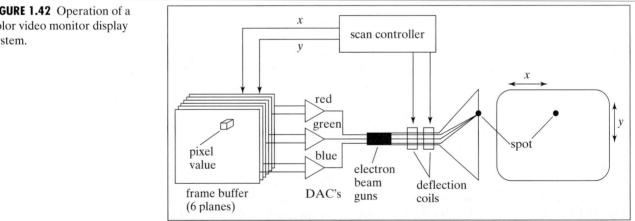

The red, green, and blue components of a pixel each use a pair of bits. These pairs are fed to three **digital-to-analog converters** (DACs), which convert logical values like 01 into actual voltages. The correspondence between digital input values and output voltages is shown in Figure 1.43, where Max is the largest voltage level the DAC can produce.

The three voltage levels drive three electron guns inside the CRT, which in turn excite three electron beams with intensities proportional to the voltages. The deflection coils divert the three beams so they stimulate three tiny phosphor dots at the proper place (x, y) on the inside of the cathode-ray tube. Because of the phosphor materials used, one dot glows red when stimulated, one glows green, and one glows blue. The dots are so close together that your eye sees one composite dot, perceiving a color that is the sum of the three component colors.

Input	Voltage/Brightness
00	0 * Max
01	0.333 * Max
10	0.666 * Max
11	1 * Max

FIGURE 1.43 Input-output characteristic of a 2-bit DAC.

Thus the composite dot can be made to glow in a total of $4 \times 4 \times 4 = 64$ different colors.

As described earlier, the scan controller addresses one pixel value mem[x][y] in the frame buffer at the same time it addresses one position (x, y) on the face of the CRT by sending the proper signal to the deflection coils. Because the glow of a phosphor dot quickly fades when the stimulation is removed, a CRT image must be **refreshed** frequently (typically 60 times a second) to prevent disturbing flicker. During each refresh interval the scan controller scans quickly through the entire frame buffer memory, sending each pixel value to its proper spot on the screen's surface.

Scanning proceeds row by row through the frame buffer, and each row provides pixel values for one **scanline** across the face of the CRT. The order of scanning is usually left to right along a **scanline** and from top to bottom by scanline. Historians say this convention has given rise to terms like scanline, as well as the habit of numbering scanlines downward with 0 at the top, resulting in upside-down coordinate systems.

Most modern systems have 24- or 32-bit displays. These were once much more expensive than those having only a few bits per color, but today they are so much more reasonable in cost it is hard to find the older kinds. With a 24-bit display each pixel can be given $2^{24} = 16,777,216$ different colors; with a 32-bit display each pixel can be given $2^{32} = 2$ billion or so colors (although 8 bits are often devoted to transparency, as we shall see subsequently.)

At the other extreme, **monochrome** video displays display a single color but at different intensities. A single DAC converts pixel values in the frame buffer to voltage levels, which drive a single electron beam gun. The CRT has only one type of phosphor, so it can produce various intensities of only one color. Note that six planes of memory in the frame buffer gives $2^6 = 64$ levels of gray.

A color display has a *fixed* (non-programmable) association with a displayed color. For instance, the pixel value 001101 sends 00 to the "red DAC," 11 to the "green DAC," and 01 to the "blue DAC," producing a mix of bright green and dark blue—a bluish-green. (See Chapter 11 on color.) Similarly, 110011 is displayed as a bright magenta, and 000010 as a medium bright blue.

Chapter 11 discusses an alternative that permits a programmable association of frame buffer values and color—the color look-up table, or LUT.

1.4.3 Video Cards/3D Accelerators

As we shall see throughout this book, there are many OpenGL commands for drawing certain shapes such as lines, circles, and rectangles. When such a command is executed, OpenGL must send a great deal of pixel data from the CPU (where the application is executing) to the monitor. This transfer of data, of course, requires some time, which, although short, can have a noticeable effect when rapid animations are desired, or when a game is being played that requires real-time computer–player interaction. Over the years, as graphics imagery has become ever more complex, it has become substantially more challenging to transfer the huge amount of data involved with each image to the monitor rapidly enough so that animations run smoothly and with sufficiently short response times.

FIGURE 1.44 A video card from ATI Technologies. (A color version is available in Plate 5). (Courtesy of ATI)

Because the two devices are not in exactly the same place, the data must travel over wires from the source to the destination. The data path, a collection of wires together with a great deal of digital logic to control the transfer, has come to be called the **bus**. Some buses are more responsive than others, and it has been an ongoing struggle to ensure that one's own bus is fast enough. (The faster the bus, the higher the cost, and the better the performance.)

Another important development is the **graphics card** or **3d graphics accelerator**. This hardware has special circuitry designed to respond very rapidly to requests for data transfer from the CPU to the display. Graphics cards are more expensive than older 'display adapters'; today's accelerators contain large amounts of on-board memory and specially crafted bus logic that speeds data transfers. (At the lowest level a transfer of data is not simply controlled by the switching of a few logic gates; a complex series of timing checks and data tests of the current bus activity must be completed before the data is 'posted' on the bus.)

Whenever an image is being formed, the geometric data that define the scene must pass through a large number of processing steps. OpenGL simply specifies the nature of these steps and the order in which they must occur. These steps are referred to as the **graphics pipeline**, which we discuss at various points throughout the book.

The stakes are high in this industry, and the strong competition between vendors has forced very rapid developments in ever-faster graphics accelerators. Inevitably the presence of a number of different possible graphics accelerators has led to the need for **standards**, so that each potential customer knows how the accelerator he/she buys will truly perform. We mention some of these standards next, but keep in mind that this is a rapidly changing field with evolving standards.

Table 1.1 lists three generations of video cards and their capabilities. Started in 1989, VESA (Video Electronic Standards Association) is an industrywide consortium monitoring display and video standards. The table provides model names and manufacturer for each standard accelerator, along with the display resolution supported, the number of colors per pixel that can be displayed, and the refresh rate (how often the entire displayed image can be rewritten). From this it is not difficult to estimate the data rate from the CPU to the display. For instance, for a VESA super VGA graphics accelerator which supports 256 colors (therefore indicating 8 bits per pixel), every 60 times per second $60 \times 1600 \times 1200 \times 8 = 921,600,000$ bits of data per second must be sent to the display!

To learn more about video cards and the trends in bus speed, use a search engine of your choice. The book's companion web site lists a number of resources.

By way of contrast, digitizing music is much simpler. High-quality music that is recorded on CD-ROMs requires a transmission rate of only 705,600 bits per second! (The bits-per-second value is based on a sampling rate of 44,100 samples per second, each sample being represented by 16 bits.)

Nonprogrammable vs. Programmable Hardware

Early graphics chips and cards had fixed-function graphics pipelines. In 1999 NVIDIA released the GeForce 256, the first video card that was programmable. Programmability allowed developers to dictate what they wanted these powerful **GPUs** to do—the actual algorithms applied to data could be programmed. With these enhancements developers are able to increase the level of realism by fashioning their own vertex and pixel programs (or shaders); as discussed in Chapter 8, they can perform per-pixel and per-vertex operations. For example, lighting, fur, and glass effects were achievable.

As graphics cards support more instructions and the developers write more complex shaders, it is no longer practical to write the shaders in a low-level assembly language. This led to the development of a series of high-level shading languages such as Cg and OpenGL 2.0's Shading Language. Cg is a language like C/C++, which, although not as efficient as assembler, allows rapid development, readable and maintainable code, and is much more platform independent than assembler.

TABLE 1.1 Some major graphics accelerators and characteristics.

Year		Model	By	Max Pixels	Colors Supported	Refresh Rate
1981	MDA	Mono Display Adapter	IBM	720×350	2	50 Hz
1990	SVGA	Super VGA	VESA	1600×1200	256	60 Hz
1997	AGP	Accelerated Graphics Port	Intel	2048×1536	16.7 million	100 Hz

A much more thorough treatment of GPUs can be found in GPU Gems series [Gems05] as well as the book's companion website.

1.4.4 Other Raster Display Devices

Video monitors are not the only raster display devices: a variety of other kinds have recently been developed. Portable laptop computers often have **flat panel** displays, as suggested in Figure 1.45. Each pixel is addressed by a horizontal grid wire and a vertical grid wire: to turn a pixel on, the corresponding horizontal and vertical grid wires are excited, producing an electric field at the pixel location. This has the effect of causing that spot to change its brightness.

FIGURE 1.45 Flat panel displays.

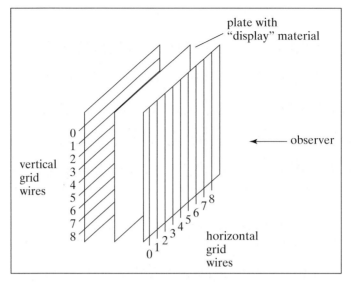

The exact mechanism of converting the electric field to a visible dot depends on the technology used. In the case of a **liquid crystal display** (LCD) the electric field alters the polarization of long crystalline molecules in the LCD material. This either allows light to pass through the panel or prevents it from passing through. **Active matrix panels** are LCD panels that have a tiny transistor at each pixel location. The transistor responds to the electric field and adjusts the liquid crystals by an amount proportional to the field, thus allowing the display of different levels of brightness. In addition, the transistors provide some memory that holds the crystals in their adjusted state, so that the display need not be refreshed. This produces a much brighter display. Color LCD panels are available that have resolutions of 800 by 1000 pixels.

The **plasma panel** display has geometry similar to that in Figure 1.45, but the material in the plate effectively places a tiny neon bulb at each pixel location. This bulb is turned on or off by the electric field, and like the active matrix display it need not be refreshed.

Several other kinds of raster displays are discussed in the references [e.g., Foley90, APeer85].

1.4.5 Hard Copy Raster Devices

One frequently wants a permanent version of an image, usually in paper form or on film. A number of raster devices produce hard copy of a raster image. Each draws pictures by transferring frame buffer information dot by dot to the display medium.

- *Laser printer* **Laser printers** also scan out raster patterns from an internal frame buffer, rapidly sweeping a laser beam over an internal drawing surface. At certain spots over which the laser beam is swept, the surface becomes electrically charged, causing toner powder to adhere to the spots. The toner is then transferred to the paper to create the picture. Laser printers offer much higher resolution than do inkjet and dot matrix printers, capitalizing on the great precision with which a laser beam can be positioned.

Figure 1.46a shows text and graphics produced on a **dot matrix printer** (the earliest type of mass-produced high-speed printer), and Figure 1.46b shows output from a laser printer. Dot matrix printers place dots at a density of only 70 or so dots per inch (dpi). Today one might find a dot matrix printer used to print receipts at a point of sale, such as a restaurant or office supply store. Laser printers, on the other hand, can produce densities of 600 or more dots per inch, and so can produce very high-quality graphics.

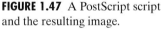

a)
```
displayed.
at we needn
to exclude
version tak
implificati
```

b)
```
esident campus
programs to t
e course to ea
ard a degree la
tes. This flexib
```

FIGURE 1.46 Blow-ups of dot matrix and laser printer images.

Even higher densities can be achieved by printers used in the publishing industry, such as the Linotronic typesetter, which prints at 2540 dots per inch. This book was printed on such a device.

Many printers today are equipped with an internal microprocessor that is programmed to interpret PostScript. PostScript[4] is a **page description language** that can generate high-quality text and graphics on a printed page. Figure 1.47a shows a brief script written in PostScript. When the file containing this script is printed, the on-board PostScript interpreter creates the picture shown in Figure 1.47b.

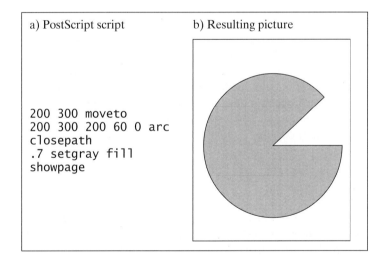

a) PostScript script

```
200 300 moveto
200 300 200 60 0 arc
closepath
.7 setgray fill
showpage
```

b) Resulting picture

FIGURE 1.47 A PostScript script and the resulting image.

- *Inkjet plotter.* **Inkjet plotters** produce hard copy raster images in color. A tiny nozzle sweeps over the paper and squirts the proper ink at each pixel position.
- *Film recorders.* In a **film recorder** the screen is a strip of photographic film, and the electron beam exposes the film as it sweeps over it (once) in a raster pattern. Sometimes film recorders are separate devices with their own frame buffers, and sometimes they are simply cameras mounted directly on a CRT display. Film recorders are frequently used to make high-quality 35-mm slides, or movies. Also, video tape recorders are available that make an electronic hard copy of the image stored in the frame buffer, to be played back on a television set.

[4] PostScript is a trademark of Adobe Systems, Inc.

1.5   GRAPHICS INPUT PRIMITIVES AND DEVICES

Many input devices are available that let the user control a computer. Whereas typing a command might be awkward, it is natural to point to a particular object displayed on the screen to make a choice for the next action.

You can look at an input device in two ways: **physically** what it *is*, and **logically** what it *does*. Each device is physically some piece of machinery like a mouse, keyboard, or trackball. It fits in the hand in a certain way and is natural for the user to manipulate. It measures these manipulations and sends corresponding numerical information back to the graphics program.

We first look at what input devices do, by examining the kinds of data each sends to the program. We then look at a number of input devices in common use today.

1.5.1   Types of Logical Input Graphics Primitives

Each device transmits a particular kind of data (e.g., a number, a string of characters, or a position) to the program. The different types of data are called **input primitives**.

The important logical input primitives are:

String   The **string** device is the most familiar, producing a **string of characters** and thus modeling the action of a keyboard. When an application requests a string, the program pauses while the user types it in, followed by a termination character. The program then resumes with the string stored in memory.

Valuator   A **valuator** produces a real value between 0.0 and 1.0, which can be used to fix the length of a line, the speed of an action, or perhaps the size of a picture. The model in the programmer's mind is a knob that can be turned from 0 to 1 in smooth gradations.

Locator   A basic requirement in interactive graphics is to enable the user to point to a position on the display. The **locator** input device performs this function, because it produces a **coordinate pair** (x, y). The user manipulates an input device (usually a mouse) in order to position a visible cursor to some spot and then triggers the choice. This returns to the application the values of x and y, along with the trigger value.

The graphics workstation is initialized when an application starts running. Among other things, each logical input function is associated with one of the installed physical devices.

Pick   The **pick** input device is used to identify a portion of a picture for further processing. Some graphics packages allow a picture to be defined in terms of **segments**, which are groups of related graphics primitives. For instance, in a restaurant a customer frequently sees the waitstaff pressing different portions of screen in order to identify food orders to the kitchen. Figure 1.48a shows an example of a restaurant's point-of-sale (POS) system. Functions within the POS system search the screen in order to determine which food item (entrees, appetizers, salads, desserts, beverages, etc) associated with the region pressed by the waitstaff. Notice that the POS system in Figure 1.48a doesn't show physical input devices other than the screen itself. This **touch screen** (shown in Figure 1.48b) of the POS system defines segments and gives the user identifying names to expedite the ordering process.

When using pick(), the user points to a part of a picture with some physical input device, and the package figures out which segment is being pointed to. pick() returns the name of the segment to the application, enabling the user to erase, move, or otherwise manipulate the segment.

b)

a)

1.5.2 Types of Physical Input Devices

We look at the other side of input devices: the physical machine that is connected to the personal computer or workstation.

Keyboard All workstations are equipped with a keyboard, which sends strings of characters to the application upon request. Hence a keyboard is usually used to produce a `string` logical device. Some keyboards have cursor keys or function keys, which are often used to produce `pick` input primitives.

Buttons Sometimes a separate bank of buttons is installed on a workstation. The user presses one of the buttons to perform a `pick` input function.

Mouse The **mouse** is perhaps the most familiar input device of all, as it is easy and comfortable to operate. As the user slides the mouse over the desktop, the mouse sends the changes in its position to the workstation. Software within the workstation keeps track of the mouse's position and moves a **graphics cursor**—a small arrow dot or cross—on the screen accordingly. The mouse is most often used to perform a `locate` function. There are usually some buttons on the mouse that the user can press to trigger the action.

Tablet Like a mouse, a tablet is used to generate `locate` input primitives. A **tablet**, as shown in Figure 1.49, provides an area on which the user can slide a stylus. The tip of the stylus contains a micro switch. By pressing down on the stylus the user can trigger the logical function.

The tablet is particularly handy for digitizing drawings: the user can tape a picture onto the tablet surface and then move the stylus over it, pressing down to send each new point to the workstation. A menu area is sometimes printed on the tablet surface, and the user selects a menu item by pressing down the stylus inside one of the menu-item boxes. Suitable software associates each menu-item box with the desired function for the application that is running. A familiar but much more compact device similar to a tablet is the **PDA** (Personal Digital Assistant), which is operated using a stylus to select specific portions of the display.

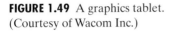

FIGURE 1.49 A graphics tablet. (Courtesy of Wacom Inc.)

Joystick and Trackball

Figure 1.50 shows three similar input devices that control the position of a cursor on the display. The arcade-style **joystick** in part a has a lever that can be pivoted in any direction to indicate position. The **trackball** in part b has a large ball that can be rotated in any direction with the palm of the hand to alter the cursor position. For each of these devices, internal circuitry converts physical motion into electrical signals, just as in the mouse. These devices are used primarily as `locator` and `valuator` devices.

a)

b)

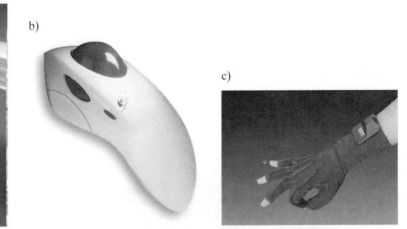

c)

FIGURE 1.50 a) A joystick, b) a trackball c) data glove (Courtesy of 5DT)

Data Glove

The **data glove** pictured in Figure 1.50c is a relatively new input device. It is designed to give a user explicit control over several variables at once, by performing natural hand and finger motions. Sensors inside the data glove pickup subtle hand motions and translate them into *valuator* values that are passed back to the application. This device is particularly suited to situations in which the hand movements themselves make sense in the context of the program (such as when the user is controlling a virtual robot hand).

Digitizing 3D Objects and Capturing Motion

Figure 1.51a shows a device that can measure the locations of points in space, allowing the capture of three-dimensional shapes. As the laser beam scans over the solid object in an *x, y* raster pattern, the distance between the image capture device and the object is stored. Figure 1.51b shows the resulting image for digitizing the human form.

a)   b)

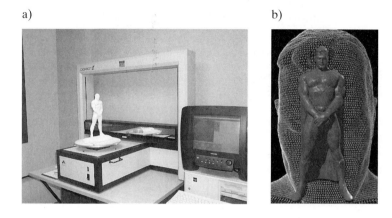

FIGURE 1.51 Digitizing a 3D shape. (Courtesy of Nvision)

Figure 1.52 shows a similar device that can track the position of many points on a moving body in real-time. This allows capture of the detailed motions of a dancer for use in animations or data analysis. Other devices have been used in the past, such as the light pen, thumbwheels, paddles, and so on. (Complete descriptions of these can be found in books such as [Foley93] and [Rogers98].)

FIGURE 1.52 Capturing a dancer's motion. (Courtesy of Ascension-Tech)

1.6 CHAPTER SUMMARY

In this chapter we introduced the field of computer graphics and showed the variety of places it is used today in the creation of pictures. We described many kinds of drawing devices, the most widely used of which are the raster video display and the ink and laser printers. We also defined the major **output primitives**—polylines, text, filled regions, and raster images—and described the attributes normally associated with each. Because of the importance in computer graphics of shaded images as a vehicle for pictures within display devices, an emphasis was placed on the raster image; such images will be discussed throughout the book. The key property of a raster image is that it consists of a collection of numbers, and each number can take on only a fixed set of values, making it discrete in two spatial dimensions as well as in the color/brightness dimension. Of equal importance is the natural association of pixel values with memory locations in a computer, which we shall exploit many times throughout the book.

We described various kinds of graphical input devices used for interactive computer graphics and discussed the **input primitives** which they normally produce.

1.7 CHAPTER EXERCISES

1.1   Name five types of logical input devices (string, and so on), and for each name a physical input device (such as keyboard) that can be used to provide the corresponding logical input data.

1.2   Name the major parts of a computer graphics system and briefly describe the function of each.

1.3   How many bits per second must be delivered to a graphics display that is refreshed 60 times per second, when the display has a resolution of 600×800 pixels, and each pixel can be displayed in one of 65,000 colors?

1.8 FOR FURTHER READING

A number of books provide a good introduction to the field of computer graphics. Hearn and Baker [Hearn04] gives a leisurely and interesting overview of the field with lots of examples. Foley and Van Dam [Foley93] and David Rogers [Rogers98] give additional technical detail on the many kinds of graphics input and output devices. An excellent series of books known as "Graphics Gems" [Gems], first published in 1990, brought together many new ideas and "gems" from graphics researchers and practitioners around the world.

There are also a number of journals and magazines that give good insight into new techniques in computer graphics. The most accessible is the *IEEE Computer Graphics and Applications*, which often features survey articles on new areas of effort with graphics. The classic repositories of new results in graphics are the annual *Proceedings of SIGGRAPH* [SIGGRAPH], and the *ACM Transactions on Graphics* [TOGS].

Chapter 2

....

Initial Steps in Drawing Figures

Machines exist; let us then exploit them to create beauty, a modern beauty, while we are about it.
For we live in the twenty-first century.

Aldous Huxley
(1894–1963)

GOALS OF THE CHAPTER

○ To get started writing programs to produce pictures.

○ To learn the basic ingredients found in every OpenGL program.

○ To develop some elementary graphics tools for drawing lines, polylines, and polygons.

○ To develop tools that allow the user to control a program with the mouse and keyboard.

Preview

Section 2.1 discusses the basics of writing a program to make simple drawings. The importance of device-independent programming is discussed, and the basics of windows-based and event-driven programs are described. Section 2.2 introduces the use of OpenGL as the device-independent application programmer interface (API) to be used throughout the book, and shows how to draw various graphics primitives. Example drawings such as a picture of the Big Dipper, the Sierpinski gasket, and plots of mathematical functions illustrate the use of OpenGL. Section 2.3 discusses how to make pictures based on polylines and polygons, and begins the building of a personal library of graphics utilities. Section 2.4 describes interactive graphics programming, whereby the user can indicate positions on the screen with the mouse, or press keyboard keys in order to control the action of a program. The chapter ends with a number of Case Studies, which embellish ideas discussed earlier in the form of design projects you will feel are beneficial to implement, and which delve deeper into the main ideas of the chapter.

2.1 TO GET STARTED MAKING PICTURES

"What is the use of a book," thought Alice, "without pictures or conversations?"

Alice in Wonderland
Lewis Carrol
(1832–1898)

Like many disciplines, computer graphics is mastered most quickly by doing it—by writing and testing programs that produce a variety of pictures. It is best to start with simple tasks. Once these are mastered, you can try variations, see what happens, and move toward drawing more complex scenes.

Note: As promised in the Preface, there is a complete listing in the book for every program discussed in any depth. The good news is that this code need only be copied and pasted in, and the program will compile and link to the appropriate OpenGL libraries. The bad news is that you, the reader, will be greatly tempted to let your eyes scan over the code to see what's there. (The same is true of equations and mathematical formulas in math books.) You are strongly urged to resist this temptation, since a quick perusal of code or an equation does you no good at all. The best course is to track through every such line of code or formula, thoroughly and carefully. When you do so, each new idea has the best chance of being understood. It's hard to do this when you are tired. OK.

To get started you need an environment that lets you write and execute programs. For graphics this environment must also include hardware to display pictures (usually a CRT or LCD display, which we shall call 'the screen'), and a library of software tools that your programs can use to perform the actual drawing of graphics primitives.

Every graphics program begins with some initializations; these establish the desired display mode and set up a coordinate system for specifying points, lines, and so on. Figure 2.1 shows some of the different variations one might encounter. In part a the entire screen is used for drawing: the display is initialized by switching it into graphics mode, and the coordinate system is established as shown. Coordinates x and y are measured in pixels, with x increasing to the right and y increasing downward.

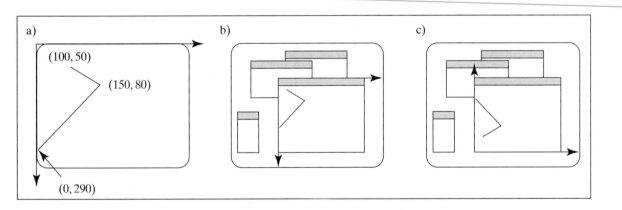

FIGURE 2.1 Some common varieties of display layouts.

In part b a more modern window-based system is shown. It can support a number of different rectangular *windows* on the display screen at one time. Initialization involves creating and opening an initial window which we shall call the **screen window**[1] for graphics. If desired, later commands are used to create other windows. Graphics commands use a coordinate system that is attached to the window: usually x increases to the right and y increases downward. Part c shows a variation where the initial coordinate system is right side up, with y increasing upward.

---

[1]   The word "window" is vastly overused in graphics. We shall take care to distinguish the various instances of the term.

Each system normally has some elementary drawing tools that help to get you started. The most basic has a name like setPixel(x, y, color): it sets the individual pixel at location (x, y) to the color specified by color. It sometimes goes by different names, such as putPixel(), SetPixel(), or drawPoint(). Along with setPixel() there is almost always a tool to draw a straight line, such as line(x1, y1, x2, y2), which draws a line between (x_1, y_1) and (x_2, y_2). In other systems it might be called drawLine() or Line(). The commands

```
line(100, 50, 150, 80);
line(150, 80, 0, 290);
```

would draw the pictures shown in each system in Figure 2.1. Practically every system has a line() command or something very similar.

Alternatively, some programmers find a slight variation of a line function very convenient. We introduce the two relevant functions here, but keep in mind that these are not essential; but they give a deeper understanding of the most basic graphics operations. They are based on the notion of a **current position** (cp), which stems from the analogy of a pen plotter. The current position reports the location of the pen at the present time. The first function, moveTo(x,y), moves the pen invisibly to the desired location (x, y) and then updates the current position to this position. The second function, lineTo(x,y), draws a straight line from the current position to (x, y) and finally updates the cp to (x, y). Each command moves the pen from its current position to a new position, one visibly, one invisibly. The new position then becomes the cp. The pictures in Figure 2.1 would be drawn using the commands

```
moveTo(100, 50);
lineTo(150, 80);
lineTo(0, 290);
```

As a further example, shown in Figure 2.2, suppose we wish to draw a square 6 units on a side with its center at location $(1, 1)$. The square is shown **aligned**—by which we mean each side is parallel to one of the axes. (We shall have frequent occasion to use the term *aligned* all through the book.) Drawing the square is easy: simply move the pen to one of the corners with a moveTo operation, and then have the pen draw out the square by tracing around the square and back to the beginning using lineTo.

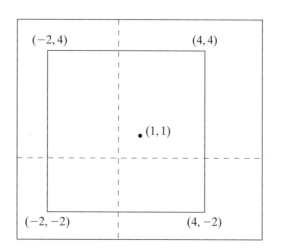

FIGURE 2.2 A square to be drawn using moveTo and lineTo commands.

Pseudocode for drawing this square might look like:

```
moveTo(4, 4);              //move to starting corner
lineTo(-2, 4);
lineTo(-2, -2);
lineTo(4, -2);
lineTo(4, 4);              //close the square
```

For a particular system, the energetic programmer can develop a whole toolkit of sophisticated functions that utilize these elementary tools, thereby building up a powerful library of graphics routines. Any number of graphics applications are then written making use of this personal library.

An obvious problem is that each graphics display uses different basic commands to drive it, and every environment has a different collection of tools for producing the graphics primitives. This could make it difficult to **port** a program from one environment to another—and hard to believe but true—sooner or later *every* programmer is faced with porting a program to a new environment. The programmer must build the necessary tools on top of the new environment's library. This may require major alterations in the overall structure of a library or application, and significant effort from the programmer.

2.1.1 Device-Independent Programming and OpenGL

It is a boon when a uniform approach to writing graphics applications is made available, such that the *same* code can be compiled and run on a variety of graphics environments, with the guarantee that it will produce nearly identical graphical output on each display, once recompiled. This is known as **device-independent** graphics programming. OpenGL offers such a tool. Porting a graphics program requires only that you install the appropriate OpenGL libraries on the new machine. The application itself requires no change: it calls the same functions in this library with the same parameters, and the same graphical results are produced. The OpenGL way of creating graphics has been adopted by a large number of industrial companies, and OpenGL libraries exist for all of the important graphics environments.[2] You may have already realized that OpenGL is an *open source graphics library*; that is, the entire program listings that go to make up the OpenGL libraries are freely available for downloading over the Internet (web site: http://www.opengl.org). This is in stark contrast to some other graphics libraries, which one must pay a fee to obtain, or which work in a somewhat restricted fashion.

OpenGL is often called an "application programming interface" (API). The interface is a collection of routines that the programmer can call, along with a model of how the routines work together to produce graphics. The programmer sees only the interface, and is therefore shielded from having to cope with the specific hardware or software idiosyncrasies on the resident graphics system.

OpenGL is at its most powerful when drawing images of complex three-dimensional (3D) scenes, as we shall see. It might be viewed as overkill for simple drawings of 2D objects. But it works well for 2D drawing, too, and affords a *unified* approach to producing pictures. We start by using the simpler constructs in OpenGL, capitalizing for simplicity on the many default states it provides. Later, when we write programs to produce elaborate 3D graphics, we tap into OpenGL's more powerful features.

Although we will develop most of our graphics tools using the power of OpenGL, we will also examine how the classical graphics algorithms work inside OpenGL. It is

---

[2]   Appendix 1 discusses how to obtain and get started with OpenGL in different environments.

important to see how such tools might be implemented, even if for most applications you use the ready-made OpenGL versions. In special circumstances you may wish to use an alternative algorithm for some task, or you may encounter a new problem that OpenGL does not solve. (Throughout the book we shall point out the few situations in which OpenGL fails to give the desired effect.)

2.1.2 Window-Based Programming

As described above, many modern graphics systems are *windows-based* and manage the display of multiple overlapping *windows*. The user can move the windows around the screen using the mouse, and can resize them. Using OpenGL, we will do our drawing in a window similar to that of Figure 2.1c.

Event-Driven Programming

Another property of most windows-based programs is that they are *event driven*. This means that the program responds to various events, such as a mouse click, the press of a keyboard key, or the resizing of the screen window. The system automatically manages an *event queue*, which receives messages that certain events have occurred and deals with them on a first-come, first-served basis. The programmer organizes a program as a collection of **callback functions** that are executed when events occur. When the callback function has finished executing, the application resumes where it left off when the event occurred. We will see examples of this in subsequent sections. The programmer must write code for *what* should happen inside each callback function, of course, but need not write instructions for *when* each callback function is to be called; this is automatically handled by the system. This is a significant advantage for the writer of the program as well as for any reader of the code.

A callback function is created for each *type* of event that might occur. Only a small number of event types exist. Throughout the book most of the callback functions are named and defined for you, but in your programs you may name and define them anyway you wish. When the system removes an event from the queue, it simply executes the callback function associated with the type of that event. For programmers accustomed to building programs with a "do this, and then do this..." structure, some rethinking is required. The new structure is more like: "do nothing until an event occurs, then do the specified thing." This kind of structure suggests an **event loop**, wherein the system waits patiently in a repeating loop until it receives an event trigger.

The method of associating a callback function with an event type is often quite system dependent. But OpenGL offers a number of supporting libraries as described next, which provide tools to assist with event management and a variety of other functions. One of these is the **GLUT** library, "the GL Utility Toolkit," which is used in connection with opening windows, managing menus and events, and so on.

Registering Callback Functions

There must be a way for the programmer to associate each type of event with the desired callback function. This is called **registering** the callback function. Each event type that is used in the application must be registered with a callback function, which has a name and definition of the programmer's choosing. For example, the way to use the GLUT to register the callback function named myMouse with a mouse event is simply:

```
glutMouseFunc(myMouse);
/* the name "myMouse" is chosen by the programmer &
"glutMouseFunc" is a name inherent to GLUT*/
```

This notifies the program that when a mouse button is depressed or clicked "glutMouseFunc" (including the capitalization) is fixed by the Glut library, but the name "my Mouse" can be chosen at the programmer's whim (the **type** of event), the callback function myMouse(), which must be written by the programmer, is to be called by the system. The programmer writes code for myMouse() to handle each of the possible mouse actions of interest. If an application does not use mouse interaction, there is no need to write glutMouseFunc() or to register it.

As an aid to the programmer, there are actually **three** libraries of utility functions available for use in developing and running applications. Each library provides welcome support to save the programmer effort. We introduce each one here briefly and elaborate on it subsequently. Here is a list of common libraries you may want to use in an OpenGL application.

The Three Main OpenGL Libraries of Interest

1. Basic **GL**: The fundamental OpenGL library. It provides functions that are a permanent part of OpenGL. As we shall see, each OpenGL function starts with the characters "GL".
2. **GLUT**, the GL Utility Toolkit, as we have discussed in connection with opening windows, developing and managing menus, and managing events. We address GLUT Menus in Section 2.5.

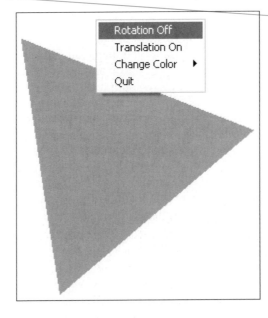

FIGURE 2.3 An example of a GLUT menu. (Courtesy of P. Rademacher)

3. **GLU**, the GL Utility Library, which provides high-level routines to handle certain matrix operations, the drawing of quadric surfaces such as spheres and cylinders (see Chapter 6). GLU also assists in the decomposition of nonconvex and nonsimple polygons (which OpenGL does not handle well) into simple shapes such as triangles, and other utilities to simplify the job of the application programmer.

Details of all these tasks will be given later and many can be found on the Internet and in the additional readings [Woo04].

4. **GLUI**, the User Interface Library, as long as GLUT is available, GLUI will operate properly. The GLUI provides programmers with the ability to add sophisticated controls and menus to their OpenGL applications. Section 2.5 covers GLUI menus and describes the available controls.

Figure 2.4 shows pseudocode for registering the essential types of callback functions for event types, basically a skeleton of a main() function for an event-driven program. We will base most of our programs in this book on this skeleton or variations of it. There are five principal types of events we will work with, and a GLUT function is available for each:

```
// include OpenGL libraries (as in Figure 2.11)
void main()
{
glutDisplayFunc(myDisplay);     // register the redraw function
glutReshapeFunc(myReshape);     // register the reshape function
glutMouseFunc(myMouse);         // register the mouse action
                                          function
  glutMotionFunc(myMotionFunc); // register the mouse motion
                                          function
  glutKeyboardFunc(myKeyboard); // register the keyboard action
                                          function
  ...perhaps initialize other things...
  glutMainLoop();                 // enter the unending main loop
}
...all of the callback functions are defined here
```

FIGURE 2.4 A skeleton of an event-driven program using OpenGL and GLUT.

- glutDisplayFunc(myDisplay); Whenever the system determines that a screen window should be redrawn it issues a redraw event. This occurs when the window is first opened, and when the window is exposed by moving another window off of it. Here the function myDisplay() is registered as the callback function for a redraw event.

- glutReshapeFunc(myReshape); Screen windows can be reshaped by the user, usually by dragging a corner of the window to a new position with the mouse. (Simply moving the window does not produce a reshape event.) Here the function myReshape() is registered with the reshape event. As we shall see, myReshape() is automatically passed arguments that report the new width and height of the reshaped window.

- glutMouseFunc(myMouse); When one of the mouse buttons is pressed and released, a mouse event is issued. Here myMouse() is registered as the callback function when a mouse event occurs. myMouse() is automatically passed arguments that describe the mouse location and the nature of the button action.

- glutMotionFunc(myMotionFunc); This function generates an event when the mouse is moved with one or more mouse buttons pressed. Notice that the mouse button need not be released for the event to be generated, as we will see in examples below. glutPassiveMotionFunc(), on the other hand, generates an event when the mouse enters the window with *no* buttons pressed.

- glutKeyboardFunc(myKeyboard); This registers the function myKeyboard() with the event of pressing and releasing some key on the keyboard. myKeyboard() is automatically passed arguments that tell which key was pressed. Conveniently, this function also makes available to the system the *x*- and *y*-coordinates (relative to the screen window) of the mouse at the time a key was pressed.

The callback functions myMouse, myKeyboard, and so on are named at the discretion of the programmer as long as they are all different. Then mouse clicks have no effect in the program. The same is true for programs that have no keyboard interaction. The programmer should be aware that glutDisplayFunc() is not automatically called when using either the keyboard or mouse functions; the display function needs to be called explicitly from within the mouse or keyboard function. Alternatively, the function glutPostRedisplay() will refresh the window and may be called from any point in the program. You can see the glutPostRedisplay() function in action in the Rubber Rectangle example in Section 2.4.

The final function shown in Figure 2.4 is glutMainLoop(). When this is executed, the program draws the initial picture and enters an unending loop, in which it simply waits for events to occur. A program is normally terminated by clicking in the close window button, which in most cases is attached to the upper right corner of each window.

2.1.3 How to Open a Window for Drawing

The first task is to open a screen window for drawing. This can be quite involved and is system dependent. Because OpenGL functions are device independent, they provide no support for window control on specific systems. But the GLUT, introduced above, *does* include functions to open a window on any system you are using.

Figure 2.5 fleshes out the skeleton above to show the entire main() function for a program that will draw graphics in a screen window. The first five function calls use the toolkit to open a window for drawing with OpenGL. In your first graphics programs you can just copy these as is. The figure also shows what the various arguments mean and how to substitute others for them to achieve certain effects. The first five functions initialize and display the screen window in which our program will produce graphics. We give a brief description of what each one does.

```
// appropriate #includes go here - see Figure 2.11

void main(int argc, char** argv)
{
        glutInit(&argc, argv); // initialize the toolkit
        glutInitDisplayMode(GLUT_SINGLE | GLUT_RGB); // set the display mode
        glutInitWindowSize(640,480); // set window size
        glutInitWindowPosition(100, 150); // set the window position on screen
        glutCreateWindow("my first attempt"); // open the screen window

        // register the callback functions
        glutDisplayFunc(myDisplay);
        glutReshapeFunc(myReshape);
        glutMouseFunc(myMouse);
        glutKeyboardFunc(myKeyboard);

        myInit();                      // additional initializations as necessary
        glutMainLoop();                // go into a perpetual loop
}
```

FIGURE 2.5 Code to open the initial window for drawing using the OpenGL utility toolkit, GLUT.

- `glutInit(&argc, argv);` This function initializes the toolkit. Its arguments are the standard ones for passing command-line information; we will make no use of them here.
- `glutInitDisplayMode(GLUT_SINGLE | GLUT_RGB);` This function specifies how the display should be initialized. The built-in constants GLUT_SINGLE and GLUT_RGB, which are OR'd together, specify that a single display buffer should be allocated and that colors are specified using desired amounts of red, green, and blue. (A discussion of *double buffering*, which creates smooth animations, is given in Chapter 3.)
- `glutInitWindowSize(640,480);` This function specifies that the screen window should initially be 640 pixels wide by 480 pixels high. When the program is running, the user can resize this window as desired.
- `glutInitWindowPosition(100, 150);` This function specifies that the window's upper left corner should be positioned on the screen 100 pixels from the left edge and 150 pixels down from the top. When the program is running, the user can move this window wherever desired.
- `glutCreateWindow("my first attempt");` This function actually opens and displays the screen window, putting the title "my first attempt" in the title bar.

The remaining functions in `main()` register the callback functions as described earlier, perform any initializations specific to the program at hand, and start the main event loop processing.

2.2 THE OPENGL BASIC GRAPHICS PRIMITIVES

Everything vanishes around me, and works are born as if out of the void. Ripe, graphic fruits fall off. My hand has become the obedient instrument of a remote will.

Paul Klee
(1879–1940)

We want to develop programming techniques for drawing a large number of geometric shapes that make up interesting pictures. The drawing commands will be placed in the callback function associated with a redraw event, such as the `myDisplay()` function mentioned above.

We first must establish the coordinate system in which we will describe graphical objects and prescribe where they will appear in the screen window. Computer graphics programming, it seems, involves an ongoing struggle with defining and managing different coordinate systems. So we start simply and work up to more complex approaches.

We begin with an intuitive coordinate system. It is tied directly to the coordinate system of the screen window (see Figure 2.1c) and measures distances in pixels. Our first example screen window, shown in Figure 2.6, is 640 pixels wide by 480 pixels high. The

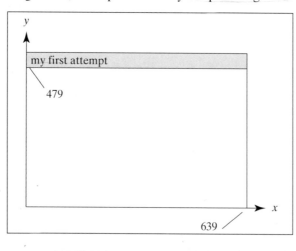

FIGURE 2.6 The initial coordinate system for drawing.

x-coordinate increases from 0 at the left edge to 639 at the right edge. The *y*-coordinate increases from 0 at the bottom edge to 479 at the top edge. We show how to establish this and other coordinate systems later, after examining some basic primitives.

OpenGL provides tools for drawing all of the output primitives described in Chapter 1. Most of them, such as points, lines, polylines, and polygons, are defined by one of more **vertices** (or corners). To draw such objects in OpenGL you pass it a list of vertices. The list occurs between the two OpenGL function calls glBegin() and glEnd(). The argument of glBegin() determines which object is to be drawn and instructs OpenGL to begin gathering primitive data that will be part of the object. The glEnd()command terminates the list of primitives to be in the object and sends all the data for the drawing down the **OpenGL graphics pipeline**.

For instance, Figure 2.7 shows three points drawn in a window 640 pixels wide and 480 pixels high (notice the ";" to terminate the statement). These dots are drawn using the command sequence:

```
glBegin(GL_POINTS);// draw individual points
   glVertex2i(100, 50);// the points
   glVertex2i(100, 130);
   glVertex2i(150, 130);
glEnd();
```

FIGURE 2.7 Drawing three dots.

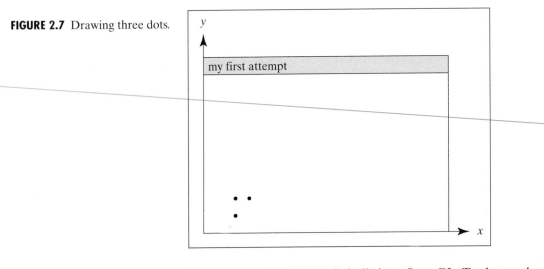

The constant GL_POINTS is built into OpenGL. To draw other primitives you re-place GL_POINTS with GL_LINES, GL_POLYGON, and so on. Each of these will be in-troduced in turn.

As we shall see, these commands send the vertex information down a **graphics pipeline**, in which they go through several processing steps. (See Chapter 5 for more detail.) Although the actual OpenGL pipeline can consist of a large number of steps, for present purposes just think of the pipeline as specifying the order of vari-ous operations to which primitives are subjected as they pass to the display.

Many functions in OpenGL, such as glVertex2i() or glColor3f(), have a num-ber of variations. The variations distinguish the number and type of arguments passed to the function. Figure 2.8 shows how the different function calls are formatted.

The prefix "gl" indicates a function from the basic OpenGL library (as op-posed to "glut" for the utility toolkit). It is followed by the basic command root (such as vertex and color), then by the number of arguments being sent to the function (this number will often be 3 and 4 in later contexts), and finally by the

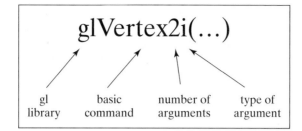

FIGURE 2.8 Format of OpenGL commands.

type of argument (i for a 32-bit integer, f for a floating-point value, and so on, as we describe later). Throughout the book, when we wish to refer to the basic command without regard to the specifics of its arguments, we will use an asterisk, as in glVertex*().

To generate the same three-dot picture above, for example, you could pass it floating-point values instead of integers, using:

```
glBegin(GL_POINTS);
  glVertex2f(100.0, 50.0);  // points specified by floats
  glVertex2f(100.0, 130.0);
  glVertex2f(150.0, 130.0);
glEnd();
```

The OpenGL DataTypes

OpenGL works *internally* with specific data types. For instance, functions such as glVertex2i() expect integers of a certain size (32 bits). It is well known that some systems treat the C or C++ data type int as a 16-bit quantity, whereas others treat it as a 32-bit quantity. We suggest that the data type GLint be used for formal parameters when defining your own functions. There is no standard size for a float or double, either. The OpenGL types are listed in Figure 2.9. Some of these types will not be encountered until later in the book.

Suffix	Data Type	Typical C or C++ Type	OpenGL Type Name
b	8-bit integer	signed char	GLbyte
s	16-bit integer	short	GLshort
i	32-bit integer	int or long	GLint, GLsizei
f	32-bit floating point	float	GLfloat, GLclampf
d	64-bit floating point	double	GLdouble, GLclampd
ub	8-bit unsigned number	unsigned char	GLubyte, GLboolean
us	16-bit unsigned number	unsigned short	GLushort
ui	32-bit unsigned number	unsigned int or unsigned long	GLuint, GLenum, GLbitfield

FIGURE 2.9 Command suffixes and argument data types.

The OpenGL State

OpenGL keeps track of many *state variables*, such as the current size of points, the current color of drawing, the current screen window size, and so on. The value of a state variable remains active until a new value is given. The size of a point can be set with glPointSize(), which takes one floating-point argument. If its argument is 3.0, the point is usually drawn as a square, three pixels on each side.

To specify the drawing color use

```
glColor3f(red, green, blue);
```

where the values of red, green, and blue vary between 0.0 and 1.0. Here we assume the reader knows that colors are made up of certain amounts of red, green, and blue. For example, some colors with familiar names consist of the following amounts of red, green, and blue (the color gray consists of equal amounts of red, green, and blue):

```
glColor3f(1.0, 0.0, 0.0);   // set drawing color to red
glColor3f(0.0, 1.0, 0.0);   // set drawing color to green
glColor3f(0.0, 0.0, 1.0);   // set drawing color to blue
glColor3f(0.0, 0.0, 0.0);   // set drawing color to black
glColor3f(0.7, 0.7, 0.7);   // set drawing color to bright gray
glColor3f(0.2, 0.2, 0.2);   // set drawing color to medium gray
glColor3f(0.1, 0.1, 0.1);   // set drawing color to dark gray
glColor3f(1.0, 1.0, 1.0);   // set drawing color to bright white
glColor3f(1.0, 1.0, 0.0);   // set drawing color to bright yellow
glColor3f(1.0, 0.0, 1.0);   // set drawing color to magenta
glColor3f(0.0, 1.0, 1.0);   // set drawing color to cyan
```

Colors are discussed in detail in Chapter 11. The background color is set with glClearColor(red, green, blue, alpha), where alpha specifies a degree of transparency and will be discussed later (use 0.0 for now.) Notice that this instruction does nothing visible but merely sets a state variable for later use. To clear the entire window to the background color, use glClear(GL_COLOR_BUFFER_BIT). The argument GL_COLOR_BUFFER_BIT is another constant built into OpenGL.

Establishing the Coordinate System

Our method for establishing our initial choice of coordinate system will seem obscure here, but it will become clearer in the next chapter when we discuss windows, viewports, and clipping. Here we just take the few required commands on faith. The myInit() function in Figure 2.10 is a good place to set up the coordinate system. As we shall see later, OpenGL routinely performs a large number of transformations. It uses matrices to do this, and the commands in myInit() manipulate certain matrices to accomplish the desired goal. The gluOrtho2D() routine as shown in Figure 2.10 sets the transformation we need for a screen window that is 640 pixels wide by 480 pixels high as we discuss in detail in subsequent chapters, the gluOrtho2D (0,640.0,0,480.0) routine, which resides in the GLU library, ... 640.0,0.0,0.0,480.0).

FIGURE 2.10 Establishing a simple coordinate system.

```
void myInit(void)
{
    glMatrixMode(GL_PROJECTION);
    glLoadIdentity();
    gluOrtho2D(0, 640.0, 0, 480.0);
}
```

Putting The Pieces Together: A Complete OpenGL Program

Figure 2.11 shows a complete program that draws the lowly three dots of Figure 2.7. It is easily extended to draw more interesting objects, as we shall see. The initialization in myInit() sets up the coordinate system, the point size, the background color, and the drawing color. The drawing (programmer-provided) function is encapsulated in the callback function myDisplay() which must, of course, be registered. As this program is noninteractive, no other callback functions are used. glFlush() is called after the dots are drawn to insure that all data are completely processed and sent to the display. This is important in some systems that operate over a network: data are buffered on the host machine and sent to the remote display only when the buffer becomes full or a glFlush() is executed.

```c
#include <windows.h>    // use as needed for your system
#include <gl/Gl.h>
#include <gl/glu.h>
#include <gl/glut.h>

//<<<<<<<<<<<<<<<<<<<<<<<<< myInit >>>>>>>>>>>>>>>>>>>>>
 void myInit(void)
 {
    glClearColor(1.0, 1.0, 1.0, 0.0);      // set the background color to a bright white
    glColor3f(0.0f, 0.0f, 0.0f);           // set the drawing color to black
    glPointSize(4.0);                      // set the point size to 4 by 4 pixels
    glMatrixMode(GL_PROJECTION);// set up appropriate matrices- to be explained
    glLoadIdentity();// to be explained
    gluOrtho2D(0.0, 640.0, 0.0, 480.0);// to be explained more fully subsequently.
}
//<<<<<<<<<<<<<<<<<<<<<<<<< myDisplay >>>>>>>>>>>>>>>>>>>
// the redraw function
void myDisplay(void)
{
    glClear(GL_COLOR_BUFFER_BIT);          // clear the screen
    glBegin(GL_POINTS);
        glVertex2i(100, 50);               // draw some points (don't know how many)
        glVertex2i(100, 130);
        glVertex2i(150, 130);
    glEnd();
    glFlush();                             // send all output to display
}
//<<<<<<<<<<<<<<<<<<<<<<<<< main >>>>>>>>>>>>>>>>>>>>>>>>>
void main(int argc, char **argv)
{
    glutInit(&argc, argv);                 // initialize the toolkit
    glutInitDisplayMode(GLUT_SINGLE | GLUT_RGB); // set the display mode
    glutInitWindowSize(640,480);           // set the window size
    glutInitWindowPosition(100, 150);      // set the window position on the screen
    glutCreateWindow("my first attempt"); // open the window with a title
    glutDisplayFunc(myDisplay);            // register the draw function
    myInit();
    glutMainLoop();                        // go into a perpetual loop
}
```

FIGURE 2.11 A complete OpenGL program to draw three dots.

2.2.1 Examples of Drawing Dot Constellations

A **dot constellation** is a (hopefully) eye-catching pattern of dots or points. We shall describe several examples of interesting dot constellations that are easily produced using variations of the basic program in Figure 2.11. In order to produce each dot constellation, changes need to be made to the myDisplay function, which is the callback function for the redraw event. You are strongly encouraged to implement and test each example, and then to fiddle around with it, in order to build up experience.

■ **EXAMPLE 2.2.1 The Big Dipper**

Figure 2.12 shows a pattern of eight dots representing the Big Dipper, a familiar sight in the night sky.

FIGURE 2.12 The Big Dipper.

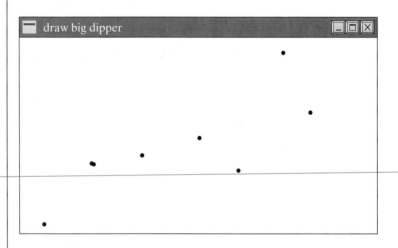

The names and positions of the eight stars in the Big Dipper (for one particular view of the night sky) are given by: {Dubhe, 289, 190}, {Merak, 320, 128}, {Phecda, 239, 67}, {Megrez, 194, 101}, {Alioth, 129, 83}, {Mizar, 75, 73}, {Alcor, 74, 74}, {Alkaid, 20, 10}. (Some people can see only seven stars in the Big Dipper with the naked eye. Apparently it was once a test of visual acuity within some Native American tribes to test whether or not all eight could be seen, which may have determined who got dinner that night.) Since so few data points are involved in this example, it is easy to list them explicitly, or **hard-wire** them into the code. On the other hand, when many points are to be drawn, it is unwieldy at best to list the points, and so the programmer would store them in a file or use a mathematical equation to calculate each point in turn. As the program proceeds, the individual points can be retrieved from a file and be drawn. We do this next. These points can replace the three points specified in Figure 2.7. It is useful to experiment with this constellation, trying different point sizes, as well as different background and drawing colors.

■ **EXAMPLE 2.2.2 Drawing the Sierpinski Gasket**

Figure 2.13 shows the fascinating Sierpinski gasket. Its dot constellation is generated **procedurally**, which means that each successive dot is determined by a procedural rule. Although the rule here is very simple, the final pattern is an infinitely complex **fractal** (see Appendix 5)! We first approach the rules for generating the Sierpinski gasket in an intuitive fashion and present a code fragment that implements the Sierpinski gasket.

FIGURE 2.13 The Sierpinski gasket.

How to Produce the Sierpinski Gasket

The Sierpinski gasket is produced by calling drawDot() many times with dot positions $(x_0, y_0), (x_1, y_1), (x_2, y_2), \ldots$, determined by a simple algorithm. A sample drawDot() function could be:

```
void drawDot( GLint x, GLint y )
{
glBegin( GL_POINTS );
    glVertex2i( x, y );
glEnd();
}
```

As for the Sierpinski algorithm, denote the kth point $p_k = (x_k, y_k)$. Each point is based on the previous point p_{k-1}. The procedure is:

1. Choose three fixed points T_0, T_1, and T_2 to form some triangle. We will call this the **parent triangle** for each Sierpinski gasket we generate, as shown in Figure 2.14a.
2. Choose the initial point p_0 to be drawn by selecting one of the points T_0, T_1, and T_2 of the parent triangle at random.

Now iterate steps 3–5 as described next until the pattern is satisfyingly filled in:

3. Choose one of the three points T_0, T_1, and T_2 also at random; call it T.
4. Construct the next point p_k as the **midpoint**[3] between T and the previously found point p_{k-1}. Hence p_k = midpoint of p_{k-1} and T.
5. Draw p_k using drawDot().

Figure 2.14b shows a few iterations of this. Suppose the initial point p_0 happens to be T_0, and that T_1 is chosen next. Then p_1 is formed so that it lies halfway between T_0 and T_1. Suppose T_2 is chosen next, so p_2 lies halfway between p_1 and T_2. Next

---

[3] To find the **midpoint** between 2 points, say (3, 12) and (5, 37), simply average their x- and y-components individually, rounding down to the nearest integer: add them and divide by 2. So the midpoint of (3, 12) and (5, 37) is ((3 + 5)/2, (12 + 37)/2) = (4, 24.5). Notice that neither coordinate needs to be an integer.

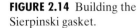

FIGURE 2.14 Building the
Sierpinski gasket.

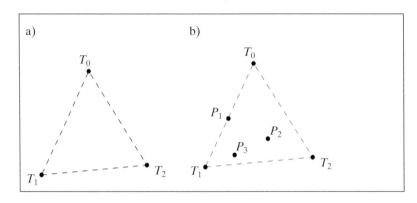

suppose T_1 is chosen again, so p_3 is formed as shown, and so on. This process goes
on generating and drawing points (conceptually forever), and the pattern of the
Sierpinski gasket quickly emerges.

It is convenient to define a simple struct GLPoint that describes a point whose
coordinates are floats:

```
struct GLPoint{
    GLfloat x, y;
};
```

We then build and initialize an array of three such points T[0], T[1], and T[2] to
hold the three corners of the triangle such as GLPoint T[3] = {{10.0,10.0},
{300.0,30.0},{200.0,300.0}}. For this example there is no need to store each
point p_k in the sequence as it is generated, since we simply want to draw it and then
move on. So we set up a variable, point, to hold this changing point. At each iteration
point is updated to hold the new value.

We use index = rand() % 3 to choose one of the points T[i] at random. rand()
returns one of the values 0, 1, or 2 with equal likelihood. Figure 2.15 shows a

```
// be sure to include math & time header files
// sierpinski_render function
void sierpinski_render() {
    glClear(GL_COLOR_BUFFER_BIT);                    //clear the screen
    GLintPoint T[3] = {{10,10},{600,10},{300,600}}; //defines the vertices of the
                                                     triangle
    int index = rand() % 3;                          //choose the initial vertex randomly
    GLintPoint point = T[index];       //creates an array of 3 vertices
    drawDot(point.x, point.y);
    for (int i = 0; i < 55000; i++)                  //draw 55000 dots of the Sierpinski Gasket
    {
            index = rand() % 3;
            point.x = (point.x + T[index].x) / 2;
            point.y = (point.y + T[index].y) / 2;
            drawDot(point.x, point.y);

    }
    glFlush();                                       //flushes all unfinished drawing
                                                     commands

}
```

FIGURE 2.15 The display
function for generating the
Sierpinski gasket.

`sierpinski_render()`, that generates 55,000 points of a Sierpinki gasket complete working function, which generates 55,000 points of the Sierpinski gasket. In your program, the function `Sierpinski()` replaces the callback function, `myDisplay()`.

What is rand()?

`rand()` is a function that returns a pseudorandom (an apparently random value) between 0 and some upper limit. Since we want to choose one of three vertices of the parent triangle, we would call `index = rand () % 3` to provide a value between 0 and 2 inclusive. `rand()` is a part of the standard C++ library and it returns a value between 0 and some upper limit (32,767 on our machine, always stored in `RAND_MAX`). As with most random number generators, the sequence of numbers generated appears random but actually is deterministic once the first number is given. Therefore, we give it an initial value, known as the "seed," to get things started properly. This seed value is based on the system clock at runtime. Because the system time is an ever-changing value, the seed is unique each time. Using system time indeed returns a different random sequence each time the program is run.

Other Interesting Variations of the Sierpinski Gasket

Many variants of the Sierpinski gasket may be made, such as varying the color of certain dots, or using the mouse to drag the vertices of the parent triangle to new positions. We describe the latter variant in subsequent sections, and provide its implementation in the book's companion web site.

■ EXAMPLE 2.2.3 Plotting Functions Using Dot Plots

Suppose you wish to learn the behavior of some mathematical function $f(x)$ as x varies. For example, how does

$$f(x) = e^{|-x|}\cos(2\pi x)$$

vary for values of x between 0 and 4? A quick plot of $f(x)$ vs. x, such as that shown in Figure 2.16, can reveal patterns and trends of information to the analyst.

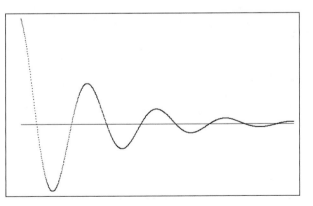

FIGURE 2.16 A dot plot of $e^{|-x|}\cos(2\pi x)$ versus x.

To plot this function, simply sample it as a collection of closely spaced x-values and plot a dot at each coordinate pair $(x_i, f(x_i))$. Choosing some suitable increment, say 0.005, between consecutive x-values, the process is basically:

```
glBegin(GL_POINTS);
   for(GLdouble x = 0; x < 4.0 ; x += 0.005)
      glVertex2d(x, f(x));
glEnd();
glFlush();
```

But there is a problem here. The picture produced will be impossibly tiny, because the total span in *x*-values is between 0 and 4, so the picture covers only the
first four pixels of the screen window, starting at the left-hand side. Further, any negative values of *f*(.) will lie below the window and will not be seen at all. We therefore
need to scale and position the values to be plotted so that they cover the screen window area appropriately. Here we do it by brute force, in essence picking some values
to make the picture show up adequately on the screen. Later we develop a general
procedure that copes with these adjustments, the so-called "mapping from world coordinates to window coordinates."

Scaling x Suppose we want the range from 0 to 4 to be scaled so that it covers the entire width of the screen window, given in pixels by `screenWidth`. We need only scale
all *x*-values by `screenWidth/4.0`, using

```
sx = x * screenWidth / 4.0;
```

which yields `sx` = 0 when *x* equals 0, and `sx` = `screenWidth` when *x* is 4.0, as
desired.

Scaling and translating y Preliminary investigation shows that the values of *f*(*x*) lie between −1.0 and 1.0, so we must scale and translate them as well for proper viewing.
Suppose the screen window has height `screenHeight` pixels. Then to place the plot
in the center of the window, scale *y*-values by `screenHeight / 2` and translate them
up by `screenHeight / 2`:

```
sy = (y + 1.0) * screenHeight / 2.0;
```

This yields `sy` = 0 when *y* equals −1.0, and `sy` = `screenHeight` when *y* is 1.0.

Note that the conversions from *x* to *sx*, and from *y* to *sy*, are of the form:

$$sx = A*x + B$$
$$sy = C*y + D \tag{2.1}$$

for properly chosen values of the constants *A*, *B*, *C*, and *D*. *A* and *C* perform scaling;
B and *D* perform translations. Scaling and translating are basically forms of *affine
transformations*. We study affine transformations in depth in Chapter 5. They provide a more consistent approach that maps any specified range in *x* and *y* to the
screen window.

We need only set the values of *A*, *B*, *C*, and *D* appropriately, and draw the dot
plot using the following code.

```
GLdouble A, B, C, D, x;
A = screenWidth / 4.0;
B = 0.0;
C = screenHeight / 2.0;
D = C;
glBegin(GL_POINTS);
   for(x = 0; x < 4.0 ; x += 0.005)
      glVertex2d(A * x + B, C * f(x) + D);
glEnd();
glFlush();
```

Figure 2.17 shows the entire program to draw the dot plot, to illustrate how the
various ingredients fit together. The initializations are very similar to those for the

program that draws three dots in Figure 2.7. Notice that the width and height of the screen window are defined as constants, and are used where needed in the code.

Figure 2.18a shows two overlapping functions, one is $f(x) = \sin(x)$, as x varies from $-\pi$ to π, and the second function (cross hatched) is $f(x) = \sin(2x)$ for the same range in x.

```c
#include <windows.h> // use proper includes for your system
#include <math.h>
#include <gl/Gl.h>
#include <gl/Glu.h>
#include <gl/Glut.h>
const int screenWidth = 640;        // width of the screen window in pixels
const int screenHeight = 480;       // height of the screen window in pixels
GLdouble A, B, C, D;  // values used for scaling and translation
//<<<<<<<<<<<<<<<<<<<<<< myInit >>>>>>>>>>>>>>>>>>>>>
 void myInit(void)
 {
    glClearColor(1.0,1.0,1.0,0.0);        // the background color is white
    glColor3f(0.0f, 0.0f, 0.0f);          // the drawing color is black
    glPointSize(2.0);                     // a 'dot' is 2 by 2 pixels
    glMatrixMode(GL_PROJECTION);
    glLoadIdentity();
    gluOrtho2D(0.0, (GLdouble)screenWidth, 0.0, (GLdouble)screenHeight);
    A = screenWidth / 4.0; // sets the values used for scaling and translating
    B = 0.0;
    C = D = screenHeight / 2.0;
 }
//<<<<<<<<<<<<<<<<<<<<<< myDisplay >>>>>>>>>>>>>>>>>>
void myDisplay(void)
{
    glClear(GL_COLOR_BUFFER_BIT);         // clear the screen
    glBegin(GL_POINTS);
    for(GLdouble x = 0; x < 4.0 ; x += 0.005)
    {
      GLdouble func = exp(-fabs(x)) * cos(2 * 3.14159265 * x);
        glVertex2d(A * x + B, C * func + D);
    }
      glEnd();
      glFlush();                          // send all output to display
}
//<<<<<<<<<<<<<<<<<<<<<< main >>>>>>>>>>>>>>>>>>>>>>>
void main(int argc, char** argv)
{
    glutInit(&argc, argv);                // initialize the toolkit
    glutInitDisplayMode(GLUT_SINGLE | GLUT_RGB); // set the display mode
    glutInitWindowSize(screenWidth, screenHeight); // set the window size
    glutInitWindowPosition(100, 150); // set the window position on screen
    glutCreateWindow("Dot Plot of a Function"); // open the screen window
    glutDisplayFunc(myDisplay);           // register the redraw function
    myInit();
    glutMainLoop();                       // go into a perpetual loop
}
```

FIGURE 2.17 A complete program to draw the dot plot of a function.

Part b in Figure 2.18 shows a curve that can be expressed simply using a parameter, a. (We will examine parametric representations for curves in detail in Chapter 3.) The x-coordinate is driven by the parameter a and is given by $x(a) = 10 + \sin(15*a)$ as a varies from 0 to 2π. The y-coordinate is given by $y(a) = \sin(a)$ as a varies over the same range, 0 to 2π. The two coordinates work together to sweep out the curve as shown. Notice that y increases toward 1, falls back to 0, decreases to -1, and finally rises to 0 again just as a sine function does over one complete period. The x-coordinate undulates back and forth 15 times along with an offset of 10.

Part c is a plot of the complex function $\sin(z^2)$ as the complex variable z varies over a square mesh. Each value of z has a real and imaginary component which maps into a real and imaginary value of $\sin(z^2)$, and which is the point plotted.

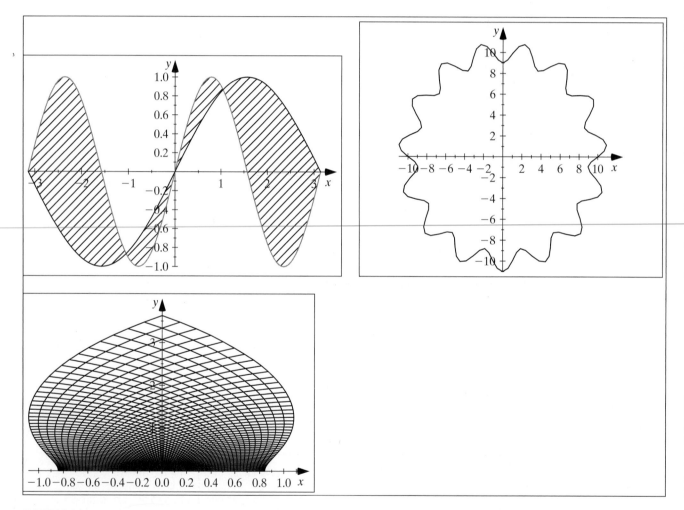

FIGURE 2.18 Three different 2D dot plots of mathematical functions. (Courtesy of MuPAD Research)

PRACTICE EXERCISE

2.2.1. Dot plots for any function f()

Consider drawing a dot plot of the function $f(x) = e^{|-x|}\cos(2\pi x)$, where it is known that as x varies from x_{low} to x_{high}, $f(x)$ takes on values between from y_{low} to y_{high}. Find the appropriate scaling and translation factors so that the dots will lie properly in a screen window with width W pixels and height H pixels.   ■

2.3 LINE DRAWINGS IN OPENGL

I prefer drawing to talking. Drawing is faster, and leaves less room for lies.

Le Corbusier
(1887–1965)

As discussed in Chapter 1, line drawings are fundamental in computer graphics, and almost every graphics system comes with driver routines to draw straight lines. OpenGL makes it easy to draw a line: use GL_LINES as the argument to glBegin(). Thus to draw a line between (40,100) and (202,96) use:

```
glBegin(GL_LINES);                // use constant GL_LINES here
    glVertex2i(40, 100);
    glVertex2i(202, 96);
glEnd();
```

This code might be encapsulated for convenience in the routine drawLine():

```
void drawLine (GLint x1, GLint y1, GLint x2, GLint y2)
{
    glBegin(GL_LINES);
    glVertex2i(x1, y1);
    glVertex2i(x2, y2);
    glEnd();
}
```

and an alternate routine, drawLineFloat(), could be implemented similarly. (How?)

If more than two vertices are specified between glBegin(GL_LINES) and glEnd(), they are taken in pairs and a separate line is drawn between each pair. The tic-tac-toe board shown in Figure 2.19a would be drawn using:

```
glBegin(GL_LINES);
    glVertex2i(10, 20);    // first horizontal line
    glVertex2i(40, 20)
    glVertex2i(20, 10);    // first vertical line
    glVertex2i(20, 40);
    <four more calls to glVertex2i() here for other two lines>
glEnd();
glFlush();
```

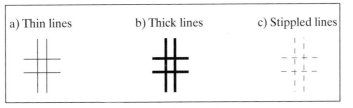

a) Thin lines   b) Thick lines   c) Stippled lines

FIGURE 2.19 Simple pictures built from four lines.

OpenGL provides tools for setting the attributes of lines. A line's color is set in the same way as for points, using glColor3f(). Figure 2.19b shows the use of thicker lines, as set by glLineWidth(4.0). The default thickness is 1.0. Figure 2.19c shows stippled (dotted and dashed) lines.

2.3.1 Drawing Polylines and Polygons

Recall from Chapter 1 that a **polyline** is a collection of line segments joined end to end. It is described by an ordered list of points, as in:

$$p_0 = (x_0, y_0), \quad p_1 = (x_1, y_1), \quad \ldots, \quad p_n = (x_n, y_n) \tag{2.2}$$

In OpenGL a polyline is called a *line strip* and is drawn by drawing lines between successive pairs of points: p_0 to p_1, p_2 to p_3, and so on as in glBegin(GL_LINE_STRIP) and glEnd(). For example, the code:

```
glBegin(GL_LINE_STRIP);   // draw an open polyline
   glVertex2i(20,10);
   glVertex2i(50,10);
   glVertex2i(20,80);
   glVertex2i(50,80);
glEnd();
glFlush();
```

produces the polyline shown in Figure 2.20a. Attributes such as color, thickness, and stippling may be applied to polylines in the same way they are applied to single lines. If it is desired to connect the last point with the first point to make the polyline into a polygon, simply replace GL_LINE_STRIP with GL_LINE_LOOP. The resulting polygon is shown as in Figure 2.20b.

FIGURE 2.20 A polyline and a polygon.

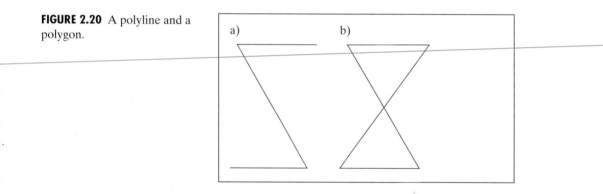

Polygons drawn using GL_LINE_LOOP cannot be filled with a color or pattern. To draw filled polygons you use glBegin(GL_POLYGON), as described later.

■ **EXAMPLE 2.3.1 Drawing Line Graphs**

In Example 2.2.3 we looked at plotting a function $f(x)$ vs. x with a sequence of dots at positions $(x_i, f(x_i))$. A line graph is a straightforward extension of this: the dots are simply joined by line segments to form a polyline. Figure 2.21 shows an example, based on the function:

$$f(x) = 300 - 100 \cos(2\pi x/100) + 30 \cos(4\pi x/100) + 6 \cos(6\pi x/100)$$

as x varies in steps of 3 for 100 steps.

The process of plotting a function with line segments is almost identical to that for producing a dot plot: the program of Figure 2.17 can be used with only slight adjustments. As with dot plots we must scale and translate the lines being drawn here, to place them properly in the window. This requires the computation of the

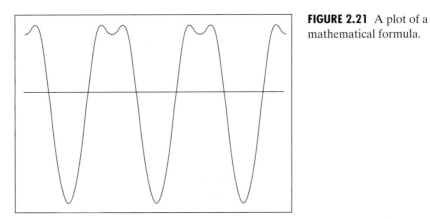

FIGURE 2.21 A plot of a mathematical formula.

constants A, B, C, and D in the same manner as we did before [see Equation (2.1)]. Figure 2.22 shows the changes necessary for the inner drawing loop in the myDisplay() function.

```
<Calculate constants A, B, C and D for scaling and translation>
glBegin(GL_LINE_STRIP);
  for(x = 0; x <= 300; x += 3)
  glVertex2d(A * x + B, C * f(x) + D);
glEnd();
glFlush;
```

FIGURE 2.22 Plotting a function using a line graph—fragment of code.

■ EXAMPLE 2.3.2 Drawing Polylines That Have Been Stored in a File

Most interesting pictures made up of polylines contain a large number of line segments. In such cases it's important to store a description of the polylines in a file, so that the picture can be redrawn at will.

It's not hard to write a routine that draws the polylines stored in a file. Figure 2.23 shows an example of what might be drawn.

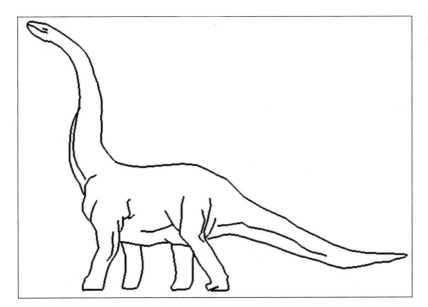

FIGURE 2.23 Drawing polylines stored in a file.

Suppose the file dino.dat contains a collection of polylines in the following format (the comments are not part of the file):

```
21                          number of polylines in the file
4                           number of points in the first polyline
169 118                     first point of first polyline
174 120                     second point of first polyline
179 124
178 126

5                           number of points in the second polyline
298 86                      first point of second polyline
304 92
310 104
314 114
314 119
29
32 435
10 439
 . . .                             etc.
```

(The entire file is given on the book's companion web site.) Figure 2.24 shows a complete function, drawPolyLineFile(), in C++ that draws pictures stored in

```cpp
void drawPolyLineFile(char * fileName)
{
   fstream inStream;
   inStream.open(fileName, ios ::in); // open the file
   if(inStream.fail())
        return;
   glClear(GL_COLOR_BUFFER_BIT);      // clear the screen
   GLint numpolys, numLines, x ,y;
   inStream >> numpolys;              // read the number of polylines
   for(int j = 0; j < numpolys; j++)  // read each polyline
   {
     inStream >> numLines;
     glBegin(GL_LINE_STRIP);          // draw the next polyline
     for (int i = 0; i < numLines; i++)
     {
        inStream >> x >> y;           // read the next x, y pair
        glVertex2i(x, y);
     }
     glEnd();
   }
//end of j loop
glFlush();
inStream.close();
}
//end of function drawPolylineFile()
```

FIGURE 2.24 A function for drawing polylines stored in a file.

such a file. The file having the name contained in the string `fileName` is read in, polyline by polyline, and each polyline is drawn. The program uses the routine, `drawPolyLineFile`, as the callback function, `myDisplay()`, for the redraw event. The values of A, B, C, and D must be chosen judiciously to scale the polylines properly. We develop a general approach to do this in Chapter 3.

This version of `drawPolyLineFile()` does very little error checking. If the file cannot be opened—perhaps the wrong name is passed to the function—the routine simply returns an error. If the file contains bad data, such as real values where integers are expected, the results are unpredictable. The routine as given should be considered only as a starting point for developing a more robust version. Some improvements to this function may be to remove the need to reread the file each time this particular function is called and to store the polyline data in memory. (Here these data are used immediately to draw the polylines and then discarded.)

■ EXAMPLE 2.3.3 Parameterizing Figures

Figure 2.25 shows a simple house consisting of a few polylines. It can be drawn using code shown partially in Figure 2.26. What code would be suitable for drawing the door and window?

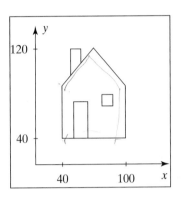

FIGURE 2.25 A house.

FIGURE 2.26 Drawing a house with hard-wired dimensions.

```
void hardwiredHouse(void)
{
  glBegin(GL_LINE_LOOP);
    glVertex2i(40, 40);      // draw the shell of house
    glVertex2i(40, 90);
    glVertex2i(70, 120);
    glVertex2i(100, 90);
    glVertex2i(100, 40);
  glEnd();
  glBegin(GL_LINE_STRIP);
    glVertex2i(50, 100);     // draw the chimney
    glVertex2i(50, 120);
    glVertex2i(60, 120);
    glVertex2i(60, 110);
  glEnd();
    . . . // draw the door
    . . . // draw the window
}
```

This is not a very flexible approach. The position of each endpoint is hardwired into this code, so `hardwirededHouse()` can draw only one house in one size and one location. More flexibility is achieved if we **parameterize** the figure, and pass the parameter values to the routine. In this way we can draw **families** of objects, which are distinguished by different parameter values. Figure 2.27 suggests the approach. The parameters specify the location of the roof peak, the width of the house, and its height. The details of drawing the chimney, door, and window are left as an exercise.

```
void parameterizedHouse(GLintPoint peak, GLint width, GLint height)
 // the top of house is at the peak; the size of house is given
 // by height and width
{
    glBegin(GL_LINE_LOOP);
      glVertex2i(peak.x,                peak.y);  // draw shell of house
      glVertex2i(peak.x + width / 2, peak.y - 3 * height /8);
      glVertex2i(peak.x + width / 2  peak.y -     height);
      glVertex2i(peak.x - width / 2, peak.y -     height);
      glVertex2i(peak.x - width / 2, peak.y - 3 * height /8);
      glEnd();
      // draw chimney in the same fashion
      // draw the door
      // draw the window

}
```

FIGURE 2.27 Drawing a parameterized house.

This routine may be used to draw a village such as that shown in Figure 2.28, by making successive calls to `parameterizedHouse()` with different parameter values. (How is a house flipped upside down? Can *all* of the houses in the figure be drawn using the routine given?)

FIGURE 2.28 A village of houses drawn using `parameterizedHouse()`.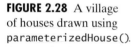

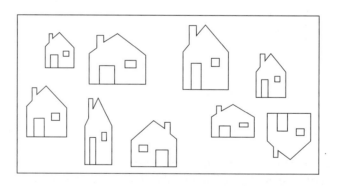

■ **EXAMPLE 2.3.4 Building a Polyline Drawer**

As we shall see, some applications compute and store the vertices of a polyline in a list. It is natural, therefore, to add to our growing toolbox of routines a function that accepts the list as a parameter and draws the corresponding polyline. The list might be in the form of an array, or a linked list. We show here the array form, and in Figure 2.29 we define the class to hold it. The figure also shows the `struct GLintPoint` being declared; this will be discussed further in subsequent sections. For those programmers wanting to deal with very large data sets, where there may be more than 10,000 points, a C++ STL (Standard Template Library) container might be a safer data structure.

```
struct GLintPoint {
GLint x, y;
};
class GLintPointArray{
  const int MAX_NUM = 10000;
//Use a symbolic constant for MAX_NUM, so you can later change it.
public:
    int num;
GLintPoint pt[MAX_NUM];
};
```

FIGURE 2.29 Data type for an array of vertices.

Figure 2.30 shows a possible implementation of the polyline drawing routine. It also takes a parameter closed: if closed is nonzero, the last vertex in the polyline is connected to the first vertex, making this a polygon. The value of closed sets the argument of glBegin(). The routine simply sends each vertex of the polyline to OpenGL.

```
void drawPolyLine(GlintPointArray poly, int closed)
{
if (closed)
      glBegin(GL_LINE_LOOP);
    //In this case a closed polyline is drawn
else
  glBegin(GL_LINE_STRIP);// In this case an open polyline is drawn
      for(int i = 0; i < poly.num; i++)
      glVertex2i(poly.pt[i].x, poly.pt[i].y);
glEnd();
glFlush();
}
```

FIGURE 2.30 A linked list data type, and drawing a polyline or polygon.

2.3.3 Line Drawing Using moveTo() and lineTo()

We saw at the start of Section 2.3 that it is easy to draw lines in OpenGL, either with an explicit glBegin(GL_LINES),...,glEnd) pair, or by a function like drawLine() as we built there.

Recall that moveTo() and lineTo() manipulate the position of a hypothetical pen, whose position is called the **current position**, or *CP*. *CP* acts very much like a state variable within OpenGL, like drawing color and background color, that is under program control. We can summarize the effects of the two functions as:

```
moveTo(x, y);    // set CP to (x, y)
lineTo(x, y);    // draw a line from CP to (x, y), and then
                    udate CP to (x, y)
```

A line from (x_1, y_1) to (x_2, y_2) is therefore drawn using the two calls moveTo(x1, y1);lineTo(x2, y2). A polyline based on the list of points $(x_0, y_0), (x_1, y_1), \ldots, (x_n, y_n)$ is easily drawn using:

```
moveTo(x[0], y[0]);
 for(int i = 1; i = n; i++)
   lineTo(x[i], y[i]);
```

It is straightforward to build moveTo() and lineTo() on top of OpenGL. To do this we must define and maintain our own *CP*. For the case of integer coordinates the implementation shown in Figure 2.31 would do the trick.

Note: Here the variable *CP* is a global variable, and therefore vulnerable to tampering from instructions at other points in your program. Therefore as always with global variables proceed with great caution.

FIGURE 2.31 Defining moveTo() and lineTo() in OpenGL.

```
GLintPoint CP;              // global current position

//<<<<<<<<<<<<<< moveTo >>>>>>>>>>>>>>>
void moveTo(GLint x, GLint y)
{
   CP.x = x; CP.y = y; // update the CP
}
//<<<<<<<<<<<<< lineTo >>>>>>>>>>>>>>>>>
void lineTo(GLint x, GLint y)
{
   glBegin(GL_LINES);   // draw the line
     glVertex2i(CP.x, CP.y);
     glVertex2i(x, y);
glEnd();
glFlush();
CP.x = x; CP.y = y; // update the CP
}
```

2.3.4 Drawing Aligned Rectangles

A special case of a polygon is the **aligned rectangle,** named this way because its sides are aligned with the coordinate axes. We could create our own function to draw an aligned rectangle, but OpenGL provides the ready-made function, glRecti():

```
glRecti(GLint x1, GLint  y1, GLint x2, GLint y2);
// draw a rectangle with opposite corners (x1, y1) and (x2, y2);
```

This command draws the aligned rectangle based on two given points. In addition the rectangle is filled with the current color. Figure 2.32 shows an example of what is drawn by the code.

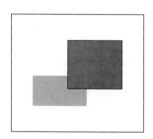

FIGURE 2.32 Two aligned rectangles filled with colors.

```
glClearColor(1.0,1.0,1.0,0.0);   // white background
glClear(GL_COLOR_BUFFER_BIT);    // clear the window
glColor3f(0.6,0.6,0.6);          // bright gray
   glRecti(20,20,100,70);
glColor3f(0.2,0.2,0.2);          // dark gray
glRecti(70, 50, 150, 130);
glFlush();
```

Notice that the second rectangle is painted over the first one.

Figure 2.33 shows two further examples. Part a is a flurry of randomly chosen aligned rectangles.

Part b is the familiar checkerboard, with alternating gray levels. The exercises ask you to generate it.

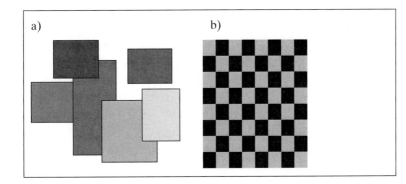

FIGURE 2.33 a) Random flurry of rectangles, b) a checkerboard.

2.3.5 On the Aspect Ratio of an Aligned Rectangle

The principal properties of an aligned rectangle are its size, position, color, and shape. Its shape is embodied in its aspect ratio, and we shall be referring to the aspect ratios of rectangles throughout the book. The aspect ratio of a rectangle is simply the ratio of its width to its height:[5]

$$\text{aspect ratio} = \frac{\text{width}}{\text{height}} \tag{2.3}$$

Rectangles with various aspect ratios are shown in Figure 2.34.

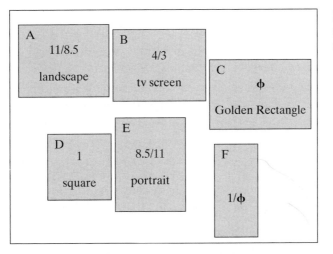

FIGURE 2.34 Examples of aspect ratios of aligned rectangles.

Rectangle A has the shape of a piece of 8.5- by 11-inch paper laid on its side in the so-called **landscape** orientation (i.e., width larger than height). It has an aspect ratio of 1.294. Rectangle B has the aspect ratio of a television screen, 4/3, and C is the famous **golden rectangle** described in Case Study 2.3. Its aspect ratio is close to $\phi = 1.618034$. Rectangle D is a square with aspect ratio equal to 1, and E has the shape of a piece of standard paper in **portrait** orientation, with an aspect ratio of .7727. Finally, F is tall and skinny with an aspect ratio of $1/\phi$. Note that a rectangle with aspect ratio r when lying on one side (and it only makes sense to talk about aspect ratio when a rectangle is aligned) has aspect ratio $1/r$ when rotated to lie on an adjacent side.

---

[5] Note: Some authors define it as height/width.

PRACTICE EXERCISES

2.3.1 Drawing the checkerboard

(Try your hand at this before looking at the answers.) Write the routine checkerboard(int size) that draws the checkerboard shown in Figure 2.33b. Place the checkerboard with its lower left corner at $(0, 0)$. Each of the 64 squares has length size pixels. Choose two nice colors for the squares.

Solution: The ijth square has lower left corner at $(i*\text{size}, j*\text{size})$ for $i = 0, \dots, 7$ and $j = 0, \dots, 7$. The color can be made to alternate between (r_1, g_1, b_1) and (r_2, g_2, b_2) using the following instructions.

```
if((i + j)%2 ==0) // if i + j is even
    glColor3f( r1, g1, b1);
else
    glColor3f(r2, g2, b2);
```

2.3.2 Alternative ways to specify a rectangle

An aligned rectangle can be described in other ways than by two opposite corners. Two possibilities are:

- its center point, height, and width;
- its upper left corner, width, and aspect ratio.

Write functions drawRectangleCenter() and drawRectangleCornerSize() that pass these alternative parameters.

2.3.3 Different aspect ratios

Write a short program that draws a filled rectangle of aspect ratio R, where R is specified by the user. Initialize the display to a drawing space of 400 by 400. Arrange the size of the rectangle so that it is as large as possible. That is, if $R > 1$, it spans across the drawing space, and if $R < 1$, it spans from top to bottom.

2.3.4 Drawing the parameterized house

Fill in the details of parameterizedHouse() in Figure 2.27 so that the door, window, and chimney are drawn in their proper proportions for given values of height and width.

2.3.5 Scaling and positioning a figure using parameters

Write the function void drawDiamond(GLintPoint center, int size) that draws the simple diamond shown in Figure 2.35, centered at center, and having size size.

Use this function to draw a flurry of diamonds as suggested in Figure 2.36.

FIGURE 2.35 A simple diamond.

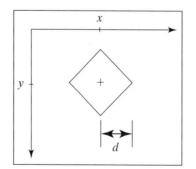

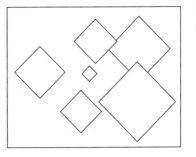

FIGURE 2.36 A flurry of diamonds.

2.3.6 Filling Polygons

So far we can draw unfilled polygons in OpenGL, as well as aligned rectangles filled with a single solid color. OpenGL also supports filling more general polygons with a pattern or color. The restriction is that the polygons must be *convex*.

> **CONVEX POLYGON:** A polygon is convex if it contains every line segment delimited by any two points on its boundary.

Several polygons are shown in Figure 2.37. Of these only D, E, and F are convex. (Check that the definition of convexity is upheld for each of these polygons.) D is certainly convex: all triangles are. A is not even simple so it cannot be convex. Both B and C "bend inward" at some point. (Find two points on B such that the line joining them does not lie entirely inside B.)

To draw a convex polygon based on vertices (x_0, y_0), (x_1, y_1), ..., (x_n, y_n) use the usual list of vertices, but place them between a glBegin(GL_POLYGON) and a glEnd():

```
glBegin(GL_POLYGON);
  glVertex2f(x0, y0);
  glVertex2f(x1, y1);
  . . .
  glVertex2f(xn, yn);
glEnd();
```

It will be filled in the current color. It can also be filled with a stipple pattern—see Case Study 2.5—and later we will paint images into polygons as part of applying a texture.

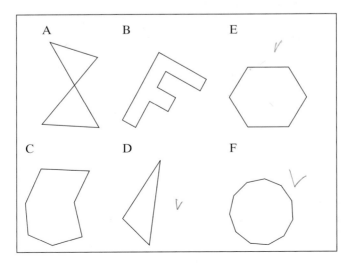

FIGURE 2.37 Convex and nonconvex polygons.

Figure 2.38 shows a number of filled convex polygons. In Chapter 9 we will examine an algorithm for filling any polygon, convex or not.

FIGURE 2.38 Several filled convex polygons.

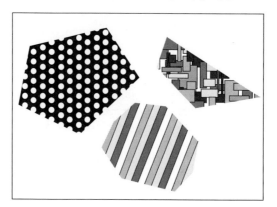

2.3.7 Other Graphics Primitives in OpenGL

OpenGL supports the drawing of five other objects as well. Figure 2.39 shows examples of each of them. To draw a particular one, the constant shown with it is used in glBegin().

- GL_TRIANGLES: takes the listed vertices three at a time and draws a separate triangle for each.
- GL_QUADS: takes the vertices four at a time and draws a separate quadrilateral for each.
- GL_TRIANGLE_STRIP: draws a series of triangles based on triplets of vertices: v_0, v_1, v_2, then v_2, v_1, v_3, then v_2, v_3, v_4, and so on (in an order so that all triangles are traversed in the same way; e.g., counterclockwise).
- GL_TRIANGLE_FAN: draws a series of connected triangles based on triplets of vertices: v_0, v_1, v_2, then v_0, v_2, v_3, then v_0, v_3, v_4, and so on.
- GL_QUAD_STRIP: draws a series of quadrilaterals based on foursomes of vertices: first v_0, v_1, v_3, v_2, then v_2, v_3, v_5, v_4, then v_4, v_5, v_7, v_6 (in an order so that all quadrilaterals are traversed in the same way; e.g., counterclockwise).

FIGURE 2.39 Other geometric primitive types.

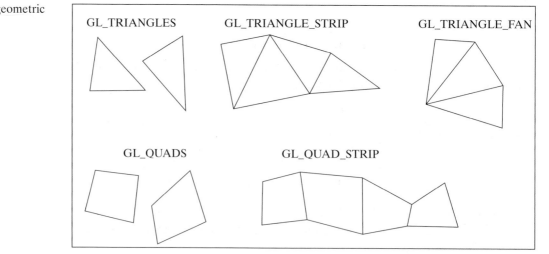

2.4 SIMPLE INTERACTION WITH THE MOUSE AND KEYBOARD

Uttering a word is like striking a note on the keyboard of the imagination.

Ludwig Wittgenstein
(1889–1951)

One of the fruitful and exciting qualities of an interactive graphics application is that the user can control the flow of a program by natural human motions: pointing and clicking the mouse and pressing various keyboard keys. The mouse position at the time of the click, or the identity of the key pressed, is made available to the application program and is processed as appropriate.

Recall from earlier in this chapter that when the user presses and releases a mouse button, moves the mouse with a button down, or presses and releases a keyboard key, an event occurs. The programmer can register a callback function with each event type, using:

- `glutMouseFunc(myMouse)`, which registers `myMouse()` with the event that occurs when the mouse button is pressed and/or released;
- `glutMotionFunc(myMovedMouse)`, which registers `myMovedMouse()` with the event that occurs when the mouse is moved while one of the buttons is held down
- `glutKeyboardFunc(myKeyboard)`, which registers `myKeyBoard()` with the event that occurs when a keyboard key is pressed and released.

Everyone wants computers to be more reactive to natural human input; such as talking and hand gestures. Computers of today are a long way from this, but moving a mouse to control a computer, although a poor second to waving your hand, is at least a far more natural method than entering obscure and arcane sequences of symbols that *nobody* understands. We shall see in this section how to use mouse movements and key presses in a program to resemble a human sitting before the computer and instructing it as to its next moves.

2.4.1 Mouse Interaction

How are data about the mouse sent to the application? It's all in the design of the callback function for the mouse, the one registered as the `glutMouseFunc`. You can give the callback function any name you wish (we often call it `myMouse`), but it must take four `int` parameters, and therefore must have the prototype:

```
void myMouse(int button, int state, int x, int y);
```

When a mouse event occurs, the system calls the registered function, supplying it with values for these parameters. The value of `button` will be one of:

`GLUT_LEFT_BUTTON`, `GLUT_MIDDLE_BUTTON`, or `GLUT_RIGHT_BUTTON`,

with the obvious interpretation, and the value of `state` will be one of: `GLUT_UP` or `GLUT_DOWN`. The values `x` and `y` report the position of the mouse at the time of the event. **Alert**: The x-value is the number of pixels from the left of the window as expected, but the y-value is the number of pixels *down* from the top of the window.

Keep in mind that the event handler itself does not cause an event redraw to the screen. Hence to see the effect of the mouse event, the mouse handler should call `glutPostRedisplay()`.

■ EXAMPLE 2.4.1 Placing Dots with the Mouse

We start with an elementary but important example. Each time the user presses down the left mouse button, a dot is drawn in the screen window at the mouse position. If the user presses the right-hand button, the color of the background changes. The version of myMouse() shown next does the job. The y-value of the mouse position is the number of pixels from the top of the screen window; we draw the dot, not at (x, y), but at (x, screenHeight – y), where screenHeight is assumed here to be the height of the window in pixels.

```
void myMouse(int button, int state, int x, int y) {
            if(state == GLUT_DOWN) {
      if(button == GLUT_LEFT_BUTTON) {
         drawDot(x, screenHeight - y);
         glFlush();
      } else if (button == GLUT_RIGHT_BUTTON) {
         glClearColor(1.0f, 0.0f, 0.0f, 0.0f); // Red
         glClear(GL_COLOR_BUFFER_BIT);
      glFlush();
            }
      }
   return;
}
```

■ EXAMPLE 2.4.2 How to Specify a Rectangle with the Mouse

Here we want the user to be able to draw rectangles whose dimensions are entered with the mouse. The user clicks the mouse at two points, which specify opposite corners of an aligned rectangle, and the rectangle is drawn. The data for each rectangle need not be retained (except through the picture of the rectangle itself): each new rectangle replaces the previous one. The user can clear the screen by pressing the right mouse button.

The routine shown in Figure 2.40 stores the corner points in a static array corner[]. It is made static so that values are retained in the array between successive calls to the routine. The variable numCorners keeps track of how many corners have been entered so far. When this number reaches two, the rectangle is drawn, and numCorners is reset to 0.

■ EXAMPLE 2.4.3 How to Control the Sierpinski Gasket with the Mouse

It is simple to extend the Sierpinski gasket routine described earlier so that the user can specify the three vertices of the initial parent triangle with the mouse. We use the same process as in the previous example and in the inside back cover: gather the three points in an array corner[ ], and when three points are available, draw the Sierpinski gasket. The meat of the myMouse() routine is therefore:

```
static GLintPoint corner[3];
static int numCorners = 0;
if(button == GLUT_LEFT_BUTTON && state == GLUT_DOWN)
   {
   corner[numCorners].x = x;
   corner[numCorners].y = screenHeight - y;
   // flip y coordinate
         if(++numCorners == 3)
            {
```

```
                    Sierpinski(corner);
                    // draw the gasket
                    numCorners = 0;
                    // back to 0 corners
                }
        }
    glFlush(); // force any drawing to complete
```

where Sierpinski() is the same as in Figure 2.13, except that the three vertices of the triangle are passed as parameters.

```
/*Upon the first left mouse click one corner of the aligned rectangle is captured; Upon
the second mouse click the opposite corner is captured, and the aligned rectangle is
drawn.*/

void myMouse(int button, int state, int x, int y){
    static GLintPoint corner[2];        // creates an array
    static int numCorners = 0;          // initial value is 0
if(state == GLUT_DOWN) {
    if(button == GLUT_LEFT_BUTTON){
        corner[numCorners].x = x;
        corner[numCorners].y = screenHeight - y;      // flip y coordinate
        if(++numCorners == 2){
        glRecti(corner[0].x, corner[0].y, corner[1].x, corner[1].y);
        numCorners = 0; // back to 0 corners
        glFlush();   }
    }
else if(button == GLUT_RIGHT_BUTTON){
            glClear(GL_COLOR_BUFFER_BIT);          // clear the window
            glFlush();                  // force all pending actions to complete
    }
}
```

Mouse Motion

Another mouse event is generated when the mouse is moved. The callback function, say myMovedMouse(), is registered with this event using one of:

```
glutMotionFunc(myMovedMouse);
glutPassiveMotionFunc(myMovedMouse);
```

The former of these functions is called when the mouse is moved across the window with one or more buttons being held down (but not released). The latter is called when the mouse moves across the window with no buttons being held down.

The callback function must take two parameters and have the prototype: myMovedMouse(int x, int y); The values of x and y are, of course, the position of the mouse when the event occurred.

An example of using glutPassiveMotionFunc() is to draw and display **rubber rectangles**, rectangles that grow and shrink as the user moves the mouse. In the following program the user clicks the mouse to establish one corner of the rectangle, and then moves the mouse around with no buttons pressed. Moving the mouse in this way generates an event that calls myPassiveMotion(int x, int y) and the current position of the mouse determines the opposite corner.

Here we set up GLUT to use double-buffered rendering for smoother animation; the mechanics of this are explained in Chapter 3. Although in previous examples some rendering took place outside of the myDisplay() function, this is something that should be avoided. Therefore we have a few global variables instead,

FIGURE 2.40 A callback routine to draw rectangles entered with the mouse.

FIGURE 2.41 A complete program to draw rubber rectangles.

```
/*A program to allow the user to draw rubber rectangles: those
that grow and shrink as the user moves the mouse.*/
//all suitable includes
struct GLintPoint {
        GLint x, y;
};
//global variables
GLintPoint    corner[2];
bool    selected = false;
int    screenWidth = 640, screenHeight = 480;
void myDisplay() {
  glClear( GL_COLOR_BUFFER_BIT );
  glMatrixMode( GL_MODELVIEW );
  glLoadIdentity();
  glColor3f( 1.0f, 1.0f, 1.0f );
  if( selected ) {
    glBegin( GL_QUADS );
    glVertex2i( corner[0].x, corner[0].y ); //draw a rectangle
    glVertex2i( corner[0].x, corner[1].y );
    glVertex2i( corner[1].x, corner[1].y );
    glVertex2i( corner[1].x, corner[0].y );
  glEnd();

}
glutSwapBuffers();

}
void myMouse( int button, int state, int x, int y ) {
  if( button == GLUT_LEFT_BUTTON && state == GLUT_DOWN ) {
    corner[0].x = x;
    corner[0].y = screenHeight - y;
    selected = true;
}
glutPostRedisplay();
}
void myPassiveMotion( int x, int y )  {
  corner[1].x = x;
  corner[1].y = screenHeight - y;
  glutPostRedisplay();
}
int main( int argc, char ** argv ) {
glutInit( &argc, argv );
// initialize window
glutInitWindowSize( screenWidth, screenHeight );
glutInitWindowPosition( 0, 0 );
glutInitDisplayMode( GLUT_RGB | GLUT_DOUBLE );
// create window
glutCreateWindow( "Rubber Rect Demo" );
// set the projection matrix
glMatrixMode( GL_PROJECTION );
glLoadIdentity();
gluOrtho2D( 0, screenWidth, 0, screenHeight );
glMatrixMode( GL_MODELVIEW );
// clear rendering surface
glClearColor(0.0f, 0.0f, 0.0f, 0.0f);  // background is black
glViewport(0, 0, screenWidth, screenHeight);
```

```
glutMouseFunc( myMouse );
glutDisplayFunc( myDisplay );
glutPassiveMotionFunc( myPassiveMotion );
glutMainLoop();
return( 0 );
}
```

FIGURE 2.41 *(Continued)*

and each time we want to render the rectangle we call `glutPostRedisplay()`, which forces GLUT to call our rendering callback, `myDisplay()`.

2.4.2 Keyboard Interaction

As mentioned earlier, pressing a key on the keyboard queues a keyboard event. The callback function `myKeyboard()` is registered with this type of event through `glutKeyboardFunc(myKeyboard)`.

It must have prototype:

```
void myKeyboard(unsigned int key, int x, int y);
```

The value of key is the ASCII value[6] of the key pressed. The values x and y report the position of the mouse at the time a keyboard key is pressed and released. (As before, y measures the number of pixels down from the top of the window.)

The programmer can capitalize on the many keys on the keyboard to offer the user a large number of choices to invoke at any point in a program. Most implementations of `myKeyboard()` consist of a large `switch` statement, with a `case` for each key of interest. **Alert:** But keep in mind that the `switch` statement is the most dangerous of any in programming: you can promise yourself that you will never forget to terminate such statements with `break`; but of course you will forget this. In the history of programming this has led to great disasters, including bringing the AT&T long distance network to its knees on January 1990. To read more on this story find a copy of the charming *Expert C Programming: Deep C Secrets*, by Peter van der Linden [van der Linden94]. Figure 2.42 shows one possibility. Pressing 'p'

```
void myKeyboard(unsigned char theKey, int mouseX, int mouseY)
{
   GLint x = mouseX;
   GLint y = screenHeight - mouseY; // flip the y value as always
   switch(theKey)
   {
     case 'p':
       drawDot(x, y);        // draw a dot at the mouse position
       break;
     case 'E':
       exit(-1);             //terminate the program
     default:
       break;                // do nothing
   }
}
```

FIGURE 2.42 An example of the keyboard callback function.

---

[6] ASCII stands for American Standard Code for Information Interchange. Tables of ASCII values are readily available on the Internet.

draws a dot at the mouse position, and pressing 'E' exits from the program. Note that if the user holds down the 'p' key and moves the mouse around, a rapid sequence of points is generated to make a freehand drawing.

2.5 INTRODUCTION TO THE DESIGN AND USE OF MENUS IN AN APPLICATION

A graphic application can be made much more congenial for the user to control if it presents menu options. As described briefly in Chapter 1, the program posts a menu at appropriate moments during its execution. The menu appears in front of the graphics already generated by the program, readily visible and offering the user a number of options. The options are of different types, as we shall see. The program then waits for the user to make one or more selections. When the user has done so, usually with the mouse or keyboard, the menu disappears, revealing the graphics that it was covering a moment before, and the program follows an execution path determined by the user's selections. (Properly designed menus are self-explanatory to the user.)

GLUT and GLUI Menus

We shall describe two levels of menu management, made available through two different OpenGL libraries, the GLUT and the GLUI libraries. GLUT menus (recall Figure 2.3) tend to be simpler than GLUI menus, but they are still very serviceable. We first describe an application which makes good use of a GLUT menu.

Example:

We will build a single menu that will allow the user to change the color of a triangle, which is rotating as the application proceeds. The user activates the menu by a right-click in the OpenGL window, at that point a choice of four colors is provided, as shown in Figure 2.43.

FIGURE 2.43 A GLUT menu in action.

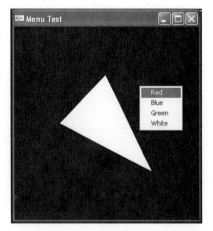

The user chooses the desired color by a left-click on one of the options. Although not included in this example, there could be additional controls, such as keyboard keystrokes that would vary certain parameters.

Code to Design and Use a GLUT Menu

Even though this menu is quite simple, it still seems that the application code to specify its shape, position, entries, and activities would present a formidable task to the application programmer. From a programming standpoint, think of drawing the menu as a square, followed by positioning and labeling menu options in a pleasing arrangement, permitting a right-click to activate the menu (make it visible) and to cause a selection of some menu option with the mouse to make the menu disappear. This would seem to be a daunting task for the application programmer, but in fact GLUT handles it all for us! With only a handful of GLUT function calls all of these tasks are easily managed.

We first must create the menu, using void glutCreateMenu(); which initializes the menu handler. Along with the glutCreateMenu() the actual menu entries need to be defined. We use the function glutCreateMenu(process MenuEvents); which has the single parameter processMenuEvents, a function which we must write and which handles the actions to be performed depending on which menu option has been selected. processMenuEvents is typically a switch statement which sets some values within the application according the menu entry that is selected.

In order to add options to your menu, use the function glutAddMenuEntry(). This is an essential part of designing the menu itself. For the example here, we add entries (using enumerated types or defines for convenience):

```
glutAddMenuEntry("Red",RED);
glutAddMenuEntry("Blue",BLUE);
glutAddMenuEntry("Green",GREEN);
glutAddMenuEntry("White",WHITE);
```

The programmer is free to add additional menu entries; there is no need to tell GLUT ahead of time how many entries to expect! Each menu entry has a string that is displayed when the user makes a selection, followed by the values produced by each mouse click. Once the menu has been designed, it is attached to the mouse button using glutAttachMenu(GLUT_RIGHT_BOTTOM); (or the designer's choice of the mouse button to be used, left, right, or middle). This is all that is required for GLUT menu handling! Notice that there is no need for a separate mouse handler. Figure 2.44 provides a complete working program incorporating a GLUT menu.

```
#include<gl/glut.h>
#include<gl/glu.h>
#include<gl/gl.h>
#define RED 1
#define GREEN 2
#define BLUE 3
#define WHITE 4
float angle = 0.0;// for rotating the triangle
float red=1.0, blue=1.0, green=1.0;  // possible triangle colors
void renderScene(void) {
// the callback to draw the triangle
  glClear(GL_COLOR_BUFFER_BIT | GL_DEPTH_BUFFER_BIT);
  glLoadIdentity();-
  glRotatef(angle,0.0,1.0,0.0);// rotate the triangle a
                                  little more
  glColor3f(red,green,blue);// change its color
```

FIGURE 2.44 A complete program to demonstrate the use of GLUT menus. (Courtesy of P. Rademacher)

```
    glBegin(GL_TRIANGLES);// draw the triangle
      glVertex3f(-0.5,-0.5,0.0);
      glVertex3f(0.5,0.0,0.0);
      glVertex3f(0.0,0.5,0.0);
    glEnd();
    angle++;
    glutSwapBuffers();
}
void processMenuEvents(int option) {
//mouse choice chooses color
    switch (option) {
      case RED : red = 1.0; green = 0.0; blue = 0.0; break;
      case GREEN : red = 0.0; green = 1.0; blue = 0.0; break;
      case BLUE : red = 0.0; green = 0.0; blue = 1.0; break;
      case WHITE : red = 1.0; green = 1.0; blue = 1.0; break;
    }
}
//---------MAIN---------
void main(int argc, char **argv) {
    glutInit(&argc, argv);
    glutInitDisplayMode(GLUT_DEPTH | GLUT_DOUBLE | GLUT_RGBA);
    glutInitWindowPosition(100,100);
    glutInitWindowSize(320,320);
    glutCreateWindow("Menu Test"); // open an OpenGL window
    glutDisplayFunc(renderScene);  // register display function
    glutIdleFunc(renderScene);
//calls to functions to create the menu
//the function called upon a right-click
//create menu and associates menu events
    glutCreateMenu(processMenuEvents);
    glutAddMenuEntry("Red",RED);
    glutAddMenuEntry("Blue",BLUE);
    glutAddMenuEntry("Green",GREEN);
    glutAddMenuEntry("White",WHITE);
    glutAttachMenu(GLUT_RIGHT_BUTTON); // attach right mouse button
to menu
    glutMainLoop();
}
```

FIGURE 2.44 (*Continued*)

GLUI Menus

GLUT menus give the user significant control over the flow of an application, but sometimes the user wants to have a finer control and a broader set of logical input devices (recall Chapter 1). We shall study the extra possibilities offered by the GLUI library (GL User Interface) here. Different kinds of controls are available when we use the GLUI. Figure 2.45 shows a rather complex menu that can be used with the GLUI; refer to this figure as we describe each item. (Some items in the list are readily apparent whereas others are rather obscure).

- **Buttons**—such as "OK" or "Cancel" buttons. Shown as "Button," "Another Button," and so on in the figure.
- **Checkboxes**—an on/off choice, such as toggling between wireframe and shaded views. Labeled "Checkbox 1" in the figure.

- **Radio Buttons**—choice device; exactly one radio button option can be selected from a radio button group at a time. Labeled "Radio Button 1," "Radio Button 2," and so on in the figure.
- **Static Text**—displays a short message to assist the user in managing the program. Static text cannot be altered by the user, so it is not an input device. Labeled "Static Text" in the figure.
- **Editable Text areas**—a string device; the user can type in a string, backspace, and otherwise change the typed string value.
- **Spinners**—value input devices; when the user clicks the mouse on the up or down arrow, the value increments or decrements rapidly to the desired value.
- **Panels**—a group of interface elements that can be minimized and maximized for easy viewing. The figure shows an example labeled "Rollout (open)." When the minus sign is pressed, the panel collapses to the single element labeled "Rollout (closed)." Not surprisingly, clicking on the plus sign expands the collapsed interface elements (such as "Hi There!" and "123") and allows each to become an input device.
- **List boxes**—a submenu of drop-down options providing a choice input device (labeled "Listbox 1" and "Listbox 2" in the figure).
- **Rotation and Translation devices**—arc ball-like devices that provide value input devices. The user moves the top of the arc ball or the head of the arrow continuously with the mouse and sees the object redrawn after a translation or rotation.
- **Separators**—visual aids (not input devices) in a program that assist the eye in organizing the many options and elements on screen. For example, the line below the "Static Text" is a separator.

Notice that GLUI menus are much more sophisticated than GLUT menus, and we would expect source code for defining and managing GLUI menus to be rather complex as well. However, GLUI handles a lot of the difficulties behind the scenes, as did

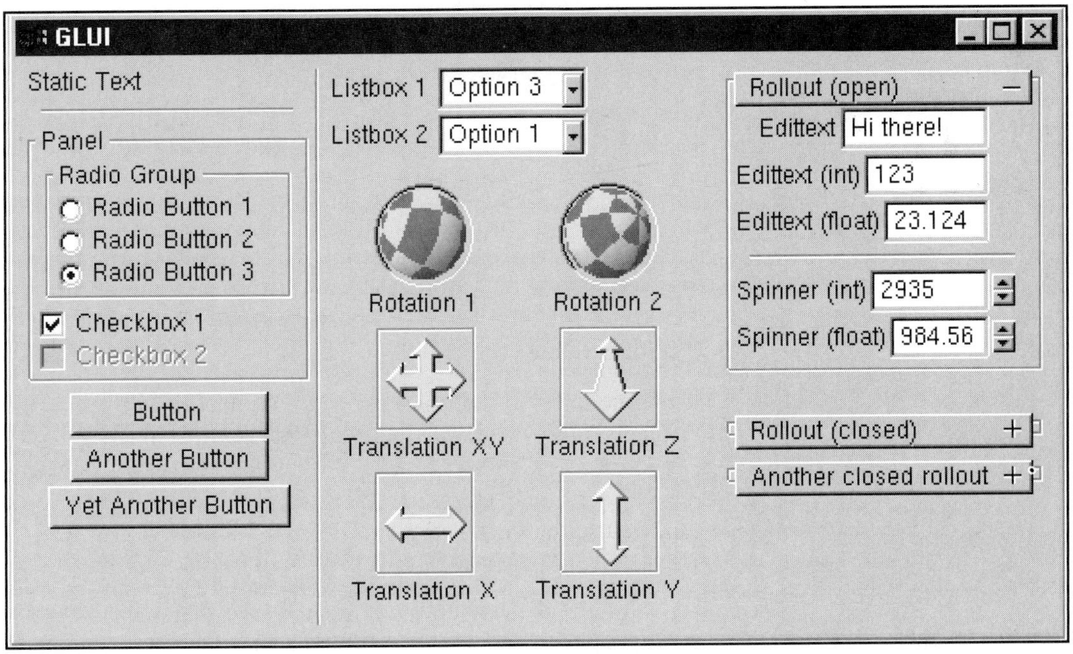

FIGURE 2.45 A sample GLUI interface. (Courtesy of P. Rademacher)

GLUT. A complete working program, courtesy of Paul Rademacher,[7] which, demonstrates the power of GLUI controls, is available on the book's companion website.

2.6 SUMMARY

Don't fear failure so much that you refuse to try new things. The saddest summary of a life contains three descriptions: could have, might have, and should have.

Louis E. Boone
(1941–2005)

The hard part in writing graphics applications is getting started—pulling together the hardware and software ingredients in a program to make the first few pictures. The OpenGL application programmer interface (API) helps enormously here, as it provides a powerful yet simple set of routines to make drawings. One of its great virtues is device independence, which makes it possible to write programs for one graphics environment, and use the same program without changes in another environment.

Most graphics applications are written today for a windows-based environment. The program opens a window on the screen that can be moved and resized by the user, and it responds to mouse clicks and keystrokes. We saw how to use OpenGL functions that make it easy to create such a program.

Primitive drawing routines were applied to making pictures composed of dots, lines, polylines, and polygons and were combined into more powerful routines that form the basis of one's personal graphics toolkit. Several examples illustrated the use of these tools and described methods for interacting with a program using the keyboard and mouse. The introduction of `moveTo()` and `lineTo()` enhanced the convenience of functions available to draw lines. Special emphasis was placed on drawing aligned rectangles, using the built-in OpenGL function, `glRecti()`.

The case studies presented next offer additional programming examples that explore more deeply the topics discussed so far, or branch out to interesting related topics.

2.7 CASE STUDIES

It is best, while using this text, to try out new ideas as they are introduced, in order to solidify the ideas presented. This is particularly true in the first few chapters, since getting started with graphics programs often presents a hurdle. To focus this effort, each chapter ends with some **Case Studies**, which describe interesting programming projects that concentrate on the ideas developed in the chapter.

Some of the Case Studies are simple exercises that only require fleshing out some pseudocode given in the text and then running the program through its paces. Others are much more challenging and could serve as the basis of a major programming project within a course. It is always difficult to judge how much time someone else will need to accomplish any project. The "**Level of Effort**" assigned to each Case Study is a rough guess at best.

Level of Effort:

I: A simple exercise. It could be assigned for the next class.
II: An intermediate exercise. It probably needs several days for completion.
III: An advanced exercise. It would probably be assigned for two weeks or so ahead.

CASE STUDY 2.1 PSEUDORANDOM CLOUDS OF DOTS

(Level of Effort: II)   The random number generator (RNG) `rand()` (a function built into the standard C++ library) produces a value between 0 and $N - 1$ each time it is called. Each value appears to be randomly selected and to have no relation to its predecessors.

Random numbers are used in a variety of computer applications in order to simulate games such as poker and craps and other situations where randomness plays a big part.

---

[7] Paul Rademacher worked with Nigel Stewart on GLUI. The GLUI project's homepage is http://glui.sourceforge.net.

In fact the successive numbers are not generated randomly at all, but rather through a very regular mechanism where each number n_i is determined from its predecessor n_{i-1} by a specific formula. A typical formula is:

$$n_i = (n_{i-1}*A + B)\%N \qquad (2.4)$$

where A, B, and N are suitably chosen constants. The operations on n_{i-1} basically appear to scramble the bits of n_{i-1} to form the new value n_i, making it *appear* to be unrelated to previous values. In fact, each number is deterministically based on the preceding value. One set of numbers in Equation 2.4 that works fairly well is: $A = 1103515245$, $B = 12345$, and $N = 32767$. Multiplying n_{i-1} by A and adding B forms a large value, and the modulo operation brings the value into the range 0 to $N - 1$. The process begins with some "seed" value chosen for n_0.

Because the numbers only give an appearance of randomness, they are called **pseudorandom** numbers. The choices of the values for A, B, and N are very important, and slightly different values give rise to very different characteristics in the sequence of numbers. More details can be found in [Knuth, Weiss98].

Scatter Plots

Some experiments yield data consisting of many pairs of numbers (a_i, b_i) and the goal is to infer visually how the a-values and b-values are related. For instance, a large number of people are measured, and one wonders whether there is a strong correlation between a person's height and weight.

A scatter plot can be used to give visual insight into the data. The data for each person are plotted as a dot at position (*height*, *weight*), so only the drawDot() tool is needed. Figure 2.46 shows an example. It suggests that a person's height and weight are roughly linearly related, although some people (such as A) are idiosyncratic, being of average height and yet unexpectedly light.

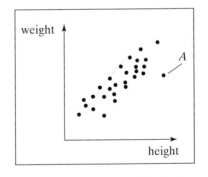

FIGURE 2.46 A scatter plot of people's height vs. weight.

We can use scatter plots visually to test the quality of a random number generator. Each time the function rand() is called, it returns a value in the range $0, \ldots, N - 1$ that is apparently chosen at random, unrelated to values previously returned from rand(). But are successive values truly unrelated?

One simple test builds a scatter plot based on pairs of successive values returned by rand(). It calls rand() twice in succession and plots the first value against the second. This can be done using drawDot():

```
for(int i = 0; i < num; i++)
    drawDot(rand(), rand());          // num is a large number
                                         chosen by the user
```

or in basic OpenGL by placing the for loop between glBegin() and glEnd():

```
glBegin(GL_POINTS);
  for(int i = 0; i < num; i++)        // do it num times
    glVertex2i(rand(), rand());
glEnd();
```

FIGURE 2.47 A constellation of 500 random dots.

It is more efficient to do it the second way, which avoids the overhead associated with making many calls to glBegin() and glEnd().

Figure 2.47 shows a typical plot that might result. There should be a uniform density of dots throughout the square, to reassure you that the values $0, \ldots, N - 1$ occur with about equal likelihood, and that there is no discernible dependence between one value and its successor.

Figure 2.48 shows what can happen with an inferior random number generator. In part a there is too high a density of certain values, so the distribution is not uniform in $0, \ldots, N - 1$. In part b there is some correlation between the x- and y-values: over a range of small and large x-values, the y-values seem to 'congregate' about a straight line aimed 45 degrees away from the x-axis. Part c shows the most unacceptable situation of all: after a few dozen values have been generated, the pattern *repeats*, and no new dots are generated!

Plotting dot constellations such as these can provide a rough first check on the uniformity of the numbers generated. It is far from a thorough test, however [Knuth97].

FIGURE 2.48 Scatter plots for inferior random number generators.

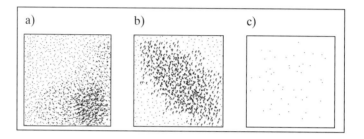

Write a program that produces random dot plots, using some different random number generators to produce the (x, y) pairs. Try different constants A, B, and N in the basic RNG and see the effect this has on the dot plot constellations generated when Equation 2.4 is used.

There is a long history of studies of RNGs which reveal some of their internal workings. We recommend using your favorite search engine to search "random number generators" and then reading the source materials found there.

CASE STUDY 2.2: INTRODUCTION TO ITERATED FUNCTION SYSTEMS

> From his paradise no one shall ever evict us.
>
> *defending Cantor's set theory*
> *David Hilbert*
> *(1862–1943),*

(Level of Effort: II)   The repetitive operation of drawing the Sierpinski gasket is an example of an **iterated function system (IFS)**, which we shall encounter surprisingly often throughout the book. Many interesting computer-generated figures (fractals, the Mandelbrot set, and so on) are based on variations of it.

A hand calculator provides a tool for experimenting with a simple IFS. Enter some (positive) number *num* and press the square root key. This produces a new number $\sqrt{num}$. Press the square root key again to take its square root, yielding $\sqrt{num}$. Keep doing this forever …, or until satisfied. We are *iterating* with the square root function, and each result is used as the input for the next square root. An initial value of *num* = 64 yields the sequence: 64, 8, 2.8284, 1.68179, …. (Is there a value to which this sequence converges?)

Figure 2.49 presents the system schematically, showing that each output value is fed back to have its square root formed, again and again.

From this we can present at least an informal definition: **Iterated function system** is a function, or collection of functions, wherein the output of each function is fed back to become the input of its corresponding function in the next iteration.

In this example the function being iterated is $f(x) = \sqrt{x}$, or symbolically $f(.) = \sqrt{\ }$, the "square-rooter." Other functions $f(.)$ can be used instead, such as:

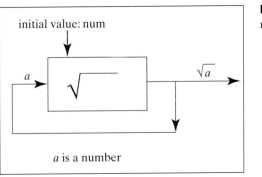

FIGURE 2.49 Taking the square root repetitively.

initial value: num

a

$\sqrt{a}$

a is a number

$f(.) = 2(.),$ the "doubler" doubles its argument

$f(.) = \cos(.),$ the "cosiner"

$f(.) = 4(.)(1 - (.)),$ the "logistic" function, used in chaos theory (see Chapter 3)

$f(.) = (.)^2 + c$ for a constant c, used to define the Mandelbrot set (see Appendix 4)

It is sometimes helpful to give a name to each number that emerges from the IFS. We call the kth such number d_k and say that the process begins at $k = 0$ by injecting the initial value d_0 into the system. Then the sequence of values generated by the IFS is:

d_0
$d_1 = f(d_0)$
$d_2 = f(f(d_0))$
$d_3 = f(f(f(d_0)))$
$\ldots$

Therefore d_3 is formed by applying function $f(.)$ three times. This is called **the third iterate** of $f()$ applied to the initial value d_0. More succinctly we can denote the **kth iterate** of $f()$ by

$$d_k = f^{[k]}(d_0) \tag{2.5}$$

meaning that the value produced after $f(.)$ has been applied k times to d_k. (**Note:** It does not mean that the value $f(d_0)$ is raised to the kth power nor does it mean the kth derivative of the function f(.)) We can also use the *recursive* form and specify how the kth value is determined by the previous $(k - 1)$st value, according to:

$$d_k = f(d_{k-1}) \quad \text{for } k = 1, 2, 3, \ldots, \quad \text{for a given value of } d_0$$

This possibly endless sequence of values $d_0, d_1, d_2, d_3, d_4, \ldots$ is called "the **orbit** of d_0" for the system.

Example: The orbit of 64 for the function $f(.) = \sqrt{.}$ is 64, 8, 2.8284, 1.68179, ..., and the orbit of 10,000 is 100, 10, 3.162278, 1.77828, ... (What is the orbit of 0? What is the orbit of 0.1?)

Example: The orbit of 7 for the "doubler" $f(.) = 2 \cdot (.)$ is 7, 14, 28, 56, 112, ... The kth iterate is $7 * 2^k$.

Example: The orbit of 1 for $f(.) = \sin(.)$ can be found using a hand calculator: 1, .8414, .7456, .6784, ..., which *very* slowly approaches the value 0. (What is the orbit of 1 for $\cos(.)$? In particular, to what value does the orbit converge?)

Project 1: Predicting the Hailstone Sequence

Consider iterating the intriguingly simple function $f(.)$:

$$f(x) = \begin{cases} \dfrac{x}{2} & \text{if } x \text{ is even} \\ 3x + 1 & \text{if } x \text{ is odd} \end{cases} \tag{2.6}$$

Even-valued arguments are cut in half, whereas odd ones are enlarged. For example, the orbit of 17 is the sequence: 17, 52, 26, 13, 40, 20, 10, 5, 16, 8, 4, 2, 1, ... Once a power of 2 is reached, the sequence falls like a hailstone to 1 and becomes trapped in a short repetitive cycle. An unanswered question in mathematics is:

Unanswered Question: Does *every* orbit fall to 1? That is, does a positive integer exist that, when used as a starting point and iterated with the hailstone function, does *not* ultimately crash down to 1? No one knows, but the intricacies of the sequence have been widely studied [Hayes 84]. As with many mathematical questions, the gigantic hurdle lurks in the single word "**every**"!

A large cash gift (plus substantial fame) has been offered to anyone who can solve this problem.

Additional resources on this problem may be found at the book's companion web site.

Write a program that plots the course of the sequence $y_k = f^{[k]}(y_0)$ vs. k. The user gives a starting value y_0 between 1 and 4,000,000,000 (unsigned long's will hold values of this size.) Each value y_k is plotted as the point (k, y_k). Each plot continues until y_k reaches a value of 1 (if it does ...).

Because the hailstone sequence can be very long, and the values of y_k can grow very large, it is essential to scale the values *before* they are displayed. Recall from Section 2.2 that appropriate values of $A, B, C,$ and D are determined so that when the value (k, y_k) is plotted at screen coordinates

$$sx = (A * k + B)$$
$$sy = (C * y_k + D) \qquad\qquad (2.7)$$

the entire sequence fits on the screen.

Note that you don't know how long the sequence will be, nor how large y_k will get, until after the sequence has been generated. A simple solution is to run the sequence *quietly* first—that is, invisibly—keeping track of the largest value yBiggest attained by y_k, as well as the number of iterations kBiggest required for the sequence to reach 1. These values are then used to determine $A, B, C,$ and D. The sequence is then rerun and plotted.

A Curious Question: What is the largest yBiggest and what is the largest kBiggest encountered for any hailstone sequence with a starting value between 1 and 1,000,000?

Iterating with Functions That Produce Points Iterating numbers through some function $f(.)$ is interesting enough, but iterating *points* through a function is even more so, since we can use drawDot() to build patterns out of the different points that emerge. So we consider a function $f(p)$ that takes one point $p = (x, y)$ as input and produces another point as its output. Each newly formed point is fed back into the same function again to generate yet another new point, as suggested in Figure 2.50. Here p_{k-1} is used to create the kth iterate $p_k = f^{[k]}(p_0)$, which is then fed back to produce p_{k+1}, and so on.

FIGURE 2.50 Iterated function sequence generator for points.

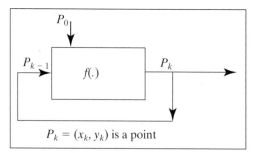

Once again, we call the sequence of points $p_0, p_1, p_2, \ldots$ the orbit of p_0.

Note: The Sierpinski gasket may be seen as an IFS.

In terms of an IFS the kth dot, p_k, of the Sierpinski gasket is formed from p_{k-1} using

$$p_k = (p_{k-1} + T[\text{random}(3)])/2; \qquad\qquad (2.8)$$

that is, it's the midpoint between the previous point p_{k-1} and a random selection of one of the three points of the parent triangle.

Here it is understood that the x- and y-components must be formed separately. Thus the function that is iterated is

$$f(.) = ((.) + T[\text{random}(3)])/2$$

Write an application that forms the Sierpinski gasket using the notions of the IFS of Equation (2.3), which expresses each new point in terms of the previous point. Draw the succession of points produced, against a white background, until some number of points, say 2000, have been drawn. Make the screen window 600 × 800 pixels in size and have it display the title "OpenGL makes this all so easy!" Is this screen window a golden rectangle? Experiment with versions of your application that use different drawing colors, point sizes, and window titles. Also, for at least one experiment, adjust the screen window so that it is a golden rectangle.

Project 2: The Gingerbread Man

The gingerbread man shown in Figure 2.51 is based on another IFS, and it can be drawn as a dot constellation. It has become a familiar creature in chaos theory [Peitgen88, Gleick87, Schroeder91] because it is a form of "strange attractor": the successive dots are attracted into a region resembling a gingerbread man, with curious hexagonal holes.

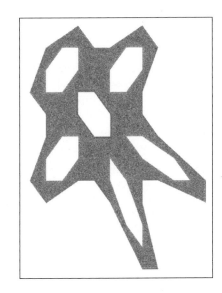

FIGURE 2.51 A typical gingerbread man.

There is no randomness in the process that generates the gingerbread man; each new point q is formed from the previous point p according to the rules:

$$q.x = M(1 + 2L) - p.y + |p.x - LM|$$
$$q.y = p.x \tag{2.9}$$

where constants M and L are carefully chosen to scale and position the gingerbread man on the display. (The values $M = 40$ and $L = 3$ might be good choices for a 640-by-480-pixel display.)

Notice that the y-coordinate of the new point, q, is simply the x-coordinate of the previous point, p.

Be sure to hand-simulate at least a few iterations of this IFS using specific numbers, in order to develop an initial understanding of the process. This familiarity will pay off handsomely.

Write a program that allows the user to choose the starting point for the iterations with the mouse, and draws the dots for the gingerbread man. Start with the suggested values of M and L, and then experiment with others as well. Using a somewhat different resolution display, say 800×600 or 1024×768, what optimum values for M and L would you recommend?

You will notice that for a given starting point only a few dots appear before the pattern repeats (so it stops changing). Certain starting points give rise to different patterns. Arrange your program so that you can add to the picture by inputting additional starting points with the mouse.

PRACTICE EXERCISE

A fixed point on the gingerbread man

Show that this process has a fixed point: $((1 + L)M, (1 + L)M)$. That is, the result of subjecting this point to the process of Equation (2.9) yields the same point. (Why would this be a very uninteresting starting point for generating the gingerbread man?) ■

CASE STUDY 2.3 THE GOLDEN RATIO AND OTHER JEWELS

(Level of Effort: I)   The aspect ratio of an aligned rectangle is one of its very important attributes. Over the centuries, one aspect ratio in particular has been has been celebrated for its pleasing qualities in works of art: that of the **golden rectangle**. The golden rectangle is considered as the most pleasing of all rectangles, being neither too tall and thin nor too short and squat. It appears in the Greek Parthenon, Leonardo da Vinci's *Mona Lisa*, Salvador Dali's *The Sacrament of the Last Supper*, and in many of M. C. Escher's works. The golden rectangle is based on a fascinating quantity, the golden ratio $\phi = 1.618033989$. This value ϕ (pronounced 'fee' or 'fie') appears in a surprising number of places in computer graphics.

The shape of the golden rectangle has the unique property (recall Figure 2.34C): if a square is removed from the rectangle, the piece that remains will again be a golden rectangle! In portrait orientation what value must ϕ have to make this work? Note in the Figure 2.34C that, after removing the square, the remaining rectangle has height 1 ϕ-1 and so to be golden must have width $1/\phi$. Thus

$$\phi = 1 + \frac{1}{\phi} \tag{2.10}$$

which leads to a quadratic equation that is easily solved to yield:

$$\phi = \frac{1 + \sqrt{5}}{2} = 1.618033989\ldots \tag{2.11}$$

This is approximately the aspect ratio of a standard 3-by-5 index card. From Equation (2.10) we see also that if 1 is subtracted from ϕ, the reciprocal of ϕ is obtained: $1/\phi = .618033989\ldots$. This is the aspect ratio of a golden rectangle standing on its short end.

The number ϕ is remarkable mathematically in many ways, two favorites being

$$\phi = \sqrt{1 + \sqrt{1 + \sqrt{1 + \sqrt{1 +}}}} \cdots \tag{2.12}$$

and the continued fraction expansion:

$$\phi = 1 + \cfrac{1}{1 + \cfrac{1}{1 + \cfrac{1}{1 + \cdots}}} \tag{2.13}$$

These formulas are *exact*, and are both easy to prove (how?), displaying a pleasing simplicity in the repeated use of the single digit 1.

The idea that each golden rectangle contains a smaller version of itself suggests a form of infinite regression of figures … within figures … within figures … *ad infinitum*. Figure 2.52 demonstrates this. Keep removing a square from the figure to produce another golden rectangle!

Write an application that draws the regression of golden rectangles centered in a screen window 600 pixels wide by 400 pixels high. (First determine where and how big the largest golden rectangle is that will fit in this screen window. Your picture should regress down until the smallest rectangle is about one pixel in size.)

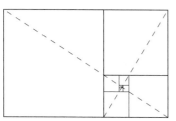

FIGURE 2.52 Infinite regressions of the golden rectangle.

There is much more to be said about the golden ratio, and many delights can be found in [Gardner61], [Hill78], [Huntley70], and [Ogilvy69]. For instance, in the next chapter we see golden pentagrams, and in Chapter 9 we see that two of the platonic solids, the dodecahedron and the icosahedron, contain three mutually perpendicular golden rectangles!

PRACTICE EXERCISES

2.7.1. Other golden things

Equation (2.10) shows ϕ as a repeated square root involving the number 1. What is the value of:

$$W = \sqrt{k + \sqrt{k + \sqrt{k + \sqrt{k + \cdots}}}}$$

2.7.2. On ϕ and golden rectangles

a. Show the validity of Equations (2.12) and (2.13).
b. Find the point at which the two dotted diagonals shown in Figure 2.52 intersect, and show that this is the point to which the sequence of golden rectangles converges.
c. Use Equation (2.10) to derive the relationship:

$$\phi^2 + \frac{1}{\phi^2} = 3 \qquad\qquad (2.14)$$

2.7.3. Golden orbits

The expressions in Equations (2.12) and (2.13) show that the golden ratio ϕ is the limiting value of applying certain functions again and again. The first function is $f(.) = \sqrt{1 + (.)}$. What is the second function? Viewing these expressions in terms of iterated functions systems, ϕ is seen to be the value to which orbits converge for some starting values. (The starting value is hidden in the "..." of the expressions.) Explore with a hand calculator what starting values one can use and still have the process converge to ϕ. ■

CASE STUDY 2.4 HOW TO BUILD AND USE POLYLINE FILES

(Level of Effort: II)   Complex pictures such as, "dino.dat" are based on a large collection of polylines. The data for the polylines are typically stored in a file, so the picture can be reconstructed at a later time by reading the polylines into a program and redrawing each line. A reasonable format for such a file was described in Section 2.3.1, and the routine drawPolyLineFile() was described that does the drawing.

The file, "dino.dat", that stores the dinosaur in Figure 2.23 is available as dino.dat on the web site for this book. Other polyline files are also available there.

a. Write a program that reads polyline data from a file and draws each polyline in turn. Generate at least one interesting polyline file of your own on a text processor, and use your program to draw it. Be sure to arrange your program so that it need not read the file of polyline data each time it needs to draw a set of polylines. An array or linked list might be found useful to store the polyline data.
b. Extend the program in the previous part to accept some other file formats. For instance, have it accept **differentially coded** x- and y-coordinates. Here the first point (x_1, y_1) of each polyline is encoded as previously but each remaining one (x_i, y_i) is encoded after subtracting the previous point from it: the file contains $(x_i - x_{i-1}, y_i - y_{i-1})$. In many cases there are fewer significant digits in the difference than in the original point values, allowing more compact files. Experiment with this format.
c. Adapt the file format above so that a color value is associated with each polyline in the file. This color value appears in the file on the same line as the number of points in the associated polyline. Experiment with several polyline files.

d. Adjust the polyline drawing routine so that it draws a closed polygon when a minus sign precedes the number of points in a polyline, as in:

```
-3              - negative: so this is a polygon
 0    0         first point in this polygon
35         3    second point in this polygon
57         8    also connect this to the first point of the polygon
 5              - positive, so leave it open as usual
 0         1
12        21
23        34
 ..  etc
```

The first polyline is drawn as a triangle: its last point is connected to its first.

CASE STUDY 2.5 HOW TO BUILD AND RUN MAZES

(Level of Effort: III)   The task of finding a path through a maze seems forever fascinating (see [Coxeter74]). You can generate an elaborate maze on a computer and use graphics to watch it be traversed. Figure 2.53 shows a rectangular maze having 100 rows and 150 columns. The goal is to find a path through a proper maze from the opening at the left edge to the opening at the right edge. Although you can traverse it manually by trial and error, it's more interesting to develop an algorithm to do it automatically.

FIGURE 2.53 A maze. (Courtesy of Dennis Chen)

Write and exercise a program that:

a. generates and displays a rectangular maze of R rows and C columns, and
b. finds and displays the path from start to end.

The mazes are generated randomly but must be **proper**; that is, every one of the R-by-C cells is connected by a unique, albeit tortuous, path to every other cell.

How should a maze be represented? One way is to state for each cell whether its north wall is intact and its east wall is intact, suggesting the following data structure:

```
char northWall[R][C], eastWall[R][C];
```

If `northWall[i][j]` is 1, the ijth cell has a solid upper wall; otherwise the wall is missing. The 0th row is a phantom row of cells below the maze whose north walls comprise the bottom edge. Similarly, `eastWall[i][0]` specifies where any gaps appear in the left edge of the maze.

How to Generate a Maze.   Start with all walls intact so that the maze is a simple grid of horizontal and vertical lines. The program draws this grid. Then an invisible mouse, whose job is to eat through walls to connect adjacent cells, is initially placed in some arbitrarily chosen cell. The mouse checks the four neighbor cells (above, below, left, and right) and for each cell asks whether it has all four walls intact. If not, the cell has previously been visited and so is already on some path. The mouse may detect several candidate cells that haven't been visited; it chooses one randomly and eats through the connecting wall, saving the locations of the other candidates on a stack. The eaten wall is erased, and the mouse repeats the process. When it becomes trapped in a dead end—surrounded by visited cells—it pops an unvisited cell and continues. When the stack is empty, all cells in the maze have been visited. A start and end cell are then chosen randomly, most likely along some edge of the maze. It is delightful to watch the maze being formed dynamically as the mouse eats through walls.

Running the Maze.   Use a backtracking algorithm. At each step, the mouse tries to move in a random direction. If there is no wall, it places its position on a stack and moves to the next cell. The cell that the mouse is in can be drawn with a red dot. When it runs into a dead end, it can change the color of the cell to blue and backtrack by popping the stack. The mouse can even put a wall up to avoid ever trying the dead-end cell again.

Note: Proper mazes aren't too challenging, because you can always traverse them using the "shoulder-to-the-wall rule." Here you trace the maze by rubbing your shoulder along the left-hand wall. At a dead end, sweep around and retrace the path, always maintaining contact with the wall. You will ultimately reach your destination. To make things more interesting, place the start and end cells in the interior of the maze and also let the mouse eat some extra walls (maybe randomly 1 in 20 times). In this way, some cycles may be formed that encircle the end cell and defeat the shoulder method.

2.8 FOR FURTHER READING

Several books provide an introduction to using OpenGL. The *OpenGL Programming Guide* by Woo, Neider, and Davis [Woo04] is an excellent source. Ball and Coxeter [74] offer a charming and readable book that addresses many topics in mathematics, revealing fresh ways to connect seemingly disparate facts, and provides a large number of engaging puzzles that everyone who likes puzzles and recreational mathematics will enjoy attacking.

There is also a wealth of information available on the Internet. See, for instance, the OpenGL main resource repository at http://www.opengl.org/. Peter Van der Linden's book, *Expert C Programming: Deep C Secrets* [Van der Linden94], provides an in depth resource on the C language.

Chapter 3

Additional Drawing Tools

"Computers are useless. They can only give you answers."

Pablo Picasso
(1881–1973)

"Even if you are on the right track, you'll get run over if you just sit there."

Will Rogers
(1879–1935)

GOALS OF THE CHAPTER

○ Introduce viewports and clipping.

○ Develop the window-to-viewport transformation.

○ Develop a classical clipping algorithm.

○ Create tools to draw in world coordinates.

○ Develop ways to select windows and viewports for optimum viewing.

○ Build figures based on regular polygons, arcs, and circles and their offspring.

○ Describe parametrically defined curves and understand techniques for drawing them.

Preview

Section 3.1 introduces world coordinates and the world window. Section 3.2 describes the window-to-viewport transformation. This simplifies graphics applications by letting the programmer work in a reasonable coordinate system, yet have all pictures mapped as desired to the display surface. The section also discusses how the programmers (and users) choose the window and viewport to achieve the desired drawings. A key property is that the aspect ratios of the window and viewport must be the same; otherwise distortion results. Figure 3.1a shows a photo of a cat with the proper aspect ratio; part b shows a photo of the same cat, but with an aspect ratio that is too small.

Some of the steps can be automated. Section 3.3 develops a classical clipping algorithm that removes any parts of the picture that lie outside the world window.

As promised in the Preface, object-oriented programming (OOP) will be used at a number of points throughout the book to simplify the task of the application programmer, or to protect the programmer from common but hard-to-find programming errors. A thorough tutorial introduction to OOP is beyond the scope of the text, but its key features are noted at each place they are used.

b)

FIGURE 3.1 a) Photo with the proper aspect ratio, b) the same photo with a too-narrow window.

a)

Section 3.4 examines how to draw interesting figures based on regular polygons, arcs, and circles. Section 3.5 describes different representations for curves and develops the very useful parametric form, which permits straightforward drawing of complex curves. Curves that reside in both 2D space and 3D space are considered. The chapter ends with several Case Studies.

3.1 INTRODUCTION

It is as interesting and as difficult to say a thing well as to paint it.

Vincent Van Gogh
(1853–1890)

In Chapter 2 our drawings used the basic coordinate system of the screen window coordinates, that are essentially in pixels, extending from 0 on the left to some value `screenWidth` -1, known as **screen coordinates**, in x, and from 0 (usually at the top) to some value `screenHeight` -1 in y. This means that we can use only positive values of x and y, and the values must extend over a large range (several hundred pixels) if we hope to get a drawing of reasonable size.

In a given problem, however, we may not want to think in terms of pixels. It may be much more natural to think in terms of x varying from, say, -1 to 1, and y varying from -100.0 to 20.0. (Recall that it was awkward to scale and translate values when making the dot plots in Figure 2.15.) Clearly we want to separate the values we use in a program to *describe* the geometrical object from those that we use to size and position the *pictures* of the objects on the display. The first is usually referred to as a **modeling** task, the second as **a viewing** task.

In this chapter we develop methods such that the programmer can describe objects in whatever coordinate system best fits the problem at hand, and the picture of the object will be automatically scaled and translated so that it comes out right in the screen window. The space in which objects are described is called **world coordinates** (by which we mean that the numbers used for *x* and *y* are those in the world where the objects in the scene are defined). It is the usual Cartesian *xy*-coordinate system used in mathematics, based on whatever units are convenient.

We define an aligned rectangular **world window**[1] in these world coordinates. The world window specifies which part of the world should be drawn. The understanding is that whatever part lies inside the window should be drawn; whatever part lies outside should be clipped away and not drawn. OpenGL does the clipping automatically.

In addition, we define a rectangular **viewport** also aligned in the screen window on the display. A **mapping** (consisting of scalings and translations) between the world window and the viewport is established automatically by OpenGL. When all the objects in the world are drawn, the parts that lie inside the world window are automatically mapped to the inside of the viewport—that is, into **screen coordinates**, which are simply pixel coordinates on the display. There are several important reasons why aligned rectangles are chosen as the shapes for the window and viewport (as well as for the screen window). Such a shape is very simple geometrically: only four parameters are required in order to describe it completely. In addition, it is very easy to determine whether a given point is inside or outside of such a window, which significantly simplifies clipping algorithms. A third important property is that an aligned rectangle is convex. This too simplifies algorithms that are used in various steps for drawing pictures. Therefore the programmer thinks in terms of looking through a window at the objects being drawn, and placing a snapshot of whatever is seen in that window into the viewport on the display. This window/viewport approach makes it much easier to do natural things like zooming in on a detail in the scene, or panning around a scene.

The principal benefit of the window/viewport paradigm is that, once the window and viewport have been specified, the application programmer can write the algorithm for the desired picture without regard for how big it is, or its location, and all of the underlying operations (scaling, positioning, and clipping) will be done automatically to place the picture in the viewport.

We first develop the mapping part that provides the automatic change of coordinates. Then we see how clipping is done.

3.2 WORLD WINDOWS AND VIEWPORTS

> But, soft! What light through yonder window breaks? It is the east, and Juliet is the sun
>
> Romeo and Juliet *(II, ii, 1–2)*
> *William Shakespeare*
> *(1564–1616)*

We use an example to motivate the use of world windows and viewports. Suppose you want to examine the nature of a certain mathematical function, the so-called "sinc" function famous in the signal-processing field. It is defined by

$$\mathrm{sinc}(x) = \frac{\sin(\pi x)}{\pi x} \qquad \text{when } x \neq 0 \text{ and } \mathrm{sinc}(0) = 1 \tag{3.1}$$

---

[1] As mentioned, the term "window" has a bewildering set of meanings in graphics, which often leads to confusion. We will try to keep the different meanings clear by saying "world window," "screen window," and so on when necessary.

The value of sinc() at 0 is 1 by definition. You want to know how sinc(*x*) bends and wiggles as *x* varies. Suppose you know that as *x* varies from $-\infty$ to ∞, the value of sinc(*x*) varies over a portion of the range -1 to 1, and (due to some genie) it is particularly interesting for values of *x* near 0. (In more complex cases you may not even know **this** much!) So you want a plot that is centered near (0, 1), and that shows sinc(*x*) for closely spaced *x*-values between, say, -4.0 and 4.0. Notice that the sinc() function must not be evaluated by the computer program at $x = 0$, as it would cause a divide by 0; therefore we initially test for the case of a zero argument.

Figure 3.2 shows an example plot of the function. Figure 3.3 is a complete program for the drawing of this figure that you might write after learning the window/viewport tools introduced later in this section. It uses `setWindow()` to establish a world window and `setViewport()` to establish the viewport. We will discuss how to define these functions directly following Figure 3.3.

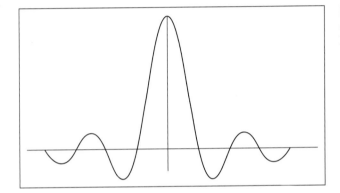

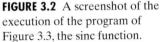

FIGURE 3.2 A screenshot of the execution of the program of Figure 3.3, the sinc function.

```
//Program to produce a sinc function, ~80 points

#include <windows.h>
#include <iostream.h>
#include <math.h>
#include <gl/GL.h>
#include <gl/GLU.h>
#include <gl/GLUT.h>
const float pi = 3.14159265358979;    // use a named constant to approximate pi.

//--------------- setWindow ----------------
void setWindow (GLdouble left, GLdouble right, GLdouble bottom, GLdouble top)

{
     // define our own function to specify the window, as explained later.
          glMatrixMode(GL_PROJECTION);
             glLoadIdentity();
                gluOrtho2D(left, right, bottom, top);
}

//--------------- setViewport ----------------
void setViewport(GLint left, GLint right, GLint bottom, GLint top)

{
// define our own function to specify the viewport, as explained later.
          glViewport(left, bottom, right - left, top - bottom);
}
```

FIGURE 3.2 A complete program to display a sinc function.

```
//<<<<<<<<<<<<<<< myDisplay >>>>>>>>>>>>>>>>>>>>>>>>>>>>>>
void myDisplay(void) // plot the sinc function, using world coordinates

{
  glClear( GL_COLOR_BUFFER_BIT );
        glMatrixMode(GL_MODELVIEW);
          glLoadIdentity();
        glBegin(GL_LINE_STRIP);
/* automatically uses the defined window and viewport, clips properly, and performs the
proper mapping */.

            for(
                float x = -4.0; x < 4.0; x += 0.1)      // draw the plot
                {
                if(x == 0.0)
                    glVertex2f(0.0, 1.0);
                else
                    glVertex2f(x, sin(3.14159 * x) / (3.14159 * x));
                }
            glEnd();
            glFlush();
}


//<<<<<<<<<<<<<<< myInit >>>>>>>>>>>>>>>>>>>>>>>>>>>>>>>>>
void myInit(void)

{
        glClearColor(1.0,1.0,1.0,0.0);   //white background
        glColor3f(0.0f,0.0f,1.0f);           //blue line
        glLineWidth(2.0);                    //line width of 2
}


//<<<<<<<<<<<<<<<main>>>>>>>>>>>>>>>>>>>>>>>>>>>>>>>>>>>>>
void main(int argc, char** argv)

{
        glutInit(&argc, argv);
        glutInitDisplayMode (GLUT_SINGLE | GLUT_RGB);
        glutInitWindowSize(640,480);
        glutInitWindowPosition(100,150);
        glutCreateWindow("The Famous Sinc Function");
        glutDisplayFunc(myDisplay);
        myInit( );
        setWindow (-5.0, 5.0, -0.3, 1.0); /* call the function to specify the
window*/.
        setViewport(0, 640, 0, 480);  /* call the function to specify the viewport*/.
        glutMainLoop( );
}
```

FIGURE 3.3 *(Continued)*

Crucial importance: When writing the program and compiling it into machine language (at what we shall call **compile time**), the programmer may have no idea of where or how big the picture of this portion of the sinc function will be. This is where the use of a world window will be particularly important.

Note that the code in these examples operates in a *natural* coordinate system for the problem: x is made to vary in small increments from -4.0 to 4.0. The key issue here is how the various (x, y) values become scaled and translated so that the picture appears properly in the screen window.

We accomplish the proper scaling and translating by setting up a world window and a viewport and establishing a suitable mapping between them. The window and viewport are both aligned rectangles specified by the programmer. The window resides in world coordinates, as shown in Figure 3.4. The viewport is a portion of the screen window. The notion is that whatever lies in the world window is scaled and translated so that it appears in the viewport; the rest is clipped off and not displayed.

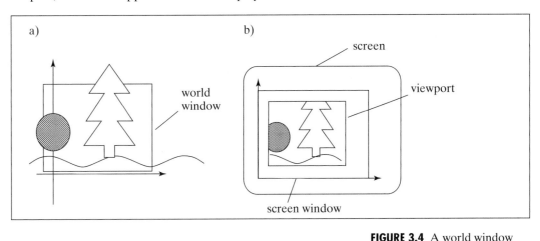

FIGURE 3.4 A world window and a viewport.

We want to describe not only how to instruct OpenGL to do this, which is very easy, but also *how* it operates under the hood, to give insight into the low-level algorithms used. We shall work with only a 2D version here, but we shall later (in Chapter 5) see how these ideas extend naturally to 3D worlds viewed with a camera.

3.2.1 The Mapping from the Window to the Viewport

Figure 3.5 shows a world window and viewport in more detail. The world window as in part a described by its *left*, *top*, *right*, and *bottom* borders as $W.l$, $W.t$, $W.r$, and $W.b$, respectively.[2] The viewport as in part b is described likewise in the coordinate system of the screen window (opened at some place on the screen), by $V.l$, $V.t$, $V.r$, and $V.b$, which are measured in pixels.

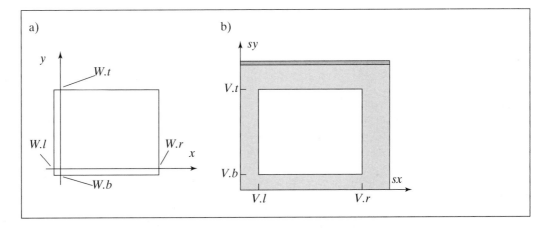

FIGURE 3.5 Specifying the a) window and b) viewport.

The world window must be an aligned rectangle, but it can have any size or position. Similarly, the viewport can be any aligned rectangle, although usually of course it is chosen to lie entirely within the screen window. Further, the world window and

---

[2] For the sake of brevity we use 'l' for 'left,' 't' for 'top,' and so on, in mathematical formulas.

viewport don't have to have the same aspect ratio, although distortion occurs if their aspect ratios differ. Distortion occurs in Figure 3.6, for instance, because the figure in the window must be stretched to fit in the viewport. We shall see later how to set up a viewport with an aspect ratio that always matches that of the window, even when the user resizes the screen window.

FIGURE 3.6 A picture mapped from a window to a viewport. Here some distortion is produced.

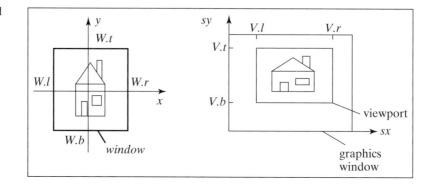

Given a description of the window and viewport, we derive a **mapping** or **transformation**, called the **window-to-viewport mapping.** This mapping is based on a formula that produces a point (sx, sy) in the screen-window coordinates for any given point (x, y) in the world. We want it to be a "proportional" mapping, in the sense that if x is, say, 40% of the way over from the left edge of the window, then sx is 40% of the way over from the left edge of the viewport. Similarly if y is some fraction, f, of the window height from the bottom, sy must be the *same* fraction f up from the bottom of the viewport.

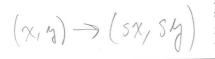

Proportionality forces the mappings to have a *linear* form:

$$sx = A*x + C$$
$$sy = B*y + D \tag{3.2}$$

for some constants A, B, C, and D. The constants A and B scale the x- and y-coordinates, and C and D translate them.

FIGURE 3.7 Proportionality in the mapping x to sx.

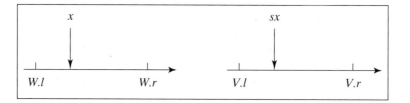

How can A, B, C, and D be determined? Consider first the mapping for x. As shown in Figure 3.7, proportionality in x dictates that

$$sx - V.l$$

must be the same fraction, f, of the total width of the viewport,

$$V.r - V.l$$

as

$$x - W.l$$

is of the total S of the width of the window is: $S\,(W.r - W.l)$

Basically, if you're halfway across the viewport, you must be halfway across the window, and similarly for every other fraction, so that

$$\frac{sx - V.l}{V.r - V.l} = \frac{x - W.l}{W.r - W.l} \qquad \text{proportionality}$$

or, after algebraic manipulation,

$$sx = \frac{V.r - V.l}{W.r - W.l}x + \left(V.l - \frac{V.r - V.l}{W.r - W.l}W.l\right).$$

Now identifying A as the part that multiplies x and C as the constant part, we obtain

$$A = \frac{V.r - V.l}{W.r - W.l}, \qquad C = V.l - A \cdot W.l$$

Similarly, proportionality in y dictates that

$$\frac{sy - V.b}{V.t - V.b} = \frac{y - W.b}{W.t - W.b}$$

and writing sy as $By + D$ yields

$$B = \frac{V.t - V.b}{W.t - W.b}, \qquad D = V.b - B \cdot W.b$$

Summarizing, the **window-to-viewport transformation** is

$$sx = Ax + C, \qquad sy = By + D \qquad\qquad\qquad (3.3)$$

with

$$A = \frac{V.r - V.l}{W.r - W.l}, \qquad C = V.l - A \cdot W.l$$

$$B = \frac{V.t - V.b}{W.t - W.b}, \qquad D = V.b - B \cdot W.b$$

Alert: Check this carefully for yourself!

The mapping can be used with *any* point (x, y) inside or outside the window. Points inside the window map to points inside the viewport, and points outside the window map to points outside the viewport.

(*Important!*) Carefully check the following properties of this mapping using Equation (3.3):

a. If x is at the window's left edge: $x = W.l$, then sx is at the viewport's left edge: $sx = V.l$.
b. If x is at the window's right edge, then sx is at the viewport's right edge.
c. If x is fraction f of the way across the window, then sx is fraction f of the way across the viewport.
d. If x is outside the window to the left, $(x < w.l)$, then sx is outside the viewport to the left $(sx < V.l)$, and similarly if x is outside to the right.

Question: Does this derivation of the transformation automatically force the aspect ratios of the window and viewport to be the same?

Also check similar properties for the mapping from y to sy.

FIGURE 3.8 An example of a window and viewport.

■ **EXAMPLE 3.2.1**

Consider the window and viewport of Figure 3.8. The window has $(W.l, W.r, W.b, W.t) = (0, 2.0, 0, 1.0)$ and the viewport has $(V.l, V.r, V.b, V.t)$ $=(40, 400, 60, 300)$.

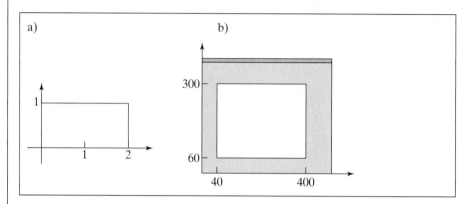

Using the formulas in Equation (3.3), we obtain

$A = 180,$ $C = 40,$
$B = 240,$ $D = 60$

Thus for this example, the window-to-viewport mapping is:

$sx = 180x + 40$
$sy = 240y + 60$

Check that this mapping properly maps various points of interest, such as:

- Each corner of the window is indeed mapped to the corresponding corner of the viewport. For example, $(2.0, 1.0)$ maps to $(400, 300)$.
- The center of the window $(1.0, 0.5)$ maps to the center of the viewport $(220, 180)$.

PRACTICE EXERCISE

3.2.1 Building the mapping

Find values of $A, B, C,$ and D for the case of a world window $(-10.0, 10.0, -6.0, 6.0)$ and a viewport $(0, 600, 0, 400)$.

"Do the window and viewport have the same aspect ratio here?
Solution: No!"   ■

Setting Up the Window-To-Viewport Mapping

OpenGL makes using the window-to-viewport mapping very easy. OpenGL automatically passes each vertex it is given through a sequence of transformations that carry out the desired mapping (via a `glVertex2*()` command). It also automatically clips off parts of objects lying outside the world window. All we need to do is set up these transformations properly, and OpenGL does the rest.

For 2D drawing the world window is set by the function `gluOrtho2D()` having the prototype:

```
void gluOrtho2D(GLdouble left, GLdouble right, GLdouble bottom,
GLdouble top);
```

In the 3D case, there are two additional parameters that need not concern us here. The viewport is set by `glViewport()` having prototype:

```
void glViewport(GLint x, GLint y, GLint width, GLint height);
```

This sets the lower left corner of the viewport, along with its width and height.

Because OpenGL uses matrices to set up all its transformations, the call to gluOrtho2D()[3] must be preceded by two setup functions: glMatrixMode (GL_PROJECTION) and glLoadIdentity(). (We discuss what is going on behind the scenes here more fully in Chapter 5.)

Thus to establish the world window and viewport used in Example 3.1 we would use:

```
glMatrixMode(GL_PROJECTION);
glLoadIdentity();
gluOrtho2D(0.0, 2.0, 0.0, 1.0);      // sets the window
glViewport(40, 60, 360, 240);        // sets the viewport
```

Hereafter every point (x, y) sent to OpenGL using glVertex2*(x, y) undergoes the mapping of Equation (3.3), and edges are automatically clipped at the window boundary. (In Chapter 7 we see the details of how this is done in 3D, where it also becomes clear how the 2D version is simply a special case of the 3D version.)

We will make programs more readable if we encapsulate the commands that set the window into a function setWindow() as shown in Figure 3.9 (also see Figure 3.3). We also show setViewport() that hides the OpenGL details of glViewport(..). To make setViewport() easier to use, we have slightly re-arranged its parameters to match those of setWindow(): they are both in the order left, right, bottom, top. Our function setViewport uses parameters left, right, bottom, top but it calls the lowest-level OpenGL function glViewport() with the parameters left, bottom, right – left, and top – bottom. (Of course right – left equals width and top – bottom equals height.)

```
//--------------setWindow----------------
void setWindow (GLdouble left, GLdouble right, GLdouble bottom, GLdouble top)
{
        glMatrixMode(GL_PROJECTION);
        glLoadIdentity();
        gluOrtho2D(left, right, bottom, top);
}
//--------------setViewport ----------------
void setViewport(GLint left, GLint right, GLint bottom, GLint top)
{
        glViewport(left, bottom, right - left, top - bottom);
}
```

FIGURE 3.9 Handy functions to set the window and viewport.

It is useful to look back and see what we used for a window and viewport in the early OpenGL programs given in Chapter 2. In Figure 2.11 (Draw Dots) the program used:

1. in main():

```
glutInitWindowSize(640,480);      // set screen window size
```

which sets the size of the screen window to 640 by 480. Since no glViewport() command was issued, the default viewport was used; the default viewport is the entire screen window.

---

[3] The root "ortho" appears because setting the window this way is actually setting up a so-called "orthographic" projection in 3D, as we'll see in Chapter 7.

2. in `myInit()`:

```
glMatrixMode(GL_PROJECTION);
glLoadIdentity();
gluOrtho2D(0.0, 640.0, 0.0, 480.0);
```

This sets the world window to the aligned rectangle with corners $(0, 0)$ and $(640.0, 480.0)$, just matching the viewport size. So the underlying window-to-viewport mappings are the same. This was a reasonable first choice for getting started.

■ **EXAMPLE 3.2.2 A Review of Plotting the Sinc Function**

An example earlier has shown *all* of the details of an OpenGL program, including all initializations, to reassure the reader that the program will compile and run properly, and that nothing vital has been omitted. One such program, for example, is the sinc function plotter shown in Figure 3.3.

■ **EXAMPLE 3.2.3 To Draw Polylines from a File**

In Chapter 2, we drew the dinosaur shown in Figure 3.10 using the routine `drawPolylineFile("dino.dat")` of Figure 2.23. The polyline data for the figure were stored in a file `"dino.dat"`. The world window and viewport had not yet been introduced, so we just took certain things on faith or by default, and luckily still got a picture of the dinosaur.

Now we can see why it worked. The world window we used happened to enclose the data for the dinosaur. All of the polylines in `dino.dat` lie inside a rectangle with corners $(0, 0)$ and $(640, 480)$, so none were clipped with this choice of a window.

Armed with tools for setting the window and viewport, we can take more control of the situation. The next two examples illustrate this.

FIGURE 3.10 The dinosaur inside its world window.

■ **EXAMPLE 3.2.4 Tiling the Screen Window with the Dinosaur Motif**

To add some interest, we can draw a number of copies of the dinosaur in some pattern. If we lay them side by side to cover the entire screen window, it's called **tiling** the screen window. The picture that is copied at different positions is often called a **motif**. Tiling a screen window is easily achieved by using a different viewport for each instance of the motif. Figure 3.11a shows a tiling involving 25 copies of the motif. The motif was generated using:

```
setWindow(0, 640.0, 0, 440.0);          // set a fixed window
for(int i = 0; i < 5; i++)              // for each column
  for(int j = 0; j < 5; j++)            // for each row
  {
    glViewport(i * 64, j * 44, 64, 44); //set the next viewport
    drawPolylineFile("dino.dat");        // draw it again
  }
```

Each copy is drawn in a viewport 64 by 44 pixels in size, whose aspect ratio 64/44 matches that of the world window. This draws each dinosaur without any distortion.

Figure 3.11b shows another tiling, but here alternate motifs are flipped upside down to produce an intriguing effect. This was done by flipping the window upside down every other iteration (when i + j is even): interchanging the

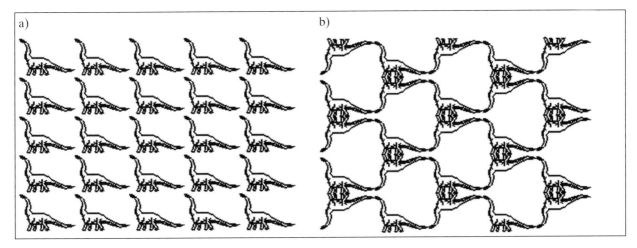

a)   b)

FIGURE 3.11 Tiling the display with copies of the dinosaur.

top and bottom values in Equation (3.3). Then the preceding double loop was changed to:

```
for(int i = 0; i < 5; i++)
  for(int j = 0; j < 5; j++)
  {
    if((i + j) % 2 == 0)                    // if (i + j) is even
      setWindow(0.0, 640.0, 0.0, 440.0); // right side up window
    else
      setWindow(0.0, 640.0, 440.0, 0.0); // upside down window
    glViewport(i * 64, j * 44, 64, 44);    // set the next viewport
    drawPolylineFile("dino.dat");          // draw it again
  }
```

Experiments like this can create pictures of great visual interest.

■ EXAMPLE 3.2.5 To Clip Parts of a Figure

A picture can also be *clipped* by proper setting of the window. OpenGL automatically clips off parts of objects that lie outside the world window. Suppose we have three viewports—the left-hand, middle, and right-hand thirds of the figure. The left-hand third of Figure 3.12 consists of a collection of hexagons of different sizes, each slightly rotated relative to its neighbor. The middle image shows what would be displayed if W1 were used as a window, and the right-hand third shows what would be displayed if W2 were used as the window. Clipping is used in all cases to prevent improper overlapping of polylines. Suppose the picture is drawn by executing some function hexSwirl() (to be described below). It is important to note that if no clipping were done, parts b and c would both show the entire hexagon swirls, crammed onto the viewport. Here the three versions in Figure 3.12 can be drawn using the code skeleton:

```
setWindow (...); // the window is changed for each picture
setViewport(...); // the same viewport is used for each picture
hexSwirl(); // the same function is called
```

What is *displayed*, on the other hand, depends on the setting of the window. We will discuss how hexSwirl() operates below.

---

[4] It might seem easier to invert the viewport, but OpenGL does not permit a viewport to have a negative height.

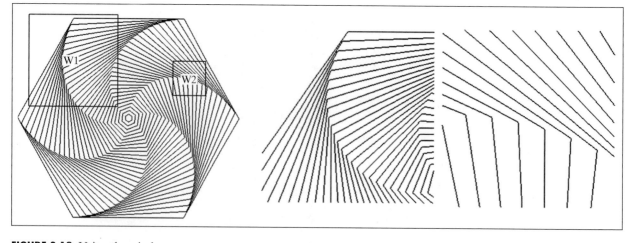

FIGURE 3.12 Using the window to clip parts of a figure.

Notice in Figure 3.12 that in moving from left to right, the window gets ever smaller. This gives the effect of zooming in on the hexagon swirl, as we discuss next.

To Zoom and Roam

The example in Figure 3.12 points out how changing the window can produce useful effects. Making the window smaller is much like **zooming in** on the object with a camera. Whatever is in the window must be stretched to fit in the fixed viewport, so when the window is made smaller, there must be greater enlargement of the portion inside. Similarly making the window larger is equivalent to **zooming out** from the object. (Visualize how the dinosaur would appear if the window were enlarged to twice the size it has in Figure 3.10.) A camera can also **roam**, which means sliding it across (sometimes called "panning") the scene, taking in different parts of it at different times. This is easily accomplished by translating the window to a new position.

■ **EXAMPLE 3.2.6 Zoom In on a Figure in an Animation**

Consider putting together an animation where the camera zooms in on some portion of the hexagons in Figure 3.12. We make a series of pictures, often called **frames**, using a slightly smaller window for each one. When the frames are displayed in rapid succession, the visual effect is of the camera zooming in on the object.

Figure 3.13 shows a few of the windows used: they are concentric and have a fixed aspect ratio, but their size diminishes for each successive frame. Visualize what is drawn in the viewport for each of these windows.

A skeleton of the code to achieve this zooming effect is shown in pseudocode in Figure 3.14. For each new frame the screen is cleared, the window is made smaller (about a fixed center, and with a fixed aspect ratio), and the figure within the window is drawn in a fixed viewport.

Achieving Smooth Animation

Because of the time it takes to draw each new figure, the previous approach isn't completely satisfying. What the user sees is a repetitive cycle of:

a. An instantaneous erasure of the current figure;
b. A (possibly) slow redraw of the new figure.

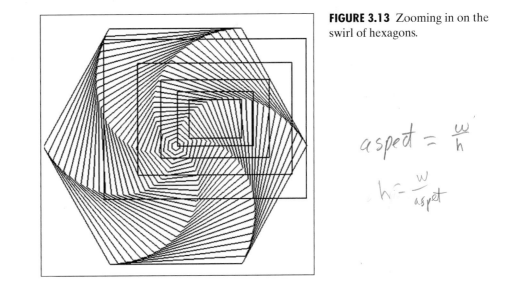

FIGURE 3.13 Zooming in on the swirl of hexagons.

$$aspect = \frac{w}{h}$$

$$h = \frac{w}{aspect}$$

```
float cx = 0.3, cy = 0.2; //center of the window
float H, W = 1.2, aspect = 0.7; // window properties

set the viewport
for(int frame = 0; frame < NumFrames; frame++) // for each frame
{
    clear the screen          // erase the previous figure
    W *= 0.7;                 // reduce the window width
    H = W / aspect;           // maintain the same aspect ratio
    setWindow (cx - W, cx + W, cy - H, cy + H); // set the next window
    hexSwirl();               // draw the object
}
```

FIGURE 3.14 Making an animation.

The problem is that the user sees the line-by-line creation of the new frame, which can be distracting and annoying. What the user would like to see is a repetitive cycle of:

a. A steady display of the current figure;
b. An instantaneous replacement of the current figure by the *finished* new figure;

The trick is to draw the new figure somewhere off screen while the user stares at the current figure, and then to move the completed new figure instantaneously onto the user's display. OpenGL offers **double buffering** to accomplish this. Memory is set aside for an extra screen window which is not visible on the actual display, and all drawing is done to this buffer. (The use of such "off-screen memory" is discussed fully in Chapter 9.) The command glutSwapBuffers() then causes the image in this buffer to be transferred onto the screen window visible to the user.

To make OpenGL reserve a separate buffer for this, use GLUT_DOUBLE rather than GLUT_SINGLE in the routine used in main() to initialize the display mode:

```
glutInitDisplayMode GLUT_DOUBLE | GLUT_RGB);    // use double
                                                   buffering
```

Then, even if it takes a substantial period for the polyline swirl to be drawn, at least the *image* will change instantaneously from one figure to the next in the animation, producing a much smoother and visually comfortable effect.

3.2.2. Whirling swirls

As another example of clipping and tiling, Figure 3.15a shows the swirl of hexagons defined with a particular window. The window is kept fixed in this example, but the viewport varies with each drawing. Figure 3.15b shows a number of copies of this figure laid side-by-side to tile the display. Try to pick out the individual swirls. (Some of the swirls have been flipped: which ones?) The result is dazzling to the eye, in part due to the eye's yearning to synthesize many small elements into an overall pattern. Except for the flipping, the code shown next creates this pattern. Function myDisplay() sets the window once, then draws the clipped swirl again and again in different viewports.   ■

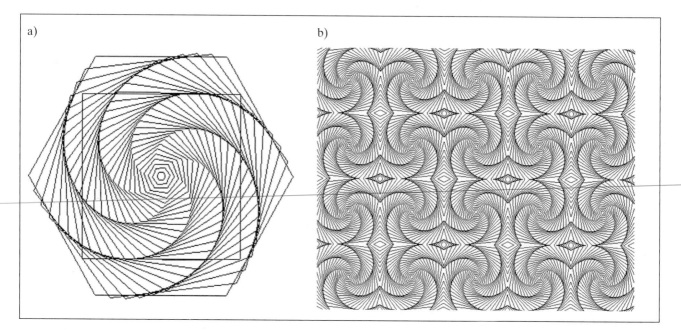

a) b)

FIGURE 3.15 a) Whirling hexagons in a fixed window b) a tiling formed using many viewports.

```
void myDisplay(void)
{
    clear the screen
    setWindow(-0.6, 0.6, -0.6, 0.6); // the portion of the
                                     //         swirl to draw
    for(int i = 0; i < 5; i++)       // make a pattern of 5-by-4
                                     //         copies
        for(int j = 0; j < 4; j++)
            {
            int L = 80; // the amount to translate each viewport
            setViewport(i * L, L + i * L, j * L, L + j * L);
            // the next viewport
            hexSwirl();
            }
```

3.3 CLIPPING LINES

Read, read, read. Read everything—trash, classics, good and bad, and see how they do it. Just like a carpenter who works as an apprentice and studies the master. Read! You'll absorb it. Then write. If it is good, you'll find out. If it's not, throw it out the window.

William Faulkner
1897–1962

Clipping is a fundamental task in graphics, needed to keep those parts of an object that lie outside a given region from being drawn. A large number of clipping algorithms have been developed. In an OpenGL environment each object is automatically clipped to the world window using a particular algorithm (which we examine in detail in Chapter 7 for both 2D and 3D objects).

Because OpenGL clips for you, there may be a temptation to skip a study of the clipping process. But the ideas that are used to develop a clipper are basic and arise in diverse situations; in later chapters we will see a variety of approaches to clipping. Next we discuss a classic line-clipping algorithm, the Cohen-Sutherland clipper.

3.3.1 How to Clip a Line

The Cohen-Sutherland clipper computes which part (if any) of a line segment with endpoints p1 and p2 lies inside the world window, and reports back the endpoints of that part.

We'll develop the routine `int clipSegment(Point2& p1, Point2& p2, Real-Rect window)` that takes two 2D points and an aligned rectangle. Parameters p1 and p2 are of type `Point2` (see Appendix 2). The routine clips the line segment defined by endpoints p1 and p2 to the window boundaries. If any portion of the line remains within the window, the new endpoints are placed in p1 and p2, and 1 is returned, indicating that some part of the segment is visible. Note that p1 and p2 are passed by reference, so that the new points will be visible outside the routine. If the line is completely clipped out, 0 is returned, reporting that no part is visible.

Figure 3.16 shows a typical situation covering some of the many possible actions for a clipper. `clipSegment( )` does one of four things to each line segment.

1. If the entire line lies within the window (e.g., segment *CD*): it returns 1.
2. If the entire line lies outside the window (e.g., segment *AB*): it returns 0.
3. If one endpoint is inside the window and one is outside (e.g., segment *ED*): it clips one end and returns 1.
4. If both endpoints are outside the window, but a portion of the segment passes through it (e.g., segment *AE*): it clips both ends and returns 1.

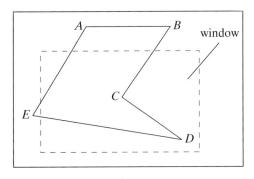

FIGURE 3.16 Clipping lines at window boundaries.

There are many possible arrangements of a segment with respect to the window. The segment can lie to the left, to the right, above, or below the window; it can cut through any one (or two) window edges, and so on. We therefore need an organized and an efficient approach that identifies the prevailing situation and computes new endpoints for the clipped segment. Efficiency is important, because a typical picture contains thousands of line segments, and each must be clipped against the window. The Cohen–Sutherland algorithm provides a rapid divide-and-conquer attack on the problem. Other clipping methods are discussed beginning in Chapter 4.

3.3.2 The Cohen-Sutherland Clipping Algorithm

The Cohen-Sutherland algorithm quickly detects and dispenses with two common cases, called **trivial accept** and **trivial reject**. As shown in Figure 3.17, both endpoints of segment *AB* lie within window *W*, and so the whole segment *AB* must lie inside. Therefore *AB* can be *trivially accepted*; it needs no clipping. This situation occurs frequently when a large window is used that encompasses most of the line segments. On the other hand, both endpoints *C* and *D* lie entirely *to one side* of *W*, and so segment *CD* must lie entirely outside. *CD* is *trivially rejected*, and nothing is drawn. This situation arises frequently when a small window is used with a dense picture that has many segments outside the window.

FIGURE 3.17 Trivial acceptance or rejection of a line segment.

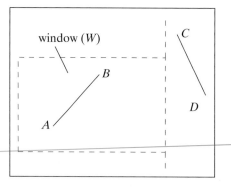

Test for a Trivial Accept or Trivial Reject

The tests for a trivial accept or trivial reject is particularly fast, because it need *only test endpoints* rather than entire line segments. We want a fast way to detect whether a line segment can be trivially accepted or rejected. To facilitate this, an "inside–outside" code is computed and attached to the point for later testing for each endpoint of the segment. Recall that inside-outside testing is particularly fast for a single point because an aligned rectangle is used for the window. Figure 3.18 shows how it is done. Point *P* is to the left and above the window *W*. There are 4 ways in which a point can be disposed relative to the window boundary (above and to the left, above and to the right, and so on), and these two facts are recorded in a four-element code word for *P*: a true (T) is seen in the first element field to indicate "is to the left of" and a T appears in the second element if P "is above." A false (F) is seen in the other two fields to indicate "is to the right of" and "is below."

FIGURE 3.18 Encoding how point *P* is disposed with respect to the window.

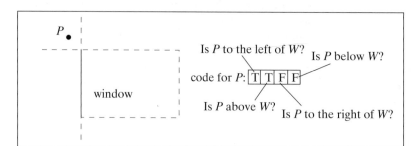

For example, if *P* is inside the window, its code is FFFF; if *P* is below but neither to the left nor to the right, its code is FFFT. Figure 3.19 shows the nine different regions possible, each with its code.

TTFF	FTFF	FTTF
TFFF	FFFF window	FFTF
TFFT	FFFT	FFTT

FIGURE 3.19 Inside–outside codes for a point.

We form a code for each of the endpoints of the line segment being tested. The conditions of trivial accept and reject are easily related to these code words:

- Trivial accept —Both code words are FFFF;
- Trivial reject —The code words have an F in the *same* element: both points are to the left of the window or both are above, and so on.

The actual formation of the code words and tests can be implemented very efficiently using the bit-manipulation capabilities of C/C++.

Chopping When There is Neither Trivial Accept Nor Trivial Reject

The Cohen-Sutherland algorithm uses a divide-and-conquer strategy. If the segment can neither be trivially accepted nor trivially rejected, it is broken into two parts at one of the window boundaries. One part lies outside the window and is discarded. The other part is potentially visible, so the entire process is repeated for this segment against another of the four window boundaries. This gives rise to the strategy:

```
do{
        form the code words for p1 and p2
        if (trivial accept) return 1;
        if (trivial reject) return 0;
        chop the line at the next window border; discard the outside part;
} while(1);
```

The algorithm terminates after at most four times through the loop, since at each iteration we retain only the portion of the segment that has survived testing against previous window boundaries, and there are only four such boundaries. After at most four iterations, trivial acceptance or rejection is assured.

Now we at look at how chopping is done at each boundary. Figure 3.20 shows an example involving the right edge of the window.

Point p1 must be computed. Its *x*-coordinate is clearly W.right, the right edge position of the window. Its *y*-coordinate requires adjusting p1.y by the amount *d* shown in the figure. But by similar triangles

$$\frac{d}{dely} = \frac{e}{delx}$$

FIGURE 3.20 Clipping a
segment against an edge.

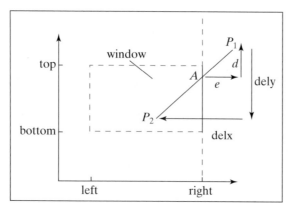

where e is `p1.x - W.right` and
```
delx = p2.x - p1.x;
dely = p2.y - p1.y;
```
$\hspace{10cm}$ (3.4)

are the differences between the coordinates of the two endpoints. Thus d is easily
determined, and the new `p1.y` is found by adding an increment to the old as
```
p1.y += (W.right - p1.x) * dely / delx
```
$\hspace{10cm}$ (3.5)

Similar reasoning is used for clipping against the other three edges of the window. In
some of the calculations the term `dely/delx` occurs, and in others it is `delx/dely`.
One must always be concerned about dividing by zero, and in fact `delx` is zero for a
vertical line, and `dely` is zero for a horizontal line. But as discussed in the exercises,
the perilous lines of code are never executed when a denominator is zero, so division by zero can not occur.

These ideas are collected in the routine `clipSegment( )`, shown in Figure 3.21.
The endpoints of the segment are passed by reference, since changes made to the
endpoints by `clipSegment()` must be visible in the calling routine. Recall that the

```
int clipSegment(Point2& p1, Point2& p2, RealRect W)
{
    do{
        if(trivial accept) return 1; // some portion survives
        if(trivial reject) return 0;  // no portion survives
        if(p1 is outside)
        {
            if(p1 is to the left) chop against the left edge, update p2
            else if(p1 is to the right) chop against the right edge, update p2
            else if(p1 is below) chop against the bottom edge, update p2
            else if(p1 is above) chop against the top edge, update p2
        }
        else                           // p2 is outside
        {
            if(p2 is to the left) chop against the left edge, update p2
            else if(p2 is to the right) chop against the right edge, update p2
            else if(p2 is below) chop against the bottom edge, update p2
            else if(p2 is above) chop against the top edge, update p2
        }
    }while(1);
}
```

FIGURE 3.21 The pseudocode
for the Cohen-Sutherland line
clipper.

type `Point2` holds a 2D point, and the type `RealRect` holds an aligned rectangle. Both types are described fully in Section 3.4.

Each time through the `do` loop the code for each endpoint is recomputed and tested. When trivial acceptance and rejection fail, the algorithm tests whether `p1` is outside, and if so, it clips that end of the segment to a window boundary. If `p1` is inside, then `p2` must be outside, so `p2` is clipped to a window boundary.

This version of the algorithm clips in the order left, then right, then bottom, and then top. The choice of order is immaterial if segments are equally likely to lie anywhere in the world. A situation that requires all four clips is shown in Figure 3.22. The first clip changes P_1 to A; the second alters P_2 to B; the third finds P_1 still outside and below and so changes A to C; and the last changes P_2 to D. For any choice of ordering for the chopping tests, there will always be a situation in which all four clips are necessary.

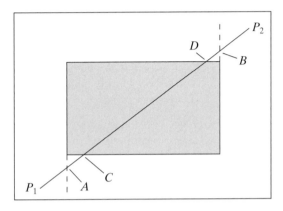

FIGURE 3.22 A segment that requires four clips.

Clipping is a fundamental operation that has received a lot of attention over the years. Several other approaches have been developed.

PRACTICE EXERCISES

3.3.1 Hand simulation of `clipSegment()`

Go through the clipping routine by hand for the case of a window given by $(left, right, bottom, top) = (30, 220, 50, 240)$ and the following line segments:

1. $P_1 = (40, 140)$, $P_2 = (100, 200)$;
2. $P_1 = (10, 270)$, $P_2 = (300, 0)$;
3. $P_1 = (20, 10)$, $P_2 = (20, 200)$;
4. $P_1 = (0, 0)$, $P_2 = (250, 250)$;

In each case determine the endpoints of the clipped segment, and for a visual check, sketch the situation on your graphing calculator.

3.3.2 Potential dividing by zero

Show that, in any situation for which the denominator in Equation (3.4) is zero, the numerator is also zero. Consequently show that the possibly dangerous operation of dividing by zero will never arise. ■

3.4 REGULAR POLYGONS, CIRCLES, AND ARCS

> To generalize is to be an idiot.
>
> *William Blake*
> *(1757–1827)*

3.4.1 The Regular Polygons

A shape often drawn in graphics is the regular polygon of n sides. A polygon is **regular** if it is simple, if all its sides have equal length, and if adjacent sides meet at equal interior angles. Recall, as discussed in Chapter 1, that a polygon is **simple** if no two of its edges cross each other. More precisely, only adjacent edges can touch, and only at their shared endpoint. We give the name **n-gon** to a regular polygon having n sides; familiar examples are a 4-gon (a square), an 8-gon (a regular octagon), and so on. A 3-gon is an equilateral triangle. Figure 3.23 shows various examples.

FIGURE 3.23 Examples of n-gons.

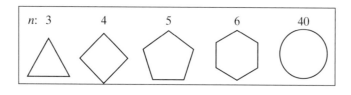

If the number of sides of an n-gon is large, the n-gon approximates a circle in appearance. In fact, this is used later as one way to implement the drawing of a circle. The vertices of an n-gon lie on a circle, the so-called "parent circle" of the n-gon, and their locations are easily calculated. The case of the hexagon is shown in Figure 3.24. The vertices lie equispaced every 60 degrees around the circle.

FIGURE 3.24 Finding the vertices of a 6-gon.

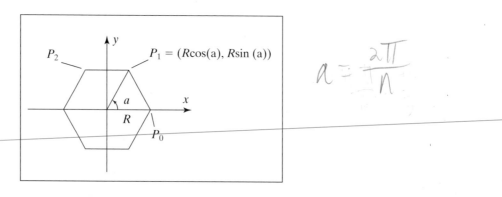

The parent circle of radius R is centered at the origin, and the first vertex P_0 has been placed on the positive x-axis. The other vertices follow accordingly, as P_i equals $(\cos(ia), \sin(ia))$ for $i = 1, \ldots, 5$, where a is equal to $\pi/3$ radians and cos and sin are the familiar cosine and sine. This 6-gon is easy to modify in order to center it at position (cx, cy); we need only add cx and cy to the x- and y-coordinates, respectively. To scale the 6-gon by factor S, we need only multiply R by S. To rotate through angle A, we need only add a to the arguments of cos() and sin(). More general methods for performing geometrical transformations are discussed in Chapter 5.

To summarize, one algorithm for drawing a circle S is to draw an n-gon with a very large number of sides. This can be done by calculating the locations of the n points around the parent circle, performing a moveTo() to one of these points, and then performing a lineTo() to each of the other points. This will draw an acceptable circle (if n is large enough) but is a very inefficient approach, because it requires so many calculations of sin() and cos(). A more efficient class of algorithms does exist, as described in the delightful article by Jim Blinn, "Home Many Ways Can You Draw a Circle?" [Blinn96].

3.4.2 Variations on n-gons

Interesting variations based on the vertices of an n-gon can also be drawn. The n-gon vertices may be connected in various ways to produce a variety of figures, as suggested in Figure 3.25. The standard n-gon is drawn in Figure 3.25a by connecting adjacent vertices, but Figure 3.25b shows a **stellation** (or starlike figure) formed by connecting every other vertex. Figure 3.25c shows the interesting **rosette**, formed by connecting each vertex to every other vertex. We discuss the rosette next. Other figures are described in the exercises.

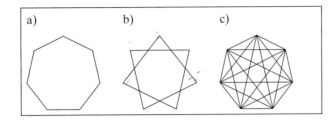

FIGURE 3.25 a) The 7-gon, b) a stellation, c) a 7-rosette.

■ EXAMPLE 3.4.1 The Rosette, and the Golden 5-Rosette

The **rosette** is an *n*-gon with each vertex joined to every other vertex. Figure 3.26 shows 5-, 11-, and 17-rosettes. A rosette is sometimes used as a test pattern for computer graphics devices. Its orderly shape readily reveals any distortions, and the resolution of the device can be determined by noting the amount of crowding and blurring exhibited by the bundle of lines that meet at each vertex.

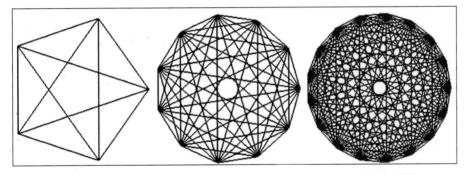

FIGURE 3.26 The 5-, 11-, and 17-rosettes.

Rosettes are easy to draw: simply connect every vertex to every other. The code for the complete rosette routine is on line and is shown in Figure 3.27.

FIGURE 3.27 A complete program for drawing a rosette.

```
#include <windows.h>
#include <gl/Gl.h>
#include <gl/Glu.h>
#include <gl/glut.h>
#include <iostream.h>
#include <math.h>

// demo program to draw a rosette based on a 5-gon

class GLintPoint
{
public:
        GLint x, y;
};

// point 2 class
class Point2
{
public:
        float x, y;
```

FIGURE 3.27 (*Continued*)

```
            void set (float dx, float dy){x = dx; y = dy;}
            void set(Point2& p) {x = p.x; y = p.y;}
            Point2(float xx, float yy){x=xx; y=yy;}
            Point2(){x=y=0;}
};

Point2 currPos;
Point2 CP;

void moveTo(Point2 p)
{
        CP.set(p);
}

void lineTo(Point2 p)
{
        glBegin(GL_LINES);
            glVertex2f(CP.x, CP.y);
            glVertex2f(p.x, p.y);
        glEnd();
        glFlush();
        CP.set(p);
}

void myInit(void)
{
        glClear(GL_COLOR_BUFFER_BIT);
        glClearColor( 1.0, 0.0, 0.0, 0.0 );
        // background is red
        glColor3f( 0.0, 0.0, 1.0 );
        // drawing color is blue
}

void rosette(int N, float radius)
{
        Point2 * pointlist = new Point2[ N ];
        GLfloat theta = ( 2.0f * 3.1415926536 ) / N;

        for( int c = 0; c < N; c++ )
        {
                pointlist[c].set( radius * sin( theta * c ),
radius * cos( theta * c ) );
                }
        for( int i = 0; i < N; i++ )
        {

                for( int j = 0; j < N; j++ )
                {

                        moveTo(pointlist[i]);
                        lineTo(pointlist[j]);
                }
        }
}
void render()
{
```

```
                //this is the callback for displays
                glClear(GL_COLOR_BUFFER_BIT);
                glViewport( 10, 10, 640, 480 );
                rosette(5, .66f);
                glFlush();
        }
        void main(int argc, char** argv) {
                glutInit(&argc, argv);
                glutInitDisplayMode(GLUT_SINGLE | GLUT_RGB);
                glMatrixMode(GL_PROJECTION);
                glLoadIdentity();
                glutInitWindowSize (640,480);
                glutCreateWindow("Rosette");
                glutDisplayFunc( render );// register the callback for
                                          the display function
                myInit();
                glutMainLoop();
        }
```

FIGURE 3.27 (*Continued*)

The 5-rosette is particularly interesting because it embodies many instances of the golden ratio φ (recall Chapter 2). Figure 3.28a shows a *5-rosette*, which is made up of an outer pentagon and an inner pentagram. The Greeks saw a mystical significance in this figure. Its segments have an interesting relationship: each segment is φ times longer than the next smaller one. Also, because the edges of the star pentagram form an inner pentagon, an infinite regression of pentagrams is possible, as shown in Figure 3.28b.

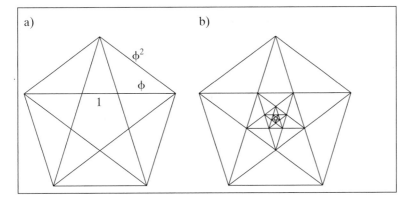

FIGURE 3.28 5-Rosette and infinite regressions—pentagons and pentagrams.

■ **EXAMPLE 3.4.2 Figures based on two concentric *n*-gons**

Figure 3.29 shows some shapes (whose main purpose is to delight the eye) built upon two concentric parent circles, the outer of radius R, and the inner of radius fR for some fraction f. Each figure uses a variation of an n-gon whose radius alternates between the inner and outer radii. Parts a and b show familiar company logos based on 6-gons and 10-gons. Part c is based on the 14-gon, and part d shows the inner circle explicitly.

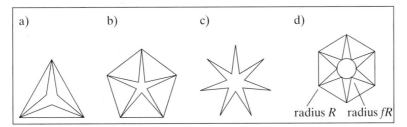

FIGURE 3.29 Interesting shapes based pn *n*-gons.

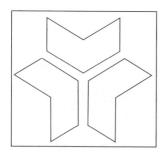

FIGURE 3.30 Logo of the
University of Massachusetts.

PRACTICE EXERCISES

3.4.1 Stellations and rosettes

The pentagram is drawn by connecting every other point as one traverses around a
5-gon. Extend this to an arbitrary odd-valued *n*-gon and develop a routine that
draws this so-called stellated polygon. Can it be done with a single initial `moveTo()`
followed only by `lineTo()`'s? What happens if *n* is even?

3.4.2 The geometry of the star pentagram

Show that the length of each segment in the 5-rosette stands in the golden ratio to
that of the next smaller one. One way to tackle this is to show that the triangles of
the star pentagram are golden triangles (see Chapter 2) with an inner angle of
$\pi/5$ radians. Show that $2*\cos(\pi/5) = \phi$ and $2*\cos(2\pi/5) = 1/\phi$. Another approach
uses only two families of similar triangles in the pentagram, along with the relationship, that is embodied in: $\phi^3 = 2\phi + 1$ satisfied by ϕ.

3.4.3 Drawing a famous logo

The esteemed logo shown in Figure 3.30 consists of three instances of a motif, rotated
a certain amount with respect to each other. Show a routine that draws this shape.   ■

3.4.3 Drawing Arcs and Circles

Many figures in art, architecture, and science involve arcs of circles placed in pleasing
or significant arrangements. An arc is conveniently described by the position of the
center, *c,* and radius, *R*, of its parent circle, along with its beginning angle *a* and the
angle *b* through which it sweeps. Figure 3.31 shows such an arc. We assume that if *b* is
positive, the arc sweeps in a counterclockwise direction from *a*. If *b* is negative, it
sweeps in a clockwise fashion. A circle is a special case of an arc, with a sweep of 360°.

FIGURE 3.31 Defining an arc.

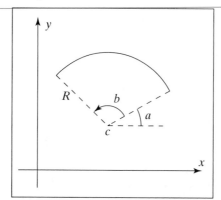

One could develop a routine `drawCircle( )` that specified the center and radius, but there are other ways to describe a circle that have important applications in
interactive graphics and computer-aided design. Two familiar ones are:

1. **The center is given, along with a point on the circle**. Here a routine that draws a
   circle can be used as soon as the radius is known. If *c* is the center and *p* is the
   given point on the circle, the radius is simply the distance from *c* to *p*, found using
   the usual Pythagorean theorem.
2. **Three points are given through which the circle must pass**. It is known that a
   unique circle passes through any three points that don't lie in a straight line. Finding the center and radius of this circle is discussed in Chapter 4.

■ **EXAMPLE 3.4.1 Blending arcs together**

More complex shapes can be obtained by using parts of two circles that are tangent
to one another. Figure 3.32 illustrates the underlying principle. The two circles are

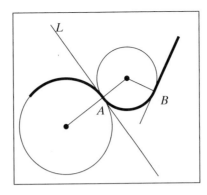

FIGURE 3.32 Blending arcs using tangent circles.

tangent at point A, where they share tangent line L. For this reason the two arcs shown by the thick curve blend together seamlessly at A with no visible break or corner. Similarly the arc of a circle blends smoothly with any tangent line, as at point B.

FIGURE 3.33 The yin–yang symbol.

PRACTICE EXERCISES

3.4.1 Circle figures in philosophy

In Chinese philosophy and religion the two principles of yin and yang interact to influence all creatures' destinies. Figure 3.33 shows the exquisite yin–yang symbol. The dark portion, yin, represents the feminine aspect, and the light portion, yang, the masculine. Describe in detail the geometry of this symbol, supposing it is centered in some coordinate system.

3.4.2 A famous logo

Figure 3.34 shows a well-known automobile logo, formed by erecting triangles inside an equilateral triangle. The outer triangle is replaced by two concentric circles. After determining the proper positions for the three inner points, write a routine to draw this logo. ■

FIGURE 3.34 A famous logo.

3.4.4 Successive Refinement of Curves

Very complex curves can be fashioned recursively by repeatedly "refining" a simple curve. The simplest example perhaps is the **Koch** curve, discovered in 1904 by the Swedish mathematician Helge von Koch. It stirred great interest in the mathematical world, because it produces an infinitely long line that unexpectedly lies completely within a region of finite area [Gardner78]. For those studying computer graphics it is a fascinating curve to generate and it is particularly easy to implement in a program.

Successive generations of the Koch curve are denoted here by $K_0, K_1, K_2, \ldots$. The 0th-generation shape K_0 is just a horizontal line of length 1. The curve K_1 is shown in Figure 3.35. To create K_1, divide the line K_0 into three equal parts and replace the middle section with a triangular bump having sides of length 1/3. The total line length is evidently 4/3. The second-order curve K_2, also shown, is formed by building a bump on each of the four line segments of K_1.

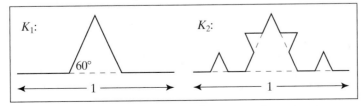

FIGURE 3.35 Two generations of the Koch curve.

We can build the K_{n+1} curve from the K_nth curve in a natural **induction** step:

Subdivide each segment of K_n into three equal parts, and replace the middle one with an equilateral triangle bump.

In this process, each segment is increased in length by a factor of 4/3, so the total curve length is 4/3 larger than that of the previous generation. Thus K_i has total length $(4/3)^i$, which increases as i increases. As i tends to infinity, the length of the curve becomes infinite.

The Koch snowflake of Figure 3.36 is another visually interesting shape formed out of three Koch curves joined together. The perimeter of the ith-generation shape S_i is three times the length of a simple Koch curve, and so it is $3(4/3)^i$, which of course grows forever as i increases. But the area inside the Koch snowflake grows quite slowly, and in fact in the limit (see the exercises) the area of S_∞ is only 8/5 the area of S_0! So the edge of the Koch snowflake gets rougher and rougher and longer and longer, but the area remains bounded. Figure 3.37 shows the fifth-generation Koch snowflake.

FIGURE 3.36 The first few generations of the Koch snowflake.

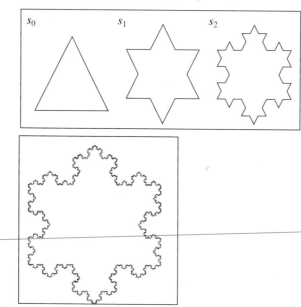

FIGURE 3.37 A Koch snowflake, S_5.

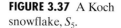

Self-Similarity

The Koch curve K_n is **self-similar** in the following sense. Place a small window about some portion of K_n and observe its ragged shape. Now choose a window a billion times smaller, and observe this blow-up. If n is very large, the curve still appears to exhibit approximately the same shape and roughness. This portion could be enlarged another billion times, and still the shape would be the same. Only the limiting case K_∞ is truly self-similar, but the effect of self-similarity can be approximated in a computer graphics setting. Just make n so large that even at the biggest blow-up to be used the smallest line segments are shorter than the spacing between pixels.

3.5 THE PARAMETRIC FORM FOR A CURVE

> In life, as in art, the beautiful moves in curves.
>
> *Edward Bulwer-Lytton*
> *(1803–1873)*

There are two principal ways to describe the shape of a curved line: *implicitly* and *parametrically*. The **implicit form** describes a curve by a function $F(x, y)$ that provides a relationship between the x- and y-coordinates: the point (x, y) lies on the curve if and only if it satisfies:

$F(x, y) = 0$ condition for (x, y) to lie on the curve   (3.6)

For example, the straight line through points A and B has implicit form:

$$F(x, y) = (y - A_y)(B_x - A_x) - (x - A_x)(B_y - A_y) \tag{3.7}$$

and the circle with radius R centered at the origin has implicit form:

$$F(x, y) = x^2 + y^2 - R^2 \tag{3.8}$$

A benefit of using the implicit form is that you can easily test whether a given point lies on the curve: simply evaluate $F(x, y)$ at the point in question. For certain classes of curves it is meaningful to speak of an inside and an outside of the curve, in which cases $F(x, y)$ is also called the **inside–outside function**. The understanding here is given in Equation (3.9).

$$
\begin{array}{lll}
F(x, y) = 0 & \text{for all } (x, y) \text{ on the curve} & \\
F(x, y) > 0 & \text{for all } (x, y) \text{ outside the curve} & \\
F(x, y) < 0 & \text{for all } (x, y) \text{ inside the curve} & \tag{3.9}
\end{array}
$$

Some curves are **single valued** in x. For instance, if $g(x)$ is single valued, there is only one value of the function for each value of x. In fact only single-valued functions are "legitimate" functions. For such curves the implicit form may be written $F(x, y) = y - g(x)$. Other curves are single valued in y, so there is a function $h(\ )$ such that points on the curve satisfy $x = h(y)$. And some curves are not single valued at all: $F(x, y) = 0$ cannot be rearranged into either of the forms $y = g(x)$ or $x = h(y)$. The circle, for instance, can be expressed as

$$y = \pm\sqrt{R^2 - x^2} \tag{3.10}$$

but here there are two functions, not one. One function uses the plus sign and the other uses the minus sign.

3.5.1 Parametric Forms for Curves

A parametric form for a curve produces different points on the curve based on the value of a parameter. Parametric forms can be developed for a wide variety of curves, and they have much to recommend them, particularly when one wants to draw or analyze the curve. A parametric form suggests the movement of a point over time, which we can translate into the motion of a pen as it sweeps out the curve. The path of the particle traveling along the curve is fixed by two functions, [$x(\ )$ and $y(\ )$], (three functions for a 3D curve, [$x(\ ), y(\ ), z(\ )$]) that determine the position of the particle at t. The parameter t is frequently referred to as time. The curve itself is the totality of points visited by the particle as t varies over some interval. For any curve, therefore, if we can dream up suitable functions $x(\ )$ and $y(\ )$ or $x(\ ), y(\ ), z(\ )$, they will represent the curve concisely and precisely.

The classic Etch-A-Sketch[5] (which remarkably is still available commercially) shown in Figure 3.38 provides a vivid 2D analogy. As knobs are turned, a stylus hidden in the box scrapes a thin visible line across the screen. One knob controls the horizontal position and the other the vertical position of the stylus. If the knobs are turned in accordance with $x(t)$ and $y(t)$, the parametric curve is swept out. Complex curves require substantial manual dexterity. A thorough treatment of curve and surface design is available in Chapter 10.

The Line and the Ellipse

The straight line of Equation (3.8) passes through points A and B. We choose a parametric form that visits A at $t = 0$ and B at $t = 1$, obtaining:

$$
\begin{aligned}
x(t) &= A_x + (B_x - A_x)t \\
y(t) &= A_y + (B_y - A_y)t
\end{aligned}
\tag{3.11}
$$

---

[5] Etch-A-Sketch is a trademark of Ohio Art.

Thus the point $P(t) = (x(t), y(t))$ sweeps through all of the points on the line between A and B as t varies from 0 to 1 (check this carefully).

Another classic example is the **ellipse**, a slight generalization of the circle. It is described parametrically by

$$x(t) = W \cos(t)$$
$$y(t) = H \sin(t), \quad \text{for } 0 \le t \le 2\pi. \tag{3.12}$$

Here W is the "half-width" and H is the "half-height" of the ellipse. Some geometric properties of the ellipse are explored in the exercises. When W and H are equal, the ellipse is a circle of radius W. Figure 3.39 shows this ellipse, along with the component functions $x(.)$ and $y(.)$.

FIGURE 3.39 An ellipse
described parametrically.

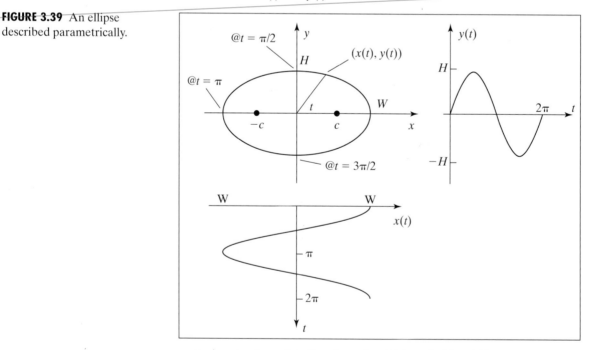

As t varies from 0 to 2π, the point $P(t) = (x(t), y(t))$ moves once around the ellipse, starting (and finishing) at $(W, 0)$. The figure shows where the point is located at various times, t. It is useful to visualize drawing the ellipse on an Etch-A-Sketch. The knobs are turned back and forth in an undulating pattern, one mimicking $W \cos(t)$ and the other $H \sin(t)$. (This is surprisingly difficult to do manually.)

Finding an Implicit Form from a Parametric Form—"Implicitization"

Suppose we want to check that the parametric form in Equation (3.12) truly represents an ellipse. How do we find the implicit form from the parametric form? The basic step is to combine the two equations for $x(t)$ and $y(t)$ to somehow eliminate the variable t. This provides a relationship that must hold for *all t*. It isn't always easy to see how to do this—no simple guidelines apply for all parametric forms. For the ellipse, however, square both x/W and y/H and use the well-known fact $\cos(t)^2 + \sin(t)^2 = 1$ to obtain the familiar equation for an ellipse:

$$\left(\frac{x}{W}\right)^2 + \left(\frac{y}{H}\right)^2 = 1 \qquad\qquad (3.13)$$

The following exercises explore properties of the ellipse and other classical curves. They develop useful facts about the **conic sections**, which will be used later. Read them over, even if you don't stop to solve each one.

PRACTICE EXERCISES

3.5.1 On the geometry of the ellipse

An ellipse is the set of all points for which the sum of the distances to two foci is constant. The point $(c, 0)$ shown in Figure 3.39 forms one focus, and $(-c, 0)$ forms the other. Show that H, W, and c are related by: $W^2 = H^2 + c^2$.

3.5.2 How eccentric

The **eccentricity**, $e = c/W$, of an ellipse is a measure of how noncircular the ellipse is, being 0 for a true circle. As interesting examples, the planets in our solar system have very nearly circular orbits, with e ranging from 1/143 (Venus) to 1/4 (Pluto). Earth's orbit exhibits $e = 1/60$. As the eccentricity of an ellipse approaches 1, the ellipse flattens into a straight line. But e has to get very close to 1 before this happens. What is the ratio H/W of height to width for an ellipse that has $e = 0.99$?

3.5.3 The other conic sections

The ellipse is one of the three conic sections, which are curves formed by cutting or sectioning a circular cone with a plane, as shown in Figure 3.40. The conic sections are:

- ellipse: if the plane cuts one "nappe" of the cone;
- parabola: if the plane is parallel to the side of the cone;
- hyperbola: if the plane cuts both nappes.

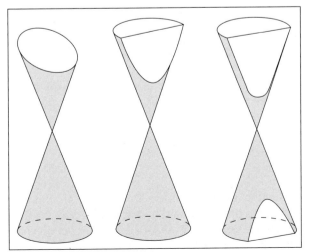

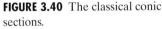

FIGURE 3.40 The classical conic sections.

The parabola and hyperbola have interesting and useful geometric properties. Both of them have simple implicit and parametric representations.

Show that the following parametric representations are consistent with the implicit forms given:

- **Parabola**:   Implicit form: $y^2 - 4ax = 0$
  Parametric Form

$$x(t) = at^2$$
$$y(t) = 2at$$

(3.14)

- **Hyperbola**:   Implicit form: $(x/a)^2 - (y/b)^2 = 1$
  Parametric Form

$$x(t) = a \sec(t)$$
$$y(t) = b \tan(t)$$

(3.15)

What range in the parameter t is used to sweep out this hyperbola? Note: A hyperbola is defined as the locus of all points for which the *difference* in its distances from two fixed foci is a constant. If the foci here are at $(-c, 0)$ and $(+c, 0)$, show that a and b must be related by $c^2 = a^2 + b^2$. ■

3.5.2 Drawing Curves Represented Parametrically

Drawing a curve is straightforward when its parametric representation is available. This is a major advantage of the parametric form over the implicit form. Suppose a curve C has the parametric representation $P(t) = (x(t), y(t))$ as t varies from 0 to T, as shown in Figure 3.41a. We want to draw a good approximation to it, using only straight lines. Just take **samples** of $P(t)$ at closely spaced instants. A sequence $\{t_i\}$ of times are chosen, and for each t_i the position $P_i = P(t_i) = (x(t_i), y(t_i))$ on the curve is found. The curve $P(t)$ is then approximated by the polyline based on this sequence of points P_i, as shown in Figure 3.41b.

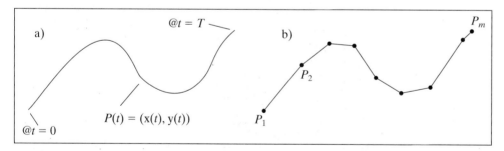

FIGURE 3.41 Approximating a curve by a polyline.

Figure 3.42 shows a code fragment that draws the curve $(x(t), y(t))$ when the desired array of sample times $t[i]$ is available.

If the samples are spaced sufficiently close together, the eye will naturally blend together the line segments and will see a smooth curve. Samples must be closely

FIGURE 3.42 Drawing a curve using points in t.

```
// draw the curve (x(t), y(t)) using
// the array t[0],..,t[n-1] of sample times

glBegin(GL_LINES);
    for(int i = 0; i < n; i++)
        glVertex2f((x(t[i]), y(t[i])));
glEnd();
```

spaced in *t*-intervals where the curve is varying rapidly, but may be placed less densely where the curve is undulating slowly. The required closeness or quality of the approximation depends on the situation.

Code can often be simplified if it is needed only for a specific curve. The ellipse in Equation (3.14) can be drawn using *n* equispaced values of *t* with:

```
#define TWOPI 2 * 3.14159265
glBegin(GL_LINES);
    for(double t = 0; t <= TWOPI; t += TWOPI/n)
        glVertex2f(W * cos(t), H * sin(t));
glEnd();
```

For drawing purposes, parametric forms circumvent all of the difficulties of implicit and explicit forms. Curves can be multivalued, and they can self-intersect any number of times. Verticality presents no special problem: $x(t)$ simply becomes constant over some interval in *t*. Later we see that drawing curves that lie in 3D space is just as straightforward: three functions of *t* are used, and the point at *t* on the curve is $(x(t), y(t), z(t))$.

PRACTICE EXERCISES

3.5.4 An example curve

Compute and plot the points that would be drawn by the fragment above for $W = 2, H = 1$, at the five values of $t = 2\pi i/9$, for $i = 0, 1, \ldots, 4$.

3.5.5 Drawing a logo

A well-known logo consists of concentric circles and ellipses, as shown in Figure 3.43. Suppose you have a drawing tool, `drawEllipse(W, H, clr)`, that draws the ellipse of Equation (3.14) filled with color, `clr`. Assume that as each color is drawn, it completely obscures any previously drawn color. Choose suitable dimensions for the ellipses in the logo and give the sequence of commands required to draw it. ■

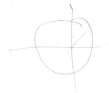

FIGURE 3.43 A familiar logo made of circles and ellipses.

Some specific examples of curves used in computer graphics will help to cement the ideas.

3.5.3 Polar Coordinate Shapes

Polar coordinates may be used to represent and draw many interesting curves. As shown in Figure 3.44, each point on the curve is represented by an angle θ (measured from the positive *x*-axis) and a radial distance *r*. If *r* and θ are each made a function of some parameter *t*, then as *t* varies the curve, $(r(t), \theta(t))$ is swept out. This curve has the Cartesian representation $(x(t), y(t))$, where

$$x(t) = r(t) \cos(\theta(t))$$
$$y(t) = r(t) \sin(\theta(t)) \tag{3.17}$$

But a simplification is possible for a large number of appealing curves. In these instances the radius *r* is expressed directly as a function of θ, and the parameter that

FIGURE 3.44 Polar coordinates.

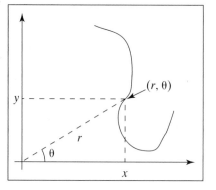

sweeps out the curve is θ itself. For each point (r, θ) the corresponding Cartesian point (x, y) is given by

$$x = f(\theta) \cdot \cos(\theta)$$
$$y = f(\theta) \cdot \sin(\theta) \tag{3.18}$$

When expressed this way, a curve can be described completely by a single function $f()$. Curves given in polar coordinates can be generated and drawn as easily as any others. The parameter is θ, which is made to vary over an interval appropriate to the shape. The simplest example is a circle with radius K: $f(\theta) = K$. Figure 3.45 shows some shapes that have simple expressions in polar coordinates:

FIGURE 3.45 Examples of curves with simple polar forms.

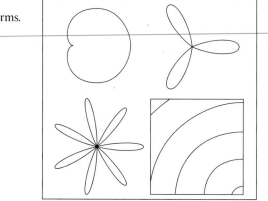

- *Cardioid:* $f(\theta) = K(1 + \cos(\theta))$.
- *Rose* curves: $f(\theta) = K \cos(n\theta)$, where n specifies the number of petals in the rose. Two cases are shown.
- *Archimedean spiral:* $f(\theta) = A\theta$ (see Figure 3.46). The parameter A dictates how rapidly the spiral grows. (Note that when theta $= 2\pi$, the spiral has radius $A2\pi$.)

In each case, constant K gives the overall size of the curve. Because the cardioid is periodic, it can be drawn by varying θ from 0 to 2π. The rose curves are periodic when n is an integer, and the Archimedean spiral keeps growing forever as θ increases from 0. The shape of this spiral has found wide use as a cam (as in an automobile camshaft) to convert rotary motion to linear motion (see [Yates46] and [Seggern90]).

The **conic sections** (the ellipse, parabola, and hyperbola) all share the following polar form:

$$f(\theta) = \frac{1}{1 \pm e \cdot \cos(\theta)} \tag{3.19}$$

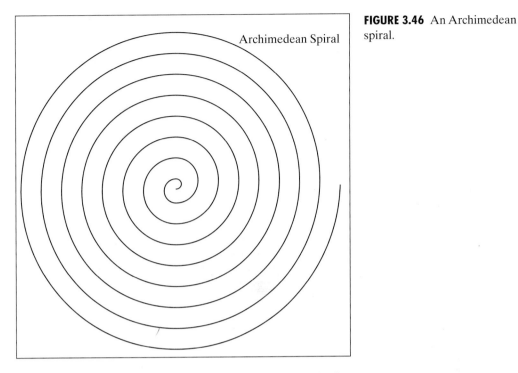

Archimedean Spiral

FIGURE 3.46 An Archimedean spiral.

where e is the eccentricity of the conic section. For $e = 1$ the shape is a parabola; for $0 \leq e < 1$ it is an ellipse; and for $e > 1$ it is a hyperbola.

The Logarithmic Spiral

The logarithmic spiral (or "equiangular spiral") $f(\theta) = Ke^{a\theta}$, shown in Figure 3.47a, is also of particular interest [Coxeter61]. This curve cuts all radial lines at a constant angle α where $a = \cot(\alpha)$. This is the only spiral that has the same shape for any change of scale. Enlarge a photo of such a spiral any amount, and the enlarged spiral will fit (after a rotation) exactly on top of the original. For this reason it is called **self-similar**, a term we have seen before and we will see in connection with the illustrious Mandelbrot set (see Appendix 4). Similarly, rotate a picture of an equiangular spiral, and it will seem to grow larger or smaller [Steinhaus69].[6]

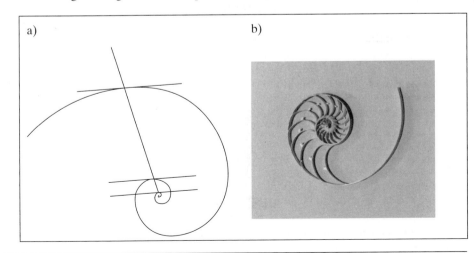

a)

b)

FIGURE 3.47 a) The logarithmic spiral, b) chambered nautilus.

---

[6] This curve was first described by Descartes in 1638. Jacob Bernoulli (1654–1705) was so taken by it that his tombstone in Basel, Switzerland, was engraved with it, along with the inscription Eadem mutata resurgo: "Though changed I shall arise the same."

This preservation of shape seems to be used by some animals such as the mollusk inside a chambered nautilus (see Figure 3.47b). As the animal grows, its shell also grows chambers along a logarithmic spiral in order to provide a home of constant shape [Gardner61]. As an intriguing side note, the ratio of the volume of each successive chamber of the chambered nautilus to that of the previous chamber appears to be the golden ratio!

Other families of curves are discussed in the exercises and Case Studies, and an exhaustive listing and characterization of interesting curves is given in [Yates46, Seggern90, Shikin95].

3.6 SUMMARY OF THE CHAPTER

In this chapter we developed several tools that allow the applications programmer to think and work directly in the most convenient world coordinate system for the problem at hand. Objects are defined or modeled using high-precision real coordinates, without concern for where or how big the picture of the object will be on the screen. These concerns are deferred to a selection of a window and a viewport—either manually or automatically—that define both how much of the object is to be drawn, and how it is to appear on the display. This approach separates the modeling stage from the viewing stage, allowing the programmer or user to focus at each phase on the relevant issues, undistracted by details of the display device.

The use of windows makes it very easy to zoom in or out on a scene, or roam around to different parts of a scene. Such actions are familiar from our everyday experience with cameras. The use of viewports allows the programmer to place pictures or collections of pictures at the desired spots on the display in order to compose the final picture. We described techniques for insuring that the window and viewport have the same aspect ratio, in order to prevent distortion.

A number of additional tools were developed for creating drawings that include regular polygons, arcs, and circles. The parametric form for a curve was introduced and shown to be a very natural description of a curve. It makes it simple to draw curves, even those that are multivalued, cross over themselves, or have regions where the curve moves vertically.

3.7 CASE STUDIES

CASE STUDY 3.1 STUDYING THE LOGISTIC MAP AND THE SIMULATION OF CHAOS

(Level of Effort: II)   Iterated function systems (IFS's) were discussed at the end of Chapter 2. Another IFS provides a fascinating look into the world of **chaos** (see [Gleick87, Hofs85]). It requires the proper setting of a window and a viewport. A sequence of values is generated by the repeated application of a function $f(.)$, called the **logistic map**. The function describes a parabola via the equation:

$$f(x) = 4\lambda x(1 - x) \tag{3.20}$$

(check that this does describe a parabola), where λ is some chosen constant between 0 and 1. Beginning at a given starting point, x_0, between 0 and 1, function $f(.)$ is applied iteratively to generate the **orbit** (recall its definition in Chapter 2):

$$x_k = f^{[k]}(x_0)$$

That is, $x_1 = f(x_0)$, $x_2 = f(f(x_0))$, $x_3 = f(f(f(x_0)))$, and so on.

Let's investigate how this sequence behaves. Recall that an orbit is formed by repeated application of a function on a value of x to form a new value of y (a vertical move from the x-axis up to $(x, f(x))$, followed by using the new value of y as the next x-value (a horizontal move from $(x, f(x))$ to $(f(x), f(x))$). In practice a world of complexity lurks here.

Figure 3.48 shows the parabola $y = 4\lambda x(1 - x)$ for $\lambda = 0.7$ as x varies from 0 to 1. (At which value of x does this curve have its maximum value?)

The starting point $x_0 = 0.1$ is chosen (somewhat arbitrarily) here, and at this x-value a vertical line is drawn up to the parabola, which it intercepts at .252 (check this value of the intercept).

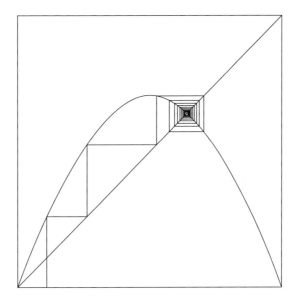

FIGURE 3.48 The logistic map for $\lambda = 0.7$.

Graphically this is drawn as a line from $(.1, 0)$ to $(.1, .252)$. Now in preparation for finding the next point on the orbit we draw a horizontal line from $(.1).252)$ to the line $y = x$, which it intercepts at $(.252, .252)$. So $x_1 = .252$. Next we must apply the function to the new value $x_1 = 0.252$. This is shown visually by moving horizontally over to the line $y = x$, as illustrated in the figure. Then to evaluate $f(\ )$ at this new value a line is again drawn up vertically to the parabola. This process repeats forever as in other IFS's. From the previous position (x_{k-1}, x_k) a horizontal line is drawn to (x_k, x_k) from which a vertical line is drawn to (x_k, x_{k+1}). The figure shows that for $\lambda = 0.7$, the values quickly converge to a stable "attractor," a fixed point so that $f(x) = x$. (What is its value for $\lambda = 0.7$?) This attractor does not depend on the starting point; the sequence always converges quickly to a final value.

If λ is set to small values, the action will be even simpler: there is a single attractor at $x = 0$. But when the "λ-knob" is increased, something strange begins to happen. Figure 3.49a shows what results when $\lambda = 0.85$. The "orbit" that represents the sequence falls into an endless repetitive cycle, never settling down to a final value. There are several attractors here, one at each vertical line in the limit cycle shown in the figure. When λ is increased beyond the *critical value* $\lambda = 0.892486418\ldots$; the process becomes truly *chaotic*.

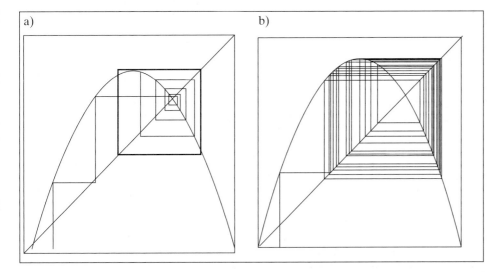

FIGURE 3.49 The logistic map for a) $\lambda = 0.85$ and b) $\lambda = 0.9$.

The case of $\lambda = 0.9$ is shown in Figure 3.49b. For most starting points the orbit is still periodic, but the number of orbits observed between the repeats is extremely large. Other starting points yield truly aperiodic motion, and very small changes in the starting point can lead to very different behavior. Prior to 1975, when the truly remarkable character of this phenomenon was first recognized and published by Mitchell Feigenbaum, most researchers believed that very small adjustments to a system (in this case adjusting the starting point slightly, or λ from 0.85 to 0.9) should produce correspondingly small changes in its behavior and that simple systems such as this could not exhibit arbitrarily complicated behavior.

Feigenbaum's work spawned a new field of inquiry into the nature of complex nonlinear systems, known as chaos theory [Gleick87]. It is intriguing to experiment with this logistic map.

Write and exercise a program that permits the user to study the behavior of repeated iterations of the logistic map, as shown in Figure 3.49. The user sets up a suitable window and viewport so that the entire logistic map can be clearly seen. Further, when the user gives the values of x_0 and λ, the program draws the limit cycles produced by the system.

CASE STUDY 3.2 IMPLEMENTATION OF THE COHEN-SUTHERLAND CLIPPER IN C/C++

(Level of Effort: II)   The basic flow of the Cohen Sutherland algorithm was described in Section 3.3.2. Here we flesh out some details of its implementation in C or C++, exploiting for efficiency the low-level bit manipulations these languages provide.

We first need to form the "inside–outside" code words that report how a point P is positioned relative to the window (see Figure 3.19). A single eight-bit word code suffices: four of its bits are used to capture the four pieces of information. Point P is tested against each window boundary in turn; if it lies outside this boundary, the proper bit of code is set to 1 to represent TRUE. Figure 3.50 shows how this can be done. code is initialized to 0, and then its individual bits are set as appropriate using a bitwise OR operation. The values 8, 4, 2, and 1 are simple masks. For instance, since 8 in binary is 00001000, bitwise OR-ing a value with 8 sets the fourth bit from the right end to 1.

FIGURE 3.50 Setting bits in the "inside–outside code word" for a point P.

```
unsigned char code = 0;          // initially all bits are 0

...

if(P.x < window.l)   code |= 8;     // set bit 3
if(P.y > window.t)   code |= 4;     // set bit 2
if(P.x > window.r)   code |= 2;     // set bit 1
if(P.y < window.b)   code |= 1;     // set bit 0
```

In the clipper both endpoints P1 and P2 (see Figure 3.20) are tested against the window, and their code words code1 and code2 are formed. We then must test for "trivial accept" and "trivial reject."

- **Trivial Accept**: Both endpoints are inside, so both codes code1 and code2 are identically 0. In C/C++ this is quickly determined using the bitwise OR: a trivial accept occurs if (code1 | code2) is 0.
- **Trivial reject**: A trivial reject occurs if both endpoints lie outside the window *on the same side*: both to the left of the window, both above, both below, or both to the right. This is equivalent to their codes having at least one 1 in the *same* bit position. For instance, if code1 is 0110 and code2 is 0100, then P1 lies both above and to the right of the window, while P2 lies above but neither to the left nor right. Since both points lie above, no part of the line can lie inside the window. Therefore trivial rejection is easily tested using the bitwise AND of code1 and code2: if they have some 1 in the same position, then code1 & code2 equals 1, and (code1 & code2) will be nonzero.

Chopping When There Is Neither Trivial Accept Nor Reject

Another implementation issue is efficient chopping of the portion of a line segment that lies outside the window. Suppose it is known that point P with code word code lies outside the window. The individual bits of code can be tested to see on which side of the window P lies, and the chopping can be accomplished as in Equation (3.5). Figure 3.51 shows a chop routine that finds the new point (such as A in Figure 3.20) and replaces P with it. It uses the bitwise AND of code with a mask to determine where P lies relative to the window. It will be passed pre-computed values for dely and delx.

```
ChopLine(Point2 &P, unsigned char code, float dely, float delx)
{
        if(code & 8){        // to the Left
                P.y += (window.l - P.x) * dely / delx);
                P.x = window.l;
        }
        else if(code & 2){        // to the right
                P.y += (window.r - P.x) * dely / delx;
                P.x = window.r;
        }
        else if(code & 1){        // below
                P.x += (window.b - P.y) * delx / dely;
                P.y = window.b;
        }
        else if(code & 4){        // above
                P.x += (window.t - P.y) * delx / dely;
                P.y = window.t;
        }
}
```

FIGURE 3.51 Chopping the segment that lies outside the window.

Write a complete implementation of the Cohen-Sutherland algorithm, putting together the pieces described here with those in Section 3.3.2. Test the algorithm by drawing a window and a large assortment of randomly chosen lines, showing the parts that lie inside the window in red, and those that lie outside in black.

PRACTICE EXERCISES

3.7.1 Why will a "divide by zero" never occur?

Consider a *vertical* line segment such that delx is zero. Why is the code P.y += (window.l - P.x) * dely / delx) that would cause a divide by zero never reached? Similarly explain why each of the four statements that compute delx/dely or dely/delx is never reached if the denominator happens to be zero.

3.7.2 Do two chops in the same iteration?

It would seem to improve performance if we replaced lines such as "else if(code & 2)" with "if(c & 2)" and tried to do two line "chops" in succession. Show that this can lead to erroneous endpoints being computed, and hence to disaster. ■

CASE STUDY 3.3 ANIMATE DINO WITH THE KEYBOARD

(Level of Effort: II)   Recall the Dinosaur polyline drawing of Figure 3.10, showing dino.dat displayed in a particular position. Arrange an application that allows the user to move Dino left and right by repeatedly pressing the 'a' and 'd' keys on the keyboard, and up and down by pressing 'w' and 's'. Be sure the motion is smooth, perhaps by using double buffering.

CASE STUDY 3.4 DRAWING ARCHES

(Level of Effort: II)   Arches have been used throughout history in architectural compositions. Their structural strength and ornamental beauty make them very important elements in structural design, and a rich variety of shapes have been incorporated into cathedrals, bridges, doorways, and so on.

Figure 3.52 shows two basic arch shapes. The arch in part a is centered at the origin and has a width of $2W$. The arch begins at height H above the base line. Its principal element is a half-circle with a radius $R = W$. The ratio H/W can be adjusted according to taste. For instance, H/W might be related to the golden ratio.

Figure 3.52b shows an idealized version of the second most famous arch shape, the **pointed** or "equilateral" arch, often seen in cathedrals.[7] Here two arcs of radius $R = 2W$ meet directly above the center. (Through what angle does each arc sweep?)

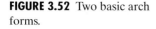

FIGURE 3.52 Two basic arch forms.

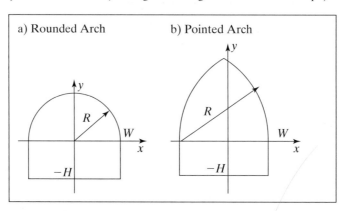

The **ogee**[8] (or "keel") arch is shown in Figure 3.53. This arch was introduced about A.D. 1300 and was popular in architectural structures throughout the late Middle Ages. Circles of radius fR rest on top of a rounded arch of radius R for some fraction f. This fixes the position of the two circles. (What are the coordinates of point C?) On each side two arcs blend together to form a smooth pointed top. It is interesting to work out the parameters of the various arcs in terms of W and f.

FIGURE 3.53 The ogee arch.

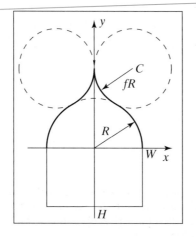

Develop routines that can draw each of the arch types described above. Also write an application that draws an interesting collection of such arches in a castle, mosque, or bridge of your design.

CASE STUDY 3.5 SOME FIGURES USED IN PHYSICS AND ENGINEERING

(Level of Effort: II)   This Case Study works with a collection of interesting pictures that arise in certain topics within physics and engineering. The first illustrates a physical principal of circles intersecting at right angles and the second creates a chart that can be used to study electromagnetic phenomena.

---

[7]   From J. Fleming, H. Honour, and N. Pevsner, *Dictionary of Architecture* (London: Penguin Books, 1980).

[8]   From the old French *ogive* meaning an S-shaped curve.

1. Electrostatic Fields

   The pattern of circles shown in Figure 3.54 is studied in physics and electrical engineering as representing the electrostatic field lines that surround electrically charged wires. It also appears in mathematics in connection with the analytic functions of a complex variable. Here we view it simply as an elegant array of circles and consider how to draw them.

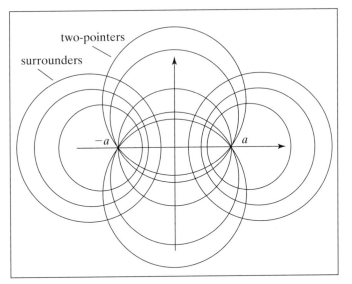

FIGURE 3.54 Families of orthogonal circles.

There are two families of circles, which we will call "two-pointers" and "surrounders." The two-pointers family consists of circles that pass through two given points. Suppose the two points are $(-a, 0)$ and $(a, 0)$. The two-pointers can be distinguished by some parameter m, and for each value of m two different circles are generated. The circles have centers and radii given by:

center $= (0, \pm a)$ and   radius $= am$

as m varies from 1 to infinity.

Circles in the surrounders family surround one of the points $(-a, 0)$ or $(a, 0)$. The centers and radii of the surrounders are also distinguished by a parameter n and have the values

center $= (\pm an, 0)$ and   radius $= a\sqrt{n^2 - 1}$

as n varies from 1 to infinity. The surrounder circles are also known as "circles of Apollonius," and they arise in problems of pursuit [Ball and Coxeter 74 for the date]. The distances from any point on a circle of Apollonius to the points $(-a, 0)$ and $(a, 0)$ have a constant ratio. (What is this ratio in terms of a and n?)

The "surrounder" family is intimately related to the two-pointer family. Every surrounder circle "cuts" through every two-pointer circle at a right angle. The families of circles are thus said to be **orthogonal** to one another.

Write and exercise a program that draws the two families of orthogonal circles. Choose sets of values of m and n so that the picture is well balanced and pleasing.

2. Smith Charts

   Another pattern of circles is found in Smith charts, familiar in electrical engineering in connection with electromagnetic transmission lines. Figure 3.55 shows the two orthogonal families found in Smith charts. Here all members of the families pass through a common point $(1, 0)$. Circles in family A have centers at $(1 - m, 0)$ and radii m, and circles in family B have centers at $(1, \pm n)$ and radii n, where both m and n vary from 0 to π. Write and exercise a program that draws these families of circles.

FIGURE 3.55 The Smith chart.

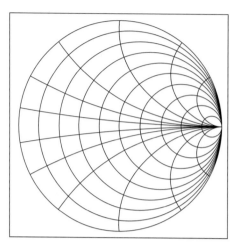

CASE STUDY 3.6 TILINGS

(Level of Effort: II)   Computer graphics offers a powerful tool for creating pleasing pictures based on geometric objects. Among the most intriguing types of pictures are those that apparently repeat forever in all directions. They are called variously **tilings** and **repeat patterns**.

a. **Basic tilings.** Figure 3.56 shows a basic tiling. A **motif**, in this case four quarter-circles in a simple arrangement, is designed in a square region of the world. To draw a tiling over the plane based on this motif, a collection of viewports is created side by side that cover the display surface, and the motif is drawn once inside each viewport.

FIGURE 3.56 A motif and the resulting tiling.

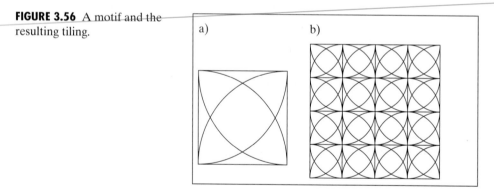

Write a program that:

a. creates a square window in the world and draws some interesting motif (possibly clipping portions of it);

b. successively draws the picture in a set of viewports that abut one another and together cover the display surface.

Exercise your program with at least two motifs.

b. **Truchet tiles.** A slight variation of the method above selects successive motifs randomly from a "pool" of candidate motifs. Figure 3.57a shows the well-known Truchet tiles,[9] which are based on two quarter-circles centered at opposite corners of a square. Tile 0 and tile 1 differ only by a 90° rotation.

Write an application that draws Truchet tiles over the entire viewport. Each successive tile uses tile 0 or tile 1, selected at random.

---

[9]   Smith, C. "The Tiling Patterns of Sebastian Truchet and the topology of structural hierarchy." Leonardo, 20:4, pp: 373–385, 1987. (refd in Pickover, p.386)

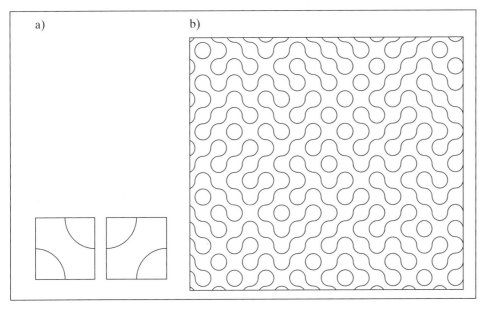

FIGURE 3.57 Truchet tiles: a) the two tiles b) a truchet pattern.

Curves other than arcs can be used as well, as suggested in Figure 3.58. What conditions should be placed on the angle with which each curve meets the edge of the tile in order to avoid sharp corners in the resulting curve? This notion can also be extended to include more than two tiles.

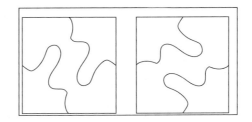

FIGURE 3.58 Extension of Truchet tiles.

Design two additional motifs and extend the program previous so that it draws Truchet tiles based on random selections (randomly rotated) of these tiles. Make sure you design motifs that blend together properly.

3.8 FOR FURTHER READING

When getting started with graphics it is very satisfying to write applications that produce fascinating curves and patterns. This leads you to explore the deep connection between mathematics and the visual arts. Many books are available that offer guidance and provide myriad examples. McGregor and Watt's *The Art of Graphics for the IBM PC* [Mcgregor86] offers many algorithms for creating interesting patterns. Some particularly noteworthy books on curves and geometry are Jay Kappraff's *Connections* [Kappraff91], Dewdney's *The Armchair Universe* [Dewdney88], Stan Ogilvy's *Excursions in Geometry* [Ogilvy69], Pedoe's *Geometry and the Visual Arts* [Pedoe76], Roger Sheperd's *Mind Sights* [Shep90], and the series of books on mathematical excursions by Martin Gardner (such as *Time Travel* [Gardner88] and *Penrose Tiles to Trapdoor Ciphers* [Gardner89]). Coxeter has written elegant books on geometry, such as *Introduction to Geometry* [Coxeter69] and *Mathematical Recreations and Essays* [Ball74], and Hoggar's *Mathematics for Computer Graphics* [Hoggar92] discusses many features of iterated function systems.

Chapter 4

Vector Tools for Graphics

The knowledge at which geometry aims is knowledge of the eternal,
and not of aught perishing and transient.

Plato
(427–347 B.C.)

GOALS OF THE CHAPTER

○ To review vector arithmetic, and to relate vectors to objects of interest in graphics.

○ To relate geometric concepts to their algebraic representations.

○ To describe lines and planes parametrically.

○ To distinguish points and vectors properly.

○ To exploit the dot product in graphics topics.

○ To develop tools for working with objects in 3D space, including the cross product of two vectors.

Preview

This chapter develops a number of useful tools for dealing with geometric objects encountered in computer graphics. Section 4.1 motivates the use of vectors in graphics and describes the principal coordinate systems used. Section 4.2 reviews the basic ideas of vectors and describes the key operations that vectors allow. Although most results apply to any number of dimensions, vectors in 2D and 3D are stressed. Section 4.3 reviews the powerful dot product operation and applies it to a number of geometric tasks, such as performing orthogonal projections, finding the distance from a point to a line, and finding the direction of a ray reflected from a shiny surface. Section 4.4 reviews the cross product of two vectors and discusses its important applications in 3D graphics.

Section 4.5 introduces the notion of a coordinate frame and homogeneous coordinates, and stresses that points and vectors are significantly different types of geometric objects. It also develops the two principal mathematical representations of a line and a plane, showing where each is useful. Further, it introduces affine combinations of points and describes an interesting kind of animation known as tweening. A preview of Bezier curves provides an application of tweening.

132

Section 4.6 examines the central problem of finding where two line segments intersect, which is vastly simplified by using vectors. It also discusses the problem of finding the unique circle determined by three points and derives an answer that further demonstrates the power of using vectors. Section 4.7 discusses the problem of finding where a ray hits a line or plane, applying the notions to the clipping problem. Section 4.8 focuses on clipping lines against convex polygons and polyhedra and develops the powerful Cyrus-Beck clipping algorithm.

The chapter ends with Case Studies that extend these tools and provide opportunities to enrich your graphics programming skills. Tasks include processing polygons, performing experiments in 2D ray tracing, entertaining experiments in animation by tweening, and developing advanced clipping tools.

4.1 INTRODUCTION

For us, whose shoulders sag under the weight of the heritage of Greek thought and who walk in the paths traced out by the heroes of the Renaissance, a civilization without mathematics is unthinkable.

Andre Weil
(1906–1998)

In computer graphics we work with objects defined in a 3D world (with 2D objects and worlds being just special cases). All objects to be drawn, and the cameras used to draw them, have shape, position, and orientation. We must write computer programs that somehow describe these objects and describe how light bounces around illuminating them, so that the final pixel values on the display can be computed. As an example, think of an animation where a camera flies through a hilly scene containing various buildings, trees, roads, and cars. What does the camera see? It all has to be converted ultimately to numbers. That's a tall order.

The two fundamental sets of tools that come to our aid in graphics are *vector analysis* and *transformations*. By studying them in detail we develop methods to describe the various geometric objects we will encounter, and we learn how to convert geometric ideas to numbers. Reducing everything to mere numbers may sound pedestrian and of little value, but two factors save the day: the "process" of finding the proper numbers is fascinating, and the final pictures are often astonishing! This leads to a collection of crucial algorithms that we can call upon in graphics programs.

In this chapter we examine the fundamental operations of vector algebra and see how they are used in graphics. Transformations are addressed in Chapter 5. We start at the beginning and develop a number of important tools and methods of attack that will appear again and again throughout the book. From previous exposure to graphics you may find several of the concepts discussed familiar, but the numerous applications of vector analysis to geometric situations are very likely new and should still be scrutinized. Having the many properties of vectors collected in one place and related to real geometric problems we encounter in graphics will certainly be found useful.

Why Are Vectors So Important?

A preview of some situations where vector analysis comes to the rescue might help to motivate the study of vectors. Figure 4.1 shows three geometric problems that arise in graphics. Many other examples could be given as well (and will be in later chapters).

Part a shows a computer-aided-design problem: the user has placed three points on the display with the mouse and wants to draw the unique circle that

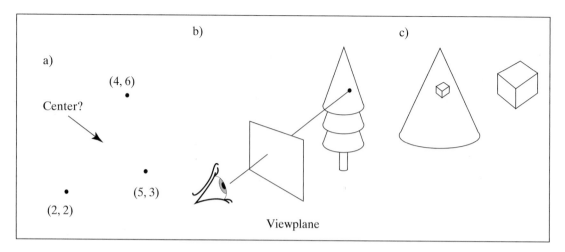

FIGURE 4.1 Three sample geometric problems that yield readily to vector analysis.

passes through them. (Can you visualize this circle?) For the coordinates given, where is the center of the circle located? We see in Section 4.6 that this problem is thorny without the use of vectors, but almost trivial when the right vector tools are used.

Part b shows a camera situated in a scene that contains a Christmas tree. The camera must form an image of the tree on its view plane (similar to the film plane of a physical camera), which will be transferred to a screen window on the user's display. Where does the image of the tree appear on this plane, and what is its exact shape? To answer this we need a detailed study of perspective projections, which will be greatly aided by the use of vector tools. If this seems too easy, imagine that you are developing an animation, and the camera is zooming in on the scene along some trajectory, rotating as it does so. Write a routine that generates the whole sequence of images!

Part c shows a shiny cone in which the reflection of a cube can be seen. Given the positions of the cone, cube, and viewing camera, where *exactly* does the reflected image appear, and what are its color and shape? When studying ray tracing in Chapter 12 we will make extensive use of vectors, and we will see that this problem is both central and is readily solved.

Some Basics

All points and vectors we work with are defined relative to some coordinate system. Figure 4.2 shows the coordinate systems that are normally used. Each system has an *origin* called O and some axes emanating from O. The axes are usually oriented at right angles to one another. Distances are marked along each axis, and a point is given coordinates according to how far along each axis it lies. Part a shows the usual two-dimensional system. When it comes to a 3D system, one finds two versions: a left-handed system (Part c) and a right-handed system (Part b). Part b shows a *right-handed* 3D coordinate system and part c a *left-handed* coordinate system.

Right-Handed and Left-Handed 3D Systems

In a right-handed system, if you rotate your *right* hand around the z-axis by sweeping from the positive x-axis around to the positive y-axis, as shown in the figure, your thumb points along the positive z-axis. In a left-handed system, you must do this

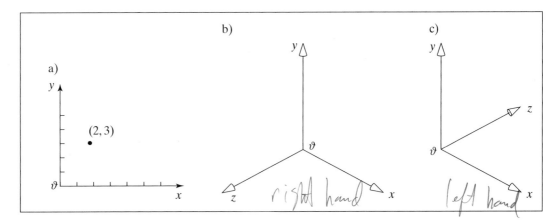

FIGURE 4.2 The familiar two- and three-dimensional coordinate systems.

with your *left* hand to make your thumb point along the positive *z*-axis. Right-handed systems are more familiar and are conventionally used in mathematics, physics, and engineering discussions. In this text we use a right-handed system when setting up models for objects. But left-handed systems also have a natural place in graphics, when dealing with viewing systems and cameras.

We first look at the basics of vectors, how one works with them, and how they are useful in graphics. In Section 4.5 we return to fundamentals and show an important distinction between points and vectors that, if ignored, can cause great difficulties in graphics programs.

Earlier we asked why vectors are so important. To return to this theme, we shall see that vectors are easy to interpret in a mathematical development. It is usually not difficult to develop some intuition about their length and direction. In addition, vectors are measured to the precision of the underlying machine in what is often called **object space**, in contrast to the pixel-based **screen space** used in applications such as ray tracing. Further, vectors are unencumbered by the need to describe their position, so it takes slightly fewer data to describe them completely.

But most importantly of all, vectors can be combined to form new objects! They may be added, subtracted, scaled, and subjected to other operations to form a scalar (the dot product) or, in the 3D case, another vector (the cross product), which has intuitively accessible properties. The operation of dividing one vector by another, however, is not defined. The vector product is easy to calculate and can help us solve many otherwise thorny geometric problems. We shall see all of these properties discussed in depth later.

4.2 REVIEW OF VECTORS

> Not only Newton's laws, but also the other laws of physics, so far as we know today,
> have the two properties which we call invariance under translation of axes and rotation
> of axes. These properties are so important that a mathematical technique has been developed
> to take advantage of them in writing and using physical law . . . called vector analysis.
>
> *Richard Feynman*
> *(1918–1988)*

Vector arithmetic provides a unified way to express geometric ideas algebraically. In graphics we work with vectors of two, three, and four dimensions, but many results need only be stated once and they apply to vectors of any dimension. This makes it possible to bring the various cases that arise in graphics together into a *single* expression, which can be applied to a broad variety of tasks.

Viewed geometrically, vectors are entities having length and direction, but no position. (In contrast, points have position, but neither length nor direction.) Vectors correspond to various physical entities such as force, displacement, and velocity. A vector is often drawn as an arrow of a certain length pointing in a certain direction. It is valuable to think of a vector geometrically as a *displacement* from one point to another.

Figure 4.3 uses vectors to show how the stars in the Big Dipper are moving over time [Kerr79]. The current location of each star is shown by a point, and a vector shows the velocity of each star. The tip of each arrow shows the point where its star will be located in 50,000 years, producing a pattern nearly unrecognizable as the Big Dipper!

FIGURE 4.3 The Big Dipper now and in A.D. 50,000.

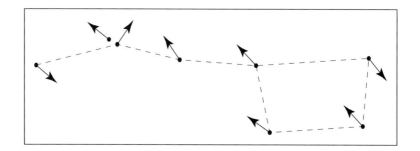

Figure 4.4a shows, in a 2D coordinate system, the two points $P = (1, 3)$ and $Q = (4, 1)$. The displacement from P to Q is a vector **v** having components $(3, -2)$,[1] calculated by subtracting the coordinates of P from those of Q individually. To get from P to Q we translate down by 2 and to the right by 3. Because a vector is a displacement, it has size and direction but no inherent location: the two arrows labeled **v** in the figure are in fact the same vector. Figure 4.4b shows the corresponding

FIGURE 4.4 A vector as a displacement.

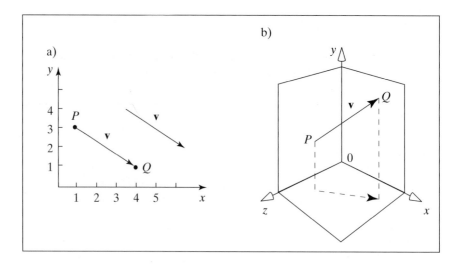

---

[1]   Upper-case letters are conventionally used for points, and boldface lower-case letters for vectors.

situation in three dimensions: $\mathbf{v}$ is the vector from point P to point Q. One often states:

The **difference** between two points is a vector: $\mathbf{v} = Q - P$.

Turning this around, we also say that a point Q is formed by displacing point P by vector $\mathbf{v}$; we say that $\mathbf{v}$ offsets P to form Q. Algebraically, Q is then the **sum**: $Q = P + \mathbf{v}$.

The **sum** of a point and a vector is a point: $P + \mathbf{v} = Q$.

At this point we represent a vector through a list of its components: an n-dimensional vector is given by an *n-tuple*:

$$\mathbf{w} = (w_1, w_2, \ldots, w_n) \tag{4.1}$$

Mostly we will be interested in 2D or 3D vectors, as in $\mathbf{r} = (3.4, -7.78)$ or $\mathbf{t} = (33, 142.7, 89.1)$. Later, when it becomes important, we will explore the distinction between a vector and its *representation*, and in fact we will use a slightly expanded notation to represent vectors (and points). Writing a vector as a *row matrix* like $\mathbf{t} = (33, 142.7, 89.1)$ fits nicely on the page, but when it matters we will instead write vectors as *column matrices*:

$$\mathbf{r} = \begin{pmatrix} 3.4 \\ -7.78 \end{pmatrix} \quad \text{or} \quad \mathbf{t} = \begin{pmatrix} 33 \\ 142.7 \\ 89.1 \end{pmatrix}$$

It matters when we want to multiply a point or a vector by a matrix, as we shall see in Chapter 5.

4.2.1 Operations with Vectors

Vectors permit two fundamental operations: you can add them, and you can multiply them by **scalars** (real numbers).[2] So if $\mathbf{a}$ and $\mathbf{b}$ are two vectors, and s is a scalar, it is meaningful to form both $\mathbf{a} + \mathbf{b}$ and the product $s\mathbf{a}$. For example, if $\mathbf{a} = (2, 5, 6)$ and $\mathbf{b} = (-2, 7, 1)$, we can form the two vectors:

$$\mathbf{a} + \mathbf{b} = (0, 12, 7)$$

$$6\mathbf{a} = (12, 30, 36)$$

always performing the operations *componentwise*. Figure 4.5 shows a two-dimensional example, using $\mathbf{a} = (1, -1)$ and $\mathbf{b} = (2, 1)$. We can represent the addition of

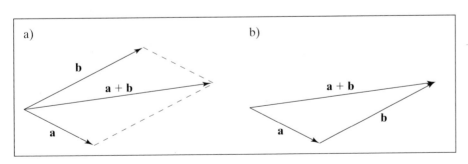

FIGURE 4.5 The sum of two vectors.

---

two vectors graphically in two different ways. In Figure 4.5a we show both vectors starting[3] at the same point, thereby forming two sides of a parallelogram. The sum of the vectors is then a diagonal of this parallelogram, the diagonal that emanates from the binding point of the vectors. This view—the *parallelogram rule* for adding vectors—is the natural picture for forces acting at a point: the diagonal gives the resultant force.

Alternatively, in Figure 4.5b we show one vector starting at the head of the other (i.e., we place the tail of **b** at the head of **a**) and draw the sum as emanating from the tail of **a** to the head of **b**. The sum completes the triangle, which is the simple addition of one displacement to another. The components of the sum are clearly the sums of the components of its parts, as the algebra dictates.

Figure 4.6 shows the effect of scaling a vector. For $s = 2.5$ the vector s **a** has the same direction as **a** but is 2.5 times as long. When s is negative, the direction of sa is opposite that of **a**. The case $s = -1$ is shown in the figure.

Subtraction follows easily, once adding and scaling have been established: **a** − **c** is simply **a** + (−**c**). Figure 4.7 shows the geometric interpretation of this operation, forming the difference of **a** and **c** as the sum of **a** and −**c** (Figure 4.7b). Using the parallelogram rule, this sum is seen to be equal to the vector that emanates from the head of **c** and terminates at the head of **a** (Figure 4.7c). This is recognized as one diagonal of the parallelogram constructed using **a** and **c**. Note, too, that it is the other diagonal from the one that represents the sum **a** + **c**.

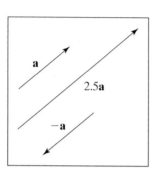

FIGURE 4.6 Scaling a vector.

FIGURE 4.7 Subtracting vectors.

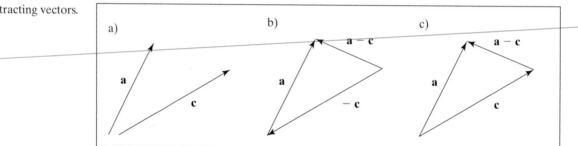

4.2.2 Linear Combinations of Vectors

With methods in hand for adding and scaling vectors, we can define a linear combination of any number of vectors. To form a **linear combination** of two vectors, **v** and **w** (having the same dimension), we scale each of them by some scalars, say a and b, and add the weighted versions to form the new vector, $a\mathbf{v} + b\mathbf{w}$. The more general definition for combining m such vectors

> **DEFINITION:** A **linear combination** of the m vectors $\mathbf{v}_1, \mathbf{v}_2, \ldots, \mathbf{v}_m$ is a vector of the form
>
> $$\mathbf{w} = a_1\mathbf{v}_1 + a_2\mathbf{v}_2 + \ldots + a_m\mathbf{v}_m \qquad (4.2)$$
>
> where $a_1, a_2, \ldots, a_m$ are scalars.

For example, the linear combination $2(3, 4, -1) + 6(-1, 0, 2)$, based on scalars 2 and 6, forms the vector $(0, 8, 10)$. In later chapters we shall deal with rather elaborate

---

[3] Since vectors have no specific location, drawing them with a location is for illustrative purposes only: the resulting vectors shown in these figures have the same coordinates.

linear combinations of vectors, especially when representing curves and surfaces using spline functions.

Two special types of linear combinations, affine and convex combinations, are particularly important in graphics.

Affine Combinations of Vectors

A linear combination is an **affine combination** (pronounced 'AFFine', with emphasis on "aff") if the coefficients $a_1, a_2, \ldots, a_m$ add up to 1. Thus the linear combination in Equation (4.2) is affine if:

$$a_1 + a_2 + \ldots + a_m = 1 \qquad \text{(4.3)}$$

affine

For example, $3\mathbf{a} + 2\mathbf{b} - 4\mathbf{c}$ is an affine combination of $\mathbf{a}, \mathbf{b}$, and $\mathbf{c}$, but $3\mathbf{a} + \mathbf{b} - 4\mathbf{c}$ is not. The coefficients of an linear combination of two vectors $\mathbf{a}$ and $\mathbf{b}$ may be chosen to create an affine combination by using an arbitrary scalar t for one vector and the scalar $(1 - t)$ for the other, as in:

$$(1 - t)\mathbf{a} + (t)\mathbf{b} \qquad \text{(4.4)}$$

Note that this condition has *nothing* to do with the vectors involved, only with the numbers used for the coefficients.

Affine combinations of vectors appear in numerous contexts, as do affine combinations of points, as we see later.

Convex Combinations of Vectors

Convex combinations have an important place in mathematics and numerous applications in graphics. A **convex combination** arises as a further restriction on an affine combination. Not only must the coefficients of the linear combination sum to one; each one must also be nonnegative. The linear combination of Equation (4.2.2) is **convex if**:

$$a_1 + a_2 + \ldots + a_m = 1 \qquad \text{(4.5)}$$

$a_i \geq 0$

and $a_i \geq 0$, for $i = 1, \ldots, m$. As a consequence all a_i must lie between 0 and 1. (Why?)

Thus $.3\mathbf{a} + .7\mathbf{b}$ is a convex combination of $\mathbf{a}$ and $\mathbf{b}$, but $1.8\mathbf{a} - .8\mathbf{b}$ is not. The set of coefficients $a_1, a_2, \ldots, a_m$ is sometimes said to form a **partition of unity**, suggesting that a unit amount of material is partitioned into pieces. Convex combinations frequently arise in applications when one is making a unit amount of some brew and can combine only positive amounts of the various ingredients. They appear in unexpected contexts. For instance, we shall see in Chapter 8 that spline curves are in fact convex combinations of certain vectors, and in our discussion of color in Chapter 11 we shall find that colors can be considered as vectors, and that any color of unit brightness may be considered to be a convex combination of three primary colors!

4.2.3 The Magnitude of a Vector and Unit Vectors

If a vector $\mathbf{w}$ is represented by the n coefficients $(w_1, w_2, \ldots, w_n)$, how might its magnitude (equivalently, its *length* or *size*) be defined and computed? We denote the magnitude by $|\mathbf{w}|$ and define it as the distance from its tail to its head. Based on the Pythagorean theorem, this becomes

$$|\mathbf{w}| = \sqrt{w_1^2 + w_2^2 + \cdots + w_n^2} \qquad (4.6)$$

For example, the magnitude of $\mathbf{w} = (4, -2)$ is $\sqrt{20}$, and that of $\mathbf{w} = (1, -3, 2)$ is $\sqrt{14}$. The vector of zero length is denoted as $\mathbf{0}$. Note that if $\mathbf{w}$ is the vector from point A to point B, then $|\mathbf{w}|$ will be the distance from A to B (why?).

It is often useful to scale a vector so that the result has unit length. This is called **normalizing** a vector, and the result is known as a **unit vector**. For example, we form the normalized version of $\mathbf{a}$ by scaling it with the value $1/|\mathbf{a}|$:

unit vector

$$\hat{\mathbf{a}} = \frac{\mathbf{a}}{|\mathbf{a}|} \quad \text{as long as } |\mathbf{a}| \neq 0 \qquad (4.7)$$

and denoting it as a normalized vector by placing a caret over the vector's name to make it very recognizable. Clearly this is a unit vector: $|\hat{\mathbf{a}}| = 1$, having the same direction as $\mathbf{a}$. For example, if $\mathbf{a} = (3, -4)$, then $|\mathbf{a}| = 5$ and the normalized version is $\hat{\mathbf{a}} = \left(\frac{3}{5}, \frac{-4}{5}\right)$. At times we refer to a unit vector as a **direction**. Note that any vector can be written as its magnitude times its direction: If $\hat{\mathbf{a}}$ is the normalized version of $\mathbf{a}$, vector $\mathbf{a}$ may always be written $\mathbf{a} = |\mathbf{a}|\hat{\mathbf{a}}$. Because things can go awry in a computer program, some vector of interest might turn out to have zero length. Therefore, always check that your vector has non-zero length before normalizing it!

PRACTICE EXERCISES

4.2.1 Normalizing vectors

Normalize each of the following vectors:

a. $(1, -2, .5)$;
b. $(8, 6)$;
c. $(4, 3)$.   ■

4.3 THE DOT PRODUCT

> We could use up two Eternities in learning all that is to be learned about our own world and the thousands of nations that have arisen and flourished and vanished from it. Mathematics alone would occupy me eight million years.
>
> Notebook #22, *Spring 1883–Sept. 1884*
> *Mark Twain*
> *(1835–1910),*

There are two other powerful tools that facilitate working with vectors: the dot (or inner) product and the cross product. The dot product produces a scalar; the cross product works only on three-dimensional vectors and produces another vector. One important property of cross products is they permit a simple test for the convexity of planar polygons. In this section we review the basic properties of the dot product, principally to develop the notion of perpendicularity. We then work with the dot product to solve a number of important geometric problems in graphics. Then we introduce the cross product and use it to solve a number of 3D geometric problems.

The **dot product** of two vectors is simple to define and compute. Dot products can be applied to vectors of any dimension. For two-dimensional vectors, (a_1, a_2) and (b_1, b_2) the dot product is simply the scalar whose value is $a_1 b_1 + a_2 b_2$. Thus, to calculate it, we multiply corresponding components of the two vectors and add the results. For example, the dot product of $(3, 4)$ and $(1, 6)$ is 27, and that of $(2, 3)$ and $(9, -6)$ is 0.

The definition of the dot product generalizes easily to n dimensions:

DEFINITION: THE DOT PRODUCT The dot product d of two n-dimensional vectors $\mathbf{v} = (v_1, v_2, \ldots, v_n)$ and $\mathbf{w} = (w_1, w_2, \ldots, w_n)$, is denoted as $\mathbf{v} \cdot \mathbf{w}$, and has the value:

$$d = \mathbf{v} \cdot \mathbf{w} = \sum_{i=1}^{n} v_i w_i \tag{4.8}$$

■ **EXAMPLE 4.3.1**

- The dot product of $(2, 3, 1)$ and $(0, 4, -1)$ is 11.
- $(2, 2, 2, 2) \cdot (4, 1, 2, 1.1) = 16.2$.
- $(22, 2, 7) \cdot (12, -9, 11) = 323$.
- $(169, 0, 43) \cdot (0, 375.3, 0) = 0$.

4.3.1 Properties of the Dot Product

The dot product exhibits four major properties that we frequently exploit and that follow easily (see the exercises) from its basic definition:

1. Symmetry: $\qquad \mathbf{a} \cdot \mathbf{b} = \mathbf{b} \cdot \mathbf{a}$
2. Linearity: $\qquad (\mathbf{a} + \mathbf{c}) \cdot \mathbf{b} = \mathbf{a} \cdot \mathbf{b} + \mathbf{c} \cdot \mathbf{b}$
3. Homogeneity: $\quad (s\mathbf{a}) \cdot \mathbf{b} = s(\mathbf{a} \cdot \mathbf{b})$
4. $|\mathbf{b}|^2 = \mathbf{b} \cdot \mathbf{b}$

Property 1 states that the order in which the two vectors are combined does not matter: the dot product is **commutative**. Properties 2 and 3 proclaim that the dot product is **linear**; that is, the dot product of a sum of vectors can be expressed as the sum of the individual dot products. Scaling a vector scales the value of the dot product. The last property is also useful, as it asserts that taking the dot product of a vector with itself yields the **square of the length** of the vector. Property 4 appears frequently in the form $|\mathbf{b}| = \sqrt{\mathbf{b} \cdot \mathbf{b}}$.

The following manipulations show how these properties can be used to simplify an expression involving dot products. The result itself will be used in the next section.

■ **EXAMPLE 4.3.2** Simplification of $|\mathbf{a} - \mathbf{b}|^2$.

Simplify the expression for the length (squared) of the difference of two vectors, $\mathbf{a}$ and $\mathbf{b}$, to obtain the following relation:

$$|\mathbf{a} - \mathbf{b}|^2 = |\mathbf{a}|^2 - 2\mathbf{a} \cdot \mathbf{b} + |\mathbf{b}|^2 \tag{4.9}$$

The derivation proceeds as follows: Give the name C to the expression $|\mathbf{a} - \mathbf{b}|^2$. By Property 4, C is the dot product:

$$C = |\mathbf{a} - \mathbf{b}|^2 = (\mathbf{a} - \mathbf{b}) \cdot (\mathbf{a} - \mathbf{b}).$$

Use linearity: $C = \mathbf{a} \cdot (\mathbf{a} - \mathbf{b}) - \mathbf{b} \cdot (\mathbf{a} - \mathbf{b})$.
Use symmetry and linearity to simplify this further: $C = \mathbf{a} \cdot \mathbf{a} - 2\mathbf{a} \cdot \mathbf{b} + \mathbf{b} \cdot \mathbf{b}$.
Use Property 4 to obtain $C = |\mathbf{a}|^2 - 2\mathbf{a} \cdot \mathbf{b} + |\mathbf{b}|^2$ gives the desired result.

By replacing the minus with a plus in this relation, the following similar and useful relation emerges:

$$|\mathbf{a} + \mathbf{b}|^2 = |\mathbf{a}|^2 + 2\mathbf{a} \cdot \mathbf{b} + |\mathbf{b}|^2 \tag{4.10}$$

4.3.2 The Angle Between Two Vectors

The most important application of the dot product is in finding the angle between two vectors, or between two intersecting lines. Figure 4.8 shows the 2D case, where vectors $\mathbf{b}$ and $\mathbf{c}$ lie at angles ϕ_b, and ϕ_c, relative to the x-axis. Now from elementary trigonometry:

$$\mathbf{b} = (|\mathbf{b}| \cos \phi_b, |\mathbf{b}| \sin \phi_b)$$
$$\mathbf{c} = (|\mathbf{c}| \cos \phi_c, |\mathbf{c}| \sin \phi_c)$$

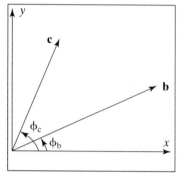

FIGURE 4.8 Finding the angle between two vectors.

We wish to find a useful form for the dot product of $\mathbf{b}$ and $\mathbf{c}$. Do this by using these forms for $\mathbf{b}$ and $\mathbf{c}$, and form their dot product by multiplying their first components and their second components. Add to obtain the dot product of $\mathbf{b}$ and $\mathbf{c}$:

$$\mathbf{b} \cdot \mathbf{c} = |\mathbf{b}||\mathbf{c}| \cos \phi_c \cos \phi_b + |\mathbf{b}||\mathbf{c}| \sin \phi_b \sin \phi_c$$

Use elementary trigonometry once more to obtain:

$$\mathbf{b} \cdot \mathbf{c} = |\mathbf{b}||\mathbf{c}| \cos(\phi_c - \phi_b)$$

So finally, for any two vectors $\mathbf{b}$ and $\mathbf{c}$, we have:

$$\mathbf{b} \cdot \mathbf{c} = |\mathbf{b}||\mathbf{c}| \cos(\theta) \qquad \theta \text{ is angle from } b \text{ to } c \tag{4.11}$$

where θ is the angle from $\mathbf{b}$ to $\mathbf{c}$. Here, θ is the smaller of the two angles between the vectors. Thus $\mathbf{b} \cdot \mathbf{c}$ varies as the cosine of the angle from $\mathbf{b}$ to $\mathbf{c}$. The same result holds for vectors of three, four, or any number of dimensions as long as $\mathbf{b}$ and $\mathbf{c}$ have the same dimensionality.

To obtain a slightly more compact form, divide through both sides by $|\mathbf{b}||\mathbf{c}|$ and use the unit vector notation $\hat{\mathbf{b}} = \mathbf{b}/|\mathbf{b}|$ to obtain

$$\cos(\theta) = \hat{\mathbf{b}} \cdot \hat{\mathbf{c}}$$

This is the desired result: The cosine of the angle between two vectors $\mathbf{b}$ and $\mathbf{c}$ is the dot product of their normalized versions.

■ **EXAMPLE 4.3.3**

Find the angle between $\mathbf{b} = (3, 4)$ and $\mathbf{c} = (5, 2)$.

SOLUTION:

Form $|\mathbf{b}| = 5$ and $|\mathbf{c}| = 5.385$ so that $\hat{\mathbf{b}} = (.6, .8)$ and $\hat{\mathbf{c}} = (.9285, .3714)$. The dot product $\hat{\mathbf{b}} \cdot \hat{\mathbf{c}} = .85422 = \cos(\theta)$, so that $\theta = 31.326°$. This can be checked by plotting the two vectors on your graphing calculator and measuring the angle between them.

4.3.3 The Sign of $\mathbf{b} \cdot \mathbf{c}$ and Perpendicularity

Recall that $\cos(\theta)$ is **positive** if $|\theta|$ is less than $90°$ (acute), **zero** if $|\theta|$ equals $90°$ (right angle), and **negative** if $|\theta|$ exceeds $90°$ (obtuse). Because the dot product of two vectors is proportional to the cosine of the angle between them, we can therefore observe that the angle between two vectors (of any nonzero length) is seen to be as in Equation (4.16).

less than $90°$	if $\mathbf{b} \cdot \mathbf{c} > 0$	
exactly $90°$	if $\mathbf{b} \cdot \mathbf{c} = 0$	(4.12)
more than $90°$	if $\mathbf{b} \cdot \mathbf{c} < 0$	

This is indicated by Figure 4.9. The sign of the dot product is used in many algorithmic tests.

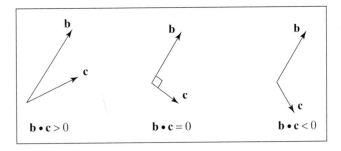

FIGURE 4.9 The sign of the dot product.

The case in which the vectors are $90°$ apart, or **perpendicular**, is of special importance.

DEFINITION: Vectors $\mathbf{b}$ and $\mathbf{c}$ are **perpendicular** if $\mathbf{b.c} = 0$. (4.13)

Other names for perpendicular are **orthogonal** and **normal**, and we shall use all three interchangeably.

The most familiar examples of orthogonal vectors are those aimed along the axes of 2D and 3D coordinate systems, as shown in Figure 4.10. In part a the 2D vectors $(1, 0)$ and $(0, 1)$ are mutually perpendicular unit vectors. The 3D versions are so commonly used that they are called the **standard unit vectors**. For our examples these vectors are given names $\mathbf{i}, \mathbf{j}$, and $\mathbf{k}$.

DEFINITION: The **standard unit vectors** in 3D have components:

$$\mathbf{i} = (1, 0, 0), \quad \mathbf{j} = (0, 1, 0), \quad \text{and} \quad \mathbf{k} = (0, 0, 1) \tag{4.14}$$

Part b of Figure 4.10 shows them for a right-handed system, and part c for a left-handed system. Note that $\mathbf{k}$ always points in the positive z-direction.

Using these definitions, we can write any 3D vector such as (a, b, c) in the alternative form:

$$(a, b, c) = a\mathbf{i} + b\mathbf{j} + c\mathbf{k} \tag{4.15}$$

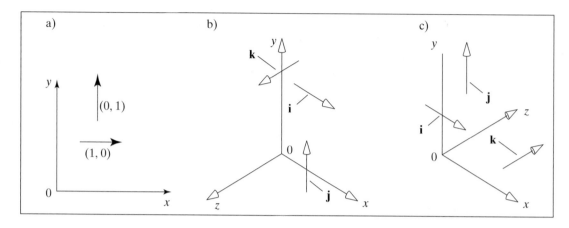

FIGURE 4.10 The standard unit vectors.

■ **EXAMPLE 4.3.4**

Notice that $\mathbf{v} = (2, 5, -1)$ is clearly the same as $2(1, 0, 0) + 5(0, 1, 0) - 1(0, 0, 1)$, which is recognized as $2\mathbf{i} + 5\mathbf{j} - \mathbf{k}$.

This form presents a vector as a sum of separate elementary component vectors, so it simplifies various pencil-and-paper calculations. It is particularly convenient when dealing with the cross product, discussed in Section 4.4.

PRACTICE EXERCISES

4.3.1 Find the angle

Calculate the angle between the vectors $(2, 3)$ and $(-3, 1)$ and determine if the angle is acute, obtuse, or right. Check the result visually, using your graphing calculator, then compute the angle between the 3D vectors $(1, 3, -2)$ and $(3, 3, 1)$.

4.3.2 Testing for perpendicularity

Which pairs of the following vectors are perpendicular to one another: $(3, 4, 1)$, $(2, 1, 1)$, $(-3, -4, 1)$, $(0, 0, 0)$, $(1, -2, 0)$, $(4, 4, 4)$, $(0, -1, 4)$, or $(2, 2, 1)$?

4.3.3 Pythagorean theorem

Refer to Equations (4.9) and (4.10). For the case in which $\mathbf{a}$ and $\mathbf{b}$ are perpendicular, these expressions have the same value, which seems to make no sense geometrically. Show that in fact it is correct and relate the result to the Pythagorean theorem. ■

4.3.4 The 2D Perp Vector

Suppose the 2D vector $\mathbf{a}$ has components (a_x, a_y). What vectors are perpendicular to it? One way to obtain such a vector is to interchange the x- and y- components and negate one of them.[4] Let $\mathbf{b} = (-a_y, a_x)$. Then the dot product $\mathbf{a} \cdot \mathbf{b}$ equals 0, so

---

[4]   This is equivalent to the familiar fact that perpendicular lines have slopes that are negative reciprocals of one another. In Chapter 5 we see the "interchange and negate" operation arises naturally in connection with a rotation of 90 degrees.

a and **b** are indeed perpendicular. For instance, if $\mathbf{a} = (4, 7)$ then $\mathbf{b} = (-7, 4)$ is a vector normal to **a**. There are infinitely many vectors normal to any **a**, since any scalar multiple of **b**, such as $(-21, 12)$ and $(7, -4)$ is also normal to **a**. (Sketch several of them for a given **a**.) Notice how easy it is to compute the perp vector for any given 2D vector.

It is convenient to have a symbol for one *particular* vector that is normal to a given 2D vector **a**. We use the symbol $\perp$ (pronounced "perp") for this.

DEFINITION: Given that

$\mathbf{a} = (a_x, a_y)$, then $\mathbf{a}^\perp = (-a_y, a_x)$ *left turn*   (4.16)

is the **counterclockwise perpendicular** to **a**.

Note that **a** and $\mathbf{a}^\perp$ have the same length: $|\mathbf{a}| = |\mathbf{a}^\perp|$. Figure 4.11a shows an arbitrary vector **a** and the resulting $\mathbf{a}^\perp$. Note that moving from the **a** direction to direction $\mathbf{a}^\perp$ requires a left turn. (Making a right turn is equivalent to turning in the direction $-\mathbf{a}^\perp$.)

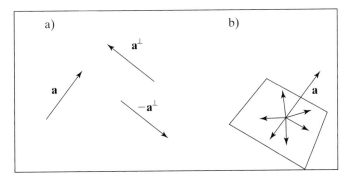

FIGURE 4.11 The vector $\mathbf{a}^\perp$ perpendicular to **a**.

We show in the next section how this notation can be put to good use. Figure 4.11b shows that in three dimensions no single vector lies in the direction perpendicular to a given 3D vector **a**, since any of the vectors lying in the plane perpendicular to **a** will do. However, the cross product developed later will provide a simple tool for dealing with such vectors.

PRACTICE EXERCISES

4.3.4 Some pleasant properties of $\mathbf{a}^\perp$.

It is useful in some discussions to view the perp symbol $\perp$ as an operator that performs a rotate 90° left operation on its argument, so that $\mathbf{a}^\perp$ is the vector produced by applying the $\perp$ to vector **a**, much as $\sqrt{x}$ is the value produced by applying the square root operator to x. Viewing $\perp$ in this way, show that it enjoys the following properties:

a. Linearity: $(\mathbf{a} + \mathbf{b})^\perp = \mathbf{a}^\perp + \mathbf{b}^\perp$ and $(A\mathbf{a})^\perp = A\mathbf{a}^\perp$ for any scalar A.

b. $\mathbf{a}^{\perp\perp} = (\mathbf{a}^\perp)^\perp = -\mathbf{a}$ (two perps make a reversal).

4.3.5 The perp dot product

Interesting things happen when we dot the perp of a vector with another vector, as in $\mathbf{a}^\perp \cdot \mathbf{b}$. We call this the perp dot product [Hill95]. Use the basic definition of $\mathbf{a}^\perp$ above to show:

- $\mathbf{a}^\perp \cdot \mathbf{b} = a_x b_y - a_y b_x$ (the value of the perp dot product).
- $\mathbf{a}^\perp \cdot \mathbf{a} = 0$ ($\mathbf{a}^\perp$ is perpendicular to $\mathbf{a}$).
- $|\mathbf{a}^\perp|^2 = |\mathbf{a}|^2$ ($\mathbf{a}^\perp$ and $\mathbf{a}$ have the same length).
- $\mathbf{a}^\perp \cdot \mathbf{b} = -\mathbf{b}^\perp \cdot \mathbf{a}$ (antisymmetric).   (4.17)

The fourth fact shows that the perp dot product is antisymmetric: moving the $\perp$ from one vector to the other reverses the sign of the dot product. Other useful properties of the perp dot product will be discussed as they are needed.

4.3.6 Calculate one

Compute $\mathbf{a} \cdot \mathbf{b}$ and $\mathbf{a}^\perp \cdot \mathbf{b}$ for $\mathbf{a} = (3, 4)$ and $\mathbf{b} = (2, 1)$.

4.3.7 It's a determinant

Show that $\mathbf{a}^\perp \cdot \mathbf{b}$ can be written as the determinant (for definitions of matrices and determinants see Appendix 2):

$$\mathbf{a}^\perp \cdot \mathbf{b} = \begin{vmatrix} a_x & a_y \\ b_x & b_y \end{vmatrix}$$

4.3.8 Other goodies

a. Show that $(\mathbf{a}^\perp \cdot \mathbf{b})^2 + (\mathbf{a} \cdot \mathbf{b})^2 = |\mathbf{a}|^2 |\mathbf{b}|^2$.
b. Show that if $\mathbf{a} + \mathbf{b} + \mathbf{c} = \mathbf{0}$, then $\mathbf{a}^\perp \cdot \mathbf{b} = \mathbf{b}^\perp \cdot \mathbf{c} = \mathbf{c}^\perp \cdot \mathbf{a}$.   ■

4.3.5 Orthogonal Projections and the Distance from a Point to a Line

Three geometric problems in particular arise frequently in graphics applications:

- **projecting** a vector onto a given vector,
- **resolving** a vector into its components in one direction and another, and
- finding the distance between a point and a line.

All three problems are simplified if we use the **perp vector** and the **perp dot product**. Recall that using perp dots requires that the relevant vectors lie in 2D.

Figure 4.12a shows the basic ingredients. We are given two points, A and C, and a vector, $\mathbf{v}$. These questions arise:

a. How far is the point C from the line L that passes through A in the direction $\mathbf{v}$?
b. If we drop a perpendicular from C onto L, where does it hit L?
c. How do we decompose the vector $\mathbf{c}$ into a part along the line L and a part perpendicular to L?

Figure 4.12b defines some additional quantities: $\mathbf{v}^\perp$ is the vector $\mathbf{v}$ rotated 90 degrees CCW. Dropping a perpendicular from C onto line L, we say that the vector $\mathbf{c}$ is **resolved** into the portion $K\mathbf{v}$ along $\mathbf{v}$ and the portion $M\mathbf{v}^\perp$ perpendicular to $\mathbf{v}$, where K and M are some constants to be determined. Then we have

$$\mathbf{c} = K\mathbf{v} + M\mathbf{v}^\perp \tag{4.18}$$

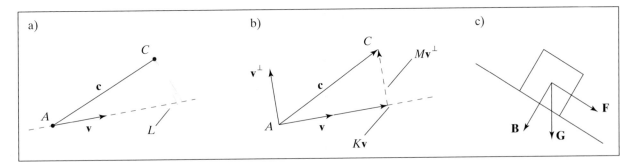

a)   b)   c)

FIGURE 4.12 Resolving a vector into two orthogonal vectors.

Given $\mathbf{c}$ and $\mathbf{v}$, we want to solve for K and M. Once found, we say that the **orthogonal projection** of $\mathbf{c}$ onto $\mathbf{v}$ is $K\mathbf{v}$ and that the distance from C to the line is $|M\mathbf{v}^{\perp}|$.

Figure 4.12c shows a situation where these questions might arise. We wish to analyze how the gravitational force vector $\mathbf{G}$ acts on the block to pull it down the incline. To do this we must resolve $\mathbf{G}$ into the force $\mathbf{F}$ acting along the incline and the force $\mathbf{B}$ acting perpendicular to the incline. That is, we must find $\mathbf{F}$ and $\mathbf{B}$ such that $\mathbf{G} = \mathbf{F} + \mathbf{B}$.

Equation (4.18) is really two equations: the left-hand and right-hand sides must agree for the x-components and also for the y-components. There are two unknowns, K and M. So we have two equations in two unknowns, and Cramer's rule can be applied. But who remembers Cramer's rule? We use a trick here that is easy to remember and immediately reveals the solution. It is equivalent to Cramer's rule, but is simpler to apply.

The trick in solving two equations in two unknowns is to eliminate one of the variables. We do this by forming the dot product of both sides with the vector $\mathbf{v}$:

$$\mathbf{c} \cdot \mathbf{v} = K\mathbf{v} \cdot \mathbf{v} + M\mathbf{v}^{\perp} \cdot \mathbf{v} \qquad (4.19)$$

Happily, the term $\mathbf{v}^{\perp} \cdot \mathbf{v}$ vanishes (why?), yielding K immediately:

$$K = \frac{\mathbf{c} \cdot \mathbf{v}}{\mathbf{v} \cdot \mathbf{v}}$$

Similarly, dot both sides of Equation (4.18) with $\mathbf{v}^{\perp}$ to obtain M:

$$M = \frac{\mathbf{c} \cdot \mathbf{v}^{\perp}}{\mathbf{v}^{\perp} \cdot \mathbf{v}^{\perp}}$$

Putting these together, we have

$$\mathbf{c} = \left(\frac{\mathbf{v} \cdot \mathbf{c}}{|\mathbf{v}|^{2}}\right)\mathbf{v} + \left(\frac{\mathbf{v}^{\perp} \cdot \mathbf{c}}{|\mathbf{v}^{\perp}|^{2}}\right)\mathbf{v}^{\perp} \qquad \text{(resolving } \mathbf{c} \text{ into } \mathbf{v} \text{ and } \mathbf{v}^{\perp}) \qquad (4.20)$$

This equality holds for any vectors $\mathbf{c}$ and $\mathbf{v}$. The part along $\mathbf{v}$ is known as the **orthogonal projection** of $\mathbf{c}$ onto the vector $\mathbf{v}$. Notice that the projection vanishes if $\mathbf{c}$ is perpendicular to $\mathbf{v}$. The second term gives the difference term explicitly and compactly. Its size is the distance from $\mathbf{c}$ to the line, given by:

$$\text{distance} = \left|\frac{\mathbf{v}^{\perp} \cdot \mathbf{c}}{|\mathbf{v}^{\perp}|^{2}}\mathbf{v}^{\perp}\right| = \frac{|\mathbf{v}^{\perp} \cdot \mathbf{c}|}{|\mathbf{v}^{\perp}|}$$

(Check that the second form really equals the first.) Referring to Figure 4.13b, we can say: **the distance from a point C to the line through A in the direction $\mathbf{v}$ is**

$$\text{distance} = \frac{|\mathbf{v}^{\perp} \cdot (C - A)|}{|\mathbf{v}^{\perp}|} \qquad (4.21)$$

■ **EXAMPLE 4.3.5**

Find the orthogonal projection of the vector $\mathbf{c} = (6, 4)$ onto $\mathbf{v} = (1, 2)$. Sketch the relevant vectors.

SOLUTION:

Evaluate the first term in Equation (4.20), obtaining the vector $(14, 28)/5$.

■ **EXAMPLE 4.3.6**

How far is the point $C = (6, 4)$ from the line that passes through $(1, 1)$ and $(4, 9)$?

SOLUTION:

Set A and $C = (6, 4)$. Then in the current notation, $\mathbf{c}$ is $(5,3)$ and $\mathbf{v}$ is $(3,8)$ $\mathbf{a} = (4, 9) - (1, 1) = (3, 8)$, and evaluate d in Equation (4.25): $d = 31/\sqrt{73}$.

PRACTICE EXERCISES

4.3.9 Resolve it!

Express vector $\mathbf{g} = (4, 7)$ as a linear combination of $\mathbf{b} = (3, 5)$ and $\mathbf{b}^{\perp}$. How far is $(4, 2) + \mathbf{g}$ from the line through $(4, 2)$ that moves in the direction $\mathbf{b}$?

4.3.10 A block pulled down an incline

A block rests on an incline tilted $30°$ from the horizontal. Gravity exerts a force of one newton on the block. What is the force that is trying to move the block along the incline?

4.3.11 How far is it?

How far from the line through $(2, 5)$ and $(4, -1)$ does the point $(6, 11)$ lie? Check your result on a graphing calculator.   ■

4.3.6 Applications of Projection: Reflections

To display the reflection of light from a mirror, or the behavior of billiard balls bouncing off one another, we need to find the direction that an object takes upon being reflected at a given surface. In a case study at the end of this chapter we describe an application to trace a ray of light as it bounces around inside a reflective chamber, or a billiard ball as it bounces around a pool table. At each bounce a reflection is made to a new direction, as derived in this section.

When light reflects from a mirror, we know from physics that the angle of reflection must equal the angle of incidence. We next show how to use vectors and projections to compute this new direction.

There are a number of different ways to derive the reflection direction; we follow a rather intuitive route suggested by [Hearn 94]. We can think in terms of two-dimensional vectors for simplicity; because the derivation does not explicitly state the dimension of the vectors involved, the same result applies in three dimensions for reflections from a surface.

Figure 4.13a shows a ray having direction $\mathbf{a}$, *away* from the light source, hitting line L, and reflecting in as yet unknown direction $\mathbf{r}$ (note: some authors assume $\mathbf{a}$ is the direction towards the light source and so equals $-\mathbf{a}$ for our approach). $\mathbf{r}$ and $\mathbf{a}$ have the same length, since for reflection from a perfect mirror the incident and reflected light have the same strength. We now find the direction of $\mathbf{r}$. The vector $\mathbf{n}$ is perpendicular to the line. Angle θ_1 in the figure must equal angle θ_2. As extreme cases, when θ_1 is $90°$, (such that the light just grazes the surface) then θ_2 must also be $90°$, and when θ_1 is 0, (the light is aimed straight down into the surface) then θ_2 is 0. (Our final formulas must apply for any values of incident angle, and so must agree

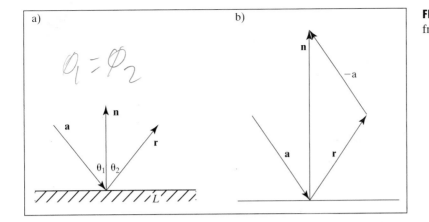

FIGURE 4.13 Reflection of a ray from a surface.

with the answers just given for these extreme cases.) A similar situation is shown in Figure 4.13b, except the vector **–a** is shown added to **r**. (It will be easier to derive the sum **r – a** first, from which r will follow immediately.) By the parallelogram rule the resultant vector **r – a** is parallel to **n**. (Check this.)

Assume, for convenience, that the vectors **a** and **n** have been normalized. Then the projection of **a** onto **n** is $- \mathbf{a} \cdot \mathbf{n}$, and the figure shows that another –a o n is added so that the resultant **r – a** lies at distance $2(\mathbf{a} \cdot \mathbf{n})$ along the direction **n**. Hence

$\mathbf{r} - \mathbf{a} = 2\,(-\mathbf{a} \cdot \mathbf{n})\,\mathbf{n}$, so that finally:
$\mathbf{r} = \mathbf{a} - 2\,(\mathbf{a} \cdot \mathbf{n})\,\mathbf{n}$. (direction of reflected ray)   (4.22)

In three dimensions, physics demands that the reflected direction **r** must lie in the plane defined by **n** and **a**. The expression for **r** above indeed supports this, as we show in Chapter 5.

The result in Equation 4.22 may appear fairly complicated and may be difficult to remember, but it bears memorization, so it will benefit from some further discussion. Looking at it broadly, it says that the reflected vector **r** is basically the same as **a**, but with a 'piece' of **n** subtracted. The size of the piece varies from 0 when **a** and **n** are orthogonal, to twice the magnitude of **a** when **a** and **n** are parallel. (Can you see that this is so?)

■ EXAMPLE 4.3.7

Let $\mathbf{a} = (4, -2)$ and $\mathbf{n} = (0, 3)$. Then Equation (4.23) yields $\mathbf{r} = (4, 2)$, as expected. Both the angle of incidence and reflection are equal to $\tan^{-1}(2)$.

PRACTICE EXERCISES

4.3.12 Find the reflected direction

For $\mathbf{a} = (2, 3)$ and $\mathbf{n} = (-2, 1)$, find the direction of the reflection.   ■

4.4 THE CROSS PRODUCT OF TWO VECTORS

> Let us grant that the pursuit of mathematics is a divine madness of the human spirit
> *Alfred North Whitehead*
> *(1861–1947)*

The **cross product** (also called the vector product) of two vectors is another 3D vector. It has many useful properties, but the one we use most often is that it is perpendicular to both of the given vectors. The cross product is defined only for three-dimensional vectors.

Given the 3D vectors $\mathbf{a} = (a_x, a_y, a_z)$ and $\mathbf{b} = (b_x, b_y, b_z)$, their cross product is denoted as $\mathbf{a} \times \mathbf{b}$. It is defined in terms of the standard unit vectors $\mathbf{i}, \mathbf{j}$, and $\mathbf{k}$ by the following definition:

Definition of $\mathbf{a} \times \mathbf{b}$:

$$\mathbf{a} \times \mathbf{b} = (a_y b_z - a_z b_y)\mathbf{i} + (a_z b_x - a_x b_z)\mathbf{j} + (a_x b_y - a_y b_x)\mathbf{k} \tag{4.24}$$

This form is rather difficult to remember, so it is often written as an easily remembered determinant (see Appendix 2 for a review of determinants):

$$\mathbf{a} \times \mathbf{b} = \begin{vmatrix} \mathbf{i} & \mathbf{j} & \mathbf{k} \\ a_x & a_y & a_z \\ b_x & b_y & b_z \end{vmatrix} \tag{4.25}$$

Remembering how to form the cross product thus requires only remembering how to form a determinant.

■ EXAMPLE 4.4.1

For $\mathbf{a} = (3, 0, 2)$ and $\mathbf{b} = (4, 1, 8)$, direct calculation shows that $\mathbf{a} \times \mathbf{b} = -2\mathbf{i} - 16\mathbf{j} + 3\mathbf{k}$. What is $\mathbf{b} \times \mathbf{a}$?

From this definition one can easily show the following algebraic properties of the cross product:

1a. $\mathbf{i} \times \mathbf{j} = \mathbf{k}$
1b. $\mathbf{j} \times \mathbf{k} = \mathbf{i}$
1c. $\mathbf{k} \times \mathbf{i} = \mathbf{j}$
2. $\mathbf{a} \times \mathbf{b} = -\mathbf{b} \times \mathbf{a}, (\mathbf{a} \cdot \mathbf{a}) \times \mathbf{b}$
    $= \mathbf{a} \cdot (\mathbf{a} \times \mathbf{b}) = -(\ )\mathbf{a} \cdot (\mathbf{b} \times \mathbf{a})$ (antisymmetry)
3. $\mathbf{a} \times (\mathbf{b} + \mathbf{c}) = \mathbf{a} \times \mathbf{b} + \mathbf{a} \times \mathbf{c}$ (linearity)   (4.26)
4. $(s\mathbf{a}) \times \mathbf{b} = s(\mathbf{a} \times \mathbf{b})$ (homogeneity)
5. $\mathbf{a} \cdot (\mathbf{a} \times \mathbf{b}) = \mathbf{b} \cdot (\mathbf{a} \times \mathbf{b}) = 0$ (normality)

These equations are true in both left-handed and right-handed coordinate systems. Note the logical (alphabetical) ordering of ingredients in the equation $\mathbf{i} \times \mathbf{j} = \mathbf{k}$, which also provides a handy mnemonic device for remembering the direction of cross products. Rule 5 states that the cross product of $\mathbf{a}$ and $\mathbf{b}$ is perpendicular to both $\mathbf{a}$ and $\mathbf{b}$. This latter rule will become important when we wish to aim a camera at a 3D scene in order to make the most desirable snapshot. This will become important in Chapters 5 and 7.

PRACTICE EXERCISES

4.4.1 Demonstrate the four properties

Prove Properties 2, 3, and 4 above for the cross product.

4.4.2 Is $\mathbf{a} \times \mathbf{b}$ perpendicular to $\mathbf{a}$ and to $\mathbf{b}$?

Show that the cross product of vectors $\mathbf{a}$ and $\mathbf{b}$ is perpendicular to both vectors $\mathbf{a}$ and $\mathbf{b}$. (*Hint*: Do not use components to do this. It can be done much more simply.)

4.4.3 Nonassociativity of the cross product

Show that the cross product is not associative—that is, that $\mathbf{a} \times (\mathbf{b} \times \mathbf{c})$ is not necessarily the same as $(\mathbf{a} \times \mathbf{b}) \times \mathbf{c}$.

4.4.4 Another useful fact

Show by direct calculation on the components that the length of the cross product has the form:

$$|\mathbf{a} \times \mathbf{b}| = \sqrt{|\mathbf{a}|^2|\mathbf{b}|^2 - (\mathbf{a} \cdot \mathbf{b})^2}$$

■

4.4.1 Geometric Interpretation of the Cross Product

By definition the cross product $\mathbf{a} \times \mathbf{b}$ of two vectors is another vector, but how is it related geometrically to the others, and why is it of interest? Figure 4.14 gives the answer. The cross product $\mathbf{a} \times \mathbf{b}$ has the following useful properties:

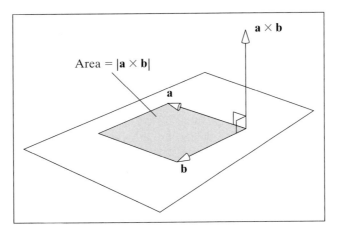

FIGURE 4.14 Interpretation of the cross product.

1. $\mathbf{a} \times \mathbf{b}$ is perpendicular (orthogonal) to both $\mathbf{a}$ and $\mathbf{b}$, as stated previously.
2. The length of $\mathbf{a} \times \mathbf{b}$ equals the area of the parallelogram determined by $\mathbf{a}$ and $\mathbf{b}$. This area is equal to

$$|\mathbf{a} \times \mathbf{b}| = |\mathbf{a}||\mathbf{b}| \sin(\theta) \qquad (4.27)$$

where θ is the angle between $\mathbf{a}$ and $\mathbf{b}$, measured from $\mathbf{a}$ to $\mathbf{b}$ or $\mathbf{b}$ to $\mathbf{a}$, whichever produces an angle less than 180 degrees. As a special case, $\mathbf{a} \times \mathbf{b} = 0$ if, and only if, $\mathbf{a}$ and $\mathbf{b}$ have the same or opposite directions or either has zero length. What is the magnitude of the cross product if $\mathbf{a}$ and $\mathbf{b}$ are perpendicular?
3. The sense of $\mathbf{a} \times \mathbf{b}$ is given by the right-hand rule when working in a right-handed system. For example, twist the fingers of your right hand from $\mathbf{a}$ to $\mathbf{b}$, and then $\mathbf{a} \times \mathbf{b}$ will point in the direction of your thumb. (When working in a left-handed system, use your left hand instead.) Note that $\mathbf{i} \times \mathbf{j} = \mathbf{k}$ supports this.

■ EXAMPLE 4.4.2

Let $\mathbf{a} = (1, 0, 1)$ and $\mathbf{b} = (1, 0, 0)$. These vectors are easy to visualize, as they both lie in the x,z-plane. (Sketch them.) The area of the parallelogram defined by $\mathbf{a}$ to $\mathbf{b}$ is easily seen to be 1. Because $\mathbf{a} \times \mathbf{b}$ is orthogonal to both $\mathbf{a}$ to $\mathbf{b}$, we expect it to be parallel to the y-axis and hence be proportional to $\pm\mathbf{j}$. In either a right-handed or a left-handed system, sweeping the fingers of the appropriate hand from $\mathbf{a}$ to $\mathbf{b}$ reveals a thumb pointed along the positive y-axis. Direct calculation based on Equation (4.24) confirms all of this: $\mathbf{a} \times \mathbf{b} = \mathbf{j}$.

PRACTICE EXERCISE

4.4.5 Proving the properties

Prove the three properties given in Equation (4.26) for the cross product.   ■

4.4.2 To Find the Normal Vector to a Plane

As we shall see in the next section, we sometimes must compute the components of the vector **n** that is normal to a plane. Supposing the plane is known to pass through three specific points, the cross product provides the tool to accomplish this.

Any three points, P_1, P_2, P_3, determine a unique plane, as long as the points don't lie in a straight line. Figure 4.15 shows this situation.

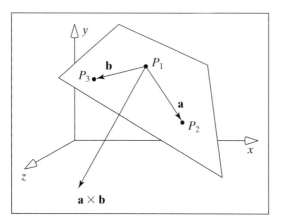

FIGURE 4.15 Finding the plane through three given points.

To find the normal vector, we build two vectors, $\mathbf{a} = P_2 - P_1$ and $\mathbf{b} = P_3 - P_1$. Their cross product, **n**, denoted by $\mathbf{a} \times \mathbf{b}$, must be normal to both **a** and **b**, so it is normal to every line in the plane (why?). It is therefore the desired normal vector. (What happens if the three points *do* lie in a straight line?) Any scalar multiple of this cross product is also a normal vector, including $\mathbf{b} \times \mathbf{a}$, which points in the opposite direction.

■ **EXAMPLE 4.4.3**

Find the normal vector to the plane that passes through the points $(1, 0, 2), (2, 3, 0)$, and $(1, 2, 4)$.

SOLUTION:

By direct calculation, $\mathbf{a} = (2, 3, 0) - (1, 0, 2) = (1, 3, -2)$, and $\mathbf{b} = (1, 2, 4) - (1, 0, 2) = (0, 2, 2)$, and so their cross product $\mathbf{n} = (10, -2, 2)$. (Note that **n** is normal to both **a** and **b**, as expected.)

Note: Since a cross product involves the subtraction of various quantities, this method for finding **n** is vulnerable to numerical inaccuracies, especially when the angle between **a** and **b** is small. We develop a more robust method in the practice exercises for finding normal vectors.

PRACTICE EXERCISES

4.4.6 Does the choice of points matter?

Is the same plane obtained as in Example 4.4.3 if we use the points in a different order, say, $\mathbf{a} = (1, 0, 2) - (2, 3, 0)$ and $\mathbf{b} = (1, 2, 4) - (2, 3, 0)$? Show that the same plane does result.

4.4.7 Finding some planes

For each of the following triplets of points, find the normal vector to the plane (if it exists) that passes through the triplet.

a. $P_1 = (1, 1, 1), P_2 = (1, 2, 1), P_3 = (3, 0, 4)$
b. $P_1 = (8, 9, 7), P_2 = (-8, -9, -7), P_3 = (1, 2, 1)$
c. $P_1 = (6, 3, -4), P_2 = (0, 0, 0), P_3 = (2, 1, -1)$
d. $P_1 = (0, 0, 0), P_2 = (1, 1, 1), P_3 = (2, 2, 2)$.

4.4.8 Finding the normal vectors.

Calculate the normal vectors to each of the faces of the two geometric objects shown in Figure 4.16. The cube has vertices $(\pm 1, \pm 1, \pm 1)$ and the tetrahedron has vertices $(0, 0, 0), (0, 0, 1), (1, 0, 0),$ and $(0, 1, 0)$. ■

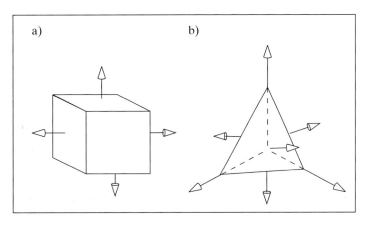

a)   b)

FIGURE 4.16 Finding the normal vectors to faces.

4.4.3 To Test the Convexity of a Planar Polygon

As we saw in Chapter 2, an important property of a polygon is whether or not it is convex. This question will be revisited in later chapters, in connection with, among other things, clipping and proper shading. We will need a simple and efficient test to determine whether a given polygon is convex.

Fortunately, the cross product provides a ready answer. It hinges on the property that as one traverses around a convex polygon from one edge to the next, either a left turn or a right turn is taken at each vertex, and they all must be the same kind of turn (all left or all right).

Figure 4.17a shows a convex polygon, and part b shows one that is not convex. The hexagon of part a is based on vertices $P_0, P_1, \ldots, P_5$, and the edge from P_0 to P_1 is labeled as vector **a**. Similarly, vector **b** points from P_1 to P_2. In total there are six vectors that lie on the edges of the polygon. We shall call these **edge vectors**. Notice that there is a right turn from each edge of the polygon to the next edge, which we will call an edge vector. For each right turn, the cross product $\mathbf{a} \times \mathbf{b}$ points into the plane of the polygon. For each left turn the cross product points out of the plane. Can you see why? By contrast, for a left turn the cross product between any edge vector and the next must point into the plane. Notice that in part b of the figure not all of the turns are the same: five of them are left turns and five of them are right turns. These turns are not all the same and in fact the polygon is not convex. This leads us to the result:

A polygon is convex if the cross products between each edge vector and the next all point into the plane or out of the plane.

FIGURE 4.17 Testing for convexity.

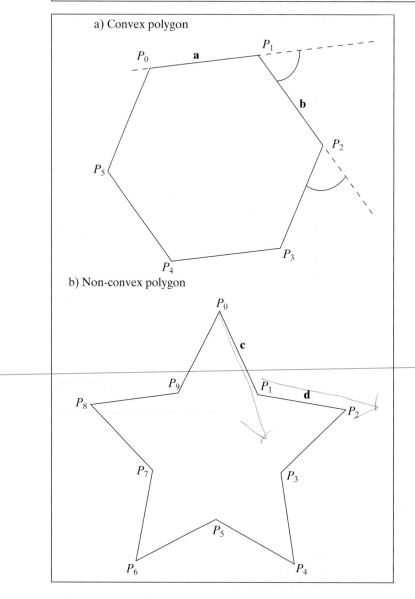

a) Convex polygon

b) Non-convex polygon

To test for this in an application requires the computation of **n** cross products and a test that their y-components all have the same sign.

4.5 REPRESENTATIONS OF KEY GEOMETRIC OBJECTS

All that transcends geometry, transcends our comprehension.

Blaise Pascal
(1623–1662)

In the preceding sections we have discussed some basic ideas of vectors and their application to important geometric problems that arise in graphics. Now we develop the fundamental ideas that facilitate working with lines and planes, which are central to graphics, and whose straightness and flatness makes them easy to represent and manipulate.

What does it mean to represent a line or plane, and why is it important? The goal is to come up with a formula or equation that distinguishes points that lie on the line from those that don't. This might be an equation that is satisfied by all points on the line, and only those points. Or it might be a function that returns different points in the line as some parameter is varied. The representation allows one to test such things as: Is point P on the line? Where does the line *intersect* another line or some other object? Very importantly, a line lying in a plane divides the plane into two parts, and we often need to ask whether point P lies on one side or the other of the line.

In order to deal properly with lines and planes we must, somewhat unexpectedly, go back to basics and review how points and vectors differ, and how each is represented. This need arises because, in order to represent a line or plane, we must add points together, and scale points—operations that for points are nonsensical. To see what is really going on we introduce the notion of a coordinate frame, which makes clear the significant difference between a point and a vector and reveals in what sense it is legitimate to add points. The use of coordinate frames leads ultimately to the notion of **homogeneous coordinates**, which is a central tool in computer graphics and greatly simplifies many algorithms. We will make explicit use of coordinate frames in only a few places in the book, most notably when changing coordinate systems and flying cameras around a scene (see Chapters 5, 6, and 7).[5] But even when not explicitly mentioned, an underlying coordinate frame will be present in every situation.

4.5.1 Coordinate Systems and Coordinate Frames

One doesn't discover new lands without consenting to lose sight of the shore for a very long time.

Andre Gide
(1869–1951)

When discussing vectors in previous sections we say, for instance, that a vector $\mathbf{v} = (3, 2, 7)$, meaning that it is a certain 3-tuple. We say the same for a point, as in point $P = (5, 3, 1)$. This makes it seem that points and vectors are the same thing. But points and vectors are very different creatures: points have location but no size or direction; vectors have size and direction but no location.

What we mean by $\mathbf{v} = (3, 2, 7)$, of course, is that the vector $\mathbf{v}$ has components $(3, 2, 7)$ in the underlying coordinate system. Similarly, $P = (5, 3, 1)$ means that point P has coordinates $(5, 3, 1)$ in the underlying coordinate system. Normally this blurring between the object and its representation presents no problem. The problem arises when there is more than one coordinate system (a very common occurrence in graphics) and when you transform points or vectors from one system into another.

We usually think of a coordinate system as three axes emanating from an origin, as in Figure 4.2b. But in fact a coordinate system is located somewhere in the world, and its axes are best described by three vectors that point in mutually perpendicular directions. In particular it is important to make explicit the location of the coordinate system. So we extend the notion of a 3D coordinate system[6] to that of a 3D coordinate frame. A **coordinate frame** consists of a specific point, ϕ, called the origin, and three mutually perpendicular unit vectors, $\mathbf{a}, \mathbf{b}$, and $\mathbf{c}$. Figure 4.18 shows a coordinate frame residing at some point ϕ within the world, with its vectors $\mathbf{a}, \mathbf{b}$, and $\mathbf{c}$ drawn so they appear to emanate from ϕ like axes.

---

[5]   This is an area where graphics programmers can easily go astray: their programs produce pictures that look OK for simple situations and become mysteriously and glaringly wrong when things get more complex.

[6]   The ideas for a 2D system are essentially identical.

FIGURE 4.18 A coordinate frame positioned in the world.

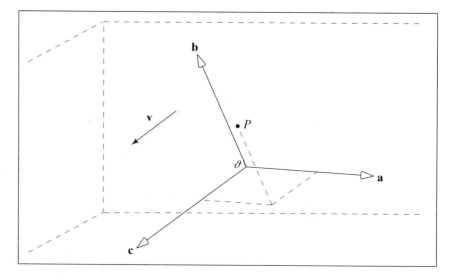

Now to represent a vector **v** we find three numbers (v_1, v_2, v_3) such that

$$\mathbf{v} = v_1\mathbf{a} + v_2\mathbf{b} + v_3\mathbf{c} \tag{4.28}$$

and say that **v** has the representation (v_1, v_2, v_3) in this system.

On the other hand, to represent a point P, we view its location as an offset from the origin by a certain amount: we represent the vector $P - \phi$ by finding three numbers (p_1, p_2, p_3) such that

$$P - \phi = p_1\mathbf{a} + p_2\mathbf{b} + p_3\mathbf{c}$$

and then equivalently write P itself as

$$P = \phi + p_1\mathbf{a} + p_2\mathbf{b} + p_3\mathbf{c} \tag{4.29}$$

The representation of P is not just a 3-tuple, but a 3-tuple along with an origin. P is at a location that is offset from the origin by $p_1\mathbf{a} + p_2\mathbf{b} + p_3\mathbf{c}$. The basic idea is to make the origin of the coordinate system *explicit*. This becomes important only when there is more than one coordinate frame, and when transforming one frame into another.

Note that when we earlier defined the standard unit vectors $\mathbf{i}, \mathbf{j}$, and $\mathbf{k}$ as $(1,0,0), (0,1,0)$, and $(0,0,1)$, respectively, we were actually defining their *representations* in an underlying coordinate frame. Since by Equation (4.32) $\mathbf{i} = 1\mathbf{a} + 0\mathbf{b} + 0\mathbf{c}$, vector $\mathbf{i}$ is actually just **a** itself! It's a matter of naming—whether you are talking about the vector or about its representation in a coordinate frame. We usually don't bother to distinguish them.

Note that you can't explicitly say where ϕ is, or cite the directions of $\mathbf{a}, \mathbf{b}$, and $\mathbf{c}$. To do so requires having some other coordinate frame in which to represent this one. In terms of its own coordinate frame, ϕ has the representation $(0,0,0)$, **a** has the representation $(1,0,0)$, and so on.

The Homogeneous Representation of a Point and a Vector

It is useful to represent both points and vectors using the *same* set of basic underlying objects, $(\mathbf{a}, \mathbf{b}, \mathbf{c}, \phi)$. From Equations (4.28) and (4.29) the vector $\mathbf{v} = v_1\mathbf{a} + v_2\mathbf{b} + v_3\mathbf{c}$ then has the four components $(v_1, v_2, v_3, 0)$, whereas the point $P = p_1\mathbf{a} + p_2\mathbf{b} + p_3\mathbf{c} + \phi$ has the four components $(p_1, p_2, p_3, 1)$. The fourth component designates whether the object does or does not include ϕ. We can formally write any **v** and P using a matrix multiplication (multiplying a row vector by a column vector—see Appendix 2):

$$\mathbf{v} = (\mathbf{a}, \mathbf{b}, \mathbf{c}, \phi) \begin{pmatrix} v_1 \\ v_2 \\ v_3 \\ 0 \end{pmatrix} \tag{4.30}$$

$$P = (\mathbf{a}, \mathbf{b}, \mathbf{c}, \phi) \begin{pmatrix} p_1 \\ p_2 \\ p_3 \\ 1 \end{pmatrix} \tag{4.31}$$

Here the row matrix captures the nature of the coordinate frame, and the column vector captures the representation of the specific object of interest. Thus vectors and points have different representations: there is a fourth component of 0 for a vector and 1 for a point. This is often called the **homogeneous representation**.[7] The use of homogeneous coordinates is one of the hallmarks of computer graphics, as it helps to keep straight the distinction between points and vectors, and provides a compact notation when we are working with affine transformations. It pays off in a computer program to represent the points and vectors of interest in homogeneous coordinates as 4-tuples, by appending a 1 or 0.[8] This is particularly true when we must convert between one coordinate frame and another in which points and vectors are represented.

It is simple to convert between the ordinary representation of a point or a vector (a 3-tuple for 3D objects or a 2-tuple for 2D objects) and the homogeneous form:

To go from ordinary to homogeneous coordinates:

If it's a point, append a 1.
If it's a vector, append a 0.

To go from homogeneous coordinates to ordinary coordinates:

If it's a vector, its final coordinate is 0. Delete the 0.
If it's a point, its final coordinate is 1. Delete the 1.

OpenGL uses 4D homogeneous coordinates for all its vertices. If you send it a 3-tuple in the form (x, y, z), it converts it immediately to $(x, y, z, 1)$. If you send it a 2D point (x, y), it first appends a 0 for the z-component and then a 1, to form $(x, y, 0, 1)$. All computations are done within OpenGL in 4D homogeneous coordinates.

Linear Combinations of Vectors

Note how nicely some things work out in homogeneous coordinates when we combine vectors coordinate-wise: all the definitions and manipulations are consistent:

- The difference of two points $(x, y, z, 1)$ and $(u, \text{``}v\text{''}, \text{``}w\text{''}, 1)$ is $(x - u, y - v, z - w, 0)$, which is, as expected, a vector.
- The sum of a point $(x, y, z, 1)$ and a vector $(d, e, f, 0)$ is $(x + d, y + e, z + f, 1)$, another point.
- Two vectors can be added: $(d, e, f, 0) + (m, n, r, 0) = (d + m, e + n, f + r, 0)$ which produces another vector.

---

[7] Actually we are only going part of the way in this discussion. As we see in Chapter 7 when studying projections, homogeneous coordinates in that context permit an additional operation, which makes them truly "homogeneous." Until we examine projections, this operation need not be introduced.

[8] In the 2D case, points are 3-tuples $(p_1, p_2, 1)$ and vectors are 3-tuples $(v_1, v_2, 0)$.

- It is meaningful to scale a vector: $3(d, e, f, 0) = (3d, 3e, 3f, 0)$.
- It is meaningful to form *any* linear combination of vectors. Let the vectors be $\mathbf{v} = (v_1, v_2, v_3, 0)$ and $\mathbf{w} = (w_1, w_2, w_3, 0)$. Then, using arbitrary scalars a and b, we form $a\mathbf{v} + b\mathbf{w} = (av_1 + bw_1, av_2 + bw_2, av_3 + bw_3, 0)$, which is a legitimate vector.

Forming a linear combination of vectors is well defined, but does it make sense for points? The answer is *no*, except in one special case, as we explore next.

4.5.2 Affine Combinations of Points

Consider forming a linear combination of two points, $P = (P_1, P_2, P_3, 1)$ and $R = (R_1, R_2, R_3, 1)$, using the scalars f and g:

$$fP + gR = (fP_1 + gR_1, fP_2 + gR_2, fP_3 + gR_3, f + g)$$

We know this is a legitimate vector if $f + g = 0$. (Why?) But we shall see that it is *not* a legitimate point unless $f + g = 1$! Recall from Equation (4.2) that when the coefficients of a linear combination sum to 1, it is called an affine combination. We will see that the only linear combination of points that is legitimate is an affine combination. Thus, for example, the object $0.3P + 0.7R$ is a legitimate point, as are $2.7P - 1.7R$ and the midpoint $0.5P + 0.5R$, but $P + R$ is not a point. For three points, P, R, and Q, we can form the legal point $0.3P + 0.9R - 0.2Q$, but not $P + Q - 0.9R$

Fact: **Any affine combination of points is a legitimate point.**

But what's wrong geometrically with forming *any* linear combination of two points, say

$$E = fP + gR \tag{4.32}$$

when $f + g$ is different from 1? The problem arises if we translate the origin of the coordinate system [Goldman85]. Suppose the origin is translated by vector $\mathbf{u}$, so that P is altered to $P + \mathbf{u}$ and R is translated to $R + \mathbf{u}$. If E is a legitimate point, it too must be translated to the new point $E' = E + \mathbf{u}$. But instead we have

$$E' = fP + gR + (f + g)\mathbf{u}$$

which is *not* $E + \mathbf{u}$, unless $f + g = 1$.

The failure of a simple sum $P_1 + P_2$ of two points to be a true point is shown in Figure 4.19. Points P_1 and P_2 are shown represented in two coordinate systems, one offset from the other. Viewing each point as the head of a vector bound to its origin, we see that the sum $P_1 + P_2$ yields two different points in the two systems. Therefore $P_1 + P_2$ depends on the choice of coordinate system. Note, by way of contrast, that the affine combination $0.5(P_1 + P_2)$ does *not* depend on this choice.

A Point Plus a Vector Is an Affine Combination of Points

There is another way of examining affine sums of points that is interesting on its own, and also leads to a useful tool in graphics. It doesn't require the use of homogeneous coordinates.

Consider forming a point as a point A offset by a vector $\mathbf{v}$ that has been scaled by scalar t: $A + t\mathbf{v}$. This is the sum of a point and a vector, so it is a legitimate point. If we take as vector $\mathbf{v}$ the difference between some other point B and A—$\mathbf{v} = B - A$—then we have the point P:

$$P = A + t(B - A) \tag{4.33}$$

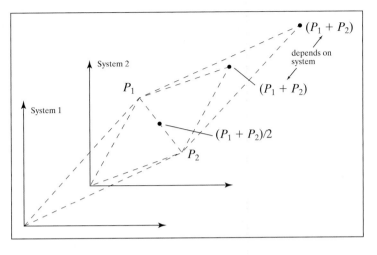

FIGURE 4.19 Adding points is not legal.

which is also a legitimate point. But now rewrite it algebraically as:

$$P = tB + (1 - t)A \tag{4.34}$$

and it is seen to be an affine combination of points. (Why?) This further legitimizes writing affine sums of points. In fact, any affine sum of points can be written as a point plus a vector (see the exercises). If you are ever uncomfortable writing an affine sum of points as in Equation (4.34) (a form we will use often), simply understand that it *means* the point given by Equation (4.33).

■ **EXAMPLE 4.5.1 The centroid of a triangle.**

Consider the triangle T with vertices A, B, and C shown in Figure 4.20. We use the ideas above to show that the three **medians** of T meet at a point that lies two-thirds of the way along each median. This is the **centroid** (center of gravity[9]) of T.

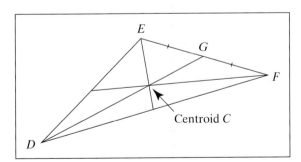

FIGURE 4.20 The centroid of a triangle as an affine combination.

By definition the median from D is the line from D to the midpoint of the opposite side. Its parametric representation is $tD + (1 - t)G$ for $t = 1/2$. Suppose a genie has stated that the centroid lies two-thirds of the way from D to G. Then we write its parametric expression as:

$$C = D\frac{1}{3} + G\frac{2}{3} \tag{4.35}$$

---

9 The reference to gravity arises because if a thin plate is cut in the shape of a T, the plate hangs level if suspended by a thread attached at the centroid. Gravity pulls equally on all sides of the centroid, so the plate is balanced.

When the form for G above is substituted for G in this expression, we get as a final result for C:

$$C = D\frac{1}{3} + \left(\frac{E + F}{2}\right)\frac{2}{3} \qquad (4.36)$$

Try it! Now how did the genie get so smart to know that the centroid lies exactly two-thirds of the way? Here's the cute part [Pedoe70]. Since this result is *symmetrical* in D, E, and F, it must also be two-thirds of the way along the median from E, and two-thirds of the way along the median from F. Hence the three medians meet there, and C is the centroid. Check that these equations are indeed affine combinations of the points involved.

This result generalizes nicely for a regular polygon of N sides: the centroid is simply the average of the N vertex locations, another affine combination. For an arbitrary polygon the formula is more complex.

4.5.3 Linear Interpolation of Two Points

The affine combination of points expressed in Equation (4.29):

$$P = A(1 - t) + Bt \quad = A + t \, (B - A)$$

performs **linear interpolation** between the points A and B. That is, the x-component $P_x(t)$ provides a value that is fraction t of the way between the values A_x and B_x. This is also true for the y-component and, in 3D, the z-component. This is a sufficiently important operation to warrant a name, and `lerp()` (for linear interpolation) has become popular. In one dimension, `lerp(a, b, t)` provides a number that is the fraction t of the way from a to b (here a and b are simply scalars, not points). Figure 4.21 provides a simple implementation of `lerp()`.

FIGURE 4.21 Linear interpolation effected by `lerp()`.

```
float lerp(float a, float b, float t)
{
       return a + (b - a) * t;   // return a float
}
```

Hence, when t is 0, lerp yields a, and when t is 1, lerp yields b. When t is one-half, lerp lies halfway between a and b.

Similarly, one often wants to compute the point $P(t)$ that is fraction t of the way along the straight line from point A to point B. This point is often called the **tween** (for in-between) at t of points A and B. Each component of the resulting point is formed as the `lerp()` of the corresponding components of A and B. A procedure called Tween() is easily written (how?) to implement tweening.

■ **EXAMPLE 4.5.2**

Let $A = (4, 9)$ and $B = (3, 7)$. Then Tween(A, B, t) returns the point $(4 - t, 9 - 2t)$, so that Tween $(A, B, 0.4)$ returns $(3.6, 8.1)$. (Check this with your graphing calculator.)

4.5.4 Tweening for Art and Animation

Recall from Chapter 3 that interesting animations can be created that show one figure being tweened into another. It's simplest if the two figures are polylines (or families of polylines) based on the same number of points. Suppose the first figure, A, is based on the polyline with points A_i, and the second polyline, B, is based on points B_i, for $i = 0, \ldots, n - 1$. We can form the polyline $P(t)$, called the tween at t, by forming the points:

$$P_i(t) = (1 - t)A_i + tB_i$$

If we look at a succession of values for t between 0 and 1, say, $t = 0, 0.1, 0.2, \ldots, 0.9, 1.0$, we see that this polyline begins with the shape of A and ends with the shape of B, but in between it is a blend of the two shapes. For small values of t it looks like A, but as t increases, it warps (smoothly) toward a shape close to B. For $t = 0.25$, for instance, point $P_i(.25)$ of the tween is 25% of the way from A to B.

Figure 4.22 shows a simple example, in which polyline A has the shape of a house, and polyline B has the shape of the letter 'T'. The point R on the house corresponds to point S on the 'T'. The various tweens of point R on the house and point S on the T lie on the line between R and S. The tween for $t = 1/2$ lies at the midpoint of RS. The in-between polylines show the shapes of the tweens for $t = 0, 0.25, 0.5, 0.75,$ and 1.0.

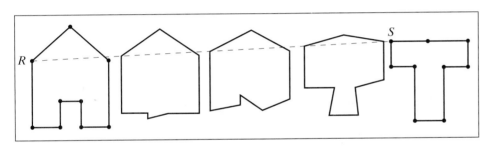

FIGURE 4.22 Tweening a T into a house.

Figure 4.23 shows drawTween(), which draws a tween of two polylines A and B, each having n vertices, at the specified value of t.

```
void drawTween(Point2 A[], Point2 B[], int n, float t)

{    // draw the tween at time t between polylines A and B
  for(int i = 0; i < n; i++)
  {
      Point2 P;
      P = Tween (A[i], B[i], t);
      if (i == 0) moveTo(P.x, P.y);
      else lineTo(P.x, P.y);
  }
}
```

FIGURE 4.23 Tweening two polylines. (Recall that in Chapter 2 lineTo() and moveTo() are defined.)

drawTween() could be used in an animation loop that tweens A and B back and forth, first as t increases from 0 to 1, then as t decreases back to 0, and so on. Double buffering, as discussed in Chapter 3, can be used to make the transition from one displayed tween to the next instantaneous.

```
for(t = 0.0, delT = 0.1; ; t += delT)
// tween back and forth forever
{
    <clear the buffer>
    drawTween(A, B, n, t);
    glutSwapBuffers();
    if( t >= 1.0 || t <= 0.0) delT = - delT;
// reverse the flow of t
}
```

Figure 4.24 shows an artistic use of this technique based on two sets of polylines; three tweens are shown for our example. Because the two sets of polylines are drawn sufficiently far apart, there is room to draw the tweens between them with no overlap, so that all five pictures fit nicely on one frame.

FIGURE 4.24 From man to woman. (Courtesy of Marc Infield)

Susan E. Brennan has produced caricatures of famous figures using this method (see [Dewdney88]). Figure 4.25 shows an example. The second and fifth faces (for which use $t = 0$ and $t = 1$, respectively) are based on digitized points for Elizabeth Taylor and John F. Kennedy. The third and fourth faces are tweens (for which $t = 1/2$), and the first and last faces are based on **extrapolation**. That is, values of t larger than 1 are used, so that the term $(1 - t)$ is negative. Extrapolation can produce caricaturelike distortions, in some sense going to the other side of polylines B from polylines A. Values of t less than 0 may also be used, with a similar effect.

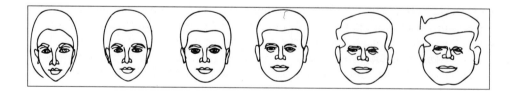

FIGURE 4.25 Face caricature: tweening and extrapolation. (Courtesy of Susan Brennan)

Tweening is used in the film industry to reduce the cost of producing animations such as cartoons. In earlier days an artist had to draw 24 pictures for each second of film, because movies display 24 frames per second. However, with the assistance of a computer, an artist need draw only the first and final pictures, called **key frames**, in certain sequences and let the others be generated automatically. For instance, if the characters are not moving too rapidly in a certain half-second portion of a cartoon, the artist can draw and digitize the first and final frames of this portion, and the computer can create 10 tweens using linear interpolation, thereby saving a great deal of the artist's time. See the Case Study at the end of this chapter for a programming project that produces these effects.

PRACTICE EXERCISES

4.5.1 A limiting case of tweening

What is the effect of tweening when all of the points A_i in polyline A are the same? How is polyline B distorted in its appearance in each tween?

4.5.2 An extrapolation

Polyline A is a square with vertices $(1, 1)$, $(-1, 1)$, $(-1, -1)$, $(1, -1)$, and polyline B is a wedge with vertices $(4, 3)$, $(5, -2)$, $(4, 0)$, $(3, -2)$. Sketch (on your graphing calculator or paper) the shape $P(t)$ for $t = -1, -0.5, 0.5$, and 1.5.

4.5.3 Extrapolation vs. tweening

Suppose that five polyline pictures are displayed side by side. From careful measurement you conclude (perhaps incorrectly) that the middle three are in-betweens of the first and the last, and you try to calculate the values of t used. But someone claims that the last is actually an extrapolation of the first and the fourth that is, the value of t is negative, or larger than 1. Is there any way to tell whether this is true? If it is an extrapolation, can the value of t used be determined? If so, what is it? ■

4.5.4 Preview: Bezier Curves Built from Quadratic and Cubic Tweening

In Chapter 8 we address the problem of designing complex shapes called *Bezier curves*. It is interesting to note here that the underlying idea is simply tweening between collections of points. With the linear interpolation above we have partition unity (that is, breaking the value 1 into the pieces that sum to 1). We can extend this to quadratic interpolation by partitioning unity into three pieces that add to 1. Just rewrite 1 as

$$1 = ((1 - t) + t)^2$$

and expand it to produce the three pieces $(1 - t)^2, 2(1 - t)t$, and t^2. They obviously sum to one, so they can be used to form the affine combination of points A, B, and C:

$$P(t) = (1 - t)^2 A + 2t(1 - t)B + t^2 C \tag{4.37}$$

This is the Bezier curve for the points A, B, and C. Figure 4.26a shows the shape of $P(t)$ as t varies from 0 to 1. It flows smoothly from A to C. (Notice that the curve does not actually touch the middle point of the segment BC: it merely gets near to it. Later we will have techniques for which the curve *does* pass through the center of BC.) Going further, one can expand $((1 - t) + t)^3$ into four pieces (which ones?) which can be used to do cubic interpolation between four points A, B, C and D, as shown in Figure 4.26b.

PRACTICE EXERCISE

4.5.4 Try it out

Using a graphing calculator, draw three points A, B, and C. For each of the values $t = 0, .1, .2, \ldots, .9, 1$ compute the position of $P(t)$ in Equation (4.37) and draw the polyline that passes through these points. Is it always a parabola? ■

FIGURE 4.26 Bezier curves as
Tweening a) a quadratic b) a
cubic.

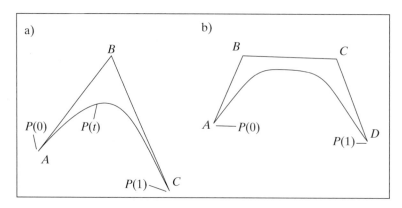

4.5.5 Representing Lines and Planes

We now turn to developing the principal forms in which lines and planes are represented mathematically. It is quite common to find data structures within a graphics
program that capture a line or plane using one of these forms.

Lines in 2D and 3D Space

A **line** is defined by two points, say C and B (see Figure 4.27a). It is infinite in
length, passing through the points and extending forever in both directions. A **line
segment** (**segment** for short) is also defined by two points, its **endpoints,** but extends only from one endpoint to the other (Figure 4.27b). Its **parent** line is the infinite line that passes through its endpoints. A **ray** is semi-infinite. It is specified by
a point and a direction. A ray starts at a point and extends infinitely far in a given
direction (Figure 4.27c).

FIGURE 4.27 Lines, segments,
and rays.

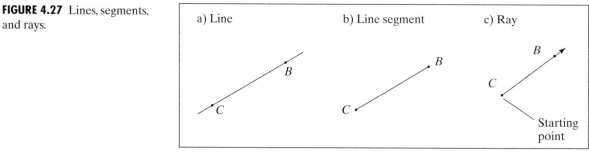

These objects, the lines segment and the ray, are very familiar, yet it is useful to
collect the important representation and properties in one place. The ray in particular is very important in the topic of **ray tracing** in 2D and 3D that we study in
Chapter 12. The reader may wish to look ahead to Chapter 12 to appreciate the
power of computer graphics in creating realistic images using ray tracing. In this
section we describe the most important representation of all for a line and a ray in
computer graphics, the **parametric representation**.

The Parametric Representation of a Line

The construction in Equations (4.32) and (4.33) is very useful, because as t varies,
the point P traces out all of the points on the straight line defined by C and B. The
construction therefore gives us a way to name and compute any point along this
line. This is done using a **parameter** t that distinguishes one point on the line from

another. Call the line L, and give the name $L(t)$ to the position associated with t. Using $\mathbf{b} = B - C$, we have:

$$L(t) = C + \mathbf{b}t \qquad\qquad b = B - C \qquad\qquad (4.38)$$

As t varies, so does the position of $L(t)$ along the line. (As we have seen before, it is very useful to think of t as time.) Figure 4.28 shows vector $\mathbf{b}$ and the line L passing through C and B. (A 2D version is shown, but the 3D version uses the same ideas.) Note where $L(t)$ is located for various values of t. If $t = 0$, $L(0)$ evaluates to C, so at $t = 0$ we are at point C. At $t = 1$ then $L(1) = C + (B - C) = B$. As t varies, we

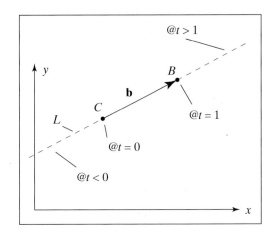

FIGURE 4.28 Parametric representation $L(t)$ of a line.

$speed = |b|$

add a longer or shorter version of $\mathbf{b}$ to the point C, resulting in a new point along the line. If t is larger than 1, this point lies somewhere on the opposite side of B from C, and when t is less than 0, it lies on the opposite side of C from B.

For a fixed value of t, say $t = 0.6$, Equation (4.38) gives a formula for exactly one point along the line through C and B—the particular point $L(0.6)$. Thus it is a description of a point. But since one can also view it as a function of t that generates the coordinates of *every* point on L as t varies, it is called the **parametric representation of line L.**

The line, ray, and segment of Figure 4.27 are all represented by the same $L(t)$ of Equation (4.38). They differ parametrically only in the values of t that are relevant:

segment:	$0 \le t \le 1$
ray:	$0 \le t < \infty$
line:	$-\infty < t < \infty$

(4.39)

C is often called the **starting point** of the ray.

A very useful fact is that $L(t)$ lies a fraction t of the way between C and B when t lies between 0 and 1. For instance, when $t = 1/2$, the point $L(0.5)$ is the **midpoint** between C and B, and when $t = 0.3$, the point $L(0.3)$ is 30% of the way from C to B. This is clear from Equation (4.38) since $|L(t) - C| = |\mathbf{b}||t|$ and $|B - C| = |\mathbf{b}|$, so the value of $|t|$ is the ratio of the distances $|L(t) - C|$ to $|B - C|$, as claimed.

One can also speak of the speed with which the point $L(t)$ moves along line L. Since it covers distance $|\mathbf{b}|t$ in time t, it is moving at constant speed $|\mathbf{b}|$. It is important to keep in mind that there is a significant difference between a parametric form for a curve ($p(t)$) and a motion path for the same curve. Just the picture of $p(t)$ swept out as t increases gives no information as to how fast the point moves along that path. (The picture for $p(t)$ is the same as that for $p(t^2)$ or $p(t^3)$.) There are an infinite number of parametric representations for a given motion path displaying a curve. Recall that the slope-intercept form for a line, such as $y = m * (x - a)$, makes use of the slope of the line as well as the value of x at which the y equals 0. For a vertical line the slope is infinite, and this form clearly cannot be used. This is one reason why the slope-intercept form is not frequently used in graphics; the parametric form for a vertical line, which presents no obstacles, is superior.

■ EXAMPLE 4.5.3 A line in 2D

Find a parametric form for the line that passes through $C = (3, 5)$ and $B = (2, 7)$.

SOLUTION:

Build vector $\mathbf{b} = B - C = (-1, 2)$ to obtain the parametric form $L(t) = (3 - t, 2 + 2t)$.

■ EXAMPLE 4.5.4 A line in 3D

Find a parametric form for the line that passes through $C = (3, 5, 6)$ and $B = (2, 7, 3)$.

SOLUTION:

Build vector $\mathbf{b} = B - C = (-1.2, -3)$ to obtain the parametric form $L(t) = (3 - t, 5 + 2t, 6 - 3t)$.

Other parametrizations for a straight line are possible, although they are rarely used. For instance, the point $W(t)$ given by

$$W(t) = C + \mathbf{b}t^3$$

also sweeps over every point on L. It lies at C when $t = 0$, and reaches B when $t = 1$. Unlike $L(t)$, however, $W(t)$ accelerates along its path from C to B.

Point Normal Form for a Line (the Implicit Form)

This is the same as Equation (4.39) for the parametric form for a line, but we rewrite it in a way that better reveals the underlying geometry. The familiar equation of a line in 2D has the form

$$fx + gy = 1 \tag{4.40}$$

where f and g are some constants. The notion is that every point (x, y) that satisfies this equation lies on the line, so it provides a condition for a point to be on the line. **Note**. This is true only for a line in 2D; a line in 3D requires two equations.

This equation can be written using a dot product: $(f, g) \cdot (x, y) = 1$, so for every point on a line a certain dot product must have the same value. We examine the geometric interpretation of the vector (f, g), and in doing so develop the point normal form of a line. A point normal form consists of any point, P, on the line and a vector, V, perpendicular to the line. Consequently the line is characterized by the pair (P, V), and no two lines have the same pair (P, V). The point normal form is useful in such tasks as clipping and ray tracing. Formally the point normal form makes no mention of dimensionality; however, a line in 2D has a point normal form, whereas a line in 3D does not.

Working in 2D, suppose that we know line L passes through points C and B, as in Figure 4.29. What is its point normal form? If we can find a vector $\mathbf{n}$ that is

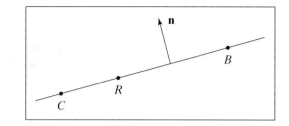

FIGURE 4.29 To find the point normal form for a 2D line.

perpendicular to the line, then for any point $R = (x, y)$ on the line, the vector $R - C$ must be perpendicular to $\mathbf{n}$, so we have the condition on R:

$$\mathbf{n} \cdot (R - C) = 0 \quad \text{(point normal form)} \qquad \text{We Know } B, C \qquad (4.41)$$

This is the **point normal** equation for the line, expressing that a certain dot product must turn out to be zero for *every* point R on the line. Two lines are distinguished by the point lying on the line and the normal vector to the line.

We still must find a suitable $\mathbf{n}$. Denote the vector from C to B by $\mathbf{b}$. Then $\mathbf{b}^\perp$ will serve well as the desired $\mathbf{n}$. For purposes of building the point normal form, any scalar multiple of $\mathbf{b}^\perp$ works just as well for $\mathbf{n}$.

■ **EXAMPLE 4.5.5 The point normal form.**

Suppose line L passes through points $C = (3, 4)$ and $B = (5, -2)$. Then $\mathbf{b} = B - C = (2, -6)$ and $\mathbf{b}^\perp = (6, 2)$ (sketch this). Choosing C as the point on the line, the point normal form is: $(6, 2) \cdot ((x, y) - (3, 4)) = 0$, or $6x + 2y = 26$. Both sides of the equation can be divided by 26 (or any other nonzero number) if desired.

It's also easy to find the normal to a line given the equation of the line, say, $fx + gy = 1$. Writing this once again as $(f, g) \cdot (x, y) = 1$, it is clear that the normal $\mathbf{n}$ is simply (f, g) (or any multiple thereof). For instance, the line given by $5x - 2y = 7$ has normal vector $(5, -2)$, or more generally $(5K, -2K)$ for any nonzero K.

It's also straightforward to find the parametric form for a line if you are given its point normal form. Suppose it is known that line L has point normal form $\mathbf{n} \cdot (P - C) = 0$, where $\mathbf{n}$ and C are given explicitly. The parametric form is then $L(t) = C + \mathbf{n}^\perp t$. (Why?) You can also obtain the parametric form if the equation of a 2D line is given in the following way:

Method #1. Find the normal $\mathbf{n}$ as in the previous paragraph, and
Method #2. Find a point (C_x, C_y) on the line by choosing any value for C_x and use the equation to find the corresponding C_y.

Planes in 3D Space

> Infinity is a floorless room without walls or ceiling.
>
> *Author Unknown*

Because such heavy use is made of polygons in 3D graphics, the plane in which each polygon lies requires a compact and easily interpreted representation. A polygon (a face of an object) lies in its **parent plane**, and we often need to clip objects against planes, or find the plane in which a certain face lies.

The Parametric Representation of a Plane

The parametric form for a plane (a plane through the origin) is built on three ingredients: one of its points, C, and two (nonparallel) vectors, **a** and **b**, that lie in the plane, as shown in Figure 4.30. If we are given the three (non-collinear) points A, B, and C in the plane, then take $\mathbf{a} = A - C$ and $\mathbf{b} = B - C$.

FIGURE 4.30 Defining a plane parametrically.

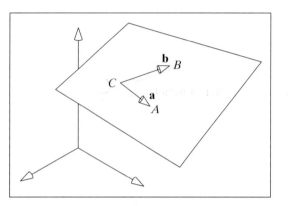

To construct a parametric form for this plane, note that any point in the plane can be represented by a sum of vectors: C plus some multiple of **a** plus some multiple of **b**. Using parameters s and t to specify the multipliers, we have $C + s\mathbf{a} + t\mathbf{b}$. This provides the desired parametric form $P(s, t)$:

$$P(s, t) = C + \mathbf{a}s + \mathbf{b}t \qquad (4.42)$$

Given any values of s and t, we can identify the corresponding point on the plane. For example, the position at $s = t = 0$ is C itself, and that at $s = 1$ and $t = -2$ is $P(1, -2) = C + \mathbf{a} - 2\mathbf{b}$.

Note that two parameters are involved in the parametric expression for a surface, whereas only one parameter is needed for a curve. In fact, if one of the parameters is fixed, say $s = 3$, then $P(3, t)$ is a function of one variable and represents a straight line: $P(3, t) = C + 3\mathbf{a} + \mathbf{b}t$.

Equation (4.43) also illustrates that we can rewrite $P(s, t)$ as an affine combination of points, further showing the value of a partition of unity (check this carefully):

$$P(s, t) = s\mathbf{a} + t\mathbf{b} + (1 - s - t)C \qquad (4.43)$$

■ **EXAMPLE 4.5.6 Find a parametric form, given three points in a plane**

Consider the plane passing through:

$A = (3, 3, 3)$, $B = (5, 5, 7)$, and $C = (1, 2, 4)$. From Equation (4.43) the vectors **a** and **b** are $\mathbf{a} = (2, 1, -1)$ and $\mathbf{b} = (4, 3, 3)$. Again, from Equation (4.43) $P(s, t) = s(2, 1, -1) + t(4, 3, 3) + (1 - s - t)(1, 2, 4)$. It has parametric form $P(s, t) = (1, 2, 4) + (2, 1, -1)s + (4, 3, 3)t$.

Planar Patches

Just as we can restrict the parameter t in the representation of a line to obtain a ray or a segment, we can restrict the parameters s and t in the representation of a plane.

In the parametric form of Equation (4.43) the values for s and t can range from $-\infty$ to ∞, and thus the plane can extend forever. In some situations we want to deal with only a *piece* of a plane, such as a parallelogram that lies in it. Such a piece is called a **planar patch**, a term that invites us to imagine the plane as a quilt of many patches joined together. In future chapters we will discuss textures mapped onto planar patches. Later we also examine curved surfaces made up of patches, which are not necessarily planar. Much of the practice of modeling solids involves piecing together patches of various shapes to form the skin of an object.

A planar patch is formed by restricting the range of allowable parameter values for s and t. For instance, one often restricts s and t to lie only between 0 and 1. The patch is positioned and oriented in space by appropriate choices of $\mathbf{a}$, $\mathbf{b}$, and C. Figure 4.31a shows the available range of s and t as a square in **parameter space**. Figure 4.31b shows the patch that results from this restriction in object space.

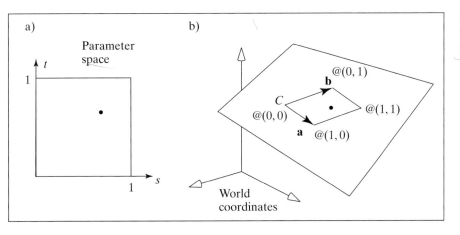

FIGURE 4.31 Mapping between two spaces to define a planar patch.

The art of mapping textures onto faces involves finding an appropriate mapping from a portion of parameter space onto object space, as we shall see later. To each point (s, t) in parameter space there corresponds one 3D point in the patch $P(s, t) = C + \mathbf{a}s + \mathbf{b}t$. The patch is a parallelogram whose corners correspond to the four corners of parameter space and are situated at

$$P(0, 0) = C$$
$$P(1, 0) = C + \mathbf{a}$$
$$P(0, 1) = C + \mathbf{b}$$
$$P(1, 1) = C + \mathbf{a} + \mathbf{b} \qquad (4.44)$$

The vectors $\mathbf{a}$ and $\mathbf{b}$ determine both the size and the orientation of the patch. If $\mathbf{a}$ and $\mathbf{b}$ are perpendicular, the grid will become rectangular, and if in addition $\mathbf{a}$ and $\mathbf{b}$ have the same length, the grid will become square. Changing C just translates the patch without changing its shape or orientation.

■ EXAMPLE 4.5.7 Make a patch.

Let $C = (1, 3, 2)$, $\mathbf{a} = (1, 1, 0)$, and $\mathbf{b} = (1, 4, 2)$. Find the corners of the planar patch.

SOLUTION:

From the preceding table we obtain the four corners: $P(0, 0) = (1, 3, 2)$, $P(0, 1) = (2, 7, 4)$, $P(1, 0) = (2, 4, 2)$, and $P(1, 1) = (3, 8, 4)$.

■ **EXAMPLE 4.5.8 Characterize a patch.**

Find **a**, **b**, and C that create a square patch of length 4 on a side centered at the origin and parallel to the x, z-plane.

SOLUTION:

The corners of the patch are at $(2, 0, 2), (2, 0, -2), (-2, 0, 2)$, and $(-2, 0, -2)$. Choose any corner, say $(2, 0, -2)$, for C. Then **a** and **b** each have length 4 and are parallel to either the x- or the z-axis. Choose **a** $= (-4, 0, 0)$ and **b** $= (0, 0, 4)$.

PRACTICE EXERCISE

4.5.9 Find a patch.

Find point C and some vectors **a** and **b** that create a patch having the four corners $(-4, 2, 1), (1, 7, 4), (-2, -2, 2)$, and $(3, 3, 5)$.   ■

4.6 FINDING THE INTERSECTION OF TWO LINE SEGMENTS

> If the facts don't fit the theory, change the facts.
>
> *Albert Einstein*
> *(1879–1955)*

We often need to compute where two line segments in 2D space intersect. It appears in many other tasks, such as determining whether or not a polygon is simple. Its solution will illustrate the power of parametric forms and dot products. We will be restricting ourselves here to finding the intersection of two lines when they are represented parametrically.

The Problem: Given two line segments, determine whether they intersect, and if they do, find their point of intersection.

Suppose one segment has endpoints A and B and the other segment has endpoints C and D. As shown in Figure 4.32, the two segments can be situated in many different ways. They can miss each other (a and b), overlap in one point (c and d), or even overlap over some region (e). They may or may not be parallel. We need an organized approach that handles all of these possibilities.

Every line segment has a **parent line**, the infinite line of which it is part. Unless two parent lines are parallel, they will intersect at some point in 2D. We first locate this point.

FIGURE 4.32 Many cases for two line segments.

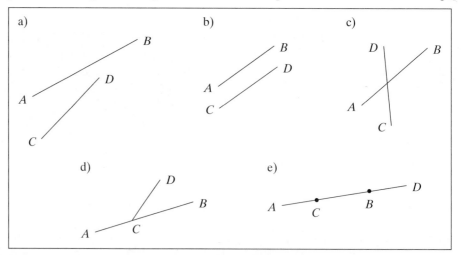

We set up parametric representations for each of the line segments in question. Call AB the segment from A to B. Then

$$AB(t) = A + \mathbf{b}t \qquad (4.45)$$

where for convenience we define $\mathbf{b} = B - A$. As t varies from 0 to 1, each point on the finite line segment is crossed exactly once.

Similarly we call the segment from C to D by the name CD, and give it parametric representation (using a *different* parameter, say, u):

$$CD(u) = C + \mathbf{d}u,$$

where $\mathbf{d} = D - C$. We use different parameters for the two lines, t for one and u for the other, in order to describe different points on the two lines independently. (If the same parameter were used, the points on the two lines would be locked together.)

For the parent lines to intersect there must be specific values of t and u for which the two equations above are equal:

$$A + \mathbf{b}t = C + \mathbf{d}u$$

Defining $\mathbf{c} = C - A$ for convenience, we can write this condition in terms of three known vectors and two unknown parameter values:

$$\mathbf{b}t = \mathbf{c} + \mathbf{d}u \qquad (4.46)$$

This provides two linear equations in two unknowns, similar to Equation (4.22). They can be solved in the usual manner.

PRACTICE EXERCISES

4.6.1 The algorithm for determining the intersection

Write the routine `segIntersect()` that would be used in the context: `if(segIntersect(A, B, C, D, &InterPt)) <do something>`.

It takes four points representing the two segments, and returns 0 if the segments do not intersect, and 1 if they do. If they do intersect, the location of the intersection is placed in `interPt`. It returns -1 if the parent lines do not intersect.

4.6.2 Testing the simplicity of a polygon

Recall that a polygon P is simple if there are no edge intersections except at the endpoints of adjacent edges. Fashion a routine `int isSimple(Polygon P)` that takes a brute-force approach and tests whether any pair of edges of the list of vertices of the polygon intersect, returning 0 if so, and 1 if not so. (`Polygon` is some suitable class for describing a polygon.) This is a simple algorithm but not the most efficient one. See [Moret91] and [Preparata85] for more elaborate attacks that involve some sorting of edges in x and y.

4.6.3 Line segment intersections

For each of the following segment pairs, determine whether the segments intersect, and if so, where.

1. $A = (1, 4)$, $B = (7, 1/2)$, $C = (7/2, 5/2)$, $D = (7, 5)$.
2. $A = (1, 4)$, $B = (7, 1/2)$, $C = (5, 0)$, $D = (0, 7)$.
3. $A = (0, 7)$, $B = (7, 0)$, $C = (8, -1)$, $D = (10, -3)$.

■

4.6.1 Application of Line Intersections: The Circle Through Three Points

Suppose a designer wants a tool that draws the unique circle that passes through three given points. The user specifies three points, A, B, and C, on the display with the mouse as suggested in Figure 4.33a, and the circle is drawn automatically as shown in Figure 4.33b. The unique circle that passes through three points is called the **excircle** or **circumscribed circle** of the triangle defined by the points. Which circle is it? Try to visualize where it lies—that is, where is its center and what is its radius? We need a routine that can calculate these data. As you follow through the development of the answer, keep in mind how difficult this problem would be without the use of vectors and the dot product!

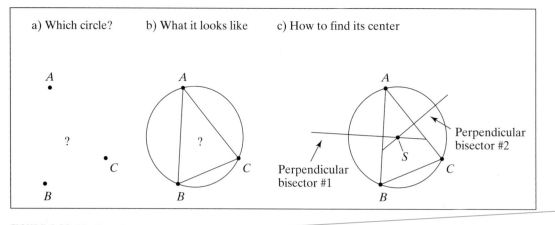

a) Which circle?   b) What it looks like   c) How to find its center

FIGURE 4.33 Finding the excircle.

The Problem

Find the unique circle that passes through the three given points A, B, and C.

The Method

Figure 4.33c shows how to find it. We work in 2D for this discussion, so that the perp vector of each vector is well defined. The center S of the desired circle must be equidistant from all three vertices, so it must lie on the **perpendicular bisector** of *each* side of triangle ABC (the perpendicular bisector, M, of segment AB, is the line perpendicular to AB and bisecting AB). Thus we can determine S if we can compute where two of the perpendicular bisectors intersect. In Figure 4.33c the perpendicular bisector of segment AC is perpendicular to AC and bisects it.

We first show how to find a parametric representation of the perpendicular bisector of a line segment. Figure 4.34 shows a segment S with endpoints A and B. Its perpendicular bisector L is the infinite line that passes through the midpoint M of segment S and is oriented perpendicular to it. But we know that midpoint M is given by $(A + B)/2$, and the direction of the normal is given by $(B - A)^{\perp}$, so the perpendicular bisector has parametric form:

$$L(t) = \frac{1}{2}(A + B) + (B - A)^{\perp} t \quad \text{(the perpendicular bisector of } AB) \quad (4.47)$$

Now we are in a position to compute the excircle of three points. We seek the intersection S of the perpendicular bisectors of AB and AC. For convenience we define the vectors:

FIGURE 4.34 The perpendicular bisector of a segment.

$$\mathbf{a} = B - A$$
$$\mathbf{b} = C - B$$
$$\mathbf{c} = A - C \qquad\qquad (4.48)$$

To find the perpendicular bisector of AB we need the midpoint of AB and a direction perpendicular to AB. The midpoint of AB is $A + \mathbf{a}/2$. (Why?) The direction perpendicular to AB is $\mathbf{a}^\perp$. So the parametric form for the perpendicular bisector is $A + \mathbf{a}/2 + \mathbf{a}^\perp t$. Check as you follow the details of this—which is well worth doing—that combinations of points always occur in *affine sums*! Similarly the perpendicular bisector of AC is $A - \mathbf{c}/2 + \mathbf{c}^\perp u$, using parameter u. Point S lies where these meet, at the solution of:

$$\mathbf{a}^\perp t = \mathbf{b}/2 + \mathbf{c}^\perp u$$

(where we have used $\mathbf{a} + \mathbf{b} + \mathbf{c} = \mathbf{0}$). To eliminate the term in u take the dot product of both sides with $\mathbf{c}$, and obtain $t = 1/2(\mathbf{b} \cdot \mathbf{c})/(\mathbf{a}^\perp \cdot \mathbf{c})$. To find S use this value for t in the representation of the perpendicular bisector $A + \mathbf{a}/2 + \mathbf{a}^\perp t$, which yields the simple *explicit* form[10]

The Result

$$S = A + \frac{1}{2}\left(\mathbf{a} + \frac{\mathbf{b} \cdot \mathbf{c}}{\mathbf{a}^\perp \cdot \mathbf{c}}\mathbf{a}^\perp\right) \quad (S \text{ is the center of the excircle; recall Figure 4.31}) \quad (4.49)$$

(Notice how difficult this calculation would be without the use of vectors.) The radius of the excircle is the distance from S to any of the three vertices, so it is $|S - A|$. Just form the magnitude of the last term in Equation (4.49). After some manipulation (check this out) we obtain:

$$radius = \frac{|\mathbf{a}|}{2}\sqrt{\left(\frac{\mathbf{b} \cdot \mathbf{c}}{\mathbf{a}^\perp \cdot \mathbf{c}}\right)^2 + 1} \quad (\text{radius of the excircle}) \qquad (4.50)$$

Result: the excircle of the triangle with vertices A, B, C has center given by Equation 4.49 and radius given by Equation 4.50.

Once S and the radius are known, use your drawCircle() from Chapter 3 to draw the desired circle.

■ EXAMPLE 4.6.1

Find the perpendicular bisector L of the segment S having endpoints $A = (3, 5)$ and $B = (9, 3)$.

SOLUTION:

By direct calculation, midpoint $M = (6, 4)$, and $(B - A)^\perp = (2, 6)$, so L has representation $L(t) = (6 + 2t, 4 + 6t)$. It is useful to plot both S and L to see this result.

Every triangle also has an **inscribed circle**, which is sometimes necessary to compute in a computer-aided design context. A Case Study examines how to do this and also discusses the beguiling **nine-point circle**.

PRACTICE EXERCISES

4.6.4 A perpendicular bisector

Find a parametric expression for the perpendicular bisector of the segment with endpoints $A = (0, 6)$ and $B = (4, 0)$. Plot the segment and the line.

---

[10] Other closed-form expressions for S have appeared previously, e.g., in [Goldman90] and [Lopez92].

4.6.5 Find the excircle

Let the three points of a triangle equal $A = (3, 6)$, $B = (4, 2)$, and $C = (8, -12)$. Calculate the center and the radius of the excircle for these three points.   ■

4.7 INTERSECTIONS OF LINES WITH PLANES, AND CLIPPING

> Rising genius always shoots out its rays from among the clouds, but these will gradually roll away
> and disappear as it ascends to its steady luster.
>
> Washington Irving
> (1783–1859)

The task of finding the intersection of a line with another line or with a plane arises in a daunting number of situations in graphics. Many clipping algorithms are used in graphics; to keep things relatively simple we will focus on one algorithm in particular, the Cyrus-Beck clipping algorithm. We have already seen one clipping approach in Section 4.6, which finds where two line segments intersect. We will pause a moment for a definition of clipping. The words "to clip a subject polygon against a window" mean to clip a subject polygon such as that of Figure 4.35a against a window such as that in Figure 4.35b to see which part of the polygon is inside the window and therefore survives. In Figure 4.35b we see the result of such a clipping. At points labeled a, b, c, d, e, f the subject polygon intersects with the window. Notice that the clipped subject polygon exits from the window and then re-enters it two more times. Contrast this with the Cohen-Sutherland clipping algorithm of Chapter 3, which had only to clip a line against a rectangular window.

FIGURE 4.35 Clipping a polygon against a window.

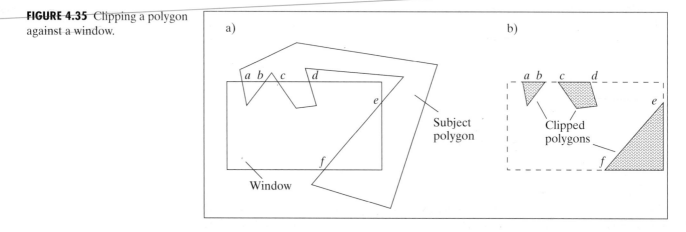

Here we develop an alternative method to clip polygons against both lines and planes. It is very direct and clearly reveals what is going on. We develop the method in Section 4.8 and then apply the results of this algorithm to the problem of clipping a line against a convex polygon in 2D, or a convex polyhedron in 3D. In Chapter 7 we see that this is an essential step in viewing 3D objects. In Chapter 12 we use the same intersection technique to develop the fundamental concepts of ray tracing.

In 2D we want to find where a line intersects another line; in 3D we want to find where a line intersects a plane. Both of these problems can be solved at once, because the formulation is in terms of dot products, and the same expressions arise whether the involved vectors are 2D or 3D.

Consider a line described parametrically as $R(t) = A + \mathbf{c}t$. We also refer to it as a *ray*. We want to compute where the ray hits a certain object shown in the figure. We focus on finding the intersections between a ray and a plane: the face of a polyhedron. In 2D this is a line: one edge of a convex polygon. In 3D it is a plane: one of the convex faces of a convex polyhedron. Suppose, point P is a point on the plane and $\mathbf{n}$ is normal to it as shown in Figure 4.36. Point P lies on the line and vector $\mathbf{n}$ is normal to it. Figure 4.36a shows the ray hitting a line and part b shows it hitting a plane. We want to find the location of the **hit point**.

P is hit point

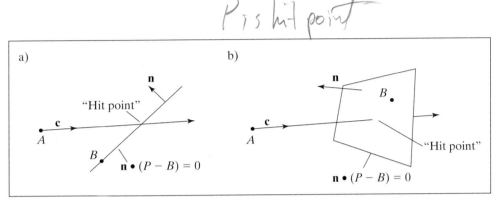

FIGURE 4.36 Where does a ray hit a line or a plane?

Suppose the ray hits at $t = t_{\text{hit}}$, the **hit time**. We first consider the 2D case, so that the line in question has a point normal form. At this value of t the line and ray and plane must have the same coordinates: so $A + \mathbf{c}t_{\text{hit}}$ must satisfy the equation of the point normal form for the plane. Therefore we substitute this unknown hit point into the point normal equation to obtain a condition on t_{hit}:

$$\mathbf{n} \cdot (A + \mathbf{c}t_{\text{hit}} - B) = 0$$

This may be rewritten as

$$\mathbf{n} \cdot (A - B) + \mathbf{n} \cdot \mathbf{c}t_{\text{hit}} = 0$$

which is a linear equation in t_{hit}. Its solution is:

$$t_{\text{hit}} = \frac{\mathbf{n} \cdot (B - A)}{\mathbf{n} \cdot \mathbf{c}} \quad \text{(hit time)} \tag{4.51}$$

As always with a ratio of terms we must examine the eventuality that the denominator of t_{hit} is zero. This occurs when $\mathbf{n} \cdot \mathbf{c} = 0$, or when the ray is aimed parallel to the object in question, in which case the ray or segment doesn't intersect the edge, but still may lie inside the polygon.[11] When the hit time has been computed, it is simple to find the location of the hit point (carefully distinguish between the *hit time* and the *hit point*). Substitute t_{hit} into the representation of the ray:

hit point: $\quad P_{\text{hit}} = A + \mathbf{c}t_{\text{hit}} \quad$ (hit spot) $\tag{4.52}$

In the intersection problems treated below we will also need to know generally the direction in which the ray strikes the line or plane—along with the normal $\mathbf{n}$ or

---

[11] If the numerator is also 0, the ray lies entirely in the line (2D) or plane (3D). (Why?)

counter to **n**. This will be important, because we will need to know whether the ray is exiting from an object or entering it. Figure 4.37 shows the two possibilities for a ray hitting a line. In part a the angle between the ray's direction, **c**, and **n** is less than 90°, so we say the ray is aimed along with **n**. In part b the angle is greater than 90°, so the ray is aimed counter to **n**.

FIGURE 4.37 The direction of the ray is a) along or b) against **n**.

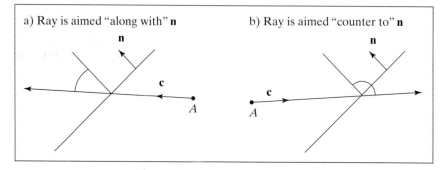

a) Ray is aimed "along with" **n**

b) Ray is aimed "counter to" **n**

It is easy to test which of these possibilities occurs, since the *sign* of **n** · **c** tells immediately whether the angle between **n** and **c** is less than or greater than 90°. Putting these ideas together, we have the three possibilities:

if $\mathbf{n} \cdot \mathbf{c} > 0$,   the ray is aimed along with the normal

if $\mathbf{n} \cdot \mathbf{c} = 0$,   the ray is parallel to the line

if $\mathbf{n} \cdot \mathbf{c} < 0$,   the ray is aimed counter to the normal   (4.53)

PRACTICE EXERCISES

4.7.1 Intersections of rays with lines and planes

Find when and where the ray $A + \mathbf{c}t$ hits the object $\mathbf{n} \cdot (P - B) = 0$ (lines in the 2D or planes in 3D).

a. $A = (2, 3), \mathbf{c} = (4, -4), \mathbf{n} = (6, 8), B = (7, 7)$.
b. $A = (2, -4, 3), \mathbf{c} = (4, 0, -4), \mathbf{n} = (6, 9, 9), B = (-7, 2, 7)$.

4.7.2 Rays hitting planes

Find the point where the ray $(1, 5, 2) + (5, -2, 6)t$ hits the plane $2x - 4y + z = 8$. This is important in a shading algorithm to tell how much light is reflected back to the viewer from a polygonal face (the plane), which describes the skin of a solid object.

4.7.3 What is the intersection of two planes?

Here we ask about a geometric problem that will be of substantial significance when we study perspective projections and hidden line removal. We know that two planes intersect in a straight line. But which line? Suppose the two planes are given by $\mathbf{n} \cdot (P - A) = 0$ and $\mathbf{m} \cdot (P - B) = 0$. Find the parametric form of the line in which they intersect. You may find it easiest to:

a. First obtain a parametric form for one of the planes, say, $C + \mathbf{a}s + \mathbf{b}t$ for the second plane.
b. Then substitute this form into the point normal form for the first plane, thereby obtaining a linear equation that relates parameters s and t.
c. Solve for s in terms of t, say, $s = E + Ft$. (Find expressions for E and F.)
d. Write the desired line as $C + \mathbf{a}(E + Ft) + \mathbf{b}t$.

Note. The perp of a 3D vector may not be used, since it is not uniquely defined.

4.8 POLYGON INTERSECTION PROBLEMS

It would be possible to describe everything scientifically, but it would make no sense; it would be without meaning, as if you described a Beethoven symphony as a variation of wave pressure.

Albert Einstein
(1879–1955)

We know polygons are the fundamental objects used in both 2D and 3D graphics. In 2D graphics their straight edges make it easy to describe and draw them. In 3D graphics an object is often modeled as a polygonal mesh—a collection of polygons that fit together to make up its skin. If the skin forms a complete surface that encloses some space, the mesh is called a **polyhedron**. In fact, it is rather difficult to assemble a completely accurate definition of a polyhedron in just a few words: we rely here on the reader's experiences with polyhedronlike shapes to approximate a familiar use of the term. We study meshes and polyhedra in depth in Chapter 6.

Figure 4.38 shows a 2D polygon and a 3D polyhedron that we might need to analyze or render in a graphics application. Three important questions that arise are:

a. Is a given point P inside or outside the object?
b. Where does a given ray R first intersect the object?
c. Which part of a given line L lies inside the object, and which part lies outside?

As a simple example, which part(s) of the line $3y - 2x = 6$ lie inside the polygon whose vertices are $(0, 3)$, $(-2, -2)$, $(-5, 0)$, $(0, -7)$, $(1, 1)$?

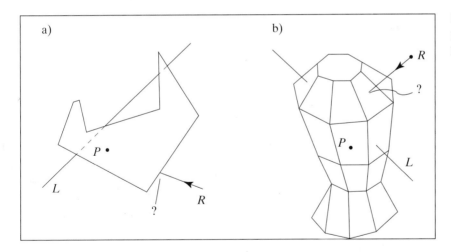

FIGURE 4.38 Intersection problems of a line and a polygonal object.

4.8.1 Working with Convex Polygons and Polyhedra

The general case of intersecting a line with any polygon or polyhedron is quite complex; we address it in Section 4.8.4. Things are much simpler when the polygon or polyhedron is convex. They are simpler because a convex polygon is completely described by a set of bounding lines; in 3D a convex polyhedron is completely described by a set of bounding planes. So we need only test the line against a set of unbounded lines or planes.

Figure 4.39 illustrates this for the 2D case. Part a shows a convex pentagon, and part b shows the bounding lines L_0, L_1, and so on, of the pentagon. Each bounding line defines two half-spaces: the inside half-space that contains the polygon, and the outside half-space that shares no points with the polygon. Part c of the figure shows a portion of the outside half space associated with the bounding line L_2.

FIGURE 4.39 Convex polygons and polyhedra.

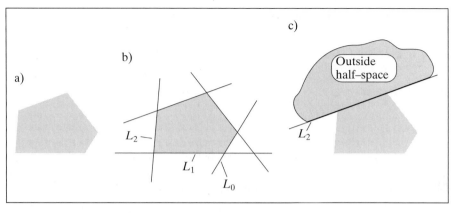

The big advantage in dealing with convex polygons is that we perform intersection tests only on infinite lines and don't need to check whether an intersection lies beyond an endpoint—recall the complexity of the intersection tests we examined earlier.

For a convex polyhedron in 3D, each plane has an inside and an outside half-space and an outward-pointing normal vector. The polyhedron is the intersection of all the inside half-spaces (the set of all points that are simultaneously in the inside half-space of every bounding plane).

4.8.2 Ray Intersections and Clipping for Convex Polygons

We developed a method in Section 4.7 that finds where a ray hits an individual line or plane. We can use this method to find where a ray hits a convex polygon or polyhedron.

The Intersection Problem

Where does the ray $A + \mathbf{c}t$ hit convex polygon P?

Figure 4.40 shows a ray $A + \mathbf{c}t$ intersecting convex polygon P. We want to know all of the places where the ray hits P. Because P is convex, the ray hits P exactly twice: it enters once and exits once. Call the values of t at which it enters and exits t_{in} and t_{out}, respectively. The ray intersection problem is to compute the values of t_{in} and t_{out}. Once these hit times are obtained, the points themselves follow immediately.

FIGURE 4.40 Ray $A + \mathbf{c}t$ intersecting a convex polygon.

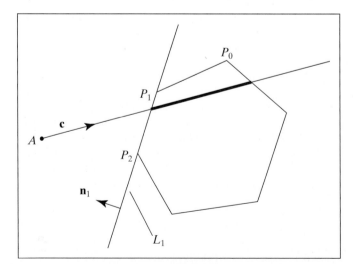

$$\begin{array}{lll}\text{Entering hit point:} & A + \mathbf{c}t_{in} \\ \text{Exiting hit point:} & A + \mathbf{c}t_{out}\end{array} \qquad (4.54)$$

The ray is inside P for all t in the interval $[t_{in}, t_{out}]$.

Note that finding t_{in} and t_{out} solves not only the intersection problem but also the clipping problem. If we know t_{in} and t_{out}, we know which part of the line $A + \mathbf{c}t$ lies inside P. Usually the clipping problem is stated as:

The Clipping Problem

For the two points A and C, which part of segment AC lies inside P?

Figure 4.41 shows several possible situations. Part a shows the case where A and C both lie outside P, but there is a portion of the segment AC that lies inside P.

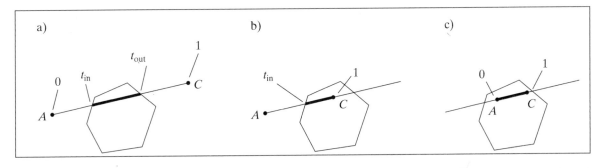

FIGURE 4.41 A segment clipped by a polygon P.

If we consider segment AC as part of a ray given by $A + \mathbf{c}t$, where $\mathbf{c} = C - A$, then point A corresponds to the point on the ray at $t = 0$, and C corresponds to the point at $t = 1$. Note the affine combinations of point that appear. These ray times are labeled in the figure. To find the clipped segment we compute t_{in} and t_{out} as described earlier. The segment that survives clipping has endpoints $A + \mathbf{c}t_{in}$ and $A + \mathbf{c}t_{out}$. In Figure 4.41b point C lies inside P and so t_{out} is larger than 1. The clipped segment has endpoints $A + \mathbf{c}t_{in}$ and C. In part c both A and C lie inside P, so the clipped segment is the same: AC.

In general we compute t_{in} and compare it to 0. The larger of the values 0 and t_{in} is used as the time for the first endpoint of the clipped segment. Similarly, the smaller of the values 1 and t_{out} is used to find the second endpoint. So the endpoints of the clipped segment are:

$$A' = A + \mathbf{c}\max(0, t_{in})$$
$$C' = A + \mathbf{c}\min(t_{out}, 1) \qquad (4.55)$$

Now how are t_{in} and t_{out} computed? We must consider each bounding line of P in turn and find where the ray $A + \mathbf{c}t$ intersects it. We suppose, as before that each polygon lies in 2D space and that each bounding line is stored in point normal form as the pair $\{B, \mathbf{n}\}$. Here B is some point on the line and $\mathbf{n}$ is the *outward-pointing normal* for the line (as in $\mathbf{n}$ of Figure 4.36a): it points to the outside of the polygon. Because it is outward pointing, the test of Equation (4.53) translates to:

$$\begin{array}{lll}\text{if } \mathbf{n} \cdot \mathbf{c} > 0, & \text{the ray is exiting from } P \\ \text{if } \mathbf{n} \cdot \mathbf{c} = 0, & \text{the ray is parallel to the line} \\ \text{if } \mathbf{n} \cdot \mathbf{c} < 0, & \text{the ray is entering } P\end{array} \qquad (4.56)$$

For each bounding line we find:

a. The hit time of the ray with the bounding line [use Equation (4.51)]
b. Whether the ray is entering or exiting the polygon [use Equation (4.56)]

If the ray is entering, we know that the time at which the ray ultimately enters P (if it enters it at all) cannot be *earlier* than this newly found hit time. We keep track of the earliest possible entering time as t_{in}. For each entering hit time, t_{hit}, we replace t_{in} by $\max(t_{in}, t_{hit})$. Similarly we keep track of the *latest* possible exit time as t_{out}, and for each exiting hit we replace t_{out} by $\min(t_{out}, t_{hit})$.

It helps to think of the interval $[t_{in}, t_{out}]$ as the **candidate interval** of t, the interval of t inside of which the ray *might* lie inside the object. Figure 4.42 shows an example for the clipping problem. We know the point $A + \mathbf{c}t$ *might be* inside P for a t that is in the candidate interval but is definitely not in P for any t outside the candidate interval. As each bounding line is tested, the candidate interval gets reduced as t_{in} is increased or t_{out} is decreased: pieces of it get chopped off. To get started we initialize t_{in} to 0 and t_{out} to 1 for the line clipping problem, so the candidate interval is $[0,1]$.

FIGURE 4.42
The candidate interval for a hit.

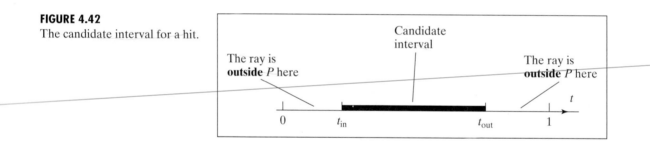

The algorithm is then:

1. Initialize the candidate interval to $[0,1]$.[12]
2. For each bounding line, use Equation (4.58) to find the hit time t_{hit} and determine whether the ray is an entering or exiting hit:

   - if it's an entering hit, set $t_{in} = \max(t_{in}, t_{hit})$
   - if it's an exiting hit, set $t_{out} = \min(t_{out}, t_{hit})$

   If at any point t_{in} becomes greater than t_{out} we know the ray misses P entirely, and testing is terminated.
3. If the candidate interval is not empty after all the edges of the polygon have been tested, then the segment from $A + \mathbf{c}t_{in}$ to $A + \mathbf{c}t_{out}$ is known to lie inside P. For the line clipping problem these are the endpoints of the clipped line. For the ray intersection problem we know the entering and exiting points of the ray.

Note that we stop further testing as soon as the candidate interval vanishes. This is called an **early out**: if we determine early in the processing that the ray is outside of the polygon, we save time by immediately exiting from the test.

---

[12] For the ray intersection problem, where the ray extends infinitely far in both directions, we set $t_{in} = -\infty$ and $t_{out} = \infty$. In practice t_{in} is set to a large negative value and t_{out} to a large positive value.

Figure 4.43 shows a specific example of clipping: we seek the portion of segment AC that lies in polygon P. We initialize t_{in} to 0 and t_{out} to 1. The ray starts at A at $t = 0$ and proceeds to point C, reaching it at $t = 1$. We test it against each bounding line $L_0, L_1, \ldots$, in turn and update t_{in} and t_{out} as necessary.

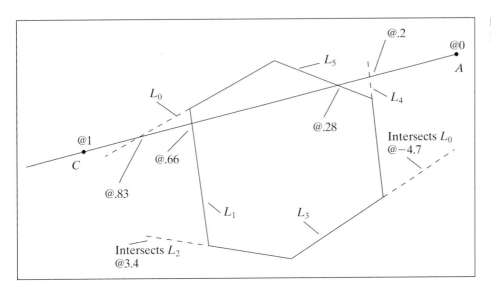

FIGURE 4.43 Testing when a ray lies inside a convex polygon.

As an example, suppose when we test it against line L_0 we find an exiting hit at $t = 0.83$. This sets t_{out} to 0.83, and the candidate interval is now $[0, 0.83]$. We then test it against L_1 and find an exiting hit at $t = 0.66$. This reduces the candidate interval to $[0, 0.66]$. The test against L_2 gives an exiting hit at $t = 3.4$. This tells us nothing new: we already know the ray is outside for $t > 0.66$. The test against L_3 gives an entering hit at $t = -4.7$, which is earlier than the current t. The test with L_4 gives an entering hit at $t = 0.2$, so t_{in} is updated to 0.2. Finally, testing against L_5 gives an entering hit at $t = 0.28$, and we are done. The candidate interval is $[0.28, 0.66]$. In fact the ray *is* inside P for all t between 0.28 and 0.66.

Based on Figure 4.43, Figure 4.44 shows the sequence of updates to t_{in} and t_{out} that occur as each of the lines above is tested.

Line Test	t_{in}	t_{out}
0	0	0.83
1	0	0.66
2	0	0.66
3	0	0.66
4	0.2	0.66
5	0.28	0.66

FIGURE 4.44 Updates on the values of t_{in} and t_{out}.

4.8.3 The Cyrus-Beck Clipping Algorithm

We build a routine from these ideas that performs the clipping of a line segment against any convex polygon. The method was originally developed by Cyrus and Beck [Cyrus78]. Later a highly efficient clipper for rectangular windows was devised by Liang and Barsky [Liang84] based on similar ideas.

The routine that implements the Cyrus-Beck clipper has interface:

```
int CyrusBeckClip(Line& seg, LineList& L);
```

Its parameters are the line segment, `seg`, to be clipped (which contains the first and second endpoints named `seg.first` and `seg.second`) and the list of bounding lines of the polygon. It clips `seg` against each line in L as described above, and places the clipped segment back in `seg`. (This is why `seg` must be passed by reference.) The routine returns:

- 0 if no part of the segment lies in P (the candidate interval became empty);
- 1 if some part of the segment does lie in P.

Figure 4.45 shows pseudocode for the Cyrus-Beck algorithm. The types LineSegment, LineList, and Vector2 are suitable data types to hold the quantities in question (see the exercises). Variables numer and denom hold the numerator and denominator for t_{hit} of Equation (4.48):

$$numer = \mathbf{n} \cdot (B - A)$$
$$denom = \mathbf{n} \cdot \mathbf{c} \qquad\qquad (4.57)$$

FIGURE 4.45 Pseudocode for Cyrus-Beck clipper for a convex polygon, 2D case.

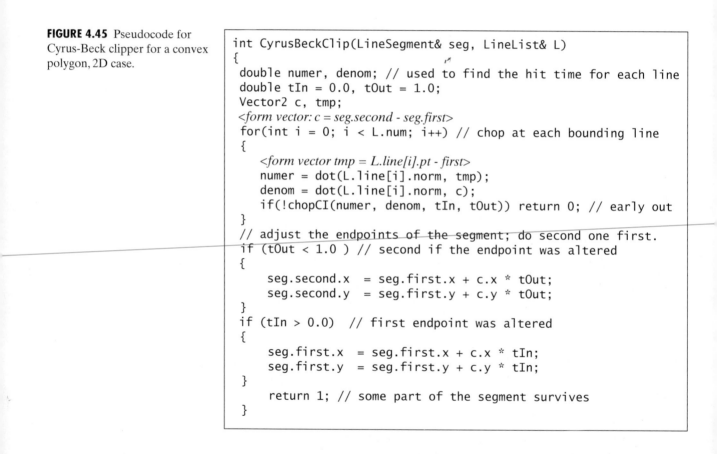

```
int CyrusBeckClip(LineSegment& seg, LineList& L)
{
  double numer, denom; // used to find the hit time for each line
  double tIn = 0.0, tOut = 1.0;
  Vector2 c, tmp;
  <form vector: c = seg.second - seg.first>
  for(int i = 0; i < L.num; i++) // chop at each bounding line
  {
      <form vector tmp = L.line[i].pt - first>
      numer = dot(L.line[i].norm, tmp);
      denom = dot(L.line[i].norm, c);
      if(!chopCI(numer, denom, tIn, tOut)) return 0; // early out
  }
  // adjust the endpoints of the segment; do second one first.
  if (tOut < 1.0 ) // second if the endpoint was altered
  {
      seg.second.x  = seg.first.x + c.x * tOut;
      seg.second.y  = seg.first.y + c.y * tOut;
  }
  if (tIn > 0.0)  // first endpoint was altered
  {
      seg.first.x  = seg.first.x + c.x * tIn;
      seg.first.y  = seg.first.y + c.y * tIn;
  }

      return 1; // some part of the segment survives
}
```

Note that the value of seg.second is updated first, since we must use the old value of seg.first in the update calculation for both seg.first and seg.second.

The routine chopCI() is shown in Figure 4.46. It uses numer and denom, whose calculation were described earlier to calculate the hit time at which the ray hits a bounding line, and to determine whether the ray is entering or exiting the polygon, and chops off the piece of the candidate interval CI that is thereby found to be outside the polygon.

If the ray is parallel to the line, it could lie entirely in the inside half-space of the line, or entirely out of it. It turns out that $numer = \mathbf{n} \cdot (B - A)$ is exactly the quantity needed to tell which of these cases occurs. See the exercises.

```
int chopCI(double& tIn, double& tOut, double numer, double denom)
{
  double tHit;
  if (denom < 0)                  // ray is entering
  {
      tHit = numer / denom;
      if (tHit > tOut) return 0;        // early out
      else if (tHit > tIn) tIn = tHit; // take larger t
  }
  else if(denom > 0)              // ray is exiting
  {
      tHit = numer / denom;
      if(tHit < tIn) return 0;        // early out
      if(tHit < tout) tOut = tHit; // take smaller t
  }
  else                  // denom is 0: ray is parallel
  if(numer <= 0) return 0;    // missed the line

  return 1;  // CI is still non-empty
}
```

FIGURE 4.46 Clipping against a single bounding line.

The 3D Case: Clipping a Line against a Convex Polyhedron

The Cyrus-Beck clipping algorithm works in three dimensions in exactly the same way. In 3D the edges of the window become planes defining a convex region in three dimensions, and the line segment is a line in 3D space. ChopCI() needs no changes at all (since it uses only the values of dot products, through numer and denom). The data types in CyrusBeckClip() must, of course, be extended to 3D types, and when the endpoints of the line are adjusted, the z-component must be adjusted as well.

PRACTICE EXERCISES

4.8.1 Data types for variables in the Cyrus-Beck clipper

Provide useful definitions for data types, either as structs or classes, for LineSegment, LineList, and Vector2 used in the Cyrus-Beck clipping algorithm.

4.8.2 What does numer < = 0 do?

Sketch the vectors involved in value of numer in chopCI() and show that when the ray $A + \mathbf{c}t$ moves parallel to the bounding line, $\mathbf{n} \cdot (P - B) = 0$. Show that, in such a case it lies wholly in the inside half-space of the line if and only if numer > 0.

4.8.3 Find the clipped line

Apply Cyrus-Beck to find the portion of the segment with endpoints $(2, 4)$ and $(20, 8)$ that lies within the quadrilateral window with corners at $(0, 7)$, $(9, 9)$, $(14, 4)$, and $(2, 2)$.   ■

4.8.4 More Advanced Clipping

Clipping algorithms are fundamental to computer graphics and a number of efficient algorithms have been developed. Figure 4.47 shows the properties and capabilities of various clipping algorithms and indicates those situations where part a names the algorithm in question, part b reveals how successful OpenGL is in performing the algorithm, and part c describes the relevant subject polygon and windows. OpenGL attempts to do the promised clipping, but may actually be unable to perform as promised (in which case the program will not crash but the final image may not be correct, particularly if the application attempts to fill the clipped polygon with a pattern). So far, we have examined clipping the Cohen-Sutherland algorithm that clips a line segment against an aligned rectangle, and the Cyrus-Beck clipper that clips a segment against any convex polygon or polyhedron. The **Cyrus-Beck** clipper generalizes this to clipping a line against any convex polygon or polyhedron. But situations arise where one needs more sophisticated clipping. We mention two such methods here, but to develop them in detail is beyond the scope of the text. j187 Further readings are suggested at the end of the chapter.

a) Clipping Algorithm	b) OpenGL Yes/No?	c) Description
Cohen-Sutherland	Yes	Line segments against a rectangle or cube (in 2D a square)
Cyrus-Beck	Tries to; results unpredictable	Line against a convex polygon
Sutherland-Hodgman	No	Any polygon (convex or nonconvex) against any convex polygon
Weiler-Atherton	No	Any polygon against any polygon

FIGURE 4.47 Description of the various clipping algorithms.

The **Sutherland-Hodgman** clipper is similar to the Cyrus-Beck method, performing clipping against a convex polygon. But instead of clipping a single line segment, it clips an entire polygon (which needn't be convex) against the convex polygon. Most importantly, its output is again a *polygon* (or possibly a set of polygons). It can be important to retain the polygon structure during clipping, since the clipped polygons may need to be filled with a pattern or color. This is not possible if the edges of the polygon are clipped individually.

The **Weiler-Atherton** clipping algorithm clips any polygon, P, against *any* other polygon, W, convex or not. It can output the part of P that lies inside W (**interior clipping**) or the part of P that lies outside W (**exterior clipping**). In addition, both P and W can have holes in them. As might be expected, this algorithm is much more complex than the others we have examined, and a thorough discussion in this book is beyond its scope.

However, in those applications where such advanced clipping algorithms are required, the Weiler-Atherton method provides a welcome addition to one's toolbox.

4.9 SUMMARY OF THE CHAPTER

Vectors provide a convenient way to express many geometric relations, and the operations they support provide a powerful way to manipulate geometric objects algebraically. Many computer graphics algorithms are simplified and made more efficient through the use of vectors.

Because most vector operations are expressed the same way independent of the dimensionality of the underlying space, it is possible to derive results that are equally true in 2D or 3D space.

The dot product of two vectors is a fundamental quantity that simplifies finding the length of a vector and the angle between two vectors. It can be used to find such things as the orthogonal projection of one vector onto another, the location of the center of the excircle of three points, and the direction of a reflected ray. It is often used to test whether two vectors are orthogonal to one another, and more generally to test when they are pointing less than, or more than, 90° from each other. It is also useful to work with a 2D vector $\mathbf{a}^\perp$ that lies 90° to the left of a given vector $\mathbf{a}$. In particular the dot product $\mathbf{a}^\perp \cdot \mathbf{b}$ reports useful information about how $\mathbf{a}$ and $\mathbf{b}$ are disposed relative to each other.

The cross product also reveals information about the angle between two vectors in 3D, and in addition evaluates to a vector that is perpendicular to them both. It is often used to find a vector that is normal to a plane.

In the process of developing an algorithm, it is crucial to have a concise representation of the graphical objects involved. The two principal forms are the parametric representation and the implicit form. The parametric representation visits each of the points on the object as a parameter is made to vary, so the parameter indexes into different points on the object. The implicit form expresses an equation that all points on the object, and only those, must satisfy. It is often given in the form $f(x, y) = 0$ in 2D, or $f(x, y, z) = 0$ in 3D, where $f()$ is some function. The value of $f()$ for a given point tells not only when the point is on the object but when a point lies off the object. The sign of $f()$ can reveal on *which* side of the object the point lies. In this chapter we addressed finding representations of the two fundamental flat objects in graphics: lines and planes. For such objects both the parametric form and implicit form are linear in their arguments. The implicit form can be revealingly written as the dot product of a normal vector and a vector lying within the object.

It is possible to form arbitrary linear combinations of vectors but not of points. For points only affine combinations are allowed, or else chaos reigns if the underlying coordinate system is ever altered, as it frequently is in graphics. Affine combinations of points are useful in graphics, and we showed that they form the basis of tweening for animations and for Bezier curves.

The parametric form of a line or ray is particularly useful for such tasks as finding where two lines intersect or where a ray hits a polygon or polyhedron. These problems are important in themselves, and they also underlie clipping algorithms that are so prominent in graphics. The Cyrus-Beck clipper finds which portion of a line segment lies inside a convex polygon or polyhedron.

In the Case Studies that are presented next, the vector tools developed so far are applied to some interesting graphics situations, and their power is seen even more clearly. Whether or not you intend to carry out the required programming to implement these mini-projects, it is valuable to read through them and visualize what process you would pursue to solve them.

4.10 CASE STUDIES

CASE STUDY 4.1 ANIMATION WITH TWEENING

(Level of Effort: II)   Devise two interesting polylines, such as A and B as shown in Figure 4.48. Ensure that A and B have the same number of points, perhaps by adding some artificial extra points in the top segment of B.

a. Develop a routine similar to routine `drawTween(A, B, n, t)` of Figure 4.21 that draws the tween at t of the polylines A and B.

Develop a routine that draws a sequence of tweens between A and B as a parameter t varies gradually from 0 to 1, and then decreases gradually back to 0, thereafter repeating this cycle indefinitely, until a key is pressed. The animation shows A mutating into B and then back into A. Use the double buffering offered by OpenGL to make the animation smooth.

FIGURE 4.48 Tweening two polylines.

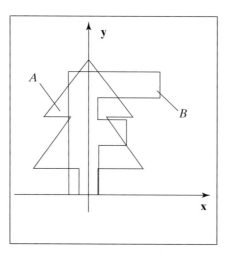

FIGURE 4.48 Tweening two polylines.

CASE STUDY 4.2 CIRCLES GALORE

(Level of Effort: II)   Write an application that allows the user to input the points of a triangle with a mouse. The program then draws the triangle along with its **inscribed** circle, its **excircle**, and its **nine-point circle**, each in a different color. Arrange matters so that the user can then move any vertex of the triangle to a new location with the mouse, after which the new triangle and its three circles are immediately redrawn.

We saw how to draw the excircle in Section 4.6.1. Here we show how to find the inscribed circle and the nine-point circle.

The inscribed circle This is the circle that just snugs up inside the given triangle and is tangent to all three sides.[13] Figure 4.49a shows a triangle ABC along with its inscribed circle.

FIGURE 4.49 The inscribed circle of ABC is the excircle of RST.

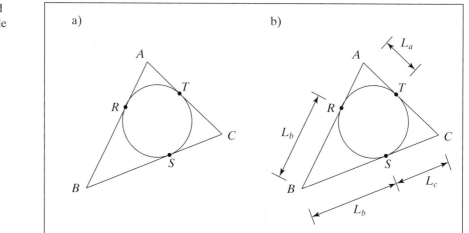

As was the case with the excircle, the hard part is finding the center of the inscribed circle. A straightforward method[14] recognizes that the inscribed circle of ABC is simply the excircle of a different set of three points, RST, as shown in Figure 4.47a.

To pursue this method we need only find the locations of R, S, and T and then use the excircle method of Section 4.6.1. Figure 4.49b shows the distances of R, S, and T from A, B, and C, respectively. By the symmetry of a circle the distances $|B - R|$ and $|B - S|$ must be equal,

---

[13]   Note: Finding the incircle also solves the problem of finding the unique circle that is tangent to three non-collinear lines in the plane.

[14]   Suggested by Russell Swan.

and there are two other pairs of lines that have the same length. We therefore have [using the definitions of Equation (4.48) for $\mathbf{a}$, $\mathbf{b}$, and $\mathbf{c}$]:

$$|\mathbf{a}| = L_b + L_a, \qquad |\mathbf{b}| = L_b + L_c, \qquad |\mathbf{c}| = L_a + L_c$$

which can be combined to solve for L_a and L_b:

$$2L_a = |\mathbf{a}| + |\mathbf{c}| - |\mathbf{b}|, \qquad 2L_b = |\mathbf{a}| + |\mathbf{b}| - |\mathbf{c}|$$

so L_a and L_b are now known. Thus R, S, and T are given by:

$$R = A + L_a \frac{\mathbf{a}}{|\mathbf{a}|}$$

$$S = B + L_b \frac{\mathbf{b}}{|\mathbf{b}|} \qquad\qquad (4.58)$$

$$T = A - L_a \frac{\mathbf{c}}{|\mathbf{c}|}$$

(Check these expressions!)

Encapsulate the calculation of R, S, and T from A, B, and C in a simple routine having usage `getTangentPoints(A, B, C, R, S, T)`. The advantage here is that if we have a routine `excircle()` that takes three points and computes the center and radius of the ex-circle defined by them, we can use the *same* routine to find the inscribed circle. Experiment with these tools.

The nine-point circle

For any triangle, there are nine particularly distinguished points:

- the midpoints of the three sides.
- the point of intersection of the line from each vertex to the midpoint of the opposite side.
- the midpoints of the lines joining the orthocenter (where the three altitudes meet) to the vertices.

Remarkably, a single circle passes through all nine points! Figure 4.50 shows **the nine-point circle**[15] for an example triangle. The nine-point circle is perhaps most easily drawn as the ex-circle of the midpoints of the sides of the triangle.

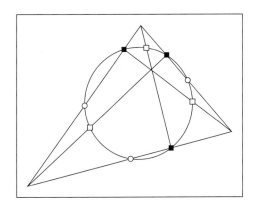

FIGURE 4.50 The nine-point circle.

---

[15] "This circle is the first really exciting one to appear in any course on elementary geometry." Daniel Pedoe. *Circles* (New York: Pergamon Press, 1957).

CASE STUDY 4.3 IS POINT Q INSIDE CONVEX POLYGON P?

(Level of Effort: II)   Suppose you are given the specification of a convex polygon, P consisting of its vertices $P_0, P_1, \ldots, P_{N-1}$. Then, given a point Q, you are asked to determine whether or not Q lies inside P. But from the discussion on convex polygons in Section 4.8.1 we know this is equivalent to asking whether Q lies on the inside half-space of *every* bounding line of P. For each bounding line L_i we need only test whether the vector $Q - P_i$ is more than 90° away from the outward pointing normal for each vertex, P_i of the polygon.

$\quad$ *Fact*: $\qquad Q$ lies in P if $(Q - P_i) \cdot n_i < 0 \qquad$ for $i = 0, 1, \ldots, N - 1 \qquad\qquad$ (4.59)

Figure 4.51 illustrates the test for the particular bounding line that passes through P_1 and P_2. For the case where point Q, which lies inside P, the angle with $\mathbf{n}_1$ is greater than 90°. For the case where Q lies outside P, of point Q', which lies outside P, the angle is less than 90°.

FIGURE 4.51 Is point Q inside polygon P?

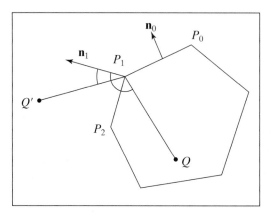

Write and test a program that chooses points at random, or allows the user to specify points with the mouse, to define polygon P, (being sure that P is convex):

a. plots the vertices of polygon P;
b. successively generates (and plots) points Q, either randomly or by the mouse, and tests each whether or not it lies inside P; plot test points, Q, with the mouse;
c. displays "*is inside*" or "*is not inside*" depending on whether the point Q is or is not inside P.

CASE STUDY 4.4 REFLECTIONS IN A CHAMBER (2D RAY TRACING)

(Level of Effort: III)   This Case Study applies some of the tools and ideas introduced in this chapter to create a fascinating yet simple simulation. The simulation performs a kind of ray tracing, based in a 2D world for easy visualization. Three-dimensional ray tracing is discussed in detail in Chapter 12.

This simulation traces the path of a single tiny pinball as it bounces off various walls inside a chamber. Figure 4.52a shows a cross section of a convex chamber W that has six walls and contains three convex pillars. The pinball begins at point S and moves in a straight line in direction $\mathbf{c}$ until it hits a barrier, whereupon it reflects off the barrier and moves in a new direction, again in a straight line. It continues to do this until the user presses a key. Figure 4.52b shows an example of the polyline path that a ray traverses.

For any given position S and direction $\mathbf{c}$ of the ray, tracing its path requires two operations:

● Finding the first wall of the chamber that is hit by the ray;
● Finding the new direction that the ray will take as it reflects off this first line.

Both of these operations have been discussed in the chapter. Note that as each new ray is created, its start point is always on some wall or pillar, the hit point of the previously hit wall.

We represent the chamber by a list of convex polygons, *pillar*$_0$, *pillar*$_1$, $\ldots$, and arrange that *pillar*$_0$ is the chamber inside which the action takes place. The pillars are stored in suitable

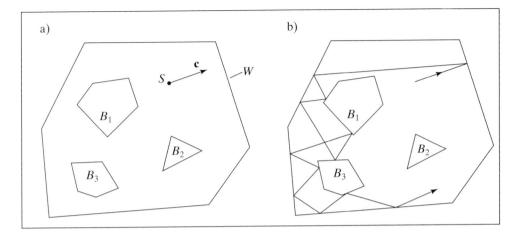

FIGURE 4.52 A 2D ray tracing experiment.

arrays of points. For each ray beginning at S and moving in direction $\mathbf{c}$, the entire array of pillars is scanned, and the intersection of the ray with each pillar is determined. This test is done using the Cyrus-Beck algorithm of Section 4.8.3. If there is a hit with a pillar, the hit time is taken to be the time at which the ray enters the pillar.

We want to know which pillar the ray hits first. This is done by keeping track of the earliest hit time as we scan through the list of pillars. Only positive hit times need to be considered: negative hit times correspond to hits at spots in the opposite direction from the ray's travel. When the earliest hit point is found, the ray is drawn from S to it.

We must find the direction of the reflected ray as it moves away from this latest hit spot. The direction $\mathbf{c}'$ of the reflected ray is given in terms of the direction $\mathbf{c}$ of the incident ray by Equation (4.23):

$$\mathbf{c}' = \mathbf{c} - 2(\mathbf{c} \cdot \hat{\mathbf{n}})\hat{\mathbf{n}} \qquad (4.60)$$

where $\hat{\mathbf{n}}$ is the unit normal to the wall or to the pillar that was hit. If a pillar inside the chamber was hit, we write and exercise a program that draws the path of a ray as it reflects off the inner walls of chamber W and the walls of the convex pillars inside the chamber. Arrange to read in the list of pillars from an external file and to have the user specify the ray's starting position and direction.

CASE STUDY 4.5 CYRUS-BECK CLIPPING

(Level of Effort: II)   Write and execute a program that clips a collection of lines against a convex polygon. The user specifies the polygon by laying down a sequence of points with the mouse (pressing key 'C' to terminate the polygon and begin clipping). Then a sequence of lines is generated, each having randomly chosen endpoints. For each such line, the whole line is first drawn in red, then the portion that lies inside the polygon is drawn in blue.

4.11 FOR FURTHER READING

Many books provide a good introduction to vectors. A favorite is Hoffmann's *About Vectors*. The *GRAPHICS and GPU Gems* series [Gems05] provides excellent sources for new approaches and results in vector arithmetic and geometric algorithms by computer graphics practitioners. Three excellent example articles are Alan Paeth's "A Half-Angle Identity for Digital Computation: The Joys of the Half Tangent" [Paeth91], Ron Goldman's "Triangles" [Goldman90], and Lopez-Lopez's "Triangles Revisited" [Lopez92]. Three books that delve more deeply into the nature of geometric algorithms are Moret and Shapiro's *Algorithms from P to NP* [Moret91], *Algorithms and Programming* [Holloway02], and Preparata and Shamos's *Computational Geometry, An Introduction* [Preparata85].

Chapter 5

Transformations of Objects

Minus times minus is plus, the reason for this we need not discuss

W. H. Auden
(1907–1973)

"If I eat one of these cakes," she thought, "it's sure to make some change in my size." So she swallowed one . . . and was delighted to find that she began shrinking directly.

Alice in Wonderland
Lewis Carroll
(1832–1898)

GOALS OF THE CHAPTER

○ Develop tools for transforming one object into another.

○ Introduce the fundamental concepts of affine transformations, which perform combinations of rotations, scalings, and translations.

○ Develop functions that apply affine transformations to objects in computer programs.

○ Develop tools for transforming coordinate frames.

○ See how to set up a camera to render a 3D scene using OpenGL.

○ Learn how to design the scenes using the Scene Design Language, SDL, and to write programs that read SDL files and draw the scenes they describe.

Preview

The main goal in this chapter is to develop techniques for working with a particularly powerful family of transformations, called **affine transformations**, in a computer program using OpenGL. Section 5.1 motivates the use of 2D and 3D transformations in computer graphics and sets up some basic definitions. Section 5.2 defines 2D affine transformations and a current transformation (CT), and establishes terminology for them in terms of a matrix. The notation of coordinate frames is used to keep clear what objects are being altered and how. The section shows how elementary affine transformations can perform scaling, rotation, translation, and shearing. Section 5.2.5 demonstrates that one can combine as many affine transformations as one wishes, and the result is another affine transformation, also characterized by a matrix. Section 5.2.7 discusses key properties of all affine transformations—most notably that they preserve straight lines, planes, and parallelism—and shows why they are so prevalent in computer graphics.

Section 5.3 extends these ideas to 3D affine transformations and shows that all of the basic 2D properties hold in 3D as well. 3D transformations—particularly 3D rotations—are more complex than 2D rotations and more difficult to visualize, so special attention is paid to describing and combining various rotations.

Section 5.4 discusses the relationship between transforming points and transforming coordinate systems. Section 5.5 shows how transformations are managed within a graphics program, and how transformations can greatly simplify many operations commonly needed in a graphics program. The modeling of transformations and the use of the *current transformation* are motivated through a number of examples. Section 5.6 discusses modeling 3D scenes and drawing them using OpenGL. A **camera** is defined that is positioned and oriented so that it takes the desired snapshot of the scene. Some people (including most people who write textbooks in computer graphics) like to think of it as an imagined pinhole **camera**, but we will use a more vivid approach that allows one to visualize an airplane moving through the scene and taking snapshot. Actually, in later discussions we will use an even more descriptive term and call this camera a "**jib camera**," borrowing terminology from the video production industry. In video production the videographer directs the motion of the jib cameras through the scene while filming. The snapshot is taken from a particular point of view, chosen by the application programmer to produce a particular visual effect. (If the desired visual effect is realism, great pains must be taken to make the objects in the scene look real, as if the objects in question are made of particular materials are bathed in light coming from light sources.) If the image is part of an animation, successive frames might show this point of view changing, as if a camera were flying through the scene. The section discusses how transformations are used to size and position objects as desired in a scene. Some example 3D scenes are modeled and rendered, and the code required to do it is examined. This section also introduces a Scene Description Language (SDL), and shows how to write an application that can draw any scene described in the language. The presentation requires the use of a number of classes (which the SDL compiler provides) to support reading and parsing SDL files and creating lists of objects that can be rendered. These classes have been compiled and tested and are available from the book's web site.

The chapter ends with a number of Case Studies that elaborate on the main ideas and provide opportunities to work with affine transformations in graphics programs. Also described are ways to decompose an affine transformation into its elementary operations, and the development of a fast routine to draw arcs of circles that capitalizes on the equivalence between a rotation and three successive shears.

5.1 INTRODUCTION

Affine transformations are a cornerstone of computer graphics and are central to OpenGL. They are also a source of difficulty for many programmers, because it is often difficult to get them right. One particularly delicate area is the confusion of points and vectors. Points and vectors seem very similar and are often expressed in a program using the same data type, perhaps a list of three numbers like $(3.0, 2.5, -1.145)$ to express them in the current coordinate system. But this practice can lead to disaster in the form of serious bugs that are very difficult to ferret out, principally because points and vectors do *not* transform the same way. We need a way to keep them straight, which is offered by using *coordinate frames* and appropriate homogeneous coordinates, as introduced in Chapter 4.

5.2 INTRODUCTION TO TRANSFORMATIONS

The universe is full of magical things, patiently waiting for our wits to grow sharper.

E. Phillpotts
(1862–1960)

We have already seen some examples of transformations, at least in 2D. In Chapter 3, for instance, the window-to-viewport transformation was used to scale and translate objects situated in the world window to their final size and position in the viewport.

We want to build on those ideas and gain more flexible control over the size, orientation, and position of objects of interest. In the following sections we develop the required tools, based on the powerful **affine transformation**, which is a staple in computer graphics. We operate in both two and three dimensions. (In the sections that follow we look at some examples that use affine transformations.)

In each example take note of how the transformations save effort for the programmer, keeping in mind that normally the hard part of creating a scene is the design of the various objects that the programmer wants to appear in the scene.

Figure 5.1a shows two versions of a simple house, drawn before and after each of its points has been transformed. Part a shows a 2D example and part b shows a 3D example. The house has been scaled down in size, rotated a small amount, and then moved up and to the right. The overall transformation here is a combination of three more elementary ones: scaling, rotation, and translation. Figure 5.1b shows a 3D house before and after it is similarly transformed: each 3D point in the house is subjected to a scaling, a rotation, and a translation.

FIGURE 5.1 Drawings of objects before and after they are transformed.

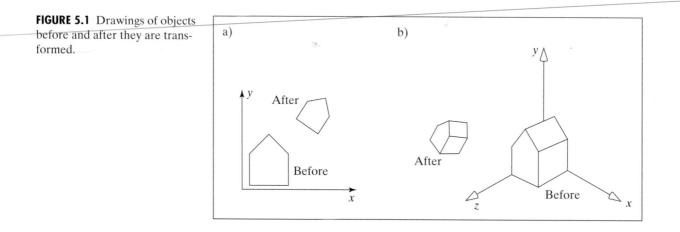

Transformations are very useful in a number of situations:

a. We can compose a scene out of a number of objects, as in Figure 5.2. Each object, such as the arch, need be designed only once in its own master coordinate system. The scene is then fashioned by placing a number of instances of the arch at different places and with different sizes, using the proper transformation for each.

Figure 5.3 shows a 3D example, where the scene is composed of many instances of cubes that have been scaled and positioned to form a city.

b. Some objects, such as the snowflake shown in Figure 5.4, exhibit certain symmetries. We can design a single **motif** and then assemble the whole shape by appropriate reflections, rotations, and translations of the motif (recall the examples from Section 3.2).

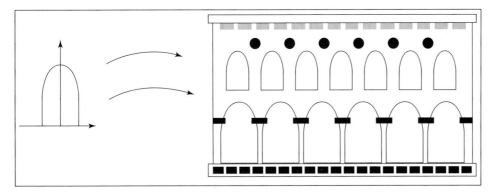

FIGURE 5.2 A picture composed from many instances of a simple form.

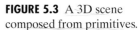

FIGURE 5.3 A 3D scene composed from primitives.

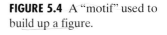

FIGURE 5.4 A "motif" used to build up a figure.

Use it 12 times

c. A designer may want to view an object from different vantagepoints and make a picture from each one. The scene can be rotated and viewed with the same camera. But, as suggested in Figure 5.5, it's more natural to leave the scene alone and move the camera to different orientations and positions for each snapshot. Positioning and reorienting a camera can be carried out through the use of 3D affine transformations.

FIGURE 5.5 A scene viewed
from different points of view.

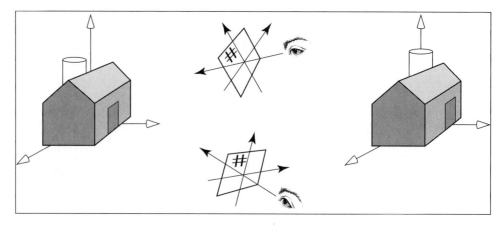

d. In a computer animation several objects frequently move relative to one another from frame to frame. This can be achieved by translating and rotating their local
coordinate systems as the animation proceeds.

Where Are We Headed? Using Transformations with OpenGL

The first few sections of this chapter present the basic concepts of affine transformations and show how they produce certain geometric effects, such as scaling, rotations,
and translations, in both 2D and 3D space. Ultimately, of course, the goal is to produce graphical drawings of objects that have been transformed to the proper size, orientation, and position so they produce the desired scene. A number of graphics
platforms, including OpenGL, provide a graphics pipeline, or sequence of operations,
that are applied to all points that are sent through it. A drawing is produced by processing each point. Figure 5.6 shows a simplified view of the OpenGL pipeline.

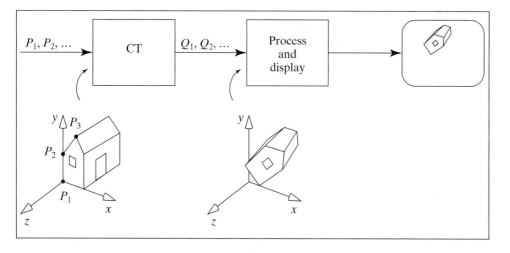

FIGURE 5.6 A simplified version
of the OpenGL pipeline.

As shown in the figure, an application sends the pipeline a sequence of points
$P_1, P_2, P_3, \ldots$, using the commands like the now familiar:

```
glBegin(GL_LINES);
    glVertex3f(...); // send P1 through the pipeline
    glVertex3f(...); // send P2 through the pipeline
    glVertex3f(...); // send P3 through the pipeline
    ...
glEnd();
```

As shown in the figure, these points first encounter a transformation that we call **the current transformation** (CT), which alters their values into a different set of points, say Q_1, Q_2, Q_3. Just as the original points P_1 describe some geometric object, the points Q_1 describe the transformed version of the same object. These points are then sent through additional steps and ultimately are used to draw the final image on the display.

The details of the pipeline omitted in Figure 5.6 will be addressed in Chapter 8. Prior to OpenGL 2.0 the pipeline was of *fixed functionality*, which means that each stage had to perform a specific operation in a particular manner. With the specification of OpenGL 2.0 and the Shading Language (GLSL) the pipeline became somewhat rearranged; the application programmer not only could change the order in which some operations were performed, but also could make the operations **programmable**. This means the application could send to the pipeline data that were highly customized to the needs of a particular application. This has allowed innovative hardware and software developers to take advantage of new algorithms and rendering techniques and still comply with OpenGL version 2.0. In Chapter 8 we introduce two programmable units, the **vertex processor** and **fragment processor,** and see how they fit into the OpenGL pipeline. (A **fragment** contains depth, color, and texture attributes for a given pixel; more on fragments can be found in Chapters 8 and 9.)

The current transformation therefore provides a crucial tool in the manipulation of graphical objects, and the application programmer must know how to adjust the CT so that the desired transformations are produced. After developing the underlying theory of affine transformations, we turn to Section 5.5 to showing how this is done.

Object Transformations vs. Coordinate Transformations

There are two ways to view a transformation: as an **object transformation** or as a **coordinate transformation**. An object transformation alters the coordinates of each point on the object according to the same rule, leaving the underlying coordinate system fixed. A coordinate transformation defines a new coordinate system in terms of the old one, then represents all of the object's points in this new system. The two views are closely connected, and each has its advantages, but they are implemented somewhat differently. We shall first develop the central ideas in terms of object transformations, and then relate them to coordinate transformations.

5.2.1 Points and Objects Transformed

We look here at the general idea of a transformation, and then specialize to affine transformations.

A transformation (call it $T(\ )$), alters each point, P, in space (2D or 3D) into a new point, Q, using a specific formula or algorithm, say $Q = T(P)$. Figure 5.7 shows 2D and 3D examples.

As Figure 5.7 illustrates, an arbitrary point P in the plane is **mapped** to Q. We say Q is the **image** of P under the mapping T. Part a shows point P lying in 2D being mapped to a new point Q; part b shows point P lying in 3D being mapped to a new Q. We transform an object by transforming each of its points, using, of course, the *same* function $T()$ for each point. We can map whole collections of points at once. The collection might be all the points on a line or a circle. The **image** of line L under T, for instance, consists of the images of *all* the individual points of L.[1]

Most mappings of interest are continuous, so the image of a straight line is still a connected curve of some shape, although it's not necessarily a straight line. Affine

---

[1] More formally, if S is a set of points, its **image**, denoted $T(S)$, is the set of all points $T(P)$, where P is some point in S.

FIGURE 5.7 Points mapped into new points.

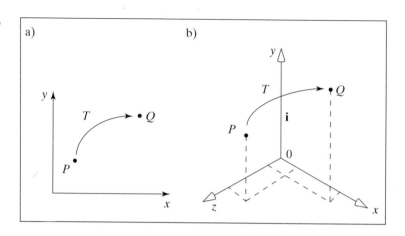

transformations, however, *do* preserve lines, as we shall see. The image under *T* of a straight line is also a straight line. This limits the richness of new shapes that you can produce with affine transformations, but this limitation is more than made up for by other properties of an affine transformation. Most of this chapter will focus on affine transformations, but other kinds can be used when desired to create special effects. Figure 5.8, for instance, shows an extreme warping of a figure that cannot be achieved with an affine transformation. (The original drawing of Leonardo appears in a circle.) This highly distorting transformation might be used for visual effect, or to emphasize important features of an object.

FIGURE 5.8 A dramatic warping of a figure.

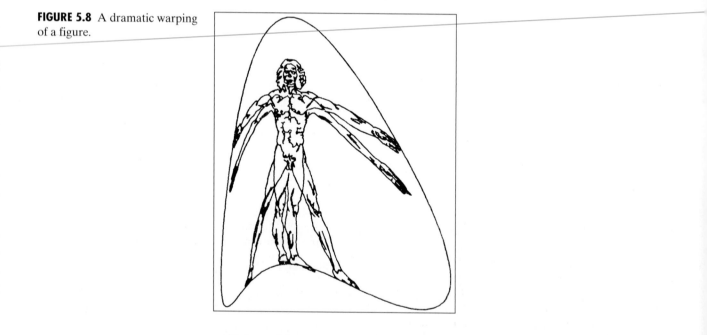

To keep things straight we use an explicit coordinate frame when performing transformations. Recall from Chapter 4 that a coordinate frame consists of a particular point, φ, called the **origin**, and some mutually perpendicular vectors (called **i** and **j** in the 2D case; **i, j**, and **k** in the 3D case) that serve as the axes of the coordinate frame.

Take the 2D case first, as it is easier to visualize. In whichever coordinate frame we are using, points *P* and *Q* have the homogeneous coordinate representations $\tilde{P}$ and $\tilde{Q}$ given by:

$$\widetilde{P} = \begin{pmatrix} P_x \\ P_y \\ 1 \end{pmatrix}, \qquad \widetilde{Q} = \begin{pmatrix} Q_x \\ Q_y \\ 1 \end{pmatrix}$$

Recall that this means that point $\widetilde{P}$ is at location $\widetilde{P} = P_x\mathbf{i} + P_y\mathbf{j} + \phi$ and similarly for $\widetilde{Q}$. P_x and P_y are the homogeneous coordinates of $\widetilde{P}$. Now to get from the origin to point $\widetilde{P}$, move amount P_x along axis $\mathbf{i}$ and amount P_y along axis $\mathbf{j}$.

Suppose that transformation T operates on any point $\widetilde{P}$ to produce point $\widetilde{Q}$:

$$\begin{pmatrix} Q_x \\ Q_y \\ 1 \end{pmatrix} = T\begin{pmatrix} P_x \\ P_y \\ 1 \end{pmatrix} \tag{5.1}$$

or more succinctly,

$$\widetilde{Q} = T(\widetilde{P}). \tag{5.2}$$

The function $T()$ could be complicated, as in

$$\begin{pmatrix} Q_x \\ Q_y \\ 1 \end{pmatrix} = \begin{pmatrix} \cos(P_x)e^{-P_y} \\ \dfrac{\ln(P_y)}{1 + P_x^2} \\ 1 \end{pmatrix}$$

so that both Q_x and Q_y are complicated mixes of P_x and P_y.

Such transformations might have interesting geometric effects, but to build affine transformations we instead restrict ourselves to much simpler families of functions, those that are *linear* in P_x and P_y. This property characterizes the affine transformations.

5.2.2 The Affine Transformations

> What is algebra, exactly? Is it those three-cornered things?
>
> *J. M. Barrie*
> *(1860–1937)*

Some Properties, Disadvantages, and Advantages of Affine Transformations

Affine transformations are the most common transformations used in computer graphics. They have many very useful properties. Among other things, they make it easy to scale, rotate, and reposition figures. A succession of affine transformations can easily be combined into a single overall affine transformation, and, very importantly, affine transformations permit a compact *matrix* representation. As we shall see, the matrix associated with an affine transformation operating on 2D vectors or points is a three-by-three matrix. This is a direct consequence of representing the vectors and points in homogeneous coordinates.

Affine transformations have a simple form. Because the coordinates of $\widetilde{Q}$ are *linear* combinations of those of $\widetilde{P}$, the transformed point $\widetilde{Q}$ may be written in the form:

$$\begin{pmatrix} Q_x \\ Q_y \\ 1 \end{pmatrix} = \begin{pmatrix} m_{11}P_x + m_{12}P_y + m_{13} \\ m_{21}P_x + m_{22}P_y + m_{23} \\ 1 \end{pmatrix} \tag{5.3}$$

for some six given constants m_{11}, m_{12}, and so on. The coordinate Q_x consists of portions of both of P_x and P_y, and so does Q_y. This *cross fertilization* between the x- and y-components gives rise to rotations and shears, as we shall see.

The affine transformation of Equation (5.3) has a useful matrix representation that helps to organize your thinking:[2]

$$\begin{pmatrix} Q_x \\ Q_y \\ 1 \end{pmatrix} = \begin{pmatrix} m_{11} & m_{12} & m_{13} \\ m_{21} & m_{22} & m_{23} \\ 0 & 0 & 1 \end{pmatrix} \begin{pmatrix} P_x \\ P_y \\ 1 \end{pmatrix} \text{ or } \tilde{Q} = \tilde{M}\tilde{P} \quad \text{(in obvious notation)} \quad (5.4)$$

To see that Q here is the same as in Equation 5.3, simply multiply P by M. In particular, note how the third row of the matrix forces the third component of $\tilde{Q}$ to be 1. For an affine transformation the third row of the matrix is always $(0, 0, 1)$.

■ **EXAMPLE 5.2.1 Apply the transformation**

An affine transformation is specified by the matrix:

$$\begin{pmatrix} 3 & 0 & 5 \\ -2 & 1 & 2 \\ 0 & 0 & 1 \end{pmatrix}.$$

Find the image Q of point $P = (1, 2, 1)$.

SOLUTION:

$$Q = \begin{pmatrix} 8 \\ 2 \\ 1 \end{pmatrix} = \begin{pmatrix} 3 & 0 & 5 \\ -2 & 1 & 2 \\ 0 & 0 & 1 \end{pmatrix} \begin{pmatrix} 1 \\ 2 \\ 1 \end{pmatrix}.$$

Check this by directly multiplying P by the matrix. Notice that Q is a point, as expected.

5.2.3 Geometric Effects of Elementary 2D Affine Transformations

What geometric effects are produced by affine transformations? They produce combinations of four elementary transformations: (1) a translation, (2) a scaling, (3) a rotation, and (4) a shear. These transformations are called *elementary* because they apply only one type of transformation at a time. Figure 5.9 shows the effect of three kinds of transformations applied individually.

Translation

You often want to translate a picture into a different position on a graphics display. One key property of a translation of point P, which must be reflected in the mathematics, is that the amount P is translated does not depend on the position of P beforehand. Furthermore it is meaningless to translate vectors, and this too should appear naturally in the representation of a translation. To translate a point P by the amount a in the x-direction and the amount b in the y-direction use the matrix:

$$\begin{pmatrix} Q_x \\ Q_y \\ 1 \end{pmatrix} = \begin{pmatrix} 1 & 0 & a \\ 0 & 1 & b \\ 0 & 0 & 1 \end{pmatrix} \begin{pmatrix} P_x \\ P_y \\ 1 \end{pmatrix}$$

[handwritten annotation: x translated a, y translated b]

---

[2] See Appendix 2 for a review of matrices.

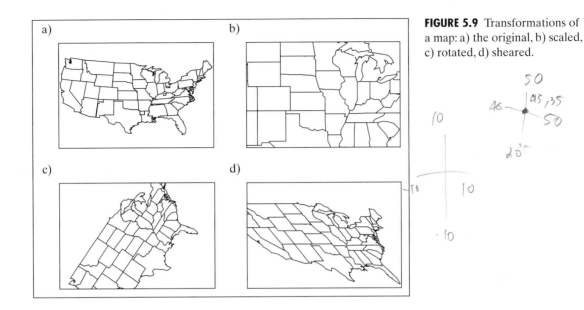

FIGURE 5.9 Transformations of a map: a) the original, b) scaled, c) rotated, d) sheared.

to produce:

$$\begin{pmatrix} P_x + a \\ P_y + b \\ 1 \end{pmatrix}$$

For example, if a is 2 and b is 3, every point will be altered into a new point that is two units farther to the right and three units above the original point. The point $(1, -5)$, for instance, is transformed into $(3, -2)$, and the point $(0, 0)$ is transformed into $(2, 3)$. Notice that if this matrix were applied to a vector (whose third coordinate is zero), the translation would have no effect on the vector, as required.

Further Justification for the Use of Homogeneous Coordinates

We hardly need to justify using homogeneous coordinates, but a brief digression will pay off later. *Without the use of homogeneous coordinates, there is no way to cause a translation using a matrix multiplication.* For example, if we use regular coordinates for P and a two-by-two matrix:

$$M = \begin{pmatrix} 1 & b \\ a & 1 \end{pmatrix} \times \begin{pmatrix} P_x \\ P_y \end{pmatrix}$$

we obtain for the transformed point:

$$\begin{pmatrix} P_x + bP_y \\ aP_x + P_y \end{pmatrix}$$

which is hardly a translation for any choice of a and b. The culprit is that the a and b terms are *multiplied* by the p_x and p_y, rather than being simply added to them. In homogeneous coordinates we are saved by the third term, *1* or zero, which adds to the other terms of the point or vector.

Scaling

A scaling changes the size of a picture and involves two scale factors, S_x and S_y, for the x- and y-coordinates, respectively:

$$(Q_x, Q_y) = (S_x P_x, S_y P_y)$$

Thus the matrix for a scaling is simply

$$\begin{pmatrix} S_x & 0 & 0 \\ 0 & S_y & 0 \\ 0 & 0 & 1 \end{pmatrix}$$ (5.5)

Scaling in this fashion is more accurately called **scaling about the origin**, because each point P is moved S_x times farther from the origin in the x-direction, and S_y times farther from the origin in the y-direction. If a scale factor is negative, then there is also a **reflection** about a coordinate axis. Figure 5.10 shows an example in which the scaling $(S_x, S_y) = (-1, 2)$ is applied to a collection of points. Each point is both reflected about the y-axis and scaled by 2 in the y-direction.

FIGURE 5.10 A scaling and a reflection.

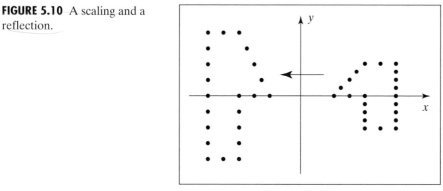

There are also pure reflections, for which each of the scale factors is $+1$ or -1. An example is

$$T(P_x, P_y) = (-P_x, P_y)$$ (5.6)

which produces a mirror image of a picture by flipping it horizontally about the y-axis, replacing each occurrence of x with $-x$. (What is the matrix of this transformation?)

If the two scale factors are the same, $S_x = S_y = S$, the transformation is a **uniform scaling**, or a magnification about the origin, with magnification factor $|S|$. If S is negative, there are reflections about both axes. A point is moved outward from the origin to a position $|S|$ times farther away from the origin. If $|S| < 1$, the points are moved closer to the origin, producing a reduction (or demagnification). If, on the other hand, the scale factors are not the same, the scaling is called a **differential scaling**.

Rotations

A fundamental graphics operation is the rotation of a figure about a given point through some angle. Figure 5.11 shows a set of points rotated about the origin through an angle of $\theta = 60°$.

When $T(\ )$ is a rotation about the origin, $Q = T(P)$ has the form, familiar from high school trigonometry:

$$Q_x = P_x \cos(\theta) - P_y \sin(\theta)$$

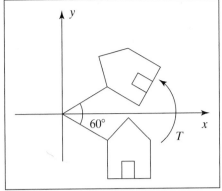

FIGURE 5.11 Rotation of points through an angle of 60°.

$$Q_y = P_x \sin(\theta) + P_y \cos(\theta) \qquad (5.7)$$

As we derive next, positive values of θ perform a counterclockwise (CCW) rotation. In terms of its matrix form, a pure rotation about the origin is given by

$$\begin{pmatrix} \cos(\theta) & -\sin(\theta) & 0 \\ \sin(\theta) & \cos(\theta) & 0 \\ 0 & 0 & 1 \end{pmatrix} \qquad CCW\ rotation \qquad (5.8)$$

■ EXAMPLE 5.2.1

Find the transformed point, Q, caused by rotating $P = (3, 5)$ about the origin through an angle of 60°.

SOLUTION:

For an angle of 60°, which is 1.047 in radians, $\cos(\theta) = .5$ and $\sin(\theta) = .866$, and Equation (5.7) yields $Q_x = (3)(0.5) - (5)(0.866) = -2.83$ and $Q_y = (3)(0.866) + (5)(0.5) = 5.098$. Check this with a graphing calculator by swinging an arc of 60° from $(3, 5)$ and reading off the position of the mapped point. Also check numerically that Q and P are at the same distance from the origin. (What is this distance? *Answer*: 5.83082. *It is* the same as the other distance!)

Derivation of the Rotation Mapping We wish to demonstrate that Equation (5.7) is correct. Figure 5.12 shows how to find the coordinates of a point Q that results from rotating point P about the origin through an angle θ. If P is at a distance R from the origin, at some angle φ, then $P = (R\cos(\phi), R\sin(\phi))$. Now Q must be at the same distance as P, and at angle $\theta + \phi$. Using trigonometry, the coordinates of Q are

$$Q_x = R\cos(\theta + \phi)$$
$$Q_y = R\sin(\theta + \phi)$$

Substitute into this equation the two familiar trigonometric relations:

$$\cos(\theta + \phi) = \cos(\theta)\cos(\phi) - \sin(\theta)\sin(\phi)$$
$$\sin(\theta + \phi) = \sin(\theta)\cos(\phi) + \cos(\theta)\sin(\phi)$$

and use $P_x = R\cos(\phi)$ and $P_y = R\sin(\phi)$ to obtain Equation (5.7).

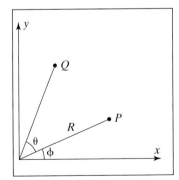

FIGURE 5.12 Derivation of the rotation mapping.

Shearing

A shear in the x-direction or along x is shown in Figure 5.13. In this case the y-coordinate of each point is unaffected, whereas each x-coordinate is translated by an amount that increases linearly with y. A shear in the x-direction is given by

$$Q_x = P_x + hP_y$$
$$Q_y = P_y$$

FIGURE 5.13 An example of shearing.

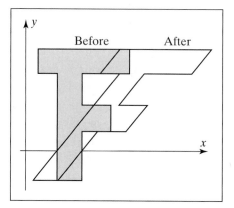

The coefficient h specifies what fraction of the y-coordinate of P is to be added to the x-coordinate. The quantity h can be positive or negative. Shearing is sometimes used to make *italic*-like letters out of regular letters. The matrix associated with this shear is:

$$\begin{pmatrix} 1 & h & 0 \\ 0 & 1 & 0 \\ 0 & 0 & 1 \end{pmatrix} \quad x-\text{shear} \tag{5.9}$$

One can also have a shear along y, in which case $Q_x = P_x$ and $Q_y = gP_x + P_y$ for some value g, so that the matrix is given by

$$\begin{pmatrix} 1 & 0 & 0 \\ g & 1 & 0 \\ 0 & 0 & 1 \end{pmatrix} \quad y-\text{shear} \tag{5.10}$$

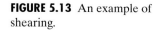

■ **EXAMPLE 5.2.2**

Into which point does $(3, 4)$ shear when $h = .3$ in Equation (5.9)?

SOLUTION:

$Q = (3 + (.3)4, 4) = (4.2, 4)$.

■ **EXAMPLE 5.2.3**

Let $g = 0.2$ in Equation (5.10). To what point does $(6, -2)$ map?

SOLUTION:

$Q = (6, 0.2 \cdot 6 - 2) = (6, -0.8)$.

A notable feature of a shear is that its matrix has a determinant of 1. As we see later, this implies that the area of a figure is unchanged when it is sheared.

PRACTICE EXERCISE

5.2.2 Sketch the effect

A pure scaling affine transformation uses scale factors $S_x = 3$ and $S_y = -2$. Find the image of each of the three objects in Figure 5.14 under this transformation, and sketch them. (Make use of the facts—to be proved later—that an affine transformations maps straight lines to straight lines, and ellipses to ellipses.)

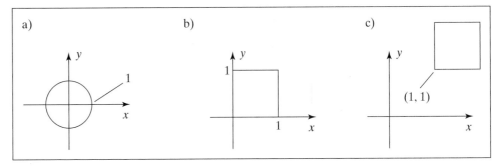

FIGURE 5.14 Objects to be scaled.

PRACTICE EXERCISE

5.2.3 Rotate a point

Use Equation (5.7) to find the image of each of the following points after rotation about the origin:

a. $(2, 3)$ through an angle of $-45°$
b. $(1, 1)$ through an angle of $-180°$.
c. $(60, 61)$ through an angle of $4°$.

In each case check the result on a graphing calculator, and compare numerically the distances of the original point and its image from the origin.

PRACTICE EXERCISE

5.2.4 To shear lines

Consider the shear for which $g = .4$ and $h = 0$. Experiment with various sets of three collinear points to build some confidence that the sheared points are still collinear. Then, assuming that lines do shear into lines, determine into what objects the following line segments shear:

a. the horizontal segment between $(-3, 4)$ and $(2, 4)$;
b. the horizontal segment between $(-3, -4)$ and $(2, -4)$;
c. the vertical segment between $(-2, 5)$ and $(-2, -1)$;
d. the vertical segment between $(2, 5)$ and $(2, -1)$;
e. the segment between $(-1, -2)$ and $(3, 2)$;   ■

5.2.4 The Inverse of an Affine Transformation

Very often when you apply a transformation, T, to a point, you may want to remove the effect of this transformation to restore the point to its previous position by applying another transformation, the so-called **inverse transformation**, which we denote T^{-1}. It is therefore valuable to know how to calculate T^{-1} easily, given the original transformation.

With affine transformations you can do these things. One agreeable property of an affine transformation is summarized by the following fact.

Fact

The inverse transformation of an affine transformation is *another* affine transformation, whose matrix is the inverse matrix of the original.

The inverse matrix exists whenever its determinant is not zero.[3]

To demonstrate this, suppose the subject affine transformation is T with associated matrix M, and apply (T) to point P to produce point Q. So $Q = T(P)$, or $Q = MP$ (This assumes we are writing points using column-matrices [why?]). Applying the inverse transform T^{-1} (if it exists) to Q yields $P = T^{-1}(Q)$. Or simply multiply both sides of the equation $Q = MP$ by the **inverse** of M, denoted M^{-1}, and write

$$P = M^{-1}Q \tag{5.11}$$

We therefore obtain the following matrices for the **elementary inverse transformations:**

- ***Translations:*** If the transformation adds the value a to the x-component and the value b to the y-component then the inverse transformation simply subtracts the offsets rather than adds them, and has the matrix:

$$M^{-1} = \begin{pmatrix} 1 & 0 & -a \\ 0 & 1 & -b \\ 0 & 0 & 1 \end{pmatrix}$$

- ***Scaling*** (use M as found in Equation (5.5)):

$$M^{-1} = \begin{pmatrix} \dfrac{1}{S_x} & 0 & 0 \\ 0 & \dfrac{1}{S_y} & 0 \\ 0 & 0 & 1 \end{pmatrix}$$

- ***Rotation*** (use M as found in Equation (5.7)):

$$M^{-1} = \begin{pmatrix} \cos(\theta) & \sin(\theta) & 0 \\ -\sin(\theta) & \cos(\theta) & 0 \\ 0 & 0 & 1 \end{pmatrix}$$

Notice, as expected, that the inverse of a rotation through angle θ is simply a rotation through angle $-\theta$.

- ***Shearing:*** (using the version of M in Equation (5.8)):

$$M^{-1} = \begin{pmatrix} 1 & -h & 0 \\ 0 & 1 & 0 \\ 0 & 0 & 1 \end{pmatrix}$$

---

[3]   See Appendix 2 for a review of inverse matrices and determinants.

PRACTICE EXERCISES

5.2.5 To invert a shear

Is the inverse of a shear also a shear? Show why or why not.

5.2.6 An inverse matrix

Compute the inverse of the matrix.

$$M = \begin{pmatrix} 3 & 2 & 1 \\ -1 & 1 & 0 \\ 0 & 0 & 1 \end{pmatrix}.$$

Assume (0,0) rator

(-10,10) × (-10,10) ■

5.2.5 To Compose Affine Transformations

> Progress might have been all right once, but it has gone on too long.
>
> *Ogden Nash*
> *(1902–1971)*

Rarely do we want to perform just one elementary transformation; usually an application requires that we build a compound transformation out of several elementary ones. For example, we may want to

- translate by $(3, -4)$
- then rotate through $30°$
- then scale by $(2, -1)$
- then translate by $(0, 1.5)$
- and finally rotate through $-30°$

How do these individual transformations combine into one overall transformation? The process of applying several transformations in succession to form one overall transformation is called **composing** (or **concatenating**) the transformations. As we shall see, when two affine transformations are composed, the resulting transformation is (happily) also affine.

Consider what happens when two 2D transformations, $T_1()$ and $T_2()$, are composed. As suggested in Figure 5.15, affine transformation $T_1()$ maps P into Q, and affine transformation $T_2()$ maps Q into point W. What is the transformation, $T()$, that maps P directly into W? That is, what is the nature of $W = T_2(Q) = T_2(T_1(P))$, and, in particular, is it affine?

Suppose the two transformations are represented by the matrices $\tilde{M}_1$ and $\tilde{M}_2$. Thus $\tilde{P}$ is first transformed to the point $\tilde{M}_1\tilde{P}$, which is then transformed to $\tilde{M}_2(\tilde{M}_1\tilde{P})$. By associativity this is just $(\tilde{M}_2\tilde{M}_1)\tilde{P}$, and so we have

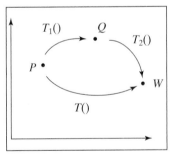

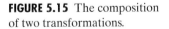

FIGURE 5.15 The composition of two transformations.

$$\tilde{W} = \tilde{M}\tilde{P} \tag{5.12}$$

where the overall transformation is represented by the single matrix

$$\tilde{M} = \tilde{M}_2\tilde{M}_1 \tag{5.13}$$

> *Therefore the composition of two affine transformations is another affine transformation, whose matrix is the product of the matrices of the individual affine transformations.*

When homogeneous coordinates are used, composing affine transformations is accomplished by a simple matrix multiplication. Notice that the matrices appear in *reverse* order to that in which the transformations are applied. If we first apply T_1 with matrix $\widetilde{M}_1$, and then apply T_2 with matrix $\widetilde{M}_2$ to the result, the overall transformation has matrix $\widetilde{M}_2\widetilde{M}_1$, with the second matrix appearing first in the product as you read from left to right. (Just the opposite order will be seen when we transform coordinate systems.)

By applying the same reasoning, we can compose any number of affine transformations simply by multiplying their associated matrices. In this way, transformations based on an arbitrary succession of rotations, scalings, shears, and translations can be formed and captured in a single matrix.

■ **EXAMPLE 5.2.4 Build one**

Build a transformation that

a. rotates through 45 degrees;
b. then scales in x by 1.5 and in y by -2;
c. then translates through $(3, 5)$.

Find the image under this transformation of the point $(1, 2)$.

SOLUTION:

Construct the three matrices and multiply them in the proper order (first one last, and so on) to form:

$$\begin{pmatrix} 1 & 0 & 3 \\ 0 & 1 & 5 \\ 0 & 0 & 1 \end{pmatrix}\begin{pmatrix} 1.5 & 0 & 0 \\ 0 & -2 & 0 \\ 0 & 0 & 1 \end{pmatrix}\begin{pmatrix} .707 & -.707 & 0 \\ .707 & .707 & 0 \\ 0 & 0 & 1 \end{pmatrix} = \begin{pmatrix} 1.06 & -1.06 & 3 \\ -1.414 & -1.414 & 5 \\ 0 & 0 & 1 \end{pmatrix}$$

Now to transform point $(1, 2)$, enlarge it to the triple $(1, 2, 1)$, multiply it by the composite matrix to obtain $(1.94, 0.758, 1)$, and drop the one to form the image point $(1.94, 0.758)$. It is instructive to use a graphing calculator to perform each of these transformations in turn to see how $(1, 2)$ is mapped.

5.2.6 Examples of Composing 2D Transformations

Art is the imposing of a pattern on experience, and our aesthetic enjoyment is recognition of the pattern.
Alfred North Whitehead
(1861–1947)

We examine some important examples of composing 2D transformations, and see how they behave.

■ **EXAMPLE 5.2.5 To Rotate Points about an Arbitrary Point**

So far all rotations have been about the origin. But suppose we wish instead to rotate points about some other point in the plane. As suggested in Figure 5.16, the desired pivot point is $V = (V_x, V_y)$, and we wish to rotate points such as P through angle θ to position Q. To do this we must relate the rotation about V to an elementary rotation about the origin.

Figure 5.16 shows that if we first translate all points so that V coincides with the origin, then a rotation about the origin (which maps P' to Q') will be appropriate. Once done, the whole plane is translated back to restore V to its original location. The rotation therefore consists of the following three elementary trans-formations:

1. Translate point P through vector $\mathbf{v} = (-V_x, -V_y)$:
2. Rotate about the origin through angle θ;
3. Translate P back through $\mathbf{v}$.

Create a matrix for each elementary transformation, and multiply the matrices to produce:

$$\begin{pmatrix} 1 & 0 & V_x \\ 0 & 1 & V_y \\ 0 & 0 & 1 \end{pmatrix} \begin{pmatrix} \cos(\theta) & -\sin(\theta) & 0 \\ \sin(\theta) & \cos(\theta) & 0 \\ 0 & 0 & 1 \end{pmatrix} \begin{pmatrix} 1 & 0 & -V_x \\ 0 & 1 & -V_y \\ 0 & 0 & 1 \end{pmatrix} = \begin{pmatrix} \cos(\theta) & -\sin(\theta) & d_x \\ \sin(\theta) & \cos(\theta) & d_y \\ 0 & 0 & 1 \end{pmatrix}$$

where the overall translation components d_x and d_y are

$$d_x = -\cos(\theta)V_x + \sin(\theta)V_y + V_x$$

$$d_y = -\sin(\theta)V_x - \cos(\theta)V_y + V_y$$

Because the same $\cos(\theta)$ and $\sin(\theta)$ terms appear in this result as in a rotation about the origin, we see that a rotation about an arbitrary point is equivalent to a rotation about the origin followed by a complicated translation through (d_x, d_y) as given.

As a specific example, we find the transformation that rotates points through $30°$ about $(-2, 3)$, and determine to which point the point $(1, 2)$ maps. A $30°$ rotation uses $\cos(\theta) = 0.866$ and $\sin(\theta) = 0.5$. The translation vector is then $(1.232, 1.402)$, and so the transformation applied to any point (P_x, P_y) is

$$Q_x = 0.866P_x - 0.5P_y + 1.232$$

$$Q_y = 0.5P_x + 0.866P_y + 1.402$$

Applying this to $(1, 2)$ yields $(1.098, 3.634)$. This is the correct result, as can be checked with a graphing calculator. (Do it!)

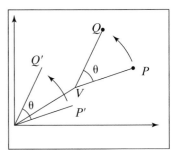

FIGURE 5.16 Rotation about a point.

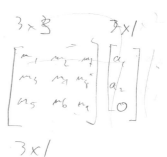

■ EXAMPLE 5.2.6 To Scale and Shear about Arbitrary Pivot Points

In a similar manner we often want to scale all points about some pivot point other than the origin. Because the elementary scaling operation of Equation (5.5) scales points about the origin, we do the same translate–transform–untranslate sequence as for rotations. This and generalizing the shearing operation are explored in the exercises.

■ EXAMPLE 5.2.7 Reflections about a Tilted Line

Consider the line through the origin that makes an angle of β with the x-axis, as shown in Figure 5.17. Point A reflects into point B, and each house shown reflects into the other. We want to develop the transformation that reflects any point P about this axis, to produce point Q. Is this an affine transformation?

To show that it is affine, we build it out of three parts:

- A rotation through angle $-\beta$ (so the rotation axis coincides with the x-axis);
- A reflection about the x-axis;
- A rotation back through β that restores the axis.

FIGURE 5.17 To reflect about a tilted axis.

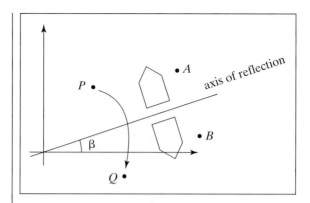

Each of these is represented by a matrix, so this *is* an affine transformation and the overall transformation is given by the product of the three matrices. Check that each of the steps is properly represented in the following three matrices, and that the product is also correct:

$$\begin{pmatrix} c & s & 0 \\ -s & c & 0 \\ 0 & 0 & 1 \end{pmatrix}\begin{pmatrix} 1 & 0 & 0 \\ 0 & -1 & 0 \\ 0 & 0 & 1 \end{pmatrix}\begin{pmatrix} c & -s & 0 \\ s & c & 0 \\ 0 & 0 & 1 \end{pmatrix} = \begin{pmatrix} c^2 - s^2 & -2cs & 0 \\ -2cs & s^2 - c^2 & 0 \\ 0 & 0 & 1 \end{pmatrix}$$

where c stands for $\cos(\beta)$ and s for $\sin(\beta)$. Using trigonometric identities, the final matrix can be written (check this out!)

$$\begin{pmatrix} \cos(2\beta) & \sin(2\beta) & 0 \\ \sin(2\beta) & -\cos(2\beta) & 0 \\ 0 & 0 & 1 \end{pmatrix} \qquad \{\text{a reflection about the axis at angle } \beta\} \qquad (5.14)$$

This has the general look of a rotation matrix, except the angle has been doubled and minus signs have crept into the second column. But in fact it is the matrix for a reflection about the axis at angle β.

PRACTICE EXERCISES

5.2.8 Fixed points of an affine transformation

A point F is a *fixed point* of the affine transformation $T(p) = Mp$ if $T(F) = F$—that is, if F satisfies $FM = F$.

a. Show that when the third column of M is $(0, 0, 1)$, such that there is no translation, the origin is always a fixed point of T.
b. Show that F must always satisfy: $F = \mathbf{d}(I - M)^{-1}$ for some vector $\mathbf{d}$. Does every affine transformation have a fixed point?
c. What is the fixed point for a scaling with scale factors S_x and S_y, about point V?

5.2.9 To find matrices

Give the explicit form of the 3-by-3 matrix representing each of the following transformations:

a. Scaling by a factor of 2 in the x-direction and then rotating about $(2, 1)$.
b. Scaling about $(2, 3)$ and following by translation through $(1, 1)$.
c. Shearing in x by 30%, scaling by 2 in x, and then rotating about $(1, 1)$ through $30°$.

5.2.10 To normalize a box

Find the affine transformation that maps the box with corners $(0, 0), (2, 1), (0, 5)$, and $(-2, 4)$ into the square with corners $(0, 0), (1, 0), (1, 1)$, and $(0, 1)$. Sketch the boxes.

5.2.11 Some transformations commute

Show that uniform scaling **commutes** with rotation, in that the resulting transformation does not depend on the order in which the individual transformations are applied. Show that two translations commute, as do two scalings. Show that differential scaling does not commute with rotation.

5.2.12 Reflection plus a rotation

Show that a reflection in x followed by a reflection in y is the same as a rotation by $180°$.

5.2.13 Two successive rotations

Suppose that $R(\theta)$ denotes the transformation that produces a rotation about the origin through angle θ. Show that applying $R(\theta_1)$ followed by $R(\theta_2)$ is equivalent to applying the single rotation $R(\theta_1 + \theta_2)$. Thus successive rotations are additive.

5.2.14 A succession of shears

Find the composition of a pure shear along the x-axis followed by a pure shear along the y-axis. Is this still a shear? Sketch on your graphing calculator an example of what happens to a square centered at the origin when subjected to a simultaneous shear vs. a succession of shears along the two axes. ▪

5.2.7 Some Useful and Pleasing Properties of Affine Transformations

We have seen how to represent 2D affine transformations with matrices, how to compose complex transformations from a sequence of elementary ones, and the geometric effect of different 2D affine transformations. Before moving on to 3D transformations, it is useful to summarize some general properties of affine transformations. These properties are easy to establish, and because no reference is made to the dimensionality of the objects being transformed, they apply equally well to 3D affine transformations. The only fact about 3D transformations we need at this point is that, like their 2D counterparts, they can be represented in homogeneous coordinates by a matrix.

1. Affine Transformations *Preserve* Affine Combinations of Points

We know that an affine combination of two points P_1 and P_2 is the point

$$W = a_1 P_1 + a_2 P_2, \qquad \text{where } a_1 + a_2 = 1$$

What happens when we apply an affine transformation $T()$ to this point W? We claim $T(W)$ is the *same* affine combination of the transformed points—that is:

Claim: $T(a_1 P_1 + a_2 P_2) = a_1 T(P_1) + a_2 T(P_2)$ (5.15)

(Think about this remarkable result: the a's are the *same* as in the previous equation!)
    For instance, $T(0.7(2, 9) + 0.3(1, 6)) = 0.7T((2, 9)) + 0.3T((1, 6))$.
    The truth of this is simply a matter of linearity. Using homogeneous coordinates, the point $T(\widetilde{W})$ is $\widetilde{M}\widetilde{W}$, and we can do the following steps using linearity of matrix multiplication:

$$\widetilde{M}\widetilde{W} = \widetilde{M}(a_1 \widetilde{P_1} + a_2 \widetilde{P_2}) = a_1 \widetilde{M}\widetilde{P_1} + a_2 \widetilde{M}\widetilde{P_2}$$

which in ordinary coordinates is just $a_1 T(P_1) + a_2 T(P_2)$, as claimed. The property that affine combinations of points are preserved under affine transformations seems fairly elementary and abstract, but it turns out to be pivotal. It is sometimes taken as the **definition** of what an affine transformation is.

2. Affine transformations preserve lines and planes

A very important property of affine transformations is that they preserve collinearity and **flatness**, so the image of a straight line is another straight line. To see this, recall that the parametric representation $L(t)$ of a line through A and B is itself an affine combination of A and B:

$$L(t) = (1 - t)A + tB$$

This is an affine combination of points, so by the previous result the image of $L(t)$ is the same affine combination of the images of A and B:

$$Q(t) = (1 - t)T(A) + tT(B) \tag{5.16}$$

This is another straight line passing through $T(A)$ and $T(B)$. In computer graphics this vastly simplifies drawing transformed line segments: we need only compute the two transformed endpoints $T(A)$ and $T(B)$ and then draw a straight line between *them*! This saves having to transform *each* of the points along the line—an obvious impossibility.

The argument is the same to show that a plane is transformed into another plane. Recall from Equation (4.45) that the parametric representation for a plane can be written as an affine combination of points:

$$P(s, t) = sA + tB + (1 - s - t)C$$

When each point is transformed, this becomes:

$$T(P(s, t)) = sT(A) + tT(B) + (1 - s - t)T(C)$$

which is clearly also the parametric representation of some plane.

Preservation of collinearity and flatness guarantees that polygons will transform into polygons, and planar polygons (those whose vertices all lie in a plane) will transform into planar polygons. In particular, triangles will transform into triangles. Yet another important property will emerge in subsequent sections: affine transformations preserve inbetweenness: If point A lies between points B and C, then point $T(A)$ lies between points $T(B)$ and $T(C)$.

3. Parallelism of Lines and Planes is Preserved

If two lines or planes are parallel, their images under an affine transformation are also parallel. This is easy to show. We first do it for lines. Take an arbitrary line $A + \mathbf{b}t$ having direction $\mathbf{b}$. It transforms to the line given in homogeneous coordinates by $\widetilde{M}(\widetilde{A} + \widetilde{\mathbf{b}}t) = \widetilde{M}\widetilde{A} + (\widetilde{M}\widetilde{\mathbf{b}})t$, which has direction vector $\widetilde{M}\mathbf{b}$. This new direction does *not* depend on point A. Thus two different lines $A_1 + \mathbf{b}t$ and $A_2 + \mathbf{b}t$ that have the same direction will transform into two lines both having the direction $\widetilde{M}\widetilde{\mathbf{b}}$, so they *are* parallel. An important consequence of this property is that *parallelograms map into other parallelograms*.

The same argument applies to planes: its direction vectors (see Equation (4.43)) transform into new direction vectors whose values do not depend on the location of the plane. A consequence of this is that parallelepipeds[4] map into other parallelepipeds.

---

[4]   As we see later, a parallelepiped is the 3D analog of a parallelogram: it has six sides that occur in pairs of parallel faces.

■ EXAMPLE 5.2.8 How Is a Grid Transformed?

Because affine transformations map parallelograms into parallelograms, they are rather limited in how much they can alter the shape of geometrical objects. To illustrate this, apply any 2D affine transformation T to a unit square grid, as in Figure 5.18. Because a grid consists of two sets of parallel lines, T maps the square grid to another grid consisting of two sets of parallel lines. Think of the grid "carrying along" whatever objects are defined in the grid, to get an idea of how the objects are warped by the transformation. This is all that an affine transformation can do: warp figures in the same way that one grid is mapped into another. The new lines can be tilted at any angle; they can be any (fixed) distance apart; and the two new axes need not be perpendicular. And of course the whole grid can be positioned anywhere in the plane.

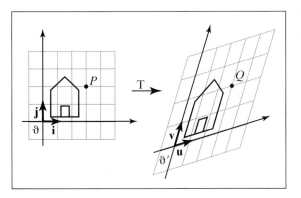

FIGURE 5.18 A transformed grid.

The same result applies in 3D: all a 3D affine transformation can do is map a cubical grid into a grid of parallelepipeds.

4. The Columns of the Matrix Reveal the Transformed Coordinate Frame

It is useful to examine the columns of the matrix M of an affine transformation, for they prescribe how the coordinate frame is transformed. Suppose the matrix M is given by

$$M = \begin{pmatrix} m_{11} & m_{12} & m_{13} \\ m_{21} & m_{22} & m_{23} \\ 0 & 0 & 1 \end{pmatrix} = (\mathbf{m}_1 \vdots \mathbf{m}_2 \vdots \mathbf{m}_3) \tag{5.17}$$

so its columns are $\mathbf{m}_1, \mathbf{m}_2$, and m_3. The first two columns are vectors (their third component is 0) and the last column is a point (its third component is a 1). As always, the coordinate frame of interest is defined by the origin ϕ, and the basis vectors $\mathbf{i}$ and $\mathbf{j}$, which have representations:

$$\phi = \begin{pmatrix} 0 \\ 0 \\ 1 \end{pmatrix}, \qquad \mathbf{i} = \begin{pmatrix} 1 \\ 0 \\ 0 \end{pmatrix} \quad \text{and} \quad \mathbf{j} = \begin{pmatrix} 0 \\ 1 \\ 0 \end{pmatrix}$$

Notice that vector $\mathbf{i}$ transforms into the vector $\mathbf{m}_1$ (check this out):

$$\mathbf{m}_1 = M\mathbf{i}$$

and similarly $\mathbf{j}$ maps into $\mathbf{m}_2$ and ϕ maps into the point m_3. This is illustrated in Figure 5.19a. The coordinate frame $(\mathbf{i}, \mathbf{j}, \phi)$ transforms into the coordinate frame $(\mathbf{m}_1, \mathbf{m}_2, m_3)$, and these new objects are precisely the columns of the matrix.

FIGURE 5.19 The transformation forms a new coordinate frame.

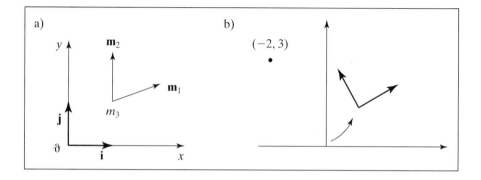

The axes of the new coordinate frame are not necessarily perpendicular, nor must they be unit length. (They are still perpendicular if the transformation involves only rotations and uniform scalings.) Any point $P = P_x\mathbf{i} + P_y\mathbf{j} + \phi$ transforms into $Q = P_x\mathbf{m}_1 + P_y\mathbf{m}_2 + m_3$. It is sometimes very revealing to look at the matrix of an affine transformation in this way.

■ **EXAMPLE 5.2.9 Rotation about a point**

The transformation explored in Example 5.2.5 is a rotation of 30° about the point $(-2, 3)$. This yielded the matrix:

$$\begin{pmatrix} .866 & -.5 & 1.232 \\ .5 & .866 & 1.402 \\ 0 & 0 & 1 \end{pmatrix}$$

As shown in Figure 5.19b, the coordinate frame therefore maps into the new coordinate frame with origin at $(1.232, 1.402, 1)$ and coordinate axes given by the vectors $(0.866, 0.5, 0)$ and $(-0.5, 0.866, 0)$. Note that these axes are still perpendicular, since only a rotation is involved.

5. Relative Ratios Are Preserved

Affine transformations have yet another useful property. Consider a point P that lies at the fraction t of the way between two given points, A and B, as shown in Figure 5.20. Apply affine transformation $T(\ )$ to A, B, and P. We claim the transformed point, $T(P)$, also lies the *same* fraction t of the way between the images $T(A)$ and $T(B)$. This is not hard to show (see the exercises).

As a special case, midpoints of lines map into midpoints. This result pops out a nice geometric result: the diagonals of any parallelogram bisect each other. (*Proof*: Any parallelogram is an affine-transformed square (why?), and the diagonals of a square bisect each other, so the diagonals of a parallelogram also bisect each other.) The same applies in 3D space: the diagonals of any parallelepiped bisect each other.

Interesting aside. In addition to preserving lines, parallelism, and relative ratios, affine transformations also preserve ellipses and ellipsoids, as we will see in Chapter 8!

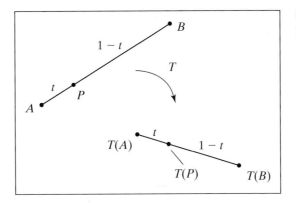

FIGURE 5.20 Relative ratios are preserved.

6. How Is the Area of a Figure Affected by an Affine Transformation?

In CAD applications it is often important to compute the area or volume of an object. For instance, how is the area of a polygon affected when all of its vertices are subjected to an affine transformation? It is clear geometrically that neither translations nor rotations have any effect on the area of a figure, but scalings certainly do, and shearing might.

The result is simple and is developed in the exercises: when the 2D transformation with matrix M is applied to an object, its area is multiplied by the *magnitude of the determinant* of M:

$$\frac{\text{area after transformation}}{\text{area before transformation}} = |\det M| \tag{5.18}$$

In 2D the determinant of M in Equation (5.6) is $|m_{11}m_{12} - m_{12}m_{21}|$.[5] Thus for a pure scaling as in Equation (5.10), the new area is $s_x s_y$ times the original area, whereas for a shear along one axis the new area is the *same* as the original area! Equation (5.21) also confirms that a rotation does not alter the area of a figure, since $\cos^2(\theta) + \sin^2(\theta) = 1$.

In 3D similar arguments apply, and we can conclude that the volume of a 3D object is scaled by $|\det M|$ when the object is transformed by the 3D transformation based on matrix M.

■ EXAMPLE 5.2.9 The Area of an Ellipse

What is the area of the ellipse that fits inside a rectangle with width W and height H?

SOLUTION:

This ellipse can be formed by scaling the unit circle $x^2 + y^2 = 1$ by the scale factors $S_x = W$ and $S_y = H$, a transformation for which the matrix M has determinant WH. The unit circle is known to have area π, and so the ellipse has area $\pi W H$.

7. Every Affine Transformation Is Composed of Elementary Operations

We can construct complex affine transformations by composing a number of elementary ones. It is interesting to turn the question around and ask: what elementary operations reside in a given affine transformation?

---

[5] The determinant of the homogeneous coordinate version is the same (see Appendix 2)

Basically a matrix $\widetilde{M}$ may be factored into a product of elementary matrices in various ways. One particular way of factoring the matrix $\widetilde{M}$ associated with a 2D affine transformation yields the result:

$$\widetilde{M} = (\text{shear})(\text{scaling})(\text{rotation})(\text{translation})$$

That is, any three-by-three matrix $\widetilde{M}$ that represents a 2D affine transformation can be written as the product of (reading right to left) a translation matrix, a rotation matrix, a scaling matrix, and a shear matrix.

In 3D things are somewhat more complicated. The 4-by-4 matrix $\widetilde{M}$ that represents a 3D affine transformation can be written as:

$$\widetilde{M} = (\text{scaling})(\text{rotation})(\text{shear}_1)(\text{shear}_2)(\text{translation})$$

the product of (reading right to left) a translation matrix, a shear matrix, another shear matrix, a rotation matrix, and a scaling matrix.

PRACTICE EXERCISES

5.2.15 The argument generalized

Show that if W is an affine combination of the N points $P_i, i = 1, \ldots, N$, and $T()$ is an affine transformation, then $T(W)$ is the same affine combination of the N points $T(P_i), i = 1, \ldots, N$.

5.2.16 Show that relative ratios are preserved

Consider P given by $A + \mathbf{b}t$, where $\mathbf{b} = B - A$. Find the distances $|P - A|$ and $|P - B|$ from P to A and B, respectively, showing that they lie in the ratio t to $1 - t$. Is this true if t lies outside of the range 0 to 1? Do the same for the distances $|T(P) - T(A)|$ and $|T(P) - T(B)|$ where T is an affine transformation.   ■

5.3 3D AFFINE TRANSFORMATIONS

> There is a fifth dimension, beyond that which is known to man. It is a dimension as vast as space and as timeless as infinity. It is the middle ground between light and shadow, between science and superstition.
>
> *Rod Serling*
> *(1924–1975)*

The same ideas apply to 3D affine transformations as apply to 2D affine transformations, but of course the expressions are more complicated, and it is considerably more difficult to visualize the effect of a 3D transformation.

Again we use coordinate frames, and suppose that we have an origin ϕ and three mutually perpendicular axes in the directions $\mathbf{i}, \mathbf{j}$, and $\mathbf{k}$ (see Figure 5.8). Point P in this frame is given by $P = \phi + P_x\mathbf{i} + P_y\mathbf{j} + P_z\mathbf{k}$, and so has as the representation

$$\widetilde{P} = \begin{pmatrix} P_x \\ P_y \\ P_z \\ 1 \end{pmatrix}$$

Suppose $T()$ is an affine transformation that transforms point $\widetilde{P}$ to point $\widetilde{Q}$. Then, just as in the 2D case, $T()$ is represented by a matrix $\widetilde{M}$, which is now 4 by 4:

$$\widetilde{M} = \begin{pmatrix} m_{11} & m_{12} & m_{13} & m_{14} \\ m_{21} & m_{22} & m_{23} & m_{24} \\ m_{31} & m_{32} & m_{33} & m_{34} \\ 0 & 0 & 0 & 1 \end{pmatrix} \tag{5.19}$$

and we can say that the representation of point $\tilde{Q}$ is found by multiplying $\tilde{P}$ by matrix $\tilde{M}$:

$$\begin{pmatrix} Q_x \\ Q_y \\ Q_z \\ 1 \end{pmatrix} = \tilde{M} \begin{pmatrix} P_x \\ P_y \\ P_z \\ 1 \end{pmatrix} \qquad (5.20)$$

Notice that once again for an affine transformation the fourth row of the matrix is a string of zeroes followed a lone one. (This will cease to be the case when we examine projective matrices in Chapter 7.)

5.3.1 The Elementary 3D Transformations

We consider the nature of elementary 3D transformations individually, and then compose them into general 3D affine transformations.

Translation

For a pure translation, the matrix $\tilde{M}$ has the simple form:

$$\begin{pmatrix} 1 & 0 & 0 & m_{14} \\ 0 & 1 & 0 & m_{24} \\ 0 & 0 & 1 & m_{34} \\ 0 & 0 & 0 & 1 \end{pmatrix}$$

Check that $\tilde{Q} = \tilde{M}\tilde{P}$ is simply a translate in $\tilde{Q}$ by the vector $\mathbf{m} = (m_{14}, m_{24}, m_{34})$.

Scaling

Scaling in three dimensions is a direct extension of the 2D case, having a matrix given by:

$$\begin{pmatrix} S_x & 0 & 0 & 0 \\ 0 & S_y & 0 & 0 \\ 0 & 0 & S_z & 0 \\ 0 & 0 & 0 & 1 \end{pmatrix} \qquad (5.21)$$

where the three constants S_x, S_y, and S_z cause scaling of the corresponding coordinates. Scaling is about the origin, just as in the 2D case. Figure 5.21 shows the effect of scaling in the z-direction by 0.5 and in the x-direction by a factor of two.

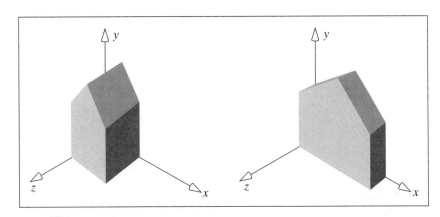

FIGURE 5.21 To scale the basic barn.

Notice that this figure shows various lines, which connect together to form the polygonal faces of the barn, before and after being transformed. It capitalizes on the important fact that straight lines transform to straight lines.

Shearing

Three-dimensional shears appear in greater variety than do their two-dimensional counterparts. The matrix for the simplest elementary shear is the identity matrix with one zero term replaced by some value, as in

$$\begin{pmatrix} 1 & 0 & 0 & 0 \\ f & 1 & 0 & 0 \\ 0 & 0 & 1 & 0 \\ 0 & 0 & 0 & 1 \end{pmatrix} \tag{5.22}$$

which produces $\widetilde{Q} = (P_x, fP_x + P_y, P_z, 1)$; that is, P_y is offset by some amount proportional to P_x, and the other components are unchanged.

Rotations

Rotations in three dimensions are common in graphics, for we often want to rotate an object or a camera in order to obtain different views. There is a much greater variety of rotations in three than in two dimensions, since we must specify an axis about which the rotation occurs, rather than just a single point. One helpful approach is to decompose a rotation into a combination of simpler ones.

Elementary Rotations about a Coordinate Axis The simplest rotation is a rotation about one of the coordinate axes. We call a rotation about the x-axis an *x-roll*, a rotation about the y-axis a *y-roll*, and one about the z-axis a *z-roll*. We present individually the matrices that produce an *x*-roll, a *y*-roll, and a *z*-roll. In each case the rotation is through an angle, β, about the given axis. We define positive angles using a looking-inward convention:

Positive values of β cause a counterclockwise (CCW) rotation about an axis as one looks inward from a point on the positive axis toward the origin.

The three basic positive rotations are illustrated in Figure 5.22.[6]

FIGURE 5.22 Positive rotations about the three axes.

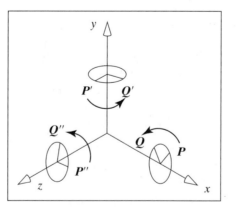

This formulation is also consistent with our notion of 2D rotations: a positive rotation in two dimensions is equivalent to a *z*-roll as we look at the *xy*-plane from a point on the positive *z*-axis.

---

[6] In a left-handed system the sense of a rotation through a positive β would be CCW looking **outward** along the positive axis from the origin. This formulation is used by some authors.

Notice what happens with this convention for the particular case of a 90° rotation:

- For a z-roll, the x-axis rotates to the y-axis.
- For an x-roll, the y-axis rotates to the z-axis.
- For a y-roll, the z-axis rotates to the x-axis.

The following three matrices represent transformations that rotate points through angle β about a coordinate axis. We use the suggestive notation $R_x()$, $R_y()$, and $R_z()$ to denote x-, y-, and z-rolls, respectively. The parameter is the angle through which points are rotated, given in radians, and c stands for $\cos(\beta)$ and s for $\sin(\beta)$.

1. An x-roll:

$$R_x(\beta) = \begin{pmatrix} 1 & 0 & 0 & 0 \\ 0 & c & -s & 0 \\ 0 & s & c & 0 \\ 0 & 0 & 0 & 1 \end{pmatrix} \tag{5.23}$$

2. A y-roll:

$$R_y(\beta) = \begin{pmatrix} c & 0 & s & 0 \\ 0 & 1 & 0 & 0 \\ -s & 0 & c & 0 \\ 0 & 0 & 0 & 1 \end{pmatrix} \tag{5.24}$$

3. A z-roll:

$$R_z(\beta) = \begin{pmatrix} c & -s & 0 & 0 \\ s & c & 0 & 0 \\ 0 & 0 & 1 & 0 \\ 0 & 0 & 0 & 1 \end{pmatrix} \tag{5.25}$$

Note that 12 of the terms in each matrix are the zeros and ones of the identity matrix. They occur in the row and column that correspond to the axis about which the rotation is being made (e.g., the first row and column for an x-roll). They guarantee that the corresponding coordinate of the point being transformed will not be altered! The c and s terms always appear in a rectangular pattern in the other rows and columns.

Aside: Why is the y-roll different? Note that the quantities c and s, or c and $-s$, appear in the rows of the preceding matrices for the elementary rotations. For an x-roll and a z-roll the row containing $-s$ appears **above** the row containing $+s$, whereas for a y-roll it appears **below** the row containing s. This suggests that there is something inherently different about a y-roll. But there isn't; a fact that we explore in the exercises.

■ **EXAMPLE 5.3.1 To rotate the barn**

Figure 5.23 shows a barn in its original orientation (part a), and after a $-70°$ x-roll (part b), a 30° y-roll (part c), and a $-90°$ z-roll (part d), each applied separately. Check these carefully!

■ **EXAMPLE 5.3.2**

Find the point Q after the point $P = (3, 1, 4)$ has been rotated 30° about the y-axis.

SOLUTION:

Using Equation (5.24) with:

FIGURE 5.23 To rotate the basic barn.

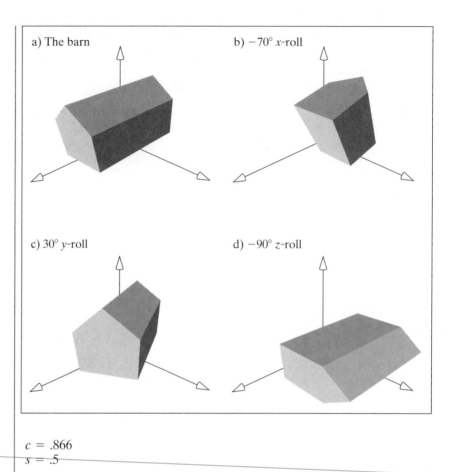

a) The barn   b) $-70°$ x-roll

c) $30°$ y-roll   d) $-90°$ z-roll

$c = .866$
$s = .5$

P is transformed into

$$Q = \begin{pmatrix} c & 0 & s & 0 \\ 0 & 1 & 0 & 0 \\ -s & 0 & c & 0 \\ 0 & 0 & 0 & 1 \end{pmatrix} \begin{pmatrix} 3 \\ 1 \\ 4 \\ 1 \end{pmatrix} = \begin{pmatrix} 4.6 \\ 1 \\ 1.964 \\ 1 \end{pmatrix}$$

As expected, the y-coordinate of the point is not altered.

PRACTICE EXERCISES

5.3.1 To visualize the 90° rotations

Draw a right-handed 3D system and convince yourself that a 90° rotation (CCW looking toward the origin) about each axis rotates the other axes into one another, as specified in the preceding list. What is the effect of rotating a point on the x-axis about the x-axis?

5.3.2 To rotate the basic barn

Sketch the basic barn after each vertex has undergone a 45° x-roll. Repeat for y- and z-rolls.

5.3.3 Do a rotation

Find the image Q of the point $P = (1, 2, -1)$ after a 45° y-roll. Sketch P and Q in a 3D coordinate system and show that your result is reasonable.

5.3.4 Test 90° rotations of the axes

This exercise provides a useful trick for remembering the form of the rotation matrices. Using a rotation of 90°, apply each of the three rotation matrices to each of the standard unit position vectors, **i**, **j**, and **k**. In each case discuss the effect of the transformation on the unit vector.

5.3.5 Is a y-roll indeed different?

The minus sign in Equation (5.24) seems to be in the wrong place—on the lower s rather than the upper one. Here you show that Equations (5.23)–(5.25) are in fact consistent. It's just a matter of how things are ordered. Think of the three axes x, y, and z as occurring cyclically: $x \to y \to z \to x \to y \dots$. If we are discussing a rotation about some current axis (x, y, or z), then we can identify the previous axis and the next axis. For instance, if x is the current axis, then the previous one is z and the next is y. Show that with this naming all three types of rotations use the same equations: $Q_{curr} = P_{curr}$, $Q_{next} = cP_{next} - sP_{prev}$, and $Q_{prev} = sP_{next} + cP_{prev}$. Write these equations out for each of the three possible current axes. ■

5.3.2 To Compose 3D Affine Transformations

Not surprisingly, 3D affine transformations can be composed, and the result is another 3D affine transformation. The thinking is exactly parallel to that which led to Equation (5.13) in the 2D case: to transform first using M_1 and then using M_2 the matrix that represents the overall transformation is the product of the individual matrices M_1 and M_2 that perform the two transformations, with M_2 *premultiplying* M_1:

$$M = M_2 M_1 \tag{5.26}$$

Any number of affine transformations can be composed in this way, and a single matrix results that represents the overall transformation.

Figure 5.24 shows an example, where a barn is first transformed using some M_1, then that transformed barn is again transformed using M_2. The result is the same as the barn transformed once using $M_2 M_1$.

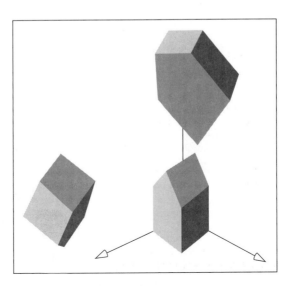

FIGURE 5.24 3D affine transformations composed.

5.3.3 A Combination of Rotations

Results! Why, man, I have gotten a lot of results. I know several thousand things that won't work.

Thomas A. Edison
(1847–1931)

One of the most important distinctions between 2D and 3D transformations is the manner in which rotations combine. In 2D two rotations, say $R(\beta_1)$ and $R(\beta_2)$, combine to produce $R(\beta_1 + \beta_2)$, and the order in which they are combined makes no difference. In 3D the situation is much more complicated, because rotations can be about different axes. The order in which two rotations about different axes are performed *does* matter: 3D rotation matrices do **not** commute. We explore some properties of 3D rotations here, investigating different ways that a rotation can be represented, and see how to create rotations that do a certain job.

It's very common to build a rotation in 3D by composing three elementary rotations: say an *x*-roll followed by a *y*-roll, and then a *z*-roll, each one about a coordinate axis. Using the notation of Equations (5.23)–(5.25) for each individual roll, the overall notation is given by

$$M = R_z(\beta_z)R_y(\beta_y)R_x(\beta_x) \tag{5.27}$$

In this context the angles β_z, β_y, and β_x are often called **Euler**[7] **angles**. We will see that *any* 3D rotation around an axis (that passes through the origin) can be obtained by the product of five matrices for the appropriate choice of Euler angles, and we will see a constructive method for forming the necessary matrices. This implies that three (and only three) values are required to specify a rotation completely!

Some people use a different ordering of rolls to create a complicated rotation. For instance, they might express a rotation as $R_x(\beta_x)R_z(\beta_z)R_y(\beta_y)$: first a *y*-roll then a *z*-roll then an *x*-roll. Because rotations in 3D do not commute this requires the use of different Euler angles β_x, β_z, and β_y to create the same rotation. For each of the possible orderings of the three individuals rolls one uses different Euler angles.

■ **EXAMPLE 5.3.3**

What is the matrix associated with an *x*-roll of 45° followed by a *y*-roll of 30° followed by a *z*-roll of 60°? Direct multiplication of the three component matrices (in the proper reverse order) yields:

$$\begin{pmatrix} .5 & -.866 & 0 & 0 \\ .866 & .5 & 0 & 0 \\ 0 & 0 & 1 & 0 \\ 0 & 0 & 0 & 1 \end{pmatrix} \begin{pmatrix} .866 & 0 & .5 & .0 \\ 0 & 1 & 0 & 0 \\ -.5 & 0 & .866 & 0 \\ 0 & 0 & 0 & 1 \end{pmatrix} \begin{pmatrix} 1 & 0 & 0 & 0 \\ 0 & .707 & -.707 & 0 \\ 0 & .707 & .707 & 0 \\ 0 & 0 & 0 & 1 \end{pmatrix} = \begin{pmatrix} .433 & -.436 & .789 & 0 \\ .75 & .66 & -.047 & 0 \\ -.5 & .612 & .612 & 0 \\ 0 & 0 & 0 & 1 \end{pmatrix}$$

Rotations about an Arbitrary Axis

When using Euler angles we perform a sequence of *x*-, *y*-, and *z*-rolls, that is, rotations about a coordinate axis, in some order. But it can be much easier to work with rotations if we have a way to rotate about an axis that points in an arbitrary direction. Visualize the earth, or a toy top, spinning about a tilted axis. In fact, Euler's theorem states that every rotation can be represented as one of this type:

---

[7] Leonhard Euler, 1707–1783, was a Swiss mathematician of extraordinary ability who made important contributions to all branches of mathematics.

EULER'S THEOREM: *Any rotation (or sequence of rotations) about a point is equivalent to a single rotation about some coordinate axis through that point.*[8]

What is the matrix for such a rotation, and can we work with it conveniently?

Figure 5.25 shows an axis represented by vector **u**, and an arbitrary point P that is to be rotated through angle β about **u** to produce point Q.

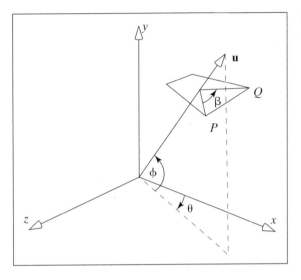

FIGURE 5.25 Rotation about an axis through the origin.

Because **u** can have any direction, it would seem at first glance to be very difficult to find a single matrix that represents such a rotation. But in fact it can be found in two rather different ways, a classic way and a constructive way.

The Classic Way

Decompose the required rotation into a sequence of known steps:

1. Perform two rotations so that **u** becomes aligned with the z-axis.
2. Do a z-roll through angle β.
3. Undo the two alignment rotations to restore **u** to its original direction.

This is reminiscent of rotating about a point in two dimensions: The first step prepares the situation for a simpler known operation; the simple operation is done; and finally the preparation step is undone. The result (discussed in the exercises) is that the transformation requires the multiplication of five matrices:

$$R_{\mathbf{u}}(\beta) = R_z(-\theta)R_y(-\phi)R_z(\beta)R_y(\phi)R_z(\theta) \qquad (5.28)$$

each being a rotation about one of the coordinate axes. This is tedious to do by hand but is straightforward to carry out in a program. However, expanding out the product gives little insight into how the ingredients go together.

The Constructive Way

Using some vector tools, we can obtain a more revealing expression for the matrix $R_{\mathbf{u}}(\beta)$. This approach has become popular recently, and versions of it are described by several authors in *GEMS I* [Glassner90]. We adapt the derivation of Maillot [Maillot90].

---

[8] This is sometimes stated alternatively as: Given two rectangular coordinate systems with the same origin and arbitrary directions of axes, one can always specify a line through the origin such that one coordinate system goes into the other by a rotation about this line [Gellert75].

Figure 5.26 shows the axis of rotation **u**, and we wish to express the operation of rotating point P through angle β into point Q. The method, spelled out in Case Study 5.5, effectively establishes a 2D coordinate system in the plane of rotation as shown. This defines two orthogonal vectors **a** and **b** lying in the plane, and as shown in Figure 5.25b, point Q is expressed as a linear combination of them. The expression for Q involves dot products and cross products of various ingredients in the problem. But because each of the terms is linear in the coordinates of P, it can be rewritten as P times a matrix.

FIGURE 5.26 P rotates to Q in the plane of rotation.

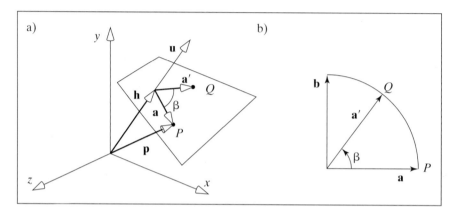

The final result is the matrix:

$$R_u(\beta) = \begin{pmatrix} c + (1-c)u_x^2 & (1-c)u_yu_x - su_z & (1-c)u_zu_x + su_y & 0 \\ (1-c)u_xu_y + su_z & c + (1-c)u_y^2 & (1-c)u_zu_y - su_x & 0 \\ (1-c)u_xu_z - su_y & (1-c)u_yu_z + su_x & c + (1-c)u_z^2 & 0 \\ 0 & 0 & 0 & 1 \end{pmatrix} \quad (5.29)$$

where $c = \cos(\beta)$, and $s = \sin(\beta)$, and (u_x, u_y, u_z) are the components of the unit vector **u**. This looks more complicated than it is. In fact, as we see later, there is so much structure in the terms that, given an arbitrary rotation matrix, we can find the specific axis and angle that produces the rotation (which **proves** Euler's theorem).

As we see later, OpenGL provides a function to create a rotation about an arbitrary axis, called by

```
glRotated(angle, ux, uy, uz);
```

This shows some of the great power of OpenGL to assist the programmer to create the desired results.

■ **EXAMPLE 5.3.4 To rotate about an axis**

Find the matrix that produces a rotation through 45° about the axis $\mathbf{u} = (1, 1, 1)/\sqrt{3} = (0.577, 0.577, 0.577)$.

SOLUTION:

For a 45° rotation, $c = s = 0.707$, and filling in the terms in Equation (5.29), we obtain:

$$R_\mathbf{u}(45°) = \begin{pmatrix} .8047 & -.31 & .5058 & 0 \\ .5058 & .8047 & -.31 & 0 \\ -.31 & .5058 & .8047 & 0 \\ 0 & 0 & 0 & 1 \end{pmatrix}$$

This has a determinant of 1 as expected. Figure 5.27 shows the basic barn translated away from the origin before it is rotated (bottom), after a rotation through 22.5° (middle), and after a rotation of 45° (top) about an axis u.

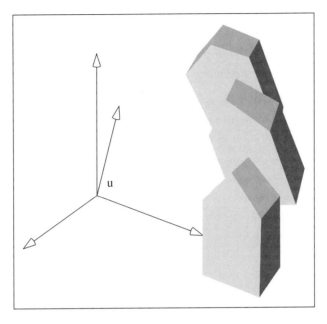

FIGURE 5.27 The basic barn rotated about axis **u**.

Finding the Axis and Angle of Rotation

Euler's theorem guarantees that any rotation is equivalent to a sequence of rotations about coordinate axes. It is useful, when presented with some rotation matrix, to determine the specific axis and angle.

Suppose we are given the nine values m_{ij} for the matrix:

$$R_{\mathbf{u}}(\beta) = \begin{pmatrix} m_{11} & m_{12} & m_{13} & 0 \\ m_{21} & m_{22} & m_{23} & 0 \\ m_{31} & m_{32} & m_{33} & 0 \\ 0 & 0 & 0 & 1 \end{pmatrix}$$

How do we extract the angle β and the unit vector $\mathbf{u}$?

This is surprisingly easy to do by examining Equation (5.29) [Watt92]. First note that the trace of $R_{\mathbf{u}}(\beta)$—that is, the sum of the four diagonal elements—is $2 + (1 + 2c) = 2 + 2\cos(\beta)$. So we can solve for $\cos(\beta)$ directly:

$$\cos(\beta) = \tfrac{1}{2}(m_{11} + m_{22} + m_{33} - 2)$$

Take the arc cosine of this value to obtain β, and use it to find $s = \sin(\beta)$ as well. Now see from Equation (5.29) how pairs of elements of the matrix combine to reveal the individual components of $\mathbf{u}$:

$$u_x = \frac{m_{32} - m_{23}}{2\sin(\beta)}$$

$$u_y = \frac{m_{13} - m_{31}}{2\sin(\beta)} \tag{5.30}$$

$$u_z = \frac{m_{21} - m_{12}}{2\sin(\beta)}$$

■ **EXAMPLE 5.3.5 Find the axis and angle**

Pretend you don't know the underlying axis and angle for the rotation matrix in
Example 5.3.3, and solve for it. The trace is 2.414, so $\cos(\beta) = 0.707$, β must be
45°, and $\sin(\beta) = 0.707$. Now calculate each of the terms in Equation (5.30): they
all yield the value 0.577, so $\mathbf{u} = (1, 1, 1)/\sqrt{3}$; just as we expected.

PRACTICE EXERCISES

5.3.6 Which ones commute?

Consider two affine transformations T_1 and T_2. Is T_1T_2 the same as T_2T_1 when:

a. They are both pure translations?
b. They are both scalings?
c. They are both shears?
d. One is a rotation and one is a translation?
e. One is a rotation and one is a scaling?
f. One is a scaling and one is a shear?

5.3.7 Special cases of rotation about a general axis u

It always helps to see that a complicated result collapses to a familiar one in special
cases. Check that this happens in Equation (5.30) when $\mathbf{u}$ is itself

a. the x-axis, $\mathbf{i}$;
b. the y-axis, $\mathbf{j}$;
c. the z-axis, $\mathbf{k}$.

Specifically, find the rotation matrix, and from it derive all of the relevant terms such
as β, and so forth.

5.3.8 Orthogonal matrices

A matrix is **orthogonal** if its columns are mutually orthogonal unit-length vectors.
Show that each of the three rotation matrices given in Equations (5.23)–(5.25) is orthogonal. What is the determinant of an orthogonal matrix? An orthogonal matrix
has a splendid property: *Its inverse is identical to its transpose* (also see Appendix 2).
Show why the orthogonality of the columns guarantees this. Find the inverse of each
of the three rotation matrices preceding, and show that the inverse of a rotation is
simply a rotation in the opposite direction.

5.3.9 The matrix is orthogonal

Show that the complicated rotation matrix in Equation (5.30) is orthogonal.

5.3.10 Structure of a rotation matrix

Show that for a 3×3 rotation M the three rows are pairwise orthogonal, and the
third is the cross product of the first two.

5.3.11 What if the axis of rotation does not pass through the origin?

If the axis does not pass through the origin but instead is given by $S + \mathbf{u}t$ for some
point S, then we must first translate to the origin through $-S$, apply the appropriate
rotation, and then translate back through S. Derive the overall matrix that results. ■

5.3.4 Summary of Properties of 3D Affine Transformations

The properties noted for affine transformations in Section 5.2.8 apply, of course, to
3D affine transformations. Stated in terms of any 3D affine transformation $T(.)$ having matrix M, they are:

- **Affine transformations preserve affine combinations of points.** If $a + b = 1$, then
  $aP + bQ$ is a meaningful 3D point, and $T(aP + bQ) = aT(P) + bT(Q)$.

- **Affine transformations preserve lines and planes.** Straightness is preserved: The image $T(L)$ of a line L in 3D space is another straight line; the image $T(W)$ of a plane W in 3D space is another plane.
- **Parallelism of lines and planes is preserved.** If W and Z are parallel lines (or planes), then $T(W)$ and $T(Z)$ are also parallel.
- **The columns of the matrix reveal the transformed coordinate frame.** If the columns of M are the vectors $\mathbf{m}_1, \mathbf{m}_2, \mathbf{m}_3$, and the point m_4, the transformation maps the frame $(\mathbf{i}, \mathbf{j}, \mathbf{k}, \phi)$ to the frame $(\mathbf{m}_1, \mathbf{m}_2, \mathbf{m}_3, m_4)$.
- **Relative ratios are preserved.** If P is fraction f of the way from point A to point B, then $T(P)$ is the *same* fraction f of the way from point $T(A)$ to $T(B)$.
- **The effect of transformations on the volumes of objects.** If 3D object D has volume V, then its image $T(D)$ has volume $|\det M|V$, where $|\det M|$ is the absolute value of the determinant of M.
- **Every affine transformation is composed of elementary operations.** A 3D affine transformation may be decomposed into a composition of elementary transformations. This can be done in several ways. See Case Study 5.2.

5.4 HOW TO CHANGE COORDINATE SYSTEMS

> *"They must often change, who would be constant in happiness or wisdom."*
>
> *Confucius*
> *(551–479 B.C.)*

There's another way to think about affine transformations. In many respects it is a more natural approach when modeling a scene. Instead of viewing an affine transformation as producing a different point in a fixed coordinate system, you think of it as producing a new coordinate system in which to represent points.

Aside: A word on notation. To make things fit better on the printed page, we shall sometimes use the notation

$$(P_x, P_y, 1)^T \qquad \text{in place of} \qquad \begin{pmatrix} P_x \\ P_y \\ 1 \end{pmatrix}$$

(Also see Appendix 2.) The superscript T denotes the **transpose**, so we are simply writing the row vector as a transposed column vector.

Suppose we have a 2D coordinate frame #1 as shown in Figure 5.28, with origin ϕ and axes $\mathbf{i}$ and $\mathbf{j}$. Further suppose we have an affine transformation $T(.)$ represented by matrix M, where $T(.)$ transforms coordinate frame #1 into coordinate frame #2, with new origin $\phi' = T(\phi)$, and new axes $\mathbf{i}' = T(\mathbf{i})$ and $\mathbf{j}' = T(\mathbf{j})$.

Now let P be a point with representation $(c, d, 1)^T$ in the new system #2. What are the values of a and b in its representation $(a, b, 1)^T$ in the original system #1? The answer: *simply premultiply* $(c, d, 1)^T$ by M:

$$\begin{pmatrix} a \\ b \\ 1 \end{pmatrix} = M \begin{pmatrix} c \\ d \\ 1 \end{pmatrix} \tag{5.31}$$

To summarize, we have the following theorem:

Suppose coordinate system #2 is formed from coordinate system #1 by the affine transformation M. Further suppose that $(P_x, P_y, P_z, 1)$ are the coordinates of a point P expressed in system #2. Then the coordinates of P expressed in system #1 are MP.

This theorem may seem obvious to some readers, but in case it doesn't, a derivation is developed in the exercises at the end of the section. This result also holds for 3D systems, of course, and we use it extensively when calculating how 3D points are transformed as they are passed down the OpenGL graphics pipeline.

FIGURE 5.28 To transform
a coordinate frame.

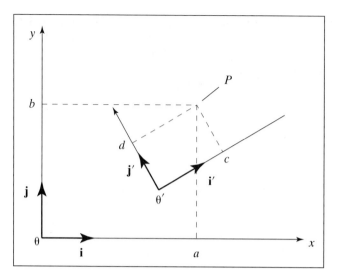

■ **EXAMPLE 5.4.1 To rotate a coordinate system**

Consider again the transformation of Example 5.2.5 that rotates points through 30° about the point $(-2, 3)$. (See Figure 5.23.) This transformation maps the origin ϕ and axes **i** and **j** into the system #2 as shown in that figure. Now consider the point P with coordinates $(P_x, P_y, 1)^T$ in the *new* coordinate system. What are the coordinates of this point expressed in the *original* system #1? The answer is simply MP. For instance, $(1, 2, 1)^T$ in the new system lies at $M(1, 2, 1)^T = (1.098, 3.634, 1)^T$ in the original system. (Sketch this in the figure.) Notice that the point $(-2, 3, 1)^T$, the center of rotation of the transformation, is a *fixed point* of the transformation: $M(2, 3, 1)^T = (2, 3, 1)^T$. Thus if we take $P = (-2, 3, 1)^T$ in the new system, it maps to $(-2, 3, 1)^T$ in the original system (check this visually).

Successive Changes in a Coordinate Frame

Now consider forming a transformation by making two successive changes of the coordinate system. What is the overall effect? As suggested in Figure 5.29, system #1 is converted to system #2 by transformation $T_1(.)$, and system #2 is then transformed to system #3 by transformation $T_2(.)$. Note that system #3 is transformed *relative* to #2.

FIGURE 5.29 To transform
a coordinate system twice.

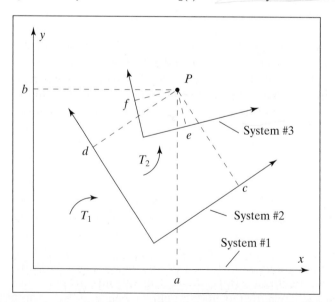

Again the question is: if point P has representation $(e, f, 1)^T$ with respect to system #3, what are its coordinates $(a, b, 1)^T$ with respect to the original system #1?

To answer this, just work backward and collect the effects of each transformation. In terms of system #2 the point P has coordinates $(c, d, 1)^T = M_2(e, f, 1)^T$. And in terms of system #1 the point $(c, d, 1)^T$ has coordinates $(a, b, 1)^T = M_1(c, d, 1)^T$. Putting these together:

$$\begin{pmatrix} a \\ b \\ 1 \end{pmatrix} = M_1 \begin{pmatrix} c \\ d \\ 1 \end{pmatrix} = M_1 M_2 \begin{pmatrix} e \\ f \\ 1 \end{pmatrix} \tag{5.32}$$

The essential point is that when determining the desired coordinates $(a, b, 1)^T$ from $(e, f, 1)^T$ we *first* apply M_2 and *then* M_1, just the *opposite* order as when applying transformations to points.

We summarize this fact for the case of three successive transformations. The result generalizes immediately to any number of transformations.

To transform points

To apply a sequence of transformations $T_1(), T_2(), T_3()$ (in that order) to a point P, where transformation T_i is represented by matrix M_i, form the matrix:

$M = M_3 \times M_2 \times M_1$.

Then P is transformed to MP. That is, to compose each successive transformation M_i you *premultiply* by M_i.

To transform the coordinate system

To apply a sequence of transformations $T_1(), T_2(), T_3()$ (in that order) to the coordinate system, form the matrix:

$M = M_1 \times M_2 \times M_3$.

Then a point P expressed in the transformed system has coordinates MP in the original system. To compose each additional transformation M_i you *postmultiply* by M_i, so that the matrices that multiply P are $M_1, M_2, \ldots, M_i$.

How OpenGL Operates

We shall see in the next section that OpenGL provides tools for successively applying transformations in order to build up an overall current transformation. In fact OpenGL is organized to *postmultiply* each new transformation matrix to combine it with the current transformation. Thus it will sometimes seem more natural to the modeler to think in terms of successively transforming the coordinate system involved, as the order in which these transformations is carried out is the *same* since the order in which OpenGL computes them.

PRACTICE EXERCISES

5.4.1 How transforming a coordinate system relates to transforming a point

We wish to show the result in Equation (5.31). To do this, show each of the following steps.

a. Show that the point P with representation $(c, d, 1)^T$ used in system #2 lies at $c\mathbf{i}' + d\mathbf{j}' + \phi'$.
b. We want to find where this point lies in system #1. Show that the representation (in system #1) of $\mathbf{i}'$ is $M(1, 0, 0)^T$, that of $\mathbf{j}'$ is $M(0, 1, 0)^T$, and that of ϕ' is $M(0, 0, 1)$.

c. Show therefore that the representation of the point $c\mathbf{i}' + d\mathbf{j}' + \phi'$ is $cM(1,0,0)^T + dM(0,1,0)^T + M(0,0,1)^T$.

d. Show that this is the same as $M(c,0,0)^T + M(0,d,0)^T + M(0,0,1)$ and that this is $M(c,d,1)^T$, as claimed.

5.4.2 Using elementary examples

Figure 5.30 shows the effect of four elementary transformations of a coordinate system. In each case the original system with axes x and y is transformed into the new system with axes x' and y'.

FIGURE 5.30 Elementary changes between coordinate systems.

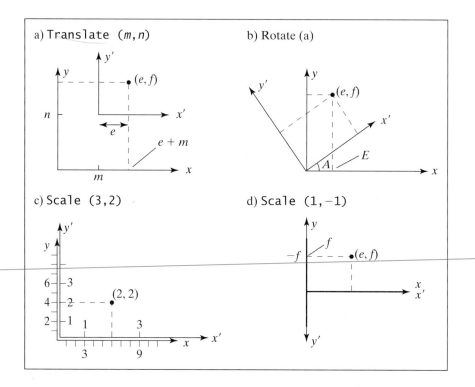

a. Part a shows the effect of a translation through (m,n). Show that point (e,f) in the new system lies at $(e+m, f+n)$ in the original system.

b. Part b shows the effect of a rotation about the origin through A degrees. Show that the point (e, f) in the new system lies at $(e\cos(a) - f\sin(a), e\sin(a) + f\cos(a))$, where $a = \pi A/180$ radians.

c. Part c shows the effect of a scaling of the axes by $(3,2)$. To make the figure clearer, the new and old axes are shown slightly displaced. Show that a point (e, f) in the new system lies at $(3e, 2f)$ in the original system.

d. Part d shows a special case of scaling, a reflection about the x-axis. Show that the point (e, f) lies in the original system at $(e, -f)$. ■

5.5 AFFINE TRANSFORMATIONS USED IN A PROGRAM

We want to see how to apply the theory of affine transformations in a program to carry out scaling, rotating, and translating of graphical objects. We investigate how it is done when OpenGL is used. We look at 2D examples first, as they are easier to visualize, and then move on to 3D examples.

To set the stage, suppose you have a routine house() that draws the house #1 in Figure 5.31. But you wish to draw the version #2 shown that has been rotated through $-30°$ and then translated through $(32, 25)$. This is a frequently encountered situation: an object is defined at a convenient size and position, but we want to draw it (perhaps many times) at different sizes, orientations, and locations.

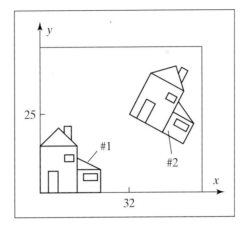

FIGURE 5.31 A rotated and translated house.

As we discussed in Chapter 3, house() would draw the various polylines of the figure. If it were written in basic OpenGL it might consist of a large number of chunks like:

```
glBegin(GL_LINES);
    glVertex2d(V[0].x, V[0].y);
    glVertex2d(V[1].x, V[1].y);
    glVertex2d(V[2].x, V[2].y);
    .... // the remaining points
glEnd();
```

based on some array V[] of points. Or if we used moveTo() and lineTo() as defined in Chapter 3, we could write this as:

```
moveTo(V[0]);
lineTo(V[1]);
lineTo(V[2]);
... // the remaining points
```

In either case we would set up a world window and a viewport with calls like:

```
setWindow(...);
setViewport(...);
```

and we would be assured that all vertex positions V[i] are quietly converted from world coordinates to screen-window coordinates by the underlying window to viewport transformation.

But how do we arrange matters so that house #2 is drawn instead? There is the hard way and the easy way.

The Hard Way

With this approach we construct the matrix for the desired transformation, say M, and build a routine, say transform2D(), that transforms one point into another, such as:

```
Q = transform2D(M, P);
```

The routine produces $\widetilde{Q} = \widetilde{M}\widetilde{P}$. To apply the transformation to each point V[i] in house() we must adjust the source code above, as in

```
moveTo(transform2D(M, V[0])); // move to the transformed point
lineTo(transform2D(M, V[1]));
lineTo(transform2D(M, V[2]));
...
```

so that the *transformed* points are sent to moveTo() and lineTo(). This is workable if the source code for house() is at hand. But it is cumbersome at best, and not *possible* at all if the source code for house() is not available. It also requires tools to create the matrix M in the first place.

The Easy Way

We cause the desired transformation to be applied automatically to each vertex. Just as we know the window-to-viewport mapping is quietly applied to each vertex as part of moveTo() and lineTo(), we can have an additional transformation applied as well. It is often called the **current transformation,** *CT*. We enhance moveTo() and lineTo() so that they first apply this transformation to the argument vertex, and then apply the window-to-viewport mapping. (Clipping is performed at the world window boundary as well.)

Figure 5.32 provides a slight elaboration of the graphics pipeline we introduced in Figure 5.6. When glVertex2d() is called with argument V, the vertex *V* is first transformed by the *CT* to form point *Q*. (In the figure the box labelled 'world-window' actually appear in the pipeline immediately after application of the *CT*.) *Q* is then passed through the window-to-viewport mapping to form point *S* in the screen window. (As we see later, clipping is also performed, inside this last mapping process.)

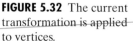

FIGURE 5.32 The current transformation is applied to vertices.

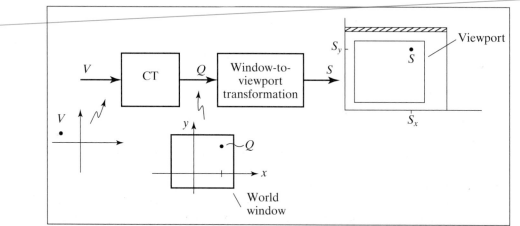

How do we extend moveTo() and lineTo() so they carry out this additional mapping? Happily the transform is done automatically by OpenGL! OpenGL maintains a so-called **modelview matrix,** and every vertex that is passed down the graphics pipeline is multiplied by this modelview matrix. We need only set up the modelview matrix *once* to embody the desired transformation.

OpenGL works entirely in 3D, so its modelview matrix produces 3D transformations. Here we work with the modelview matrix in a restricted way to perform 2D transformations. Later we use its full power. Figure 5.33 shows how we restrict the 3D transformations to carry out the desired 2D transformations. The main idea is that 2D drawing is done in the *xy*-plane: the *z*-coordinate is understood to be zero. Therefore when we transform 2D points, we set the part of the underlying 3D transformation that affects the *z*-coordinate so that it has no effect at all. For example, rotating

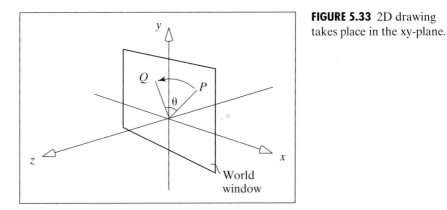

FIGURE 5.33 2D drawing takes place in the xy-plane.

about the origin in 2D is equivalent to rotating about the *z*-axis in 3D, as shown in the figure. Further, although a scaling in 3D takes three scale factors, *Sx*, *Sy*, and *Sz* to scale in the *x*-, *y*-, and *z*-dimensions, respectively, we set the scale factor $Sz = 1$.

The principal routines for altering the modelview matrix are `glRotated()`,[9] `glScaled()`, and `glTranslated()`. These don't set the *CT* directly; instead each one *postmultiplies* the *CT* (the modelview matrix) by a particular matrix, say *M*, and puts the result back into the *CT*. That is, each of these routines creates a matrix *M* as required for the new transformation, and performs:

$$CT = CT*M \qquad\qquad (5.33)$$

The order is important. As we saw earlier, applying *CT* * *M* to a point is equivalent to first performing the transformation embodied in *M*, followed by performing the transformation dictated by the previous value of *CT*. Or if we are thinking in terms of transforming the coordinate system, it is equivalent to performing one additional transformation to the existing current coordinate system.

OpenGL routines for applying transformations in the 2D case are:

- `glScaled(sx, sy, 1.0);` Postmultiply *CT* by a matrix that performs a scaling by *sx* in *x* and by *sy* in *y*. Put the result back in *CT*.

  It is best, but really a matter of taste, to pronounce 'gl' scaled' as 'GL SCALE DEE' since the 'D' specifies the data type of the argument (double), just as it does in "glVertex 2f" or "glColor 3f".
- `glTranslated(dx, dy, 0);` Postmultiply *CT* by a matrix that performs a translation by *dx* in *x* and by *dy* in *y*. Put the result back in *CT*.
- `glRotatef(angle, x, y, z);` Postmultiply *CT* by a matrix that performs a rotation through *angle* degrees about the axis given by the vector with coordinates (*x*, *y*, and *z*). If the vector (*x*, *y*, *z*) is not normalized, OpenGL will normalize it.[10] Put the result back in *CT*. There are two forms of glRotate:

  a. glRotated takes double arguments for angle, *x*, *y*, and *z*, whereas
  b. glRotated takes float arguments for angle *x*, *y*, and *z*.

Since these routines only *compose* a transformation with the *CT*, we need some way to get started: to initialize the *CT* to the identity transformation. OpenGL provides `glLoadIdentity()` and, because these functions can be set to work on any of the matrices that OpenGL supports, we must inform OpenGL which matrix we are altering. This is accomplished using `glMatrixMode(GL_MODELVIEW)`.

Figure 5.34 shows suitable definitions of four new user-defined functions that manage the *CT* and allow us to build up arbitrarily complex 2D transformations. Their pleasing simplicity is possible because OpenGL is doing the hard work.

```
//<<<<<<<<<<<<<<< initCT >>>>>>>>>>>>>>>>>
void initCT(void)
{
        glMatrixMode(GL_MODELVIEW);
        glLoadIdentity();          // set CT to the identity matrix
}
//<<<<<<<<<<<<<<< scale2D >>>>>>>>>>>>>>>>>>>>
void scale2D(double sx, double sy)
{
        glMatrixMode(GL_MODELVIEW);
        glScaled(sx, sy, 1.0); // set CT to CT * (2D scaling)
}
//<<<<<<<<<<<<<<< translate2D >>>>>>>>>>>>>>>>>>
void translate2D(double dx, double dy)
{
        glMatrixMode(GL_MODELVIEW);
        glTranslated(dx, dy, 1.0); // set CT to CT * (2D translation)
}
//<<<<<<<<<<<<<<< rotate2D >>>>>>>>>>>>>>>>>>>>>
void rotate2D(double angle)
{
        glMatrixMode(GL_MODELVIEW);
        glRotated(angle, 0.0, 0.0, 1.0); // set CT to CT * (2D rotation)
}
```

FIGURE 5.34 Routines to manage the *CT* for 2D transformations.

We are now in a position to use 2D transformations. To draw version #2 of the house in Figure 5.35, we next show the code that first rotates the house through −30° and then translates it through (32, 25) the functions used are those just defined in Figure 5.34. Notice that, to get the ordering straight, it calls the operations in opposite order to the way they are applied: *first* the translation operation, and *then* the rotation operation.

FIGURE 5.35 The same transformation viewed as a sequence of coordinate system changes.

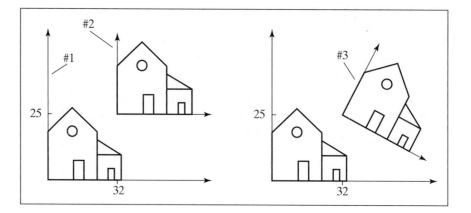

```
setWindow(...);
setViewport(..);      // set the window-to-viewport mapping
initCT();             // get started with the identity
                         transformation
house();              // draw the untransformed house first
translate2D(32, 25);  // CT now includes translation
rotate2D(-30.0);      // CT now includes translation and rotation
house();              // draw the transformed house
```

Notice that we can scale, rotate, and position the house in any manner we choose, and never need to go inside the routine house() or alter it. (In particular, the source code for house() need not be available.)

Some people find it more natural to think in terms of transforming the coordinate system. As shown in Figure 5.35 they would think of first translating the coordinate system through (32, 25) to form system #2, and then rotating *that* system through −30° to obtain coordinate system #3. Because OpenGL applies transformations in the order that coordinate systems are altered, the code for doing it this way first calls translate2D(32, 25) and then calls rotate2D(-30.0). This is, of course, identical to the code obtained doing it in the reverse order, but it has been arrived at through a different thinking process.

We give some further examples to show how easily the *CT* is manipulated to produce various effects.

■ EXAMPLE 5.5.1 To capitalize on rotational symmetry

Figure 5.36a shows a star made of stripes that seem to interlock with one another. This is easy to draw using rotate2D(). Suppose that routine starMotif() draws a part of the star, the polygon shown in Figure 5.36b. (Determining the positions of this polygon's vertices is challenging, and is addressed in Case Study 5.1.) To draw the whole star we just draw the motif five times, each time rotating the motif through an additional 72° or one-fifth of a circle:

```
for(int count = 0; count < 5; count++)
{
   starMotif();
   rotate2D(72.0); // concatenate another rotation
}
```

Visualize what is happening during each of these steps.

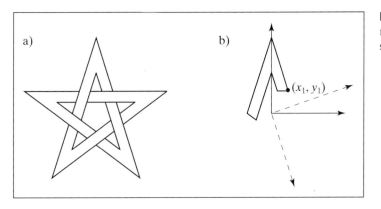

FIGURE 5.36 Successive rotations of the coordinate system.

■ EXAMPLE 5.5.2 Snowflakes

The beauty of a snowflake arises in good measure from its high degree of symmetry. A snowflake has six identical spokes oriented 60° apart, and each spoke is symmetrical about its own axis. It is easy to produce a complex snowflake by designing one-half of a spoke and drawing it 12 times. Figure 5.37a shows a snowflake, based on the motif shown in Figure 5.37b. The motif is a polyline that meanders around above the positive *x*-axis. (To avoid any overlap with other parts of the snowflake, the polyline is kept below the 30° line shown in the figure.)

FIGURE 5.37 Design a snowflake.

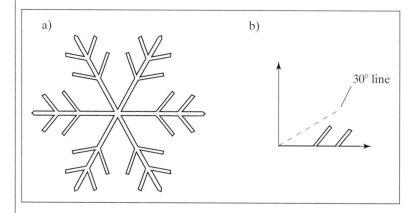

a)

b)

30° line

Each spoke of the snowflake is a combination of the motif and a reflected version. A reflection about the *x*-axis is achieved by the use of scale2D(1,-1)(why?), so the motif plus its reflection can be drawn using

```
flakeMotif();            // draw the top half
scale2D(1.0,-1.0);       // flip it vertically
flakeMotif();            // draw the bottom half
scale2D(1.0,-1.0);       // restore the original axis
```

To draw the entire snowflake just do this six times, with intervening rotations of 60°:

```
void drawFlake()
{
   for(int count = 0; count < 6; count++) // draw a snowflake
   {
      flakeMotif();
      scale2D(1.0,-1.0);
      flakeMotif();
      scale2D(1.0,-1.0);
      rotate2D(60.0);                      // concatenate a 60-
                                           // degree rotation

   }
}
```

■ EXAMPLE 5.5.4 A pattern made from Dino

Figure 5.38 shows two configurations of the dinosaur motif. The dinosaurs are distributed around a circle in both versions, but in one case each dinosaur is

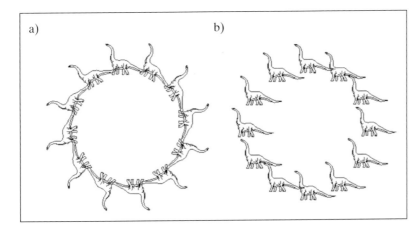

FIGURE 5.38 Two patterns based on a motif. a) each motif is rotated separately b) all motifs are upright.

rotated so that its feet point toward the origin, and in the other all the dinosaurs are upright. In both cases a combination of rotations and translations is used to create the pattern. It is interesting to see how the ordering of the operations affects the picture.

Suppose that drawDino() draws an upright dinosaur centered at the origin. In part a the coordinate system for each motif is first rotated about the origin through a suitable angle (such that the y-axis points directly up through Dino's spine,) and then this coordinate system is translated along its y-axis by H units. Note that the CT is reinitialized each time through the loop so that the transformations don't accumulate. (Think through the transformations you would use if, instead, you took the point of view of transforming points of the motif.)

An easy way to keep the motifs upright as in part b is to prerotate each motif rather than the coordinate system before translating it. If a particular motif is to appear finally at 120°, it is first rotated (while still at the origin) through −120°, then translated up by H units, and then rotated through 120°.

5.5.1 The CT Saved for Later Use

A program can involve rather lengthy sequences of calls to rotate2D(), scale2D(), and translate2D(). These functions make additional or relative changes to the CT, but sometimes we may need to back up to some prior CT in order to follow a different path of transformations for the next instance of a picture. In order to remember the desired CT we make a copy of it and store it in a convenient location. Then at a later point we can restore this matrix as the CT, effectively returning to the transformation that was in effect at that point. We may even want to keep a collection of prior CT's, and return to selected ones at key moments.

To do this you can work with a **stack of transformations**, as suggested by Figure 5.39. The top matrix on the stack is the actual CT, an and operations like rotate2D() compose their transformation with it in the manner described earlier. To save this CT for later use, a copy of it is made and *pushed* onto the stack using a routine pushCT() to be defined in Figure 5.40. This makes the top two items on the stack identical. The top item can now be altered further with additional calls to scale2D() and the like. To return to the previous CT, the top item is simply *popped* off the stack, using popCT(), and discarded. This way we can return to the most recent *CT*, the next most recent *CT*, and so forth, in a last-in, first-out order.

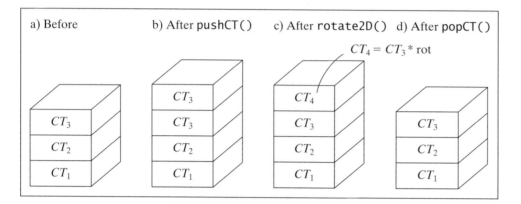

a) Before   b) After pushCT()   c) After rotate2D()   d) After popCT()

$$CT_4 = CT_3 * \text{rot}$$

FIGURE 5.39 A stack of *CT*'s.

The implementation of pushCT() and popCT() is simple, since OpenGL has routines glPushMatrix() and glPopMatrix() to manage several different stacks of matrices. Figure 5.40 shows the required functions. *Caution*: Note that each of them must inform OpenGL which matrix stack is being affected. Additionally, when working with stacks there is a problem with popping an empty stack. In the case of OpenGL, popping a stack that contains only a single matrix is an error, so it is important to test the number of matrices on the stack before popping. Happily, OpenGL provides a query function to determine how many matrices remain on the stack, using glGet(GL_MODELVIEW_STACK_DEPTH). So the pseudocode that follows prevents serious stack underflow errors.

```
void pushCT(void)
{
        glMatrixMode(GL_MODELVIEW);
        glPushMatrix();              // push a copy of the top matrix
}
void checkStack(void)
{
   // pop the CT stack only if the stack depth is greater than 1
        if (glGet (GL_MODELVIEW_STACK_DEPTH() = 1) )
                // do something different
        else
                popCT();
}
void popCT(void)
{
        glMatrixMode(GL_MODELVIEW);
        glPopMatrix(); // pop the top matrix from the stack
}
```

FIGURE 5.40 Routines to check stack depth, save and restore *CT*'s.

■ **EXAMPLE 5.5.5 Tilings made easy**

Many beautiful designs called **tilings** appear on walls, pottery, and fabric all over the world. They are based on the repetition, both horizontally and vertically, of a basic motif. Consider tiling the window with some motif, as suggested in Figure 5.41. The motif is drawn centered in its own coordinate system as shown in part a, using some routine `motif()`. Copies of the motif are drawn L units apart in the x-direction, and D units apart in the y-direction, as shown in part b.

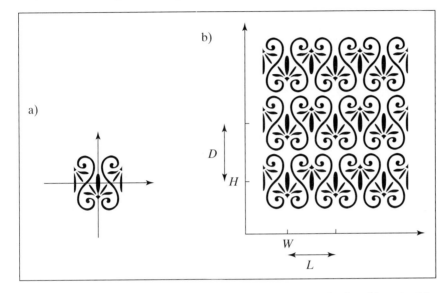

FIGURE 5.41 A tiling based on a motif. a) the motif, b) the tiling.

Figure 5.42 shows how easily the coordinate system can be manipulated in a double loop to draw the tiling. The CT is restored after drawing each row, so it returns to the start of that row, ready to move up to start the next row. In addition, the whole block of code is surrounded with a `pushCT()` and a `popCT()`, so that after the tiling has been drawn the CT is returned to its initial value, in case more drawing needs to be done.

FIGURE 5.42 A hexagonal tiling

```
pushCT();                    // so we can return here
translate2D(W, H);              // position for the first motif
for(row = 0; row < 3; row++) // draw each row
{
   pushCT();
   for(col = 0; col < 4; col++)// draw the next set of columns
   {
      motif();
      translate2D(L, 0);       // move to the right
   }
   popCT();                   // back to the start of this row
   translate2D(0, D);         // move up to the next row
}
popCT();                      // back to where we started
```

PRACTICE EXERCISES

5.5.1 A hexagonal tiling

A hexagonal pattern provides a rich setting for tilings, since regular hexagons fit together neatly as in a beehive. Figure 5.43 shows 9 columns of stacked 6-gons. Here the hexagons are shown empty, but we could draw interesting figures inside them. Write code that will draw this pattern of hexagons. ■

5.5.2

Repeat the previous exercise, but prompt the user to enter values for the number of rows and columns to appear in the tiling.

5.5.3

Repeat the previous exercise, but draw a tiling consisting of tightly packed squares instead of hexagons, with a user-supplied number of rows and columns, and draw a simple polyline drawing inside of each square.

FIGURE 5.43 A simple hexagonal tiling.

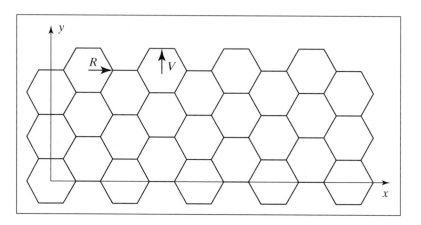

5.6 TO DRAW 3D SCENES WITH OPENGL

Many of the brightly colored tile-covered walls and floors of the Alhambra in Spain show us that the Moors were masters in the art of filling a plane with similar interlocking figures, bordering each other without gaps. What a pity that their religion forbade them to make images!

M. C. Escher
(1898–1972)

We introduced the drawing of 2D objects in Chapter 3. These functions establish a window and viewport, and they do line drawing through moveTo() and lineTo(). So far in this chapter we have added the notion of the *CT*, and provided functions that perform 2D rotations, scalings, and translations. These 2D transformations are really just special cases of 3D transformations: they basically ignore the third dimension.

In this section we examine how 3D affine transformations are used in an OpenGL-based program. The main emphasis is on transforming objects in order to orient and position them as desired in a 3D scene. Not surprisingly it is all done with matrices, and OpenGL provides the necessary functions to build and use the required matrices. Further, the matrix stacks maintained by OpenGL make it easy to set up a transformation for one object, and then return to a previous transformation, in preparation for transforming another object.

It is very satisfying to build a program that draws different scenes using a collection of 3D transformations. Experimenting with such a program also improves your ability to visualize what the various 3D transformations do. (These 3D transformations are notoriously difficult to visualize, involving the several rotations and translations, so any help we can glean from OpenGL is very welcome.)

OpenGL makes it easy for the programmer to set up a camera that takes a snapshot of the scene from a particular point of view. The camera is created with a matrix as well, and we study the details of how this is done in Chapter 7. Here we just use an OpenGL tool to set up a reasonable camera, so that attention can be focused on transforming objects. Granted we are using a tool before seeing exactly how it operates, but the payoff is high: you can make impressive pictures of 3D scenes with a few simple calls to OpenGL functions.

5.6.1 An Overview of the Viewing Process and the Graphics Pipeline

All of our 2D drawing so far has actually used a special case of 3D viewing, based on a simple parallel projection. We have been using the camera suggested in Figure 5.44. The camera has an eye along with a distinguished point called **look**. (Since the programmer knows the scene it is not difficult to identify the look point as a point of particular interest). Keep in mind that, although we draw the eye as if it belonged to some person or animal, this is just to assist in developing intuition. In fact, eye is simply a point located somewhere in 3D space. we say it is *oriented* in a certain direction; this, too, is designed to assist the reader better to understand the viewing process. The **view volume** (discussed more thoroughly in Chapter 7) of the camera is a rectangular parallelepiped, whose four side walls are determined by the border of the window, and whose other two walls are determined by a **near plane** and a **far plane**. Points lying inside the view volume are projected onto the window along lines parallel to the z-axis; the 3D point (x_1, y_1, z_1) projects to $(x_1, y_1, 0)$. Points lying outside the view volume are clipped off. A separate **viewport transformation** maps the projected points from the window to the viewport on the display device.

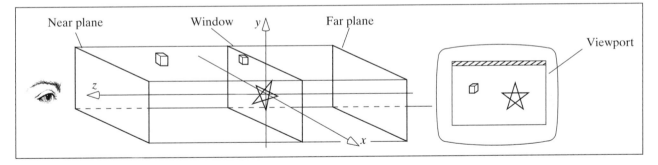

FIGURE 5.44 Simple viewing used in OpenGL for 2D drawing.

Now we move into 3D graphics and place 3D objects in a scene. For the examples here we continue to use a parallel projection. (The more realistic and familiar **perspective projection**, for which more remote objects appear smaller than nearby objects, is introduced in Chapter 7.) Therefore we use the same camera as in Figure 5.44, but allow it to have a more general position and orientation in the 3D scene, in order to produce better views of the scene.

Figure 5.45 shows such a camera immersed in a scene; the scene consists of a block, part of which lies outside the view volume. The image produced by this camera is also shown.

FIGURE 5.45 A camera to produce parallel views of a scene.

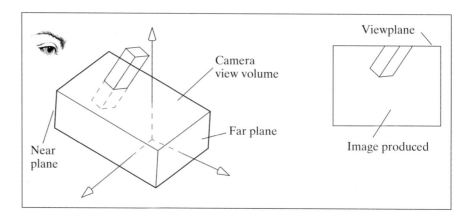

We saw in the previous section that OpenGL provides the three functions `glScaled(..)`, `glRotated(..)`, and `glTranslated(..)` for applying modeling transformations to a shape. The block in Figure 5.45 is in fact a cube that has been stretched, rotated, and translated as shown. OpenGL also provides functions for defining the view volume and its position in the scene.

The graphics pipeline implemented by OpenGL does its major work through matrix transformations, so we first give insight into each of the matrices in the pipeline. At this point it is important only to grasp the basic idea of how each matrix operates; in Chapter 7 we give a detailed discussion. Figure 5.46 shows the simplified pipeline. Each vertex of an object is passed through this pipeline with a call such as `glVertex3d(x, y, z)`. The vertex is multiplied by the various matrices shown; it is clipped if necessary, and if it survives clipping it is ultimately mapped onto the viewport. Each vertex encounters three matrices:

FIGURE 5.46 The OpenGL pipeline (slightly simplified).

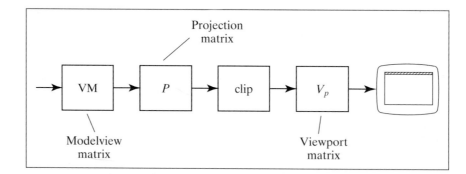

- The **modelview matrix**
- The **projection matrix**
- The **viewport matrix**

The **modelview matrix** basically provides what we have been calling the *CT*. It combines two effects: the sequence of modeling transformations applied to objects, and the transformation that orients and positions the camera in space (hence its peculiar name *modelview*). Although it is a single matrix in the actual pipeline, it is easier to think of it as the product of two matrices—a modeling matrix M and a viewing matrix V. The modeling matrix is applied first, and then the viewing matrix, so the modelview matrix is in fact the product VM. (Why?)

Figure 5.47 suggests what the *M* and *V* matrices do, for the situation shown in Figure 5.45 where a camera is oriented down on a scene consisting of a block. Part a shows a unit cube centered at the origin. A modeling transformation based on *M* scales, rotates, and translates the cube into block shown in part b. Part b also shows the relative position of the camera's view volume.

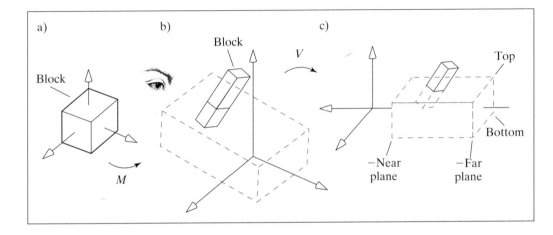

FIGURE 5.47 Effect of the modelview matrix in the graphics pipeline. a) before the transformations, b) after the modeling transformation, c) after the modelview transformation.

The *V* matrix is now used to rotate and translate the block into a new position. The specific transformation used is that which would carry the camera from its position in the scene to its generic position. This generic position has the camera's eye at the origin and the view volume aligned with the *z*-axis, as shown in part c. The vertices of the block are now positioned (that is, their coordinates have the proper values) so that projecting them onto a plane such as the near plane yields the proper values for displaying the projected image. So the matrix *V* in fact effects a change of coordinates of the scene vertices into the **camera's coordinate system**. (Camera coordinates are sometimes also called **eye coordinates**.) To inform OpenGL that we wish it to operate on the modelview matrix we call `glMatrixMode(GL_MODELVIEW)`.

In the camera coordinate system the edges of the view volume are parallel to the *x*-, *y*-, and *z*-axes. The view volume extends from *left* to *right* in *x*, from *bottom* to *top* in *y*, and from *near* to *far* in *z*, as shown. When the vertices of the original cube have passed through the entire modelview matrix, they are located as shown in part c.

The **projection matrix** scales and translates each vertex in a particular way, so that all those that lie inside the view volume will lie inside a *standard cube* that extends from −1 to 1 in each dimension. (When perspective projections are being used, this matrix does quite a bit more, as we will see in Chapter 7.) This matrix effectively squashes the view volume into the cube centered at the origin. This cube is a particularly efficient boundary against which to clip objects, as we see in Chapter 7. Scaling the block in this fashion might badly distort the picture, of course, but this distortion will be compensated for in the viewport transformation. The projection matrix also reverses the sense of the *z*-axis, so that increasing values of *z* now represent increasing values of depth of a point from the eye. Figure 5.48 shows how the block is transformed into a different block by this transformation. To inform OpenGL that we wish it to operate on the projection matrix we call `glMatrixMode(GL_PROJECTION)`.

(Notice that the view volume of the camera need never be created or modeled as a parallelepiped itself. It is defined only as the particular shape that the projection matrix converts into the standard cube!)

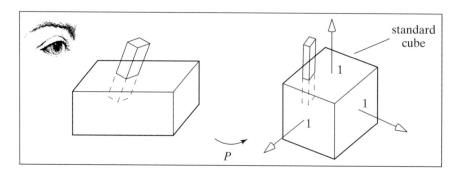

Clipping is now performed automatically, which eliminates the portion of the
block that lies outside the standard cube.

Finally, the **viewport matrix** maps the surviving portion of the block into a 3D viewport. This matrix maps the standard cube into a block shape whose x- and y-values extend across the viewport (in screen coordinates), and whose z-component extends
from 0 to 1 and retains a measure of the depth of each point, as shown in Figure 5.49.
This measure of depth makes hidden surface removal particularly efficient.

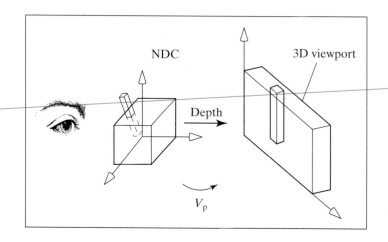

Summary of the Modelview Process

This overview has outlined how the OpenGL graphics pipeline operates, showing
that transformations are a central ingredient. Each vertex of an object is subjected
to a sequence of transformations that carry it from world coordinates into eye coordinates, then into a neutral system specially designed for clipping, and finally into
the right coordinate system for proper display. Each transformation is effected by a
matrix multiplication.

Aside: Some important details of the pipeline have been suppressed in this first
overview. When perspective projections are used, we need to include a *perspective
division* that capitalizes on a property of homogeneous coordinates. And of course
many interesting details lurk in the last step of actually rendering the image, such as
computing the color of pixels in between vertices.

5.6.2 Some OpenGL Tools for Modeling and Viewing

We now some functions that OpenGL provides for modeling and setting the camera,
and how to use them. It turns out to be very useful to use an aviation analogy when you

are trying to develop intuition as to where the camera is located and how it is pointed. This replaces the camera that takes the picture with an airplane that is flying through some point aimed in some direction. Figure 5.51 shows such an airplane, and it might be used by the programmer to conjure up a vivid image of how the camera is positioned and oriented. Because there are so many terms used for planes, it is best to avoid too much use of the term plane here; the same can be said about the term camera. So we introduce a different term, which is already a familiar staple in the television industry: the **jib camera**. Figure 5.50 shows a jib camera which is suspended at the of a long boom; the boom in turn rides on a powered tripod that can be wheeled through the scene by the cinematographer, who rides atop the tripod and controls both the path of the tripod and the exact positioning of the camera. The cinematographer rides on the apex of the tripod around the jib camera as it wheels through the scene, bobbing up and down to get the desired shots.

FIGURE 5.50 A jib camera used in television production.

1. Three functions are used to set viewing transformations

The following functions are normally used to modify the modelview matrix, so the modelview matrix is first made current by executing: `glMatrixMode(GL_MODELVIEW);`

- `glScaled(sx, sy, sz);` Postmultiply the current matrix by a matrix that performs a scaling by sx in x, by sy in y, and by sz in z. Put the result back in the current matrix.
- `glTranslated(dx, dy, dz);` Postmultiply the current matrix by a matrix that performs a translation by dx in x, by dy in y, and by dz in z. Put the result back in the current matrix.
- `glRotated(angle, ux, uy, uz);` Postmultiply the current matrix by a matrix that performs a rotation through *angle* degrees about the axis that passes through the origin and the point (ux, uy, uz). Put the result back in the current matrix.

2. Set the camera in OpenGL (for a parallel projection)

`glOrtho(left,right,bottom,top,near,far);` establishes as a view volume a parallelepiped that extends from[11] `left` to `right` in x, from `bottom` to `top` in y, and from `near` to `far` in z. (Since this definition operates in eye coordinates, the camera's eye is at the origin, oriented down the negative z-axis.) This function creates a matrix and postmultiplies the current matrix by it. (We show in Chapter 7 precisely what values this matrix contains.)

---

[11] All parameters of `glOrtho()` are of the `GLdouble`.

Thus to set the projection matrix use:

```
glMatrixMode(GL_PROJECTION); // make the projection matrix
                                current
glLoadIdentity();               // set it to the identity matrix
glOrtho(left, right, bottom, top, near, far); // multiply it by
                                the new matrix
```

Because the default camera is located at the origin oriented down the negative z-axis, using a value of 2 for near means to place the near plane at $z = -2$—that is, 2 units in front of the eye. Similarly, using 20 for far places the far plane 20 units in front of the eye.

3. To position and aim the camera

OpenGL provides a function that makes it easy to set up a basic camera:

```
gluLookAt(eye.x, eye.y, eye.z, look.x, look.y, look.z, up.x,
up.y, up.z);
```

creates the view matrix and postmultiplies the current matrix by it. Its ultimate goal is to establish a coordinate system—that is, to compute the directions of three mutually orthogonal unit vectors, which we shall call **u**, **v**, and **n**. **n** is the normalized version of eye (the eye location) – look (the look at position); this is a vector pointing from the jet intake to its exhaust. We call **n** the **longitudinal axis** and call the axis through the plane from one wing to the other the **transverse axis**. The vectors are based on information that must be reasonably simple for the application programmer to enter into the program.

The function gluLookAt() takes as parameters the eye position, eye, of the camera and the look-at point, look. It also takes an approximate up direction, up. The first two are simple. Since the programmer knows where the interesting parts of the scene are situated, it is usually straightforward to choose reasonable values for eye and look for good starting camera positions of the scene. Figure 5.51 shows a plane's orientation relative to the world, along with the **n**, **v**, and **u** vectors. The aviation terms, **pitch**, **roll**, and **yaw** are used here to describe the airplane's rotations.

- **Pitch**—the angle between the longitudinal axis and world horizontal (Figure 5.51a).
- **Roll**—the angle between the transverse axis and the world (Figure 5.51b).
- **Yaw**—the angle between the longitudinal axis and some basic "compass" direction in the world the longitudinal axis causing a change in the direction of the plane's flight (Figure 5.51c).

FIGURE 5.51 A description of the airplane's rotations: pitch, roll, and yaw.

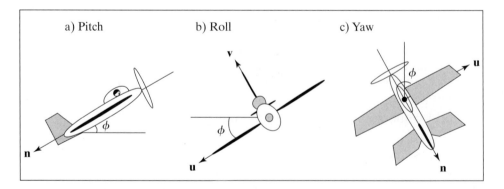

It is much more difficult to choose a proper direction for **up**. Recall that when the code is written, the programmer may have little idea of the plane's orientation in the running program at any particular point since the plane may have been flown through complicated loops and rolls. As a first guess up_{guess} is most often set to $(0, 1, 0)$; this suggests an **up** direction parallel to the *y*-axis. On the other hand given any orientation of the plane, with its vector **n** running from jet intake to tailpipe, we must be able to compute two mutually orthogonal unit vectors **u** and **v** in order to construct a coordinate system for the plane(see Figure 5.51.) For an airplane, visualize that *n* points from the jet intake (front of plane) to the tailpipe. Each rotation is through the angle ϕ about the axis suggested in the figure. The figure shows each rotation through the angle ϕ.

Be aware that an up vector perpendicular to **n** is very difficult for the application programmer to estimate. The **n** vector is simply a normalized version of eye – look. We see next how to implement an appropriate up vector, up_{true}. We start by setting it to be parallel to the *y*-axis, $up_{guess} = (0, 1, 0)$.

We want gluLookAt (...) to set the *V* part of the modelview matrix *VM*. Therefore it is invoked before any modeling transformations are added, since subsequent modeling transformations will postmultiply the modelview matrix. Consequently to use gluLookAt() follow the sequence:

```
glMatrixMode(GL_MODELVIEW);      // make the modelview matrix
                                 current
glLoadIdentity();                // start with a unit matrix
gluLookAt(eye.x, eye.y, eye.z,   // the eye position
     look.x, look.y, look.z,     // the "look at" point
     0, 1, 0)                    // approximation to the uptrue
                                 direction
```

■ EXAMPLE 5.6.1 Set up a typical camera

Cameras are often set to look down on the scene from some nearby position. Figure 5.52 shows the camera with its eye situated at eye $= (4, 4, 4)$ oriented at the origin with look $= (0, 1, 0)$. The up_{guess} direction is set initially to $up_{guess} = (0, 1, 0)$. Suppose we also want the view volume to have a width of 6.4, a height of 4.8 (so its aspect ratio is 640/480), and to set near to 1 and far to 50. This camera would be established using:

```
glMatrixMode(GL_PROJECTION);  // set the view volume
glLoadIdentity();
glOrtho(-3.2, 3.2, -2.4, 2.4, 1, 50);
glMatrixMode(GL_MODELVIEW);   // place and aim the camera
glLoadIdentity();
gluLookAt(4, 4, 4, 0, 1, 0, 0, 1, 0);
```

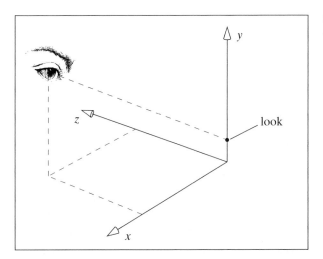

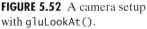

FIGURE 5.52 A camera setup with gluLookAt().

The exercises show the specific values that get placed in the modelview matrix. Notice that since the eye is above the origin oriented down the negative z-axis, the vector up_{true} will not be along the y-axis, but instead tilted forward. Visualize the plane oriented straight down, in which case up_{true} is parallel to the ground! In Chapter 7, we discuss how this function operates and also develop flexible tools for establishing the camera. For those curious about what values gluLookAt() actually places in the modelview matrix, see the exercises.

PRACTICE EXERCISES

5.6.1 What does gluLookAt() do?

We know that gluLookAt() builds a matrix that converts world coordinates into eye coordinates. Figure 5.53 shows the camera as a coordinate system suspended in the world, with its origin at *eye*, and oriented according to its three mutually perpendicular unit vectors **u**, **v**, and **n**. The eye is oriented in the direction −**n**. gluLookAt() uses the parameters *eye*, *look*, and **up**guess to create **u**, **v**, and **n**. The formulas it uses are developed in Chapter 7.

FIGURE 5.53 A world coordinate system transformed into camera coordinates.

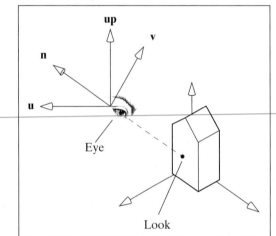

5.6.3 To Draw Elementary Shapes Provided by OpenGL

We see in the next chapter how to create our own 3D objects, but at this point we need some 3D objects to draw, in order to experiment with setting and using cameras. The GLUT provides several ready-made 3D objects (Figure 5.54). These include a sphere, a cone, a torus, the five Platonic solids (discussed in Chapter 6), and the famous teapot. Each is available as a **wireframe** model (one appearing as a collection of wires connected end to end) and as a solid model with faces that can be shaded.

FIGURE 5.54 Shapes available in the GLUT.

- **cube:** glutWireCube(GLdouble size) **Each side is of length** size
- **sphere:** glutWireSphere(GLdouble radius, GLint nSlices, GLint nStacks)
- **torus:** glutWireTorus(GLdouble inRad, GLdouble outRad, GLint nSlices, GLint nStacks)
- **teapot:** glutWireTeapot(GLdouble size)

There is also a `glutSolidCube()`, `glutSolidSphere()`, and so on, that we use later. The shape of the torus is determined by its inner radius `inRad` and its outer radius `outRad`. The sphere and torus are approximated by polygonal faces; you can adjust the parameters `nSlices` and `nStacks` to specify how many faces to use in the approximation. The view of Figure 5.55 is oriented along the z-axis with the x-axis pointing to the right and the y-axis pointing up. Envision a pizza or donut; nSlices specifies the number of slices into which you have cut the pizza around the z-axis. In the figure nSlices is 8.

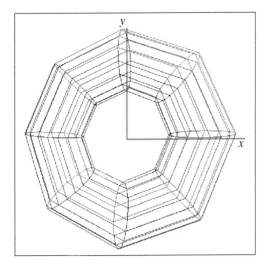

FIGURE 5.55 A torus. How many **nSlices?**

If you rotate the torus so that its z-axis is oriented upward, either side is an approximate circle in the form of a polygon with a certain number of segments. This number is called nStacks and in Figure 5.56 `nStacks` is 16.

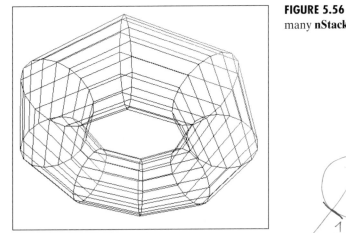

FIGURE 5.56 A torus. How many **nStacks?**

The GLUT provides four additional Platonic solids, which are discussed in Chapter 6. These are generated by the functions:

- **tetrahedron:** `glutWireTetrahedron()`
- **octahedron:** `glutWireOctahedron()`

- **dodecahedron:** `glutWireDodecahedron()`
- **icosahedron:** `glutWireIcosahedron()`

Others, generated by both the GLUT and GLU, are also of great interest:

- **cone:** `glutWireCone(GLdouble baseRad, GLdouble height, GLint nSlices, GLint nStacks)`
- **tapered cylinder:** `gluCylinder(GLUquadricObj * qobj, GLdouble baseRad, GLdouble topRad, GLdouble height, GLint nSlices, GLint nStacks)`

The axes of the cone and tapered cylinder coincide with the z-axis. Their bases rest on the $z = 0$ plane, and they extend to $z = $ `height` along the z-axis. The radius of the cone and tapered cylinder at $z = 0$ is given by `baseRad`. The radius of the tapered cylinder at $z = $ `height` is `topRad`. As with the torus and sphere there are nSlices subdivisions about the z- axis of the cone and cylinder, and nStacks polygons along the z-axis of these objects.

> The **tapered cylinder** is actually a *family* of shapes, distinguished by the value of `topRad`. When `topRad` is 1, there is no taper: this is the classic **cylinder**. When `topRad` is 0, the tapered cylinder is identical to the **cone**.

Note that drawing the tapered cylinder in OpenGL requires some extra work, because it is a special case of a quadric surface, as we shall see in Chapter 6. To draw it you must 1) define a new quadric object, 2) set the drawing style (`GLU_LINE` for a wireframe, `GLU_FILL` for a solid rendering), and 3) draw the object:

```
GLUquadricObj * qobj = gluNewQuadric(); // make a quadric object
gluQuadricDrawStyle(qobj,GLU_LINE);     // set style to wireframe
gluCylinder(qobj, baseRad, topRad, nSlices, nStacks); // draw the cylinder
```

We next employ some of these shapes in two substantial examples that focus on using affine transformations to model and view a 3D scene. The complete program to draw each scene is given. A great deal of insight can be obtained if you enter these programs and produce the figures, and then see the effect of adjusting the various parameters.

■ **EXAMPLE 5.6.2 A scene composed of wireframe objects**

Figure 5.57 shows a scene with several objects disposed at the corners of a unit cube. The cube has one corner at the origin. Seven objects appear at various corners of the cube, all drawn as **wireframes**.

The camera is given a view volume that extends from −2 to 2 in y, with an aspect ratio of aspect = 640/480. Its near plane is at $N = 0.1$, and its far plane is at $F = 100$. This is accomplished using:

```
glOrtho(-2.0* aspect, 2.0* aspect, -2.0, 2.0, 0.1, 100);
```

The camera is positioned with $eye = (2, 2, 2)$, $look = (0, 0, 0)$, and $up = (0, 1, 0)$ using:

```
gluLookAt(2.0, 2.0, 2.0, 0.0, 0.0, 0.0, 0.0, 1.0, 0.0);
```

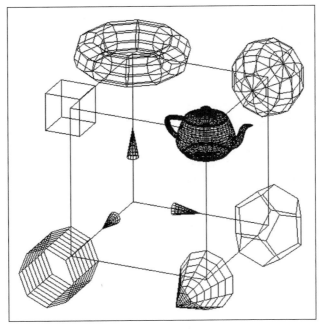

FIGURE 5.57 Wireframe drawing of various primitive shapes.

Figure 5.58 shows the complete program to produce the drawing. The main() routine initializes a 640-by-480-pixel screen window, sets the viewport and background color, and specifies displayWire() as the display function to be called to perform the drawing. In displayWire() the camera shape and position are established first. Then each object is drawn in turn. Most objects need their own modeling matrix, in order to rotate and position them as desired. Before each modeling transformation is established, a glPushMatrix() is used to remember the current transformation, and after the object has been drawn, this prior current transformation is restored with a glPopMatrix(). Thus the code to draw each object is imbedded in a glPushMatrix(), glPopMatrix() pair. Check each transformation carefully to see that it places its object at the proper place.

Also shown in the figure are the *x*-, *y*-, and *z*- drawn with conical arrow heads. Displaying the underlying coordinate system can help to orient the viewer. Because our function axis() draws a *z*-axis, it is hard from the viewpoint to see the *x*-axis. It is made easier if we first rotate the *x* and *z*-axes 90° about the *y*-axis so that the rotated system is plainly visible, and the axis is redrawn in its new orientation. Note that this axis is drawn without immersing it in a glPushMatrix(), glPopMatrix() pair, so the next rotation to produce the *y*-axis takes place in the already rotated coordinate system. Check that it's the proper rotation.

```
#include <windows.h> //suitable when using Windows 95/98/NT/2000/XP
#include <gl/Gl.h>
#include <gl/Glu.h>
#include <gl/glut.h>
//<<<<<<<<<<<<<<<<<<< axis >>>>>>>>>>>>>
void axis(double length)
{ // draw a z-axis, with cone at end
```

FIGURE 5.58 A complete program to draw Figure 5.57 using OpenGL

```
    glPushMatrix();
    glBegin(GL_LINES);
        glVertex3d(0, 0, 0); glVertex3d(0,0,length); // along the z-axis
    glEnd();
    glTranslated(0, 0,length -0.2);
    glutWireCone(0.04, 0.2, 12, 9);
    glPopMatrix();
}
//<<<<<<<<<<<<<<<<<<<<<<<<<<< displayWire >>>>>>>>>>>>>>>>>>>>>>>>>
void displayWire(void)
{
    glMatrixMode(GL_PROJECTION);  // set the view volume shape
    glLoadIdentity();
    glOrtho(-2.0*64/48.0, 2.0*64/48.0, -2.0, 2.0, 0.1, 100);
    glMatrixMode(GL_MODELVIEW);   // position and aim the camera
    glLoadIdentity();
    gluLookAt(2.0, 2.0, 2.0, 0.0, 0.0, 0.0, 0.0, 1.0, 0.0);

    glClear(GL_COLOR_BUFFER_BIT); // clear the screen
    glColor3d(0,0,0); // draw black lines
    axis(0.5);                          // x-axis
    glPushMatrix();
    glRotated(90, 0,1.0, 0);
    axis(0.5);                          // y-axis
    glRotated(-90.0, 1, 0, 0);
    axis(0.5);                          // z-axis
    glPopMatrix();

    glPushMatrix();
    glTranslated(0.5, 0.5, 0.5); // big cube at (0.5, 0.5, 0.5)
    glutWireCube(1.0);
    glPopMatrix();

    glPushMatrix();
    glTranslated(1.0,1.0,0);       // sphere at (1,1,0)
    glutWireSphere(0.25, 10, 8);
    glPopMatrix();

    glPushMatrix();
    glTranslated(1.0,0,1.0);       // cone at (1,0,1)
    glutWireCone(0.2, 0.5, 10, 8);
    glPopMatrix();

    glPushMatrix();
    glTranslated(1,1,1);
    glutWireTeapot(0.2); // teapot at (1,1,1)
    glPopMatrix();

    glPushMatrix();
    glTranslated(0, 1.0 ,0); // torus at (0,1,0)
    glRotated(90.0, 1,0,0);
    glutWireTorus(0.1, 0.3, 10,10);
    glPopMatrix();

    glPushMatrix();
    glTranslated(1.0, 0 ,0); // dodecahedron at (1,0,0)
```

FIGURE 5.58 (*Continued*)

```
        glScaled(0.15, 0.15, 0.15);
        glutWireDodecahedron();
        glPopMatrix();

        glPushMatrix();
        glTranslated(0, 1.0 ,1.0); // small cube at (0,1,1)
        glutWireCube(0.25);
        glPopMatrix();

        glPushMatrix();
        glTranslated(0, 0 ,1.0);  // cylinder at (0,0,1)
        GLUquadricObj * qobj;
        qobj = gluNewQuadric();
        gluQuadricDrawStyle(qobj,GLU_LINE);
        gluCylinder(qobj, 0.2, 0.2, 0.4, 8,8);
        glPopMatrix();
        glFlush();
}
//<<<<<<<<<<<<<<<<<<<<< main >>>>>>>>>>>>>>>>>>>>>>>>>>>>>
void main(int argc, char **argv)
{
        glutInit(&argc, argv);
        glutInitDisplayMode(GLUT_SINGLE | GLUT_RGB );
        glutInitWindowSize(640,480);
        glutInitWindowPosition(100, 100);
        glutCreateWindow("Transformation Test - wireframes");
        glutDisplayFunc(displayWire);
        glClearColor(1.0f, 1.0f, 1.0f,0.0f); // background is white
        glViewport(0, 0, 640, 480);
        glutMainLoop();
}
```

FIGURE 5.58 (*Continued*)

Notice that the sides of the large cube which are parallel in 3D, are also displayed as parallel. This is a result of using a parallel projection. The cube looks slightly unnatural, because we are used to seeing the world with a perspective projection. As we see in Chapter 7, if a perspective projection were used instead, these parallel edges would *not* be drawn parallel.

■ EXAMPLE 5.6.3 A 3D scene rendered with shading

We develop a somewhat more complex scene to illustrate further the use of modeling transformations. We also show how easy OpenGL makes it to draw much more realistic drawings of solid objects by incorporating shading, along with proper hidden surface removal.

Two views of a scene are shown in Figure 5.59. Both views use a camera set by gluLookAt(2.3, 1.3, 2, 0, 0.25, 0, 0.0, 1.0, 0.0). Part a uses a large view volume that encompasses the whole scene; part b uses a small view volume that encompasses only a small portion of the scene, thereby providing a close-up view.

The scene contains three objects resting on a table in the corner of a room. Each of the three walls is made by flattening a cube into a thin sheet and moving it into position. (Again, they look somewhat unnatural due to the use of a parallel

FIGURE 5.59 A simple 3D scene: a) using a large view volume, b) using a small view volume.

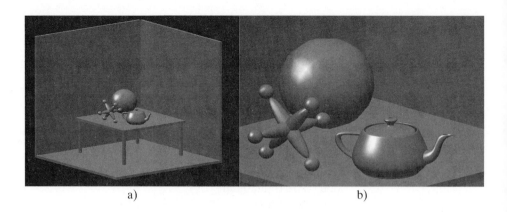

a)   b)

projection.) The jack is composed of three stretched spheres oriented at right angles plus six small spheres at their ends.

The table consists of a table top and four legs. Each of the table's five pieces is a cube that has been scaled to the desired size and shape. The layout for the table is shown in Figure 5.60. It is based on four parameters that characterize the size of its parts: `topWidth`, `topThick`, `legLen`, and `legThick`. A routine `tableLeg()` draws each leg and is called four times within the routine `table()` to draw the legs in the four different locations. The different parameters used produce different modeling transformations within `tableLeg()`. As always, a `glPushMatrix()`, `glPopMatrix()` pair surrounds the modeling functions to isolate their effect.

FIGURE 5.60 The design of a table.

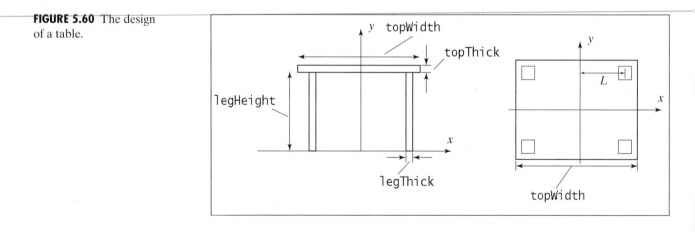

The complete code for this program is shown in Figure 5.61. Note that the solid version of each shape, such as `glutSolidSphere()`, is used here, rather than the wire version. Check the assorted transformations used to orient and position each object in the scene. Check the jack model particularly. This example is designed to whet your appetite for trying out scenes on your own and practicing with transformations.

The code also shows the various things that must be done to create shaded images. The position and properties of a light source must be specified, along with certain properties of the objects' surfaces, in order to describe how they reflect light. Since we discuss the shading process in Chapter 8, we just present the various function calls here; using them as shown will generate shading.

```
#include <windows.h>
#include <iostream.h>
#include <gl/Gl.h>
#include <gl/Glu.h>
#include <gl/glut.h>
//<<<<<<<<<<<<<< wall >>>>>>>>>>>>>>>>
void wall(double thickness)
{ // draw thin wall with top = xz-plane, corner at origin
      glPushMatrix();
      glTranslated(0.5, 0.5 * thickness, 0.5);
      glScaled(1.0, thickness, 1.0);
      glutSolidCube(1.0);
      glPopMatrix();
}
//<<<<<<<<<<<<<<<<< tableLeg >>>>>>>>>>>>>>>>>>>
void tableLeg(double thick, double len)
{
      glPushMatrix();
      glTranslated(0, len/2, 0);
      glScaled(thick, len, thick);
      glutSolidCube(1.0);
      glPopMatrix();
}
//<<<<<<<<<<<<<<<<<<<< jack part >>>>>>>>>>>>>>
void jackPart()
{ // draw one axis of the unit jack - a stretched sphere
      glPushMatrix();
      glScaled(0.2,0.2,1.0);
      glutSolidSphere(1,15,15);
      glPopMatrix();
      glPushMatrix();
      glTranslated(0,0,1.2); // ball on one end
      glutSolidSphere(0.2,15,15);
      glTranslated(0,0, -2.4);
      glutSolidSphere(0.2,15,15); // ball on the other end
      glPopMatrix();
}
//<<<<<<<<<<<<<<<<<< jack >>>>>>>>>>>>>>>>>>>>>>
void jack()
{ // draw a unit jack out of spheroids
      glPushMatrix();
      jackPart();
      glRotated(90.0, 0, 1, 0);
      jackPart();
      glRotated(90.0, 1,0,0);
      jackPart();
      glPopMatrix();
}
//<<<<<<<<<<<<<<<<<<<<<< table >>>>>>>>>>>>>>>>>>>>>>
void table(double topWid, double topThick, double legThick, double legLen)
{ // draw the table - a top and four legs
```

FIGURE 5.61 Complete program to draw the shaded scene.

```
       glPushMatrix(); // draw the table top
       glTranslated(0, legLen, 0);
       glScaled(topWid, topThick, topWid);
       glutSolidCube(1.0);
       glPopMatrix();
       double dist = 0.95 * topWid/2.0 - legThick / 2.0;
       glPushMatrix();
       glTranslated(dist, 0, dist);
       tableLeg(legThick, legLen);
       glTranslated(0, 0, -2 * dist);
       tableLeg(legThick, legLen);
       glTranslated(-2 * dist, 0, 2*dist);
       tableLeg(legThick, legLen);
       glTranslated(0, 0, -2*dist);
       tableLeg(legThick, legLen);
       glPopMatrix();
}
//<<<<<<<<<<<<<<<<<<<<< displaySolid >>>>>>>>>>>>>>>>>>>>>>>
void displaySolid(void)
{
       // set properties of the surface material
       GLfloat mat_ambient[] = { 0.7f, 0.7f, 0.7f, 1.0f}; // gray
       GLfloat mat_diffuse[] = {0.6f, 0.6f, 0.6f, 1.0f};
       GLfloat mat_specular[] = {1.0f, 1.0f, 1.0f, 1.0f};
       GLfloat mat_shininess[] = {50.0f};
       glMaterialfv(GL_FRONT,GL_AMBIENT,mat_ambient);
       glMaterialfv(GL_FRONT,GL_DIFFUSE,mat_diffuse);
       glMaterialfv(GL_FRONT,GL_SPECULAR,mat_specular);
       glMaterialfv(GL_FRONT,GL_SHININESS,mat_shininess);
       // set the light source properties
       GLfloat lightIntensity[] = {0.7f, 0.7f, 0.7f, 1.0f};
       GLfloat light_position[] = {2.0f, 6.0f, 3.0f, 0.0f};
       glLightfv(GL_LIGHT0, GL_POSITION, light_position);
       glLightfv(GL_LIGHT0, GL_DIFFUSE, lightIntensity);
       // set the camera
       glMatrixMode(GL_PROJECTION);
       glLoadIdentity();
       double winHt = 1.0; // half-height of the window
       glOrtho(-winHt*64/48.0, winHt*64/48.0, -winHt, winHt, 0.1, 100.0);
       glMatrixMode(GL_MODELVIEW);
       glLoadIdentity();
       gluLookAt(2.3, 1.3, 2, 0, 0.25, 0, 0.0,1.0,0.0);

       // start drawing
       glClear(GL_COLOR_BUFFER_BIT|GL_DEPTH_BUFFER_BIT); // clear the screen
       glPushMatrix();
       glTranslated(0.4, 0.4, 0.6);
       glRotated(45,0,0,1);
       glScaled(0.08, 0.08, 0.08);
       jack();            // draw the jack
       glPopMatrix();
       glPushMatrix();
       glTranslated(0.6, 0.38, 0.5);
       glRotated(30,0,1,0);
```

FIGURE 5.61 (*Continued*)

```
        glutSolidTeapot(0.08);       // draw the teapot
        glPopMatrix();
        glPushMatrix();
        glTranslated(0.25, 0.42, 0.35); // draw the sphere
        glutSolidSphere(0.1, 15, 15);
        glPopMatrix();
        glPushMatrix();
        glTranslated(0.4, 0, 0.4);
        table(0.6, 0.02, 0.02, 0.3); // draw the table
        glPopMatrix();
        wall(0.02);    // wall #1: in xz-plane
        glPushMatrix();
        glRotated(90.0, 0.0, 0.0, 1.0);
        wall(0.02);    // wall #2: in yz-plane
        glPopMatrix();
        glPushMatrix();
        glRotated(-90.0,1.0, 0.0, 0.0);
        wall(0.02);    // wall #3: in xy-plane
        glPopMatrix();
        glFlush();
}
//<<<<<<<<<<<<<<<<<<<<< main >>>>>>>>>>>>>>>>>>>>>>>>>>>>>
void main(int argc, char **argv)
{
        glutInit(&argc, argv);
        glutInitDisplayMode(GLUT_SINGLE | GLUT_RGB| GLUT_DEPTH);
        glutInitWindowSize(640,480);
        glutInitWindowPosition(100, 100);
        glutCreateWindow("shaded example - 3D scene");
        glutDisplayFunc(displaySolid);
        glEnable(GL_LIGHTING); // enable the light source
        glEnable(GL_LIGHT0);
        glShadeModel(GL_SMOOTH);
        glEnable(GL_DEPTH_TEST); // for hidden surface removal
        glEnable(GL_NORMALIZE);  // normalize vectors for proper shading
        glClearColor(0.1f,0.1f,0.1f,0.0f);  // background is light gray
        glViewport(0, 0, 640, 480);
        glutMainLoop();
}
```

PRACTICE EXERCISES

FIGURE 5.61 (*Continued*)

5.6.3 Inquiring of the values in a matrix in OpenGL

Test some of the assertions above that put specific values into the modelview matrix. You can see what is stored in the modelview matrix in OpenGL by defining an array `GLfloat mat[16]` and using `glGetFloatv(GL_MODELVIEW_MATRIX,mat)`, which copies into `mat[]` the 16 values in the modelview matrix. $M[i][j]$ is copied into the element `mat[4j+i]`, for $i, j = 0, 1, \ldots, 3$. ■

5.6.4 Reading a Scene Description from a File using SDL

In the previous examples the scene was described through specific OpenGL calls that transform and draw each object, as in the following code:

```
glTranslated(0.25, 0.42, 0.35);
glutSolidSphere(0.1, 15, 15); // draw a sphere
```

The objects in the scene were therefore "hard-wired" into the program. This way of specifying a scene is cumbersome and error prone. It is a boon when the designer can specify the objects in a scene through a simple language, and place the description in a file. The drawing program becomes a (much simpler) general-purpose program: it reads a scene file at runtime and draws whatever objects are encountered in the file.

The **Scene Description Language (SDL)** described in Appendix 3 provides such a tool. We define a Scene class, also described in Appendix 3 and on the book's web site, that supports the reading of an SDL file and the drawing of the objects described in the file. It is very simple to use the Scene class in an application, when the following sequence of commands is used. Create a global Scene object:

```
Scene scn; // create a scene object
```

Read in a scene file using the read method of the class:

```
scn.read("example.dat");
// read the scene file and build an object list
```

Figure 5.62 shows the data structure for the scn object, after the following simple SDL file has been read.

FIGURE 5.62 An object of the Scene class.

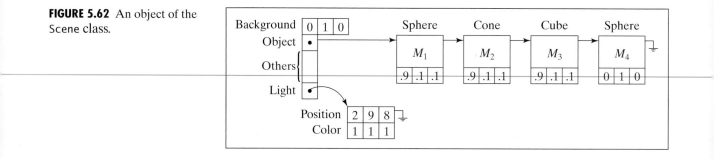

```
! example.dat: a simple scene having one light and four shapes
background 0 0 1              ! give the scene a blue background
light 2 9 8 1 1 1            ! put a white light at (2, 9, 8)
diffuse .9 .1 .1             ! make the following objects reddish
translate 3 5 -2 sphere     ! put a sphere at 3 5 -2
translate -4 -6 8 cone      ! put a cone in the scene
translate 1 1 1 cube        ! add a cube
diffuse 0 1 0                ! make the following objects green
translate 40 5 2 scale .2 .2 .2 sphere !add a tiny sphere
```

The first line is a comment; comments extend to the end of the line. This scene has a bright blue background color $(red, green, blue) = (0, 0, 1)$, a bright white $(1, 1, 1)$ light situated at $(2, 9, 8)$, and four objects: two spheres, a cone, and a cube. The light field points to the list of light sources, and the obj field points to the object list. Each shape object has its own affine transformation M that describes how it is scaled, rotated, and positioned in the scene. It also contains various data fields that specify its material properties, which are important when we want to render it faithfully as discussed in Chapter 8. Only the diffuse field is shown in the figure.

Once the light list and object list have been built, the application can render the scene:

```
scn.makeLightsOpenGL();
scn.drawSceneOpenGL(); // render the scene using OpenGL
```

The first instruction passes a description of the light sources to OpenGL. The second uses the method drawSceneOpenGL() to draw each object in the object list. The code for this method is very simple:

```
void Scene :: drawSceneOpenGL()
{
        for(GeomObj* p = obj; p ; p = p->next)
                p->drawOpenGL(); // draw it
}
```

The function moves a pointer through the object list, calling drawOpenGL() for each object in turn. It's a nice example of using polymorphism, which is a foundation stone of object-oriented programming. Each different shape knows how to draw itself: it has a method drawOpenGL() that calls the appropriate routine for that shape. So when p points to a sphere, the drawOpenGL() routine for a sphere is called automatically; when p points to a cone, the drawOpenGL() routine for a cone is called; and so on. Figure 5.63 shows the methods for the Sphere and Cone classes; they differ only in the final OpenGL drawing routine that is called. Each first passes the object's material properties to OpenGL, then updates the modelview matrix with the object's specific affine transformation. The original modelview matrix is pushed and later restored, to protect it from being affected after this object has been drawn. In programming Figures 5.63 and 5.64 you will see how materials, color, and light are specified and used in an OpenGL application; these topics will be discussed further in Chapter 8.

Figure 5.64 shows the program that reads an SDL file and draws the scene. It is very short, but of course the code for the classes Scene, Shape, and so on must be available in a header file included at compile time. It reads the particular SDL file myScene1.dat, which recreates the same scene as in Figure 5.59. Note that by simply changing the SDL file that is read, this program can draw *any* scene described in SDL, without any changes in its code.

```
void Sphere :: drawOpenGL()
{
  tellMaterialsGL(); // pass material data to OpenGL
  glPushMatrix();
  glMultMatrixf(transf.m); // load this object's matrix
  glutSolidSphere(1.0,10,12); // draw a sphere
  glPopMatrix();
}
void Cone :: drawOpenGL()
{
  tellMaterialsGL(); // pass material data to OpenGL
  glPushMatrix();
  glMultMatrixf(transf.m);  // load this object's matrix
  glutSolidCone(1.0,1.0, 10,12); // draw a cone
  glPopMatrix();
}
```

FIGURE 5.63 The drawOpenGL() methods for two shapes.

```
#include "basicStuff.h"
#include "Scene.h"
//######################### GLOBALS #######################
Scene scn; // construct the scene object
//<<<<<<<<<<<<<<<<<<<<<< displaySDL >>>>>>>>>>>>>>>>>>>>>>>>>>
void displaySDL(void)
{
      glMatrixMode(GL_PROJECTION); // set the camera
      glLoadIdentity();
      double winHt = 1.0; // half-height of the window
      glOrtho(-winHt*64/48.0, winHt*64/48.0, -winHt, winHt, 0.1, 100.0);
      glMatrixMode(GL_MODELVIEW);
      glLoadIdentity();
      gluLookAt(2.3, 1.3, 2, 0, 0.25, 0, 0.0,1.0,0.0);
      glClear(GL_COLOR_BUFFER_BIT|GL_DEPTH_BUFFER_BIT);      // clear screen
      scn.drawSceneOpenGL();
} // end of display
//<<<<<<<<<<<<<<<<<<<<<< main >>>>>>>>>>>>>>>>>>>>>>>>>>>>>>>
void main(int argc, char **argv)
{
      glutInit(&argc, argv);
      glutInitDisplayMode(GLUT_RGB |GLUT_DEPTH);
      glutInitWindowSize(640, 480);
      glutInitWindowPosition(100, 100);
      glutCreateWindow("read and draw an SDL scene");
      glutDisplayFunc(displaySDL);
      glShadeModel(GL_SMOOTH);
      glEnable(GL_DEPTH_TEST);
      glEnable(GL_NORMALIZE);
      glViewport(0, 0, 640, 480);
      scn.read("myScene1.dat"); // read the SDL file and build the objects
      glEnable(GL_LIGHTING);
      scn.makeLightsOpenGL();   // scan the light list and make OpenGL lights
      glutMainLoop();
}
```

FIGURE 5.64 A program reading an SDL file.

The SDL file that describes the scene of Figure 5.59 is shown in Figure 5.65. It defines the jack shape of nine spheres by first defining a jackPart and then using it three times, as explained in Appendix 3. Similarly a leg of the table is first defined as a unit, and then used four times.

```
! - myScene1.dat
light 20 60 30 .7 .7 .7 ! put a light at (20,60,30),color:(.7, .7, .7)
ambient .7 .7 .7 ! set material properties for all of the objects
diffuse .6 .6 .6
specular 1 1 1
exponent 50

def jackPart{ push scale .2 .2 1 sphere pop
push translate 0 0 1.2 scale .2 .2 .2 sphere pop
push translate 0 0 -1.2 scale .2 .2 .2 sphere pop
}
```

FIGURE 5.65 An example SDL file.

```
def jack{ push use jackPart
rotate 90 0 1 0 use jackPart
rotate 90 1 0 0 use jackPart pop
}

def wall{push translate 1 .01 1 scale 1 .02 1 cube pop}
def leg {push translate 0 .15 0 scale .01 .15 .01 cube pop}

def table{
push translate 0 .3 0 scale .3 .01 .3 cube pop !table top
push
translate .275 0 .275 use leg
translate 0 0 -.55 use leg
translate -.55 0 .55 use leg
translate 0 0 -.55 use leg pop
}
!now add the objects themselves
push translate .4 .4 .6 rotate 45 0 0 1 scale .08 .08 .08 use jack pop
push translate .25 .42 .35 scale .1 .1 .1 sphere pop
push translate .6 .38 .5 rotate 30 0 1 0 scale .08 .08 .08 teapot pop
push translate 0.4 0 0.4 use table pop

use wall
push rotate 90 0 0 1 use wall pop
push rotate -90 1 0 0 use wall pop
```

FIGURE 5.65 (*Continued*)

With a scene description language like SDL available, along with tools to read and parse it, the scene designer can focus on creating complex scenes without having to work at the application code level. The scene being developed can be edited and tested again and again until it is right. The code developer puts the initial effort into constructing an application that can render any scene describable in SDL.

5.7 SUMMARY OF THE CHAPTER

Affine transformations are a staple in computer graphics, for they offer a unified tool for manipulating graphical objects in important ways. Affine transformations are defined by matrices, and applying an affine transformation to a point or vector is equivalent to a matrix multiplication. A designer always needs to scale, orient, and position objects in order to compose a scene as well as an appropriate view of the scene, and affine transformations make this simple to manage in a program.

Affine transformations convert one coordinate frame into another, and when homogeneous coordinates are used, an affine transformation is captured in a single matrix form. A sequence of such transformations can be combined into a single transformation whose matrix is simply the product of the individual transformation matrices. Significantly, affine transformations preserve straightness, so the image of a line is another line, and the image of a plane is a plane. This vastly simplifies working with lines and planes in a program, where one benefits from the simple representations of a line (its two endpoints) and a plane (by three points or four coefficients). In addition, parallelism is preserved, so that parallelograms map to parallelograms, and in 3D parallelepipeds map to parallelepipeds. This makes it simpler to visualize the geometric effects of affine transformations.

Three-dimensional affine transformations are much more complex than their 2D counterparts, particularly when it comes to visualizing a combination of rotations. A given rotation can be viewed as three elementary rotations through Euler angles, or a rotation about some axis, or simply as a matrix that has special properties. (Its columns are orthogonal unit vectors.) It is often important to move between these different forms.

OpenGL and other graphics packages offer powerful tools for manipulating and applying transformations. In OpenGL all points are passed through several transformations, and the programmer can exploit this to define and manipulate a camera, as well as to size and position different objects into a scene. Two of the matrices used by OpenGL (the modelview and viewport transformations) define affine transformations, whereas the projection matrix normally defines a perspective transformation, to be examined thoroughly in Chapter 7. OpenGL also maintains a stack of transformations, which make it easy for the scene designer to control the dependency of one object's position on that of another, and to create objects that are composed of several related parts.

The SDL language, along with the Scene and Shape classes, make it much simpler to separate programming issues from scene design issues. An application is developed once that can draw any scene described by a list of light sources and a list of geometric objects. This application is then used over and over again with different scene files. A key task in the scene design process is applying the proper geometric transformations to each object. Since a certain amount of trial and error is usually required, it is convenient to be able to express these transformations in a concise and readable way.

The next section presents a number of Case Studies that elaborate on the main ideas of the chapter and suggest ways to practice with affine transformations in a graphics program. These range from plunging deeper into the theory of transformations to actual modeling and rendering of objects, such as electronic CAD circuits and robots.

5.8 CASE STUDIES

CASE STUDY 5.1 DRAW THE STAR OF FIGURE 5.36. USING MULTIPLE ROTATIONS

(Level of Effort: II)   Develop a function that draws the polygon in Figure 5.36b that is one-fifth of the star. Use it with rotation transformations to draw the whole star.

CASE STUDY 5.2 DECOMPOSING A 3D AFFINE TRANSFORMATION

(Level of Effort: III)   This Case Study looks at several broad families of affine transformations.

What Is in a 3D Affine Transformation?

Once again we ignore the translation portion of an affine transformation and focus on the linear transformation part represented by the 3×3 matrix M. What kinds of transformations are imbedded in it? It is somewhat more complicated than its 2D counterpart. Goldman [*GEMS III*, p. 108] shows that every such M is the product of a scaling S, a rotation R, and two shears H_1 and H_2.

$$M = SRH_1H_2 \qquad\qquad\qquad (5.34)$$

Every 3D affine transformation, then, can be viewed as this sequence of elementary operations, followed by a translation. In this Case Study we explore the mathematics behind this form and see how an actual decomposition might be carried out.

Useful Classes of Transformations

It is useful to categorize affine transformations, according to what they "do" or "don't do" to certain properties of an object when it is transformed. We know they always preserve parallelism of edges of an object, but which transformations also preserve the length of each edge, and which ones preserve the angles between each pair of edges?

1. Rigid Body Motions

It is intuitively clear that translating an object, or rotating it, will not change its shape or size. In addition, reflecting it about a plane has no effect on its shape or size. Since the shape is not affected by any of these transformations alone, it is also not affected by an arbitrary composition of them. We denote by

$T_{\text{rigid}} = \{\text{rotations, reflections, translations}\}$

the collection of all affine transformations that consist of any sequence of rotations, reflections, and translations. These are known classically as the **rigid body motions**, since an object is moved rigidly from one position and orientation to another. Such transformations have *orthogonal* matrices in homogeneous coordinates. These are matrices for which the inverse is the same as the transpose:

$$\widetilde{M}^{-1} = \widetilde{M}^{T}$$

2. Angle-Preserving Transformations

A uniform scaling (having equal scale factors $S_x = S_y = S_z$) expands or shrinks an object, but does so uniformly, so there is no change in the object's shape. Thus the angle between any two edges is unaffected. We can denote such a class as

$T_{\text{angle}} = \{\text{rotations, reflections, translations, uniform scalings}\}$

This class is larger than the rigid body motions, because it includes uniform scaling. It is an important class because, as we see in Chapter 8, lighting and shading calculations depend on the dot products between various vectors. If a certain transformation does not alter angles, then it does not alter dot products, and lighting calculations can take place in either the transformed or the untransformed space.

(Estimate of time required: three hours.) Given a 3D affine transformation $\{M, \mathbf{d}\}$ we wish to see how it is composed of a sequence of elementary transformations. Following Goldman [*GEMS III*, p. 108] we develop the steps required to decompose the 3-by-3 matrix M into the product of a scaling S, a rotation R, and two shears H_1 and H_2:

$$M = SRH_1H_2 \tag{5.35}$$

You are asked to verify each step along the way and to develop a routine that will produce, from a given matrix M, the individual matrices S, R, H_1, and H_2.

Suppose the matrix M has rows $\mathbf{u}, \mathbf{v}$, and $\mathbf{w}$, each a 3D vector:

$$M = \begin{pmatrix} \mathbf{u} \\ \mathbf{v} \\ \mathbf{w} \end{pmatrix}$$

Goldman's approach is based on the classical Gram-Schmidt orthogonalization procedure, whereby the rows of M are combined in such a way that they become mutually orthogonal and of unit length. The matrix composed of these rows is therefore orthogonal and so represents a rotation (or a rotation with a reflection). Goldman shows that the orthogonalization process is in fact two shears. The rest is detail.

The steps are as follows. Carefully follow each step, and do each of the tasks given in brackets.

1. Normalize $\mathbf{u}$ to $\mathbf{u}^* = \mathbf{u}/S_1$, where $S_1 = |\mathbf{u}|$.
2. Subtract a piece of $\mathbf{u}^*$ from $\mathbf{v}$ so that what is left is orthogonal to $\mathbf{u}^*$. Call $\mathbf{b} = \mathbf{v} - d\mathbf{u}^*$, where $d = \mathbf{v} \cdot \mathbf{u}^*$. [Show that $\mathbf{b} \cdot \mathbf{u}^* = 0$.]
3. Normalize $\mathbf{b}$: set $\mathbf{v}^* = \mathbf{b}/S_2$, where $S_2 = |\mathbf{b}|$.

4. Set up some intermediate values: $m = \mathbf{w} \cdot \mathbf{u}^*$ and $n = \mathbf{w} \cdot \mathbf{v}^*$, $e = \sqrt{m^2 + n^2}$, and $\mathbf{r} = (m\mathbf{u}^* + n\mathbf{v}^*)/e$.
5. Subtract a piece of $\mathbf{r}$ from $\mathbf{w}$ so that what is left is orthogonal to both $\mathbf{u}^*$ and $\mathbf{v}^*$. Call $\mathbf{c} = \mathbf{w} - e\mathbf{r}$. [Show that $\mathbf{c} \cdot \mathbf{u}^* = \mathbf{c} \cdot \mathbf{v}^* = 0$.]
6. Normalize $\mathbf{c}$: set $\mathbf{w}^* = \mathbf{c}/S_3$, where $S_3 = |\mathbf{c}|$.
7. The matrix

$$R = \begin{pmatrix} \mathbf{u}* \\ \mathbf{v}* \\ \mathbf{w}* \end{pmatrix}$$

is therefore orthogonal, and so represents a rotation. (Compute its determinant: if it is -1, then simply replace $\mathbf{w}*$ with $-\mathbf{w}*$.)

8. Define the shear matrix $H_1 = I + \dfrac{d}{S_2}(\mathbf{v}* \otimes \mathbf{u}*)$, where

   $(\mathbf{v}* \otimes \mathbf{u}*) = (\mathbf{v}*)^T\mathbf{u}*$ is the **outer product** (see Appendix 2) of $\mathbf{v}*$ and $\mathbf{u}*$.

9. Define the shear matrix $H_2 = I + \dfrac{e}{S_3}(\mathbf{w}* \otimes \mathbf{r})$, where $(\mathbf{w}* \otimes \mathbf{r} = (\mathbf{w}*)^T\mathbf{r}$.

10. [Show that $\mathbf{u}*H_1 = \mathbf{u}*$, $\mathbf{v}*H_1 = \mathbf{v}* + d\mathbf{u}*/S_2 = \mathbf{v}/S_2$, and $\mathbf{w}*H_1 = \mathbf{w}*$. First show the property of the outer product that for any vectors $\mathbf{a}, \mathbf{b}$, and $\mathbf{c}$: $\mathbf{a}(\mathbf{b} \otimes \mathbf{c}) = (a \cdot b)c$. Then use this property, along with the orthogonality of $\mathbf{u}*$, $\mathbf{v}*$ and $\mathbf{w}*$, to show the three relations.]

11. [Show that $\mathbf{u}*H_2 = \mathbf{u}*$, $\mathbf{v}*H_2 = \mathbf{v}*$, $\mathbf{w}*H_2 = \mathbf{w}* + e\mathbf{r}/S_3 = \mathbf{w}/S_3$.]

12. [Put these together to show that $M = SRH_1H_2$.] S is defined to be

$$S = \begin{pmatrix} S_1 & 0 & 0 \\ 0 & S_2 & 0 \\ 0 & 0 & S_3 \end{pmatrix}$$

Note that the decomposition is not unique, since the vectors $\mathbf{u}, \mathbf{v}$, and $\mathbf{w}$ could be orthogonalized in a different order. For instance, we could first form $\mathbf{w}*$ as $\mathbf{w}/|\mathbf{w}|$, then subtract a piece of $\mathbf{v}$ from $\mathbf{w}*$ to make a vector orthogonal to $\mathbf{w}*$, then subtract a vector from $\mathbf{u}$ to make a vector orthogonal to the other two. Write the routine:

```
void decompose(DBL m[3][3],DBL S[3][3],DBL R[3][3],DBL H1[3][3],DBL
H2[3][3])
```

where **DBL** is defined as `double`, that takes matrix M and returns the matrices S, R, H_1 and H_2 as described above. Test your routine on several matrices to insure that their product results in the original matrix M.

Other ways to decompose a 3D transformation have been found as well. See for instance, [Thomas, GEMS II, p. 320] and [Shoemaker, GEMS IV, p. 207].

CASE STUDY 5.3 INTERACTION AND CREATION OF OBJECTS WITHIN A SCENE

(Level of Effort: III)   A facility within an interactive program that can add a great deal of excitement, particularly in games, is the ability to add or remove objects from a scene. Examples are the use of the mouse and keyboard to add a robot or table to the scene, or to have one of these objects suddenly disappear. Another element of interest would be to make the robot's head pivot left or right, or to make the robot wave its forearm. How are these done in a 3D OpenGL program? Write the keyboard handler that controls the creation and deletion of objects from a scene and write the mouse handler which controls the direction in which a robot is looking. The robot's head need not be developed in detail; it could be a simple cylinder or cone. Manage the mouse callback function so that a left mouse click on the desired object causes its display to toggle between wireframe and solid polygon.

CASE STUDY 5.4 FLYING THROUGH PRIMITIVE SHAPES

(Level of Effort: II)   Using Figure 5.57 as your guide, develop an application that allows the user to control the camera in order to fly it through the scene. The plane should be stationary when the program starts as well as when no key is pressed. The mouse movement left or right should change the yaw of the camera; forward and backward mouse motions should change the pitch of the camera (no mouse buttons need be pressed). Have the keyboard controls 'a' and 'd' slide the camera left and right respectively; and 'w' and 's' slide the camera forward and back. If the 'r' key and the left mouse button are pressed simultaneously, with the mouse at any location, the plane rolls CCW. If, instead, the right mouse button is pressed and the 'r' key, the camera rolls CW.

CASE STUDY 5.5 DRAW 3D SCENES DESCRIBED BY SDL

(Level of Effort: II) Develop a complete application that uses the Scene, Shape, Affine4, and so on classes and supports reading in and drawing the scene described in an SDL file. To assist you, use any classes provided on the book's web site. Flesh out any drawOpenGL() methods that are needed. Develop a scene file that contains descriptions of the jack, a wooden chair, and several walls.

5.9 FOR FURTHER READING

There are some excellent books on transformations that supplement the treatment here. George Martin's *Transformation Geometry* [Martin82] is superb, as is Yaglom's *Geometric Transformations* [Yaglom62]. Hogar also provides a fine chapter on vectors and transformations [Hoggar92]. Also see Foley, van Dam, Feiner, and Hughes' *Computer Graphics: Principles and Practice* [VanDam95] for a comprehensive treatment of graphics in general and transformations in particular. Several of Blinn's engaging articles in *Jim Blinn's Corner—A Trip Down the Graphics Pipeline* [Blinn96] provide excellent discussions of homogeneous coordinates and transformations in computer graphics.

Chapter 6

Modeling Shapes with Polygonal Meshes

Try to learn something about everything and everything about something.

T. H. Huxley
(1825–1895)

GOALS OF THE CHAPTER

○ To develop tools for working with objects in 3D space.

○ To represent solid objects using polygonal meshes.

○ To draw simple wireframe views of mesh objects.

○ To introduce particle systems and describe how they operate.

○ To introduce physically based systems and describe how an application can generate and display them.

Preview

Section 6.1 gives an overview of the 3D modeling process. Section 6.2 describes polygonal meshes that allow you to capture the shape of complex 3D objects in simple data structures. The properties of such meshes are reviewed, and algorithms are presented for viewing them.

Section 6.3 describes families of interesting 3D shapes, such as the Platonic solids, the Buckyball, geodesic domes, and prisms. Section 6.4 examines the family of extruded or swept shapes and shows how to create 3D letters for flying logos, tubes and snakes that undulate through space, and surfaces of revolution.

Section 6.5 discusses building meshes to model solids that have smoothly curved surfaces. The meshes approximate some smooth **underlying surface**. A key ingredient is the computation of the normal vector to the underlying surface at any point. Several interesting families of smooth solids are discussed, including quadric, ruled surfaces and Coons patches, explicit functions of two variables, and surfaces of revolution.

Section 6.6 describes the fascinating area of **particle systems**, which are most interesting when viewed as animations. In such systems the scene consists of hundreds or thousands of elementary particles, sometimes modeled as simple dots. The dots exist in 3D space and have certain attributes such as color, lifetime, velocity, and size. In the animation they are born at some point and made to expire at some later time. Examples include grass, water being ejected from a fountain, star clutters zooming by the observer, clouds, and fog. Figure 6.1a shows a fountain where the

a)   b)

FIGURE 6.1 a) Particle system showing water droplets in a fountain (Courtesy of Philipp Crocoll/CodeColony.de), b) starfield simulation (Courtesy of Ge Wang).

particles are droplets of water being shot up into the air. In the corresponding animation the droplets fall back into the pool of water below, causing ripples. Part b shows a cluster of stars flying by the observer, familiar from television and movies. Both programs are available on the book's web site.

Section 6.6.2 also introduces **physically based systems** in which the various objects in a scene are modeled as being connected by springs, gears, electrostatic forces, gravity, or other mechanisms. The application programmer includes routines that make the objects react properly to these forces. Physically based systems are most vivid when we view them in an animation, watching the objects bob around, swing back and forth, and rotate as if controlled by invisible but well-known forces.

The Case Studies at the end of the chapter explore several ideas further and request that you develop applications to test things out. Some of the case studies are more practical, such as reading mesh data from a file and creating beautiful 3D shapes such as tubes and arches.

6.1 INTRODUCTION

In this chapter we examine ways to describe 3D objects using **polygonal meshes**. Polygonal meshes are simply collections of polygons, or faces that fit together to form the skin of the object. They have become a standard way of representing a broad class of solid shapes in graphics. Previously we have seen several examples of polygonal meshes, such as the cube and icosahedron, as well as approximations to smooth shapes like the sphere, cylinder, and cone. In this chapter we shall see many more examples. Their prominence in graphics stems from the simplicity of using polygons. Polygons are easy to represent (by a sequence of vertices) and transform, they have simple properties (a single normal vector, a well-defined inside and outside, and so on), and they are easy to draw (using a polygon-fill routine, or by mapping texture onto the polygon).

Many rendering systems, including OpenGL, are based on drawing objects by drawing a sequence of polygons. Each polygonal face is sent through the graphics pipeline, where its vertices undergo various transformations, until finally the portion of the face that survives clipping is colored in, or shaded, and shown on the display device.

We want to see how to design complicated 3D shapes by defining an appropriate set of faces. Some objects can be perfectly represented by a polygonal mesh, whereas others can only be approximated. The barn of Figure 6.2a, for example, naturally has flat faces, so that in a rendering the edges between faces will be visible, as desired. But the situation is different for the cylinder in part b: the cylinder in Figure 6.2b should appear to have a smoothly rounded wall, but this roundness cannot be achieved if we use only polygons: the individual flat faces are quite visible, as are the edges between them. We must develop rendering techniques that make a mesh like this *appear* to be smooth, as in Figure 6.2c. We examine the details of such a technique in Chapter 8.

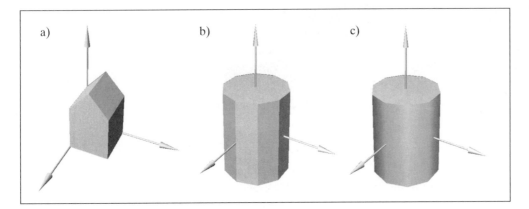

FIGURE 6.2 Various shapes modeled by meshes.

We begin by describing polygonal meshes in some generality, and by seeing how to define and manipulate them in a program with OpenGL. We apply these ideas to modeling polyhedra, which have inherently flat faces, and study a number of interesting families of polyhedra. We then tackle the problem of using a mesh to approximate a smoothly curved shape, and we develop the necessary tools to create and manipulate such models.

6.2 INTRODUCTION TO SOLID MODELING WITH POLYGONAL MESHES

> I never forget a face, but in your case I'll be glad to make an exception.
>
> *Groucho Marx*
> *(1890–1977)*

We shall use meshes to model both solid shapes and thin skins. The object is considered to be **solid** if the polygonal faces fit together to enclose space. In other cases the faces fit together without enclosing space, and so they represent an infinitesimally thin surface. In both cases we call the collection of polygons a **polygonal mesh** (or simply a **mesh**).

A polygonal mesh is given by a list of polygons, along with information about the direction in which each polygon is facing. The important directional information is often simply directional information is often simply the outward-pointing **normal vector** to the plane of the face, and it is used in the shading process to determine how much light from a light source is scattered in various directions by the face, as discussed in Chapter 8. Figure 6.3 shows the normal vectors for various faces of the barn. As we discuss in Chapter 8, the brightness of a face is taken to be proportional to the cosine of the angle (shown as θ in the figure) between the outward normal to the face and a vector to a light source. Thus the orientation of a surface with respect to light sources plays an important part in the final drawing and texturing. We discuss the new ideas behind OpenGL's Shading Language in Chapter 8.

Vertex Normals vs. Face Normals

For some objects, it turns out to be beneficial to associate a *normal vector* to each vertex of a face, rather than one vector to an entire face. This approach facilitates both the clipping and shading processes for smoothly curved shapes. We shall have frequent need to consider mesh objects that are intended to represent shapes with smoothly curved faces, such as a sphere or cylinder. Because it is so efficient to use a polygonal skin for such objects, we will still refer to their faces but with the understanding that there is a "*smooth underlying surface.*" When we display such an object, we will want to de-emphasize its individual faces, in order to make the object look smooth. In computer graphics a number of algorithms have been developed to assist this. For other shapes, such as the barn or a die for playing dice, the edges between individual faces *should* be visible, and we will seek a different reflected light intensity for each.

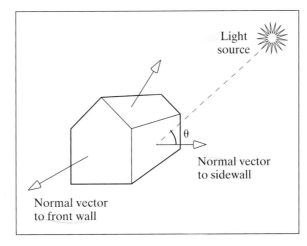

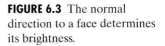

FIGURE 6.3 The normal direction to a face determines its brightness.

For flat surfaces such as the wall of a barn, this means that each of the vertices V_1, V_2, V_3, and V_4 that define the side wall of the barn will be associated with the *same* normal $\mathbf{n}_1$, the normal vector to the side wall itself (see Figure 6.4a). But vertices of the *front* wall, such as V_5, will use normal $\mathbf{n}_2$. (Note that vertices V_1 and V_5 are located at the same point in space, but use different normals.)

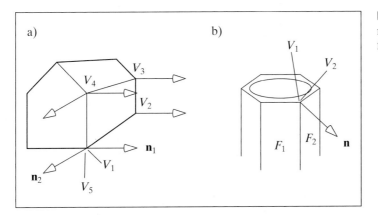

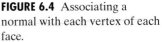

FIGURE 6.4 Associating a normal with each vertex of each face.

For a smoothly curved surface such as the cylinder in Figure 6.4b on the other hand, both vertex V_1 of face F_1 and vertex V_2 on face F_2 use the same *normal $\mathbf{n}$*, which is the vector perpendicular to the underlying smooth surface. We see how to compute this vector conveniently in Section 6.2.2.

6.2.1 To Define a Polygonal Mesh

A polygonal mesh is a collection of polygons along with a normal vector associated with each vertex of each polygon. We begin with an example.

■ EXAMPLE 6.2.1 The basic barn

Figure 6.5 shows a simple shape we call the basic barn. It has seven polygonal faces and a total of 10 vertices (each of which is shared by three faces). For convenience it has a square floor one unit on a side. (The barn could be scaled and oriented appropriately before being placed in a scene.) Because the barn is assumed to have flat walls, there are only seven distinct normal vectors involved, the normal to each face as shown.

FIGURE 6.5 Introducing the basic barn.

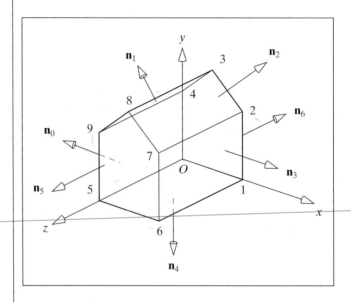

There are various ways to store mesh information in a file or program. For the barn you could use a list of seven polygons, and list for each one where its vertices are located and the direction in which the normal for each of its vertices points (a total of 30 vertices and 30 normals). This would be quite redundant and bulky, however, since there are only 10 distinct vertices and seven distinct normals.

A more efficient approach uses three separate lists, a **vertex list**, **normal list**, and **face list**. The vertex list reports the locations of the distinct vertices in the mesh. The list of normals reports the directions of the distinct normal vectors that occur in the model. The face list simply indexes into the vertex and normal lists. As we see next, the barn is thereby captured with 10 vertices, seven normals, and a list of seven simple face descriptors.

The three lists work together: The vertex list contains locational or **geometric** information, the normal list contains **orientation** information, and the face list contains connectivity or **topological** information.

The vertex list for the barn is shown in Figure 6.6. The list of the seven distinct normals is shown in Figure 6.7. The vertices have indices 0 through 9 and the normals have indices 0 through 6. The vectors shown have already been normalized, since most shading algorithms require unit vectors. (Recall that a cosine can be found as the dot product between two unit vectors.)

Vertex	x	y	z
0	0	0	0
1	1	0	0
2	1	1	0
3	0.5	1.5	0
4	0	1	0
5	0	0	1
6	1	0	1
7	1	1	1
8	0.5	1.5	1
9	0	1	1

FIGURE 6.6 Vertex list for the basic barn.

Normal	n_x	n_y	n_z
0	−1	0	0
1	−0.707107	0.707107	0
2	0.707107	0.707107	0
3	1	0	0
4	0	−1	0
5	0	0	1
6	0	0	−1

FIGURE 6.7 The list of distinct normal vectors involved.

Figure 6.8 shows the barn's face list: each face has a list of vertices and the normal vector associated with each vertex. To save space, only the indices of the proper vertices and normals are used. (Since each surface is flat, all of the vertices in a face are associated with the same normal.) The list of vertices for each face begins with any vertex in the face and then proceeds around the face, vertex by vertex, until a complete circuit has been made. There are two ways to traverse a polygon: clockwise and counterclockwise. For instance, face #5 above could be listed as (5, 6, 7, 8, 9) or (9, 8, 7, 6, 5). Either direction could be used, but we follow a convention that proves handy in practice:

Traverse the polygon counterclockwise as seen from outside the object.

Using this order, if you traverse around the face by walking on the outside surface from vertex to vertex, the interior of the face is on your left. We later design algorithms that exploit this ordering. Because of it, the algorithms are able to distinguish with ease the front from the back of a face.

Face	Vertices	Associated Normal
0 (left)	0, 5 ,9 ,4	0, 0, 0, 0
1 (roof left)	3, 4, 9, 8	1, 1, 1, 1
2 (roof right)	2, 3, 8, 7	2, 2, 2, 2
3 (right)	1, 2, 7, 6	3, 3, 3, 3
4 (bottom)	0, 1, 6, 5	4, 4, 4, 4
5 (front)	5, 6, 7, 8, 9	5, 5, 5, 5, 5
6 (back)	0, 4, 3, 2, 1	6, 6, 6, 6, 6

FIGURE 6.8 Face list for the basic barn.

The barn is an example of a data-intensive model, where the position of each vertex is entered by the designer. In contrast, we see later some models that are generated algorithmically. For instance, some prospective home owners may wish to design the floorplan of their dream house and let a CAD software program or an architect flesh out the actual 3D contours or a full-color rendition of the house. For some buildings such as a house or hospital, or the Pentagon in Washington, it would be an enormous task to fill in the tables by hand. A likely substitute would be to have the table data stored in files. Having these files it isn't too hard to come there, it isn't too hard to come up with the vertices for the basic barn or house.

Some CAD and 3D graphics programs, such as AutoCAD and 3D Studio Max, automatically create lists such as those described in the previous tables. The designer of the hospital, factory, or church can save all of the data in a file with a simple command and later make it available for rendering in an application.

6.2.1 Sample 3D File Formats

You may be curious as to how some popular CAD and 3D graphics programs store their descriptions of 3D mesh objects in files. There is no standard file format, but some file formats have been found to be particularly efficient and easy to use. For example, Figure 6.9 shows three different views of one 3D mesh model file, a .qs file format developed by the Stanford University Computer Graphics Laboratory. This particular mesh model has 2,748,318 points (about 5,500,000 triangles) and is based on 566,098 vertices.[1] Imagine plotting those points out in your head!

OpenGL has the capability to load a variety of 3D model formats, such as, but not limited to, 3DS, VRML, PLY, MS3D, and OBJ. A number of resources are available on the book's companion web site that covers loading 3D mesh models into OpenGL.

 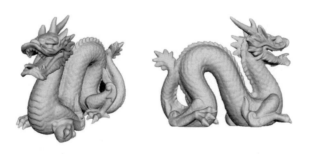

FIGURE 6.9 Three views of a 3D mesh model. (Courtesy of Stanford Univ. Computer Graphics Lab)

6.2.2 To Find the Normal Vectors

It may be possible to set vertex positions by hand, but it is not so easy to calculate the normal vectors. In general each face will have three or more vertices, and a designer would find it challenging to jot down the normal vectors. It's best to let the computer do it during the creation of the mesh model.

If the face is considered flat, as in the case of the barn, we need only find the normal vector to the face itself and associate it with each of the face's vertices. One direct way uses the vector cross product to find the normal, as in Figure 4.14. Take any three adjacent points on the face, V_1, V_2, and V_3, and compute the normal as their cross product $\mathbf{m} = (V_1 - V_2) \times (V_3 - V_2)$. This vector can now be normalized to unit length.

---

[1]   Source: Stanford University Computer Graphics Laboratory

There are two problems with this simple approach.

1. If the two vectors $V_1 - V_2$ and $V_3 - V_2$ are nearly parallel, the cross product will be very small (Why?), and numerical inaccuracies may result.
2. As we see later, it may turn out that the polygon is not perfectly planar, i.e., that all of the vertices do not lie in the same plane. Thus the surface represented by the vertices cannot be truly flat. We need to form some average value for the normal to the polygon, one that takes into consideration all of the vertices.

A robust method is presented and derived in Case Study 6.2, which, solves both of these problems, was devised by Martin Newell [Newell79]. It computes the components m_x, m_y, m_z of the normal **m** according to the formulas:

$$m_x = \sum_{i=0}^{N-1} (y_i - y_{\text{next}(i)})(z_i + z_{\text{next}(i)})$$

$$m_y = \sum_{i=0}^{N-1} (z_i - z_{\text{next}(i)})(x_i + x_{\text{next}(i)})$$

$$m_z = \sum_{i=0}^{N-1} (x_i - x_{\text{next}(i)})(y_i + y_{\text{next}(i)}) \tag{6.1}$$

where N is the number of vertices in the face, (x_i, y_i, z_i) is the position of the ith vertex, and $\text{next}(j) = (j + 1) \bmod N$ is the index of the next vertex around the face after vertex j. The modulo operation ensures that the vertex after vertex number $(N - 1)$is vertex 0. The computation requires only one multiplication per edge for each component of the normal, and no testing for collinearity is needed.

The vector **m** computed by the Newell method could point toward the inside or toward the outside of the polygon. If the vertices of the polygon are traversed (as i increases) in a CCW direction as seen from outside the polygon, then **m** points toward the outside of the face.

■ **EXAMPLE 6.2.2**

Consider the polygon with vertices $P_0 = (6, 1, 4)$, $P_1 = (7, 0, 9)$, and $P_2 = (1, 1, 2)$. Find the normal to this polygon using the Newell method. Being a triangle, this polygon must be planar.

SOLUTION:

Direct use of the cross product gives $((7, 0, 9) - (6, 1, 4)) \times ((1, 1, 2) - (6, 1, 4))$ $= (2, -23, -5)$. Application of the Newell method yields the same result: $(2, -23, -5)$.

PRACTICE EXERCISES

6.2.1 Using the Newell method

For the three vertices $(6, 1, 4), (2, 0, 5)$, and $(7, 0, 9)$, compare the normal found using the Newell method with that found using the usual cross product. Then use the Newell method to find (n_x, n_y, n_z) for the polygon having the vertices $(1, 1, 2), (2, 0, 5), (5, 1, 4), (6, 0, 7)$. Is the polygon planar? If so, find its true normal using the cross product, and compare it with the result of the Newell method.

6.2.2 What about a nonplanar polygon?

Consider the quadrilateral shown in Figure 6.10 that has the vertices $(0, 0, 0), (1, 0, 0), (0, 0, 1)$, and $(1, a, 1)$. When a is nonzero, this is a nonplanar polygon. Find the normal to it using the Newell method, and discuss how good an estimate it is for different values of a.

FIGURE 6.10 A nonplanar polygon.

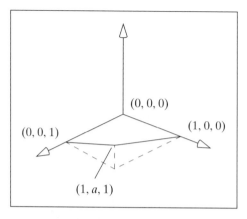

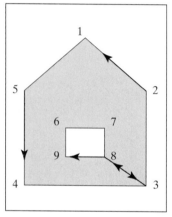

FIGURE 6.11 A face containing a hole.

6.2.3 Represent the generic cube

Make vertex, normal, and face lists for the "generic" cube, which is centered at the origin, has its edges aligned with the coordinate axes, and has edges of length two. The eight vertices of this generic cube therefore lie at $(-1,-1,-1)$, $(-1,-1,1)$, $(-1,1,-1)$, $(-1,1,1)$, $(1,-1,-1)$, $(1,-1,1)$, $(1,1,-1)$, and $(1,1,1)$.

6.2.4 Faces with holes

Figure 6.11 shows how a face containing a hole can be captured in a face list. A pair of imaginary edges is added that bridge the gap between the outer edge of the face and the hole, as suggested in the figure. The face is traversed so that (when walking along the outside surface) the interior of the face lies to the left. Thus a hole is traversed in the CW direction. Assuming we are looking at the face in the figure from its outside, the list of vertices would be: 5 4 3 8 9 6 7 8 3 2 1. Sketch this face with an additional hole in it, and give the proper list of vertices for the face. What normals would be associated with each vertex? ■

6.2.3 Properties of Meshes

Given a mesh specified by its vertex, normal, and face lists, we might wonder what kind of an object it represents. Some properties of interest are:

- **Solidity**: As mentioned earlier, a mesh represents a solid object if its faces together enclose a positive and finite amount of space.
- **Connectedness:** A mesh is **connected** if every face shares at least one edge with some other face. (If a mesh is not connected, it is usually considered to represent more than one object.)
- **Simplicity**: A mesh is **simple** if the object it represents is solid and has no holes through it; it can be deformed into a sphere without tearing. (Note that the term simple is being used here in quite a different sense from that for a simple polygon.)
- **Planarity**: A mesh is planar if every face is a **planar** polygon: the vertices of each face then lie in a single plane. Some graphics algorithms work much more efficiently if a face is planar. Triangles are inherently planar, and some modeling software takes advantage of this by using only triangles. Quadrilaterals, on the other hand, may or may not be planar. The quadrilateral in Figure 6.10, for instance, is planar if and only if $a = 0$.
- **Convexity**: A mesh represents a **convex** object if the line connecting any two points within the object lies wholly inside the object. Convexity was first discussed

in Section 2.3.6 in connection with polygons. Figure 6.12 shows some convex and some nonconvex objects. For each nonconvex object an example line is shown whose endpoints lie in the object but which is not itself contained within the object.

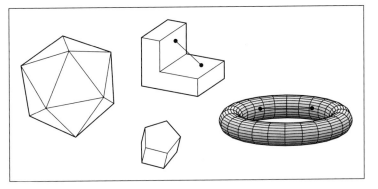

FIGURE 6.12 Examples of convex and nonconvex 3D objects.

PRACTICE EXERCISE:

6.2.3

1. Identify the objects in Figure 6.12 that are convex, and those that are not.

The basic barn possesses all of the properties in the preceding list (check this). For a given mesh some of these properties are easy to determine in a program, in the sense that a simple algorithm exists that does the job. (We discuss some subsequently.) Other properties, such as solidity, are quite difficult to establish.

The polygonal meshes we choose to use to model objects in graphics may have some or all of these properties: the choice depends on how one is going to use the mesh. If the mesh is supposed to represent a physical object made of some material, perhaps to determine its mass or center of gravity, we may insist that it be at least connected and solid. If we just want to draw the object, however, much greater freedom is available, since many objects can still be drawn, even if they are *nonphysical*.

Figure 6.13 shows some examples of objects we might wish to represent by meshes. Pyramid is made up of triangular faces which are necessarily planar. It is not only convex; in fact it has all of the properties above.

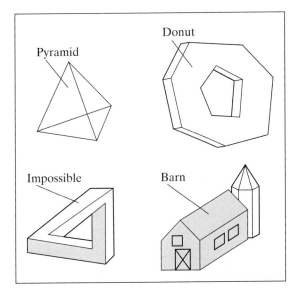

FIGURE 6.13 Examples of solids to be described by meshes.

Donut is connected and solid, but it is neither simple (there is a hole through it) nor convex. Two of its faces themselves have holes. Whether or not its faces are planar polygons cannot be determined from a figure alone. Later we give an algorithm for determining planarity from the face and vertex lists.

The figure labeled Impossible looks impossible but is not. This object can even be represented by a mesh. Gershon Elber's research web site (http:// www.cs.technion.ac.il/~gershon/EscherForReal/) presents a collection of apparently impossible objects, but describes how in fact they can be modeled.

Barn seems to be made up of two parts, but it could be contained in a single mesh. Whether it is connected would then depend on how the faces were defined at the juncture between the silo and the main building. Barn also illustrates a situation often encountered in graphics. Some faces have been added to the mesh that represent windows and doors, to provide texture to the object. For instance, the side of Barn is a rectangle with no holes in it, but two squares have been added to the mesh to represent windows. These squares are made to lie in the same plane as the side of Barn. This then is not a connected mesh, but it can still be displayed on a graphics device.   ■

6.2.4 Mesh Models for Nonsolid Objects

Figure 6.14 shows examples of other objects that can be characterized by polygonal meshes. These are surfaces and are best thought of as infinitesimally thick shells. Part a is a box whose lid has been raised. Part b is a structure some of whose faces are being used to approximate a smooth underlying surface. Part c is a Face based on digitized points of a person's face.

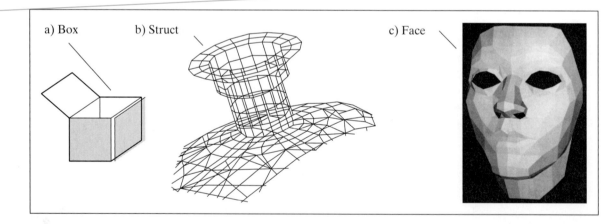

FIGURE 6.14 Some surfaces describable by meshes. (Part c is courtesy of the University of Utah.)

If each face of the mesh is drawn as a shaded polygon, the picture will look artificial, as seen in Face. Later we shall examine tools that attempt to draw the smooth underlying surface based only on the mesh model.

Many geometric modeling software packages construct a model from some object—a solid or a surface—that tries to capture the true shape of the object in a polygonal mesh. The problem of composing the lists can be difficult. As an example, consider creating an algorithm that generates vertex and face lists to approximate the shape of an engine block, a prosthetic limb, or a building. By using a sufficient number of faces, a mesh can approximate the underlying surface to any degree of accuracy desired.

6.2.5 Working with Meshes in a Program

We want an efficient way to capture a mesh in a program that makes it easy to create and draw the object. Since mesh data are frequently stored in a file, we also need simple ways to read and write mesh files.

It is natural to define a class Mesh and to imbue it with the desired functionality. Figure 6.15 shows the declaration of the class Mesh, along with those of two simple helper classes, VertexID and Face.[2] A Mesh object has a vertex list, a normal list, and a face list, represented simply by arrays pt, norm, and face, respectively. These arrays are allocated dynamically at runtime, when it is known how large they must be. Their lengths are stored in numVerts, numNormals, and numFaces, respectively. Additional data fields can be added later that describe various physical properties of the object, such as weight and type of material.

```
//################# VertexID #################
class VertexID{
    public:
        int vertIndex;    // index of this vertex in the vertex list
        int normIndex;    // index of this vertex's normal
};
//################### Face ##################
class Face{
    public:
        int nVerts;      // number of vertices in this face
        VertexID * vert;      // the list of vertex and normal indices
        // constructor
        // destructor
};
//##################### Mesh #####################
class Mesh{
    private:
        int numVerts;      // number of vertices in the mesh
        Point3* pt;       // array of 3D vertices
        int numNormals;   // number of normal vectors for the mesh
        Vector3 *norm;    // array of normals
        int numFaces;     // number of faces in the mesh
        Face* face;       // array of face data
        // ... others to be added later
    public:
        Mesh();           // constructor
        ~Mesh();          // destructor
        int readFile(char * fileName);    // to read in a filed mesh
        .. others ..
};
```

The Face data type is basically a list of vertices and the normal vector associated with each vertex in the face. It is organized here as an array of index pairs: the normal to the vth vertex of the fth face has value normal vector norm[face[f].vert[v].normIndex]. This appears cumbersome at first exposure, but the indexing scheme is quite orderly and easy to manage, and it has the advantage of efficiency, allowing rapid random access indexing into the pt[] array.

FIGURE 6.15 Proposed data type for a mesh.

---

[2] Definitions of the basic classes Point3 and Vector3 have been given previously, and they also appear in Appendix 3.

FIGURE 6.16 Data for the tetrahedron.

■ **EXAMPLE 6.2.3 Data for the tetrahedron**

Figure 6.16 presents the specific data structure for the tetrahedron shown, which has vertices at $(0,0,0)$, $(1,0,0)$, $(0,1,0)$, and $(0,0,1)$. Check the values reported in each field. (We discuss how to find the normal vectors later.)

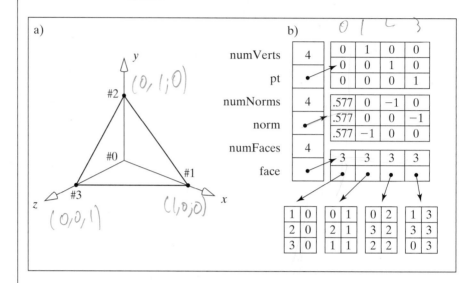

The first task is to develop a method for drawing such a mesh object. It's a matter of drawing each of its faces, of course. An OpenGL-based implementation of the `Mesh::draw()` method must traverse the array of faces in the mesh object, and for each face send the list of vertices and their normals down the graphics pipeline. In OpenGL you specify that subsequent vertices are associated with normal vector **m** by executing `glNormal3f(m.x, m.y, m.z)`.[3] So the basic flow of `Mesh::draw()` is:

```
for (each face, f, in the mesh)
{
        glBegin(GL_POLYGON);
        for (each vertex, v, in face, f)
        {
            glNormal3f(normal at vertex v);
            glVertex3f(position of vertex v);
        }
glEnd();
}
```

The implementation is shown in Figure 6.17.

We also need methods to create a particular mesh and to read a predefined mesh into memory from a file. We consider reading from and writing to files in Case Study 6.1. We next examine a number of interesting families of shapes that can be stored in a mesh and see how to create them.

To Create and Draw a Mesh Object Using SDL

It is convenient in a graphics application to read in mesh descriptions using the SDL language introduced in Chapter 5. To use SDL, simply develop the `Mesh` class from

---

[3] For proper shading these vectors must be normalized. To accomplish this place `glEnable(GL_NORMALIZE)` in the `init()` function. This requests that OpenGL automatically normalize all normal vectors.

```
void Mesh:: draw()        // use OpenGL to draw this mesh
{
   for (int f = 0; f < numFaces; f++)      // draw each face
   {
      glBegin (GL_POLYGON);
         for (int v = 0; v < face[f].nVerts; v++)     // for each one..
         {
            int in = face[f].vert[v].normIndex ;   // index of this normal
            int iv = face[f].vert[v].vertIndex ;   // index of this vertex
            glNormal3f(norm[in].x, norm[in].y, norm[in].z);
            glVertex3f(pt[iv].x, pt[iv].y, pt[iv].z);
         }
      glEnd();
   }
}
```

FIGURE 6.17 Method to draw a mesh using OpenGL.

the Shape class (as SDL does for you) and add the method drawOpenGL(). The book's companion web site gives full details on the Shape class and SDL's supporting classes. This idea becomes more important as we near our ray tracing discussion in Chapter 12.

The Scene class that reads SDL files is already set to accept the keyword mesh, followed by the name of the file that contains the mesh description. Thus to create and draw a pawn with a certain translation and scaling, use:

push translate 3 5 4 scale 3 3 3 mesh pawn.3vn pop

(A number of such files having suffix .3vn, are available on the book's web site.) The file pawn.3vn is used in tellMaterialsGL(); as the list of vertices, normals to each vertex, and various reflection coefficients to be discussed in Chapter 8.

6.3 POLYHEDRA

Often it is convenient to restrict the data in a mesh so that they represent a **polyhedron**. A very large number of solid objects of interest are indeed polyhedra, and algorithms for processing a mesh can be greatly simplified if they need only process meshes that represent a polyhedron.

Slightly different definitions for a polyhedron are used in different contexts [Coxeter69, Hilbert50, Foley90], but we use the following:

> **DEFINITION:** A **polyhedron** is a connected mesh of simple planar polygons that enclose a finite amount of space.

So by definition a polyhedron represents a single solid object. This requires that:

- every edge is shared by exactly two faces;
- at least three edges meet at each vertex;
- faces do not interpenetrate: two faces either do not touch at all, or they touch only along their common edge.

In Figure 6.13 Pyramid is clearly a polyhedron. Donut evidently encloses space, so it is a polyhedron if its faces are in fact planar. It is not a simple polyhedron, since there is a hole through it. In addition, two of its faces themselves have holes. Is Impossible a polyhedron? Why? If the texture faces (the windows and doors) are omitted, Barn might be modeled as two polyhedra, one for the main part and one for the silo.

Euler's Formula

Euler's formula (which is very easy to prove—see, for instance, [Courant and Robbins, 61, p. 236]) provides a fundamental relationship between the number of faces, edges, and vertices (F, E, and V, respectively) of a simple polyhedron:

$$V + F - E = 2 \tag{6.1}$$

For example, a cube has $V = 8$, $F = 6$, and $E = 12$.

The structure of a polyhedron is often nicely revealed by a **Schlegel diagram**. This is based on a view of the polyhedron from a point just outside the center of one of its faces, as suggested in Figure 6.18a. Viewing a cube in this way produces the Schlegel diagram shown in Figure 6.18b. The front face appears as a large polygon surrounding the rest of the faces.

FIGURE 6.18 The Schlegel diagrams for a cube.

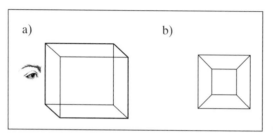

Figure 6.19 shows further examples. Part a shows the Schlegel diagram of Pyramid shown in Figure 6.13, and parts b and c show two quite different Schlegel diagrams for the basic Barn. (Which faces are closest to the eye?)

FIGURE 6.19 Schlegel diagrams for Pyramid and the basic Barn.

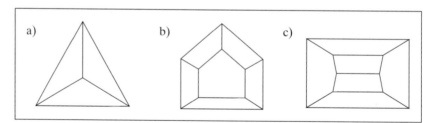

6.3.1 Prisms

A prism is a particular type of polyhedron that embodies certain symmetries and therefore is quite simple to describe. As shown in Figure 6.20, a prism is defined by **sweeping** (or **extruding**) a polygon along a straight line, turning a 2D polygon into a 3D polyhedron. In Figure 6.20a polygon P is swept along vector **d** to form the polyhedron shown in part b. When **d** is perpendicular to the plane of P, the prism is a **right prism**. Figure 6.20c shows some block letters of the alphabet swept to form prisms.

FIGURE 6.20 Using extrusion to form a prism.

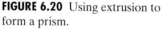
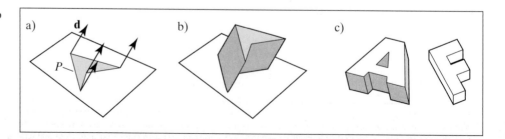

PRACTICE EXERCISES

6.3.1 Build the lists for a prism

Give the vertex, normal, and face lists for the prism shown in Figure 6.21. Assume the base of the prism (face #4) lies in the xy-plane, and vertex 2 lies on the z-axis at $z = 4$. Further assume vertex 5 lies 3 units along the x-axis, and that the base is an equilateral triangle.

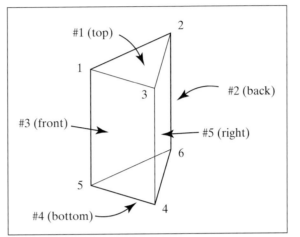

FIGURE 6.21 An example polyhedral object.

6.3.2 Build meshes

For the donut and barn objects in Figure 6.13, assign numbers to each vertex and then write a face list. ■

6.3.2 The Platonic Solids

If all of the faces of a polyhedron are identical and each is a regular polygon, the object is a **regular polyhedron**. These symmetry constraints are so severe that only five such objects can exist, the **Platonic solids**[4] shown in Figure 6.22 [Coxeter61]. The Platonic solids exhibit a sublime symmetry and a fascinating array of properties. They make interesting objects of study in computer graphics, and often appear in solid modeling CAD applications.

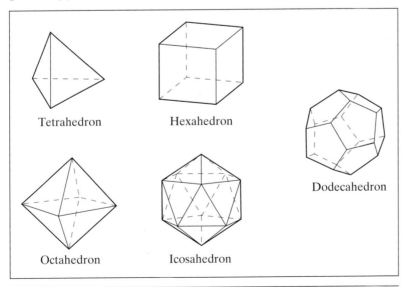

Tetrahedron   Hexahedron   Dodecahedron   Octahedron   Icosahedron

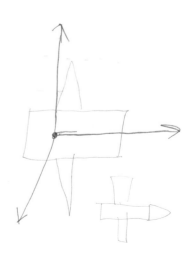

FIGURE 6.22 The five Platonic solids.

---

4 Named in honor of Plato (427–347 B.C.), who commemorated them in his *Timaeus*. But they were known before this: for instance a toy dodecahedron was found near Padua in Etruscan ruins that date from 500 B.C.

Three of the Platonic solids have equilateral triangles as faces, one has squares, and the dodecahedron has pentagons. The cube and octahedron are variations of the regular prism.

It is straightforward to build mesh lists for the cube and octahedron (see the exercises). We give example vertex and face lists for the tetrahedron and icosahedron below, and we discuss how to compute normal lists. We also show how to derive the lists for the dodecahedron from those of the icosahedron, making use of their duality, which we define next.

Dual Polyhedra

Each of the Platonic solids P has a **dual** polyhedron D. The vertices of D are the *centers* of the faces of P, so edges of D connect the midpoints of adjacent faces of P. Figure 6.23 shows the dual of each Platonic solid inscribed within it.

FIGURE 6.23 Dual Platonic solids.

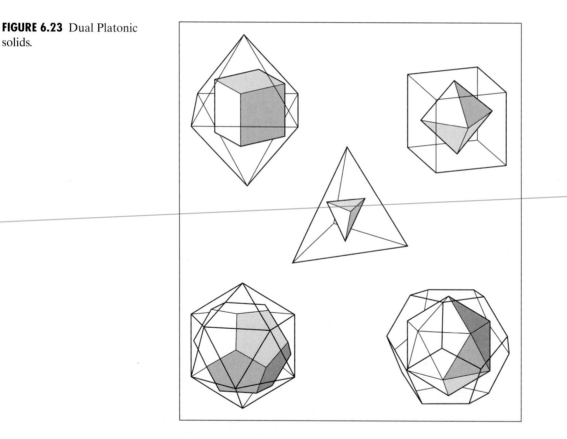

- The dual of a tetrahedron is also a tetrahedron.
- The cube and octahedron are duals.
- The icosahedron and dodecahedron are duals.

The number of vertices for one is the number of faces for the dual. Duals have the same number, E, of edges, and the number of vertices, V, for one is the number of faces, F, for the other. If we know the vertex list of one Platonic solid P, we can immediately build the vertex list of its dual D, since vertex k of D lies at the center of face k of P. Building D in this way actually builds a version that inscribes P.

To keep track of vertex and face numbering we use a **model**, which is fashioned by slicing along certain edges of each solid and unfolding it to lie flat, so that all the faces are seen from the outside. Models for three of the Platonic solids are shown in Figure 6.24.

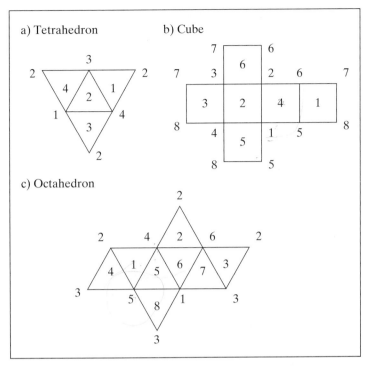

a) Tetrahedron

b) Cube

c) Octahedron

FIGURE 6.24 Models for the tetrahedron, cube, and octahedron.

Each of the vertices and each of the faces of the model are then numbered, as you wish. Much greater attention to numbering must be paid when drawing the model of the dual polyhedra, however, as we see next. Consider the dual pair of the cube and octahedron. Face 4 of the cube is seen to be surrounded by vertices 1, 5, 6, and 2. By duality vertex 4 of the octahedron is surrounded by faces 1, 5, 6, and 2. Note for the tetrahedron that since it is self-dual, the list of vertices surrounding the kth face is identical to the list of faces surrounding the kth vertex.

The position of vertex 4 of the octahedron is the center of face 4 of the cube. Recall from Chapter 5 that the center of a face is just the *average* of the vertices belonging to that face. So if we know the vertices V_1, V_5, V_6, and V_2 for face 4 of the cube, we have immediately for the octahedron:

$$V_4 = \tfrac{1}{4}(V_1 + V_5 + V_6 + V_2) \tag{6.3}$$

PRACTICE EXERCISES

6.3.3 The octahedron

Consider the octahedron that is the dual of the cube. Build vertex and face lists for this octahedron.

6.3.4 Check duality

Beginning with the face and vertex lists of the octahedron in the previous exercise, find the dual of this polyhedron, and check that this dual is (a scaled version of) the cube. ■

Normal Vectors for the Platonic Solids

If we wish to build meshes for the Platonic solids, we must compute the normal vector to each face. Since we want to display Platonic solids as having flat faces with visible edges, it is appropriate to use face normals rather than vertex normals. This can be done in the usual way using Newell's method, but the high degree of symmetry of a Platonic solid offers a much simpler approach. Assuming the solid is centered at the origin, the normal vector to each face is the vector from the origin to the *center* of the face, which is formed as the average of the vertices which is, of course, an affine combination of points. Figure 6.25 shows this for the octahedron. The normal to the face shown is simply:

FIGURE 6.25 Symmetry used to find the normal to a face.

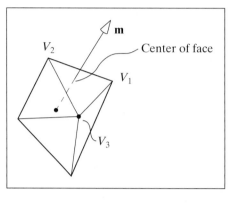

$$\mathbf{m} = (V_1 + V_2 + V_3)/3 \qquad\qquad (6.4)$$

(*Note*: This vector is also the same as that from the origin to the appropriate vertex on the dual Platonic solid.)

The Tetrahedron

The vertex list of a tetrahedron depends, of course, on how the tetrahedron is positioned, oriented, and sized. It is interesting that a tetrahedron can be inscribed in a cube (such that its four vertices lie in corners of the cube, and its four edges lie in faces of the cube). Consider the unit cube having vertices ($\pm 1, \pm 1, \pm 1$), and choose the tetrahedron that has one vertex at (1,1,1). Then it has vertex and face lists given in Figure 6.26 [Blinn87].

FIGURE 6.26 Vertex list and face list for a tetrahedron.

vertex list				face list	
Vertex	**x**	**y**	**z**	**Face number**	**Vertices**
0	1	1	1	0	1, 2, 3
1	1	−1	−1	1	0, 3, 2
2	−1	−1	1	2	0, 1, 3
3	−1	1	−1	3	0, 2, 1

The Icosahedron

The vertex list for the icosahedron presents more of a challenge, but we can exploit a remarkable fact to make it simple. Figure 6.27 shows that three mutually perpendicular **golden rectangles** inscribe the icosahedron! A vertex list may be read directly from this picture. We choose to align each golden rectangle with a coordinate axis. For convenience, we define one rectangle so that its longer edge extends from −1 to 1 along the *x*-axis and its shorter edge extends from −φ to φ, where $\phi = (\sqrt{5} - 1)/2 = 0.618$ is the reciprocal of the golden ratio φ.

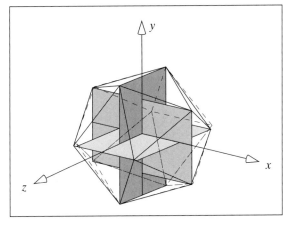

FIGURE 6.27 Golden rectangles defining the icosahedron.

From this it is just a matter of listing vertex positions, as shown in Figure 6.28.

A model for the icosahedron is shown in Figure 6.29. The face list for the icosahedron can be read directly. (*Question*: What is the normal vector to face 8?)

FIGURE 6.28 Vertex list for the icosahedron.

Vertex	*x*	*y*	*z*
0	0	1	φ
1	0	1	−φ
2	1	φ	0
3	1	−φ	0
4	0	−1	−φ
5	0	−1	φ
6	φ	0	1
7	−φ	0	1
8	φ	0	−1
9	−φ	0	−1
10	−1	φ	0
11	−1	−φ	0

FIGURE 6.29 Model for the icosahedron.

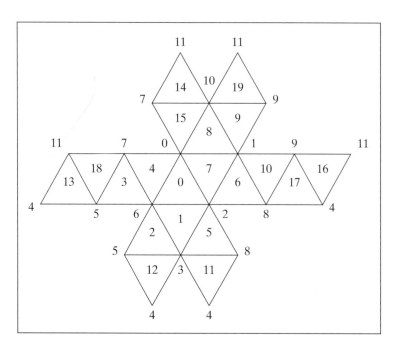

Some people prefer to adjust the model for the icosahedron slightly into the form shown in Figure 6.30. This makes it clearer that an icosahedron is made up of a type of prism (shown shaded) and two pentagonal pyramids on its top and bottom.

FIGURE 6.30 An icosahedron is a prism with a cap and base.

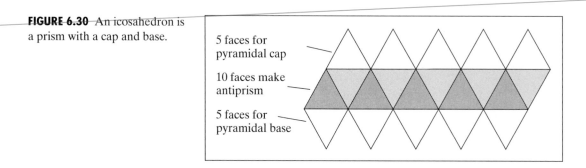

The Dodecahedron

The dodecahedron is dual to the icosahedron, so all the information needed to build lists for the dodecahedron is buried in the lists for the icosahedron. But it is convenient to see the model of the dodecahedron laid out, as in Figure 6.31.

Using duality again, we know vertex k of the dodecahedron lies at the center of face k of the icosahedron: just average the three vertices of face k. All of the vertices of the dodecahedron are easily calculated in this fashion.

6.3.3 Other Interesting Polyhedra

There are endless varieties of polyhedra (see for instance [Wennington71] and [Coxeter63]), but one class is particularly interesting. Whereas each Platonic solid has the same type of n-gon for all of its faces, the **Archimedean** (also **semiregular**) solids have more than one kind of face, although they are still regular polygons. In addition it is required that every vertex is surrounded by the same collection of polygons in the same order.

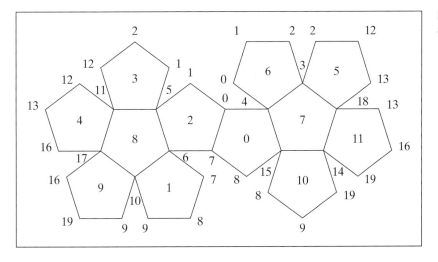

FIGURE 6.31 Model for the dodecahedron.

For instance, the **truncated cube**, shown in Figure 6.32a, has 8-gons and 3-gons for faces, and around each vertex one finds one triangle and two 8-gons. This is summarized by associating the symbol $3 \cdot 8 \cdot 8$ with this solid.

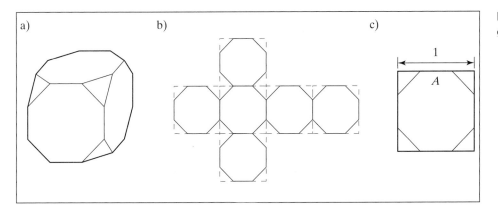

FIGURE 6.32 The truncated cube.

The truncated cube is formed by slicing a portion off each corner of a cube in just the right fashion. The model for the truncated cube, shown in Figure 6.32b, is based on that of the cube. Each edge of the cube is divided into three parts, the middle part is of length $A = 1/(1 + \sqrt{2})$ (Figure 6.32c), and the middle portion of each edge is joined to its neighbors. Thus if an edge of the cube has endpoints C and D, two new vertices V and W are formed as the affine combinations

$$V = \frac{1 + A}{2} C + \frac{1 - A}{2} D$$

$$W = \frac{1 - A}{2} C + \frac{1 + A}{2} D \tag{6.5}$$

Based on this it is straightforward to build vertex and face lists for the truncated cube.

Given the constraints that faces must be regular polygons, and that they must occur in the same arrangement about each vertex, there are only 13 possible Archimedean solids. Archimedean solids still enjoy enough symmetry that the normal vector to each face is found using the center of the face.

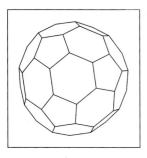

FIGURE 6.33 The Buckyball.

One Archimedean solid of particular interest is the truncated icosahedron $5 \cdot 6^2$ shown in Figure 6.33, which consists of regular hexagons and pentagons. The pattern is familiar from soccer balls used around the world. More recently this shape has been named the **Buckyball** after Buckminster Fuller because of his interest in geodesic structures similar to this. Crystallographers have recently discovered that 60 atoms of carbon can be arranged at the vertices of the truncated icosahedron, producing a new kind of carbon molecule that is neither graphite nor diamond. The material has many remarkable properties, such as high-temperature stability and superconductivity [Browne90], and has acquired the name **Fullerene**.

The Buckyball is interesting to model and view on a graphics display. To build its vertex and face lists, draw the model of the icosahedron given in Figure 6.29 and divide each edge into three equal parts. This produces two new vertices along each edge, whose positions are easily calculated. Number the 60 new vertices according to taste to build the vertex list of a Buckyball. Figure 6.34 shows a partial model of the icosahedron with the new vertices connected by edges. Note that each old face of the icosahedron becomes a hexagon, and that each old vertex of the icosahedron has been snipped off to form a pentagonal face. Building the face list is just a matter of listing what is seen in the model.

FIGURE 6.34 To build a Buckyball.

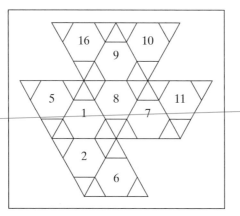

6.4 EXTRUDED SHAPES

The object of art is to give life a shape.

William Shakespeare
(1564–1616)

A large class of shapes can be generated by **extruding** or **sweeping** a 2D shape through space. The prism shown in Figure 6.20 is an example of sweeping linearly, which is in a straight line. As we shall see, the tetrahedron and octahedron of Figure 6.24 are also examples of extruding a shape through space in a certain way. In addition, surfaces of revolution can also be approximated by extrusion of a polygon, once we slightly broaden the definition of extrusion.

In this section we examine some ways to generate meshes by sweeping polygons in discrete steps. In Section 6.5 we develop similar tools for building meshes that attempt to approximate smoothly swept shapes.

6.4.1 Creating Prisms

We begin with the prism, which is formed by sweeping a polygon in a straight line. Figure 6.35 shows a prism based on an ARROW polygon P we shall call ARROW,

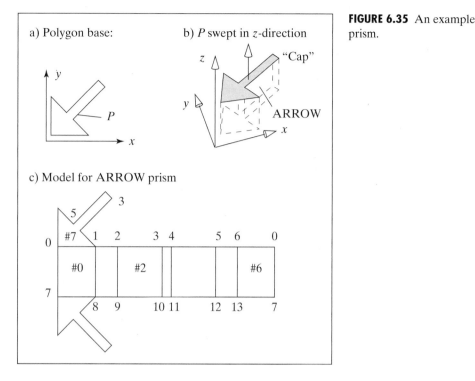

FIGURE 6.35 An example prism.

having seven vertices that lie in the xy-plane. P is swept through a distance H along the z-axis, forming the ARROW prism shown in Figure 6.35b. (More generally, the sweep could be along a vector **d**, as in Figure 6.19.) As P is swept along, an edge in the z-direction is created for each vertex of P. Here this creates another seven vertices, so the prism has 14 vertices in all. They appear in pairs: if $(x_i, y_i, 0)$ is one of the vertices of the base P, then the prism also contains the vertex (x_i, y_i, H).

What face list describes ARROW? The prism is unfolded into the model shown in Figure 6.35c to expose its nine faces as seen from the outside. There are seven rectangular sides plus the bottom **base** P and the top **cap**. Face 2, for instance, is defined by vertices 2, 9, 10, and 3.

Because the prism has flat faces, we associate the same normal vector with every vertex of a face: the normal vector to the face itself.

To Build a Mesh for the Prism

We want a tool to make a mesh for the prism based on an arbitrary polygon. Suppose the prism's base is a polygon with N vertices (x_i, y_i). We number the vertices of the base $0, \ldots, N-1$ and those of the cap $N, \ldots, 2N-1$, so that an edge joins vertices i and $i + N$, as in the example. The vertex list is then easily constructed to contain the points $(x_i, y_i, 0)$ and (x_i, y_i, H), for $i = 0, 1, \ldots, N-1$.

The face list is also straightforward to construct. We first make the side faces or walls and then add the cap and base. For the jth wall ($j = 0, \ldots, N-1$) we create a face with the four vertices having indices $j, j + N, next(j) + N$, and $next(j)$ where $next(j)$ is $j + 1$ unless j equals $N - 1$, whereupon it is 0. This takes care of the wraparound from the $(N - 1)$st to the 0th vertex. In terms of program code, we say:

```
if (j < n-1)
     next = j+1;
else
     next = 0;
```

Each face is inserted in the face list as it is created. The normal vector to each face is easily found using the Newell method described earlier. We then create the base and cap faces and insert them in the face list. Case Study 6.2 provides more details for building mesh models of prisms.

PRACTICE EXERCISE

6.4.1 Develop a mesh model

1. Develop a mesh model for the prism of Figure 6.35. Invent a pleasing shape of your choice for the arrow of Figure 6.35b that is swept in the z-direction, which will determine the positions of the vertices.   ∎

6.4.2 Arrays of Extruded Prisms—"Brick Laying"

Some rendering tools, like OpenGL, can reliably draw only convex polygons. OpenGL might fail, for instance, to draw the arrow of Figure 6.35 correctly; it might instead draw an imperfect version of the arrow. If this is so, the polygon can be decomposed (tessellated) into a set of convex polygons, and each one can be extruded. Figure 6.36 shows an example; an extruded letter, F, decomposed so that its four pieces are convex.

FIGURE 6.36 Extruded objects based on a collection of convex prisms.

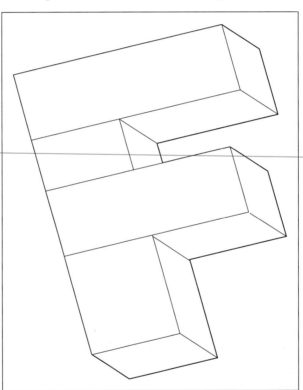

Prisms like this are composed of an array of convex prisms. Some of the component prisms abut one another and therefore share all or parts of some walls. Because vertex positions are being computed at a high precision, the crease where two walls adjoin will usually be invisible.

For this family of shapes we need a method that builds a mesh out of an array of prisms, say

```
void Mesh:: makePrismArray(...)
```

which would take as its arguments a suitable list of (convex) base polygons (assumed to lie in the xy-plane), and perhaps a vector **d** that describes the direction and amount of extrusion. The vertex list would contain the vertices of the cap and base polygons for each prism, and the individual walls, base, and cap of each prism would be stored in the face list. Drawing such a mesh would involve some wasted effort, since walls that abut would be drawn (twice), even though they are ultimately invisible.

Special Case: Extruded Quad-Strips

A simpler but very interesting family of such prisms can be built and manipulated more efficiently. These are prisms for which the base polygon can be represented by a *quad-strip*. The quad-strip is an array of quadrilaterals connected in a chain, like bricks laid in a row, such that neighboring faces coincide completely, as shown in Figure 6.37a. Recall from Figure 2.39 that the quad-strip is an OpenGL geometric primitive. A quad-strip is described by a sequence of vertices:

$$\text{quad-strip} = \{p_0, p_1, p_2, \ldots, p_{M-1}\} \tag{6.7}$$

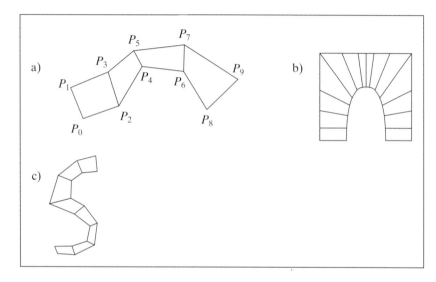

FIGURE 6.37 Quad-strips and prisms built upon quad-strips.

The vertices are understood to be taken in pairs, with the odd ones forming one edge of the quad-strip and the even ones forming the other edge. Each 'brick' reuses the previous pair of vertices, plus two more from the list. Not every polygon can be represented as a quad-strip. (Which of the polygons in Figure 6.36 are not quad-strips? What block letters of the alphabet can be drawn as quad-strips?)

When a mesh is formed as an extruded quad-strip, only $2M$ vertices are placed in the vertex list, and only the outside walls are included in the face list. There are $2M - 2$ faces in all. (Why?) Thus no redundant walls are drawn when the mesh is rendered.

Figure 6.38 shows an example of an interesting extruded quad-strip. Case Study 6.4 considers how to make such meshes in more detail.

6.4.3 Extrusions with a "Twist"

So far an extrusion just shifts the base polygon to a new position to define the cap polygon. It is easy to generalize on this in a way that produces a much broader family of shapes; create the cap polygon as an enlarged or shrunk, and possibly rotated, version of the base polygon. Specifically, if the base polygon is P, with vertices $\{p_0, p_1, \ldots, p_{N-1}\}$, the cap polygon has vertices

$$P' = \{M_{p0}, M_{p1}, \ldots, M_{pN-1}\} \tag{6.8}$$

FIGURE 6.38 Extruded quad-
strips—arches.

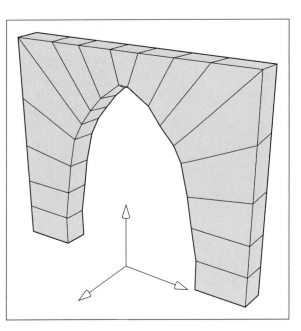

where *M* is some 4-by-4 matrix representing an affine transformation. Figure 6.39
shows some examples.

FIGURE 6.39 Pyramids and
twisted prisms.

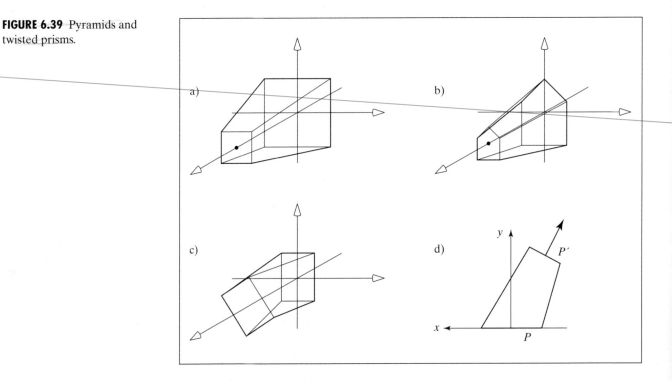

Parts a and b show pyramids, or tapered cylinders (also truncated cones), where
the cap is a smaller version of the base. The transformation matrix for this is:

$$M = \begin{pmatrix} 0.7 & 0 & 0 & 0 \\ 0 & 0.7 & 0 & 0 \\ 0 & 0 & 1 & H \\ 0 & 0 & 0 & 1 \end{pmatrix}$$

based simply on a scaling factor of 0.7 and a translation by H along z. Part c shows a cylinder where the cap has been rotated through an angle θ about the z-axis before translation, using the matrix:

$$M = \begin{pmatrix} \cos(\theta) & \sin(\theta) & 0 & 0 \\ -\sin(\theta) & \cos(\theta) & 0 & 0 \\ 0 & 0 & 1 & H \\ 0 & 0 & 0 & 1 \end{pmatrix}$$

And part d shows in cross section how cap P' can be rotated arbitrarily before it is translated to the desired position.

Prisms such as these are just as easy to create as those that use a simple translation for M: the face list is identical to the original; only the vertex positions (and the values for the normal vectors) are altered.

PRACTICE EXERCISES

6.4.2 The tapered cylinder

Describe in detail how to make vertex, normal, and face lists for a tapered cylinder having regular pentagons for its base and cap, where the cap is one-half as large as the base.

6.4.3 The tetrahedron as a tapered cylinder

Describe how to model a tetrahedron as a tapered cylinder with a triangular base. Is this an efficient way to obtain a mesh for a tetrahedron? ■

6.4.4 To Build Segmented Extrusions—Tubes and Snakes

Another rich set of objects can be modeled by employing a sequence of extrusions, each with its own transformation, and laying them end to end to form a tube. Figure 6.40a shows a tube made by extruding a square P three times, in different directions with different tapers and twists. The first segment has end polygons M_0P and M_1P, where the initial matrix M_0 positions and orients the starting end of the tube. The second segment has end polygons M_1P and M_2P, and so on. We shall call the various transformed polygons the "**waists**" of the tube. In this example the vertex list of the mesh contains the 16 vertices M_0p_0, M_0p_1, M_0p_2, M_0p_3, M_1p_0, M_1p_1, M_1p_2, M_1p_3, ..., M_3p_0, M_3p_1, M_3p_2, M_3p_3. Figure 6.40b shows a "snake," so called because the matrices M_i cause the tube to grow and shrink to represent the body and head of a snake. Note the various shades of the snake segments. We will see how to do shading algorithmically in Chapter 8

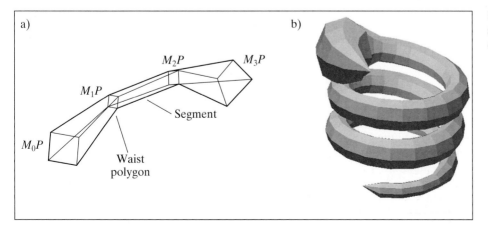

FIGURE 6.40 A tube (a) and a snake (b) made from successive extrusions of a polygon.

Tubes Based on 3D Curves—Frenet Frames

How do we design interesting and useful tubes and snakes? We could choose the individual matrices M_i by hand, but this is awkward at best. This is a perfect application for CAD, to automate the task. It is much easier to think of the tube as wrapped around a curve, which we shall call the **spine** of the tube, that undulates through space in some organized fashion. We shall represent the curve parametrically as $C(t)$. For example, the **helix** (recall Section 3.8) shown in stereo in Figure 6.41a, has the parametric representation

$$C(t) = (\cos(t), \sin(t), bt) \tag{6.9}$$

for some constant b.

FIGURE 6.41 A helix stereo pair.

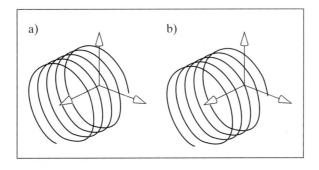

To form the various waist polygons of the tube we sample $C(t)$ at a set of t-values, $\{t_0, t_1, \dots\}$, and build a transformed polygon in the plane perpendicular to the curve at each point $C(t_i)$, as suggested in Figure 6.42. It is convenient to think of erecting a local coordinate system at each chosen point along the spine: the local z-axis points along the curve, and the local x- and y-axes point in directions normal to the z-axis (and normal to each other). The waist polygon is set to lie in the local xy-plane. All we need is a straightforward way to determine the vertices of each waist polygon.

FIGURE 6.42 Local coordinate systems constructed along the spine curve.

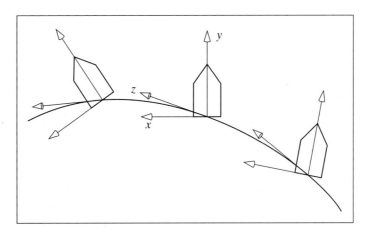

It is most convenient to let the curve $C(t)$ *itself* determine the local coordinate systems. A method well known in differential geometry creates the **Frenet frame** at each point along the spine [Gray93]. At each value t_i of interest a vector $\mathbf{T}(t_i)$ that is tangent to the curve is computed. Then two vectors, $\mathbf{a}(t_i)$ and $\mathbf{b}(t_i)$, which are perpendicular to $\mathbf{T}(t_i)$ and to each other, are computed. These three vectors constitute the **Frenet frame** at t_i.

Once the Frenet frame is computed, it is easy to find the transformation matrix M that transforms the base polygon of the tube to its position and orientation in this frame. It is the transformation that carries the world coordinate system into this new coordinate system. (The reasoning is very similar to that used in Exercise 5.6.1 on transforming the camera coordinate system into the world coordinate system.) The matrix M_i must carry $\mathbf{i}, \mathbf{j}$, and $\mathbf{k}$ into $\mathbf{b}(t_i)$, $\mathbf{a}(t_i)$, $\mathbf{T}(t_i)$, respectively, and must carry the origin of the world into the spine point $C(t_i)$. Thus the matrix has columns consisting directly of $\mathbf{N}(t_i)$, $\mathbf{B}(t_i)$, $\mathbf{T}(t_i)$, and $C(t_i)$ expressed in homogeneous coordinates:

$$M_i = (\mathbf{N}(t_i) \mid \mathbf{B}(t_i) \mid \mathbf{T}(t_i) \mid C(t_i)) \tag{6.10}$$

Forming the Frenet Frame

The Frenet frame at each point along a curve depends on how the curve twists and undulates. It is derived from certain derivatives of $C(t)$, and so it is easy to form if these derivatives can be calculated.

Specifically, if the formula that we have for $C(t)$ is differentiable, we can take its derivative and form the tangent vector to the curve at each point, $\dot{\mathbf{C}}(t)$. (Suppose $C(t)$ has components $C_x(t), C_y(t)$, and $C_z(t)$. Then this derivative is simply $\dot{\mathbf{C}}(t) = (\dot{C}_x(t), \dot{C}_y(t), \dot{C}_z(t))$. This vector points in the direction the curve is headed at each value of t—that is, in the direction of the **tangent** to the curve. We normalize it to unit length to obtain the **unit tangent vector** at t. For example, the helix of Equation (6.9) has the unit tangent vector given by

$$\mathbf{T}(t) = \frac{1}{\sqrt{1 + b^2}}(-\sin(t), \cos(t), b) \tag{6.11}$$

This tangent is shown at four values of t in Figure 6.43a. Visualize how the frame rotates as it moves along the curve.

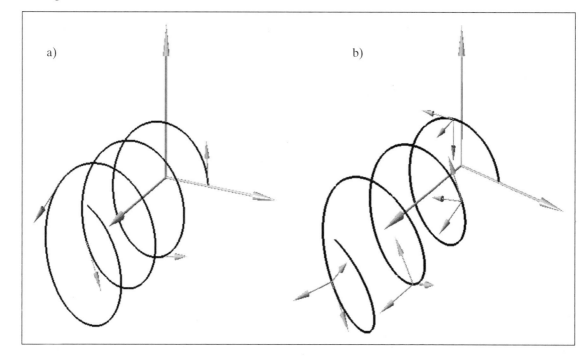

a) b)

FIGURE 6.43 a) Tangents to the helix, b) Frenet frame at various values of t, for the helix.

Given the unit tangent vector $\mathbf{T}(t)$ we need another vector, say $\mathbf{a}(t)$, that is normal to $\mathbf{T}(t)$. With these two vectors in hand it will be simple to complete the coordinate system: a third vector, say $\mathbf{b}(t)$, normal to them both can be found by taking their cross product, $\mathbf{b}(t) = \mathbf{a}(t) \times \mathbf{T}(t)$.

How can we find a vector normal to $\mathbf{T}(t)$? The classical way [Gray93] to develop the Frenet frame is to compute a second derivative vector, and to use suitable cross products to find $\mathbf{a}(t)$ and $\mathbf{b}(t)$. Finding the second derivative may be awkward to do, however, for some intricate curves. In 2D we could enlist the perp vector (see Chapter 4), which is a unique vector perpendicular to a given vector. But what can we do in 3D, where the perp vector itself is inapplicable? Note that we don't need a unique vector here, just some vector that is normal to $\mathbf{T}(t)$. Can we find one simply and inexpensively?

Suppose $\mathbf{T}(t)$ has components we shall call a, b, c (each of these is a function of t, of course). Then by inspection the vector

$$\mathbf{n} = (-b, a, 0) \tag{6.12}$$

is perpendicular to $\mathbf{T}(t)$ (check this). Normalize $\mathbf{n}$ and $\mathbf{T}(t)$, and take their cross product to form a third product, say a, and we have the desired coordinate system: three mutually perpendicular unit vectors!

$$\mathbf{a} = n \times \mathbf{T} \tag{6.13}$$

Some readers might argue that it is restrictive forcing the third component of $\mathbf{n}$ to be 0. For those who find it bothersome, the restriction can be lifted by using a different value, say d, for the third component, and then adjusting the second component (a) to force once again the dot product of $\mathbf{n}$ with $\mathbf{T}$ to be 0. (Work out these details if you are curious.) For the helix example these vectors are given by:

$$\mathbf{n}(t) = \frac{1}{\sqrt{1 + b^2}}(b\sin(t), -b\cos(t), 1) \tag{6.14}$$

Figure 6.43b shows the Frenet frame at various values of t along the helix.

> There is nothing quite as annoying as a good example.
>
> *Mark Twain*
> *(1835–1910)*

Aside: Finding the Frenet frame numerically.

If the formula for $\mathbf{C}(t)$ is complicated, it may be awkward to form its successive derivatives in closed form, such that formulas for $\mathbf{T}(t)$, $\mathbf{B}(t)$, and $\mathbf{N}(t)$ can be hardwired into a program. As an alternative, it is possible to approximate the derivatives numerically using:

$$\dot{\mathbf{C}}(t) = \frac{C(t + \varepsilon) - C(t - \varepsilon)}{2\varepsilon}$$

$$\ddot{\mathbf{C}}(t) = \frac{C(t - \varepsilon) - 2C(t) + C(t + \varepsilon)}{\varepsilon^2} \tag{6.15}$$

This computation will usually produce acceptable directions for $\mathbf{T}(t)$, $\mathbf{B}(t)$, and $\mathbf{N}(t)$, although the user should beware that numerical differentiation is an inherently unstable process [Burden85].

Figure 6.44 shows the result of wrapping a decagon about the helix in this way. The helix was sampled at 30 points, a Frenet frame was constructed at each point, and the decagon was erected in the new frame. Try to visualize the local coordinate systems as you move along the spine, and note how they "drift" and rotate about the spine along the way.

Figure 6.45 shows other interesting examples, based on the toroidal spiral (which we first saw in Section 3.8.) [Gray93, p. 212]. The edges of the individual faces are

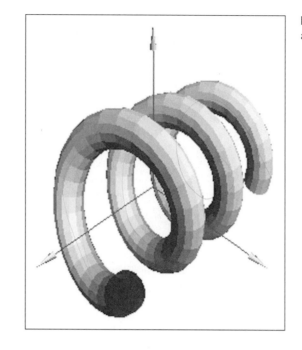

FIGURE 6.44 A tube wrapped along a helix.

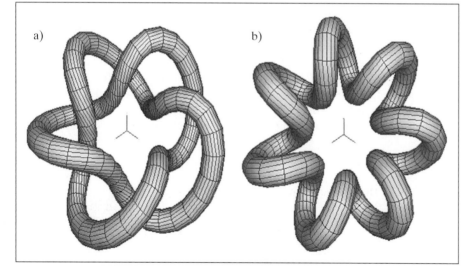

FIGURE 6.45 Tubes based on toroidal spirals.

drawn to clarify how the tube twists as it proceeds. Drawing the edges of a mesh is considered in Case Study 6.7. A toroidal spiral is formed when a spiral is wrapped about a torus (try to envision the underlying invisible torus here), and it is given by

$$C(t) = ((a + b\cos(qt))\cos(pt), (a + b\cos(qt))\sin(pt), c\sin(qt)) \qquad (6.16)$$

for some choice of constants $a, b, p,$ and q. For part a the parameters p and q were chosen as 2 and 5, and for part b they are chosen to be 1 and 7.

Figure 6.46 shows a sea shell, formed by wrapping a tube with a growing radius about a helix. To accomplish this, the matrix of Equation (6.10) was multiplied by a scaling matrix, where the scale factors also depend on t:

$$M' = M \begin{pmatrix} g(t) & 0 & 0 & 0 \\ 0 & g(t) & 0 & 0 \\ 0 & 0 & 1 & 0 \\ 0 & 0 & 0 & 1 \end{pmatrix}$$

FIGURE 6.46 A sea shell.

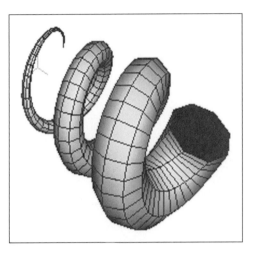

Here $g(t) = t$. It is also possible to add a rotation to the matrix, so that the tube appears to twist more vigorously as one looks along the spine.

One problem with using Frenet frames for sweeping curves is that the local frame sometimes twists in such a way as to introduce undesired knots in the surface. Recent work, such as [Wang97], finds alternatives to the Frenet frame that produce less twisting and therefore more graceful surfaces.

Another interesting application for Frenet frames is analyzing the motion of a car moving along a roller coaster. Figure 6.47 shows an example roller coaster and illustrates how complicated the path of the car can be. If we assume that a motor within the car is able to control its speed at any instant, then knowing the shape of the car's path is enough to specify $C(t)$. Now if suitable derivatives of $C(t)$ can be taken, the normal and binormal vectors for the car's motion can be found and a Frenet frame for the car can be constructed for each relevant value of t. This will allow us to develop formulas for the forces operating on both the wheels and the passengers of each car.

FIGURE 6.47 A model of a roller coaster. (Courtesy of Ing.-Büro Stengel GmbH)

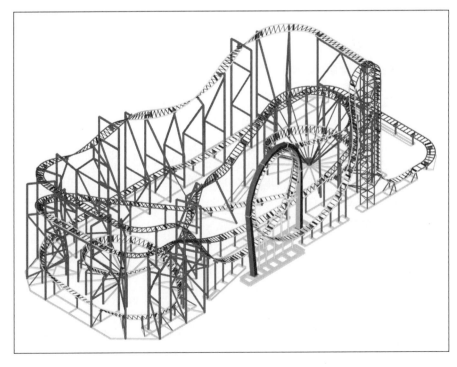

PRACTICE EXERCISES

6.4.4 What is N(*t*)?

Show that $\mathbf{N}(t)$ is parallel to $\ddot{\mathbf{C}}(t) - (\dot{\mathbf{C}}(t) \cdot \ddot{\mathbf{C}}(t))\dot{\mathbf{C}}(t)/|\dot{\mathbf{C}}(t)|^2$, so it points in the direction of the acceleration when the velocity and acceleration at *t* are perpendicular.

6.4.5 The frame for the helix

Consider the circular helix treated in the preceding example. Show that the formulas above for the unit tangent, binormal, and normal vectors are correct. Also show that these are unit length and mutually perpendicular. Describe how this local coordinate system orients itself as you move along the curve. ■

Figure 6.48 shows additional examples. Part a shows a hexagon wrapped about an elliptical spine to form a kind of elliptical torus, and part b shows segments arranged into a knot along a Lissajous figure given by:

$$C(t) = (r\cos(Mt + \phi), 0, r\sin(Nt)) \tag{6.17}$$

with $M = 2$, $N = 3$, $\phi = 0$.

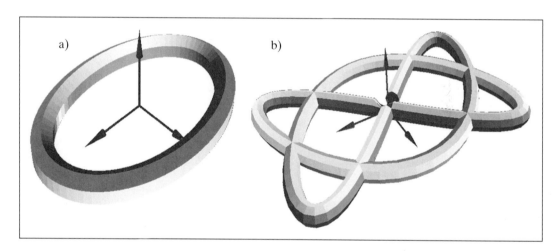

FIGURE 6.48 a) A hexagon wrapped about an elliptical torus, b) a 7-gon wrapped about a Lissajous figure.

Case Study 6.5 examines more details of forming meshes that model tubes based on a parametric curve.

6.4.5 Discretely Swept Surfaces of Revolution

The tubes above use affine transformations to fashion a new coordinate system at each spine point. If we use pure rotations for the affine transformations, and place all spine points at the origin, a rich set of polyhedral shapes can be created. Figure 6.49 shows an example, where a base polygon—now called the **profile**—is initially positioned 3 units out along the *x*-axis, and then is successively rotated in steps about the *y*-axis to form an approximation of a torus.

This is equivalent to **circularly sweeping** a shape about an axis, and the resulting shape is often called a **surface of revolution**. We examine true surfaces of revolution in Section 6.5; here we are forming only a discrete approximation to them, since we are sweeping in discrete steps.

Figure 6.50 shows an example that produces pictures of a martini glass. The profile here is not a closed polygon but a simple polyline based on points $P_j = (x_j, y_j, 0)$. If we choose to place this polyline at K equispaced angles about the *y*-axis, we set the transformations to have matrices:

$$\widetilde{M}_i = \begin{pmatrix} \cos(\theta_i) & 0 & \sin(\theta_i) & 0 \\ 0 & 1 & 0 & 0 \\ -\sin(\theta_i) & 0 & \cos(\theta_i) & 0 \\ 0 & 0 & 0 & 1 \end{pmatrix}$$

FIGURE 6.49 Rotational sweeping in discrete steps.

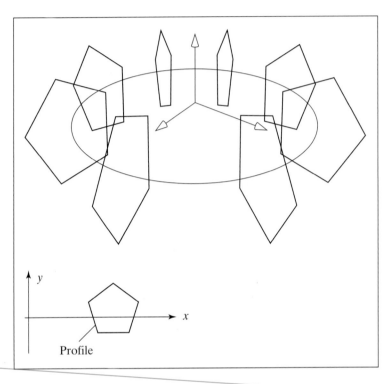

FIGURE 6.50 Approximating a martini glass with a discretely swept polyline: a) the profile, b) the swept surface.

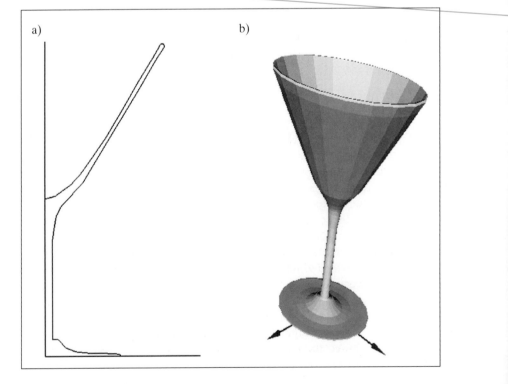

where $\theta_i = 2\pi i/K, i = 0, 1, \ldots, K - 1$. Note there is no translation involved. This transformation is simple enough that we can write the positions of the vertices directly. The rotation sets the points of the ith waist polyline at:

$$(x_j \cos(\theta_i), y_j, x_j \sin(\theta_i)) \tag{6.18}$$

Building meshes that model surfaces of revolution is treated further in Section 6.5.7 and Case Study 6.6.

6.5 MESH APPROXIMATIONS TO SMOOTH OBJECTS

So far we have built meshes to represent polyhedra, where each shape is a collection of flat polygonal faces. They tend to be data intensive, specified by listing the vertices of each face individually. Now we want to build meshes that attempt to approximate inherently smooth shapes like a sphere or torus. These shapes are normally defined by formulas rather than data. We also want to arrange matters so that these meshes can be *smoothly shaded*: even though they are represented by a collection of flat faces as before. The proper algorithm (Gouraud shading) draws them with smooth gradations in shading, and the individual faces are invisible (recall Figure 6.1). All this requires is that we find the proper normal vector at each vertex of each face. Specifically, we compute the normal vector to the underlying smooth surface. We discuss the Gouraud shading algorithm in Chapter 8.

The basic approach for each type of surface is to **polygonalize** (also called **tesselate**) it into a collection of flat faces. If the faces are small enough and there is a graceful change in direction from one face to the next, the resulting mesh will provide a good approximation to the underlying surface. The faces have vertices that are found by evaluating the surface's parametric representation at discrete points. A mesh is created by building a vertex list and face list in the usual way, except here the vertices are computed from formulas. The same is true for the vertex normal vectors: they are computed by *evaluating formulas* for the normal to the surface at discrete points.

6.5.1 Representations for Surfaces

To set the stage, recall that in Section 4.5.5 we examined the planar **patch**, given parametrically by

$$P(u, v) = C + \mathbf{a}u + \mathbf{b}v \tag{6.19}$$

where C is a point, and $\mathbf{a}$ and $\mathbf{b}$ are vectors. The range of values for the parameters u and v is usually restricted to $[0, 1]$, in which case the patch is a parallelogram in 3D with corner vertices $C, C + \mathbf{a}, C + \mathbf{b}$, and $C + \mathbf{a} + \mathbf{b}$.

Here we enlarge our interests to nonlinear forms to represent more general surface shapes. We introduce three functions $X()$, $Y()$, and $Z()$ so that the surface has parametric representation in point form

$$P(u, v) = (X(u, v), Y(u, v), Z(u, v)) \tag{6.20}$$

with u and v restricted to suitable intervals. Different surfaces are characterized by different functions, X, Y, and Z. The notion is that the surface is at $(X(0, 0), Y(0, 0), Z(0, 0))$ when both u and v are zero, at $(X(1, 0), Y(1, 0), Z(1, 0))$ when $u = 1$ and $v = 0$, and so on. Keep in mind that two parameters are required when representing a surface, whereas a curve in 3D requires only one. Letting u vary while keeping v constant generates a curve called a v-**contour**. Similarly, letting v vary while holding u constant produces a u-**contour**. (Look ahead to Figure 6.51 to see examples of u- and v-contours.)

The Implicit Form of a Surface

Although we are mainly concerned with parametric representations of different surfaces, it will prove useful to keep track of an alternative way to describe a surface, through its **implicit form.** Recall from Section 3.8 that a curve in 2D has an implicit form $F(x, y)$, which must evaluate to 0 for all points (x, y) that lie on the curve, and for only those. For surfaces in 3D a similar function $F(x, y, z)$ exists that evaluates to 0 if and only if the point (x, y, z) is on the surface. The surface therefore has an **implicit equation** given by

$$F(x, y, z) = 0 \qquad\qquad (6.21)$$

that is satisfied for all points on the surface, and only those (Note the distinction between "implicit equation" and "implicit form".) The equation constrains the way that values of x, y, and z must be related to confine the point (x, y, z) to the surface in question. For example, recall (from Chapter 4) that the plane that passes through point B and has normal vector $\mathbf{n}$ is described by the equation $n_x x + n_y y + n_z z = D$ (where $D = \mathbf{n} \cdot B$), so the implicit form for this plane is $F(x, y, z) = n_x x + n_y y + n_z z - D$. Sometimes it is more convenient to think of F as a function of a point P, rather than a function of three variables x, y, and z, and we write $F(P) = 0$ to describe more compactly all points that lie on the surface. For the example of the plane here, we would define $F(P) = \mathbf{n} \cdot (P - B)$ and say that P lies in the plane if and only if $F(P) = \mathbf{n} \cdot (P - B)$ is zero. If we wish to work with coordinate frames (recall Section 4.5) so that $\widetilde{P}$ is the 4-tuple $\widetilde{P} = (x, y, z, 1)^T$, the implicit form for a plane is even simpler: $F(\widetilde{P}) = \widetilde{n} \cdot \widetilde{P}$, where $\widetilde{n} = (n_x, n_y, n_z, -D)$ captures both the normal vector and the value $-D$.

It is not always easy to find the function $F(x, y, z)$ or $F(P)$ from a given parametric form (nor can you always find a parametric form when given $F(x, y, z)$). But if both a parametric form **and** an implicit form are available, it is simple to determine whether they describe the same surface. Simply substitute $X(u, v)$, $Y(u, v)$, and $Z(u, v)$ for x, y, and z, respectively, in $F(x, y, z)$ and check that F is 0 for all values of u and v of interest.

For some surfaces like a sphere that enclose a portion of space it is meaningful to define an inside region and an outside region. Other surfaces like a plane clearly divide 3D space into two regions, but one must refer to the context of the application to tell which half-space is the inside and which the outside. There are also many surfaces, such as a strip of ribbon candy, for which it makes little sense to name an inside and an outside.

When it is meaningful to designate an inside and outside to a surface, the implicit form $F(x, y, z)$ of a surface is also called its **inside outside function**. We then say that a point (x, y, z) is

inside the surface if:	$F(x, y, z) < 0$
on the surface if:	$F(x, y, z) = 0$
outside the surface if:	$F(x, y, z) > 0$

(6.22)

This provides a quick and simple test for the disposition of a given point (x', y', z') relative to the surface: Just evaluate $F(x', y', z')$ and test whether it is positive, negative, or zero. There has also been vigorous recent activity in rendering surfaces directly from their implicit forms: see [Bloomenthal97].

6.5.2 The Normal Vector to a Surface

As described earlier, we need to determine the direction of the normal vector to a surface at any desired point. Here we present one way based on the parametric expression, and one based on the implicit form, of the surface. As each surface type is examined later, we find the suitable expressions for its normal vector at any point.

The normal direction to a surface can be defined at a point, $P(u_0, v_0)$, on the surface by considering a very small region of the surface around $P(u_0, v_0)$. If the region is small enough and the surface varies smoothly in the vicinity, the region will be essentially flat. Thus it behaves locally like a tiny planar patch and has a well-defined normal direction. Figure 6.51 shows a surface patch with the normal vector drawn at various points. The direction of the normal vector is seen to be different at different points on the surface.

We use the name $\mathbf{n}(u, v)$ for the normal at (u, v). We now examine how it can be calculated.

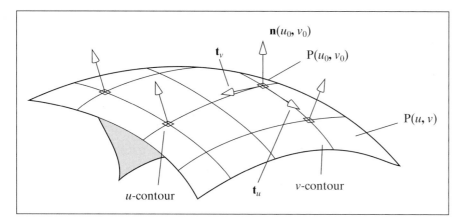

FIGURE 6.51 The normal vector to a surface.

The Normal Vector for a Surface that is specified Parametrically

Not surprisingly, $\mathbf{n}(u_0, v_0)$ is a cross product between two vectors that lie in the tiny planar patch near (u_0, v_0). Being a cross product, it is guaranteed to be perpendicular to both vectors. The two vectors in the plane (indicated as $\mathbf{t}_u$ and $\mathbf{t}_v$ in Figure 6.51) are certain tangent vectors. Calculus texts show that they are simply related to partial derivatives of $\mathbf{p}(u, v)$ (the vector from the origin to the surface point $P(u, v)^5$), evaluated at the point in question [Thomas53]. An expression for the normal vector is therefore

$$\mathbf{n}(u_0, v_0) = \left(\frac{\partial \mathbf{p}}{\partial \mathbf{u}} \times \frac{\partial \mathbf{p}}{\partial \mathbf{v}} \right)\Bigg|_{u=u_0, v=v_0} \tag{6.23}$$

where the vertical bar $|$ indicates that the derivatives are evaluated at $u = u_0, v = v_0$. Formed this way, $\mathbf{n}(u_0, v_0)$ is not automatically a unit-length vector, but it can be normalized if desired.

■ EXAMPLE 6.5.1 Does this work for a plane?

Consider the plane given parametrically by $P(u, v) = C + \mathbf{a}u + \mathbf{b}v$. The partial derivative of this with respect to u is just $\mathbf{a}$, and that with respect to v is $\mathbf{b}$. Thus according to Equation (6.23), $\mathbf{n}(u, v) = \mathbf{a} \times \mathbf{b}$, which we recognize as the correct result.

More generally, the partial derivatives of $\mathbf{p}(u, v)$ exist whenever the surface is smooth enough. Most of the surfaces of interest to us in modeling scenes have the

---

5 Since $\mathbf{p}(u, v)$ is simply the difference $P(u, v) - (0, 0, 0)$, the derivative of $\mathbf{p}()$ is the same as that of $P()$.

necessary smoothness and have simple enough mathematical expressions so that finding the required derivatives is not difficult. Because $\mathbf{p}(u, v) = X(u, v)\mathbf{i} + Y(u, v)\mathbf{j} + Z(u, v)\mathbf{k}$, the derivative of a vector is just the vector of the individual derivatives:

$$\frac{\partial \mathbf{p}(u, v)}{\partial u} = \left(\frac{\partial X(u, v)}{\partial u}, \frac{\partial Y(u, v)}{\partial u}, \frac{\partial Z(u, v)}{\partial u}\right) \tag{6.24}$$

We apply these formulas directly to each surface type we examine later.

The Normal Vector for a Surface Given Implicitly

An alternative expression is used if the surface is given by an implicit form, $F(x, y, z) = 0$. The normal direction at the surface point, (x, y, z), is found using the three partial derivatives—commonly called the **gradient**, ∇F, of F, which is given by [Thomas53]:

$$\mathbf{n}(x_0, y_0, z_0) = \nabla F|_{x-x_0, y-y_0, z-z_0} = \left(\frac{\partial F}{\partial x}, \frac{\partial F}{\partial y}, \frac{\partial F}{\partial z}\right)\Bigg|_{x=x_0, y=y_0, z=z_0} \tag{6.25}$$

where each partial derivative is evaluated at the desired point, (x_0, y_0, z_0). If the point (x_0, y_0, z_0) for the surface in question corresponds to the point $P(u_0, v_0)$ of the parametric form, then $\mathbf{n}(x_0, y_0, z_0)$ has the same direction as $\mathbf{n}(u_0, v_0)$ in Equation (6.17), but it may have a different length. Again, it can be normalized if desired.

■ **EXAMPLE 6.5.2 The plane again**

Consider once again the plane with normal $\mathbf{n}$ that passes through point A, given implicitly by $F(x, y, z) = \mathbf{n} \cdot ((x, y, z) - A) = 0$, or $n_x x + n_y y + n_z z - \mathbf{n} \cdot A = 0$. This has gradient $\nabla F = \mathbf{n}$ as expected.

Note that the gradient-based form gives the normal vector as a function of x, y, and z, rather than of u and v. Sometimes for a surface we know *both* the inside–outside function, $F(x, y, z)$, and the parametric form, $\mathbf{p}(u, v) = X(u, v)\mathbf{i} + Y(u, v)\mathbf{j} + Z(u, v)\mathbf{k}$. In such cases it may be easiest to find the parametric form, $\mathbf{n}(u, v)$, of the normal at (u, v) by a two-step method: (1) Use Equation (6.20) to obtain the normal at (x, y, z) in terms of x, y, and z, and then (2) substitute the known functions $X(u, v)$ for x, $Y(u, v)$ for y, and $Z(u, v)$ for z. Some of the later examples illustrate this method.

6.5.3 The Effect of an Affine Transformation

We shall need on occasion to work with the implicit and parametric forms of a surface after the surface has been subjected to an affine transformation. We will also want to know how the normal to the surface is affected by the transformation.

Suppose the transformation is represented by a 4-by-4 matrix M, and that the original surface has implicit form (in terms of points in homogeneous coordinates) $F(\widetilde{P})$ and parametric form $\widetilde{P}(u, v) = (X(u, v), Y(u, v), Z*(u, v), 1)^T$. Then it is clear that the transformed surface has parametric form $M\widetilde{P}(u, v)$ (Why?). It is also easy to show (see the exercises that follow) that the transformed surface has implicit form $F'(\widetilde{P})$ given by:

$$F'(\widetilde{P}) = F(M^{-1}\widetilde{P})$$

Further, if the original surface has normal vector $\mathbf{n}(u, v)$, then the transformed surface has:

- normal vector: $M^{-T}\mathbf{n}(u, v)$

For example, suppose we wish to transform the plane examined above, given by $F(\widetilde{P}) = \widetilde{n} \cdot \widetilde{P}$, that has normal vector with $\widetilde{n} = (n_x, n_y, n_z, -D)$. The transformed plane has implicit form $F'(\widetilde{P}) = \widetilde{n} \cdot (M^{-1}\widetilde{P})$. This can be written (see the exercises) as $(M^{-T}\widetilde{n}) \cdot \widetilde{P}$, so the normal vector of the transformed plane involves the inverse transpose of the matrix, consistent with the claimed form for the normal to a general surface.

PRACTICE EXERCISES

6.5.1 The implicit form of a transformed surface

Suppose all points on a surface satisfy $F(P) = 0$, and that M transforms $\widetilde{P}$ into $\widetilde{Q}$; i.e., $\widetilde{Q} = M\widetilde{P}$. Then argue that any point $\widetilde{Q}$ on the transformed surface comes from a point $M^{-1}\widetilde{Q}$, and those points all satisfy $F(M^{-1}\widetilde{Q}) = 0$. Show that this proves that the implicit form for the transformed surface is $F(\widetilde{Q}) = F(M^{-1}\widetilde{Q})$.

6.5.2 How are normal vectors affected?

Let $\mathbf{n} = (n_x, n_y, n_z, 0)^T$ be the normal at P and let $\mathbf{v}$ be any vector tangent to the surface at P. Then $\mathbf{n}$ must be perpendicular to $\mathbf{v}$ and we can write $\mathbf{n} \cdot \mathbf{v} = 0$.

a. Show that the dot product can be written as a matrix product: $\mathbf{n}^T\mathbf{v} = 0$ (see Appendix 2).
b. Show that this dot product is still 0 when the matrix product $M^{-1}M$ is inserted: $\mathbf{n}^T M^{-1}M\mathbf{v} = \mathbf{0}$.
c. Show that this can be rewritten as $(M^{-T}\mathbf{n})(M\mathbf{v}) = 0$, so $M^{-T}\mathbf{n}$ is perpendicular to $(M\mathbf{v})$. Now since the tangent $\mathbf{v}$ transforms to $M\mathbf{v}$, which is tangent to the transformed surface, show that this dictates $M^{-T}\mathbf{n}$ must be normal to the transformed surface, which we wished to show.
d. The normal to a surface is also given by the gradient of the implicit form, so the normal to the transformed surface at point P must be the gradient of $F(M^{-1}P)$. Show (by the chain rule of calculus) that the gradient of this function is M^{-T} multiplied onto the gradient of $F()$.

6.5.3 The tangent plane to a transformed surface

To find how normal vectors are transformed, we can also find how the tangent plane to a surface is mapped to the tangent plane on the transformed surface. Suppose the tangent plane to the original surface at point P has parametric representation $P + a\mathbf{u} + b\mathbf{v}$, where $\mathbf{a}$ and $\mathbf{b}$ are two vectors lying in the plane. The normal to the surface is therefore $\mathbf{n} = \mathbf{a} \times \mathbf{b}$.

a. Show that the parametric representation of the transformed plane is $MP + Ma\mathbf{u} + Mb\mathbf{v}$, and that this plane has normal $\mathbf{n}' = (M\mathbf{a}) \times (M\mathbf{b})$.
b. Referring to Appendix 2, show the following identity:

$$(M\mathbf{a}) \times (M\mathbf{b}) = (\det M)M^{-T}(\mathbf{a} \times \mathbf{b})$$

This relates the cross product of transformed vectors to the cross product of the vectors themselves.
c. Show that $\mathbf{n}'$ is therefore parallel to $M^{-T}\mathbf{n}$.   ■

6.5.4 Three "Generic" Shapes: the Sphere, Cylinder, and Cone

We begin with three classic objects, "generic" versions of the sphere, cylinder, and cone. We develop the implicit and parametric forms for each of these, and see how one might make meshes to approximate them. By **generic** we mean that the object is *basic* or *fundamental* in size, orientation, and position. An alternative, but rough, way to say this is that they require a minimum number of parameters to describe them: most of the usual parameters are zero. For instance, generic spheres are centered at the origin and have unit radius; generic cones have a circular base of unit radius that coincides with the xy-plane, and an axis of unit length along the z-axis. We describe the other two major generic shapes, the generic cylinder and the tapered cylinder, shortly. We also derive formulas for the normal direction at each point on these objects. Note that we have already used OpenGL functions in Chapter 5 to draw these shapes. Developing our own tools has advantages, however: a) we have much more control over the detailed nature of the shape being created; b) we have the object as an actual mesh that can be operated upon by methods of the Mesh class.

The Generic Sphere

We call the sphere of unit radius centered at the origin the generic sphere (see Figure 6.52a). It forms the basis for all other spherelike shapes we use. It has the familiar implicit form

$$F(x, y, z) = x^2 + y^2 + z^2 - 1 \tag{6.26}$$

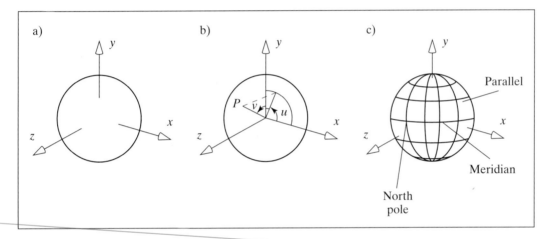

FIGURE 6.52 a) The generic sphere, b) a parametric form, c) parallels and meridians.

In the alternate notation $F(P)$ we obtain the more elegant $F(P) = |P|^2 - 1$. (What would these forms be if the sphere has radius R?)

A parametric description of this sphere arises immediately from the basic description of a point in spherical coordinates (see Appendix 2). We choose to let u correspond to azimuth or **longitude** and v to **latitude**. Then any point $P = (x, y, z)$ on the sphere has a parametric representation $(\cos(v)\cos(u), \cos(v)\sin(u), \sin(v))$ in spherical coordinates (see Figure 6.52b).

$$P(u,v) = (\cos(u)\cos(v), \cos(u)\sin(v), \sin(v)).$$

We let u vary over $(0, 2\pi)$ and v vary over $(-\pi/2, \pi/2)$ to cover all such points.

It's easy to check that this is consistent with the implicit form: substitute terms of Equation (6.27) into corresponding terms of Equation (6.26) and see that zero is obtained for *any* value of u and v.

(*Question*: What is the corresponding parametric form if the sphere instead has radius R and is centered at (a, b, c)?)

For geographical reasons certain contours along a sphere are given common names. For this parameterization u-contours are called **meridians**, and v-contours are known as **parallels**, as suggested in Figure 6.52c.

Question: For what values of u and v does a point $P(u, v)$ lie on the Earth's equator? Where in u and v, is the south pole? Where is the north pole?

Different parametric forms are possible for a given shape. An alternative parametric form for the sphere is examined in the exercises.

The Normal Vector to a Surface

What is the normal direction $\mathbf{n}(u, v)$ of the sphere's surface at any point specified by parameters (u, v)? Intuitively the normal vector is always aimed radially outward, so it must be parallel to the vector from the origin to the point itself. This is confirmed by Equation (6.19): the gradient is simply $2(x, y, z)$, which is proportional to P. Working with the parametric form, Equation (6.17) yields $\mathbf{n}(u, v) = -\cos(v)\mathbf{p}(u, v)$, so $\mathbf{n}(u, v)$ is parallel to $\mathbf{p}(u, v)$ as expected. The uninteresting scale factor $-\cos(v)$ will disappear when we normalize $\mathbf{n}$. We must make sure to use $\mathbf{p}(u, v)$ rather than $-\mathbf{p}(u, v)$ for the normal, so that it does indeed point radially outward rather than inward. Suppose, that you are asked the longitude and latitude of the normal vector to your ship (the direction from the deck straight up through the peak of the mast) when your ship lies at 50 degrees 25 minutes north latitude and 4 degrees 26 minutes west longitude. First, is the question well defined, and, if so, what is the answer?

The Generic Cylinder

We adopt as the **generic cylinder** the cylinder whose axis coincides with the z-axis, has a circular cross section of radius 1, and extends in z from 0 to 1, as pictured in Figure 6.53a.

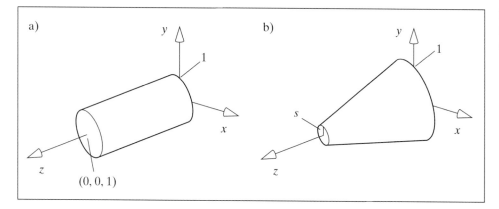

FIGURE 6.53 The generic cylinder and the tapered cylinder.

It is convenient to view this cylinder as one member of the large family of **tapered cylinders**, as we did in Chapter 5. This only requires the introduction of one parameter to distinguish an infinite number of different shapes. Figure 6.53b shows the generic tapered cylinder, having a radius of s when $z = 1$. Parameter s is usually smaller than 1, but it might just as well be larger than 1 just as well. (Visualize both situations.) The generic cylinder is simply a tapered cylinder with $s = 1$. Further, the generic **cone** to be examined next is simply a tapered cylinder with $s = 0$. We develop formulas for the tapered cylinder with an arbitrary value of s. These also provide formulas for the generic cylinder and cone by setting s to 1 or 0, respectively.

If we consider the tapered cylinder to be a thin hollow shell, its **wall** (ignoring for a moment the possible presence of a cap or a base on the cylinder) is given by the implicit form

$$F(x, y, z) = x^2 + y^2 - (1 + (s - 1)z)^2 \qquad \text{for } 0 < z < 1 \qquad (6.28)$$

and by the parametric form

$$P(u, v) = ((1 + (s - 1)v)\cos(u), \qquad (1 + (s - 1)v)\sin(u), v) \qquad (6.29)$$

for appropriate ranges of u and v. (Which ones?) What are these expressions for the generic cylinder with $s = 1$?

When it is important to model the tapered cylinder as a solid object, we add two circular discs at its ends: a **base** and a **cap**. The cap is a circular portion of the plane $z = 1$, characterized by the inequality $x^2 + y^2 < s^2$, or given parametrically by $P(u, v) = (v \cos(u), v \sin(u), 1)$ for v in $[0, s]$. (What is the parametric representation of the base?)

The normal vector to the wall of the tapered cylinder is found using Equation (6.25). (Be sure to check this). It is

$$\mathbf{n}(x, y, z) = (x, y, -(s - 1)(1 + (s - 1)z)) \tag{6.30}$$

or in parametric form $\mathbf{n}(u, v) = (\cos(u), \sin(u), 1 - s)$. For the generic cylinder the normal is simply $(\cos(u), \sin(u), 0)$. This agrees with intuition: the normal is directed radially away from the axis of the cylinder. For the tapered cylinder it is also directed radially, but shifted by a constant z-component. (What are the normals to the cap and base?)

The Generic Cone

We take as the generic cone the cone whose axis coincides with the z-axis, has a circular cross section of maximum radius 1, and extends in z from 0 to 1, as pictured in Figure 6.54. It is a tapered cylinder with small radius of $s = 0$. Thus its wall has implicit form

$$F(x, y, z) = x^2 + y^2 - (1 - z)^2 = 0 \qquad \text{for } 0 < z < 1 \tag{6.31}$$

and parametric form $P(u, v) = ((1 - v) \cos(u), (1 - v) \sin(u), v)$ for azimuth u in $[0, 2\pi]$ and v in $[0, 1]$. Using the results for the tapered cylinder again, the normal vector to the wall of the cone is $(x, y, 1 - z)$. What is it parametrically?

FIGURE 6.54 The generic cone.

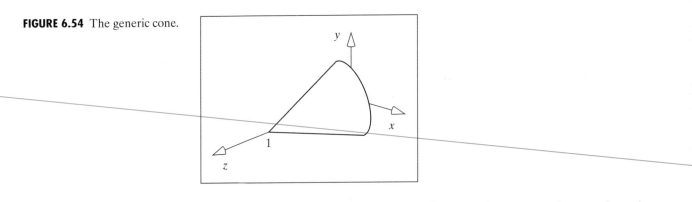

For easy reference Figure 6.55 shows the normal vectors to the generic surfaces we have discussed.

FIGURE 6.55 Normal vectors to the generic surfaces.

Surface	$\mathbf{n}(u, v)$ at $\mathbf{p}(u, v)$	$\nabla F(x, y, z)$
Sphere	$\mathbf{p}(u, v)$	(x, y, z)
Tapered cylinder	$(\cos(u), \sin(u), 1 - s)$	$(x, y, -(s - 1)(1 + (s - 1)z))$
Cylinder	$(\cos(u), \sin(u), 0)$	$(x, y, 0)$
Cone	$(\cos(u), \sin(u), 1)$	$(x, y, 1 - z)$

PRACTICE EXERCISES

6.5.4 Alternative representation for the generic sphere

We can associate different geometric quantities with the parameters u and v to obtain a different parametric form for the sphere. We again use parameter u for azimuth, but now use v for the height of the point above the xy-plane. All points at height v lie on a circle of radius $\sqrt{1 - v^2}$, so this parametric form is given by:

$$P_2(u, v) = \left(\sqrt{1 - v^2} \cos(u), \quad \sqrt{1 - v^2} \sin(u), v \right) \tag{6.32}$$

for u in $[0, 2\pi]$ and v in $[-1, 1]$. Show that P_2 lies unit distance from the origin for all u and v.

6.5.5 What's the surface?

Let A have position $\mathbf{a}$, and P have position $\mathbf{p}$. Describe in words and sketch the surface described by: a) $\mathbf{p} \cdot \mathbf{a} = 0$; b) $\mathbf{p} \cdot \mathbf{a} = |\mathbf{a}|$; c) $|\mathbf{p} \times \mathbf{a}| = |\mathbf{a}|$; d) $\mathbf{p} \cdot \mathbf{a} = \mathbf{p} \cdot \mathbf{p}$; e) $\mathbf{p} \cdot \mathbf{a} = |\mathbf{a}||\mathbf{p}|/2$.

6.5.6 Find the normal vector to the generic cylinder and cone

Derive the normal vector to any point on the generic tapered cylinder and the generic cone in two ways:

a. Using the parametric representation.
b. Using the implicit form, and then expressing the result parametrically.

6.5.7 Transformed spheres

Find the implicit form for a generic sphere that has been scaled in x by 2 and in y by 3, and then rotated $30°$ about the z-axis. ■

6.5.5 To Form a Polygonal Mesh for a Curved Surface

Now we examine how to make a mesh object that approximates a smooth surface such as the sphere, cylinder, or cone. The process is called **polygonalization** or **tesselation**, and it involves replacing the surface by a collection of triangles and quadrilaterals. The vertices of these polygons lie in the surface itself, and they are joined by straight edges (which usually do not lie wholly in the surface). One proceeds by choosing a number of values of u and v and sampling the parametric form for the surface at these values to obtain a collection of vertices. These vertices are placed in a vertex list. A face list is then created: each face consists of three or four indices pointing to suitable vertices in the vertex list. Associated with each vertex in a face is the normal vector to the surface. This normal vector is the normal direction to the true underlying surface at each vertex location. (Note how this contrasts with the normal used when representing a flat-faced polyhedron: there the vertex of each face is associated with the normal to the face.)

Figure 6.56 shows how this works for the generic sphere, as viewed looking up at the south pole. We think of slicing up the sphere along azimuth lines *and latitude* lines. Using OpenGL terminology of slices and stacks (see Section 5.6.3), we choose to slice the sphere into nSlices slices around the equator, and nStacks stacks from the south pole to the north pole. The figure shows the example of 12 slices and 8 stacks. The larger nSlices and nStacks are, the better the mesh approximates a true sphere.

To make slices we need nSlices values of u *around the equator* between 0 and 2π. Usually these are chosen to be equispaced: $u_i = 2\pi i/\text{nSlices}$, $i = 0, 1, \dots$, nSlices $- 1$. As for stacks, we normally put half of them above the equator and half below. The top and bottom stacks will consist of triangles; all other faces will be quadrilaterals. This requires we define (nStacks $+ 1$) values of latitude: between $-\pi/2$ and $\pi/2$ $v_j = \pi - \pi j/\text{nStacks}$, $j = 0, 1, \dots$, nStacks.

The vertex list can now be created. The figure shows how we might number the vertices (the ordering is a matter of convenience). We put the south pole in pt[0], the bottom points $v_j = -\pi/2 + \pi \times j/\text{nStacks}$, of the next stack into the next 12 vertices, and so on. With 12 slices and 8 stacks there will be a total of 98 points. (Why?)

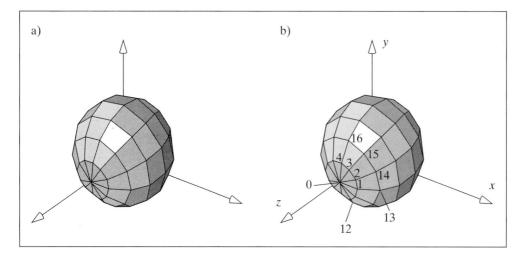

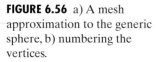

FIGURE 6.56 a) A mesh approximation to the generic sphere, b) numbering the vertices.

The normal vector list is also easily created: `norm[k]` will hold the normal for the sphere at vertex `pt[k]`. `norm[k]` is computed by evaluating the parametric form of $\mathbf{n}(u,v)$ at the same (u,v) used for the points. For the sphere this is particularly easy, since `norm[k]` is the same as `pt[k]`.

For this example the face list will have 96 faces, of which 24 are triangles. We can put the top triangles in the first 12 faces, the 12 quadrilaterals of the next stack down in the next 12 faces, and so on. The first few faces will contain the data:

Number of vertices:	3	3	3	. . .
Vertex indices:	0 1 2	0 2 3	0 3 4	. . .
Normal indices:	0 1 2	0 2 3	0 3 4	. . .

Note that for all meshes that try to represent smooth shapes the `normIndex` is always the same as the `vertIndex`, so the data structure holds redundant information. (Because of this, one could use a more streamlined data structure for such meshes. What would it be?) Polygonalization of the sphere in this way is straightforward, but for more complicated shapes it can be very tricky. See Further Readings for additional discussions.

Ultimately we need a method, such as `makeSurfaceMesh()`, that generates appropriate meshes for a given surface $P(u, v)$.

Note that some graphics packages have routines that are highly optimized when they operate on triangles. To exploit these we might choose to polygonalize the sphere into a collection of triangles, subdividing each quadrilateral into two triangles.

A simple approach would use the same vertices as above but alter the face list, replacing each quadrilateral with two triangles. For instance, a face that uses vertices 2, 3, 15, 14 might be subdivided into two triangles, one using 2, 3, 15 and the other using 2, 15, 14.

The sphere is a special case of a surface of revolution. The tapered cylinder is also a surface of revolution. It is straightforward to develop a mesh model for the tapered cylinder. Figure 6.57 shows the tapered cylinder approximated with `nSlices` = 8 and `nStacks` = 1. An octagon is used for its cap and base. (If you prefer to use only triangles in a mesh, the walls, the cap, and the base could be dissected into triangles. (How?))

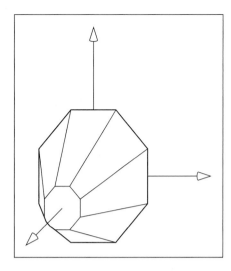

FIGURE 6.57 A mesh approximation to the tapered cylinder.

PRACTICE EXERCISES

6.5.8 The mesh for a given sphere

Write out the vertex, normal, and face lists for the generic sphere, when `nSlices` = 6 and `nStacks` = 4, choosing a convenient numbering scheme.

6.5.9 Restricting the mesh to triangular faces

Adjust the lists in the previous exercise for the case where all faces are triangles.

6.5.10 The mesh for a cylinder and cone

Write out vertex, normal, and face lists for the generic tapered cylinder that uses `nSlices` = 4 and `nStacks` = 2. ■

6.5.6 Ruled Surfaces

Next we define and discuss two important classes of surfaces that enlarge the families we can model and analyze with meshes. One is the "**ruled surface**" that is often encountered in nature, and one is the family of true surfaces of revolution. By definition a ruled surface is one for which, at any point, it is possible to find a straight line through that point that lies entirely within the surface. For example, the cone and the generic tapered cylinder, being linearly extruded shapes, are certainly ruled surfaces. But the sphere is not a ruled surface (Why?)

Cones

A cone is a ruled surface for which one of the curves, say, $P_0(u)$, is a *single* point $P_0(u) = P_0$, the apex of the cone, as suggested in Figure 6.58.

For this parameterization all lines pass through P_0 at $v = 0$, and through $P_1(u)$ at $v = 1$. Certain special cases are familiar. A *circular cone* results when $P_1(u)$ is a circle, and a *right circular cone* results when the circle lies in a plane that is perpendicular to the line joining the circle's center to P_0. The specific example shown in Figure 6.59b uses $P_1(u) = (r(u) \cos u, r(u) \sin u, 1)$ where the radius curve $r(u)$ varies sinusoidally: $r(u) = 0.5 + 0.2 \cos(5u)$.

Recalling that a cone is formed by linearly extruding a curve, say P sub 0(u), which collapses to a single dot at $v = 0$, points on the cone, P(u, v), may be represented as in Equation 6.33.

$$P(u, v) = (1 - v)P_0 + vP_1(u) \qquad \{\text{a general cone}\} \qquad (6.33)$$

FIGURE 6.58 A cone.

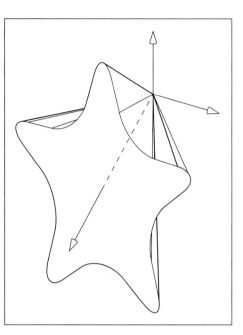

FIGURE 6.59 a) A cylinder, b) ribbon candy cylinder.

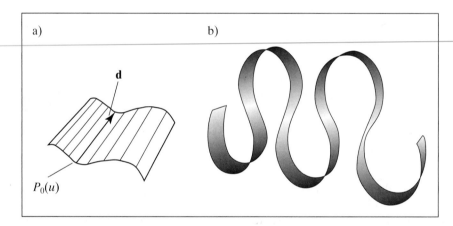

Cylinders

A cylinder is a ruled surface for which $P_1(u)$ is simply a translated version of $P_0(u)$: $P_1(u) = P_0(u) + \mathbf{d}$, for some vector $\mathbf{d}$, as shown in Figure 6.59a. Sometimes one speaks of sweeping the line with endpoints $P_0(0)$ and $P_0(0) + \mathbf{d}$ (often called the *generator*) along the curve $P_0(u)$ (often called the *directrix*), without altering the direction of the line.

The general cylinder therefore has the parametric form

$$P(u, v) = P_0(u) + \mathbf{d}v \tag{6.34}$$

To be a true cylinder, the curve $P_0(u)$ is confined to lie in a plane. If $P_0(u)$ is a circle, the cylinder is a **circular cylinder**. The direction $\mathbf{d}$ need not be perpendicular to this plane, but if it is, the surface is called a **right cylinder**. This is the case for the generic cylinder. Figure 6.59b shows a "ribbon candy cylinder" where $P_0(u)$ undulates back and forth like a piece of ribbon. The ribbon shape is explored in the exercises.

Other Ruled Surfaces

There are many other interesting ruled surfaces. Figure 6.60a shows a double helix formed when $P_0(u)$ and $P_1(u)$ are both helixes that wind around each other. Part b

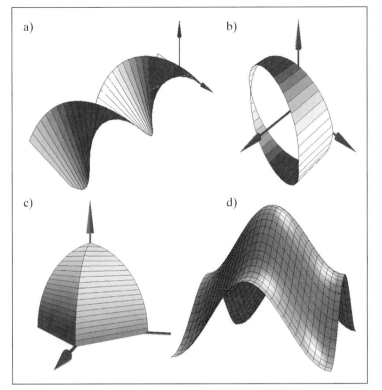

FIGURE 6.60 a) Double helix, b) möbius strip, c) vaulted roof, d) Coons patch.

shows the intriguing Möbius strip that has only one edge. The exercises explore the parametric representation of these surfaces. Part c shows a vaulted roof made up of four ruled surfaces. Case Study 6.8 examines modeling such vaulted domes of a cathedral. Part d is a **Coons patch** named after the legendary graphicist Steven Coons.

PRACTICE EXERCISES

6.5.11 A pyramid is a cone

What shape should $P_1(u)$ have to create a ruled surface that is a pyramid (such as the pyramid of Gizeh) with a square base? Give specific expressions for the curve and the point P_0 so that the square base of the pyramid lies in the xz-plane, centered at the origin, with sides of length 2. The pyramid should have height 1.5.

6.5.12 Ribbon candy cylinders

Find a parametric form for $P_0(u)$ that produces a good approximation to the ribbon candy cylinder shown in Figure 6.59b. Consider the ribbon as wrapped about a succession of abutting circular cylinders of radius 1. The center of the ith cylinder lies at $(x_i, y_i) = (id, \pm r)$, where the + and − alternate, and $d^2 = 1 - r^2$. Choose some value of r between 0 and 1.

6.5.13 The double helix

The parametric form for a helix is $(\cos(t), \sin(t), t)$. Find expressions for two helices, $P_0(u)$ and $P_1(u)$, both of which wind around the z-axis yet are 180° out of phase so that they wind around each other. Write the parametric form for the ruled surface formed using these two curves.

6.5.14 The Möbius strip

Find a parametric form for the Möbius strip shown in Figure 6.60.

Hint: Revolve a line about the z-axis, but put in a twist as it goes around. Does the following attempt do the job: $P_0(u) = (\cos(2pu)), \sin(2pu), u)$, and $P_1(u) = (\cos(2pu)), \sin(2pu), 1 - u)$?

6.5.16 Does it really interpolate?

Check that $P(u, v)$ of Equation (6.31) interpolates (tweens) each of the four boundary curves, and therefore interpolates each of the four corners.   ■

6.5.7 Surfaces of Revolution

As described earlier, a surface of revolution is formed by a **rotational sweep** of a profile curve, C, around an axis. Suppose we place a profile in the xz-plane and represent it parametrically by $C(v) = (X(v), Z(v))$. To generate the surface of revolution we sweep the profile about the z-axis under control of the u-parameter, with u specifying the angle through which each point has been swept about the axis. As before, the different positions of the curve C around the axis are called **meridians**. Sweeping it completely around generates a full circle, so contours of constant v are circles, called **parallels** of the surface.[6] The parallel at v has radius $X(v)$ and lies at height $Z(v)$ above the xy-plane. Thus the general point on the surface is

$$P(u, v) = (X(v) \cos(u), X(v) \sin(u), Z(v)) \tag{6.35}$$

The generic sphere, tapered cylinder, and cone are all familiar special cases. (What are their profiles?) The normal vector to a surface of revolution is easily found by directly applying Equation (6.38) to Equation (6.23) (see the exercises). This yields

$$\mathbf{n}(u, v) = X(v)(\dot{Z}(v) \cos(u), \dot{Z}(v) \sin(u), -\dot{X}(v)) \tag{6.36}$$

where the dot denotes the first derivative of the function. The scaling factor $X(v)$ disappears upon normalization of the vector. This result specializes to the forms we found previously for the simple generic shapes (see the exercises).

For example, the **torus** is generated by sweeping a displaced circle about the z-axis, as shown in Figure 6.61a. The circle has radius A and is displaced along the x-axis by D, so that its profile is $C(v) = (D + A \cos(v), A \sin(v))$. Therefore the torus (Figure 6.61b) has representation

$$P(u, v) = ((D + A \cos(v)) \cos(u), (D + A \cos(v)) \sin(u), A \sin(v)) \tag{6.37}$$

Its normal vector is developed in the exercises.

FIGURE 6.61 A torus.

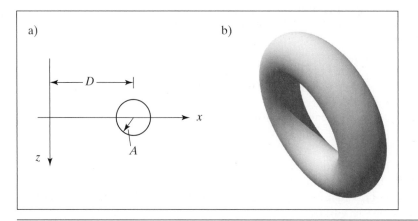

---

[6]   More formally, a **meridian** is the intersection of the surface with a plane that contains the axis of revolution, and a **parallel** is the intersection of the surface with a plane perpendicular to the axis.

We usually sweep a curve lying in a plane about an axis that lies in that plane, but a surface of revolution can be formed by sweeping about any axis. Choosing different axes for a given profile can lead to interesting families of surfaces. The general form for $P(u, v)$ for the surface of revolution about an arbitrary axis is developed in the exercises.

A mesh for a surface of revolution is built in a program in the usual way (see Section 6.5.4). We choose a set of u and v values, $\{u_i\}$ and $\{v_j\}$, and compute a vertex at each from $P(u_i, v_j)$, and a normal direction from $\mathbf{n}(u_i, v_j)$. Polygonal faces are built by joining four adjacent vertices with straight lines. A method to do this is discussed in Case Study 6.13.

Figure 6.62 shows another example in which we model an approximation of the dome of the exquisite Taj Mahal in Agra, India, part a shows a photo of this dome. Part b shows the profile curve in the xz-plane, and part c shows the resulting surface of revolution. Here we describe the profile by a collection of data points $C_i = (X_i, Z_i)$, since no suitable parametric formula is available. (We rectify this limitation in Chapter 8 by using a B-spline curve to form a smooth parametric curve based on a set of data points.)

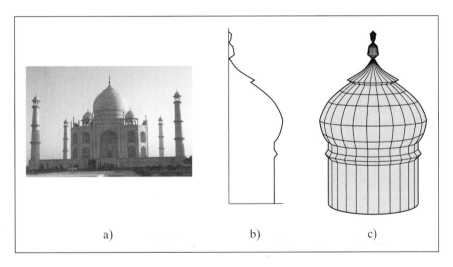

a)   b)   c)

FIGURE 6.62 A surface of revolution—the dome of the Taj Mahal.

To build a surface of revolution when the profile consists of discrete points, simply take as the ijth vertex the slightly different form of Equation (6.38):

$$P_{i,j} = (X_j \cos(u_i), X_j \sin(u_i), Z_j)$$

PRACTICE EXERCISES

6.5.17 The generic shapes as surfaces of revolution

Describe the profiles of the generic sphere, cylinder, and cone parametrically, and then express them as surfaces of revolution.

6.5.18 Rotation about other axes

Consider a profile curve $C(v) = (X(v), Z(v))$, lying in the xz-plane, and an arbitrary axis through the origin given by unit vector $\mathbf{r}$. We know from Equation (5.31) that the matrix $R_r(\theta)$ performs a rotation of a point through θ radians about the axis $\mathbf{r}$.

a. From this show that the surface of revolution formed by sweeping $C(v)$ about axis **r** is

$$(X(u, v), Y(u, v), Z(u, v), 1) = R_r(u)\begin{pmatrix} X(v) \\ 0 \\ Z(v) \\ 1 \end{pmatrix}$$

b. Check this for the special case of rotation about the z-axis.
c. Repeat part b for rotations about the x-axis, and about the y-axis.

6.5.19 Find the normal vectors

a) Apply Equation (6.38) to Equation (6.23) to derive the form in Equation (6.39) for the normal vector to a surface of revolution. b) Use this result to find the normal to each of the generic sphere, cylinder, and cone, and show that the results agree with those found in Section 6.5.2. Show that the normal vector to the torus has the form

$$\mathbf{n}(u, v) = (\cos(v)\cos(u), \cos(v)\sin(u), \sin(v))(D + A\cos(v)).$$

Also, find the inside–outside function for the torus, and compute the normal using its gradient.

6.5.20 An elliptical torus

Find the parametric representation for the following two surfaces of revolution: a) The ellipse given by $(a\cos(v), b\sin(v))$ is first displaced R units along the x-axis and then revolved about the y-axis. b) The same ellipse is revolved about the x-axis.

6.5.21 A Lissajous of revolution

Sketch what the surface would look like if the Lissajous figure of Equation (6.17) with $M = 2$, $N = 3$, and $\phi = 0$ were rotated about the y-axis. ▨

6.5.8 Tubes Based on 3D Curves

In Section 6.4.4 we studied tubes that were based on a "spine" curve $C(t)$ meandering through 3D space. A polygon was stationed at each of a selection of spine points, and oriented according to the Frenet frame computed there. Then corresponding points on adjacent polygons were connected to form a flat-faced tube along the spine.

Here we do the same thing, except we compute the normal to the surface at each vertex, so that smooth shading can be performed. Figure 6.63 shows the example of a tube wrapped around a helical shape. Compare this with Figure 6.40.

If we wish to wrap a circle $(\cos(u), \sin(u), 0)$ about the spine $C(t)$, the resulting surface has parametric representation

$$P(u, v) = C(v) + \cos(u)\mathbf{a}(v) + \sin(u)\mathbf{b}(v) \tag{6.38}$$

where the vector $\mathbf{a}(v)$ is normal to the curve and $\mathbf{b}(v)$ is normal to both the curve and $\mathbf{a}(v)$. Now we can build a mesh for this tube in the usual way, by taking samples of $P(u, v)$, building the vertex, normal, and face lists, and so on.

6.5.9 Surfaces Based on Explicit Functions of Two Variables

Many surface shapes are **single-valued** in one dimension, so their position can be represented as an explicit function of two of the independent variables. For instance, there may be a single value of height of the surface above the xz-plane for each point (x, z), as suggested in Figure 6.64. We can then say that the height of the surface at (x, z) is some $f(x, z)$. Such a function is sometimes called a **height field** [Bloomenthal97]. A height field is often given by a formula such as the Gaussian shape of Equation(6.39):

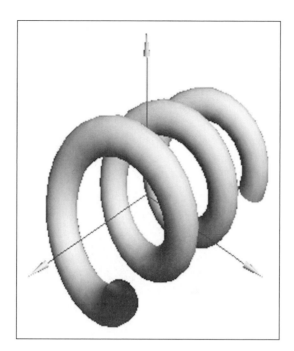

FIGURE 6.63 A helical tube undulating through space.

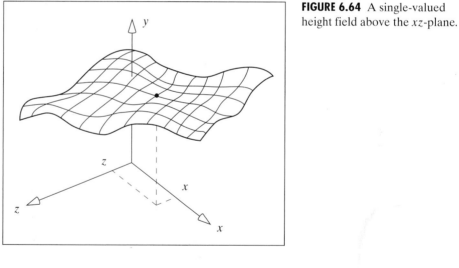

FIGURE 6.64 A single-valued height field above the xz-plane.

$$f(x, z) = e^{-ax^2 - bz^2} \tag{6.39}$$

(where a and b are given constants), or the circularly symmetric *sinc* function

$$f(x, z) = \frac{\sin\left(\sqrt{x^2 + z^2}\right)}{\sqrt{x^2 + z^2}} \tag{6.40}$$

and the undulating surface

$$f(x,z) = e^{-2|x|-.5|z|} \cos(4x - 12z)$$

Contrast this with surfaces such as the sphere, for which more than one value of y is associated with each point (x, z). Single-valued functions permit a simple parametric form:

$$P(u, v) = (u, f(u, v), v) \tag{6.41}$$

and their normal vector can be found by a direct application of Equation 6.23. (Check this.) That is, u and v can be used directly as the dependent variables for the function. Thus u-contours lie in planes of constant x, and v-contours lie in planes of constant z. Figure 6.65a shows a view of the example in Equation (6.39), and Figure 6.65b shows the function of Equation (6.40).

FIGURE 6.65 Two height fields: a) gaussian, b) sinc function.

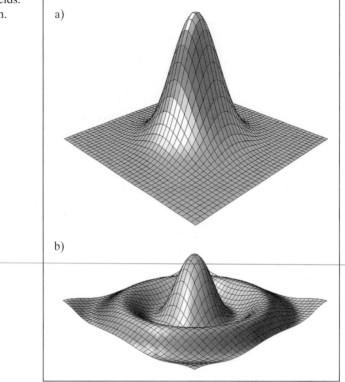

a)

b)

Each line is a trace of the surface cut by a plane, $x = k$ or $z = k$, for some value of k. Plots such as these can help illustrate the behavior of a mathematical function.

PRACTICE EXERCISE

6.5.22 The quadrics as explicit functions

The elliptic paraboloid can be written as $z = f(x, y)$, so it has an alternate parametric form $(u, v, f(u, v))$. What is $f()$? In what ways is this alternate parametric form useful? What other quadrics can be represented this way?   ■

6.6 PARTICLE SYSTEMS AND PHYSICALLY BASED SYSTEMS

> I think that a particle must have a separate reality independent of the measurements.
>
> That is, an electron has spin, location and so forth even when it is not being measured.
>
> I like to think that the moon is there even if I am not looking act it.
>
> *Albert Einstein*
> *(1879–1955)*

6.6.1 Particle Systems

Figure 6.66a shows a screenshot from an animation that simulates fire using a **particle system**. Recall from this chapter's preview that a particle system has the capability to keep track of an enormous number of particles. Each particle has a position and velocity in the scene, and may in addition have a color, lifetime, and in some cases a size, a degree of transparency, and even a shape. Any of these attributes might be randomly chosen by a random number generator, depending on the needs of the application.

a)   b)

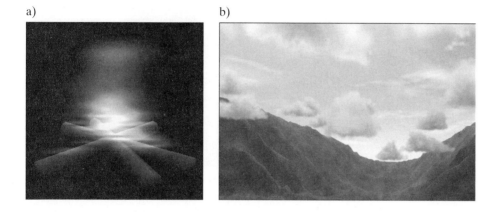

FIGURE 6.66 a) A fire simulation using particles to simulate fire, (Courtesy of Jeremy Allard) b) clouds as clumps of particles (Courtesy of Rob Hall).

It is usually important that a compelling application model each particle with its own set of attributes; in particular you want to track and update the position and velocity of each particle so that its movement appears natural, so that for instance water droplets fly out of a fountain and then fall back down gracefully the way real droplets do. Because each particle must be tracked accurately, one of the difficulties in creating a successful particle system application is the amount of memory required to store this information. A natural data structure is to store the state of the particles in a very large list of records array, and use some reasonable laws or rules to update each particle's state as times passes. For instance, if some particles are assumed to have mass, they may be influenced by gravity, and their acceleration would be determined by Newton's laws such as the familiar f = ma. Some particle systems, on the other hand, consider the particles to be so small that they are massless, in which case gravity has no effect. Figure 6.66b shows a possible simulation where the clouds in the scene have little to no mass. A number of great particle-system tutorials are available online; one excellent resource is www.nehe.com.

6.6.2 Physically Based Systems

There is a subfield of modeling systems known as **Physically based modeling** for which there is an attempt to describe in mathematical terms how various objects in a scene behave under the control of forces that act between them. Some examples of the systems to which physically based modeling are applied are pieces of cloth as in the flag of Figure 6.67a blowing in the wind. In Figure 6.67b a stick with a metal ball is shown being buffeted by the magnetic attractions of three magnetized blocks. The motion of the pendulum is determined not only by the magnetic forces but also by the usual Newtonian laws that predict how the acceleration of the stick must respond to the net force acting on it ($f = ma$).

Additional examples are blobs of gelatin being deformed as they hit each other, and then bouncing back to their original shapes hitting each other, being deformed, and then bouncing apart; clouds, waves, and other turbulent objects; and even living things. In these examples one of the key ingredients is that different objects collide with one another and are possibly deformed in the process. The desire to represent the action of such systems leads to very complex mathematics, and in fact a distinguishing characteristic of physically based systems is the difficulty of working with the mathematics involved (ordinary differential equations, partial differential equations, and so on). These often must be solved numerically, which tends to make the associated algorithms rather slow.

FIGURE 6.67 a) Flag blowing in the wind (Courtesy of Philip Crocoll/CodeColony.de), b) a pendulum buffeted by magnetized blocks.

a)   b)

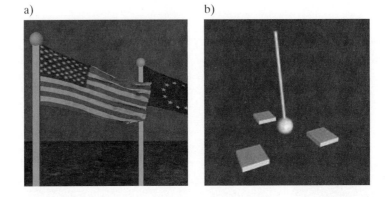

One particularly intriguing family of examples, a favorite among players of computer games, is the modeling and viewing of *terrain*. As an animation proceeds, the observer can fly over simulated terrain, there can be realistic ripples in an ocean below or in a waterfall, smoke and debris can gush out of a mountain top from a volcano, and many other physically based phenomena can be seen in action.. The terrain often consists of mountains rising from the sea, each mountain consisting of a range of peaks creating massive valleys, with the whole mountain range surrounding by oceanlike bodies of water. Figure 6.68 shows a screenshot from such a simulation.

Terrain is often modeled as a mesh object: a surface, based perhaps on a height field such as the one given in Equation (6.39), is defined and then successively refined by subdividing certain quadrilateral faces into smaller versions, until they are small enough to provide the desired level of detail. These faces are then rendered as filled shaded polygons, as we detail in Chapter 9.

FIGURE 6.68 A terrain simulation (Courtesy of Rob Hall).

Terrain imagery can be pleasing to the eye, it is even more engaging to fly over terrain in combination with undulating waves. We examine how to fly an observer over terrain in Chapter 7. A number of such animations are located on the book's accompanying web site.

6.7 SUMMARY

This chapter is concerned with modeling and drawing a wide variety of surfaces of 3D objects. This involves finding suitable mathematical descriptions for surface shapes, and creating efficient data structures that hold sufficient detail about a surface to facilitate rendering of the surface. We developed the Mesh class, whose data fields include three lists: the vertex, normal vector, and face lists. This data structure can efficiently hold all relevant geometric data about a flat-faced object such as a polyhedron, and it can hold sufficient data to model a polygonal skin that approximates other smoothly curved surfaces.

We showed that once a mesh data structure has been built, it is straightforward to render it in an OpenGL environment. It is also easy to store a mesh in a file, and to read it back again into a program.

Modern shading algorithms use the normal vector at each vertex of each face to determine how light or dark the different points within a face should be drawn. If the face should be drawn flat, the same normal vector—the normal vector to the face itself—is used for every vertex normal. If the mesh is designed to represent an underlying smoothly curved surface, the normal vector at each vertex is set to the face normal of the underlying surface at that point, and rendering algorithms use a form of interpolation to produce gracefully varying shades in the picture (as we discuss in Chapter 10). Thus the choice of what normal vectors to store in a mesh depends on how the designer wishes the object to appear.

A wide variety of polyhedral shapes that occur in popular applications were examined, and techniques were developed that build meshes for several polyhedral families. Here special care was taken to use the normal to the face in each of the face's vertex normals. We also studied large families of smoothly varying objects, including the classical quadric surfaces, cylinders, and cones, and discussed how to compute the direction of the normal vector at each point by suitable derivatives of the parametric form for the surface.

The Case Studies in the next section elaborate on some of these ideas, and should not be skipped. Some of them probe further into theory. A derivation of the Newell method to compute a normal vector is outlined, and you are asked to fill in various details. Other Case Studies ask that you develop methods or applications to create and draw meshes for the more interesting classes of shapes described.

6.8 CASE STUDIES

CASE STUDY 6.1. MESHES STORED IN FILES

(Level of Effort: II) We want the Mesh class to support writing of Mesh objects to a file, and reading of filed Mesh objects back into a program. We choose a simple format for such files. The first line lists the number of vertices, number of normals, and number of faces in the mesh. Then each vertex in the mesh is listed as a triple of floating-point values, (x_i, y_i, z_i). Several vertices are listed on each line. Then each normal vector is listed, also as a triple of floating-point numbers. Finally, each face is listed, in the format:

- number of vertices in this face
- the list of indices in the vertex list for the vertices in this face
- the list of indices in the normal list for the vertices in this face

For example, the simple barn of Figure 6.5 could be stored as:

```
10 7 7
0 0 0   1 0 0   1 1 0   1 1.5 0   0 1 0
0 0 1   1 0 1   1 1 1   1 1.5 1   0 1 1
-1 0 0 -0.477 0.8944 0 0.447 0.8944 0
1 0 0  0 -1 0   0 0 1  0 0 -1
4    0 5 9 4    0 0 0 0
4    3 4 9 8    1 1 1 1
4    2 3 8 7    2 2 2 2
4    1 2 7 6    3 3 3 3
4    0 1 6 5    4 4 4 4
5    5 6 7 8 9  5 5 5 5 5
5    0 4 3 2 1  6 6 6 6 6
```

Here the first face is a quadrilateral based on the vertices numbered 0, 5, 9, 4, and the last two faces are pentagons.

To read a mesh into a program from a file you might wish to use the code along the lines of Figure 6.69. Given a filename, it opens and reads the file into an existing `Mesh` object, and returns 0 if it can do this successfully. It returns nonzero if an error occurs, such as when the named file cannot be found. (Additional testing should be done within the method to catch formatting errors, such as a floating-point number when an integer is expected.)

```cpp
int Mesh:: readmesh(char * fileName)
{
      fstream infile;
      infile.open(fileName, ios::in);
      if(infile.fail()) return -1; // error - can't open file
      if(infile.eof()) return -1;  // error - empty file
      infile >> numVerts >> numNorms >> numFaces;
      pt = new Point3[numVerts];
      norm = new Vector3[numNorms];
      face = new Face[numFaces];
      //check that enough memory was found:
      if( !pt || !norm || !face)return -1; // out of memory
      for(int p = 0; p < numVerts; p++) // read the vertices
            infile >> pt[p].x >> pt[p].y >> pt[p].z;
      for(int n = 0; n < numNorms; n++) // read the normals
            infile >> norm[n].x >> norm[n].y >> norm[n].z;
      for(int f = 0; f < numFaces; f++) // read the faces
      {
            infile >> face[f].nVerts;
            face[f].vert = new VertexId[face[f].nVerts];
            for(int i = 0; i < face[f].nVerts; i++)
                  infile >> face[f].vert[i].vertIndex
                         >> face[f].vert[i].normIndex;
      }
      return 0; // success
}
```

FIGURE 6.69 Read a mesh file into memory.

Because no knowledge of the required mesh size is available before `numVerts`, `numNorms`, and `numFaces` is read, the arrays that hold the vertices, normals, and faces are allocated dynamically at runtime with the proper sizes.

A number of files in this format are available on the internet site for this book. (They have the suffix .3vn)

It is equally straightforward to fashion the method `int Mesh:: writeMesh(char* fileName)` that writes a mesh object to a file.

Write an application that reads mesh objects from files and draws them in the manner of Figure 6.17, and also allows the user to write a mesh object to a file. As examples of simple files for getting started, arrange that the application can create meshes for a tetrahedron and the simple barn.

CASE STUDY 6.2 DERIVATION OF THE NEWELL METHOD

(Level of Effort: II) This study develops the theory behind the **Newell method** for computing the normal to a polygon based on its vertices, leading to Equation (6.1). The necessary mathematics is presented as needed as the discussion unfolds; you are asked to show several of the intermediate results. Note, you need only show the steps marked explicitly with the phrase "as part of this case study, show that". Other steps along the way are for your guidance.

In these discussions we work with the polygonal face (convex or nonconvex) P given by the N 3D vertices:

$$P = \{P_0, P_1, \ldots, P_{N-1}\} \tag{6.42}$$

We want to show why the formulas in Equation (6.1) provide an exact computation of the true normal vector $\mathbf{m} = (m_x, m_y, m_z)$ to P when P is planar, and a good direction to use as an average normal when P is nonplanar.

Derivation:

Figure 6.70 shows P projected (orthographically—along the principal axes as in Chapter 5) onto each of the principal planes: the $x = 0$, $y = 0$, and $z = 0$ planes. Each projection is a 2D polygon. We first show that the components of $\mathbf{m}$ are proportional to the areas, A_x, A_y, and A_z, respectively, of these projected polygons.

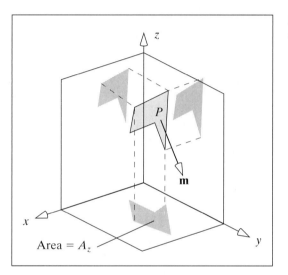

FIGURE 6.70 Using projected areas to find the normal vector.

For simplicity consider the case where P is a triangle that we shall call T, as shown in Figure 6.71. Suppose its unit normal vector is some $\mathbf{m}$. Further, let T' be the projection of T onto the plane with unit normal $\mathbf{n}$. We show that the area of T', denoted Area(T'), is a certain fraction of the area Area(T) of T, and that the fraction is a simple dot product:

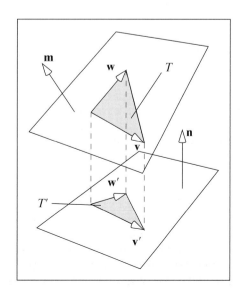

FIGURE 6.71 Effect of orthographic projection on area.

$$\text{Area}(T') = (\mathbf{m} \cdot \mathbf{n}) \, \text{Area}(T)$$

Suppose triangle T has edges defined by the vectors $\mathbf{v}$ and $\mathbf{w}$ as shown in the figure.

As part of this case study, use the familiar size and direction of the cross product (recall Chapter 4) to show that the area of T is $\text{Area}(T) = \frac{1}{2}|\mathbf{w} \times \mathbf{v}|$, also as part of this case study, show that $\mathbf{v} \times \mathbf{w} = 2 \, \text{Area}(T)\mathbf{m}$. Now since triangle T is defined by the vectors $\mathbf{v}$ and $\mathbf{w}$, the projection T' is defined by the projected vectors $\mathbf{w'}$ and $\mathbf{v'}$. As part of this case study, find an expression for the area of T' in terms of a cross product between $\mathbf{w'}$ and $\mathbf{v'}$. Our key goal is to express the area of T' in terms of the original v and w, however, rather than their projected versions. But from Chapter 4 we know how to form orthogonal projections, and so this should present little problem.

As part of this case study, express the projected vectors $\mathbf{w'}$ and $\mathbf{v'}$ in terms of the original $\mathbf{v}$ and $\mathbf{w}$, and use them to show that the area of T' is: $\text{Area}(T')\mathbf{m.n}$.

As part of this case study, show that this result generalizes to the areas of any planar polygon P and its projected image P'.

As part of this case study, recalling that a dot product is proportional to the cosine of an angle, show that $\text{Area}(T') = \text{Area}(T) \cos \phi$ and state what the angle ϕ is.

As part of this case study, show that the areas A_x, A_y, A_z defined above are simply $Km_x, Km_y,$ and Km_z, respectively, where K is some constant. Hence the areas $A_x, A_y,$ and A_z are in the same ratios as $m_x, m_y,$ and m_z.

So to find $\mathbf{m}$ we need only compute the vector (A_x, A_y, A_z) and normalize it to unit length. We now show how to compute the area of the projection of P of Equation (6.42) onto the xy-plane directly from its vertices. The other two projected areas follow similarly.

Each 3D vertex $P_i = (x_i, y_i, z_i)$ projects onto the xy-plane as $V_i = (x_i, y_i)$. Figure 6.72 shows an example projected polygon P'. Each edge of P' defines a trapezoidal region lying between it and the x-axis.

FIGURE 6.72 Computing the area of a polygon.

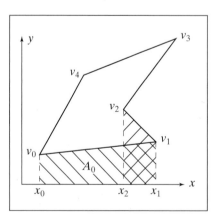

The area of such a trapezoid is the width of the base times the midpoint of the edge. For instance, the area A_0 in the figure is $A_0 = 0.5(x_0 - x_1)(y_0 + y_1)$. This quantity is negative if x_0 lies to the left of x_1, and is positive otherwise. We use this same form for each edge. For the ith edge define

$$A_i = \frac{1}{2}(x_i - x_{\text{next}(i)})(y_i + y_{\text{next}(i)})$$

where $\text{next}(i)$ is 0 if i is equal to $N - 1$, and is $i + 1$ otherwise. Since this is essentially the desired expression for the normal of polygon P first presented in Equation 6.1, it completes the derivation of the Newell method.

If two adjacent edges of the polygon are collinear (which would make a cross product based on them zero), the area contributed by these edges is still properly accounted for.

The sum of the A_i properly adds the positive and negative contributions of area to form a resultant sum that is either the area of the polygon, or its negative.

Now we ask, in which of the two basic directions does **m** point? That is, if you circle the fingers of your right hand around the vertices of the polygon moving from P_0 to P_1, to P_2, and so on, the direction of the arrow in Figure 6.73, does **m** point along your thumb or in the opposite direction?

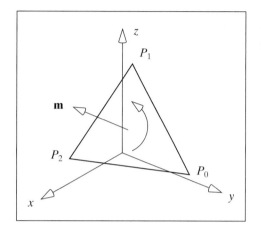

FIGURE 6.73 The direction of the normal found by the Newell method.

m *does* point as shown in Figure 6.73. Thus for a mesh that has a well-defined inside–outside, we can say that **m** is the outward-pointing normal if the vertices are labeled CCW as seen from the outside.

CASE STUDY 6.3 THE PRISM

(Level of Effort: III) Write an application that allows the user to specify the polygonal base of a prism using the mouse. It then creates the vertex, normal, and face lists for the prism, and displays it.

Figure 6.74a shows the user's drawing area; a square presented on the screen. The user lays down a sequence of points in this square with the mouse, terminating the process with a right-click.

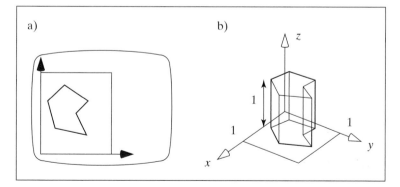

FIGURE 6.74 Designing and building a prism mesh.

In 3D space the corresponding square is considered to be a unit square lying in the xy-plane as suggested in Figure 6.74b, and the base of the prism lies within it. This establishes the size of the base in the 3D world. The prism is considered to be the base polygon after it is swept one unit in the direction of the z-axis. Exercise the program on several prisms input by the user. See if your implementation of OpenGL properly draws nonconvex base polygons.

CASE STUDY 6.4 PRISM ARRAYS AND EXTRUDED QUAD-STRIPS

(Level of Effort: III) Write the two methods described in Section 6.4.2:

```
void Mesh:: makePrismArray(<... suitable arguments ..>);
void Mesh:: makeExtrudedQuadStrip(Point2 p[], int numPts, Vec-
tor3 d);
```

that create meshes for an array of prisms, and for an extruded quad-strip.

a) **Arrays of prisms:** Choose an appropriate data type to represent an array of prisms. Note that makePrismArray() is similar to the method that makes a mesh for a single prism. Exercise the first method on at least the two block letters with the shapes 'K' and 'W'. (Try 'D' also if you wish.)

b) **Extruded quad-strips used to form tubes:** The process of building the vertex, normal, and face lists of a mesh is really a matter of keeping straight the many indices for these arrays. To assist in developing this method, consider a quad-strip base polygon described as in Equation (6.7) by the vertices

$$\text{quad-strip} = \{p_0, p_1, \ldots, p_{M-1}\}$$

where $p_i = (x_i, y_i, 0)$ lies in the xy-plane, as shown in Figure 6.75a. When extruded, each successive pair of vertices forms a waist of the tube, as shown in Figure 6.75b. There are $num = M/2 - 1$ segments in the tube.

FIGURE 6.75 Building a mesh from a quad-strip base polygon.

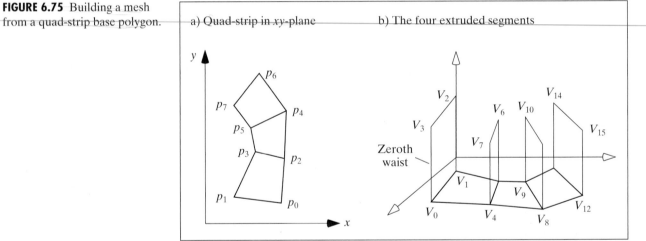

a) Quad-strip in xy-plane   b) The four extruded segments

The 0th waist consists of vertices p_0, p_1, $p_1 + \mathbf{d}$, and $p_0 + \mathbf{d}$, where $\mathbf{d}$ is the extrusion vector. We add vertices to the vertex list as suggested in Figure 6.75b.

Now for the face list. We first add all of the outside walls of each segment of the tube, and then append the end walls (i.e., the first end wall uses vertices of the first waist). Each of the num segments has four walls. For each wall we list the four vertices in CCW order as seen from the outside. There are patterns in the various indices encountered, but they are complicated.

What are indices of the two end faces of the tube?

Each face has a normal vector determined by the Newell method, which is straightforward to calculate at the same time the vertex indices are placed in the face list. All vertex normals of a face use the same normal vector: face[L].normindex = {L,L,L,L}, for each L.

Exercise the make ExtrudedQuadStrip() method by modeling and drawing some arches, such as the one shown in Figure 6.38, as well as some block letters that permit the use of quad-strips for their base polygon.

CASE STUDY 6.5 TUBES AND SNAKES BASED ON A PARAMETRIC CURVE

(Level of Effort: III) Write and test a method

```
void Mesh:: makeTube(Point2 P[], int numPts, float t[], int num-
Times)
```

that builds a flat-faced mesh based on wrapping the polygon with vertices $P_0, P_1, \ldots, P_{N-1}$ about the spine curve $C(t)$. The waists of the tube are formed on the spine at the set of instants $t_0, t_1, \ldots, t_{M-1}$, and a Frenet frame is constructed at each $C(t_i)$. The function $C(t)$ is "hard-wired" into the method as a formula.

Experiment with the method by wrapping polygons taken from Example 3.5.5 that involve a line jumping back and forth between two concentric circles. Try at least the helix and a Lissajous figure as example spine curves.

CASE STUDY 6.6 BUILDING DISCRETE-STEPPED SURFACES OF REVOLUTION

(Level of Effort: III) Write an application that allows the user to specify the profile of an object with the mouse, as in Figure 6.76. It then creates the mesh for the surface of revolution, and displays it. The program also writes the mesh data to a file in the format described in Case Study 6.1.

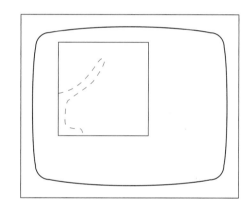

FIGURE 6.76 Designing a profile for a surface of revolution.

Figure 6.76 shows the user's drawing area: a square presented on the screen. The user lays down a sequence of points in this square with the mouse.

In 3D space the corresponding square is considered to be a unit square lying in the xz-plane. This establishes the size of the profile in the 3D world. The surface of revolution is formed by sweeping the profile about the z-axis, in a user-defined number of steps.

Exercise the program on several surfaces of revolution input by the user.

CASE STUDY 6.7 ON EDGE LISTS AND WIREFRAME MODELS

(Level of Effort: II) A wireframe version of a mesh can be drawn by drawing a line for each edge of the mesh. Write a routine `void Mesh:: drawEdges(void)` that does this for any given mesh. It simply traverses each face, connecting adjacent vertices with a line. This draws each line twice. (Why?)

In some time critical situations this inefficiency might be intolerable. In such a case an **edge list** can be built for the mesh which contains each edge of the mesh only once. An edge list is an array of index pairs, where the two indices indicate the two endpoints of each edge. Describe an algorithm that builds an edge list for any mesh. It traverses each face of the mesh, noting each edge as it is found, but adding it only if that edge is not already on the list.

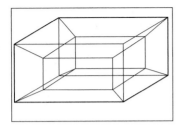

FIGURE 6.77 An ambiguous object.

Note that it is usually impossible to build a face list from an edge list and a vertex list. Figure 6.77 shows the classic example. From an edge list alone there is no way to tell where the faces are: even a wireframe model for a cube could be a closed box or an open one. A face list has more information, therefore, than does an edge list.

CASE STUDY 6.8 VAULTED CEILINGS

(Level of Effort: III) Many classic buildings have arched ceilings or roofs shaped as a **vault**. Figure 6.78a shows a domical vault [Fleming66] built on a square base. Four webs, each a ruled surface, rise in a circular sweep to meet at the peak. Part b shows a domical vault built on an octagon, having eight webs. Write a function that creates and draws the associated wireframe mesh model for a domical vault built on a cube, and on an octagon.

FIGURE 6.78 Examples of vaulted ceilings.

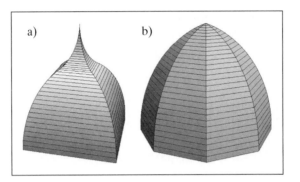

CASE STUDY 6.9 ON PLATONIC SOLIDS

(Level of Effort: II) Create files (in the format described in Case Study 6.1) for each of the Platonic solids. Experiment by reading each file into an application and drawing the associated object.

6.9 FOR FURTHER READING

A number of books are available that treat the definition and generation of surfaces and solids. Rogers and Adams *Mathematical Elements for Computer Graphics* [Rogers90] provides a clear introduction to curves and surfaces, as does the classic and older Faux and Pratt's *Computational Geometry for Design and Manufacture* [Faux79]. Gray's *Modern Differential Geometry of Curves and Surfaces with Mathematica* [Gray93] offers a rigorous mathematical treatment of curve and surface shapes, and provides code in *Mathematica* for drawing them. Mortenson's *Geometric Modeling* [Mortenson85] also provides an excellent discussion of solid modeling used in the CAD industry. Hearn and Baker [Hearn03] offer an introduction to computer graphics and develop many topics related to the current literature.

Chapter 7

Three-Dimensional Viewing

Surely it is the total projection of an individual creative mind that really counts.

Gerald Finzi
(1901–1956)

GOALS OF THE CHAPTER

○ To develop tools for creating and manipulating a camera that produces pictures of a 3D scene in various perspective views.

○ To see how to fly a camera through a scene interactively, and to make animations.

○ To learn the mathematics that describes various kinds of projections.

○ To see how each operation in the OpenGL graphics pipeline operates, and why it is used.

○ To build a powerful clipping algorithm for 3D objects.

○ To devise a means for producing stereo views of objects.

Preview

Section 7.1 provides an overview of the additional tools that are needed to build an application that lets a camera fly through a scene. Recall that we use the term "camera" to describe the airplanelike synthetic camera that is commonly used in television production for the same purpose. Section 7.2 defines a camera that produces perspective views and shows how to make such a camera using OpenGL. It introduces aviation terminology, "pitch, roll, and yaw," which helps to describe ways to manipulate a camera in intuitive ways. It develops some of the mathematics needed to describe a camera's orientation by means of a matrix. Section 7.3 defines the Camera class to encapsulate information about a camera and develops methods that create and adjust a camera in an application.

Section 7.4 examines the geometric nature of perspective projections and describes mathematical tools to characterize perspective. It shows how to incorporate perspective projections in the graphics pipeline and describes how OpenGL does it. An additional property of homogeneous coordinates is introduced to facilitate this. The section also develops a powerful clipping algorithm that operates in homogeneous coordinate space, showing how its efficiency is a result of proper transformations applied to points before clipping begins.

Section 7.5 shows how to produce stereo views of a scene in order to make them more intelligible and engaging. The chapter closes with a number of Case Studies that focus on applications for developing applications to test the techniques discussed.

7.1 INTRODUCTION

We are now in a position to create pictures of elaborate 3D objects residing in a scene. As we saw in Chapter 5, OpenGL provides tools for establishing a jib camera in the scene, for projecting the scene onto the jib camera's viewplane, and for rendering the projection in the viewport. So far our jib camera only produces parallel projections. In Chapter 6 we described several classes of interesting 3D shapes that can be used to model the objects we want in a scene, and through the Mesh class we have ways of drawing any of them with basic shading.

So what is left to do? We want to develop a deeper understanding of what is going on behind the scenes. This deeper understanding will allow us to create better bug-free applications in shorter periods of time. An increased understanding of the mathematics behind the formulas offers new approaches for the application programmer. For greater realism we want to create and control a camera that produces perspective projections. We want ways to provide the user with more control of the camera's position and orientation, so that he or she can fly the camera through the scene in an animation. This requires developing more controls than OpenGL provides, and hopefully in a more intuitive manner. We also need to achieve precise control over the camera's view volume, which is determined in the perspective case, as it was when forming parallel projections, by a certain matrix. This requires a deeper utilization of homogeneous coordinates than we have needed so far, so we develop the mathematics of perspective projections from the beginning, and see how they are incorporated in the OpenGL graphics pipeline. We also describe how clipping is done against the camera's view volume, which again requires some detailed working with homogeneous coordinates. So at the end of this adventure we shall finally see how it is all done, from start to finish!

7.2 THE CAMERA REVISITED

It adds a precious seeing to the eye.

William Shakespeare,
Love's Labours Lost
(1562–1616)

In Chapter 5 we used a camera that produces parallel projections. Its view volume is a parallelepiped bounded by six walls, including a near plane and a far plane. OpenGL also supports a camera that creates **perspective views** of 3D scenes. It is similar in shape to the camera used before, except that its view volume has a different shape.

Figure 7.1 shows its general form. It has an **eye (or view reference point**, VRP) positioned at some point in space, and its **view volume** is a portion of a pyramid, whose apex is at the eye. The straight line from a point P to the eye is called the **projector** of P. (All projectors of a point meet at the eye.) The axis of the view volume is called the **viewplane normal**, **VPN**. The opening of the pyramid is set by the **view angle**, θ (see part b of the figure). Three planes are defined perpendicular to the VPN: the **near plane**, the **viewplane**, and the **far plane**. Where these planes intersect the VPN, they form rectangular windows. The windows have a certain **aspect ratio**, which can be set in a program. OpenGL clips off any points of the scene that lie outside the view volume. Points P lying inside the view volume are projected onto the **viewplane** to a corresponding point P', as suggested in part c. (We can always think in terms of projecting *points*; when projecting a larger, more complex object, each of its points is projected.)

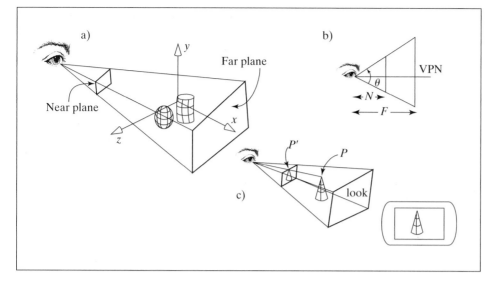

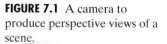

FIGURE 7.1 A camera to produce perspective views of a scene.

The main point: Any point P projects to point P', which is located where the projector from P intersects the view plane.

A suggestion to the reader: try to memorize and become familiar with these various terms; they will be used very frequently in the ensuing chapter.

Finally, the image formed on the view plane is mapped into the viewport as shown in part c, and becomes visible on the display device.

7.2.1 To Set the View Volume

Figure 7.2 shows the camera in its default position, with the eye at the origin and the **VPN** aligned with the z-axis. Some students find it useful to think of the eye as "looking" in some direction. This might be useful in developing intuition about the camera; however, keep in mind that the eye is simply a point and consequently is not *looking* at anything. On the contrary, the programmer defines a *look* point (part c of Figure 7.1) as a point of particular interest in the scene, and together the two points **eye** and **look** define the **VPN** as *eye – look*. This is later normalized to become the vector **n**, which is pivotal for properly specifying the camera. (From our knowledge of vectors keep in mind that with this definition, both the **VPN** and **n** point from *look* to *eye*.)

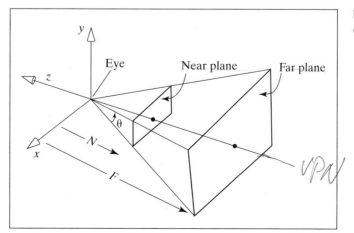

FIGURE 7.2 The camera in its default position.

OpenGL provides a simple way to set the view volume in a program, which we examine in detail in subsequent sections.

7.2.2 To Position and Point the Camera

In order to obtain the desired view of a scene, we move the camera away from its default position shown in Figure 7.2 and aim it in a particular direction. We do this by performing a rotation and a translation; these transformations become part of the **modelview matrix**, as we discuss in later Sections.

Happily, we set up the camera's position and orientation in *exactly* the same way we did for the parallel-projection camera. (The only difference between a parallel- and perspective-projection camera resides in the projection matrix, which determines the *shape* of the view volume.) The simplest function to use is again gluLookAt(), using the sequence

```
glMatrixMode(GL_MODELVIEW);   // make the modelview matrix
                                  current
glLoadIdentity();              // start with a unit matrix
gluLookAt(eye.x, eye.y, eye.z, look.x, look.y, look.z, up.x,
up.y, up.z);
```

As before, this moves the camera so that its eye resides at point eye, and it "looks" toward the point of interest, look. The "upward" direction is generally suggested by the vector up, which is most often set simply to $(0, 1, 0)$. In Chapter 5 we took these parameters and the whole process of setting the camera pretty much for granted. In this chapter we will probe deeper, both to see how it is done and to take finer control over setting the camera. We also develop tools to make *relative* changes to the camera's direction, such as rotating it slightly to the left, tilting it up, or sliding it forward.

The Camera with Arbitrary Orientation and Position

A camera can have any position in the scene, and any orientation. Imagine a transformation that picks up the camera of Figure 7.2 and moves it somewhere in space, then rotates it around so that it is aimed as desired. We need a way to describe this precisely, and to determine what the resulting modelview matrix will be.

It will serve us well to attach an explicit coordinate system to the camera, as suggested by Figure 7.3.

FIGURE 7.3 Attach a coordinate system to the camera.

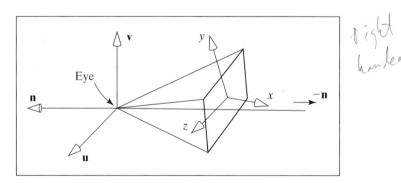

This coordinate system has its origin at the eye and has three axes, usually called the u-, v-, and n- axes, that define its orientation. The axes are pointed in directions given by the vectors **u**, **v**, and **n**, as shown in the figure. Note that this is a right-handed system. The camera is oriented by default down the negative z-axis, so we say in

[handwritten: camera oriented down negative n-axis]

general that the camera is oriented down the negative *n*-axis, in the direction −**n**. The direction **u** points off to the right of the camera, and direction **v** points upward. Think of the *u*-, *v*-, and *n*-axes as clones of the *x*-, *y*-, and *z*-axes of Figure 7.2, that are moved and rotated as we move the camera into position.

Position is easy to describe, but orientation is difficult. It helps if we specify orientation using the flying terms **pitch**, **heading**, **yaw**, and **roll**, as suggested in Figure 7.4. The *pitch* of an airplane is the angle that its longitudinal axis (running from tail to nose and having direction −**n**) makes with the horizontal plane. An airplane *rolls* by rotating about this longitudinal axis; its *roll* is the amount of this rotation relative to the horizontal. An airplane's *heading* is the direction in which it is headed. (Other terms are *azimuth* and *bearing*.) To find the heading and pitch given **n**, simply express −**n** in spherical coordinates, as shown in Figure 7.5. (See Appendix 2 for a review of spherical coordinates.) The vector −**n** has longitude and latitude given by angles θ and φ, respectively. The heading of a plane is given by the longitude of −**n**, and the pitch is given by the latitude of −**n**. Formulas for roll, pitch, and heading in terms of the vectors **u** and **n** are developed in the exercises.

[handwritten: r =]

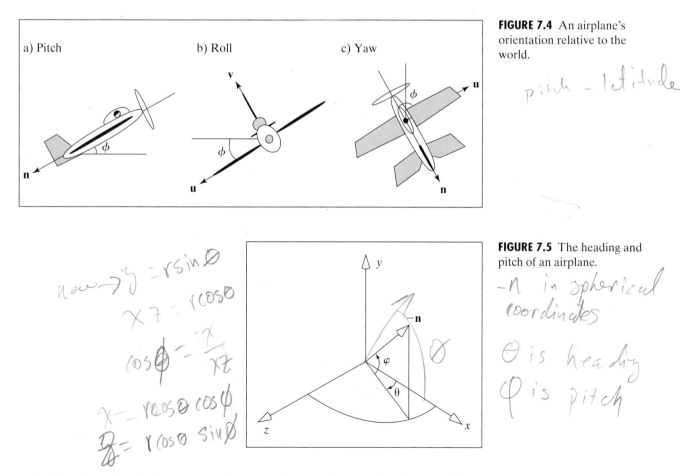

FIGURE 7.4 An airplane's orientation relative to the world.

[handwritten: pitch − latitude]

a) Pitch   b) Roll   c) Yaw

FIGURE 7.5 The heading and pitch of an airplane.

[handwritten: −n in spherical coordinates]

[handwritten: θ is heading]

[handwritten: φ is pitch]

*[handwritten equations:
new → y = r sin φ
x z = r cos φ
cos φ = x / xz
x = r cos φ cos θ
z = r cos φ sin θ]*

Pitch and *roll* are both nouns and verbs: when used as verbs, they describe a change in the airplane's orientation. You can say an airplane pitches up when it increases its pitch (rotates about its *u*-axis), and that it rolls when it rotates about its *n*-axis. The common aviation term for changing heading is *yaw*: to yaw left or right it is rotated about its *v*-axis.

These terms can be used with a camera as well. Figure 7.6a shows a familiar camera with the same coordinate system attached: it has *u*-, *v*-, and *n*-axes, and its origin is at position *eye*. The camera in part b has some nonzero roll, whereas the one in part c has zero roll. We most often set a camera to have zero roll and call it a "**no-roll**" camera. The *u*-axis of a no-roll camera is horizontal—that is, perpendicular to the *y*-axis of the world. Note that a no-roll camera can still have an arbitrary *n* direction, so it can have any pitch or heading.

FIGURE 7.6 Various camera orientations.

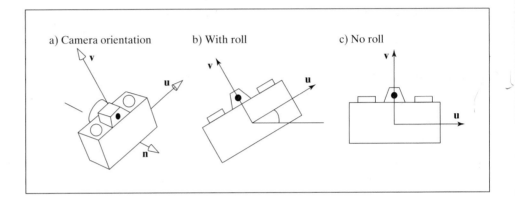

How do we control the roll, pitch, and heading of our camera? `gluLookAt()` is handy for setting up an initial camera, since we usually have a good idea of how to choose *eye* and *look*. But it's harder to visualize how to choose **up** to obtain a certain roll, and it's hard to make later relative adjustments to the camera using only `gluLookAt()`. (`gluLookAt()` works with Cartesian coordinates, whereas orientation deals with angles and rotations about axes.) OpenGL doesn't give direct access to the *u*-, *v*-, and *n*-directions, so we'll maintain them ourselves in a program. This will make it much easier to describe and adjust the camera.

What `gluLookAt()` Does: Some Mathematical Underpinnings

What, then, are the directions **u**, **v**, and **n** when we execute `gluLookAt()` with given values for *eye*, *look*, and **up**? Let's see exactly what `gluLookAt()` does, and why it does it.

As shown in Figure 7.7a, we are given the locations of *eye* and *look*, and the **up** direction. We know that **n** is parallel to the vector *eye* – *look*, as shown in Figure 7.7b, so we set **n** = *eye* – *look*. (We'll normalize this and the other vectors later as necessary.)

FIGURE 7.7 Build the vectors **u**, **v**, and **n**.

$n = eye - look$

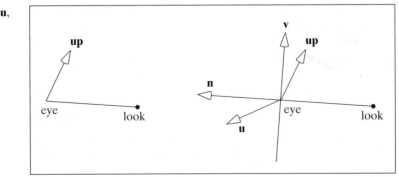

We now need to find **u** and **v** that are perpendicular to **n** and to each other. The **u** direction points off to the side of a camera, so it is (fairly) natural to make it perpendicular to **up**, which the user has said is the upward direction. This is the assumption gluLookAt() makes in any case, and so the direction **u** is made perpendicular to **n** and **up**. An excellent way to build a vector that is perpendicular to two given vectors is to form their cross product, so we set **u** = **up** × **n**. (The user should not choose an **up** direction that is parallel to **n**, as then **u** would have zero length—why?) We choose **u** = **up** × **n** rather than **n** × **up** so that **u** will point to the right as we look along −**n**.

With **u** and **n** in hand, the final chore is to form **v**; it must be perpendicular to both **u** and **v**, so use a cross product again: **v** = **n** × **u**. Notice that **v** will usually not be aligned with **up**: **v** must be aimed perpendicular to **n**, whereas the user provides **up** as a suggestion of upwardness.

Summarizing: Given *eye*, *look*, and **up**, we form

$$\mathbf{n} = eye - look$$
$$\mathbf{u} = \mathbf{up} \times \mathbf{n}$$
$$\mathbf{v} = \mathbf{n} \times \mathbf{u} \tag{7.1}$$

and then normalize all three to unit length.

Note how this plays out for the common case where **up** = $(0, 1, 0)$. Convince yourself that in this case $\mathbf{u} = (n_z, 0, -n_x)$ and $\mathbf{v} = (-n_x n_y, n_x^2 + n_z^2, -n_z n_y)$. Notice in particular that **u** does have a y-component of 0, so it is horizontal. Further, **v** has a positive y-component, so it is pointed more or less upward.

■ EXAMPLE 7.2.1 Find the camera coordinate system

Consider a camera with *eye* = $(4, 4, 4)$ that looks down on a look-at point *look* = $(0, 1, 0)$. Further suppose that **up** is initially set to $(0, 1, 0)$. Find **u, v**, and **n**. Repeat for **up** = $(2, 1, 0)$.

SOLUTION:

From Equation (7.1) we find before any vectors have been normalized: $\mathbf{u} = (4, 0, -4)$, $\mathbf{v} = (-12, 32, -12)$, $\mathbf{n} = (4, 3, 4)$, which are easily normalized to unit length. (Sketch this situation.) Note that **u** is indeed horizontal. Check that these are mutually perpendicular. For the case of **up** = $(2, 1, 0)$ (try to visualize this camera before working out the arithmetic. We find, again before normalizing the vectors, that), $\mathbf{u} = (4, -8, 2)$, $\mathbf{v} = (38, 8, -44)$, and $\mathbf{n} = (4, 3, 4)$. Sketch this situation. Check that these vectors are mutually perpendicular.

■ EXAMPLE 7.2.2 To build intuition with cameras

To assist in developing geometric intuition when setting up a camera, Figure 7.8 shows two example cameras—each depicted as a coordinate system with a view volume—positioned above the world coordinate system, which is made more visible by grids drawn in the *xz*-plane. One camera is set with *eye* = $(-2, 2, 0)$, *look* = $(0, 0, 0)$, and **up** = $(0, 1, 0)$. For this camera, we find from Equation (7.1) before normalization that $\mathbf{n} = (-2, 2, 0)$, $\mathbf{u} = (0, 0, 2)$, and $\mathbf{v} = (4, 4, 0)$. The figure shows these vectors as well as the **up** vector. The second camera uses *eye* = $(2, 2, 0)$, *look* = $(0, 0, 0)$, and **up** = $(0, 0, 1)$. In this case $\mathbf{u} = (-2, 2, 0)$ and $\mathbf{v} = (0, 0, 8)$. The direction **v** is parallel to **up** here. Note that this camera appears to be on its side: (Check that all of these vectors appear drawn in the proper directions.)

FIGURE 7.8 Two example settings of the camera.

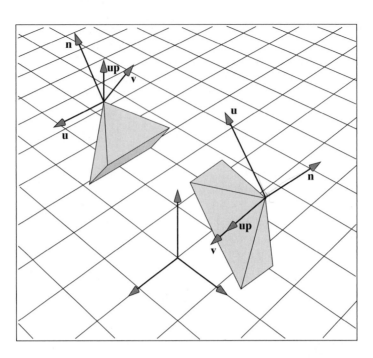

FIGURE 7.8 Two example settings of the camera.

Finally, we want to see what values `gluLookAt()` places in the modelview matrix. From Chapter 5 we know that the modelview matrix is the product of two matrices—the matrix V that accounts for the transformation of world points into camera coordinates, and the matrix M that embodies all of the modeling transformations applied to points. `gluLookAt()` builds the V matrix using Equation 7.1 and postmultiplies the current matrix by it. Because the job of the V matrix is to convert world coordinates to camera coordinates, it must transform the camera's coordinate system into the generic position for the camera, as shown in Figure 7.9. This means it must transform *eye* into the origin, $\mathbf{u}$ into the vector $\mathbf{i}$, $\mathbf{v}$ into $\mathbf{j}$, and $\mathbf{n}$ into $\mathbf{k}$. There are several ways to derive what V must be, but it's easiest to check that the following matrix does the trick:

$$V = \begin{pmatrix} u_x & u_y & u_z & d_x \\ v_x & v_y & v_z & d_y \\ n_x & n_y & n_z & d_z \\ 0 & 0 & 0 & 1 \end{pmatrix} \tag{7.2}$$

FIGURE 7.9 The transformation that `gluLookAt()` sets up.

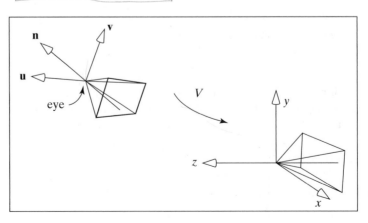

where $(d_x, d_y, d_z) = (-eye \cdot \mathbf{u}, -eye \cdot \mathbf{v}, -eye \cdot \mathbf{n})$. Check that in fact

$$V \begin{pmatrix} eye_x \\ eye_y \\ eye_z \\ 1 \end{pmatrix} = \begin{pmatrix} 0 \\ 0 \\ 0 \\ 1 \end{pmatrix}$$

as desired, where we have extended point *eye* to homogeneous coordinates. Also check that

$$V \begin{pmatrix} u_x \\ u_y \\ u_z \\ 0 \end{pmatrix} = \begin{pmatrix} 1 \\ 0 \\ 0 \\ 0 \end{pmatrix},$$

and that V maps $\mathbf{v}$ into $(0, 1, 0, 0)^T$ and maps $\mathbf{n}$ into $(0, 0, 1, 0)^T$. The matrix V is created by gluLookAt() and is postmultiplied with the current matrix. We will have occasion to do this same operation later when we maintain our own camera in a program.

7.3 TO SPECIFY A CAMERA IN A PROGRAM

Writing has laws of perspective, of light and shade just as painting does, or music. If you are born knowing them, fine. If not, learn them. Then rearrange the rules to suit yourself.

Truman Capote
(1924–1984)

In order to have fine control over camera movements, we create and manipulate our own camera in a program. After each change to this camera is made, the camera tells OpenGL what the new camera is. We create a Camera class that knows how to do all the things a camera does. Because so many variables and vectors are involved in the calculations needed to establish a camera, we need an organized way to control and manipulate the ingredients of the camera. The obvious answer, as mentioned, is to define a Camera class. It's very simple to do so and the payoff is high. In a program we create a Camera object called, say, cam, and adjust it with functions such as:

```
cam.set(eye, look, up);    // initialize the camera - similar to
                              gluLookAt()
cam.slide(-1,0,-2); // slide the camera forward and to the left
cam.roll(30); // roll it through 30° CCW as seen by the pilot
cam.yaw(20); // yaw it through 20° to the left
cam.pitch (15); // pitch it up through 15°
etc.
```

Figure 7.10 shows a portion of the definition of the Camera class. (A more complete definition appears on the book's companion web site. The Camera class contains fields for eye, look, up, and other relevant points, which are of type Point3, and for vectors $\mathbf{u}$, $\mathbf{v}$, and $\mathbf{n}$, which are of type Vector3. The types Point3 and Vector3 have been defined previously and are also given in Appendix 3.

---

[1] A technicality: since it's not legal to dot a point and a vector, *eye* should be replaced here by the vector $(eye - (0, 0, 0))$.

```
class Camera{
  private:
      Point3 eye, look, up;
      Vector3 u, v, n;
      double viewAngle, aspect, nearDist, farDist; // view volume shape
      void setModelviewMatrix(); // tell OpenGL where the camera is

  public:
      Camera(); // constructor
      void set(Point3 eye, Point3 look, Vector3 up); // like gluLookAt()
      void roll(float angle); // roll it
      void pitch(float angle); // increase pitch
      void yaw(float angle); // yaw it
      void slide(float delU, float delV, float delN); // slide it
      void setShape(float vAng, float asp, float nearD, float farD);
      void getShape(float &vAng, float &asp, float &nearD, float &farD);
};
```

FIGURE 7.10 The Camera class definition.

It also has fields that describe the shape of the view volume: viewAngle, aspect, nearDist, and farDist.

The utility routine setModelviewMatrix() communicates the modelview matrix to OpenGL. It is used only by member functions of the class. The modelview matrix needs to be updated after each change is made to the camera's position or orientation. Figure 7.11 shows a possible implementation. It computes the matrix of Equation (7.2) based on current values of *eye*, look, **u**, **v**, and **n**, and loads the matrix directly into the modelview matrix using glLoadMatrixf().

```
void Camera :: setModelviewMatrix(void)
{ // load modelview matrix with existing camera values
      float m[16];
      Vector3 eVec(eye.x, eye.y, eye.z); // constructor of a vector version of eye
      m[0] = u.x; m[4] = u.y; m[8] = u.z; m[12] = -eVec.dot(u);
      m[1] = v.x; m[5] = v.y; m[9] = v.z; m[13] = -eVec.dot(v);
      m[2] = n.x; m[6] = n.y; m[10] = n.z;m[14] = -eVec.dot(n);
      m[3] = 0; m[7] = 0; m[11]    = 0;  m[15] = 1.0;
      glMatrixMode(GL_MODELVIEW);
      glLoadMatrixf(m); // load OpenGL's modelview matrix
}
void Camera:: set(Point3 Eye, Point3 look, Vector3 up)
{ // create a modelview matrix and send it to OpenGL
      eye.set(Eye); // store the given eye position
      n.set(eye.x - look.x, eye.y - look.y, eye.z - look.z); // make n
      u.set(up.cross(n)); // make u = up X n
      n.normalize(); u.normalize(); // make them unit length
      v.set(n.cross(u)); // make v = n X u
      setModelViewMatrix(); // tell OpenGL
}
```

FIGURE 7.11 The utility routines set() and setModelviewMatrix().

The method set() acts just like gluLookAt(): it uses the values of eye, look, and up to compute **u**, **v**, and **n** according to Equation (7.1). It communicates this information into the fields of the camera object and communicates these values to OpenGL.

The routine setShape() is even simpler: it puts the four argument values into the appropriate camera fields and then calls gluPerspective(viewAngle,aspect, nearDist, farDist) (along with glMatrixMode   (GL_PROJECTION) and glLoadIdentity()) to set the projection matrix.

The central camera methods are slide(), roll(), yaw(), and pitch(), which make *relative* changes to the camera's position and orientation. The function slide() moves the camera without changing its orientation. (The whole reason for maintaining the eye, u, v, and n fields in our Camera data structure is so that we have a record of the current camera and can therefore alter it, perhaps interactively.) We next examine how the camera methods operate.

7.3.1 To Fly the Camera Interactively

The user flies the camera through a scene **interactively** by pressing keys or clicking the mouse. For instance, pressing 'u' might slide the camera up some amount, pressing 'y' might yaw it to the left, and pressing 'f' might slide it forward. The user can see how the scene looks from one point of view, then change the camera to a better viewing spot and direction and produce another picture. Or the user can fly around a scene taking different snapshots in rapid succession. If the snapshots are stored and then played back rapidly, an animation is produced of the camera flying around the scene.

There are six degrees of freedom for adjusting a camera: its position can be varied in three dimensions, and it can be rotated about any of three coordinate axes. We first develop the slide() function.

Slide the Camera

Sliding a camera means to move it along one of its *own* axes—that is, in the **u**, **v**, or **n** direction, without rotating it. Since the camera is looking along the negative **n**-axis, movement along **n** is forward or back. Similarly, movement along **u** is left or right, and along **v** is up or down.

It is simple to move the camera along one of its axes. To move it distance D along its **u**-axis, set *eye* to $eye + D\mathbf{u}$ and alter look in the same way. Make no change to up. For convenience we can combine the three possible slides in a single function. slide(delU, delV, delN) slides the camera amount delU along **u**, delV along **v**, and delN along **n**:

```
void Camera:: slide(float delU, float delV, float delN)
{
    eye.x += delU * u.x + delV * v.x + delN * n.x;
    eye.y += delU * u.y + delV * v.y + delN * n.y;
    eye.z += delU * u.z + delV * v.z + delN * n.z;
    look.z += delU * u.z + delV * v.z + delN * n.z;
    look.z += delU * u.z + delV * v.z + delN * n.z;
    look.z += delU * u.z + delV * v.z + delN * n.z;
    setModelViewMatrix();
}
```

Rotate the Camera

We want to roll, pitch, or yaw the camera. This involves a rotation of the camera about one of its own axes. We look at rolling in detail; the other two types of rotation are similar.

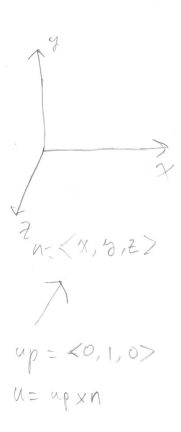

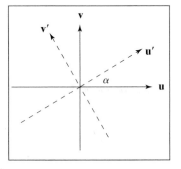

FIGURE 7.12 Roll the camera.

To roll the camera is to rotate it about its own **n** axis. This means that both the directions **u** and **v** must be rotated, as shown in Figure 7.12. We form two new axes **u′** and **v′** that lie in the same plane as **u** and **v** yet have been rotated through the angle α degrees.

So we need only form **u′** as the appropriate linear combination of **u** and **v**, and form a similarly combination for **v′**:

$$\mathbf{u}' = \cos(\alpha)\mathbf{u} + \sin(\alpha)\mathbf{v}$$
$$\mathbf{v}' = -\sin(\alpha)\mathbf{u} + \cos(\alpha)\mathbf{v} \tag{7.3}$$

The new axes **u′** and **v′** then replace **u** and **v** in the camera. This is straightforward to implement.

```
void Camera :: roll(float angle)
{ // roll the camera through angle degrees
      float cs = cos(3.14159265/180 * angle);
  // convert degrees to radians
      float sn = sin(3.14159265/180 * angle);
      Vector3 t(u); // remember old u
      u.set(cs*t.x - sn*v.x, cs*t.y - sn*v.y, cs*t.z - sn*v.z);
      v.set(sn*t.x + cs*v.x, sn*t.y + cs*v.y, sn*t.z + cs*v.z);
      setModelViewMatrix();
}
```

The functions `pitch()` and `yaw()` are implemented in a similar fashion. See the exercises.

Put It All Together

We show in Figure 7.13 how the `Camera` class can be used with OpenGL to fly a camera through a scene. The scene consists of the lone teapot here. The camera is a global object and is set up in `main()` with a good starting view and shape. When a key is pressed, `myKeyboard()` is called, and the camera is slid or rotated, depending on which key was pressed. For instance, if 'P' is pressed, the camera is pitched up by 1 degree. If CTRL F is pressed[2] (hold down the control key and press 'f'), the camera is pitched down by 1 degree. After the keystroke has been processed, `glutPostRedisplay()` causes `myDisplay()` to be called again to draw the new picture.

Notice the call to `glutSwapBuffers()` and NOTE the argument GLUT_DOUBLE to the function `glutInitDisplayMode()`.[3] This application uses **double buffering** (see Chapter 3, "Achieving Smooth Animation") to produce a rapid and smooth transition between one picture and the next. Two memory buffers are used to store the generated pictures. The display switches from showing one buffer to showing the other under the control of `glutSwapBuffers()`. Each new picture is drawn in the invisible buffer, and when the drawing is complete, the display switches to it. Thus the viewer doesn't see the screen erased and the new picture slowly emerge line by line, which is visually annoying. Instead the old picture is displayed steadily while the picture is being composed off screen, and then the display switches very rapidly to the newly completed picture.

---

2   On most keyboards pressing CTRL and a letter key returns an ASCII value that is 64 less than the ASCII value returned by the letter itself.

3   `glutInitDisplayMode()` must have an argument of GLUT_DOUBLE to enable double buffering.

```
// the usual includes
#include "camera.h"

Camera cam; // make a global camera object

//<<<<<<<<<<<<<<<<<<<<<<< myKeyboard >>>>>>>>>>>>>>>>>>>>>>>
void myKeyboard(unsigned char key, int x, int y)
{
  switch(key)
  {
      // controls for camera
      case 'F':    cam.slide(0,0, 0.2); break; // slide camera forward
      case 'F'-64: cam.slide(0,0,-0.2); break; //slide camera back
      // add up/down and left/right controls
      case 'P':     cam.pitch(-1.0); break;
      case 'P' - 64: cam.pitch( 1.0); break;
      // add yaw controls
      case 'Y':     cam.yaw(-1.0); break;
      case 'Y' - 64: cam.yaw( 1.0); break;
      // add roll controls
      case 'R':     cam.roll(1.0); break;
      case 'R' - 64: cam.roll( 1.0); break;
}

      glutPostRedisplay(); // draws it again
}
//<<<<<<<<<<<<<<<<<<<<<<< myDisplay >>>>>>>>>>>>>>>>>>>>>>>>>>
void myDisplay(void)
{
      glClear(GL_COLOR_BUFFER_BIT||GL_DEPTH_BUFFER_BIT);
      glutWireTeapot(1.0); // draw the teapot
      glFlush();
      glutSwapBuffers(); // display the screen just made
}
//<<<<<<<<<<<<<<<<<<<<<<< main >>>>>>>>>>>>>>>>>>>>>>>>>>>>>>>
void main(int argc, char **argv)
{
      glutInit(&argc, argv);
      glutInitDisplayMode(GLUT_DOUBLE | GLUT_RGB); // double buffering
      glutInitWindowSize(640,480);
      glutInitWindowPosition(50, 50);
      glutCreateWindow("fly a camera around a teapot");
      glutKeyboardFunc(myKeyboard);
      glutDisplayFunc(myDisplay);
      glClearColor(0.0f,1.0f,0.0f,0.0f);  // background is green
      glColor3f(0.0f,0.0f,0.0f);    // set color of stuff
      glViewport(0, 0, 640, 480);
      cam.set(4, 4, 4, 0, 0, 0, 0, 1, 0); // make the initial camera
      cam.setShape(30.0f, 64.0f/48.0f, 0.5f, 50.0f);
      glutMainLoop();
}
```

FIGURE 7.13 A complete program to fly a camera around the teapot using the Camera class.

To Draw SDL Scenes Using a Camera

It is just as easy to incorporate a camera in an application that reads SDL files, as described in Chapter 5. There are then two global objects:

```
Camera cam;
Scene scn;
```

and in `main()` an SDL file is read and parsed using `scn.read("myScene.dat")`. Finally, in `myDisplay(void)`, simply replace the call to the function that draws the scene with `scn.drawSceneOpenGL();`

PRACTICE EXERCISES

7.3.1 Implement `pitch()` and `yaw()`

Write the functions void `Camera::pitch(float angle)` and void `Camera::yaw(float angle)` that respectively pitch and yaw the camera. Arrange matters so that a positive yaw yaws the camera to the left and a positive pitch pitches the camera up.

7.3.2 Build a universal `rotate()` method

Write the function void `Camera::rotate(Vector3 axis, float angle)` that rotates the camera through `angle` degrees about `axis`. It rotates all three axes **u**, **v**, and **n** about the eye. ■

7.4 PERSPECTIVE PROJECTIONS OF 3D OBJECTS

> Treat them in terms of the cylinder, the sphere, the cone, all in perspective.
>
> *Ashanti proverb*

With the `Camera` class in hand, we can navigate around 3D scenes and readily create pictures. Using OpenGL, each picture is created by passing vertices of objects (such as a mesh representing a teapot or chess piece) down the graphics pipeline, as we described in Chapter 5. Figure 7.14 shows the graphics pipeline again, with one new element.

Recall that each vertex v is multiplied by the modelview matrix (VM). The modeling part (M) embodies all of the modeling transformations for the object; the viewing part (V) accounts for the transformation set by the camera's position and orientation. When a vertex emerges from this matrix, it is in **eye coordinates**—that is, in the coordinate system of the eye. Figure 7.15 shows this system, for which the

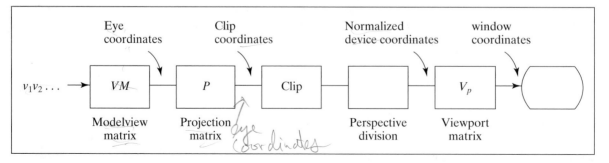

FIGURE 7.14 The graphics pipeline revisited.

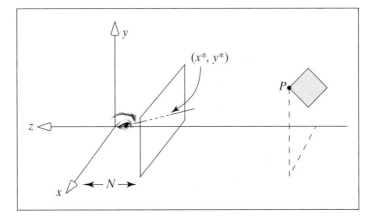

FIGURE 7.15 Perspective projection of vertices expressed in eye coordinates.

eye is at the origin, and the near plane is perpendicular to the z-axis residing at $z = -N$. A vertex located at P in eye coordinates is passed through the next stages of the pipeline, where it is (somehow) projected to a certain point (x^*, y^*) on the near plane, clipping is carried out, and finally the surviving vertices are mapped to the viewport on the display.

At this point we must look more deeply into the process of forming perspective projections. We need answers to a number of questions. What operations constitute forming a perspective projection, and how does the pipeline perform these operations? What's the relationship between perspective projections and matrices? How does the projection map the view volume into a canonical view volume for clipping? How is clipping done? How do homogeneous coordinates come into play in the process? How is the depth of a point from the eye retained so that proper hidden surface removal can be done? And what is that *perspective division* step?

We start by examining the nature of perspective projection, independent of specific processing steps in the pipeline. Then we see how the steps in the pipeline are carefully crafted to produce the numerical values required for a perspective projection.

7.4.1 Perspective Projection of a Point

The fundamental operation is projecting a 3D point to a 2D point on a plane. Figure 7.16 elaborates on Figure 7.15 to show point $P = (P_x, P_y, P_z)$ projecting onto the near plane of the camera to a point (x^*, y^*). We erect a local coordinate system on the near plane, with its origin on the camera's z-axis. Then it is meaningful to talk about the point x^* units over to the right of the origin, and y^* units above the origin.

The first question is then, what are the values x^* and y^*? It's simplest to use similar triangles, and say x^* is in the same ratio to P_x as the distance N is to the distance $|P_z|$. Or since P_z is negative, we can say

$$\frac{x^*}{P_x} = \frac{N}{-P_z}$$

or $x^* = NP_x/(-P_z)$. Similarly $y^* = NP_y/(-P_z)$. So we have that P projects to the point on the viewplane:

$$(x^*, y^*) = \left(N\frac{P_x}{-P_z}, N\frac{P_y}{-P_z} \right) \qquad \text{(the projection of } P \text{)} \qquad (7.4)$$

An alternate (analytical) method for arriving at this result is given in the exercises.

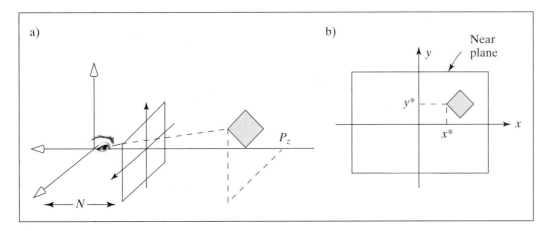

FIGURE 7.16 To find the projection of a point P in eye coordinates.

■ EXAMPLE 7.4.1

Where on the viewplane does $P = (1, 0.5, -1.5)$ lie for the camera having a near plane at $N = 1$?

SOLUTION:

Direct use of Equation (7.4) yields $(x^*, y^*) = (0.666, 0.333)$.

We can make some preliminary observations about how points are projected.

1. Note the denominator term $-P_z$. It is larger for more remote points (those farther along the negative z-axis), which reduces the values of x^* and y^*. This introduces **perspective foreshortening** and makes remote parts of an object appear smaller than nearer parts.
2. Denominators have a nasty way of evaluating to zero, and P_z becomes 0 when P lies in the same plane as the eye: the $z = 0$ plane. Normally we use clipping to remove such offending points before trying to project them.
3. If P lies behind the eye, there is a reversal in sign of P_z, which causes further trouble, as we see later. These points, too, are usually removed by clipping.
4. The effect of the near plane distance N is simply to *scale* the picture (both x^* and y^* are proportional to N). So if we choose some other plane (still parallel to the near plane) as the view plane onto which to project pictures, the projection will differ only in size from that onto the near plane. Since we ultimately map this projection to a viewport of a fixed size on the display, the size of the projected image makes no difference. This shows that any view plane parallel to the near plane would work just as well, so we might as well use the near plane itself.
5. Straight lines project to straight lines. Figure 7.17 provides the simplest proof. Consider the line in 3D space between points A and B. A projects to A' and B projects to B'. But do points *between* A and B project to points directly between A' and B'? Yes: just consider the plane formed by A, B, and the origin. Since any two planes intersect in a straight line, this plane intersects the near plane in a straight line. Thus line segment AB projects to *line segment* $A'B'$.

Recall that the goal here is to calculate appropriate values for the P matrix so that OpenGL can use them as needed. This process takes place at different points in the graphics pipeline. It begins as in Figure 7.17, with geometry that shows where a

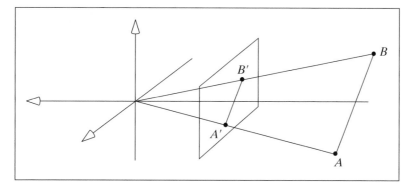

FIGURE 7.17 Proof that a straight line projects to a straight line.

point along the line AB projects. The projected point is converted to an arithmetic expression for each projected point, which is then loaded into the P matrix. Of particular importance is that calculating the projected point requires a division, known as *perspective division*, which introduces and stresses the use of *homogenous coordinates*. Details of these steps now follow.

■ **EXAMPLE 7.4.2 Three projections of the barn**

A lot of intuition can be acquired by seeing how a simple object is viewed by different cameras. Here we examine how the edges of the barn defined in Chapter 6 and repeated in Figure 7.18 are projected onto three cameras. The barn has 10 vertices, 15 edges, and seven faces.

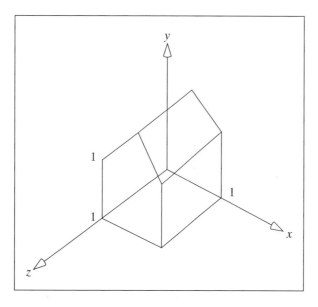

FIGURE 7.18 The basic barn revisited.

View #1: We first set the camera's *eye* at $(0, 0, 2)$ and set look to $(0, 0, 0)$, to cause $\mathbf{u} = (1, 0, 0)$ and $\mathbf{n} = (-1, 0, 0)$. We will set the near plane at distance 1 from the eye. (The near plane happens therefore to coincide with the front of the barn.) In terms of camera coordinates, all points on the front wall of the barn have $P_z = -1$ and those on the back wall have $P_z = -2$. So from Equation (7.4) any point (P_x, P_y, P_z) on the front wall projects to:

$$P' = (P_x, P_y) \qquad \{\text{projection of a point on the front wall}\}$$

and any point on the back wall projects to

$$P' = (P_x/2, P_y/2) \qquad \{\text{projection of a point on the back wall}\}$$

The foreshortening factor is two for those points on the back wall. Figure 7.19a shows the projection of the barn for this view. Note that edges on the rear wall project at half their true length. Also note that edges of the barn that are actually parallel in 3D *need not* project as parallel. (We shall see that edges that are parallel to each other and are also parallel to the viewplane *do* project as parallel, but parallel edges that are not parallel to the viewplane are not parallel: they recede to a **vanishing point**.)

FIGURE 7.19 Projections of the barn for views #1 and #2.

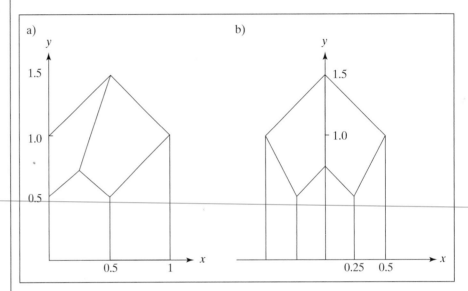

View #2: Here the camera has been slid over so that *eye* $= (0.5, 0, 2)$, but we suppose **u** and **n** are the same as in view #1. Figure 7.19b shows the projection.

View #3: Here we use the camera with *eye* $= (2, 5, 2)$ and *look* $= (0, 0, 0)$, resulting in Figure 7.20. The world axes have been added as a guide. This view shows the barn from an informative point of view. From a wireframe view it is difficult to discern where each face truly is.

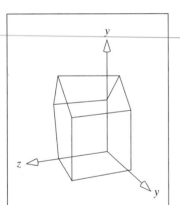

FIGURE 7.20 A third view of the barn.

PRACTICE EXERCISES

7.4.1 Sketch a cube in perspective

Draw (on your graphing calculator or paper) the perspective view of a **cube** C (axis-aligned and centered at the origin, with sides of length 2) when the eye is at $E = 5$ on the z-axis. Repeat when C is translated so that its center is at $(1, 1, 1)$.

7.4.2 Where does the ray hit the viewplane? (Don't skip this one.)

We want to derive Equation (7.4) by finding where the ray from the origin to P intersects the near plane.

a. Show that if this ray is at the origin at $t = 0$ and at P at time $t = 1$, then it has parametric representation $r(t) = Pt$.
b. Show that it hits the near plane at $t = N/(-P_z)$.
c. Show that the hit point is $(x^*, y^*) = (NP_x/(-P_z), NP_y/(-P_z))$. ■

7.4.2 Perspective Projection of a Line

We develop here some interesting properties of perspective projections by examining how straight lines project.

1. We know that lines that are parallel in 3D project to lines, but these lines aren't necessary parallel. If not parallel, they meet at some vanishing point.
2. Lines that pass behind the eye of the camera cause a catastrophic passage through infinity. (Such lines should be clipped off.)
3. Perspective projections usually produce geometrically realistic pictures. But realism is strained for very long lines parallel to the viewplane.

1. Projecting Parallel Lines

We suppose the line in 3D passes (using camera coordinates) through point $A = (A_x, A_y, A_z)$ and has direction vector $\mathbf{c} = (c_x, c_y, c_z)$. It therefore has parametric form $P(t) = A + \mathbf{c}t$. Substituting this form in Equation (7.4) yields the parametric form for the projection of this line:

$$p(t) = \left(N\frac{A_x + c_x t}{-A_z - c_z t}, N\frac{A_y + c_y t}{-A_z - c_z t} \right) \tag{7.5}$$

(This may not look like the parametric form for a straight line, but it is. See the exercises.) Thus the point A in 3D projects to the point $p(0)$, and as t varies, the projected point $p(t)$ moves across the screen (in a straight line). We can discern several important properties directly from this formula.

Suppose the line $A + \mathbf{c}t$ is parallel to the viewplane. Then $c_z = 0$ and the projected line is given by:

$$p(t) = \frac{N}{-A_z}(A_x + c_x t, A_y + c_y t)$$

This is the parametric form for a line with slope c_y/c_x. This slope does not depend on the position of the line, only on its direction $\mathbf{c}$. Thus all lines in 3D with direction $\mathbf{c}$ will project with this slope, so their projections are parallel. We conclude:

> **If two lines in 3D are parallel to each other *and* to the viewplane, they project to two parallel lines.**

Contrariwise, consider the case where the direction $\mathbf{c}$ is not parallel to the viewplane. For convenience suppose $c_z < 0$, so that as t increases, the line recedes farther and farther from the eye. At very large values of t, Equation (7.5) becomes (because the terms multiplying t dominate the other terms):

$$p(\infty) = \left(N\frac{c_x}{-c_z}, N\frac{c_y}{-c_z} \right) \quad \text{(the vanishing point for the line)} \tag{7.6}$$

This is called the **vanishing point** for this line: the point to which the projected line approaches as t gets larger and larger. Notice that it depends only on the direction $\mathbf{c}$ of the line and not on its position (which is embodied in A). Thus all parallel lines share the same vanishing point. In particular, these lines project to lines that are *not* parallel, of course, since they meet at a point.

Figure 7.21a makes this more vivid for the example of a cube. Several edges of the cube are parallel: there are those that are horizontal, those that are vertical, and

FIGURE 7.21 The vanishing point for parallel lines.

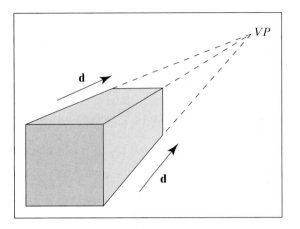

those that recede from the eye. This picture was made with the camera oriented so that its near plane was parallel to the front face of the cube. Thus in camera coordinates the z-component of **c** for the horizontal and vertical edges is 0. The horizontal edges therefore project to parallel lines, and so do the vertical edges. The receding edges, however, are not parallel to the view plane and hence converge onto a vanishing point (VP). Artists often set up drawings of objects this way, choosing the vanishing point and sketching parallel lines as pointing at the VP. We shall see more on vanishing points as we proceed.

Figure 7.22 suggests what a vanishing point is geometrically. Looking down onto the camera's xz-plane from above, we see the eye at the origin is viewing various points on the line AB. A projects to A', B projects to B', and so on. Very remote points on the line project to VP as shown. The line from the eye through VP must be parallel to the line AB. (Why?)

FIGURE 7.22 The geometry of a vanishing point.

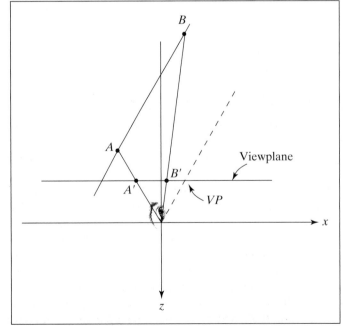

2. Lines That Pass Behind the Eye

We saw earlier that trying to project a point that lies in the plane of the eye ($z = 0$ in eye coordinates) results in a denominator of 0, and would surely spell trouble if we try to project it. We now examine the projection of a line segment where one endpoint lies in front of the eye, and one endpoint lies behind.

Figure 7.23 again looks down on the camera from above. Point A lies in front of the eye and projects to A' in a very reasonable manner. Point B, on the other hand, lies behind the eye, and projects to B', which seems to end up on the wrong side of the viewplane! Consider a point C that moves from A to B, and sketch how its projection moves. As C moves back towards the plane of the eye, its projection slides farther and farther along the viewplane to the right. As C approaches the plane of the eye, its projection spurts off to infinity, and as C moves behind the eye, its projection reappears from far off to the left on the viewplane! You might say that the projection has "wrapped around infinity" and has come back from the opposite direction [Blinn96]. If we tried to draw such a line in an algorithm, there would most likely be chaos. Normally all parts of the line closer to the eye than the near plane are clipped off before the projection is attempted.

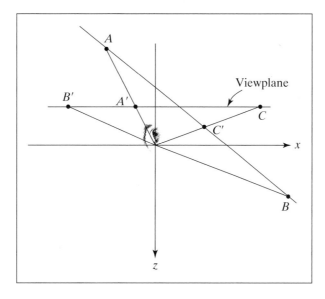

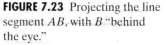

FIGURE 7.23 Projecting the line segment AB, with B "behind the eye."

■ EXAMPLE 7.4.3 The classic horizontal plane in perspective

A good way to gain insight into vanishing points is to view a grid of lines in perspective, as in Figure 7.24. Grid lines here lie in the xz-plane and are spaced 1 unit apart. The eye is perched 1 unit above the xz-plane, at $(0, 1, 0)$, and looks along $-\mathbf{n}$, where $\mathbf{n} = (0, 0, 1)$. As usual we take $\mathbf{up} = (0, 1, 0)$. N is chosen to be 1.

The grid lines of constant x have parametric form in eye coordinates of $(i, 0, t)$, where $i = \ldots, -2, -1, 0, 1, 2, \ldots$, and t varies from 0 to ∞. By Equation (7.4) the ith line projects to $(-i/t, 2/t)$, which is a line through the vanishing point $(0, 0)$, so all of these lines converge on the same vanishing point, as expected.

The grid lines of constant z are given by $(t, 0, -i)$, where $i = 1, 2, \ldots, N$ for some N, and t varies from $-\infty$ to ∞. These project to $(-t/i, -2/i)$, which appear as horizontal straight lines (check this). Their projections are parallel, since the gridlines themselves are parallel to the viewplane. The more remote ones (larger values of i) lie closer together, providing a vivid example of perspective foreshortening. Many of the remote contours are not drawn here, as they become so crowded they cannot be drawn clearly. The **horizon** consists of all the contours where z is very large and negative; it is positioned at $y = 0$.

FIGURE 7.24 Viewing a horizontal grid on the xz-plane.

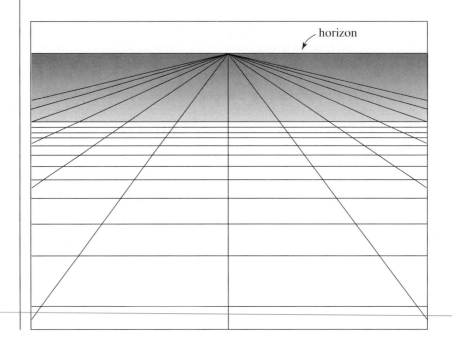

3. The Anomaly of Viewing Long Parallel Lines

Perspective projections seem to be a reasonable model for the way we see. But there are some anomalies, mainly because our eyes do not have planar view screens. The problem occurs for very long objects. Consider an experiment, for example, where you look up at a pair of parallel telephone wires, as suggested in Figure 7.25a.

For the perspective view, if we orient the viewplane to be parallel to the wires, we know the image will show two straight and parallel lines (part b). But what you see is quite different. The wires appear curved as they converge to vanishing points in both directions (part c)! In practice this anomaly is barely visible, because the

FIGURE 7.25 Viewing very long parallel wires.

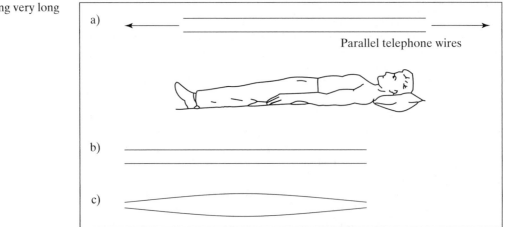

window or your eye limits the field of view to a reasonable region. (To see different parts of the wires you have to roll your eyes up and down, which of course rotates your viewplanes.)

PRACTICE EXERCISES

7.4.3 Straight lines project as straight lines: the parametric form

Show that the parametric form in Equation (7.5) is that of a straight line. *Hint*: For the x-component divide the denominator into the numerator to get $-A_x N / A_z + Rg(t)$, where R depends on the x-components of A and $\mathbf{c}$, but not the y-components, and $g(t)$ is some function of t that depends on neither the x nor the y-components. Repeat for the y-component, obtaining $-A_y N / A_z + Sg(t)$ with similar properties. Argue why this is the parametric representation of a straight line (albeit one for which the point does not move with constant speed as t varies).

7.4.4 Derive results for horizontal grids

Derive the parametric forms for the projected grid lines in Example 7.4.3. ▪

7.4.3 To Incorporate Perspective in the Graphics Pipeline

> Only a fool tests the depth of the river with both feet.
>
> *Paul Cezanne*
> *(1839–1907)*

We want the graphics pipeline to project vertices of 3D objects onto the near plane, then map them to the viewport. After passing through the modelview matrix, the vertices are represented in the camera's coordinate system, and Equation (7.4) shows the values we need to compute for the proper projection. We need to do clipping, and then map what survives to the viewport. But we need a little more as well.

Adding Pseudodepth

Taking a projection discards depth information—that is, how far the point is from the eye. But we mustn't discard this information completely, or it will be impossible to do hidden surface removal later.

The actual distance of a point P from the eye in camera coordinates is $\sqrt{P_x^2 + P_y^2 + P_z^2}$, which would be cumbersome and slow to compute for each point of interest. All we really need is some measure of distance that tells, when two points project to the *same* point on the near plane, which is the closer. Figure 7.26 shows points P_1 and P_2 that both lie on a line from the eye, and therefore project to the same point. We must be able to test whether P_1 obscures P_2 or vice versa. So for each point P that we project we compute a value called the **pseudodepth** that provides an adequate measure of depth for P. We then say that P projects to (x^*, y^*, z^*), where (x^*, y^*) is the value provided in Equation (7.4) and z^* is its pseudodepth.

What is a good choice for the pseudodepth function? Notice that if two points project to the same point, the farther one always has a more negative value of P_z, so we might use $-P_z$ itself for pseudodepth. But it will turn out to be very harmonious and efficient to choose a function with the *same denominator* $(-P_z)$ as occurs with x^* and y^*. So we try a function that has this denominator, and a numerator that is linear in P_z, and say that P "projects to"

$$(x^*, y^*, z^*) = \left(N \frac{P_x}{-P_z}, N \frac{P_y}{-P_z}, \frac{aP_z + b}{-P_z} \right) \tag{7.7}$$

FIGURE 7.26 Is P_1 closer than P_2 or farther away?

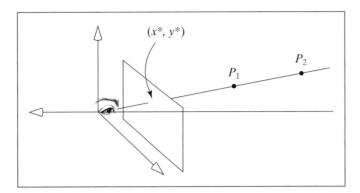

for some choice of the constants a and b. Although many different choices for a and b will do, we choose them so that the pseudodepth varies between -1 and 1 (we see later why these are good choices). Since depth increases as a point moves farther down the negative z-axis, we *decide* that the pseudodepth is -1 when $P_z = -N$, and is $+1$ when $P_z = -F$. With these two conditions we can easily solve for a and b, obtaining:

$$a = -\frac{F + N}{F - N}, \qquad b = \frac{-2FN}{F - N} \qquad\qquad (7.8)$$

Figure 7.27 plots pseudodepth versus $(-P_z)$. As we insisted, it grows from -1 for a point on the near plane up to $+1$ for a point on the far plane. As P_z approaches 0 (so that the point is just in front of the eye), pseudodepth plummets to $-\infty$. For a point just behind the eye, the pseudodepth is huge and positive. But we will clip off points that lie closer than the near plane, so this catastrophic behavior will never be encountered.

FIGURE 7.27 Pseudodepth grows as P_z becomes more negative.

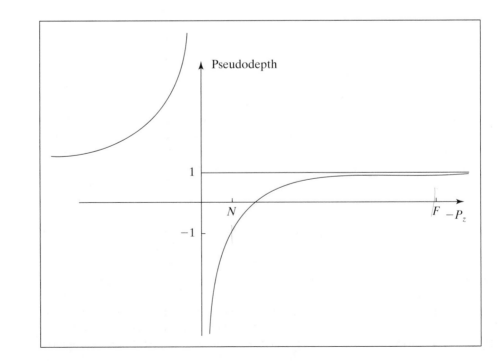

Also notice that pseudodepth values bunch together as $(-P_z)$ gets closer to F. Given the finite-precision arithmetic of a computer, this can cause a problem when you must distinguish the pseudodepth of two points during hidden surface removal: the points have different true depths from the eye, but their pseudodepths come out with the same value!

Note that defining pseudodepth as in Equation (7.7) causes it to become more positive as P_z becomes more negative. This seems reasonable, since depth from the eye increases as P_z moves farther along the negative z-axis.

■ **EXAMPLE 7.4.4 Pseudodepth varies slowly as $(-P_z)$ approaches F**

Suppose $N = 1$ and $F = 100$. This produces $a = -101/99$ and $b = -200/99$, so pseudodepth is given by

$$\text{pseudodepth}\big|_{N=1,F=100} = \frac{101P_z + 200}{99P_z}$$

This maps appropriately to -1 at $P_z = -N$, and 1 at $P_z = -F$. But close to $-F$ it varies quite slowly with $(-P_z)$. For $(-P_z)$ values of 97, 98, and 99, for instance, this evaluates to 1.041028, 1.040816, and 1.040608.

A little algebra (see the exercises) shows that when N is much smaller than F as it normally will be, pseudodepth can be approximated by

$$\text{pseudodepth} \approx 1 + \frac{2N}{P_z} \tag{7.9}$$

Again you see that it varies more and more slowly as $(-P_z)$ approaches F. But its variation is increased by using large values of N. N should be set as large as possible (but of course not so large that objects nearest to the camera are clipped off!).

Using Homogeneous Coordinates

Why did we consider having the same denominator for each term in Equation (7.7)? As we now show, this makes it possible to represent all of the steps so far in the graphics pipeline as matrix multiplications, offering both processing efficiency and uniformity. (Chips on some graphics cards can multiply a point by a matrix in hardware, making this operation extremely fast!) Doing it this way will also allow us to set things up for a highly efficient and reliable clipping step.

The new approach requires that we represent points in homogeneous coordinates. We have been doing that anyway, since this makes it easier to transform a vertex by the modelview matrix. But we are going to expand the notion of the homogeneous coordinate representation beyond what we have needed before now, and therein find new power. In particular, a matrix will be able to perform not only an affine transformation but also a *perspective transformation*.

Up to now we have said that a point $P = (P_x, P_y, P_z)$ has the representation $(P_x, P_y, P_z, 1)$ in homogeneous coordinates, and that a vector $\mathbf{v} = (v_x, v_y, v_z)$ has the representation $(v_x, v_y, v_z, 0)$. That is, to form the homogeneous representation from the ordinary version, we have simply appended a 1 or 0. This made it possible to use coordinate frames as a basis for representing the points and vectors of interest, and it allowed us to represent an affine transformation by a matrix.

Now we extend the idea, and say that a point $P = (P_x, P_y, P_z)$ has a whole family of homogeneous representations (wP_x, wP_y, wP_z, w) for *any* value of w except 0. For example, the point $(1, 2, 3)$ has the representations $(1, 2, 3, 1)$, $(2, 4, 6, 2)$, $(0.003, 0.006, 0.009, 0.001)$, $(-1, -2, -3, -1)$, and so forth. If someone hands you a point in this form, say $(3, 6, 2, 3)$ and asks what point is it, just divide through by

(handwritten margin note: (wP_x, wP_y, wP_z, w))

the last component to get $\left(1, 2, \frac{2}{3}, 1\right)$, then discard the last component: the point in ordinary coordinates is $\left(1, 2, \frac{2}{3}\right)$. Thus:

- To convert a point from *ordinary coordinates* to *homogeneous coordinates*, append a 1.[4]
- To convert a point from *homogeneous coordinates* to *ordinary coordinates*, divide all components by the last component, and discard the fourth component.

The additional property of being able to scale all the components of a point without changing the point is really the basis for the name "homogeneous." Up until now we have always been working with the special case where the final component is 1.

We examine homogeneous coordinates further in the exercises, but now we focus on how they operate when transforming points. Affine transformations work fine when homogeneous coordinates are used. Recall that the matrix for an affine transformation always has $(0, 0, 0, 1)$ in its fourth row. Therefore if we multiply a point P in homogeneous representation by such a matrix M, to form $MP = Q$ [recall Equation (5.24)], as in the example

$$\begin{pmatrix} 2 & -1 & 3 & 1 \\ 6 & .5 & 1 & 4 \\ 0 & 4 & 2 & -3 \\ 0 & 0 & 0 & 1 \end{pmatrix} \begin{pmatrix} wP_x \\ wP_y \\ wP_z \\ w \end{pmatrix} = \begin{pmatrix} wQ_x \\ wQ_y \\ wQ_z \\ w \end{pmatrix}$$

the final component of Q will always be unaltered: it is still w. Therefore we can convert the Q back to ordinary coordinates in the usual fashion.

But something new happens if we deviate from a fourth row of $(0, 0, 0, 1)$. Consider the important example that has a fourth row of $(0, 0, -1, 0)$, (which is close to what we shall later call the "projection matrix"):

$$\begin{pmatrix} N & 0 & 0 & 0 \\ 0 & N & 0 & 0 \\ 0 & 0 & a & b \\ 0 & 0 & -1 & 0 \end{pmatrix} \qquad \text{(the projection matrix—version 1)} \qquad (7.10)$$

for any choices of N, a, and b. Multiply this by a point represented in homogeneous coordinates with an arbitrary w:

$$\begin{pmatrix} N & 0 & 0 & 0 \\ 0 & N & 0 & 0 \\ 0 & 0 & a & b \\ 0 & 0 & -1 & 0 \end{pmatrix} \begin{pmatrix} wP_x \\ wP_y \\ wP_z \\ w \end{pmatrix} = \begin{pmatrix} wNP_x \\ wNP_y \\ w(aP_z + b) \\ -wP_z \end{pmatrix}$$

This corresponds to an ordinary point, but which one? Divide through by the fourth component and discard it, to obtain

$$\left(N\frac{P_x}{-P_z}, N\frac{P_y}{-P_z}, \frac{aP_z + b}{-P_z} \right)$$

which is precisely what we need according to Equation (7.7). Thus using homogeneous coordinates allows us to capture perspective using a matrix multiplication! To make it work we must always divide through by the fourth component, a step which is called **perspective division**.

---

[4]   And, if you wish, multiply all four components by any nonzero value.

A matrix that has values other than $(0, 0, 0, 1)$ for its fourth row does not perform an affine transformation. It performs a more general class of transformation called a **perspective transformation**. It is a transformation, not a projection. A projection reduces the dimensionality of a point, to a 3-tuple or a 2-tuple, whereas a perspective transformation takes a 4-tuple and produces a 4-tuple.

Consider the algebraic effect of putting nonzero values in the fourth row of the matrix of Equation (7.10), such as (A, B, C, D). When you multiply the matrix by $(P_x, P_y, P_z, 1)$ (or any multiple thereof), the fourth term in the resulting point becomes $AP_x + BP_y + CP_z + D$, making it linearly dependent on each of the components of P. After perspective division, this term appears in the denominator of the point. Such a denominator is exactly what is needed to produce the geometric effect of perspective projection onto a general plane, as we show in the exercises.

The perspective transformation therefore carries a 3D point P into another 3D point P', according to:

$$(P_x, P_y, P_z) \rightarrow \left(N\frac{P_x}{-P_z}, N\frac{P_y}{-P_z}, \frac{aP_z + b}{-P_z} \right) \qquad \text{``the perspective transformation''} \qquad (7.11)$$

Where does the projection part come into play? Further along the pipeline the first two components of this point are used for drawing: to locate in screen coordinates the position of the point to be drawn. The third component is peeled off to be used for depth testing. As far as locating the point on the screen is concerned, ignoring the third component is equivalent to replacing it by 0, as in:

$$\left(N\frac{P_x}{-P_z}, N\frac{P_y}{-P_z}, \frac{aP_z + b}{-P_z} \right) \rightarrow \left(N\frac{P_x}{-P_z}, N\frac{P_y}{-P_z}, 0 \right) \qquad \text{``the projection''} \qquad (7.12)$$

This is just what we did in Chapter 5 to project a point orthographically (meaning perpendicularly to the viewplane) when setting up a camera for our first efforts at viewing a 3D scene. We will study orthographic projections in full detail later. For now we can conclude:

(perspective projection) = (perspective transformation) + (orthographic projection)

This decomposition of a perspective projection into a specific transformation followed by a (trivial) projection will prove very useful, both algorithmically and for understanding better what each point actually experiences as it passes through the graphics pipeline. OpenGL does the transformation step separately from the projection step. In fact it inserts clipping, perspective division, and one additional mapping between them.

One final emphasis. When we wish to display a mesh model, we must send thousands or even millions of vertices down the graphics pipeline. Clearly it will be far superior in terms of efficiency if we can subject each vertex to a *single* matrix multiplication rather than to a sequence of matrix multiplications. Thus the ability to combine all of the matrix multiplications that a vertex must undergo into a single matrix will increase efficiency dramatically. This is what OpenGL does: it multiplies all of the required matrices into a single matrix *once* and then multiplies each vertex by this combined matrix.

We next look deeper into the transformation part of the process.

The perspective transformation alters 3D point P into another 3D point according to Equation (7.11), to prepare it for projection. It is useful to think of it as causing a warping of 3D space and to see how it warps one shape into another. Very importantly, it preserves straightness and flatness, so lines transform into lines, planes into planes, and polygonal faces into other polygonal faces. It also preserves inbetweenness, so if point a is inside an object, the transformed point will also be inside the transformed object. (Our choice of a suitable pseudodepth function was guided by the need to preserve these properties.) The proof of these properties is developed in the exercises.

Of particular interest is how it transforms the camera's view volume, because, if we are going to do clipping in the warped space, we will be clipping against the warped view volume. The perspective transformation shines in this regard: the warped view volume is a perfect shape for simple and efficient clipping! Figure 7.28 suggests how the view volume and other shapes are transformed. The near plane W at $z = -N$ maps into the plane W' at $z = -1$, and the far plane maps to the plane at $z = +1$. The top wall T is tilted into the horizontal plane T' so that it is parallel to the z-axis. The bottom wall S becomes the horizontal S', and the two side walls become parallel to the z-axis. The camera's view volume is transformed into a parallelepiped!

FIGURE 7.28 The view volume warped by the perspective transformation.

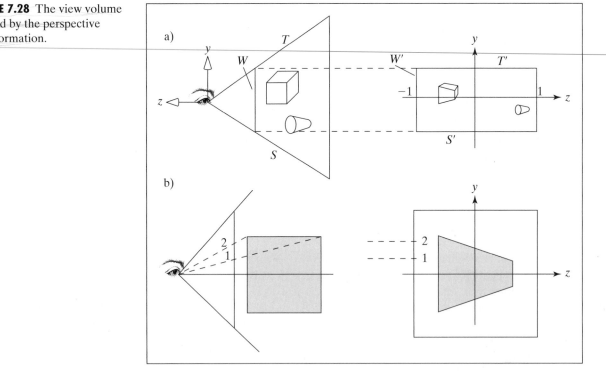

The Geometric Nature of the Perspective Transformation

It's easy to prove how these planes map, because they all involve lines that either are parallel to the near plane or pass through the eye. Check these carefully:

Fact: Lines through the eye map into lines parallel to the z-axis.
Proof: All points of such a line project to a single point, say (x^*, y^*), on the viewplane. So all of the points along the line transform to all of the points (x, y, z) with $x = x^*$, $y = y^*$, and z taking on all pseudodepth values between -1 and 1.

Fact: Lines perpendicular to the z-axis map to lines perpendicular to the z-axis.
Proof: All points along such a line have the same z-coordinate, so they all map to points with the same pseudodepth value.

Using these facts, it is straightforward to derive the exact shape and dimensions of the warped view volume.

The transformation also warps objects, like the blocks shown, into new shapes. Figure 7.28b shows a block being projected onto the near plane. Suppose the top edge of its front face projects to $y = 2$ and the top edge of its back face projects to $y = 1$. When this block is transformed, it becomes a truncated pyramid: the top edge of its front face lies at $y = 2$ and the top edge of its back face at $y = 1$. Things closer to the eye than the near plane become bigger, and things beyond the near plane become smaller. The transformed object is smaller at the back than the front because the original object projects that way. The x- and y-coordinates of the transformed object are the x- and y-coordinates of the *projection* of the original object. These are the coordinates you would encounter upon making an orthographic projection of the transformed object. In a nutshell:

The perspective transformation warps objects so that, when viewed with an orthographic projection, they appear the same as the original objects do when viewed with a perspective projection.

So all objects are warped into properly foreshortened shapes according to the rules of perspective projection. Thereafter they can be viewed with an orthographic projection, and the correct picture is produced.

We look more closely at the specific shape and dimensions of the transformed view volume.

Details of the Transformed View Volume and Mapping into the Canonical View Volume

We want to put some numbers on the dimensions of the view volume before and after it is warped. Consider the top plane, and suppose it passes through the point $(left, top, -N)$ at $z = -N$ as shown in Figure 7.29. Because it is composed of lines that pass through the eye and through points in the near plane all of which have a y-coordinate of top, it must transform to the plane $y = top$. Similarly,

- the bottom plane transforms to the $y = bott$ plane;
- the left plane transforms to the $x = left$ plane;
- the right plane transforms to the $x = right$ plane.

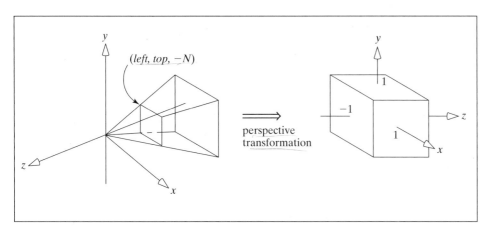

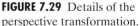

FIGURE 7.29 Details of the perspective transformation.

We now know the transformed view volume precisely: a parallelepiped with dimensions that are related to the camera's properties in a very simple way. This is a splendid shape to clip against, as we shall see, because its walls are parallel to the coordinate planes. But it would be an even better shape for clipping if its dimensions didn't depend on the particular camera being used. OpenGL composes the perspective transformation with another mapping that scales and translates this parallelepiped into the **canonical view volume**, a cube that extends from −1 to 1 in each dimension. Because this scales things differently in the x- and y-dimensions, as it squashes the scene into a fixed volume it introduces some distortion, but the distortion will be eliminated in the final viewport transformation.

The transformed view volume already extends from −1 to 1 in z, so it only needs to be scaled in the other two dimensions. We therefore include a scaling and translation in both x and y to map the parallelepiped into the canonical view volume. We first translate by $-(right + left)/2$ in x and by $-(top + bott)/2$ in y. Then we scale by $2/(right - left)$ in x and by $2/(top - bott)$ in y. When the matrix multiplications are done (see the exercises) we obtain the final matrix:

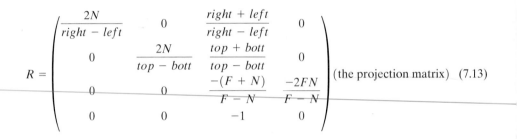

$$R = \begin{pmatrix} \dfrac{2N}{right - left} & 0 & \dfrac{right + left}{right - left} & 0 \\[2ex] 0 & \dfrac{2N}{top - bott} & \dfrac{top + bott}{top - bott} & 0 \\[2ex] 0 & 0 & \dfrac{-(F + N)}{F - N} & \dfrac{-2FN}{F - N} \\[2ex] 0 & 0 & -1 & 0 \end{pmatrix} \quad \text{(the projection matrix)} \quad (7.13)$$

This is known as the **projection matrix**, and it performs the perspective transformation plus a scaling and translation to transform the camera's view volume into the canonical view volume. It is precisely the matrix that OpenGL creates (and by which it multiplies the current matrix) when `glFrustum(left, right, bott, top, N, F)` is executed. Recall that `gluPerspective(viewAngle, aspect, N, F)` is usually used instead, as its parameters are more intuitive. This sets up the same matrix, after computing values for *top*, *bott*, and so on, using

$$top = N \tan\left(\frac{\pi}{180} viewAngle/2 \right)$$

$$bott = -top, \quad right = top * aspect, \quad \text{and} \quad left = -right$$

Clipping Faces Against the View Volume

Recall from Figure 7.14 that clipping is performed after vertices have passed through the projection matrix. It is done in this warped space because the canonical view volume is particularly well suited for efficient clipping. Here we show how to exploit this, and we develop the details of the clipping algorithm.

Clipping in the warped space works because a point lies inside the camera's view volume if and only if its transformed version lies inside the canonical view volume. Figure 7.30a shows an example of clipping in action. A triangle has vertices v_1, v_2, and v_3. Vertex v_3 lies outside the canonical view volume, CVV. The clipper works on edges: it first clips edge v_1v_2 and finds that the entire edge lies inside CVV. Then it clips edge v_2v_3, and records the new vertex a formed where the edge exits from the CVV. Finally it clips edge v_3v_1 and records the new vertex where the edge enters the

CVV. At the end of the process the original triangle has become a quadrilateral with vertices $v_1 v_2 ab$. (We will see later that, in addition to identifying the locations of the new vertices, the pipeline also computes new color and texture parameters at these new vertices.)

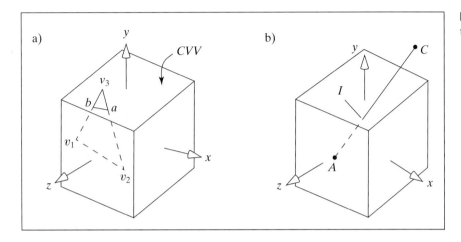

FIGURE 7.30 Clipping against the canonical view volume.

The clipping problem is basically the problem of clipping a line segment against the *CVV*. We examined such an algorithm, the Cyrus-Beck clipper, in Section 4.8.3. The clipper we develop here is similar to that one, but of course it works in 3D rather than 2D.

Actually, it works in 4D. We will clip in the 4D homogeneous coordinate space called "clip coordinates" in Figure 7.14. This is easier than it might seem, and it will nicely distinguish between points in front of, and behind, the eye.

Suppose we want to clip the line segment *AC* shown in Figure 7.30b against the *CVV*. This means we are given two points in homogeneous coordinates, $A = (a_x, a_y, a_z, a_w)$ and $C = (c_x, c_y, c_z, c_w)$, and we want to determine which part of the segment lies inside the *CVV*. If the segment intersects the boundary of the *CVV*, we will need to compute the intersection point $I = (I_x, I_y, I_z, I_w)$.

As with the Cyrus-Beck algorithm, we view the CVV as six infinite planes and consider where the given edge lies relative to each plane in turn. We can represent the edge parametrically as $A + (C - A)t$. It lies at *A* when *t* is 0, and at *C* when *t* is 1. For each wall of the *CVV* we first test whether *A* and *C* lie on the same side of a wall: if they do, there is no need to compute the intersection of the edge with the wall. If they lie on opposite sides, we locate the intersection point and clip off the part of the edge that lies outside.

So we must be able to test whether a point is on the *outside* or *inside* of a plane. For example, take the plane $x = -1$. Point *A* lies to the right of (on the inside) this plane if

$$\frac{a_x}{a_w} > -1 \quad \text{or} \quad a_x > -a_w \quad \text{or} \quad (a_w + a_x) > 0 \qquad (7.14)$$

When you multiply both sides of an inequality by a negative term, you must reverse the direction of the inequality. But we are ultimately dealing with only positive values of a_w here (see the exercises). Similarly *A* is inside the plane $x = 1$ if

$$\frac{a_x}{a_w} > 1 \quad \text{or} \quad (a_w - a_x) > 0$$

Blinn [Blinn96] calls these quantities the "boundary coordinates" of point A, and he lists the six such quantities that we work with as in Figure 7.31.

FIGURE 7.31 The boundary codes computed for each end point of an edge.

Boundary Coordinate	Homogeneous Value	Clip Plane
BC_0	$w + x$	$X = -1$
BC_1	$w - x$	$X = 1$
BC_2	$w + y$	$Y = -1$
BC_3	$w - y$	$Y = 1$
BC_4	$w + z$	$Z = -1$
BC_5	$w - z$	$Z = 1$

We form these six quantities for A and again for C. If all six are positive, the point lies inside the *CVV*. If any are negative, the point lies outside. If both points lie inside, we have the same kind of "trivial accept" we had in the Cohen-Sutherland clipper of Section 3.3. If A and C lie outside on the same side (corresponding BC's are negative), the edge must lie wholly outside the *CVV*.

> *Trivial accept: both endpoints lie inside the CVV (all 12 BC's are positive).*
> *Trivial reject: both endpoints lie outside the same plane of the CVV.*

If neither condition prevails, we must clip segment AC against each plane individually. Just as with the Cyrus-Beck clipper, we keep track of a **candidate interval** (*CI*) (see Figure 4.45), an interval of time during which the edge *might* still be inside the *CVV*. Basically we know the converse: if t is outside the *CI*, we know for sure the edge is *not* inside the *CVV*. The *CI* extends from $t = t_{in}$ to t_{out}.

We test the edge against each wall in turn. If the corresponding boundary codes have opposite signs, we know the edge hits the plane at some t_{hit}, which we then compute. If the edge is entering (is moving into the inside of the plane as t increases), we update $t_{in} = \max(\text{old } t_{in}, t_{hit})$, since it could not possibly be entering at an earlier time than t_{hit}. Similarly, if the edge is exiting, we update $t_{out} = \min(\text{old } t_{out}, t_{hit})$. If at any time the *CI* is reduced to the empty interval (t_{out} becomes $> t_{in}$), we know the entire edge is clipped off and we have an "early out," which saves unnecessary computation.

It is straightforward to calculate the hit time of an edge with a plane. Write the edge parametrically in homogeneous coordinates:

$$\text{edge}(t) = (a_x + (c_x - a_x)t, a_y + (c_y - a_y)t, a_z + (c_z - a_z)t, a_w + (c_w - a_w)t)$$

For a hit between the edge and the $X = 1$ plane, for instance, when the x-coordinate of $A + (C - A)t$ is 1:

$$\frac{a_x + (c_x - a_x)t}{a_w + (c_w - a_w)t} = 1$$

This is easily solved for t, yielding

$$t = \frac{a_w - a_x}{(a_w - a_x) - (c_w - c_x)} \tag{7.15}$$

Note that t_{hit} depends on only two boundary coordinates. Intersections with other planes yield similar formulas.

This is easily put into code, as suggested in the pseudocode of Figure 7.32. This is basically the **Liang-Barsky** algorithm [Liang84], with some refinements suggested by Blinn [Blinn96]. The routine clipEdge(Point4 A, Point4 C) takes two points in homogeneous coordinates (having fields x, y, z, and w) and returns 0 if no part of AC lies in the CVV, and 1 otherwise. It also alters A and C so that when the routine is finished, A and C are the endpoints of the clipped edge.

```
int clipEdge(Point4& A, Point4& C)
{
    double tIn = 0.0, tOut = 1.0, tHit;
    double aBC[6], cBC[6];
    int aOutcode = 0, cOutcode = 0;
    <.. find BC's for A and C ..>
    <.. form outcodes for A and C ..>

    if((aOutcode & cOutcode) != 0) // trivial reject
            return 0;
    if((aOutcode | cOutcode) == 0) // trivial accept
            return 1;

    for(int i = 0; i < 6; i++) // clip against each plane
    {
        if(cBC[i] < 0) // exits: C is outside
        {
          tHit = aBC[i]/(aBC[i] - cBC[i]);
          tOut = MIN(tOut,tHit);
        }
        else if(aBC[i] < 0) //enters: A is outside
        {
          tHit = aBC[i]/(aBC[i] - cBC[i]);
          tIn = MAX(tIn, tHit);
        }
        if(tIn > tOut) return 0; //CI is empty early out
    }
    // update the endpoints as necessary
    Point4 tmp;
    if(aOutcode != 0) // A is out: tIn has changed
    { // find updated A, (but don't change it yet)
        tmp.x = A.x + tIn * (C.x - A.x);
        tmp.y = A.y + tIn * (C.y - A.y);
        tmp.z = A.z + tIn * (C.z - A.z);
        tmp.w = A.w + tIn * (C.w - A.w);
    }
    if(cOutcode != 0) // C is out: tOut has changed
    { // update C (using original value of A)
        C.x = A.x + tOut * (C.x - A.x);
        C.y = A.y + tOut * (C.y - A.y);
        C.z = A.z + tOut * (C.z - A.z);
        C.w = A.w + tOut * (C.w - A.w);
    }
    A = tmp; // now update A
    return 1; // some of the edge lies inside the CVV
}
```

FIGURE 7.32 The edge clipper (as refined by Blinn).

The routine finds the six boundary coordinates for each endpoint and stores them in aBC[] and cBC[]. For efficiency it also builds an **outcode** for each point, which holds the *signs* of the six boundary codes for that point. Bit i of A's outcode holds a 0 if aBC[i] > 0 (A is inside the ith wall) and a 1 otherwise. Using these, a trivial accept occurs when both aOutcode and cOutcode are 0. A trivial reject occurs when the bitwise AND of the two outcodes is nonzero.

In the loop that tests the edge against each plane, at most one of the BC's can be negative. (Why?) If A has a negative BC, the edge must be entering at the hit point; if C has a negative BC, the edge must be exiting at the hit point. (Blinn uses a slightly faster test by incorporating a mask that tests one bit of an outcode.) Each time tIn or tOut is updated, an early out is taken if tIn has become greater than tOut.

When all planes have been tested, one or both of tIn and tOut have been altered. A is updated to $A + (i - A)tIn$ if tIn has changed, and C is updated to $A + (C - A)tOut$ if tOut has changed.

Blinn suggests precomputing the BC's and outcode for every point to be processed. This eliminates the need to recompute these quantities when a vertex is an endpoint of more than one edge, as is often the case.

Why Did We Clip Against the Canonical View Volume?

Now that we have seen how easy it is to do clipping against the canonical view volume, we can see the value of having transformed all objects of interest into clip coordinates prior to clipping. There are two important features of the CVV:

1. It is parameter free: the algorithm needs no extra information to describe the clipping volume. It uses only the values -1 and 1. So the code itself can be highly tuned for maximum efficiency.
2. Its planes are aligned with the coordinate axes (after the perspective transformation is performed). This means that we can determine which side of a plane a point lies on using a single coordinate, as in $a_x > -1$. If the planes were not aligned, an expensive dot product would be needed.

Why Did We Clip in Homogeneous Coordinates, Rather Than After the Perspective Division Step?

This isn't completely necessary, but it makes the clipping algorithm clean, fast, and simple. Doing the perspective divide step destroys information: if you have the values a_x and a_w explicitly, you know, of course, the signs of both of them. But given only the ratio a_x/a_w you can tell only whether a_x and a_w have the same or opposite signs, and their relative sizes. Keeping values in homogeneous coordinates and clipping points closer to the eye than the near plane automatically removes points that lie behind the eye, such as B in Figure 7.23.

Some perverse situations that necessitate clipping in homogeneous coordinates are described in [Blinn96, Foley90]. They involve peculiar transformations of objects, or construction of certain surfaces, where the original point (a_x, a_y, a_z, a_w) has a negative fourth term, even though the point is in front of the eye. None of the objects we discuss modeling here involve such cases. We conclude that clipping in homogeneous coordinates, although usually not critical, makes the algorithm fast and simple, and brings it almost no cost.

Following the clipping operation **perspective division** is finally done (as in Figure 7.14), and the 3-tuple (x, y, z) is passed through the viewport transformation. As we discuss next, this transformation sizes and translates the *x*- and *y*-values so they are placed properly in the viewport, and makes minor adjustments on the *z*-component (pseudodepth) to make it more suitable for depth testing.

The Viewport Transformation

As we have seen, the perspective transformation squashes the scene into the canonical cube, as suggested in Figure 7.33. If the aspect ratio of the camera's view volume (that is, the aspect ratio of the window on the near plane) is 1.5, there is obvious distortion introduced when the perspective transformation scales objects into a window with aspect ratio 1. But the viewport transformation can undo this distortion by mapping a square into a viewport of aspect ratio 1.5. of whatever aspect ratio is desired.

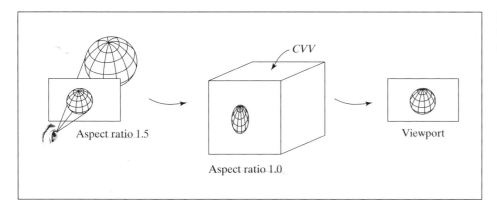

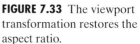

FIGURE 7.33 The viewport transformation restores the aspect ratio.

We have encountered the OpenGL function `glViewport(x, y, wid, ht)` often before. It specifies that the viewport will have lower left corner (x,y) in screen coordinates, and will be `wid` pixels wide and `ht` pixels high. It thus specifies a viewport with aspect ratio `wid/ht`. The viewport transformation also maps pseudodepth from the range −1 to 1 into the range 0 to 1.

Review Figure 7.14, which reveals the entire graphics pipeline. In OpenGL each point *P* (which is usually one vertex of a polygon) is passed through the following steps:

- *P* is **extended** to a homogeneous 4-tuple by appending a 1;
- This 4-tuple is multiplied by the **modelview matrix**, producing a 4-tuple giving the position in eye coordinates;
- The point is then multiplied by the **projection matrix**, producing a 4-tuple in clip coordinates;
- The edge having this point as an endpoint is **clipped**;
- Perform hidden surface removal (see Section 8.4);
- **Perspective division** is performed, returning a 3-tuple;
- The **viewport transformation** multiplies the 3-tuple by a matrix: the result (sx, sy, dz) is used for drawing and depth calculations. (sx, sy) is the point in screen coordinates to be displayed; dz is a measure of the depth of the original point from the eye of the camera.

PRACTICE EXERCISES

7.4.5 Where does point P project?

Suppose the viewplane is given in camera coordinates by the equation $Ax + By + Cz = D$. Show that any point P (P_x, P_y, P_z) projects onto this plane at the point given in homogeneous coordinates

$$P' = (DP_x, DP_y, DP_z, AP_x + BP_y + CP_z)$$

7.4.6 A revealing approximate form for pseudodepth

Show that pseudodepth $a + b/(-P_z)$, where a and b are given in Equation (7.8), is well approximated by Equation (7.9) when N is much smaller than F.

7.4.7 Points at infinity in homogeneous coordinates

Consider the nature of the homogeneous coordinate point (x, y, z, w) as w becomes smaller and smaller. For $w = .01$ it is $(100x, 100y, 100z, w)$, for $w = 0.0001$ it is $(10000x, 10000y, 10000z, w)$, and so on. It progresses out "toward infinity" in the direction (x, y, z). The point with representation $(x, y, z, 0)$ is in fact called a "point at infinity." It is one of the advantages of homogeneous coordinates that such an idealized point has a perfectly finite representation: in some mathematical derivations this removes many awkward special cases. For instance, two lines will always intersect, even if they are parallel [Ayers67, Semple52]. But other things don't work as well. What is the difference of two points in homogeneous coordinates?

7.4.8 How does the perspective transformation affect lines and planes?

We must show that the perspective transformation preserves flatness and inbetweenness.

a. Argue why this is proven if we can show that a point P lying on the line between two points A and B transforms to a point P' that lies between the transformed versions of A and B.
b. Show that the perspective transformation does indeed produce a point P' with the property just stated.
c. Show that each plane that passes through the eye maps to a plane that is parallel to the z-axis.
d. Show that each plane that is parallel to the z-axis maps to a plane parallel to the z- axis.
e. Show that relative depth is preserved.

7.4.9 The details of the transformed view volume

Show that the warped view volume has the dimensions given in the five points in the preceding exercise. You can use the facts developed in the preceding exercise.

7.4.10 Show the final form of the projection matrix

The projection matrix is basically that of Equation (7.10), followed by the translation and scaling described. If the matrix of Equation (7.10) is denoted as M, and T represents the translating matrix, and S the scaling matrix, show that the matrix product STM is that given in Equation (7.13).

7.4.11 What becomes of points behind the eye?

If the perspective transformation moves the eye off to $-$infinity, what happens to points that lie behind the eye? Consider a line, $P(t)$, that begins at a point in front of the eye at $t = 0$ and moves to one behind the eye at $t = 1$.

a. Find its parametric form in homogeneous coordinates.
b. Find the parametric representation after it undergoes the perspective transformation.
c. Interpret it geometrically. Specifically state what the fourth homogeneous coordinate is geometrically. A valuable discussion of this phenomenon is given in [Blinn78].   ∎

PLATE 1: A ray traced image including reflections and shadows.
(Courtesy of Sven Maerivoet.)

PLATE 2: Shows a screenshot from a 3D computer-based game. *(Courtesy of High Moon Studios, Inc.)*

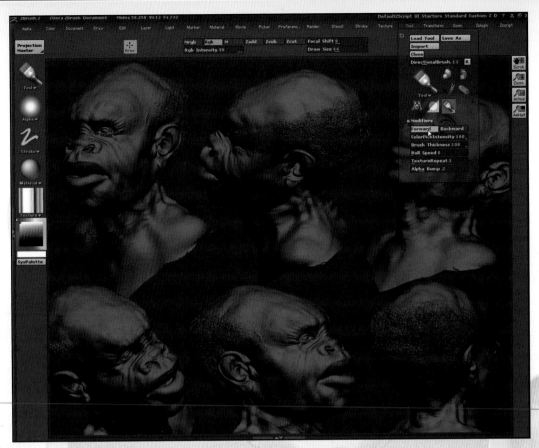

PLATE 3: Screenshot of a paint system with drawing tools and menus. *(Courtesy of Pixologic, Inc.)*

PLATE 4: An enhanced view of the Mars landscape. *(Courtesy of NASA/NSSDC/Mary A. Dale-Bannister, Washington University in St. Louis.)*

PLATE 5: A video card from ATI Technologies. *(Courtesy of ATI.)*

PLATE 6: A complex OpenGL menu system. *(Courtesy of Unigine.)*

PLATE 7: A sphere reflecting off a shiny surface. *(Courtesy of Sven Maerivoet.)*

PLATE 8: The classic teapot, sphere, and jack on a table. *(Courtesy of Sven Maerivoet.)*

PLATE 9: A water fountain animation. *(Courtesy of Phillipp Crocoll.) Program available online.*

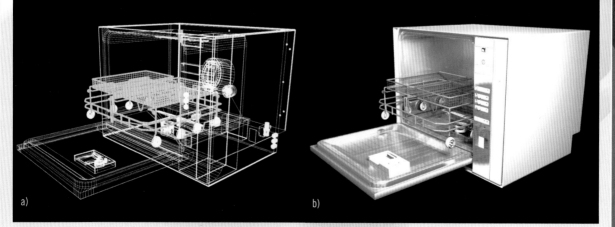

a)

b)

PLATE 10: Part a) The wire-frame mesh model for a household appliance. Part b) A shaded version of the mesh model. *(Courtesy of Lamont Gilkey.)*

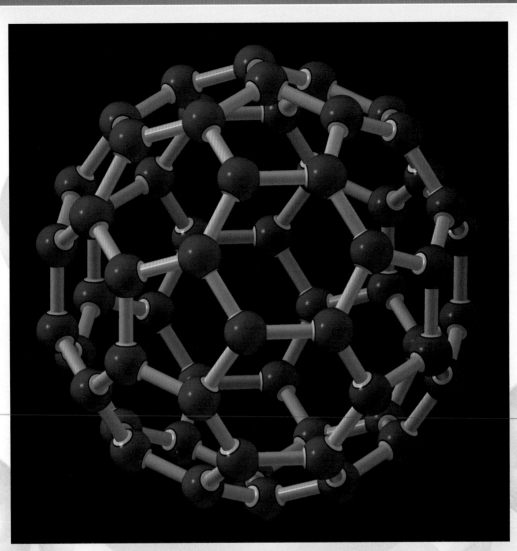

PLATE 11: A view of a fullerine molecule *(Courtesy of Dr. Koch/Lauher, SUNY.)*

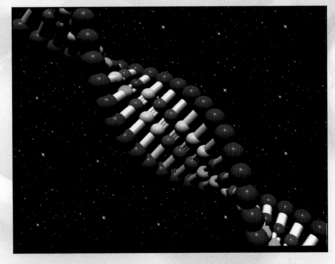

PLATE 12: A double helix model. *(Courtesy of Sven Maerivoet.)*

PLATE 13: Part a) An actal photograph of the Taj Mahal. Part b) A screenshot showing mesh model fo the Taj Mahal.

PLATE 14: An image of terrain using mesh models for the mountains and hills and particles for the clouds.
(Courtesy of Rob Hall.)

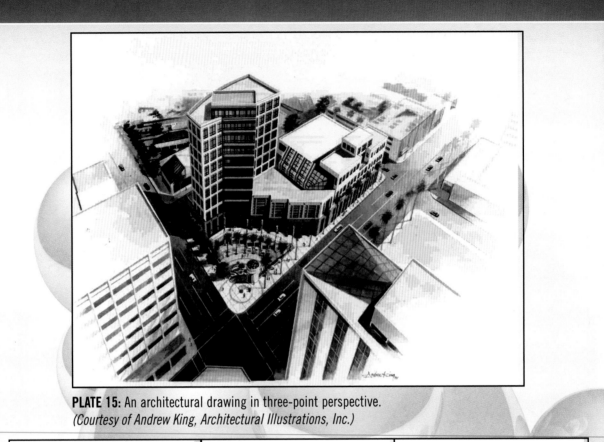

PLATE 15: An architectural drawing in three-point perspective.
(Courtesy of Andrew King, Architectural Illustrations, Inc.)

PLATE 16: Three renderings of a model frog using shading models to suggest gold, silver, and copper.
(Courtesy of Lutz Latta and Anto Matkovic)

PLATE 17: Light sources in a scene. *(Courtesy of Unigine.)*

PLATE 18: A chessboard showing marbleized texture, along with wood grain and metallic texture on chess pieces. *(Courtesy of Sven Maerivoet.)*

PLATE 19: Wrapping a texture map onto each octant of a billiard ball. *(Courtesy of Sven Maerivoet.)*

PLATE 20: A chrome environment map. *(Courtesy of Eric Boissard.)*

PLATE 21: Examples of chrome mapping. *(Courtesy of L.Latta & P. Debevec.)*

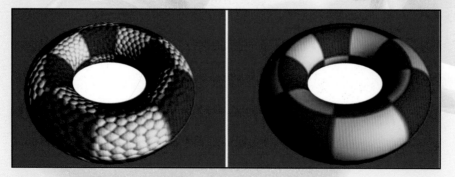

PLATE 22: An example of bump mapping.

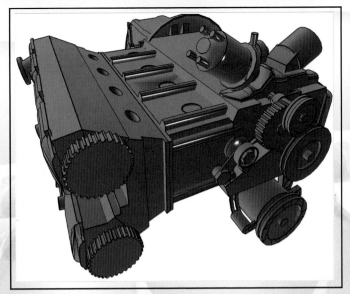

PLATE 23: A cartoon rendering of an engine.
(Courtesy of L. Molnar and J. Sun, The Ohio State University.)

PLATE 24: A non-photorealistic rendering.
(Courtesy of Kontantinos Sakelllis.)

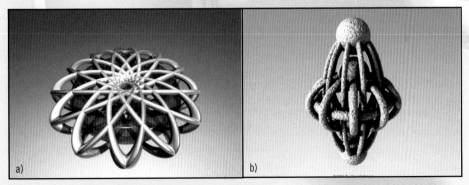

PLATE 25: Part a) An object built from Bezier patches. Part b) A complex shape representing intricate bonds. *(Courtesy of Tor Olav Kristensen, subcube.com. All images generated with POV-Ray.)*

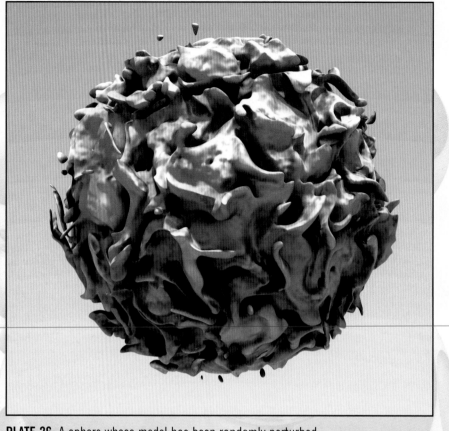

PLATE 26: A sphere whose model has been randomly perturbed.
(Courtesy of Tor Olav Kristensen, subcube.com. All images generated with POV-Ray.)

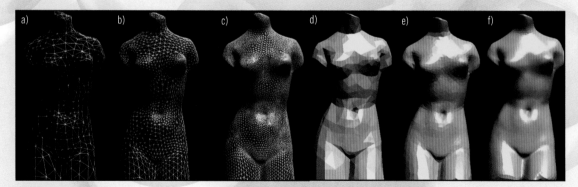

PLATE 27: Successive subdivisions of a mesh model. Parts a)-c) Wireframe views. Part d)-f) Shaded views.
(Courtesy of Jian Zhang.)

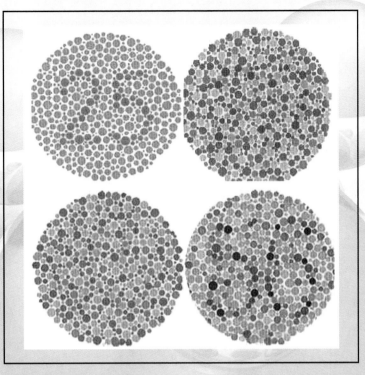

PLATE 28: A test for color blindness.
(Courtesy of Terrance L. Waggoner, O.D. Copyright owner Color Vision Testing Made Easy and the PIPIC Color Vision Tests.)

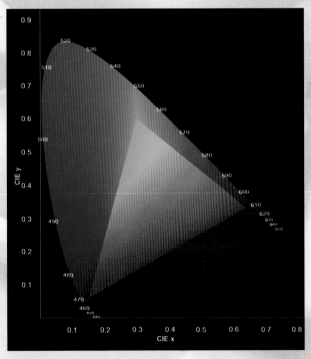

PLATE 29: CIE Chromacity Diagram. *(Courtesy of TechMind.)*

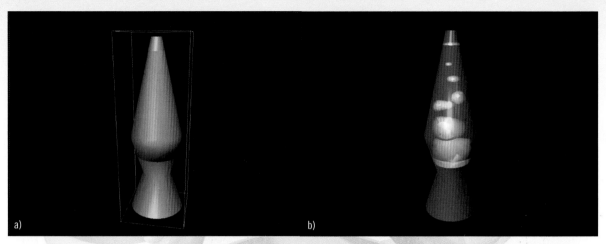

PLATE 30: Part a) A lava lamp mesh model with a box extent (OpenGL shading). Part b) A ray traced version of the image in Part a *(Courtesy of Sven Maerivoet.)*

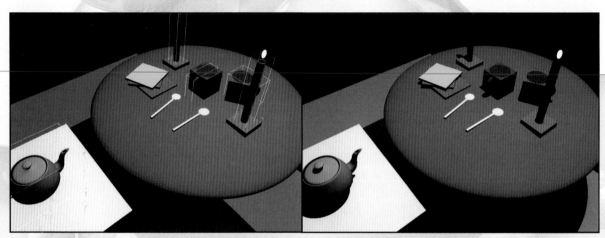

PLATE 31: A scene ray traced to exhibit shadows. *(Courtesy of Sven Maerivoet.)*

PLATE 32: Ray tracing in progress: part preview and part final rendering. *(Courtesy of Sven Maerivoet.)*

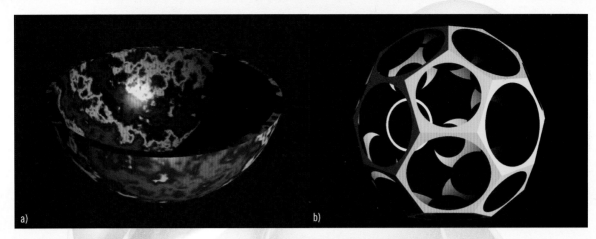

PLATE 33: Part a) A ray traced CSG object. Part b) A ray traced CSG object; the intersection of a shpere with a BuckyBall. *(Courtesy of Sven Maerivoet.)*

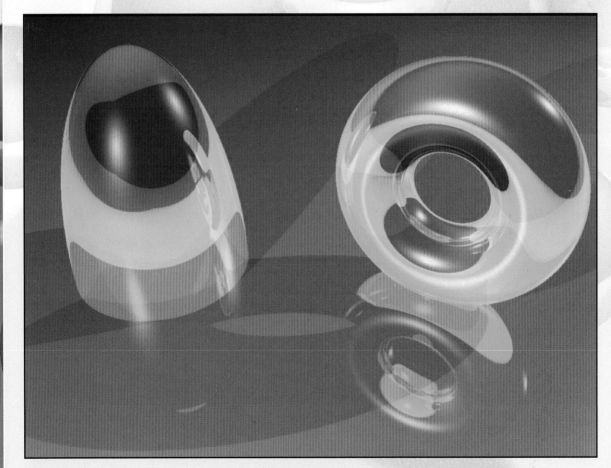

PLATE 34: Two glass objects with reflection, refraction, and shadows. *(Courtesy of Sven Maerivoet.)*

PLATE 35: A ray traced image with shadows, textures and refraction. *(Courtesy of Sven Maerivoet.)*

PLATE 36: Iridescence viewed in a car's window. *(Courtesy of Emmanuel Agu.)*

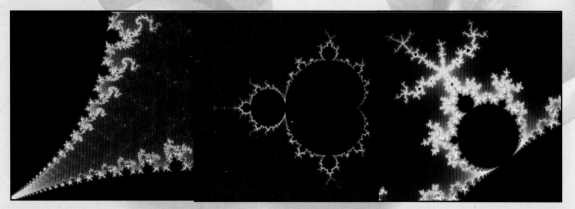

PLATE 37: Various views of the extraordinary Mandelbrot Set. *(Courtesy of Anton Feenstra.)*

7.5 TO PRODUCE STEREO VIEWS

I love 5.1. Sometimes you can't squeeze everything in comfortably into a stereo picture.
There is a lot more space in a 5.1 environment.

Peter Gabriel
(1950–)

We digress briefly to use the camera controls developed earlier for producing stereo views of a scene. A stereo view can make a picture much more intelligible; when it is viewed properly the viewer obtains a sense of depth in a picture, which not only makes it much more interesting and realistic, but also reduces the visual ambiguity in the picture (such as which lines lie in front of others.) All of the stereo figures in this book were made using the following technique.

We might call the camera used so far a "cyclops" camera, after the one-eyed monster polyphemus, son of Poseidon, in greek mythology." Also, replace "fabled" with "storied". To get a sense of its limitations, keep one eye closed as you walk around a room and try to do simple tasks. Our natural stereoscopic eye–brain system provides a tremendous amount of information by adding a visual sense of depth. We want to add this capability to computer graphics pictures.

To make a stereo view, two pictures, a left and a right picture, are made using slightly different cameras, as suggested in Figure 7.34. The cameras are built using the same `lookAt` point but different eye positions. Two viewports are created side by side on the display as in Figure 7.34b. The left picture is displayed in the left viewport, and the right picture in the right viewport.

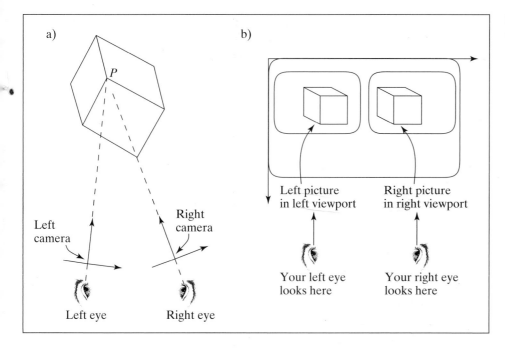

FIGURE 7.34 Creating stereo views.

To view a stereo picture, let your left eye look at the left picture and your right eye look at the right picture. When you do this properly, the two images fuse into a single image that appears to have depth. This may take some practice. (The preface describes a method for learning how to do this.)

Figure 7.35 shows a stereo wireframe view of the Buckyball described in Chapter 6. The two pictures are evidently quite different, and there is significant visual ambiguity (which edges are in front; which behind?) when only one of the pictures is

FIGURE 7.35 Stereo view of the Buckyball.

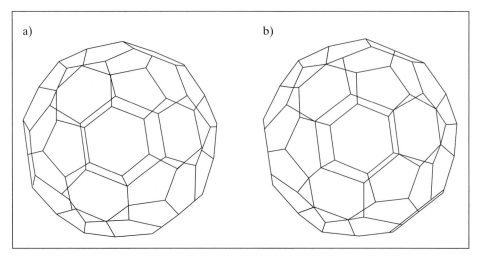

a)   b)

viewed. A stereo view, however, disambiguates the various edges, making the picture easily intelligible.

Figure 7.36 shows stereo views of the barn. In part a the camera is rolled by 40°. Note that the orientation of the barn is difficult to comprehend without the stereo effect. Part b shows a close-up of one corner of the barn, and the severe perspective distortion produced is clearly visible.

FIGURE 7.36 Close-up views of the barn.

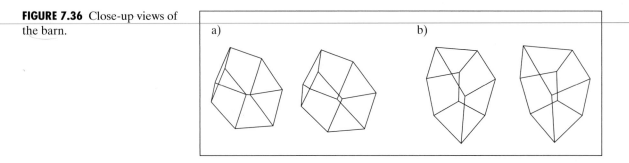

a)   b)

To build the two cameras we must decide where to put the left and right eyes. A simple approach begins with a regular camera based on a single lookAt point and a single initial cyclops eye, as suggested in Figure 7.37. Along with a choice of **up**, these establish the cyclops camera, with its **u**, **v**, and **n** directions.

FIGURE 7.37 Setting the two eye positions for stereo viewing.

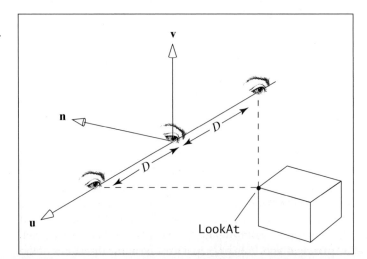

The left and right eyes are defined at slight displacements of the cyclops eye, at some distance D along $-\mathbf{u}$ and $\mathbf{u}$, respectively. The choice of D depends on the unit of measure being used in the application. If all lengths and distances are being thought of as inches, then the user will probably set up the camera at an appropriate number of inches from the desired lookAt point. Human eyes are about 3 inches apart, so a good first choice of D would be 1.5. If things were measured in meters instead, you might use the distance in meters between eyes. In those cases where the scene is fanciful and has no inherent scale, some experimentation would be needed to achieve the desired visual effect. Case Study 7.2 suggests a project to produce stereo views.

7.6 TAXONOMY OF PROJECTIONS

As lines, so loves oblique, may well Themselves in every angle greet; But ours, so truly parallel, Though infinite, can never meet.

The Definition of Love
Andrew Marvell
(1621–1678),

We examined the basic ideas of *planar projections*, where points are projected in one way or another onto a plane. We looked at parallel projections in Chapter 5, and at perspective projections in this chapter. There are many special cases that have been used in art, architecture, and engineering drawings, and we now look to see what their characteristics are, and how they fit together.

Planar projections fall naturally into the tree structure shown in Figure 7.38. Each child of a projection type represents a special case of its parent in the tree. The first fundamental split is between parallel and perspective projections. We shall first examine classes of perspective projections.

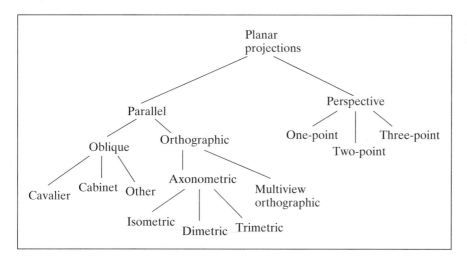

FIGURE 7.38 A taxonomy of popular projections.

7.6.1 One-, Two-, and Three-Point Perspective

Perspective projections divide nicely into three classes: one-point, two-point, and three-point. They are distinguished by the orientation of the camera relative to the world coordinate system. The names derive from the situation of viewing the unit cube shown in Figure 7.39. The unit cube is nestled into the positive x-, y-, z-octant with one corner at the origin. Most important, its edges are aligned with the world coordinate axes, which in this discussion are called **principal axes**. The principal axes lie in the directions of the unit vectors **i**, **j**, and **k**. Similarly, the three planes $x = 0$, $y = 0$, and $z = 0$ are called the **principal planes**, and the cube has its six faces aligned with them.

FIGURE 7.39 The unit cube, the principal axes, and the principal planes.

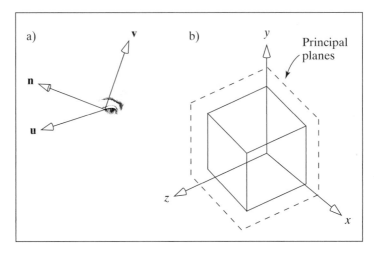

The camera can be oriented in an infinite number of ways relative to this coordinate system. For some of these the *n*-axis of the camera is perpendicular to one principal axis or another. Traditionally, perspective projections are categorized by counting the number of **finite vanishing points** that the principal axes produce. Recall that if a line is perpendicular to **n**, its vanishing point is at infinity; otherwise it is finite. So we can also count the number of principal axes that are *not* perpendicular to **n**. This is also the number of principal axes that **pierce** the viewplane of the camera. (Why?)

1. **One-point perspective**: Exactly one principal axis has a finite vanishing point. Thus **n** is not perpendicular to exactly one of the three directions **i**, **j**, or **k**. But it is perpendicular to the other two directions, so it is perpendicular to one of the principal planes. Two of its three components, n_x, n_y, or n_z, must be 0.

   Figure 7.40a shows a one-point perspective view, in which the camera has been oriented with its viewplane parallel to the *xy*-plane. The receding lines of the cube converge to a finite vanishing point. The camera here has **n** = $(0, 0, 1)$. In camera coordinates the receding lines have direction **c** = $(0, 0, -1)$, so by Equation (7.6) the vanishing point lies at $(0, 0)$. On the other hand the lines parallel to the *x*- and *y*-axes have vanishing points at infinity.

FIGURE 7.40 One-point perspective views.

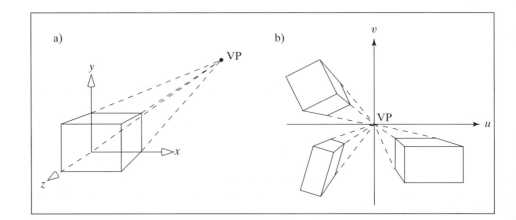

The location of the vanishing point does not depend on the position of the camera relative to a cube. Figure 7.40b shows several blocks in one-point perspective. Each block may be considered to have its own principal axes, and in this picture the front face of each block is parallel to the viewplane. All receding lines share the same vanishing point $(0, 0)$.

Revisit Figure 7.24, which shows two sets of grid lines on a horizontal plane. The grid lines run parallel to the principal axes (the world coordinate axes). Another set of grid lines, not shown, would run vertically, parallel to the world y-axis. The figure looks like a one-point perspective, since there seems to be a single finite vanishing point at the horizon. But the camera could be aimed downward, making it a two-point perspective, as we discuss next. You can't tell from the figure alone. (If you are told that the horizon projects to $y = 0$, you can then conclude that the camera is level and that this is indeed a one-point perspective.)

2. **Two-point perspective**. Exactly two principal axes have finite vanishing points. Thus the camera's **n** direction is *not* perpendicular to two of these axes; it is perpendicular to only one. One of its three components must be 0.

Figure 7.41a shows a cube in two-point perspective: there are two finite vanishing points, since both axes **i** and **k** pierce the viewplane. The camera was set up as suggested in Figure 7.41b, with its **n** making an angle of θ with the z-axis, so that $\mathbf{n} = (\sin(\theta), 0, \cos(\theta))$. Here **n** is perpendicular to **j**, so the vertical principal axis has an infinite vanishing point.

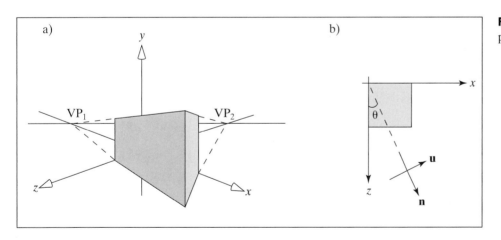

FIGURE 7.41 A two-point perspective view.

It's not hard to compute where the finite vanishing points are located (see the exercises).

It is interesting to see what happens if we view the infinite grid scene, first seen in Figure 7.24, in two-point perspective. Figure 7.42 shows the case where the eye is still at $y = 1$ oriented horizontally, but the camera has been yawed to the left so that $\mathbf{n} = (.74, 0, .67)$. Now both sets of lines recede to the horizon, producing two widely separated vanishing points on the horizon. (What are the vanishing points numerically?) Many of the more remote lines are not drawn here, as they are so crowded together that they cannot be seen clearly.

3. **Three-point perspective**. All three principal axes have finite vanishing points: all three pierce the viewplane. **n** is not perpendicular to any axes, so all of its components are nonzero.

FIGURE 7.42 The infinite grid in two-point perspective.

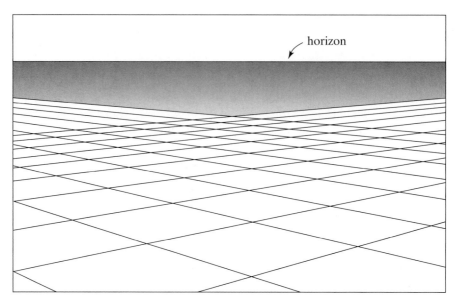

Figure 7.43 shows the cube in three-point perspective. The three finite vanishing points are also shown.

FIGURE 7.43 Three-point perspective.

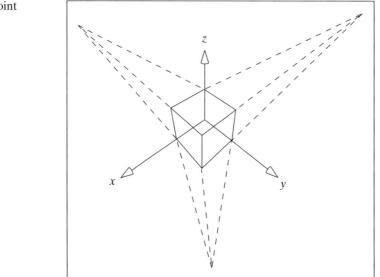

Artists often use vanishing points in perspective drawings, in order to highlight features or to increase dramatic effect. Figure 7.44 shows a building viewed in three-point perspective that illustrates this. (Where are the three vanishing points in this drawing?) The notable Dutch artist M. C. Escher is well known for dazzling and beguiling three-dimensional drawings, some of which use three-point perspectives.

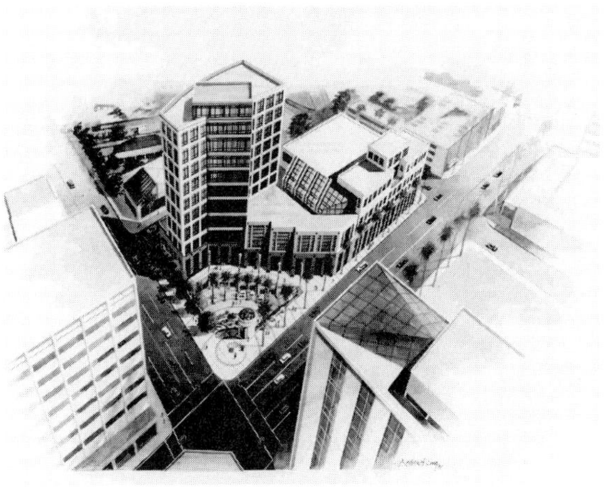

FIGURE 7.44 An illustration in three-point perspective. (Courtesy of Andrew King, Architectural Illustrations Inc.)

PRACTICE EXERCISES

7.6.1 Setting up a one-point perspective

In an application we choose eye and look to establish the desired camera, and **n** is determined from eye - look. Give three examples of eye and the corresponding look that produce interesting one-point perspective views of the unit cube.

7.6.2 Position of the vanishing point

Draw by hand the unit cube and the world coordinate axes in one-point perspective for a camera with: eye = $(2, 3, 4)$.

7.6.3 Calculating vanishing points

Find the locations of the two vanishing points in Figure 7.41a for an arbitrary value of θ.

7.6.4 Creating two-point perspective views

Give three examples of eye and the corresponding look for a camera that produces interesting two-point perspective views of the unit cube. For each example compute the actual positions of the vanishing points. ■

7.6.2 Types of Parallel Projections

We shall continue exploring the taxonomy of projections with parallel projections. So far we only introduced parallel projections in Chapter 5 as a simple way to get started viewing objects. glOrtho() was used to establish a view volume, and OpenGL did the rest. Now we shall look a little deeper at the nature of parallel projections, and distinguish the various types that are used in practice.

We know that with a perspective projection all points P in the scene are projected onto the viewplane along **projectors** that converge on the eye: each projector is determined by P itself and the eye, and they have assorted directions. In contrast, with a parallel projection, all of the projectors are given the same direction, say **d**. Figure 7.45 shows two arbitrary points being projected. P projects to p on the viewplane, and Q projects to q, both along vector **d**.

FIGURE 7.45 Parallel
projections.

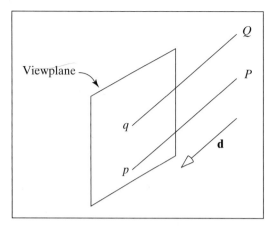

Some Theory of Parallel Projections

To what point p does P project? Assume the plane has normal vector $\mathbf{n}$ and passes
through some point B. Then p lies on the plane at the spot where a ray from P along
$\mathbf{d}$ hits the plane. We've done this calculation in several places earlier. If the ray has
parametric form $P + \mathbf{d}t$, substitute this into the plane equation $\mathbf{n} \cdot (P - B) = 0$
and solve for t. Use this t in $P + \mathbf{d}t$ to obtain the hit point:

$$p = P + \mathbf{d}\frac{\mathbf{n} \cdot (B - P)}{\mathbf{n} \cdot \mathbf{d}} \tag{7.16}$$

This is quite different from the expression we obtain when perspective projection is
used; in particular, there is no foreshortening with distance: there is no occurrence of
a P term in the denominator. (Notice in addition that $\mathbf{d}$ can be replaced with $-\mathbf{d}$
with no effect on the resulting projection.)

   We specialize to the familiar camera to see what this formula reveals. Assume we
are working in camera coordinates, so $\mathbf{n} = (0, 0, 1)$, and consider projecting onto
the xy-plane for which $B = (0, 0, 0)$. (This makes things a little simpler than projecting onto the near plane.) Then p is given by (check this):

$$p = \left(P_x - d_x\frac{P_z}{d_z}, P_y - d_y\frac{P_z}{d_z}, 0 \right) \tag{7.17}$$

Parallel projections split into two principal types, as illustrated in Figure 7.46.

FIGURE 7.46 Parallel
projections working in camera
coordinates: a) a general $\mathbf{d}$, b) $\mathbf{d}$
parallel to $\mathbf{n}$.

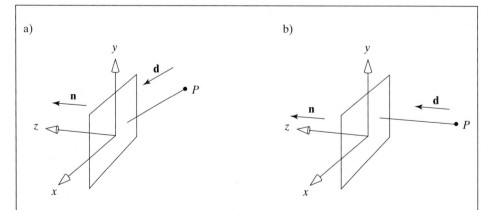

1. *Oblique*: the projection direction **d** is not parallel to **n**.
2. *Orthographic*: the projection direction **d** is parallel to **n**.

Part a shows the case of a general direction **d**, not necessarily parallel to **n**. (We will, of course, not choose to make d_z equal to 0.) Part b shows the case where **d** is parallel to **n**, so d_x and d_y are equal to 0. We will examine only the orthographic case, since oblique projections are not used as much in practice.

1. Orthographic Projections

This occurs when both d_x and d_y are 0. Then p becomes $p = (P_x, P_y, 0)$. Thus projecting orthographically is a matter of just dropping the third component of P in camera coordinates.

It is interesting to see how OpenGL carries out orthographic projection. Recall that OpenGL uses the projection matrix to describe the view volume of the camera. Specifically, the projection matrix specifies how to transform vertices to squash them into the canonical view volume (CVV). Suppose the actual view volume extends from l to r (short for *left* and *right*) in x, from b to t (short for *bottom* and *top*) in y, and from n to f (short for *near* and *far*) in z. To transform this parallelepiped into the CVV we must translate and scale so that the CVV extends from -1 to 1 in each dimension. It is easy to check (see the exercises) that the matrix

$$\begin{pmatrix} \dfrac{2}{r-l} & 0 & 0 & -\dfrac{r+l}{r-l} \\ 0 & \dfrac{2}{t-b} & 0 & -\dfrac{t+b}{t-b} \\ 0 & 0 & \dfrac{-2}{f-n} & -\dfrac{f+n}{f-n} \\ 0 & 0 & 0 & 1 \end{pmatrix} \quad \begin{array}{l}\text{(OpenGL projection matrix} \\ \text{for orthographic projection)}\end{array} \qquad (7.18)$$

does indeed map the view volume into the CVV. This is the one formed by `glOrtho()`. If you multiply it by P (expressed in homogeneous coordinates) you get the actual point p OpenGL submits for clipping and mapping to the viewport. Notice that OpenGL itself does not set the z-component to 0 as suggested in the preceding paragraph. Instead, it performs a transformation, not a projection. Ultimately it does the actual projection by separating off the z-component at the very end, using the x- and y-components in screen coordinates for drawing, and the z-component for depth testing.

Types of Orthographic Projection

There are various kinds of orthographic projection, as seen in the taxonomy. The different types are distinguished by different orientations of the camera in the world. Specifically they are named according to how the camera's **n** direction is aimed relative to the world coordinate axes (an aspect we examined in Figure 7.40 when discussing k-point perspective).

Multiview Orthographic Projections These are traditionally presented as the top, front, and side views of an object. **n** is made parallel to **k**, **i**, and **j** in turn, and the object of interest is drawn. Figure 7.47 shows an example. These views are especially suited to engineering drawings, as you can measure dimensions of an object directly from the piece of paper on which the drawing is made, particularly when the object is "cubelike," so its various faces are aligned with the world axes.

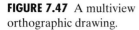

FIGURE 7.47 A multiview orthographic drawing.

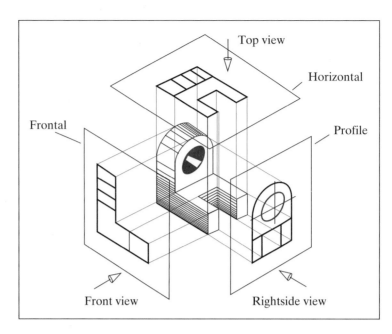

Axonometric Views For an axonometric view **n** is chosen to obtain a better 3D sense of the shape of the object. In such a view, **n** is usually not parallel to any principal axis; rather, it is oriented so that three adjacent faces of the (cubelike) object are visible. The choice of which faces to make visible depends on which faces of the object are important and should be emphasized. In addition, one of the principal axes is usually chosen to be vertical. Parallel lines in the object are, of course, viewed as parallel, but if a line recedes, it is **foreshortened** by some factor. Figure 7.48 shows **n** tilted to form angle α with the *x*-axis.

FIGURE 7.48 The foreshortening factor.

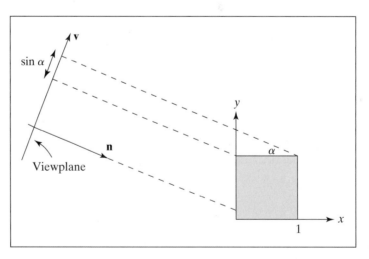

A line of unit length oriented α radians from the viewplane normal is viewed as having a length of $\sin(\alpha)$, and so the **foreshortening factor** is $\sin(\alpha)$.

Axonometric projections fall into three classes, depending on how many principal axes are *equally* foreshortened:

1. Isometric ("equal measure"): All three principal axes are foreshortened equally.
2. Dimetric ("two measures"): Two principal axes are foreshortened equally.
3. Trimetric ("three measures"): All three principal axes are foreshortened unequally.

Isometric Views An **isometric** view of a cube is shown in Figure 7.49a, looking in a direction along one of the cube's eight diagonals. All three axes are foreshortened by the same amount. As shown in Figure 7.49b, an isometric view of a transparent cube is just a regular hexagon with three diagonal lines.

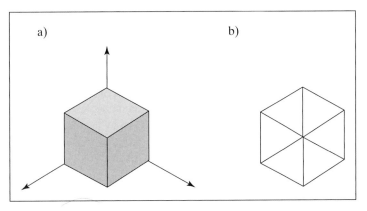

FIGURE 7.49 An isometric view of a cube.

The condition for an isometric view is $n_x = \pm n_y = \pm n_z$. In an isometric view the angles between the projections of the principal axes are equal. The length of any line that lies in a principal plane can be measured directly from the drawing, and this length can then be scaled by a fixed amount (how much?) to obtain the true length.

Dimetric Views When only two of the axes make the same angle with **n**, the view is called **dimetric**. For a dimetric view, two of the direction cosines must have the same size, so that $n_x = \pm n_y$, $n_x = \pm n_z$, or $n_y = \pm n_z$. A sequence of dimetric views is shown in Figure 7.50; the third one is almost isometric. For each view, $n_x = n_y$, and both are negative. (What is n_z approximately in the first figure? In the last one?) The different orientations place differing amounts of emphasis on the faces.

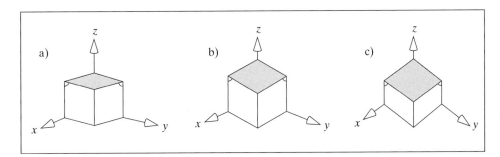

FIGURE 7.50 Several dimetric views of a cube.

Trimetric Views Finally, if the three axes make different angles with **n**, the view is called **trimetric**. Figure 7.51 provides an example, in which there is almost complete freedom of choice for the components of **n**. When the proper orientation is chosen, a trimetric view can look the most natural.

7.7 SUMMARY

In this chapter we saw how to define and manipulate a "viewing system" in a program, so a user can make pictures of how a 3D scene looks from various points of view, and fly a camera through a scene in an animation. The camera is modeled as an eye and a view volume residing in its own coordinate system. It generally resembles a **pinhole camera** and projects points onto a flat viewplane. Points lying inside the view volume are projected onto the viewplane; those lying outside are clipped away.

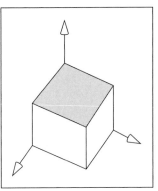

FIGURE 7.51 A trimetric view.

Much of the mathematics of the viewing process revolves around geometric transformations that relate the positions of points in different spaces. The graphics pipeline employed by OpenGL performs a sequence of transformations on the vertices fed into it. Each transformation embodies separate properties of the camera and the projection mechanism. Through the use of homogeneous coordinates all of these transformations can be performed by matrix multiplication. Points are ultimately mapped into a special space that is ideally suited for efficient clipping of edges, and in addition a single clipping algorithm suffices for any camera.

The geometry of perspective projections is essentially one of similarity, and happily it preserves flatness and inbetweenness, so the projection of an entire line can be computed simply by projecting two points on the line. The central transformation that a point undergoes when being projected involves a division by the depth of the point, which makes more remote objects appear smaller. This division of spatial coordinates by a common divisor makes the transformation well suited for expression in homogeneous coordinates, where the fourth coordinate is the divisor. The transformation can therefore be implemented by a matrix multiplication followed by a division step, and so the geometric details that distinguish one projection from another simply determine the parameters of a matrix.

The full graphics pipeline can now be seen to be a matrix multiplication followed by a clip operation, then by a perspective division step, and finally by a matrix multiplication into screen coordinates. The first matrix is often separated into a modelview matrix and a projection matrix, as this allows the camera's orientation and position to be specified independently of its view volume. We have seen before that the modelview matrix combines two transformations: the transformation that places an object in the scene at the desired position and size, and the transformation that reflects the position and orientation of the camera in the scene.

7.8   CASE STUDIES

CASE STUDY 7.1 FLYING A CAMERA THROUGH A SCENE

(Level of Effort: II) Write an application that allows the user to fly a camera through some scene. The user presses keys to control the camera. At each keystroke the camera is slid in one of the three dimensions, or is rotated about one of its axes (through function calls similar to those used in Figure 7.13), and the scene is redrawn from the camera's new point of view. (You should decide which keystrokes to use for sliding the camera, and which to use for rotating it.) Also allow the user to change the view angle and aspect ratio of the camera with other keystrokes.

Experimentation with a camera is made much more intelligible if you cover the horizontal plane with a set of **grid lines**, as in Figure 7.24. This is easily done in a loop such as:

```
for(int x = -100; x < 100; x++)
{
      glBegin(GL_LINES);
            glVertex3d(x,0,100); glVertex3d(x,0,-100);
      glEnd();
}
```

that draws a set of 200 x-contours. A similar loop draws the z-contours. Add a keystroke control so the user can toggle the grid lines on and off.

OpenGL offers primitives that can be used to model interesting scenes. Use several of the objects described in Chapter 5, such as spheres, cones, dodecahedra, and the teapot, to make such a scene. Use the wireframe versions. Later we discuss the solid versions, which establish a light source and assign material properties to objects. Use the examples in Chapter 5 as a guide.

CASE STUDY 7.2 STEREO VIEWS

(Level of Effort: II) Extend your mesh viewer so that it can produce stereo views of objects, as described in Figure 7.34. Three **Camera** objects are created. The *cyclops* camera is first created as a regular camera, then the left-eye and right-eye cameras are constructed using information (*eye*, the direction **u**, and so on) stored in the cyclops camera.

The images formed by the two cameras are placed side by side in two viewports within the screen window. Practice allowing your eyes to drift so you can see the stereo effect.

Allow the user to move the left-eye and right-eye cameras (locked together) around the scene to obtain good views. Experiment to find the most natural interocular distance, both for objects close to the cameras and for those far away.

CASE STUDY 7.3 BACK FACE REMOVAL FOR GREATER EFFICIENCY

(Level of Effort: II) When we render a mesh object, each of its faces is sent down the graphics pipeline, its vertices are transformed, and the face is rendered. But for any orientation of the object there are many faces that are pointed away from the viewer. These are called **back faces**, and there is no need to send them through the pipeline, since they will not be visible: there will be some other face that is closer to the eye and therefore obscures them. Figure 7.52 shows the classic barn being viewed by a certain camera. For any position of the camera some of the barn's faces will be back faces: two are labeled in the figure.

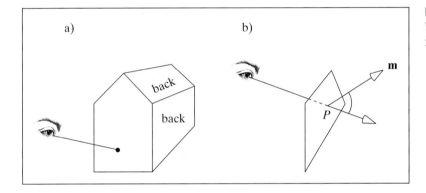

FIGURE 7.52 a) Back faces of a barn. b). Definition of a back face.

We call a face a back face if its outside surface is pointed away from the eye. This means that its outward-pointing normal vector, say **m**, is pointing less than 90° away from the vector from the eye to any point P on the face (see part b). If an angle between two vectors is less than 90°, the dot product between them is positive. So the test for a face to be a back face is:

F is *a back face* if $(P - eye) \cdot \mathbf{m} > 0$

This test is inexpensive computationally to perform. Therefore it might speed up the drawing of a complex mesh object significantly to first test whether a face is a back face, and if so, to skip it.

Adapt the code of Figure 6.15: `Mesh :: draw()` that draws only the front faces of a mesh object, skipping those faces it determines are back faces by inserting the test `if(isBackFace(f,…)) continue`. Develop the code for `int isBackFace(. f.)`, which returns 1 if f is a back face and 0 otherwise, using the simplest set of parameters that must be passed to it. Develop an application that draws meshes with an arbitrary camera, and test its speed both with and without back face removal.

7.9 FOR FURTHER READING

As mentioned throughout the chapter, the *OpenGL Programming Guide* [Woo04] provides a clear introduction to setting up and controlling a viewing system for 3D graphics. Foley et al. [Foley03] go into additional detail. Several articles in *Jim Blinn's Corner—A Trip Down the Graphics Pipeline* [Blinn96] offer clear and entertaining discussions of projections, viewing transformations, and clipping methods. Also see Angel [Angel03] for a good description of camera adjustments and the viewing system.

Chapter 8

Rendering Faces for Visual Realism

My most recent paintings are a mixture of realism and futurism, representation and geometrical distortion to reflect movement.

Ralph Allen
(1693–1764)

GOALS OF THE CHAPTER

○ To add realism to drawings of 3D scenes.

○ To examine ways to determine how light reflects off surfaces.

○ To render polygonal meshes that are bathed in light.

○ To see how to make a polygonal mesh object appear smooth.

○ To develop methods for adding textures to the surfaces of objects.

○ To add shadows of objects to a scene.

Preview

Section 8.1 motivates the need for enhancing the realism of pictures of 3D objects. Section 8.2 introduces various shading (or illumination) models used in computer graphics, and develops tools for computing the ambient, diffuse, and specular light contributions to an object's color. It also describes how to set up light sources in OpenGL, how to describe the material properties of surfaces, and how the OpenGL graphics pipeline operates when rendering polygonal meshes.

Section 8.3 focuses on rendering objects modeled as polygon meshes. Flat shading, as well as Gouraud and Phong shading, are described. Section 8.4 develops a simple hidden surface removal technique based on a depth buffer, like the one OpenGL uses. Proper hidden surface removal greatly improves the realism of pictures.

Section 8.5 develops methods for painting texture (such as images, clip art, or labels) onto the surface of an object, to make the object appear as if a label were actually affixed to its surface, or to give the impression that it is made of a real material such as brick or wood. Procedural generation of a texture map, which creates textures through a routine, is also described. Section 8.5.4 presents a complete program that uses OpenGL to add texture to objects. Section 8.5.6 discusses mapping textures onto "reflective" curved surfaces that make the object appear to be immersed within a scene. This provides more tools for making a 3D scene appear real.

Section 8.6 describes techniques for adding shadows to pictures, and compares OpenGL's (rather less powerful methods) for doing so. Section 8.7 introduces and develops the topic of bump mapping, which produces images of objects that appear to have a rough or bumpy surface, yet spares the programmer from the difficult task of having to make the *actual* surface of the object (such as a mesh) rough or bumpy. The chapter finishes with a number of Case Studies that delve deeper into some of these topics, urging the reader to experiment with them.

8.1 INTRODUCTION

In previous chapters we have fashioned tools for **modeling** mesh objects and for manipulating a jib camera to view them and make pictures. Now we want to add tools to make these objects and others look visually interesting, realistic, or both. Some examples in Chapter 5 invoked a number of OpenGL functions to produce shiny teapots and spheres apparently bathed in light, but we did not examine any of the underlying theory of how this is done. Here we rectify this and examine how to render a lore of **rendering** a picture of the objects of interest. This is the business of *computing* how each pixel of a picture should look. Much of it is based on different **shading models**, which attempt to describe how light that emanates from light sources would interact with objects in a scene. Owing to practical limitations one usually doesn't try to simulate all of the physical principles of light scattering and reflection; this is very complicated and would lead to lengthy development periods (the most expensive part within a development organization) and very slow algorithms. But a number of approximate models have been invented that do a good job and produce various levels of realism.

We start by describing a hierarchy of techniques that provide increasing levels of realism, in order to show the basic issues involved. Then we examine how to incorporate each technique in an application, and also how to use OpenGL to do much of the hard work for us.

At the bottom of the hierarchy, offering the lowest level of realism, is **wireframe** rendering. Figure 8.1 shows a chaotic jumble of 540 cubes rendered as wireframes. Only the edges of each object are drawn, and you can see right through an object. It is nearly impossible to see what's what. (A stereo view would help only a little.)

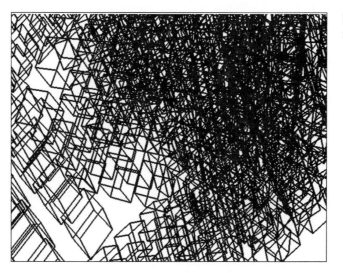

FIGURE 8.1 A wireframe rendering of a scene.

Figure 8.2 makes a significant improvement by omitting the drawing of those edges that lie behind a face. We can call this a "wireframe with hidden surface removal" rendering (More accurately it should be called: a visible edge wireframe rendering.) Even though only edges are drawn, the objects now look solid, and it is easy to tell where one stops and the next begins. Notice that some edges are only partly drawn, terminating abruptly as they slip behind an obscuring face.

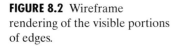

FIGURE 8.2 Wireframe rendering of the visible portions of edges.

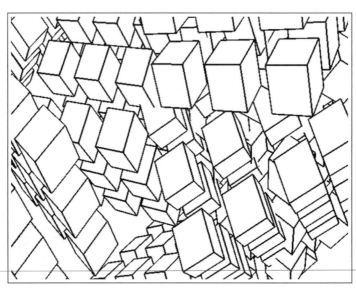

For the curious: This picture was made using OpenGL with its depth buffer enabled. For each mesh object the faces were drawn in white using drawMesh(), and then the edges were drawn in black using drawEdges(). Both routines were discussed in Chapter 6.

The next step in the hierarchy toward realism produces pictures where objects appear to be in a scene as well as illuminated by some light sources. Different parts of each object reflect different amounts of light, depending on the properties of the surfaces involved and on the positions of the sources. The proper drawing of such a scene requires computing the color of each portion of each face in some automated way, using a shading model.

Figure 8.3 shows a scene modeled with polygonal meshes: a jack (recall Example 5.6.3) and a Buckyball rest atop a tapered cylinder, which in turn rests on a cylinder of its own. Part a shows the **wireframe** version, and part b shows a shaded version (with hidden surfaces removed). Those faces aimed toward the light source (which is located above the main objects) appear brighter than those aimed away from the source. (Study this carefully.) This picture shows flat shading: the calculation of how much the computation of the amount of light scattered from each face is computed at only a single point on the face. Therefore all points on a face are rendered with the same gray level.

The next step in complexity should reveal the use of color. Color will be covered in Section 8.2.6.

In Chapter 6 we discussed building a mesh approximation to a smoothly curved object. A picture of such an object should show this smoothness, revealing the smooth "underlying surface" rather than the individual polygons. In Figure 8.4 the spheres and cylinders of the jack are smoothly shaped objects, whereas the Buckyball and table are not. Figure 8.3b shows the scene rendered using flat shading, whereas Figure 8.4 shows the same scene rendered using **smooth shading**. Here different points of a face are drawn with different gray levels found through an interpolation scheme known as **Gouraud shading**. The variation in gray levels for the inherently smooth objects is much smoother (although not perfectly smooth), and the edges of polygons disappear, giving the impression of a smooth, rather than a faceted, surface. Note that the Buckyball is not a smoothly shaped surface, so that even a smooth rendering leaves the individual faces visible. We examine Gouraud shading in Section 8.3.

a)

b)

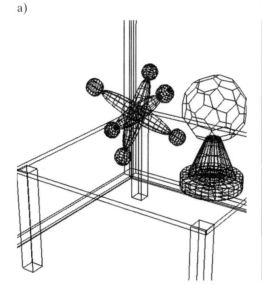

FIGURE 8.3 A mesh approximation shaded with a shading model: a) wireframe view, b) flat shading.

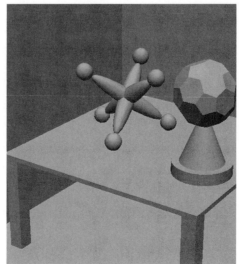

FIGURE 8.4 The scene rendered with smooth shading.

Highlights (shiny glints) can be added to make objects look glossy. Figure 8.5 shows the scene with **specular light** components added. Specular light is discussed in Section 8.2. The shinier objects possesses brighter but more localized specular highlights, which often give them a plastic appearance.

FIGURE 8.5 The scene with specular highlights added.

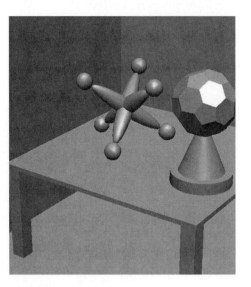

Shadowing is another effect that improves the realism of a picture. Figure 8.6 shows the scene of Figure 8.6 with shadows properly rendered, where one object casts a shadow onto a neighboring object (Count the shadows.) We discuss how to do this algorithmically in Section 8.6 and in Chapter 12.

FIGURE 8.6 The scene rendered with shadows.

Adding texture to an object can produce a big step in realism. Figure 8.7 shows the scene with different textures painted onto the different surfaces. The back wall has a repeating pattern painted on it that seems to arise from tiling the pattern seen on each square. These textures can make the various surfaces appear to be made of such materials as wood, marble, or copper. Another use of texture wraps an image around an object like a decal.

FIGURE 8.7 Textures mapped onto surfaces.

There are additional techniques that improve realism. In Chapter 12 we study **ray tracing** in depth. Although ray tracing is a expensive computationally approach, it is easy to program and can produce pictures that show proper shadows, mirrorlike reflections, and the passage of light through transparent objects.

In this chapter we describe a number of methods for rendering scenes with various levels of realism. We first look at the classical lighting models used in computer graphics that make an object appear bathed in light from one or more light sources, and see how to draw a polygonal mesh so that it appears to have a smoothly curved surface. We then examine a particular hidden surface removal method—the one that OpenGL uses—and see how it is incorporated into the rendering process. In general we shall see that there is a price to be paid for choosing one shading model over another in order to obtain greater realism: the algorithm runs more slowly. This may or may not be important when creating your OpenGL applications.

8.2 ■ INTRODUCTION TO SHADING MODELS

Children need models rather than critics.

Joseph Joubert
(1754–1824)

The mechanism of light reflection from an actual surface is very complicated; it depends on many factors. Some of these are geometric, such as the relative directions of the light source, the observer's eye, and the normal to the surface at each point. Others are related to the characteristics of the surface, such as its roughness and color.

A shading model dictates how light is scattered or reflected from a surface. We shall examine some simple shading models here, focusing on achromatic light. **Achromatic** light has brightness but no color; it is only a shade of gray. Hence it is described by a single value: its intensity. We shall see how to calculate the intensity of the light reaching the eye of the camera from each portion of the object. We then extend the ideas to include colored lights and colored objects. The computations are almost identical to those for achromatic light, except that separate intensities of red, green, and blue components are calculated.

A shading model frequently used in graphics supposes that two types of light sources illuminate the objects in a scene: point light sources and **ambient** light. These light sources "shine" on the various surfaces of the objects. Incident light interacts with the surface in three different ways:

- Some is absorbed by the surface and is converted to heat;
- Some is reflected from the surface;
- Some is transmitted into the interior of the object, as in the case of a piece of glass.

If all incident light is absorbed, the object appears black and is known as a **black body**. If all of the incident light is transmitted, the object is visible only through the effects of reflection (or **refraction** if the camera is poised to look through the object at a scene behind it), which we shall discuss in Chapter 12.

Here we focus on the part of the light that is reflected or scattered from the surface. Some amount of this reflected light travels in just the right direction to reach the eye, causing the object to be seen. The amount of light that reaches the eye depends on the orientation of the surface, light sources, and observer. We assume that there are two types of reflection of incident light: diffuse scattering and specular reflection.

- **Diffuse scattering** occurs when some of the incident light slightly penetrates the surface and is re-radiated uniformly in all directions. Scattered light interacts strongly with the surface, and so its color is usually affected by the nature of the surface material.
- **Specular reflections** are more mirrorlike and are highly directional. Incident light does not penetrate the object but instead is reflected directly from its outer surface. This gives rise to highlights and makes the surface look shiny. In the simplest model for specular light the reflected light has the same color as the incident light. This tends to make the material look like plastic. In a more complex model the color of the specular light varies over the highlight, providing a better approximation to the shininess of metal surfaces. We discuss both models for specular reflections.

Most surfaces produce some combination of the two types of reflection, depending on surface characteristics such as roughness and type of material. We say that the total light reflected from the surface in a certain direction is the sum of the diffuse component and the specular component. For each surface point of interest we compute the size of each component that reaches the eye. Algorithms are developed next that accomplish this.

8.2.1 Geometric Ingredients for Finding Reflected Light

On the outside grows the furside, on the inside grows the skinside;
So the furside is the outside, and the skinside is the inside.

The Sleeping Bag
Herbert George Ponting
(1870–1935)

We need to find three vectors in order to compute the diffuse and specular components. Figure 8.8 shows the three principal vectors (**s**, **m**, and **v**) required to find the amount of light that reaches the eye from a point P.

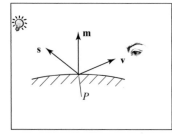

FIGURE 8.8 Important directions in computing the reflected light.

1. The normal vector, **m**, to the surface at P.
2. The vector **v** from P to the viewer's eye (vector **v** short for viewer).
3. The vector **s** from P to the light source (vector **s** short for source).

The angles between these three vectors form the basis for computing light intensities. These angles are normally calculated using world coordinates, because some transformations (such as the perspective transformation) do not preserve angles.

Each face of a mesh object has two sides. If the object is solid, one is usually the "inside" and one is the "outside." The eye can then see only the outside (unless the eye is inside the object!), and it is this side for which we must compute light contributions. But for some objects, such as the open box of Figure 8.9, the eye might be able to see the inside of the lid. This depends on the angle between the normal to that side, m_2, and the vector to the eye, v. If the angle is less than 90° this side is visible. Since the cosine of that angle is proportional to the dot product $v \cdot m_2$, the eye can see this side only if $v \cdot m_2 > 0$.

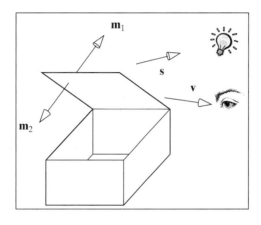

FIGURE 8.9 Light computations are made for one side of each face.

We shall develop the shading model for a given side of a face. If that side of the face is turned away from the eye, there is normally no light contribution. In an actual application the rendering algorithm must be told whether to compute light contributions from one side or both sides of a given face. We shall see that OpenGL supports this.

8.2.2 How to Compute the Diffuse Component

Suppose that light falls from a point source onto one side of a face (a small piece of a surface). A fraction of it is re-radiated diffusely in all directions from this side. Some fraction of the re-radiated part reaches the eye, with an intensity denoted by I_d. How does I_d depend on the directions m, v, and s?

An important property assumed for diffuse scattering is that it is independent of the direction from the point, P, to the location of the viewer's eye. This is often called **omnidirectional scattering**. Because the scattering is uniform in all directions, the orientation of the face, F, relative to the eye is not significant. Therefore, I_d is independent of the angle between m and v (unless $v \cdot m < 0$, whereupon I_d is zero.) On the other hand, the amount of light that illuminates the face *does* depend on the orientation of the face relative to the point source: The amount of light is proportional to the area of the face that it sees—that is, the area *subtended* by a face.

Figure 8.10a shows in cross section a point source illuminating a face S when m is aligned with s. In Figure 8.10b the face is turned partially away from the light source through angle θ. The area subtended is now only $\cos(\theta)$ as much as before, so that the brightness of S is reduced by this same factor. This relationship between brightness and surface orientation is often called **Lambert's law** [after Johann Heinrich Lambert, 1728–1777]. Notice that for θ near 0, brightness varies only slightly with

FIGURE 8.10 The brightness depends on the area of the face subtended.

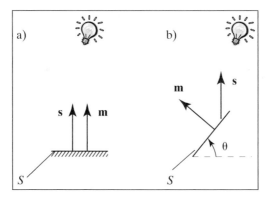

angle, because the cosine changes slowly there. As θ approaches 90°, however, the brightness falls rapidly to 0.

Now we know that $\cos(\theta)$ is the dot product between normalized versions of $\mathbf{s}$ and $\mathbf{m}$. We can therefore adopt as the strength of the diffuse component:

$$I_d = I_s \rho_d \frac{\mathbf{s} \cdot \mathbf{m}}{|\mathbf{s}||\mathbf{m}|}$$

In this equation, I_s is the intensity of the light source, and ρ_d is the **diffuse reflection coefficient**. Note that if the facet is aimed away from the eye, this dot product is negative, and we want I_d to evaluate to 0. So a more precise computation of the diffuse component is:

$$I_d = I_s \rho_d \max\left(\frac{\mathbf{s} \cdot \mathbf{m}}{|\mathbf{s}||\mathbf{m}|}, 0\right) \tag{8.1}$$

Figure 8.11 shows how a sphere appears when it reflects diffuse light incident from above, for six reflection coefficients: 0, 0.2, 0.4, 0.6, 0.8, and 1. In each case the source intensity is 1.0 and the background intensity is set to 0.4. Note that the sphere is totally black when ρ_d is 0.0, and the shadow in its bottom half (where the dot product above is negative) is also black.

FIGURE 8.11 Some spheres having various reflection coefficients illuminated by diffuse light.

In reality the mechanism behind diffuse reflection is much more complex than the simple model we have adopted here. The reflection coefficient ρ_d depends on the wavelength (color) of the incident light, the angle θ, and various physical properties of the surface. But for simplicity and to reduce computation time, these effects are usually suppressed when rendering images. A "reasonable" value for ρ_d is chosen for each surface, sometimes by trial and error according to the realism observed in the resulting image.

In some shading models the effect of distance is also included, although it is somewhat controversial. The light intensity falling on face S in Figure 8.10 from the point source is known to fall off as the inverse square of the distance between S and the source. But experiments have shown that using this law yields pictures with exaggerated depth effects. What is more, it is sometimes convenient to model light sources as if they were situated "at infinity." Using an inverse-square law in such a case would quench the light entirely! The problem is thought to be in the model: we model light sources as point sources for simplicity, but most scenes are actually illuminated by additional reflections from the surroundings, which are difficult to model. (These effects are lumped together into an ambient light component.) It is not surprising, therefore, that strict adherence to a physical law based on an unrealistic model can lead to unrealistic results.

The realism of most pictures is enhanced rather little by the introduction of a distance term. Some approaches force the intensity to be inversely proportional to the distance between the eye and the object, but this is not based on physical principles. It is interesting to experiment with this effect, and OpenGL provides some control over it, as we see in Section 8.2.8, but in the following development we don't include a distance term.

8.2.3 Specular Reflection

Real objects do not scatter light uniformly in all directions, and so a specular component is added to the shading model. Specular reflection causes highlights, which can add significantly to the realism of a picture when objects are shiny. In this section we discuss a simple model for the behavior of specular light due to Phong [Phong75]. It is easy to apply, and the highlights generated by Phong specular light give an object a plasticlike appearance, so the Phong model is good when you intend the object to be made of shiny plastic or glass. The Phong model is less successful with objects that are supposed to have a shiny metallic surface, although you can roughly approximate them with OpenGL by careful choices of certain color parameters. More advanced models of specular light have been developed that do a better job of modeling shiny metals. These are not supported directly by OpenGL's rendering process, so we defer a detailed discussion of them to Chapter 12 on ray tracing.

Figure 8.12a shows a situation where light from a source impinges on a surface and is reflected in different directions. In the **Phong model** we discuss here, the amount of light reflected is greatest in the direction of *perfect mirror reflection* (discussed in Chapter 4), **r**, where the angle of incidence θ equals the angle of reflection. This is the direction in which all light would travel if the surface were a perfect mirror. At other nearby angles the amount of light reflected diminishes rapidly, as indicated by the relative lengths of the reflected vectors. Part b shows this in terms of a "beam pattern" familiar in radar circles. The distance from P to the beam envelope shows the relative strength of the light scattered in that direction.

Part c shows how to quantify this beam pattern effect. We know from Chapter 4 that the direction **r** of perfect reflection depends on both **s** and the normal vector **m** to the surface, according to:

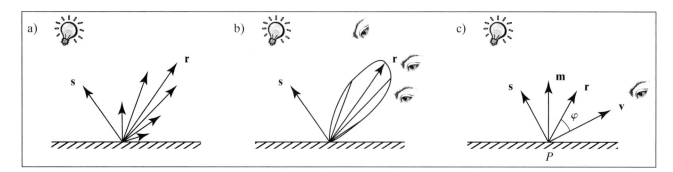

FIGURE 8.12 Specular reflection from a shiny surface.

$$\mathbf{r} = -\mathbf{s} + 2\frac{(\mathbf{s} \cdot \mathbf{m})}{|\mathbf{m}|^2}\mathbf{m} \qquad \text{(the mirror-reflection direction)} \tag{8.2}$$

For surfaces that are shiny but not true mirrors, the amount of light reflected falls off as the angle ϕ between $\mathbf{r}$ and $\mathbf{v}$ increases. The actual amount of falloff is a complicated function of ϕ, but in the Phong model it is said to vary as some power f of the cosine of ϕ—that is, according to $(\cos(\phi))^f$, in which f is chosen experimentally and usually lies between 1 and 200.

Figure 8.13 shows how this intensity function varies with ϕ for different values of f. As f increases, the reflection becomes more mirrorlike and is more highly concentrated along the direction $\mathbf{r}$. A perfect mirror could be modeled using $f = \infty$, but pure reflections are usually handled in a different manner, as described in Chapter 12.

FIGURE 8.13 The falloff of specular light with angle.

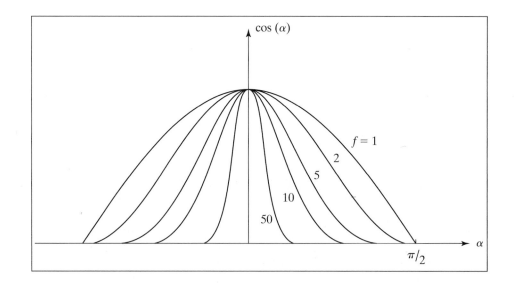

Using the equivalence of $\cos(\phi)$ and the dot product between $\mathbf{r}$ and $\mathbf{v}$ (after they are normalized), the contribution I_{sp} due to specular reflection is modeled by

$$I_{sp} = I_s\rho_s\left(\frac{\mathbf{r}}{|\mathbf{r}|} \cdot \frac{\mathbf{v}}{|\mathbf{v}|}\right)^f \tag{8.3}$$

where the new term ρ_s is the **specular reflection coefficient**. Like most other coefficients in the shading model, it is usually determined experimentally. (As with the diffuse term, if the dot product $\mathbf{r} \cdot \mathbf{v}$ is found to be negative, I_{sp} is set to zero.)

The complexity of the method for calculating the specular component should be examined. It involves several dot products, vector normalizations, and exponentiation. It is natural to look for a simpler method for finding the same term.

A Boost in Efficiency Using the Halfway Vector

It can be expensive to compute the specular term in Equation (8.3), since it requires first finding vector **r** and normalizing it. The halfway vector partially alleviates this inadequacy. In practice an alternate term, apparently first described by Blinn [Blinn77], is used to speed up computation. Instead of using the cosine of the angle between **r** and **v**, one finds a vector halfway between **s** and **v**—that is, **h** = **s** + **v**—as suggested in Figure 8.14. If the normal to the surface were oriented along **h**, the viewer would see the brightest specular highlight. Therefore the angle β between **m** and **h** can be used to measure the falloff of specular intensity that the viewer sees. The angle β is not the same as φ (in fact β is twice φ if the various vectors are coplanar—see the exercises), but this difference can be compensated for by using a different value of the exponent f. (The specular term is not based on physical principles anyway, so it is at least plausible that our adjustment to f yields acceptable results.) Thus it is common practice to base the specular term on $\cos(β)$ using the dot product of **h** and **m**:

$$I_{sp} = I_s \rho_s \max\left(0, \left(\frac{\mathbf{h}}{|\mathbf{h}|} \cdot \frac{\mathbf{m}}{|\mathbf{m}|}\right)^f\right) \qquad \{\text{adjusted specular term}\} \qquad (8.4)$$

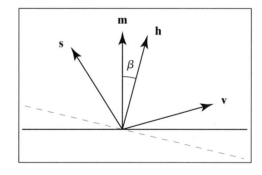

FIGURE 8.14 The halfway vector.

Note that with this adjustment the reflection vector **r** need not be found, saving computation time. In addition, if both the light source and viewer are very remote, then **s** and **v** are constant over the different faces of an object, so **h** · **m** need be computed only once.

Figure 8.15 shows a sphere reflecting different amounts of specular light. The reflection coefficient ρ_s varies from top to bottom with values 0.25, 0.5, and 0.75, and the exponent f varies from left to right with values 3, 6, 9, 25, and 200. (The ambient and diffuse reflection coefficients are 0.1 and 0.4 for all spheres. The light source has the same location in all cases.)

The physical mechanism for secularly reflected light is actually much more complicated than the Phong model suggests. A more realistic model makes the specular reflection coefficient dependent on both the wavelength λ (i.e., the color) of the incident light and the angle of incidence $θ_i$ (the angle between vectors **s** and **m** in Figure 8.10). This effect, which attempts to describe how light is reflected from different materials (such as zinc vs. pewter), is discussed briefly in connection with Equation 8.9. We also address these issues, in Chapter 12 in order to examine how rainbows and prisms operate.

FIGURE 8.15 Specular reflection from a shiny surface.

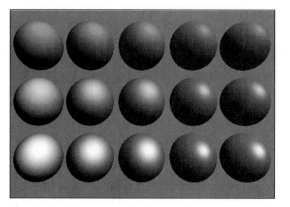

PRACTICE EXERCISES

8.2.1 On the halfway vector

By examining the geometry displayed in Figure 8.14, show that $\beta = 2\phi$ if the vectors involved are coplanar.

8.2.2 A specular speed-up

Schlick [Schlick94] has suggested an alternative to the exponentiation required when computing the specular term. Let D denote the dot product $\mathbf{r} \cdot \mathbf{v}/|\mathbf{r}||\mathbf{v}|$ in Equation (8.3). Schlick suggests replacing D^f with

$$\frac{D}{f - fD + D}$$

which is faster to compute. Plot these two functions for values of D in [0,1] for various values of f and compare them. Pay particular attention to values of D near 1, since this is where specular highlights are brightest.   ■

8.2.4 The Role of Ambient Light and Exploiting Human Perception

The diffuse and specular components of reflected light are found by simplifying the rules by which physical light reflects from physical surfaces. The dependence of these components on the relative positions of the eye, model, and light sources greatly improves the realism of a picture over renderings that simply fill a wireframe with a shade.

But our desire for a simple reflection model leaves us with far from perfect renderings of a scene. As an example, shadows are seen to be unrealistically deep and harsh. To soften these shadows, we can add a third light component called *ambient light*.

With only diffuse and specular reflections, any parts of a surface that are shadowed from the point source receive no light and so are drawn black! But this is not our everyday experience. The scenes we observe around us always seem to be bathed in some soft nondirectional light. This light arrives by multiple reflections from various objects in the surroundings and from light sources that populate the environment, such as light coming through a window, fluorescent lamps, and the like. But it would be computationally very expensive to model this kind of light precisely.

Ambient Sources and Ambient Reflections

To overcome the problem of totally dark shadows, we imagine that a uniform background glow called **ambient light** exists in the environment. This ambient light source is not situated at any particular place, and it spreads in all directions uniformly. The source is assigned an intensity, I_a. Each face in the model is assigned a value for its **ambient reflection coefficient**, ρ_a (often this is the same as the diffuse reflection coefficient, ρ_d), and the term $I_a\rho_a$ is simply added to whatever diffuse and specular light is reaching the eye from each point P on that face. I_a and ρ_a are usually arrived at experimentally, by trying various values and seeing what looks best. Too little ambient light makes shadows appear too deep and harsh; too much makes the picture look washed out and bland.

Figure 8.16 shows the effect of adding various amounts of ambient light to the diffuse light reflected by a sphere. In each case both the diffuse and ambient sources have intensity 1.0, and the diffuse reflection coefficient is 0.4. Moving from left to right, the ambient reflection coefficient takes on values 0.0, 0.1, 0.3, 0.5, and 0.7. With only a modest amount of ambient light the harsh shadows on the underside of the sphere are softened and look more realistic. Too much ambient reflection, on the other hand, suppresses the shadows excessively.

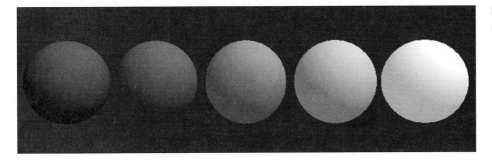

FIGURE 8.16 On the effect of ambient light.

8.2.5 How to Combine Light Contributions

We can now sum the three light contributions—diffuse, specular, and ambient—to form the total amount of light I that reaches the eye from point P:

$$I = \text{ambient} + \text{diffuse} + \text{specular}$$

$$I = I_a\rho_a + I_d\rho_d \times lambert + I_{sp}\rho_s \times phong^f \tag{8.5}$$

where we define the values

$$lambert = \max\left(0, \frac{\mathbf{s} \cdot \mathbf{m}}{|\mathbf{s}||\mathbf{m}|}\right) \quad \text{and} \quad phong = \max\left(0, \frac{\mathbf{h} \cdot \mathbf{m}}{|\mathbf{h}||\mathbf{m}|}\right) \tag{8.6}$$

I depends on the various source intensities and reflection coefficients, as well as on the relative positions of the point P, the eye, and the point light source. Here we have given different names, I_d and I_{sp}, to the intensities of the diffuse and specular components of the light source, because OpenGL allows you to set them individually, as we see later. In practice they usually have the same value.

To gain some insight into the variation of I with the position of P, consider again Figure 8.10. I is computed for different points P on the face shown. The ambient component shows no variation over the face; $\mathbf{m}$ is the same for all P on the face, but the directions of both $\mathbf{s}$ and $\mathbf{v}$ depend on P. (For instance, $\mathbf{s} = S - P$, where S is the location of the light source. How does $\mathbf{v}$ depend on P and the eye?) If the light source is fairly far away (the typical case), $\mathbf{s}$ will change only slightly as P changes, so that the diffuse component will change only slightly for different points P. This is especially true when $\mathbf{s}$ and $\mathbf{m}$ are nearly aligned, as the value of cos() changes slowly for small angles. For remote light sources, the variation in the direction of the halfway vector **h** is also slight as P varies. On the other hand, if the light source is close to the face, there can be substantial changes in **s** and **h** as P varies. Then the specular term can change significantly over the face, and the bright highlight can be confined to a small portion of the face. This effect is increased when the eye is also close to the face—causing large changes in the direction of **v**—and when the exponent f is very large.

PRACTICE EXERCISE

8.2.4 The effect of the eye distance

Describe (based on intuition) how much the various light contributions change as P varies over a face a) when the eye is far away from the face and b) when the eye is near the face.   ■

8.2.6 To Add Color

It is straightforward to extend this shading model to the case of colored light reflecting from colored surfaces. Again it is an approximation born from simplicity, but it offers reasonable results and is serviceable.

Chapter 11 provides more detail and background on the nature of color, but we know colored light can be constructed by adding certain amounts of red, green, and blue light. When dealing with colored sources and surfaces, we calculate each color component individually and simply add them to form the final color of reflected light. So Equation (8.5) is applied three times:

$$I_r = I_{ar}\rho_{ar} + I_{dr}\rho_{dr} \times lambert + I_{spr}\rho_{sr} \times phong^f$$
$$I_g = I_{ag}\rho_{ag} + I_{dg}\rho_{dg} \times lambert + I_{spg}\rho_{sg} \times phong^f$$
$$I_b = I_{ab}\rho_{ab} + I_{db}\rho_{db} \times lambert + I_{spb}\rho_{sb} \times phong^f \qquad (8.7)$$

[where $lambert$ and $phong^f$ are given in Equation (8.6)] to compute the red, green, and blue components of reflected light. Note that we say the light sources have three types of color: ambient = (I_{ar}, I_{ag}, I_{ab}), diffuse = (I_{dr}, I_{dg}, I_{db}), and specular = $(I_{spr}, I_{spg}, I_{spb})$. Usually the diffuse and specular light colors are the same. Note also that the $lambert$ and $phong^f$ terms do not depend on which color component is being computed (except through the dependence of the reflection coefficient), so they need only be computed once. To pursue this approach we need to define nine reflection coefficients:

ambient reflection coefficients:	ρ_{ar}, ρ_{ag}, and ρ_{ab}
diffuse reflection coefficients:	ρ_{dr}, ρ_{dg}, and ρ_{db}
specular reflection coefficients:	ρ_{sr}, ρ_{sg}, and ρ_{sb}

The ambient and diffuse reflection coefficients are based on the color of the surface itself. By "color of a surface" we mean the diffuse color that is reflected from it when the illumination is *white* light: a surface is red if it appears red when bathed in white light. If bathed in some other color, it can exhibit an entirely different color. The following examples illustrate this.

■ **EXAMPLE 8.2.1 The color of an object**

If we say that the color of a sphere is 30% red, 45% green, and 25% blue, it makes sense to set its ambient and diffuse reflection coefficients to $(0.3K, 0.45K, 0.25K)$, respectively, where K is some scaling value that determines the overall fraction of incident light that is reflected from the sphere. Now if it is bathed in white light having equal amounts of red, green, and blue ($I_{sr} = I_{sg} = I_{sb} = I$), the individual diffuse components have intensities $I_r = 0.3KI$, $I_g = 0.45KI$, $I_b = 0.25KI$, so as expected we see a color that is 30% red, 45% green, and 25% blue.

■ EXAMPLE 8.2.2 A reddish object bathed in greenish light

Suppose a sphere has ambient and diffuse reflection coefficients (0.8, 0.2, 0.1), so it appears mostly red when bathed in white light. We illuminate it with a greenish light $I_s = (0.15, 0.7, 0.15)$. The reflected light is then given by (0.12, 0.14, 0.015), which is a fairly even mix of red and green, and would appear yellowish (as we discuss further in Chapter 11).

The Color of Specular Light Because specular light is mirrorlike, the color of the specular component is often the same as that of the light source. For instance, it is a matter of experience that the specular highlight seen on a glossy red apple when illuminated by a yellow light is yellow rather than red. This is also observed for shiny objects made of plasticlike material. To create specular highlights for a plastic surface the specular reflection coefficients, ρ_{sr}, ρ_{sg}, and ρ_{sb} used in Equation (8.7) are set to the same value, say ρ_s, so that the reflection coefficients are 'gray' in nature and do not alter the color of the incident light. The designer might choose $\rho_s = 0.5$ for a slightly shiny plastic surface, or $\rho_s = 0.9$ for a highly shiny surface.

Objects Made of Different Materials

A careful selection of reflection coefficients can make an object appear to be made of a specific material such as copper, gold, or pewter, at least approximately. McReynolds and Blythe [McReynolds97] have suggested using the reflection coefficients given in Figure 8.17. Figure 8.18 shows several spheres modeled using these coefficients (a color version, in which the spheres rather faithfully resemble the stated materials, is available at the companion web site). Note that the specular reflection coefficients have different red, green, and blue components, so the color of specular light is not simply that of the incident light. But McReynolds and Blythe caution users that, because OpenGL's shading algorithm incorporates a Phong specular component, the visual effects are not completely realistic. We shall revisit the issue in Chapter 12 and describe the more realistic Cook-Torrance shading approach.

8.2.7 Shading and the Graphics Pipeline

At which step in the graphics pipeline is shading performed? And how is it done? Figure 8.19 shows the pipeline again. The key idea is that the vertices of a mesh are sent down the pipeline along with their associated vertex normals, and all shading calculations are done on *vertices*. (Recall that the draw() method in the Mesh class sends a vertex normal along with each vertex, as in Figure 6.15.)

The figure shows a triangle with vertices v_0, v_1, and v_2 being rendered. Vertex v_i has the normal vector $\mathbf{m}_i$ associated with it. These quantities are sent down the pipeline with calls such as:

```
glBegin(GL_POLYGON);
      for(int i = 0; i < 3; i++)
      {
          glNormal3f(m[i].x, m[i].y, m[i].z);
          glVertex3f(v[i].x, v[i].y, v[i].z);
      }
glEnd();
```

Material	Ambient: ρ_{ar}, ρ_{ag}, ρ_{ab}	Diffuse: ρ_{dr}, ρ_{dg}, ρ_{db}	Specular: ρ_{sr}, ρ_{sg}, ρ_{sb}	Exponent: f
Black Plastic	0.0 0.0 0.0	0.01 0.01 0.01	0.50 0.50 0.50	32
Brass	0.329412 0.223529 0.027451	0.780392 0.568627 0.113725	0.992157 0.941176 0.807843	27.8974
Bronze	0.2125 0.1275 0.054	0.714 0.4284 0.18144	0.393548 0.271906 0.166721	25.6
Chrome	0.25 0.25 0.25	0.4 0.4 0.4	0.774597 0.774597 0.774597	76.8
Copper	0.19125 0.0735 0.0225	0.7038 0.27048 0.0828	0.256777 0.137622 0.086014	12.8
Gold	0.24725 0.1995 0.0745	0.75164 0.60648 0.22648	0.628281 0.555802 0.366065	51.2
Pewter	0.10588 0.058824 0.113725	0.427451 0.470588 0.541176	0.3333 0.3333 0.521569	9.84615
Silver	0.19225 0.19225 0.19225	0.50754 0.50754 0.50754	0.508273 0.508273 0.508273	51.2
Polished silver	0.23125 0.23125 0.23125	0.2775 0.2775 0.2775	0.773911 0.773911 0.773911	89.6

FIGURE 8.17 Parameters for common materials [McReynolds97].

FIGURE 8.18 A rendition of Shiny spheres made of different materials.

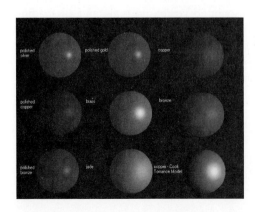

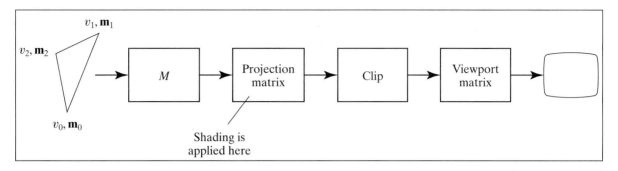

The call to glNormal3f() sets the "current normal vector," which is applied to all vertices subsequently sent using glVertex3f(). The current normal vector remains current until changed with another call to glNormal3f(). For the preceding code example a new normal is associated with each vertex.

FIGURE 8.19 The graphics pipeline revisited.

The vertices are transformed by the modelview matrix, M, so they are then expressed in camera (eye) coordinates. The normal vectors are also transformed, but vectors transform differently from points. As shown in Section 6.5.3, transforming points of a surface by a matrix M causes the normal $\mathbf{m}$ at any point to become the normal $M^{-T}\mathbf{m}$ on the transformed surface, where M^{-T} is the transpose of the inverse of M. OpenGL automatically performs the proper calculation on normal vectors.

As we discuss in the next section, OpenGL allows you to specify various light sources and their locations. Lights are objects, too, and the light source positions are also transformed by the modelview matrix.

All quantities end up after the modelview transformation expressed in camera coordinates. At this point the shading model of Equation (8.7) is applied, and a color is attached to each vertex. The computation of this color requires knowledge of vectors $\mathbf{m}$, $\mathbf{s}$, and $\mathbf{v}$, but these are all available at this point in the pipeline. (Convince yourself of this.)

Progressing farther down the pipeline, the pseudodepth term is created and the vertices are passed through the projection matrix. The color information tags along with each vertex. The clipping step is performed in homogeneous coordinates, as described in the preceding. This may alter some of the vertices. Figure 8.20 shows the case where vertex v_1 of a triangle is clipped off, and two new vertices, a and b, are created. The triangle becomes a quadrilateral. The color at each of the new vertices must be computed, since it is needed in the actual rendering step.

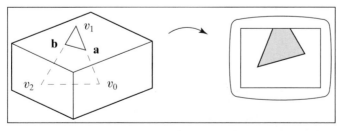

FIGURE 8.20 Clipping a polygon against the (warped) view volume.

The color at each new vertex is sometimes found by interpolation, as we do with Gouraud shading. For instance, suppose that the color at v_0 is (r_0, g_0, b_0) and the color at v_1 is (r_1, g_1, b_1). If the point a is 40% of the way from v_0 to v_1, the color associated with a is a blend of 60% of (r_0, g_0, b_0) and 40% of (r_1, g_1, b_1). This is expressed as

$$\text{color at point } a = (\text{lerp}(r_0, r_1, 0.4), \text{lerp}(g_0, g_1, 0.4), \text{lerp}(b_0, b_1, 0.4)) \tag{8.8}$$

where we use the convenient function lerp() (short for "linear interpolation") used in Chapter 4 in connection with tweening.

Define by:

$$\text{lerp}(G, H, f) = G + (H - G)f \qquad (8.9)$$

Its value lies at fraction f of the way from G to H.[1]

The vertices are finally passed through the viewport transformation, where they are mapped into screen coordinates (along with pseudodepth, which now varies between 0 and 1). The quadrilateral is then rendered (with hidden surface removal), as suggested in Figure 8.20. We shall say much more about the actual rendering step.

8.2.8 To Use Light Sources in OpenGL

OpenGL provides a number of functions for setting up and using light sources, as well as for specifying the surface properties of materials. It can be daunting to absorb all of the many possible variations and details, so we describe the basics here. We discuss how to establish different kinds of light sources in a scene. In the next section we look at ways to characterize the reflective properties of the surfaces of an object.

Create a Light Source

OpenGL allows you to define up to eight sources, which are referred to through names GL_LIGHT0, GL_LIGHT1, and so on. Each source is invested with various properties and must be enabled. Each property has a default value. For example, to create a source located at $(3, 6, 5)$ in world coordinates, use:[2]

```
GLfloat myLightPosition[] = {3.0, 6.0, 5.0, 1.0};
glLightfv(GL_LIGHT0, GL_POSITION, myLightPosition);
glEnable(GL_LIGHTING); // enable lighting in general
glEnable(GL_LIGHT0);   // enable source GL_LIGHT0
```

The array myLightPosition[] (use any name you wish for this array) specifies the location of the light source. This position passed to glLightfv() along with the name GL_LIGHT0 to attach it to the particular source GL_LIGHT0.

Some sources, such as a desk lamp, are in the scene, whereas others, like the sun, are infinitely remote. OpenGL allows you to create both types by using homogeneous coordinates to specify light position:

$(x, y, z, 1)$: a local light source at the position (x, y, z)
$(x, y, z, 0)$: a vector to an infinitely remote light source in the direction (x, y, z)

Figure 8.21 shows a local source positioned at $(0, 3, 3, 1)$ and a remote source "located" along vector $(3, 3, 0, 0)$. Infinitely remote light sources are often called **"directional."** There are computational advantages to using directional light sources, since the direction **s** in the calculations of diffuse and specular reflections is *constant* for all vertices in the scene. But directional light sources are not always the correct choice: some visual effects are properly achieved only when a light source is close to an object.

You can also spell out different colors for a light source. OpenGL allows you to assign a different color to three types of light that a source emits: ambient, diffuse, and specular. It may seem strange to say that a source emits ambient light. It

---

[1]   In Section 8.5 we discuss replacing linear interpolation by "hyperbolic interpolation" as a more accurate way to form the colors at the new vertices formed by clipping.

[2]   Here and elsewhere the type float would most likely serve as well as Glfloat. But using Glfloat makes your code more portable to other OpenGL hardware.

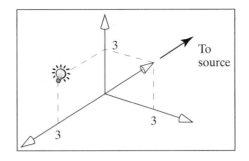

FIGURE 8.21 A local source and an infinitely remote source.

is still treated as in Equation (8.7): a global omnidirectional light that bathes the entire scene. The advantage of attaching it to a light source is that it can be turned on and off as an application proceeds. (OpenGL also offers a truly ambient light, not associated with any source, as we discuss later in connection with "lighting models.")

Arrays are defined to hold the colors emitted by light sources, and they are passed to glLightfv().

```
GLfloat amb0[] = {0.2, 0.4, 0.6, 1.0}; // define some colors
GLfloat diff0[] = {0.8, 0.9, 0.5, 1.0};
GLfloat spec0[] = {1.0, 0.8, 1.0, 1.0};
glLightfv(GL_LIGHT0, GL_AMBIENT, amb0); // attach them to LIGHT0
glLightfv(GL_LIGHT0, GL_DIFFUSE, diff0);
glLightfv(GL_LIGHT0, GL_SPECULAR, spec0);
```

Colors are specified in so-called **RGBA** format, meaning red, green, blue, and "alpha." The alpha value is sometimes used for blending two colors on the screen. We discuss it in Chapter 9. For our purposes here it is normally 1.0.

Light sources have various default values. For all sources:

default ambient $= (0, 0, 0, 1)$;   ← dimmest possible: black

For light source LIGHT0:

default diffuse $= (1, 1, 1, 1)$;   ← brightest possible: white

default specular $= (1, 1, 1, 1)$;   ← brightest possible: white

whereas for the other sources the diffuse and specular values have defaults of black.

Spotlights

Light sources are *point sources* by default, meaning that they emit light uniformly in all directions. But OpenGL allows you to make them into spotlights, so they emit light in a restricted set of directions. Figure (8.22) shows a spotlight aimed in direction **d**, with a "cutoff angle" of α.

No light is seen at points lying outside the cutoff cone. For vertices such as P that lie inside the cone, the amount of light reaching P is attenuated by the factor $\cos^{\varepsilon}(\beta)$, where β is the angle between **d** and a line from the source to P, and ε is an exponent chosen by the user to give the desired fall-off of light with angle.

The parameters for a spotlight are set using glLightf() to set a single value, and glLightfv() to set a vector:

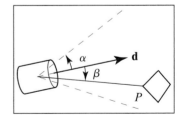

FIGURE 8.22 Properties of an OpenGL spotlight.

```
glLightf(GL_LIGHT0, GL_SPOT_CUTOFF, 45.0); // a cutoff angle of 45°
glLightf(GL_LIGHT0,GL_SPOT_EXPONENT, 4.0); // ε = 4.0
GLfloat dir[] = {2.0, 1.0, -4.0}; // the spotlight's direction
glLightfv(GL_LIGHT0,GL_SPOT_DIRECTION, dir); // send the
direction vector, dir
```

The default values for these parameters are $\mathbf{d} = (0, 0, -1)$, $\alpha = 180°$, and $\varepsilon = 0$, which makes a source an omnidirectional point source.

Attenuation of Light with Distance

OpenGL also allows you to specify how rapidly light diminishes with distance from a source. Although we have downplayed the importance of this dependence, it can be interesting to experiment with different fall-off rates and to fine-tune a picture. OpenGL attenuates the strength of a positional[3] light source by the following attenuation factor:

$$atten = \frac{1}{k_c + k_l D + k_q D^2} \tag{8.10}$$

where k_c, k_l, and k_q are coefficients and D is the distance between the light's position and the vertex in question. This expression is rich enough to allow you to model any combination of constant, linear, and quadratic (inverse square law) dependence on distance from a source. These parameters are controlled by function calls:

```
glLightf(GL_LIGHT0, GL_CONSTANT_ATTENUATION, 2.0);
```

and similarly for GL_LINEAR_ATTENUATION and GL_QUADRATIC_ATTENUATION. The default values are $k_c = 1$, $k_l = 0$, and $k_q = 0$, which eliminate any attenuation.

Lighting Model

OpenGL allows three parameters to be set that specify general rules for applying the lighting model. These parameters are passed to variations of the function glLightModel.

a. The color of global ambient light.
   You can establish a global ambient light source in a scene that is independent of any particular source. To create this light, specify its color using:

```
GLfloat amb[] = {0.2, 0.3, 0.1, 1.0};
glLightModelfv(GL_LIGHT_MODEL_AMBIENT, amb);
```

   This sets the ambient source to the color $(0.2, 0.3, 0.1)$. The default value is $(0.2, 0.2, 0.2, 1.0)$, so this ambient light is always present unless you purposely alter it. This makes objects in a scene visible even if you have not invoked any of the lighting functions.

b. Is the viewpoint local or remote?
   OpenGL computes specular reflections using the "halfway vector"

   $$\mathbf{h} = \mathbf{s} + \mathbf{v} \text{ (to compute the halfway vector)} \tag{8.11}$$

   developed in Section 8.2.3. The true directions $\mathbf{s}$ and $\mathbf{v}$ are normally different at each vertex in a mesh (visualize this). If the light source is directional, then $\mathbf{s}$ is constant, but $\mathbf{v}$ still varies from vertex to vertex. Rendering speed is increased if $\mathbf{v}$ is made constant for all vertices. This is the default: OpenGL uses $\mathbf{v} = (0, 0, 1)$, which points along the positive z-axis in camera coordinates. You can force the pipeline to compute the true value of $\mathbf{v}$ for each vertex by executing:

```
glLightModeli(GL_LIGHT_MODEL_LOCAL_VIEWER, GL_TRUE);
```

c. Are both sides of a polygon shaded properly?
   Each polygonal face in a model has two sides. When modeling, we tend to think of them as the "inside" and "outside" surfaces. The convention is to list the vertices of a face in counterclockwise (CCW) order as seen from outside the object. Most

---

[3]   This attenuation factor is disabled for directional light sources, since they are infinitely remote.

mesh objects represent solids that enclose space, so there is a well-defined inside and outside. For such objects the camera can see only the outside surface of each face (assuming the camera is not inside the object). With proper hidden surface removal, the inside surface of each face is hidden from the eye by some closer face.

OpenGL has no notion of inside and outside. It can only distinguish between "front faces" and "back faces." A face is a **front face** if its vertices are listed in counterclockwise (CCW) order as seen by the eye.[4] Figure 8.23a shows the eye viewing a cube, which we presume was modeled using the CCW ordering convention. Arrows indicate the order in which the vertices of each face are passed to OpenGL (in a `glBegin(GL_POLYGON);...; glEnd()` block). For a space-enclosing object all faces that are visible to the eye are therefore front faces, and OpenGL draws them properly with the correct shading. OpenGL also draws the back faces,[5] but they are ultimately hidden by closer front faces.

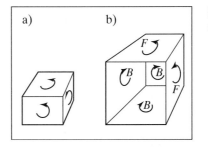

FIGURE 8.23 OpenGL's definition of a front face.

Things are different in part b, which shows a box with a face removed. Again arrows indicate the order in which vertices of a face are sent down the pipeline. Now three of the visible faces are back faces. By default OpenGL does not shade these properly. To coerce OpenGL to do proper shading of back faces, use:

```
glLightModeli(GL_LIGHT_MODEL_TWO_SIDE, GL_TRUE);
```

Then OpenGL reverses the normal vectors of any back face so that they point toward the viewer, and it performs shading computations properly. Replace GL_TRUE with GL_FALSE (the default) to turn off this facility.

Note. Faces drawn by OpenGL do not cast shadows, so the back faces receive the same light from a source, even though there may be some other face between them and the source.

Moving Light Sources

Recall that light sources pass through the modelview matrix just as vertices do. Therefore lights can be repositioned by suitable uses of `glRotated()` and `glTranslated()`. The array `position` specified using `glLightfv(GL_LIGHT0, GL_POSITION, position)` is modified by the modelview matrix in effect at the time `glLightfv()` is called. So to modify the light position with transformations, and independently move the camera, imbed the light-positioning command in a push/pop pair, as in:

---

[4] You can reverse this sense with `glFrontFace(GL_CW)`, which decrees that a face is a front face only if its vertices are listed in clockwise order. The default is `glFrontFace(GL_CCW)`.

[5] You can improve performance by instructing OpenGL to skip rendering of back faces, with `glCullFace(GL_BACK); glEnable(GL_CULL_FACE);`

```
void display()
{
    GLfloat position[] = {2, 1, 3, 1}; //initial light position
    <.. clear color and depth buffers ..>
    glMatrixMode(GL_MODELVIEW);
    glLoadIdentity();
    glPushMatrix();
      glRotated(...); // move the light
      glTranslated(...);
      glLightfv(GL_LIGHT0, GL_POSITION, position);
    glPopMatrix();

    gluLookAt(...); // set the camera position
    <.. draw the object ..>
    glutSwapBuffers();
}
```

On the other hand, to have the light move with the camera, use:

```
GLfloat pos[] = {0,0,0,1};
glMatrixMode(GL_MODELVIEW);
glLoadIdentity();
glLightfv(GL_LIGHT0, GL_POSITION, pos);// light at (0,0,0)
gluLookAt(...); // move the light and the camera
    <.. draw the object ..>
```

This establishes the light to be positioned at the eye (like a minor's lamp), and the light moves with the camera.

8.2.9 To Work with Material Properties in OpenGL

You can see the effect of a light source only when light reflects off an object's surface. OpenGL provides ways to specify the various reflection coefficients that appear in Equation (8.7). They are set with variations of the function glMaterial, and they can be specified individually for front faces and back faces (see the discussion concerning Figure 8.23). For instance,

```
GLfloat myDiffuse[] = {0.8, 0.2, 0.0, 1.0};
glMaterialfv(GL_FRONT, GL_DIFFUSE, myDiffuse);
```

sets the diffuse reflection coefficient $(\rho_{dr}, \rho_{dg}, \rho_{db}) = (0.8, 0.2, 0.0)$ for all subsequently specified front faces. Reflection coefficients are specified as a 4-tuple in RBGA format, just like a color. The first parameter of glMaterialfv() can take on values:

GL_FRONT: set the reflection coefficient vector for front faces
GL_BACK: set it for back faces
GL_FRONT_AND_BACK: set it for both front and back faces

The second parameter can take on values:

GL_AMBIENT: set the ambient reflection coefficients
GL_DIFFUSE: set the diffuse reflection coefficients
GL_SPECULAR: set the specular reflection coefficients
GL_AMBIENT_AND_DIFFUSE: set both the ambient and diffuse reflection coefficients to the same values. This is for convenience, since the ambient and diffuse coefficients are so often chosen to be the same.
GL_EMISSION: set the emissive color of the surface.

The last choice sets the **emissive color** of a face, causing it to "glow" in the specified color, independent of any light source.

Putting It All Together

We now extend Equation (8.7) to include the additional contributions that OpenGL actually calculates. The total red component is given by:

$$I_r = e_r + I_{mr}\rho_{ar}$$

$$+ \sum_i atten_i \times spot_i \times (I_{ar}^i\rho_{ar} + I_{dr}^i\rho_{dr} \times lambert_i + I_{spr}^i\rho_{sr} \times phong_i^f) \quad (8.12)$$

Expressions for the green and blue components are similar. The emissive light is e_r, and I_{mr} is the global ambient light introduced in the lighting model. The summation states that the ambient, diffuse, and specular contributions of all light sources are summed. For the ith source $atten_i$ is the attenuation factor as in Equation (8.10), $spot_i$ is the spotlight factor (see Figure 8.22), and $lambert_i$ and $phong_i$ are the familiar diffuse and specular dot products. All of these terms must be recalculated for each source.

Note: If I_r turns out to have a value larger than 1.0, OpenGL clamps it to 1.0: the brightest any light component can be is 1.0.

8.2.10 Shading of Scenes Specified by SDL

The scene description language SDL introduced in Chapter 5 and Appendix 3 supports the loading of certain material properties into objects, so that they can be shaded properly. For instance,

```
light 3 4 5 .8 .8 .8 ! bright white light at (3, 4, 5)
background 1 1 1 ! white background
globalAmbient .2 .2 .2 ! a dark gray global ambient light
ambient .2 .6 0
diffuse .8 .2. 1 ! red material
specular 1 1 1 ! bright specular spots - the color of the source
exponent 20 !set the Phong exponent
scale 4 4 4 sphere
```

describes a scene containing a sphere with material properties [see Equation (8.7)]:

- ambient reflection coefficients: $(\rho_{ar}, \rho_{ag}, \rho_{ab}) = (0.2, 0.6, 0)$
- diffuse reflection coefficients: $(\rho_{dr}, \rho_{dg}, \rho_{db}) = (0.8, 0.2, 1.0)$
- specular reflection coefficients: $(\rho_{sr}, \rho_{sg}, \rho_{sb}) = (1.0, 1.0, 1.0)$
- and *Phong* exponent $f = 20$.

The light source is given a color of $(0.8, 0.8, 0.8)$ for both its diffuse and specular components. There is a global ambient term $(I_{ar}, I_{ag}, I_{ab}) = (0.2, 0.2, 0.2)$.

The current material properties are loaded into each object's mtrl field at the time it is created (see the end of Scene :: getObject() in the source example Shape.cpp of Appendix 3 and online). When an object draws itself using its drawOpenGL() method, it first passes its material properties to OpenGL (see Shape:: tellMaterialsGL()), so that at the moment it is actually drawn, OpenGL has these properties in its current state.

When we describe ray tracing in Chapter 12 we shall use each object's material field in a similar way to acquire the material properties and do proper shading.

8.3 FLAT SHADING AND SMOOTH SHADING

*I never saw an ugly thing in my life: for let the form of an object be what it may, light, shade,
and perspective will always make it beautiful.*

John Constable
(1776–1837)

Different objects require different shading effects. In Chapter 6 we modeled a variety of shapes using polygonal meshes. For some, like the barn or Buckyball, we want to see the individual faces in a picture, but for others, like the sphere or chess pawn, we want to see the surface that the faces approximate, and we want the visibility of the edges to be suppressed.

In the modeling process we attached a normal vector to each vertex of each face. To recapitulate, if a certain face is to appear as a distinct polygon, we attach the *same* normal vector to all of its vertices; the normal vector chosen is the normal direction to the plane of that face. On the other hand, if the face is supposed to approximate an underlying surface, we attach to each vertex the normal to the underlying surface at that point.

We examine now how the normal vector information at each vertex is used to perform different kinds of shading. The main distinction is between a shading method that accentuates the individual polygons (flat shading) and a method that blends the faces to de-emphasize the edges between them (smooth shading). There are two kinds of smooth shading, called *Gouraud* and *Phong* shading. We shall discuss both. Notice that some authors prefer to use the term "illumination model" rather than "shading model" when discussing these topics.

For both kinds of shading the vertices are passed down the graphics pipeline, illumination calculations are performed to attach a color to each vertex, and ultimately the vertices of the face are converted to screen coordinates and the face is painted pixel by pixel with the appropriate color.

Painting a Face

The face is colored using a polygon-fill routine. Filling a polygon is very simple, although fine-tuning the fill algorithm for highest efficiency can be very complex. (See Chapter 9.) Here we look at the basics, focusing on how the color of each pixel is set.

A polygon-fill routine is sometimes called a **tiler**, because it moves over the polygon pixel by pixel, coloring each pixel as appropriate, as one might lay down tiles on a parquet floor. Specifically, the pixels in a polygon are visited in a regular order, usually scanline by scanline from the bottom to the top of the polygon, and across each scanline from left to right.

We assume here that the polygons of interest are *convex*. A tiler designed to fill only convex polygons can be made highly efficient, since at each scanline there is a single unbroken run of pixels that lie inside the polygon. Most implementations of OpenGL exploit this and always fill convex polygons correctly, but do not guarantee to fill nonconvex polygons properly. See the exercises for more thoughts on convexity.

Figure 8.24 shows an example where the face is a convex quadrilateral. The screen coordinates of each vertex are noted. The lowest and highest points on the face are y_{bot} and y_{top}, respectively. The tiler first fills in the row at $y = y_{bot}$ (in this case a single pixel), then the one at $y_{bot} + 1$, and so on. At each scanline, say y_s in the figure, there is a leftmost pixel, at x_{left}, and a rightmost pixel, at x_{right}. The tiler moves from x_{left} to x_{right}, placing the desired color in each pixel. So the tiler is implemented as a simple double loop, looking in pseudocode like:

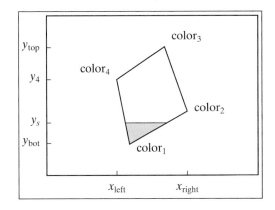

FIGURE 8.24 Filling a polygonal face with color.

```
for (int y = ybot; y <= ytop; y++)    // for each scanline
{
    <.. find xleft and xright ..>
    for (int x = xleft; x <= xright; x++) // for each relevant pixel
    across this scanline
    {
        <.. find the color c for this pixel ..>
        <.. put c into the pixel at (x, y) ..>
    }
}
```

Hidden surface removal is also easily accomplished within this double loop. The principal difference between flat and smooth shading is the manner in which the color c is determined at each pixel.

8.3.1 Flat Shading and Mach Banding

When a face is flat (like the roof of a barn) and the light sources are quite distant, the diffuse light component varies little over different points on the roof. The *lambert* term in Equation (8.6) is nearly the same at each vertex of the face, since the vector from each point to the source is approximately the same. In such cases it is reasonable to use the same color for every pixel within the convex face. OpenGL offers a rendering mode in which the entire face is drawn with the same color. Although a color is passed down the pipeline as part of each vertex of the face, the painting algorithm uses only one of them (usually that of the first vertex in the face). So the command in the preceding pseudocode, `<find the color c for this pixel>`, is not inside both loops but instead appears just prior to the inside loop, setting c to the color of one of the vertices. (Using the same color for every pixel tends to make flat shading quite fast.)

OpenGL can be instructed to do flat shading using:

```
glShadeModel(GL_FLAT);
```

Figure 8.25 shows a Buckyball and a sphere rendered using flat shading. The individual faces of the Buckyball in part a are clearly visible, as desired. The sphere might instead be considered as a smooth object, but no smoothing takes place when we use `glShadeModel(GL_FLAT);` since the color of an entire face is set to that of only one vertex.

An illusion, the origin of which is not completely understood, causes the edges between faces actually to appear more pronounced than they "are", due to a phenomenon in the eye known as **lateral inhibition**, first described by Ernst Mach.[6] When there is a discontinuity in the gradient of intensity across an object, the eye manufactures a

---

[6] Ernst Mach (1838–1916) was an Austrian physicist whose early work strongly influenced the theory of relativity his name is also used as a measure of the speed of planes and rockets, relative to the speed of sound, as in "Mach 2" and "Mach 4."

FIGURE 8.25 Two meshes rendered using flat shading. a) a buckyball; b) a sphere.

a)   b)

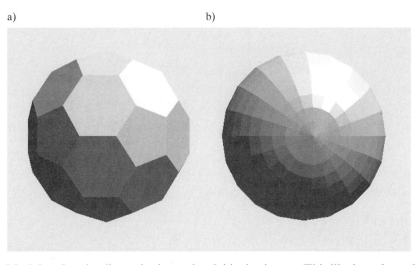

Mach band at the discontinuity, and a vivid edge is seen. This illusion of an edge can be distracting.

(*Experiment for seeing Mach bands:* Choose a face and an edge on the Buckyball for which the left neighboring face is darker than the right neighboring face. Can you see the narrow band close to and parallel to the edge that is darker on the *left* face (surprisingly) than on the right face? It's quite subtle.) This exaggerates the polygonal look of mesh objects rendered with flat shading. Mach bands are also clearly visible in the sphere of part b.

Specular highlights are rendered poorly with flat shading, again because an entire face is filled with a color that was computed at only one vertex. If there happens to be a large specular component at the representative vertex, that brightness is drawn uniformly over the entire face. If a specular highlight doesn't fall on the representative point, it is missed entirely. For this reason, there is little incentive for including the specular reflection component in the shading computation.

8.3.2 Smooth Shading

Smooth shading attempts to de-emphasize edges between faces by computing colors at more points on each face. There are two principal types of smooth shading, Gouraud shading and Phong shading [Gouraud71, Phong75]. These techniques should more properly be called "Gouraud and Phong interpolation", as they deal with blending colors at different points. OpenGL performs only Gouraud shading, but we describe both of them.

Gouraud shading computes a different value of c for each pixel. For the scanline at y_s (in Figure 8.24) it finds the color at the leftmost pixel, $color_{left}$, by linear interpolation of the colors at the top and bottom of the left edge.[7] For the scanline at y_s the color at the top is $color_4$ and that at the bottom is $color_1$, so $color_{left}$ would be calculated as [recall Equation (8.9)]:

$$color_{left} = \text{lerp}(color_1, color_4, f) \qquad (8.13)$$

where f is the fraction of the way that y_s lies between y_4 and y_{bot};

As y_s varies between y_4 and y_{bot}, f varies between 0 and 1. Note that Equation (8.13) involves three calculations, since each color quantity has a red, green, and blue component.

---

[7] We shall see later that, although colors are usually interpolated *linearly* as we do here, better results can be obtained by using so-called *hyperbolic interpolation*. For simple shading the distinction is minor; for texture mapping it is crucial.

Similarly $color_{right}$ is found by interpolating the colors at the top and bottom of the right edge. The tiler then fills across the scanline, linearly interpolating between $color_{left}$ and $color_{right}$ to obtain the color at pixel x:

$$c(x) = \text{lerp}\left(color_{left}, color_{right}, \frac{x - x_{left}}{x_{right} - x_{left}}\right) \qquad (8.14)$$

To increase efficiency this color is computed incrementally at each pixel. That is, there is a constant difference between $c(x + 1)$ and $c(x)$, so

$$c(x + 1) = c(x) + \frac{color_{right} - color_{left}}{x_{right} - x_{left}} \qquad (8.15)$$

Gouraud shading is modestly more expensive computationally than flat shading. Gouraud shading is established in OpenGL using:

```
glShadeModel(GL_SMOOTH);
```

Figure 8.26 shows a Buckyball and a sphere rendered using Gouraud shading. The Buckyball looks the same as when it was flat shaded in Figure 8.25, because the same color is associated with each vertex of a face, so interpolation changes nothing. But the sphere looks much smoother. There are no abrupt jumps in color between neighboring faces. The edges of the faces (and the Mach bands) are gone, replaced by a smoothly varying color across the object. Along the silhouette, however, you can still see the bounding edges of individual faces.

a)   b)

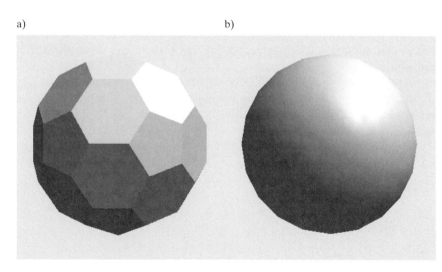

FIGURE 8.26 Two meshes rendered using smooth shading. a) a buckyball; b) a sphere.

Why do the edges disappear with this technique? Figure 8.27a shows two faces, F and F', that share an edge when the object is supposed to exhibit its individual faces. When rendering F the colors c_L and c_R are used, and when rendering F' the colors c_L' and c_R' are used. But since c_R' equals c_L', there is an abrupt change in color at the edge along the scanline as desired. Both c_L and c_R are calculated using normals that are found by averaging the face normals of all the faces that abut the edge.

Figure 8.27b suggests how this technique reveals the underlying surface approximated by the mesh, when a picture of a smooth object is desired. The polygonal surface is shown in cross section, with vertices V_1, V_2, and so on marked. The imaginary smooth surface that the mesh supposedly represents is suggested as well. Properly computed vertex normals $\mathbf{m}_1, \mathbf{m}_2$, and so on point perpendicularly to this imaginary surface, so the normal for correct shading is being used at each vertex, and the color thereby found is correct. The color is then made to vary smoothly between vertices, following no physical law but rather a simple mathematical one; based on interpolation.

FIGURE 8.27 Continuity of color across a polygon edge. a) a 3D view of an object with sharp edges; b) a cross-sectional view of a smoothly curved object.

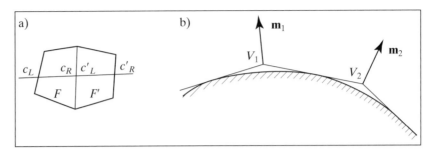

Because colors are formed by interpolating rather than by computation at every pixel, Gouraud shading does not picture highlights well. Therefore, when Gouraud shading is used, one normally suppresses the specular component of intensity in Equation (8.12). Highlights are better reproduced using Phong shading, discussed next.

Phong Shading

Greater realism can be achieved—particularly with regard to highlights on shiny objects—by a better approximation of the normal vector to the face at each pixel. This type of shading is called **Phong shading**, after its inventor Phong Bui-tuong [Phong75].

When computing Phong shading we find the normal vector *at each point* on the face and we apply the shading model there to find the color. We compute the normal vector at each pixel by interpolating the normal vectors at the vertices of the polygon.

Figure 8.28 shows a projected face, with the normal vectors m_1, m_2, m_3, and m_4 indicated at the four vertices. For the scanline y_s as shown, the vectors m_{left} and m_{right} are found by linear interpolation.

FIGURE 8.28 Interpolating normals.

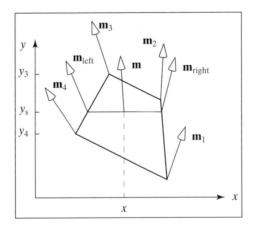

This interpolated vector must be normalized to unit length before its use in the shading formula. Once m_{left} and m_{right} are known, they are interpolated to form a normal vector at each x along the scanline. This vector, once normalized, is used in the shading calculation to form the color at that pixel.

Figure 8.29 shows an object rendered using Gouraud shading and Phong shading. Because the direction of the normal vector varies smoothly from point to point and

a)   b)

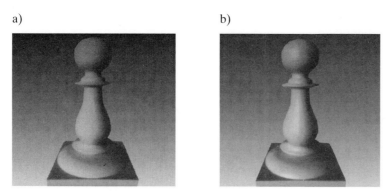

FIGURE 8.29 Comparison of a) Gouraud and b) Phong shading. (Courtesy of Bishop and Weimar, 1986)

more closely approximates that of an underlying smooth surface, the production of specular highlights is much more faithful than with Gouraud shading, and more realistic renderings are produced.

The principal drawback of Phong shading is the amount of computation required per pixel: such that a Phong shading can take six to eight times longer than Gouraud shading to perform. A number of approaches have been suggested to speed up the process [Bishop86, Claussen90].

OpenGL is not set up to do Phong shading, since it applies the illumination model once per vertex right after the modelview transformation, and normal vector information is not passed to the rendering stage following the perspective transformation and perspective divide. We will see in Section 8.5, however, that an approximation to Phong shading can be created by mapping a highlight texture onto an object using the environment mapping technique.

PRACTICE EXERCISES

8.3.1 Filling your face

Fill in details of how the polygon-fill algorithm operates for the polygon with vertices $(x, y) = (23, 137), (120, 204), (200, 100), (100, 25)$, for scanlines $y = 136$, $y = 137$, and $y = 138$. Specifically write the values of x_{left} and x_{right} in each case.

8.3.2 Retaining edges with Gouraud shading

In some cases we may want to show specific creases and edges in the model. Discuss how this can be controlled by the choice of the vertex normal vectors. For instance, to retain the edge between faces F and F' in Figure 8.27, what should the vertex normals be? Other tricks and issues can be found in the references [e.g., Rogers85].

8.3.3 Faster Phong shading with fence shading

To increase the speed of Phong shading, Behrens [Behrens94] suggests interpolating normal vectors between vertices to get $\mathbf{m}_L$ and $\mathbf{m}_R$ in the usual way at each scanline, but then computing colors only at these left and right pixels, interpolating them along a scanline as in Gouraud shading. This so-called "fence shading" speeds up rendering dramatically, but does less well in rendering highlights than true Phong shading. Describe general directions for the vertex normals $\mathbf{m}_1, \mathbf{m}_2, \mathbf{m}_3$, and $\mathbf{m}_4$ in Figure 8.28 such that

a. Fence shading produces the same highlights as Phong shading;
b. Fence shading produces very different highlights from Phong shading.

8.3.4 The Phong shading algorithm

Make the necessary changes to the tiling code to incorporate Phong shading. Assume the vertex normal vectors are available for each face. Also discuss how Phong shading can be approximated by OpenGL's smooth shading algorithm. *Hint:* Increase the number of faces in the model. ▪

8.4 ADDING HIDDEN SURFACE REMOVAL

> Three things cannot be long hidden: the sun, the moon, and the truth.
>
> *Gautama Buddha*
> *(563–483* B.C.*)*

It is very simple to incorporate hidden surface removal in the rendering process discussed earlier if enough memory is available to have a **depth buffer** (also called a "z-buffer"). Because it fits so easily into the rendering mechanisms we are discussing, we include it here.

8.4.1 The Depth-Buffer Approach—The Method OpenGL Uses

The depth-buffer (or z-buffer) algorithm is one of the simplest and most easily implemented hidden surface removal methods. It is the method used by OpenGL. Its principal limitations are that it requires a large amount of memory and it often renders an object that is later obscured by a nearer object (so time spent rendering the more remote object is wasted).

Figure 8.30 shows a depth buffer associated with the frame buffer. For every pixel $p[i][j]$ on the display the depth buffer stores a b bit quantity $d[i][j]$. The value of b is usually chosen to lie the range of 12 to 30 bits.

FIGURE 8.30 Conceptual view of the depth buffer.

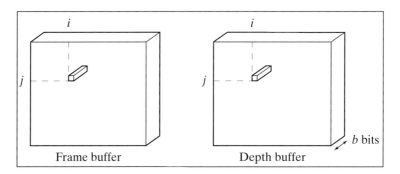

| Frame buffer | Depth buffer |

During the rendering process the depth-buffer value $d[i][j]$ contains the pseudodepth of the closest object encountered (so far) (this is what requires memory of the closest object) at that pixel. As the tiler proceeds pixel by pixel across a scanline filling the current face, it tests whether the pseudodepth of the current face is less than the depth $d[i][j]$ stored in the depth buffer at that point. If so, the color of the closer surface replaces the color $p[i][j]$, and this smaller pseudodepth replaces the old value in $d[i][j]$. Faces can be drawn in any order. If a remote face is drawn first, some of the pixels that show that face will later be replaced by the colors of a nearer face. The time spent rendering the more remote face is therefore wasted. Note that this algorithm works for objects of any shape, including curved surfaces, because it finds the closest surface based on a point-by-point test.

To summarize

- *at each pixel ij, p[i][j] holds the color of the nearest face found so far at that point on the screen;*
- *d[i][j] holds the pseudodepth of the nearest face found so far at that point on the screen.*

8.5 TO ADD TEXTURE TO FACES

I found Rome a city of bricks and left it a city of marble.

from Suetonius, Lives of the Caesars
Caesar Augustus
(c. 63 B.C.–A.D. *14),*

The realism of an image, as well as its charm and appeal to the observer, are greatly enhanced by adding surface texture to the various faces of a mesh object. Figure 8.32 show some examples. In part a images have been pasted onto some of the faces of a cube. In part b a label has been wrapped around a cylindrical can, and the wall behind the can appears to be made of bricks.

a)   b)

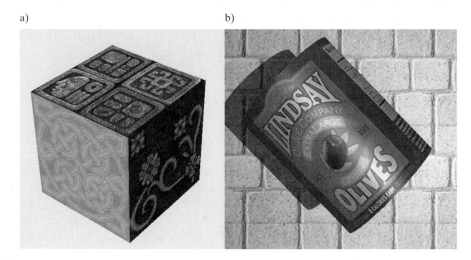

FIGURE 8.32 Examples of texture mapped onto surfaces. a) a texture images mapped onto the surfaces of a cube; b) a texture image wrapped about a can, and pasted onto a wall behind the can.

The basic technique begins with a collection of texture functions defined in "**texture space**," such as those shown in Figure 8.33. Texture space is conventionally marked off by parameters named s and t. The texture is a function texture(s, t) that produces a color or intensity value for each value of s and t between 0 and 1.

We must see how texture is attached to points on an object, but first we look at some sources of different kinds of textures.

Various Sources of Textures

The most common sources of textures are bitmaps (a matrix-like array of pixels) and computed functions. Figure 8.33a shows another example of a bitmap, whereas part b shows an (artificial) image formed according to some calculated function.

Bitmap Textures

Textures are often formed from bitmap representations of images (such as a digitized photo, digital camera image, clip art, or an image previously generated in some program.) In addition, the World Wide Web famously offers a gigantic number of interesting textures. Such a texture consists of a 2D array, say `txtr[r][c]`, of color values (often called "**texels**"). Our first task is to associate the proper item in the array `txtr[r][c]` with given values of s and t between 0 and 1. Suppose the array `txtr[][]` has c columns and r rows.

a)

b)

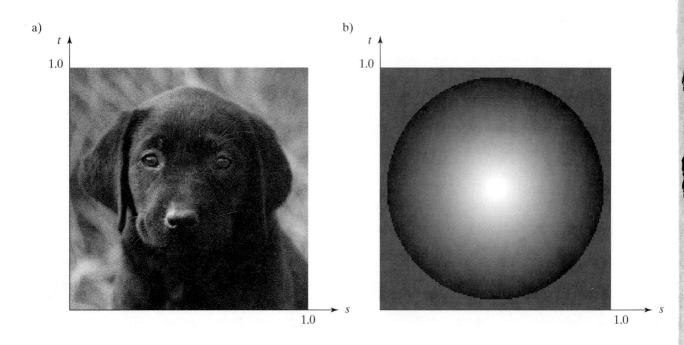

FIGURE 8.33 Examples of textures: a) image texture, b) procedural generation of a texture map.

Procedural Generation of a Texture Map

Alternatively, we can define a texture by a mathematical function or procedure. Because such functions are usually created in the mind of the programmer, there is a lot of freedom in describing them. For instance, the sphere shown in Figure 8.33b is centered, at least in 2D at $(s, t) = (0.5, 0.5)$ and has a radius of 0.5, so the distance from its center to the point (s, t) is:

$$\sqrt{(s - 0.5)^2 + (t - 0.5)^2}$$

The spherical texture in Figure 8.31b could be generated by the function:

```
float fakeSphere (float s, float t)
{
   float r = sqrt((s-0.5)*(s-0.5)+(t-0.5)*(t-0.5));
/* distance from sphere's center to (s,t). */
   if(r < 0.3) return 1 - r/0.3;
/* sphere intensity brightest at the center; dark along the edges */
   else return 0.2; // dark background
}*/
```

This function varies from 1 (white) at the center to 0 (black) at the edges (along the axes) of the apparent sphere. The value 0.3 in the preceding function allows the darkest intensity in the sphere to blend smoothly with the background intensity. Another example that mimics a checkerboard is examined in the exercises. Any function that can be computed for each value of s and t can provide a texture: smooth blends and swirls of color, the Mandelbrot set (discussed in the appendix), wireframe drawings of solids, and so on.

We see later that the value texture(s, t) can be *used* in a variety of ways: it can be used as the color of the face itself as if the face were glowing; it can be used as the ambient, diffuse, or specular reflection coefficients to modulate the amount of light reflected from the face; it can be used to alter the normal vector to the surface to give the object a bumpy appearance.

PRACTICE EXERCISE

8.5.1 The classic checkerboard texture

Figure 8.34 shows a checkerboard consisting of 5-by-5 squares with brightness levels that alternate between 0 (for black) and 1 (for white).

a. Write the function `float texture(float s, float t)` for this texture. (See also Exercise 2.3.1.) ■

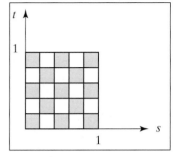

FIGURE 8.34 A classic checkerboard pattern.

With a texture function in hand, the next step is to map it properly onto the desired surface, and then to view it with a camera. Figure 8.35 shows an example that illustrates the overall problem. Here a single example of texture is mapped onto two different objects: a planar polygon and a cylinder. For each object there is some transformation, say T_{tw} (for texture to world) that maps texture (s, t) values to points (x, y, z) on the object's surface. The camera takes a snapshot of the scene from some angle, producing the view shown. We call the transformation from points in 3D to points on the screen T_{ws} (from world to screen), so a point (x, y, z) on a surface is seen at pixel location $(sx, sy) = T_{ws}(x, y, z)$. So overall, the value (s^*, t^*) on the texture finally arrives at pixel $(sx, sy) = T_{ws}(T_{tw}(s^*, t^*))$.

The rendering process actually goes the other way: for each pixel at (sx, sy) there is a sequence of questions:

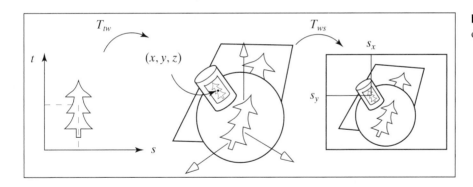

FIGURE 8.35 Drawing texture onto a cylinder and plane.

a. What is the closest surface seen at (sx, sy)? To answer this requires solving the hidden surface removal problem, at least for this pixel, in order to determine which texture is relevant.
b. To what point (x, y, z) on this surface does (sx, sy) correspond?
c. To which texture coordinate pair (s, t) does this point (x, y, z) correspond?

So we need the inverse transformation, something like $(s, t) = T_{tw}^{-1}(T_{ws}^{-1}(sx, sy))$, that reports (s, t) coordinates given pixel coordinates. This inverse transformation can be hard to obtain or easy to obtain, depending on the surface shapes.

8.5.1 Paste the Texture onto a Flat Surface

We first examine the most important case: mapping texture onto a flat surface. This is a modeling task. We tackle the viewing task subsequently to see how the texture is actually rendered. We then discuss mapping textures onto more complicated surface shapes.

Pasting Texture onto a Flat Face

Since texture space itself is flat, it is simplest to paste texture onto a flat surface. Figure 8.36 shows a texture image (inside a pentagon) mapped to a portion of a planar polygon (another pentagon) F. We must specify how to associate points on the texture with points on F. In OpenGL we associate a point in texture space $P_i = (s_i, t_i)$ with each *vertex* V_i of the face using the function $\texttt{glTexCoord2f()}$. The function $\texttt{glTexCoord2f(s,t)}$ sets the current texture coordinates to (s, t), and they are attached to subsequently defined vertices. Normally each call to $\texttt{glVertex3f()}$ is preceded by a call to $\texttt{glTexCoord2f()}$, whereupon each vertex gets a new pair of texture coordinates. For example, to define a quadrilateral face and to position a texture on it, we send OpenGL four texture coordinates and the four 3D points, as in:

```
gBegin(GL_QUADS); // define a quadrilateral and position our
                  // texture on it
    glTexCoord2f(0.0, 0.0); glVertex3f(1.0, 2.5, 1.5);
    glTexCoord2f(0.0, 0.6); glVertex3f(1.0, 3.7, 1.5);
    glTexCoord2f(0.8, 0.6); glVertex3f(2.0, 3.7, 1.5);
    glTexCoord2f(0.8, 0.0); glVertex3f(2.0, 2.5, 1.5);
glEnd();
```

FIGURE 8.36 Mapping texture onto a planar polygon.

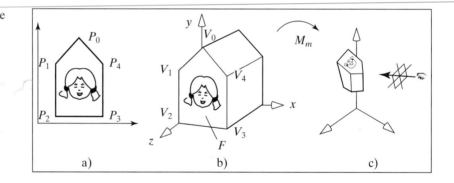

a)   b)   c)

Visualize the effect of altering the texture coordinates above that are associated with each of the four vertices.

Attaching a P_i to each V_i is equivalent to prescribing a polygon P in texture space that has the same number of vertices as F. Usually P has the same shape as F as well: then the portion of the texture that lies inside P (say, the upper left quadrant of the dog image in Figure 8.31a) is pasted without distortion onto the whole of F. When P and F have the same shape, the mapping is clearly affine: it is a scaling, possibly accompanied by a rotation and a translation.

Figure 8.37 shows a common case where the four corners of a texture rectangle are associated with the four corners of a face in the 3D scene. (The texture coordinates (s, t) associated with each corner are noted on the 3D face.) In this example the texture is a 640-by-480 pixel bitmap, and it is pasted onto a rectangle with aspect ratio 640/480, so it appears without distortion. (*Note:* The texture coordinates s and t still vary from 0 to 1.) Figure 8.38 shows the use of texture coordinates that **tile** the texture, making it repeat. To do this, some texture coordinates that lie outside of the interval [0,1] are used. When the renderer encounters a value of s and t outside of

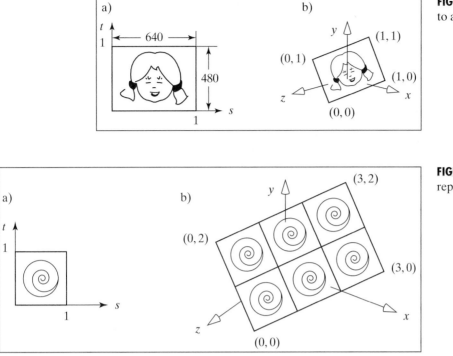

FIGURE 8.37 Mapping a square to a rectangle.

FIGURE 8.38 Producing repeated textures.

the unit square, such as $s = 2.67$, it ignores the integral part and uses only the fractional part, 0.67. Thus, the point on a face that requires $(s, t) = (2.6, 3.77)$ is textured with texture(0.6, 0.77). By default OpenGL tiles texture this way. If desired, it may be set to "clamp" texture values instead; see the exercises.

Thus a coordinate pair (s, t) is sent down the pipeline along with each vertex of the face. As we describe in the next section, the notion is that points inside F will be filled with texture values lying inside P, by finding the internal coordinate values (s, t) using interpolation. This interpolation process is described in the next section.

To Add Texture Coordinates to Mesh Objects

Recall from code from Chapter 6 that a mesh object has three lists: the vertex list, the list of normal vectors, and the face list. We must add to this a texture coordinate list that stores the coordinates (s_i, t_i) to be associated with various vertices. To this end we add an array of elements. Each element is a pair of float numbers from the class TxtrCoord, whose definition begins with

```
class TxtrCoord { public: float s, t; };
```

The array holds all of the coordinate pairs of interest for the mesh. There are several different ways to treat texture for an object, each having implications for how texture information is organized in the model. The two most important ways are:

1. The mesh object consists of a small number of flat faces, and a different texture is to be applied to each face. Here each face has only a single normal vector but its own list of texture coordinates. So the data associated with each face would be:
   • the number of vertices in the face;
   • the index of the normal vector to the face;
   • a list of indices of the vertices;
   • a list of indices of the texture coordinates.

2. The mesh represents a smooth underlying object, and a single texture is to be wrapped around it (or a portion of it). Here each vertex has associated with it a specific normal vector and a particular texture coordinate pair. A single index into the vertex, normal, and texture lists is used for each vertex. The data associated with each face would then be:
   - the number of vertices in the face;
   - a list of indices of the vertices.

The exercises take a further look at the required data structures for these types of meshes.

8.5.2 To Render the Texture

Rendering texture in a face F is similar to Gouraud shading: the renderer moves across the face pixel by pixel. For each pixel it must determine the corresponding texture coordinates (s, t), access the texture and set the pixel to the proper texture color. We shall see that finding the coordinates (s, t) must be done very carefully.

Figure 8.39 shows the camera taking a snapshot of face F with texture pasted onto it, and the rendering in progress. Scanline y is being filled from x_{left} to x_{right}. For each x along this scanline we must compute the correct position (shown as $P(x, y)$) on the face, and from this obtain the correct position (s^*, t^*) within the texture.

FIGURE 8.39 Rendering the face in a camera snapshot.

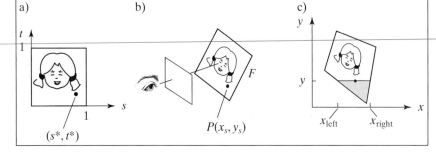

Having set up the texture-to-object mapping, we know the texture coordinates at each of the vertices of F, as suggested in Figure 8.40. The natural thing is to compute (s_{left}, t_{left}) and (s_{right}, t_{right}) for each scanline in a rapid incremental fashion and to interpolate between these values moving across the scanline. But we must be careful: simple increments from s_{left} to s_{right} as we march across scanline y from x_{left} to x_{right} won't work, since equal steps across a projected face do *not* correspond to equal steps across the 3D face.

FIGURE 8.40 Incremental calculation of texture coordinates.

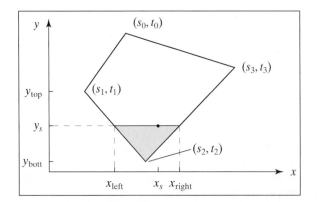

Figure 8.41 illustrates the problem. Part a shows face F viewed so that its left edge is closer to the viewer than its right edge. Part b shows the projection F' of this face on the screen. At scanline $y = 170$ we mark points equally spaced across F', suggesting the positions of successive pixels on the face. The corresponding positions of these marks on the actual face are shown in part a. They are seen to be more closely spaced at the farther end of F. This is simply the effect of perspective foreshortening.

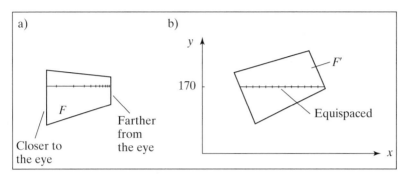

FIGURE 8.41 Spacing of samples with linear interpolation.

If we use simple linear interpolation and take equally spaced steps in s and t to compute texture coordinates, we sample into the texture at the wrong spots, and a distorted image results. Figure 8.41a shows what happens with a simple checkerboard texture mapped onto a rectangle. Linear interpolation is used in part a, producing palpable distortion in the texture. This distortion is particularly disturbing in an animation where the polygon is rotating, as the texture appears to warp and stretch dynamically. Correct interpolation is used in Figure 8.42, and the checkerboard looks as it should. In an animation this texture would appear to be firmly attached to the moving or rotating face. A complete working program is available online (`RotatingCube.cpp`), showing a rotating cube with different textures painted on each of the six sides. Figure 8.32 is a screen shot of the Rotating Cube program in action. As the cube rotates and incorrect interpolation is used, the six pasted images are seen to become distorted. With correct interpolation, however, there is no distortion on any face. We discuss next how code should be written properly to produce correct interpolation.

Several approaches have appeared in the literature that develop the proper interpolation method. Heckbert and Moreton [Heckbert91] and Blinn [Blinn92] describe an elegant development based on the general nature of affine and projective mappings. Segal et al. [Segal92] arrive at the same result using a more algebraic derivation based on the parametric representation for a line segment. We follow the latter approach here.

Figure 8.43 shows the situation to be analyzed. We know that affine and projective transformations preserve straightness, so line L_e in eye space projects to line L_s in screen space, and similarly the texels we wish to draw on line L_s lie along the line L_t in texture space that maps to L_e. The key question is this: if we move in equal steps across L_s on the screen, how should we step across texels along L_t in texture space?

We develop a general result next that summarizes how interpolation works: it all has to do with the effect of perspective division. Then we relate the general result to the transformations performed in the graphics pipeline, and we see precisely where extra steps must be taken to do proper mapping of texture.

FIGURE 8.42 Images formed using linear interpolation and correct interpolation.

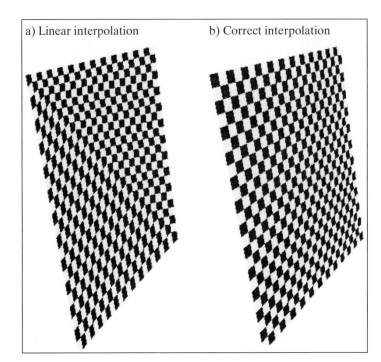

a) Linear interpolation   b) Correct interpolation

FIGURE 8.43 Lines in one space map to lines in another.

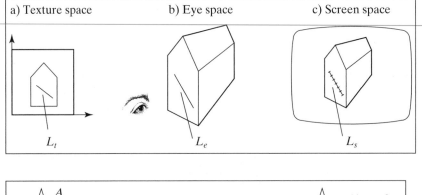

a) Texture space   b) Eye space   c) Screen space

L_t L_e L_s

FIGURE 8.44 How does motion along corresponding lines operate?

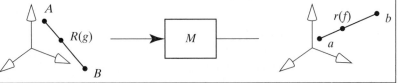

Figure 8.44 shows the line AB in 3D being transformed into the line ab in 3D by matrix M. (M might represent an affine transformation, or a more general perspective transformation.) Point A maps to a, B maps to b. Consider the point $R(g)$ that lies fraction g of the way between A and B. It maps to some point $r(f)$ that lies fraction f of the way from a to b. The fractions f and g are *not* the same, as we shall see. The question is, as f varies from 0 to 1, how exactly does g vary? That is, how does motion along ab correspond to motion along AB?

Deriving How g and f Are Related

We denote the homogeneous coordinate version of a by $\tilde{a}$, and name its components $\tilde{a} = (a_1, a_2, a_3, a_4)$. (We use subscripts 1, 2, 3, and 4 instead of x, y, and so on to prevent ambiguity, since there are so many different "x, y, z" spaces.) So point a is found from $\widetilde{a}$ by perspective division:

$$a = \left(\frac{a_1}{a_4}, \frac{a_2}{a_4}, \frac{a_3}{a_4}\right)$$

Since M maps $A = (A_1, A_2, A_3)$ to a, we know $\widetilde{a} = M(A, 1)^T$, where $(A, 1)^T$ is the column vector with components A_1, A_2, A_3, and 1. Similarly, $\widetilde{b} = M(B, 1)^T$. (Check each of these relations carefully.) Now using lerp() notation to keep things succinct, we have defined $R(g) = \text{lerp}(A, B, g)$, which maps to $M(\text{lerp}(A, B, g), 1)^T = \text{lerp}(\widetilde{a}, \widetilde{b}, g) = (\text{lerp}(a_1, b_1, g), \text{lerp}(a_2, b_2, g), \text{lerp}(a_3, b_3, g), \text{lerp}(a_4, b_4, g))$. (Check these, too.) This is the homogeneous coordinate version $\widetilde{r}(f)$ of the point $r(f)$. We recover the actual components of $r(f)$ by perspective division. For simplicity write just the first component $r_1(f)$, which is:

$$r_1(f) = \frac{\text{lerp}(a_1, b_1, g)}{\text{lerp}(a_4, b_4, g)} \tag{8.16}$$

But since by definition $r(f) = \text{lerp}(a, b, f)$, we have another expression for the first component $r_1(f)$:

$$r_1(f) = \text{lerp}\left(\frac{a_1}{a_4}, \frac{b_1}{b_4}, f\right) \tag{8.17}$$

Expressions (what are they?) for $r_2(f)$ and $r_3(f)$ follow similarly. Equate these two versions of $r_1(f)$ and do a little algebra to obtain the desired relationship between f and g:

$$g = \frac{f}{\text{lerp}\left(\dfrac{b_4}{a_4}, 1, f\right)} \tag{8.18}$$

Therefore the point $R(g)$ maps to $r(f)$, but g and f aren't the same fraction. g matches at $f = 0$ and at $f = 1$, but its growth with f is tempered by a denominator that depends on the ratio b_4/a_4. If a_4 equals b_4 then g is identical to f (check this). Figure 8.45 shows how g varies with f, for different values of b_4/a_4.

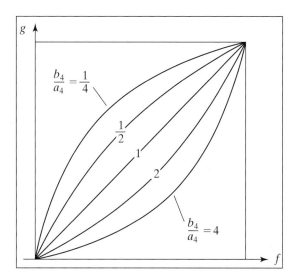

FIGURE 8.45 How g depends on f.

We can go the final step and show where the point $R(g)$ is on the 3D face that maps into $r(f)$. Simply use Equation (8.17) in $R(g) = A(1 - g) + Bg$ and simplify algebraically (check this out) to obtain for the first component:

$$R_1 = \frac{\text{lerp}\left(\dfrac{A_1}{a_4}, \dfrac{B_1}{b_4}, f\right)}{\text{lerp}\left(\dfrac{1}{a_4}, \dfrac{1}{b_4}, f\right)} \tag{8.19}$$

with similar expressions resulting for the components R_2 and R_3 (which have the *same* denominator as R_1). This is a key result. It tells which 3D point (R_1, R_2, R_3) corresponds (in eye coordinates) to a given point that lies (fraction f of the way) between two given points a and b in screen coordinates. So any quantity (such as texture) that is attached to vertices of the 3D face and varies linearly between them will behave the same way.

The two cases of interest for the transformation with matrix M are:

- The transformation is affine.
- The transformation is the perspective transformation.

a. When the transformation is affine, then a_4 and b_4 are both 1 (why?), so the formulas above simplify immediately. The fractions f and g become identical, and R_1 above becomes $\text{lerp}(A_1, B_1, f)$. We can summarize this as:

> **Fact**: If M is *affine*, equal steps along the line ab *do* correspond to equal steps along the line AB.

b. When M represents the perspective transformation from eye coordinates to clip coordinates, the fourth components a_4 and b_4 are no longer 1. We developed the matrix M in Chapter 7. Its basic form, given in Equation (7.10), is:

$$M = \begin{pmatrix} N & 0 & 0 & 0 \\ 0 & N & 0 & 0 \\ 0 & 0 & c & d \\ 0 & 0 & -1 & 0 \end{pmatrix}$$

where c and d are constants that make pseudodepth work properly. What is $M(A, 1)^T$ for this matrix? It's $\tilde{a} = (NA_1, NA_2, cA_3 + d, -A_3)$, the crucial part being that $a_4 = -A_3$. This is the position of the point along the z-axis in camera coordinates—that is, the depth of the point in front of the eye.

So the relative sizes of a_4 and b_4 lie at the heart of perspective foreshortening of a line segment: they report the "depths" of A and B, respectively, along the camera's viewplane normal. If A and B have the same depth (i.e., they lie in a plane parallel to the camera's viewplane), there is no perspective distortion along the segment, so g and f are indeed the same. Figure 8.46 shows in cross section how rays from the eye through evenly spaced spots (those with equal increments in f) on the viewplane correspond to unevenly spaced spots on the original face in 3D. For the case shown, A is closer than B, causing $a_4 < b_4$, so the g-increments grow in size as they move across the face from A to B.

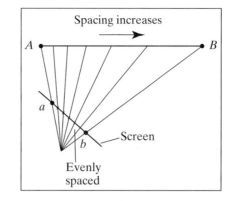

FIGURE 8.46 The values of a_4 and b_4 are related to the depths of points.

Rendering Incrementally

We now put these ingredients together and find the proper texture coordinates (s, t) at each point on the face being rendered. Figure 8.47 shows a face of the barn being rendered. The left edge of the face has endpoints a and b. The face extends from x_{left} to x_{right} across scanline y. We need to find appropriate texture coordinates $(s_{\text{left}}, t_{\text{left}})$ and $(s_{\text{right}}, t_{\text{right}})$ to attach to x_{left} and x_{right}, respectively, which we can then interpolate across the scanline. Consider finding $s_{\text{left}}(y)$, the value of s_{left} at scanline y. We know that texture coordinate s_A is attached to point a, and s_B is attached to point b, since these values have been passed down the pipeline along with the vertices A and B. If the scanline at y is fraction f of the way between y_{bott} and y_{top} (so that $f = (y - y_{\text{bott}})/(y_{\text{top}} - y_{\text{bott}})$), then we know from Equation (8.19) that the proper texture coordinate to use is:

$$s_{\text{left}}(y) = \frac{\text{lerp}\left(\dfrac{s_A}{a_4}, \dfrac{s_B}{b_4}, f\right)}{\text{lerp}\left(\dfrac{1}{a_4}, \dfrac{1}{b_4}, f\right)} \tag{8.20}$$

and similarly for t_{left}. Notice that s_{left} and t_{left} have the same denominator—a linear interpolation between values $1/a_4$ and $1/b_4$. The numerator terms are linear interpolations of texture coordinates which have been divided by a_4 and b_4. This is sometimes called *rational linear rendering* [Heckbert91] or "hyperbolic interpolation" [Blinn92]. To calculate (s, t) efficiently as f advances, we need to store values of s_A/a_4, s_B/b_4, t_A/a_4, t_B/b_4, $1/a_4$, and $1/b_4$, as these don't change from pixel to pixel. Both the numerator and denominator terms can be found incrementally for each y,

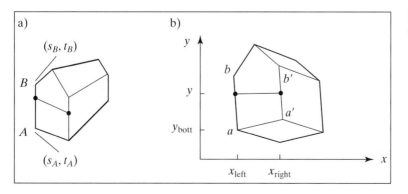

FIGURE 8.47 Rendering the texture on a face.

just as we did for Gouraud shading [see Equation (8.15)]. But to find s_{left} and t_{left} we must still perform an explicit division at each value of y.

The pair (s_{right}, t_{right}) is calculated in a similar fashion. They have denominators that are based on values of a_4' and b_4' that arise from the projected points a' and b'.

Once (s_{left}, t_{left}) and (s_{right}, t_{right}) have been found, the scanline can be filled. For each x from x_{left} to x_{right} the values s and t are found, again by hyperbolic interpolation. (What is the expression for s at x?)

Why Use Hyperbolic Interpolation and How Costly Is It Computationally?

What are the implications of having to use hyperbolic interpolation to render texture properly? And does the clipping step need any refinement? As we shall see, we must send certain additional information down the pipeline and calculate slightly different quantities than supposed so far.

Figure 8.48 shows a refinement of the pipeline. Various points are labeled with the information that is available at that point. Each vertex V is associated with a texture pair (s, t) as well as a vertex normal. The vertex is transformed by the modelview matrix (and the normal is multiplied by the inverse transpose of this matrix), producing vertex $A = (A_1, A_2, A_3)$ and a normal $\mathbf{n}'$ in eye coordinates. Shading calculations are done using this normal, producing the color $\mathbf{c} = (c_r, c_g, c_b)$. The texture coordinates (s_A, t_A) (which are the same as (s, t)) are still attached to A. Vertex A then undergoes the perspective transformation, producing $\tilde{a} = (a_1, a_2, a_3, a_4)$. The texture coordinates and color $\mathbf{c}$ are not altered.

FIGURE 8.48 Refinement of the graphics pipeline to include hyperbolic interpolation.

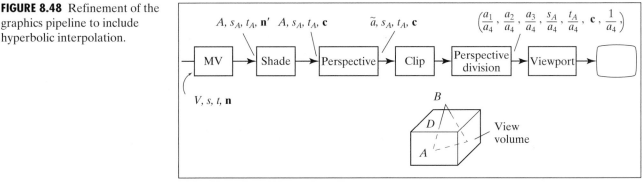

Now clipping against the view volume is done, as discussed in Chapter 7. As the figure suggests, this can cause some vertices to disappear and others to be formed. When a vertex such as D is created, we must determine its position (d_1, d_2, d_3, d_4) and attach to it the appropriate color and texture point. By the nature of the clipping algorithm the position components d_i are formed by linear interpolation: $d_i = \text{lerp}(a_i, b_i, t)$, for $i = 1, \ldots, 4$, for some t. Notice that the fourth component d_4 is also formed this way. It is natural to use linear interpolation here also to form both the color components and the texture coordinates. (The rationale for this is discussed in the exercises.) Therefore, after clipping, the face still consists of a number of vertices, and to each are attached a color and a texture point. For point A the information is stored in the array $(a_1, a_2, a_3, a_4, s_A, t_A, \mathbf{c}, 1)$. A final term of 1 has been appended: we will use it in the next step.

Now perspective division is done. Since for hyperbolic interpolation we need terms such as s_A/a_4, $1/a_4$, and t_A/a_4 [see Equation (8.20)], we divide *every* item in the array that we wish to interpolate hyperbolically by a_4 to obtain the array $(x, y, z, 1, s_A/a_4, t_A/a_4, \mathbf{c}, 1/a_4)$. (We could also divide the color components in order to obtain slightly more realistic Gouraud shading. See the exercises.) The first three, $(x, y, z) = (a_1/a_4, a_2/a_4, a_3/a_4)$, report the position of the point in normalized device coordinates. The third component is pseudodepth. The first two components are scaled and shifted by the viewport transformation. To simplify notation we shall continue to call the screen coordinate point (x, y, z).

So finally the renderer receives the array $(x, y, z, 1, s_A/a_4, t_A/a_4, \mathbf{c}, 1/a_4)$ for each vertex of the face to be rendered. Now it is simple to render texture using hyperbolic interpolation as in Equation (8.20): the required values s_A/a_4 and $1/a_4$ are available for each vertex.

PRACTICE EXERCISES

8.5.1 Data structures for mesh models with textures

Discuss the specific data types needed to represent mesh objects in the two cases:

a. A different texture is to be applied to each face.
b. A single texture is to be wrapped around the entire mesh.

Draw templates for the two data types required, and for each show example data in the various arrays when the mesh holds a cube.

8.5.2 Pseudodepth calculations are correct

Show that it is correct, as claimed in Section 8.4, to use linear (rather than hyperbolic) interpolation when finding pseudodepth. Assume point A projects to a, and B projects to b. With linear interpolation we compute pseudodepth at the projected point lerp(a, b, f) as the third component of this point. This is the correct thing to do only if the resulting value equals the true pseudodepth of the point that lerp(A, B, g) (for the appropriate g) projects to. Show that it is in fact correct. [*Hint:* Apply Equations (8.16) and (8.17) to the third component of the point being projected.]

8.5.3 Wrapping and clamping textures in OpenGL

To make the pattern "wrap" or "tile" in the s-direction use: glTexParameteri (GL_TEXTURE_2D, GL_TEXTURE_WRAP_S, GL_REPEAT). Similarly use GL_TEXTURE_WRAP_T for wrapping in the t-direction. This is actually the default, so you needn't do this explicitly. To turn off tiling replace GL_REPEAT with GL_CLAMP. Refer to the OpenGL web site for more details, and experiment with different OpenGL settings to see their effect.

8.5.4 Rationale for linear interpolation of texture during clipping

New vertices are often created when a face is clipped against the view volume. We must assign texture coordinates to each vertex. Suppose a new vertex V is formed that is fraction f of the way from vertex A to vertex B on a face. Further suppose that A is assigned texture coordinates (s_A, t_A), and similarly for B. Argue why, if a texture is considered as pasted onto a flat face, it makes sense to assign texture coordinates $(\text{lerp}(s_A, s_B, f), \text{lerp}(t_A, t_B, f))$ to V.

8.5.5 Computational burden of hyperbolic interpolation

Compare the amount of computation required to perform hyperbolic interpolation vs. linear interpolation of texture coordinates. Assume multiplication and division each require ten times as much time as addition and subtraction. ■

8.5.3 What Does the Texture Modulate?

How are the values in a texture map applied in the rendering calculation? We examine three common ways to use such values in order to achieve different visual effects. We do it for the simple case of the grayscale intensity calculation of Equation (8.5). For full color the same calculations are applied individually for the red, green, and blue components.

1. Create a Glowing Object

This is the simplest method computationally. The visible intensity I is set equal to the texture value at each spot:

$$I = \text{texture}(s, t)$$

(or to some constant multiple of it). The object appears to emit light or glow: lower texture values emit less light and higher texture values more light. No additional lighting calculations need be done.

(For colored light the red, green, and blue components are set separately: for instance, the red component is $I_r = \text{texture}_r(s, t)$.)

To cause OpenGL to do this type of texturing, specify:

```
glTexEnvf(GL_TEXTURE_ENV,GL_TEXTURE_ENV_MODE, GL_REPLACE);
```
[8]

2. Paint the Texture by Modulating the Reflection Coefficient

We noted earlier that the color of an object is the color of its diffuse light component (when bathed in white light). Therefore we can make the texture appear to be painted onto the surface by varying the diffuse reflection coefficient, and perhaps the ambient reflection coefficient as well. We say that the texture function modulates the value of the reflection coefficient from point to point. Thus we replace Equation (8.5) with:

$$I = \text{texture}(s, t)[I_a \rho_a + I_d \rho_d \times lambert] + I_{sp} \rho_s \times phong^f$$

for appropriate values of s and t. Since Phong specular reflections are the color of the source rather than the object, highlights do not depend on the texture.

To cause OpenGL to do this type of texturing, specify:

```
glTexEnvf(GL_TEXTURE_ENV,GL_TEXTURE_ENV_MODE, GL_MODULATE);
```

8.5.4 A Texture Example Using OpenGL

To illustrate how to invoke the texturing tools that OpenGL provides, we show an application that displays a rotating cube having different images painted on its six sides. Figure 8.49 shows a snapshot from the animation created by this program. The texture is mapped onto each face using hyperbolic interpolation.

The code for the application is shown in Figure 8.50. It uses a number of OpenGL functions to establish the six textures and to attach them to the walls of the cube. There are many variations of the parameters shown here that one could use to map textures. The version shown works well, but careful adjustment of some parameters (using the OpenGL documentation as a guide) can improve the images or increase performance. We discuss only the basics of the key routines.

One of the first tasks when adding texture to pictures is to create a **pixmap** of the texture in memory. OpenGL uses textures that are stored in **pixel maps**, or pixmaps for short. These are discussed in depth in Chapter 9, and the class RGBpixmap is developed that provides tools for creating and manipulating pixmaps. Here we view a pixmap as a simple array of pixel values, each pixel value being a triple of bytes to hold the red, green, and blue color values:

FIGURE 8.49 The textured cube generated by the example code.

---

[8]   Use either GL_REPLACE or GL_DECAL.

```
// <... the usual includes ...>
#include "RGBpixmap.h"
//###################### GLOBALS ######################
RGBpixmap pix[6]; // make six (empty) pixmaps
float xSpeed = 0, ySpeed = 0, xAngle = 0.0, yAngle = 0.0;
//<<<<<<<<<<<<<<<<<<<<<<<<<< myinit >>>>>>>>>>>>>>>>>>>>>>>>>>>>>.
void myInit(void)
{
    glClearColor(1.0f,1.0f,1.0f,1.0f); // background is white
    glEnable(GL_DEPTH_TEST);
    glEnable(GL_TEXTURE_2D);

    pix[0].makeCheckerboard();          // make pixmap procedurally
    pix[0].setTexture(2001);                // create texture
    pix[1].readBMPFile("Mandrill.bmp");  // make pixmap from image
    pix[1].setTexture(2002);   // create texture
    //< ...similarly for other four textures ...>

    glViewport(0, 0, 640, 480); // set up the viewing system
    glMatrixMode(GL_PROJECTION);
    glLoadIdentity();
    gluPerspective(60.0, 640.0/ 480, 1.0, 30.0); // set camera shape
    glMatrixMode(GL_MODELVIEW);
    glLoadIdentity();
    glTranslated(0.0, 0.0, -4); // move camera back
}
//<<<<<<<<<<<<<<<<<<<<<<<<<< display >>>>>>>>>>>>>>>>>>>>>>>>
void display(void)
{
    glClear(GL_COLOR_BUFFER_BIT | GL_DEPTH_BUFFER_BIT);
    glTexEnvf(GL_TEXTURE_ENV, GL_TEXTURE_ENV_MODE, GL_DECAL);
    glPushMatrix();
    glRotated(xAngle, 1.0,0.0,0.0); glRotated(yAngle, 0.0,1.0,0.0); // rotate

    glBindTexture(GL_TEXTURE_2D,2001); // top face: 'fake' checkerboard
    glBegin(GL_QUADS);
    glTexCoord2f(-1.0, -1.0); glVertex3f(-1.0f, 1.0f, -1.0f);
    glTexCoord2f(-1.0, 2.0); glVertex3f(-1.0f, 1.0f, 1.0f);
    glTexCoord2f(2.0, 2.0); glVertex3f( 1.0f, 1.0f, 1.0f);
    glTexCoord2f(2.0, -1.0); glVertex3f( 1.0f, 1.0f, -1.0f);
    glEnd();

    glBindTexture(GL_TEXTURE_2D,2002);    // right face: mandrill
    glBegin(GL_QUADS);
    glTexCoord2f(0.0, 0.0); glVertex3f(1.0f, -1.0f,  1.0f);
    glTexCoord2f(0.0, 2.0); glVertex3f(1.0f, -1.0f, -1.0f);
    glTexCoord2f(2.0, 2.0); glVertex3f(1.0f,  1.0f, -1.0f);
    glTexCoord2f(2.0, 0.0); glVertex3f(1.0f,  1.0f,  1.0f);
    glEnd();
```

FIGURE 8.50 A complete working program of a rotating textured cube.

```
      // <… similarly for other four faces …>
      glFlush();
      glPopMatrix();
      glutSwapBuffers();
}
//<<<<<<<<<<<<<<<<<<<<<<<<<<<<<<<< spinner >>>>>>>>>>>>>>>>>>>>>>
void spinner(void)
{ // alter angles by small amount
      xAngle += xSpeed; yAngle += ySpeed;
      display();
}
//<<<<<<<<<<<<<<<<<<<<< main >>>>>>>>>>>>>>>>>>>>>>>>>>>>>>>>>>
void main(int argc, char **argv)
{

      GlutWin win( 600, 800,100, 100,GLUT_DOUBLE | GLUT_RGB,"Rotating Cube Demo" );
      //creates a new object glutWin object
      win.glutDisplayFunc(display);
      win.myInit();
      win.glutIdleFunc(spinner);
      win.glutMainLoop();
}
```

FIGURE 8.50 (*Continued*)

```
class RGB{ // holds a color triple – each with 256 possible
                    intensities
      public: unsigned char r,g,b;
};
```

The RGBpixmap class stores the number of rows and columns in the pixmap, as well as the address of the first pixel in memory:

```
class RGBpixmap{
  public:
      int nRows, nCols; // dimensions of the pixmap
      RGB* pixel;        // array of pixels
      int readBMPFile(char * fname);  // read BMP file into this
                                           pixmap
      void makeCheckerboard();
      void setTexture(GLuint textureName);
};
```

We show it here as having only three methods that we need for mapping textures. Other methods and details are discussed in Chapter 9. The method readBMPFile() reads a BMP file[9] and stores the pixel values in its pixmap object; its implementation is available on the book's companion web site. The other two methods are discussed next.

Our example OpenGL application will use six textures. To create them we first make an RGBpixmap object for each:

```
RGBpixmap pix[6]; // create six (empty) pixmaps
```

and then load the desired texture image into each one. Finally each one is passed to OpenGL to define a texture.

---

[9] This is a standard device-independent image file format from Microsoft. Many images are available on the internet in BMP format, and tools are readily available on the Internet to convert other image formats to BMP files.

1. Making a Procedural Texture

We first create a checkerboard texture using the method `makeCheckerboard()`. The checkerboard pattern is familiar and easy to create, and its geometric regularity makes it a good texture for testing correctness. The application generates a checkerboard pixmap in `pix[0]` using: `pix[0].makeCheckerboard()`. The method itself follows:

```
void RGBpixmap:: makeCheckerboard()
{   // make checkerboard pattern
      nRows = nCols = 64;
      int numBytes = 3 * nRows * nCols; // number of bytes in
                                          the pixmap
      RGB * pixel = new RGB[numBytes]; // allocate the pixmap
      if(!pixel) {cout << "out of memory!"; return;}
      long count = 0;
      for(int i = 0; i < nRows; i++)
            for(int j = 0; j < nCols; j++)
            {
                  int c = (((i/8) + (j/8)) %2) * 255; 10
                  pixel[count].r = c;     // red
                  pixel[count].g = c;     // green
                  pixel[count++].b = 0;   // blue
            }
}
```

It creates a 64-by-64-pixel array, where each pixel is an RGB triple. OpenGL up to version 1.5 required that texture pixel maps have a width and height that are both some power of two. OpenGL 2.0 has removed this restriction. The pixel map is laid out in memory as one long array of bytes: row by row from bottom to top, left to right across a row. Here each pixel is loaded with the value $(c, c, 0)$, where c jumps back and forth between 0 and 255 every 8 pixels. (We used a similar jumping method in Exercise 2.3.1.) The two colors of the checkerboard are black: $(0, 0, 0)$, and yellow: $(255, 255, 0)$. The function sets the address of the first pixel of the pixmap, which is later passed to `glTexImage2D()` to create the actual texture for OpenGL.

Once the pixel map has been formed, we must bind it to a unique integer (its name) so that it can be referred to in OpenGL without ambiguity. We arbitrarily assign the names $2001, 2002, \ldots, 2006$ to our six textures in this example.[11] The texture is created by making certain calls to OpenGL, which we encapsulate in the method:

```
void RGBpixmap :: setTexture(GLuint textureName)
{
  glBindTexture(GL_TEXTURE_2D,textureName);
  glTexParameteri(GL_TEXTURE_2D,GL_TEXTURE_MAG_FILTER,GL_NEAREST);
  glTexParameteri(GL_TEXTURE_2D,GL_TEXTURE_MIN_FILTER,GL_NEAREST);
  glTexImage2D(GL_TEXTURE_2D, 0, GL_RGB,nCols,nRows,0, GL_RGB,
               GL_UNSIGNED_BYTE, pixel);
}
```

---

[10] A faster way that uses C++'s bit-manipulation operators is `c = ((i&8)^(j&8))*255;`

[11] To avoid overlap in (integer) names in an application that uses many textures, it is better to let OpenGL supply unique names for textures using `glGenTextures()`. If we need six unique names, we can build an array to hold them: `GLuint name[6];` and then call `glGenTextures(6,name)`. OpenGL places six heretofore unused integers in `name[0]`,…,`name[5]`, and we subsequently refer to the Ith texture using `name[i]`.

The call to `glBindTexture()` binds the given name to the texture being formed. When this call is made at a later time, it will make this texture the active texture, as we shall see.

The calls to `glTexParameteri()` specify that a pixel should be filled with the texel whose coordinates are nearest the center of the pixel, when the texture needs to be either magnified or reduced in size. This is fast but can lead to aliasing effects. We discuss filtering of images and antialiasing further in Chapter 9. Finally, the call to `glTexImage2D()` associates the pixmap with this current texture. This call describes the texture as 2D consisting of RGB byte-triples, and gives its width and height and the address in memory (`pixel`) of the first byte of the bitmap.

2. Making a Texture from a Stored Image

OpenGL offers no support for reading an image file and creating the pixel map in memory. The method `readBMPFile()`, available on the book's companion web site provides a simple way to read a BMP image into a pixmap. For instance,

```
pix[1].readBMPFile("mandrill.bmp");
```

reads the file `mandrill.bmp` and creates the pixmap in `pix[1]`.

Once the pixel map has been created, `pix[1].setTexture()` is used to pass the pixmap to OpenGL to make a texture.

Texture mapping must also be enabled with `glEnable(GL_TEXTURE_2D)`. In addition, the routine `glHint(GL_PERSPECTIVE_CORRECTION_HINT,GL_NICEST)` is used to request that OpenGL render the texture properly (using hyperbolic interpolation), so that it appears correctly attached to faces even when a face rotates relative to the viewer in an animation.

The texture creation, enabling, and hinting needs to be done only once, in an initialization routine. Then, each time through the display routine, the texture is actually applied. In `display()` the cube is rotated through angles `xAngle` and `yAngle`, and the six faces are drawn. This requires simply that the appropriate texture be bound to the face and that within a `glBegin()`/`glEnd()` pair the texture coordinates and 3D positions of the face's vertices be specified, as shown in the code.

Once the rendering (off screen) of the cube is complete, `glutSwapBuffers()` is called to make the new frame visible. The animation is controlled by using the callback function `spinner()` as the "idle function." Whenever the system is idle—not responding to user input—`spinner` is called automatically. It alters the rotation angles of the cube slightly and calls `display()` once again. The effect is an ongoing animation showing the cube rotating, so that its various faces come into view and rotate out of view again and again.

8.5.5 Wrap Texture on Curved Surfaces

We have seen how to paste a texture onto a flat surface. Now we examine how to wrap texture onto a curved surface, such as a beer can or a chess piece. We assume as before that the object is modeled by a mesh, so it consists of a large number of small flat faces. As discussed at the end of Section 8.5.1, each vertex of the mesh has an associated texture coordinate pair (s_i, t_i), although we may not yet know them. The main question is finding the proper texture coordinate (s, t) for each vertex of the mesh.

We present examples of mapping textures onto "cylinderlike" objects and "spherelike" objects and see how a modeler might deal with each one.

■ EXAMPLE 8.5.1 Wrapping a label around a can

Suppose that we want to wrap a label about a circular cylinder, as suggested in Figure 8.51a. It's natural to think in terms of cylindrical coordinates. The label is to extend from θ_a to θ_b in azimuth and from z_a to z_b along the z-axis. The cylinder is modeled as a polygonal mesh, so its walls are rectangular strips, as shown in part b. For vertex V_i of each face we must find suitable texture coordinates (s_i, t_i), so that the correct "slice" of the texture is mapped onto the face.

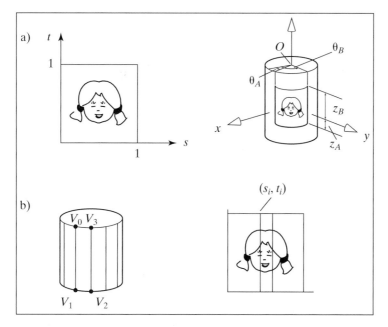

FIGURE 8.51 To wrap a label around a cylinder.

The geometry is simple enough here that a solution is straightforward. There is a direct linear relationship between (s, t) and the azimuth and height (θ, z) of a point on the cylinder's surface:

$$s = \frac{\theta - \theta_a}{\theta_b - \theta_a}, \qquad t = \frac{z - z_a}{z_b - z_a} \tag{8.23}$$

So, if there are N faces around the cylinder, the ith face has left edge at azimuth $\theta_i = 2\pi i / N$, and its upper left vertex has texture coordinates $(s_i, t_i) = ((2\pi i / N - \theta_a)/(\theta_b - \theta_a), 1)$. Texture coordinates for the other three vertices follow in a similar fashion. This association between (s, t) and the vertices of each face is easily put in a loop in the modeling routine (see the exercises).

Things get more complicated when the object isn't a simple cylinder. We see next how to map texture onto a more general surface of revolution.

■ EXAMPLE 8.5.2 Shrink wrapping a label onto a surface of revolution

Recall from Chapter 6 that a surface of revolution is defined by a profile curve $(x(v), z(v))$,[12] as shown in Figure 8.52a, and the resulting surface—here a vase—is given parametrically by $P(u, v) = (x(v) \cos u, x(v) \sin u, z(v))$. The shape is modeled as a

---

[12] We revert to calling the parameters u and v in the parametric representation of the shape, since we are using s and t for the texture coordinates.

FIGURE 8.52 To wrap a label around a vase.

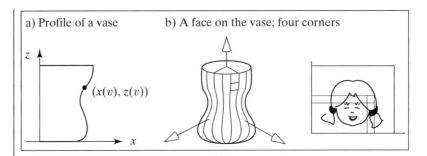

a) Profile of a vase

b) A face on the vase; four corners

collection of faces with sides along contours of constant u and v (see Figure 8.52b). So a given face F_i has four vertices, $P(u_i, v_i)$, $P(u_{i+1}, v_i)$, $P(u_i, v_{i+1})$, and $P(u_{i+1}, v_{i+1})$. We need to find the appropriate (s, t) coordinates for each of these vertices.

One natural approach is to proceed as above and to make s and t vary linearly with u and v in the manner of Equation (8.23). This is equivalent to wrapping the texture about an imaginary rubber cylinder that encloses the vase (see Figure 8.53a) and then letting the cylinder collapse, so that each texture point slides radially (and horizontally) until it hits the surface of the vase. This method is called "shrink wrapping" by Bier and Sloane [Bier86], who discuss several possible ways to map texture onto different classes of shapes. They view shrink wrapping along the imaginary cylinder's *normal* vector (see Figure 8.53b): texture point P_i is associated with the object point V_i that lies along the normal from P_i.

FIGURE 8.53 Shrink wrapping texture onto the vase.

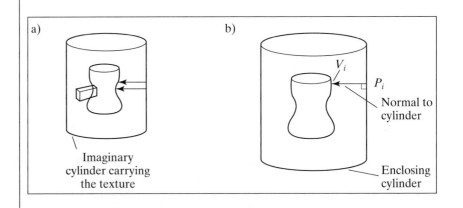

a)

b)

V_i

P_i

Normal to cylinder

Imaginary cylinder carrying the texture

Enclosing cylinder

Shrink wrapping works well for cylinderlike objects, although the texture pattern will be distorted if the profile curve has a complicated shape.

Bier and Sloane suggest some alternate ways to associate texture points on the imaginary cylinder with vertices on the object. Figure 8.54 shows two other possibilities.

In part a, a line is drawn from the object's centroid C, through the vertex V_i, to its intersection with the cylinder P_i. In part b the normal vector to the object's surface at V_i is used: P_i is at the intersection of this normal from V_i with the cylinder. Notice that these three ways to associate texture points with object points can lead to very different results, depending on the shape of the object (see the exercises). The designer must choose the most suitable method based on the object's shape and the nature of the texture image being mapped. (What would be appropriate for a chess pawn?)

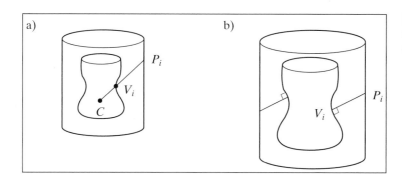

FIGURE 8.54 Alternative mappings from the imaginary cylinder to the object.

■ EXAMPLE 8.5.3 Map a texture onto a sphere

It was easy to wrap a texture rectangle around a cylinder: topologically a cylinder can be sliced open and laid flat without distortion. A sphere is a different matter. As all map makers know, there is no way to show accurate details of the entire globe on a flat piece of paper: if you slice open a sphere and lay it flat, some parts always suffer serious stretching. (Try to imagine a checkerboard mapped over an entire sphere!)

It's not hard to paste a rectangular texture image onto a *portion* of a sphere, however. To map the texture square to the portion lying between azimuth θ_a to θ_b and latitude ϕ_a to ϕ_b, just map linearly as in Equation (8.23): if vertex V_i lies at (θ_i, ϕ_i), associate it with texture coordinates $(s_i, t_i) = ((\theta_i - \theta_a)/((\theta_b - \theta_a), (\phi_i - \phi_a)/(\phi_b - \phi_a))$. Figure 8.55 shows an image pasted onto a band around a sphere. Only a small amount of distortion is seen.

Figure 8.55b shows how one might cover an entire sphere with texture: map eight triangular texture maps onto the eight octants of the sphere.

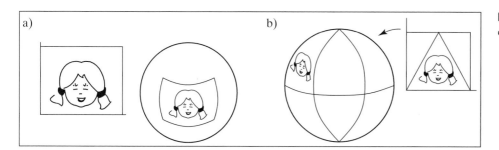

FIGURE 8.55 Mapping texture onto a sphere.

■ EXAMPLE 8.5.4 Mapping texture to spherelike objects

We discussed adding texture to cylinderlike objects in preceding paragraphs above. But some objects are more spherelike than cylinder-like. Figure 8.56a shows the Buckyball, whose faces are pentagons and hexagons. One could devise a number of pentagonal and hexagonal textures and manually paste one on each face, but for some scenes it may be desirable to wrap the whole Buckyball in a single texture.

It is natural to surround a spherelike object with an imaginary sphere (rather than a cylinder) that has texture pasted to it, and use one of the association methods discussed above. Figure 8.56b shows the Buckyball surrounded by such a sphere in cross section. The three ways of associating texture points P_i with object vertices V_i are sketched:

FIGURE 8.56 Spherelike objects.

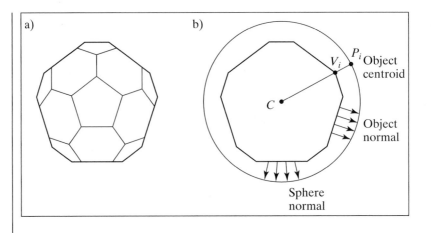

- object-centroid: P_i is on a line from the centroid C through vertex V_i;
- object-normal: P_i is the intersection of a ray from V_i in the direction of the face normal;
- sphere-normal: V_i is the intersection of a ray from P_i in the direction of the normal to the sphere at P_i.

(*Question*: Are the object-centroid and sphere-normal methods the same if the centroid of the object coincides with the center of the sphere?) The object-centroid method is most likely the best, and it is easy to implement. As Bier and Sloane argue, the other two methods usually produce unacceptable final renderings.

Bier and Sloane also discuss using an imaginary box rather than a sphere to surround the object in question. Figure 8.57a shows the six faces of a cube spread out over a texture image, and part b shows the texture wrapped about the cube, which in turn encloses an object. Vertices on the object can be associated with texture points in the three ways discussed above: the object-centroid and cube-normal are probably the best choices.

FIGURE 8.57 Using an enclosing box.

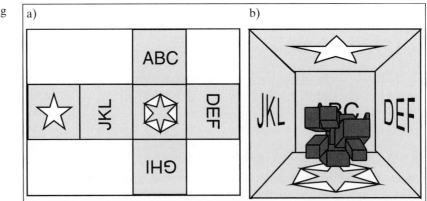

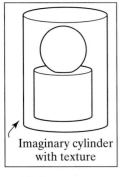

FIGURE 8.58 A surface of revolution surrounded by an imaginary cylinder.

PRACTICE EXERCISE

8.5.7 How to associate P_i and V_i.

Surface of revolution S shown in Figure 8.58 consists of a sphere resting on a cylinder. The object is surrounded by an imaginary cylinder having a checkerboard texture pasted on it. Sketch how the texture will look for each of the following methods of associating texture points to vertices:

a. shrink wrapping.
b. object centroid.
c. object normal. ■

8.5.6 Reflection Mapping

The class of techniques known as **reflection mapping** can significantly improve the realism of pictures, particularly in animations. The basic idea is to see reflections in an object that suggest the world that surrounds that object.

The two main types of reflection mapping are called **chrome mapping** and **environment mapping**. In the case of **chrome mapping** a rough and usually blurry image that suggests the surrounding environment is reflected in the object, as you would see in a surface coated with chrome, such as a trailer hitch. Television commercials abound with animations of shiny letters and logos flying around in space, where the chrome map includes occasional spotlights for dramatic effect. Figure 8.59 offers an example. Part a shows an example of chrome mapping; the overall image clearly shows a shiny stick man sitting on a stool, with dark and light regions, but the reflections themselves are unrecognizable. The reflection provides a rough suggestion of the world surrounding the object.

a)   b)

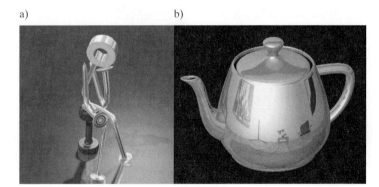

FIGURE 8.59 Example of a) chrome mapping, b) environment mapping (Courtesy of Okino Computer Graphics).

In the case of **environment mapping** (first introduced by Blinn and Newell [Blinn76]), a *recognizable* image of the surrounding environment is seen reflected in the object. We get valuable visual cues from such reflections, particularly when the object moves about. Everyone has seen the classic photographs of an astronaut walking on the moon with the moonscape reflected in his face mask. Similarly, in movies you sometimes see close-ups of a character's reflective dark glasses (Darth Vader, for instance), in which the world is reflected. Figure 8.60 shows two examples where a cafeteria is reflected in a sphere and a torus. The cafeteria texture is wrapped about a large sphere that surrounds the object, so that the texture coordinates (s, t) correspond to azimuth and latitude about the enclosing sphere.

Figure 8.61 shows the use of a surrounding cube rather than a sphere. Part a shows the map, consisting of six images of various views of the interior walls, floor, and ceiling of a room. Part b shows a shiny object reflecting different parts of the room. The use of an enclosing cube was introduced by Greene [Greene86] and generally produces less distorted reflections than are seen with an enclosing sphere. The six maps can be generated by rendering six separate images from the point of view of the object (with the object itself removed, of course). For each image a synthetic camera is set up and the

FIGURE 8.60 Example of environment mapping. (Courtesy of Haeberli and Segal)

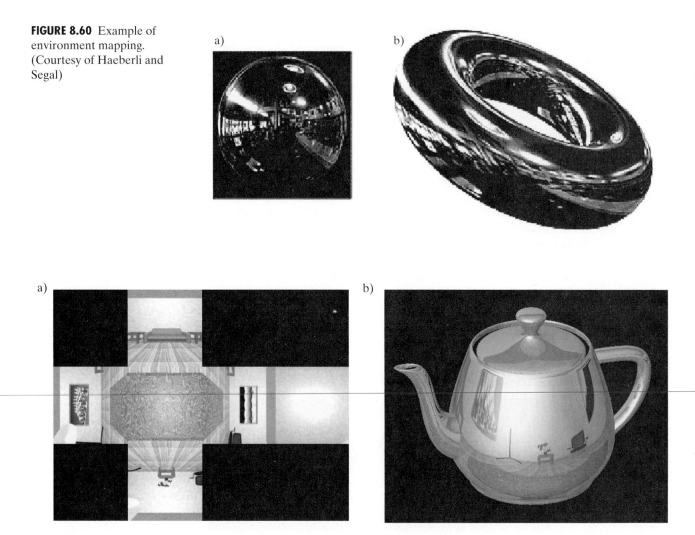

a)

b)

a)

b)

FIGURE 8.61 Environment mapping based on a surrounding cube.

appropriate window is set. Alternatively, the textures can be digitized from photos taken by a real camera that looks in the six principal directions inside an actual room or scene.

Chrome and environment mapping differ most dramatically from normal texture mapping in an animation when the shiny object is moving. The reflected image will flow over the moving object, whereas a normal texture map will be attached to the object and move with it. If a shiny sphere rotates about a fixed spot, a normal texture map spins with the sphere, but a reflection map stays fixed.

How to Program Chrome and Environment Maps

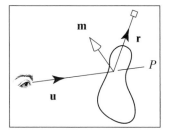

FIGURE 8.62 Finding the direction of the reflected ray.

How is environment mapping done? What you see at point P on the shiny object is what has arrived at P from the environment in just the right direction to reflect into your eye. To find that direction, trace a ray from the eye to P, and determine the direction of the reflected ray. Trace this ray to find where it hits the texture (on the enclosing cube or sphere). Figure 8.62 shows a ray emanating from the eye to point V. If the direction of this ray is $\mathbf{u}$ and the unit normal at P is $\mathbf{m}$, we know from Equation (8.2) that the reflected ray has direction $\mathbf{r} = \mathbf{u} - 2(\mathbf{u} \cdot \mathbf{m}) \, \mathbf{m}$. (Recall Chapter 4.) The reflected ray moves in direction $\mathbf{r}$ until it hits the hypothetical surface with its attached texture. It is easiest computationally to suppose that the shiny object is centered in, and much smaller than, the enclosing cube or sphere. Then the reflected ray emanates approximately from the object's center, and its direction **r** can be used directly to index into the texture.

OpenGL provides a tool to perform approximate environment mapping for the case where the texture is wrapped about a large enclosing cube. It is invoked by setting a mapping mode for both *s* and *t* using:

```
glTexGenf(GL_S,GL_TEXTURE_GEN_MODE, GL_CUBE_MAP);
glTexGenf(GL_T,GL_TEXTURE_GEN_MODE, GL_CUBE_MAP);
glEnable(GL_TEXTURE_GEN_S);
glEnable(GL_TEXTURE_GEN_T);
```

Now when a vertex *P* with its unit normal **m** is sent down the pipeline, OpenGL calculates a texture coordinate pair (s, t) suitable for indexing into the texture attached to the surrounding cube. This is done for each vertex of the face on the object, and the face is drawn as always using interpolated texture coordinates (s, t) for points in between the vertices.

How does OpenGL rapidly compute a suitable coordinate pair (s, t)? As shown in Figure 8.63a, it first finds (in eye coordinates) the reflected direction **r** (using the formula above), where **u** is the unit vector (in eye coordinates) from the eye to the vertex *V* on the object, and **m** is the normal at *V*.

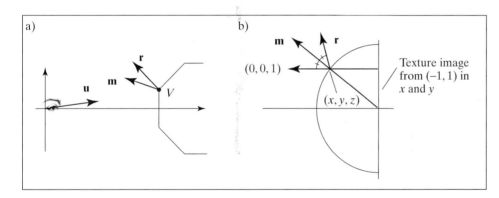

FIGURE 8.63 OpenGL's computation of the texture coordinates.

It then simply uses the expression:

$$(s, t) = \left(\tfrac{1}{2}\left(\frac{r_x}{p} + 1\right), \tfrac{1}{2}\left(\frac{r_y}{p} + 1\right) \right) \tag{8.24}$$

where *p* is a mysterious scaling factor $p = \sqrt{r_x^2 + r_y^2 + (r_z + 1)^2}$. The derivation of this term is developed in the exercises. We must precompute a texture that shows what you would see of the environment in a perfectly reflecting cube, from an eye position far removed from the cube [Haeberli93]. This maps the part of the environment that lies in the hemisphere behind the eye into a circle in the middle of the texture, and the part of the environment in the hemisphere in front of the eye into an annulus around this circle (visualize this). This texture must be recomputed if the eye changes position.

Recall that we introduced the concept of **extensions** to OpenGL in the Preface; a number of extensions can be implemented in OpenGL programs that make environment mapping a simpler task.[13]

---

[13] The OpenGL Extension Registry is online at: http://oss.sgi.com/projects/ogl-sample/registry/

To Simulate Highlights Using Environment Mapping

Reflection mapping can be used in OpenGL to produce specular highlights on a surface. A texture map is created that has an intense concentrated bright spot. Reflection mapping paints this highlight onto the surface, making it appear to be an actual light source situated in the environment. The highlight created can be more concentrated and detailed than those created using the Phong specular term with Gouraud shading. Recall that the Phong term is computed only at the vertices of a face, and it is easy to miss a specular highlight that falls between two vertices. With reflection mapping the coordinates (s, t) into the texture are formed at each vertex and then interpolated in between. So if the coordinates indexed by the vertices happen to surround the bright spot, the spot will be properly rendered inside the face.

PRACTICE EXERCISE

8.5.9 OpenGL's computation of texture coordinates for environment mapping

Derive the result in Equation (8.24). Figure 8.63b shows in cross-sectional view the vectors involved (in eye coordinates). The eye is looking from a remote location in the direction $(0, 0, 1)$. A sphere of radius 1 is positioned on the negative z-axis. Suppose light comes in from direction $\mathbf{r}$, hitting the sphere at the point (x, y, z). The normal to the sphere at this point is (x, y, z), which also must be just right so that light coming along $\mathbf{r}$ is reflected into the direction $(0, 0, 1)$. This means the normal must be halfway between $\mathbf{r}$ and $(0, 0, 1)$, or must be proportional to their sum, so $(x, y, z) = K(r_x, r_y, r_z + 1)$ for some K.

a. Show that the normal vector has unit length if K is $1/p$, where p is given as in Equation (8.24).
b. Show that therefore $(x, y) = (r_x/p, r_y/p)$.
c. Suppose for the moment that the texture image extends from -1 to 1 in x and from -1 to 1 in y. Argue why what we want to see reflected at the point (x, y, z) is the value of the texture image at (x, y).
d. Show that if instead the texture uses coordinates from 0 to 1—as is true with OpenGL—we want to see at (x, y) the value of the texture image at (s, t) given by Equation (8.24).   ■

8.6 TO ADD SHADOWS OF OBJECTS

> To think of shadows is a serious thing.
>
> *Victor Hugo*
> *(1802–1885)*

8.6.1 Introduction to Shadows

Shadows make an image much more realistic. From everyday experience the way one object casts a shadow on another object gives important visual cues as to how they are positioned. Figure 8.64 shows two images involving a cube and a sphere suspended above a plane. Shadows are absent in part a, and it is impossible to see how far above the plane the cube and sphere are floating. By contrast, the shadows seen in part b give useful hints as to the positions of the objects. A shadow conveys a lot of information; similar to your getting a second look at the object (from a viewpoint near the light source).

There are several methods for generating shadows in an image, as we shall see. Unfortunately, the tools we develop in this chapter will be useful only for generating shadows cast by a point light source onto a flat surface. In Chapter 12 ray tracing tools will allow us to show accurate shadow shapes for *any* light source shining on *any* surface shape.

FIGURE 8.64 The effect on shadows. a) floating cube and sphere, with no shadows; b) with shadows

Shadows as Texture

This technique displays shadows that are cast onto a flat surface by a point light source. The problem is to compute the shape of the shadow that is cast. Figure 8.65a shows a box casting a shadow onto the floor. The shape of the shadow is determined by the projections of each of the faces of the box onto the plane of the floor, using the source as the center of projection. In fact the shadow is the union[14] of the projections of the six faces. Figure 8.65b shows the superposed projections of two of the faces: the top face projects to *Top'* and the front face to *Front'*. (Sketch the projections of the other four faces, and see that their union is the required shadow.[15])

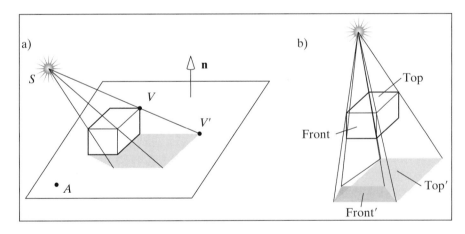

FIGURE 8.65 Computing the shape of a shadow.

This is the key to drawing the shadow. After drawing the plane using ambient, diffuse, and specular light contributions, redraw the six projections of the box's faces on the plane using only ambient light. This will draw the shadow in the right shape and color. Finally draw the box. (If the box is near the plane, parts of it might obscure portions of the shadow.)

Building the "Projected" Face

To make the new face F' produced by F, project each of its vertices onto the plane in question. We need a way to calculate these vertex positions on the plane. Suppose, as in Figure 8.65a, that the plane passes through point A and has normal vector $\mathbf{n}$. Consider projecting vertex V, producing point V'. The mathematics here are

---

14   The set-theoretic union: a point is in the shadow if it is in one or more of the projections.

15   You need to form the union of the projections of only the three "front" faces—those facing toward the light source. (Why?)

familiar: Point V' is the point where the ray from the source at S through V hits the plane. As developed in the exercises, this point is:

$$V' = S + (V - S)\frac{\mathbf{n} \cdot (A - S)}{\mathbf{n} \cdot (V - S)} \tag{8.25}$$

The exercises show how this can be written in homogeneous coordinates as V times a matrix, which is handy for rendering engines, like OpenGL, that support convenient matrix multiplication.

PRACTICE EXERCISES

8.6.1 Shadow shapes

Suppose a cube is floating above a plane. What is the shape of the cube's shadow if the point source lies a) directly above the top face? b) along a main diagonal of the cube (as in an isometric view)? Sketch shadows for a sphere and for a cylinder floating above a plane for various source positions.

8.6.2 Making the shadow face

a) Show that the ray from the source point S through vertex V hits the plane $\mathbf{n} \cdot (P - A) = 0$ at $t^* = \mathbf{n} \cdot (A - S)/\mathbf{n} \cdot (V - S)$. b) Show that this defines the hit point V' as given in Equation (8.25).

8.6.3 It's equivalent to a matrix multiplication

a) Show that the expression for V' in Equation (8.25) can be written as a matrix multiplication: $V' = M(V_x, V_y, V_z, 1)^T$, where M is a 4-by-4 matrix. b) Express the terms of M in terms of A, S, and $\mathbf{n}$.   ■

8.6.2 Shadows Using a Shadow Buffer

A rather different method for drawing shadows uses a variant of the depth buffer that performs hidden surface removal. It uses an auxiliary second depth buffer, called a **shadow buffer**, for each light source. This requires a lot of memory, but this approach is not restricted to casting shadows onto planar surfaces.

The method is based on the principle that any points in the scene that are "hidden" from the light source must be in shadow. On the other hand, if no object lies between a point and the light source, the point is not in shadow. The shadow buffer contains a "depth picture" of the scene from the point of view of the light source: each of its elements records the distance from the source to the *closest* object in the associated direction.

Rendering is done in two stages:

1. Shadow buffer loading

   The shadow buffer is first initialized with 1.0 in each element, the largest pseudodepth possible. Then, using a camera positioned at the light source, each face in the scene is scan converted, but only the pseudodepth of the point on the face is tested. Each element of the shadow buffer keeps track of the smallest pseudodepth seen so far.

   To be more specific, Figure 8.66 shows a scene being viewed by the usual "eye camera" as well as a "source camera" located at the light source. Suppose point P is on the ray from the source through shadow buffer "pixel" $d[i][j]$, and that point B on the pyramid is also on this ray. If the pyramid is present, $d[i][j]$ contains the pseudodepth to B; if it happens to be absent, $d[i][j]$ contains the pseudodepth to P.

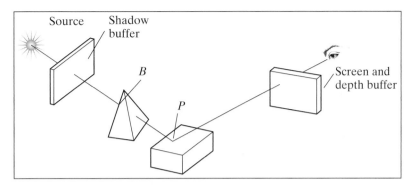

FIGURE 8.66 Using the shadow buffer.

Note that the shadow buffer calculation is independent of the eye position, so in an animation where only the eye moves, the shadow buffer is loaded only once. The shadow buffer must be recalculated, however, whenever the objects move relative to the light source.

2. Rendering the scene

Each face in the scene is rendered using the eye camera as usual. Suppose the eye camera sees point P through pixel $p[c][r]$. When rendering $p[c][r]$, we must find:[16]

- the pseudodepth D from the source to P;
- the index location $[i][j]$ in the shadow buffer that is to be tested;
- the value $d[i][j]$ stored in the shadow buffer.

If $d[i][j]$ is less than D, the point P is in shadow, and $p[c][r]$ is set using only ambient light. Otherwise P is not in shadow and $p[c][r]$ is set using ambient, diffuse, and specular light.

How are these steps done? As described in the exercises, to each point on the eye camera viewplane there corresponds a point on the source camera viewplane.[17] For each screen pixel this correspondence is invoked to find the pseudodepth from the source to P as well as the index $[i][j]$ that yields the minimum pseudodepth stored in the shadow buffer.

PRACTICE EXERCISES

8.6.4 Finding pseudodepth from the source

Suppose the matrices M_c and M_s map the point P in the scene to the appropriate (3D) spots on the eye camera's viewplane and the source camera's viewplane, respectively.

a. Describe how to establish a source camera and how to find the resulting matrix M_s.
b. Find the transformation that, given position (x, y) on the eye camera's viewplane, produces the position (i, j) and pseudodepth on the source camera's viewplane.
c. Once (i, j) are known, how are the index $[i][j]$ and the pseudodepth of P on the source camera determined?

8.6.5 Extended light sources

We have considered only point light sources in this chapter. Greater realism is provided by modeling extended light sources. As suggested in Figure 8.67a, such sources cast more complicated shadows, having an **umbra** within which no light from the

---

[16] Of course, this test is made only if P is closer to the eye than the value stored in the normal depth buffer of the eye camera.

[17] Keep in mind these are 3D points: two-position coordinates on the viewplane, and pseudodepth.

FIGURE 8.67 Umbra and penumbra for extended light sources.

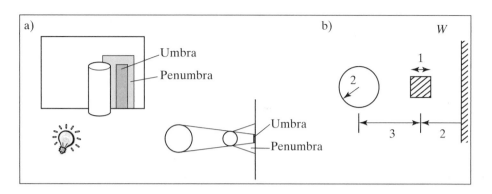

source is seen, and a lighter **penumbra** within which a part of the source is visible. In part b a glowing sphere of radius 2 shines light on a unit cube, thereby casting a shadow on the wall W. Make an accurate sketch of the umbra and penumbra that is observed on the wall. As you might expect, algorithms for rendering shadows due to extended light sources are complex. See [Watt92] for a thorough treatment. ■

Next we will introduce the **radiosity** method for image generation and contrast it with the ray tracing method. We shall give only a brief overview of the radiosity method here, since the numerous details needed to explain it fully are beyond the scope of the text.

8.6.3 A Brief Look at Radiosity

Recall that the inclusion of ambient light in the calculation of the light components that reflect from each face of an object is a "catch-all." It attempts to summarize the many beams of light that make multiple reflections off the various surfaces in a scene. One source of its improved realism is that it attempts to form an accurate model of the amount of light energy arriving at each surface vs. the amount of light leaving that surface. It would be too expensive to trace each individual light contribution, so instead they are all lumped together into the single ambient light component. Ambient is a concocted light attribute and does not exist in real life. Figure 8.68 shows an example where a scene is ray traced; part a shows the scene using radiosity, whereas part b shows it ray traced but without radiosity.

FIGURE 8.68 a) With radiosity, b) without radiosity.

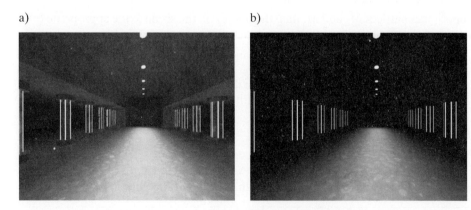

We will see in Chapter 12 that the use of ray tracing raises the level of realism dramatically, permitting a number of specific effects to be included. Radiosity in particular is an alternative to ray tracing that produces very high levels of realism, but at the cost of significantly increased computation.

A number of resources are available on the book's companion web site. There is also a fine article by Paul Nettle[18] which provides an excellent overview of the calculations involved with radiosity and its complexities.

8.7 OPENGL 2.0 & THE SHADING LANGUAGE (GLSL)

Recall from the Preface that there are mechanisms for enhancing **core** functionality in OpenGL:

- **Extensions**—These allow changes and improvements to be made to OpenGL. Extensions are created and specified by companies who wish to test and implement innovations in OpenGL, such as new sets of algorithms, functions, and access to the latest hardware capabilities.

For example, programmable shading, not to be confused with shadowing, was an extension, which provided the application programmer with function calls directly to the graphics card. In OpenGL 2.0 the programmable shading extension was promoted to the core of OpenGL. The addition of these new function calls allowed the application programmer to control shading operations directly, avoiding the fixed pipeline shading functions. Some of the most difficult shading approaches are bump mapping and 3D textures, but the OpenGL Shading Language (GLSL) removes much of the burden of accomplishing these from the application programmer. Figure 8.69 is a simplified version of the OpenGL pipeline with the addition of the GLSL. The pipeline begins with a collection of polygons (vertices) as input, followed by a **vertex processor**. The vertex processor runs **vertex shaders**. Vertex shaders are pieces of code which take vertex data as input; the data include position, color, normals, and so on. With a vertex shader an application program can perform tasks such as:

- vertex position transformations, controlled by the modelview and projection matrices,
- transforming the normal vectors and normalizing them if appropriate,
- generating and transforming texture coordinates,
- applying a light model per vertex (ambient, diffuse, and specular),
- computing color.

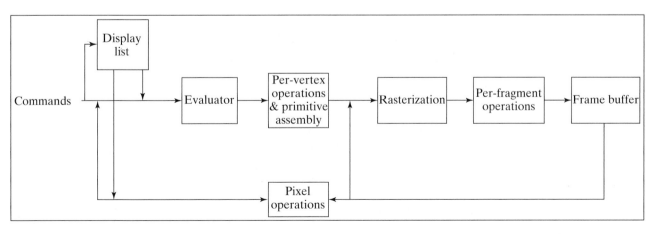

FIGURE 8.69 A portion of the OpenGL pipeline with the addition of vertex and fragment processing.

---

18 Paul Nettle's article is available at http://www.flipcode.com/articles/article_radenglish.shtml

Note. When the application programmer designs a custom vertex shader, the fixed functionality of OpenGL's vertex processor is replaced. If a custom vertex shader is enabled, it becomes accountable for replacing all the needed functionality for vertex processing.

Once the vertices have been transformed into the viewplane, primitives are rasterized and **fragments** are formed. For instance, a primitive such as a point might cover a single pixel on the screen, or a line might cover five pixels on a screen. The fragment resulting from the point consists of a window's coordinate and depth information, as well as other associated attributes including color, texture coordinates, depth, and so forth. Rasterization also determines the pixel position of the fragment. The values for each such attribute are found by interpolating between the values encountered at the vertices. A line primitive that stretches across five pixels results in five fragments, and the attributes of these fragments are found by interpolating between the corresponding values at the endpoints of the line. Some primitives don't yield any fragments at all, whereas others generate a large number of fragments. With regard to the OpenGL pipeline in Figure 8.69 the output of the "rasterization" stage is a flow of fragments (the pipeline here is actually a suggestion to how OpenGL operates).

8.7.1 Bump Mapping

The technique of bump mapping was first reported by Jim Blinn [Blinn88]. It is a highly effective method for adding complex texture to objects, without having to alter their underlying geometry. For example, Figure 8.70 shows a close-up view of an orange with a rough pitted surface. However, the actual geometry of the orange is a smooth sphere, and the texture has been painted on it. At each point the texture perturbs the natural normal vector to the surface and consequently perturbs the normal direction that is so important in the calculation of each specular highlight.

FIGURE 8.70 Bump mapping applied to an orange. (Courtesy of Ozan Uzel)

It is important to note that the geometry of the object is still a simple sphere (easily modelled), whereas the perturbing texture can be an image or other source of randomized texture, as we have discussed previously.

Figure 8.71 shows another example, where the surface appears to have been engraved with the dates, "1914–1918". However, the object is in fact a smooth rectangle, and the indentations of the engraving are created by perturbing the normal vector. Consider how complicated it would be to alter the underlying geometry (possibly a complex mesh) in order to produce similar results.

How is bump mapping done? Given an initial perturbation map with which we wish to perturb the surface normal of an object, we must calculate its effect pixel by pixel on the actual surface normal. As Blinn described it, the derivation of this normal perturbation requires the repeated use of partial derivatives and cross products between them.

FIGURE 8.71 An apparent engraving into a flat surface. (Courtesy of Chris Eyles)

The calculations are beyond the scope of this book. Fortunately certain extensions to OpenGL offer some assistance in bump mapping, sparing the application programmer from having to use the underlying mathematics (partial derivatives, and so on). There is also an excellent tutorial on this subject by Paul Baker at www.paulsprojects.net. Figure 8.72 shows an example of a torus with and without bump mapping that he develops carefully in the tutorial.

a)   b)

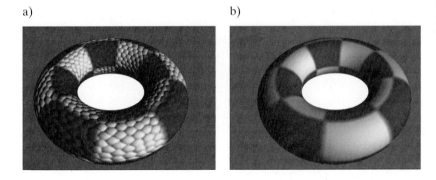

FIGURE 8.72 a) Example bump mapping of a torus, b) torus without bump mapping.

Another excellent article on bump mapping is available by Mark Kilgard of NVIDIA, who has been instrumental in implementing GLUT and continues to research OpenGL. Mark's paper, "A Practical and Robust Bump-Mapping Technique for Today's GPUs" (which can be found at www.nvidia.com), is a wonderful treatment of bump mapping and its underlying theories.

8.7.2 Nonphotorealistic Rendering

The emphasis in this book is on photorealistic rendering of scenes so that the final image is as natural looking as possible. But there are situations when realism is not the most desirable attribute of an image. Instead, one might want to emphasize a particular message in an image, or omit details that are expensive to render and of little interest to the intended audience. For example, one might want to produce a cartoonlike rendering of an engine as shown in Figure 8.73. This image gives the impression that it could have been done by hand with a paintbrush.

In another situation one might want to generate a highly detailed and precise technical drawing of some machine or a blueprint, without regard to the fineries of shading, shadows, and antialiasing. This technique has been called **pen-and-ink rendering** (could be called engraving as well). Figure 8.74 shows a pen-and-ink rendering of sailboat scene.

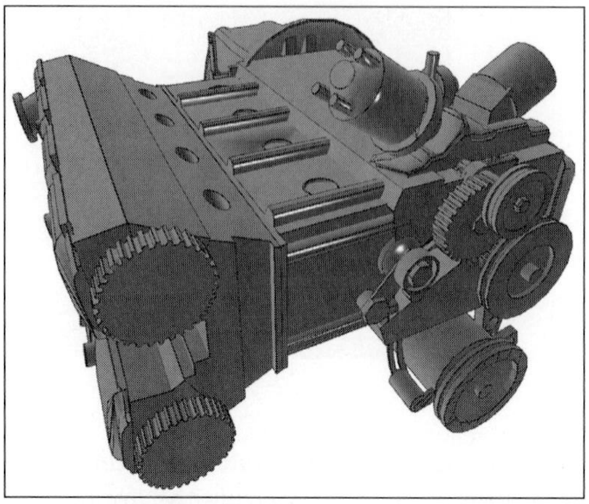

FIGURE 8.73 A cartoonlike rendering of an engine. (Courtesy of L. Molnar and J. Sun, The Ohio State University)

FIGURE 8.74 A pen-and-ink rendering of a sailboat scene. (Courtesy of Kostas Sakellis).

Figure 8.75 shows three additional examples of nonphotorealistic rendering. Note that these images must be very suggestive of what they represent, even though they clearly do not look like actual photographs of the objects.

FIGURE 8.75 Nonphotorealistic renderings of a tractor, motorcycle, and plane. (Courtesy of L. Molnar and J. Sun, The Ohio State University)

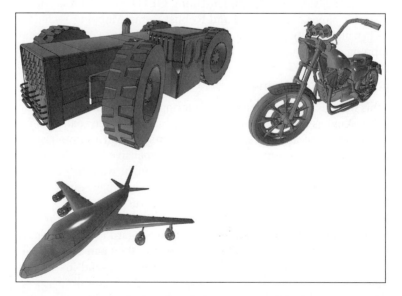

Check the book's companion web site for additional links and resources on non-photorealistic rendering.

8.8 SUMMARY

Since the beginning of computer graphics there has been a relentless quest for greater realism when rendering 3D scenes. Wireframe views of objects can be drawn very rapidly but are difficult to interpret, particularly if several objects in a scene overlap. Realism is greatly enhanced when the faces are filled with some color and surfaces that should be hidden are removed, but pictures rendered this way still do not give the impression of objects residing in a scene, illuminated by light sources.

What is needed is a shading model, which describes how light reflects off a surface depending on the nature of the surface and its orientation to both light sources and the camera's eye. The physics of light reflection is very complex, so programmers have developed a number of approximations and tricks that do an acceptable job most of the time and are reasonably efficient computationally. The model for the diffuse component is the one most closely based on reality, and it becomes extremely complex as more and more ingredients are considered. Specular reflections are not modeled on physical principles at all, but they can do an adequate job of recreating highlights on shiny objects. Ambient light is purely an abstraction, a shortcut that avoids dealing with multiple reflections from object to object, and prevents shadows from being too deep.

Even simple shading models involve several parameters such as reflection coefficients, descriptions of a surface's roughness, and the color of light sources. OpenGL provides ways to set many of these parameters. There is little guidance for the designer in choosing their values; they are often determined by trial and error until the final rendered picture looks right.

In this chapter we focused on rendering of polygonal mesh models, so the basic task was to render a polygon. Polygonal faces are particularly simple and are described by a modest amount of data, such as vertex positions, vertex normals, surface colors and material. In addition there are highly efficient algorithms for filling a polygonal face with calculated colors, especially if it is known to be convex. Algorithms can also capitalize on the flatness of a polygon to interpolate depth in an incremental fashion, making the depth-buffer hidden surface removal algorithm simple and efficient.

When a mesh model is supposed to approximate an underlying smooth surface, the appearance of a face's edges can be objectionable. Gouraud and Phong shading provide ways to draw a smoothed version of the surface (except along silhouettes). Gouraud shading is very fast but does not reproduce highlights very faithfully; Phong shading produces more realistic renderings but is computationally quite expensive. For further reading the OpenGL Architecture Review Board (ARB) has developed a shading language to produce more realistic images. Go to www.opengl.org for more details.

The realism of a rendered scene is greatly enhanced by the appearance of texturing on object surfaces. Texturing can make an object appear to be made of some material such as brick or wood, and labels or other figures can be pasted onto surfaces. Environment mapping gives the viewer an impression of the environment that surrounds a shiny object, and this can make scenes more realistic, particularly in animations. Texture mapping must be done with care, however, using proper interpolation and antialiasing (as we discuss in Chapter 9).

The chapter closed with a discussion of the effects of shadows produced by objects. This is a complex subject, and many techniques have been developed. Greater realism can be attained with more elaborate techniques such as ray tracing. Chapter 12 develops the key ideas of these techniques.

8.9 CASE STUDIES

CASE STUDY 8.1 CREATING SHADED OBJECTS USING OPENGL

(Level of Effort: II) Develop an application that flies a camera through space looking at various polygonal mesh objects. Extend it by establishing a point light source in the scene, and assigning various material properties to the meshes. Include ambient, diffuse, and specular light components. Provide a keystroke that switches between wireframe, flat, and smooth shading.

CASE STUDY 8.2 TEXTURE RENDERING

(Level of Effort: II) Enhance the program of Case Study 8.1 so that textures can be painted on the faces of the mesh objects. Assemble a routine that can read a BMP image file and attach it to an OpenGL texture object. Experiment by putting five different image textures and one procedural texture on the sides of a cube and arranging to have the cube rotate in an animation. Provide a keystroke that lets the user switch between linear interpolation and correct interpolation for rendering textures.

CASE STUDY 8.3 EXTENDING SDL TO INCLUDE TEXTURING

(Level of Effort: III) The SDL scene description language does not yet include a means to specify the texture that one wants applied to each face of an object. The keyword `texture` is currently in SDL, but it does nothing when encountered in a file. Do a careful study of the code in the `Scene` and `Shape` classes, available on the book's companion web site, and design an approach that permits a syntax such as

```
texture giraffe.bmp p1 p2 p3 p4
```

to create a texture from a stored image (here `giraffe.bmp`) and paste it onto certain faces of subsequently defined objects. Determine how many parameters `texture` should require, and how they should be used. Extend `drawOpenGL()` for two or three shapes so that it properly pastes such texture onto the objects in question.

8.10 FOR FURTHER READING

For an in-depth look into the very recent OpenGL Shading Language book, see "OpenGL Shading Language" by Randi J. Post [Post02]. For another very recent book on vertex and fragment shaders see *GPU Gems 2*, edited by Matt Pharr [Pharr05]. The classic books on graphics include Jim Blinn's *A Trip Down the Graphics Pipeline* [Blinn96] and *Dirty Pixels* [Blinn98], which offer numerous articles that lucidly explain the issues of drawing shadows and the hyperbolic interpolation used in rendering texture.

Chapter 9

....

Tools for Raster Displays

A designer knows he has achieved perfection not when there is nothing left to add, but when there is nothing left to take away.

Antoine de Saint-Exupèry
(1900–1944)

GOALS OF THE CHAPTER

○ To describe pixmaps and useful operations on them.

○ To develop tools for copying, scaling, and rotating pixmaps.

○ To discuss different drawing modes, such as XOR mode.

○ To develop tools for compositing images.

○ To develop ways to define and manipulate regions.

○ To develop Bresenham's line-drawing algorithm.

○ To build tools for filling regions—particularly polygon-defined ones.

○ To discuss aliasing, and develop antialiasing methods.

○ To introduce dithering and error-diffusion tools for creating more colors.

Preview

Sections 9.1 and 9.2 revisit the pixmap as a fundamental object for storing and manipulating images, and develop several operations on pixmaps. Section 9.3 describes ways to combine pixmaps. Drawing modes such as "exclusive-or" mode, which offer additional ways to combine pixmaps, are also discussed.

Section 9.4 develops Bresenham's line-drawing algorithm, and the next three sections examine ways to describe "regions" in a pixmap, to fill them with a color or pattern, and to manipulate them in various ways. Sections 9.5 through 9.7 offer other ways to characterize and fill regions. Section 9.8 discusses the phenomenon of aliasing (familiarly known as the "jaggies") that is inherent in pictures displayed on a raster device, and develops techniques for ameliorating its visual effect.

Section 9.9 describes ways to make a raster display appear to have more colors than it really has, using dithering and error diffusion. The Case Studies elaborate on these topics and suggest several important programming projects.

9.1 INTRODUCTION

In this chapter we examine details of how an image is formed from graphics primitives, and how an image can be manipulated to achieve an assortment of visual effects. The images in question are composed of arrays of pixels and are commonly viewed on a raster display.

There are two principal ways to create an image:

1. Scan (and digitize) an existing photograph or television image.
2. Compute pixel values procedurally, as when rendering a scene.

In previous chapters we have focussed on the second route: generating graphics primitives such as lines or polygons, and seeing how to attach colors and texture coordinates to each. Using OpenGL, we simply sent them to the viewport, where they were displayed on the screen. We glossed over the key step of setting the individual pixel values inside the line or polygon to their proper colors, letting OpenGL do the difficult work.

This process of taking high-level information such as vertex position and color and determining the colors of many pixels in a region of the frame buffer is called **scan conversion** or **rasterization**. Figure 9.1 shows a back-end portion of the graphics pipeline where rasterization is performed. When vertices emerge from the viewport transformation, OpenGL assembles them into the appropriate primitive (as determined by glBegin (GL_POLYGON) or the like) and then rasterizes the primitive, determining the properties of those pixels that lie inside the primitive. In this chapter we examine how this is done, showing ways to draw lines and to fill polygons with colors and textures.

FIGURE 9.1 The rasterization step in the graphics pipeline.

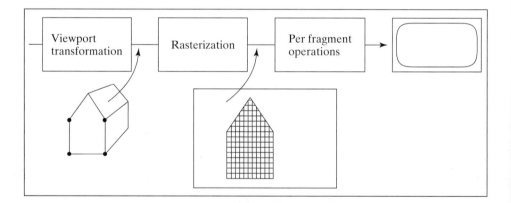

Actually, the rasterization process doesn't produce just simple pixels; as described at the end of Chapter 8 it produces **fragments**, which consist of a color, a depth, and a texture coordinate pair. A number of steps and tests (denoted in the figure as "per-fragment operations") are performed on fragments before they are written into the frame buffer as simple pixel values. We describe various possibilities for these operations, and discuss how they are useful.

We also describe how to perform various operations on an image once it has been created. This involves calculating new pixel values based on certain related pixel values in an existing image (or in several images that are being combined). OpenGL performs these manipulations in the "per-fragment operations" portion of the pipeline.

Chapter 1 introduced raster images and some of the devices that display them. Recall that the image is stored in memory in the form of a **pixmap** (short for "pixel map")—a rectangular array of numerical values. Pixmaps can be stored in arbitrary regions of a computer's memory and copied from one place to another. When a pixmap is copied to the frame buffer, the scan controller orchestrates the conversion of pixel values to dots of colored light, and the pixmap becomes visible on the display. What you see on the screen is a picture of what is stored in the frame buffer. The term *pixels* often refers both to the numerical values stored in the pixmap and to the dots of light themselves.

Also recall that each pixel value in a pixmap consists of a fixed. The number of bits used to represent each pixel value is called its **color depth**. If a pixel has a color depth of b bits, then it can take on 2^b different values, and thus can represent a maximum of 2^b different colors. If b is 1, only two colors are possible; such as black and white. But because of shrinking costs many video displays use 32 bits, thereby providing 2^{32} or more than 81 quadrillion possible colors!

Raster images and displays therefore deal with data that are **discrete** both spatially and in (color) value. This discreteness, coupled with the ability of a program to operate directly on pixel values in memory, leads to a special collection of tools for generating and processing images.

9.2 MANIPULATING PIXMAPS

> Things equal to nothing else are equal to each other.
>
> *Murphy's laws of computers*

In this section we examine a number of tools for manipulating pixmaps, both on screen (when they reside in the frame buffer) and off screen (in regular memory), and describe the visual effects these manipulations produce. We also see what tools OpenGL provides for working with pixmaps.

9.2.1 Operations of Interest for Pixmaps

We first outline what you can do with pixmaps. Then in subsequent sections we discuss how to do each of them and how well they work in different situations.

Drawing a Picture

Rendering operations that draw into the frame buffer change the particular pixmap that is visible on the display.[1] So, for instance, when OpenGL is used to render a scene, the writing is done directly into the frame buffer's pixmap.

Copying a Pixmap from One Place to Another

You can copy a pixmap from one section of memory to another. Figure 9.2 shows four kinds of copying. Four visible pixmaps are shown, along with their off-screen copies. The *copy* operation copies an image from one place on the display to another. The *read* operation copies a portion of the displayed image to off-screen memory. The *draw* operation copies a pixmap from off-screen memory onto the display. An operation we will call *memCopy* copies an image from one part of off-screen memory ro another.

As we shall see in more detail later, OpenGL offers several functions for performing these copying operations:

- `glReadPixels();` ← reads a region of the frame buffer into off-screen memory
- `glCopyPixels();` ← copies a region of the frame buffer into another part of the frame buffer
- `glDrawPixels();` ← draws a given pixmap into the frame buffer

---

[1] Frame-buffer memory is sometimes called on-screen memory, due to the close connection between pixel values and what is seen on the screen.

FIGURE 9.2 Varieties of copy operations for a pixmap.

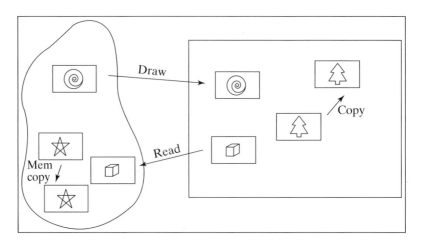

Scaling and Rotating a Pixmap

It is often necessary to magnify or reduce an image, and to rotate it. This can be a simple or rather complex process, depending on the magnification factor and the rotation angle involved.

We discuss many details later.

Comparing Two Pixmaps

Another important task is to compare two pixmaps to see how they differ. For instance, two digitized x-rays can be compared to see if a tumor has changed over time. Usually the two pixmaps are compared pixel by pixel, and some mathematical operation is performed on pairs of corresponding pixels.

Representing and Coloring Regions in a Pixmap

Some pixmaps contain clearly identifiable objects, such as circles, polygons, or certain **regions** of pixels that are in some way homogeneous. (Think of an x-ray of a heart, a brain, or a jaw.) We need ways to describe regions in a pixmap and to represent them in a higher-level, more abstract, or symbolic form. In addition we often want to color all of the pixels that lie inside some region with a given color or pattern, a process known as **region filling**.

9.2.2 Useful Data Types for Pixmaps

A man's work is nothing but this slow trek to rediscover, through the detours of art, those two or three great and simple images in whose presence his heart first opened.

Albert Camus
(1913–1960)

It is natural to design some classes to support pixmap manipulations. A pixmap has a certain number of rows and columns, and each of its pixels contains a specified amount of data. Important examples are:

- The **bitmap:** Each pixel is stored in a single bit, so each pixel is either "on" or "off".
- The **grayscale** pixmap: Each pixel is stored in a single byte, representing levels of gray from 0 for black up to 255 for white.
- **LUT indices**: Each pixel contains a number that represents an index into a color look-up table (LUT), as described in Chapter 1.

- The **RGB pixmap:** Each pixel consists of three bytes, one each for the red, green, and blue components. Such pixels are considered to represent "true color."
- The **RGBA pixmap**: Each pixel consists of four bytes; the fourth byte contains the "alpha value," which represents opacity. We shall discuss the use of the alpha channel in Section 9.3.

In order to work with pixmaps we fashion a class that holds a pixmap's data and provides methods to manage and manipulate the images. We'll develop the details for RGB pixmaps, and extend them as needed to other types of pixmaps. In order to capitalize on OpenGL's image manipulations tools we shall store the pixmap data in the same way OpenGL does[2].

We first define a type called RGB that holds a single pixel value as an RGB triple:

```
struct RGB{unsigned char r,g,b;};
```

Figure 9.3 shows the beginning of our RGBpixmap class. We follow OpenGL and represent a pixmap as a simple array pixel of pixel values stored row by row from bottom to top, and across each row from left to right.

Several methods are outlined in the figure. The default RGBpixmap constructor makes an empty pixmap, and the other constructor creates a pixmap having r rows and c columns. The methods setPixel() and getPixel() respectively set and read a specific pixel values.

The methods draw(), read(), and copy() are implemented directly in terms of OpenGL functions.

- draw() copies the pixmap to the frame buffer, placing its lower left corner at the "current raster position," a variable that can be set using glRasterPos2i (x, y).
- read() copies in the other direction, from a rectangular region in the frame buffer into the pixmap. The lower left corner of this region lies at point pt, and wid and ht specify the size of the region. read() allocates the necessary memory to hold the pixels, and glReadPixels() does the actual copying.
- copy() copies one region of the frame buffer into another, effectively performing both a read() and a draw() but without creating an intermediate pixmap. The region has lower left corner at point (x, y) and a size given by wid and ht. The region is copied to a new position in the frame buffer, whose lower left corner lies at the current raster position. This is a form of the "**bitblt**" operation we shall examine in Section 9.3.4.

The utilities readBMPFile() and writeBMPFile() allow easy creation and storage of pixmaps. readBMPFile() reads an image stored as a BMP file into the pixmap, allocating storage as necessary. writeBMPFile() creates a BMP file that contains the pixmap. Code for both of these functions is given on line at the book's companion web site. Another option is the loadBMP() function developed at http://nehe.gamedev.net; several tutorials are available there which provide a slightly different approach to pixmap functions.

This class is simple yet powerful. In the following example we show how it may be used.

---

[2] OpenGL actually offers a number of ways to "pack" data for a pixmap in memory. We work with the most commonly used format.

```
class RGBpixmap{
    private:
        int nRows, nCols; // dimensions of the pixmap
        RGB* pixel; // array of pixels
    public:
        RGBpixmap() {nRows = nCols = 0; pixel = 0;}
        RGBpixmap(int r, int c) // constructor
        {
           nRows = r;
           nCols = c;
           pixel = new RGB[r*c];// allocate memory for the pixel array
        }
        void setPixel(int x, int y, RGB color)
        {
           if(x >= 0 && x < nCols && y >= 0 && y < nRows)
               pixel[nCols * y + x] = color;
        }
        RGB getPixel(int x, int y)// read pixel value stored in memory
        {
               return pixel[nCols * y + x];
        }
    //*** draw this pixmap at the current raster position(CRP)
    void draw(){
        glDrawPixels(nCols, nRows, GL_RGB, GL_UNSIGNED_BYTE,pixel);
    }
    //*** read a rectangle of pixels into this pixmap
    void read(int x, int y, int wid, int ht){
        nRows = ht;
        nCols = wid;
        pixel = new RGB[nRows *nCols]; if(!pixel)exit(-1);
        glReadPixels(x, y, nCols, nRows, GL_RGB,
        GL_UNSIGNED_BYTE, pixel);
    }
    //*** copy a region of the display back onto the display
    void copy(int x, int y, int wid, int ht){
        glCopyPixels(x, y, wid, ht, GL_COLOR);
    }
    //*** read BMP file into this pixmap
    int readBmpFile(char * fname);
    //*** write this pixmap to a BMP file
    void writeBmpFile(char * fname);

    // ...others ...
}; // end of the RGBpixmap class
```

FIGURE 9.3 The RGBpixmap class for manipulating RGB images.

■ **EXAMPLE 9.2.1 A test bed for manipulating pixmaps**

Figure 9.4 shows an application that uses the pixmap class to control the reading and drawing of pixmaps with the mouse and keyboard. It is very informative to experiment with this program. Two pixmaps, Pic[0] and Pic[1], are created at startup and loaded with two BMP images. One is displayed at the initial raster position. A left mouse click draw()'s it again at the mouse position. If the left button is held down, the pixmap is drawn again and again as the mouse is swept around the screen window. Pressing the 's' key toggles between the two pixmaps that are drawn in this way. Pressing 'r' read()'s whatever has been drawn in a

200-by-200-pixel region in the screen window and places the data in pic[0], destroying the previous contents of pic[0]. A right mouse click clears the screen.

```
//necessary includes
RGBpixmap pic[2]; // create two (empty) global pixmaps
 int screenWidth = 640, screenHeight = 480;
IntPoint rasterPos(100,100);
int whichPic = 0; // which pixmap to display
//<<<<<<<<<<<<<<<<<<<<<<< myMouse >>>>>>>>>>>>>>>>>>>>>>>>
void myMouse(int button, int state, int mx, int my)
{ // set raster position with a left click
  if(button == GLUT_LEFT_BUTTON && state == GLUT_UP)
  {
     rasterPos.x = mx; rasterPos.y = screenHeight - my;
     glRasterPos2i(rasterPos.x, rasterPos.y);
     glutPostRedisplay();
  }
 else glClear(GL_COLOR_BUFFER_BIT); // clear with right click
}
//<<<<<<<<<<<<<<<<<<<<<<< mouseMove >>>>>>>>>>>>>>>>>>
void mouseMove(int x, int y)
{// set raster position with mouse motion
    rasterPos.x = x; rasterPos.y = screenHeight - y;
    glRasterPos2i(rasterPos.x, rasterPos.y);
    glutPostRedisplay();
}
//<<<<<<<<<<<<<<<<<<<<<<< myReshape >>>>>>>>>>>>>>>>>>>>>
void myReshape(int w, int h)
{
    screenWidth = w; screenHeight = h;
}
//<<<<<<<<<<<<<<<<<<<<<<< myDisplay >>>>>>>>>>>>>>>>>>>>>>>>
void myDisplay(void)
{
    pic[whichPic].draw(); //draw it at the raster position
}
//<<<<<<<<<<<<<<<<<<<<<<< myKeys >>>>>>>>>>>>>>>>>>>>>>>>
void myKeys(unsigned char key, int x, int y)
{
 switch(key)
 {
    case 'q': exit(0);
    case 's': whichPic = 1 - whichPic; break; // switch pixmaps
    case 'r': pic[0].read(0,0,200,200); break; // grab a piece
 }
 glutPostRedisplay();
}
//<<<<<<<<<<<<<<<<<<<<< main >>>>>>>>>>>>>>>>>>>>>>>>>>
void main(int argc, char **argv)
{
 glutInit(&argc, argv);
 glutInitDisplayMode(GLUT_SINGLE | GLUT_RGB);
 glutInitWindowSize(screenWidth, screenHeight);
 glutInitWindowPosition(30, 30);
 glutCreateWindow("Experiment with images");
 glutKeyboardFunc(myKeys);
 glutMouseFunc(myMouse);
```

FIGURE 9.4 A test-bed application for manipulating pixmaps.

FIGURE 9.4 (*Continued*)

```
    glutMotionFunc(mouseMove);
    glutDisplayFunc(myDisplay);
    glutReshapeFunc(myReshape);
    glClearColor(0.9f, 0.9f, 0.9f, 0.0); //background color
    glClear(GL_COLOR_BUFFER_BIT);
    pic[0].readBmpFile("CokeCan2.bmp"); //make a pixmap
    pic[1].readBmpFile("Mandrill.bmp"); // make another one
    glutMainLoop();
}
```

We show in subsequent examples how variants of the draw(), read(), and copy() functions can be used to accomplish frequently needed tasks. These utilities are also exercised in Case Study 9.1.

▪ EXAMPLE 9.2.2 Writing text to the screen

One common way to draw text characters on a raster display is to build a different pixmap for each possible character. Figure 9.5 shows several examples. These pixmaps provide pictures of characters defined in a cell of a certain size, say 12 by 8, typically by making some pixels 0 and the rest 1. A large cell size allows more freedom in placing the 0 pixels in each cell and thereby managing the shape of each character, so that pleasing fonts can be fashioned.

FIGURE 9.5 Individual text characters can be formed in arrays of binary cells: larger arrays allow more pleasing shapes to be formed. Left-to-right, arrays of size 4 by 6, 6 by 8, 8 by 12, and 12 by 16.

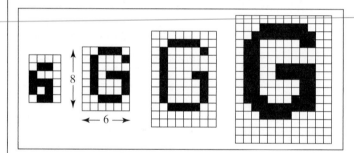

When a workstation is initialized, a variety of fonts can be loaded from disk into off-screen memory to make them readily available. To draw a string of characters, each character is draw()'n into the frame buffer at the proper spot. After each character is drawn, the *x*-position is incremented by the width of that character. With a **proportionally spaced** font each character has a specific width ("i" is usually the narrowest, and "W" the widest). This gives text the most pleasing appearance.

▪ EXAMPLE 9.2.3 Window scrolling

In applications such as word processors, the screen usually fills with text, line by line. To make room for a new line of text at the bottom, all of the text above it must be scrolled up one line (discarding the top line of text, of course), as suggested in Figure 9.6. To do this, the rectangle containing all but the top line is copy()'d up one line, overwriting what was previously there. Then a blank line is draw()'n into the position of the last row.

FIGURE 9.6 Scrolling text in a window.

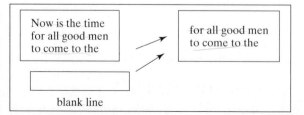

■ EXAMPLE 9.2.4 Pop-up, pull-down menus, and dialog boxes

Most interaction with a computer today is through a graphical user interface (GUI), as discussed in Chapter 2. Among other things, such an interface presents menus and dialog boxes, and the user employs the mouse to choose each action desired.

When a menu is activated, it pops into view, temporarily covering some part of the screen. Figure 9.7a shows a part of the screen obscured by a **pull-down menu**. After the user makes a choice the menu disappears, and the portion that was hidden by the menu is again revealed (Figure 9.7b). This hidden portion must first be stored in off-screen memory, so that it can later be restored. This is done with the sequence described in Chapter 2:

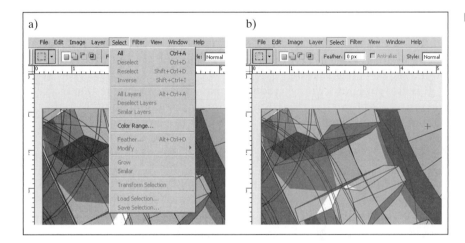

FIGURE 9.7 A pull-down menu.

1. The user selects a menu header;
2. The program determines the rectangular region that is about to be obscured;
3. A copy of this region is read() to a pixmap off screen;
4. The picture of the menu is draw()'n in its place;
5. The user moves the cursor to the desired menu item and releases the button;
6. The application restores the obscured portion by copying the off-screen pixmap to its original position.

9.2.3 To Scale and Rotate Images

> Never wear earmuffs in a bed full of rattlesnakes.
>
> *Murphy's laws of computers*

Images often must be scaled or rotated. For instance, a satellite image of the earth might show Europe in a 1200-by-1600-pixel pixmap, and we may wish to compare this with a previously scanned 1540-by-1880-pixel image of India. Before the pixmaps can be compared, the smaller one must be enlarged to make corresponding parts of the images line up properly. Similarly, in compiling a collection of digitized fingerprints we may find that some fingerprint images are rotated slightly relative to the others. To compare different fingerprints we must rotate the images into the same alignment. We look briefly at some of the simple types of scaling and rotation.

When scaling a pixmap by some scaling factor, say s, the notion is to create a pixmap that has s times as many pixels in both x and y. In photography parlance, when s is larger than 1, the pixmap is **enlarged**; otherwise it is **reduced**. The pixels themselves, of course, don't change size. When s is an integer, it is easy to

FIGURE 9.8 Pixel doubling to scale characters.

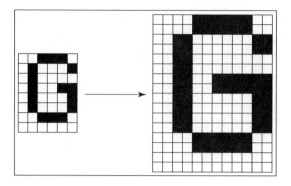

scale a pixmap by **pixel replication**. Figure 9.8 shows an example of *pixel doubling* of a character bitmap. Each pixel in the smaller character produces a 2-by-2 array of pixels. For other integer values of *s*, each pixel produces an *s*-by-*s* array of pixels.

It is also straightforward to reduce a pixmap by some integer factor (i.e., $s = 1/n$, where *n* is an integer). For $s = 1/3$, for instance, we could build the reduced pixmap by simply retaining only every third row and column of the original. "Sampling" the original pixmap in this way usually loses information, so the reduced image may be far inferior to the original. It is usually better, if possible, to compute the average color of the nine pixels and place this average in the remaining representative pixel. We discuss this and other antialiasing techniques in Section 9.7.

OpenGL provides a simple mechanism to scale the picture drawn by a pixmap through either glDrawPixels() or glCopyPixels() (so the methods draw() and copy() will show the effects of the scaling). The function

    glPixelZoom(float sx, float sy);

sets scale factors in *x* and *y* by which subsequent drawing of pixmaps takes place. The pixmaps themselves are not scaled; rather the pictures produced from the pixmaps are scaled. Any floating-point values are allowed for sx and sy, even negative ones. The default values are 1.0.

The scaling takes place about the current raster position, *pt*. Consider the pixel in row *r* and column *c* of the pixmap. Roughly speaking, it will be drawn as a rectangle of width *sx* and height *sy* screen pixels, with lower left corner at screen pixel ($pt.x + sx*r$, $pt.y + sy*c$). More precisely, any screen pixels whose centers lie in this rectangle are drawn in the color of this pixmap pixel. For example, if *sx* is 2 and *sy* is 3, the pixmap is drawn with true pixel replication and will be twice as wide and three times as high as the unscaled pixmap. Its lower left corner remains at the current raster position. If *sx* and/or *sy* have fractional values, the image will be correspondingly reduced and may experience a loss in quality, since the color of each screen pixel is simply the color of the "rectangular" pixel in which its center lies.

If *sx* or *sy* is negative, the image is flipped about the current raster position. This can be useful for flipping a pixmap upside down (using glPixelZoom(1.0, −1.0)) and producing special visual effects. Figure 9.9 shows a snapshot from the preceding test bed program, in which six scaled versions of a cat are seen placed about the current raster position (using the sequence of scale factors $sx = -1.5, -1.0, -0.5, 1.5, 1.0, 0.5$). To produce each image the new value of *sx* was set, and glPixelZoom(sx, 1); glutPostRedisplay(); was executed.

FIGURE 9.9 Multiple versions of a pixmap formed by scaling in x.

Quarter-Turn Rotations

The process of rotating a pixmap through 90°, 180°, or 270° is very simple. A new pixmap is created, and pixels are copied from one to the other using `getPixel()` and `setPixel()`. See the exercises.

More General Scaling and Rotations

Things are more complicated when an arbitrary scaling and/or rotation is desired. Suppose we wish to create a pixmap that contains a transformed version of some original pixmap. Figure 9.10 shows a pixmap S (the source) that we wish to alter with a transformation T, perhaps an affine transformation that involves some mix of scaling and rotation. The result will be the pixmap D (the destination). The issue is to compute the proper pixel color at each point p in D. The simplest approach finds, for the center point p of each pixel in D, the color of the pixel in S that covers the point $T^{-1}(p)$. This color is then used for the pixel at p in D. Using just these samples can lead to poor results with severe aliasing. This is again a form of antialiasing.

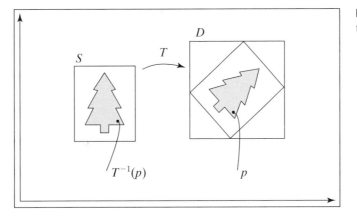

FIGURE 9.10 Computing the transformed image.

PRACTICE EXERCISES

9.2.1 Design the letter 'R'

Design and sketch an 8-by-16 bilevel image that displays the letter 'R'. Show both the pattern of 1's and 0's, and the picture that results when 0 stands for white and 1 for black.

9.2.2 Designing characters

Design the most pleasing-looking characters, a, A, r, R, &, and 3, inside cells of r rows and c columns. Do this for each of the following cell sizes:

a. $(r, c) = (6, 4)$.
b. $(r, c) = (10, 8)$.
c. $(r, c) = (14, 12)$.

9.2.3 Reducing characters

One way to reduce the size of a character defined in a rectangular pixmap is to cut the cell size in half in both dimensions. Then each pixel in the reduced pixmap must mimic what was a 2-by-2 array of pixels in the original cell. Develop an algorithm that produces a 6-row by 5-column pixel pattern from a 12-row by 10-column pixmap. One approach sets each new pixel to 1 if two or more pixels in the 2-by-2 array are 1. Is this a good rule?

9.2.4 Rotation through 90°

Consider the square pixmap represented by the array `A[i][j]`, where i and j vary from 0 to `N-1`. Express the value `B[col][row]` of the pixmap formed by rotating A through 90° counterclockwise. ■

9.3 COMBINING PIXMAPS

> Your life story would not make a good book. Don't even try.
>
> *Metropolitan Life*
> *Fran Lebowitz*
> *(1950–)*

There are circumstances where we wish to combine two pixmaps to produce a third. This is useful for such things as moving cursors around a screen, comparing two images, and morphing one image into another. We look at several examples of practical importance.

Pixmaps are usually combined *pixelwise*—that is, by performing some operation between corresponding pixels in the old and new pixmaps. Specifically, pixmaps A and B are combined to form pixmap C according to:

$$C[i][j] = A[i][j] \otimes B[i][j] \qquad \text{for each } i, j$$

where $\otimes$ denotes some operation. Examples of different operations are:

- Averaging two images—here $\otimes$ means to form the sum of one half of A plus one half of B:

$$C[i][j] = \tfrac{1}{2}(A[i][j] + B[i][j])$$

- Differencing two images, to determine how different they are—here $\otimes$ means subtraction:

$$C[i][j] = A[i][j] - B[i][j]$$

- Finding where one image is brighter than another—here $>$ means "is greater than":

$$C[i][j] = A[i][j] > B[i][j]$$

  giving each pixel in C the value 1 if the corresponding pixel in A is brighter than that in B, and 0 otherwise.

A generalization of averaging two images is to form their **weighted average**. Pixmap A is weighted by $(1 - f)$ and B is weighted by f, for some fraction f:

$$C[i][j] = (1 - f)A[i][j] + fB[i][j] \tag{9.1}$$

For instance, if the RGB components of $A[i][j]$ are $(14, 246, 97)$ and those of $B[i][j]$ are $(82, 12, 190)$, then for $f = 0.2$ we have $C[i][j] = (27, 199, 115)$. A weighted average of two RGBpixmaps can be achieved using the modification of the `setPixel()` function given in Figure 9.3.

■ **EXAMPLE 9.3.1 Dissolving one image into another**

An interesting application of a weighted average occurs when you wish to **dissolve** between two images. First image A is fully displayed, but as time passes A slowly fades and image B emerges superimposed on A, until finally only B is displayed. If t represents time, then at time t the image:

$$A(1 - t) + Bt$$

is displayed, as t moves smoothly from 0 to 1. This is very similar to tweening, which we described in Chapter 4. Figure 9.11 shows five stages of the displayed image, for values of $t = 0, 0.25, 0.5, 0.75$, and 1. Case Study 9.2 discusses an easy way to dissolve between two images, using the alpha channel facility of OpenGL, as we describe in Section 9.3.2.

FIGURE 9.11 Dissolving between two images.

9.3.1 The Read–Modify–Write Cycle

We looked at forming a new pixmap C as a combination of two pixmaps—say, D and S. A special case occurs when C is the same as D, so the result is placed back into D. This can be represented as $D = D \otimes S$: the pixels in pixmap D (for "destination") are combined with those in S (for "source"), and the result is put back into D. This is called a **read–modify–write** cycle, because the pixels in D are first read from memory, then modified by combining them with those of S, and then the result is written back into D. Figure 9.12 suggests symbolically how this works when D is the frame buffer itself. The cycle is applied for each pixel of D in turn. Some hardware configurations make this a very efficient operation. OpenGL provides tools to do this to an entire pixmap in one instruction, as we shall see.

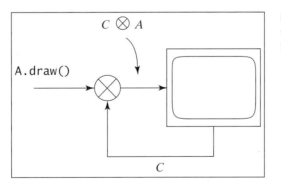

FIGURE 9.12 A read–modify–write cycle applied to the frame buffer.

9.3.2 The Alpha Channel and Image Blending

Forming a weighted sum of two images is actually a special case of a more general operation, which is variously called **blending** or **compositing** of images. Blending allows you to draw a partially transparent image over another image.

The key is to add a fourth component, the so-called **alpha value**, to *each* RGB color. In terms of data types to hold pixels, we extend the previous RGB type to the RGBA type:

```
struct RGBA{
unsigned char r, g, b, a;
};
```

and assign each pixel an alpha value a between 0 and 255. The usual interpretation is that the alpha value specifies how "opaque" each pixel is: a value of 0 indicates complete transparency, and a value of 255 indicates total opacity. Note that it takes 4/3 as much memory to store an RGBA pixmap as it does to store an RGB pixmap. Taken together, the collection of alpha values present in a pixmap is often called the **alpha channel**.

As we see next, the alpha component is most frequently used as a scaling factor that lies between 0 and 1, so the actual value used is the fraction $a/255$.

■ EXAMPLE 9.3.2 Overlaying an image with a partially transparent image

Figure 9.13 shows an example of overlaying an image S of a mask and a dragon onto an ocean background image D. When the source image S was created, the dragon pixels were given alpha values of 255 (the dragon is always opaque), the mask pixels were given alpha values of 128 (half opaque), and all other pixels were given alpha values of 0. When S is blended with D, the result shows the dragon in the foreground on top of the background D, and some of the background color "seeps through" the mask.

FIGURE 9.13 Compositing image S onto image D.

Alpha blending can be accomplished in a read–modify–write cycle by forming a weighted average of the source and destination pixels and putting this average back into the destination. Symbolically, $D = aS + (1 - a)D$, where a is the alpha value of the source, considered as some fraction between 0 and 1. But the alpha value varies from pixel to pixel, and both S and D have red, green, and blue components, so a more precise writing of, say, the green component of the final destination pixel at row j and column i, is:

$$D[i][j] \cdot g = aS[i][j] \cdot g + (1 - a)D[i][j] \cdot g \tag{9.2}$$

where the fraction a is

$$a = \frac{S[i][j] \cdot a}{255}$$

Note particularly the dependence of a on i and j: the alpha value varies from pixel to pixel. Similar expressions hold for the red and blue components.

To do this kind of blending in a program we would first extend the RGBpixmap class described earlier to the class RGBApixmap (see the exercises) and then add a method blend() that performs this overlaying in a read–modify–write cycle. Then blending the pixmap S with pixmap D would be carried out using:

```
D.draw(); // draw D opaquely as usual
S.blend(); // use alpha values in S: form a weighted average with D
```

OpenGL offers tools that make it easy to implement blend(): you simply set a *blend mode* that specifies how it determines the source scaling factor and the destination scaling factor. To set *a* to the source's alpha value, simply specify:

```
glBlendFunc(GL_SRC_ALPHA, GL_ONE_MINUS_SRC_ALPHA);
```

This command sets the source scale factor to the alpha value of the source itself, and the destination scale factor to 1 minus the source's alpha value, as desired. Figure 9.14 shows a simple implementation of blend().

```
void RGBApixmap :: blend()
{
    glBlendFunc(GL_SRC_ALPHA, GL_ONE_MINUS_SRC_ALPHA);
    glEnable(GL_BLEND); // enable blending
    draw(); // draw this pixmap blended with the destination
}
```

FIGURE 9.14 Blending a source and destination image using the source's alpha channel.

■ **EXAMPLE 9.3.3 Simulating ChromaKey: forcing certain colors to be transparent**

A familiar sight on television is the weather announcer standing in front of a map pointing at various weather conditions. In fact, the person is standing in front of a blue background (Figure 9.15a), and a separate weather map is filmed simultaneously. The television signal switches between the person image and the map image on the fly: when the blue color is encountered during a line scan, the map signal is switched in; otherwise the person signal is switched in.

FIGURE 9.15 ChromaKey used in television.

We can simulate this with pixmaps and make a specific color in the source pixmap transparent by setting its alpha value to 0. The following routine scans through a pixmap, setting the alpha value of each pixel to 0 if the pixel's color matches the chosen color, and to 1 otherwise.

```
void RGBApixmap::setChromaKey(RGB c)
{   long count = 0;
    for(int row = 0; row < nCols; row++)
     for(int col = 0; col < nRows; col++)
     {
    RGBA p = pixel[count];
    if(p.r == c.r && p.g == c.g && p.b == c.b)
            pixel[count++].a = 0;
        else pixel[count++].a = 255;
    }
}
```

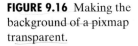

FIGURE 9.16 Making the background of a pixmap transparent.

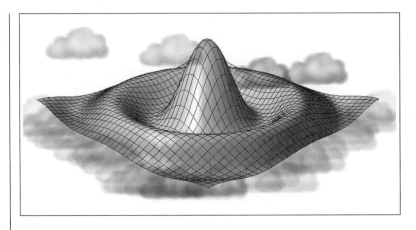

Figure 9.16 shows a pixmap S that has a background of color c. The method setChromaKey(c) was applied to this pixmap to make pixels of color c have alpha values of 0. The result of blend()ing pixmap S with a pixmap D is shown in part b.

■ EXAMPLE 9.3.4 Applying paint with a paintbrush

In a paint program the mouse cursor acts like a paintbrush, and you can lay down a swatch of color with each "brush stroke." This can be done by blend()ing the pixmap of the paintbrush with the destination image, using an alpha of 10% or so for the paintbrush pixels. At each brushstroke a little more of the paintbrush color is blended into the destination. (See the exercises for an estimate of how the amount of the new color grows with each brushstroke.) Pixels near the center of the brush can be given a higher alpha than those near the edges, so color is added more rapidly near the center of the brush.

■ EXAMPLE 9.3.5 Cursor management

When the user moves the mouse, the mouse cursor is swept across the display. At each position the cursor obscures the part of the display that it covers. When the mouse moves on, this part must be restored.

The process to do this is similar to that required for a pull-down menu, as we now show in Figure 9.17. Before the cursor is drawn on the screen, a copy (shown as pixmap *Pix1*) is made of the rectangular piece of the image that is about to be covered by the cursor. The cursor pixmap is then blended at that spot. This pixmap has an alpha of 1 in the opaque part of the cursor arrow, and an alpha of 0 elsewhere, so when blended, the arrow appears to float over the background image. When the cursor is moved to a new position, three things happen:

1. *Pix1* is draw()n (with an alpha of 1) to cover the current cursor image and to restore the original image.
2. A copy of the part about to be obscured (*Pix2*) is read() into off-screen memory.
3. The cursor is again blended at the new position.

Note that this works even if the cursor is moved only a very small distance.

Extensions Available in OpenGL

OpenGL offers several tools for setting and using alpha channel.

1. *Setting Alpha Values* While rendering a scene, you can explicitly set alpha values of subsequently drawn graphics objects by specifying the fourth color component using glColor4f(r,g,b,a), where a ranges from 0.0 (total transparency) to 1.0 (total opacity). The default alpha value is 1.0.

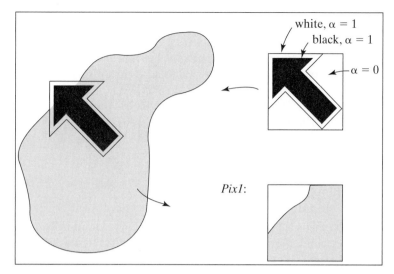

FIGURE 9.17 Managing the moving cursor.

You can also give a 3D object a "semitransparent material," so that all pixels drawn for this object have specific alpha values. This is done by specifying an alpha value in the diffuse reflection coefficient for each vertex of the object, using

```
glMaterialfv(GL_FRONT, GL_DIFFUSE, refl);
```

where `refl` is a 4-tuple giving the color of the diffuse component, as in `float refl[4] = {0.5, 0.3, 0.8, 0.4}`. This assigns an alpha value of 0.4 to subsequently defined vertices.

2. *Setting Blending Methods* We saw the use of `glBlendFunc(GL_SRC_ALPHA, GL_ONE_MINUS_SRC_ALPHA)` to produce the weighted average $D = aS + (1 - a)D$ of the source and destination pixmaps. OpenGL allows the source and destination scaling factors to be set to different values by choosing different parameters for `glBlendFunc()`, such as `GL_ZERO`, `GL_ONE`, `GL_DST_ ALPHA`, `GL_SRC_COLOR`, and so on.

For example, `glBlendFunc(GL_DST_ALPHA, GL_ONE_MINUS_DST_ALPHA)` weights the source and destination pixels by a_D and $(1 - a_D)$, respectively, where a_D is now the alpha of the destination rather than that of the source. And `glBlendFunc(GL_DST_COLOR, GL_ZERO)` modulates (multiplies) each color component of a source pixel by the level of the corresponding component in the destination.

PRACTICE EXERCISES

9.3.3 Extend the `RGBpixmap` class to include an alpha component

Make adjustments to the `RGBpixmap` class defined in Section 9.2.2 so that pixmaps support an alpha channel. Add the `blend()` and `setChromaKey()` methods, and test them by: a) reading a BMP image into a pixmap (it is most interesting if the image has a uniform background of some color); b) making a certain color transparent using `setChromaKey()`; c) blending this pixmap with some other to see the transparency in action.

9.3.4 Applying new color with "brushstrokes"

Consider a "paintbush" pixmap that has small alpha values near the center of the brush and 0 alpha values elsewhere. Each time the paintbrush is applied, it blends the brush color C with whatever color image D is in the destination, so D becomes $aC + (1 - a)D$. Repeated applications increase the amount of paintbrush color. a) Show that after the ith application the destination color is $D_i = aC + (1 - a)D_{i-1}$. b) Solve for the fraction of the destination color that is due to the source color C after eight applications. ■

9.3.3 Logical Combinations of Pixmaps

Other ways of combining pixmaps treat each pixel value simply as a collection of bits, paying no attention to the numerical value that the bits represent. The pixmaps are combined pixel by pixel as before, but the bits in a pixel are combined **logically** bit by bit. For instance, they might be OR-ed, AND-ed, or EXCLUSIVE OR-ed together.

Suppose, for example, that pixel A has RGB components $(21, 127, 0)$. Writing the components in binary form, A is $(00010101, 01111111, 00000000)$. Suppose further that pixel B in binary is $(01010101, 11110000, 10000101)$. If these are OR-ed together, the result is shown as C:

A: (00010101, 01111111, 00000000)
B: (01010101, 11110000, 10000101)
C: (01010101, 11111111, 10000101)   ← the OR of A and B

Each bit of C is a 1 if either (or both) of the corresponding bits in A and B is 1. If, on the other hand, they are EXCLUSIVE OR-ed (XOR-ed) together, we get:

A: (00010101, 01111111, 00000000)
B: (01010101, 11110000, 10000101)
C: (01000000, 10001111, 10000101)   ← the XOR of A and B

In this case each bit of C is 1 if exactly one of the corresponding bits in A and B is 1—i.e., if one but not both are 1. The color C = A XOR B depends on both A and B in a complex manner—see the exercises. What is A XOR B if B is black: $(0, 0, 0)$? What is A XOR B if B is white: $(255, 255, 255)$? An interesting property of the XOR operation is that applying it twice is equivalent to not applying it at all: that is, if we form C = A XOR B, and then XOR this with B to form (A XOR B) XOR B, the result is A again! (See the exercises.) We exploit this later when doing rubber banding.

Languages like C++ directly support executing bitwise logical operations, so it is straightforward to perform them in a routine. To OR the green components of A and B, for instance, simply execute: `C.g = A.g | B.g`. Similarly, to XOR the red bytes, execute `C.r = A.r ^ B.r`.

Other operators include AND, NOT, and combinations of these. If two values are AND-ed, represented in C++ for the green component as `C.g = A.g & B.g`, each bit in `C.g` is a 1 only if both the corresponding bits in A and B are 1. If a value is NOT-ed or complemented, represented in C++ as `C.g = ~A.g`, each bit in C is 1 if and only if the corresponding bit in A is 0.

We could use these logical operators in C++ to combine two pixmaps pixel by pixel, but happily OpenGL provides a mechanism for combining two pixmaps all at once. Once a logical operation is chosen and enabled, all subsequent drawing performs a read–modify–write cycle of the source pixels with the pixels currently stored in the frame buffer.

The use of logical operations is enabled using `glEnable(GL_COLOR_LOGIC_OP)`. The operator is selected using `glLogicOp()` with one of the arguments shown in Figure 9.18, where S stands for the source pixel and D for the destination pixel. The default is `GL_COPY`, which simply replaces the destination with the source.

Figure 9.19 shows examples of logically combining two 8-by-8-pixel pixmaps A and B, for the case of binary-valued pixels. The association of pixel value to color here is black for 0 and white for 1. (What do the pixmaps look like for the GL_AND and GL_EQUIV operators?)

Next we describe the classic application of XOR drawing, **rubber rectangles**, and show how it is implemented using OpenGL. It exploits the fact that two successive drawings of an object in XOR mode erase the object, leaving the original image untouched. Other examples are considered in the exercises.

Parameter Value	Value written to Destination
GL_CLEAR	0
GL_COPY	S
GL_NOOP	D
GL_SET	1
GL_COPY_INVERTED	NOT S
GL_INVERT	NOT D
GL_AND_REVERSE	S OR NOT D
GL_AND	S AND D
GL_OR	S OR D
GL_NAND	NOT(S AND D)
GL_NOR	NOT(S OR D)
GL_XOR	S XOR D
GL_EQUIV	NOT(S XOR D)
GL_AND_INVERTED	NOT S AND D
GL_OR_INVERTED	NOT S OR D

FIGURE 9.18 Possible logical operations in OpenGL.

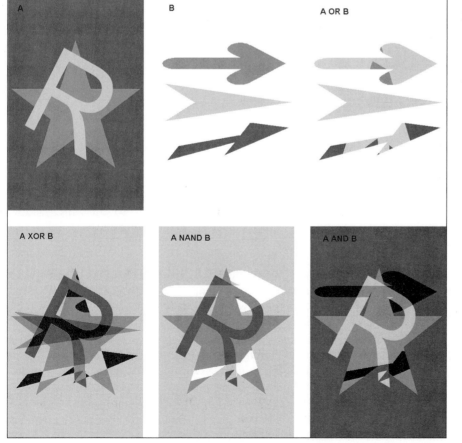

FIGURE 9.19 Effect of various logical operations.

▪ EXAMPLE 9.3.6 Rubber rectangle drawing

"Rubber rectangles" and "rubber-band lines" provide valuable feedback to a user who wishes to draw precise figures on the display with the mouse. Figure 9.20 shows examples. When drawing a rubber rectangle as in part a, the user first points the mouse at the spot where one corner of the rectangle is desired and presses a mouse button. This defines a "pivot" point. Then, as the user moves the mouse away from the pivot (with the button depressed), an "elastic" rectangle is seen that always has one corner at the pivot and the opposite corner at the current mouse position. As the rectangle changes, it appears to pass over whatever is drawn on the screen without altering it. The rectangle lets the user adjust the rectangle back and forth until it covers exactly the region desired. When the button is released, the final rectangle remains visible, and its coordinates can be used by the program to do further drawing. A rubber band (part b) is an elastic line that extends from the pivot to the mouse position, growing and shrinking as the mouse is moved. It is just a variation of the rubber rectangle, produced by drawing only the diagonal of the rectangle.

FIGURE 9.20 Rubber rectangles and rubber-band lines.

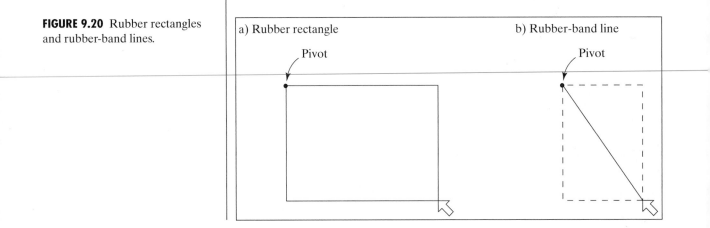

A rubber rectangle (or rubber-band line) must be continually erased and redrawn at slightly different positions. The rectangle cannot simply be erased by redrawing it in the background color, as this would destroy the image lying beneath the line. Drawing in XOR mode provides the solution. To erase the rectangle we simply draw it a second time, which restores the original image.

Figure 9.21 shows mouse routines that create and manage a rubber rectangle (recall Section 2.4). These callback routines are registered in main() in the usual way: glutMouseFunc(myMouse) to make myMouse() the callback for a mouse keypress or release, and glutMouseMotionFunc (mouseMove) to make mouseMove() the callback for a mouse motion event with the button down. A global rectangle object rr is used and referred to by both routines. The initial rectangle (of zero size) is established by myMouse(). Be sure not to draw the rectangle using black (all 0's) for the drawing color! (Why?)

It will be noticed that when drawing in XOR mode, the rubber rectangle does not have a uniform color. Instead, each pixel along the rectangle is drawn in the color that results from XOR-ing the true rectangle color with the background at that point. This is usually not too annoying. It can even be useful, because any objects under the rectangle are plainly visible.

```
IntRect rr; // create and draw a rubber rectangle

//<<<<<<<<<<<<<<<< myMouse >>>>>>>>>>>>>>>>
void myMouse(int button, int state, int mx, int my)
{
  if(button == GLUT_LEFT_BUTTON && state == GLUT_DOWN)
  {
        glEnable(GL_COLOR_LOGIC_OP); // enable logical operations
        glLogicOp(GL_XOR);           // set it to XOR mode
        rr.left = rr.right = mx; // set the pivot
        rr.top = rr.bott = screenHeight - my;
  } // end of if block
  if(button == GLUT_LEFT_BUTTON && state == GLUT_UP) // end of if block
    glDisable(GL_COLOR_LOGIC_OP); // disable logical operations
}
//<<<<<<<<<<<<<<<< mouseMove >>>>>>>>>>>>>>>>
void mouseMove(int mx, int my)
{
    rr.draw(); // erase the old: works only in XOR mode
    rr.right = mx; // set the new opp. corner
    rr.bott = screenHeight - my; // flip y-coord.
    rr.draw(); // draw the new
}
```

FIGURE 9.21 Mouse routines for a rubber rectangle.

PRACTICE EXERCISES

9.3.5 Drawing multiple colors in XOR mode

Suppose the frame buffer supports 3 bits per pixel. Describe what color is observed when the pixel value 110 is XOR-ed with each of the possible pixel values.

9.3.6 Drawing twice in XOR mode equals not drawing at all

Show, for any pixel colors A and B, that drawing B twice in XOR mode leaves A unchanged. That is, show that: (A XOR B) XOR B is A itself.

9.3.7 Symmetric operators

Note that the OR operator is symmetric: A OR B is the same as B OR A. Which of the 16 operators $\oplus$ is symmetric in the sense that a $\oplus$ b = b $\oplus$ a?

9.3.8 Swapping two images in place

Show that two pixmaps A and B may be interchanged by performing the following three XOR combinations. When the process is complete, A contains the pixel values originally held by B, and vice versa.

    A = A XOR B
    B = A XOR B
    A = A XOR B

9.3.9 Reverse-mode drawing

Drawing a pattern in reverse mode can also be used to erase a line and restore the original pixel values. A b-bit frame buffer has $N = 2^b$ possible pixel values, ranging from 0 to $2^b - 1$. To draw a pixel d in reverse mode replace d with the value

$f(d) = N - d$. Note that this drawing function is an *involution*: drawing twice restores the original, because $f(f(d)) = N - f(d) = N - (N - d) = d$. Describe how this technique operates for rubber-band drawing, and what colors are seen along the rubber-band line as it crosses pixels of various colors. Is it the same as drawing in XOR mode? For a single bit-plane, ($b = 1$), what is the difference between reverse mode and XOR drawing?   ■

9.3.4 The BitBLT Operation

The routines `draw()`, `read()`, and `copy()` can be integrated into a single function with some added capabilities that vastly increase their power and applicability. The operation has become known as **BitBLT** (pronounced "bitblit"), which stands for Bit boundary Block Transfer. It is also called a **raster op** [Inga78, Newell79]. BitBLTs are sometimes called **pixelBLTs** when more than one bit per pixel is involved. We use "BitBLT" to denote both kinds.

A BitBLT is sometimes performed in software, but it has become such a pervasive operation that specially designed VLSI chips have been crafted to perform BitBLTs at very high speeds (hundreds of millions of pixels per second). A few parameters are written to the BitBLT chip, which then takes over and interacts directly with the system bus to move the data.

Definition of the BitBLT Operation

There are several versions of the BitBLT, which differ in various details. In its simplest form, BitBLT copies a **source rectangle** of pixels to a **destination rectangle** of the same height and width. The source and the destination may reside in either on- or off-screen memory. The BitBLT processor keeps track of the two rectangles in a simple manner: It stores the x- and y-coordinates of the upper left corner of each rectangle and also records their height and width (in pixels). The processor makes all necessary conversions between an (x, y) pair and the corresponding address in memory.

The BitBLT copies source pixels S to the destination rectangle D using the logical combination method described earlier: $D = D \otimes S$. Various choices for $\otimes$ are available.

Some versions of BitBLT allow the user to "premix" the image in the source rectangle with some other predefined pixmap, referred to as a **halftone pattern**, and this premixed version becomes the source S that is copied to the destination. The halftone pattern is stored in a pixmap of some size, such as 16 by 16 pixels. It might be, for instance, a checkerboard pattern of 0's and 1's that simulates a shade of gray. If the mask is smaller than the source, it is replicated (tiled) until it attains the size of the source. The user has four choices for the source pixmap S:

- the AND of the source and the halftone pattern.
- the source alone (so the halftone pattern is ignored).
- the halftone pattern alone.
- solid black.

Most BitBLT processors also maintain a **clipping** rectangle. Before each pixel in the destination is drawn, its coordinates are compared with the boundaries of the clipping rectangle, and the pixel is drawn only if it lies within the boundaries. This can be done rapidly in hardware within the processor. The clipping rectangle effectively limits the region of the destination in which drawing can take place.

9.4 DO IT YOURSELF LINE DRAWING: BRESENHAM'S ALGORITHM

What a pity, when Christopher Columbus discovered America, that he ever mentioned it.

Margo Asquith
(1864–1945)

Most graphics environments come with a built-in tool that draws straight lines. Every environment has at least some form of line() or lineto(). OpenGL, of course, goes much further. We usually aren't concerned, therefore, with the details of how such a tool works—how it determines which pixels to turn on between the two endpoints of the line.

But line drawing is fundamental to computer graphics, and it is enlightening to see how such a routine operates. In fact programmers still need to write such routines when developing or optimizing new commercial graphics packages.

We start with a straightforward but dreadfully inefficient method to set forth the main ideas. Then we present a much faster method known as **Bresenham's line-drawing algorithm**.

Suppose we want to set pixel values so that a line appears on the screen between integer coordinates (a_x, a_y) and (b_x, b_y). Figure 9.22 shows that certain pixels along the mathematical ideal line from (a_x, a_y) to (b_x, b_y) are set to "on". Hopefully these pixels can be chosen efficiently, and together they will give the appearance of a straight line (albeit with some inevitable "jaggies").

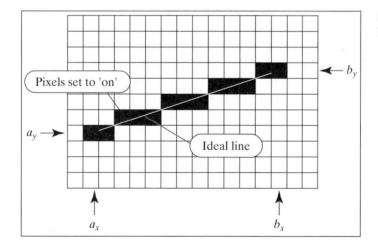

FIGURE 9.22 Drawing a straight line segment.

From elementary algebra the ideal line satisfies the equation:

$$y = m(x - a_x) + a_y \qquad (9.3)$$

where x varies between a_x and b_x, and m is the **slope** of the line, given by:

$$m = \frac{b_y - a_y}{b_x - a_x} \qquad (9.4)$$

For example, given $(a_x, a_y) = (23, 41)$ and $(b_x, b_y) = (125, 96)$, then $m = 55/102 = 0.5392$. The slope is meaningful only for nonvertical lines, where a_x and b_x are different. If the line is horizontal or vertical, it is clear which pixels to turn on, but for other lines we need an algorithm that computes which ones to turn on.

The simple but inefficient first approach just steps across in x from a_x to b_x in steps of one, and at each step **rounds** the corresponding value of $m(x - a_x) + a_y$ to the nearest integer. For the case where a_x is less than b_x this leads to:

```
float y = a.y;        // initial value
for (int x = a.x; x <= b.x ; x++, y += m)
        setPixel(x, round(y));
```

where, as before, `setPixel(x, y)` writes the current color into the pixel in column x and row y in the frame buffer. The y-value must be rounded to the nearest integer value, a fairly expensive operation.

9.4.1 Bresenham's Line-Drawing Algorithm

Bresenham's algorithm offers a significant advantage over the previous method, as it avoids floating-point arithmetic and rounding. The ideas behind it are important also, because they appear in other types of utilities such as circle- and ellipse-drawing algorithms. It is a classic example of an **incremental algorithm** that computes the location of each pixel along the line based on information about the previous pixel.[3] It uses only integer values and avoids any multiplications. It has a tight and efficient innermost loop that generates the proper pixels.

Several variations of Bresenham's algorithm do the job in slightly different ways. We describe the version known as the midpoint algorithm. It produces the same pixels as Bresenham's algorithm for straight lines, and its approach can be extended directly to the drawing of more complex shapes such as circles and ellipses.

Suppose that, as before, we are given the integer-valued endpoints (a_x, a_y) and (b_x, b_y). We want to determine the best sequence of intervening pixels.

To simplify our discussion, we shall examine the special case in which $a_x < b_x$ (i.e., b lies to the right of a) and the slope of the line lies between 0 and 1. (We remove these restrictions later.) We define for convenience the extents of the segment in x and y—say, W for "width" and H for "height":

$$W = b_x - a_x$$
$$H = b_y - a_y \tag{9.5}$$

Under our assumptions, both are positive, with $H < W$. Therefore, as x increases from a_x to b_x, the corresponding y increases from a_y to b_y, but y increases less rapidly than does x. As x steps across in unit increments from a_x to b_x, the best integer y-value will sometimes stay the same and sometimes increment by one. The midpoint algorithm quickly determines which of these should occur. (Note that y never needs to either decrement, or to increment, by more than 1. Why?)

From Chapter 4 we know that the equation of the ideal line through (a_x, a_y) and (b_x, b_y) is

$$-W(y - a_y) + H(x - a_x) = 0$$

The left-hand side is 0 for all points (x, y) that lie on the ideal line.

We give a name to this expression for later use. Actually it is strategic to double the expression first, and then give it a name. (As we shall see, this prevents an awkward factor of 1/2 from appearing in key formulas.) So we define the function $F(x, y)$ according to:

$$F(x, y) = -2W(y - a_y) + 2H(x - a_x) \tag{9.6}$$

---

[3] It is sometimes called a **digital differential analyzer** (DDA) algorithm, after a mechanical device used to solve differential equations in an incremental fashion.

The important property of $F(x, y)$ is that its sign tells whether (x, y) lies above or below the ideal line:

- If (x, y) lies above the line, then $F(x, y) < 0$.
- If (x, y) lies below the line, then $F(x, y) > 0$.

[*Hint*: Suppose (x, y) is on the line, so that we know $F(x, y)$ is 0. Adjust y upward slightly, keeping x the same. This makes the value of $F(.,.)$ smaller. Hence increasing y above the line makes F negative.]

PRACTICE EXERCISE

9.4.1 Experiment with Bresenham's algorithm.

For the line segment between $(3, 7)$ and $(9, 11)$, $F(x, y)$ is given by:

$$F(x, y) = (-12)(y - 7) + (8)(x - 3)$$

and points on the line, such as $(7, 29/3)$, satisfy $F(x, y) = 0$. What is the sign of $F(x, y)$ for the points $A = (4, 4)$ and $B = (5, 9)$, and where do they lie relative to the line segment?

Answer: A lies below the line and F is 44 there. B lies above the line and F is -8 there. ■

Now how do we decide which pixels to turn on? Figure 9.23 shows some pixels near the ideal line. The circles at each intersection in the grid represents the center of a pixel. Suppose we somehow know that at p_x the best y-value is p_y, and we want to determine the best y-value at the next x-value given by $p_x + 1$. We wish to know whether the line at $p_x + 1$ is closer to the point L (for "lower") given by $L = (p_x + 1, p_y)$, or to U (for "upper") given by $U = (p_x + 1, p_y + 1)$. The figure shows one possible position of the ideal line, but it could also pass slightly below L or slightly above U. (Why?)

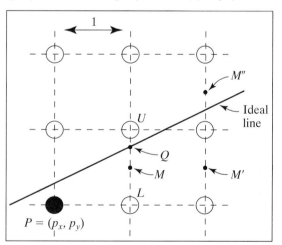

FIGURE 9.23 The configuration for deriving the midpoint technique.

We decide to turn on pixel U or L according to whether the ideal line lies above or below the midpoint M between U and L. M is given by $M = (p_x + 1, p_y + 1/2)$. If we evaluate the function $F(\,,)$ at M, its sign will tell whether the ideal line lies above or below M:

- If $F(M_x, M_y) < 0$, then M lies above the ideal line, so choose L.
- If $F(M_x, M_y) > 0$, then M lies below the ideal line, so choose U.

Thus if $F(M_x, M_y) > 0$, the pixel to be turned on is one higher than before, so we increment y. Otherwise we don't increment y. The rest is algebra—determining how to compute $F(\,,)$ quickly. The key is to compute it incrementally, according to how much its value must *change* from one step to the next.

For later reference we note that at M the value of $F(M_x, M_y)$ is:

$$F(M_x, M_y) = -2W(p_y + 1/2 - a_y) + 2H(p_x + 1 - a_x) \qquad (9.7)$$

Consider how $F(\ ,\ )$ changes as we move from $x = p_x + 1$ to the next x-value: $p_x + 2$. The M in question is either M' or M'', as shown in Figure 9.23. It is $M' = (p_x + 2, p_y + 1/2)$ if we did not increment on the previous step, whereas it is $M'' = (p_x + 2, p_y + 3/2)$ if we did increment.

Case 1: If F was negative on the previous step (so that no increment was done at this step), then

$$F(p_x + 2, p_y + 1/2) = -2W(p_y + 1/2 - a_y) + 2H(p_x + 2 - a_x)$$

We subtract Equation (9.7) to find out how much bigger this is than $F(M_x, M_y)$:

$$F(p_x + 2, p_y + 1/2) = F(M_x, M_y) + 2H$$

Case 2: If F was positive on the previous step (an increment *was* done at this step), then

$$F(p_x + 2, p_y + 3/2) = -2W(p_y + 3/2 - a_y) + 2H(p_x + 2 - a_x)$$
$$= F(M_x, M_y) - 2(W - H)$$

In either case the value of the test quantity has a constant added to it: $2H$ if we did not increment, and $-2(W - H)$ if we did.

The only question remaining is how to start the process. When $x = a_x$, we know $y = a_y$. The first instance of M is therefore $M = (a_x + 1, a_y + 1/2)$, so

$$F(x, y) = -2W(a_y + 1/2 - a_y) + 2H(a_x + 1 - a_x)$$
$$= 2H - W \qquad (9.8)$$

Note: If we hadn't doubled the function earlier, this result would be $H - 0.5W$, preventing the use of integer values for all quantities involved.

Summarizing: We initialize F to $2H - W$, x to a_x, and y to a_y. Then at each step:

1. set the pixel at (x, y) to the desired color value;
2. increment x by 1;
3. if $F < 0$, just update F by adding $2H$; otherwise increment y by 1 and update F by adding $-2(W - H)$.

Putting all this together, we get Bresenham's algorithm (for this special case):

FIGURE 9.24 The midpoint algorithm (special case).

```
bresenham(IntPoint a, IntPoint b)
{ // restriction: a.x < b.x and 0 < H/W < 1
    int y = a.y, W = b.x - a.x, H = b.y - a.y;
    int F = 2 * H - W;        // current error term
    for(int x = a.x; x <= b.x; x++) // inner loop
    {
        setPixel(x, y);
        if(F< 0)
            F += 2 * H;        // set up for next pixel
        else{
            y++;
            F += 2 * (H - W);
        }
    }
}
```

Because the algorithm reinitializes itself for each new line and depends only on the endpoint data, it is *repeatable*. Redrawing a line in a different color completely replaces the first line pixel by pixel; for instance, drawing in the background color totally erases a previously drawn line.

This algorithm is extremely simple, with an inner loop that has only a few comparisons and a few additions. It can be easily implemented in assembly language to achieve the greatest speed. Special-purpose graphics hardware is often available that implements this algorithm for even higher performance.

■ **EXAMPLE 9.4 Example**

It is instructive to watch how F varies in a specific example. Let $(a_x, a_y) = (4, 1)$ and $(b_x, b_y) = (16, 4)$. Then $W = 12$ and $H = 3$. Because this line has a slope of 1/4, we expect the y-value to increment only every fourth step or so in x. F is initialized to -6. Each time x is incremented, we do one of two things: if F is negative, we add 6 to it; otherwise we both subtract 18 and increment y.

The resulting sequence of values (viewed just after the setPixel(x,y) command) is:

x:	4	5	6	7	8	9	10	11	12	13	14	15	16
y:	1	1	2	2	2	2	3	3	3	3	4	4	4
F:	-6	0	-18	-12	-6	0	-18	-12	-6	0	-18	-12	-6

The behavior of the algorithm for this example is shown in Figure 9.25, which illustrates both the resulting line and the variation in F. The "jaggies" are clearly visible for the line, where each short horizontal line segment breaks to the next higher one.

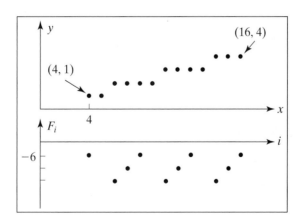

FIGURE 9.25 An example of the midpoint algorithm in action.

Removing the Restrictions on Bresenham's Algorithm

The preceding algorithm copes only with the special case $a_x < b_x$ and a slope between 0 and 1. The remaining cases are easily handled as well, by adding code that copes with each case as it arises.

To Get the Same Line when $a_x > b_x$. The midpoint algorithm sets whichever pixel is on the proper side of the midpoint between the two choices at each step. Thus we need only adjust the code above so that it carries out the midpoint algorithm in the case where $a_x > b_x$. This requires only slight adjustments (see the exercises). One detail to note: the code above distinguishes between the cases $F < 0$ and $F \geq 0$, so the $F = 0$ case is "combined" with the $F > 0$ case (where y is incremented). We must make sure, when tracing the line in the other direction, that we combine the $F = 0$ case with the case that causes a decrement in y.

An alternate method just tests whether $a_x > b_x$, and if so swaps a_x with b_x, and a_y with b_y, thereafter using the steps in Figure 9.24. In effect it never draws toward the left. Instead it redefines the endpoints so it doesn't have to. This is not very successful, however, if the algorithm is to be used to draw connected line segments as in a polyline. Swapping endpoints would obliterate the natural order in which the segments of a polyline are drawn. The order can be important when drawing lines as dotted or dashed.

Lines Having Slope Greater than 1 Simply interchange the roles of x and y, step in y from a_y to b_y, and use the same test to determine when to increment (the less rapidly changing) x.

Lines with Negative Slopes If the slope is between 0 and -1, H automatically takes on the proper sign. Step in x using exactly the same tests, but decrement the dependent variable rather than increment it. If the slope is more negative than -1, replace W with $-W$, and interchange the roles of x and y, as in the case where the slope is greater than 1.

Horizontal and Vertical Lines These occur so frequently in graphics that it may increase performance to test for them (e.g., `if(a.x == b.x)...`) and to use a simplified algorithm when they occur. The improvement in performance for a vertical line would be marginal; most of the time is spent in `setPixel( )`, anyway. For a horizontal line you might use a routine that writes many bits along a scanline at once, thereby significantly increasing the drawing speed.

See the exercises for implementing these generalizations.

Summary of Properties a Drawn Line Should Have

What properties should we require of a line-drawing algorithm? The lines should be as straight as possible and should reliably pass through both of the given endpoints. The lines should be smooth and have uniform brightness along their length. Lines of different slopes should have the same brightness. The process should also be repeatable: if at a later time we apply the algorithm to the same endpoint data, it should produce exactly the same pixels. This is important for erasing the line, which is accomplished by redrawing it in the background color or in XOR drawing mode. It also shouldn't matter in which direction the line is drawn: if drawn from (b_x, b_y) to (a_x, a_y), exactly the same pixels should be turned on. If this is so, the application can erase a previously drawn line without regard for how it was originally drawn.

To Draw Lines in Patterns and Draw Stippled Lines

You may have occasion to draw lines or polygons that are dotted or dashed using some pattern. As mentioned in Chapter 1, a dashing pattern is stored as a sequence of bits, such as 0011111100111111.

It is simple to incorporate such patterns into Bresenham's algorithm. Each time x is incremented, a pointer into the pattern can be incremented as well, and the corresponding bit value can be used to set the current drawing color used by `setPixel()`.

For long lines the pattern is used repeatedly by incrementing cyclically from the end of the pattern back to its beginning.

When a polyline is to be drawn dashed or in some pattern, you may want the pattern to be continuous from segment to segment. To do this, the pattern and the pointer into it are made globally available to Bresenham's algorithm so that it can be accessed during successive calls to the algorithm. See the exercises for other issues concerning drawing in patterns.

OpenGL makes it easy to draw stippled lines and polygons. The function glEnable (GL_LINE_STIPPLE) enables the stippling for all lines to follow. Stippling can be disabled with a glDisable(GL_LINE_STIPPLE). Once line stippling has been enabled, subsequent lines are drawn by calling glLineStipple (factor, pattern). The argument factor is of type int and determines the number of times a pattern is repeated. For example, a factor of 2 causes each bit in the pattern to be used twice before the next bit is used. Factor can range from 1 to 256. Figure 9.26 shows three lines, each drawn with a factor of 1, 2, and 3 respectively.

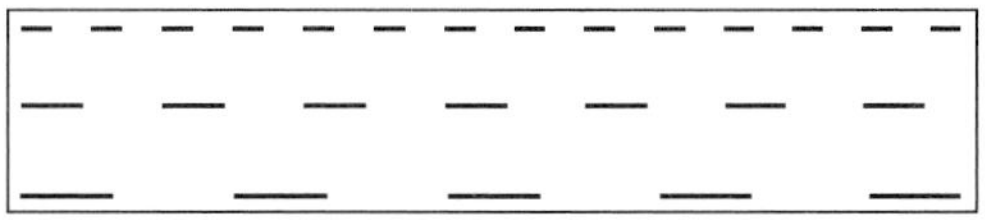

FIGURE 9.26 Three stippled lines using different factor values.

The argument pattern is an array of gluByte, where each element of the pattern is a string of zeros and ones (1 = pixel on, 0 = pixel off). To make things simpler the programmer usually specifies elements of pattern in hexadecimal format, understanding that each hex value will be converted automatically to four binary bits. For instance, a stipple pattern with a hex value of 0x0000 has a binary equivalent of 0000000000000000, so all these 16 pixels are black. On the other hand, the pattern 0x0101 (binary equivalent is 0000000100000001) will produce a dotted line, and the pattern 0x0F0F (binary equivalent is 0000111100001111) will produce a line with wider dashes. Figure 9.27 shows a complete working program from the OpenGL Red Book [Woo04].

Polygon Stippling

OpenGL also offers a mechanism for stippling a polygon as an alternative to filling it with a solid color. Polygon stippling is very similar to line stippling. The programmer must first enable polygon stippling with glEnable (GL_POLYGON_STIPPLE);. Next an

```
#include <GL/glut.h>
#include <stdlib.h>

#define drawOneLine(x1,y1,x2,y2) glBegin(GL_LINES);  \
    glVertex2f ((x1),(y1)); glVertex2f ((x2),(y2)); glEnd();

void init(void)
{
    glClearColor (1.0, 1.0, 1.0, 0.0); // use a white opaque background.
    glShadeModel (GL_FLAT);
}
```

FIGURE 9.27 A complete working program to demonstrate line stippling. [Woo04]

```
void display(void)
{
   int i;

   glClear (GL_COLOR_BUFFER_BIT);

/* select black for lines      */
   glColor3f (0.0, 0.0, 0.0);

/* in first row, 3 lines, each with a different stipple   */
   glEnable (GL_LINE_STIPPLE);

   glLineStipple (1, 0x0F0F); /* dotted   */
   drawOneLine (50.0, 125.0, 150.0, 125.0);
   glLineStipple (2, 0x0F0F);  /* dashed   */
   drawOneLine (150.0, 125.0, 250.0, 125.0);
   glLineStipple (3, 0x0F0F);  /* dash/dot/dash  */
   drawOneLine (250.0, 125.0, 350.0, 125.0);

   glDisable (GL_LINE_STIPPLE);
   glFlush ();
}

void reshape (int w, int h)
{
   glViewport (0, 0, (GLsizei) w, (GLsizei) h);
   glMatrixMode (GL_PROJECTION);
   glLoadIdentity ();
   gluOrtho2D (0.0, (GLdouble) w, 0.0, (GLdouble) h);
}

void keyboard(unsigned char key, int x, int y)
{
 //escape key to exit
   switch (key) {
      case 27:
         exit(0);
         break;
   }
}

int main(int argc, char** argv)
{
   glutInit(&argc, argv);
   glutInitDisplayMode (GLUT_SINGLE | GLUT_RGB);
   glutInitWindowSize (400, 150);
   glutInitWindowPosition (100, 100);
   glutCreateWindow (argv[0]);
   init ();
   glutDisplayFunc(display);
   glutReshapeFunc(reshape);
   glutKeyboardFunc(keyboard);
   glutMainLoop();
   return 0;
}
```

FIGURE 9.27 (*continued*)

array of hex values that define the stipple pattern is specified using glPolygonStipple (bug);—again similar to line stippling. Here we call our stipple pattern, bug, a sample of which is shown in part b of Figure 9.28. Part C shows a halftone pattern that the programmer might want to use in order to achieve a smooth gray effect.

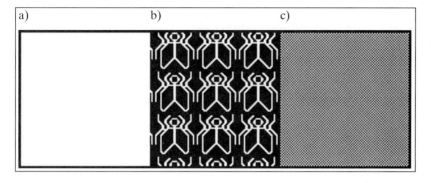

FIGURE 9.28 Three rectangles: a) one nonstippled, b) "bug" stippling, c) halftone stippling.

The bug and halftone stipple patterns are defined as arrays and take the form [Woo04]:

```
GLubyte bug[] = {
    0x00, 0x00, 0x00, 0x00, 0x00, 0x00, 0x00, 0x00,
    0x03, 0x80, 0x01, 0xC0, 0x06, 0xC0, 0x03, 0x60,
    0x04, 0x60, 0x06, 0x20, 0x04, 0x30, 0x0C, 0x20,
    0x04, 0x18, 0x18, 0x20, 0x04, 0x0C, 0x30, 0x20,
    0x04, 0x06, 0x60, 0x20, 0x44, 0x03, 0xC0, 0x22,
    0x44, 0x01, 0x80, 0x22, 0x44, 0x01, 0x80, 0x22,
    0x44, 0x01, 0x80, 0x22, 0x44, 0x01, 0x80, 0x22,
    0x44, 0x01, 0x80, 0x22, 0x44, 0x01, 0x80, 0x22,
    0x66, 0x01, 0x80, 0x66, 0x33, 0x01, 0x80, 0xCC,
    0x19, 0x81, 0x81, 0x98, 0x0C, 0xC1, 0x83, 0x30,
    0x07, 0xe1, 0x87, 0xe0, 0x03, 0x3f, 0xfc, 0xc0,
    0x03, 0x31, 0x8c, 0xc0, 0x03, 0x33, 0xcc, 0xc0,
    0x06, 0x64, 0x26, 0x60, 0x0c, 0xcc, 0x33, 0x30,
    0x18, 0xcc, 0x33, 0x18, 0x10, 0xc4, 0x23, 0x08,
    0x10, 0x63, 0xC6, 0x08, 0x10, 0x30, 0x0c, 0x08,
    0x10, 0x18, 0x18, 0x08, 0x10, 0x00, 0x00, 0x08
};
GLubyte halftone[] = {
    0xAA, 0xAA, 0xAA, 0xAA, 0x55, 0x55, 0x55, 0x55,
    0xAA, 0xAA, 0xAA, 0xAA, 0x55, 0x55, 0x55, 0x55,
    0xAA, 0xAA, 0xAA, 0xAA, 0x55, 0x55, 0x55, 0x55,
    0xAA, 0xAA, 0xAA, 0xAA, 0x55, 0x55, 0x55, 0x55,
    0xAA, 0xAA, 0xAA, 0xAA, 0x55, 0x55, 0x55, 0x55,
    0xAA, 0xAA, 0xAA, 0xAA, 0x55, 0x55, 0x55, 0x55,
    0xAA, 0xAA, 0xAA, 0xAA, 0x55, 0x55, 0x55, 0x55,
    0xAA, 0xAA, 0xAA, 0xAA, 0x55, 0x55, 0x55, 0x55,
    0xAA, 0xAA, 0xAA, 0xAA, 0x55, 0x55, 0x55, 0x55,
    0xAA, 0xAA, 0xAA, 0xAA, 0x55, 0x55, 0x55, 0x55,
    0xAA, 0xAA, 0xAA, 0xAA, 0x55, 0x55, 0x55, 0x55,
    0xAA, 0xAA, 0xAA, 0xAA, 0x55, 0x55, 0x55, 0x55,
    0xAA, 0xAA, 0xAA, 0xAA, 0x55, 0x55, 0x55, 0x55,
    0xAA, 0xAA, 0xAA, 0xAA, 0x55, 0x55, 0x55, 0x55,
    0xAA, 0xAA, 0xAA, 0xAA, 0x55, 0x55, 0x55, 0x55,
    0xAA, 0xAA, 0xAA, 0xAA, 0x55, 0x55, 0x55, 0x55
};
```

FIGURE 9.29 A polygon stippling code fragment.

```
glRectf (25.0, 25.0, 125.0, 125.0); // plain white rect ...rect1
glEnable (GL_POLYGON_STIPPLE);
glPolygonStipple (bug);
glRectf (125.0, 25.0, 225.0, 125.0); // stippled fly ...bug rect2
glPolygonStipple (halftone);
glRectf (225.0, 25.0, 325.0, 125.0); // halftone's rect ...rect3
glDisable (GL_POLYGON_STIPPLE);
```

Suppose the programmer wants to display parts a, b, and c of Figure 9.28, three separate rectangles in all. Figure 9.29 shows a code fragment for polygon stippling.

The rectangle in part a is drawn solid using the familiar function glRectf (...), then stippling is enabled and the pattern is changed to the bug using glPolygon-Stipple(bug); and the rectangle is drawn again using another glRectf call. Finally, the stipple pattern is changed to the halftone pattern and the rectangle is drawn once more.

PRACTICE EXERCISES

9.4.2 Removing restrictions on Bresenham's algorithm

Work out the variations of Bresenham's algorithm for the cases of: a) $a_x > b_x$; b) lines with slopes > 1; c) lines with negative slopes, and combine them into a single algorithm that works for any line segment. Try to make the routine as efficient as possible.

9.4.3 Numerical example

For endpoints $(8, 23)$ and $(21, 11)$ calculate using your graphing calculator and show the sequences of x, y, and F that evolve as Bresenham's algorithm is applied. Demonstrate that the same pixels are illuminated when the algorithm is started from the opposite endpoint.

9.4.4 Drawing in patterns

Extend Bresenham's algorithm to draw lines using a pattern of 16 bits. Arrange it so that if a polyline is drawn, the pattern will continue uninterrupted from one line segment to the next.   ■

9.5 TO DEFINE AND FILL REGIONS OF PIXELS

Architecture is the art of wasting space.

Philip Johnson
(1906–2005)

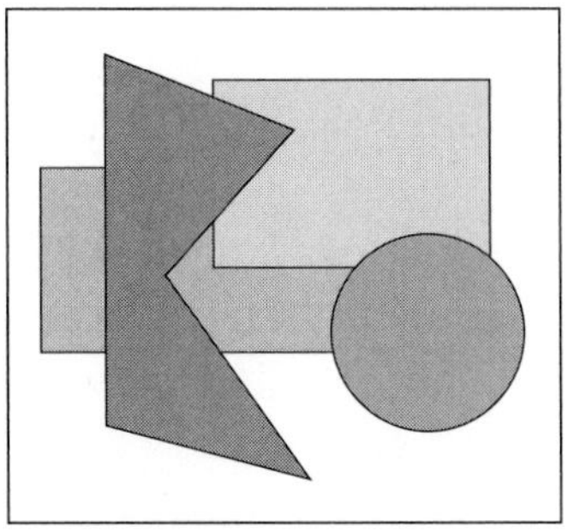

A raster display can show regions of pixels **filled** with a solid color or a pattern of colors. By a **region** we mean a collection of pixels lying next to one another in some fashion, or being associated by some common property. Figure 9.30 shows an image having a number of regions filled with various color patterns.

Paint programs are widely available today that allow one to create pictures interactively (recall Chapter 1.) They all include a tool that allows the user to point with a mouse at a region and then select a new pattern, whereupon the region is instantly flooded with the new pattern. We want to see how this is done.

FIGURE 9.30 Several regions filled with patterns.

9.5.1 To Define Regions

There are various ways to define a region. One important distinction is whether the description is "pixel defined" or "symbolic."

- A **pixel-defined** region is characterized by the actual pixel colors in a pixmap. The description of a region R might list each pixel considered to lie in R: $(34, 12)$, $(34, 13)$, $(34, 14)$, and so on. Or R could be defined as consisting of all pixels having value 77 that are "connected" in some way to pixel $(43, 129)$. The notion of "connected" has to be spelled out carefully. To see what the region R is, you must scrutinize the pixmap and see just which pixels are in R according to this definition. In any case the enumeration of pixels for a region is tedious at best and certainly error prone.
- A **symbolic** description does not enumerate the pixels but rather provides some property that all the pixels in region R enjoy. Such descriptions tend to be "higher level," or more abstract, than pure pixel enumeration. Some possible ways to describe regions symbolically are:
  - All pixels that are closer to a given point $(23, 47)$ than to any of the given points $(12, 14)$, $(22, 56)$, or $(35, 45)$.
  - All pixels lying within a circle of radius 8 centered at $(5, 23)$.
  - All pixels inside the polygon with vertices at $(32, 56)$, $(120, 546)$, and $(345, 1129)$, and $(80, 87)$. This **polygon-defined** region is a particularly important case, which we discuss in detail later.

  The programmer who wishes to manipulate or analyze regions would most likely choose quite different data structures and algorithms, depending on how the regions of interest are described.

We do not pay much attention to the pixel-defined method; instead we discuss various methods for manipulating symbolically defined and polygon-defined regions.

9.6 MANIPULATING SYMBOLICALLY DEFINED REGIONS

> You do live longer with bran, but you spend the last fifteen years on the toilet.
>
> *Alan King*
> *(1927–2004)*

Some region-filling algorithms read the frame buffer pixel by pixel in order to identify each pixel's color, and thus feel their way across a region. One might suspect that a fill algorithm would be much more efficient if it had access to a higher-level, more symbolic, description of the region than a pixel-by-pixel enumeration.

We examine some ways to capture a region symbolically, each with its advantages and disadvantages. The most widely used method in graphics defines a region as the interior of a **polygon**; this is the approach used by OpenGL. This approach is described in detail.

The methods fall into two classes. The first represents a region by a collection of **rectangles**, and the second captures a region by a **path** that defines its boundary.

9.6.1 Rectangle-Defined Regions

This method describes a region as a list of rectangles. The rectangles may be as small as a single pixel, or as large as an entire pixmap. The region may have holes and even isolated blobs.

Figure 9.31 shows a simple example where each pixel value is black or white. We decompose the region into a collection of aligned rectangles. The representation is just a list of the various rectangles found. (A quick scan by eye of Figure 9.31 shows that about 11 rectangles will do the job, and that the decomposition can be done in different ways.)

FIGURE 9.31 A region to be represented by rectangles.

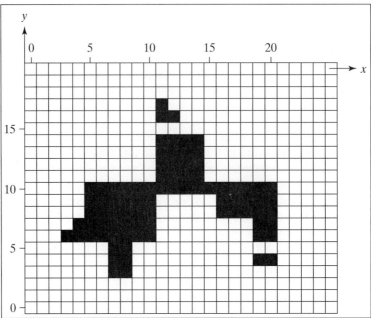

We describe an organized way to decompose the pixmap into a list of rectangles. The method is simple and efficient; it allows rapid building of a shape from a pixmap, and rapid filling of a region described by a shape.

Start at the top and move down scanline by scanline, identifying rectangles. Whenever the set of runs in a scanline differs from those in the scanline above, a new set of rectangles begins. A **run** is a group of adjacent pixels of the same color that lie on the same scanline.

This representation of a pixmap is sometimes called its **shape** representation [Steinhart92]. Note that this form can describe any set of pixels in a pixmap, including a collection of separate regions.

Regions represented using this method are most compact when they exhibit span coherence and scanline coherence. **Span coherence** is the property wherein many pixels along a scanline tend to have the same value. **Scanline coherence** is the property wherein the pattern of pixels of one scanline tends to be similar to the pattern of pixels on the next scanline below. Regions that exhibit high degrees of coherence require fewer data "per pixel" to characterize them.

Scaling and Translating Regions

The shape representation can also be useful when we want to manipulate regions in other ways.

- *Translate a region.* To translate a region represented in shape form by 30 pixels in x and 55 pixels in y, simply traverse the list, incrementing all x-values by 30 and all y-values by 55.
- *Double its size.* To double the size of the region, first translate it so that the first run is at the origin $(0, 0)$, then double all values in the data structure. Finally, translate it to the desired position.

9.6.2 Path-Defined Regions

It is natural to specify a region by its boundary, which we usually take to be a path of some sort. There are many ways to describe a path. Some useful ones are:

- **By a mathematical formula** The formula $(x - 122)^2 + (y - 36)^2 = 25$, for instance, defines a circular path 10 pixels in diameter.
- **By a polyline** A sequence of pixel locations $(x_1, y_1), (x_2, y_2), \ldots, (x_n, y_n)$ defines a polyline path which, if closed $((x_1, y_1) = (x_n, y_n))$, specifies a polygon.
- **By a sequence of adjacent pixels** One particularly appealing way to represent a path of adjacent pixels is by a **chain code**. Here the path is specified by a starting pixel, say $(34, 67)$, and a sequence of moves from pixel to pixel, such as "go up, go right, go down, ..." The set of possible moves can be encoded in various ways.

Figure 9.32 shows two versions. The first, shown in Figure 9.32a, admits moves in the four "compass" directions, and each direction is associated with a number between 0 and 3. Thus a sequence of such steps defines a continuous path. Path A is specified by the sequence shown in the figure, beginning at its lower right. This path happens to be closed, but in general it need not be. (What is a condition on the numbers of 0's, 1's, 2's, and 3's for a path to be closed?) Note that, since only four possible direction values are used, each can be represented by only two bits.

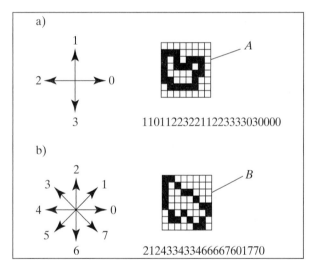

FIGURE 9.32 Defining a path by chain codes.

The version given in Figure 9.32b permits eight directions. A '1' indicates that the next pixel on the path is "up-one" and "over-one-to-the-right," with similar combinations for the other three diagonal directions. (Where is the starting point for the sequence shown?) Chain codes are reminiscent of the *relative* draws that we mentioned in Chapter 3 and shall discuss further in Appendix 5.

Figure 9.33 shows a possible data structure to store a path. The first two elements give its starting pixel, followed by the number of steps, and then a list of the steps themselves.

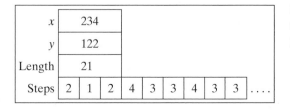

FIGURE 9.33 Suitable data structure for a chain-encoded path.

Chain codes can offer a very compact representation for certain paths and regions. (How many bits per step are needed for the eight-way code?) In addition, some processing tasks are easily performed:

1. **Translate** a path. This is trivial: just change the starting pixel.
2. **Scale** a path by scale factor k. Repeat each symbol k times;
3. **Rotate** a path 90° CCW. For the four-direction chain code, increment each step value by 1, properly incrementing 3 to the value 0. For the 8-direction use a similar increment in the direction number.

On the other hand, some operations are difficult. For instance, filling a region defined by a chain code is complicated, since runs of pixels along scanlines are not easily identified. One would most likely first convert the chain-code representation into a "shape table."

PRACTICE EXERCISE

9.6.1 Chain-code path

Write the code that represents an aligned square using 3-bit codes for each step in the path. Choose a starting point so that the overall length of the chain code needed for the square is a minimum.

9.6.2 The chain code for a rotated square

Repeat Exercise 9.6.1 for the case of a square that has been rotated through 45 degrees. If the representation cannot bed one perfectly, find the closest approximation. ■

9.7 FILLING POLYGON-DEFINED REGIONS

> For most men life is a search for the proper manila envelope in which to get themselves filed.
>
> *Clifton Fadiman*
> *(1902–1999)*

Regions are often defined by polygons, and efficient algorithms have been developed for filling them with a solid color or a pattern. Some graphics packages provide efficient filling routines for you. We examine how to do it in one's own package.

Suppose that the region to be filled is a polygon P described by a set of pixel addresses, $p_i = (x_i, y_i)$, for $i = 1, \ldots, N$, that specifies the sequence of P's vertices. Figure 9.34 shows an example having seven vertices. To fill P we progress through the frame buffer scanline by scanline, filling in the appropriate portions of each line. As shown in the figure, the proper portions are determined by finding the intersections of the scanline, say, $y = 3$, with all the edges of P. The runs of pixels that lie between pairs of edges must lie inside P and are filled with the desired color.

The following pseudocode suggests the filling process:

```
for(each scanline L)
{
        <Find intersections of L with all edges of P>
        <Sort the intersections by increasing x-value>
        <Fill pixel runs between all pairs of intersections>
}
```

For example, in Figure 9.34 the scanline at $y = 3$ intersects the four edges e_2, e_3, e_4, and e_5. The four intersection x-values are rounded up or down to integers as described next, and sorted to yield the sequence 1, 2, 7, 9. Then two runs are filled: the first from column 1 to 2 and the second from column 7 to 9.

Note that taking the sorted edge intersections in pairs uses a form of **inside–outside** test. Moving along a scanline, we pass either into or out of P at each intersection; the

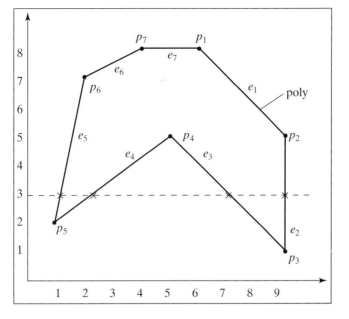

FIGURE 9.34 Filling proper portions of a scanline.

"insideness" changes at each intersection. (Insideness is sometimes called "**parity**" in this context, and we say the parity changes at each intersection.) If we pass to the inside, the subsequent pixels will be filled; if to the outside, they will not. If P lies wholly to the right of the start of each scanline, the parity is initially *out*. The algorithm exploits **span coherence**, the tendency for several consecutive pixels along a scanline to lie next to an interior pixel. Hence an entire run can be filled with minimal calculation.

9.7.1 Which Pixels on an Edge Belong to a Polygon?

It is common for a scene to consist of several polygons, and for some of the polygons to lie next to one another and therefore share an edge. Such polygons are said to abut one another. If we are not careful, the algorithm could set pixels on the common edge first to the color of one polygon and then to the color of the other. Drawing the edge twice in this fashion could lead to a visually disturbing result: the edge could have a bizarre color if the application happened to be drawing in XOR mode, or it could be drawn twice too bright if the drawing were sent to a photo recorder. The algorithm must therefore decide which polygon "owns" each edge, so that each edge belongs to only one of the two polygons.

A rule that works well is that a polygon owns its left edges (or in the case of horizontal edges it owns its bottom ones). So when two polygons abut, as in Figure 9.35, the edge belongs to the "right-hand" polygon, and this edge is drawn only once in the right-hand polygon's color. If a shared edge is horizontal, it is drawn in the upper polygon's color. Figure 9.35 uses simple triangles to show the four possible ways that two polygons can share an edge. In each case the shared edge should be drawn in the color of polygon B.

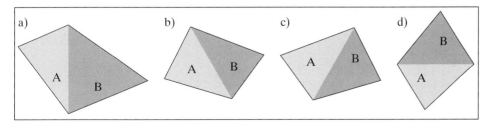

FIGURE 9.35 The shared edge belongs to polygon B.

FIGURE 9.36 Filling in spans of internal pixels.

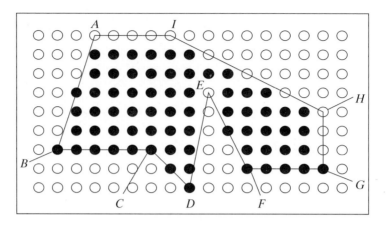

How do we apply this rule when executing the command to fill pixel runs between all pairs of intersections? Figure 9.36 shows a sample polygon P with nine vertices. Pixels whose centers lie in the interior of P are colored, but which pixels with centers lying *on* the edges should be colored? Since the left and bottom edges are owned by P, pixels lying on these edges are colored, while those lying on the right and top edges are not.

Thus when filling each span along a scanline between two intersections, the span includes its leftmost pixel if that pixel lies on an edge, but not its right pixel. This leaves unaffected any pixels that are owned by other polygons above and to the right of P. (Check that Figure 9.36 shows this.)

Since intersections will normally occur at some x that lies between integer values, we round up or down to the proper pixel to start and end each span. Suppose that the left intersection of a run lies at the real value xLeft and the right intersection at xRight. We want to compute the first and last pixels in the run, xFirst and xLast, respectively. By the rule above xFirst is the smallest integer that is greater than or equal to xLeft. Similarly, xLast is the largest integer strictly less than xRight.

Handling Intersections with Edge Endpoints

It can happen that a scanline passes directly through an endpoint (since endpoints of an edge are integers). In order to achieve the correct change in parity, we must count this passage as an intersection; others we don't.

For instance, the scanline that passes through vertex H in Figure 9.36 apparently sees two intersections (one with edge GH and one with HI), so the parity on both sides of H seems to be the same. But this would cause us to fill to the right of H, which is clearly wrong. Further, the polygon owns its bottom horizontal edge BC, so we want to see one intersection at B. (Why?) But it doesn't own its top horizontal edge AI, so we want to see an even number of intersections at A. There are so many different cases that it appears a complex set of rules is required.

However, one simple rule that works well in every case is to ignore intersections of a scanline with the *upper* endpoint of an edge, and to ignore horizontal edges altogether in intersection calculations. Thus in Figure 9.36 there are no intersections at A and I, one at B and one at H, just as we hoped. Figure 9.37 shows other situations that can occur and shows a count of the number of intersections that are "seen" by scanlines that pass through vertices of the polygon. In each case the parity to the right of the intersection has the proper value for filling. (Check this out.) Note that one inconsequential effect of this rule is that the pixel at E in Figure 9.36 is not drawn, being at the upper end of both edges.

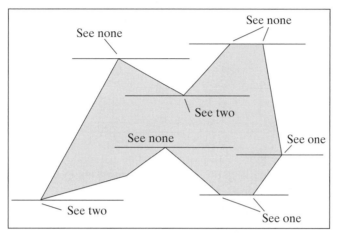

FIGURE 9.37 Number of intersections seen with edges of a polygon.

We therefore adjust the instruction in the fill algorithm, *Find intersections of L with all edges of P*; to include the refinement:

> *Find the intersections of the scanline with all edges of P;*
> *Discard intersections with horizontal edges and with the upper endpoint of any edge.*

PRACTICE EXERCISE

9.7.1 Testing the method

Consider the example polygon Q of Figure 9.38, which has the 16 vertices:

A: (52, 30) B: (74, 43) C: (60, 60) D: (38, 60) E: (30, 50)
F: (10, 50) G: (10, 28) H: (22, 41) I: (33, 10) J: (50, 10)
K: (39, 30) L: (40, 44) M: (54, 44) N: (46, 34) O: (45, 42)
P: (33, 34)

where the last five vertices constitute a hole in Q. Sketch this on your graphing calculator and determine that it is filled properly, using the method above. ■

9.7.2 Improving the Algorithm's Performance

To improve the performance of this method we look for the most time-consuming part. Here it is the large number of intersection calculations between scanlines and edges. To reduce this burden, we build and maintain a simple list so that we

FIGURE 9.38 Example polygon
to be filled.

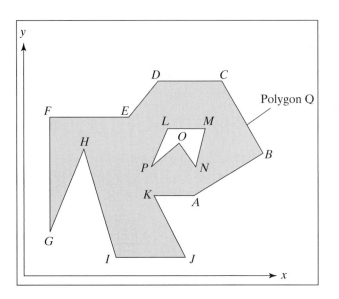

FIGURE 9.38 Example polygon
to be filled.

can locate intersections rapidly. The list, called the *active edge list* (AEL), allows the algorithm to capitalize on **edge coherence**, which has two parts:

- The tendency for many of the edges intersected by scanline y to be intersected as well by scanline $(y + 1)$;
- The property (of a straight line) that the x-value of the intersection migrates *in uniform increments* from scanline to scanline.

During the filling process, the appropriate runs of pixels along each scanline are filled simply by referring to the AEL. The AEL contains the x-values of all the edge intersections for the current scanline (the line currently being filled). The x-values are maintained in sorted order, so that according to the parity rule the first two x-values define the first run; the next two define the next run; and so on.

For example, suppose we are filling the polygon shown in Figure 9.39, and have reached scanline $y = 50$. This scanline intersects four edges of the polygon. The x-values of the intersections are easily calculated to be 45, 56.66, 70, and 100 in sorted order. The two spans from 45 to 56, and from 70 to 99, are now easily filled in.

FIGURE 9.39 Example of filling
a polygon.

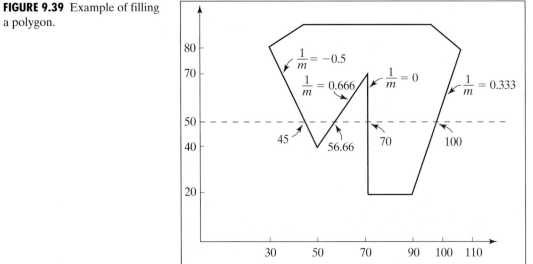

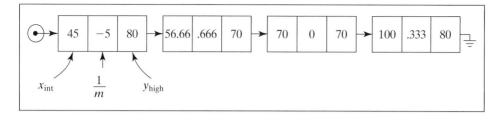

FIGURE 9.40 The AEL for scanline $y = 50$.

A linked-list form of the AEL for this situation is suggested in Figure 9.40, showing the four current intersections stored in order, along with some other data that let the algorithm quickly update the AEL for use on the next scanline.

Specifically, the AEL contains three items for each currently intersected edge:

1. The x-value, x_{int}, of the intersection with the current scanline.
2. The reciprocal, $1/m$, of the edge's slope m.
3. The y-value, y_{high}, of the upper endpoint of the edge.

The second item is used to locate the intersections that scanline $y = 51$ makes with each edge. Note that if an edge has slope m, then moving up by 1 unit causes the intersection x-value to increase by $1/m$ (check this out). The value $1/m$ is stored directly in the AEL for each edge, as seen in Figure 9.40. (For instance, the leftmost edge spans 20 units in x and 40 in y, so its inverse slope is 20/40. Check the other values shown in the figure.) Thus a single addition of x_{int} and $1/m$ finds the intersection point for the next scanline above, capitalizing on edge coherence.

Note that incrementing by $1/m$ and rounding is basically what Bresenham's line algorithm does to migrate from point to point along a line. In fact Bresenham's method (incrementing based on the sign of an "error term," then updating the error term) would most likely be used here to maximize efficiency.

As we move to the next scanline in the filling process, several things can happen in addition to an incremental move along an edge.

1. The new scanline may now lie just beyond (above) an edge represented in the AEL. The y-value of the top endpoint of each edge is kept on the AEL to make this situation easy to identify. If the new y exceeds this upper value, the edge is deleted from the AEL.
2. One or more new edges may be encountered, as y becomes equal to the y-value of the lower endpoint of some edges in the polygon. Edge records for such edges are added to the AEL by referring to a separate table, as we shall describe next.
3. The order of x-values of edge intersections may become reversed if two edges cross (for nonsimple polygons). The list of intersections must be resorted if this happens.

So, after the runs have been filled for the current scanline, y is incremented, x-intersections are updated, some edges are dropped off the AEL, others are added, and the x-intersections are sorted if necessary. The runs along this next scanline can now be filled in a similar manner.

The Edge Table

To find which edges must be added as we proceed to the next scanline, we could test each vertex in P to determine which edges have been reached while incrementing y, but this is inefficient. Instead, information is gathered about each edge in P ahead of time and cleverly placed in an **edge table** (ET). The ET provides rapid access to the required information during the AEL's updating.

FIGURE 9.41 Edge table characterizing the polygon Q.

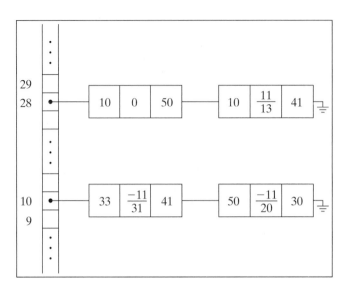

The edge table is fashioned as an array of lists, `edgetable[]`, one list for each scanline. A portion of the ET for polygon Q in Figure 9.38 is shown in Figure 9.41. It is formed while initially traversing the polygon to eliminate horizontal edges and shorten others.

The list for each scanline contains information about any edge of Q that has its *lower* endpoint at that scanline. (This effectively sorts the edges of Q by their lower y-values; one says that the ET performs a **bucket sort** of the polygon's edges.) Thus many of the lists in the *ET* are empty.

Each edge is characterized by a record of the same type as used in the AEL. The y_{lower} and $1/m$ fields are loaded with the proper values, and the x_{int} field is loaded with the x-value of the lower endpoint of the edge in question.

The edge table makes it simple to identify those edges that must be added to the AEL during updating. For the new current scan line at row y, all edges pointed to by `edgetable[y]` have been reached and are added to the AEL. The x_{int} value automatically contains the initial intersection value, and the other fields are already properly loaded. Therefore, only a few pointers must be adjusted to insert the new edge records. Before filling pixel runs, the AEL is resorted into ascending x_{int} values to maintain parity.

A skeleton of the overall algorithm is shown in Figure 9.42. It begins with an empty AEL and successively fills each scanline, starting at $y = 0$. It moves quickly through the main loop, drawing nothing until the first edges are added to the AEL.

FIGURE 9.42 Skeleton of the polygon-fill algorithm.

```
AEL = NULL;
for(y = 0; y <= maxRow; y++)
{                                        // AEL is initially empty
    <add all edges in edgetable[y] to AEL>
    if( AEL != NULL)   // any edges to process?
    {
        <sort AEL by xInt value>
        <fill pixel values along y using AEL info>
        <delete from AEL any records for which yupper == y>
        <update each xInt value by its inverse slope>
    }
}
```

Lui et al. have recently [Lui00] described a highly efficient polygon-fill algorithm which uses a data structure based on "triples" to describe each line segment of the polygon. (Each triple consists of a y-value, an x-value for the left end of the segment, and an x-value for the right end of the segment.)

PRACTICE EXERCISES

9.7.2 Table-fill algorithm

The table-fill algorithm provides very fast filling of a certain class of polygons. Each edge of the polygon is first scan converted (perhaps using Bresenham's algorithm) pixel by pixel to generate the (x, y) pairs that occur along its edges. As each pair (x, y) is formed, it is tested against two arrays, min[y] and max[y], that contain for each y-value the minimum and maximum x-values encountered so far. If $x < $ min[y], then min[y] is updated to contain the new x-value, and similarly for max[y]. The polygon is then filled by drawing in the run of pixels from min[y] to max[y] for each scanline y. No sorting is required, and so this algorithm is fast.

What are the geometric conditions on a polygon that guarantee it will be filled correctly? Give several examples of polygons for which the method works and several for which it fails.

9.7.3 Fence-fill algorithm

The fence-fill method for polygonal regions uses the notion of complementing or reversing certain pixels in the picture. For a bilevel display, a pixel of 1 (white) is set to 0 (black), and vice versa. The essential property of complementing is that doing it twice restores the original value.

It works as follows. Erect a vertical "fence"— perhaps through some vertex of the polygon to be filled. Set all pixels to 0. Now for each edge of the polygon do the following. On each scanline through the edge, complement all pixels from the edge to the fence. Pixels along a scanline that lie outside the polygon are complemented an even number of times and so are 0. Those that lie inside are complemented an odd number of times and so are 1 (filled). This is independent of where the fence lies.

Draw example polygons on paper and use the fence-fill method to fill the polygons by hand. Show that the method works for multiple polygons and for polygons with holes. What will happen if the method is used on a single line rather than on a polygon having a true inside and outside? ▪

9.8 ALIASING AND ANTIALIASING TECHNIQUES

> We often plough so much energy into the big picture, we forget the pixels.
> *Dame Silvia Cartwright*

The notion of the jaggies has appeared in various preceding discussions. Jaggies are a form of **aliasing**, which is an inherent property of raster displays. They occur because of the discrete nature of pixels; that is, pixels occur on a display in a fixed rectangular array. Figure 9.43 shows an aliased image of the letter 'a'.

As an example, a black rectangle is shown in Figure 9.44a. If this rectangle covers a large number of pixels, its border will appear relatively smooth, although still somewhat jagged. But if it covers only a few pixels, as in part b, the jaggies will be very prominent and disturbing to the eye. In this figure each pixel is set to black based on whether (or measures the presence of) the rectangle covers one particular spot: the pixel's center. Effectively each pixel "samples" the rectangle at a single point, its center, asking whether the rectangle is present there. Based on this sample, the color of the entire pixel area is set to white or black.

FIGURE 9.43 An aliased image of the letter 'a'.

FIGURE 9.44 Aliasing of a rectangle. a) A shape that covers many pixels; b) A shape that covers relatively few pixels.

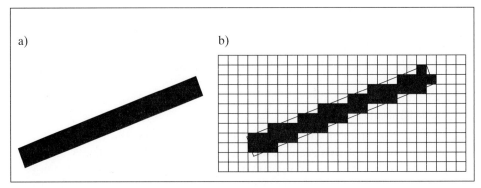

This sampling policy can cause small objects (e.g., distant objects in a 3D scene) to disappear entirely, as suggested in Figure 9.45a. If the object lands between pixel centers, it will not be displayed at all. Part b shows how an object can blink on and off objectionably in an animation. The object might cover a pixel center in one frame but miss it in the next.

FIGURE 9.45 Small objects missed by aliasing.

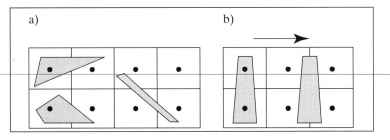

Roughly speaking, if signal that varies rapidly across the screen is sampled too infrequently, the samples appear to represent a signal that varies at a lower frequency: the frequency of the original appears replaced by its lower "alias" frequency. Figure 9.46a shows a rapidly varying square wave, which is sampled uniformly the at the pixels shown by dots. Based on these samples alone, the signal appears to be its "alias": a square wave with lower frequency, as shown in part b.

FIGURE 9.46 Sampling too slowly makes a signal look like its alias.

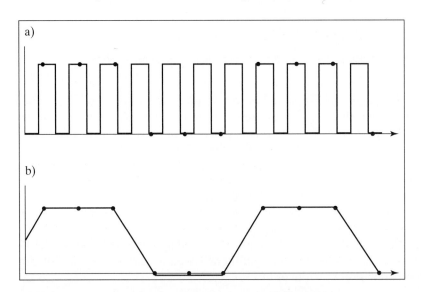

9.8.1 Antialiasing Techniques

How can one reduce the aliasing produced by insufficient sampling? A higher-resolution display, coupled with better algorithms, helps, because the jags are then smaller relative to the object. But some of the jaggies still remain. We therefore look for other ways to deal with aliasing.

Antialiasing techniques involve one form or another of blurring to smooth the image. In the case of a black rectangle against a white background, the sharp transition from black to white is softened by using a mixture of gray pixels near the rectangle's border. When the picture is looked at from afar, the eye blends together the gracefully varying shades of gray and sees a smoother edge.

Three approaches to antialiasing are commonly used: **prefiltering**, **supersampling**, and **postfiltering**.

Prefiltering

Prefiltering techniques compute pixel colors based on an object's *coverage*: the fraction of the pixel area that is covered by the object. Consider scan-converting a white polygon in a black background, as in Figure 9.47a. Suppose the intensity values are 0 for black and 1 for white. The polygon is situated in a square grid, where the center of each square corresponds to the center of a pixel on the display. A pixel that is half-covered by the polygon should be given the intensity 1/2; one that is one-third covered should be given the intensity 1/3; and so forth. If the frame buffer has 4 bits per pixel, so that black is represented by 0 and white by 15, a pixel that is one-quarter covered by the polygon should be given the value of (1/4)15, which rounds up to 4. Figure 9.47b shows the pixel values that result when the coverage of each pixel is calculated. (What would this array of pixel values be if we instead just *sampled* the polygon at each pixel center, using level 15 when the rectangle covers the center, and 0 otherwise?)

a) White : 1   Black : 0

b)

0	0	0	0	1	6	0	0
0	0	0	6	13	15	8	0
0	3	11	15	15	9	7	3
3	11	14	15	12	2	0	0
0	0	1	6	5	0	0	0

FIGURE 9.47 Using the fraction of pixel area covered by the object.

The geometric computations required to find the coverage for each pixel can, of course, be rather time consuming. A number of efficient approaches have been developed, such as those by Pitteway and Watkinson [Pitteway80] and more recently by Xiaolin Wu [Wu91]. These algorithms calculate the coverage of each pixel in an incremental fashion, using only integer arithmetic.

In summary, prefiltering operates on the detailed geometric shape of the object(s) being scan converted and computes an average intensity for each pixel based on the objects found lying within each pixel's area. For shapes other than polygons, it can be an expensive technique computationally, and so we shall seek alternative approaches to antialiasing.

Supersampling

Since aliasing arises from sampling an object at too few points, we can try to reduce its effects by sampling more densely than one sample per pixel. This is called **supersampling**: taking more intensity samples of the scene than are displayed. Each display pixel value is formed as the average of several samples.

Figure 9.48 shows an example of double sampling: The object (in this case a tilted bar) is sampled twice more densely in both x and y than it is displayed. The squares indicate display pixels, and the x's denote spots at which the scene is sampled. Each final display pixel is formed as the average of the nine neighbor samples: the center one and the eight surrounding ones. Some samples are reused in several pixel calculations. (Which ones?) The display pixel centered at A "sees" six is based on six samples within the bar and three samples of background. Its color is set to the sum of two-thirds the bar's color and one-third the background's color. The pixel at B is based on all nine samples within the bar. Its color is set to that of the bar.

FIGURE 9.48 Antialiasing using supersampling.

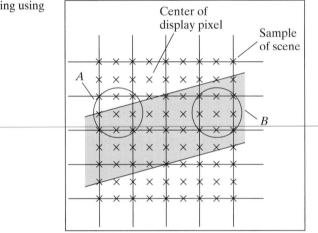

The lefthand side of Figure 9.49 shows a scene displayed at a resolution of 300 by 400 pixels. The jaggies are readily apparent in the left-hand side, particularly near the profiles of objects. The right-hand side of Figure 9.49 shows the benefits of double sampling. The same scene was sampled at a resolution of 600-by-800 samples, and each of the 300-by-400 display pixels is an average of nine neighbors. The jaggies have been softened considerably, although there is some apparent blurring.

FIGURE 9.49 Objects rendered at two different sample sizes left panel without antialiasing; right panel: with double sampling.

In general, supersampling computes N_s scene samples in both x and y for each display pixel, averaging some number of neighbor samples to form each display pixel value. Supersampling with $N_s = 4$, for example, averages 16 samples for each display pixel.

One can do antialiasing even with no supersampling ($N_s = 1$). The scene is sampled at the corner of each display pixel, as suggested in Figure 9.50. The intensity of each display pixel is set to the average of the four samples taken at its corners. Some softening of the jaggies is still observed, even though there is no supersampling.

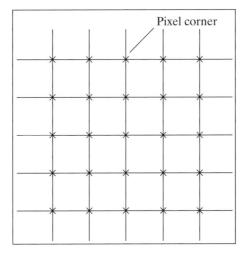

Pixel corner

FIGURE 9.50 Antialiasing by corner sampling.

Postfiltering

In the double-sampling method, nine neighboring samples are averaged to compute each display pixel's intensity, giving each neighbor equal importance. This form of blurring or filtering might be improved by giving the center sample more weight and the eight neighbors less weight. Or it may help to include more neighbors in the averaging computation.

Postfiltering computes each display pixel as a **weighted average** of an appropriate set of neighboring samples of the scene. Figure 9.51 shows the situation for double sampling. Each value represents the intensity of a scene sample, the ones in gray indicating the centers of the various display pixels. The square **mask** or **window function** of weights is laid over each gray square in turn. Then each window weight is multiplied by its corresponding sample, and the nine products are summed to form the display pixel intensity. For example, when the mask shown is laid over the sample of intensity 30, the weighted average is found to be

$$(30)/2 + (28 + 16 + 4 + 42 + 17 + 53 + 60 + 62)/16 = 32.625$$

which rounds to intensity 33. This mask gives eight times as much weight to the center as to the other eight neighbors. The weights always sum to 1.

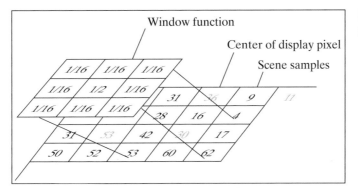

Window function

Center of display pixel

Scene samples

FIGURE 9.51 Postfiltering a graphics image.

Note that supersampling as we have described it is just a special case of postfiltering, in which all the weights have value 1/9. Sampling and filter theory from the signal processing field provide analytical methods for determining how different classes of window functions perform as postfilters. Sometimes larger masks, 5-by-5 or even 7-by-7, are used. These look farther into the neighborhood of the center sample and can provide additional smoothing.

Postfiltering can be performed for any value of oversampling N_s. If $N_s = 4$ is used, a 5-by-5, 7-by-7, or even 9-by-9 mask is appropriate. If $N_s = 1$, as in the case of corner sampling, one might use a 3-by-3 mask that weights the center pixel most heavily. This blurring may or may not pay off, depending on the scene being rendered.

More advanced techniques for antialiasing are discussed in Chapter 12 in connection with ray tracing and are also discussed on line.

PRACTICE EXERCISES

9.8.1 Supersampling

For the case of $N_s = 1$ show a grid of pixels similar to Figure 9.53. Place an '×' at the center of each display pixel, and the letter s at each pixel corner, indicating the location of the scene sample. Sketch this situation.

9.8.2 Antialiasing a polygon

For a frame buffer that holds values from 0 to 15, find the pixel values that result when prefiltering is used when scan converting each edge of the white polygon with vertices $(1, 3), (6, 7), (15, 4), (11, 15)$, and $(1, 8)$. Assume a black background. Then fill the polygon with white using a boundary-fill algorithm. Is there any chance that if a hole appeared in the polygon's edge, the fill routine would fail? If so, how could this be fixed?

9.8.3 Corner sampling

For a raster having R rows and C columns, how many samples of the scene must be computed when corner sampling is used? That is, how many corners are there? Compare this with center-of-pixel sampling and with double sampling.   ■

a)

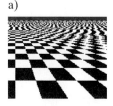

b)

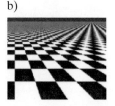

FIGURE 9.52 Example of aliasing, and improvement due to antialiasing. (Courtesy of Paul Heckbert)

9.8.2 Antialiasing of Texture

In Chapter 8 we examined how to map textures onto surfaces to achieve greater realism. Mapped textures are particularly prone to aliasing effects, because we usually expect the texture to represent some pattern or image faithfully. In addition, the texture itself is usually defined as a pixmap, and there is often a complex geometric relationship between pixels on the display and pixels in the pixmap. We describe the specific issues that arise when drawing textures, and we examine some solutions.

Figure 9.52a shows a classic case of aliasing: texture painted onto a tilted plane. The checkerboard squares that are far away are severely aliased, giving rise to various moiré patterns. In part b the image has been antialiased as described below, and the result is substantially better.

Recall that the texture is defined as a function texture(s, t) in texture space, and that it undergoes a complex sequence of mappings before it is finally depicted on the display. The rendering task is to work the other way, and, for each given display pixel at coordinates (x, y), find the corresponding color in the texture() function.

Figure 9.53 shows a particular pixel at (x, y) being rendered, and the corresponding value (s^*, t^*) in texture space that is accessed. For convenience we will give the name $T()$ to the overall mapping from pixel space to texture space, so $(s^*, t^*) = T(x, y)$. (The components of this mapping were developed in Chapter 8.)

Because pixels are not single points but have area, we should more properly think of how the whole square pixel centered at (x, y) maps to texture space. This is

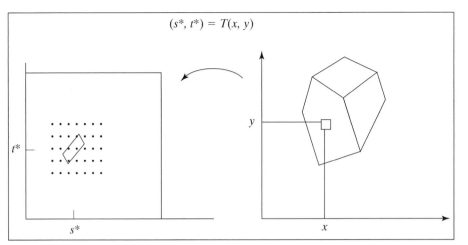

FIGURE 9.53 Cause of aliasing in texture rendering.

also shown in Figure 9.53 as a quadrilateral.[4] We will call this the *texture quad* corresponding to the screen pixel in question. Think of the texture space as being covered with such quads, each arising from a screen pixel. The size and shape of each texture quad depends on the nature of $T()$ and can be costly to find. If *texture(,)* varies inside the quad, yet the screen pixel is colored using only the single sample *texture*(s^*, t^*), significant information is missed, and there is substantial aliasing.

To reduce the effects of aliasing we should color each screen pixel with some form of average of the colors lying in the corresponding texture quad. Figure 9.54 shows a texture quad superimposed on the individual texture elements, or texels, of the pixmap `txtr[][]` that defines the texture(s, t). If there were a simple way to find the area of each texel that lies inside this texture quad, the average would be easy to find: weigh each `txtr[r][c]` by this area, sum the results, and divide by the area of the quad. This is analogous to the prefiltering technique used for antialiasing earlier. Unfortunately such a calculation hinders performance; it might be hard to find the area of each texel covered by the quad.

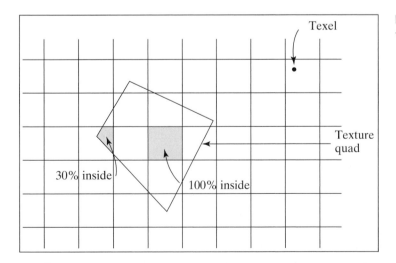

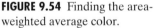

FIGURE 9.54 Finding the area-weighted average color.

Some time ago Heckbert surveyed the various methods researchers have developed to approximate this prefiltering [Heckbert86]. One method in particular, the elliptical weighted average (EWA) filter, was found to be effective. As suggested in

---

[4] If the 3D surface being viewed were curved, the sides of this quadrilateral would be curved. Visualize this.

Figure 9.55, it imagines each screen pixel to be covered by a circularly symmetric filter function. The concentric circles indicate different weighting levels (like a topographic map) and map the filter function into texture space. Once in texture space, the levels become a form of ellipse, roughly resembling the shape of the texture quad. Samples of the filter function, stored in a look-up table, are used to weigh different points within the ellipse, and these weighted values are summed to form the average. This can all be done incrementally and very efficiently (capitalizing on the controlled transformation of the filter function from one space to the other) at the cost of a few arithmetic operations per texel. Figure 9.52b shows the receding checkerboard rendered using an EWA filter.

FIGURE 9.55 Elliptical weighted area filtering.

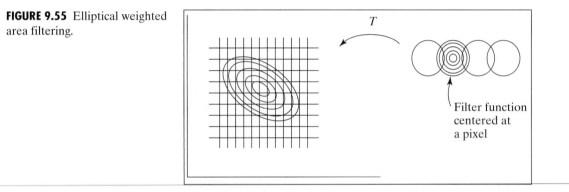

A second approach, known as **stochastic sampling** and fully described in [Watt&Watt92], avoids difficult geometric calculations in forming an average texture color by sampling texels in a randomized pattern. Figure 9.56 shows the texture quad with center (s^*, t^*) associated with a particular screen pixel. The texture quad itself is not used directly: instead, the region around (s^*, t^*) is sampled at a number of points, and the texel colors are averaged to form the color:

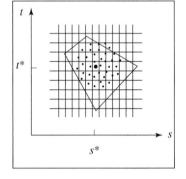

$$\text{average} = \frac{1}{N} \sum_k \text{texture}(s^* + \alpha_k, t^* + \beta_k)$$

FIGURE 9.56 Antialiasing using stochastic sampling.

The values α_k and β_k are small random quantities that are easy to create using a random number generator, and their distribution can be tuned if desired to the general size of the texture quad.

We will see stochastic sampling appear again in Chapter 12, where it offers a powerful tool for ray tracing.

9.8.3 Antialiasing Using OpenGL

OpenGL provides some tools to perform antialiasing. The simplest to use employs an **accumulation buffer**, which is an extra storage area similar to the frame buffer that OpenGL can create and draw into. The antialiasing method resembles stochastic sampling. It draws a scene multiple times at slightly different positions (which differ by just fractions of a pixel) and adds the results into the accumulation buffer. When all of the slightly perturbed drawings have been added to the accumulation buffer, the results are copied over into the frame buffer and the antialiased drawing is displayed. Thus the method forms in each pixel an average value based on colors in the projected scene that lie in the immediate vicinity of the pixel.

The following code shows how an example of how this can be done when a camera is taking a picture of a 3D scene. The accumulation buffer is created at startup[5] and initially zeroed out (using glClear(GL_ACCUM_BUFFER_BIT). Then the scene is drawn eight times, each time translating the camera in x and y (recall Chapter 5 and 7) by a small displacement stored in an array jitter[] of vectors. Each new drawing is scaled by 1/8 and added pixel by pixel to the accumulation buffer using glAccum(GL_ACCUM, 1/8.0). When the eight renditions have been drawn, the accumulation buffer is copied into the frame buffer using glAccum (GL_RETURN, 1.0).

```
glClear(GL_ACCUM_BUFFER_BIT); // clear the accumulation buffer
for(int i=0; i < 8; i++)
{
    cam.slide(f * jitter[i].x, f * jitter[i].y,0); // slide the
                                                       camera
    display(); // draw the scene
    glAccum(GL_ACCUM, 1/8.0); // add to the accumulation buffer
}
glAccum(GL_RETURN, 1.0); // copy accumulation buffer into frame
                           buffer
```

The jitter vector contains eight points that lie in x and y between -0.5 and 0.5. The header file jitter.h[6] uses the values: $(-0.3348, 0.4353)$, $(0.2864, -0.3934)$, $(0.4594, 0.1415)$, $(-0.4144, -0.1928)$, $(-0.1837, 0.0821)$, $(-0.0792, -0.3173)$, $(0.1022, 0.2991)$, $(0.1642, -0.0549)$. These mimic eight randomly chosen offsets from a circularly symmetric probability distribution, reminiscent of the EWA method described earlier. jitter.h also contains other jitter vectors, both shorter and longer, that can be used to try different levels of antialiasing.

Figure 9.57 shows a 3D scene rendered two ways: the left half shows the scene without antialiasing; the right half shows the improvement afforded by averaging eight jittered versions in the accumulation buffer. The jaggies in the antialiased version are noticeably reduced. This method can reduce performance, since the scene is rendered eight times for each frame.

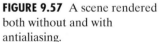

FIGURE 9.57 A scene rendered both without and with antialiasing.

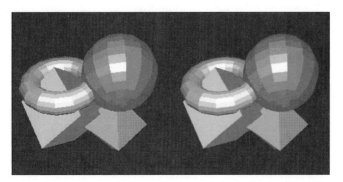

---

[5] It is created by including GL_ACCUM in the initialization: glutInitDisplayMode(GLUT_SINGLE| GLUT_RGB| GLUT_ACCUM| GLUT_DEPTH);

[6] Available as part of the download package of the GLUT.

9.9 CREATING MORE SHADES AND COLORS

I have dreamed in my life, dreams that have stayed with me ever after, and changed my ideas; they have gone through and through me, like wine through water, and altered the color of my mind.

Emily Bronte
(1818–1848)

In the early days of graphics, displays were expensive, particularly those that supported full color. Today such displays have become much less costly, and it is common to have full-color (32-bits per pixel) displays both at home and work. In the late 1980s a number of researchers invented methods for making one-bit-per-pixel images appear to show multiple shades per pixel.

We shall look briefly at one or two of these methods, both to give historical perspective on the problem and to delve deeper into the ways that the human perceptual system interacts with an image.

One method is **halftoning**, which trades spatial resolution for color resolution. [Ulichney87, Knuth87]. Newspapers provide a familiar example. Only black ink is used, yet an image seen in a newspaper appears to have many levels of gray. This is achieved by using smaller or larger blobs of black ink spaced closely together. Areas over which most of the blobs are large appear darker to the eye, because the average level of blackness is higher. Places where the blobs are smaller appear as a lighter shade of gray. The eye combines the blobs and perceives an average darkness over small regions. The spatial resolution of a newspaper picture is much less than that of a photograph, however, because it is made up of distinct blobs, which cannot be arbitrarily small.

In a computer graphics context **digital halftoning**, or **patterning**, uses arrays of small dots instead of variable-sized blobs. Figure 9.58a shows an example where 2-by-2 arrays of dots (each dot being 0 or 1) are used to simulate larger blobs having five possible intensity levels. For this discussion we adopt the printing analogy and associate level 0 with white (no ink) and 4 with black. The notion is that the eye sees the average intensity in each 2-by-2 blob, and so can see five levels.

FIGURE 9.58 2-by-2 patterns.

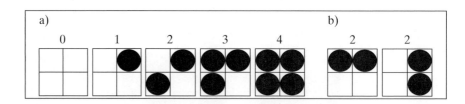

To put this in context, suppose the original grayscale image uses a 100-by-100 array of pixels whose intensity values range from 0 to 4. We have only a bilevel display available, so we display the image using a 200-by-200 pixel area. We shade each 2-by-2 block of pixels appropriately to create a semblance of one of the gray shades 0, . . . , 4. Again spatial resolution is exchanged for intensity resolution.

The positions of the black elements in the cell in Figure 9.58a were chosen to be as irregular as possible so as to avoid streaks or other artifacts in the image. If, instead, either of the patterns shown in Figure 9.58b was used for level 2, the image might exhibit horizontal or vertical stripes in certain patterns.

Figure 9.59 shows two examples; the left image is shown in grayscale with 256 levels. The right-hand version is viewed on a bilevel display when 2-by-2 patterning is used. The five effective gray levels are clearly visible.

Larger cell sizes can be used to create a larger number of gray levels. Figure 9.60 shows a pattern using a 3-by-3 cell, which achieves 10 gray levels. In general, an n-by-n cell of zeros and ones can produce $n^2 + 1$ gray levels. (Can you prove that $n^2 + 1$ gray levels can be produced?) Patterning is most applicable when the original image is of lower resolution than is the display device to be used.

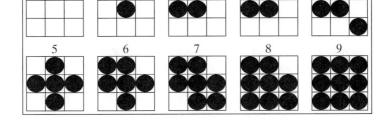

FIGURE 9.60 3-by-3 patterns.

For more information on digital halftoning, see [Knuth87].

In the previous subsection we looked briefly at a technique called halftoning that can be used to make the eye see more gray levels than are actually present. Here we give an equally brief overview of another method intended to do aimed at doing the same thing, **error diffusion**.

9.9.1 Error Diffusion

Error diffusion provides another thresholding technique for displaying multilevel pixmaps on a display that supports a small number of colors (although today these displays are uncommon). Again suppose each pixel of the original pixmap has intensities between 0 and 255, and that we need to replace each pixel by 0 or 1 in a judicious fashion.

If a pixel has intensity A, pure thresholding dictates that we replace it by 0 if $A < 128$, and by 1 if $A \geq 128$. When A is anything other than exactly 0 or 255, this produces some error between the truth and the displayed values. If $A = 42$, for instance, we set the display pixel to 0, which is too low by the amount 42. If $A = 167$, we display a 1 (the highest intensity, corresponding to a pixel value of 255), which is too high by the amount $255 - 167 = 88$. What is to be done with this error?

With error diffusion we try to compensate for the unavoidable errors by subtracting them from some neighboring pixels in the pixmap. We pass portions of the error on to neighboring pixels that haven't been thresholded yet, so that when they get thresholded later, the *new* adjusted value is tested against the threshold. In this way the error diffuses through the image, maintaining proper values of average intensity.

Figure 9.61 shows a portion of the original (multilevel) pixmap, which we assume is processed in the usual order of top to bottom and left to right. Suppose the shaded pixels have been processed. Pixel *p* has just been compared with 128, and either 0 or 1 has been output.

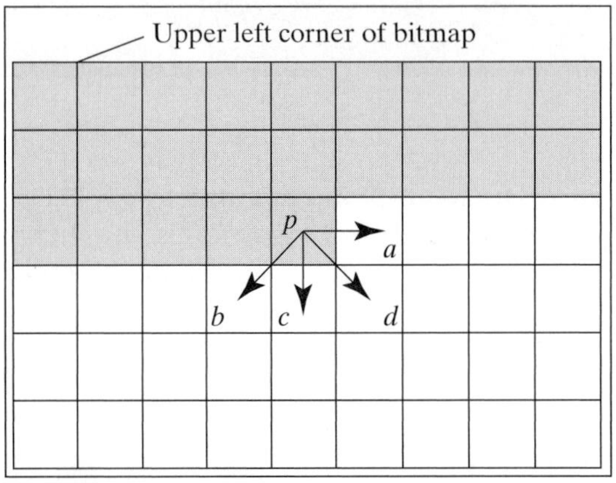

FIGURE 9.61 The error-diffusion process.

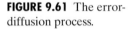

Let *A* denote the value of this pixel. If *A* is less than 128, the display pixel is set to 0 and the error *E* is −*A* (we are displaying a value *A* too low). If *A* is greater than or equal to 128, the display pixel is set to 1 and the error *E* is 255 − *A* (we are displaying a value too high by the amount 255 − *A*).

Fractions of the resulting error *E* are now passed to pixels *a*, *b*, *c*, and *d* as suggested in the figure. Old values of *a*, *b*, *c*, and *d* are replaced with:

$$a = a - f_a E \quad \{\text{adjust pixel to the right}\}$$
$$b = b - f_b E \quad \{\text{adjust pixel at lower left}\}$$
$$c = c - f_c E \quad \{\text{adjust pixel below}\}$$
$$d = d - f_d E \quad \{\text{adjust pixel at lower right}\} \qquad (9.12)$$

where f_a, f_b, and so on are constants. A typical choice of the fractions is $(f_a, f_b, f_c, f_d) = (7/16, 3/16, 5/16, 1/16)$. These values sum to one, so the entire amount of error has been passed off to neighbors of *p*. This acts to preserve the average intensity of a region.

When the end of a scanline is reached, the errors that would go to *a* and *d* are not passed on to the start of the next scanline. (Why?) Instead they might be discarded, or the algorithm could diffuse the entire error to pixels *b* and *c*. Experience shows that it is best to alternate the direction in which successive scanlines are processed: first left to right then right to left, so the pattern in Figure 9.61 reverses on the next line (e.g., *a* is to the left). The snakelike shape of this scanning has become known as a **serpentine raster pattern**.

Figure 9.62 shows a 512 × 512 pixmap after error diffusion, viewed on an outdated display. The error-diffusion method used the serpentine raster and the coefficients cited in Equation (9.12).

Extending this technique to displays that support more than two colors is trivial. At each pixel the closest displayable level is found, and the resulting error is passed on as described above. For color images each of the three color components is error diffused independently.

FIGURE 9.62 A pixmap viewed after error diffusion.

The techniques of halftoning and error diffusion have been combined by Knuth into a method he calls "dot diffusion," which is only slightly more complex than either method alone and can produce better images. Details can be found in [Knuth87].

PRACTICE EXERCISES

9.9.4 Doing it by hand

Carry out the error-diffusion process on the top scanline of an image, where all pixels in the top scanline have value 130, and all those on the next scanline have value 132. Discuss what happens.

9.9.5 Diffusing other amounts of error

Explain the effect of error diffusion when we diffuse all of the error to the right pixel. Explain the case where 1/2 is diffused to the right pixel and 1/2 is diffused down. ■

9.10 SUMMARY

In this chapter we looked at problems and opportunities that arise when you use a raster display to view an image. The fundamental property of a raster display is **discreteness**: the viewed image consists of many glowing pixels arranged in discrete rows and columns, each pixel glowing in one of several discrete colors. The image is discrete in three dimensions: horizontal, vertical, and color value. But since the pixel dots are very close together, and there are (usually) many possible color values, your eye–brain system blends neighboring dots and tends to see average values, thereby fusing the array of glowing dots into recognizable patterns.

This blending sanctions a fundamental property of raster displays: regions of the image can appear to be filled in a solid color or pattern, something that is very difficult to do using a line-drawing device such as a pen plotter. We discussed a number of methods to fill regions, paying particular attention to those described by a polygon.

Discreteness is both good and bad. Discreteness in space (horizontal and vertical) gives rise to aliasing (the jaggies). A diagonal line appears to jerk abruptly along its path, which can be disturbing to the eye. So antialiasing methods have been developed to ameliorate the visual effect of aliasing. Excessive discreteness in color—as when a display has only two color values—produces images with artificial bands or islands of color, and much of the information in the intended image is lost. So dithering techniques have been developed that exploit the nature of the eye to blend closely spaced dots, tricking it into seeing more colors than are really there.

Raster display systems have another fundamental property: pixels are represented by numbers, and numbers are stored in memory. A raster display is almost literally a window into a huge array of system memory, and hence into a huge array of numbers: a **pixmap**. The display maps numbers into colors, making the pixmap palpable. Computer instructions manipulate numbers easily, which opens the door to a host of techniques. Cursors can be swept across the screen with a mouse, windows can scroll, images can be "blitted" back and forth from on-screen to off-screen memory, and so forth.

A characteristic of modern raster displays is that there are very many pixels to deal with, sometimes even millions. This allows rich images but also increases the time required to perform certain operations. Copying large numbers of pixel values is often facilitated with specialized hardware, as with bitBLT chips. And people have been compelled to invent ever more efficient algorithms in an attempt to improve performance. Many of these algorithms capitalize on **coherence**, a notion that pervades much of graphics. **Span coherence**, for example, is the tendency of many adjacent pixels on a scanline to be of the same color. And **scanline coherence** is the tendency for pixels on neighboring scanlines to be similar.

The various techniques discussed in this chapter operate at the pixel level to fashion or enhance a picture viewed on a raster display. They all work either to exploit the positive effects of the discreteness of the raster or to counteract its negative effects. Because there are so many pixels in a given image, the efficiency of each algorithm is important.

9.11 CASE STUDIES

CASE STUDY 9.1 READING AND DISPLAYING BMP IMAGE FILES

(Level of Effort: II). Write an application that fills in the details of the `RGBpixmap` methods `draw()`, `read()`, `copy()`, `readBMPFile()`, and `writeBMPFile()` and allows the user to read an image stored as a BMP file and to display it using OpenGL. Further, the user can designate a rectangle on the display with the mouse, and the portion of the pixmap inside the rectangle is written to a BMP file. And if the user presses the 'f' key, the displayed pixmap is flipped about its horizontal centerline, thereby appearing upside down. Pressing 'v' flips the image about its vertical centerline. Experiment with several BMP files of your choice.

CASE STUDY 9.2 DISSOLVING BETWEEN TWO PIXMAPS WITH OPENGL

(Level of Effort: II). As discussed in Section 9.3, it is straightforward to dissolve between two images. Figure 9.12 showed an example. If the two images are stored in pixmaps A and B, we need only draw the weighted averages $A(1 - t) + Bt$ of them for a succession of t-values.

In this case study we use the alpha blending capability of OpenGL, and the method `blend()` of Figure 9.15, to form the weighted averages. The basic steps are:

For each of a set of t-values, say, 0, 0.2, 0.4, 0.6, 0.8, and 1.0:

a. Read two image files to create two pixmaps, A and B, of the same size
b. Set the proper blending function `glBlendFunc()`;
c. Erase the display;
d. Set the alpha of A to the value t;
e. Draw B, fully opaque;
f. Blend in A;
g. Pause to admire the latest blended image;
h. Go to e.

We need to set a global alpha value in one of the images—that is, set the alpha for every pixel to the *same* value. This is easily done by adding a method `setAlpha(float alpha)` to the `RGBApixmap` class.

1. Write the method `setAlpha(float alpha)`. It simply traverses all the pixel values in the pixmap, setting the alpha component of each to the fraction `alpha` of its maximum values (of 255).
2. Using Example 9.3.2 as a guide, write a program that dissolves between images A and B. Arrange matters so that pressing the key 'd' begins a dissolve from A to B, and pressing the key 'b' begins a dissolve from B to A. Exercise it on several image pairs.

CASE STUDY 9.3 WORKING WITH THE SHAPE DATA STRUCTURE

(Level of Effort: III) Section 9.6.1 described a data structure that represents a region in terms of a collection of rectangles. Here you are asked to work out the programming details for actually working with such creatures.

1. **Creating a shape.** Write the routine

   ```
   void pixmap2Shape(RGBpixmap& pixmap,Shape& shape, Color3 color);
   ```

   that creates a shape data structure from a pixmap. The shape structure accurately represents all of the region(s) described by the pixels having color `color` in the pixmap.

2. **Making pixmaps from shapes.** The inverse of the previous operation is to create a pixmap that contains the region(s) described by a shape. Write the routine

   ```
   void shape2Pixmap(Shape& shape, RGBpixmap& pixmap, Color3 fore,
   Color3 back);
   ```

   that creates a pixmap of sufficient size to hold the region(s) described by `shape`. It fills all pixels inside the shape in the color `fore`, and all the remaining pixels in color `back`.

CASE STUDY 9.4 GENERAL POLYGON FILLING

(Level of Effort: III) Write the routine

```
short fillPoly(IntPolyArray& poly)
```

that fills the polygon `poly`. It returns −1 if the polygon is degenerate or ill formed, or if the filling process is unsuccessful. It returns 0 otherwise. It uses the fill algorithm described in Section 9.7, and for efficiency it employs an edge table and an active edge list.

Test polygons are easily generated randomly. The user inputs the desired number of vertices, and the vertices are generated randomly and make sure the polygon is indeed closed. The application then fills the polygon. *Extra credit*: Fill your polygon with a stippled pattern.

CASE STUDY 9.5 ERROR DIFFUSION

(Level of Effort: II) Write the routine `errorDiffuse(IntRect r)` that performs error diffusion as described in Equation (9.9.2) on the portion of the screen image lying inside rectangle `r`. The rectangles of interest are filled with an image as in Case Study 9.1. The rectangles display the rectangles before and after error diffusion. Results will be most noticeable if the display supports only a few intensities or colors. The routine uses the serpentine pattern for scanning adjacent scanlines. Test the routine on several pictures.

9.12 FURTHER READING

Jim Blinn provides a very readable discussion of several of the topics introduced here in the so-called Jim Blinn's Corner, *Dirty Pixels* [Blinn98], including antialiasing, dithering, and compositing. Ulichney's *Digital Halftoning* [Ulichney87] provides a thorough treatment of dithering, and Knuth offers a broad perspective on the topic as well [Knuth87]. Also see a new approach to region filling presented in the paper by Lui et al. [Lui00], "A New Polygon Based Algorithm for Filling Regions." The OpenGL "Red Book" provides a lot of detail on how to control in applications many of the effects discussed in the chapter [Wu04].

Chapter 10

· ·

Curve and Surface Design

Whose woods these are I think I know;
His house is in the village though;
He will not see me stopping here
To watch his woods fill up with snow.

Robert Frost
(1874–1963)

GOALS OF THE CHAPTER

○ To develop tools for representing and designing curves.

○ To determine and describe mathematically key properties of useful curves such as their smoothness.

○ To develop the mathematical properties of Bezier and B-spline curves.

○ To develop tools to design Bezier, B-spline, and NURBS surface patches.

Preview

Section 10.1 reviews some important properties of parametric representations for curves and develops ways to measure the smoothness of such curves. Section 10.2 focuses on representing curves by polynomials and ratios of polynomials and describes the classes of shapes one can obtain from them.

Section 10.3 introduces the main ideas of interactive curve design, wherein a designer specifies a set of control points with a mouse, uses a curve generation algorithm to preview a curve, and then edits the control points in order to improve the curve's shape. Emphasis is placed on the distinction between curves that interpolate the points and those that only approximate the points.

Section 10.4 introduces Bezier curves in this context, and Section 10.5 discusses the properties of Bezier curves that have made them so popular in computer-aided design (CAD). Section 10.6 discusses the limitations of Bezier curves and begins the search for better methods for curve design, focusing on piecewise polynomials. This leads to a discussion of spline functions.

B-splines are introduced in Section 10.7, and their useful properties are developed in Section 10.8. Section 10.9 describes curves based on nonuniform rational B-splines (NURBS). Section 10.10 discusses some methods for finding curves that interpolate control points.

Section 10.11 addresses the design of complex surface shapes and extends the discussion of Chapter 6 to surfaces that are built upon Bezier, B-spline, and NURBS curves. It confronts the issue of joining two surface patches together seamlessly and uses the classical teapot as an example of blending surface patches. Several examples of surface designs are presented.

The Case Studies present projects for describing and drawing a variety of parametric curves and surfaces. The ElliptiPool game is introduced, as well as projects for drawing Bezier, B-spline, and NURBS curves and surfaces.

10.1 INTRODUCTION

Music is the expression of the movement of the waters, the play of curves described by changing breezes.
Claude Debussy
(1862–1918)

So far we have dealt mainly with two types of simple geometric objects: a collection of polypoints, which in turn consist of collections of points or straight lines, and meshes, which consist of a collection of faces (recall Chapter 6). We want an organized way to describe and represent a much richer set of shapes that occur in computer graphics and in computer-aided design programs.

Certain shapes are of particular interest because they are aesthetically pleasing to behold, or because they represent the shape of some actual object found in nature. Other shapes are computed by some analysis program as the best possibility for a particular job, such as the sweep of an airplane wing to give maximum lift. Still other shapes, like the curve of a car fender, are designed by a person, based on a complex combination of engineering utility, ease of manufacture, and an intuitive sense of what is appealing to customers.

Some shapes, like logarithmic spirals and path of a planet as it sweeps about its sun, have a concise mathematical formulation that makes them easy to analyze, but is of little help when we want to write a routine to draw them. Thus we need ways to convert from one kind of representation to another that is more suited to certain tasks. Other shapes are more free-form and are based on data rather than on mathematical expressions. Those we want to handle in a program also, perhaps in order to find where one such curve intersects another.

10.1.1 Parametric Curves as Trajectories

An important application of representing curves parametrically arises in describing the path that an object takes as it moves in time. For instance, when designing an animation, the trajectory of the camera through the scene must be specified at each instant. Figure 10.1 shows a camera moving through a scene. It is located at $P(t)$ at time t. The designer chooses a suitable function $P(t)$ so that the camera moves as desired, perhaps taking snapshot #1 at $t = 0.1$, snapshot #2 at $t = 0.2$, and so on. The view direction of the camera must also be specified at each instant. (See the exercises.)

In addition to having the camera be at specific positions at specific times, the designer must insure that the camera moves smoothly as it progresses along $P(t)$, without any disturbing jerks that will show up when the animation is played back. This imposes certain conditions on the velocity of the camera, as we consider next. Other objects might be moving in the animation as well: in Figure 10.1 the car might move along the road, the boat might change its course, and a person might come out of the house. As discussed in Chapter 6, the legs and arms of the person might have their own motions as well. The movement of each of these objects must be described in a suitable manner.

FIGURE 10.1 Specifying the path of a camera in an animation.

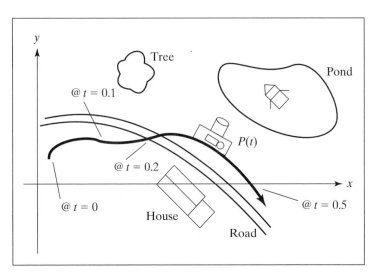

Animations usually take place in a 3D world, of course, where the camera moves along a 3D path and each snapshot is formed by projecting the scene onto the film of the camera.

10.1.2 Smoothness of Motion

Consider the parameter t as indicating the passage of time, and view the point $P(t)$ as moving along the curve as t increases. It is then natural to ask what the velocity of the point $P(t)$ is along the curve at each instant. The **velocity** $\mathbf{v}(t)$ is a vector that describes the speed and direction of $P(t)$ as it traverses the curve. From elementary calculus it is given for curves lying in 2D by

$$\mathbf{v}(t) = \frac{dP(t)}{dt} = \left(\frac{dx(t)}{dt}, \frac{dy(t)}{dt} \right) \tag{10.1}$$

For example, the ellipse given by $P(t) = (W \cos(t), H \sin(t))$ has velocity at t given by $\mathbf{v}(t) = (-W \sin(t), H \cos(t))$. The size of $\mathbf{v}(t)$ is often called the **speed** at t. Figure 10.2 shows the velocity at several points along the ellipse. Both the size and direction change as t varies. (Where is the speed the greatest?)

The **tangent line** to the curve $P(t)$ at $t = t_0$ can be given in parametric form $L(u)$, having parameter u, as follows. It clearly passes through $P(t_0)$ at $u = t_0$ and moves in the direction $\mathbf{v}(t_0)$. So it is given by:

$$L(u) = P(t_0) + \mathbf{v}(t_0)u \tag{10.2}$$

FIGURE 10.2 The velocity of $P(t)$ along a curve.

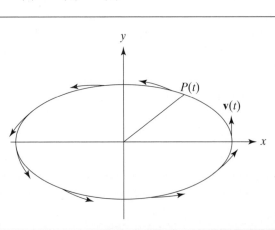

These formulas make it straightforward to compute and draw tangent lines to curves in various applications.

The **normal** direction to a curve may also be found at each point. It is defined as the direction perpendicular to the tangent line at the point of interest. Thus if the tangent line has direction $\mathbf{v}(t_0)$ at time t_0 as above, the normal direction at t_0 is any multiple of the vector $\mathbf{v}$ of Chapter 4. Using K as the multiplicative constant, the normal vector is:

(Note: the sign of the multiple K chosen will distinguish the **inward pointing normal** from the outward pointing normal. Reverse the sign of K as needed in a particular analysis.)

$$\mathbf{n}(t_0) = \mathbf{v}^\perp(t_0) = (-dy/dt, dx/dt)|t = t_0 \qquad (10.3)$$

So the ellipse of Equation 10.1 in the example just given above, for example, has normal vector $(-H \cos(t), -W \sin(t))$ or any multiple thereof. This is an inward pointing normal: multiply it by –1 to obtain the outward pointing normal. In the special case of a circle, $\mathbf{n}(t_0)$ is a multiple of $P(t_0)$ itself, so the normal points in the same direction as the radius vector from $\mathbf{0}$ to the point $P(t_0)$. (Note that this is *not* the case for an ellipse.)

When a curve $P(t_0)$ is used to describe how an object such as a camera moves in time, the issue arises: Does the object move jerkily or smoothly along its trajectory? The object can move in an infinite variety of ways along a given path, starting, stopping, accelerating, temporarily retracing a portion of the curve, and so on. If we are only drawing the curve, this motion is irrelevant: all trajectories have the same picture. But it's a very different story when the parametric function represents camera motion: the details of movement along the trajectory are recorded in the sequence of snapshots taken. Abrupt accelerations or jumps have a distinctive visual effect which can be normally undesirable.

As an example, consider a camera that moves along an elliptical trajectory, but with an altered parametric representation: at $t = a$ the speed of motion suddenly increases by a factor of 3:

$$P(t) = (x(t), y(t)) = \begin{cases} (W \cos(t), H \sin(t)) & \text{for } 0 < t < a \\ (W \cos(3t - 2a), H \sin(3t - 2a)) & \text{for } a < t < \frac{2(\pi + a)}{3} \end{cases} \qquad (10.4)$$

The situation is shown in Figure 10.3. The trajectory is still elliptical, but at $t = a$ both $x(t)$ and $y(t)$ start to vary three times faster, so there is a discontinuity in the derivative at $t = a$. The time axis appears to be suddenly compressed by a factor of three, starting at this instant.

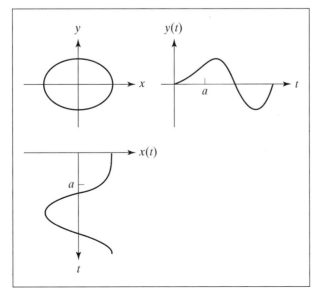

FIGURE 10.3 A trajectory with a sudden change in speed of motion.

The shape of the parametric curve is unaffected by this jump, but the nature of the motion of the point $P(t)$ along the curve is dramatically different before and after $t = a$.

PRACTICE EXERCISE

10.1.1 Formulas for the velocity of the point along the ellipse

For the curve in Equation (10.4) give formulas for the first derivative $P'(t) = (x'(t), y'(t))$ for t just before a and just after a. Is the velocity the same? Is the speed the same? ■

$$P'(t) = (x'(t), y'(t)) \tag{10.5}$$

As we study the smoothness of curves and of camera motion, it will be handy to have vocabulary that describes different kinds of smoothness of curves. We will be interested in two kinds of smoothness, often called **parametric continuity** and **geometric continuity**.

Parametric Continuity

We say a curve $P(t)$ has kth-order parametric continuity everywhere in the t-interval $[a, b]$ if all derivatives of the curve, up through the kth, exist and are continuous at all points inside $[a, b]$. To express this briefly we say

$$P(\ ) \text{ is } k\text{-smooth in } [a, b] \tag{10.6}$$

As an example, the ellipse in Figure 10.4 is 0-smooth everywhere, since the function $P(t)$ itself is continuous everywhere. But it is not 1-smooth everywhere, because there is a discontinuity in $P'(t)$ at $t = a$. (It *is* 1-smooth everywhere except at $t = a$.) To avoid jerky animations it is usually desirable that we insist that camera motion be 1-smooth.

FIGURE 10.4 What is the parametric representation?

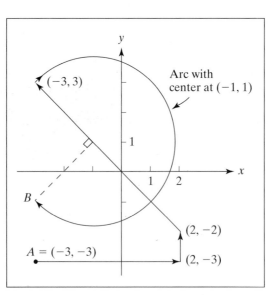

A curve with a continuous velocity and acceleration is 2-smooth. Note that a *2-smooth* function $[a, b]$ is necessarily 1-smooth *and* 0-smooth. However, a 1-smooth function may or may not also be 2-smooth.

Recall the three classes of spirals we discussed in Chapter 3 (Archimedean, logarithmic, and equiangular). We are curious about the degrees of smoothness of these curves. For example, the logarithmic spiral can house the chambered nautilus. It has the parametric polar form $f(\theta) = Ke^{a\theta}$ for all θ. By inspection it is 0-smooth, and direct calculation shows that its velocity vector is:

$$f'(\theta) = (-Ke^{a\theta}\sin(\theta) + Ke^{a\theta}\cos(\theta)ae^{a\theta}$$
$$f'(\theta) = Ke^{a\theta}\cos(\theta) + Ke^{a\theta}\sin(\theta)ae^{a\theta})$$

Since all terms in this expression are continuous, the logarithmic spiral is 1-smooth. Figure 10.5 shows a picture of a logarithmic spiral which in nature houses a chambered nautilus.

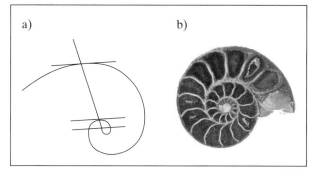

FIGURE 10.5 A logarithmic spiral and chambered nautilus.

In this section we discuss different degrees of another kind of smoothness, based on the visual smoothness of a curve rather than the smoothness of motion along a curve.

- A curve is **0-smooth** in an interval if it is continuous.
- A curve is **1-smooth** in an interval if its first derivative exists and is continuous throughout the given interval.
- A curve is **2-smooth** if its first and second derivatives exist and are continuous throughout the given interval.
- A curve is **3-smooth** if its first, second, and third derivatives exist and are continuous throughout the given interval.

Geometric Continuity (G^k continuity)

Basically geometric continuity requires that various derivative vectors have a continuous direction even though they might have discontinuity in speed. The ellipse in Equation (10.4) has a continuous derivative except at $t = a$.

The example in Equation (10.4) also suggests that it's the strange parameterization (at $t = a$) that causes this kind of smoothness to fail. This is true. For our purposes in this book the following definitions suffice:

- G^0 continuity is the same as 0-smoothness: it simply means that $P(t)$ is continuous with respect to t throughout the interval $[a, b]$ of interest.
- G^1 continuity in $[a,b]$ means that $P'(c-) = kP'(c+)$ for some constant k and for every c in the interval $[a, b]$. Thus at any point (c) in the interval of interest the velocity vector may jump in size by some amount k, but its direction is continuous.
- G^2 continuity in $[a, b]$ means that both first and second derivatives have continuous directions: $P'(c-) = kP'(c+)$ and $P''(c-) = mP''(c+)$ for constants k and m and for every c in the interval $[a, b]$.

Note: from these definitions that geometric continuity requires the speed, or size of the velocity vectors (and their derivatives) to be continuous.

PRACTICE EXERCISES

10.1.2 Drawing tangent lines to an ellipse

Write a routine that draws a short line segment tangent to the ellipse produced by the fragment in Figure 10.3 at parameter value t.

10.1.3 Tangents and normals to the conic sections

Find expressions for the tangent line and the normal vector at any value of t for the parabola and for the hyperbola.

10.1.4 Find the parametric representation

Find a parametric representation $P(t)$ for the curve shown in Figure 10.4. The curve starts at point A at $t = 0$ and moves at *constant speed* over the entire shape shown, reaching point B at $t = 20$.

10.1.5 Another parametric form for the circle

In addition to the variety of representations produced by time warps, some curves permit simple representations that differ greatly in character, such as this next one. Show that the following form generates part of a circle as t varies from 0 to infinity.

$$x(t) = a\frac{1 - t}{1 + t}$$

$$y(t) = 2a\frac{\sqrt{t}}{1 + t} \tag{10.7}$$

What is its center and radius? What portion is generated as t varies from 0 to 1?
[*Hint*: Recall the relations $T = \tan(b/2)$ for some parameter b. Then

$$\sin(b) = 2T/(1 + T^2) \text{ and } \cos(b) = (1 - T^2)/(1 + T^2). \tag{10.8}$$

10.2 DESCRIBING CURVES USING POLYNOMIALS

It seems that if one is working from the point of view of getting beauty in one's equations, and if one has really a sound insight, one is on a sure line of progress.

Paul Dirac
(1902–1984)

Polynomials are fundamental mathematical objects and are frequently used in computer graphics because they are well behaved and efficient to compute. In the rest of the chapter we will focus on particular forms of polynomials: here we examine the interplay between implicit forms and parametric forms that are simple polynomials.

First a reminder: An ***L*th-degree polynomial in t** is a function given by

$$a_0 + a_1t + a_2t^2 + \cdots + a_Lt^L \tag{10.9}$$

where the constants $a_0, a_1, \ldots, a_L$ are its **coefficients**, each associated with one of the powers of t. The **degree** of the polynomial is the highest power to which t is raised. For this to be Lth degree, we insist that a_L not equal 0. The **order** is the number of coefficients in the polynomial ($L + 1$ here). It is always one greater than the degree.

Polynomial Curves of Degree 1

We have already examined **linear** polynomials and know that a linear parametric form for $x(t)$ and $y(t)$ yields a **straight line**, and the corresponding implicit form is linear in x and y. For example, the curve whose parametric representation is $P(t) = a_0 + a_1t$ is a straight line which passes through a_0 at time 0, and through $a_0 + a_1$ at time $t = 1$. Notice that the equation for $P(t)$ is actually two equations, one for $x(t)$ and one for $y(t)$. In 3D there would, of course, be a third equation for z(t).

Polynomial Curves of Degree 2

We naturally ask what curve shapes are attainable using quadratic polynomials $x(t)$ and $y(t)$:

$$x(t) = at^2 + 2bt + c$$
$$y(t) = dt^2 + 2et + f \tag{10.10}$$

where a, b, and so on are constants. The answer is simple (but perhaps disappointing): this curve is always a **parabola**, for any choice of constants $a, b, \ldots, f$. So there is no way to generate an ellipse or hyperbola using this form. Visualize what the parabola looks like for two cases:

- Case #1: $a = b = 0, c = d = -2$ and $e = f = -6$
- Case #2: $a = b = 3, c = d = 8$, and $e = f = 4$

Implicit Forms of Degree 2

Going the other way, we look at quadratic implicit forms—that is, polynomials of degree 2 in both x and y. Recall from analytic geometry that the general second-degree implicit form is given by:

$$F(x, y) = Ax^2y + Cy^2 + Dx + Ey + F \tag{10.11}$$

(Note: some authors write this second-degree implicit form with an additional term in both x and y, as in $+Bxy$. Such a term can be removed, however, with a suitable rotation of coordinate axes.)

for constants $A, C, \ldots, F$. It is assumed that A and C are not both 0, which produces a degenerate curve. Also recall that the shape of the curve $F(x, y) = 0$ so described is a conic section. The particular conic that is represented is easily determined by examining the signs of the coefficients A and C, as follows:

if $AC > 0$, it is an **ellipse** (10.12)
if $AC = 0$, it is a **parabola**
if $AC < 0$, it is a **hyperbola** (10.13)

Therefore it is a parabola if one of A or C but not both is 0, an ellipse if A and C have the same sign, and a hyperbola if they have the opposite sign.

The conic that it describes depends on the value of the **eccentricity**[1] ε, as suggested in Figure 10.6.

The exercises explore possible choices of parameterization for drawing this set of curves. Note that we are unable to find a polynomial **parametric** form for the conic sections, beyond the parabola. For this we must wait until the next subsection and the inroduction of a **ratio** of polynomials.

Polynomial Curves of Degree 3 and Higher

Parametric-to-Implicit Forms versus Implicit-to-Parametric Forms

We have seen that the situation is well understood if we restrict ourselves to curves parameterized with first- and second-degree polynomials. Things get more complicated when the polynomials are of higher degree, however. In early curve design research, Sederberg et al. [Sederberg85] showed that it is always possible to find an implicit form given polynomial functions for $x(t)$ and $y(t)$, but that a parametric form can in general be found when given an implicit form that is of degree only one or two.

Our main workhorse in this chapter with Bezier and B-spline curves is cubic polynomials, and we will see that it provides a powerful approach to curve design.

---

[1] As a point of interest, the eccentricity of earth's orbit is .0167 and that of Pluto is .25.

FIGURE 10.6 The conic sections with different eccentricities.

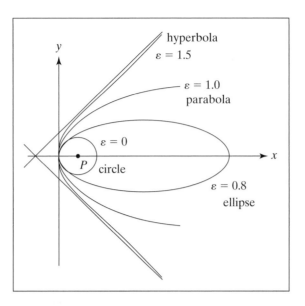

But the methods won't start with an implicit form and try to parameterize it. Rather they will start with a collection of control points laid down by the designer and allow a specific algorithm to generate points along the curve, so that the designer if necessary can edit the positions of the control points and view the curve again. In many ways this is a more natural approach to curve design than a purely mathematical one because it is very visual, allowing the designer to see the progress of the curve design as the process takes shape.

Before leaving this analytical approach to curve design, however, we preview briefly the class of **rational polynomial** functions, which we examine later. (As we'll see, they are the basis for NURBS.) This first look shows how the definition of a few *points* can determine a curve shape. It also produces an important result: the conic sections can be represented *exactly* by a ratio of two quadratic *polynomials*.

Rational Parametric Forms

Consider parametrizations where $x(.)$ and $y(.)$ are each defined as a **ratio** of two polynomials. The linear case is explored in the exercises. Equation (10.14) shows a parametric form comprised of the ratio of two quadratic polynomials. We look here at the quadratic polynomial case and focus on the particular parametric form:

$$P(t) = \frac{P_0(1-t)^2 + 2wP_1t(1-t) + P_2t^2}{(1-t)^2 + 2wt(1-t) + t^2} \tag{10.14}$$

where P_0, P_1, and P_2 are any three points in the plane. They are called **control points** in this context, as they control the shape of the curve. Equation (10.14) is actually two equations, of course, being shorthand for

$$(x(t), y(t)) = \left(\frac{x_0(1-t)^2 + 2x_1wt(1-t) + x_2t^2}{(1-t)^2 + 2wt(1-t) + t^2}, \frac{y_0(1-t)^2 + 2y_1wt(1-t) + y_2t^2}{(1-t)^2 + 2wt(1-t) + t^2} \right) \tag{10.15}$$

where x_0 and y_0 are the components for P_0, and similarly for the other two points. The coefficients of the quadratic polynomials in the numerators are the components of the control points. The denominator polynomials are the *same* for $x(.)$ and $y(.)$.

They are also quadratic but do not depend on the points. They do depend on a **weight parameter,** w, however, to be discussed.

Note that $P(t)$ is a linear combination of control points. As we saw in Section 4.5.2, in order to make sense as a point it must be an affine combination of these points. Happily this is so, as discussed in the exercises.

Note that if we evaluate this form at $t = 0$, the right-hand side collapses simply to (x_0, y_0), so this curve passes through, or **interpolates**, the point P_0. Similarly at $t = 1$ it passes through P_2. For t in between, $P(t)$ depends on all three points in a complicated way.

Figure 10.7a shows three sample control points and shows how the curve emerges from P_0 as t increases from 0 and ends up at P_2 as t approaches 1. It asks what the shape in between is. Part b shows the answer: the curve is one of the conic sections, and the type depends on the values of w:

if $w < 1$, it is an **ellipse**
if $w = 1$, it is a **parabola**
if $w > 1$, it is a **hyperbola** (10.16)

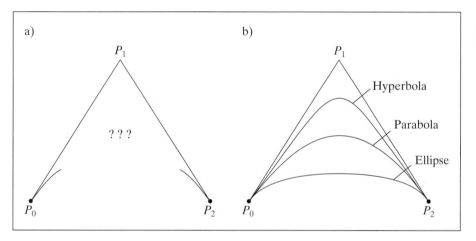

FIGURE 10.7 Generating conics with rational quadratics.

So we have a way of generating the conic sections parametrically, without recourse to the trigonometric functions needed earlier. The exercises show how to generate the other half of each of these curves and also how to generate a circle using this parametric form.

PRACTICE EXERCISES

10.2.1 Degenerate quadratics

Give examples of the coefficients $A, B, \ldots, F$ in Equation (10.11) such that the curve $F(x, y) = 0$ is:

a. nothing (i.e., no points satisfy $F(x, y) = 0$);
b. a single point;
c. a straight line;
d. two parallel lines.

10.2.2 Linear rational parameterizations

Discuss the class of curves that can be generated by the parameterizations:

$$x(t) = \frac{a + bt}{e + ft}$$

$$y(t) = \frac{c + dt}{g + ht} \qquad\qquad (10.17)$$

for constants $a, b, \ldots, h$. Can curves that are not straight be generated? Give some examples that show how rich this class is.

10.2.3 Is it straight?

From Figure 10.7 it appears that if P_0, P_1, and P_2 lie in a straight line, the whole curve should be a straight line. Show whether this is true or not.

10.2.4 Using rational quadratics to draw conic sections

Figure 10.8a shows a circle inscribed in an equilateral triangle. One third of the circle can be drawn using the parametric form of Equation (10.14) based on the points P_0, P_1, and P_2 as shown. Thus the whole circle can be drawn as three arcs, each generated using three points. It can be shown [Farin90] that the proper weight w to use for a circle is $w = \cos(a)$, where a is the angle $P_2P_0P_1$. The angle is 60° for the equilateral triangle.

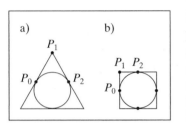

FIGURE 10.8 A circle viewed as three or four arcs.

a. Plot the point $P(t)$ of Equation (10.7) for five values of t, such that the points are approximately equispaced along the arc from P_0 to P_2.
b. Is this a more efficient way to draw a circle than using samples of $(\cos(.), \sin(.))$? Discuss.
c. Repeat parts a and b for one of the four arcs shown in part b. What is angle $P_2P_0P_1$ in this case? ■

10.3 ON INTERACTIVE CURVE DESIGN

> *I could never make out what those damned dots meant.*
>
> *Lord Randolph Churchill*
> *(1849–1895)*

The curves considered so far have been based on relatively simple mathematical formulas. Now we want to broaden the task and develop more complex curves that serve a certain purpose. In particular we want to develop tools that allow a designer to fashion a large variety of shapes by simply specifying a small collection of control points.

Assume, for example, that the designer wishes to create a computer representation of the curve of Figure 10.9a. It might be a part of an emerging design for a car fender, a turbine blade, or the casing of an electric drill. Or it might be the trajectory of a camera as it sweeps through a scene taking snapshots. The goal is to capture the shape of this curve in a form that permits it to be reproduced at will, adjusted in shape and size as desired, sent to a machine for automatic cutting or molding, and so on. Probably there is no simple formula that matches it very closely.

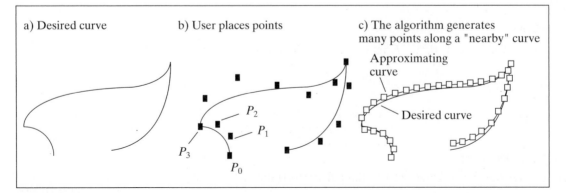

a) Desired curve   b) User places points   c) The algorithm generates many points along a "nearby" curve

FIGURE 10.9 A curve design scenario.

To enter the curve the designer tapes a sketch of the figure onto a drawing tablet, and then moves the pointer along the curve clicking at a set of **control points** $P_0, P_1, \ldots$ close to the curve, as shown in Figure 10.9b. The sequence of control points is often called the **control polygon**.[2] The designer enters the control polygon based on a lot of experience, along with a clear understanding of the characteristics of the curve generation algorithm—the algorithm that will later be used to regenerate the curve from the data points.

As suggested in Figure 10.10, the role of the algorithm is to produce a point $P(t)$ for any value of t given to it. The data for the algorithm are the set of control points, which together determine the curve along which the points $P(t)$ will fall.

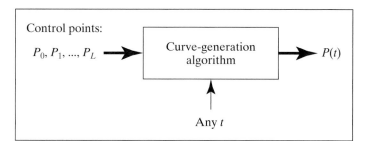

FIGURE 10.10 The curve generation algorithm.

The algorithm is usually implemented as a function

```
Point2 curvePt(double t, RealPointArray pts)
```

that returns a point for any value of t in a certain interval. To draw the curve the user can choose a sequence of t-values, evaluate `curvePt()` at each of them, and connect the points with line segments to form a polyline. Figure 10.9c shows a collection of small squares, indicating the points that might be returned by a reasonable algorithm that is given the set of control points in Figure 10.9b.

Hopefully the polyline defined by these points will closely approximate the original curve the designer had in mind when entering the control points. If the generated curve does not provide an adequate approximation to the original curve, the designer will edit the control points, presumably with the mouse, translating them this way and that and generating the curve again with many calls to `curvePt()`. This iterative process continues until the designer is satisfied. Interactive design therefore consists of the following steps:

The interactive design process:

1. Lay down the initial control points.
2. Use the algorithm to generate the curve.
3. If the curve is satisfactory, stop.
4. Adjust some control points.
5. Go to step 2.

Interpolation vs. Approximation

Figure 10.11 distinguishes between two main classes of curve generation algorithms. Part a shows an algorithm that generates a curve $P(t)$ that **interpolates** the control points: $P(t)$ passes exactly through the control points and forms a smooth curve for points in between. Part b uses an algorithm that generates a curve $R(t)$ that **approximates** the control points. $R(t)$ is attracted toward each control point in turn, but

---

[2] The control points usually designate a polyline rather than a closed polygon, but we shall continue to use "polygon" since the terminology has become common.

FIGURE 10.11 Interpolating vs. approximating curve generation methods.

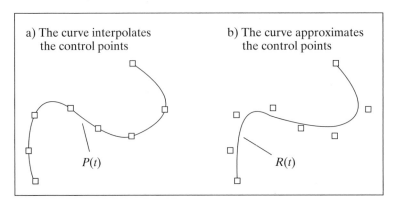

a) The curve interpolates the control points

b) The curve approximates the control points

$P(t)$

$R(t)$

doesn't actually pass through all of them. In our study of various algorithms subsequently we will see that each kind of algorithm has advantages and disadvantages.

This scenario of iterative curve design is a staple in the field of computer-aided design (CAD) and is often used when designing an item to be manufactured.

In the next sections we shall build up a set of techniques for curve design as well as surface design. Choosing from the many approaches one might take, the emphasis is placed on *interactive* curve design using Bezier and B-spline curves. These families of curves have become very popular in CAD applications. Our presentation will necessarily be brief, but we shall provide enough detail to enable you to write programs to perform interactive curve design and to create drawings of the objects so designed.

We first examine some techniques for curve approximation focusing on Bezier curves and B-spline curves. Although it might seem that a designer would always want to interpolate the control points, we will see that there are advantages to the curve approximation approach. We then study how to adjust algorithms to insure interpolation of the control points.

10.4 BEZIER CURVES FOR CURVE DESIGN

We begin with the simple and elegant **de Casteljau** algorithm that produces Bezier curves, which are fundamental to CAD. Bezier curves were developed by Paul de Casteljau in 1959 and independently by Pierre Bezier around 1962. They were formulated as ingredients in CAD systems at two automobile companies, Citroen and Renault, to help design shapes for car bodies.

10.4.1 The de Casteljau Algorithm

The de Casteljau algorithm uses a sequence of points, P_0, P_1, and $P_2, \ldots$, to construct a well-defined value for the point $P(t)$ at each value of t from 0 to 1. Thus it provides a way to generate a curve from a set of points. Changing the points changes the curve. The construction is based on a sequence of familiar tweening steps (recall Chapter 5) that are easy to implement. Because *tweening* is such a well-behaved procedure, it is possible to deduce many valuable properties of the curves that it generates.

Tweening Three Points to Create a Parabola

Start with three points, P_0, P_1, and P_2, as shown in Figure 10.12a. Choose some value of t between 0 and 1, say $t = 0.3$, and locate the point A that is fraction t of the way along the line from P_0 to P_1. Similarly, locate B at fraction t along the line between the endpoints P_1 and P_2 (using the same t). From Chapter 5 we know that the new points can be expressed as

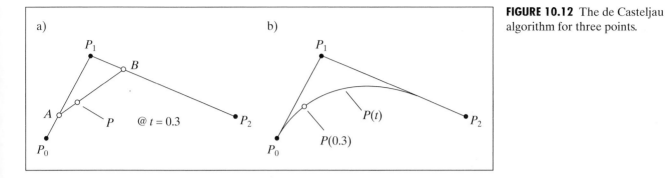

FIGURE 10.12 The de Casteljau algorithm for three points.

$$A(t) = (1 - t)P_0 + tP_1$$
$$B(t) = (1 - t)P_1 + tP_2 \qquad\qquad (10.18)$$

Now repeat the linear interpolation step on these points (again using the same t). Find the point, $P(t)$, that lies fraction t of the way between A and B:

$$P(t) = (1 - t)A + tB \qquad\qquad (10.19)$$

as shown. As an example, for $t = .5$, $P(0.5)$ is simply the "midpoint between midpoints" for the three given points. If this process is carried out for *every* t between 0 and 1, the curve $P(t)$ will be generated, as shown in Figure 10.12b. What is the parametric form for this curve? By direct substitution of Equation (11.18) into Equation (11.19), we obtain

$$P(t) = (1 - t)^2 P_0 + 2t(1 - t)tP_1 + t^2 P_2 \qquad\qquad (10.20)$$

It can be expressed in terms of the Tween() function of Chapter 5—see the exercises.

The parametric form for $P(t)$ is quadratic in t, so we know from Section 10.2 that the curve is a parabola. It will still be a parabola even if t is allowed to vary from $-$infinity to infinity. It clearly passes through P_0 at $t = 0$ and through P_2 at $t = 1$. (Why?) We thus have a well-defined process that can generate a smooth parabolic curve based on three given points.

What if more than three control points are used? The most commonly used family of Bezier curves are those based on four control points. Figure 10.13a shows how the de Casteljau algorithm is applied to the points P_0, P_1, P_2, and P_3.

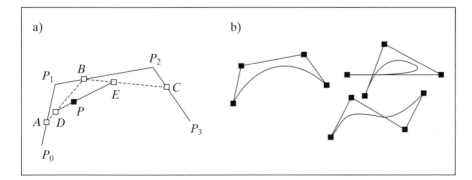

FIGURE 10.13 The Bezier curve based on four points.

For a given value of t point A is placed fraction t of the way from P_0 to P_1, and similarly for points B and C. Then D is placed fraction t of the way from A to B, and similarly for point E. Finally, the desired point P is located fraction t of the way from D to E. If this is done for *every* t between 0 and 1, the curve $P(t)$ is formed that starts at P_0, is attracted toward P_1 and P_2, and ends at P_3. It is the **Bezier** curve determined by the four points. Figure 10.13b shows the Bezier curves defined by different configurations of four points. To see these four curves clearly, let your eyes peruse them while ignoring the control polygon—that is, just think of the final resulting curve in each case.

It is easy to work out (see the exercises) that the Bezier curve based on four points has the parametric form:

$$\mathbf{P}(t) = \mathbf{P}_0(1 - t)^3 + \mathbf{P}_1 3(1 - t)^2 t + \mathbf{P}_2 3(1 - t)t^2 + \mathbf{P}_3 t^3 \tag{10.21}$$

which is a cubic polynomial in t. Note from Equation (10.21) that $P(t)$ involves the four control points, each weighted by a cubic polynomial, and that the weighted terms are then added. The terms involved here are known as **Bernstein polynomials**. The four cubic Bernstein polynomials (What are their order, and what are their co-efficients?) are:

$$\begin{aligned}
B_0^3(t) &= (1 - t)^3 \\
B_1^3(t) &= 3(1 - t)^2 t \\
B_2^3(t) &= 3(1 - t)t^2 \\
B_3^3(t) &= t^3
\end{aligned} \tag{10.22}$$

The cubic Bernstein polynomials are easily remembered as the terms one gets by raising the expression $a(t) = (1 - t + t)$, which of course is simply 1 for all values of t, to the third power. Now expand $a^3(t)$ and then collect terms in the various powers of $(1 - t)$ and t.

$$((1 - t) + t)^3 = (1 - t)^3 + 3(1 - t)^2 t + 3(1 - t)t^2 + t^3$$

This immediately yields an important property of the Bernstein polynomials: they add to unity at *every* t. (Why?)

$$\sum_{k=0}^{3} B_k^3(t) = 1 \tag{10.23}$$

For this reason $P(t)$ of Equation (10.21) is clearly an affine combination of points, so it is legitimate to add the weighted points together. (Recall the issue of adding points in Chapter 5.)

Figure 10.14 plots the shapes of the four Bernstein polynomials of degree 3 as t varies between 0 and 1. They are seen to undulate smoothly versus t. Later we see just how "smooth" they are.

FIGURE 10.14 The Bernstein polynomials of degree 3.

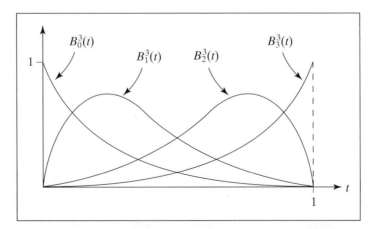

Figure 10.15 illustrates geometrically how the four points $P_0, \ldots, P_3$ in Equation (10.21) are blended together to form $P(t)$. View the points as vectors bound to the origin (so we write P_0 as $\mathbf{p}_0$, and so on) and let $t = 0.3$. Then Equation (10.21) becomes

$$\mathbf{p}(0.3) = 0.343\mathbf{p}_0 + 0.441\mathbf{p}_1 + 0.189\mathbf{p}_2 + 0.027\mathbf{p}_3$$

In the figure the four vectors are weighted and the results are added using the parallelogram rule (recall Chapter 4) to form the vector $\mathbf{p}(0.3)$. It is seen that at $t = 0.3$ the main contributors are $\mathbf{p}_0$ and $\mathbf{p}_1$. Even though the weights are very small for the third and fourth terms, these terms still have an effect on $\mathbf{p}(0.3)$ since the vectors $\mathbf{p}_2$ and $\mathbf{p}_3$ are rather large.

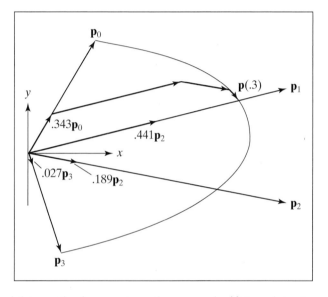

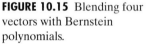

FIGURE 10.15 Blending four vectors with Bernstein polynomials.

As t varies, the relative weights on the four vectors change, and $\mathbf{p}(t)$ translates to different positions. Try to visualize how the vectors would be weighted at $t = 0.5$, and how the four contributions would collaborate to form the vector $\mathbf{p}(0.5)$.

Extending the de Casteljau Algorithm to Any Number of Points

We have seen that the de Casteljau algorithm uses tweening to produce quadratic parametric representations when three points are used, and cubic representations when four points are used. It generalizes gracefully to the case in which $L + 1$ control points $P_0, P_1, \ldots, P_L$ are used. For each value of t a succession of generations are built up, each one by tweening adjacent points produced in the previous generation:

$$\mathbf{P}_i^4(t) = (1 - t)\mathbf{P}_i^3(t) + t\mathbf{P}_{i+1}^3(t)$$

$$\ldots$$

$$\mathbf{P}_i^L(t) = (1 - t)\mathbf{P}_i^{L-1}(t) + t\mathbf{P}_{i+1}^{L-1}(t) \tag{10.24}$$

for $i = 0, \ldots, L$. The superscript k in $\mathbf{P}_i^k(t)$ denotes the generation. The process starts with $\mathbf{P}_i^0(t) = P_i$ and ends with the final Bezier curve $P(t) = P_\mathrm{i}^\mathrm{L}(t)$. The resulting Bezier curve can be written in terms of Bernstein polynomials

$$P(t) = \sum_{k=0}^{L} P_k B_k^L(t) \tag{10.25}$$

where the kth Bernstein polynomial of degree L is defined as[3]

$$B_k^L(t) = \binom{L}{k}(1 - t)^{L-k}t^k \qquad (10.26)$$

Here $\binom{L}{k}$ is the **binomial coefficient function**, given by

$$\binom{L}{k} = \frac{L!}{k!(L - k)!} \qquad \text{for } L <= k \qquad (10.27)$$

The value of this term is 0 if $L < k$. Each of the Bernstein polynomials is seen to be of degree L. As before, the Bernstein polynomials are the terms one gets when expanding $[(1 - t) + t]^L$, so we are assured that

$$\sum_{k=0}^{L} B_k^L(t) = 1 \qquad \text{for all } t \qquad (10.28)$$

and that $P(t)$ is a legitimate affine combination of points.

PRACTICE EXERCISES

10.4.1 Generate the curve with a graphing calculator

Using the de Casteljau method with the three points $(0, 0)$, $(2, 4)$, and $(6, 1)$, locate $P(t)$ on a graphic calculator for the t-values 0, .2, .4, .6, .8, and 1.

10.4.2 Quadratic curves must be planar

Justify the assertion that there is a unique quadratic curve that passes through a set of three (distinct) points. Remembering that three (noncollinear) points determine a plane, show that the quadratic they determine never leaves this plane. Thus a parabola can never deviate from a plane. For extra benefit, show that a cubic curve *can* be nonplanar.

10.4.3 A Bezier curve in terms of Tween()

Recall the function Tween() in Section 4.5.3. It takes two points as arguments and returns the tween of these points at a given value of t. Show that $P(t)$ of Equation (10.20) can be written as Tween(Tween(P0,P1,t),Tween(P1,P2,t),t), or a tween of two tweens. Write a similar expression for the cubic version.

10.4.4 The cubic Bezier curve

By writing out a succession of tweens as in the previous exercise, show that the parametric form of the Bezier curve given in Equation (10.21) is correct.

10.4.5 Building intuition about Bezier curves

Using Equation (10.21), compute the position of $P(t)$ at the times $t = 0.2, 0.5, 0.9$, when the four control points are $(2, 3)$, $(6, 6)$, $(8, 1)$, and $(4, -3)$. Sketch the weighted vectors, as in Figure 10.15, that contribute to the final value of $P(t)$.

10.4.6 The quartic and quintic Bezier curves

Write out the Bernstein functions in Equation (10.26) for the case of $L = 4$. Show that they are the terms one gets upon expanding $[(1 - t) + t]^4$. Repeat for $L = 5$.

10.4.7 Recursion relation for the Bernstein polynomials

Show that the nth-order Bernstein polynomial can always be formed from $(n - 1)$th-order versions using

---

[3] Readers familiar with probability theory will also notice a strong resemblance between this form and the binomial probability distribution.

$$B_i^n(t) = (1 - t)B_i^{n-1}(t) + tB_{i-1}^{n-1}(t) \tag{10.29}$$

where $B_0^0(t) = 1$, and where $B_j^n(t) = 0$ when j is not in the range $0, \ldots, n$.

$$\textit{Hint:} \begin{pmatrix} n \\ i \end{pmatrix} = \begin{pmatrix} n-1 \\ i \end{pmatrix} + \begin{pmatrix} n-1 \\ i-1 \end{pmatrix}.$$

10.4.8 Bezier curves interpolate at both ends

Show that the general L-degree Bezier curve passes through the two outermost control points: $P(0) = P_0$ and $P(1) = P_L$. Do this by examining the values of the Bernstein polynomials at $t = 0$ and $t = 1$, and showing that all but one term vanishes at these endpoints. ■

10.5 PROPERTIES OF BEZIER CURVES

A little inaccuracy sometimes saves a ton of explanation.

H. H. Munro (Saki)
(1870–1916)

Bezier curves have some important properties that make them well suited for CAD. We will find later that these properties apply to B-splines as well. Exploring these properties and their proofs provides a great deal of insight into Bezier curves.

Endpoint Interpolation

The Bezier curve $P(t)$ based on control points $P_0, P_1, \ldots, P_L$ does not generally pass through, or interpolate, all of the control points. But we have seen that it always does interpolate P_0 and P_L. This is a very useful property, because a designer who is inputting a sequence of points thereby knows precisely where the Bezier curve will begin and end.

Affine Invariance

It is often necessary to subject a Bezier curve to an affine transformation in order to scale it, orient it, or position it for subsequent use. Suppose we wish to transform point $P(t)$ on the Bezier curve of Equation (10.25) to the new point $Q(t)$, using the affine transformation T. (T is represented by a 3-by-3 matrix in the 2D case and by a 4-by-4 matrix in the 3D case.) So $Q(t) = T(P(t))$. It appears that to find $Q(t)$ at any given value of t we must first evaluate $P(t)$, and then transform it, effectively starting over fresh for each new t. But this isn't so. We need only transform the control points (once), and then use these new control points in the same Bernstein form to re-create the transformed Bezier curve at any t! That is:

$$Q(t) = \sum_{k=0}^{L} T(P_k) B_k^L(t) \tag{10.30}$$

Affine invariance means that the transformed curve is identical to the curve based on the transformed control points.

Figure 10.16 shows a Bezier curve based on four control points $P_0, \ldots, P_3$. These points are rotated, scaled, and translated to the new control points Q_k, and the Bezier curve determined by them is drawn. This curve is identical point by point to the result of transforming the original Bezier curve.

Bezier curves are affine invariant for a very simple reason: they are formed as an affine combination of points, and from Section 5.2 we know that an affine transformation preserves affine combinations.

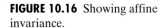

FIGURE 10.16 Showing affine invariance.

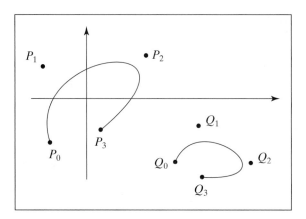

Convex Hull Property

Another property that designers may rely on is that a Bezier curve, $P(t)$, never wanders outside its convex hull. Recall from Chapter 5 that the convex hull of a set of points $P_0, P_1, \ldots, P_L$ is the set of all *convex combinations* of the points—that is, the set of all points given by

$$\sum_{k=0}^{L} \alpha_k P_k \tag{10.31}$$

where each α_k is nonnegative, and they sum to 1.

But $P(t)$ of Equation (10.33) *is* a convex combination of its control points for every t, since no Bernstein polynomial is ever negative, and they sum to 1. Thus every point on the Bezier curve is a convex combination of its control points, so it must lie within the convex hull of the control points.

The convex hull property also follows immediately from the fact that each point on the curve is the result of tweening two points that are themselves tweens, and the tweening of two points forms a convex combination of them. Figure 10.17 illustrates how the designer can use the convex hull property. Even though the eight control points form a jagged control polygon, the designer knows the Bezier curve will flow smoothly between the two endpoints, never extending outside the convex hull.

Derivatives of Bezier Curves

Because a curve can exhibit corners and other abrupt changes when its derivatives with respect to t have discontinuities, we must investigate the various derivatives of $P(t)$ in Equation (10.25).

FIGURE 10.17 Using the convex hull property.

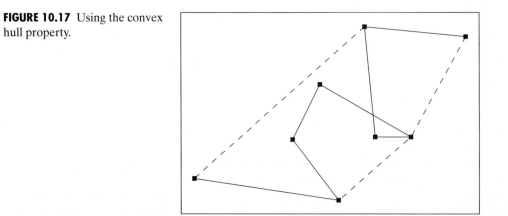

For a Bezier curve one can show that the first derivative is

$$\mathbf{p}'(t) = L \sum_{k=0}^{L-1} \Delta P_k B_k^{L-1}(t) \tag{10.32}$$

where

$$\Delta P_k = P_{k+1} - P_k \tag{10.33}$$

(See the exercises.) So the velocity is another Bezier curve, built on a new set of control vectors ΔP_k. We simply *difference* the original control points, $\Delta P_k = P_{k+1} - P_k$, in pairs to form the control vectors of the velocity. Note from the form $B_k^{L-1}(t)$ that taking the derivative lowers the order of the curve by 1. For instance, the derivative of a cubic Bezier curve is a quadratic Bezier curve. The smoothness of Bezier curves is addressed in the exercises.

Creating and Drawing Bezier Curves

Suppose we wish to build an application that draws a Bezier curve from a sequence of control points. How might it be organized? The Bezier curve, $P(t)$, of Equation (10.25) will be drawn by an approximating polyline. The function $P(t)$ is sampled at closely spaced values of t—say at $t_i = i/N$ for $i = 0, 1, \ldots, N$—and the points, $P(t_i)$, are connected with straight lines. The only issue is the evaluation of $P(t)$ at each desired value of t, which we suppose is performed in the following function:

```
Point2 bezier(RealPointArray poly, double t);
/* compute position P(t) of the Bezier curve based on a control
polygon */
```

This routine uses the point array (called the **control polygon**) stored in `poly` to evaluate Equation (10.25) for the given value of t and returns the resulting point. Notice that the degree of the Bernstein polynomials is stored in `poly.num`. Implementing this routine is left as a (valuable) exercise. A great deal of insight is gained by experimenting with a Bezier curve design application, to see the effect of using different control polygons. Figure 10.18 shows a complete working program which the user can then indicate additional control points. After each group of three points is placed, another Bezier curve is drawn. Further extensions to the program are addressed in the Case Studies.

```
#include <windows.h>
#include <math.h>
#include <gl/Gl.h>
#include <gl/Glu.h>
#include <gl/glut.h>

int SCREEN_HEIGHT = 480;
// Keep track of times clicked, on 3 clicks draw.
int NUMPOINTS = 0;

// Point class to keep it a little cleaner.
class Point {
public:
        float x, y;
        void setxy(float x2, float y2) { x = x2; y = y2; }
        const Point & operator=(const Point &rPoint) {
```

FIGURE 10.18 A complete Bezier curve application.

```
            x = rPoint.x;
            y = rPoint.y;

            return *this;
        }
};

Point abc[3];

void myInit() {
        glClearColor(0.0,0.0,0.0,0.0);
        glColor3f(1.0,0.0,0.0);
        glPointSize(4.0);
        glMatrixMode(GL_PROJECTION);
        glLoadIdentity();
        gluOrtho2D(0.0,640.0,0.0,480.0);

}

void drawDot(int x, int y) {
        glBegin(GL_POINTS);
          glVertex2i(x,y);
        glEnd();
        glFlush();
}

void drawLine(Point p1, Point p2) {
        glBegin(GL_LINES);
           glVertex2f(p1.x, p1.y);
           glVertex2f(p2.x, p2.y);
        glEnd();
        glFlush();
}
// Calculate the next bezier point.
Point drawBezier(Point A, Point B, Point C, double t) {

        Point P;
        P.x = pow((1 - t), 2) * A.x + 2 * t * (1 -t) * B.x + pow(t, 2) * C.x;
        P.y = pow((1 - t), 2) * A.y + 2 * t * (1 -t) * B.y + pow(t, 2) * C.y;
        return P;
}

void myMouse(int button, int state, int x, int y) {
  // If left button was clicked
  if(button == GLUT_LEFT_BUTTON && state == GLUT_DOWN) {
        // Store where the user clicked, note Y is backward, note that y = 0
        lies at the top of the screen.
        abc[NUMPOINTS].setxy((float)x,(float)(SCREEN_HEIGHT - y));
        NUMPOINTS++;

        // Draw the red  dot.
        drawDot(x, SCREEN_HEIGHT - y);

        // If 3 points are drawn do the curve.
        if(NUMPOINTS == 3) {
```

FIGURE 10.18 (*Continued*)

```
                    glColor3f(1.0,1.0,1.0);
                    // Draw two legs of the triangle
                    drawLine(abc[0], abc[1]);
                    drawLine(abc[1], abc[2]);
                    Point POld = abc[0];
                    /* Draw each segment of the curve.  Make t increment in
                        smaller amounts for a more detailed curve. */
                    for(double t = 0.0;t <= 1.0; t += 0.1) {
                            Point P = drawBezier(abc[0], abc[1], abc[2], t);
                            drawLine(POld, P);
                            POld = P;
                    }
                    glColor3f(1.0,0.0,0.0);
                    NUMPOINTS = 0;
            }
        }
}

void myDisplay() {
        glClear(GL_COLOR_BUFFER_BIT);
        glFlush();
}

int main(int argc, char *argv[]) {
        glutInit(&argc, argv);
        glutInitDisplayMode(GLUT_SINGLE|GLUT_RGB);
        glutInitWindowSize(640,480);
        glutInitWindowPosition(100,150);
        glutCreateWindow("Bezier Curve");
        glutMouseFunc(myMouse);
        glutDisplayFunc(myDisplay);

        myInit();
        glutMainLoop();

        return 0;
}
```

FIGURE 10.18 (*Continued*)

PRACTICE EXERCISES

10.5.1 Draw the velocity

Plot four points on a graphing calculator or graph paper, plot out the Bezier curve, and carefully calculate its velocity and acceleration vectors as functions of *t*. ■

10.6 FINDING BETTER BLENDING FUNCTIONS

> I was gratified to be able to answer promptly.
> I said I didn't know.
>
> *Mark Twain*
> *(1835–1910)*

It might appear that Bezier curves provide the ultimate tool for designing curves. An endless variety of smooth curves can be fashioned by placing control points judiciously in the plane.

But we see next that Bezier curves by themselves do not provide enough flexibility in curve design. One problem is that the degree of the Bernstein polynomials used is coupled to the number of control points: a Bezier curve based on $L + 1$ control points is a combination of L-degree polynomials. High-degree polynomials are expensive to compute and are vulnerable to numerical round-off errors. We want the designer to be free to use as many control points as desired, even 40 or more.

10.6.1 The Problem of Local Control

An even more significant problem is that Bezier curves do not offer enough **local control** of the curve shape. Figure 10.19 shows a situation where five control points are used to fashion a Bezier curve (solid line), which deviates somewhat from the desired curve (dashed line) near $t = 1$.

FIGURE 10.19 Editing portions of a curve.

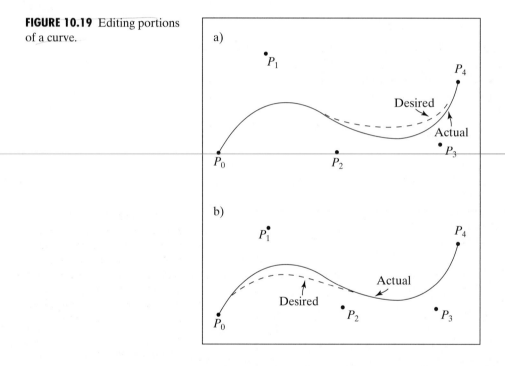

To correct this the user would move P_2 and P_3 up to force the Bezier curve closer to the desired curve. But, as shown in Figure 10.19, this also affects the shape of the first half of the curve, forcing it away from the desired version.

The problem is that a change to any control point alters the *entire* curve. This arises from the nature of Bernstein polynomials (recall Figure 10.14): each one is "active" (meaning nonzero) over the entire interval $[0, 1]$. The interval over which a function is nonzero is often called its **support**. Because every Bernstein polynomial has support over the entire interval $[0, 1]$, and the curve is a blend of these functions, it follows that each control point has an effect on the curve at all t-values between 0 and 1. Therefore, adjusting any control point affects the shape of the curve everywhere, with no local control.

Contrast that with the more favorable set of hypothetical blending functions illustrated in Figure 10.20. The six blending functions, $R_0(t), R_1(t), \ldots, R_5(t)$, (to be defined shortly[4]) are shown, each having support that is only a part of the interval

[4] (preview): These are in fact quadratic B-splines, developed later.

[0, 1]. For instance, the support of $R_0(t)$ is $[0, .25]$ and that of $R_3(t)$ is $[.25, 1.0]$. In fact, at any value of t no more than three of the blending functions are active.

Consider using these blending functions to build a curve, $V(t)$, based on six given control points, $P_0, P_1, \ldots, P_5$. We use the same kind of parametric form as for Bezier curves:

$$V(t) = \sum_{k=0}^{5} P_k R_k(t) \tag{10.35}$$

but seek a better set of funtions $R_k(t)$ Figure 10.20b shows the curve for an example set of control points. At each t the position $V(t)$ depends on no more than three of the control points. In particular, for all t in $[0.75, 1.0]$ only the points P_3, P_4, and P_5 control the shape of the curve. If the single control point P_4 is moved to P'_4, only a portion of the curve, shown dashed, will change. Thus this set of blending functions *does* give some local control to the control points.

10.6.2 Wish List for a Set of Blending Functions

The shapes of the blending functions in Figure 10.20 were apparently concocted just to illustrate the property of local control. But they are in fact based on functions that are often used for curve design. Their detailed nature is described later, but we scrutinize them further here to get a sense of what properties a set of blending functions should have.

As always, we suppose that the curve generation algorithm to be used blends control points $P_0, \ldots, P_L$ according to:

$$V(t) = \sum_{k=0}^{L} P_k R_k(t), \qquad \text{for } t \text{ in } [a, b] \tag{10.36}$$

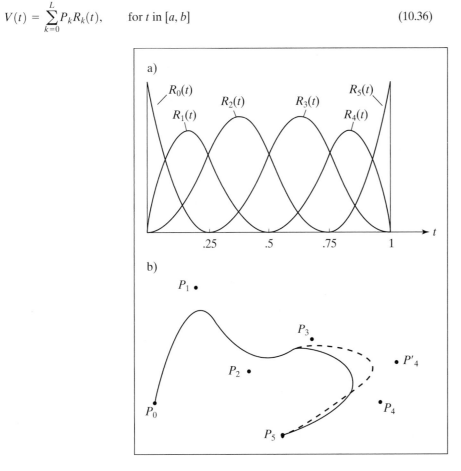

FIGURE 10.20 Blending functions having concentrated support. a) A more promising set of hypothetical blending functions that have concentrated support; b) an example curve before (solid) and after (dashed) a control point is adjusted.

where the blending functions $R_0(t), \dots, R_L(t)$ have certain properties that produce better curves and/or make the design process more intuitive. We construct a wish list of such properties. The blending functions should:

- be easy to compute and numerically stable;
- sum to one at every t in $[a, b]$;
- have small support to offer local control;
- interpolate certain control points, chosen by the designer;
- be smooth enough.

We consider each property individually.

The Functions Should be Easy to Compute and Numerically Stable

For rapid curve generation we want the blending functions to be computationally simple. We also want them to be minimally susceptible to numerical round-off error. These considerations lead one to choose polynomials for the blending functions, and to choose polynomials having the smallest degree possible consistent with producing the desired curves. Other kinds of functions, such as sines and cosines, would be too expensive to use.

The Functions Must Sum to One at Every t in $[a, b]$

$V(t)$ is a weighted sum of points at each t, which makes sense only if it is an *affine* sum of points at every t in $[a, b]$ (otherwise it is not a point). Thus we insist that:

$$\sum_{k=0}^{L} R_k(t) = 1 \tag{10.37}$$

You can see that the candidate functions in Figure 10.20 appear to enjoy this propert. The functions we actually will use will indeed sum to one.

The Functions Should have Small Support for Local Control

This was discussed earlier: to achieve local control we want each blending function to be concentrated in t, having support over only a small portion of the interval $[a, b]$.

The Functions Should Interpolate Certain Control Points

The designer may want $V(t)$ to pass through some of the control points, but only be attracted toward others. The shapes in Figure 10.20 cause the first and last control points to be interpolated. This is apparent because at both $t = 0$ and $t = 1$ all but one of the blending funtions is seen to be 0, forcing the remaining one to be 1 (why), which forces interpolation (why?) We will see shortly how to provide a mechanism that adjusts the blending functions so that certain additional control points are interpolated.

The Functions Should have Sufficient Smoothness

The designer normally wants $V(t)$ to be a smooth curve for any set of control points. Typically $V(t)$ should be at least 1-smooth, maybe even 2-smooth, to produce curve shapes of the desired smoothness. The smoothness of $V(t)$ depends on the smoothness of the blending functions. Specifically, if every blending function is 1-smooth in $[a, b]$, then $V(t)$ will also be 1-smooth in $[a, b]$.

Notice that the blending functions in Figure 10.20 appear to be smooth in their interior. It's also important that they start and stop gracefully. Figure 10.21 shows a blending function along with its first derivative.

The derivative of the function varies continuously from 0 at $t = c$, where the function starts. But where it ends at d its derivative is discontinuous, jumping abruptly from a negative value to 0. This function is 1-smooth everywhere except at $t = d$. A curve that used

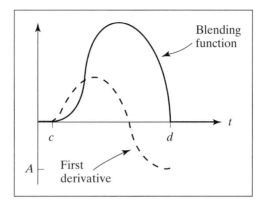

FIGURE 10.21 A candidate blending function and its derivative.

this blending function would not be 1-smooth at $t = d$. Thus it is desirable for blending functions to be smooth internally, and also to start and end with derivatives of 0.

Some of the shapes in Figure 10.20 start and stop with zero derivatives, while others do not. The shapes that begin and end inside the interval [0, 1] do so with zero derivatives, so the curve $V(t)$ will be 1-smooth inside (0,1). It is acceptable for derivatives to be discontinuous at the ends of the interval [0, 1] because we never use values of t beyond 0 or 1.

10.6.3 Piecewise Polynomial Curves and Splines

We start looking for good candidate blending functions, say polynomials of low degree. For instance, is there some cubic polynomial that has the shape suggested in Figure 10.22 that will satisfy all our needs?

To explore this we define the function:

$$R(t) = at^3 + bt^2 + ct + d$$

and see if there is a choice of coefficients that makes $R(t)$ and its first derivative to both be 0 at $t = 0$ and $t = 1$. This leads to four conditions on the coefficients to:

$$R(0) = d = 0$$
$$R(1) = a + b + c + d = 0$$
$$R'(0) = c = 0$$
$$R'(1) = 3a + 2b + c = 0$$

Unfortunately these conditions force $a = b = c = d = 0$, so there is no such shape. There just isn't enough flexibility in a cubic to do the bending we need. (The exercises ask whether a quadric polynomial would work.)

To attain more flexibility we try piecing together several low-degree polynomials. Such curves are defined by different polynomials in different t-intervals, and are called **piecewise polynomials**.

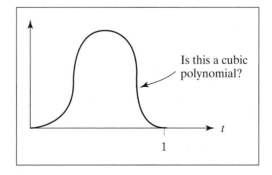

FIGURE 10.22 Can we find a cubic polynomial like this?

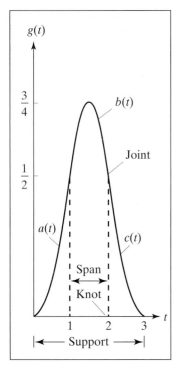

FIGURE 10.23 Ingredients of a piecewise polynomial.

The example shape, $g(t)$, shown in Figure 10.23 helps establish some nomenclature. We see that $g(t)$ consists of three polynomial **segments**, $a(t), b(t),$ and $c(t)$, defined as

$$a(t) = \frac{1}{2}t^2$$

$$b(t) = \frac{3}{4} - \left(t - \frac{3}{2}\right)^2$$

$$c(t) = \frac{1}{2}(3 - t)^2 \tag{10.38}$$

The support of $g(t)$ is $[0, 3]$; $a(t)$ is defined on the **span** $[0, 1]$, $b(t)$ on the span $[1, 2]$, and $c(t)$ on the span $[2, 3]$. The points at which a pair of the individual segments meet are called **joints**, and the values of t at which this happens are called **knots**. There are four knots in this example: $0, 1, 2,$ and 3.

To repeat for emphasis:

- Knots are values of t where segments meet:
- joints are values of the function of adjacent segments.

Is $g(t)$ continuous everywhere over its support? Because it is built from polynomials, it is certainly continuous inside each span, and so we need only check that the segments meet properly at the joints. This is easily checked from Equation (10.37): $a(1) = b(1) = 1/2$, and $b(2) = c(2) = 1/2$.

Going further, the derivative of $g(t)$ is continuous everywhere, so $g(t)$ is 1-smooth in $[0, 3]$. To see this, note that the derivative is necessarily continuous inside each span (why?), and so we need to check its continuity only at the knots. Direct calculation shows that $a'(1) = b'(1) = 1$, and $b'(2) = c'(2) = -1$. Thus as we move from one polynomial piece to the next, the slope does not jump abruptly.

The second derivative is not continuous, however, but does jump abruptly between two values (which ones?) at the knots.

The shape $g(t)$ here is an example of a **spline function**, a piecewise polynomial function that enjoys enough smoothness. Specifically, we have

Definition of a Spline Function

An Mth-degree **spline function** is a piecewise polynomial of degree M that is $(M - 1)$-smooth at each knot.

Evidently our example $g(t)$ is a quadratic spline: it is a piecewise polynomial of degree 2 and has a continuous first derivative everywhere.

10.6.4 To Build a Set of Blending Functions Out of $g(t)$

How can we use the spline function $g(t)$ above as a blending function to represent a curve? One way is to use *translated* versions of $g(t)$, where each blending function $g_k(t)$ is formed by translating the basic shape $g(t)$ by a certain amount. Figure 10.24 shows seven blending functions $g_0(t), \ldots, g_6(t)$ formed by translating $g(.)$ by integer amounts:

$$g_k(t) = g(t - k), \quad \text{for } k = 0, 1, \ldots \tag{10.39}$$

Since the knots of the various versions of $g()$ occur at integers, this is equivalent to translating so that the knots of one curve line up with knots of the next curve. These translated versions will form a legitimate set of blending functions only if they add up exactly to 1 at every t. But they do indeed do this for all t between 2 and 7! (See the exercises.)

$$\sum_{k=0}^{6} g(t - k) = 1, \quad \text{for } t \text{ in } [2, 7] \tag{10.40}$$

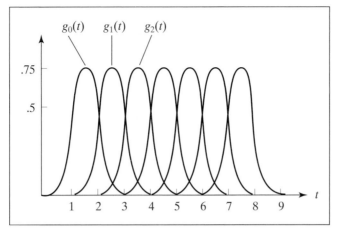

FIGURE 10.24 Blending functions representing a spline curve.

This may seem like magic, but we will see that it is a general property of the blending functions we ultimately develop. Here it is crucial that we translate each function by an integer, to make the shapes line up properly so they sum to 1.

So the designer chooses seven control points and generates the curve using the algorithm:

$$V(t) = \sum_{k=0}^{6} P_k g(t - k) \qquad (10.41)$$

Only values of t between 2 and 7 can be used. (Why?) In that range note that exactly three of the blending functions are active at any value of t, so there is good local control of the curve's shape. In addition note that at the specific times $t = 2, 3, \ldots$, and 7 only two of the functions are active and they both have value 0.5. Therefore at these t-values $V(t)$ will lie at the *midpoint* of the line between two of the control points.

Figure 10.25 shows an example placement of the seven control points, and the resulting curve. The curve begins at $t = 2$ at the midpoint of $P_0 P_1$, and fluctuates smoothly, passing through subsequent midpoints of the edges of the control polygon. As t increases, the various blending functions rise and fall, and the major influence on the curve is passed on from point to point.

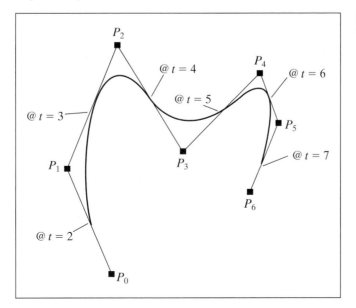

FIGURE 10.25 Curve design using translates of $g(.)$.

What are some properties of curves based on this set of blending functions?

- The designer has a good measure of local control of the curve shape, because the interval of support for each blending function is limited to length 3.
- The designer will lay down points exploiting the knowledge that the curve must pass through midpoints of the control polygon edges. So the algorithm has some intuitive geometric properties.
- Because each blending function is 1-smooth, the whole curve is 1-smooth.
- No control points on the curve are interpolated except P_0 and P_6.
- All polynomials are of degree 2, so they are fast and stable to compute. The degree of the polynomials does not depend on the number of control points. The technique works for any number of control points.

The curve generation algorithm just described can easily be implemented in the routine

```
Point2 curvePt(double t, RealPointArray pts)
```

that returns the point $V(t)$ for each value of t input to it. This is further discussed in Case Study 10.4.

■ EXAMPLE 10.6.1 Extension to drawing closed curves

It is not difficult to extend the technique above to the generation of closed curves such as those shown in Figure 10.26a. Figure 10.26b shows the closed version of the curve in Figure 10.25. All you must do to achieve this is to add two more terms to the sum in Equation (10.41), with two additional control points that *duplicate* P_0 and P_1. We know that at $t = 7$ the previous curve passed through the midpoint of leg P_5P_6. Thus at $t = 8$ the curve passes through the midpoint of P_6P_7, and at $t = 9$ it passes through the midpoint of P_7P_8, thus closing the curve. An alternative method is given in the exercises.

FIGURE 10.26 Generating closed curves. a) examples of closed curves; b) a technique for generating a closed curve.

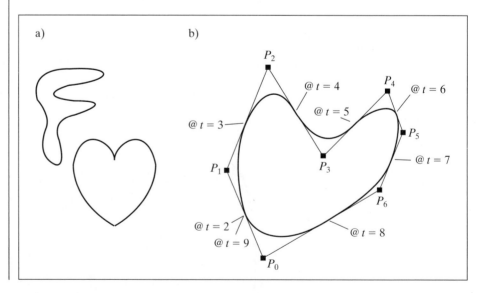

PRACTICE EXERCISES

10.6.1 Is there a quadric polynomial blending function?

Consider the quadric polynomial $r(t) = at^4 + bt^3 + ct^2 + dt + e$. Are there values of a, b, c, d, and e that cause this function to pass through 0, and have first derivatives equal to 0, at both $t = 0$ and $t = 1$? If so, find suitable values and sketch the curve.

10.6.2 Show that the g(.) translates add to 1 at every t

Consider the sum of translates $g(t) + g(t-1) + g(t-2)$, where $g(t)$ is the piecewise polynomial defined in Equation (10.38). Show that this sum is one for every t between 2 and 3.

10.6.3 Are Bernstein polynomials splines?

Show that the Bernstein polynomials $B_k^L(t)$ are indeed splines. How many polynomials are pieced together to form each one? Where are the knots? What degree is the spline? Is it sufficiently continuously differentiable?

10.6.4 Develop intuition about quadratic splines curves

Draw 12 control points in some complex pattern, and sketch a rough version of the curve generated using the quadratic spline functions as in Equation (10.38). Use the fact that the curve passes through the midpoint of certain edges of the control polygon.

10.6.5 Building closed curves with no extra control points

Show that a slight variation on Equation (10.41):

$$V(t) = \sum_{k=0}^{6} P_k g((t-k) \bmod 7) \tag{10.42}$$

creates a closed curve based on seven (distinct) control points as t varies from 0 to 7. No duplicate control points are required. The modulo function mod effectively folds the blending functions into the interval $[0, 7]$, making them active in different parts of the interval. To see how this works, sketch for $L = 4$ the five functions $g((t-k) \bmod(L+1))$ for $k = 0, 1, 2, 3, 4$ as t varies from 0 to 5. ■

10.6.5 Spline Curves and Basis Functions

The method above, which involves translations of the quadratic $g(t)$, seems to give us a fine curve design tool. Why go further? The issue is that we need more control of the curve shape: it must bend more and be smoother than just 1-smooth. This suggests moving to cubic polynomials. We also want the designer to be able to specify which control points are interpolated. It would also be beneficial to have a *single* algorithm that would encompass all of the design techniques described above—including Bezier curves.

So we want to develop more general families of blending functions that meet all the properties discussed in the wish list given earlier. We continue to use the same parametric form

$$P(t) = \sum_{k=0}^{L} P_k R_k(t) \tag{10.43}$$

based on $L + 1$ control points and $L + 1$ blending functions $R_0(t), \ldots, R_L(t)$. We continue to require that $P(t)$ be an affine sum of points. We also continue to use piecewise polynomials for the blending functions, but now they are defined on a more general sequence of knots, called the **knot vector, T:**

$$\text{knot vector:} \qquad \mathbf{T} = (t_0, t_1, t_2, \ldots) \tag{10.44}$$

which is simply a list of knot values $t_0, t_1, \ldots$ which is assumed to be nondecreasing: $t_i \leq t_{i+1}$. Some of the knots might have the same value but are still given distinct names. The number of knots involved in $\mathbf{T}$ is discussed later.

Figure 10.27 illustrates the situation. Each blending function $R_k(t)$ is a piecewise polynomial that is zero up to time t_k, is nonzero over several spans in the knot vector, and then returns to zero again. We insist further that each $R_k(t)$ be a spline function, so that it enjoys a certain level of smoothness at all t in its support.

FIGURE 10.27 Generalizing on the knot vector and blending functions.

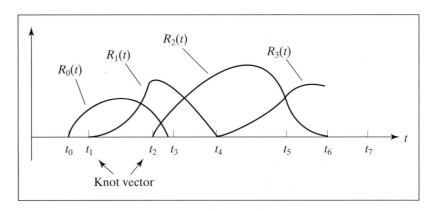

Notice that both the Bezier curve formulation and the translates of $g(t)$ formulation fit into this more general scheme:

- Bezier: There is one span from 0 to 1, all the Bernstein polynomials are of degree L, there are $L + 1$ knots having the value $t = 0$, and $L + 1$ more knots at $t = 1$. The Bernstein polynomials are splines, since they have continuous derivatives of order L.
- Translates of $g(t)$: The knot values are the integers $0, 1, \ldots, L + 2$; each translate $g(t - k)$ is a spline, consisting of three polynomials of degree 2 and covering a span of 3.

Because each $R_k(t)$ is a piecewise polynomial, the whole curve $P(t)$ is a sum of piecewise polynomials, weighted by the control points. For instance, in some span the curve might be given by

$$P(t) = P_0(3t^2 - 4t + 2) + P_1(8t^2 - 7.3t - 7.99) + \cdots \qquad (10.45)$$

In an adjacent span it is given by a different sum of polynomials, but we know that all segments meet to make the curve continuous. Such a curve is known as a **spline curve** [Farin88].[5]

The question can now be posed: Given a knot vector, can some family of blending functions be used to generate every possible spline curve that can be defined on that knot vector? Such a family is called a **basis** for the splines, meaning that any spline curve whatsoever can be matched by the sum in Equation (10.43) by choosing the proper control polygon.

The answer is that there are many such families, but there is one basis in particular whose blending functions have the smallest support and therefore offer the greatest local control. These are the **B-splines**, the 'B' derived from the word *basis*.

10.7 THE B-SPLINE BASIS FUNCTIONS

The chief function of the body is to carry the brain around.

Thomas A. Edison
(1847–1931)

We wish to define the B-spline blending functions, $R_k(t)$, in a way that lends some intuition to them and, in addition, leads to a straightforward computer implementation. Although the literature offers many different approaches to formulating B-splines,

---

[5] Note the difference between a *spline function* as defined in Section 10.6.3 and a *spline curve*. A spline function is simply a piecewise polynomial having a certain level of smoothness. A spline curve is an affine blend of points using piecewise polynomial blending functions. A spline curve must be continuous at knots but might have discontinuous derivatives at its knots.

there is a single formula that defines all the B-spline functions of any order. It is a recursive relation that is easy to implement in a program and is numerically well behaved. (Some other methods are more computationally efficient—see the exercises.)

Each B-spline function is based on polynomials of a certain order, m. If $m = 3$, the polynomials will be of order 3 and thus of degree 2, and so they will be quadratic B-splines. If the order is $m = 4$, the underlying polynomials will be of degree 3, or cubic. These are the two most important cases, although the formulation allows us to construct B-splines of *any* order.

10.7.1 Definition of B-Spline Functions

It is useful to make the order of a B-spline function explicit in the notation, and so instead of saying simply $R_k(t)$, we denote the kth B-spline blending function of order m by $N_{k,m}(t)$. Hence for B-spline curves Equation (10.43) becomes

$$P(t) = \sum_{k=0}^{L} P_k N_{k,m}(t) \tag{10.46}$$

Summarizing the ingredients to this point, we have

- a knot vector $\mathbf{T} = (t_0, t_1, t_2, \dots)$
- $(L + 1)$ control points P_k
- the order m of the B-spline functions

The fundamental formula for the B-spline function $N_{k,m}(t)$ is the somewhat formidable expression, (but don't be alarmed):

$$N_{k,m}(t) = \left(\frac{t - t_k}{t_{k+m-1} - t_k}\right) N_{k,m-1}(t) + \left(\frac{t_{k+m} - t}{t_{k+m} - t_{k+1}}\right) N_{k+1,m-1}(t) \tag{10.47}$$

for $k = 0, 1, \dots, L$. This is a recursive definition, specifying how to construct the mth-order function from two B-spline functions of order $(m - 1)$. To get things started, the first-order function must be defined. It is simply the constant function 1 within its span:

$$N_{k,1}(t) = \begin{cases} 1 & \text{if } t_k < t \leq t_{k+1} \\ 0 & \text{otherwise} \end{cases} \tag{10.48}$$

Note that this set of functions automatically sums to one at every t, so it is legitimate to use them in forming combinations of points.

■ EXAMPLE 10.7.1 Linear B-splines

What shape does $N_{0,2}(t)$, which is the first ($k = 0$) B-spline function of order $m = 2$, have when the knots are equispaced: $\mathbf{T} = (t_0 = 0, t_1 = 1, t_2 = 2, \dots)$? With these parameters Equation (10.47) becomes

$$N_{0,2}(t) = \frac{t}{1} N_{0,1}(t) + \frac{2 - t}{1} N_{1,1}(t) \tag{10.49}$$

We see that a linear up ramp (given by the term t) multiplies $N_{0,1}(t)$ and that a linear down ramp $(2 - t)$ multiplies $N_{1,1}(t)$, as shown in Figure 10.28a. When these are summed, the result is a triangular pulse (Figure 10.28b). Notice the similarity to tweening here: $N_{0,2}(t)$ is an affine combination of $N_{0,1}(t)$ and $N_{1,1}(t)$. So $N_{0,2}(t) = t$ for $0 \leq t \leq 1$; it is $2 - t$ for $1 \leq t \leq 2$; and it is 0 otherwise.

The construction of other linear B-splines follows similarly. For instance, $N_{1,2}(t)$ is a triangular pulse beginning at $t = 1$ and ending at $t = 3$. It is just a translated version of the first. More generally, every linear spline is a translated version of the zeroth one when equispaced knots are used: $N_{i,2}(t) = N_{0,2}(t - i)$.

FIGURE 10.28 Construction of linear B-splines.

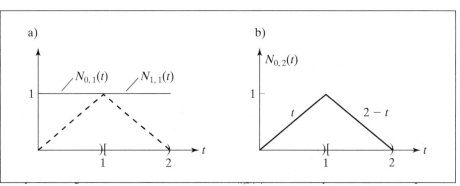

overlap in just the right way to insure they sum to 1 at all t. (Try it!)

Note that a curve built on linear B-splines is the control polyline itself. (Is this also true if the knots are not equispaced?) Because linear splines offer nothing beyond simple straight lines, they are normally not used for curve design. But they arise, of course, in the process of constructing higher-order B-splines.

■ EXAMPLE 10.7.2 Quadratic B-splines

Suppose we wish to determine the shape of the quadratic ($m = 3$) B-spline functions $N_{i,3}(t)$ based on the same equispaced knots. We need build only $N_{0,3}(t)$, as the others are simple translations of this one. Equation (10.47) shows that $N_{0,3}(t)$ is the sum:

$$N_{0,3}(t) = \frac{t}{2}N_{0,2}(t) + \frac{3-t}{2}N_{1,2}(t) \tag{10.50}$$

(Notice again the tweening of the two lower-order spline functions.) The first term is an up ramp times the first triangular pulse, and the second is a down ramp times the second pulse. As shown in Figure 10.29a, a ramp times a triangular pulse produces two parabolas that meet at a corner. But when the two terms in Equation (10.47) are summed, the corners vanish and the resulting pulse shape, $N_{0,3}(t)$ (see Figure 10.29b), has a continuous derivative.

Equation (10.50) can be used to determine the algebraic form of the quadratic spline for each segment. The middle segment involves the sum of two quadratics, and the result is

FIGURE 10.29 The first quadratic B-spline shape.

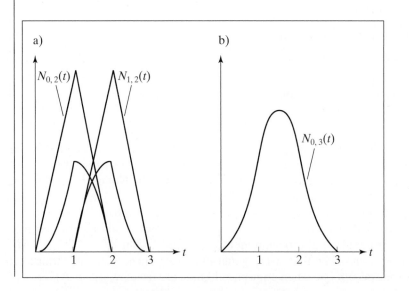

$$N_{0,3}(t) = \begin{cases} \dfrac{1}{2}t^2 & \text{for} \quad 0 \le t \le 1 \\[2mm] \dfrac{3}{4} - \left(t - \dfrac{3}{2}\right)^2 & \text{for} \quad 1 \le t \le 2 \\[2mm] \dfrac{1}{2}(3 - t)^2 & \text{for} \quad 2 \le t \le 3 \\[2mm] 0 & \text{otherwise} \end{cases}$$

(10.51)

Note that it depends on the four knots $0, 1, 2,$ and 3 and that its support is the interval $[0, 3]$.

Compare $N_{0,3}(t)$ with $g(t)$ of Equation (10.39); they are *precisely* the same. This is because $g(t)$ was (secretly) chosen to be a B-spline function. Its first derivative has already been checked and found to be continuous. Its second derivative is not. Thus quadratic B-splines (at least on equispaced knots) are in fact splines.

The other quadratic spline shapes, $N_{k,3}(t)$, are obtained easily when the knots are equispaced. Because the first-order splines are simple translations of one another, and all the ramp terms in Equation (10.47) involve only differences among knot values, the quadratic B-splines must also be simple translations of one another. In fact, this is true for any order B-spline on equally spaced knots:

if knot $t_k = k,$ then $N_{k,m}(t) = N_{0,m}(t - k)$ (10.52)

This form can be substituted directly into Equation (10.46) when the knots are equispaced.

We claimed earlier that the quadratic splines of Equation (10.47) sum to 1 at all t. This is true even if the knots are not equispaced, as we show in the exercises.

■ EXAMPLE 10.7.3 Cubic B-splines

The cubic B-spline is perhaps the most frequently used. $N_{0,4}(t)$ is shown in Figure 10.30a. Its form is found in the same fashion as before. (See the exercises) $N_{0,4}(t)$ is symmetrical about $t = 2$ and can be written compactly as

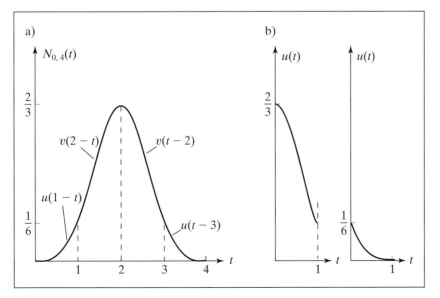

FIGURE 10.30 The cubic B-spline on equispaced knots.

$$N_{0,4}(t) = \begin{cases} u(1-t) & \text{for} \quad 0 \le t \le 1 \\ v(2-t) & \text{for} \quad 1 \le t \le 2 \\ v(t-2) & \text{for} \quad 2 \le t \le 3 \\ u(t-3) & \text{for} \quad 3 \le t \le 4 \\ 0 & \text{otherwise} \end{cases} \tag{10.53}$$

where the two segments $u(\ )$ and $v(\ )$ are shown in Figure 10.30b and are given by

$$u(t) = \frac{1}{6}(1-t)^3$$

$$v(t) = \frac{1}{6}(3t^3 - 6t^2 + 4) \tag{10.54}$$

Direct calculation of derivatives shows that the first and second derivatives of the cubic spline are everywhere continuous, so cubic spline curves are 2-smooth, at least on equispaced knots.

Based on the reasoning here, one can show (see the exercises) that in general the function $N_{k,m}(t)$ begins at t_k and ends at t_{k+m}: its support is $[t_k, t_{k+m}]$. It is also never negative.

One must always be alert to a potential division by zero. One or both denominators in Equation (10.47) might become zero for certain choices of knot values. But whenever this happens, the corresponding lower-order function, $N_{k,m} - 1(t)$ or $N_{k+1,m-1}(t)$, is also always zero. So we can adopt the rule that any term having a zero denominator is evaluated as 0.

It is easy to implement the recursive formulation of the function $N_{k,m}(t)$ in program code and therefore to compute its value at any t for any given knot vector. Note that the code fragment in Figure 10.31 is a direct translation of Equation (10.47).

```
float bSpline(int k, int m, float t, float knot[])
{
    float denom1, denom2, sum = 0.0;
    if(m == 1)
        return (t >= knot[k] && t < knot[k+1]); // 1 or 0
    // m exceeds 1.. recurse
    denom1 = knot[k + m -1] - knot[k];
    if(denom1 != 0.0)
        sum = (t - knot[k]) * bSpline(k,m-1,t, knot) / denom1;
    denom2 = knot[k + m] - knot[k+1];
    if(denom2 != 0.0)
        sum += (knot[k+m] - t) * bSpline(k+1,m-1,t,knot) / denom2;
    return sum;
}
```

FIGURE 10.31 Computing
B-spline blending functions.

PRACTICE EXERCISES

10.7.1 Potential division by zero

Show that when two knots have the same value, a denominator term in Equation (10.47) has value 0. Show that in this case the term in which this zero denominator appears is always 0 also.

10.7.2 B-spline support

Show that in general $N_{k,m}(t)$ is zero outside the interval $[t_k, t_{k+m}]$, and so the support of an mth-order B-spline is m spans in the knot vector. Also show that this function is nonnegative for all t.

10.7.3 Quadratic B-spline functions always sum to unity

We have already shown that the linear B-spline functions sum to unity. Show this is true as well for the quadratic B-splines. *Hint*: The following sequence of steps might help. You want to show that

$$\sum_{k=-\infty}^{\infty} N_{k,3}(t) = \sum_{k=-\infty}^{\infty} \frac{t - t_k}{t_{k+2} - t_k} N_{k,2}(t) + \sum_{k=-\infty}^{\infty} \frac{t_{k+3} - t}{t_{k+3} - t_{k+1}} N_{k+1,2}(t)$$

is 1 for all t (so we sum from $-\infty$ to ∞), where we have just applied Equation (10.47) directly here. Simply make a change of variable on the second sum ($k \rightarrow k - 1$), then combine the sums into one and note that the coefficient of $N_{k,2}(t)$ is always unity. Since the second-order B-splines sum to unity everywhere, you are done.

10.7.4 Computation of the cubic B-spline

Verify the formulas in Equation (10.53) for the cubic B-spline based on equispaced knots. Also calculate the first and second derivatives for the cubic B-spline, and show that they are continuous everywhere.

10.7.5 Periodic B-spline curves

Show that the curve

$$P(t) = \sum_{k=0}^{L} P_k N_{0,m}((t - k) \bmod(L + 1)) \tag{10.55}$$

based on $L + 1$ control points and mth-order B-splines closes on itself and is therefore periodic in t. ▪

10.7.2 How to Use Multiple Knots in the Knot Vector

Up to this point we have used only B-splines based on equispaced knots. By varying the spacing between knots, the curve designer acquires much greater control of the shape of the final curve.

A central question is: what happens to the shapes of the blending functions when two knots are set very close to one another? Figure 10.32 shows the situation when the knot vector is $\mathbf{T} = (0, 1, 2, 3, 3 + \varepsilon, 4 + \varepsilon, \ldots)$, where ε is a small positive number.

Now the piece of each piecewise polynomial lying in the interval $[3, 3 + \varepsilon]$ has become squeezed into a very narrow span. The blending functions will clearly no longer be translations of one another. If ε is set to zero, this span will vanish altogether, and a **multiple knot** will occur at $t = 3$. This knot is said to have a "multiplicity of 2."

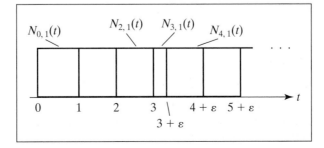

FIGURE 10.32 Moving knots close together.

Figure 10.33 shows the resulting blending functions. Now two of the linear B-spline shapes are discontinuous (part b), and the quadratic shapes have a discontinuous derivative at $t = 3$ (part c). In general, an i-smooth curve is reduced to an $(i - 1)$-smooth curve at the multiple knot value. The cubic B-spline curves (part d) are 1-smooth everywhere, but not 2-smooth at $t = 3$. But notice in part c that if quadratic B-splines are used, the curve will interpolate control point P_2, because the blending function $N_{2,3}(t)$ reaches value 1 at $t = 3$ and all the other blending functions are zero there. In general, when t approaches a knot of multiplicity greater than one, there is a stronger attraction to the governing control point. (Which one?)

Going further, quadratic splines become discontinuous near a knot of multiplicity 3. Cubic splines exhibit a discontinuous derivative near a knot of multiplicity 3, but they also interpolate one of the control points. By adjusting the multiplicity of each knot, the designer can therefore change the shape of the curve in a predictable fashion.

Neither Equation (10.47) nor the code fragment in Figure 10.31 need be altered when the knot vector contains multiple knots. As we mentioned, some of the denominators in Equation (10.47) become zero, but the code automatically handles this situation, and no adjustments need be made.

10.7.3 Open B-Spline Curves: Standard Knot Vector

One special choice of knot vector has become a standard for curve design. With this arrangement, the curve interpolates the first and last control points, thus better enabling the designer to predict where the computed curve will lie.

FIGURE 10.33 B-spline shapes near a knot of multiplicity 2.

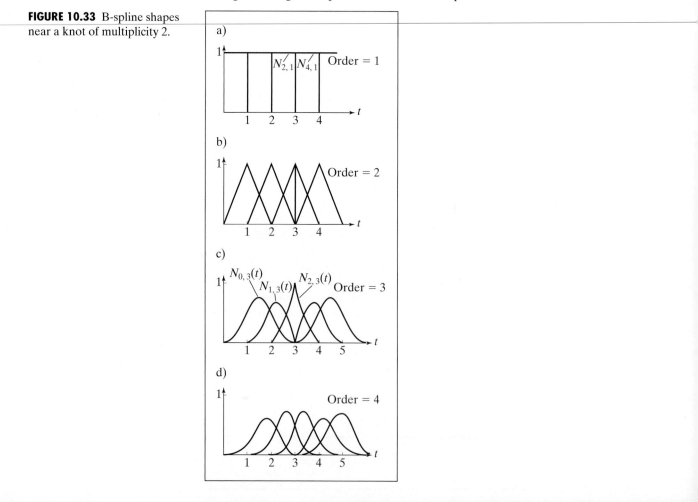

The **standard knot vector** for a B-spline of order m begins and ends with a knot of multiplicity m and uses unit spacing for the remaining knots. We start with an example and then see how it arises. Suppose there are eight control points and we want to use cubic ($m = 4$) B-splines. The standard knot vector turns out to be

$$\mathbf{T} = (0, 0, 0, 0, 1, 2, 3, 4, 5, 5, 5, 5)$$

The eight blending functions, $N_{0,4}(t), \dots, N_{7,4}(t)$, are defined on these knots using Equation (10.47) and are shown in Figure 10.34a. $N_{0,4}(t)$ and $N_{7,4}(t)$ are discontinuous and have a support of only one unit span. Only $N_{3,4}(t)$ and $N_{4,4}(t)$ have the usual span of four units. The remaining blending functions have two or three unit spans, and their shapes become more distorted as they approach the first and last knots. The specific polynomial functions that comprise the blending functions are requested in the exercises.

Notice that, taken together, this set of functions always insures interpolation of the first and last control points. For example, at $t = 0$, all blending functions are zero except for $N_{0,4}(t)$, which equals one. It is also not hard to show that the initial direction of the B-spline curve at $t = 0$ is along the first segment of the control polygon, and similarly for the final direction (see the exercises).

Figure 10.34b shows an example of a curve based on eight control points. Clearly the first and last points are interpolated and the curve directions at these points are as promised.

Note that a B-spline curve can cross itself when the control polygon does.

The standard knot vector for $(L + 1)$ control points and order-m B-splines is described as follows (comments about the corresponding blending functions appear in parentheses)

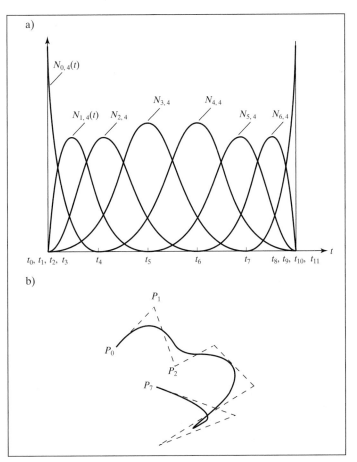

FIGURE 10.34 Eight cubic B-spline blending functions. a) Defined on the standard knot vector. b) The resulting curve based on 8 control points.

1. There are $L + m + 1$ knots all together, denoted as $t_0, \ldots, t_{L+m}$.
2. The first m knots, $t_0, \ldots, t_{m-1}$, all share the value 0. (The first m blending functions start at $t = 0$.)
3. Knots $t_m, \ldots, t_L$ increase in increments of 1, from value 1 through value $L - m + 1$. (The final blending function, $N_{L,m}(t)$, begins at $t_L = L - m + 1$ and has a support of width 1.)
4. The final m knots, $t_{L+1}, \ldots, t_{L+m}$, all equal $L - m + 2$.

From these rules, it is easy to compose a procedure that generates the standard knot vector for given values of m and L, as shown by the following code fragment:

```
void buildKnots(int m, int L, double knot[])
{
    // Build the standard knot vector for L+1 control points
    // and B-splines of order m
    int i;
    if(L < (m - 1)) return;              // too few control points
    for(i = 0; i <= L + m; i++){
        if (i < m) knot[i] = 0.0;
        else if (i <= L) knot[i] = i - m + 1; // i is at least m here
        else knot[i] = L - m + 2;}       // i exceeds L here
}
```

Note that the error condition is based on the values of m and L. For a given m there must be enough control points so that there will be room for at least one span of width 1. This leads to the following constraint:

The order m cannot exceed the number of control points $(L + 1)$.

Bezier Curves Are B-Spline Curves

Bezier curves were introduced earlier through two approaches: the de Casteljau algorithm and the Bernstein polynomials. We can now state a third approach: Bezier curves are also a special case of B-splines. This is so because the B-spline blending functions defined on the standard knot vector are in fact Bernstein polynomials when $m = L + 1$! That is,

$$N_{k,L+1}(t) = B_k^L(t)$$

for $k = 0, \ldots, L$. (Note that by convention the superscript parameter of $B()$ is **degree**, while the second parameter of $N()$ is **order**.)

To see this, note what happens to the standard knot vector as the order m is increased up to $L + 1$. (See the exercises.) The first m knots have value 0; the last m have value 1; and t varies only over $[0, 1]$. For example, if $L = 5$ and $m = 6$, we obtain $\mathbf{T} = (0, 0, 0, 0, 0, 0, 1, 1, 1, 1, 1, 1)$. Thus each piecewise polynomial has only a single span, and each is a polynomial of order $m = L + 1$. This is precisely how the Bernstein polynomials behave. In fact, one can derive the Bernstein polynomials directly from Equation (10.47).

Recall that the prime motivation for going beyond Bezier curves to B-spline curves was the desire to obtain local control of the curve's shape. When the order of the B-spline polynomials is increased by 1, the support of each B-spline blending function extends one span further, reducing the amount of local control. When m reaches the bound of $L + 1$, the Bezier case is obtained, and local control is at a minimum. Figure 10.35 shows how B-spline curves become more "taut," thereby permitting less local control, as their order increases. There are eight control points, and so the order $m = 8$ curve is the Bezier curve. All of these curves were generated using the fragment of Figure 10.31. (What is the $m = 2$ curve?)

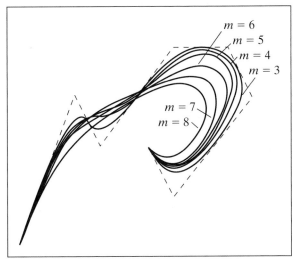

FIGURE 10.35 Curves based on splines of different orders.

PRACTICE EXERCISES

10.7.7 Standard knots for quadratic B-spline curves

Show that the standard knot vector for an order $m = 3$ B-spline curve based on eight control points is $\mathbf{T} = (0, 0, 0, 1, 2, 3, 4, 5, 6, 6, 6)$.

10.7.8 Knot vectors as order m is increased

What is the standard knot vector when seven control points are used for B-splines of order a) $m = 3$, b) $m = 4$, c) $m = 5$, d) $m = 6$, and e) $m = 7$?

10.7.9 Quadratic B-splines on standard knot vectors

Using Equation (10.47), find explicit expressions for the piecewise polynomials that describe the quadratic B-spline blending functions when defined on the standard knot vector.

10.7.10 Cubic B-splines

Find analytically the first four cubic B-splines defined on a standard knot vector. Find also their derivatives at $t = 0$ and show that the initial direction of the B-spline curve is along the first segment of the control polygon.

10.7.11 Deriving the Bernstein polynomials

Show that when $m = L + 1 = 4$, the B-spline functions of Equation (10.47) are the Bernstein polynomials.

10.7.12 On the efficient computation of B-splines

When drawing a B-spline curve, many points have to be formed, and so values $N_{k,m}(t)$ must be computed at a large number of t-values. Using the recursive form of Figure 10.58 at each t makes many redundant calls to lower-order B-spline functions. It is much more efficient, therefore, to compute values of each $N_{k,m}(t)$ once and store them in arrays, such as the array $N[k, i]$, which holds $N_{k,m}(t)$ evaluated at $t_i = i \, \Delta t$, where Δt is the fixed difference between the t-values desired. Samples of each $N[k, i]$ need only be formed over the support of the corresponding B-spline function. Furthermore, only a few different shapes, $N[k, i]$, are needed, since many are just translations of one another and have the same shape. If there are 55 control points, how many different cubic B-spline functions will be needed?

Once stored, each point on the curve can be fashioned by accessing the proper samples of the functions: $P(t_i)$ is formed as the vector sum of the terms $C[k]N[n,j]$, where $C[k]$ is a control point, and proper values of n and j are selected. Determine, for the case of cubic splines, the proper values of n and j to be used, for each k and t_i. Note that when j is outside a certain region, it is known that the function $N[k,j]$ is certainly 0, and so the array is not accessed.   ■

10.8 USEFUL PROPERTIES OF B-SPLINE CURVES FOR DESIGN

> When a man is wrapped up in himself
> he makes a pretty small package.
>
> *John Ruskin*
> *(1819–1900)*

It is useful to summarize the principal properties of B-splines and the curves they generate. We shall also see that many of the desirable properties attributed to Bezier curves carry over intact to B-spline curves.

1. The mth-order B-spline functions are piecewise polynomials of order m. They are $(m-2)$-smooth splines: They exhibit $(m-2)$ orders of continuous derivatives at every point in their support. They form a basis for any spline of the same order defined on the same knots; i.e., any spline can be represented as a linear combination of B-splines. Of all spline bases, the B-splines are the most concentrated, having the shortest supports.
2. The B-spline blending function, $N_{k,m}(t)$, begins at t_k and ends at t_{k+m}. Its support is $[t_k, t_{k+m}]$. The support of the family of functions, $N_{k,m}(t)$, for $k = 0,\ldots,L$ is the interval $[t_0, t_{m+L}]$.
3. A closed B-spline curve based on $L+1$ control points may be obtained using Equation (10.55) (assuming evenly spaced knots in the definition of $N_{0,m}(.)$).
4. If the standard knot vector is used, the B-spline curve will interpolate the first and last control points. Its initial and final directions are along the first and last edges of the control polygon, respectively.
5. Each B-spline function, $N_{k,m}(t)$, is nonnegative for every t, and the family of such functions sums to 1:

$$\sum_{k=0}^{L} N_{k,m}(t) = 1 \tag{10.56}$$

for every $t\epsilon[t_0, t_{m+L}]$. As we have seen for the low-order cases, this can be proved by induction from Equation (10.47.)
6. Curves based on B-splines are affine invariant. To transform a B-spline curve, simply transform each control point, and generate the new curve based on the transformed control points. This follows because a B-spline curve is an affine sum of points, and affine transformations preserve affine combinations.
7. According to property 5, a B-spline curve is a convex combination of its control points and so lies in their convex hull. A stronger statement is possible: at any t only m B-spline functions are active (nonzero). Thus at each t the curve must lie in the convex hull of at most m consecutive active control points. Figure 10.36 shows a quadratic B-spline curve based on the standard knot vector. At most three control points are active at each t, and so the relevant convex hulls are triangles. As t increases, $P(t)$ progressively passes out of each triangle of the convex hull and into the next as each new blending function becomes active in turn. At which t-value does the curve enter and exit the shaded convex hull?

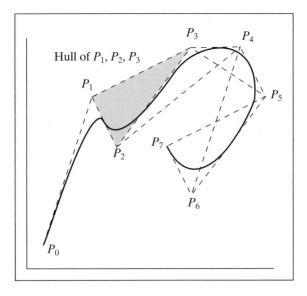

FIGURE 10.36 Convex hulls for the quadratic B-spline curve.

Convex hulls based on m control points are typically smaller regions than the hull based on all the control points. The curve is therefore trapped in a smaller region than is the case for a Bezier curve. The narrow support of the B-splines not only gives local control to the designer but also provides more insight into the nature of the curve.

8. B-spline curves exhibit **linear precision**: if m consecutive control points are collinear, their convex hull will be a straight line, and the curve will be trapped within it.

9. B-spline curves are variation diminishing: a B-spline curve does not pass through any line more times than does its control polygon [Farin88].

10.8.1 Using Multiple Control Points

The designer can usefully alter the shape of a B-spline curve by placing several control points at the same spot, producing a **multiple control point**, which attracts the curve more strongly to the control polygon.

Figure 10.37 shows an example that uses cubic B-spline curves. The curve based on control points A, B, C, D, E, F, and G exhibits the usual behavior for cubic

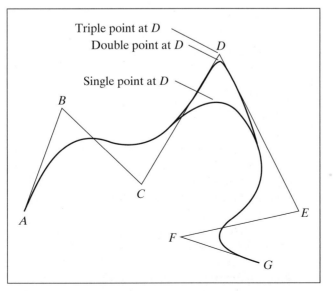

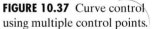

FIGURE 10.37 Curve control using multiple control points.

splines. When a double point is used at D, so that the control polygon is $A, B, C, D,$ $D, E, F, G,$ the curve is pulled more strongly toward D. When a triple point is placed at D, making the control polygon $A, B, C, D, D, D, E, F, G,$ the curve must actually interpolate the point!

The interpolation effect is easily explained from Figure 10.34a. Note that at t-values such as t_5 and t_6, exactly three B-spline functions are nonzero and that they sum to one. If they are all weighted by the same control point, the weighted sum will be the control point itself. More generally, recall that a cubic B-spline is always trapped within some convex hull based on four consecutive control points. When a triple point is used at D, the convex hulls that surround D consist of edges of the control polygon, and so the curve is trapped in this edge for one span of the polynomials.

Notice that the use of multiple control points is not the same as the use of multiple knots, although their effects are similar. It is usually easier for a designer to increase the multiplicity of a control point than that of a knot, because control points are plainly visible and can be pointed to. (The designer could click on a point multiple times to specify its multiplicity.)

PRACTICE EXERCISES

10.8.1 Sketching the convex hull property

Draw several example control polygons of eight points. Consider quadratic B-splines based on the standard knot vector. Draw the successive convex hulls, and determine the values of t for which the curve enters and exits. Sketch the resulting B-spline curve, labeling various t-values along it. Be sure it also passes through the midpoints of each inner edge of the control polygon.

10.8.2 Multiple control points with quadratic B-splines

Explain the effect of a double control point on a quadratic B-spline curve. Sketch an interesting control polygon having no multiple control points; show the sequence of convex hulls that trap the curve; and sketch the curve. Then increase the multiplicity of one of the control points and repeat.   ■

10.9 RATIONAL SPLINES AND NURBS CURVES

Whose afraid of NURBS, anyway?

Overheard on a bus at SIGGRAPH '98

In Section 10.2 we looked briefly at rational parametric forms and noted that conic sections (the ellipse, hyperbola, and parabola) can be generated exactly by the ratio of polynomials in Equation (10.14). Here we take a more detailed look at rational polynomial forms based specifically on B-splines.

A rational spline curve is very similar to its B-spline counterpart. It is formed as the familiar blending of control points:

$$P(t) = \sum_{k=0}^{L} P_k R_k(t) \tag{10.57}$$

but uses a different set of blending functions. The designer conjures up a set of **weights,** $\{w_0, w_1, ..., w_L\}$ and control points, $P_0, \ldots, P_L$, and creates the curve:

$$P(t) = \frac{\sum_{k=0}^{L} \overline{w}_k P_k N_{k,m}(t)}{\sum_{k=0}^{L} \overline{w}_k N_{k,m}(t)} \tag{10.58}$$

where the $N_{k,m}(t)$ are kth order B-splines. The weights are often called *shape parameters* and are usually set by the designer to be nonnegative to insure that the denominator is never zero. Because the knot vector used to define the B-spline functions is usually nonuniform (i.e., not equispaced) this family of curve shapes has come to be called the **nonuniform rational B-splines**, or simply **NURBS**.[6]

By inspection of Equation (10.58) the numerator of $P(t)$ is a linear combination of the control points. As we saw in Chapter 4, for this to make sense it must be an affine combination of the P_k. Hence we scale them all such that they sum to 1, in which case the $P(t)$ *is* an affine combination of the P_k as desired.

Equation (10.58) also reveals that if all the weights are made the *same,* the denominator becomes a constant (why?), and this collapses to the earlier B-spline form of Equation (10.46). So when the weights are different, $R_k(t)$ is a true extension of Equation (10.46).

It helps to see where these blending functions come from. As discussed in the exercises, work in homogeneous coordinates and use each weight w_k to give a weight to the kth control point. Then convert back into ordinary coordinates, and you have the NURBS curve. NURBS curves attain their desirable properties through the weighting of points in a higher-dimensional space.

Two Principal Advantages to NURBS Curves

1. With properly chosen control points and weights, $P(t)$ is *exactly* a conic section. See Example 10.9.2. This is in contrast to the nonrational B-spline curves, which can only *approximate* a true conic.
2. NURBS curves are invariant under so-called **projective transformations**, which we studied in Chapter 7. These are transformations like the perspective transformation that produce a perspective view of a scene. They are generalizations of affine transformations. The matrix for an affine transformation has a fourth row of $(0, 0, 0, 1)$, but a projective transformation can have a more general fourth row. Recall that normal B-spline curves are invariant under only affine transformations. This means that they are invariant to rotations, scalings, translations, or any combination of these, but NURBS curves are invariant under a *larger* class of transformations.

Among other things this invariance means that you can draw a perspective projection of a NURB curve simply by finding the perspective projection of each of its control points, and then fashioning the curve according to Equation (10.57). (The weights must be adjusted as well.) This is far more efficient than finding the perspective projection of *every* point on the curve individually. By contrast, nonrational B-spline curves are invariant under affine transformations, but *not* under projective transformations.

Projective Invariance

We fill in some details of the projective invariance property for NURB curves (in 2D or 3D). The derivation is given in Case Study 10.9. The main idea is that when a NURB curve is transformed by a general 4-by-4 matrix (which may produce perspective distortion), the result is another NURB curve, and its control points are simply transformed versions of the original control points. To make things work the weights must also be adjusted.

Specifically, consider the case of 3D points, and let T be the transformation represented by the general 4-by-4 matrix M. Denote its rows by $\mathbf{m}_1, \mathbf{m}_2, \mathbf{m}_3$, and $\mathbf{m}_4$, so that in partitioned form $M = (\mathbf{m}_1|\mathbf{m}_2|\mathbf{m}_3|\mathbf{m}_4)^T$. ($T$ as always, represents the transpose.) If

---

[6] NURBS have become so popular for designers in the gaming industry, movies, and CAD that they are the basic geometric element in numerous software packages.

the last row is $(0, 0, 0, 1)$, the transformation specializes to an affine transformation and so produces no perspective distortion. The result is that the curve $T(P(t))$ obtained by applying $T()$ to the NURB curve of Equation (10.57) is identical to the NURB curve based on transformed control points $T(P_k)$ [Piegl91]

$$T(P(t)) = \frac{\sum_{k=0}^{L} \overline{w}_k T(P_k) N_{k,m}(t)}{\sum_{k=0}^{L} \overline{w}_k N_{k,m}(t)} \tag{10.59}$$

where the adjusted weights are

$$\overline{w}_k = w_k(\widetilde{P}_k \cdot \mathbf{m}_4) \tag{10.60}$$

(where $\widetilde{P}_k = (P_x, P_y, P_z, 1)^T$ is the version of P with an appended 1 to produce its form in homogeneous coordinates). Note that the weights depend on the positions of the control points, as well as on the fourth column of the matrix. If the transformation is affine, so that $(P_k \cdot \mathbf{m}_4) = 1$, the weights need no adjustment.

PRACTICE EXERCISES

10.9.1 Fashioning generic surface shapes

Discuss how you could create each of the following surfaces using NURBS curves.

a. a circular cylinder
b. a circular cone
c. a planar patch
d. a sphere.

See Case Study 10.10 for more details. Can an arbitrary Coon's patch be created?

10.9.2 What if the weights are equal?

Suppose a NURB curve $q(t)$ happens to have all its weights equal so that it is a B-spline curve. Is it still a NURB curve after it has been transformed by M (where M is any 4-by-4 matrix)? Is it still a B-spline curve?

10.9.3 Forming NURBS curves in homogeneous coordinates

Consider forming a B-spline curve based on control points P_k that have been weighted by a chosen set of weights $\{w_k\}$. This B-spline curve is formed in homogeneous coordinates as:

$$\widetilde{R}(t) = \sum_{k=0}^{L} w_k \widetilde{P}_k N_{k,m}(t) \tag{10.61}$$

Here $\widetilde{P}_k$ denotes the homogeneous coordinate form for P_k (i.e., $\widetilde{P}_k = (x_k, y_k, z_k, 1)^T$ for a 3D point).

a. Write out the individual components $x(t)$, $y(t)$, $z(t)$, and w_k of $\widetilde{R}(t) = (x(t), y(t), z(t), w_k)^T$, paying particular attention to the form of w_k.
b. Convert the expression to ordinary coordinates by dividing through by w_k. Show that this produces

$$P(t) = \frac{\sum_{k=0}^{L} w_k P_k N_{k,m}(t)}{\sum_{k=0}^{L} w_k N_{k,m}(t)} \tag{10.62}$$

c. Show that this is the same form as in Equations (10.57) and (10.58).   ■

■ **EXAMPLE 10.9.1 How to obtain the conics**

To see the special case of Equation (10.14) emerge, let $m = 3$ (quadratic B-splines) and choose the knot vector so we obtain the Bernstein polynomials. (How?) Now set $w_0 = w_2 = 1$ and $w_1 = w$ and you have Equation (10.14).

■ **EXAMPLE 10.9.2 How to make a perfect circle**

There are several ways to create an exact circle with a NURB curve [Piegl89]. We examine a basic one based on quadratic B-splines using seven control points. Figure 10.38a shows the control points $P_0, \ldots, P_6$ situated about a square, along with the full circle generated. The proper weights are also labeled; note they are either 1 or 1/2. The knot vector is given by:

$$T = \{0, 0, 0, \tfrac{1}{4}, \tfrac{1}{2}, \tfrac{1}{2}, \tfrac{3}{4}, 1, 1, 1\}$$

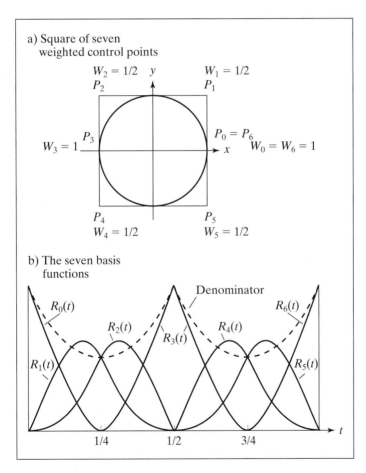

a) Square of seven weighted control points

b) The seven basis functions

FIGURE 10.38
Curve control using multiple control points. a) NURBS forming a circle; b) the corresponding basis functions.

Note the double knot at $t = \tfrac{1}{2}$. Figure 10.38b shows the seven basis functions that weight the control points. See the exercises for a valuable process to determine the actual formulas for each of the basis functions in each knot interval, and to assure yourself that $x^2(t) + y^2(t)$ is 1 for all t.

■ **EXAMPLE 10.9.3 How to see the effect of weight factors**

Figure 10.39a shows a cubic B-spline curve based on six control points (with equispaced knots). This is the usual nonrational B-spline (or equivalently a NURB with equal weights w_i). Figure 10.39b shows what happens when the weights are made unequal: the curve is more attracted to those points with higher weights. (What if some point has zero weight?)

FIGURE 10.39 Effect of unequal weights in the NURB curve. [Farin90]

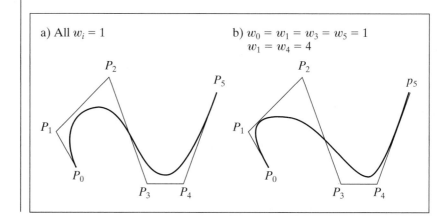

a) All $w_i = 1$

b) $w_0 = w_1 = w_3 = w_5 = 1$
$w_1 = w_4 = 4$

NURBS have become popular with curve designers due to their generality and flexibility. Because they include B-splines as a special case, a single curve creation algorithm can be used to create a broad family of shapes, including the conic sections. Thus a designer does not need a toolbox containing many different curve algorithms; a single method is available.

A number of other curve design techniques are available, some of which give the user even greater control over the shape of the curve. For example, one can vary the separation between knots (here taken to be the same) in the knot vector or add extra "ghost" points to the given data in order to control the curve's behavior at its endpoints. The reader interested in the various generalizations should search the Internet for many additional resources on B-splines and NURBS.

PRACTICE EXERCISE

10.9.4 Is it really a circle?

Show that the NURB curve described in Example 10.9.2 is truly a circle. Do this by finding expressions for the basis function polynomials in each knot interval, evaluating $x^2(t) + y^2(t)$ and showing it is 1 at all t.   ■

10.10 A GLIMPSE AT INTERPOLATION

> When the only tool you own is a hammer,
> every problem begins to resemble a nail.
>
> *Abraham Maslow*
> *(1908–1970)*

Sometimes the designer wants the curve design algorithm to produce a curve that passes *through all* of the control points. This might seem more natural than using an algorithm that just attracts the curve to the control points, but we will see that constraining a curve to pass through a set of points can result in shapes with too little local control, or undesired extra wiggles between control points. In spite of such limitations, we want to provide the designer with an interpolating tool for those situations that benefit from them.

The designer already has one way of achieving interpolation using B-splines: if the designer lays down control points of sufficient multiplicity, the B-spline curve is guaranteed to interpolate them.

In Case Study 10.6 we will see another method based on B-splines. The designer lays down points, and the algorithm figures out a different set of points such that a B-spline curve generated by them happens to pass through the designer's points.

In this section we look briefly at curve generation algorithms that directly interpolate all of the control points laid down by the user. This is a large topic with a long history; we examine only a restricted class of methods. Farin [Farin88] discusses interpolation in a more general setting and provides many details.

10.10.1 Interpolation Using Piecewise Cubic Polynomials

Here we describe interpolation of a set of control points using piecewise cubic polynomials. We restrict ourselves to piecewise cubics because they offer enough richness and flexibility for our needs, yet are simple enough that they can be used effectively.

The Problem: Figure 10.40a shows the basic design problem. The user places a sequence of control points $P_0, P_1, \ldots, P_L$ (here $L = 4$), and desires a sufficiently smooth curve to be generated that passes through all of them in turn.

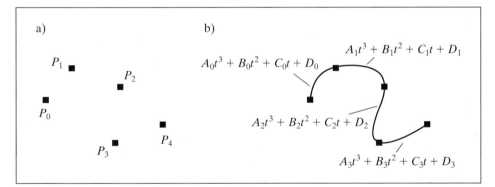

FIGURE 10.40 Interpolating with piecewise cubic polynomials.

Figure 10.40b shows a curve $R(t)$ that achieves this. The curve consists of four segments, each a cubic polynomial:

$$R_k(t) = A_k t^3 + B_k t^2 + C_k t + D_k, \ k = 0, 1, \ldots, L - 1, \ \text{for } t \text{ in } [0, 1] \qquad (10.63)$$

Each of the elements has both an x- and a y-component, of course. The question is: what should the coefficients A_k, B_k, C_k, and D_k be?

Notice that we are using a slightly different formulation than earlier to simplify the notation: each segment uses the same t-interval 0 to 1. Thus to draw this curve we would draw four separate curves as in:

```
for(k = 0; k < L; k++)
{
    Retrieve the coefficients A[k], B[k],C[k],D[k]
    Draw the curve R_k(t) using these coefficients in short line segments, as t goes from 0 to 1
}
```

The segment $R_k(t) = (x(t), y(t))$ is a 2D curve as always. If $R(t)$ interpolates a point $P = (x, y)$, then $x(t)$ must interpolate x and $y(t)$ must interpolate y. So we can consider how interpolation works separately for the x- and the y-components. The notation is simplified by doing this, and it is easier to visualize what is happening.

Figure 10.41a shows the interpolation problem for the y-coordinate alone. A sequence of y-values $y_0, y_1, \ldots, y_L$ is given, and we want $y(t)$ to be a piecewise cubic polynomial that passes through the y-values and is 1-smooth (in some cases we will force it to be 2-smooth as well: i.e., to be a spline).

FIGURE 10.41 The y-component of the interpolating curve.

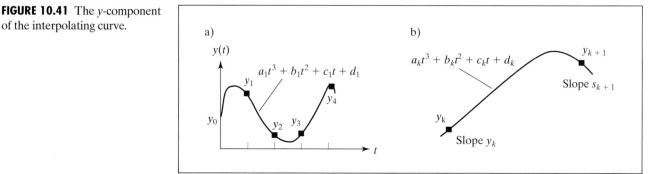

The kth cubic segment of the curve is shown in Figure 10.41b and is given by:

$$y_k(t) = a_k t^3 + b_k t^2 + c_k t + d_k, \quad k = 0, 1, \ldots, L, \quad \text{for } t \text{ in } [0, 1] \tag{10.64}$$

We denote the value of its derivative by s_k (i.e., $y_k'(0) = s_k$). As we discuss shortly, in some cases the values s_k are given (i.e., input by the user), and in others they are computed from other required properties of the curve. Again we ask, what are the coefficients?

10.10.2 Hermite Interpolation

We develop conditions on the coefficients a_k, b_k, c_k, and d_k so that each segment interpolates the given value y_k at $t = 0$ and the value y_{k+1} at $t = 1$:

at $t = 0$: (note from Equation (10.64): when $t = 0$ y_k equals d_k itself.) $d_k = y_k$
at $t = 1$: $\quad a_k + b_k + c_k + d_k = y_{k+1}$

for $k = 0, \ldots, L - 1$. This provides $2L$ conditions. We also force the derivative of $y_k(t)$ to equal the given values s_k and s_{k+1} at $t = 0$ and $t = 1$, respectively. Since the derivative is $y_k'(t) = 3a_k t^2 + 2b_k t + c_k$, this gives the conditions:

at $t = 0$: $\quad c_k = s_k$
at $t = 1$: $\quad 3a_k + 2b_k + c_k = s_{k+1}$

for $k = 0, \ldots, L - 1$. This provides another $2L$ conditions, so we have a total of $4L$ conditions on the $4L$ unknown coefficients. Notice that setting the derivatives to the given slope values in this fashion automatically forces the slope to be continuous at the joints, so the curve is 1-smooth.

It is straightforward based on Equations (10.61) and (10.62) to solve for the coefficients symbolically in terms of the values y_k and s_k (check this out):

$$a_k = s_{k+1} + s_k - 2(y_{k+1} - y_k)$$
$$b_k = 3(y_{k+1} - y_k) - 2s_k - s_{k+1}$$
$$c_k = s_k$$
$$d_k = y_k$$

for $k = 0, \ldots, L - 1$. This specifies the components of $y_k(t)$ for each segment. A similar process yields the coefficients of $x_k(t)$, and the cubic curve segments can be drawn as noted earlier to produce the piecewise cubic curve.

This would complete the solution if we knew the slope values s_k at each y_k. There are several approaches to determining them. We first see what effect s_k has on the shape of the curve. We then examine what it takes to make the curve 2-smooth. This leads to the "natural" cubic spline.

■ EXAMPLE 10.10.1 On tangents and slopes

In order to gain insight into how the many ingredients above fit together, consider a curve consisting of two cubic segments, $R_0(t)$ and $R_1(t)$, with the following properties.

Segment 0: $R_0(t)$ passes through $(1,1)$ at $t = 0$, and through $(4,3)$ at $t = 1$. In addition, its velocity is $(1,0)$ at $t = 0$ and is $(0,S)$ at $t = 1$, where S is some value we will vary to see the effect of slope changes in the curves.

Segment 1: $R_1(t)$ passes through $(4,3)$ at $t = 0$ and through $(0,3)$ at $t = 1$. Its velocity is $(0,S)$ at $t = 0$ and $(0,1)$ at $t = 1$. The resulting curve for the specific case $S = 1$ is shown in Figure 10.42. The parametric segments are shown in the xy-plane, and in addition the figure shows the components $x_0(t)$, $x_1(t)$, $y_0(t)$, and $y_1(t)$ that make up the curve.

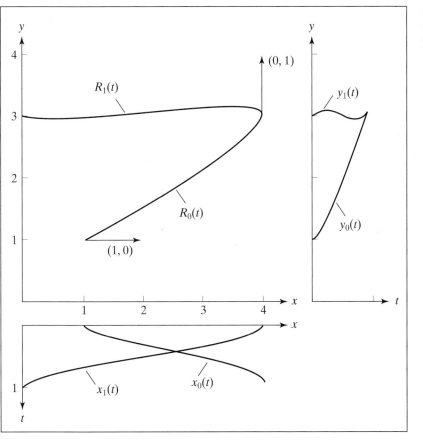

FIGURE 10.42 Two cubic segments meeting with a prescribed velocity.

Carefully trace how the curve shape derives from the shapes of the individual components. Note that the curve makes a smooth transition from one segment to the next, since its velocity is continuous there. This results because both $x(t)$ and $y(t)$ are continuous and have continuous slopes at the joint, so the curve is 1-smooth. The slope of $x(t)$ is 0 at the joint for both segments, so both segments are level just to the left and to the right of the joint. $y(t)$ also moves smoothly from one segment to the other: its slope is $S = 1$ just to the left and to the right of the joint.

To see the exact nature of the segments we apply Equation (10.63) to the data. For the y-component:

Segment 0: $y_0 = 1$, $y_1 = 3$, $s_0 = 0$, $s_1 = S$, which leads to the cubic:

$$y_0(t) = (S - 4)t^3 + (6 - S)t^2 + 1$$

Segment 1: $y_1 = 3$, $y_2 = 3$, $s_1 = S$, $s_2 = 1$, which leads to the cubic:

$$y_1(t) = (S + 1)t^3 - (2S + 1)t^2 + St + 3$$

Similarly for the x-component we have:

Segment 0: $x_0 = 1$, $x_1 = 4$, $s_0 = 1$, $s_1 = 0$, which leads to the cubic:

$$x_0(t) = -5t^3 + 7t^2 + t + 1$$

Segment 1: $x_1 = 4$, $x_2 = 0$, $s_1 = 0$, $s_2 = 0$, which leads to the cubic:

$$x_1(t) = 8t^3 - 12t^2 + 4.$$

Thus the two segments have the shape:

$$R_0(t) = -5t^3 + 7t^2 + t + 1, (S - 4)t^3 + (6 - S)t^2 + 1$$
$$R_1(t) = 8t^3 - 12t^2 + 4, (S + 1)t^3 - (2S + 1)t^2 + St + 3$$

It is illuminating to observe the effect of changing the slope S of the $y()$-component at the joint. This alters only the magnitude of the velocity at the joint, not its direction. From the formulas it is evident that S affects the coefficients of $y_0(t)$ and $y_1(t)$ but has no effect on the x-component functions. Figure 10.43 shows the $y(t)$ functions and the parametric curve for various example values of S.

FIGURE 10.43
The effect of varying a slope value.

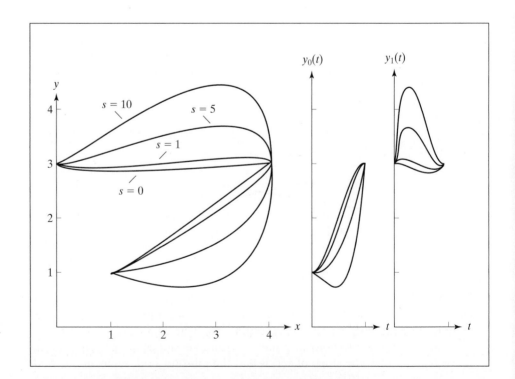

For large values of S the curve has a high speed at the joint. To accommodate this the curve has to bulge out before and after the joint to "prepare" for the rapid passage through the joint in the vertical direction. This illustrates how "elastic" a cubic curve is: it can't bend arbitrarily rapidly—there aren't enough degrees of freedom—so its shape throughout the interval adjusts to meet the slope constraint at one end.

The case of $S = 0$ produces a corner at the joint (see the exercises). The speeds of both $R_0(t)$ and $R_1(t)$ go to zero as they approach the joint, so even though the velocity of the curve changes direction abruptly at the joint, it is still continuous and the curve is 1-smooth. (Is it G^1-continuous?)

PRACTICE EXERCISES

10.10.1 When the speed is zero

Suppose a cubic curve segment has a speed of 0 at both ends. Show that the segment is a straight line.

10.10.2 Scrutinize the curves

Write a short program that generates the curves in Figures 10.41 and 10.42, and exercise it with different values of S. To assist this, it is convenient to define the function:

```
Point2 y(float t, float S, int seg)
{
// return y(t) for segment k when initial derivative has value S.
}
```

and a similar one for $x(.)$.

10.10.3 Make a loop

Show that if $S = -1$, the curve in Figure 10.42 has a loop in it. ■

10.10.3 The Natural Cubic Spline

As one approach to setting the derivative values s_k in the Hermite formulation, we find the specific values of the s_k that will cause the *second* derivative of $y(t)$ to be continuous at each of the "inner" joints, where $k = 1, 2, \ldots, L - 1$. (At the ends of the whole curve there is no need for continuity of derivatives.) The second derivative in each segment is $y_k''(t) = 6a_k t + 2b_k$, so matching the second derivative $y_{k-1}''(1)$ with $y_k''(0)$, we get:

$$6a_{k-1} + 2b_{k-1} = 2b_k \qquad (10.65)$$

for $k = 1, \ldots, L - 1$. Using the coefficient values in Equation (10.73) and simplifying, this imposes the following conditions on the slopes:

$$s_{k-1} + 4s_k + s_{k+1} = 3(y_{k+1} - y_{k-1}) \qquad (10.66)$$

for $k = 1, \ldots, L - 1$. This shows how the various neighboring slopes must be related to insure a continuous second derivative at the inner joints. We still need to fix the first and last slopes, s_0 and s_L. A classic approach chooses them so that the second derivatives are 0 at the two ends of the curve: $y_0''(0) = 0$ and $y_{L-1}''(1) = 0$. The first sets b_0 to 0, the second sets $3a_{L-1} + b_{L-1}$ to 0. (Why?) Again using Equation (10.63) we obtain the final two conditions:

$$\begin{aligned} 2s_0 + s_1 &= 3(y_1 - y_0) \\ 2s_L + s_{L-1} &= 3(y_L - y_{L-1}) \end{aligned} \qquad (10.67)$$

Together Equations (10.65) and (10.66) provide L linear equations in the unknown slopes s_k. As explored in the exercises, the nature of these equations makes them rather easy to solve.

Figure 10.44 shows a set of control points and the natural cubic spline that interpolates them. Note that visually the curve is smooth everywhere, and that at the ends of the curve it straightens out so that the second derivative vanishes. The dashed line shows the effect of moving one of the control points. The shape of the curve is affected everywhere. There is no local control with natural splines, since the constraint of a continuous second derivative couples together the first-order derivatives at the knots, making a change in one derivative ripple through all of the others.

FIGURE 10.44 Natural cubic splines interpolating control points.

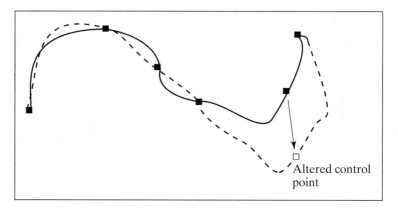

Altered control point

PRACTICE EXERCISE

10.10.4 Solving the equations for the natural spline slopes

It is revealing to write the Equations (10.65) and (10.66) in matrix form. For the case $L = 4$ we have:

$$(s_0, s_1, s_2, s_3, s_4) \begin{pmatrix} 2 & 1 & 0 & 0 & 0 \\ 1 & 4 & 1 & 0 & 0 \\ 0 & 1 & 4 & 1 & 0 \\ 0 & 0 & 1 & 4 & 1 \\ 0 & 0 & 0 & 1 & 2 \end{pmatrix} = 3(y_1 - y_0, y_2 - y_0, y_3 - y_1, y_4 - y_2, y_4 - y_3)$$

This matrix is **tridiagonal**: its nonzero terms are confined to three diagonals. This allows the set of equations to be solved in two easy steps, which we now outline.

a. You first perform a **forward elimination** pass through the set of equations to eliminate the upper strip of ones. To do this, divide the first equation through by 2 so that its leading term is 1. Then, beginning with the second equation, subtract from each equation in turn the proper amount of the previous equation to eliminate the 1, and then scale the equation so a 1 appears in the diagonal term. Show that this converts the set of equations into the lower triangular form (having all zeros above the major diagonal):

$$(s_0, s_1, s_2, s_3, s_4) \begin{pmatrix} 1 & 0 & 0 & 0 & 0 \\ v_0 & 1 & 0 & 0 & 0 \\ 0 & v_1 & 1 & 0 & 0 \\ 0 & 0 & v_2 & 1 & 0 \\ 0 & 0 & 0 & v_3 & 1 \end{pmatrix} = (q_0, q_1, q_2, q_3, q_4) \qquad (10.68)$$

and show how the v_i and q_i terms are easily computed.

b. Show that Figure 10.45 properly represents pseudocode to do this based on arrays $v[\ ]$ and $q[\ ]$.

```
v[0] = 0.25;
q[0] = 3.0  * (y[1] - y[0]) * v[0];
for(i = 1; i < L; i++)
{
    v[i] = 1.0 / (4.0 - v[i - 1]);
    q[i] = (3.0 *(y[i]-y[i-1]) - q[i - 1]) * v[i];
}
```

FIGURE 10.45 A possible implementation (in pseudocode) for the forward elimination step.

c. To obtain the desired s[ ] terms, perform a **backward substitution** step. The matrix in Equation (10.79) has a single term in the rightmost column, so $s_4 = g_4$. Show that you can back up through the equations to obtain each s_i using the following fragment:

```
s[L] = q[L];
for(i = L - 1; i > 0; i- -) s[i] = q[i] - v[i] * s[i+1];
```

10.10.4 How to Compute the Slopes in Cubic Interpolation

Several other approaches can be used to fix the slopes at the joints. We look briefly at one of the most popular, the **Catmull-Rom**[7] family of splines [Bartels87, Farin88], along with its variations.

We still want the curve to be 1-smooth at the inner joints, but we now forfeit the requirement that it be 2-smooth there. The hope is that giving up this extra level of smoothness will afford the designer greater local control of the curve's shape.

In contrast with setting the slope values s_k in order to force a continuous second derivative, here we set them based on the positions of their neighboring control points.

The (simplest) Catmull-Rom approach is to force the velocity vector at P_k to be a value $\mathbf{P}'(t_k)$ based on the positions of the two neighboring points. As shown in Figure 10.46, it is simply made proportional to the vector from P_{k-1} to P_{k+1}. This influences the curve at P_k to be moving parallel to the direction between the previous and next points. So we insist that

$$\mathbf{P}'(t_k) = m(P_{k+1} - P_{k-1}) \tag{10.69}$$

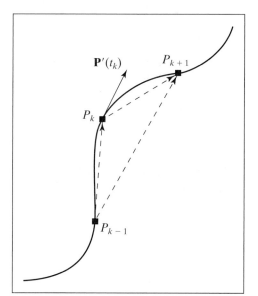

FIGURE 10.46 Determining slopes based on neighboring data values.

---

[7] These are also called **cardinal** splines by some, and **Overhauser** splines by others. They are in fact special cases of a larger family of Catmull-Rom curves.

for some scalar m. (We examine below the effect of the coefficient m; $m = 1/2$ is often used.) In terms of previous quantities this sets the slope of the y-component s_k to be $m(y_{k+1} - y_{k-1})$, and similarly for the x-component.

At this point we have set the values of the slopes s_k for each inner joint, so that the coefficients of the various cubic polynomials in Equation (10.32) can be determined for $k = 1, \ldots, L - 2$. We still need two additional conditions to set the unspecified end slopes s_0 and s_L. To do this we can use the same condition of vanishing second derivatives at the ends that leads to Equation (10.35). Other possibilities are considered in the exercises. Figure 10.47 shows an example of the curve that is generated using this method. Note that at the joints the curve 'straightens out' as a result of having a second derivative of 0.

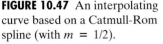

FIGURE 10.47 An interpolating curve based on a Catmull-Rom spline (with $m = 1/2$).

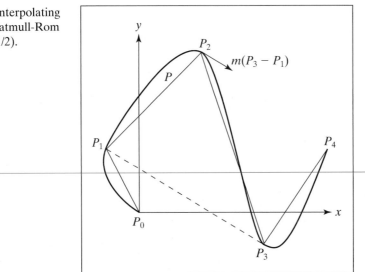

Adding Tension Control

To give the designer greater control of the curve's shape at each joint the Catmull-Rom method introduces a "tension" parameter, v_k. It gives the designer control over the constant m in Equation (10.69), adjusting the magnitude of the velocity $\mathbf{P}'(t)$ at a joint, without altering its direction.

In this method the velocity at the kth joint is set to

$$\mathbf{P}'(t_k) = \frac{1}{2}(1 - v_k)(P_{k+1} - P_{k-1}) \tag{10.70}$$

for $k = 1, \ldots, L - 1$. (What value does this cause s_k to have?)

Although the tension v_k is normally set between -1 and 1, it can have any value. The case $c_k = 0$ corresponds to $m = \frac{1}{2}$ in Equation (10.69). Figure 10.48 shows the influence of tension at vertex P_2 on the shape of the curve. In part a the tension v_2 is 1, so the speed is made zero at the joint. This straightens out the curve as it approaches the joint. (Why?) In part b v_2 is -1 and the curve is more "slack" at the joint.

Adding Bias Control

The class of curves known as the **Kochanek-Bartels splines** adds additional parameters to further assist the control of curve shape [Kochanek84]. One of these is "bias". Notice that we can rewrite Equation (10.69) (using $m = 1/2$) as

$$\mathbf{P}'(t_k) = \frac{1}{2}(P_k - P_{k-1}) + \frac{1}{2}(P_{k+1} - P_k) \tag{10.71}$$

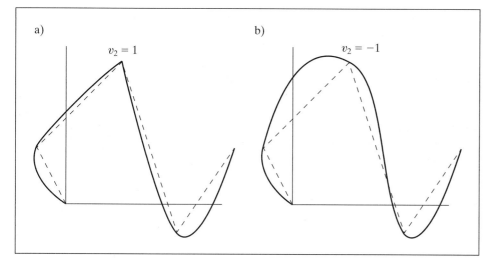

FIGURE 10.48 Effect of tension at vertex 2: (a) tension = 1, (b) tension = −1.

which is seen to be the average of the two neighboring vectors $P_k - P_{k-1}$ and $P_{k+1} - P_k$ (observe these in Figure 10.46). The **bias** parameter b_k weights these two contributions unequally:

$$\mathbf{P}'(t_k) = \frac{1}{2}(1 - b_k)(P_k - P_{k-1}) + \frac{1}{2}(1 + b_k)(P_{k+1} - P_k) \qquad (10.72)$$

so the actual velocity specified at the joint is determined more by one of these neighboring vectors than by the other. When $b_k = 0$, the two vectors are weighted equally. Figure 10.49 shows the effect of bias for a two-segment curve.

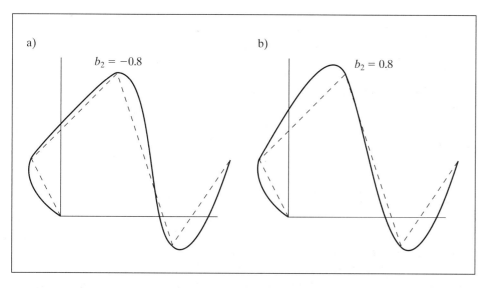

FIGURE 10.49 Effect of bias: a) bias = −0.8, b) bias = 0.8.

Adding Continuity Control

Instead of forcing the velocity to be continuous at P_k, Kochanek and Bartels introduce another parameter to let the designer make the velocity just before a joint differ from that just after the joint. Consider the joint at P_k. The $(k - 1)$st segment, $R_{k-1}(t)$ [recall Equation (10.59)] reaches P_k at $t = 1$. We set its velocity at $t = 1$ to be:

$$\mathbf{R}'_{k-1}(1) = \frac{1}{2}(1 - c_k)(P_k - P_{k-1}) + \frac{1}{2}(1 + c_k)(P_{k+1} - P_k) \qquad (10.73)$$

using some value for c_k, the "continuity parameter." (c_k looks at this point like the bias parameter: larger values of c_k bias the velocity toward $P_{k+1} - P_k$.) Similarly the kth segment, $R_k(t)$, leaves P_k at $t = 0$. We set its velocity at $t = 0$ to be:

$$\mathbf{R}'_k(0) = \frac{1}{2}(1 + c_k)(P_k - P_{k-1}) + \frac{1}{2}(1 - c_k)(P_{k+1} - P_k) \qquad (10.74)$$

using the same value c_k. Again this is like a bias: larger values of c_k bias the velocity toward $P_k - P_{k-1}$. If $c_k = 0$, the two velocities are equal and the curve is 1-smooth at the joint. As c_k deviates from 0, the two velocities have different magnitudes and directions. Figure 10.50 shows the effect of varying the continuity parameter.

FIGURE 10.50 Effect of the continuity parameter: a) $c_2 = 1$, b) $c_2 = -1$.

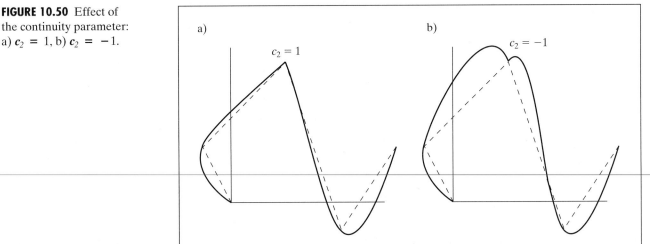

In practice the three parameters of tension, bias, and continuity are used together (see the exercises), and the designer can set them individually for each joint. In a typical scenario the designer might follow the steps:

1. Lay down initial choices for the control points with the mouse.
2. Examine the resulting curve. If satisfactory, stop.
3. Edit the control points, and adjust tension, bias, and continuity for each. (The designer might click on a control point and drag it to a new position. Then to adjust the various parameters at that joint a sequence of keystrokes could be made. For instance, the key 'b' might be pressed to reduce the bias, or 'B' to increase it.)
4. Go to step 2.

PRACTICE EXERCISES

10.10.5 Putting the Kochanek-Bartels splines together

Put the three influences of tension, bias, and continuity together to write a formula for $\mathbf{R}'_{k-1}(1)$ and $\mathbf{R}'_k(0)$ for the Kochanek-Bartels splines.

10.10.6 Choosing the end conditions

Recall that when cubic interpolation is to be performed on $L + 1$ control points, we must determine $4L$ coefficients. Since $4L - 2$ are set by interpolation and slope constraints, 2 must still be fixed. In Equation (10.66) they were fixed by requiring the second derivative at the end segments to vanish, but other conditions can be used to fix them. We need to determine only two equations that are linear in the coefficients and independent of the other $4L - 2$ equations. Determine the equations that arise for each of the conditions below.

a. Fix the first derivatives at the endpoints P_0 and P_L to be zero.
b. Require that the third derivatives at P_1 and at P_{L-1} be continuous. This is known as de Boor's "not-a-knot" constraint; it makes the first two segments into a single polynomial, and the last segments also.
c. Add two "ghost" points, (effectively P_{-1} and P_{L+1}) at the ends of the control polygon. The curve is still drawn starting at P_0, and ends at P_L, but we can derive velocity values at these two points.

10.10.7 Pass a parabola through the control points

To find the slope at P_k, we can find the unique parabola that passes through P_{k-1}, P_k, and P_{k+1}, and compute its velocity at P_k. For any three such control points, find the formula for this velocity. ◾

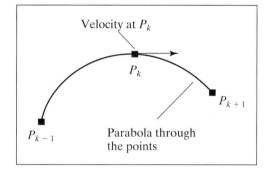

FIGURE 10.51 Setting the velocity by the parabola through three points.

10.10.5 How to Specify the Tangent Vectors Interactively

A CAD drawing program might offer the designer visual handles for setting the tangent vectors, as suggested in Figure 10.52. The user lays down the control points, and an initial interpolating curve is drawn. At this point the user can depress the mouse button on one of the (circular) handles and pull it to a new spot. When released the curve is redrawn—still interpolating the control point—with a tangent vector determined by the (new) straight line through the control point and the handle. This step can be repeated as needed.

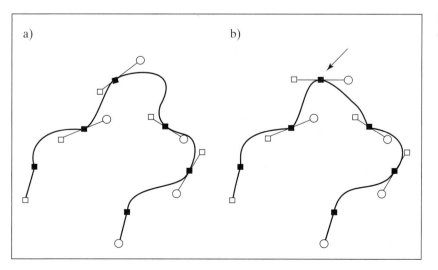

FIGURE 10.52 Interactive design of the cubic segments.

10.11 MODELING CURVED SURFACES

I think there is a world market for maybe five computers.

Thomas Watson
(1874–1956)

So far we have been striving to represent and generate 2D and 3D curves. It is straightforward to extend these ideas to the generation of curved surfaces. In Chapter 6 we examined a variety of surface types, such as ruled surfaces, bilinear and Coons patches, and surfaces of revolution. Now we consider how to use Bezier and B-spline curves to design these surfaces, thereby developing powerful tools for creating a rich set of curved surfaces.

10.11.1 Ruled Surfaces Based on B-splines

It is particularly easy to work with ruled surfaces. Recall from Section 6.5.6 that a ruled surface is defined by two end curves, $P_0(u)$ and $P_1(u)$, which are connected at each value of u by a straight line. Therefore the parametric expression for a ruled surface is just a linear interpolation (or a tweening) between corresponding points on the two curves. Repeating Equation (6.35) for convenience, we have:

$$P(u, v) = (1 - v)P_0(u) + vP_1(u) \tag{10.75}$$

The extension here is to choose $P_0(u)$ and $P_1(u)$ to be B-spline (or Bezier) curves. Figure 10.53 shows a ruled surface where both of the end curves $P_0(u)$ and $P_1(u)$ are cubic Bezier curves. $P_0(u)$ is based on the four control points $P_0^0, P_1^0, P_2^0, P_3^0$, and $P_1(u)$ is based on the four control points $P_0^1, P_1^1, P_2^1, P_3^1$. Using Equation (10.25) for a Bezier curve, we write this surface as

$$P(u, v) = \sum_{k=0}^{3} ((1 - v)P_k^0 + vP_k^1)B_k^3(u) \tag{10.76}$$

FIGURE 10.53 A ruled surface based on Bezier curves.

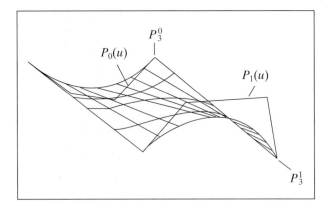

Visualize how this shape behaves. Its u-contours are straight lines joining corresponding points on the two Bezier curves. Its v-contours are Bezier curves whose control points are tweens $(1 - v)P_k^0 + vP_k^1$ of the control points of the two Bezier curves. B-spline or NURBS curves could be used just as well for the end curves; they can even be defined on different knot vectors, as long as their u parameter varies over the same interval.

All of the special cases of ruled surfaces, such as cones and cylinders, are also easily obtained. For instance, what does the surface become if $P_0(u)$ is a version of $P_1(u)$ that has been translated through space?

10.11.2 Surfaces of Revolution Based on B-splines

Recall from Section 6.5.7 that a surface of revolution is formed when a **profile** swept about an axis. $C(v) = (X(v), Z(v))$ is swept about the z-axis. If we suppose that the profile in question has x- and y-components given parametrically by $P(u) = (x(u), y(u))$, then after sweeping about the y-axis the surface has parametric form: $P(u,v) = (x(u,v), y(u,v), v(u,v)) = (x(u)\cos(v), y(u), x(u)\sin(v))$.

$$P(u, v) = (X(v)\cos(u), X(v)\sin(u), Z(v)) \qquad (10.77)$$

It is often convenient to express the profile using Bezier or B-spline curves. We do this by selecting $L + 1$ control points (X_k, Z_k) and using them to create the curve:

$$(X(v), Z(v)) = \sum_{k=0}^{L}(X_k, Z_k)N_{k,m}(v) \qquad (10.78)$$

Figure 10.54a shows an example profile for a goblet defined by a cubic B-spline curve. Figure 10.54b shows the resulting surface of revolution. (A mesh object for the surface of revolution was created as discussed in Chapter 6, and the mesh was drawn using the Mesh :: draw() method.)

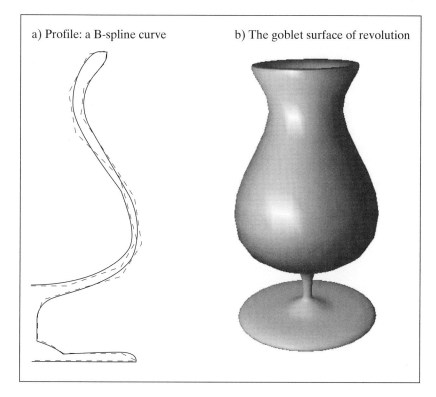

a) Profile: a B-spline curve   b) The goblet surface of revolution

FIGURE 10.54 The profile as a B-spline curve. a) the goblet profile; b) the goblet rendered as a surface of revolution.

■ **EXAMPLE 10.11.1 The classic teapot**

Bezier curves may also be used for profile design. Figure 10.55a shows the profile of the body of the teapot originally designed by Martin Newell [Blinn96]. The body profile consists of three Bezier curves, based on the 10 points displayed in Figure 10.56. The first Bezier curve is defined by points 0, 1, 2, and 3, the second by points 3, 4, 5, and 6, and the third by points 6, 7, 8, and 9. Notice that the last segment of each curve is collinear with the first segment of the next curve. This

FIGURE 10.55 Bezier-based profiles for the teapot body.

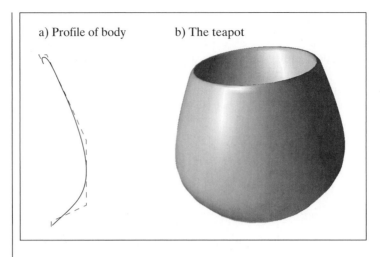

a) Profile of body　　　　b) The teapot

I	X	Z
0	1.4	2.25
1	1.3375	2.38125
2	1.4375	2.38125
3	1.5	2.25
4	1.75	1.725
5	2	1.2
6	2	0.75
7	2	0.3
8	1.5	0.075
9	1.5	0

FIGURE 10.56 Data for the body profile of the teapot.

condition insures that the different Bezier curves blend together with a continuous derivative (recall Section 10.1.2).

The lid of the teapot is also a surface of revolution, and is described in Case Study 10.8.

10.11.3 Bezier Surface Patches

Figure 10.53 showed a ruled patch based on two Bezier curves. For greater design flexibility, we can replace the linear u-contours in Equation (10.76) with Bezier or B-spline curves. A Bezier patch uses Bezier curves for *both* the u- and v-contours. For example, if the u-contours are quadratic Bezier curves and the v-contours are cubic Bezier curves, the Bezier patch has the representation:

$$P(u, v) = \sum_{k=0}^{3} P_k(v) B_k^3(u) = \sum_{k=0}^{3} \left(\sum_{i=0}^{2} P_{i,k} B_i^3(v) \right) B_k^3(u) \tag{10.79}$$

where u and v vary as usual between 0 and 1. Figure 10.57 shows an example.

Each v-contour is a Bezier curve in u based on four control points, which themselves lie along a quadratic Bezier curve. (How would you describe each u-contour?) The 12 control points together constitute the **control polyhedron**, which determines the shape of the patch. The equation for the patch is given in Equation (10.80).

FIGURE 10.57 An example of a Bezier patch.

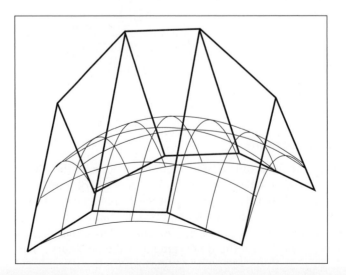

$$P(u, v) = \sum_{k=0}^{L} \sum_{i=0}^{M} P_{i,k} B_i^M(u) B_k^L(v) \qquad (10.80)$$

In general, the control polyhedron is a network of $(M + 1)(L + 1)$ vertices. To create a patch, the designer carefully specifies the positions of these vertices to define the shape of the surface.

Figure 10.58 shows an example of a **bicubic** Bezier patch (for which L and M are both 3), along with its control polyhedron. For more detail on Bezier surfaces, see [Rogers90]. ATI (www.ati.com) and NVIDIA (www.nvidia.com) both provide interesting and in-depth discussions of modeling Bezier surfaces.

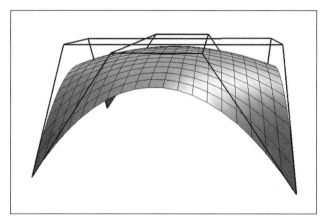

FIGURE 10.58 A bicubic Bezier patch with its control polyhedron.

PRACTICE EXERCISES

10.11.1 Normals to Bezier patches

Apply the parametric form for a Bezier patch to Equation (6.25) to obtain a (complicated) expression for the normal vector to a Bezier patch. Simplify it symbolically as much as possible. Does the normal vector vary continuously at all (u and v)? ▪

10.11.4 To Patch Together Bezier Patches

The designer might want to model a complex shape out of several Bezier surface patches and have the patches meet smoothly at their common boundaries. Figure 10.59 shows two control polyhedra, one in black, one in gray, that define two Bezier patches. Equation (10.80) is used for both patches, and both u and v vary from 0 to 1 to generate each patch. Only the control polyhedra differ.

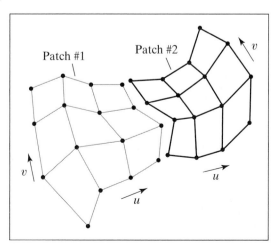

FIGURE 10.59 Two Bezier patches meeting continuously.

What conditions must the designer impose on the two control polyhedra so that the two patches will meet seamlessly? It is simple to make the two patches meet at all points along a common boundary: make their control polyhedra coincide at the boundary. This is so because the shape of the boundary Bezier curve depends only on the boundary polygon of the control polyhedron. [See what happens when $u = 0$ in Equation (10.80).] So the designer chooses these boundary control polygons to be identical for the two patches.

It is more difficult to achieve tangent continuity at the join of the two patches. (But once achieved, it will also guarantee continuity of the normal vector to the surface at the join—why?) One sufficient condition is illustrated in Figure 10.60: each pair of polyhedron edges that meet at the boundary, such as E and E^1, must be collinear. This can be awkward for a designer to satisfy. Other slightly different conditions are discussed in Faux and Pratt [Faux79] as well.

FIGURE 10.60 Achieving tangent continuity across the boundary.

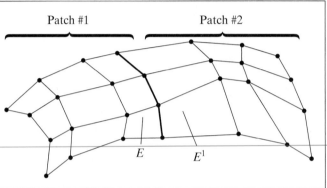

■ **EXAMPLE 10.11.2 Designing the handle of the teapot**

We have seen that the body and the lid of the teapot are surfaces of revolution based on Bezier curves. The handle and the spout, on the other hand, each consist of four Bezier patches. We show how the handle is constructed here [Blinn96]; the spout is described in Case Study 10.8.

Figure 10.61a shows a 3D view of the handle of the teapot. Part b shows the handle in cross section, along with a cross-sectional view of the control polyhedron for the patches.

FIGURE 10.61 Design of the handle of the teapot.

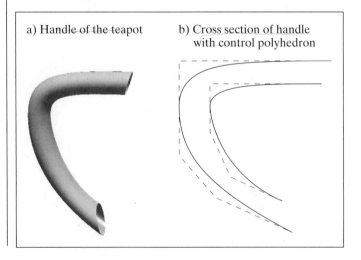

a) Handle of the teapot   b) Cross section of handle with control polyhedron

The handle's surface is symmetrical about the xz-plane. There are an upper and a lower patch on the positive y-side of the xz-plane, and mirror upper and lower patches on the negative y-side of the xz-plane. The control polyhedron for the upper "positive y" patch consists of four rectangles erected on the xz-plane that extend distance 0.3 into the positive xzy-octant. The first such rectangle uses point A_0 once with $y = 0$ and once with $y = 0.3$, and similarly it uses point B_0 once with $y = 0.3$ and once with $y = 0$. With $A_0 = (-1.65, 1.875)$ and $B_0 = (-1.5, 2.1)$ we thus have the four control points $(-1.65, 0.0, 1.875)$, $(-1.65, 0.3, 1.875)$, $(-1.5, 0.3, 2.1)$, $(-1.5, 0.0, 2.1)$.

The entire upper positive-y patch has the 16 control points:

based on A_0, B_0: $(-1.6, 0.0, 1.875), (-1.6, 0.3, 1.875), (-1.5, 0.3, 2.1), (-1.5, 0.0, 2.1)$
based on A_1, B_1: $(-2.3, 0.0, 1.875), (-2.3, 0.3, 1.875), (-2.5, 0.3, 2.1), (-2.5, 0.0, 2.1)$
based on A_2, B_2: $(-2.7, 0.0, 1.875), (-2.7, 0.3, 1.875), (-3.0, 0.3, 2.1), (-3.0, 0.0, 2.1)$
based on A_3, B_3: $(-2.7, 0.0, 1.65), (-2.7, 0.3, 1.65), (-3.0, 0.3, 1.65), (-3.0, 0.0, 1.65)$

Similarly, the lower positive-y patch has the 16 control points:

based on A_3, B_3: $(-2.7, 0.0, 1.65), (-2.7, 0.3, 1.65), (-3.0, 0.3, 1.65), (-3.0, 0.0, 1.65)$
based on A_4, B_4: $(-2.7, 0.0, 1.425), (-2.7, 0.3, 1.425), (-3.0, 0.3, 1.2), (-3.0, 0.0, 1.2)$
based on A_5, B_5: $(-2.5, 0.0, 0.975), (-2.5, 0.3, 0.975), (-2.65, 0.3, 0.7875), (-2.65, 0.0, 0.7875)$
based on A_6, B_6: $(-2.0, 0.0, 0.75), (-2.0, 0.3, 0.75), (-1.9, 0.3, 0.45), (-1.9, 0.0, 0.45)$

Case Study 10.8 exhorts you to write a program to draw the teapot from different points of view using these data.

10.11.5 B-Spline Patches

B-spline functions can be used in place of Bernstein polynomials to achieve greater local control in surface design. The equation is

$$P(u, v) = \sum_{i=0}^{M} \sum_{k=0}^{L} P_{i,k} N_{i,m}(u) N_{k,n}(v) \tag{10.81}$$

where $N_{i,m}(u)$ and $N_{k,n}(v)$ are B-spline basis functions (possibly of different order) defined in Equation (10.47). Usually the standard knot vector is chosen for both B-spline forms, so that the corners of the polyhedron are properly interpolated. Closed surfaces (in u or v or both) will be formed if control points are duplicated or if a periodic form like that in Equation (10.55) is used. The control polyhedron consists of $(L + 1)(M + 1)$ control points, and u and v each vary from 0 to the maximum knot value in their respective knot vectors. Cubic B-splines (for which $m = n = 4$) are again a popular choice, and because there is no limit on the number of control points (since this number does not affect the order of the polynomials as it does for Bezier curves), one can fashion extremely complex surface shapes. As before, the designer must choose the knot polyhedron to create a surface having the desired shape.

Figure 10.62 shows an example of a B-spline surface. It is periodic in one of the parameters. (See the exercises.) It is valuable to identify visually the various control polyhedra, for both the 'u' and 'v' contours.

FIGURE 10.62 Example of a B-spline surface.

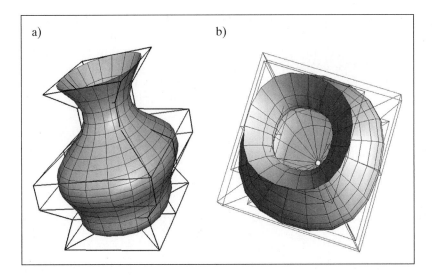

PRACTICE EXERCISE

10.11.4 Periodic B-spline surfaces

Specialize Equation (10.81) to the case where the surface is periodic in u. You may find Equation (10.55) helpful for this. What would useful knot vectors for the two kinds of B-splines be here?   ■

10.11.6 NURBS Surfaces

In Section 10.9 we looked briefly at curves based on rational parametric B-splines. As seen in Equation (10.57), the shape of such curves depends on both a set of control points and a set of weights w_i. These parameters are set by the designer to achieve the desired curve shape.

We can extend NURBS curves to NURBS surfaces just as we did for B-splines in Equation (10.81). [Rogers00] uses the form:

$$P(u, v) = \frac{\sum_{i=0}^{M} \sum_{k=0}^{L} w_{i,k} P_{i,k} N_{i,m}(u) N_{k,n}(v)}{\sum_{i=0}^{M} \sum_{k=0}^{L} w_{i,k} N_{i,m}(u) N_{k,n}(v)} \tag{10.82}$$

Here points $P_{i,k}$ are control points of the **control polyhedron**, the weights $w_{i,k}$ are the weights and the $N_{i,k}$ are B-splines. As in the case of B-spline curves, if all of the weights are equal, this surface simplifies to the B-spline surface of Equation (10.81). (Check this.)

As discussed earlier, there are two principal advantages to NURBS surfaces.

1. With properly chosen control points and weights, the contours of $P(u, v)$ are exactly quadric surfaces. This is in contrast to the nonrational B-spline patches, whose contours can only approximate true quadrics. We see some design examples next that produce conic sections.
2. NURBS surfaces are invariant under **projective transformations**. This invariance means that you can draw a perspective projection of a NURBS patch simply by finding the perspective projection of each of its control points, adjusting the weights somewhat, and then using Equation (10.82). By contrast, nonrational B-spline patches are invariant under affine transformations but *not* under projective transformations.

Owing to their generality and flexibility, NURBS surfaces have become popular with curve and surface designers.

Fashioning Commonly Used NURBS Surfaces

The NURBS family of surfaces offers a tremendous variety of shapes. This family also includes some of the surface types discussed earlier in the chapter. Examples are shown in Figure 10.63 of:

- **Extruded surfaces** (Figure 10.63a). The prism shape is determined by a NURBS curve in parameter u; the straight sides are produced by a first-order NURBS curve in v.
- **Ruled surfaces.** The two edge curves are NURBS curves in u; the rulings are first-order NURBS curves in v.
- **Surfaces of revolution.** (Figure 10.63b). The profile is a NURBS curve lying in the xz-plane; the circular cross sections parallel to the $z = 0$ plane exploit the ability of NURBS curve to create true conic sections.
- **Quadric surfaces.** Quadrics that are surfaces of revolution use conic sections for their profiles. To distort such a surface so that it is no longer circularly symmetric, use an affine transformation on the NURBS surface.

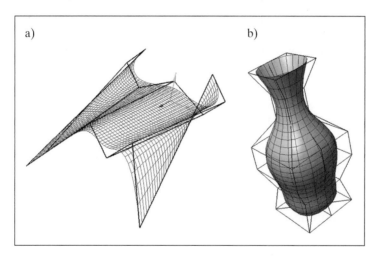

a)   b)

FIGURE 10.63 Example NURBS surfaces.

We emphasize that the single NURBS design tool offers enough flexibility to create all of these surface types. Case Study 10.10 addresses the details of designing and building such surfaces.

Many other techniques have been developed for defining surfaces and operating on them. Check the companion web site for resources and links to see other examples and details.

PRACTICE EXERCISE

10.11.5 Fashioning generic surface shapes

Discuss how you could create each of the following surfaces using NURBS surfaces: a) a circular cylinder, b) a circular cone, c) a planar patch, d) a sphere. See Case Study 10.8 for more details. Can an arbitrary Coon's patch be created? ■

10.11.7 Subdivision of Surfaces

Some mesh models, particularly those that are purchased from a third-party vendor and are available on line, provide a geometry that is rough and not detailed enough for some applications. For example, there may not be enough faces in a model of terrain to hide the individual faces and thereby distinguish properly between the smooth undulations of a hill (when seen from afar) and the craggy buttes of a mountain (when seen close by from an airplane). Or you may wish to have a smoothly crafted chess piece, as in Figure 10.64, to represent a bishop or pawn and the only file available may offer too few faces (as in the leftmost panel of the figure) to be convincing.

FIGURE 10.64 Two levels of refinement in wireframe, and a shaded view of a chess piece. (Courtesy of Scott Cooper)

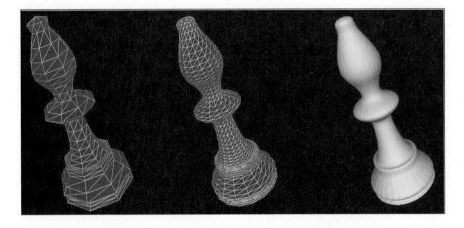

Given such a file, how can the modeler adjust it to create a more convincing mesh model? One very promising approach, which is still a subject of ongoing research, subdivides the mesh faces in order to create additional faces. The subdivision process can be very simple, as we describe next. Figure 10.65 shows a certain triangular face of a mesh model. A simple method to create additional faces is to add edges between the midpoints of each face, thus causing each triangular face to become four triangular faces. (Keep in mind during this discussion how this can be done algorithmically, given the basic vertex, normal list, and face list data structure introduced in Chapter 6 for mesh models.) In particular, note that forming these new faces requires *no* new data—the refined mesh is an inherent part of the original mesh.

FIGURE 10.65 Left: the original triangle. Right: after first subdivision.

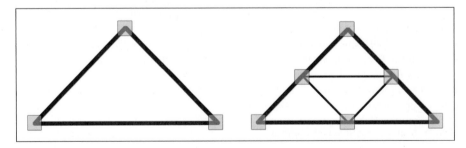

Creating four faces from a single face might be called a "single level of refinement." Evidently it is straightforward to continue this process to greater levels of refinement. Figure 10.66 shows three levels of refinement of the female torso in a wireframe view, where the facets in the left mesh model are clearly visible.

Figure 10.67 shows the same three levels of refinement but in a shaded view. The difference in quality from left to right is clearly visible.

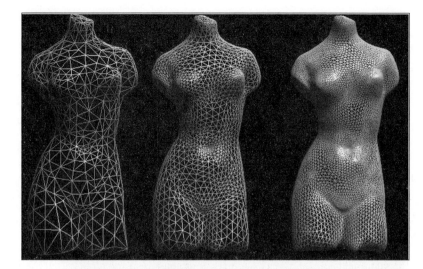

FIGURE 10.66 Three levels of refinement of a mesh model—wireframe views. (Courtesy of Jian Zhang)

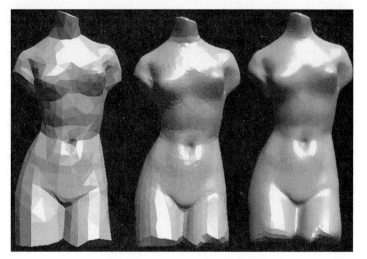

FIGURE 10.67 Three levels of refinement of a mesh model—shaded views. (Courtesy of Jian Zhang)

10.12 SUMMARY

This chapter discussed several techniques for representing and manipulating complex curves and surfaces. The two principal uses of such curves are for rendering them in a graphics application and for modeling the motion of objects such as a camera in an animation. We based most of the designs on the parametric representation for a curve, first described in Chapter 3. Parametric forms are more natural than implicit equations when manipulating and drawing curves that can cross over themselves at certain points or move vertically.

Some important properties of curves were studied. Of particular interest are the velocity of a curve and the normal vector to a curve at each point. The property of the smoothness of a curve was defined and shown to be rather subtle.

A number of example families of curves were examined. The conic sections were discussed, and curves based on polynomials as well as ratios of polynomials were examined.

We also discussed how to generate smoothly varying curves by means of a set of control points. This approach is a staple in the field of computer-aided geometric design (CAD). A designer can specify a small set of points that acts as data to control the shape of a curve as they are blended numerically. The distinction between curves that interpolate the points and those that only approximate the points was emphasized. In either case the small set of control points, along with an algorithm, produces an infinite set of points along the curve, one for each value of the parameter t.

Bezier curves were defined first because of their simplicity. They arise from the iterative de Casteljau process of tweening, which lends a great deal of intuition to their properties. They were shown to have an assortment of desirable properties that make their shape predictable, thereby guiding the designer when laying down control points.

Bezier curves are useful in many design situations, but they suffer from lack of local control, because the Bernstein polynomials on which they are based have support over the entire parametric interval. Another complication is that the order of the underlying polynomials increases as the number of control points is increased. This tends to "quench" the intended variation and can make the curves more expensive and less stable computationally.

We therefore examined a richer class of blending functions based on splines, which are piecewise polynomials that piece together in such a way that various orders of derivatives are everywhere continuous. A particular family of basis functions, the B-splines, can generate any spline and are the most concentrated of such shapes. They therefore offer the designer the strongest measure of local control, and they also exhibit the same desirable properties seen in Bezier functions. When the order of the B-spline polynomials is increased to the number of control points being used, the B-splines become identical to Bernstein polynomials.

Additional control over curve shape is attained by using NURBS curves. These are more complicated, but they include B-splines as a special case and can represent conic sections perfectly. A CAD environment that supports the NURBS algorithm gives the designer a single unified tool for creating a very large variety of curve shapes.

We examined algorithms for forcing a curve to interpolate the given control points instead of only being attracted to them. We focused on piecewise cubic polynomial curves, and developed conditions on the various coefficients so that the curve not only interpolates the points but also has a prescribed velocity at each joint. The velocity can be fixed by the user, by a constraint of greater smoothness at the joints, or by local geometric information based on neighboring control points. Additional parameters such as tension and bias can be introduced that afford the designer a great deal of control over the final shape of the curve.

Another approach to interpolation uses B-splines, which do not usually cause the curve to interpolate any but the first and last control points. The trick here is to compute a second set of control points cleverly positioned so that the B-spline curve based on them passes through every one of the original control points.

We extended the curve design techniques to the design of different families of surfaces, including ruled surfaces, surfaces of revolution, and quadric surfaces. We also considered surface design using Bezier, B-spline, and rational B-spline functions. One may think of generating a Bezier patch by sweeping a Bezier curve of changing shape through space. Each point on the moving Bezier curve moves along a trajectory that is itself a Bezier curve. Bezier patches may be pieced together if certain conditions on their control polyhedra are met. B-spline surfaces were also discussed and shown to offer more flexibility to the designer. Because the order of the polynomials involved does not increase as the number of control points increases, very complex surface shapes can be fashioned.

The final extension was to the family of NURBS surfaces, which, by allowing the designer to vary a set of weights to alter the shape of the patch, provide an additional degree of design flexibility. NURBS surfaces are invariant under both affine and projective transformations. In addition, NURBS surfaces specialize to many other families of surfaces, so a designer armed with a NURBS surface algorithm can fashion many types of surfaces.

Surface subdivision was also introduced as a method for refining a mesh model in a simple and organized fashion. Refining a model in this way creates new faces for the model such that, when rendered, the model appears much smoother.

This chapter only touched on the fundamentals of surface design. Many variations of these techniques have been developed, and large computer-aided design and 3D modeling packages often include an assortment of methods. The designer can choose from among these methods and iteratively fine-tune the shapes they produce until the design goals are met. Some shapes, such as the wing of an airplane or the hull of a sailboat, are fashioned from a complex mixture of principles, aesthetics, intuition, and experience.

10.13 CASE STUDIES

CASE STUDY 10.1 A POTPOURRI OF INTERESTING PARAMETRIC CURVES

(Level of Effort: II) **A. A Generalization of the Ellipse.** An ellipse is formed using a single sine and cosine for the parametric representation. An interesting family of curves may be generated by superimposing several ellipses that are traversed at different speeds. The summing of harmonics in this way is similar to the Fourier series plots seen in Chapter 3, but now it is done in two dimensions. We start with two terms and then generalize. Consider the family of curves described by

$$x(t) = X_1 \cos(2\pi t) + X_2 \cos(2\pi k t)$$
$$y(t) = Y_1 \sin(2\pi t) + Y_2 \sin(2\pi k t) \tag{10.83}$$

The first term in each formula represents an ellipse, to which is added a second, "piggyback" ellipse that is traced out k times as fast. As t varies from 0 to 1, the first ellipse is traced out once, whereas the other is traced out k times. If k is an integer, the figure will close exactly. Write a program that draws such periodic figures, using as input the values of X_1, X_2, Y_1, Y_2, and k. Generalize further by adding more terms to $x(t)$ and $y(t)$.

B. The Involute of the Circle. Grab a point P on a piece of thread wound round a broomstick. Keeping the thread taut, unwrap it by circling the broomstick with your hand. The path taken by P is a spiral known as the "involute of a circle." The thread connecting the circle (broomstick) to P forms a tangent to the circle. Evidently this tangent is always perpendicular to the spiral. In addition, successive coils of the spiral are parallel and separated by the same distance. (Which distance?) A family of such spirals is formed by rotating the figure (or by choosing different points P on the thread). Each spiral is orthogonal to all lines tangent to the circle. The parametric form for this curve is

$$x(t) = \cos(2\pi t) + 2\pi t \sin(2\pi t)$$
$$y(t) = \sin(2\pi t) - 2\pi t \cos(2\pi t) \tag{10.84}$$

Write a program that draws involutes of a circle.

C. Other Sinusoidal-Type Curves. Slight adjustments to $x(t)$ and $y(t)$ in the previous exercises can produce remarkably different shapes. For instance, the curve in Figure 10.68 (contributed by Professor Robert Weaver of Mount Holyoke College) results from the following functions:

$$x(t) = \cos(t) + \sin(8t)$$
$$y(t) = 2\sin(t) + 7\sin(7t) \tag{10.85}$$

Write a routine that produces this curve, and try other variations as well. Under what conditions on the arguments of the trigonometric functions does the curve always form a closed (periodic) figure?

D. Lissajous Figures. A variation on the ellipse is provided if the frequencies of the two sinusoids are allowed to differ:

$$x(t) = \cos(2\pi M t + angle)$$
$$y(t) = \sin(2\pi N t) \tag{10.86}$$

where M and N are the new frequencies and *angle* is a "phase offset" between the two components. These shapes are called "Lissajous figures" and are sometimes viewed on an oscilloscope while testing electrical circuits. Write a program that takes M, N, and *angle* as parameters and displays the resulting Lissajous figures. Experiment with large increments in t between points chosen on the curves to see the variety of shapes that result. Interesting symmetries can be observed if the values of the x- and y-variables are interchanged after each line is drawn.

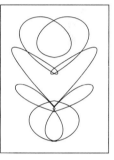

FIGURE 10.68 Genie rising. (Courtesy of Robert Weaver)

CASE STUDY 10.2 ELLIPTIPOOL

(Level of Effort: III) In Case Study 4.4 we examined how rays bounce off the walls of a polyg-onal chamber. It is interesting to consider other chamber shapes. Elliptical pool tables went on sale in the United States in 1964 under the name Elliptipool [Gardner71, Steinhaus69]. We can simulate Elliptipool by tracing rays bouncing inside an elliptical chamber, as suggested in Figure 10.69.

FIGURE 10.69 Example simulation of Elliptipool.

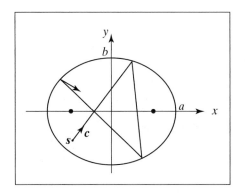

An initial ray $S + \mathbf{c}t$ is given, with starting point S inside the ellipse. The point P where it hits the ellipse is determined, and the direction $\mathbf{r}$ of the reflected ray is also found. A line is drawn from S to P to "trace" the ray. Then the next ray is set as $P + \mathbf{r}t$, and the process repeats.

Suppose the ellipse has the implicit form

$$F(P) = \left(\frac{x}{a}\right)^2 + \left(\frac{y}{b}\right)^2 - 1 = 0$$

and that a ray is given by $S + \mathbf{c}t$.

To intersect a ray with an ellipse:

If the ray intersects the ellipse at all, it must be at some value of t that produces a point $S + \mathbf{c}t$ lying on the curve $F(P) = 0$. This produces a condition on t: $F(S + \mathbf{c}t) = 0$. So for the el-lipse we obtain the equation

$$\left(\frac{S_x + c_x t}{a}\right)^2 + \left(\frac{S_y + c_y t}{b}\right)^2 - 1 = 0$$

which is a *quadratic* equation in t. Quadratic equations are easily solved and have zero, one, or two solutions.

- no solutions: the ray misses the ellipse.
- one solutions: the ray grazes the ellipse.
- two solutions: the ray enters the ellipse and later exits from it.

If the ray starts out in the interior of the chamber, one of the solutions is positive and one is negative. (Why?) Use the positive one, and call it t_{hit}.

We must find the direction of the reflected ray at the hit point. Use $x(t) = a \cos(t)$ and $y(t) = b \sin(t)$ in Equation (10.3) to obtain the normal vector $(-b \cos(t), -a \sin(t))$, which can be written in terms of x and y as $(-bx/a, -ay/b)$. Since only its direction is important, it's convenient to scale this to $(-b^2 x, -a^2 y)$. Now we want the inner normal, as the ray bounces off the inside wall of the ellipse. By inspection of Figure 10.69, both the x- and y-components of the inner normal are negative when x and y are positive, so the form

$$\mathbf{n} = (-b^2 x, -a^2 y) \tag{10.87}$$

does indeed have the direction of the inner normal. The reflected ray $\mathbf{r}$ may be obtained by using this in Equation (4.27).

A simulation of Elliptipool reveals some fascinating behavior: there are only three types of ray paths [Steinhaus69].

- If the ray passes over either focus, it will rebound and pass over the other focus. This is due, of course, to the reflection property of ellipses: that a ray leaving one focus always bounces off the elliptical wall and goes to the other focus. The ray will pass over alternating foci forever. After a few passes the path will become indistinguishable from the *x*-axis.
- If the ray does not pass between the foci on its initial path, it will never pass between them thereafter. Instead, it will move along paths that are tangent to a smaller ellipse having the same foci, as shown in Figure 10.70.

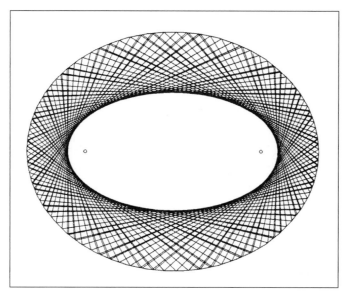

FIGURE 10.70 Rays tangent to a second ellipse.

- If the ray starts off passing between the foci, it will trace out an endless path that will never get closer to the foci than a hyperbola with the same foci, as shown in Figure 10.71.

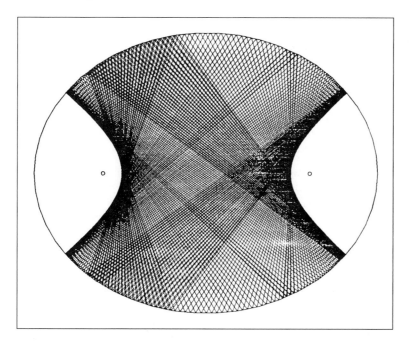

FIGURE 10.71 Rays tangent to a hyperbola.

Write and exercise a program that simulates Elliptipool. The user indicates the starting position and direction of the ray in some fashion, and the ray is traced for a large number of bounces. Allow the user to specify the case of the ray passing through a focus. (Beware that for this situation, an arithmetic round-off error may cause some unpredicted effects. How can it be counteracted?) Have the ray change color occasionally so that its current path remains apparent as the display fills in with paths. Experiment with ellipses of different eccentricity, including circular pool tables.

(Optional) Enhance the experiment by placing circles or other barriers (ellipses?) inside the elliptical pool table. Do any recognizable patterns emerge in the ray paths in this case?

CASE STUDY 10.3 BEZIER CURVES

(Level of Effort: II) Write a program that takes as input a sequence of control points laid down by the user with the mouse, and draws the Bezier curve based on these points. Points along the curve are computed at closely spaced values of t, and these points are joined by straight line segments. Exercise the program with different numbers of control points. Notice how the computation slows down for larger numbers of control points, since the polynomials are then of higher degree.

CASE STUDY 10.4 A QUADRATIC SPLINE CURVE GENERATOR

(Level of Effort: II) Equation (10.41) represents a curve as a weighted sum of blending functions $g(t - k)$:

$$V(t) = \sum_{k=0}^{6} P_k g(t - k)$$

where $g(t)$ is a quadratic spline function defined in Equation (10.38) . Write and exercise a program that lets the user lay down a sequence of control points P_k with the mouse, and then draws the curve $V(t)$ given above. This is aided by developing a function `double g(double t)` that returns the value of $g(t)$, in particular returning 0 if t lies outside of the interval $[0, 3]$.

CASE STUDY 10.5 BUILDING A SPLINE CURVE EDITOR

(Level of Effort: III) Design and exercise a program that allows the user to create a control polygon **P** using the mouse. On request the program draws the B-spline curve determined by **P**. The program should implement the following commands, which are executed by pressing suitable keys on the keyboard ('b' for begin, 'd' for delete, and so on):

- `b)egin:` (begin a new control polygon **P**)
- `d)elete:` (delete the closest point in **P** pointed to)
- `m)ove:` (drag the point of **P** pointed at to a new location)
- `r)efresh:` (draw **P**)
- `o)rder ('1'..'9'):` (draw the spline curve of this order based on **P**)
- `c)losed ('-1',..,'-9'):` (draw the *closed* B-spline curve based on **P**)
- `e)rase:` (erase the screen)
- `q)uit:` (exit from the program)

1. **(Optional) Having several control polygons.** Extend the program so that you can have up to 10 different control polygons on the display at one time, and edit each one at will.
2. **(Optional) Can B-splines make circles?** Experiment with four and eight control points that lie on a circle to see how closely a closed cubic B-spline curve based on these points approximates a circle. Develop a reasonable numerical measure of the error between the curve and the circle, and try different configurations to determine the best curve.
3. **(Optional). Transforming B-spline curves.** Extend the program so that the user can specify an affine transformation (perhaps from a menu of prestored versions) and point to a control polygon, after which the B-spline curve is drawn based on the transformed polygon.

CASE STUDY 10.6 INTERPOLATION OF CONTROL POINTS WITH B-SPLINES

(Level of Effort: III) A curve based on B-spline blending functions and the standard knot vector interpolates only the first and last control point. However, a preprocessing step can be applied to the control points so that the B-spline curve interpolates all of them. During pre-processing, a new set of control points is carefully fashioned out of the given set. This new set has the property that when a B-spline curve is formed from it, the curve passes through all of the points in the original set.

We develop the central idea through a specific example, interpolating a set of six data points, $y_0, \ldots, y_5$, at equispaced values of t with cubic B-splines, as shown in Figure 10.72a.

Instead of the standard knot vector, knots are made equispaced, so that $N_{0,4}(t)$ begins at $t = 0$ and "bulges up" at $t = 2$, $N_{1,4}(t)$ begins at $t = 1$ and "bulges up" at $t = 3$, and so on. Thus we attempt to interpolate y_0 at $t = 2$, y_1 at $t = 3$, and so forth.

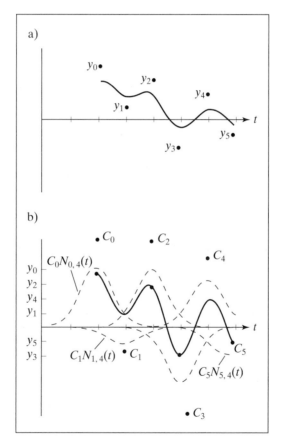

FIGURE 10.72 Attempt to interpolate six points with cubic B-splines.

As shown in Figure 10.72b, the sum

$$y(t) = \sum_{i=0}^{5} y_i N_{i,4}(t)$$

does not pass through the points. Because the B-spline functions overlap, the various terms in the sum interact in such a way that $y(t)$ falls short of the data values. To correct this, a different set of values, $c_0, \ldots, c_5$, is used instead of the y_i, so that the curve based on them:

$$p(t) = \sum_{i=0}^{5} c_i N_{i,4}(t) \tag{10.87}$$

does indeed interpolate the y_i's, as shown in Figure 10.72b. We must find just the right set of c_i values to accomplish this. It is done by solving a set of linear equations. The conditions for interpolating the six points are $p(2) = y_0$, $p(3) = y_1$, $p(4) = y_2, \ldots, p(7) = y_5$. Because at integer values of t the only values taken on by the B-splines functions are 0, 1/6, and 4/6, these six conditions have the form

$$
\begin{aligned}
4c_0 + c_1 &= 6y_0 \\
c_0 + 4c_1 + c_2 &= 6y_1 \\
c1 + 4c_2 + c3 &= 6y2 \\
\cdots &= \cdots \\
c_4 + 4c_5 &= 6y_5
\end{aligned}
\tag{10.88}
$$

These equations are nearly identical to Equations (10.65) and (10.66), so they can be solved using the techniques described in Section 10.10.3.

These ideas extend immediately to any number of data points, $y_0, y_1, \ldots, y_L$, simply by choosing the proper L. Write a function, `void adjust(double y[], double c[], int L)`, that produces the array `c[]` given the array `y[]`.

To interpolate points $p_i = (x_i, y_i)$ the preceding process is performed once for the x-components and once for the y-components, producing the two arrays `x_new[]` and `y_new[]`. Then the interpolating curve is given by

$$
P(t) = \sum_{i=0}^{L} W_i N_{i,4}(t)
$$

FIGURE 10.73 Example of 2D interpolation with B-splines. (Courtesy of Tuan Le Ngoc)

where $W_i = $ `(x_new[i], y_new[i])`. An example is shown in Figure 10.73.

Write a program that allows the user to lay down a sequence of $(L + 1)$ control points with the mouse, and then draws the interpolating curve based on cubic B-splines. Experiment with different values of L.

(Optional). Extend the program so that it draws *closed* curves that interpolate the control points. What adjustments are needed in Equation (10.88) to do this?

CASE STUDY 10.7 INTERPOLATING WITH CUBIC POLYNOMIALS

(Level of Effort: III) Write a program that allows the user to lay down a sequence of $(L + 1)$ control points with the mouse, and then draws the interpolating curve based on cubic polynomials. The velocities at the inner joints are set using the Kochanek-Bartels approach, with specified values of tension, bias, and continuity. The remaining two conditions on the cubic coefficients are set by forcing the second derivatives at the end control points to 0.

Allow the user to adjust the tension, bias, and continuity at each inner control point using keystrokes. For instance, to change the tension the user clicks on the control point in question and taps the key 'v' to decrease tension there by some small fixed amount, or 'V' to increase it. Similarly, 'b' or 'B' is tapped to change bias, and 'c' or 'C' to adjust continuity.

CASE STUDY 10.8 THE VENERABLE TEAPOT

(Level of Effort: II) Write a program that uses OpenGL to draw the classical teapot from different points of view. Do not use the GLUT version of the teapot: fashion your own teapot out of surface patches.

The teapot has four major parts. The **body is** a surface of revolution whose profile consists of 3 Bezier curves in the x z-plane, as described in Section 10.10.2. The **handle** consists of four Bezier patches, as described in Section 10.10.3. The **lid** is a surface of revolution whose profile is described by two Bezier curves, as shown in Figure 10.74, with data points given in Figure 10.75.

The **spout** is similar to the handle, also consisting of four Bezier patches. Figure 10.76a shows the spout in cross section, along with a cross-sectional view of the control polyhedron for the patches.

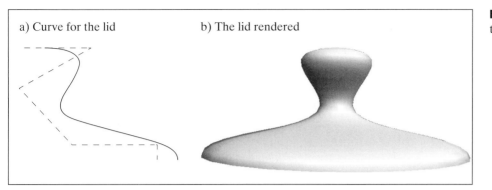

a) Curve for the lid   b) The lid rendered

FIGURE 10.74 The lid of the teapot.

Similar to the handle, the spout's surface is symmetrical about the xz-plane. The entire upper positive-y patch has the 16 control points:

based on C_0, D_0: $(1.7, 0.0, 0.45)(1.7, 0.66, 0.45)(1.7, 0.66, 1.275)(1.7, 0.0, 1.275)$
based on C_1, D_1: $(3.1, 0.0, 0.675)(3.1, 0.66, 0.675)(2.6, 0.66, 1.275)(2.6, 0.0, 1.275)$
based on C_2, D_2: $(2.4, 0.0, 1.875)(2.4, 0.25, 1.875)(2.3, 0.25, 1.95)(2.3, 0.0, 1.95)$
based on C_3, D_3: $(3.3, 0.0, 2.25)(3.3, 0.25, 2.25)(2.7, 0.25, 2.25)(2.7, 0.0, 2.25)$

The lower positive-y patch has the 16 control points:

based on C_3, D_3: $(3.3, 0.0, 2.25)(3.3, 0.25, 2.25)(2.7, 0.25, 2.25)(2.7, 0.0, 2.25)$
based on C_4, D_4: $(3.525, 0.0, 2.34375)(3.525, 0.25, 2.34375)(2.8, 0.25, 2.325)(2.8, 0.0, 2.325)$
based on C_5, D_5: $(3.45, 0.0, 2.3625)(3.45, 0.1, 2.3625)(2.9, 0.1, 2.325)(2.9, 0.0, 2.325)$
based on C_6, D_6: $(3.2, 0.0, 2.25)(3.2, 0.15, 2.25)(2.8, 0.15, 2.25)(2.8, 0.0, 2.25)$

i	x	z
0	0	3
1	0.8	3
2	0	2.7
3	0.2	2.55
4	0.4	2.4
5	1.3	2.4
6	1.3	2.25

FIGURE 10.75 Data for the lid profile of the teapot.

FIGURE 10.76 Design of the spout of the teapot.

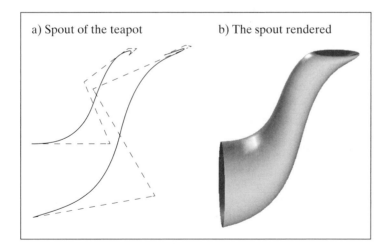

a) Spout of the teapot   b) The spout rendered

CASE STUDY 10.9 NURBS: INVARIANCE TO PROJECTIVE TRANSFORMATIONS

(Level of Effort: I) A. This case study provides a step-by-step demonstration that NURBS curves are invariant under a projective transformation. Show the details leading to each of the steps. Suppose the NURBS curve is given by Equation (10.57), and the transformation has 4-by-4 matrix M whose rows are the vectors $\mathbf{m}_1, \mathbf{m}_2, \mathbf{m}_3,$ and $\mathbf{m}_4$, respectively.

a. Show that the homogeneous coordinate version, $\widetilde{P}(t)$, of the curve in Equation (10.57), when transformed by T, becomes the curve $M\widetilde{P}(t)$ given by:

$$M\widetilde{P}(t) = \sum_{k=0}^{L} w_k (\widetilde{P}_k \cdot \mathbf{m}_1, \widetilde{P}_k \cdot \mathbf{m}_2, \widetilde{P}_k \cdot \mathbf{m}_3, \widetilde{P}_k \cdot \mathbf{m}_4)^T N_{k,m}(t)$$

where $\widetilde{P}_k = (P_x, P_y, P_z, 1)^T$ is the homogeneous coordinate version of P_k.

b. Show that in ordinary coordinates this becomes

$$T(p(t)) = \frac{\displaystyle\sum_{k=0}^{L} w_k (\widetilde{P}_k \cdot \mathbf{m}_1, \widetilde{P}_k \cdot \mathbf{m}_2, \widetilde{P}_k \cdot \mathbf{m}_3)^T N_{k,m}(t)}{\displaystyle\sum_{k=0}^{L} w_k (\widetilde{P}_k \cdot \mathbf{m}_4) N_{k,m}(t)} \tag{10.89}$$

c. Show that each control point P_k is transformed to

$$T(P_k) = \left(\frac{\widetilde{P}_k \cdot \mathbf{m}_1}{\widetilde{P}_k \cdot \mathbf{m}_4} \frac{\widetilde{P}_k \cdot \mathbf{m}_2}{\widetilde{P}_k \cdot \mathbf{m}_4} \frac{\widetilde{P}_k \cdot \mathbf{m}_3}{\widetilde{P}_k \cdot \mathbf{m}_4} \right)^T$$

d. Show that building a NURB curve with weights, say v_k, on these transformed control points yields the curve:

$$\frac{\displaystyle\sum_{k=0}^{L} v_k \left(\frac{\widetilde{P}_k \cdot \mathbf{m}_1}{\widetilde{P}_k \cdot \mathbf{m}_4} \frac{\widetilde{P}_k \cdot \mathbf{m}_2}{\widetilde{P}_k \cdot \mathbf{m}_4} \frac{\widetilde{P}_k \cdot \mathbf{m}_3}{\widetilde{P}_k \cdot \mathbf{m}_4} \right)^T N_{k,m}(t)}{\displaystyle\sum_{k=0}^{L} v_k N_{k,m}(t)}$$

e. Show that this agrees with Equation (10.59) for the choice of v_k equal to the $\overline{w}_k$ of Equation (10.60).

B. Why B-splines aren't projectively invariant. Show where the derivation in the previous exercise fails for B-splines.

C. Extension to surfaces. Work through steps similar to those above to show that NURBS surfaces are also projectively invariant.

CASE STUDY 10.10 DRAWING NURBS PATCHES

(Level of Effort: II)

a. Write and experiment with an application that draws u- and v-contours of NURBS surfaces. The core of such an application is a function that evaluates points on the surface $P(u, v)$, whose prototype might be:

```
Point3 nurbsPoint(Point3 P[][],   // matrix of control points
          int L, int M,           // # of control pts = (L+1)(M+1)
          float w[],              // vector of weights
          float knot[],           // knot vector
          int m, int n,           // orders of B-splines
          float u,  v);           // values of parameters u and v
```

b. Experiment with the control polyhedron shown in plan view in Figure 10.77, where the label 0, a, or b gives the height of each point above the xy-plane. Figure 10.77b shows an example of the "**domelike**" shape produced by a NURBS patch for certain choices of weights and heights a and b.

Build and draw patches formed this way for user-specified values of a and b. Try various cases of weight selection:

    i.   All weights are equal.

    ii. Points at height 0 each have weight W, and all the others have weight sW, where the user enters a values of s.

    iii. Other interesting arrangements of weights.

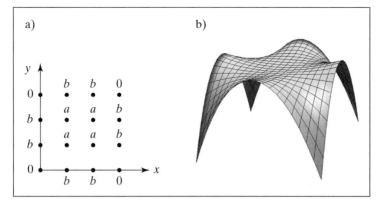

FIGURE 10.77 Designing a dome.

Does any combination you come upon produce a dome that is nearly a hemisphere? What adjustments might produce a more hemispherical dome?

c. Building extruded surfaces and ruled surfaces. Experiment with creating extruded (linearly swept) surfaces using NURBS surfaces. A contour, $C(u)$, described as a NURBS curve, is swept in a direction perpendicular to the plane of the contour. The straight sides are produced by a first-order NURBS curve in v. Also experiment with a ruled surface, where the two edge curves are NURBS curves in u, and the rulings are first-order NURBS curves in v.

10.14 FOR FURTHER READING

An excellent early book by Faux and Pratt [Faux79] develops the mathematical foundations of curve and surface design. The book by Rogers and Adams [Rogers90] provides a wealth of techniques for designing surfaces, and Farin [Farin90] offers a lucid treatment of the underlying mathematics of surfaces. Bartels, Beatty, and Barsky [Bartels87] discuss the many varieties of splines that you can use in curve and surface design, and describe their different properties. The book edited by Bloomenthal [Bloomenthal97] has several fine chapters on curve and surface design, including one by Blinn on second-order surfaces and one by Bajaj on implicitly defined surface patches. Rogers provides an excellent introduction and historical perspective on NURBS curves and surfaces [Rogers00]. See also recent reports on subdivision research by M. Bunnel in *GPU Gems 2, Adaptive Tesselation of Subdivision Surfaces with Displacement Mapping*, as well as *Compressed Progressive Meshes* by R. Pajarola and J. Rossignac in *IEEE CG&A* [Pajarola00]

Chapter 11

....

Color Theory

Colors and textures will become important to you.
Found in fortune cookie, Amherst, Mass.

GOALS OF THE CHAPTER

○ To study the nature of color and its numerical description.

○ To examine some standards for color representation.

○ To define and use various color spaces.

○ To describe different methods for reducing the number of colors in an image.

○ To develop methods for programming the color look-up table.

Preview

Section 11.1 describes some of the intricacies of the human color vision system and introduces the problem of describing colors numerically in a reliable and reproducible way. Section 11.2 discusses the process of color matching, and the representation of any color as a linear combination of three primary colors. The issue of choosing good primary colors is addressed. Section 11.3 develops central ideas of the CIE standard chromaticity diagram, showing how it is useful in color calculations. The notion of a gamut of colors is also discussed. Section 11.4 describes different color spaces and gives some tools for converting a color between spaces. Section 11.5 discusses methods used for color quantization: reducing the number of different colors in an image without destroying its visual quality.

11.1 INTRODUCTION

The illumination models discussed in the previous chapter computed colors by working separately with three basic primaries, red, green, and blue. This is serviceable, and we show below that it is in fact related to the manner in which the eye operates. In addition, it is consistent with the way most common graphics displays used today generate color by mixing amounts of some built-in red, green, and blue colors.

But the subject of color is much more complex than this simple approach would suggest. Color depends on subtle interactions between the physics of light radiation and the eye–brain system. See [Feynman63] for a superb discussion.

From the point of view of writing computer graphics applications, we must be able to answer several questions:

- How are colors described accurately in numerical terms?
- How do these descriptions relate to everyday ways of describing color?
- How does one compare colors?
- What range of colors can a CRT display or a printed page exhibit?
- How can color look-up tables be loaded to produce the colors required?
- How do we deal with a range of color when a device can display only, say, 256 colors?

In order to write applications that produce the proper colors we need convenient tools to describe and control color, so much of this chapter will deal with this rather thorny issue.

Light itself is an electromagnetic phenomenon, like television waves, infrared radiation, and x-rays. By light, we mean those waves that lie in a narrow band of **wavelengths**[1] in the so-called *visible spectrum*. Figure 11.1 shows the location of the visible spectrum (for humans) within the entire electromagnetic spectrum, along with the spectra of some other common phenomena. The frequency of vibration f increases to the right, whereas wavelength λ increases to the left.[2] The eye responds to light with wavelengths between approximately 400 and 700 nm (nanometers).

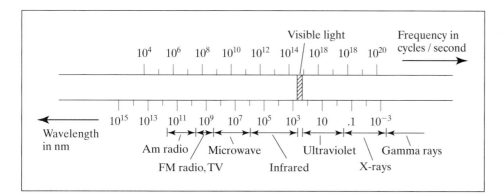

FIGURE 11.1 Electromagnetic spectrum.

11.1.1 The Eye: Physiologic Basis for Human Color Perception

The retina of the eye is its light-sensitive membrane. It lines the posterior portion of the eye's wall and contains two kinds of receptor cells, cones and rods.

The **cones** are the color-sensitive cells, each responding to a particular color, red, green, or blue. According to the tri-stimulus theory (which we examine below), the color we see is the result of our cones' relative responses to red, green, and blue light. The human eye can distinguish about 200 intensities of red, green, and blue, each. Each eye has 6 to 7 million cones, concentrated in a small portion of the retina called the **fovea**. Each cone has its own nerve cell, thereby allowing the eye to discern tiny details. To see an object in detail, the eye looks directly at it in order to bring the image onto the fovea.

---

[1] The wavelength of a wave is the distance light travels during one cycle of its vibration.

[2] Wavelength λ and frequency f are inversely related by $\lambda = v/f$, where v is the speed of light in the medium of interest. In air (or a vacuum) $v = 300,000$ km/sec; in glass it is about 65 percent as fast.

By contrast, the **rods** cannot distinguish colors, nor can they see fine detail. Seventy-five million to 150 million rods are crowded onto the retina surrounding the fovea. Moreover, many rods are attached to a single nerve cell, preventing the discrimination of fine detail [Gonzalez and Wintz87]. So what do rods do? They are very sensitive to low levels of light and can see things in dim light that the cones miss. At night, for instance, it is best to look slightly away from an object so that the image falls outside the fovea. Detail and color are lost, but at least the general form of an object is visible. Indeed, the sensitivity of our peripheral vision to dim light was probably instrumental in our evolution.

Some light sources, such as lasers, emit light of essentially a single wavelength, or "pure spectral" light. We perceive 400-nm light as violet and 620-nm light as red, with the other pure colors lying in between these extremes. Figure 11.2 shows some example **spectral densities** $\mathbf{S}(\lambda)$ (power per unit wavelength) for pure lights and the common names given to their perceived colors.

FIGURE 11.2 Spectra for some pure colors.

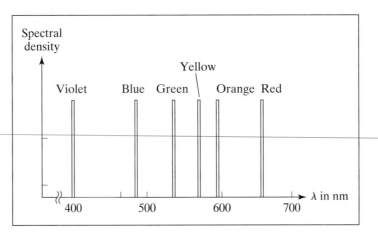

The light from most sources does not consist of only one wavelength; instead, it contains varying amounts of power in a continuous set of wavelengths. Their set of spectral densities (or **spectra**) covers a band of wavelengths. The total power of the light in any band of wavelengths is found as the *area* under the density curve over that band. Figure 11.3 shows several example spectra for lights of familiar colors.

The label for each indicates the color that we perceive when we look at such light. Note that white light contains approximately equal amounts of power at all frequencies, whereas reds tend to have more power concentrated at the longer wavelengths. Gray light also exhibits a "flat" spectral density, but at a lower intensity. These examples highlight one of the difficulties of trying to describe color numerically: *an enormous variety of spectral density functions is perceived by the eye as having the same color.* For example, a given color sample can be matched by many different spectral density shapes, such that the colors of the sample and any of the spectral densities are indistinguishable when placed side by side.

11.1.2 RGB Color Blindness

Some people's visual system cannot distinguish red and green light. Approximately 10% of males and far fewer females are "color-blind" in the sense that they cannot distinguish certain colors from others. Tests have been devised to determine whether a given individual suffers from this lack of perception. Our companion web site illustrates such a test by placing a large number of circles in a large circle.

precise characterization of the color you have in mind. If you knew the spectral density curve of the desired color, as in Figure 11.3, you could try to describe its level at a dozen or so wavelengths, but that is clearly awkward and seems too specific, as many different spectral shapes produce the same color. Ideally, you would be able to recite a few numbers, such as "the target color is 3.24 at 400 nm, 1.6 at 500 nm, 85 at 600 nm, and 1.117 at 680 nm," and you could be assured that *exactly* the same color could be reproduced by the listener from this description.

How many numbers taken from the spectrum are required, and what do they mean? Remarkably, the answer is three numbers: human **color perception** is three dimensional. But we still must agree on what coding scheme is to be used to map colors into numbers, and vice versa. We shall examine some conventional schemes in the following sections and then discuss the ideas behind the current international standard.

11.2.1 Dominant Wavelength

One simple way to describe a color capitalizes on the variety of spectra that produce the same (perceived) color. It specifies a spectrum having the very simple shape shown in Figure 11.4 by stating three numbers: dominant wavelength, saturation, and luminance.

FIGURE 11.4 Spectrum of a color using a dominant wavelength.

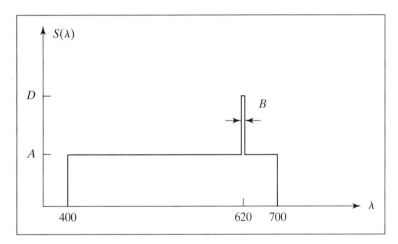

The spectrum consists of a spike located at a dominant wavelength—620 nm in the example. The location of the **dominant wavelength** specifies the **hue** of the color, in this case red. In addition, a certain amount of white light is present, represented by the rectangular pedestal that desaturates the light from a pure red toward a light red , making it appear pink.

The total power in the light, known as its **luminance**, is given by the area L under the entire spectrum. Because of the rectangular shapes of the various spectra involved, this calculation is particularly simple: $L = (700 - 400)A + DB$. The **saturation** (or purity) of the light is defined as the percentage of luminance that resides in the dominant component [Billmeyer81]:

$$\text{purity} = \frac{(D - A)B}{L} \times 100\% \tag{11.1}$$

If $D = A$, the purity is 0, and white light is observed without any trace of red. If $A = 0$, no white light is present, and a pure red light is seen. Pastel colors contain a large amount of white and are said to be **unsaturated**. When two colors differ only in hue, the eye can distinguish about 128 different hues. When two colors differ only in saturation, the eye can distinguish about 20 different saturations, depending on the hue.

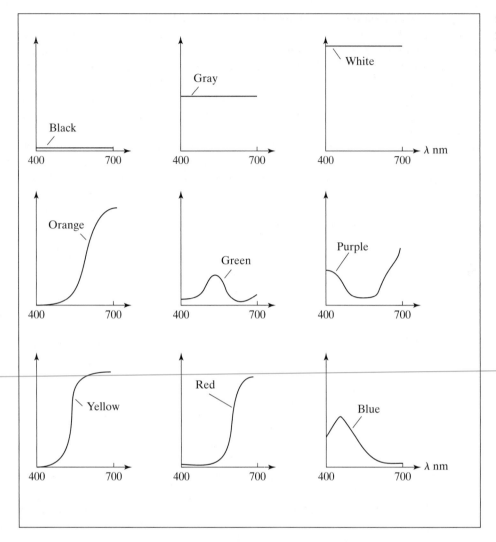

FIGURE 11.3 Example spectra for light and their perceived colors.

(Can you see the numbers?) The small circles are rendered with slightly different colors, cleverly chosen so that a person with normal vision will see numerical patterns in the large circle but a color-blind person will see only a random pattern of circles.

The color-blind person should be particularly careful when crossing streets, where a red traffic light looks the same as a green traffic light! Computer graphics could be perceived as a strange profession for a color-blind person.

11.2 COLOR DESCRIPTION

Nature always wears the colors of the spirit.

Ralph Waldo Emerson
(1803–1882)

Suppose that you want to describe a color precisely over the telephone, where all descriptions must be verbal. Perhaps you need to describe a desired color to a dye manufacturer or to the production manager in a publishing company. It isn't enough to say "a bright robin's egg blue"; you must make sure that the listener receives a

By contrast, the **rods** cannot distinguish colors, nor can they see fine detail. Seventy-five million to 150 million rods are crowded onto the retina surrounding the fovea. Moreover, many rods are attached to a single nerve cell, preventing the discrimination of fine detail [Gonzalez and Wintz87]. So what do rods do? They are very sensitive to low levels of light and can see things in dim light that the cones miss. At night, for instance, it is best to look slightly away from an object so that the image falls outside the fovea. Detail and color are lost, but at least the general form of an object is visible. Indeed, the sensitivity of our peripheral vision to dim light was probably instrumental in our evolution.

Some light sources, such as lasers, emit light of essentially a single wavelength, or "pure spectral" light. We perceive 400-nm light as violet and 620-nm light as red, with the other pure colors lying in between these extremes. Figure 11.2 shows some example **spectral densities** $S(\lambda)$ (power per unit wavelength) for pure lights and the common names given to their perceived colors.

FIGURE 11.2 Spectra for some pure colors.

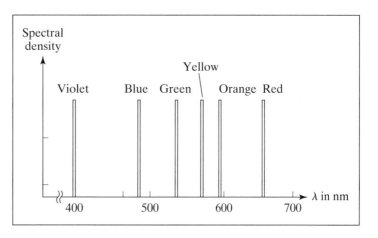

The light from most sources does not consist of only one wavelength; instead, it contains varying amounts of power in a continuous set of wavelengths. Their set of spectral densities (or **spectra**) covers a band of wavelengths. The total power of the light in any band of wavelengths is found as the *area* under the density curve over that band. Figure 11.3 shows several example spectra for lights of familiar colors.

The label for each indicates the color that we perceive when we look at such light. Note that white light contains approximately equal amounts of power at all frequencies, whereas reds tend to have more power concentrated at the longer wavelengths. Gray light also exhibits a "flat" spectral density, but at a lower intensity. These examples highlight one of the difficulties of trying to describe color numerically: *an enormous variety of spectral density functions is perceived by the eye as having the same color.* For example, a given color sample can be matched by many different spectral density shapes, such that the colors of the sample and any of the spectral densities are indistinguishable when placed side by side.

11.1.2 RGB Color Blindness

Some people's visual system cannot distinguish red and green light. Approximately 10% of males and far fewer females are "color-blind" in the sense that they cannot distinguish certain colors from others. Tests have been devised to determine whether a given individual suffers from this lack of perception. Our companion web site illustrates such a test by placing a large number of circles in a large circle.

From the point of view of writing computer graphics applications, we must be able to answer several questions:

- How are colors described accurately in numerical terms?
- How do these descriptions relate to everyday ways of describing color?
- How does one compare colors?
- What range of colors can a CRT display or a printed page exhibit?
- How can color look-up tables be loaded to produce the colors required?
- How do we deal with a range of color when a device can display only, say, 256 colors?

In order to write applications that produce the proper colors we need convenient tools to describe and control color, so much of this chapter will deal with this rather thorny issue.

Light itself is an electromagnetic phenomenon, like television waves, infrared radiation, and x-rays. By light, we mean those waves that lie in a narrow band of **wavelengths**[1] in the so-called *visible spectrum*. Figure 11.1 shows the location of the visible spectrum (for humans) within the entire electromagnetic spectrum, along with the spectra of some other common phenomena. The frequency of vibration f increases to the right, whereas wavelength λ increases to the left.[2] The eye responds to light with wavelengths between approximately 400 and 700 nm (nanometers).

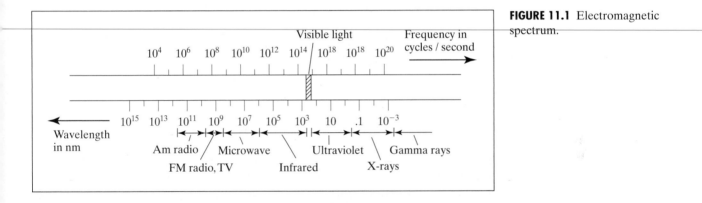

FIGURE 11.1 Electromagnetic spectrum.

11.1.1 The Eye: Physiologic Basis for Human Color Perception

The retina of the eye is its light-sensitive membrane. It lines the posterior portion of the eye's wall and contains two kinds of receptor cells, cones and rods.

The **cones** are the color-sensitive cells, each responding to a particular color, red, green, or blue. According to the tri-stimulus theory (which we examine below), the color we see is the result of our cones' relative responses to red, green, and blue light. The human eye can distinguish about 200 intensities of red, green, and blue, each. Each eye has 6 to 7 million cones, concentrated in a small portion of the retina called the **fovea**. Each cone has its own nerve cell, thereby allowing the eye to discern tiny details. To see an object in detail, the eye looks directly at it in order to bring the image onto the fovea.

---

[1] The wavelength of a wave is the distance light travels during one cycle of its vibration.

[2] Wavelength λ and frequency f are inversely related by $\lambda = v/f$, where v is the speed of light in the medium of interest. In air (or a vacuum) $v = 300,000$ km/sec; in glass it is about 65 percent as fast.

The notions of saturation, luminance, and dominant wavelength are useful for describing colors. However, when presented with a sample color, it is not clear how to measure their values. We shall thus consider some more effective ways to describe color. To get started, we need a way of testing when two colors are the same. This leads to the area of **color matching**, which is the basis for specifying all colors.

11.2.2 Color Perception and Color Matching

Colors are often described by comparing them with a set of standard color samples and finding the closest match. Many such standard sets have been devised and are widely used in the dyeing and printing industries [Munsell41]. One can also try to produce a sample color by matching it to the proper combination of some test lights, as shown in Figure 11.5.

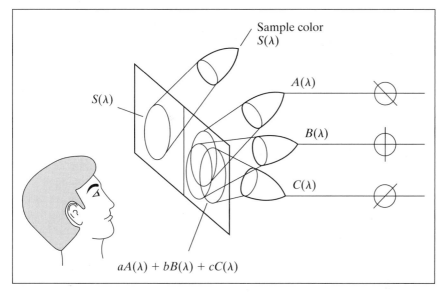

FIGURE 11.5 Color matching using superposition of test lights.

As shown in this figure, the sample color has spectral density we shall call $S(\lambda)$, and it is projected onto one part of a screen. The other part of the screen is bathed in the superposition of three test lights, with spectral densities $A(\lambda)$, $B(\lambda)$, and $C(\lambda)$. The observer adjusts the intensities (a, b, and c) of the test lights until the test color $T(\lambda) = aA(\lambda) + bB(\lambda) + cC(\lambda)$ is indistinguishable from the sample color, even though the two spectra, $S(\lambda)$ and $T(\lambda)$, may be quite different. The temptation is then to say that the sample color consists of a sum of the amounts a, b, and c of the three test colors. In what sense is this meaningful?

Our brains exhibit a remarkable algebra of color superposition [Feynman63]. Suppose that two spectral shapes, $S(\lambda)$ and $P(\lambda)$, have the same (perceived) color, a fact that we denote as $S = P$. Now add a third color, N, to both of these, by superposing light with spectrum $N(\lambda)$ on both. It is an experimental fact that these two new colors will still be indistinguishable!

Along with the symbol =, which means that two colors are indistinguishable, we define the meaning of + for colors so that $S + N$ denotes the color observed when the spectra $S(\lambda)$ and $N(\lambda)$ are added. This experimental fact can then be written as

$$\text{if } (S = P) \qquad \text{then } (N + S = N + P) \tag{11.2}$$

The same goes for *scaling* colors, or scaling their spectral densities or overall brightness: If $S = P$, then $aS = aP$ for any (positive) scalar a. And it is meaningful to write *linear combinations* of two colors, A and B, as in $T = aA + bB$, where a and b are scalars (recall similar operations on vectors in Chapter 4). Thus there is an experimentally verified *vector algebra* of colors, in which we treat colors as vectors, add them, scale them, decompose them into their components, and so forth.

As we mentioned, another remarkable fact of human color perception is that it is *three dimensional*.[3] Any color, C, can be constructed as the superposition of just three primary colors, say R, G, and B:

$$C = rR + gG + bB \qquad (11.3)$$

where r, g, and b are scalars describing the amounts of each of the primaries contained in C. The symbols R, G, and B are suggestive of red, green, and blue, which are often used as the primaries in a discussion. The reason for stressing red, green, and blue originates from the high sensitivity of our cones is to these three colors. But Equation (11.3) works with any choice of primaries, as long as one of them is not just a combination of the other two.

Given a set of three primary colors, R, G, and B, any other color, $C = rR + gG + bB$, can be represented in three-dimensional space by the point (r, g, b). For instance, if R, G, and B correspond to some versions of what we normally call red, green, and blue, then $(0, 1, 0)$ will be perceived as a pure green of unit brightness, and $(.2, .3, .5)$ will be perceived as a yellow. If we double each component, we will obtain a color that is twice as bright but appears as the same color.

Experiments have been run to see how people match colors. Of particular interest is one that combines three specific choices of R, G, and B in order to produce a (perceived) **pure spectral color** of wavelength, which is a totally saturated monochromatic color having its power concentrated at a single wavelength λ. (In dominant-wavelength terms it is 100 percent saturated and has dominant wavelength λ.) Figure 11.6 shows the results of experiments run on a large number of observers. The primaries used were pure monochromatic red, green, and blue lights at wavelengths 700 nm, 546 nm, and 436 nm, respectively. The functions $r(\lambda)$, $g(\lambda)$, and $b(\lambda)$ show how much of these red, green, and blue lights are needed to match the pure spectral color at λ. We shall call this pure spectral color $mono(\lambda)$. So we have:

$$mono(\lambda) = r(\lambda)R + g(\lambda)G + b(\lambda)B \qquad (11.4)$$

FIGURE 11.6 Color matching functions for RGB primaries.

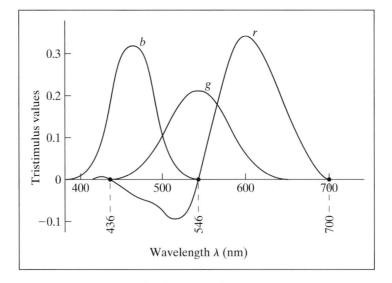

---

[3] Another way of saying this is that any four colors are always linearly related; that is, any one of them can be represented as a combination of the other three.

For example, a pure orange color *mono*(600) looks (to the average observer) identical to the combination $0.37R + .08G$. Obviously the spectrum of the orange light is not the same as the spectrum of this sum, but the two lights look exactly the same.

But there is a rub: for this set of choices of R, G, and B, some of the scalars r, g, and b must be *negative* to make Equation (11.4) correct! For instance, $r(\lambda)$ is negative at $\lambda = 520$. What is the physical meaning of the minus sign in a color such as $C = 0.7R + 0.5G - 0.2B$? One cannot remove light that isn't there. Fortunately this contradiction disappears if we rewrite the equation as $C + 0.2B = 0.7R + 0.5G$. Whereas C alone cannot be constructed as the superpositions of positive amounts of the primaries, the color $C + 0.2B$ can be matched by positive amounts of R and G. This is in fact what happens with any choice of visible primaries R, G, and B. Many colors can be fabricated (using positive coefficients r, g, and b), but some cannot, and one primary must be put on the other side of the equation. Roughly speaking, the problem is that when two colors are added, the result is a less saturated color, and so it is impossible to form a highly saturated color by superposing two others. This is particularly obvious for any of the pure spectral colors, which are themselves saturated.

It's useful to scale the color matching functions so that they add to one, so we define:

$$\bar{r}(\lambda) = \frac{r(\lambda)}{r(\lambda) + g(\lambda) + b(\lambda)}, \bar{g}(\lambda) = \frac{g(\lambda)}{r(\lambda) + g(\lambda) + b(\lambda)}, \bar{b}(\lambda) = \frac{b(\lambda)}{r(\lambda) + g(\lambda) + b(\lambda)}$$

and therefore know that $\bar{r}(\lambda) + \bar{g}(\lambda) + \bar{b}(\lambda) = 1$. These relative weights are called *chromaticity values* for *mono*(λ). They give the amounts of each of the primaries required to match a unit brightness light at λ. Removing variations in brightness allows us to specify colors with only two numbers, say $(\bar{r}(\lambda), \bar{g}(\lambda))$, as we can always determine $\bar{b}(\lambda)$ through $\bar{b}(\lambda) = 1 - \bar{r}(\lambda) - \bar{g}(\lambda)$.

We can plot the position of the 3D point $(\bar{r}(\lambda), \bar{g}(\lambda), \bar{b}(\lambda))$ as λ varies across the visible spectrum, as shown in Figure 11.7. Because of the normalization, all points on this curve lie on the $r + g + b = 1$ plane as shown. Notice that because some coordinates are negative at certain values of λ, the curve does not lie totally inside the positive octant in this space. The CIE standard, to be discussed next, provides a variation of this curve that *does* lie totally inside the positive octant, with all three coordinates everywhere positive.

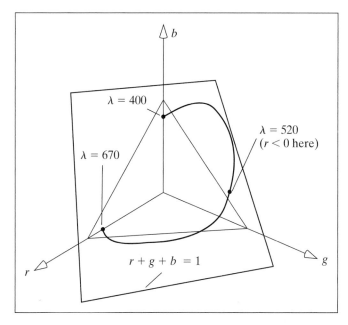

FIGURE 11.7 The pure-spectral-color curve for the RGB primaries.

11.3 THE CIE STANDARD

In our life there is a single color, as on an artist's palette, which provides the meaning of life and art.
It is the color of love.

Marc Chagall
(1887–1985)

How can colors be specified precisely in a way that everyone agrees on? Because color perception is three dimensional, we need only agree on three primaries and describe any color desired by the proper 3-tuple, as in (r, g, b). What primaries are to be used? Unfortunately, all visible primaries require using negative coefficients for at least some visible colors.

To circumvent this awkwardness, a standard was devised in 1931 by the International Commission on Illumination (Commission Internationale de l'éclairage, or CIE). The CIE defined three special supersaturated primaries, X, Y, and Z. The CIE standard is often called the **XYZ model**. The primaries don't correspond to real colors, but they do have the property that *all* real colors can be represented as *positive* combinations of them. They are defined through color matching functions like those in Figure 11.6.

Figure 11.8 shows the color matching functions adopted by the CIE. The notion is the same as Equation (11.4): a monochromatic light at wavelength λ is matched by the specified linear combination of these special primaries:

$$mono(\lambda) = x(\lambda)X + y(\lambda)Y + z(\lambda)Z \tag{11.5}$$

FIGURE 11.8 Color matching functions for primaries X, Y, and Z.

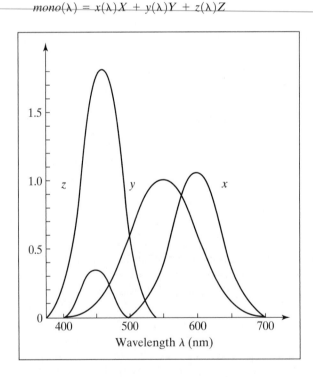

Notice that all three functions are positive at every λ, so $mono(\lambda)$ is always a positive linear combination of the primaries.

How were the X, Y, and Z primaries determined? They were defined by means of an affine transformation applied to color matching functions like $r(\lambda)$, $g(\lambda)$, and $b(\lambda)$ in Equation (11.4); $x(\lambda)$ is a particular linear combination of these shapes, and so are $y(\lambda)$ and $z(\lambda)$. For convenience $y(\lambda)$ was chosen to have the same shape as the **luminous efficiency function**, which is the eye's measured response to monochromatic light of fixed strength at different wavelengths. This causes the amount of the Y primary present in a light to equal the overall intensity of the light.

It's useful to work again with normalized chromaticity values to maintain unit brightness, so we define

$$\overline{x}(\lambda) = \frac{x(\lambda)}{x(\lambda) + y(\lambda) + z(\lambda)}, \overline{y}(\lambda) = \frac{y(\lambda)}{x(\lambda) + y(\lambda) + z(\lambda)}, \overline{z}(\lambda) = \frac{z(\lambda)}{x(\lambda) + y(\lambda) + z(\lambda)}$$

and of course $\overline{z}(\lambda) = 1 - \overline{x}(\lambda) - \overline{y}(\lambda)$. Figure 11.9 shows the parametric $\mathbf{s}(\lambda) = (\overline{x}(\lambda), \overline{y}(\lambda), \overline{z}(\lambda))$, which now lies in the positive octant of the xyz-plane.

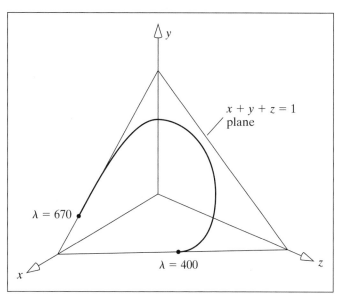

FIGURE 11.9 Building the CIE standard.

The specific nature of the original primaries used, and the details of deriving the transformation, can be found in various references—for example, [Billmeyer81], [Conrac85]. However, you need not know this in order to understand and use the CIE standard.

11.3.1 Constructing the CIE Chart

The spectral color curve $\mathbf{s}(\lambda)$ lies in three-dimensional space, but because it lies on the $x + y + z = 1$ plane, it is easy to represent its shape in a two-dimensional chart that can be printed on a page for reference. Only x and y are needed to specify a (unit intensity) color, because given (x, y) we can find z trivially. (How?)

Thus the standard **CIE Chromaticity Diagram** is the curve $\mathbf{s}'(\lambda) = (\overline{x}(\lambda), \overline{y}(\lambda))$, shown in Figure 11.10.

(Think of viewing the 3D curve of Figure 11.9 in an orthographic projection looking along the z-axis.) The diagram displays the horseshoe-shaped locus of all pure spectral colors, labelled according to wavelength. Inside the horseshoe lie all other visible colors. Points outside the horseshoe region do not correspond to visible light.

Various regions are labelled in the figure with names that people commonly use to describe the colors found there. For example, points near $(0.6, 0.3)$ are perceived as red. Unfortunately, equal distances between points in the chart do not correspond to equal differences in perceived color. For instance, small changes in position in the G region cause only slight changes in perceived color. On the other hand, rather small changes in position in the B or Y regions cause large changes in perceived color.

FIGURE 11.10 The CIE Chromaticity Diagram.

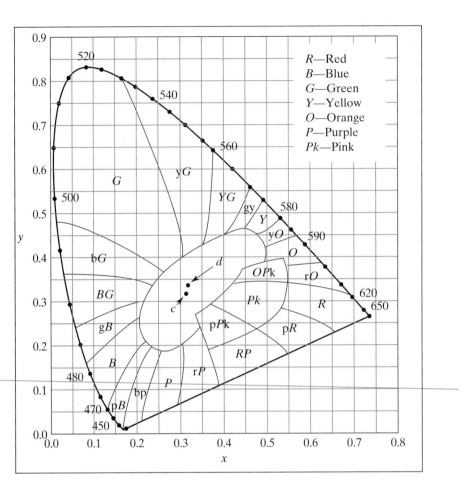

The CIE Chromaticity Diagram defines certain special points. Point c at $(x, y) = (0.310, 0.316)$ is a white color known as **Illuminant C**, which is taken to be the fully un-saturated color. It is often used as the reference color white in aligning some graphics monitors. Illuminant C has the color of an overcast sky at midday. Point d at $(0.313, 0.329)$ is the color that an ideal black-body radiator emits when raised to the "white-hot" temperature of 6504° Kelvin. It is a little greener than Illuminant C. Many other colors, such as those emitted by a tungsten filament light bulb, moonlight, red-hot steel at certain temperatures, and so on have been carefully measured [Conrac85], [Rogers85].

The great value of the CIE Chromaticity Diagram is that it provides a worldwide standard for describing any color. Instruments have been devised that can generate the color represented by any (x, y, z) inside the horseshoe, and so by careful match-ing one can measure the value for any color desired. Instruments also exist that au-tomatically measure (x, y, z) for a given color sample. The chart also permits important calculations to be performed on colors, as we shall see.

Doing It Yourself: Testing Out the Control of Colors

We now describe an application with which you can directly control the individual r, g, and b values of a color with the mouse and see the resulting color. Figure 11.11 shows the color swatch exhibited by this program, along with three sliders which ad-just the r, g, and b levels. It is amusing and instructive to fine-tune the sliders from left to right to vary each color value from 0 to 255.

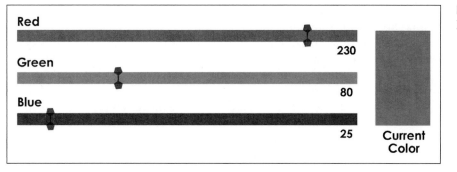

FIGURE 11.11 Color Demonstration.

See Practice Exercise 11.3.1, which requests that you write the entire program in C++ using OpenGL.

11.3.2 Using the CIE Chromaticity Diagram

The CIE chromaticity diagram has many uses. Several of them stem from the ease with which we can interpret straight lines on the chart, as suggested in Figure 11.12.

Consider line l between the two colors a and b. All points on l are convex combinations (recall Chapter 4) of a and b, having the form $(\alpha)a + (1 - \alpha)b$ for $0 \le \alpha \le 1$. Each point is a legitimate color (its x, y, and z components sum to 1—why must they sum to 1?), so we can assert that any color on the straight line (and only these) can be generated by shining various amounts of colors a and b onto a screen.

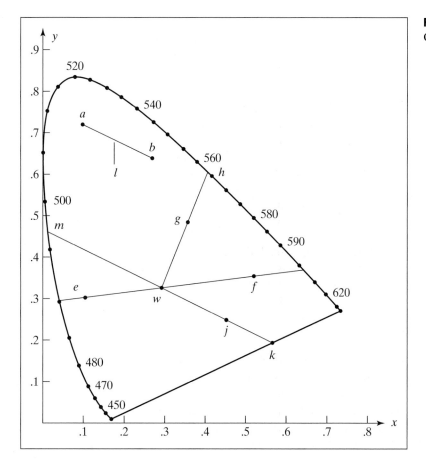

FIGURE 11.12 Uses for the CIE Chromaticity Diagram.

red	⇔	cyan
green	⇔	magenta
blue	⇔	yellow

FIGURE 11.13
Complementary colors.

When two colors are added and their sum turns out to be white, we say that the colors are **complementary** (with respect to the choice of white). Thus in Figure 11.10 *e* (blue-green) and *f* (orange-pink) are seen to be complementary colors with respect to *w*, because proper amounts of them added together form white, *w*. Some familiar pairs of complementary colors, to be discussed further, are listed in Figure 11.13.

The diagram can also be used to measure the dominant wavelength and purity of a given color, such as *g* in the figure. Accordingly, *g* must be the linear combination of some pure spectral color (found on the edge of the horseshoe) and a standard white, *w*. To find which spectral color is involved, just draw a line from *w* through *g* (to *h* here) and measure the wavelength at *h*—in this case 564 nm, a yellowish green. Similarly, the saturation or purity is just the ratio of distances *gw/hw*. The color at *j* has no dominant wavelength, because extending line *wj* hits *k* on the so-called purple line, which does not correspond to a single pure spectral color. (Colors along this line are combinations of red and violet.) In such a case the dominant wavelength is specified by finding the complement of *j* at *m* and using its wavelength with a *c* suffix, 498_c.

11.3.3 Color Gamuts

The CIE diagram is especially useful in defining *color gamut*, the range of colors that can be produced on a device. For instance, a CRT monitor can produce combinations of only the basic red, green, and blue primaries that its three phosphor types can generate. Figure 11.14 shows the locations of phosphor colors *r*, *g*, and *b* for a typical color CRT monitor.

FIGURE 11.14 Gamut for typical CRT monitor.

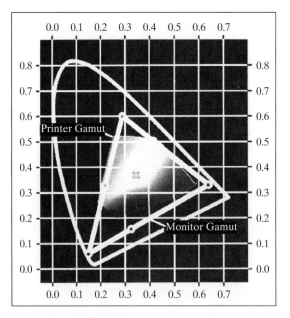

Primary	*x*	*y*
red	.628	.330
green	.258	.590
blue	.1507	.060

FIGURE 11.15 CIE coordinates for typical CRT monitor primaries.

Figure 11.15 shows these positions for a CRT monitor. (see [Stone88]).

The three points define the triangular region shown. Any color within this triangle is a convex combination of the three primaries and can be displayed.[4] Colors outside this triangle are not in the gamut of the display and thus cannot be displayed. White falls within the gamut, reflecting the well-known fact that appropriate amounts of red plus green plus blue yield white.

---

[4] The National Television Standards Committee (NTSC) defines the following standard primaries in CIE co-ordinates: red = (.670, .330), green = (.210, .710), and blue = (.140, .080) [Rogers85].

Also shown is the gamut for a color printing process. Because of the mechanism by which color is placed on paper, colors are not directly additive (see Section 11.4.2), and so the gamut is not a simple triangle. It is somewhat smaller than the gamut for a CRT monitor, and so some colors that can be reproduced on this monitor cannot be displayed by a printer. On the other hand, some points that the printer gamut can reach lie outside the monitor gamut. Therefore, some colors can be printed but not observed on the CRT monitor.

Note that for any choice of three primaries, even the pure spectral colors on the horseshoe edge, a triangular gamut can never encompass all visible colors, because the horseshoe bulges outside any triangle whose vertices are within it. Red, green, and blue are natural choices for primaries, as they lie far apart in the CIE chart and therefore produce a gamut that covers a large part of the chart's area. If yellow, cyan, and magenta were used as primaries, for instance, the gamut would be much smaller. (Could white still be produced?)

PRACTICE EXERCISE

11.3.1 Controlling the color swatch

Using Figure 11.11 as your guide, develop a program in C++ and OpenGL which allows the user to adjust the values of r, g, and b in the sample color swatch.

11.3.2 Why red, green, and blue?

Provide physical and philosophical arguments why the cones in our eyes have peak sensitivities to red, green, and blue lights.   ▪

11.4 COLOR SPACES

> There is no blue without yellow and without orange.
>
> *Vincent Van Gogh*
> *(1853–1890)*

The CIE's specification of color is precise and standard, but it is not necessarily the most natural. In computer graphics, particularly, it is most natural to think of combining red, green, and blue to form the colors desired. Other people are more comfortable thinking in terms of hue, saturation, and lightness, and artists frequently refer to tints, shades, and tones to describe color. These all are examples of **color models**, choices of three *descriptors* used to describe colors. If one can quantify the three descriptors, one can then describe a color by means of a 3-tuple of values, such as (tint, shade, tone) = (.125, 1.68, .045). This establishes a 3D coordinate system in which to describe color. The different choices of coordinates then give rise to different **color spaces**, and we need ways to convert color descriptions from one color space to another.

11.4.1 The RGB Color Spaces

The RGB (short for red, green, blue) color model describes colors as positive combinations of three appropriately defined red, green, and blue primaries, as in Equation (11.3). If the scalars r, g, and b are confined to values between 0 and 1, all definable colors will lie in the cube shown in Figure 11.16.

Unlike the CIE diagram, there is no normalization for the intensity of the color here. Points close to $(0, 0, 0)$ are dark, and those farther out are lighter. For example, $(1, 1, 1)$ corresponds to pure white. This color space is the most natural for computer graphics, in which a color specification such as (.3, .56, .9) can be directly translated

FIGURE 11.16 The RGB color cube.

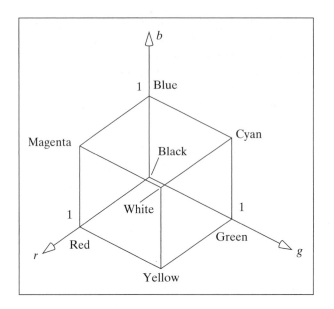

into values stored in a color look-up table. Note that the corner marked magenta properly signifies that red light plus blue light produces magenta light, and similarly for yellow and cyan. Colors at diagonally opposite corners are complementary.

When normalized to unit intensity, all of the colors that can be defined here will of, course, lie in the CIE Chromaticity Diagram, once suitable positions of red, green, and blue have been provided. (What shape is the gamut?) It is not hard to convert a color specified in CIE coordinates (x, y, z) into (r, g, b) space, and vice versa. Because the R, G, B primaries are linear combinations of the X, Y, and Z CIE primaries, a linear transformation suffices. The mapping depends on the definition of the primaries R, G, and B and on the definition of white. For the primaries given in Figure 11.14 and the white given by point d in Figure 11.10, the transformation is as follows (see [Rogers85] for the details):

$$(r, g, b) = (x, y, z) \begin{pmatrix} 2.739 & -1.110 & .138 \\ -1.145 & 2.029 & -.333 \\ -.424 & .033 & 1.105 \end{pmatrix} \tag{11.6}$$

The conversion from RGB to XYZ, of course, uses the inverse of this matrix.

PRACTICE EXERCISES

11.4.1 Converting from RGB to CIE space

Find the inverse of the preceding matrix to provide the transformation from RGB coordinates to CIE space. An important property of CIE space is that all colors can be expressed as positive linear combinations of the X, Y, and Z primaries. What property does this impose on the inverse matrix? Does the inverse you calculate satisfy this condition?

11.4.2 Derive the ingredients

Derive the ingredients in the matrix of Equation (11.6) and find its inverse.   ■

11.4.2 The Additive and Subtractive Color Systems

So far we have considered summing contributions of colored light to form new colors, an *additive* process. An **additive color system** expresses a color, D, as the sum of certain amounts of primaries, usually red, green, and blue: $D = (r, g, b)$. An additive system can use any three primaries, but because red, green, and blue are situated far apart in the CIE chart, they provide a large gamut.

Subtractive color systems are used when it is natural to think in terms of removing colors. When light is reflected (diffusely) from a surface or is transmitted through a partially transparent medium (as when photographic filters are used), certain colors are absorbed by the material and thus removed. This is a *subtractive* process.

A **subtractive color system** expresses a color, D, by means of a 3-tuple, just as an additive system does, but each of the three values specifies how much of a certain color (the complement of the corresponding primary) to *remove* from white in order to produce D. To clarify this, consider the most common subtractive system, the CMY system, which uses the subtractive primaries cyan, magenta, and yellow. If we say that $D = (c, m, y)_{CMY}$, we are saying that D is formed from white by subtracting amount c of the complement of cyan (i.e., red), amount m of the complement of magenta (green), and amount y of the complement of yellow (blue). Thus we immediately have the following relationship between the RGB and CMY systems:

$$(r, g, b)_{RGB} = (1, 1, 1) - (c, m, y)_{CMY} \tag{11.7}$$

That is, the amount of blue b in a color is reduced by increasing y, as y specifies the amount of yellow's complement to remove from white.

Figure 11.17 illustrates this. The three glass slides are described in the CMY system by $(.4, .5, .2)_{CMY}$. When white light, given by $(1, 1, 1)_{RGB}$ in the RGB additive system, penetrates the cyan-colored slide, 40 percent of the red component is absorbed, and a "cyanish" light containing $(.6, 1, 1)_{RGB}$ emerges. When this light penetrates the magenta slide, 50 percent of the green light is removed, and the color $(.6, .5, 1)_{RGB}$ emerges. (What color is it now?) Finally, this light penetrates the yellow slide, and 20 percent of the blue component is absorbed, and the color $(.6, .5, .8)_{RGB}$ emerges.

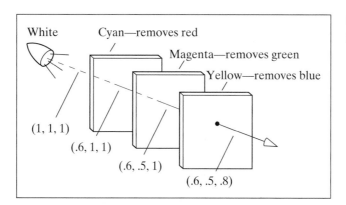

FIGURE 11.17 The subtractive process.

A similar description applies to light scattering from a colored surface. In a three-color printing process, for instance, cyan, magenta, and yellow pigments are suspended in a colorless paint. Each subtracts a portion of the complement component of its incident light. For example, if magenta particles are mixed into a colorless paint, the particles will subtract the green portion of the white light and reflect only the red and blue components. The subtractive system is used for color hard-copy devices to fashion colors by mixing the three CMY primaries.

Figure 11.18 shows the additive and subtractive primaries and their interaction. In part a, red, green, and blue beams of light shine on a white surface. Where the two beams overlap, their lights combine to form a new color. For instance, red and green add to form yellow light. Where all three overlap, white light is formed.

FIGURE 11.18 Additive and subtractive color systems.

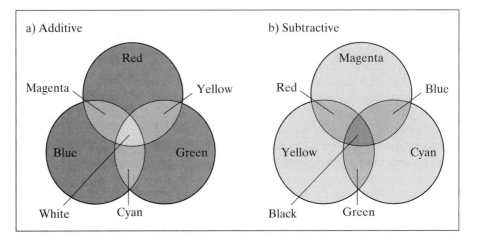

a) Additive

Red
Magenta
Yellow
Blue
Green
White   Cyan

b) Subtractive

Magenta
Red
Blue
Yellow
Cyan
Black   Green

Part b of Figure 11.18 shows a different situation. Each circle is formed by laying down ink in the color shown. Be sure to view it in white light. One disk appears yellow because its pigment subtracts the complement (blue) from the incident white light. When the yellow and cyan pigments are blended, one sees green, as both the blue and the red components have been removed. The center is black because all the components have been removed.

11.4.3 The HLS Color Model

A more intuitive color model uses coordinates hue (H), lightness (L), and saturation (S) to describe colors, because these are qualities that the human eye easily recognizes and can distinguish. The model arises from a distortion of the RGB cube into a double cone, as shown in Figure 11.19.

FIGURE 11.19 Warping the RGB system to the HLS system.

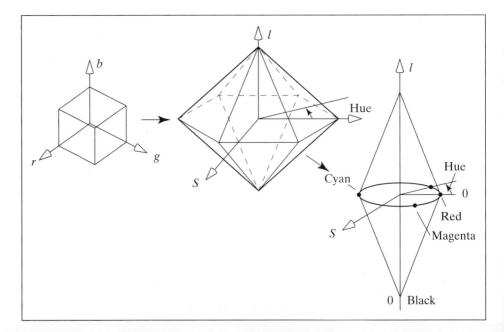

By looking along the diagonal from $(1, 1, 1)$ to $(0, 0, 0)$ of the RGB cube, we see that the six principal hues (R, G, B, and their three complements) lie on the vertices of a hexagon. Thus hue can be associated with an angle between 0 and 360 degrees. Convention puts 0 degrees at red. Lightness varies from 0, when all the RGB components are 0 to 1, when they all are 1. This corresponds nicely to the distance along the diagonal of the RGB cube from black to white. Saturation, which is roughly the distance a color lies away from the diagonal of the RGB cube, is mapped into radial distance from the lightness axis of the HLS cones.

The HLS color space is based on a distortion of the RGB space, leading us to seek an algorithm that maps from one system to the other. The distortion is quite complex, and so we don't insist on an exact geometric transformation. The principal algorithm converting from RGB into HLS coordinates pays the most attention to the largest and smallest of the R, G, and B components, but it provides a useful conversion and is invertible.

PRACTICE EXERCISES

11.4.3 Perform some conversions

Find (H, L, S) for each of the following cases, and explain why the result is reasonable.

$(r, g, b) = (.2, .8, .1)$
$(r, g, b) = (0, 0, .8)$
$(r, g, b) = (1, 1, 1)$
$(r, g, b) = (0, .7, .7)$

11.4.4 HLS-to-RGB conversion

Work out an algorithm, $HLS\_to\_RGB(\ )$, that converts from HLS into RGB coordinates. It should provide an inverse transformation to the RGB-to-HLS conversion that we discussed, in that it recovers the original R, G, B values when applied to the H, L, S values.

11.4.5 The HSV color model

Another color model, the hue (H), saturation (S), and value (V) system, is also based on a warped version of the RGB cube but is a single cone rather than a double cone, as suggested in Figure 11.20. In this model, the hue is again mapped to angle, with the hexagon distorted into a circle, as in the HLS system, and the saturation having the same interpretation as with the HLS system. The light's intensity is captured in the value V, which varies from 0 to 1, as shown. Develop an algorithm that converts from RGB into HSV coordinates. ■

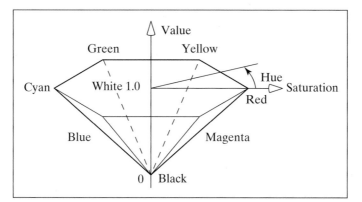

FIGURE 11.20 The HSV color model.

11.5 INDEXED COLOR AND THE LUT

Some systems are built using an alternative method of associating pixel values with colors. They use a **color look-up table** (or **LUT)**, which offers a *programmable* association between pixel value and final color. Figure 11.21 shows a simple example. The color depth is again six, but the six bits stored in each pixel go through an intermediate step before they drive the CRT. They are used as an *index* into a table of 64 values, say LUT[0]...LUT[63]. (Why are there exactly 64 entries in this LUT?) For instance, if a pixel value is 39, the values stored in LUT[39] are used to drive the DACs, as opposed to having the bits in the value 39 itself drive them. As shown, LUT[39] contains the 15-bit value 01010 11001 10010. Five of these bits (01010) are routed to drive the "red DAC," five others drive the "green DAC," and the last five drive the "blue DAC."

FIGURE 11.21 A color display system that incorporates a LUT.

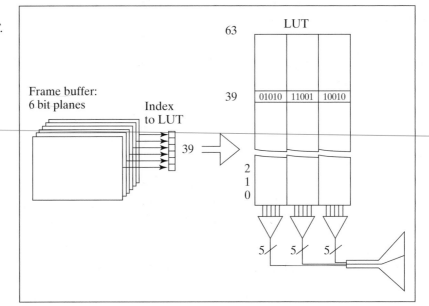

Each of the LUT[ ] entries can be set under program control, using some system routine such as setPalette(). For example, the instruction:

```
setPalette(39, 17, 25, 4);
```

would set the value in LUT[39] to the 15-bit quantity 10001 11001 00100 (since 17 is 10001 in binary, 25 is 11001, and 4 is 00100).

To make a particular pixel glow in this color, say the pixel at location $(x, y) = (479, 532)$, the value 39 is stored in the frame buffer, using drawDot() defined earlier:

```
drawDot(479, 532, 39);   // set pixel at (479, 532) to value 39
```

Each time the frame buffer is "scanned out" to the display, this pixel is read as value 39, which causes the value stored in LUT[39] to be sent to the DACs.

This programmability offers a great deal of flexibility in choosing colors, but of course it comes at a price: the program (or programmer) has to figure out which colors to use!

What is the potential of this system for displaying colors? In the system each entry of the LUT consists of 15 bits, so each color can be set to one of $2^{15} = 32$ K = 32,768 possible colors. The set of 2^{15} possible colors displayable by the system is called its **palette**, so we say this display "has a palette of 32K colors."

The problem is that each pixel value lies in the range $0\ldots63$, and only 64 different colors can be stored in the LUT at one time. Therefore this system can display a maximum of 64 different colors *at one time*. "At one time" here means during one scan-out of the entire frame buffer—something like a sixtieth of a second. The contents of the LUT are not changed in the middle of a scan-out of the image, so one whole scan-out uses a fixed set of 64 palette colors. Usually the LUT contents remain fixed for many scan-outs, although a program can change the contents of a small LUT during the brief dormant period between two successive scan-outs.

In more general terms, suppose that a raster display system has a color depth of b bits (so there are b bit planes in its frame buffer), and that each LUT entry is w bits wide. Then we have a system that can display 2^w colors, any 2^b at one time.

■ EXAMPLES

1. A system with $b = 8$ bit planes and a LUT width $w = 12$ can display 4096 colors, any 256 of them at a time.
2. A system with $b = 8$ bit planes and a LUT width $w = 24$ can display $2^{24} = 16{,}777{,}216$ colors, any 256 at a time.
3. If $b = 12$ and $w = 18$, the system can display $256\text{K} = 262{,}144$ colors, $2^{12} = 4096$ at a time.

There is no enforced relationship between the number of bit planes, b, and the width of the LUT, w. Normally w is a multiple of 3, so the same number of bits ($w/3$) drives each of the three DACs. Also, b never exceeds w, so the palette is at least as large as the number of colors that can be displayed at one time. (Why would you never design a system with $w < b$?)

Note that the LUT itself requires very little memory, only 2^b words of w bits each. For example, if $b = 12$ and $w = 18$, there are only 9,216 bytes of storage in the LUT.

So what is the motivation for having a LUT in a raster display system? It is usually a need to reduce the cost of memory. Increasing b increases significantly the amount of memory needed for the frame buffer, mainly because there are so many pixels. The tremendous amount of memory needed can add significantly to the cost of the overall system.

11.6 COLOR QUANTIZATION

> Life is like a rainbow. You need both the sun and the rain to make its colors appear.
>
> *Anonymous*

When rendering a scene, an enormous number of floating-point color triples (I_r, I_g, I_b) are generated, one for each pixel in the image. Chapter 9 discussed strategies for converting such color triples to binary values that can be sent to a display or placed in a file for later use. A common approach is to convert each floating-point value to a single byte, so the image is represented by true-color pixel values, with 24 bits/pixel. It is also common for scanners to produce true-color image files when digitizing a photograph.

But two problems must be dealt with.

- Some devices (such as PDAs or GPS systems) can't handle 24-bit colors. Plummeting memory costs ensure that displays for general workstations have sufficient color resolution, although many devices have limits to color resolution. They might be built to handle only 5 bits each for red, green, and blue, or they might be built with a look-up table that has only 256 entries (the example of an airport or supermarket kiosk comes to mind), where each entry allows, say, 6 bits each for red, green, and blue.

- True-color images can be very large, requiring large amounts of disk space, or taking inordinate amounts of time to transmit over a network.

We therefore need methods for reducing the size of color images and for reducing the number of colors contained in them. For instance, we need a way of choosing the *best* 256 colors found in a true-color image, and replacing all the other colors in the image with *good* substitutes from this list of 256. This process is commonly known as **color quantization**.

The Problem

Given N color triples, find K colors that do the best job of representing the original colors. (Normally K is much smaller than N.) For each original color find the closest *representative*. If desired, replace the original color triple by the index $0, 1, \ldots, K - 1$ of its best representative.

There are many questions to be answered, such as what *best* and *good* mean here. Also, since N is so large, any worthwhile algorithm must be efficient.

We look at four different methods for reducing the colors in an image. In each case we assume that the image is stored in a file of RGB color triples[5]—either floating-point triples or byte triples.

A useful first preprocessing step is sometimes used. The 3-tuple file is scanned to determine the range of pixel 3-tuples residing in the image. In particular the scan looks for the extreme values for each of the three color components: r_{min} and r_{max} for the r component, g_{min} and g_{max} for the green, and so forth. These values define a parallelepiped in RGB-space, as suggested by Figure 11.22. The entire **color population** resides within this block.

FIGURE 11.22 A color population residing in a color block.

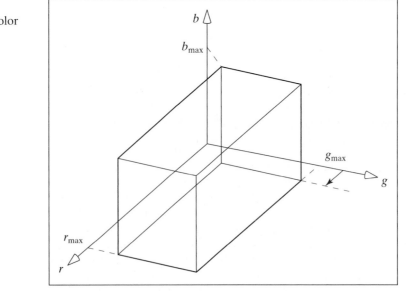

---

5   Alternatively it might improve things to convert the RGB colors into some other system, such as HSV or CIE, and then to quantize values in this new system.

Think of a large number of dots, each representing a color, scattered in different regions of the block. Some colors may be repeated many times; others might lie in tight clusters; still others might be loners, with no neighbors over a significant portion of the block. Questions abound: If many dots lie in a compact region, should we replace them all by a color near the center of the cluster? If a color occurs many times, but has no nearby neighbors, should we attempt to represent it with high precision?

11.6.1 Uniform Quantization

The simplest approach is to subdivide the color block along color axes into a number of nonoverlapping subblocks and to choose as the representative of each subblock a color value near its center.

How should the color block be subdivided? Here we describe only the simplest approach. The block is subdivided by slicing it along each of the three axes, as shown in Figure 11.23. This allows the red, green, and blue components of the color representatives to be chosen independently. For instance, if $K = 256$, the red range $r_{min}, \ldots, r_{max}$ might be divided into 8 slices, the green into 8, and the blue into 4, creating exactly 256 subblocks. Alternatively, we might break both the red and blue into 6 slices and the green into 7 slices, to produce a total of 252 subregions. (If a LUT is being loaded, four entries could go unused, or they could be loaded with colors for some border or text annotation.)

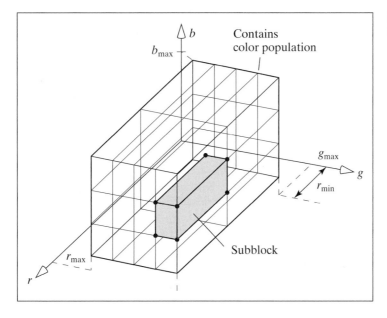

FIGURE 11.23 Slicing the color block.

An equally important consideration is where to locate the color representatives, which are digital values that must fit in the LUT entries. For instance, suppose there are 4 bits in each entry for the green value, permitting green intensities from 0 to 15 (0000 to 1111 in binary). If we decide on six slices for green, which six values between 0 and 15 should we select? Note that the actual green brightness that corresponds to level 15 can be set independently on most raster displays by adjusting a control knob in its front panel. For such terminals, only the relative intensities must be encoded. An example will help clarify how the various ingredients interact.

■ **EXAMPLE 11.6.1**

Consider a typical case in which the LUT has $K = 256$ entries, each of which contains 4 bits for each of the red, green, and blue intensities. The 3-tuple image file is scanned, and it is found that r_{min}, g_{min}, and b_{min} all are very close to 0 and that $r_{max} = 4.0$, $g_{max} = 7.0$, and $b_{max} = 3.0$. How can we map 3-tuples into LUT values?

We decide to use 7 representatives for green and 6 each for red and blue. We also choose, for simplicity, to space the representative values as evenly as possible over the 16 possible LUT values. For the red and blue colors, the 6 values 0, 3, 6, 9, 12, 15 do a fine job. For green, we can't achieve an equal spacing, but 0, 3, 5, 8, 11, 13, 15 provide a reasonable choice.

Now how are these values stored in LUT entries? An array int r[6] is created to store the 6 red values, and similarly for the arrays g[] and b[]. For instance, r[] holds the 6 values 0, 3, 6, 9, 12, and 15. As shown next, three embedded loops cycle through all combinations of the values stored in these arrays, and for each combination a single 12-bit number is created and stored in the LUT[ ] array:

FIGURE 11.24 Loading the LUT.

```
#define numRed 6
#define numGreen 7
#define numBlue 6
#define pack(r,g,b) (256 * (r)+ 16 * (g) + (b))

for(rd = 0; rd < numRed; rd++)
  for(grn = 0; grn < numGreen; grn++)
    for(blu = 0; blu < numBlue; blu++)
    {
        index = numRed * numGreen * rd + numBlue * grn + blu;
        LUT[index] = pack(r[rd],g[grn],b[blu]);
    }
```

The macro pack multiplies the red value by 256 to shift it into the upper 4 most significant bits of the LUT entry. It shifts the green value similarly. For instance, when rd, grn, and blu are 3, 2, and 5, respectively, the index into the LUT is 133, and the value composed from r[3] = 9, g[2] = 5, and b[5] = 15 is 2399, which in hexadecimal is 95*f*, as desired.

Now when the 3-tuple pixel list, (r_i, g_i, b_i), for the image file is rescanned, each r_i is compared with the 6 red representatives, and the nearest one is identified: Find *j_r* such that r_i is closest to $r[j\_r]$. For instance, if $r_i = 8.23$, the closest value will be 9, and so *j r* = 3. Do the same to identify index values *j_g* and *j_b*. Then compute the index value into the LUT itself as $j = 42*j\_r + 6*j\_g + j\_b$.

This uniform quantization approach is rather hapless; it takes no account of the color population, and learns nothing from scanning the original file of colors (except for the values of r_{max}, g_{max}, and b_{max}). It can work adequately for some images, however, particularly if the number of bits per pixel is large and the LUT offers a large palette.

Figure 11.25 shows an original image, and Figure 11.26 shows the result of uniform quantization (color versions of these images are available on the book's companion web site). Notice large amounts of **banding** in regions of the image where there is a color gradient (a smooth variation of color across the image): many slightly different color neighbors are replaced by a single representative, leading to regions of a fixed color when there should be a smooth variation in color.

FIGURE 11.25 The original image of the authors of this book.

FIGURE 11.26 The authors in an image after uniform quantization to 256 colors. (A color version is available online.)

PRACTICE EXERCISE

11.6.1 Trying out some values

For Example 11.5.1, show the first 20 entries of the LUT. Does this seem like an orderly arrangement? What is stored in LUT[29]? What about LUT[231]? ■

11.6.2 The Popularity Algorithm

The popularity algorithm [Heckbert82] at least tries to determine which colors occur often in the file. It gives them greater priority, even if many of the most popular colors lie very close together.

The basic method is to form a list of the number of times each color occurs in the file, and to sort this list. Then the first K colors in the sorted list are the K most popularly occurring colors.

Because there are so many possible values for a true-color 3-byte value (2^{32} of them), the problem is simplified by first truncating each red, green, and blue byte to

5 bits, leaving $2^{15} = 32K$ possible color values. An array of length 32K is allocated and its elements are set to 0. The file is scanned, and as each color is read, the corresponding element in the array is incremented. When all N color values have been read, the array is sorted, and the K most frequent colors are accepted as the color representatives.

Now when the file is rescanned, each color encountered must be replaced by the closest representative $(r, g, b)[i]$ in the popularity list. Minimum mean-squared distance is often taken as a measure of "closest":

> **Find *i* for which $(rd - r[i])^2 + (grn - g[i])^2 + (blu - b[i])^2$ is the smallest**

This can be an expensive operation.

11.6.3 The Median Cut Algorithm

The median cut algorithm was introduced by Heckbert [Heckbert82]. It subdivides the color block into K subblocks, each having approximately the same number of color dots. Figure 11.27 shows the basic process in 2D for clarity. (Suppose colors have only a red and a green component.) In Figure 11.27a the original color cube is first subdivided along its longest dimension: the *median* value r_1 is found such that $N/2$ dots occur in one subblock, and $N/2$ in the other. Then each of these subblocks is processed similarly—sliced at the median along its longest dimension. This process continues until there are K subblocks. The color representative for each subblock is taken as the center of the subblock. Figure 11.27b shows example subblocks after nine cuts have been made.

FIGURE 11.27 The median cut process at work (for 2D colors).

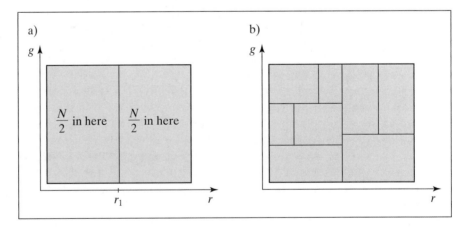

One simple way to organize the process is to use a queue of subblocks. An appropriate data structure is defined that holds the dimensions of the block and a pointer to the list of colors it contains. At each stage one subblock is dequeued, and split at the median of the longest dimension into two subblocks. Each of these is then enqueued for later processing.

At this juncture we have K subblocks, which can be numbered $0, 1, \ldots, K - 1$. Now the file is read again and each color is tested to see which subblock it lies within. Heckbert [Heckbert82] suggests efficient ways to do this.

Figure 11.28 shows the same image as Figure 11.25, after the median cut algorithm has been used to reduce the number of colors to 256. (Again, the color versions are on line.) There is still some banding visible.

FIGURE 11.28 The image after quantization to 256 colors by the median cut algorithm. (A color version is available online.)

11.6.4 Octree Quantization

Gervautz [Gervautz90] suggested an efficient method based on an octree (a tree data structure where each node has up to eight children) for reducing to K the number of colors in a file. In essence it reads the color file and builds an octree of colors, representing colors perfectly until K different colors have been encountered. Then as each additional new color is read, it is added to the octree, but the octree is then "reduced" so it again contains no more than K different colors. The reduction process forces certain colors to be "lumped together" (into their color representative) and thus replaces colors by some nearby approximation. When all N colors in the file have been read, the octree contains K (or slightly fewer) color representatives. The octree is traversed and an index is assigned to each color representative.

The file is then read again, and as each color is encountered, it is inserted back into the tree and quickly finds its place, either at its perfect representation at the bottom of the tree, or at some intermediate node where its best color representative resides. The index of this node is then returned, denoting which color this is.

It is interesting to see how the octree structure is exploited to make this process efficient without excessive demands for memory. Figure 11.29 shows a portion of the octree: each node contains some information about the colors that have been added to the octree, and eight pointers to its children.

When a color is inserted into the tree, its existence is recorded by "growing" a path down to level eight. Figure 11.30 shows a specific example, where the R, G, and B bytes are displayed (in binary notation). Examine individual bits of the (R, G, B) triple, starting at the most significant bit each of R, G, and B, here given by 101. This represents five in binary, so the path follows child #5. If child #5 is so far empty, a new node is created and attached. The process then repeats with the next most significant bit triple (011), so the path looks at child #3. After five more iterations the least significant bits (110) of the color are examined, and the path follows child #6. If a leaf node is present there (because this color has been encountered before in the file), the number of colors (which is one of the fields of a node) is incremented. Otherwise a leaf node is created, with a color count of 1. Note that the depth of the octree never exceeds eight, and inserting a color is fast: it requires no more than eight calculations of a child index.

FIGURE 11.29 The octree containing four colors.

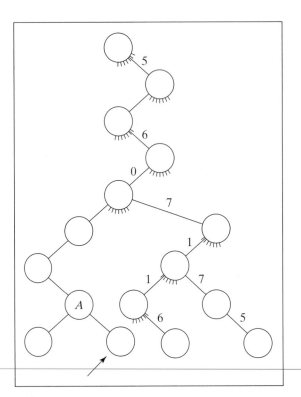

FIGURE 11.30 An example path from the root to the color's leaf.

$R =$	1	0	1	0	1	0	0	1
$G =$	0	1	1	0	1	0	0	1
$B =$	1	1	0	0	1	1	1	0
Child:	5	3	6	0	7	1	1	6

Each node at depth 8 represents a color perfectly (to 8 bits of precision), whereas interior nodes represent subblocks of colors. For instance, a node at level 3 represents all colors having a specific set of three most significant bits for R, G, and B, but arbitrary succeeding bits.

When the octree contains more than K colors, it is reduced. A "reducible" node (one with at least two children) is found at the lowest level possible. (The node marked A in Figure 11.29 is a reducible node.) To reduce the octree, the children of the reducible node are deleted (which releases storage for use by future nodes), and the node is marked as a leaf. It already contains summary information about the color occurrences that resided in its children. Each reduction reduces the total number of different colors in the octree by one less than the number of children deleted. Now additional colors can be inserted into the octree.

As described more fully in Case Study 11.7, each node keeps track of certain information, which includes:

```
long numTimes;              // # colors seen in this sub-block
long rSum, gSum, bSum;      // sum of color values accumulated
int isLeaf;                 // 1 if this node is a leaf
```

As each color (R, G, B) is inserted in the octree, every node in its path gets updated information:

```
numTimes++;      // encountered another color in this sub-block
rSum += R;       // total amount of red encountered
gSum += G;
bSum += B;
```

Therefore when a node is reduced (its children are deleted), it already contains the required information about everything that happened in the subtree below it. Later when the tree is scanned to associate an index with each leaf, the color representative of the leaf is simply the average color:

$$\text{color representative} = \left(\frac{rSum}{numTimes}, \frac{gSum}{numTimes}, \frac{bSum}{numTimes} \right)$$

Finally, when the N colors are read from the file a second time, each color is traced down its path until it finds a leaf, and the index is retrieved. Since each path is no longer than 8 nodes, this process is fast.

Gervautz and Purgathofer provide some opinions and estimates of the computer resources required for each method. They claim that the octree method produces results that are comparable in quality to those formed using the median cut algorithm, but at much less cost in processing time and memory.

Figure 11.31 shows the same image as Figure 11.25, after the octree quantization method has been used to reduce the number of colors to 256. There is still some banding visible, but the reproduction of color is noticeably superior to that in Figure 11.26.

FIGURE 11.31 The image after quantization to 256 colors by the octree quantization method.

11.7 SUMMARY

The eye–brain system perceives colors in a complex way. The color of a light may be specified precisely according to its spectral density function, but this is an inconvenient format for communicating color information. In addition the same perceived color can arise from myriad different spectral densities. In fact, our perception of color is three dimensional, and so we need methods for describing color through a 3-tuple of numbers.

The CIE standard provides a precise approach to specifying colors. Any color, S, of unit brightness is described by two numbers, (x, y). The notion is that S is created by adding the proper amounts of three special primary lights, X, Y, and Z, as defined by the standard.

Specifically, $S = xX + yY + (1 - x - y)Z$. The special primaries—which are supersaturated and cannot actually be seen—are chosen so that any pure spectral color (based on a single wavelength of light) can be formed using positive amounts of x and y. The CIE Chromaticity Diagram provides a useful worldwide standard for describing colors and calculating the ingredients of a given color. It is also used to display the gamut of colors that can be formed by adding together various amounts of available primaries.

Some methods convert the colors described in one color system into those of another system, so that one can convert from CIE coordinates into more familiar RGB coordinates and vice versa. Other color spaces are commonly used as well, such as hue, saturation, and lightness.

When computing colored images (based, for instance, on an illuminated 3D scene), the range of colors that the renderer produces is not known until rendering is finished, so it is difficult to display an image while rendering is underway. A good approach is to file all of the pixel 3-tuples as they are calculated, and then to scan this file to determine the color population of the image. Once the color population is known, one can set up appropriate mappings between color 3-tuples and values that a display device can handle. This may involve choosing a set of colors to load into a LUT. Because some devices can display only a limited number of colors, it is often necessary to reduce the number of colors found in an image. Several methods for color quantization have been developed. They vary in the difficulty of implementing them in a program, their computational efficiency, and the quality of the final image they can produce.

11.8 CASE STUDIES

CASE STUDY 11.1 DRAWING RGB SPACE

(Level of Effort: II) Write a program that displays a "slice" through the RGB color cube of Figure 11.16. Points on the slice are shown in their proper color. Arrange so the user can choose the slicing plane with the keyboard (i.e., choose the constants a, b, c, and d of the plane $aR + bG + cB = d$).

CASE STUDY 11.2 HSV TO RGB

(Level of Effort: II) Write a program that presents a GLUI menu, including the spinner input device from Chapter 2, and allows the user to choose values for H, S, and V. The values are selected with the mouse, and the program displays the corresponding RGB representations for the specific color in a properly colored rectangle.

CASE STUDY 11.3 UNIFORM COLOR QUANTIZATION

(Level of Effort: III) Write a program that lets you experiment with uniform color quantization. An image is read in from a file and two versions are displayed side by side on the screen: the full color on the left and the quantized version on the right. The user chooses the allowed number of red, green, and blue values (e.g., 8, 7, and 4, respectively), and the program computes the quantized colors and recalculates the image to be displayed.

CASE STUDY 11.4 POPULARITY COLOR QUANTIZATION

(Level of Effort: III) Write a program that lets you experiment with the popularity color quantization method. A true-color image is read in from a file. The user then chooses the allowed number K of different colors. The program scans the image, quantizing RGB triples to 15 bits, computes the histogram of color values, sorts the array, and uses the most popular K values. The image is then rescanned, and for each pixel the best match of the K representatives is displayed. Two versions of the image are displayed side by side on the screen: the full color on the left and the quantized version on the right.

CASE STUDY 11.5 MEDIAN CUT COLOR QUANTIZATION

(Level of Effort: III) Write a program that lets you experiment with the median cut color quantization algorithm. Obtain code that performs the algorithm either from the Internet or from a book such as [Lindley92]. A true-color image is read in from a file. The user then chooses the allowed number K of different colors. The program scans the image and finds the K representatives determined by the median cut method. The image is then rescanned, and for each pixel the best match of the K representatives is displayed. Two versions are displayed side by side on the screen: the full color on the left and the quantized version on the right.

CASE STUDY 11.6 OCTREE COLOR QUANTIZATION

(Level of Effort: III) Write a program that lets you experiment with the octree color quantization algorithm. Either write the algorithm yourself, or obtain code exactly as you did in the previous case study. A true-color image is read in from a file. The user then chooses the allowed number K of different colors. The program scans the image, builds the octree with K representatives, and then traverses the octree to attach an index to each leaf. The image is then rescanned, and for each pixel the appropriate index is found in the octree and that color is displayed. Two versions are displayed side by side on the screen: the full color on the left and the quantized version on the right.

A useful data type for an octree node is:

```
class Node{
  public:
    int isLeaf;            // 1 if this node is a leaf
    int whichLevel;        // the level this node is at
    int index;             // its LUT index - assigned in pass 1
    int numChildren;       // number of children this node has
    long numTimes;         // # colors seen in this sub-block
    long Rsum, Gsum, BSum; // sum of color values accumulated
    Node* nextCand; // candidate for reducing at this level
    Node* child[8]; // the 8 children of this node
};
```

Skeletons of some of the key routines are given below.

```
insertTree(Node& node, BYTE rgb[])
{ // insert 24-bit color rgb into subtree tree
    if(node == NULL)
            makeNewNode(node); // make & initialize a new node
    if(node.isLeaf)
    {
            node.numTimes++;   // inc # of pixels represented
            addColors(node, rgb); // sum the color values
    }
    else
            childIndex = 4 * rgb[0] + 2 * rgb[1] + rgb[2];
            insertTree(childIndex, rgb);
}
```

How to find a reducible node? Maintain an array, reducible[], of seven stacks, one for each level of the tree. reducible[i] contains pointers to tree nodes at level i that are known to be reducible (they have more than one child). As each color is inserted into the octree, it follows a specific path and/or builds new nodes in the path toward a leaf. At each node visited (except the final leaf node) the number of children is incremented by one and then tested: if the number of children is exactly 2, the node has just become reducible, and a pointer to it is pushed onto the appropriate stack.

When the tree must be reduced, the stacks are tested, working back from $i = 7$ to smaller i: the first nonempty stack reducible[i] points to a reducible node, which is popped from that stack and reduced.

```
void reduceTree(void)
{
    thisNode = findReducibleNode();
    thisNode.isLeaf = 1;
    numLeaves -= (thisNode.numChildren - 1);
    freeChildren(thisNode);
}
```

11.9 FOR FURTHER READING

The Feynman chapter on color [Feynman63] is beautifully written and is a classic introduction to color theory. Bill Meyer gives a very thorough discussion of the technology of color theory [Meyer81]. Rogers [Rogers90] also provides a solid introduction to color and it management in computer graphics. Hall's [Hall88] *Illumination and Color in Computer Generated Imagery* gives more detail on color production and conversion.

Chapter 12

Introduction to Ray Tracing

We attempt to abstract from the complexity of phenomena some simple systems whose properties are susceptible of being described mathematically. This power of abstraction is responsible for the amazing mathematical description of nature.

Morris Kline
(1908–1992)

Ye little stars! hide your diminish'd rays.

Alexander Pope
(1688–1777)

GOALS OF THE CHAPTER

○ To develop the fundamental concepts of ray tracing.

○ To set up the mathematics and algorithms to perform ray tracing.

○ To build and render scenes of spheres, cones, cylinders, convex polyhedra, and other solids.

○ To create highly realistic images, which include transparency and refraction of light.

○ To develop tools for working with solid 3D texture and bitmapped images.

○ To add surface texture to objects in the scene, in order to enliven them.

○ To study the creation of solid (3D) textures, such as wood grain and marble, in objects, and to see how to ray trace such objects.

○ To create a much richer class of object shapes, based on constructive solid geometry (CSG), and to learn how to ray trace scenes populated with such objects.

Preview

Section 12.1 introduces the ray tracing technique, and Section 12.2 establishes the camera and scene geometry needed for ray tracing. Section 12.3 shows how an application performs ray tracing. Section 12.4 describes various primitive shapes that are easy to ray trace, and develops the heart of ray tracing, the technique of intersecting an object with a ray. The advantages accrued by transforming the ray into the generic coordinate system of the object is discussed.

Section 12.5 develops various classes and routines that make up a ray tracer, introducing some principles and techniques of object-oriented programming (OOP), and discusses how the various players interact. One of the foundations of OOP is **polymorphism**, and we show in this section how the use of polymorphism not only saves the writing of a large amount of code, but also leads to much more reliable and maintainable code. A complete, albeit primitive, ray tracer is developed. Section 12.6 considers how to intersect rays with an extended set of shapes, including tapered cylinders and convex polyhedra.

Section 12.7 uses the shading models of Chapter 8 to develop a full-color ray tracer that handles ambient, diffuse, and specular reflections from surfaces. Section 12.8 explores techniques for painting texture onto surfaces when rendering. It develops the painting of both 2D texture, derived from images, and 3D textures such as marble or wood grain. The issue of antialiasing ray tracings is addressed in Section 12.9. Section 12.10 discusses how to speed up ray tracing dramatically by judicious use of bounding boxes and other kinds of extents to eliminate many costly ray intersections.

Section 12.11 describes how to spawn secondary rays in order to enhance the realism of a ray tracer. A method for the faithful generation of shadows is described. Section 12.12 describes the details of generating secondary rays to simulate the reflection of light from a shiny surface, and the refraction of light as it passes through a transparent object.

Section 12.13 extends the class of objects that can be ray traced to compound objects defined through constructive solid geometry (CSG). Methods are developed for ray tracing objects with arbitrarily complex shapes. The chapter closes with a number of Case Studies that guide the development and testing of working ray tracers.

12.1 INTRODUCTION

> Full many a gem of purest ray serene
> The dark, unfathomed caves of ocean bear.
>
> *Elegy,* stanza 14
> *Thomas Gray*
> *(1716–1761)*

In Chapters 6 through 8 we described methods for rendering scenes composed of polygonal meshes, including shading models that represent—at least approximately—how light reflects from the surface of a polygon. In addition, the Gouraud and Phong interpolation schemes were applied to suppress the faceted nature of the mesh model. Pictures formed in this way show a smooth surface (except along silhouette edges), even though the model consists of discrete faces.

Ray tracing provides a related but even more powerful approach for rendering scenes. Figure 12.1 shows the basic idea. Think of the frame buffer as the now familiar array of pixels positioned in space, with the eye looking through it into the scene. For each pixel in the frame buffer the question is asked: What does the eye see through this pixel? One can think of a ray of light arriving at the eye (or, more importantly, on the viewport) through this pixel from some point P in the scene. The color of the pixel is set to that of the light that emanates along the ray from point P in the scene.

An aspect that often confuses students, and to which we will devote considerable discussion throughout this chapter, is that in actuality the process is a slight variation of that described above. A ray is thought to be cast from the eye through the pixel center and out into the scene. Its path is tested against each object in the scene to see which object (if any) it hits first and at what point. A parameter t is used to associate the ray's position with our abstract notion of time, so that we can say "The ray is here now" or "The ray reaches this point first." We shall see a remarkable property of

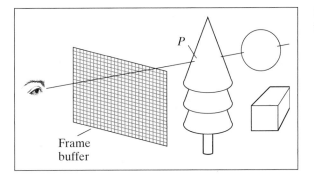

FIGURE 12.1 To view a point in the scene through a pixel.

ray tracing: it automatically solves the *hidden surface removal problem*, since the first surface hit by the ray is the closest object to the eye. More remote surfaces are ignored. Armed with a description of light sources in the scene, the same shading model as before is applied to the first hit point, and the ambient, diffuse, and specular components of light are computed. The resulting color is then displayed at the pixel.

Because the path of a ray is traced through the scene, interesting visual effects such as shadowing, reflection, and refraction are easy to incorporate, producing images of dazzling realism that are difficult to create by any other method. Another feature of ray tracing is its ability to work comfortably with a richer class of geometric objects than polygon meshes. Solid objects are constructed out of various geometric primitives, such as spheres, cones, and cylinders. Each shape is represented *exactly* through a mathematical expression: it need not be (but could be if desired). The shapes can also be subjected to transformations to alter their size and orientation before they are added to the scene, providing more modeling power for complex scenes. Our Scene Description Language (SDL) proves very useful in describing the objects in a scene.

In this chapter we shall describe the algorithmic artillery needed to produce high-quality ray traced images of complex scenes. Our development will be incremental, so that we can produce simple images with little programming after only a few sections. Additional tools are developed as needed to build up a repertoire of more advanced techniques. To provide some inspiration to your examining this chapter in depth, Figures 12.52 and a number of color inserts (Plate 33, for example) display the stunning quality of the images that ray tracing can produce.

12.2 SETTING UP THE GEOMETRY OF RAY TRACING

> O Life! how pleasant is thy morning,
> Young Fancy's rays the hills adorning!
> Cold-pausing Caution's lesson scorning,
> We frisk away,
> Like schoolboys at th' expected warning,
> To joy and play.
>
> *Robert Burns*
> *(1759–1796)*

In order to trace rays, we need a convenient representation for the ray (a parametric representation will be the most serviceable by far) that passes through a particular pixel. For easy reference, we gather together the required ingredients from Chapters 6 and 7 of the viewing process. By way of warning, in order to describe exactly the geometry of the ray tracing process, a large number of parameters will be necessary, which may seem overwhelming at first. You may find it helpful to keep some sketches of the key ingredients nearby. Ultimately, with familiarity, the many parameters will fit together and make more sense.

We use the same camera as in Chapter 7: its eye is at point *eye*, and the axes of the camera are along the vectors **u**, **v**, and **n** as shown in Figure 12.2. The near plane lies at distance N in front of the eye, and the frame buffer lies in the near plane. The shape of the camera is also the same as in Chapter 7, as shown in Figure 12.3: it has a view angle of θ, and the window in the near plane has aspect ratio *aspect*. Thus it extends from $-H$ to H in the **v**-direction, and from $-W$ to W in the **u**-direction, where H and W are given by the expressions:

$$H = N \times \tan(\theta/2)$$
$$W = H \times aspect \tag{12.1}$$

FIGURE 12.2 Setting up the camera for ray tracing.

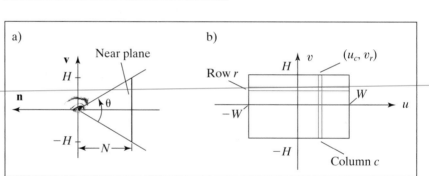

FIGURE 12.3 The shape of the camera. a) the shape of the camera; b) describing pixels on the screen window

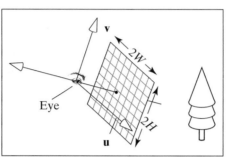

Recall from Chapter 7 that the viewport transformation sets up a correspondence between points on the near plane and pixels in the viewport. Here we use the same correspondence, but without using an explicit viewport transformation. In fact, it is simplest to think of the viewport being pasted onto the screen window in the near plane, so that the eye is looking through individual pixels out into the scene. Suppose there are $nCols$ by $nRows$ of pixels in the viewport, and consider the pixel at row r and column c, where r varies from 0 to $nRows - 1$ and c varies from 0 to $nCols - 1$. We'll call this the "rcth pixel." We shall do all computations for the path of a ray in terms of the ray through the rcth pixel. As always, we count rows from bottom to top and columns from left to right. This is shown in part b of Figure 12.3. Where on the near plane does this pixel appear?

As Figure 12.3 reveals, the pixel has lower left corner at (u_c, v_r), given by

$$u_c = -W + W\frac{2c}{nCols}, \quad \text{for } c = 0, 1, \ldots, nCols - 1$$

$$v_r = -H + H\frac{2r}{nRows}, \quad \text{for } r = 0, 1, \ldots, nRows - 1 \tag{12.2}$$

In order to develop an expression for a ray that passes through this point we will need to express where it lies in 3D: the actual point on the near plane. But this is easy: find how far this point is from the eye. Start at *eye* and determine how far you must go in each of the directions **u**, **v**, and **n** to reach the pixel corner. Some readers might argue that we should compute the path of the ray through the *center* of this pixel rather than through its corner. This is certainly satisfactory; however, pixels are so tiny that the image would be indistinguishable if we were to do it this way. You must go distance N in the negative **n**-direction, distance u_c along **u**, and distance v_r along **v**. Thus the 3D point is given by Equation (12.3):

$$eye - N\mathbf{n} + u_c\mathbf{u} + v_r\mathbf{v} \qquad \leftarrow \text{the location of the pixel corner in space} \qquad (12.3)$$

The position of a ray along its path will be parameterized using the familiar parameter t, which is conveniently taken to be time. We use the notion that as t increases, the ray moves further and further along its path. By design it starts at the eye at $t = 0$ and reaches the lower left corner of the rcth pixel at $t = 1$. The basic operation of ray tracing is to compute where this ray lies at each instant t between 0 and 1, and specifically to find which objects it hits. The ray of interest moves at constant speed in straight line segments and passes through a given pixel on the near plane. Along this path we must determine whether the ray hits any object in the scene. Speaking very roughly in pseudocode form (we shall clarify this formula next), the parametric expression for the ray is:

$$r(t) = eye(1 - t) + pixelcorner \ t \qquad (12.4)$$

Substituting the variable on which *pixelcorner* depends, we get the detailed parametric form for the **rcth ray**:

$$r(t) = eye(1 - t) + (eye - N\mathbf{n} + u_c\mathbf{u} + v_r\mathbf{v})t \qquad (12.5)$$

Check carefully that this ray is indeed located at the eye at $t = 0$ and at the lower left-hand corner of the rcth pixel at $t = 1$. It is useful to isolate the *starting point* and *direction* of this ray, as $r(t) = eye + \mathbf{dir}_{rc}t$. Simple manipulation of the previous expressions gives the ray through the rcth pixel as:

$$r(t) = eye + \mathbf{dir}_{rc}t$$

where

$$\mathbf{dir}_{rc} = -N\mathbf{n} + W\left(\frac{2c}{nCols} - 1\right)\mathbf{u} + H\left(\frac{2r}{nRows} - 1\right)\mathbf{v} \qquad (12.6)$$

We will be referring to this description of the rcth ray throughout the chapter, and when programming a ray tracing application you will incorporate these expressions directly, so you are urged to study them carefully.

Note an important property of each ray in this family: as t increases from 0, the ray point moves farther and farther from the eye. Convince yourself of this by examining this distance: it's the magnitude of the vector $r(t)$ - eye. If the ray strikes two objects in its path, say at times t_a and t_b, the object lying closer to the eye will be the one hit at the lower value of t. Therefore, as each ray is traced and tested against all of the objects in the scene, we need keep track only of the smallest hit time encountered. The pixel for that ray is ultimately rendered according to the object with the smallest hit time. This automatically makes more remote surfaces invisible, and solves the "hidden surface removal problem", which over the years has been a major issue in computer graphics!

PRACTICE EXERCISES

12.2.1 Work out the details

Develop Equations (12.1)–(12.6) in detail, and justify that the rcth ray truly has the direction shown. Where is this ray at $t = 2$, and at $t = -1$, in terms of the ingredients of the problem?

12.2.2 Numerical calculation of a ray

Suppose the camera has $eye = (0, 0, -5)$, $\mathbf{u} = (1, 0, 0)$, $\mathbf{v} = (0, 1, 0)$, and $\mathbf{n} = (0, 0, -2)$. Further suppose its view angle is $30°$ and its *aspect* is 1.5. For $nRows = 480$ and $nCols = 640$ find the parametric expression for the rcth ray, when $r = 100$ and $c = 200$.

12.2.3 Where are the pixel corners?

Find formulas for the (u, v) coordinates corresponding to the *center* of the rc-th pixel rather than its lower left corner.

12.2.4 Incremental calculation of rays

Note from Equation 12.6 that along a scan line, the direction of one ray can be found incrementally from that of the previous one by means of a single (vector) addition: Express $\mathbf{dir}_{r,c+1}$ in terms of $\mathbf{dir}_{r,c}$. ■

12.3 OVERVIEW OF THE RAY TRACING PROCESS

In Tracings of Eternal Light, ...

J. C. F. von Schiller
(1759–1805)

We first develop an overview of a ray tracer to describe the basic operations required. Later we describe how to implement the key ingredients in a program.

Figure 12.4 shows the basic steps in a ray tracer. The scene to be ray traced is inhabited by various geometric objects and light sources. A typical scene may contain spheres, cones, boxes, cylinders, and the like, each having a specified shape, size, and position. These objects are described in some fashion and stored in an object list. The camera as described earlier is also created. Then for each pixel in turn we construct a ray that starts at the eye and passes through the lower left corner of the pixel. This involves simply evaluating the direction $\mathbf{dir}_{rc}$ for the rcth ray. This process in pseudocode takes the shape shown in Figure 12.4.

```
<define the objects and light sources in the scene>
<set up the camera>
for(int r = 0; r < nRows; r++)
  for(int c = 0; c < nCols; c++)
  {
    < 1. Build the rc-th ray >
    < 2. Find all intersections of the rcth ray with objects in the scene >
    < 3. Identify the intersection that lies closest to, and in front of, the eye >
    < 4. Compute the hit point where the ray hits this object, and the normal vector at that point >
    < 5. Find the color of the light returning to the eye along the ray from the point of intersection >
    < 6. Place the color in the rc-th pixel. >
  }
```

FIGURE 12.4 Pseudocode skeleton of a ray tracer.

Steps 3–5 are new and are described in detail in the following sections. We first find whether the rcth ray intersects each object in the list, and if so we note the "hit time"—the value of t at which the ray $r(t)$ coincides with the object's surface. When all objects have been tested, the object with the smallest hit time is the closest to the eye. The location of the hit point on the object is then found, along with the normal vector to this object's surface at the hit point. The color of the light that reflects off this object, in the direction of the eye, is then computed and stored in the pixel.

Figure 12.5 shows a simple example scene consisting of some cylinders and spheres, and three cones. The snowman consists mainly of spheres. (What are the primitive shapes that make up his hat?) Two light sources are also shown. Notice that the objects in the scene can interpenetrate. As far as a picture is concerned, however, we are interested only in the outermost surfaces.

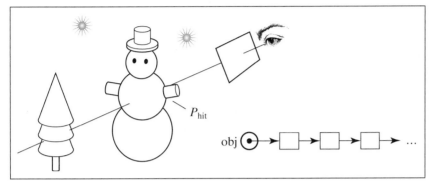

FIGURE 12.5 Ray tracing a scene.

Descriptions of all the objects are stored in an **object list**, suggested in the figure by the linked list of descriptive records. The ray shown intersects a sphere, a cylinder, and two cones. All the other objects are missed. The object with the smallest hit time—a cylinder in the example—is identified. The hit spot, P_{hit}, is then easily found *from the ray itself* by evaluating the ray of Equation (12.6) at the hit time, t_{hit}:

$$P_{hit} = eye + \mathbf{dir}_{r,c} t_{hit} \qquad \{\text{hit spot}\} \tag{12.7}$$

(Be sure you understand this equation: it will recur many times in this chapter.) In some cases a ray will not hit *any* object in the object list, in which case the ray will contribute only background light to the relevant pixel.

From this description it is clear that the fundamental operation in ray tracing is the calculation of intersections between a ray and a given object. We shall devote considerable time in this chapter to discussions of how to find such intersections algorithmically, and how to make such computations efficient.

12.4 INTERSECTION OF A RAY WITH AN OBJECT

Nothing puzzles me more than time and space; and yet nothing troubles me less, as I never think of them.
Charles Lamb
(1775–1834)

Recall from Chapter 5 that we developed the Scene class that can read a file in the SDL language and build a list of the objects in the scene. We will use this tool for ray tracing as well, building the scene with:

```
Scene scn;              // instantiate a scene object
scn.read("myScene.dat"); // read the SDL scene file
```

The objects in the scene are created and placed on a list. Each object is an instance of a generic shape such as a sphere or cone (we shall discuss the exact meaning of generic for each class of shapes), along with an affine transformation that specifies how it is scaled, oriented, and positioned in the scene. We introduced several generic shapes in Chapter 6. Figure 12.6 shows some of the generic shapes we shall be ray tracing. Note in particular the presence of a sphere, cylinder, cone, cube, square, and tetrahedron.

FIGURE 12.6 Some common generic shapes used in ray tracing.

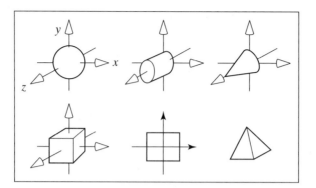

Whereas in Chapter 5 we used OpenGL to draw each of the objects (using the method `drawOpenGL()` that we developed for each type of shape), here we will be ray tracing them. This involves finding where a ray intersects each object in the scene. As we discuss next, this is most easily accomplished by using the *implicit form* for each shape, discussed in Section 6.5.1. For example, the **generic sphere** is a sphere of radius 1 centered at the origin. It has implicit form:

$$F(x, y, z) = x^2 + y^2 + z^2 - 1 \quad \text{\{generic sphere\}} \tag{12.8}$$

If we use for convenience the notation $F(P)$, where the argument of the implicit function is a point, the implicit form for the generic sphere becomes:

$$F(P) = |P|^2 - 1 \quad \text{\{generic sphere\}} \tag{12.9}$$

The **generic cylinder** as pictured in Figure 12.6 has radius 1; it is aligned along the z-axis with its longitudinal axis of length 1 and has the implicit form:

$$F(x, y, z) = x^2 + y^2 - 1 = 0 \quad \text{for } 0 < z < 1 \quad \text{\{generic cylinder\}} \tag{12.10}$$

In a real scene each generic shape is transformed by its affine transformation into a shape that has a quite different implicit form. But, as we see shortly, it turns out, surprisingly, that we need only figure out how to intersect rays with generic objects! Thus the implicit form of each generic shape will be of fundamental importance in ray tracing.

How do we find the intersection of a ray with a shape whose implicit form is $F(P)$? Suppose the ray has starting point S and direction $\mathbf{c}$. This is simpler notation to use here at first than a starting point *eye* and a direction $\mathbf{dir}_{rc}$. The ray is therefore given by:

$$r(t) = S + \mathbf{c}t \tag{12.11}$$

It is easy to state the general theory. All points on the surface of the shape satisfy $F(P) = 0$, and the ray hits the surface whenever the point $r(t)$ coincides with the surface. A condition for $r(t)$ to coincide with a point on the surface is therefore $F(r(t)) = 0$. This will occur at the hit time t_{hit}. To find t_{hit} we must therefore solve the equation:

$$F(S + \mathbf{c}t_{\text{hit}}) = 0 \tag{12.12}$$

Much of the effort in ray tracing lies in trying to solve this equation efficiently for interesting objects. It is easy to do it for simple shapes such as a plane or a sphere, as we now develop.

12.4.1 Intersection of a Ray with the Generic Plane

A scene often includes floors and walls of some room. These are easily modeled as planes. They sometimes have a uniform color, or they might be covered with texture such as a checkerboard pattern or a digitized image.

The generic plane is the xy-plane or the $z = 0$, so its implicit form is $F(x, y, z) = z$. The ray $S + \mathbf{c}t$ therefore intersects this plane when $S_z + c_z t_h = 0$. This is a simple linear equation in t_h with solution:

$$t_h = -\frac{S_z}{c_z} \tag{12.13}$$

If $c_z = 0$, the ray is moving parallel to the plane, and there is no intersection (unless, of course, S_z is also 0, in which case the ray hits the plane end-on and cannot be seen anyway). Otherwise the ray hits the plane at the point $P_{hit} = S - \mathbf{c}(S_z/c_z)$.

■ **EXAMPLE 12.4.1 Where does a certain ray hit a certain plane?**

Where does the ray $r(t) = (4, 1, 3) + (-3, -5, -3)t$ hit the generic plane?

SOLUTION:

Equation (12.13) yields $t_h = -3/-3 = 1$. The hit point is found as $S + \mathbf{c} = (1, -4, 0)$. Note that this point does indeed lie in the $z = 0$ plane as we would expect.

12.4.2 Intersection with a Generic Sphere

Where then does the ray $S + \mathbf{c}t$ intersect the generic sphere whose implicit form is given in Equation (12.9)? Substituting $S + \mathbf{c}t$ in $F(P) = 0$, we obtain $|S + \mathbf{c}t|^2 - 1 = 0$, or [recall Equation (4.10)][1]

$$|\mathbf{c}|^2 t^2 + 2(S \cdot \mathbf{c})t + (|S|^2 - 1) = 0 \tag{12.14}$$

This is a *quadratic* equation in t: $At^2 + 2Bt + C = 0$, where the quantities A, B, and C are recognized to be

$$\begin{aligned} A &= |\mathbf{c}|^2 \\ B &= S \cdot \mathbf{c} \\ C &= |S|^2 - 1 \end{aligned} \tag{12.15}$$

We solve the equation using the quadratic formula:

$$t_h = -\frac{B}{A} \pm \frac{\sqrt{B^2 - AC}}{A} \tag{12.16}$$

If the *discriminant* $B^2 - AC$ is negative, there can be no solutions, and the ray **misses** the sphere. If the discriminant is zero, the ray **grazes** the sphere at one point, and the hit time is $-B/A$. If the discriminant is positive, there are two hit times, t_1 and t_2, which use the '+' and '−' in Equation (12.16), respectively. (Some issues of numerical accuracy are addressed in the exercises.)

The pleasant aspect of intersecting a ray with a plane or a sphere is that a simple equation in t results, either linear or quadratic, which is easily solved. Some other simple shapes also yield reasonable equations in t, but many don't. We explore some in the exercises.

---

[1] Notice some abuse of notation here for compactness. S is a point, not a vector, so we technically can't use it in a dot product. Think of the notation $|S|^2$ simply as shorthand for $S_x^2 + S_y^2 + S_z^2$.

■ **EXAMPLE 12.4.2 Where does an example ray hit the generic sphere?**

Where does the ray $r(t) = (3, 2, 3) + (-3, -2, -3)t$ hit the generic sphere?

SOLUTION:

From Equation (12.15) $A = 22, B = -22$, and $C = 21$. Then Equation (12.16) yields $t_1 = 0.7868$ and $t_2 = 1.2132$. The two hit points are $S + \mathbf{c}t_1 = (3, 2, 3)(1 - 0.7868) = (0.6393, 0.4264, 0.6396)$ and $S + \mathbf{c}t_2 = (3, 2, 3)(1 - 1.2132) = (-0.6393, -0.4264, -0.6396)$. Both of these points are easily seen to be exactly unit distance from the origin, as expected. Notice the pleasant symmetry of points here. It arises because this ray goes through the origin, and the generic sphere is centered at the origin.

12.4.3 Intersection of the Ray with Transformed Objects

According to the scene designer's wishes, each object in the scene has an associated affine transformation T that places it in the scene with the desired size, orientation, and position. What does transforming an object do to the equations and the results just developed? If the implicit form for the transformed object is very complicated, it could make Equation (12.12) extremely difficult to solve. This could be quite worrisome. Here, however, we show that this situation need never arise!

Figure 12.7 illustrates the issue: transformation T maps a generic sphere W' into an ellipsoid W. When does the ray $S + \mathbf{c}t$ hit W? Suppose we can find the implicit form, say $G()$, for the transformed object W. We must solve $G(S + \mathbf{c}t) = 0$ for the hit time.

FIGURE 12.7 Intersecting a ray with an ellipsoid.

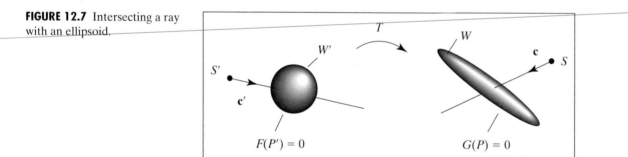

So it comes down to finding the implicit form for a transformed object. But we saw in Section 6.5.3 that if the original generic object has implicit function $F(P)$, the transformed object has implicit function $F(T^{-1}(P))$, where T^{-1} is the inverse transformation to T. (That is, if T has matrix M, then T^{-1} has matrix M^{-1}.) We therefore must solve the equation:

$$F(T^{-1}(S + \mathbf{c}t)) = 0 \tag{12.17}$$

for the hit time t. This could be a very messy equation. But in fact it simply says: solve for the time at which the *inverse transformed ray* $T^{-1}(S + \mathbf{c}t)$ hits the original generic object! Because transformation T is linear, the inverse transformed ray is:

$$T^{-1}(S + \mathbf{c}t) = (T^{-1}S) + (T^{-1}\mathbf{c})t$$

which we denote as $S' + \mathbf{c}'t$ in Figure 12.7. (Not surprisingly, the inverse transformed ray is still a ray—a straight line emanating from S' in direction $\mathbf{c}'$). Suppose the matrix associated with transformation T is M. Using homogeneous coordinates, the inverse transformed ray has parametric expression:

$$\tilde{r}(t) = M^{-1}\begin{pmatrix} S_x \\ S_y \\ S_z \\ 1 \end{pmatrix} + M^{-1}\begin{pmatrix} c_x \\ c_y \\ c_z \\ 0 \end{pmatrix} t = \tilde{S}' + \tilde{c}'t \qquad \{\text{inverse transformed ray}\} \qquad (12.18)$$

Note that M^{-1} multiplies a point in one case and a vector in the other. S' is formed from $\tilde{S}'$ by dropping the 1; $\mathbf{c}'$ is formed from $\tilde{\mathbf{c}}'$ by dropping the 0.

Thus instead of trying to intersect a ray with a transformed object, we intersect an inverse transformed ray with the generic object. The technique is the following sequence of steps. Each object on the object list has its own affine transformation. To intersect ray $S + \mathbf{c}t$ with the transformed object:

1. Inverse transform the ray (obtaining $S' + \mathbf{c}'t$).
2. Find its intersection time t_h with the *generic object*.
3. Use the *same* t_h in $S + \mathbf{c}t$ to identify the actual hit point.

The beauty of this approach is that we need only work up code that intersects a ray with a *generic* object. It's a win-win situation—the programmer wins by being able to use simpler code and the computer wins by having less of a computational burden. We can apply affine transformations to objects for modeling purposes in order to create interesting scenes, yet not pay the price of more complex code in the intersection routines. The affine transformation burden is shifted simply to transforming the ray. This rather dramatic benefit arises simply because rays are based on straight lines!

■ EXAMPLE 12.4.3 Where does a specific ray hit a transformed sphere?

Suppose ellipsoid W is formed from the generic sphere using the SDL commands:

```
translate 2 4 9
scale 1 4 4
sphere
```

so the generic sphere is first scaled and then translated. Its transformation and inverse transformation have matrices (check these):

$$M = \begin{pmatrix} 1 & 0 & 0 & 2 \\ 0 & 4 & 0 & 4 \\ 0 & 0 & 4 & 9 \\ 0 & 0 & 0 & 1 \end{pmatrix}, \qquad M^{-1} = \begin{pmatrix} 1 & 0 & 0 & -2 \\ 0 & \frac{1}{4} & 0 & -1 \\ 0 & 0 & \frac{1}{4} & -\frac{9}{4} \\ 0 & 0 & 0 & 1 \end{pmatrix}$$

respectively. Find where the ray $(10, 20, 5) + (-8, -12, 4)t$ intersects W.

SOLUTION:

The inverse transformed ray is $(8, 4, -1) + (-8, -3, 1)t$. (Check this, too.) Use this in Equation (12.15) to obtain $(A, B, C) = (74, -77, 80)$, so the discriminant is 9. Hence there are two intersections. From Equation (12.16) we obtain the hit times 1.1621 and 0.9189. The hit spot is found by using the smaller hit time in the ray representation, $(10, 20, 5) + (-8, -12, 4)0.9189 = (2.649, 8.97, 8.67)$. How would you check that this point lies on the transformed sphere?

PRACTICE EXERCISES

12.4.1 Find the intersection points

Find the times and points of intersection of the ray $(3, 5, 8) + (-4, -2, -6)t$ with the sphere of radius 5 centered at $(1, 2, 1)$.

12.4.2 Does it hit the plane?

When and where does the ray $(10 - t, 8 - 2t, 3 + t)$ hit the plane created in SDL by: `translate 4 5 6 rotate 90 1 0 0 plane`?   ■

12.5 ORGANIZING A RAY TRACER APPLICATION

> Each life sends out a trillion rays,
> But most die in a background hue
> Never to be seen.
> Some lucky few who meet a stranger on their path
> Return such heav'nly jewels,
> As only gods may understand.
>
> *Anonymous*

With this theory in hand we can construct an actual ray tracer based on the skeleton of Figure 12.4. We shall use the Scene class and the SDL language first encountered in Chapter 5, since they provide convenient tools to describe a complex scene. Thus we begin with an already constructed object list for the scene, where each object has an associated affine transformation.

A ray tracer has to deal with several different interacting objects: the camera that is viewing the scene; the screen on which the image is created; rays that emanate from the camera and migrate through the scene; and the scene itself, which contains many geometric objects and light sources. An object-oriented approach should carefully define what types of objects are involved and decide which actions each data type must perform, as well as what information each object must have in order to perform it. We define one top-down approach here, but you might choose to divide up the tasks in a different manner.

In this approach the camera is given the task of doing the ray tracing, for which we add a method to the existing Camera class:

```
void Camera :: raytrace(Scene& scn, int blockSize);
```

The camera is passed a scene to ray trace and a certain **blocksize**, to be described. It generates a ray from its eye through each pixel corner into the scene and determines the color of the light coming back along that ray. It then draws the pixel in that color.

We will use OpenGL to do the actual pixel drawing, and we will have raytrace() set up the modelview and projection matrices to draw directly on the display, as explained later. This makes the display() function in the main loop of the application very simple: it need only clear the screen and tell the camera object cam to ray trace according to code such as:

```
void display(void)
{
    glClear(GL_COLOR_BUFFER_BIT);      // clear the screen
    cam.raytrace(scn, blockSize);      // ray trace the scene
}           //set the color of this pixel as appropriate
            //draw a dot in the correct color at this pixel
```

A slight variation of this will make a big difference while developing your ray tracer. We already have in place a tool that draws an SDL scene using OpenGL's drawing functions, so there is no harm in drawing a coarse *preview* of the scene, as long as this is followed by the detailed ray-tracing desired. The preview is rendered rapidly and can reassure the user that the camera is aimed properly and the objects are in their proper places. If either the camera or the scene are improperly constructed, the user interrupts the process and fixes it, then tries again. If things are set up correctly, the ray traced objects will line up exactly with the previewed objects. Any bugs in the ray tracer are immediately apparent.

To add a preview of the scene, simply extend `display()` to:

```
void display(void)
{
   // clear the screen and reset the depth buffer
   glClear(GL_COLOR_BUFFER_BIT|GL_DEPTH_BUFFER_BIT);
   cam.drawOpenGL(scn); // draw the preview
   cam.raytrace(scn, blockSize); // ray trace over the preview
}
```

Figure 12.8 shows an example of ray tracing in progress: the preview has been drawn, over the entire screen, and is quite crude, whereas only the bottom half of the screen has been fully ray-traced. The important point here is that the ray tracing *exactly* overlays the preview scene.

FIGURE 12.8 A ray tracing in progress over a previewed scene.

Putting It All Together: The Ingredients of raytrace()

The `Camera` class's `raytrace()` method implements the steps of Figure 12.4. For each row *r* and column *c* a ray object is created that emanates from the eye and passes through the lower left corner of the *rc*th pixel into the scene. We need a `Ray` class for this, the beginnings of which are shown in Figure 12.9. It has a field to hold the start point of the ray, and a field to hold its direction. We shall add other fields later. Two methods set the start point and direction of a given ray.

FIGURE 12.9 Beginning of the Ray class.

```
class Ray{
public:
   Point3 start;
   Vector3 dir;
   void setStart(point3& p{start.x = p.x; etc..}
   void setDir(Vector3& v){dir.x = v.x; etc..}
   // other fields and methods
};
```

A skeleton of `raytrace()` is shown in Figure 12.10. It sets the start point of theRay once to the camera's eye, and then for each pixel it computes and sets the direction of the *rc*th ray [according to Equation (12.3)]. The Scene object scn is then told to find the color coming back along this ray: clr = scn.shade(theRay). The method shade() does the hard work: it casts the ray into the scene, determines intersections, computes the color of the light coming back along the ray, and returns it. We develop it in the remainder of this chapter.

```
void Camera :: raytrace(Scene& scn, int blockSize)
{
    Ray theRay;
    theRay.setStart(eye);
    // set up OpenGL for simple 2D drawing
    glMatrixMode(GL_MODELVIEW);
    glLoadIdentity();
    glMatrixMode(GL_PROJECTION);
    glLoadIdentity();
    gluOrtho2D(0,nCols,0,nRows); // whole screen is the window
    glDisable(GL_LIGHTING); // so glColor3f() works properly
    // begin raytracing
    for(int row = 0; row < nRows; row += blockSize)
    for(int col = 0; col < nCols; col += blockSize)
    {
        compute the ray's direction
        theRay.setDir(<direction>); // set the ray's direction
        Color3 clr = scn.shade(theRay);          // find the color
        glColor3f(clr.red, clr.green, clr.blue);
        glRecti(col,row,col + blockSize, row + blockSize);
    }
}
```

FIGURE 12.10 Skeleton of raytrace().

Drawing Pixel Blocks for Previewing

The blockSize parameter determines the size of the block of pixels being drawn at each step. Displaying pixel blocks is simply a time saver for the viewer during the development of a ray tracer. The images formed are rough but they appear rapidly: instead of tracing a ray through every pixel, wherein the picture emerges slowly pixel by pixel, rays are traced only through the lower left corner of each block of pixels.

Figure 12.11a shows how this works for a simple example of a display that has 16 rows and 32 columns of actual pixels, where blockSize is set to 4. Each block consists of 16 pixels. The color of the ray through the corner of the block is determined, and the entire block (all 16 pixels) is set to this uniform color. The image appears as a raster of four-by-eight blocks, giving only a very rough approximation to the full-resolution ray tracing. But it draws very quickly. If this rough image suggests that everything is working correctly, the viewer can retrace the scene at full resolution by setting blockSize to 1. Figure 12.11b shows a simple scene ray traced with block size of 4, 2, and 1. The first version is rendered 16 times faster than the last. Note that when the block size is 4 the image is rougher than that with a block size of 1, but the texture on the globe and floor is still clearly visible.

Note that `raytrace()` sets up OpenGL matrices for drawing the pixel blocks. The modelview matrix is set to the identity matrix, and the projection matrix does simple scaling of the window to the viewport with no projection. These steps effectively make the OpenGL pipeline transparent, so that a square can be drawn directly into the viewport using `glRecti()`. We assume the viewport has already been set to the full screen

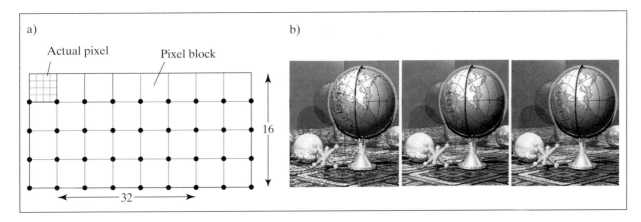

a) Actual pixel   Pixel block

16

32

b)

FIGURE 12.11 (a) The setup for preview ray tracing with blocks of pixels; (b) ray tracings with blocks of size 4, 2, and 1.

window with a glViewport(0,0,nCols,nRows) when the program is first started. OpenGL's lighting must also be disabled so that glColor3f() will work properly.

The Basics of shade(ray)

The meat of a ray tracer resides in shade(), a Pseudocode skeleton of which is shown in Figure 12.12. Its first job is to determine whether the ray hits some object, and if so, which one. To do this, it uses a routine getFirstHit(ray, best), which puts data about the first hit into an *intersection record* named best. We describe intersection records and getFirstHit() in more detail next. Once information about the first hit is available, shade() proceeds to find the color of the ray. If no object was hit, this is simply the background color, which shade() returns. On the other hand, if the ray did hit an object, shade() accumulates the various contributions in the variable color. These consist of the color emitted by the object if it is glowing, the ambient, diffuse, and specular components that are part of the classical shading model that are described in Chapter 8. In addition, shade() accumulates any color that might originate by reflection from a shiny surface, or from refraction through a transparent object.

```
Color3 Scene :: shade(Ray& ray)
{       // return the color of this ray
  Color3 color;      // total color to be returned
  Intersection best;  // data for the best hit so far
  getFirstHit(ray, best);   // fill the 'best' record
  if(best.numHits == 0)          // did the ray miss every object?
     return background;
  color.set (the emissive color of the object);
  color.add (ambient, diffuse, and specular components); // add more contributions
  color.add (reflected and refracted components);
  return color;
}
```

FIGURE 12.12 Skeleton of shade().

The routine getFirstHit() finds the object hit first by the ray, and returns the information in the intersection record best. We implement intersection records using the class Intersection, which is given in pseudocode by:

```
class Intersection{
 public:
  int numHits;      // # of hits at positive hit times
  HitInfo hit[8]; // list of hits - may need more than 8 later
  ... various methods  ...
};
```

It has two fields—the number of times the ray hits the object, and an array holding data about each hit. We shall only consider as legitimate those intersections that occur at positive hit times (in front of the ray's start point); hits behind the eye are of no interest. We are particularly interested in the first hit of the ray with an object. If `inter` is an intersection record, and `inter.numHits` is greater than 0, information concerning the first hit is stored in `inter.hit[0]`.

Why keep information on *all* of the hits the ray makes with an object at positive hit times, rather than just the first? One of the powerful advantages of the ray tracing approach is the ability to render *boolean* objects (see Section 12.12). To handle booleans we must keep a record of all the hits a ray makes with an object, so we take pains now to set things up properly. Normally the eye is outside all objects and a ray hits just twice: once upon entering the object and once upon exiting it. In such cases `inter.numHits` is 2, `inter.hit[0]` describes where the ray enters the object, and `inter.hit[1]` describes where it exits. But some objects, like the torus and booleans shown in Figure 12.13, can have more than two hits. In part a of the figure there are four hits with positive hit times, so `inter.numHits` is 4, and we store hit information in `inter.hit[0]`, ..., `inter.hit[3]`. In part b the ray hits the object (assumed to be transparent) eight times, but the eye is inside the object just after the first, third, fifth, and seventh hits, and only these three hits occur with positive hit times (so `inter.numHits` is 3).

FIGURE 12.13 Multiple hits with an object, some occurring at negative hit times.

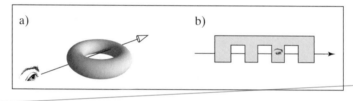

Information about each hit is stored in a record of type `HitInfo` form looks like:

```
class HitInfo { // data for each hit with a surface
    public:
    double hitTime;         // the hit time
    GeomObj* hitObject;     // the object hit
    bool isEntering;        // is the ray entering or exiting?
    int surface;            // which surface is hit?
    Point3 hitPoint;        // hit point
    Vector3 hitNormal;      // normal at hit point
    ... other fields and methods  ...
};
```

A hit record contains several fields that describe the hit: the hit time, a pointer to the object that was hit, whether the ray was entering or exiting the object at the hit, the location of the hit point, and the normal vector to the surface at that point. All of these fields will be important at various points in the ray tracing process.

The routine `getFirstHit()` is shown in pseudocode in Figure 12.14. It scans through the entire object list using pointer `pObj` to each object in turn, testing whether the ray hits the object. To do this it uses each object's own `hit()` method, as we describe starting in the next section. Each `hit()` method returns `true` if there is a legitimate hit, and `false` otherwise. If there is a hit, the method builds an entire intersection record describing all of the hits with this object, and places it in `inter`. Then `getFirstHit()` compares the first positive hit time in `inter` with that of `best`, the record of the best so far hit. If an earlier hit time is found, the data in `inter` is copied into `best`. The value of `best.numHits` is initialized to 0, so that the first real hit will be counted properly as `pObj` loops through the object list.

Notice that `getFirstHit()` passes the burden of computing ray intersections onto the `hit()` routine that each object possesses. We shall develop a `hit()` method for each

```
void Scene:: getFirstHit(Ray& ray, Intersection& best)
{
   Intersection inter;            // make intersection record
   best.numHits = 0;              // no hits yet

   For each object in turn, pointed to by pObj
   {       // test each object in the scene
     if(!pObj->hit(ray, inter))   // does the ray hit pObj?
            continue;             // miss: test the next object
     if(best.numHits == 0 ||      // best has no hits yet
       inter.hit[0].hitTime < best.hit[0].hitTime)
            best.set(inter);      // copy inter into best

   }

}
```

FIGURE 12.14 The method getFirstHit().

type of object. For the sake of efficiency it will be finely tuned to exploit special knowledge of the shape of the generic object. This is an excellent example of using **polymorphism** to simplify code and make it more robust and efficient. Polymorphism allows us to use the *same* name 'hit' for all hit() routines between rays and object types. The compiler can't tell which hit routine will be needed, since it doesn't even know what object types will be in the object list; instead, the proper hit routine is chosen at run time by the system to do the actual intersection calculations.

The job of hit() in a given class is to take a ray and build an intersection record, loading the record with all the details of the hits that the ray makes with the object. We develop hit() for a sphere next to show what is involved.

12.5.1 A Routine to Compute Ray–Sphere Intersections

Figure 12.15 shows the hit() method for the Sphere class. It first transforms the ray r into the generic coordinates of this sphere, using this sphere's particular inverse transformation. xfrmRay() transforms the ray according to Equation (12.18) (see the exercises). Next the coefficients A, B, and C of the quadratic equation of Equation (12.12) are found, and the discriminant $B^2 - AC$ is tested. If it is negative, there are no real solutions to the equation, and we know the ray must miss the sphere. Therefore hit() returns false, and inter is never used.

On the other hand, if the discriminant is positive, the two hit times are computed as in Equation (12.16). Call the earlier hit time t_1 and the later one t_2. As shown in Figure 12.16, there are three possibilities. The sphere can be in front of the eye, in which case both hit times are positive; the eye can be inside the sphere, in which case t_1 is negative but t_2 is positive; the sphere can be behind the eye, so that both times are negative.

If t_1 is strictly positive, then t_2 must also be data for the first hit are placed in inter.hit[0], and variable num is set to one to indicate there has been a hit. If t_2 is positive, data for the next hit are placed in inter.hit[num]. (If the first hit time is negative, the second hit time could be positive or negative and is automatically placed in hit[0].)

The data that are placed in each hit record use knowledge about a sphere. For instance, because the sphere is a convex object, the ray must be entering at the earlier hit time, and exiting at the later hit time. The value of surface is set to 0, as there is only one surface for a sphere: we address the issue wherein a ray can hit several possible surfaces later. The points, in generic coordinates, where the ray hits the sphere are also recorded in the hitPoint field. The hit spot is always (by definition) the same as the position of the ray at the given hit time, which is found by the function (see the exercises):

```
Point3 rayPos(Ray& r, float t);//returns the ray's location at
time t
```

FIGURE 12.15 The hit() method for the Sphere class.

```cpp
bool Sphere:: hit(Ray &r, Intersection& inter)
{
 Ray genRay; // need to make the generic ray
 xfrmRay(genRay,invTransf,r);
 double A, B, C;
 A = dot3D(genRay.dir, genRay.dir); assert(A > 0);
 B = dot3D(genRay.start, genRay.dir);
 C = dot3D(genRay.start, genRay.start) - 1.0;
 double discrim = B * B - A * C;
 if(discrim < 0.0) // ray misses
    return false;
 int num = 0;   // the # of hits so far
 double discRoot = sqrt(discrim);
 double t1 = (-B - discRoot)/A;            // the earlier hit
 if(t1 > 0.00001)    // is hit in front of the eye?
 {
    inter.hit[0].hitTime = t1;
    inter.hit[0].hitObject = this;
    inter.hit[0].isEntering = true;
    inter.hit[0].surface = 0;
    Point3 P(rayPos(genRay, t1)); // hit spot
    inter.hit[0].hitPoint.set(P);
    inter.hit[0].hitNormal.set(P);
    num = 1;      // have a hit
 }
 double t2 = (-B + discRoot)/A;   // the later hit
 if( t2 > 0.00001)
 {
    inter.hit[num].hitTime = t2;
    inter.hit[num].hitObject = this;
    inter.hit[num].isEntering = false;
    inter.hit[num].surface = 0;
    Point3 P(rayPos(genRay, t2)); // hit spot
    inter.hit[num].hitPoint.set(P);
    inter.hit[num].hitNormal.set(P);
    num++;      // have another hit
 }
 inter.numHits = num;
 return (num > 0); // true or false
}
```

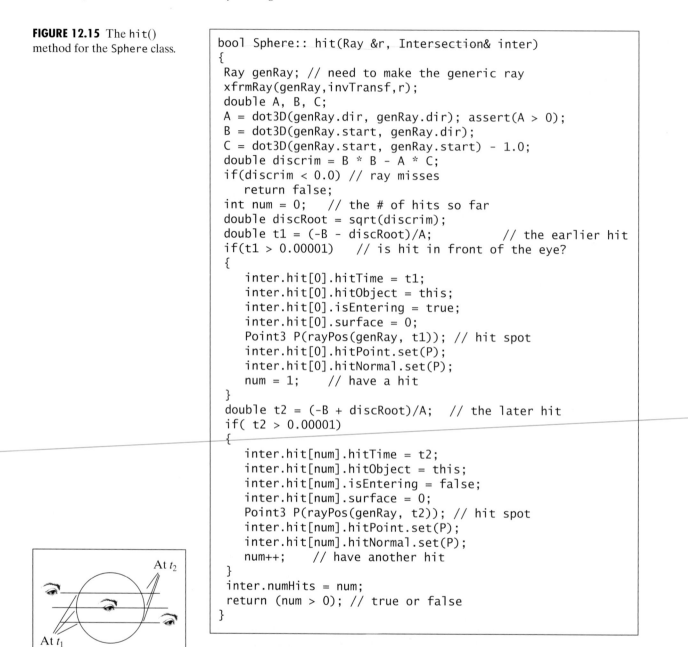

At t_2

At t_1

FIGURE 12.16 Which hits are in front of the eye?

The calculation of the normal vector at the hit spot is also simple for a sphere: because the normal points outward radially from the center of the sphere, it has coordinates *identical* to the hit point itself.

PRACTICE EXERCISE

12.5.1 Convert a ray from scene to generic coordinates

Write the routine xfrmRay() that hit() uses to transform a ray into the generic coordinates of a sphere. Give careful attention to the difference between transforming a point and a vector.

12.5.2 The function rayPos()

Implement the function rayPos() as described earlier that is given a ray and a time, and returns the position of the ray at that instant.

12.5.3 When the ray grazes the sphere

Discuss what values will be computed and stored for the case where the ray just grazes the sphere.

12.5.4 On computational complexity

How costly is it to intersect a ray with a sphere? How many multiplications, divisions, and square roots are required when the ray hits the sphere? ■

12.5.2 A Complete Ray Tracer for Emissive Sphere Scenes

In full-orbed glory, yonder moon divine
Rolls through the dark blue depths;
Beneath her steady ray
The desert circle spreads
Like the round ocean, girdled with the sky.
How beautiful is night!

Robert Southey
(1774–1843)

We have enough tools in place to put together a simple ray tracer for scenes composed of spheres and, of course, ellipsoids. It is very useful to get this much working before things get more complicated, to see how all of the ingredients discussed go together. Nothing is wasted in the process, as all of these tools are needed later.

So far we can only make an object glow in some color by setting its emissive component (recall Chapter 8) in the SDL file to some nonzero color, as in: emissive 0.3 0.6 0.2

It is simple to adjust Scene:: shade() of Figure 12.12 so that it handles only emissive light: just remove the color.add() lines that find other light contributions:

```
Color3 Scene :: shade(Ray& ray)
{
  Color3 color;
  Intersection best;
  getFirstHit(ray, best);
  if(best.numHits == 0) return background;
  Shape* myObj = (Shape*)best.hit[0].hitObject; // the hit object
  color.set(myObj->mtrl.emissive);
  return color;
}
```

The only parts of Camera :: raytrace() of Figure 12.10 that need fleshing out are the computation of the ray's direction for each pixel block.[2] What is the parametric form for the ray that passes through the lower left corner of the *ik*th pixel block; Equation (12.2) may be of some assistance in this calculation. Case Study 12.1 discusses in more detail the implementation of a simple ray tracer for sphere scenes.

12.6 INTERSECTING RAYS WITH OTHER PRIMITIVES

The color of the object illuminated partakes of the color of that which illuminates it.

Leonardo da Vinci
(1452–1519)

We need to develop the hit() method for other shape classes. All the hit() methods are similar: the ray is first transformed into the generic coordinates of the object in

---

[2] Note that the computation of several of these variables can be removed from the inner loop for efficiency.

question, and the various intersections with the generic object are computed. We need only work out the specific details of intersection for each generic shape.

12.6.1 Intersecting with a Square

A square is a useful generic shape. The generic square lies in the $z = 0$ plane and extends from -1 to 1 in both x and y. Its implicit form is $F(P) = P_z$ for $|P_x| \leq 1$ and $|P_y| \leq 1$. It can be transformed into any parallelogram positioned in space, and so it is often used in scenes to provide thin flat surfaces such as walls and windows. hit() first finds where the ray hits the generic plane [see Equation (12.10) for a guide] and then tests whether this hit spot also lies within the square, as suggested in Figure 12.17.

```
//<<<<<<<<<<<<<<<<<<< hit for Square >>>>>>>>>>>>>>>>>.
bool Square:: hit(Ray &r, Intersection& inter)
{
    Ray genRay; // need to make the generic ray
    inter.numHits = 0; // initial assumption
    xfrmRay(genRay, invTransf, r);
    double denom = genRay.dir.z; // denominator
    if(fabs(denom) < 0.0001) return false; // ray parallel to plane: miss
    double time = -genRay.start.z/denom; // hit time
    if(time <= 0.0) return false; // it lies behind the eye
    double hx = genRay.start.x + genRay.dir.x * time;// x at hit
    double hy = genRay.start.y + genRay.dir.y * time;// y at hit
    if((hx > 1.0) || (hx < -1.0)) return false; // misses in x-direction
    if((hy > 1.0) || (hy < -1.0)) return false; // misses in y-direction
    inter.numHits = 1;   // have a hit
    inter.hit[0].hitObject = this;
    inter.hit[0].hitTime = time;
    inter.hit[0].isEntering = true;
    inter.hit[0].surface = 0;
    inter.hit[0].hitPoint.set(hx,hy,0);
    inter.hit[0].hitNormal.set(0,0,1);
    return true;
}
```

FIGURE 12.17 The hit() method for the Square class.

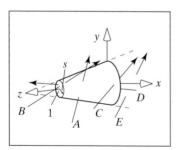

FIGURE 12.18 The generic tapered cylinder.

12.6.2 Intersecting with a Tapered Cylinder

The generic tapered cylinder is shown in Figure 12.18, along with several rays. The side of the cylinder is part of an infinitely long wall, hereafter called the wall, with a radius of 1 at $z = 0$ and a small radius of s at $z = 1$. From Equation (6.30) we know that this wall has the implicit form:

$$F(x, y, z) = x^2 + y^2 - (1 + (s - 1)z)^2 \qquad \text{for } 0 < z < 1$$

If $s = 1$, the shape becomes the generic cylinder; if $s = 0$, it becomes the generic cone. We develop a hit() method for the tapered cylinder, which provides as well a hit() method for the cylinder and cone.

Several rays are also shown in the figure, illustrating the variety of ways in which a ray can hit or miss this object. Ray A hits the wall twice on the actual cylinder (for brevity we will often refer to a tapered cylinder as simply a cylinder), whereas B passes through the wall before entering the cylinder through its cap, and exits through the side. C hits the wall first, then exits through the base, and D enters through the base and exits through the cap. Ray E hits the wall but outside the extent of the cylinder, and so misses. Not shown are rays that miss the cylindrical wall entirely.

With this many possibilities we need an organized approach that avoids an unwieldy number of if()..else tests. The solution is to identify hits in whatever order is convenient and to put them in the inter.hit[] list regardless of order. At the end, if inter.hit[] holds two hits out of order, the two items are swapped. It's handy that we already have a list available to put these hits in.

The individual tests are straightforward. To determine whether the ray strikes the wall, substitute $S + \mathbf{c}t$ into the implicit form for the tapered cylinder to obtain the quadratic equation $At^2 + 2Bt + C = 0$. It is straightforward to show that

$$A = c_x^2 + c_y^2 - d^2$$
$$B = S_x c_x + S_y c_y - Fd$$
$$C = S_x^2 + S_y^2 - F^2 \qquad\qquad (12.19)$$

where $d = (s - 1)c_z$ and $F = 1 + (s - 1)S_z$. What do these parameters become for the cylinder and the cone?

We use the coefficients in the same manner as for a sphere. If the discriminant $B^2 - AC$ is negative, the ray passes by the tapered cylinder's wall. If the discriminant is not negative, the ray does strike the wall, and the hit times can be found by solving the quadratic equation. To test whether each hit is on the actual cylinder wall, find the z-component of the hit spot. The ray hits the cylinder only if the z-component lies between 0 and 1.

To test for an intersection with the base, intersect the ray with the plane $z = 0$. Suppose it hits at the point $(x, y, 0)$. The hit spot lies within the cap if $x^2 + y^2 < 1$. Similarly, to test for an intersection with the cap, intersect the ray with the plane $z = 1$. Suppose it hits at the point $(x, y, 1)$. The hit spot lies within the cap if $x^2 + y^2 < s^2$.

A cylinder has more than one surface, and we will later want to know which surface is hit. For instance, we may want to paste a different texture on the wall than on the cap. Therefore we adopt the following numbering: the wall is surface 0, the base is surface 1, and the cap is surface 2. The appropriate value is placed in the surface field of each hit record.

It is not difficult, but is lengthy, to bring these ideas together and to create code for intersecting a ray with a tapered cylinder. In the service of compactness these details are requested in the exercises.

Keep in mind that the normal vector must be found at the two hit points. As we discussed in Chapter 6, the normal to the cylinder wall at point (x, y, z) is simply $(x, y, -(s - 1)(1 + (s - 1)z))$. The normals to the cap and base are $(0, 0, 1)$ and $(0, 0, -1)$, respectively. The hitNormal fields are filled with the appropriate values by hit().

PRACTICE EXERCISES

12.6.1 Implementation of hit() for the tapered cylinder

Check that the coefficients of the quadratic equation in Equation (12.19) are correct. Flesh out the code for TaperedCylinder ::hit(Ray& r, Intersection& inter).

12.6.2 Implementation of hit() for intersecting a cone

If you wanted to have a hit() routine specially crafted for a Cone class, how would it differ from that for the TaperedCylinder class? Show which lines of code would be changed to increase efficiency.

12.6.3 On computational complexity

How many adds/subtracts and multiplies/divides are required to intersect a ray with a square and a tapered cylinder?   ■

12.6.3 Intersecting with a Cube (or Any Convex Polyhedron)

Convex polyhedra prove useful in many graphics situations and have been treated in several places in the book. (See, for example, the Platonic solids in Chapter 6.) Because they are defined in terms of bounding planes, it is easy to develop an intersection routine for a ray with any convex polyhedron. We do this later in this section.

One particular convex polyhedron, the **generic cube**, deserves special attention. It is centered at the origin and has corners at $(\pm 1, \pm 1, \pm 1)$, using all eight combinations of $+1$ and -1. Thus its edges are aligned with the coordinate axes, and its six faces lie in the planes specified in Figure 12.19. To aid visualization a name is given to each of the planes of this cube as viewed from a point such as $(0, 0, 10)$. For instance, the plane named *top* lies on top of the cube, and so on. The figure also shows the outward-pointing normal vector to each plane and a typical point, *spot*, that lies in the plane.

The generic cube is important for two reasons:

1. A large variety of interesting boxes can be modeled and placed in a scene by applying an affine transformation to a generic cube. Then, when ray tracing, each ray can be inverse transformed into the generic cube's coordinate system, and we can use a *ray-with-generic-cube* intersection routine which can be made very efficient.

2. The generic cube can be used as an **extent** for the other generic primitives in the sense of a **bounding box**: each generic primitive like the cylinder fits snugly inside it. As we discuss later, it is often efficient to test whether a ray intersects the extent of an object before testing whether it hits the object itself, particularly if the ray-with-object intersection is computationally expensive. If a ray misses the extent, it *must* miss the object. So there is a strong advantage in having available a highly efficient algorithm for intersecting a ray with the generic cube.

FIGURE 12.19 The six planes that define the generic cube.

Plane	Name	Equation	Outward Normal	Spot
0	top	$y = 1$	$(0, 1, 0)$	$(0, 1, 0)$
1	bottom	$y = -1$	$(0, -1, 0)$	$(0, -1, 0)$
2	right	$x = 1$	$(1, 0, 0)$	$(1, 0, 0)$
3	left	$x = -1$	$(-1, 0, 0)$	$(-1, 0, 0)$
4	front	$z = 1$	$(0, 0, 1)$	$(0, 0, 1)$
5	back	$z = -1$	$(0, 0, -1)$	$(0, 0, -1)$

The Intersection Algorithm for the Generic Cube

The process of intersecting a ray with a cube is essentially the Cyrus-Beck algorithm described in Section 4.8.3, in which a line is clipped against a convex window in 2D space. It was also used for clipping a line against the camera's view volume in Chapter 8. The basic idea is that each plane of the cube defines an inside half-space and an outside half-space. A point on a ray lies inside the cube if and only if it lies on the inside of every half-space of the cube. So, intersecting a ray with a cube is a matter of finding the interval of time in which the ray lies inside all the planes of the cube.

Call the cube P. We test the ray against each of the planes of P in turn, in some chosen order, computing the time at which the ray either enters or exits the inside half-space for that plane. We keep track of a *candidate interval, CI*: the interval of time in which, based on our tests so far, the ray *could* be inside the object. It is bracketed by the values t_{in} and t_{out}: $CI = [t_{in}, t_{out}]$. Values inside the CI 'might-be-inside' the half-space in question, although we usually think of it the other way around: values of t not inside the CI are definitely *not* inside this half-space. The ray, if it is entering, must be outside the relevant plane for all $t < t_{in}$ and, if it is exiting, for all $t > t_{out}$. As each plane of P is tested, we chop away at this interval, either increasing t_{in} or reducing t_{out}. If at any point the CI becomes empty, the ray must miss the object, giving an early out. If, after testing all of the planes of P, the remaining CI is nonempty, the ray enters the object at t_{in} and exits at t_{out}.

To assist in visualizing this process, Figure 12.20 shows the example of a ray entering the generic cube at $t = 3.6$ and exiting at $t = 4.1$. In this example, when testing is complete, the remaining CI is [3.6, 4.1] and the ray definitely hits the cube. Figure 12.21 shows a 2D version for simplicity, where we wish to find the intersection of a ray with a square. The order in which the planes of the cube are tested against the ray makes a difference during testing, although after all planes have been tested the result will be the same. Now suppose we test the sides of the square in the order shown beginning with #1 and proceeding to #4. The CI is initially set to $CI = (-\infty, \infty)$. The hit with plane #1 shows an exit time of 2.9, so we know the ray *must be outside* the square beyond 2.9, and so the CI becomes $(-\infty, 2.9]$. The test with plane #2 reveals that the ray actually exits earlier, at 2.7, so t_{out} is set to 2.7. The test with plane #3 shows that the ray cannot possibly enter earlier than $t = 1.6$, so t_{in} is set to 1.6. Finally the test with plane #4 shows that t_{in} is actually 1.8. The final CI is [1.8, 2.7].

At each step t_{in} and t_{out} are adjusted according to the following pseudocode algorithm.

```
initialize t_in at -∞, and t_out at ∞ (for each CI)
if(the ray is entering at t_hit)
      t_in = max(t_in, t_hit)
else if(the ray is exiting at t_hit)
      t_out = min(t_out, t_hit)
```

As for the details, let the ray be $S + \mathbf{c}t$ and suppose the plane in question has outward-pointing normal $\mathbf{m}$ and contains the point B. The implicit form for this

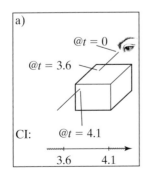

FIGURE 12.20 A ray pierces the generic cube.

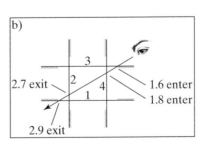

FIGURE 12.21 The 2D version.

plane is $F(P) = \mathbf{m} \cdot (P - B)$, so the ray hits it when $\mathbf{m} \cdot (S + \mathbf{c}t - B) = 0$ or at the hit time:

$$t = \frac{numer}{denom}$$

where

$$numer = \mathbf{m} \cdot (B - S)$$

$$denom = \mathbf{m} \cdot \mathbf{c} \tag{12.20}$$

The ray is passing into the outside half-space of the plane if $denom > 0$ (since then $\mathbf{m}$ and $\mathbf{c}$ are less than 90° apart), and passing into the inside half-space if $denom < 0$. If $denom = 0$, the ray is parallel to the plane, and the value of $numer$ determines whether it lies wholly inside or wholly outside, as discussed in Section 4.8.3. These four possibilities are summarized in Figure 12.22.

FIGURE 12.22 Interaction of a ray and a plane's inside half-space.

Situation	Condition
Pass to inside	$denom < 0$
Pass to outside	$denom > 0$
Wholly inside	$denom = 0$, $numer > 0$
Wholly outside	$denom = 0$, $numer < 0$

All of these ideas work just as well in 3D as 2D. For the generic cube the quantities $numer$ and $denom$ can be computed very quickly: the dot products are trivial to find, because each vector $\mathbf{m}$, in the cube's generic coordinates, has two components of zero. The planes in Figure 12.20 yield the values (check these):

Plane	numer	denom
0	$1 - S_y$	c_y
1	$1 + S_y$	$-c_y$
2	$1 - S_x$	c_x
3	$1 + S_x$	$-c_x$
4	$1 - S_z$	c_z
5	$1 + S_z$	$-c_z$

Figure 12.23 shows the routine hit() in pseudocode for the Cube class, which implements the required tests. As with the other hit() routines, the ray is converted to the object's generic coordinates, and all testing is then done using the generic object. The six planes are then tested in a loop, using the proper values of $numer$ and $denom$. The initially infinite CI is chopped down to its final value (tIn, tOut), unless it becomes empty after one of the tests, indicating that the ray misses the cube. Because it is important to keep track of which plane is associated with the current values of tIn and tOut, this information is stored in the variables surfIn and surfOut.

```
bool Cube:: hit(Ray& r, Intersection& inter) // in condensed pseudocode
{
    double tHit, numer, denom;
    double tIn = -100000.0, tOut = 100000.0; // plus-minus infinity
    Ray genRay;
    int inSurf, outSurf; // which of the six surfaces
    xfrmRay(genRay, invTransf, r);
    for (int i = 0; i < 6; i++)
    {
      switch(i) // which plane of cube to test
      {
      case 0: numer = 1.0 - genRay.start.y; denom = genRay.dir.y; break;
        case 1, case 2, case 3, case 4 similarly
      case 5: numer = 1.0 + genRay.start.z; denom = -genRay.dir.z; break;
      }
     if(fabs(denom) < 0.00001)    // ray is parallel
          if(numer < 0) return false; // ray is out;
          else;                   // ray inside, no change to tIn,tOut
        else                      // ray is not parallel
      {
         tHit = numer / denom;
         if(denom > 0){  // exiting
           if(tHit < tOut){ // a new earlier exit
               tOut = tHit; outSurf = i;
           }
         }
       else { // denom is negative: entering
         if(tHit > tIn){  // a new later entrance
             tIn = tHit; inSurf = i;
         }
       }
      }
     }
     if(tIn >= tOut) return false; // it's a miss - early out
} // end of the for loop
  int num = 0; // no positive hits yet
  if(tIn > 0.00001) // is first hit in front of the eye?
  {
     inter.hit[0].hitTime = tIn;
     inter.hit[0].surface = inSurf;
     inter.hit[0].isEntering = 1; // is entering
     inter.hit[0].hitObject = this;
     inter.hit[0].hitPoint.set(rayPos(genRay.start, genRay.dir,tIn));
     inter.hit[0].hitNormal.set(cubeNormal(inSurf));
     num++; //have a hit
  }
  if(tOut > 0.00001)
  {
     inter.hit[num].hitTime = tOut;
     inter.hit[num].surface = outSurf;
     inter.hit[num].isEntering = 0; // is exiting
     inter.hit[num].hitObject = this;
```

FIGURE 12.23 The hit()
method for the Cube class.

```
        inter.hit[num].hitPoint.set(rayPos(genRay.start,genRay.dir,tOut));
        inter.hit[num].hitNormalset(cubeNormal(outSurf));
        num++;
    }
    inter.numHits = num; // number of hits in front of eye
    return (num > 0);
}
```

FIGURE 12.23 (*Continued*)

When all planes have been tested, we know the hit times tIn and tOut. If tIn is positive, the data for the hit at tIn are loaded into inter.hit[0], and the data for the hit at tout are loaded into inter.hit[1]. If only tOut is positive, the data for its hit are loaded into inter.hit[0].

The normal vector to each hit surface is set using a helper function cubeNormal(i), which returns the outward normal vector given in Figure 12.20. For instance, cubeNormal(0) returns $(0, 1, 0)$, and cubeNormal(3) returns $(-1, 0, 0)$. See the exercises.

The Intersection Algorithm for Any Convex Polyhedron

The extension of hit() for any convex polyhedron is very straightforward. Suppose there are N bounding planes, and the ith plane contains point B_i and has (outward) normal vector m_i. Everything in hit() for the cube remains the same except that Equation (12.20) is used for the calculation of numer and denom. Now two expensive dot products must be performed, and the for loop becomes:

```
for (int i = 0; i < N; i++) // for each plane of the polyhedron
{
    numer = dot3(m_i, B_i - S);
    denom = dot3(m_i, c);
    if(fabs(denom) < eps) … as before
    … same as before ..
}
```

The Intersection Algorithm for a Mesh Object

Since we have a rich assortment of mesh objects to use from Chapter 6, and we already have a drawOpenGL() method for any mesh, it is natural to consider ray tracing meshes. We use the previous approach to develop a hit() method for meshes. Recall that Mesh objects are described by a list of faces, and each face is a list of vertices along with a normal vector at each vertex. We shall take each face of the mesh in turn and treat it as a bounding plane. Call the plane associated with each face its *face plane*. The object that is ray traced, therefore, is the shape that is the intersection of the inside half-spaces of each of its face planes.

Figure 12.24 shows two shapes (in 2D for simplicity) with their face planes marked. The object in part a is convex, so its face planes are the same as its bounding planes. This shape will be ray traced correctly. Part b shows a nonconvex object. The portion that is inside all of its face planes is shown shaded. This is what the ray tracer—which does not know the object fails to be convex and will proceed blindly with the Cyrus Beck algorithm—will display! So using this method for a mesh will work only if the mesh represents a truly convex object.

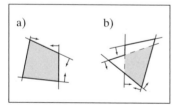

FIGURE 12.24 Objects (in 2D) and their face planes: a) convex, b) nonconvex.

To build hit() for a mesh, we form numer and denom for each face in turn. We use as the representative point on the face plane the 0th vertex of the face: pt[face[f].vert[0].vertIndex], and use as the normal to the face plane the normal associated with this 0th vertex: norm[face[f].vert[0].normIndex].

PRACTICE EXERCISES

12.6.5 Setting the normal vector for a cube intersection

Write the function Vector3 cubeNormal(int which) that returns the outward normal vector to face which of a cube, according to Figure 12.20. It's probably most readable to use a single six-way switch statement that sets the vector to one of six hard-wired values. A slightly briefer approach recognizes a pattern in the normals, and computes them using:

```
int m = which/2,n = (which%2)? -1:1;
if(m == 0)v.set( 0, n, 0);
else if(m == 1) v.set( n, 0, 0);
else v.set( 0, 0, n);
```

Determine how this method works, and rewrite the cubeNormal function to employ it.

12.6.6 The planes of a tetrahedron

Using Figure 6.27 as a guide, show the ingredients of the list of planes for the regular tetrahedron.

12.6.7 Fine tuning of hit() for a convex polyhedron

Fill in the details of the ConvexPolyhedron :: hit() method for intersecting a ray with a convex polyhedron. See the Shapes class in the book's companion web site for more details on the ConvexPolyhedron class.

12.6.8 Intersection with a tetrahedron

Find the t-interval for which the ray: $(0, 0, 0) + (1, 2, 3)t$ is inside the tetrahedron with vertices $(1, 0, 0)$, $(-1, 0, -1)$, $(-1, 0, 1)$, and $(0, 1, 0)$.

12.6.9 On computational complexity

How many multiplications/divisions are required to test each plane of a convex polyhedron? Sometimes tIn exceeds tOut after only a few planes have been tested. What is a good rule of thumb for the average number of plane tests that are made for an N-plane convex polyhedron when a randomly chosen ray is tested? Compare this complexity with that for determining a ray–sphere intersection. ■

12.6.4 Adding More Primitives

One can go beyond the generic primitives considered so far to include other kinds of shapes. We need to have in hand only the implicit form $F(P)$ of the shape. Then, as before, to find where the ray $S + \mathbf{c}t$ intersects the surface, we substitute $S + \mathbf{c}t$ for P in $F(P)$, forming a function of time t:

$$d(t) = F(S + \mathbf{c}t) \tag{12.21}$$

This function is:

- positive at those values of t for which the point on the ray is outside the object,
- zero when the ray coincides with the surface of the object,
- negative when the ray is inside the surface.

When seeking intersections, we look for values of t that make $d(t) = 0$, so intersecting a ray is equivalent to solving this equation. For the sphere and other quadric surfaces we have seen that this leads to a simple quadratic equation.

A *torus* is a different matter. The generic torus has the implicit function

$$F(P) = \left(\sqrt{P_x^2 + P_y^2} - d\right)^2 + P_z^2 - 1 \tag{12.22}$$

so the resulting equation $d(t) = 0$ is quartic (fourth-order). This is much harder to solve, although closed-form solutions may be found in various mathematical handbooks.

More generally, consider the general shape of $d(t)$ as t increases. If the ray is aimed toward the object in question, and the start point S lies outside the object, we get shapes similar to those in Figure 12.25.

The value of $d(0)$ is positive, since the ray starts outside the object. As the ray approaches the surface, $d(t)$ decreases, reaching 0 if the ray intersects the surface at t_1 in the figure. There is a period of time during which the ray is inside the object and is $d(t) < 0$. When the ray emerges again, $d(t)$ passes through 0 and increases thereafter. For an object like a torus the ray might re-enter the object—sketch a typical shape for $d(t)$ in such a case. If instead the ray misses the object (as in the dashed curve), $d(t)$ decreases for a while, but then increases forever without reaching 0.

For quadrics such as the sphere, $d(t)$ has a parabolic shape, and for the torus, a quartic shape. For other surfaces $d(t)$ may be so complicated that we have to search numerically to locate t's for which $d(.)$ equals 0.

To find the smallest positive value of t that yields 0, we evaluate $d(t)$ at a sequence of t-values, searching for one that makes $d(t)$ very small. Techniques such as Newton's method [Acton70, Conte and deBoor80] provide clever ways to progress toward better and better t-values, but in general these numerical techniques require many iterations. This, of course, significantly slows down the ray tracing process.

Techniques have been developed for ray tracing a variety of other objects. Notable among these are fractal surfaces, surfaces of revolution, and prismlike cylinders [Kajiya83]. See Case Study 12.2 for approaches to ray tracing these objects. The search for efficient algorithms to ray trace ever-larger collections of shapes is an ongoing subject of research in graphics.

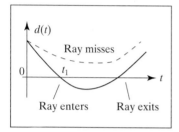
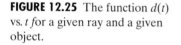

FIGURE 12.25 The function $d(t)$ vs. t for a given ray and a given object.

PRACTICE EXERCISES

12.6.11 Intersections with a torus

Determine from a mathematical handbook how to find the solutions to a quartic equation, and set up the steps necessary to find the intersection(s) of a ray, $S + \mathbf{c}t$, with the torus in Equation (12.22).   ■

12.7 TO DRAW SHADED PICTURES OF SCENES

> If I wish to explain what it is to him who asks me, I do not know.
>
> *on the nature of time*
> *St. Augustine*
> *(354–430)*

A ray tracer that draws emissive objects provides a good way to get started, but is soon found to be inadequate when what you want are pictures of stunning realism. To produce such pictures we must determine the nature of the light that is reflected toward the eye from the hit point. We will begin with the shading model that OpenGL uses, as discussed in Chapter 8, to guide the calculations. We then discuss how the model can be refined to achieve greater realism.

OpenGL draws scenes by combining the ambient, diffuse, and specular components of light that illuminate a vertex of an object. It uses the Gouraud model to calculate a smoothly varying diffuse light component. Figure 12.26 summarizes the main ingredients. The rcth ray is seen intersecting a spheroid at hit point P_h. A light source is located at L. We wish to compute the amount of light that travels back from P_h to the eye. The principal vectors of interest are shown as **s**, **v**, and **m**. Vector **s** points to the light source and is therefore given by $\mathbf{s} = L - P_h$; Vector **v** points to the viewer and so is just the negative of the ray's direction **dir**; and **m** is the normal to the surface at P_h.

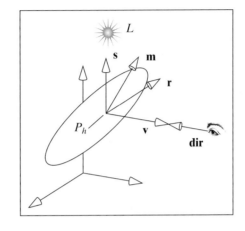

FIGURE 12.26 Applying the shading model.

As we developed in Chapter 8, the total monochromatic light intensity observed by the eye, consisting of the ambient, diffuse, and specular components, is:

$$I = I_a\rho_a + I_d\rho_d \times lambert + I_{sp}\rho_s \times phong^f \qquad (12.23)$$

where we define the values

$$lambert = \max\left(0, \frac{\mathbf{s}\cdot\mathbf{m}}{|\mathbf{s}||\mathbf{m}|}\right) \quad \text{and} \quad phong = \max\left(0, \frac{\mathbf{h}\cdot\mathbf{m}}{|\mathbf{h}||\mathbf{m}|}\right) \qquad (12.24)$$

I_a is the ambient intensity and I_s is the intensity of the light source. The terms I_a, I_d, and I_s are the intensities of the ambient, diffuse, and specular light sources, respectively. Vector **h** is the half-way vector given by $\mathbf{h} = \mathbf{s} + \mathbf{v}$.

If several light sources are present in the scene, there will be a diffuse and specular contribution from each, and these are summed to form I. Recall that the ambient term is an approximation that lumps together diverse contributions from multiple reflections off neighboring bodies throughout the scene. We shall see later that we must trace some rays individually through multiple reflections when an object is shiny enough. The ambient term still helps approximate the effect of all the less prominent rays circulating about the scene, which are too numerous to trace individually.

As we did in Chapter 8, we extend this formulation to colored lights and objects. The light that reaches the eye will then have red, green, and blue components given by

$$I_r = I_{ar}\rho_{ar} + I_{dr}\rho_{dr} \times lambert + I_{spr}\rho_{sr} \times phong^f$$
$$I_g = I_{ag}\rho_{ag} + I_{dg}\rho_{dg} \times lambert + I_{spg}\rho_{sg} \times phong^f$$
$$I_b = I_{ab}\rho_{ab} + I_{db}\rho_{db} \times lambert + I_{spb}\rho_{sb} \times phong^f \qquad (12.25)$$

where the various I's and ρ's are intensities and reflection coefficients for the individual color components. Note in particular that the *same* terms *lambert* and *phong* (and the same vectors **m**, **s**, and **h**) are used for the three color contributions, so a ray need be traced only once, and the *lambert* and *phong* terms need be evaluated only once.

Shading calculations require that we know the hit point P_h as well as the vectors: **v**, **s**, and **m**. We address next the problem of computing **m**, which requires several pieces of information, all of which are stored in the intersection record.

12.7.1 To Find the Normal at the Hit Spot

The vector **m** is the normal vector to the hit surface at the hit spot. How is it determined? First we find it most easily in generic coordinates, and then transform it into world coordinates. In Section 6.5.3 we showed that if one object is transformed into another by a transformation with matrix M, the normal vector **m′** is transformed into the normal vector **m** given by

$$\mathbf{m} = M^{-T}\mathbf{m} \tag{12.26}$$

where M^{-T} denotes the transpose of the inverse of M. The desired normal **m** is therefore found by computing the normal vector to the surface of the generic object at the hit spot and then multiplying this by M^{-T}.

Happily we have already computed and stored the normal vector at the hit point in generic coordinates; it resides in the `hitNormal` field of the intersection record for the hit in question.

12.7.2 Color Objects According to Their Surface Materials

The color seen at the hit point depends on the combination of the ambient, diffuse, and specular light contributions. The reflection coefficients ρ_{ar}, ρ_{dg}, and so forth are stored with the object that is hit, available in the `mtrl.ambient`, `mtrl.diffuse`, and `mtrl.specular` fields. These fields are loaded up when the SDL file is first read.

A common practice is to make the Phong specular light the same color as the light source. To do this the `mtrl.specular` reflection coefficient is given equal red, green, and blue components, as in (0.9, 0.9, 0.9), so its product with the source color reproduces the source color, albeit slightly diminished. This tends to make the material look like a shiny plastic.

It is not difficult to add ambient, diffuse, and specular light computations in a ray tracer. Figure 12.27 shows a pseudocode skeleton of what needs to be added in the `shade()` method of Figure 12.12.

The best intersection record `best` formed in `getFirstHit()` is examined to collect data for the first hit of the ray with an object. A convenient copy of `best.hit[0]` is put in `HitInfo` record h. The position of the hit point `hitPoint` is computed using the ray and `h.hitTime`. The generic coordinate normal vector at the hit point, stored in `h.hitNormal`, is then converted to world coordinates using Equation (12.26). The various contributions to the total color returning along the ray are then computed in `color`. The emissive and ambient components are found, and then for each light source the diffuse and specular contributions arising from that light source are found and added into the growing `color`. If the light source is shadowed by some object at the hit point, there is no contribution from that source. We discuss shadowing in Section 12.10. Simply omit the line `if(isInShadow(…)) continue;` to remove any shadow testing for now.

The specular component is found according to Equation (12.23), which requires computing the vectors **v** and **h** and using the specular reflection coefficient (and exponent f) stored in `myObj->mtrl.specular`.

```
Color3 Scene :: shade(Ray& r)
{
  Get the first hit using getFirstHit(r, best);
  Make handy copy h = best.hit[0]; // data about the first hit
  Form hitPoint based on h.hitTime
  Form v = - ray.dir; // direction to viewer
  v.normalize();
  Shape* myObj = (Shape*)h.hitObject; // point to the hit object
  Color3 color(myObj->mtrl.emissive) ³; // start with emissive part
  color.add(ambient contribution); // compute ambient color
  Vector3 normal;
  // transform the generic normal to the world normal
  xfrmNormal(normal, myObj->invTransf, h.hitNormal);
  normal.normalize(); // normalize invTransfTransposed
  for(each light source, L) // sum over all sources
  {
    if(isInShadow(...)) continue; // skip this source if in shadow
    Form s = L.pos - hitPoint; // vector from hit point to source
    s.normalize();
    float mDotS = s.dot(normal); // the Lambert term
    if(mDotS > 0.0) // hit point is turned toward the light
    Form diffuseColor = mDotS * myObj->mtrl.diffuse * L.color;
    color.add(diffuseColor);   // add the diffuse part
    Form h = v + s;  // the halfway vector
    h.normalize();
    float mDotH = h.dot(normal); // part of phong term
    if(mDotH <= 0) continue; // no specular contribution
    float phong = pow(mDotH, myObj->mtrl.specularExponent);
    specColor = phong * myObj->mtrl.specular * L.color;
    color.add(specColor);
  }
  return color;
}
```

FIGURE 12.27 Adding shading calculations to shade()—pseudocode.

Figure 12.28 shows a scene where objects have been rendered using ambient, diffuse, and specular light (but with no shadows computed). The specular highlights make the objects appear to be composed of a shiny plastic material.

PRACTICE EXERCISE

12.7.1 Transforming the normal vector

Write the routine void xfrmNormal(Vector3& res, Affine4& aff,Vector3& v) that multiplies the vector v by the *transpose* of the matrix stored in aff, and produces vector res. It is used in the ray tracer by calling xfrmNormal(normal, myObj->inv Transf, h.hitNormal). That is, the normal vector h.hitNormal in generic coordinates is transformed using the *inverse* matrix myObj-> invTransf stored in the hit object, to produce the normal vector normal in world coordinates. ■

FIGURE 12.28 Objects illuminated with ambient, diffuse, and specular light.

---

³ We assume that some handy constructors have been added to the Vector3 and Color3 classes: Vector3 s(A,B) constructs a vector as the difference of two points A and B, and Color3 col(f, d, c) constructs a color having red component f * d.red * c.red, and similarly for the green and blue components.

12.7.3 Physically Based Shading Models—Cook Torrance Shading

Phong highlights are easy to generate but tend to give objects a "shiny plastic" look. If OpenGL is used for shading, one is forced to settle for Phong highlights, but if we render by ray tracing, we have more options and can consider different algorithms for computing specular highlights.

In a quest for greater realism many researchers have developed more elaborate shading models. These models start from physical principles that characterize how light reflects from an actual surface, and develop mathematical expressions for the intensity and color of the reflected light that reaches the viewer. The models pay attention to the "balance" of light energy at the surface: the incident light energy is separated into a part that is absorbed in the material as heat, a part that interacts with the surface and is scattered back as diffuse light, and a part that reflects from the surface as specular light. Different materials split the incident light up differently: a rough surface produces more diffuse light and less specular light than a smooth shiny one.

In early contributions by Torrance and Sparrow [Torr67] and Trowbridge and Reitz [Trowbridge75] a rough surface was modeled conceptually as a collection of shiny "microfacets" oriented in different directions, as suggested in Figure 12.29. Incident light arrives at angle φ from the average normal direction **m** and reflects in different directions, depending on the microfacets that it hits. A fraction of it reflects toward the viewer.

FIGURE 12.29 Modeling a rough surface as a collection of randomly oriented microfacets.

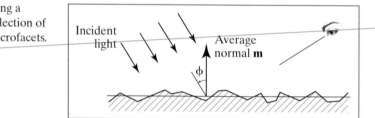

Blinn [Blinn77] used this model to develop an algorithm suitable for computer graphics, showing that it produced specular highlights quite different from Phong highlights. Cook and Torrance [Cook82] extended and refined Blinn's model, showing that there is a color shift in the specular highlights, which does a better job of matching how light reflects off real materials.

We describe the major ingredients of the Cook-Torrance model and show how it can be incorporated into a ray tracer. We discuss the three principal aspects of this model and the effects they have on the amount of specular light that is reflected. Each aspect attempts to represent accurately a physical phenomenon involved in light reflection, in a way that can be built into an algorithm.

1. The Distribution of Facet Orientations

The model assumes that each microfacet acts as a tiny perfect mirror, and only those facets that are oriented perfectly contribute to the light that is reflected in a particular direction. As suggested in Figure 12.30a, only those oriented with their normal in the direction **h** = **s** + **v** contribute to the light seen in direction **v** (the vector in the direction of the viewer). It is necessary, therefore, to know what fraction of the microfacets have this orientation. Statistical studies have been made of how randomly oriented microfacets might actually arrange themselves on a surface made of a certain material. The studies yield a distribution function $D(\delta)$ that reports the fraction of microfacets that are aimed with their normals at angle δ relative to the surface normal **m**. As shown in Figure 12.30b, if the incident angle is ϕ and the viewer lies at angle θ then only facets lying at angle $\delta = (\theta - \phi)/2$ have the right orientation to reflect light to the viewer. (See the exercises.) The fraction of facets having this orientation is $D(\delta)$.

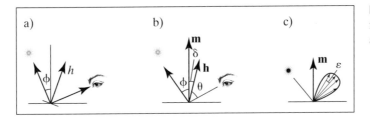

FIGURE 12.30 Finding the fraction of microfacets oriented at angle δ.

Various distribution functions have been developed. Cook and Torrance use the Beckmann distribution [Beckmann63] given by

$$D(\delta) = \frac{1}{4m^2 \cos^4(\delta)} e^{-\left(\frac{\tan(\delta)}{m}\right)^2} \qquad (12.27)$$

where the parameter m is a measure of the surface roughness. Specifically it is the root-mean-square slope of the microfacets. The Beckmann distribution has shown to be a good mathematical fit for many actual rough surfaces. $D(\delta)$ has its peak value at $\delta = 0$, falling off as δ moves away from 0. (What is the peak value?) Its value would be around 0.2 for a nearly smooth surface, and around 0.6 for a rough surface. $D(\delta)$ falls off more rapidly with δ at smaller values of m.

Cook and Torrance incorporate $D(\delta)$, with δ set equal to the angle between **h** and **m**, as a scaling factor on the specular contribution in different directions. Figure 12.30c shows how the specular intensity varies at different viewing directions for $m = 0.3$. The figure shows a "beam pattern" similar to that in Figure 8.12. The relative size of the specular component in each direction is shown by the length of the arrow. It is strongest in the direction of perfect(mirror-like) reflection (at angle ϕ) because the facets are most likely to have normals parallel to **m**. It is smaller in the direction, say ε away from this perfect mirror direction because the facet would have to have a normal ε away from **m**, and the distribution function dictates that on average fewer of them do. (See the exercises.)

2. Shadowing and Masking

Torrance and Sparrow also considered the effects of "masking" or "shadowing" that would occur on a microfaceted surface. This results in a "geometry term," G, that scales the strength of the specular component. Figure 12.31 suggests how this effect is related to the geometry of a typical facet. In part a, light arrives at the facet at such an angle that the entire facet is illuminated, and all of the reflected light "escapes" from the facet. G would equal 1 in this case. In part b the reflection direction relative to **h** is such that part of the light leaving the facet is masked off by the neighboring edge of the facet. This reduces the value of G accordingly. Finally in part c only a portion of the facet is illuminated, the rest being shadowed by the edge of the neighboring facet. Again this makes G less than 1.0.

FIGURE 12.31 Masking and shadowing of light at the facet level.

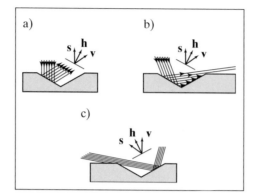

Blinn related these geometric phenomena to simple terms involving only dot products. The geometric factor uses the smallest of three values: $1, G_s$, and G_m:

$$G = \min(1, G_m, G_s) \tag{12.28}$$

where G_m is the fraction of light that is not masked out, and G_s is the fraction of light that is not shadowed. These terms are given by:

$$G_m = \frac{2(\mathbf{m}\cdot\mathbf{h})(\mathbf{m}\cdot\mathbf{s})}{\mathbf{h}\cdot\mathbf{s}}, \quad G_s = \frac{2(\mathbf{m}\cdot\mathbf{h})(\mathbf{m}\cdot\mathbf{v})}{\mathbf{h}\cdot\mathbf{s}} \tag{12.29}$$

3. The Fresnel Coefficient

The third factor in the Torrance-Sparrow model also modulates the amount of specular light. The shiny microfacets are not perfect mirrors, but like real materials reflect only a fraction of the incident light, with the remainder being transmitted into the surface. The fraction that is reflected is given by the Fresnel coefficient[4] $F(\phi, \eta)$. Here ϕ is the angle of incidence as in Figure 12.30 (the angle between $\mathbf{m}$ and $\mathbf{s}$), and η is the index of refraction of the material. Later, when ray tracing transparent materials[5] in Section 12.11, we will work with the index of refraction, but it comes into play also with opaque materials such as metals.

The Fresnel coefficient $F(\phi, \eta)$ can be derived from first principles of electromagnetic reflection from a surface having index of refraction η. Computationally it is given by:

$$F = \frac{1}{2}\frac{(g-c)^2}{(g+c)^2}\left\{1 + \left(\frac{c(g+c)-1}{c(g-c)+1}\right)^2\right\} \tag{12.30}$$

where $c = \cos(\phi) = \mathbf{m}\cdot\mathbf{s}$ and $g^2 = \eta^2 + c^2 - 1$. Note that the intermediate term g depends on the index of refraction of the material. For many materials the index of refraction varies with the wavelength of the light in a complex way. This makes the dependence of F on wavelength particularly complicated.

Figure 12.32 shows the basic shape of F versus ϕ for various values of η. The Fresnel coefficient is seen to have some material-dependent value at "normal

---

[4] Augustin Jean Fresnel (1788–1827), a French physicist, developed a number of basic results for the reflection, refraction, and polarization of light.

[5] The index of refraction of a material is the ratio of the speed of light in air divided by that in the material. It typically depends on the wavelength of the light. The relationship between the wavelength and color of light is described later in this chapter.

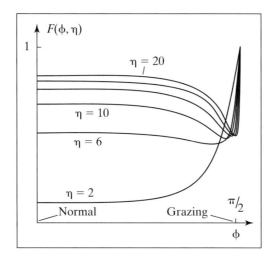

FIGURE 12.32 The Fresnel coefficient vs. angle of incidence.

incidence" ($\phi = 0$), and to vary smoothly up to the value 1.0 at a "grazing angle" ($\phi = \pi/2$). The Fresnel coefficient can never exceed one (why?)

- At normal incidence: $F(0, \eta)$ is always less than 1.
- At grazing incidence: $F(\pi/2, \eta)$ is always 1.

Torrance and Sparrow [Torrance67] put these factors together for the microfacet model and formed a physically based model for specular reflections. They derived the relative amount of specular light reflected to be the product of the three terms, F, D, and G as just discussed, divided by $\mathbf{m} \cdot \mathbf{v}$:

$$spec = \frac{F(\phi, \eta)DG}{(\mathbf{m} \cdot \mathbf{v})} \tag{12.31}$$

The denominator term $\mathbf{m} \cdot \mathbf{v}$ (which is $\cos(\theta)$; see Figure 12.31b) arises from the following argument. When viewing a surface at a grazing angle (large θ and therefore small cosine) more of the microfacets are seen within a given viewing solid angle than is the case with a view having a small angle θ. Seeing more facets produces more light, and so a smaller value of $\mathbf{m} \cdot \mathbf{v}$ produces a larger resulting intensity.

Blinn [Blinn77] adapted this model to computer graphics and compared it with Phong specular highlights. Of particular interest was the different way this specular light behaves at different angles of incidence ϕ. With Phong shading the specular highlight is always strongest in the direction of "perfect reflection" and falls off rapidly at viewing angles slightly off this direction. Figure 12.33a shows the "beam pattern" that describes how the strength of Phong highlights fall off with angle. The shape of the beam pattern is the same regardless of the angle of incidence ϕ. The beam patterns for the microfacet model are shown in part b of the figure. (The exercises develop the expression for these beam patterns.) When angle ϕ is small, the beam shape is similar to that of Phong highlights. But for grazing incidence angles the beam not only has a different shape, but the direction of greatest intensity is no longer the direction of mirrorlike reflection! This causes the "halo" of light around a specular glint to vary quite differently from the one seen about a Phong glint—a phenomenon observed with light reflecting off real surfaces.

Cook and Torrance [Cook82] extended this model in two directions. First, they took into account how incident light energy is divided into the ambient, diffuse, and

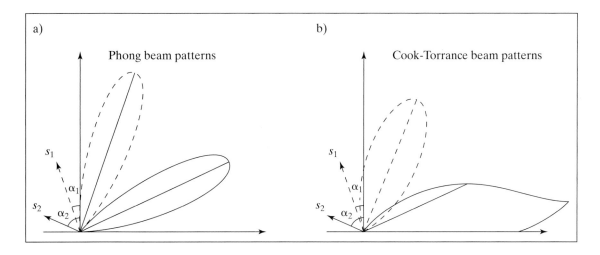

FIGURE 12.33 A contrast of
how specular intensity varies
with incident angles.

specular portions. Second, they took into account the variation in real materials of
the index of refraction with the wavelength of incident light. This variation causes
the Fresnel coefficient to vary with wavelength as well, which in turn causes the
specular light to *change* color at different incidence angles. This variation of color
with angle, or "color shift," is also observed with real materials.

When suitable expressions for each of these phenomena are combined appropriately to describe this model, the final result has the general form:

$$I_r = I_{ar}k_aF(0, \eta_r) + I_{sr}\,d\omega k_dF(0, \eta_r) \times lambert + I_{sr}k_s\,d\omega\frac{F(\phi, \eta_r)DG}{(\mathbf{m} \cdot \mathbf{v})} \qquad (12.32)$$

The expression just gives the strength of the red color component; the green and
blue components are the same except that η_g and η_b are used. The ambient source
and light source have red strengths I_{ar} and I_{sr}, respectively, and the three contributions; ambient, diffuse, and specular, are recognizable. I_{ar} is usually taken to be a
small fraction of I_{sr}. (If there is more than one light source, there is a similar diffuse
and specular term for each source, and all contributions are summed.)

The ambient and diffuse reflection coefficients are based on the Fresnel coefficient $F(0, \eta_r)$ at normal incidence. This is an approximation Cook and Torrance use
for simplicity, noting that $F(\phi, \eta_r)$ varies only slightly over a range of values of ϕ
near 0, so a reasonable approximation uses just the value at $\phi = 0$. Notice that this
coefficient *is* different at different wavelengths (it "has a color"): the green and blue
components depend on $F(0, \eta_g)$ and $F(0, \eta_b)$, respectively, and these values are different because the index of refraction is different at different colors.

The diffuse term has the familiar Lambert term [see Equation (12.24)], along
with two other factors. The term $d\omega$ is the solid angle subtended at the hit point by
the light source (see Figure 12.34). For simplicity this is assumed to be constant at all
points in the scene, and is usually chosen as a small constant, such as 0.0001. (The
sun when viewed from Earth subtends a solid angle of 0.000068 steradian.) The factor k_d (and its mate k_s in the specular term) report how the incident light is divided
between diffuse and specular reflections. They sum to one: $k_d + k_s = 1$, and are a
property of the material. The specular term is the same as *spec* of Equation (12.31),
with the explicit dependence of the Fresnel coefficient on wavelength.

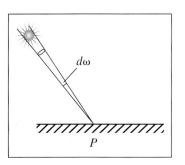

FIGURE 12.34 The source
subtends a solid angle $d\omega$.

To use these formulas we must know the index of refraction of the material in question at different wavelengths. This information is generally not available. What is available are measurements of the "normal reflectance" of different materials— that is, values for $F(0, \eta)$ at different wavelengths. Cook and Torrance infer the index of refraction from these measured values using the following argument. If we evaluate $F(\phi, \eta)$ in Equation (4.28) at $\phi = 0$, then $c = 1$ and $g = \eta$ (check this). Therefore, the whole expression collapses to:

$$F_0 = \frac{(\eta - 1)^2}{(\eta + 1)^2}$$

where F_0 denotes the value of the normal reflectance $F(0, \eta)$. This is easily inverted to expose η:

$$\eta = \frac{1 + \sqrt{F_0}}{1 - \sqrt{F_0}} \tag{12.33}$$

So, given values F_0, we can solve for the corresponding index of refraction. Figure 12.35 shows some measured values of F_0 for four polished metals [Touloukian70]

	F_0 at Red	F_0 at Green	F_0 at Blue
Gold	0.989	0.876	0.399
Silver	0.95	0.93	0.88
Copper	0.755	0.49	0.095
Iron	0.53	0.505	0.480

FIGURE 12.35 Measured normal reflectances at different wavelengths.

The Cook-Torrance shading model is computationally more expensive than the Phong model, but many people are willing to accept this cost in order to achieve the greater realism it offers. For even greater realism, scenes should be rendered at many more than three wavelengths, and the colors combined. Using only the red, green, and blue colors that more or less match those of a CRT display places an inherent limitation on the ultimate realism of computer-generated images.

PRACTICE EXERCISES

12.7.2 What angle is right for specular reflection?
Show that the angle δ in Figure 12.30b must be $\delta = (\theta - \phi)/2$ to cause light to be reflected from the source at angle ϕ to the viewer at angle θ.

12.7.3 Beam patterns for the microfacet model
Since incident and reflected light lies in the same plane, the terms G, D, F, etc used in Equation (12.31) can all be expressed in terms of the incident angle θ and the viewer angle ϕ.

a. Show that G of Equation (12.28) can be written as:

$$G(\phi, \theta) = \min\left(1, \frac{\cos\left(\dfrac{\theta - \phi}{2}\right)\cos(\phi)}{\cos\left(\dfrac{\theta + \phi}{2}\right)}, \frac{\cos\left(\dfrac{\theta - \phi}{2}\right)\cos(\theta)}{\cos\left(\dfrac{\theta + \phi}{2}\right)}\right)$$

b. Show that *spec* of Equation (12.31) is therefore given by:

$$spec = \frac{F(\phi, \eta)D\left(\dfrac{\theta - \phi}{2}\right)G(\phi, \theta)}{\cos(\theta)}.$$

c. Make your own plots of *spec* vs. θ for various values of φ, roughness *m*, and index of refraction.   ■

12.8 ADDING SURFACE TEXTURE

> Success is transient, evanescent.
> The real passion lies in the poignant acquisition of knowledge about all the shading
> and subtleties of the creative secrets.
>
> *Konstantin Stanislavsky*
> *(1863–1938)*

As we saw in Chapter 8, we can make computer-generated images much more lively and realistic by painting textures on various surfaces. Figure 12.36 shows a ray traced scene with several examples of textures.

In Chapter 8 the surfaces were polygons, and OpenGL was used to render each face. For each face *F* a pair of texture coordinates was attached to each vertex of *F*, and OpenGL painted each pixel inside the face by using the color of the corresponding point within a texture image.

FIGURE 12.36 A scene with several textured surfaces.

We want to see how to incorporate texturing into a ray tracer. Two principal kinds of texture are used:

1. *Image texture*: A 2D image is pasted onto each surface of the object.
2. *Solid texture*: The object is considered to be carved out of a block of some material. The material itself has texturing. The ray tracer reveals the color of the texture at each surface point on the object.

Solid texture is the simplest to work with, so we begin with it. We discussed a method to apply solid texture in Case Study 8.5 when using OpenGL to draw polygonal faces, but it was somewhat contrived. By contrast, it fits very naturally within a ray tracing framework.

12.8.1 Solid Texture

Solid texture is sometimes called 3D texture. It was first reported simultaneously by Perlin and Peachey [Perlin85, Peachey85]. We view an object as being carved out of some textured material such as marble or wood. The texture is represented by a function texture(*x, y, z*) that produces an (*r, g, b*) color value at every point in space. Think of this texture as a color or inkiness that varies with position; if you look (with x-ray vision) at different points (*x, y, z*), you see different colors. When an object of some shape is defined in this space, and all the material outside of the shape is chipped away to reveal the object's surface, the point (*x, y, z*) on the surface is revealed and has the specified texture.

We first elaborate on some interesting examples that were mentioned in Case Study 8.5, and then show how to incorporate such texture in a ray tracer. Next we develop some richer types of materials, such as wood grain and marble.

■ EXAMPLE 12.8.1 A 3D checkerboard that fills space

Imagine a 3D checkerboard made up of alternating red and black cubelets stacked up throughout all of space. We position one of the cubelets with a vertex at $(0, 0, 0)$ and size it so that its diagonally opposite vertex lies at point $S = (S.x, S.y, S.z)$. All other cubes have this same size (a width of $S.x$, a height of $S.y$, and so on) and they are placed adjacent to one another in all three dimensions. It's easy to write an expression for such a checkerboard texture: add together the integer parts of $x/S.x$, $y/S.y$, and $z/S.z$ and reduce the sum modulo 2:

$$\text{jump}(x, y, z) = ((\text{int})(x/S.x) + (\text{int})(y/S.y) + (\text{int})(z/S.z)) \% 2 \qquad (12.34)$$

We then set texture(x, y, z) to return black if jump() is 0, and red if jump() is 1.

Figure 12.37 shows a generic sphere and generic cube composed of material with this solid texture. Also shown, similarly textured, are a collection of interpenetrating planes and a tapered cylinder. The color of the texture is used to set the diffuse reflection coefficient of the surface. Hence the color of the material is the color of the texture. The diffuse component varies at different positions relative to the light source, and the Phong specular component is the color of the light source. Notice that the sphere and cube are clearly made up of solid cubelets. Contrast how these objects would look if a 2D checkerboard image were pasted onto them.

FIGURE 12.37 Ray tracing of some objects with checkerboard solid texture.

■ EXAMPLE 12.8.2 A stack of color cubes of smoothly varying colors

You can also stack up copies of a single unit cube. One interesting cube exhibits a smoothly varying color over the entire spectrum as you move around inside it. All eight corners are black, and the center point $(0.5, 0.5, 0.5)$ of the cube is white. In between the color varies smoothly. To make the red component rise to 1 and then fall back to 0 along the x-dimension use $red = 1 - |2*x - 1|$. The green component is similarly driven by y, and the blue component by z. To stack an infinite number of copies of this cube together in space use the fractional part of x, y, and z, giving finally:

$$\text{texture}(x, y, z) = (1 - |2*\text{fract}(x) - 1|, 1 - |2*\text{fract}(y) - 1|, 1 - |2*\text{fract}(z) - 1|) \qquad (12.35)$$

where fract(x) is $1-(\text{int})x$ and the fractional part of x. Visualize what a sphere of radius 100 would look if made of this material.

Ray Tracing Objects Composed of Solid Texture

Once the function texture() is available, almost nothing else is required to incorporate solid texture in a ray tracer. There are various ways that the texture can alter the light coming from a surface point:

1. The light can be set equal to texture() itself, as if the object were glowing with that color.
2. The texture can *modulate* (recall Chapter 8) the ambient and diffuse reflection coefficients, so that

$$I = \text{texture}(x, y, z)(I_a\rho_a + I_s\rho_d lambert) + I_s\rho_s phong \qquad (12.36)$$

where texture(x, y, z) is evaluated at the hit point (x, y, z) of the ray. This is the most common use of texture: the surface looks as if its inherent color were lighter or darker at different points, according to the fluctuations in texture(). Here the specular highlight has the color of the source and is not affected by the texture. This makes the textured object appear to be shiny, as if made of plastic.

The hit point (x, y, z) used in this formula could be either in generic coordinates or in world coordinates. Usually it is in generic coordinates, in which case the object carries the texture along with it when it is rotated or moved to its final position in the scene. In an animation where the object is rotating or moving from frame to frame, the texture will be solidly attached to the object.

If, on the other hand, (x, y, z) is the world-coordinate version, the texture is fixed in space. Now when the object rotates or moves in an animation the texture will sweep over it, making it appear to be carved out of new material at each new position. This can produce an interesting visual effect.

Rich and varied solid textures are easy to create, and some can faithfully model actual materials. The two classic examples are wood grain and marble.

Wood Grain Texture

The grain in a log of wood is due to concentric cylinders of varying color, corresponding to the rings seen where a log is cut. As the distance of points from some axis varies, the function jumps back and forth between two values. This can be simulated with a modulo function:

```
rings(r) = ((int)r) % 2
```

where, for rings about the z-axis, radius r is $r = \sqrt{x^2 + y^2}$. The value of `rings % 2` jumps between 0 and 1 as r increases from 0. The texture can be made to jump between two preset values, say D and $D + A$, using:

```
simple_wood(x, y, z) = D + A * rings(r/M) % 2);
```

where again $r = \sqrt{x^2 + y^2}$. This produces rings of thickness M concentric about the z-axis.

Things get more interesting if we wobble, skew, and rotate the rings [Watt92]. To wobble the rings add a component that varies with azimuth θ about the z-axis:

$$\text{rings}\left(\frac{r}{M} + K \sin\left(\frac{\theta}{N}\right)\right)$$

Now even when the radius is held constant there is a fluctuation of the rings as θ varies, making the rings wobble in and out N times as you look around the axis. Note that we are nesting functions within functions to add more effects: the argument of rings() is not just r but is the sum of r/M and a sinusoid, which is itself the quotient of an angle and N. Perlin [Perlin85] made powerful use of this functional composition to create many interesting visual effects. We can go further and add a twist to the wobbling wood grain using

$$\text{rings}\left(\frac{r}{M} + K \sin\left(\frac{\theta}{N} + Bz\right)\right) \tag{12.37}$$

so that the phase of the sinusoid varies with z, effectively rotating the wobble as height varies. And if you want to tilt this grain so that it is concentric about some axis other than the z-axis, apply a rotation before evaluating r and θ. For instance, form r as $\sqrt{x'^2 + y'^2}$, where $(x', y', z') = T(x, y, z)$ for some rotation transformation $T()$.

FIGURE 12.38 Objects apparently carved out of wood.

Figure 12.38 shows some objects that appear to be carved out of wood, having wood grain defined in these ways.

3D Noise and Marble Texture

The grain in materials such as marble is quite chaotic, as suggested in Figure 12.39. There are turbulent rivulets of dark material coursing through the stone, with random whirls and blotches, as if the stone were formed of some violently stirred molten material.

We can simulate turbulence by building a noise function that produces an apparently random value at each point (x, y, z) in space. This noise field is then stirred up in a well-controlled way to give the appearance of turbulence.

The noise field itself is easy to program. Imagine defining a random value at each *integer* position in space—that is, at $(x, y, z) = (i, j, k)$ for every combination of integers i, j, and k. Such an arrangement of points is called an **integer lattice**. Figure 12.40a shows a 2D version, where various points in a 2D integer lattice are labeled with noise values between 0 and 1. For instance, point $(1, 2)$ has noise value 0.653 and point $(3, 1)$ has value 0.129. Part b shows a 3D integer lattice. Visualize every integer point having some fixed noise value, such as 0.7341 at $(2, 2, 1)$.

FIGURE 12.39 Materials carved from marble.

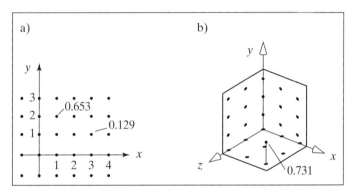

FIGURE 12.40 Defining noise values at each point in a 3D integer lattice.

The collection of noise values could be stored in a huge array `float N[10000]` `[10000][10000]`, but this would require an unacceptable amount of memory. It is far simpler to generate each noise value each time it is needed. For this approach we need a function, say `float latticeNoise(int i,int j,int k)`, that returns an apparently random value given the integers i, j, and k that specify the position in the lattice. The function must be efficient and completely *repeatable*, always returning the same noise value for a given (i, j, k). Several of the authors in the excellent text *Texturing and Modeling* [Ebert98] describe suitable approaches. We focus on the one introduced by Perlin and elaborated on by Peachey.

Generating Repeatable Random Values

The trick is to set up a fixed array, say `noiseTable[]`, of pseudorandom noise values in an initialization step. Arrays of length 256 have been found to be quite adequate, so we use this length.

Now the main function, `latticeNoise(i, j, k)`, simply indexes into `noiseTable[]` in a repeatable way. To insure that there is little or no pattern in the noise values as i, j, or k varies, the indexing function effectively scrambles or hashes the (i, j, k) combination into a value between 0 and 255. This is easy to accomplish using a second array, `index[]`, that contains the values 0 through 255 randomly permuted. Peachy suggests defining the two macros

```
#define PERM(x) index[(x) & 255]
#define INDEX(ix, iy, iz) PERM( (ix) + PERM((iy) + PERM(iz)) )
```

The PERM macro takes an integer value of x and performs a bitwise AND operation on it with 255, effectively retaining only its low-order 8 bits, so it is hashed into a value between 0 and 255. The value of PERM is therefore one of the values selected from the index array. The INDEX macro uses PERM to dip into the index array three times, in each case choosing an element of index[] based on one of the values ix, iy, or iz. Note that this is a repeatable and efficient operation, and that there is plenty of scrambling taking place. The latticeNoise() function then is simply:

```
float latticeNoise(int i, int j, int k)
{
    return noiseTable[INDEX(i,j,k)];
}
```

Developing the Noise Class

It is convenient to encapsulate all of this action into a class Noise that we will use to generate marble and other noiselike textures. Figure 12.41 shows the declaration of this class (also see the book's companion web site).

```
class Noise{
public:
    Noise() // a constructor
    {
        int i;
        index = new unsigned char[256];
        for(i = 0; i < 256; i++) index[i] = i; // fill array with indices
        for(i = 0; i < 256; i++) // shuffle it
        {
            int which = rand() % 256; // choose random place in array
            unsigned char tmp = index[which]; // swap them
            index[which] = index[i];
            index[i] = tmp;
        }
        noiseTable = new float[256];
        for(i = 0; i < 256; i++) noiseTable[i] = rand()/32767.99;
    } // end of constructor

    float noise(float x, float y, float z);
    float noise(float scale, Point3& p);
    float turbulence(float s, Point3& p);
    float marble(float x, float y, float z);
    float marble(float strength,Point3& p);

private:
    float* noiseTable;        // array of noise values
    unsigned char * index;    // pseudorandom indices
    float mySpline(float x);  // used for marble
    float latticeNoise(int i, int j, int k)
    { // return noise value on an integer lattice
        #define PERM(x) index[(x) & 255]
        #define INDEX(ix, iy, iz) PERM( (ix) + PERM((iy) + PERM(iz)) )
        return noiseTable[INDEX(i,j,k)];
    }
};
```

FIGURE 12.41 Generating repeatable noise values.

The method of greatest interest in the class is `marble()`, which returns a position-dependent value of brightness between 0 and 1 that mimics the rivulets of dark and light stone in marble. We develop its details later. It would be used to generate a greenish marble by constructing a noise object at the start of the ray tracing with:

```
Noise n; // create and construct a noise object
```

and thereafter obtaining the texture(x, y, z) value at each point (x, y, z) desired as simply `n.marble(x, y, z)`;

The method `marble()` uses `noise()` and `turbulence()`, also developed shortly, as well as the helper function `latticeNoise()`. The class constructor creates and fills the arrays `noiseTable[]` and `index[]`. The random values that are put into `noiseTable[]` are simply created using the standard C function `rand()`, scaling the values to lie between 0.0 and 1.0. The array index[] is first loaded with values 0 to 255 in order, and then this array is shuffled by swapping each of its elements in turn with some randomly selected element.

With the function `latticeNoise()` in hand that produces random values at integer lattice points, we want a function noise(x, y, z) that produces randomlike values at points in between—in fact at *any* point in space. We also want the noise to vary smoothly as x, y, and z vary.

Simple linear interpolation between the lattice values gives acceptable results.[6] Figure 12.42 shows interpolation in 2D; the 3D case is similar. Here we wish to evaluate noise at say (x, y) = (0.6, 1.4), given the noise values on the four surrounding corners of the lattice. First interpolate in x along y = 1 and y = 2 to form the values[7]

$$n(0.6, 1) = \text{lerp}(0.6, n_{01}, n_{11})$$
$$n(0.6, 2) = \text{lerp}(0.6, n_{02}, n_{12})$$

and then interpolate these in y to form

$$n(0.6, 1.4) = \text{lerp}(0.4, n(0.6, 1), n(0.6, 2))$$

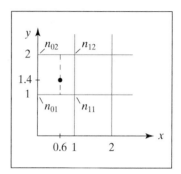

FIGURE 12.42 Linear interpolation of noise values—2D case.

Figure 12.43 shows a possible implementation of the function `noise()` for the 3D case. It has an extra parameter `scale` that scales the given 3D point (x, y, z); this will prove handy when we are creating turbulence. The scaled point is first offset by 1000 in x, y, and z so that all components will be positive. (Since the lattice values are random anyway, this shift doesn't change the statistical nature of the noise generated.) Then noise values are generated at the eight lattice vertices that surround the point. Finally seven `lerp`s are used to find the interpolated noise value.

Figure 12.44a shows a plot of the function `noise(20, x, y, 0)`, using black for 0.0 and white for 1.0. In the figure both x and y range from −1 to 1. Some structure is apparent in the noise field, due to the vagaries of the random number generation process, but it is not excessive.

Turbulence

Perlin [Perlin85, Ebert98] described a method for generating more interesting noise than that above. The idea is to mix together several noise components, one that fluctuates slowly as you move slightly through space, one that fluctuates twice as rapidly, one that fluctuates four times as rapidly, and so on. The more rapidly varying components are given progressively smaller strengths. The function `turb()`:

$$\text{turb}(s, x, y, z) = \frac{1}{2}\text{noise}(s, x, y, z) + \frac{1}{4}\text{noise}(2s, x, y, z) + \frac{1}{8}\text{noise}(4s, x, y, z) \qquad (12.38)$$

---

[6] Perlin and Peachey argue that cubic interpolation gives more realistic results [Ebert98].

[7] Recall the lerp() function introduced in Chapter 5: lerp(f, A, B) = A + (B − A)f is the value that lies fraction f of the way from A to B.

```
float Noise:: noise(float scale, Point3& p)
{ // linearly interpolated lattice noise
  #define lerp(f, A, B) A + f * (B - A)
    float d[2][2][2];
    Point3 pp;
    pp.x = p.x * scale + 10000; // offset avoids negative values
    pp.y = p.y * scale + 10000;
    pp.z = p.z * scale + 10000;
    long ix = (long)pp.x; long iy = (long)pp.y; long iz = (long)pp.z;
    float tx,ty,tz, x0,x1,x2,x3, y0,y1;
    tx = pp.x - ix; ty = pp.y - iy; tz = pp.z - iz; // fractional parts
    float mtx = 1.0 - tx, mty = 1.0 - ty, mtz = 1.0 - tz;

    for(int k = 0; k <= 1; k++) // get noise at 8 lattice points
    for(int j = 0; j <= 1; j++)
    for(int i = 0; i <= 1; i++)
       d[k][j][i] = latticeNoise(ix + i, iy + j,iz + k);

    x0 = lerp(tx, d[0][0][0],d[0][0][1]);
    x1 = lerp(tx, d[0][1][0],d[0][1][1]);
    x2 = lerp(tx, d[1][0][0],d[1][0][1]);
    x3 = lerp(tx, d[1][1][0],d[1][1][1]);
    y0 = lerp(ty, x0, x1);
    y1 = lerp(ty, x2, x3);
    return lerp(tz, y0, y1);
}
```

FIGURE 12.43 A function to generate noise at any point p.

FIGURE 12.44 Sample plots of a) noise() and b) turb().

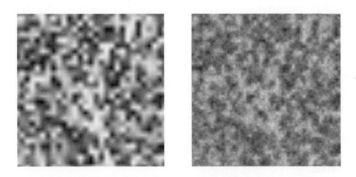

adds three such components: each is half as strong, and varies twice as rapidly, as its predecessor. Parameter s scales distances just as it does in noise(). Figure 12.45 suggests a way in 2D to see how turb() fluctuates. Think of the xy-plane covered with fixed values of noise(1, x, y, 0). For each point $P = (x, y)$, turb(1, x, y, 0) sums together three noise values, at the points (x, y), $(2x, 2y)$, and $(4x, 4y)$ shown. At nearby P' the value noise(1, x', y', 0) is very similar to noise(1, x, y, 0), but noise(2, x', y, 0') will be quite different from noise(2, x, y, 0), and noise(4, x', y', 0) will be still more different. Features in the first noise component will appear at half size in the next component, and at quarter size in the next.

The size of each component is half as large as its predecessor at each scale of detail, but its frequency (or rate of fluctuation) is twice that of the previous component. This

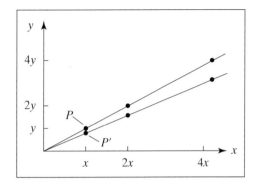

FIGURE 12.45 On the behavior of turb().

gives rise to the kind of **self-similarity** we study in Appendix 5, and in fact under certain conditions turb() produces a useful approximation to so-called "1/f noise" that seems to show up in various naturalistic shapes. Figure 12.44b shows a plot of turb() generated from the noise() field of part a, when $M = 3$. The greater level of detail is apparent, and the fluctuations seem softer and more cloudlike. The turbulence that is provided by a function like turb() can be used to perturb some attribute of a shape or texture to give it a more realistic appearance, as we see next for the case of marble.

Marble Texture

Marble shows veins of dark and light material that have some regularity, but the veins also exhibit some chaotic irregularities. Following Watt and Watt [Watt92] we can build up a marblelike 3D texture by giving the veins a smoothly fluctuating behavior in, say, the z-direction, and then perturbing it chaotically using turb(). We start with a texture that is constant in x and y and smoothly varying in z. The function marble is given by:

$$\text{marble}(x, y, z) = \text{undulate}(\sin(z))$$

where undulate() is the spline-shaped function shown in Figure 12.46a [Watt92] that varies between some dark and some light value as its argument varies from -1 to 1. The spline function is discussed in the exercises. Using $\sin(z)$ for this argument produces a periodic ripple in z that moves back and forth across the spline curve, once each period, producing the fluctuation in intensity shown in Figure 12.46b. The vertical veins of color in the marble are, of course, much too regular. So the argument of sin() is modulated with some turbulence:

$$\text{marble}(x, y, z) = \text{undulate}(\sin(z + A \, \text{turb}(s, x, y, z)))$$

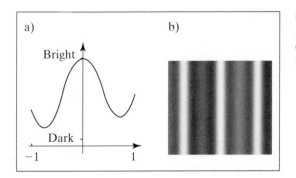

FIGURE 12.46 Constructing marble texture: a) a spline curve, b) unperturbed marble texture.

The phase of the sin() is offset different amounts at different positions in the marble. This produces much more realistic veins. Parameter s makes the turbulence vary more or less rapidly at different points; parameter A changes the amount of the perturbation. Watt demonstrates that if undulate() were replaced by a simple straight line, the effect would be much less satisfactory.

Figure 12.47 shows the marble texture seen on the face of a cube. The function plotted is:

$$g = \text{spline}(\sin(2\pi z + A \times \text{turb}(5, x, y, z)))$$

where z moves from 0 at the right to 1 at the left, and y points upward. The amplitude A is 1 in part a, so only a little turbulence is present. In parts b and c A is 3 and 6, respectively, and the turbulence is much more pronounced.

FIGURE 12.47 Marble texture: a) $A = 1$, b) $A = 3$, c) $A = 6$.

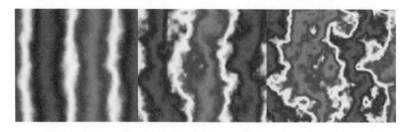

The value of marble() would be used as a reflection coefficient in Equation (12.36) to modulate the amount of light returning from different points in the object hit by different rays. It is straightforward to extend marble() to return red, green, and blue components for full-color ray tracers.

Figure 12.48 shows a ray traced scene containing a number of marble objects. The effect is quite convincing.

FIGURE 12.48 A scene with marble objects.

12.8.2 To Paste Images onto Surfaces

We examined in Chapter 8 how to paste images onto polygonal surfaces using OpenGL. Now we examine how to paste images onto arbitrary curved surfaces in a ray tracer. The routines for doing so are simple, and results can be excellent, but more execution time is usually required than with OpenGL. Among other burdens, each pixel is computed individually, and no scanline coherence can be exploited.

As in Chapter 8 we assume that a 2D texture function texture(u, v) has been defined, as u and v vary from 0 to 1, that produces an intensity or color at each point (u, v). texture(u, v) might be a procedural texture such as the checkerboard or a Mandelbrot set, or it might be an image texture stored in a pixmap. Suppose the pixmap is arranged as an *N*-by-*M* array of pixel values called `txtr[][]`. Then, given values for *u* and *v* between 0 and 1, we can index into the appropriate pixel of `txtr` simply using

`txtr[(int)(u/N)] [(int)(v/M)].`

It is simplest to paste a texture to a generic object rather than its transformed version in scene coordinates. The designer associates texture coordinates with coordinates on the generic object in such a way that when the object is transformed into the scene, the texture appears correctly and with the proper aspect ratio on the transformed object.

Wrapping Texture onto Surfaces

We need a way to associate points (x, y, z) on a generic object's surface to texture coordinates (u, v). Different mappings are needed for different generic shapes.

■ **EXAMPLE 12.8.3 Textures for the square and plane**

The generic plane is the *xy*-plane, and the generic square lies in this plane. Thus there is a natural association between the image plane of texture(u, v) and the generic square or plane. As shown in Figure 12.49, the designer simply chooses a window on the plane (*left, top, right, bottom*), and if the ray hits within this window it is easy to compute which point (u, v) in the texture is to be used.

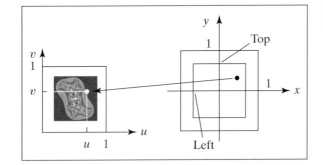

FIGURE 12.49 Mapping textures onto the square or plane.

Specifically, given hit point $(x, y, 0)$ in generic coordinates, the corresponding texture coordinates are as follows.

$$u = \frac{x - left}{right - left}, \quad v = \frac{y - bottom}{top - bottom} \tag{12.39}$$

The designer must also decide how to handle hit points that fall outside the window. A common approach is to specify some fixed value that is used for the texture value when this occurs.

■ **EXAMPLE 12.8.4 Textures for the cylinder**

Wrapping a texture around a generic cylinder is almost as easy. Recall the discussion in Section 8.5.5 about wrapping a texture about a cylindrical surface. The generic tapered cylinder is shown in Figure 12.50, with a window specified on its surface. The window extends in azimuth from a_1 to a_2, and in *z* from z_1 to z_2. When a ray hits a cylinder at (x, y, z) we simply compute the azimuth as $\theta = \arctan(y, x)$ and compute the texture coordinates (u, v) using

$$u = \frac{\theta - a_1}{a_2 - a_1}, \quad v = \frac{z - z_1}{z_2 - z_1} \tag{12.40}$$

FIGURE 12.50 Wrapping a texture about a cylinder.

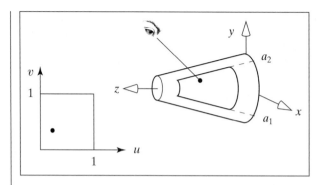

If the hit point lies outside of the designated window, the designer must choose the color to use for the texture. Notice that if the cylinder is highly tapered, there will be distortion in the mapped texture image. Pasting texture onto the cap or base of a cylinder is addressed in the exercises. Also addressed there is the problem of wrapping a texture about a sphere or cone.

PRACTICE EXERCISES

12.8.1 Wrapping a texture on the cap and base of a cylinder

Discuss in detail how to paste a texture onto the cap and base of a cylinder. A portion of a bitmap is to be pasted so that it covers the cap or base completely.

12.8.2 Wrapping a texture about a sphere

Discuss in detail how to wrap a texture about a portion of a generic sphere. The texture window extends from azimuth a_1 to a_2, and from latitude l_1 to l_2. Discuss the severity of the distortion a bitmap will suffer if l_1 or l_2 is set too close to $\pm 90°$. If a texture function is used instead of a bitmap, can the function be defined so that it produces no distortion, even near the poles of the sphere?

12.8.3 Wrapping the world around a sphere

Suppose you have a geographical database for the borders of all the countries of the world. It consists of a large number of polylines whose endpoints are given as (*longitude*, *latitude*). Can this be used to wrap a geographically accurate map of the world about the generic sphere? If so, describe how to do it.

12.8.4 Wrapping a texture about a cone

Discuss in detail how to wrap a texture about a portion of the wall of a generic cone. What is a natural interpretation of the window parameters? Discuss the nature of the distortion a bitmap will suffer in various situations. Describe how to map a texture onto the base of the cone.   ■

12.9 ANTIALIASING RAY TRACINGS

Ray tracing is inherently a point-sampling process—taking discrete looks at a scene along individual rays. So it is not surprising that aliasing effects often degrade the quality of ray traced images.

As we saw earlier, aliasing effects can be reduced by sampling a scene at more points, often called **supersampling**. This is true for ray tracing, too: several rays per pixel are traced into the scene, and the intensities that are returned along the ray are averaged. This is, of course, costly in execution time.

Figure 12.51a shows a sampling pattern where rays are shot through the corners of the pixels. The final color given to each pixel is the average of the colors found at its four corners. This level of antialiasing is easy to do and only costs a little in time. Supersampling can involve many more rays per pixel. An example of shooting nine rays through parts of a pixel is shown in Figure 12.51b. The light returned along all nine rays is averaged to form the final pixel value.

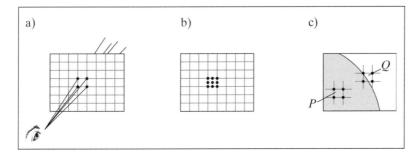

FIGURE 12.51 Supersampling techniques for antialiasing.

Several more sophisticated techniques have been developed that do a better job. Whitted [Whitted80] suggested an adaptive procedure that shoots more rays into regions where antialiasing is more needed—where there are abrupt changes in the image.

In Whitted's method, rays are shot through the four corners of each pixel and the average intensity is formed, but then this average is compared with the four individual intensities. If a corner intensity differs too much from the average, the pixel is subdivided into quadrants, and additional rays are sent through the corners of the quadrant. This is illustrated in Figure 12.51c. The four rays for pixel P return nearly the same intensity because the scene is not changing in that region, but one of the rays for pixel Q sends back an intensity very different from the others. Therefore three new rays are shot through the corners of the lower left-hand quadrant of Q, and again the intensity from each is compared with the average. Subdivision is performed recursively until either a prefixed recursion level has been reached, or the four intensities are sufficiently close to the average to make the intensity acceptable as close enough. When this has been done to the four quadrants of a pixel as needed, the final pixel value is formed as a weighted average of the quadrant averages.

Another technique is based on distributed sampling [Cook84]. It uses a form of stochastic sampling, which we saw in Chapter 9 in connection with antialiasing of texture. A random pattern of rays is shot into the scene for each pixel, and the resulting intensities are averaged. For instance, a pixel can be subdivided into a regular 4-by-4 grid. But instead of rays being shot exactly through these grid points, a ray is shot through displaced or jittered grid points. Jittering the sample points adds a measure of noise to the image, but this noise can be less intrusive to the eye than aliasing errors. A smaller grid of samples can be used with jittering than without it.

Figure 12.52 shows a ray traced billiard ball that illustrates the use of stochastic sampling. There is noticeable aliasing, particularly noticeable around the edge of the ball.

FIGURE 12.52 The jitter effect on a billiard ball. (Courtesy of Sven Maerivoet)

12.10 USING EXTENTS

Real knowledge is to know the extent of one's ignorance.

Confucius
(551–479 B.C.)

Ray tracing is very repetitive, performing the same set of operations again and again for a very large number of rays. Each ray must be intersected with every object, amounting to an enormous number of intersection calculations. Matters will get much worse when we incorporate shadows, reflections, and refractions. We welcome any technique that reduces the number of objects that must be completely scrutinized and processed. The use of extents can speed up the ray tracing process significantly.

An **extent** of an object is a shape that encloses that object. It accelerates the ray tracing process by quickly revealing when the current ray *could not possibly hit* a particular object. The notion is that if a ray misses the extent, it must perforce miss the object. If the extent has a simple shape, it may be inexpensive to intersect a ray with it, whereas it may be very expensive to intersect a ray with the enclosed object.

Figure 12.53 shows an example where a torus (expensive to intersect) is enclosed in a box-like extent (inexpensive to intersect). When the ray is tested against the extent, three things can happen:

1. The ray misses the box. Therefore the test against the torus is skipped.
2. The ray hits the box, so the full test against the torus is performed, revealing that the ray misses the torus. (This might be called a false alarm; the first test indicated the ray could hit the torus, but in fact it did not.)

FIGURE 12.53 Enclosing a torus in a box extent.

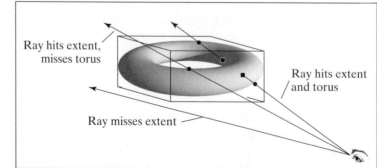

Ray hits extent, misses torus

Ray hits extent and torus

Ray misses extent

3. The ray hits the box, so the full test against the torus is performed, revealing that the ray hits the torus.

If the cost of the full hit test is much greater than that of the extent test, the savings in the frequent cases where the ray does miss the extent can more than offset that list.

Aside: A little analysis of the cost saving:

Suppose it costs T time units to test a ray against the extent, and mT time units to test it against the torus. Suppose further that N rays are cast to create the image, and only fraction f of them hit the box. It follows that N tests are made against the extent, at a cost of NT, and fN tests are made against the torus, at a cost of $fNmT$. So the total cost is $NT(1 + fm)$. On the other hand, if extents are not used, all N rays must be tested against the torus, at a total cost of mNT. This yields the ratio

$$\text{speed ratio} = \frac{\text{cost without extents}}{\text{cost with extents}} = \frac{m}{1 + f \cdot m} \qquad (12.41)$$

For example, if $m = 20$ and $f = 1/40$ (each object in a typical scene covers only a small fraction of the image area), this ratio is about 13, so it would take 13 times as long to trace this scene if extent testing were disabled.

Note from this analysis that we want f to be as small as possible. That is, we want each extent to be as small as possible so that the fewest rays will hit it. This agrees with our intuition that extents should be as tight fitting about their parent objects as possible.

Where does extent testing fit into the ray tracing process? Arvo and Kirk [Arvo89] made an excellent survey of possible approaches, including the use of hierarchical extents that enclose whole groups of objects within an extent. We focus on improving the basic `hit()` method that every object in the scene possesses. Recall the basic routine `getFirstHit()` of Figure 12.4 that must test the current ray against every object, using the specific `hit()` method for the object:

```
for(each object, obj)
{
    if(!obj->hit(ray,inter)) continue;
        compare this hit time with the best so far,etc.
}
```

We shall use extent testing inside `hit()` to accelerate each individual test. If we can quickly determine that the ray does *not* hit the object before we perform the entire intersection calculation, the overall speed of the ray tracer will increase significantly. One advantage of putting extent testing inside each `hit()` method is that the testing can be fine-tuned to the specific geometric shape in question.

There are several ways to create and use extents in ray tracing. Some are easy to implement, while others require more programming but yield better performance. We examine a handful of different simple methods, showing how they fit into the logical flow in a ray tracer. Others are described in the exercises.

12.10.1 Box and Sphere Extents

The two shapes most often used for extents are the sphere and an aligned box:

- **Sphere extent**: a sphere that completely encloses the given object; it is specified by (C, r), its center point C and radius r.
- **Box extent**: a rectangular parallelepiped whose sides are aligned with the coordinate axes. It is specified by six numbers: (*left, top, right, bottom, front, back*)

We have seen that intersecting each of these shapes with a ray is reasonably fast. For the sphere we must form a quadratic equation and test whether the discriminant is positive (see Figure 12.15). For an aligned box we must intersect the ray with six planes (or fewer, if lucky enough to get an 'early out'), and test whether the candidate interval (t_{in}, t_{out}) vanishes (see Figure 12.23). Each of the plane intersections is very fast, since no dot products need to be formed.

There are two coordinate spaces in which we can do extent testing, world coordinates and generic coordinates. Recall that each object is transformed from some generic shape into the scene by an affine transformation. To intersect the ray with the object we first inverse-transform the ray into generic coordinates and intersect the generic ray with the generic object. But we can place an extent about the object in the scene itself and test the current ray against it. If the ray misses this extent, the generic ray need not be computed, which saves a transformation. We can also place an extent about the generic object and test the inverse transformed ray against it. If the ray misses this extent, a full intersection test is avoided.

Extents in world coordinates might not fit particularly well about their objects. Figure 12.54a shows a tapered cylinder positioned in some scene being ray traced. Part b shows the cylinder, in 2D for simplicity, surrounded by a sphere extent and a box extent. If the cylinder is long and thin, the sphere extent doesn't fit particularly closely, and using it would lead to many false alarms (where the ray hits the extent but doesn't hit the cylinder). The box extent fits closely about the cylinder even if it is long and thin, unless the cylinder is rotated away from alignment with the coordinate axes. The exercises ask you to estimate the likelihood of false alarms for various cases.

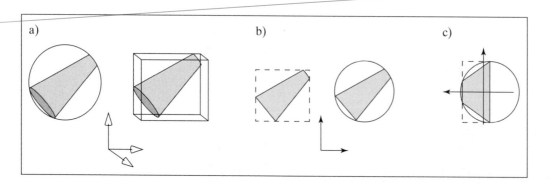

FIGURE 12.54 Extents formed in world and generic coordinates.

Extents in generic coordinates usually fit more snugly. Figure 12.54c shows the generic tapered cylinder, surrounded by a sphere extent and a box extent. The sphere extent fits reasonably snugly, and the box extent fits very tightly about the cylinder.

There is a trade-off to consider when deciding whether to do extent testing in world coordinates or in generic coordinates. Testing in world coordinates is fast, because there is no need to compute the inverse-transformed ray, but extents may not fit very tightly about their objects. Testing in generic coordinates requires finding the generic ray, but extents fit more tightly. It is difficult to say in general which kind of test is superior. It is also difficult to generalize on the advantage of sphere extents over box extents. People do elaborate timing tests on sample scenes, using one or more of the methods, and decide on the best combination to use in their ray tracers. One informal test on a scene of 100 randomly scaled and oriented tapered cylinders showed that the use of sphere extents in world coordinates reduced the ray tracing time by 27%, whereas the use of any other combination of extents *increased* the ray tracing time. But as we shall see later, when we incorporate more features in a ray tracer, the results can be quite different.

Figure 12.55 shows in pseudocode how extent testing fits into a hit() method, for the case of the tapered cylinder. Sphere extent testing is shown, and the test is done in both world and generic coordinates to show where the testing is done. Probably only one of the tests would be used in an actual ray tracer. The routine rayHitsSphereExtent() is called to see whether the ray hits the sphere extent, and if not, there is an early out from hit(). It is called first with the ray in world coordinates and tested against a worldSphereExtent. If the ray hits this extent, it is inverse transformed. The routine is then called a second time to see if the generic ray hits the generic sphere extent. Again, if it misses, there is an early out, and the elaborate intersection test of a ray with the generic cylinder is skipped.

```
bool TaperedCylinder::hit(Ray &r, Intersection &inter)
{
  if(!rayHitsSphereExtent(r,worldSphereExtent)) return false;

  Ray genRay; // make the generic ray
  xfrmRay(genRay,invTransf,r); // expensive

  if(!rayHitsSphereExtent(genRay,genSphereExtent)) return false;
  ...The ray hit the extent; you have to do expensive full testing with the generic cylinder...

}
```

FIGURE 12.55 Testing against sphere extents within the hit() method for the cylinder.

If it were felt that box extents would be more efficient than sphere extents for the tapered cylinder, we could replace the rayHitsSphereExtent() routine with a rayHitsBoxExtent() routine. We could even put *both* extent tests inside hit(), although this would most likely produce a net loss in speed.

We must choose which tests to include in each hit() method for the different shape classes. Some choices are obvious. For a Sphere object there is no sense in doing a sphere extent test in generic coordinates (why?), and similarly you would never do a box extent test in generic coordinates for the Cube object. There are no extents for a Plane, so no tests are included in Plane :: hit(). For a Square it is meaningful to build an extent, but the intersection test is so simple anyway that little or no gain would be expected in using an extent test. A Mesh object, on the other hand, has a large number of bounding planes and is expensive to intersect, so extent testing can yield significant gains.

How to Implement Extent Testing

How are extents formed for each geometric shape, and how is each extent test carried out? It is natural to store the extent information of an object inside the object itself, so we add some fields to the GeomObj class (see book's companion web site). We may want to do any one of the four types of extent testing, so we add fields for each:

```
SphereInfo genSphereExtent, worldSphereExtent;
Cuboid genBoxExtent, worldBoxExtent;
```

The SphereInfo class (see book's companion web site) holds a description of a sphere in two fields: center, which holds the location of the center of the sphere extent, and radSq, which holds the square of its radius. It could instead hold the radius, but only the square of the radius is required for the extent test. The Cuboid class has six fields: left, top, right, bottom, front, back. The box extent is understood to extend from left to right along the *x*-axis, from bottom to top along the *y*-axis, and from back to front along the *z*-axis.

After the object list has been built but before ray tracing begins, data are placed in these fields for each object in the object list. Then during ray tracing some combination of the routines rayHitsSphereExtent() and rayHitsBoxExtent() is called inside each hit() method, as shown in Figure 12.55. The test of a ray with a sphere extent is particularly easy to implement (see the exercises).

It tests whether the discriminant of the appropriate quadratic equation is positive. Eleven multiplications are required to compute the discriminant, so this test is not entirely without cost.

The rayHitsBoxExtent() test is an adaptation of the hit() method of the Cube class to work with a box extent described in a Cuboid data structure. It should be finely tuned for maximum speed.

To Build the Sphere and Box Extents

We need to create the sphere and box extents for each given object. The generic extents need be made only once for each type of shape, but the world extents must be made for each object instance, taking into account the affine transformation associated with the instance. The involvement of a transformation makes the computation of the extent more difficult. For instance, how do we find a sphere extent for a cylinder that has been scaled and rotated in a complex way?

For the cylinder a particularly straightforward method associates a **point cluster** with each shape. This is a set of points whose convex hull encloses the object. Recall an intuitive way to envision the convex hull of a set of points fixed in space: place a balloon about the points and let the balloon collapse onto the points. The resulting polyhedron is the convex hull. With a point cluster in hand it is easy to construct a sphere that just encloses the cluster. And certainly such a sphere would enclose the original object. We can also obtain a convex hull for the object after it is transformed: just transform each point in the point cluster, and use the new points to define the transformed convex hull. Since affine transformations preserve insideness, if object *A* lies inside the convex hull *B*, then the transformed object *T(A)* must lie inside the convex hull *T(B)* built on the transformed points.

We therefore need to build a point cluster for each shape type. This is easy for the Cube and the Square: their own vertices provide the points. It is also simple for a Mesh: just use the vertex list itself as the point cluster.

The Sphere and the TaperedCylinder present more of a problem, since they are defined by various symmetry properties rather than by points. A reasonable approach wraps each shape in a tightly enclosing polyhedron and uses the vertices of the polyhedron as the point cluster. Figure 12.56a shows the generic tapered cylinder wrapped in a prism based on a hexagon at each end. The hexagon at the base must have a radius of 4/3 in order to fit snugly about the circular. The hexagon at the cap has a radius of 4/3 times the radius of the cap. Note that this point cluster is constructed individually for each instance of a tapered cylinder, and that it is designed specially for the specific shape of the cylinder. Figure 12.56b shows the generic sphere wrapped in an icosahedron, whose 12 vertices comprise the point cluster. The vertices of the icosahedron must be placed at a radius of about 1.26 to ensure that the unit sphere is properly enclosed.

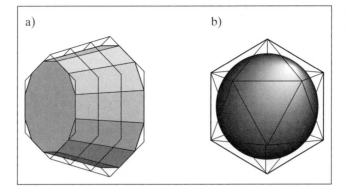

a) b)

FIGURE 12.56 Defining point clusters for the cylinder and the sphere.

The point clusters for each shape type can be stored in a simple `PointCluster` data structure containing a field `num` for the number of points in the cluster, and an array `pt[]`. A method `makeExtentPoints(PointCluster& clust)` is developed for each shape class and called once during a preprocessing step for each object in the scene.

Once the point cluster is available for a generic object, it is easy to find the box and sphere extents. Each field of the box extent holds the largest or smallest coordinate found among the cluster points, so all fields can be found within a single loop over the cluster points. This would be done in a routine `void makeBoxExtent (PointCluster& clust, Cuboid& cub)` that takes a point cluster and generates a `Cuboid` data structure, which is then stored in the object.

Building the sphere extent takes only a little more work. The center of the sphere extent is chosen to be the *centroid* of the point cluster, since this is a nice centralized point. To find the centroid, just add up all of the points componentwise and divide by the number of points. Then the radius of the enclosing sphere is found as the largest distance from this center to any one of the points in the cluster. Based on this approach, the routine `void makeSphereExtent (PointCluster& clust, SphereInfo& sph)` is easily fashioned.

Finally, it is easy to form the world box extent and world sphere extent. Simply transform each of the points of the generic object's point cluster to form a point cluster in world coordinates. Then use the same routines as above to form the desired extents.

PRACTICE EXERCISES

12.10.1 Testing a ray with a sphere extent

a. Show that the smallest enclosing sphere about the generic cylinder (with small radius of 1) is centered at $(0, 0, 0.5)$ and that its radius is $\sqrt{1.25}$.
b. Show that this sphere therefore has implicit form $F(x, y, z) = x^2 + y^2 + \left(z - \frac{1}{2}\right)^2 - 1.25$.
c. Show that solving $F(S + \mathbf{c}t) = 0$ as usual results in the quadratic equation $At^2 + 2Bt + C = 0$, where $A = |\mathbf{c}|^2, B = c \cdot S, C = |S|^2 - 1.25$, where we have defined $S' = (S_x, S_y, S_z - 0.5)$.

12.10.2 Implementing the generic box extent test

Adjust the `Cube :: hit()` method to develop the routine `bool rayHitsBoxExtent(Ray& ray, Cuboid& cub)` that tests whether the given ray intersects the extent described in cub. This entails simplifying hit() without altering its logic. Show how the numer and denom values needed for each plane of the box depend on the data in cub. The top plane, for instance, uses numer = cub.top - ray.start.y; denom = ray.dir.y. As each plane of the box is intersected by the ray, the candidate interval (t_{in}, t_{out}) is updated, and if the interval vanishes, an early out occurs and the test returns true.

12.10.3 The point cluster for the sphere

Using the vertex list of the icosahedron given in Figure 6.28, determine how much it must be scaled so the icosahedron just encloses the generic sphere. (Is a scale factor of $f = 1.071$ sufficient?)

12.10.4 Routines to create the sphere and box extents

Write the routines: void makeSphereExtent(PointCluster& clust, SphereInfo& sph) and void makeBoxExtent(PointCluster& clust, Cuboid& cub) that build a sphere extent and a box extent from a given point cluster. ■

12.10.2 Using Projection Extents

There is another kind of extent whose use provides a dramatic gain in the speed of a ray tracer. In contrast with box and sphere extents, which operate in 3D space, this extent is a rectangular region on the screen.

The **projection extent** of an object is an aligned rectangle on the screen that encloses the projection of an object, as suggested in Figure 12.57a. Part b shows the resulting projection extent in more detail. The projection extent is captured by four numbers {*left, top, right, bottom*}.

FIGURE 12.57 The projection extent of an object.

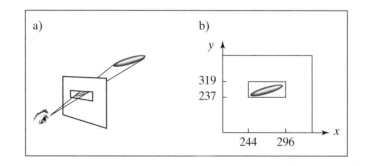

It is very easy to use projection extents while ray tracing. Each ray passes through the screen at a certain row and column value, say (r, c). If (r, c) lies outside the projection extent of an object, the ray cannot possibly intersect the object. For the example in Figure 12.57b, if c is less than 244 or larger than 296, or if r is less than 237 or larger than 319, the ray definitely misses the object.

Because projection extents are intimately coupled to the geometry of the camera and the position of the eye, they can be used only for **eye rays**, those that emanate from the eye. In later sections we will be generating rays for shadowing, reflections, and refraction, and since these emanate from arbitrary points in the scene, there is no screen on which to place a projection. But for eye rays the technique works superbly and can speed up ray tracing by a substantial factor.

We construct the projection extent for each object in the scene in a preprocessing step, and store the extent with the object just as we did with the box and sphere extents. To accommodate this we add an `IntRect screenExtent` field to the `GeomObj` class. We also extend the `Ray` class so that a ray knows which row and column on the display it is passing through. And we give it one more piece of information: its so-called **recursion level**. This will play a big part later when we work with reflection and refraction. Here the level simply keeps track of whether this ray is an eye ray. Eye rays are given a level of 0.

During ray tracing a new test is performed at the start of the `hit()` method for each object type, before any sphere or box extent tests. Figure 12.58 shows where this test is located for the `TaperedCylinder` class. This same test is used for all object types—except for the plane. Compare this with Figure 12.55. The test checks whether this ray is an eye ray, and if so, it tests the ray's row and column against the projection extent stored in the object. If the row or column is outside the projection extent, the ray must miss the object, and `hit()` immediately returns `false`. The test is very fast indeed.

```
bool TaperedCylinder::hit(Ray &r, Intersection &inter)
{
  if(r.recurseLevel == 0 &&
     r.col < projExtnt.left ||
     r.col > projExtnt.right ||
     r.row < projExtnt.bottom ||
     r.row > projExtnt.top ) return false; // misses screen extent
     if(!rayHitsSphereExtent(r,worldSphereExtent)) return false;
     make, and inverse transform, the generic ray
     if(!rayHitsSphereExtent(genRay,genSphereExtent)) return
false;
     …do expensive full testing with the generic cylinder…
}
```

FIGURE 12.58 Testing against sphere extents within the `hit()` method for the cylinder.

Computing Projection Extents

The preprocessing step must compute the projection extent for each object in the scene. The extent is easily computed, given the point cluster of the object. The point cluster of the generic object is transformed into world coordinates using the object's transformation, just as we did for world sphere and box extents. Figure 12.59 shows the 12 points of the cluster for a transformed cylinder.

Now each of the points is projected onto the near plane of the camera. Given a general point p in the scene, we can find its projection p' by a calculation based on the location of p and the camera geometry. The projected point p' is associated with a particular row r and column c.

Figure 12.60 shows a ray traced scene with each object's projection extent superimposed on the object. For debugging purposes, some programmers like to draw the projection extents of every object before ray tracing starts. These rectangles disappear when the final pixel colors are painted in during ray tracing.

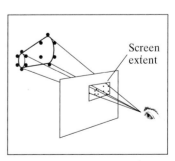

FIGURE 12.59 Building the projection extent.

FIGURE 12.60 A ray traced scene with projection extents made visible.

12.10.3 Alternative Method for Accelerating Ray Tracing: BSP Trees

We have seen how time consuming it is to ray trace a scene, owing to the large number of rays that must be cast and the large number of objects that are typically in a scene. The problem is clearly the large number of intersection tests that must be performed for each ray and each object. The use of extents helps somewhat to increase efficiency but is of little service for secondary (spawned) rays.

We therefore seek other ways for accelerating ray tracing. One elegant method for accelerating ray tracing makes use of binary space partition (BSP) trees [Arvo88]. It builds a hierarchical data structure for each ray that eliminates a large number of intersection tests by quickly determining which objects could not possibly intersect that ray. Binary space partition trees are data structures which can be constructed rapidly and then traversed. The BSP tree is **traversed** by visiting each of its nodes in turn (in some order) and testing for an intersection between the ray and the node object. At each node the ray is intersected with the object but needs only a coarse intersection test.

Building a BSP Tree

For ease of visualization we introduce BSP trees using a 2D example involving edges. Because the organization of the tree does not depend on the dimensionality of the objects it contains, the extension to a BSP of 3D polygons is immediate.

Figure 12.61 shows three polygons in the plane, and an eye positioned at a certain point. The question is: what is seen from the ray origin? If you prefer to think in 3D, imagine an observer standing in front of three large stone pillars rising out of the ground. The pillars have the cross-sectional shapes shown in the figure. Again, which parts of the walls of the pillars are visible, and which are obscured? Sketch the resulting scene for this example. Each edge is given a number, and its outward-pointing normal vector is indicated. We wish to insert each edge into a tree in such a way that the plane is partitioned (or tesselated) into nonoverlapping polygonal regions.

FIGURE 12.61 A set of edges in 2D to be arranged in a BSP tree.

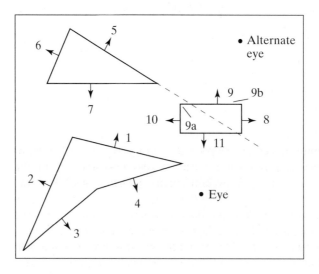

To begin building the tree for this set of edges, take an edge, say #1. Extending it in both directions, edge #1 splits the plane (in which the polygons lie) into two half-spaces, its outside (the side pointed to by the outward-pointing normal) and its inside. We put edge #1 into the root of the tree, as shown in Figure 12.62a. Now we insert each of the other edges into the tree in turn. Consider edge #2, for instance,

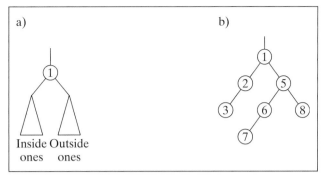

FIGURE 12.62 Building the BSP tree.

and compare it with edge #1. If edge #2 lies in the outside half space of edge #1 it is placed in the right subtree, labelled `outsideOnes`. Otherwise, it is placed in the left subtress, labelled `insideOnes`. As each edge is inserted, it finds its way down the tree, comparing itself with each node it reaches. It goes to the `outsideOnes` subtree of the node if it lies on the outside of that node, and to the `insideOnes` subtree otherwise, until it becomes attached to the tree as a new leaf.

Figure 12.62b shows the status after seven more edges, #2, . . . , #8, have been inserted. Edge #2 lies on the inside half-space of #1, so it is placed in the `insideOnes` subtree. Edge #3 lies on the inside of both #1 and #2, so it finds its way to the position shown. (Check this.) Edge 4 is not shown. Where does it go in the tree?

When we insert edge #9, something new happens. It lies on the outside of #1 but lies in both half-spaces of #5. It is therefore **split** by #5 into two edges, #9a and #9b, as shown in Figure 12.61, and each piece finds its way further down in the tree. Edge #9a lies on the inside of #5, so it goes down to the left and is tested against #6 and #7; edge #9b lies on the outside of #5 but the inside of #8. Edges #10 and #11 are inserted in like manner, and don't require splitting. (What does the final tree look like?)

The BSP tree lists the edges in a particular way, so that for any edge you can quickly tell (by its position in the tree) in which part of space it lies (e.g., edge #6 lies on the outside of #1 and on the inside of #5).

Notice that the order in which edges are inserted in the tree has a profound effect on the "shape" of the final tree. Some choices of ordering can make the tree full and "shallow" (a small number of nodes from the root to the deepest leaf), whereas others make it scrawny and "deep". Shallow trees are more efficient to deal with. The worst case is a BSP tree in the shape of a single chain from top to bottom.

BSP Trees for 3D Scenes

These ideas extend immediately to scenes composed of 3D polygon meshes. Consider the block shown in Figure 12.63a. Each of its eight faces is numbered, and the outward-pointing normal vector is indicated. Part b shows another view of the same block. If the faces are inserted into a BSP tree in the order #1, #2, . . . , #8, the tree shown in part c is formed. (A face finds its way down the tree in the same way as for the 2D case: if it lies in the outside half-space of the node face, it goes to the `outsideOnes` subtree, and so on) Face #7 is the only one that must be split: it is split into #7a and #7b by the plane of #3, as the dashed line in the figure indicates. (Is there an order for inserting these faces such that *no* splits are necessary?)

Here we see how the BSP tree is used to draw a scene flawlessly.

Traversing the Tree (to Ray Trace the Scene)

We now must determine which object the ray hits first. We know that this ray hits some object and that the hit times are smaller for each left child in the tree than for

FIGURE 12.63 Building the BSP tree.

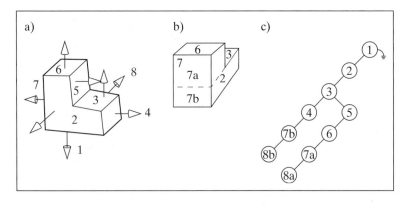

the right child at the same level. Thus to find the smallest time, simply trace the tree down from the root, always moving to the left child. We finally reach the leaf marked 8b in Figure 12.63, which must be the closest object to the eye.

For the 3D scene in Figure 12.63a the tree in part c can be traversed using this scheme, and the block will be drawn properly. Figure 12.64a shows arrows to indicate the order in which nodes of the BSP tree of Figure 12.63c are visited, for the particular view of the block shown in Figure 12.63a. The order of increasing hit times is shown in part b. Those faces which are underlined are never drawn.

FIGURE 12.64 Drawing order for the faces, given the position of the eye.

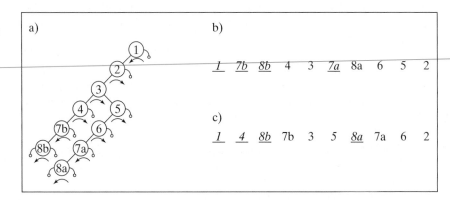

For additional reading on the use of BSP trees for ray tracing see *Graphics Gems III* [Kirk92], especially the two articles "Use of Residency Masks and Object Space Partitioning to Eliminate Ray–Object Intersection Calculations" and "Ray Tracing with BSP Trees."

12.11 ADDING SHADOWS FOR GREATER REALISM

> Misled by fancy's meteor ray,
> By passion driven;
> But yet the light that led astray
> Was light from heaven.
>
> *Robert Burns*
> *(1759–1796)*

The presence of shadows of the proper shape and darkness adds a great deal of realism to computer-generated images. We saw in Chapter 8 that OpenGL offers some rudimentary mechanisms to produce shadows, but it is awkward at best to use these tools, and they produce shadows only in limited situations. Ray tracing, on the other hand, produces shadows with very little programming effort. Unfortunately it slows down the ray tracing process. Figure 12.65 shows a scene rendered with and without shadows. Notice that in part b it is difficult to see how far above the platform the Buckyball lies, whereas in part a our eye can see this immediately.

a)   b)

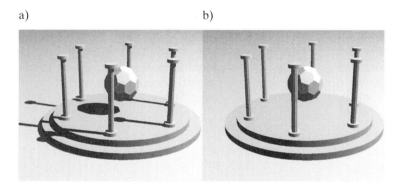

FIGURE 12.65 a) Rendering with shadows, b) rendering without shadows.

The light intensities we have calculated up to now have assumed that the hit point, P_h, of the ray with the first object hit is in fact bathed in light from the various light sources. But this is not the case if some other object happens to lie between P_h and a light source. In that case P_h is in shadow with respect to that light source, and both the diffuse and specular contributions are therefore absent. This leaves only the ambient light component.

Figure 12.66 shows various shadowing situations. Point P is able to see source L_1, so P is not in shadow with respect to L_1. But P *is* in the shadow of the cube with respect to source L_2. Further, source L_3 is so positioned that the hit object itself hides the source from P; this is called **self-shadowing**. For this configuration, therefore, the only light that P can see is the light from source L_1.

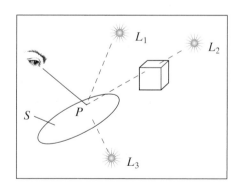

FIGURE 12.66 Various cases of shadowing the hit point.

Spawning Additional Rays—"Shadow Feelers"

In order to compute shadows accurately we need to know when a hit point is in shadow with respect to a light source. So we need a routine, isInShadow(), that returns true if any part of *any* object lies between the hit point and a given source, and false otherwise. To do this we spawn a new ray, often called a **shadow feeler**, that emanates from P_h at $t = 0$ and reaches L at $t = 1$. The shadow feeler thus has the parametric representation $P_h + (L - P_h)t$. To see whether it hits anything, the entire object list is scanned, and each object is tested for an intersection with this ray. If any intersection is found to lie between $t = 0$ and $t = 1$, isInShadow() returns true. This seems like a tall order, but the basic mechanism of ray tracing, using a ray to probe the scene, again comes to our rescue.

A thorny problem lurks in a naïve use of this approach. The problem is in self-shadowing. If the shadow feeler really starts at P_h, then there is *always* an intersection between the feeler ray and the object itself: at $t = 0$! Thus isInShadow() would always return true, which is clearly wrong. Some people try to cope with this by accepting intersections only if they occur at some t strictly greater than 0. But, as shown in Figure 12.67a, this will miss a true intersection with the square or plane if the source is on the opposite side of the square from the eye. The feeler from P to source L_1 correctly reports no intersection, but the feeler from P to L_2 would also report no intersection, whereas the square itself shadows point P. Why does this anomaly not arise for other shapes such as spheres and cones?

FIGURE 12.67 Shadow-feeler strategies.

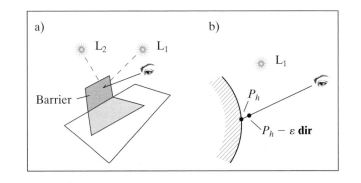

A strategy that works reliably sends an adjusted shadow feeler to isInShadow(), as shown in Figure 12.67b. The start point of the shadow feeler is shifted toward the eye by a small amount. If the ray has direction **dir** and hits at point P_h, the start point of the shadow feeler is offset to $P_h - \varepsilon$ **dir**, where ε is a small positive number. This puts the starting point slightly in front of ("on the eye side of") the object that is hit by the ray. Using this start point for the shadow feeler, there is no intersection with the object at $t = 0$, and the problem is solved.

This approach fits into the Scene :: shade(ray) method in the following way. When getFirstHit() has returned the best intersection record, the hit point and the normal vector at the hit point are determined. The ambient light color is found for this ray. Then a feeler ray is constructed and its start point is set to $P_h - \varepsilon$ **dir**. Its recurseLevel is set to 1, so that projection extents will be disabled in the various hit() methods.

Then for each light source L the feeler direction is computed as L.pos - feeler.start, and isInShadow(feeler) is called to see if the feeler hits any object. If it does, the computation of the diffuse and specular light contributions is skipped for this light source. The shadow-related part of this process takes the following form in pseudocode:

```
feeler.start = hitPoint - ε ray.dir;
feeler.recurselevel = 1;
color = ambient part;
for(each light source, L)
{
        feeler.dir = L.pos - hitPoint;
        if(isInShadow(feeler))continue;
        color.add(diffuse light);
        color.add(specular light);
}
```

The following code shows one possible implementation of isInShadow() itself. It simply scans through the object list looking for a hit, and if one is found, it returns false. If no hits are found, it returns true.

```
bool Scene :: isInShadow(Ray& f)
{
  for(GeomObj* p = obj; p; p = p->next)
    if(p->hit(f))return true;
  return false;
}
```

It uses a simplified version of hit() for each object type that takes only one argument—it doesn't need to build an intersection record. This version of hit() differs in three ways from the version we have been using up to now.

1. It only accepts a hit for which the hit time lies between 0 and 1, since an object lying beyond the light source does not cast a shadow.
2. If it detects such a hit, it returns immediately, without computing any data about the hit itself.
3. It cannot use projection extents, since shadow feelers can originate anywhere in the scene. Therefore it should perform some carefully selected combination of sphere and/or box extent tests for each object type.

12.12 REFLECTIONS AND TRANSPARENCY

> Beauty is a form of genius—is higher, indeed, than genius, as it needs no explanation.
> It is of the great facts in the world like sunlight, or springtime, or the reflection in dark water
> of that silver shell we call the moon.
>
> *Oscar Wilde*
> *(1854–1900)*

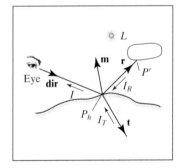

FIGURE 12.68 Including reflected and refracted light.

One of the great strengths of the ray-tracing method is the ease with which it can handle both the reflection and the refraction of light. This allows one to build scenes of exquisite realism,[8] containing mirrors, fishbowls, lenses, and the like. There can be multiple reflections in which light bounces off several shiny surfaces before reaching the eye, or elaborate combinations of refraction and reflection. Each of these processes requires the spawning and tracing of additional rays.

Figure 12.68 shows a ray emanating from the eye in the direction **dir** and hitting a surface at the point P_h. The figure shows the key ingredients in 2D, which is acceptable because the nature of reflection and refraction causes all vectors to lie in the same plane. All formulas we develop operate in 3D. When the surface is mirrorlike or transparent, or both, the light I that reaches the eye may have five components:

$$I = I_{amb} + I_{diff} + I_{spec} + I_{refl} + I_{tran} \qquad (12.42)$$

The first three are the familiar ambient, diffuse, and specular contributions. The diffuse and specular parts arise from light sources in the environment that are visible at P_h. I_{refl} is the reflected light component, arising from the light, I_R, that is incident at P_h along direction $-$**dir**. This direction is such that the angles of incidence and reflection are equal, so **r** is given according to the following equation:

$$\mathbf{r} = \mathbf{dir} - 2(\mathbf{dir} \cdot \mathbf{m})\,\mathbf{m} \qquad (12.43)$$

(where we assume the normal vector **m** at P_h has been normalized).

---

[8] Some people say "super-realistic" [watt92].

Similarly, I_{tran} is the transmitted light component, arising from the light, I_T, that is transmitted through the transparent material to P_h along direction $-\mathbf{t}$. A portion of this light passes through the surface and in so doing is bent. It then continues its travel along $-\mathbf{dir}$. The refraction direction, $\mathbf{t}$, depends on several factors, and its details are developed in the next section.

Just as I is a sum of various light contributions, I_R and I_T each arise from their own five components: ambient, diffuse, and so on. As the figure shows, I_R is the light that would be seen by an eye at P_h along a ray from P′ to P_h. To determine I_R, we do in fact spawn a secondary ray from P_h in the direction $\mathbf{r}$, find the first object it hits, and repeat the same computation of light components as in Equation (12.42). This may in turn require spawning additional rays. Similarly, I_T is found by casting a ray in direction $\mathbf{t}$ and seeing what surface is hit first, then computing the light contributions there, and so forth.

Figure 12.69 shows how the number of contributions of light grows at each contact point. The final light that reaches the eye is named I; it is a combination of a large number of contributions, consisting of reflected and refracted light from various points in the scene in addition to a number of ambient, diffuse, and specular components.

FIGURE 12.69 The tree of light.

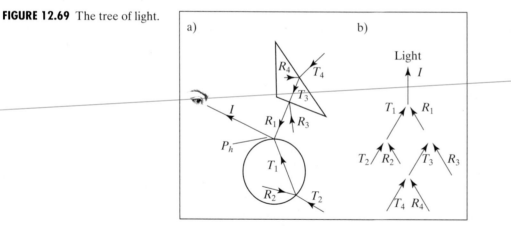

As seen in part a, I is the sum of three components, the reflected component R_1, the transmitted component T_1 from the refraction, and the local component L_1 (not labelled). The *local components are simply* the sum of the usual ambient, diffuse, and specular reflections at P_h. Local components depend only on actual light sources; they are not computed based on casting secondary rays. Recall that the role of the ambient term is to approximate the effect of diffuse and specular reflections off other surfaces. R_1 is in turn the sum of R_3, T_3, and the local L_3. And T_3 is the sum of R_4, T_4, and L_4. Each contribution is the sum of three others, possibly ad infinitum. This suggests a recursive approach to computing light intensity.

Figure 12.69b abstracts the various light components into a tree of light contributions, with the transmitted components arriving on the left branches, and the reflected components arriving on the right branches [Whitted80]. At each node a local component must also be added, but for simplicity it is not shown.

To incorporate these visual effects, Scene::shade() is extended so that it can call itself recursively. Figure 12.70 shows a skeleton of shade(), emphasizing what is added to the version of shade() of Figure 12.12. Under the right conditions shade() calls itself twice to accumulate reflected and transmitted light contributions.

FIGURE 12.70 Skeleton of recursive shade().

```
Color3 Scene :: shade(Ray& r)
int recurseLevel = 0; // set recursion level to 0
{
  Get the first hit, and build hitInfo h
  Shape* myObj = (Shape*)h.hitObject; // pointer to the hit object
  Color3 color.set(the emissive component);
  color.add(ambient contribution);
  get the normalized normal vector  m  at the hit point
  for(each light source)
      add the diffuse and specular components
  // now add the reflected and transmitted components

  if(r.recurseLevel == maxRecursionLevel)
     return color; // don't recurse further

  if(hit object is shiny enough) // add any reflected light
  {
  get reflection direction
  build reflected ray, refl
     refl.recurseLevel = r.recurseLevel + 1;
     color.add(shininess * shade(refl));
  }
  if(hit object is transparent enough)
  {
   get transmited direction
   build transmitted ray, trans
   trans.recurseLevel = r.recurseLevel + 1;
   color.add(transparency * shade(trans));
  }
  return color;
}
```

If the hit object is shiny enough to warrant the effort of deeper ray tracing, then a reflected ray is spawned, and shade() is used to compute how much light comes back along the reflection direction. The amount of light shade() finds is tempered by the reflection coefficient, shininess, of the hit object. This reflection coefficient is stored in one of the fields of the object. The user specifies it in an *SDL* file using, say, shininess 0.8. It is used for the "if shiny enough" test, as in if(shininess > 0.6).

Similarly, if the hit object is transparent enough to warrant further ray tracing, then a transmitted ray is spawned, and shade() is used to compute how much light comes back along the transmitted direction. The amount of light found is scaled by the transmission coefficient, transparency, of the hit object. This coefficient is also stored with the object, and it is used for the "if transparent enough" test, as in if(transparency > 0.5).

Because there is the possibility that rays would keep spawning new reflected or transmitted rays forever, some limit must be imposed on the depth of recursion. Consider a scene consisting of four perfect mirrors set at such angles that a ray perpetually bounces around them. This could lead to endless recursion, which must therefore be controlled. To control this we let each ray keep track of how deep it is; the recurseLevel field mentioned in connection with shadowing is part of each ray. Eye rays that emanate from the eye have a recurseLevel of 0. This level is incremented each time a reflected or transmitted ray is formed. If the level of a ray is already at the limit maxRecursionLevel (which is stored in a field in the Scene object and specified in an *SDL* file as maxRecursionDepth 5), no further reflected or transmitted rays are spawned. Usually a maximum recursion depth of 4 or 5 gives very realistic images.

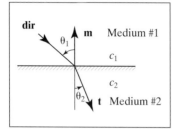

FIGURE 12.71 The refraction of light in a transparent medium.

12.12.1 The Refraction of Light

> *Be thou the rainbow to the storms of life,*
> *The evening beam that smiles the clouds away,*
> *And tints to-morrow with prophetic ray!*
>
> *Lord George Gordon Byron*
> *(1788 - 1824)*

When a ray of light strikes a transparent object, a portion of the ray penetrates the object, as shown in Figure 12.71. The ray will change direction from **dir** to **t** if the speed of light is different in medium 1 and medium 2. Vector **t** still lies in the same plane as **dir** and the normal **m**. If the angle of incidence of the ray is θ_1, **Snell's law** states that the angle of refraction θ_2 will be given by the following equation [Halliday70, Rogers92]:

$$\frac{\sin(\theta_2)}{c_2} = \frac{\sin(\theta_1)}{c_1}$$

(12.44)

where c_1 is the speed of light in medium 1 and c_2 is the speed of light in medium 2, as shown in the figure. Only the ratio c_2/c_1 is important. It is often called the **index of refraction** of medium 2 with respect to medium 1.[9] Note that if θ_1 equals 0, so does θ_2; light hitting an interface at right angles is not bent.

■ EXAMPLE 12.12.1 Find the angle

Suppose medium 2 is some form of glass, in which light travels only 54% as fast as in a vacuum. Further suppose that the angle of incidence of the impinging light is 60° from the vertical. What is the angle of the transmitted light?

SOLUTION:

Evaluate $\sin(\theta_2)$ in Equation (12.44), using $c_2/c_1 = 0.54$, and $\sin(\theta_1) = 0.866$, to get $\sin(\theta_2) = (0.54)(0.866) = 0.4676$, so $\theta_2 = 27.88°$. Light is bent *closer* to the normal as it moves from a faster medium into a slower medium.

Figure 12.72 shows the speed of light in various media relative to that in a vacuum (or air). This table is something of a simplification, because the speed of light generally varies with the wavelength of the light. For instance, the relative speed in fused quartz varies from 0.680 at λ = 400 nm (red) to 0.685 at λ = 520 nm (green), to 0.687 at λ = 680 nm (blue) [Halliday97]. This variation causes the familiar effect where a beam of white light is split into its rainbow of spectral colors when it passes through a glass prism.

FIGURE 12.72 Relative speed of light in various media.

In air: 99.97%
In glass: 52.2% to 59%
In water: 75.19%
In a 30% sugar solution: 72.46%
In acetone and ethyl alcohol: 73.5%
In sodium chloride: 64.93%
In benzene: 55.5%
In sapphire: 56.50%
In diamond: 41.33%

---

[9]   Since "index of refraction" is defined by some as c_1/c_2 and by others as c_2/c_1, we will avoid using it by name in formulas, and will explicitly use c_2/c_1.

The Critical Angle

Example 12.12.1 noted that rays of light are bent more toward the normal direction when they enter a medium with a lower speed of light: (i.e., $c_2/c_1 < 1$). This is clear from Equation (12.44), because $\sin(\theta_2)$, which equals $c_2/c_1 \sin(\theta_1)$, is less than $\sin(\theta_2)$, so θ_2 must be less than θ_1.

The reverse is true when light enters a medium with a higher speed of light: light is bent further away from the normal. Snell's law is completely symmetrical when subscripts 1 and 2 are interchanged. Figure 12.73a shows light moving from the faster medium to the slower, and part b shows light moving from the slower medium to the faster. The angles pair together in the same way in both cases; only the names change. Parts c and d show similar situations, but the larger angle has become nearly 90°. The smaller angle is near the so-called **critical angle**. When the smaller angle (associated with the slower medium) gets large enough, it forces the larger angle to 90°. A larger value is impossible, so no light is transmitted into the second medium. This is called **total internal reflection**. Consider the situation in part d, where light is coming from the slower to the faster medium. Since $\sin(\theta_1)$ equals $(c_1/c_2) \sin(\theta_2)$, angle θ_1 takes on its largest possible value when $\theta_2 = 90°$, or $\theta_1 = \sin^{-1}(c_1/c_2)$. For example, when light moves from water into air we have $c_1/c_2 = 0.7519$, so the critical angle for water is 48.75°.

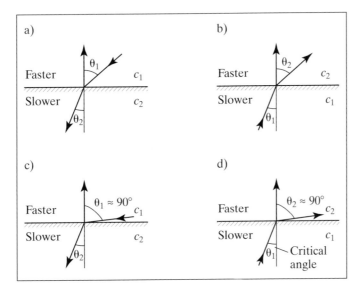

FIGURE 12.73 Symmetry of light transmission, and the critical angle.

The critical angle appears in an interesting setting. When you are underwater in a pond looking up at the surface, you can see the whole world above water within a limited solid angle from the vertical. If you look up at about 48° you see the edge of the pond (sketch this). On the other hand, if you are in a boat looking down into the pond, what range of angles can you see? Is there a limited cone of view, outside which you can't see objects? (See the exercises at the end of the section.)

■ EXAMPLE 12.12.2 What is the shape of a rainbow?

The speed of light in water varies with the light's wavelength, and this is the genesis of rainbows. Figure 12.74a shows several spherical droplets suspended in air. A ray of sunlight coming from the left is refracted slightly as it enters a droplet and experiences a total internal reflection before exiting. The angle between the

FIGURE 12.74 The genesis of a rainbow.

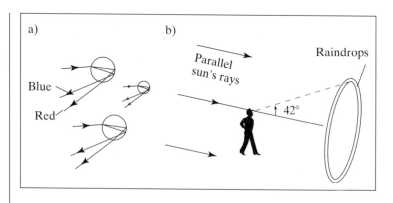

incident and exiting rays is about 42°. Red light is refracted a little less than blue light, so the directions of the exiting rays are slightly different. Thus red rays pour out of the myriad raindrops in one direction, and blue rays in a slightly different direction.

In 1637 Descartes used a simple ray tracing argument to explain the shape of a rainbow. Figure 12.74b shows an observer with his back to the sun, looking at a mist of rain drops. When the observer looks about 42° off the sun's direction, she sees rings of light. Raindrops situated along a cone of a certain angle reflect back light of one color; change the angle slightly and the color is slightly different. Thus a rainbow is a collection of circular rings, and each observer has her own private rainbow.

Finding the Direction of Transmission, t

For ray tracing purposes we must find the direction, **t**, (see Figure 12.71) given the surface normal, **m**, and the ray direction, **dir**. We shall do this in a coordinate-free form using only dot products, so that it applies to any directions for **dir** and **m**. As we develop in the exercises, the vector **t** that results is a linear combination of **m** and **dir** (assuming both have been normalized to unit length):

$$\mathbf{t} = \frac{c_2}{c_1}\mathbf{dir} + \left(\frac{c_2}{c_1}(\mathbf{m}\cdot\mathbf{dir}) - \cos(\theta_2)\right)\mathbf{m} \tag{12.45}$$

where $\cos(\theta_2)$ is found from Snell's law:

$$\cos(\theta_2) = \sqrt{1 - \left(\frac{c_2}{c_1}\right)^2(1 - (\mathbf{m}\cdot\mathbf{dir})^2)} \tag{12.46}$$

Check that **t** has the correct value when either a) the speed of light is the same in the two media or b) the incident angle is 0°.

There will be total internal reflection if the quantity in the square root of $\cos(\theta_2)$ becomes negative, in which case **t** becomes irrelevant. This happens at the critical angle. The exercises request an implementation of the routine `transmitDirection()` that computes **t**.

Because the derivation of **t** uses only dot products, it is equally applicable to a 2D situation. See Case Study 12.8 for an interesting 2D demonstration program of refraction.

When developing a ray tracer, it is simplest to model transparent objects so that their index of refraction does not depend on wavelength. In this case the *same* rays are used to trace the red, green, and blue color components. To do otherwise would require tracing separate rays for each of the color components, as they would refract in somewhat different directions. This would be expensive computationally and would still provide only an approximation, because an accurate model of refraction should take into account a large number of colors, not just the three primaries.

PRACTICE EXERCISES

12.12.1 On the effects of refraction

Figure 12.75a shows an eye at height H looking from air into a pool of water. A fish at horizontal distance L from the eye is located at depth D. Where does the eye see the fish if light travels twice as fast in air as in water?

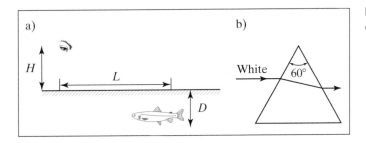

FIGURE 12.75 Some experiments with refraction.

12.12.2 Making a rainbow

Figure 12.75b shows a beam of white light entering a prism having an internal angle of 60°. The prism is made of fused quartz. Calculate and sketch the paths of the red, green, and blue components of light as they pass through and emerge from the prism. If the white beam passes instead through a slab of fused quartz having parallel walls, will a rainbow be seen as the light emerges?

12.12.3 Deriving the refraction direction

Figure 12.76 shows a clever way to derive the transmission direction **t** that also results in an efficient algorithm [Heckbert89]. The unit vectors **dir** and **m** together determine a plane, in which both the reflected ray and the transmitted ray lie. The figure shows a unit circle drawn in this plane. Because all vectors are unit vectors, their various components along **m** and perpendicular to **m** have lengths that are simple sines and cosines of the angles θ_1 and θ_2.

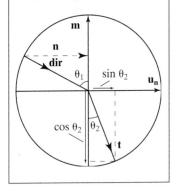

FIGURE 12.76 Deriving the transmission direction t.

a. Show that the vector named **n** in the figure is

$$\mathbf{n} = \cos(\theta_1)\mathbf{m} + \mathbf{dir}$$

and that its length is $\sin(\theta_1)$, so that its normalized version $\mathbf{u}_n$ is $\mathbf{n}/\sin(\theta_1)$. Prove with dot products that **n** lies in the plane of **m** and **dir** and is perpendicular to **m**.

b. Show that

$$\mathbf{t} = \sin(\theta_2)\mathbf{u}_n - \cos(\theta_2)\mathbf{m} = \frac{c_2}{c_1}\mathbf{dir} + \left(\frac{c_2}{c_1}\cos(\theta_1) - \cos(\theta_2)\right)\mathbf{m}$$

and that this is the same as Equation (12.45).

c. Using Snell's law, show that $\cos(\theta_2) = \sqrt{1 - \left(\frac{c_2}{c_1}\right)^2 \sin^2(\theta_1)}$, and that Equation (12.46) follows immediately.

12.12.4 A routine to compute the transmission direction

Write `Vector3 transmitDirection(Vector3 m, Vector3 dir, float c1, float c2)` that computes the direction **t**, given the unit normal vectors **m** and **dir** and the speed of light in the two media.   ■

12.12.2 Dealing with Refraction in `shade()`

When ray tracing scenes that include transparent objects, we must keep track of the medium through which a ray is passing, so that we can determine the value c_2/c_1 at the next intersection where the ray either exits from the current object or enters another one. This is most easily accomplished by adding a field to the ray that holds a pointer to the object within which the ray is traveling.

How does `shade()` deal with rays that are inside objects? The answer depends on how much freedom is given to the modeler for describing scenes. We can think of several *design policies* the modeler might agree to.

Design Policy 1: No Two Transparent Objects May Interpenetrate

Suppose first that the modeler promises never to let two transparent objects interpenetrate. There can be no glass marble placed inside another, no cube of water inside a glass box. Then each ray is either in air alone or inside a *single* object.

a. Suppose the current ray in `shade()` is outside all objects, and upon hitting an object, say A, finds that A is transparent enough. It computes the direction **t** of the transmitted ray from Equation (12.45), using $c_1 = 1$ for air and obtaining c_2 from the properties of A. The new ray is built, with its `recurseLevel` duly incremented, and containing a pointer to A. `shade()` is then called recursively and ultimately returns a color, which is scaled by the `transparency` of A and added to the colors accumulated so far.

b. Suppose, on the other hand, that the current ray is inside some object A and hits another surface. Since it must be a surface of A, the ray is exiting into air. The routine can check that the ray hits the same object that it is currently in. Because the ray is inside the object, the normal at the hit point must be reversed in sign; we want it to be pointing *into* the medium in which the ray is traveling. When a ray is inside an object, it is usually considered not to be bathed in light, so no local ambient, diffuse, and specular intensities are computed. The inside wall of A might be considered shiny enough to warrant casting a reflected ray back into A. In that case the reflected ray is created and cast as usual. As for the refracted ray, A is obviously transparent enough, so the value of c_1 is taken from the properties of A, and c_2 is set to 1 for air. If the angle of incidence is less than the critical angle, a new ray is spawned (with its pointer set to `NULL`, since it is not inside any object now) and sent on its way, to gather more light contributions.

Design Policy 2: Transparent Objects May Interpenetrate

Things get a little more complicated if we allow the modeler to place transparent objects in the scene so that they interpenetrate. Figure 12.77 shows a glass cube with several objects imbedded in it: a quartz spherical marble, a cylindrical air hole, a cube filled with water, and a partially imbedded glass cone. We shall see how to model such **Boolean objects** in Section 12.13. Each has its own speed of light. Figure 12.77b shows in cross section a ray traveling through a set of transparent objects. The ray enters and exits from objects in a complex sequence. A list of objects is shown with each segment of the ray, reporting which objects the ray is traveling in. As you read along the ray's path, notice the complicated sequence of additions and deletions from the list. This is admittedly a contrived scene, but it's worth seeing what it costs to insure

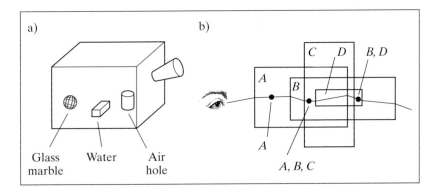

FIGURE 12.77 Several interpenetrating transparent objects.

that shade() will always handle it correctly. This extra capability could then be included or left out of a particular ray tracer.

What does it mean to be inside two transparent objects at once, such that certain points in space are owned by two objects? In the modeling phase you have to decide what the nature of the material is inside each joint region. If a green marble is completely enclosed in a blue marble, it makes sense to say that the joint region belongs to the blue marble, and assign it the color blue. But if objects partially interpenetrate, as in Figure 12.77b, there is no obvious way to decide whose properties to use in the joint regions. The designer must assign a priority to each object, with the understanding that the color of the object with the highest priority dominates in each joint region.

One way to handle this is to add a field to each object instance providing its priority, and to augment the pointer in the Ray data structure so it becomes a list of pointers. At any instant the ray is inside a certain set of objects, and the list reports this set. If the list is empty, the ray is outside all objects. So we might enhance the Ray type as shown in Figure 12.78. The list is implemented as an array rather than a linked list to facilitate copying the whole object at once when making a new ray.

FIGURE 12.78 Augmenting the Ray type.

```
class Ray{
public:
        Point3 start;
        Vector3 dir;
        int recurseLevel;
        int row, col; // to assist with screen extents
        int numInside; // number of objects on the list
        GeomObj* inside[8]; // array of object pointers
        Ray(){recurseLevel = numInside = 0;} // constructor
        ...other methods  ...
};
```

How is this inside list used in shade()? At any moment the current ray is inside some collection of objects, as reported by the list. When it hits the next surface of some object, say B, we take different actions depending on whether the ray is entering or exiting B, which is determined from the isEntering field of the hit record.

a. Suppose the ray is entering B. If B is not transparent enough, stop spawning refracted rays, but do spawn a reflected ray if B is shiny enough. If B is transparent enough, use for c_1 the speed of light of the highest-priority object currently on the list. If B has a higher priority, then use its speed of light for c_2; otherwise set c_2 equal to c_1. Add B to the list. Make a new transmitted ray, copying the current list (with B added) into it. Call shade() recursively.

b. Suppose the ray is exiting B. For c_1 use the speed of light of the highest-priority object in the list. Remove B from the list. For c_2 use the speed of light of the highest-priority object still on the list. Make a new transmitted ray, and copy the current inside list into it. Call shade() recursively.

Figure 12.79 shows a scene containing several transparent objects. The globe and jack are transparent, whereas the floors and walls are not. The distortions produced when light is refracted through a transparent object are apparent.

FIGURE 12.79 Scenes with and without refraction.

PRACTICE EXERCISES

12.12.5 Another possible design policy: If two transparent objects interpenetrate, one must contain the other

Suppose the modeler promises not to position two transparent objects so that they partially overlap: either they are disjoint, or one encloses the other. In set terminology, their intersection is empty or is identical to one of them. Discuss what implications this has on the logic of shade(). Specifically, show that the list processing becomes simpler: no priorities are needed, and the list can be treated like a stack. Describe how this is done.

12.12.6 Light transmission through colored glass

Discuss how to include the effect of refracted light that passes through an orange glass sphere.   ■

12.13 COMPOUND OBJECTS: BOOLEAN OPERATIONS ON OBJECTS

So far we can ray trace only a limited variety of shapes: transformed spheres, planes, cones, and so on. But if a way can be found to combine these simple shapes into more complex ones, and to develop a ray tracing method for them, much richer and more interesting scenes can be ray traced (Figure 12.80).

The method known as **constructive solid geometry** (CSG) provides such a method. Arbitrarily complex shapes are defined by set operations, also called **Boolean operations**, on simpler shapes [Ballard82, Mortenson85]. Objects such as lenses and hollow fishbowls, and objects with holes, are easily formed by combining the generic shapes

FIGURE 12.80 Ray tracing of a complicated Boolean shape. (Courtesy of Noel Llopis)

treated so far. Such objects are variously called **compound, Boolean**, or **CSG** objects. The ray tracing method extends in a very organized way to compound objects: it is one of the great strengths of ray tracing that it fits so naturally with CSG models.

We look at examples of the three boolean operators: **union**, **intersection**, and **difference**. Figure 12.81 shows two compound objects built from spheres. Figure 12.81a is a lens shape constructed as the **intersection** of two spheres. That is, a point is in the lens if and only if it lies in *both* spheres. Symbolically one writes that L is the intersection of the spheres S_1 and S_2 using the notation of Equation (12.47).

$$L = S_1 \cap S_2 \tag{12.47}$$

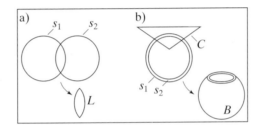

FIGURE 12.81 A lens and a fishbowl.

Part b shows a bowl, constructed using the difference operation. A point is in the **difference** of sets A and B, denoted $A - B$, if it is in A and not in B. Differencing is analogous to removing material, to cutting or carving. The bowl is specified by Equation (12.48).

$$B = (S_1 - S_2) - C \tag{12.48}$$

The solid globe, S_1, is hollowed out by removing all the points of the inner sphere, S_2. This forms a hollow spherical shell. The top is then opened by removing all points in the cone, C.

A point is in the **union** of two sets A and B, denoted $A \cup B$, if it is in A or in B or in both. Forming the union of two objects is analogous to gluing them together. Figure 12.82 shows a rocket constructed as the union of two cones and two cylinders and is represented mathematically as in Equation (12.49).

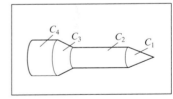

FIGURE 12.82 A union of four primitives.

$$R = C_1 \cup C_2 \cup C_3 \cup C_4 \tag{12.49}$$

Cone C_1 rests on cylinder C_2. Cone C_3 is partially embedded in C_2 and rests on the fatter cylinder C_4.

PRACTICE EXERCISE

12.13.1 Decomposing compound shapes

Give an equation that expresses each of the objects shown in Figure 12.83 in terms of set operations on spheres, cones, cylinders, and rectangular parallelepipeds. Notice that different expressions are possible for some objects.

FIGURE 12.83 Various shapes made from primitives.

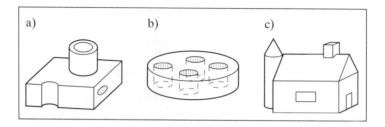

12.13.2 Composing compound shapes

Consider the type of bowling ball that has three finger holes for you to use in order to keep a firm grip on the ball. Express it as the appropriate CSG combination of a sphere and cylinders.　■

12.13.1 Ray Tracing CSG Objects

How do we ray trace objects that are boolean combinations of simpler objects? This might seem on first exposure to be a daunting task, but in fact, owing to the nature of the ray tracing process, it can be handled with surprising ease. In fact the intersection of a ray with a 3D CSG object is reduced to the intersection of an ordered list of one-dimensional *numbers* with one-dimensional *parts* of a CSG object! First consider the preceding examples. Figure 12.84 shows a ray entering and exiting the spheres S_1 and S_2 at the times indicated.

FIGURE 12.84 Ray tracing the lens and fishbowl.

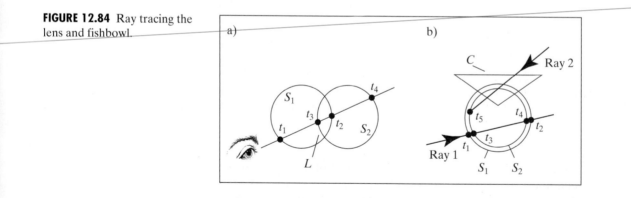

It is therefore inside lens L from t_3 to t_2, and the hit time is t_3. If the lens is opaque, the familiar shading rules will be applied to find what color the lens has at the hit spot. If it is mirror-like or transparent, spawned rays are generated with the proper directions and are traced farther.

The situation is similar for the bowl in Figure 12.84b. Ray 1 first strikes the bowl at t_1, the smallest of the times for which it is in S_1 but not in either S_2 or C. Ray 2, on the other hand, first hits the bowl at t_5. Again this is the smallest time for which the ray is in S_1 but in neither the other sphere nor the cone. The hits at earlier times are hits with component parts of the bowl, but not the bowl itself.

We organize these ideas into an algorithm to ray trace any compound object [Roth82]. Consider two objects, A and B, and a ray. Build a list of times at which the ray enters and exits from A, ordered so that the times are increasing. Because the object is solid, enter and exit times alternate. Build a similar list of enter and exit times for B. Two such lists are shown in Figure 12.85.

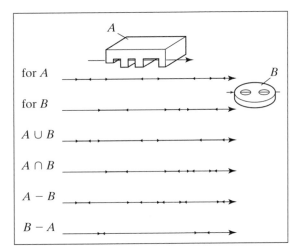

FIGURE 12.85 Lists of *t*-values for a ray with two objects.

The interval between each enter time and the next exit time is shown solid; otherwise it is shown dashed. The ray is inside the object throughout each solid interval. Call the set of *t*-values for which the ray is inside the object its **inside set**. An inside set is specified by an ordered list that contains the alternating enter and exit times of the ray $(t_1, t_2, \dots)$, where t_1 is an enter time, t_2 is an exit time, and so forth. This is sometimes called the ray's **t-list**.

Given the inside sets for a ray with compound objects A and B, we want to find the inside set for the ray with a compound object built from A and B. The four new objects we can build are $A \cup B$, $A \cap B$, $A - B$, and $B - A$. Consider $A \cup B$. The ray is inside the union of the objects if it is inside either of the objects. Thus the inside set for $A \cup B$ is simply the union of the individual inside sets. The same thinking applies to the other three objects. The inside set for $A \cap B$ is the intersection of the individual inside sets; the inside set for $A - B$ is composed of the difference of the inside set for A and that for B, and similarly for $B - A$ (just reversing the roles of A and B). In general, if we denote by $T(A)$ and $T(B)$ the inside sets of two objects, A and B, as shown in Equation (12.50),

$$T(A \text{ op } B) = T(A) \text{ op } T(B) \tag{12.50}$$

where op is one of the boolean operators $\cup$, $\cap$, or $-$, then the inside set for the compound object, $T(A) \text{ op } T(B)$, is simply $T(A) \text{ op } (B)$. In general, as shown here, the operation of performing boolean operations on objects is equivalent to performing boolean operations on lists of intervals!

Notice that although we are ultimately interested in only the first item in the inside set—the first hit time—we must retain *entire lists* for inside sets during the list-building process, because the ultimate *first* hit time may reside deep within one of the intermediate lists. Happily, we already have the artillery in place for creating inside sets in a ray tracer: the `hit()` method for each type of shape carefully collects all the hits that a ray experiences with an object in the `inter.hit[]` array in time-sorted order. Up to this point we have made use only of the first hit time in the list. As we begin to ray trace Boolean objects, however, we will utilize the entire list.

■ EXAMPLE 12.13.1 To Form Inside Sets

Consider the following two lists that represent inside sets:

A_list: 1.2 1.5 2.1 2.5 3.1 3.8
B_list: 0.6 1.1 1.8 2.6 3.4 4.0

We apply the preceding rules to build four new inside sets (check their accuracy):

$$A \cup B = 0.6, 1.1, 1.2, 1.5, 1.8, 2.6, 3.1, 4.0$$
$$A \cap B = 2.1, 2.5, 3.4, 3.8$$
$$A - B = 1.2, 1.5, 3.1, 3.4$$
$$B - A = 0.6, 1.1, 1.8, 2.1, 2.5, 2.6, 3.8, 4.0$$

To construct new inside sets, we need a function `combineLists()` that takes as arguments an operator and two t-lists and creates a new list of t-values according to one of the preceding four combining methods. We discuss later how this routine operates.

The ray tracing process for a compound object boils down to ray tracing its component objects, building inside sets for each, and finally combining them. The first positive hit time on the combined list yields the point on the compound object that is hit first by the ray. The usual shading is then done, including the casting of secondary rays if the surface is shiny or transparent.

PRACTICE EXERCISE

12.13.2 Find the inside sets

Suppose that for a given ray the objects C and D have the t-lists:

C_list: 0.8 1.7 2.2 2.9 4.7 5.55
D_list: 1.2 1.5 2.1 2.5 3.1 3.8 4.7 8.3

Find the t-list for each of the four possible Boolean combinations of C and D.   ■

12.13.2 Data Structure for Boolean Objects

> So, naturalists observe, a flea
> Hath smaller fleas that on him prey;
> And these have smaller still to bite 'em;
> And so proceed ad infinitum.
>
> *"On Poetry, A Rhapsody"*
> *Jonathan Swift*
> *(1667–1745)*

How do we represent a compound object such as $((A \cap B) - C) - D$ in a program? Since a compound object is always the combination of two other (possibly compound) objects, Obj_1 op Obj_2, a binary tree structure provides a natural description. Figure 12.86 shows the tree corresponding to the object $(((B_1 \cap B_2) \cup C_2) \cup ((S_1 - S_2) - B_3)) - C_1)$. Each internal node (shown as a circle) represents an operator, and each leaf (shown as a square) is a primitive shape. A tree is made up by combining subtrees, which are in turn primitive objects or subtrees (*and so proceed ad infinitum*). When a node contains the difference operator, it is understood that the node produces the (left subtree) − (right subtree), as opposed to (right subtree) − (left subtree).

The expression for a compound object can be rearranged to some degree without altering the ultimate shape of the object being represented. Each rearrangement gives rise to a different tree. Therefore there is not a unique tree for a given compound object.

Currently, all the object types like `Sphere` and `Cube` are derived from the `Shape` class, which is in turn derived from the basic `GeomObj` class (see the inheritance hierarchy in Appendix 3). It seems natural to derive a new class `Boolean` from `GeomObj`, so that the object list (which is a list of `GeomObjs`) can hold a `Boolean` object. A

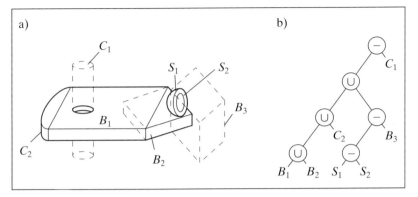

FIGURE 12.86 A compound object and its CSG tree.

`Boolean` object must be able to hold a binary tree, so we give it pointers `left` and `right` to point to its child subtrees. These must be pointers to `GeomObjs`, since in some places they point to geometric shapes and in others to `Boolean` trees. So a first cut at the `Boolean` class is as follows.

```
class Boolean: public GeomObj{
public:
        GeomObj *left, *right; // pointers to the children
        Boolean(){left = right = NULL;} // constructor
        virtual bool hit(Ray &r, Intersection &inter);
        ... other methods ...
};
```

Because `GeomObjs` have sphere and box extents, so do `Boolean`'s, which is useful since `Booleans` are expensive to ray trace, and anything that speeds this up is a blessing. We shall design a special `hit()` routine for `Booleans` that understands how to intersect a ray with a `Boolean`, which capitalizes again on polymorphism to simplify code. Actually, since `hit()` must operate differently for unions, intersections, and differences, it will improve matters to derive separate classes for the three kinds of `Booleans`: `UnionBool`, `IntersectionBool` and `DifferenceBool`. The definition of `UnionBool` is simply the following.

```
class UnionBool : public Boolean{
public:
        UnionBool(){Boolean();} // constructor
        virtual bool hit(Ray &r, Intersection &inter);
        ... other methods ...
};
```

The other definitions are nearly identical. Each type will have a `hit()` routine that is finely tuned to handle its specific nature.

Notice that `Booleans` do not have their own affine transformation; only `Shapes` do. This causes a Boolean tree to have transformations only at its leaves. This is a design decision that offers both advantages and disadvantages, and in fact some modeling systems and ray tracers operate differently. To understand the distinction, consider Figure 12.87a, which shows a tree for a Boolean object that *does* have a transformation at each internal node, as well as one at each leaf. The effect of each transformation is felt by all nodes beneath it in its subtrees. As discussed in the exercises, this tree is equivalent geometrically to the tree in part b, in the sense that both trees represent the same shape. Here the transformations have been percolated down to the leaf nodes and combined to form a single transformation at each leaf.

FIGURE 12.87 Including transformations at internal nodes of compound objects.

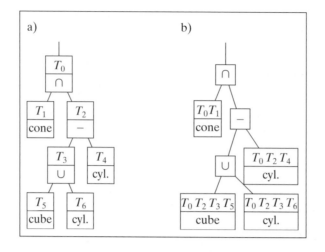

One advantage of keeping explicit transformations in internal nodes is that the designer can separately alter a particular transformation deep within a tree to adjust the shape of a CSG object after it has been created. It is also possible to have more control over the tightness of various extents for Boolean objects. A significant disadvantage, on the other hand, is the speed of ray tracing, since a ray must be inverse transformed at every node of the tree, not just at the leaves.

The way to specify a Boolean in an *SDL* file is to use one of the key words `union`, `intersection`, or `difference`, followed by the specification of the left geometric object, then the specification of the right one (which can themselves be Booleans). As an example, the fishbowl shape of Figure 12.84b, given by $(S_1 - S_2) - C$, can be specified by the following *SDL* code.

```
!make a fish bowl
rotate -90 1 0 0
difference
   difference
      sphere ! outer sphere
      push scale 0.9 0.9 0.9 sphere pop !inner sphere
   push translate 0 0 1.3 rotate 180 1 0 0 cone pop
```

The first transformation rotates the whole bowl about the *x*-axis. The difference is then formed between the left object (which is itself a difference of two spheres) and the cone. Because transformations given to *SDL* postmultiply the current transformation, and the current transformation is placed in a shape object at the time it is created, transformations are automatically percolated down the tree.

PRACTICE EXERCISES

12.13.3 Rearranging expressions for booleans

Because there is some flexibility in writing expressions for a compound object, more than one tree can represent it. For instance, both $\cup$ and $\cup$ commute, so $A \cup B = B \cup A$. Prove or disprove the following assertions.

a. $(A - B) - C = A - (B \cup C)$
b. $(A \cup B) - (A \cup C) = A \cup (B - C)$
c. $(A \cup B) \cap (A \cup C) = A \cap (B \cup C)$

12.13.4 How transformations percolate down a boolean tree

Consider the tree of Figure 12.84a, which supports a transformation at each internal node.

a. Prove (or disprove) that the geometric shape represented by this tree is the same as that represented by the tree in part b. Does the proof depend on the transformations being affine?

b. If transformation T_i in the figures is represented in homogeneous coordinates by matrix M_i, is the combined matrix for the cube in part b equal to $M_0 M_2 M_3 M_5$ or to $M_5 M_3 M_2 M_0$?

Hint: Prove that, in general, $T(A \text{ op } B) = T(A) \text{ op } T(B)$, where $T()$ represents a one-to-one transformation, A and B are sets of points, and op represents one of the operators $\cap$, $\cup$, or $-$.

12.13.5 Why does ray tracing handle unions automatically?

Explain why ray tracing the union of two objects (whether or not they interpenetrate) is equivalent to ray tracing their union.

12.13.6 The whole scene as one CSG object

Discuss the pros and cons of modeling an entire scene as one compound object, rather than using a list of simpler compound objects. ■

12.13.3 Intersecting Rays with Boolean Objects

We need to develop a `hit()` method to work with each type of boolean object. It must form the inside set for the ray with the left subtree, the inside set for the ray with the right subtree, and then combine the two sets appropriately.

A skeleton of `hit()` is shown in Figure 12.88 for the case of an intersection operation. Extent tests are first made to see if there is an early out (as discussed in the next section). Then the proper `hit()` is called for the left subtree, and unless the ray misses this subtree, the hit list `lftInter` is formed. If there is a miss, `hit()` returns false, immediately producing an early out, because the ray must hit both subtrees in order to hit their intersection. Then the hit list `rtInter` is formed, and finally the two hit lists are combined using the intersection operation.

The code is similar for the `UnionBool` and `DifferenceBool` classes.

```
bool IntersectionBool:: hit(Ray &r, Intersection &inter)
{
    Intersection lftInter, rtInter;
    if(ray misses the extents) return false;
    if((!left->hit(r,lftInter))||(!right->hit(r,rtInter)))
        return false; // early out
    make the combined list: place it in inter
    return(inter.numHits > 0); // true if inter is not empty
}
```

FIGURE 12.88 A skeleton of `hit()` for an intersection boolean object.

To Combine *t*-lists

Combining *t*-lists is intricate but logical. Consider the two example hit lists, L and R (standing for left and right), shown in Figure 12.89. For brevity we call the left list simply $L[]$ rather than `leftInter.theHit[]`, and similarly for the right list. In addition, the `hitObject` and `surface` fields are not shown. L shows 8 hits for its object, and R shows 5 hits. Each list contains the positive hit times and is ordered in time, and the entering field of the zeroth element shows whether the first hit that has a positive hit time, in front of the eye, occurs with the ray entering or exiting the object. Since all objects are solid, the entering values alternate after the zeroth.

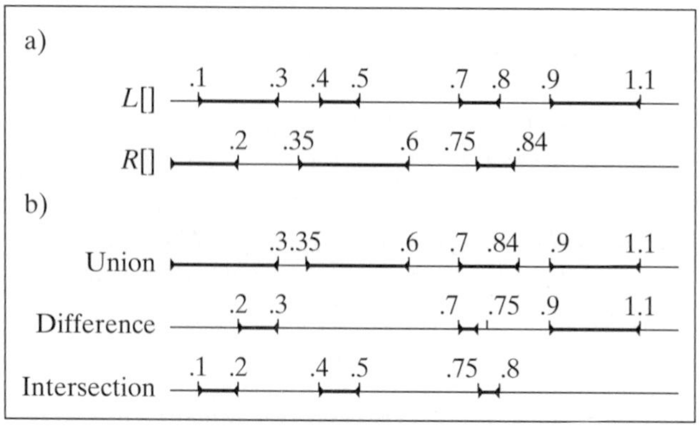

FIGURE 12.89 Example intersection records.

The lists are combined by scanning through both lists, noting at each step which next item in the two lists has the smaller hit time, and keeping track of whether the ray is inside or outside the object just before this next hit. These pieces of information are combined in a manner appropriate to the operator involved: *union*, *intersection*, or *difference*. Figure 12.89b shows the resulting *t*-list after combination, for each of the Boolean operators.

Consider a specific example of the logic used when combining the lists. Suppose that the operator is *difference* and that just before the next hit time the ray is inside the left object and outside the right object, so it must be inside the difference. The next hit time on each list is examined; suppose the right one is found to be smaller. This means that just after this next hit time the ray is inside the right object, so it must now be outside the difference. At this instant the state of the ray in the combined object changes from inside to outside.

We keep track of the state of the ray (whether it is inside or outside the object at the current time) as it progresses through the subtrees with the following variables.

```
bool lftInside;    // true if ray is inside left object;
bool rtInside;     // true if ray is inside right object;
bool combInside;   // true if ray is inside combined object;
```

These are the states of the ray *between* hits—that is, just before the next hit to be considered. `lftInside` is initialized according to whether the ray enters or exits the left object at the first hit—that is, according to `L[0].isEntering`. Specifically, `lftInside` is `false` if the first hit is entering (because before the hit the ray must be outside) and is `true` if the first hit is exiting. So we can initialize `lftInside` to `!L[0].isEntering`, and similarly for `rtInside`. Then `combInside` is found as a logical combination of `lftInside` and `rtInside`; if the operator is *union*, `combInside` is `true` if `lftInside` or `rtInside` or both are `true`. This is nicely captured using the logical operators: `combInside = lftInside || rtInside`. Similarly if the operator is *intersection*, we use `combInside = lftInside && rtInside`, and if it is *difference*, we use `combInside = lftInside && !rtInside`.

The algorithm proceeds by incrementing through both the L[] and R[] lists, at each step noting the smaller of the hit times, and using it to update `lftInside`, `rtInside`, and `combInside`. If `combInside` *changes* at any point, the latest hit event is added to the C[] list.

When either L[] or R[] has been consumed (when its final hit time has been examined), the other unconsumed list may or may not need to be considered:

- for **intersection**: ignore the unconsumed list;
- for **union**: increment through the unconsumed list, adding hit events as appropriate;
- for **difference**: if the left list is the unconsumed one, increment through it adding hit events as appropriate; if the right list is unconsumed, ignore it.

Note that when combining lists, we must take care to put the all necessary information into each new hit[] record. Specifically, the isEntering and hitObject fields must be properly filled, because if a hit ever becomes the first hit of the ray, we will be gleaning properties about the surface hit from the hitObject itself. When an exiting hit on the right object causes the ray to be entering the object itself, we must be sure the hit information points to the left object, so that what we see in the hole are the properties of the left object.

We also must make sure that the logic of hit() for CSG objects works properly when the object is transparent and the ray is traveling inside the boolean (as when the ray passes through a martini glass). Check that for the difference object above, the correct hit information is placed on the hit list even when rays begin inside an object.

Figure 12.90 shows an example of various compound objects that have been ray traced using these techniques. Full-color ray traced images of CSG objects are given in Plate 33. Try to identify the specific shapes out of which each boolean object was formed.

FIGURE 12.90 Example of ray traced compound objects.

PRACTICE EXERCISE

12.13.7 Hand simulate the algorithm

Hand simulate the list-combining algorithm of Figure 12.88 for the examples in Example 12.13.1.

12.13.8 Writing the hit() methods

Implement the hit() methods for the UnionBool and IntersectionBool classes. Each should be fine-tuned to the specific requirements of its boolean operator. ■

12.13.4 Building and Using Extents for CSG Objects

One issue remaining is the creation of projection, sphere, and box extents for CSG objects. During a preprocessing step the tree for the CSG object is scanned, and extents are built for each node and stored within the node itself. Later during ray tracing the ray can be tested against each extent encountered, with the potential benefit of an early out in the intersection process if it becomes clear the ray cannot hit the object. This can save the cost of combining lists further up the CSG tree.

Extents are tested as always inside the `hit()` method of the object's class, as was suggested in Figure 12.88. If the ray hits the extent for this node of the tree, it is intersected with the left and right subtrees in the usual manner.

To Make Box Extents

What is a reasonable definition of a box extent for a CSG node? We mean, of course, world box extents, since a boolean object doesn't have a generic version. Suppose the node represents the object A op B, where A and B are shapes and op is one of the Boolean operators. The box extent for this object must enclose the object, so that we can rest assured the ray misses the object if it misses the box. The shape of the object might be quite complicated (e.g., the intersection of a rotated torus with a skewed cube), so it will be very difficult to find the tightest aligned box automatically without an inordinate amount of processing.

We take the simplest approach and create the box extent of L op R out of the box extent, $E(L)$, of L and the box extent, $E(R)$, of R. We define the box extent differently for the different operators.

a. **union:** Take as the box extent the aligned box that fits about both $E(L)$ and $E(R)$ simultaneously. This is equivalent to $E(E(L) \cup E(R))$. (*Questions:* Is this always the same as $E(L \cup R)$? Would it be much more efficient to test $E(L)$ and $E(R)$ separately? If the ray misses both extents separately, does it necessarily miss $L \cup R$?)

b. **intersection:** Take as the box extent the intersection of $E(L)$ and $E(R)$. The intersection of two aligned boxes is always an aligned box, and it is easy to compute its (*left, top, right, bottom, front, back*) components. (*Question:* Are you sure the ray will miss $L \cap R$ if it misses this extent?) This extent will most likely be reasonably tight if the extents of L and R are tight.

c. **difference:** Take as the box extent simply $E(L)$. This is very conservative, as we are failing to take advantage of the possibility that $(E(L) - E(R))$ may be considerably smaller than $E(L) - E(R)$. We may have chopped out a lot of space from $E(L)$. But to do a more thorough analysis would be very costly.

Box extents would be formed recursively, because the box extent for an internal node of a boolean tree would be constructed out of the box extents of its children nodes. For shape objects the box extent would be constructed nonrecursively, as we discussed above: finding the cloud of points for the object in world coordinates, and building an aligned box around it. Each type of shape would have its own `makeBoxExtent()` method. Each method would build the box extent, store it within the object, and return it for use by other objects. The `UnionBool` class, for example, might use the following code.

```
Cuboid UnionBool :: makeBoxExtent()
{
    Cuboid lft = left->makeBoxExtent();
    Cuboid rt = right->makeBoxExtent();
    Cuboid tmp;
    tmp.left = min(lft.left,rt.left); // form the union
    tmp.top = max(lft.top,rt.top);
    // etc. for the other four values
    worldBoxExtent = tmp; // store it in the object
    return tmp;
}
```

The preprocessing step would call makeBoxExtent() for each object on the object list. When this method is called for a Boolean object, it creates and stores a box extent at the root node of the tree, as well as at each internal node.

To Make Sphere Extents

World sphere extents would be built in a similar way to box extents. As discussed earlier, for shapes, the cloud of points is found in world coordinates, and the sphere extent is the closest-fitting sphere about this cloud. For Boolean objects we must decide how to form the sphere extent for a union, difference, and intersection of two objects.

The difference is easy; use the sphere extent for the left object itself. It won't be too tight, but it is serviceable. The same choice could be made for intersections, as it is very difficult to compute the true sphere extent for an intersection. For unions it is probably simplest to combine the clouds of points for the left and right objects and then to form a single sphere about it.

To Make Projection Extents

There is strong motivation to use projection extents for CSG objects, owing to the cost of ray tracing them. A projection extent can be built for each node of a CSG object in much the same way as we built box extents. The projection extent of a node is formed by a combination of the projection extents of the left and right sub-objects. Using $P(object)$ to mean the projection extent of $object$, we have, according to the rules above, the following:

$$P(L \cup R) = P(P(L) \cup P(R))$$
$$P(L \cap R) = P(L) \cap P(R)$$
$$P(L - R) = P(L)$$

As before, each class has its own makeProjectionExtent() method (for eye rays only).

12.14 RAY TRACING VS. RAY CASTING

The ray casting technique began in 1992 with the appearance of the game Wolfenstein 3D from ID Software. In Wolfenstein 3D the player was placed into a 3D maze-like environment where the player could move through rooms battling demons and enemies.

Although ray tracing is a method that produces very high quality images of any scene desired, it is rather time consuming and therefore not usually suitable for real-time applications, such as games or simulations. On the other hand, ray casting is a much faster technique, but it suffers from severe geometric constraints on the scene of interest, and the resulting images are blocky and nonrealistic.

Figure 12.91 shows screenshots from Wolfenstein 3D that illustrates the type of scene which can be ray cast. Notice the blocky and coarse quality of the image and its texture. Ray casting has largely fallen out of favor in recent years, as innovations in graphics hardware have made some of the limitations of ray tracing unimportant. The companion web site links to a fine tutorial on ray casting by F. Permadi.

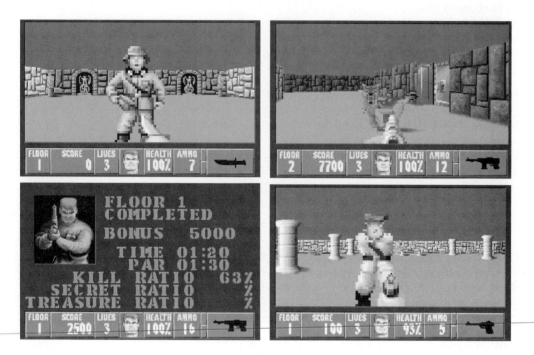

FIGURE 12.91 A screen shot of the ray-cast game Wolfenstein 3D. (Courtesy of I.D. software)

12.15 SUMMARY

> For tribal man space was the uncontrollable mystery.
> For technological man it is time that occupies the same role.
>
> *Marshall McLuhan*
> *(1911–1980)*

Ray tracing offers a conceptually simple and uniform approach to creating dazzlingly realistic images. A large collection of relevant rays of light is traced through a scene composed of various objects, and each is analyzed to find how much light it returns to the observer's eye. This mechanism makes possible many visual effects. In addition to the usual simulation of ambient, diffuse, and specular light components, ray tracing can, with relative ease, simulate shadows, reflections from mirror-like surfaces, and transmission of refracted light through transparent objects. Ray tracing also provides a natural approach to applying both 2D and 3D texture to objects.

The heart of a ray tracing application is the routine that finds the intersections between a ray and an object. A huge number of rays is cast to create a high-resolution image, and many of these rays spawn several secondary rays, so that much of the computation time is spent in finding intersections. Because each ray is tested against each object in the scene, the time required for ray tracing grows nearly linearly with the complexity of the scene. The judicious use of extents can produce many early outs and relieve a large number of objects from requiring a more complete intersection test, vastly speeding up the ray tracing process.

Ray tracing automatically solves the problem of removing hidden surfaces, because the hit times that various objects make with a ray are a direct measure of their distance from the observer. Thus the object with the smallest hit time is the closest one and cannot be obscured by any other object. This same principle also makes it straightforward to calculate shadows. A shadow feeler is cast from the ray's intersection point with an object to each light source, and the presence of any intersections with objects is tested. If there is an object positioned between a point of interest and a light source, *that point* is in shadow with respect to the source. Thus, determining such shadowing is equivalent to determining whether an object has a hit time with a shadow feeler between 0 and 1.

Some object shapes are easy to ray trace, because finding their intersection with a ray is equivalent to solving a linear or quadratic equation. Typical among these are planes, spheres, cylinders, and cones. The scene designer starts with generic versions of each of these and transforms them into their desired sizes, orientations, and positions, using an affine transformation. This can change spheres into ellipsoids, cubes into parallelepipeds, and so forth, thereby enlarging the class of objects that appear in the scene. It is also simple to model and ray trace any convex polyhedron, because its interior is merely the intersection of a number of half-spaces.

Rays are simple things that are easy to work with and have the desirable property that, when subjected to an affine transformation, they are still legitimate rays. Therefore it is not difficult to carry out the spawning of new rays from a given start point in some new direction, and to test what objects in the scene they hit. This provides a direct way to gather light contributions from reflections off shiny surfaces, and from transmission through transparent bodies. The programming effort to implement these techniques is very modest.

Adding methods to ray trace CSG objects dramatically increases the variety of scenes that can be rendered. Highly complex shapes can be modeled and ray traced. The internal logic of a ray tracing algorithm for CSG objects is straightforward and easy to manage in a program.

Ray tracing offers one of the most powerful approaches to computer-synthesized images today. Although the enormous amount of computation involved makes it one of the slower methods for generating images, the images that result offer a degree of realism that is hard to match with any other technique.

12.16 CASE STUDIES

CASE STUDY 12.1 AN EMISSIVE RAY TRACER

(Level of Effort: II) Write and exercise an application that ray traces a scene described in SDL. This ray tracer properly handles emissive objects that glow with their own light. It need not reflect ambient, diffuse, and specular light contributions. It should properly ray trace at least the following shapes: sphere, tapered cylinder, cube, square, and plane. Other shapes noted in the SDL scene file are simply ignored. A preview of the scene is drawn before ray tracing begins, using the `Scene::drawOpenGL()` method.

Keystrokes are used to control the action. The key strokes '1', '2', '4', '8' set the size of pixel blocks, as discussed in Section 12.5, permitting experimentation at different resolutions. Other keystrokes adjust the position and orientation of the camera.

Also create a scene in SDL that contains several *jacks* and *octos*, arranged so you can ray trace them. A jack consists of three mutually perpendicular bars, where a bar is an elongated sphere with a small sphere at each end. An octo consists of a small sphere positioned at the six vertices of an octohedron, and of 12 edges between the vertices made up of elongated spheres.

CASE STUDY 12.2 A RENAISSANCE RAY TRACER

(Level of Effort: II—given that the emissive ray tracer of Case Study 12.1 is available) Enhance the previous ray tracer so that it properly handles ambient and diffuse reflections and Phong specular highlights. It need not handle reflections, refractions, or shadowing. It properly ray traces all of the generic primitives, as well as meshes that represent convex polyhedra. The scene information is read in from an SDL file. As with the previous ray tracer, a preview of the scene is drawn before each ray tracing.

For extra control, implement code so that the user can indicate a rectangular region of the display using the mouse, after which the designated region is ray traced at full resolution (block size = 1). The region outside the rectangular region is not ray traced. This is a boon to a user who wants rapid ray tracing but needs full resolution only at limited places in a scene.

CASE STUDY 12.3 IMPLEMENTING SHADOWS IN A RAY TRACER

(Level of Effort: I—given that the ray tracer of Case Study 12.2 is available) Enhance the previous ray tracer so that it properly displays shadows.

CASE STUDY 12.4 USING EXTENTS TO SPEED UP RAY TRACING

(Level of Effort: II—given that the ray tracer of Case Study 12.3 is available) Implement the use of sphere extents, box extents, and projection extents in the previous ray tracer, and make a study of the relative speedup that the use of each type of extent provides. Allow the user to turn each kind of extent on and off with individual keystrokes and to see (on your wristwatch) the elapsed time that each ray tracing requires.

CASE STUDY 12.5 RAY TRACING WITH 3D TEXTURES

(Level of Effort: II—given that the ray tracer of Case Study 12.2 is available) Enhance the Renaissance ray tracer above to support the display of several 3D textures, including a checkerboard pattern, wood grain, and marble. The user can choose which texture to employ using different keystrokes, and all objects in the scene are rendered with the chosen texture.

Determine a way to extend SDL and the `Scene  :read()` method so that parameters can be specified in an SDL file and attached to subsequently defined objects. Use the parameters to choose which texture each object is composed of and to specify some of the numerical parameters inherent in the definition of these textures. For instance, the SDL lines:

```
parameter 3 12.6 -91
cube
```

might attach the three parameters shown to the cube, denoting the association of texture #3 to this object.

CASE STUDY 12.6 ANTIALIASING

(Level of Effort: II—given that the ray tracer of Case Study 12.2 is available) Extend the ray tracer of Case Study 12.2 so that it antialiases a ray traced scene. For each major ray it shoots N rays in slightly altered directions and averages the colors that return along the rays. Experiment with different amounts of jitter in the ray directions and with different values of N.

CASE STUDY 12.7 RAY TRACING OTHER PRIMITIVES

(Level of Effort: III—given that the ray tracer of Case Study 12.2 is available) Do a thorough study of the paper by Jim Kajiya [Kajiya83] on ray tracing complex shapes such as prisms, mountainous terrain, and surfaces of revolution. Implement at least the fractal mountain technique, and extend SDL with the key word `mountain` followed by some parameters that specify the nature of the mountain that is to be ray traced.

CASE STUDY 12.8 A 2D RAY TRACER TO EXPLORE REFRACTION

(Level of Effort: II) Because the formula for the refracted direction, **t**, in Equation (12.45) uses only dot products, it is as correct for two-dimensional vectors as for three-dimensional vectors. Write and exercise a program that generates pictures such as that in Figure 12.63. The user gives the index of refraction and the angle of incidence, and the program draws the incident and refracted rays.

CASE STUDY 12.9 REFLECTED AND REFRACTED LIGHT

(Level of Effort: III—given that the ray tracer of Case Study 12.2 is available) Extend the ray tracer of Case Study 12.2 so that it properly handles reflections from shiny surfaces and refraction of light through transparent objects. Experiment with different transparent shapes and different indices of refraction to explore the basic properties of refraction.

CASE STUDY 12.10 RAY TRACING BOOLEAN COMBINATIONS OF OBJECTS

(Level of Effort: III—given that the ray tracer of Case Study 12.2 is available) Extend the ray tracer of Case Study 12.2 so that it properly ray traces boolean objects (whose tree is at least 3 deep, as in Figure 12.74). Build an interesting scene that includes several boolean objects, including:

- an object with a cylindrical hole through it,
- a spherical lens $A \cap (B - C)$ (formed as the intersection of two spheres),
- an object given by: $A \cap (B - C)$, where A, B and C are shapes.

Arrange so that you can see some object through the holes in other objects, and some object through the lens.

12.17 FOR FURTHER READING

An Introduction to Ray Tracing, edited by Andrew Glassner [1989], provides an excellent collection of survey papers that explore the essential algorithms for ray tracing, along with methods for speeding up the ray tracing process. *Graphic Gems III* [Kirk92] contains several articles on ray tracing and radiosity that may serve useful. Watt and Watt [Watt92] offer a broad perspective on ray tracing and ray tracing methods. The Internet Ray Tracing Competition (http://www.irtc.org/) has a collection of ray traced images which offer ideas and motivation to get ray tracing.

Appendix 1

···

Graphics Tools: How to Obtain and Install OpenGL

Most of the code discussed in this book is based on using OpenGL as the application programming interface (API). In this appendix we describe how to acquire the OpenGL tools that you will need to build your own applications using OpenGL.

A1.1 OBTAIN AND INSTALL OPENGL

It is straightforward and cost free to obtain the necessary OpenGL software for almost any computer platform in common use today. We discuss how to access the software for each of the major platforms. Also, an enormous amount of supplementary information about OpenGL is available through the Internet.

Information Repositories for OpenGL

A rich source of general information on OpenGL and a starting point for downloading software is _http://www.opengl.org/_. A great deal of information, including some on-line manuals, also is available at _http://opengl.org/documentation/_. The Internet site (see the Preface) for this book provides additional information and links on OpenGL. The excellent book _OpenGL Programming Guide_ (often called "The Red Book"), published by the OpenGL Architecture Review Board (ARB) and currently in its fifth edition, is an essential source of information about using OpenGL and gives pointers on obtaining and installing the software.

What You Need

With any system, you start with a good C/C++ compiler and install appropriate OpenGL header files and libraries. Three libraries with associated files are required to use OpenGL as it is described in this book:

> OpenGL (the basic API tool);
> **GLU** (the OpenGL Utility Library);
> **GLUT** (the OpenGL Utility Toolkit, a windowing tool kit that handles window system operations).

Typically, several files are associated with each library: a header file (.h), a library file (.lib), and in some systems a dynamically linked library file (.dll).

Adding Header Files Place the three files Gl.h, Glu.h, and Glut.h in a gl subdirectory (newly created by you) of the include directory of your compiler. In each application you write the following include statements:

```
#include <gl/Gl.h>
#include <gl/Glu.h>
#include <gl/glut.h>
```

Linking Library Files Each application will be part of a project that is compiled and linked. In addition to the (.c or .cpp) files that you write, add the appropriate OpenGL library (.lib) files to your project so that the linker can find them.

We next discuss the individual requirements for each major type of system.

Microsoft Windows 98/NT/2000/XP

Much of OpenGL comes already installed on a Windows machine. At the time of writing, OpenGL comes installed on a Windows XP machine.

A suitable environment for using OpenGL on Windows systems is Microsoft's Visual C±± 6.0 or later. (If you declare the application to be a "win32 console application," there is no need to build a graphical user interface (GUI): input from the keyboard and output of text take place through the separate console window.)

See "Download OpenGL Specs" at http://www.opengl.org/documentation/spec.html for the latest specifications on OpenGL and the Utility Libraries for Windows. The libraries are also available as the self-extracting archive file on the Microsoft ftp site at ftp://ftp.microsoft.com/softlib/mslfiles/opengl95.exe. Included are gl.h, glu.h, glu32.lib, opengl32.lib, glu32.dll, and opengl32.dll. (Do not use older .aux files.)

The glut library is available at http://www.opengl.org/resources/libraries/glut.html. Included are glut.h, glut32.lib, and glut32.dll. (Do not use the glut.lib and glut.dll files.) When these files have been downloaded and extracted, place the .lib files in some convenient directory, from which you will add them to each of your projects.

Place the .dll files in the Windows/System directory (if they aren't already there). Write the following include statements to include the designated files in your applications:

```
#include <windows.h>
#include <gl/Gl.h>
#include <gl/Glu.h>
#include <glut/glut.h>
```

If you have stored the .h files in a different folder from that shown, such as 'myglut', the include directive would be #include <myglut/glut.h>.

Macintosh

The principal source for OpenGL for Macintosh systems is http://www.apple.com/macosx/features/graphicsandmedia/. OS 9 and X users should note that basic OpenGL libraries and GLUT are automatically installed! Opengl.org also has information on how to get OpenGL running on earlier Macintosh platforms. Every iMac, iBook, PowerBook, PowerMac G4, and PowerMac G5 has OpenGL Hardware acceleration built in.

UNIX and X Window Systems

OpenGL is supported on all UNIX workstations. GLX provides the connection between OpenGL® and the X Window System. It is required by any OpenGL implementation using X. Resources and download information can be found at http:// www.sgi.com/products/software/opensource/glx/. GLX extends OpenGL to Linux, FreeBSD, and other operating systems using the popular XFree86 implementation of X.

Mesa 3D

Mesa is an OpenGL lookalike library that is available for free. Currently, the best place to obtain it is at http://www.mesa3d.org/#Systems. Follow the directions bundled with each downloadable version. Another option is Cygwin under Windows. Cygwin is Linux that runs under Windows. Cygwin allows the application programmer to link to Windows dll's. Cygwin runs faster than the Mesa and allows access to video hardware that may not be available on the native Linux video drivers.

Appendix 2

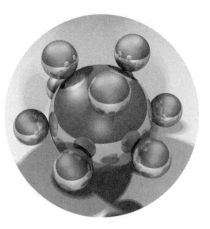

Some Mathematics for Computer Graphics

Mathematics, rightly viewed, possess not only truth, but supreme beauty
—a beauty cold and austere, like that of sculpture.

Bertrand Russell
(1872–1970)

This appendix draws together and summarizes various mathematical results that are referred to throughout the book. In some cases a brief derivation of a result is given, but that material here is mainly for convenient reference.

A2.1 SOME KEY DEFINITIONS PERTAINING TO MATRICES AND THEIR OPERATIONS

In this appendix we review some fundamental concepts of matrices and ways to manipulate them. More general treatments are available in many other books (for instance, Birkhoff76, Faux79).

A matrix is a rectangular array of elements, most commonly numbers. A matrix with m rows and n columns is said to be an m-by-n matrix. For example,

$$A = \begin{pmatrix} 3 & 2 & -5 \\ -1 & 8 & 0 \\ 6 & 3 & 9 \\ 1 & 21 & 2 \end{pmatrix} \tag{A2.1}$$

is a four-by-three matrix of integers, and $B = [1.34, -6.275, 0.0, 81.6]$ is a one-by-four matrix, also called a **quadruple** or a vector. In common parlance, a 1-by-n matrix is a **row vector**, and an n-by-1 matrix is a **column vector**.

The individual elements of a matrix are conventionally given lowercase symbols and distinguished by subscripts. The ijth element of matrix B is denoted as b_{ij}. This is the element in the ith row and jth column, so for the matrix of Equation (A2.1), $a_{32} = 3$. A matrix is **square** if it has the same number of rows as columns. In graphics, we frequently work with two-by-two, three-by-three, and four-by-four matrices. Two common square matrices are the **zero matrix** and the **identity matrix**. All of the elements of the zero matrix are zero. All are zero for the identity matrix, too, except those along the **main diagonal** (those elements a_{ij} for which $i = j$), which have the value unity. The three-by-three identity matrix is therefore given by

$$I = \begin{pmatrix} 1 & 0 & 0 \\ 0 & 1 & 0 \\ 0 & 0 & 1 \end{pmatrix}$$

A2.1.1 Manipulations with Matrices

A matrix B of numbers may be **scaled** by a number s. Each element of B is multiplied by s. The resulting matrix is denoted sB. Using matrix A of Equation (A2.1), for instance, we may have

$$6A = \begin{pmatrix} 18 & 12 & -30 \\ -6 & 48 & 0 \\ 36 & 18 & 54 \\ 6 & 126 & 12 \end{pmatrix}$$

Two matrices C and D having the same number of rows and columns are said to have the same **shape** and may be added together. The ijth element of the sum $E = C + D$ is simply the sum of the corresponding elements: $e_{ij} = c_{ij} + d_{ij}$. Thus,

$$\begin{pmatrix} 3 & 2 & -5 \\ -1 & 8 & 0 \\ 6 & 3 & 9 \\ 1 & 21 & 2 \end{pmatrix} + \begin{pmatrix} 0 & 5 & -1 \\ 9 & 8 & -3 \\ 2 & 6 & 18 \\ 4 & 2 & 7 \end{pmatrix} = \begin{pmatrix} 3 & 7 & -6 \\ 8 & 16 & -3 \\ 8 & 9 & 27 \\ 5 & 23 & 9 \end{pmatrix}$$

Since matrices can be scaled and added, it is meaningful to define linear combinations of matrices (of the same shape), such as $2A - 4B$. The following facts about three matrices A, B, and C of the same shape result directly from these definitions:

$$A + B = B + A$$
$$A + (B + C) = (A + B) + C$$
$$(f + g)(A + B) = fA + fB + gA + gB$$

The **transpose** of a matrix M, denoted M^T, is formed by interchanging the rows and columns of M. The ijth element of M^T is the jith element of M. Thus, the transpose of matrix A of Equation (A2.1) is

$$A^T = \begin{pmatrix} 3 & -1 & 6 & 1 \\ 2 & 8 & 3 & 21 \\ -5 & 0 & 9 & 2 \end{pmatrix} \tag{A2.2}$$

The transpose of a row vector is a column vector. For example,

$$(3, 2, -5)^T = \begin{pmatrix} 3 \\ 2 \\ -5 \end{pmatrix}$$

A matrix is **symmetric** if it is identical to its own transpose. Only square matrices can be symmetric. Thus, an n-by-n matrix M is symmetric if $m_{ij} = m_{ji}$ for i and j between 1 and n.

A2.1.2 Multiplying Two Matrices

The transformations initially discussed in Chapter 5 involve multiplying a vector by a matrix and multiplying two matrices together. The first is a special case of the second.

The **product** AB of two matrices A and B is defined only if the matrices **conform**. That means that the number of columns of the first matrix, A, equals the number of rows of the second one, B. Thus, if A is 3 by 5 and B is 5 by 2, then AB is defined, but BA is not. **Each term** of the product $C = AB$ of A with B is simply the dot product of some row of A with some column of B. Specifically, the ijth element c_{ij} of the product is the dot product of the ith row of A with the jth column of B. Thus, the product of an n-by-n matrix with an m-by-r matrix is an n-by-r matrix. For example, we might have

$$\begin{pmatrix} 2 & 0 & 6 & -3 \\ 8 & 1 & -4 & 0 \\ 0 & 5 & 7 & 1 \end{pmatrix} \begin{pmatrix} 6 & 2 \\ -1 & 1 \\ 3 & 1 \\ -5 & 8 \end{pmatrix} = \begin{pmatrix} 45 & -14 \\ 35 & 13 \\ 11 & 20 \end{pmatrix}$$

Here, for instance, $c_{12} = -14$, since $(2, 0, 6, -3) \cdot (2, 1, 1, 8) = -14$. A much simpler case is the multiplication of a row matrix by column matrix, as in

$$(4, 5)\begin{pmatrix} 2 \\ 3 \end{pmatrix} = 23$$

This results because the dot product between $(4, 5)$ and $(2, 3)^T$ is 23. The multiplication of a *one*-by-*one* matrix by another *one*-by-*one* matrix is, of course, simply the product of the two numbers involved.

A routine to multiply square matrices is given on the book's companion web site and is easily extended to find the product of any two matrices that conform.

We list some useful properties of matrix multiplication. Suppose that matrices A, B, and C conform properly. Then

$$(AB)C = A(BC)$$
$$A(B + C) = AB + AC$$
$$(A + B)C = AC + BC$$
$$(AB)^T = B^T A^T$$

and

$$A(sB) = sAB$$

where s is a number. In forming a product of two matrices A and B, the order in which the matrices are taken makes a difference. For the expression AB, we say "A **premultiplies** B" or "A is **postmultiplied** by B." If A and B are both square matrices of the same size, they conform both ways, so AB and BA are both well defined, but the two products may contain different elements. If $AB = BA$ for two matrices, we say that they **commute**. (Do two symmetric matrices always commute?)

Multiplying a Vector by a Matrix

A special case of matrix multiplication occurs when one of the matrices is a row vector or column vector. In graphics, we often see a column vector $\mathbf{w}$ being premultiplied by a matrix M in the form $M\mathbf{w}$. For example, let

$$w = \begin{pmatrix} 2 \\ 5 \\ -3 \end{pmatrix} = (2, 5, -3)^T$$

and

$$M = \begin{pmatrix} 2 & 0 & 6 \\ 8 & 1 & -4 \\ 0 & 5 & 7 \end{pmatrix}$$

Then **w** conforms with M, and we can form

$$M\mathbf{w} = \begin{pmatrix} 2 & 0 & 6 \\ 8 & 1 & -4 \\ 0 & 5 & 7 \end{pmatrix} \begin{pmatrix} 2 \\ 5 \\ -3 \end{pmatrix} = \begin{pmatrix} -14 \\ 33 \\ 4 \end{pmatrix}$$

By the same rules as those given previously, each component of $M\mathbf{w}$ is the dot product of the appropriate row of M with **w**. One can also premultiply a matrix by a row vector **v**, as in

$$\mathbf{v}M = (3, -1, 7) \begin{pmatrix} 2 & 0 & 6 \\ 8 & 1 & -4 \\ 0 & 5 & 7 \end{pmatrix} = (-2, 34, 71)$$

A2.1.3 Partitioning a Matrix

It is sometimes convenient to subdivide a matrix into blocks of elements and to give names to the various blocks. For example,

$$M = \begin{pmatrix} 2 & 0 & 6 \\ 8 & 1 & -4 \\ 3 & 2 & 7 \end{pmatrix} = \left(\begin{array}{c|c} M_1 & M_2 \\ \hline M_3 & M_4 \end{array} \right)$$

where the blocks are identified as

$$M_1 = \begin{pmatrix} 2 & 0 \\ 8 & 1 \end{pmatrix}, \qquad M_2 = \begin{pmatrix} 6 \\ -4 \end{pmatrix}, \qquad M_3 = (3 \quad 2)$$

and M_4, consisting of the single element 7. This is called a **partition** of M into the four blocks shown. Note that when one block is positioned above another, the two blocks must have the same number of columns. Similarly, when two blocks lie side by side, they must have the same number of rows. Two matrices that have been partitioned in the same way (corresponding blocks have the same shape) may be added by adding the blocks individually. To transpose a partitioned matrix, transpose each block individually, and then transpose the arrangement of blocks. Thus,

$$\left(\begin{array}{c|c} M_1 & M_2 \\ \hline M_3 & M_4 \end{array} \right)^T = \left(\begin{array}{c|c} M_1^T & M_3^T \\ \hline M_2^T & M_4^T \end{array} \right)$$

You can also multiply two partitioned matrices by multiplying their submatrices in the usual way, as long as the submatrices conform:

$$\left(\begin{array}{c|c} M_1 & M_2 \\ \hline M_3 & M_4 \end{array} \right) \left(\begin{array}{c|c} M_5 & M_6 \\ \hline M_7 & M_8 \end{array} \right) = \left(\begin{array}{c|c} M_1M_5 + M_2M_7 & M_1M_6 + M_2M_8 \\ \hline M_3M_5 + M_4M_7 & M_3M_6 + M_4M_8 \end{array} \right)$$

A2.1.4 The Determinant of a Matrix

Every square matrix M has a number associated with it called its **determinant** and denoted by $|M|$. The determinant describes the volume of certain geometric shapes and provides information concerning the effect that a linear transformation has on areas and volumes of objects.

For a two-by-two matrix M, the determinant is simply the difference of two products:

$$|M| = \begin{vmatrix} m_{11} & m_{12} \\ m_{21} & m_{22} \end{vmatrix} = m_{11}m_{22} - m_{12}m_{21}$$

If M is a three-by-three matrix, its determinant has the form

$$|M| = \begin{vmatrix} m_{11} & m_{12} & m_{13} \\ m_{21} & m_{22} & m_{23} \\ m_{31} & m_{32} & m_{33} \end{vmatrix} = m_{11} \begin{vmatrix} m_{22} & m_{23} \\ m_{32} & m_{33} \end{vmatrix} - m_{12} \begin{vmatrix} m_{21} & m_{23} \\ m_{31} & m_{33} \end{vmatrix} + m_{13} \begin{vmatrix} m_{21} & m_{21} \\ m_{31} & m_{32} \end{vmatrix}$$

Accordingly,

$$\begin{vmatrix} 2 & 0 & 6 \\ 8 & 1 & -4 \\ 0 & 5 & 7 \end{vmatrix} = 294$$

Note that $|M|$ here is the sum of three terms, $m_{11}M_{11} - m_{12}M_{12} + m_{13}M_{13}$, so it has the form of a dot product: $|M| = (m_{11}, -m_{12}, m_{13}) \cdot (M_{11}, M_{12}, M_{13})$. What are the M_{ij} terms? M_{ij} is called the **cofactor** of element m_{ij} for matrix M. Since we shall see cofactors emerging when we seek the inverse of a matrix, it is convenient to define them formally.

> **DEFINITION:** Each element m_{ij} of a square matrix M has a corresponding **cofactor** M_{ij} that is $(-1)^{i \pm j}$ times the determinant of the matrix formed by deleting the ith row and the jth column from M.

Note that as one moves along a row or column, the value of $(-1)^{i+j}$ alternates between 1 and -1. One can visualize a checkerboard pattern of 1's and -1's distributed over the matrix. The general rule for finding the determinant $|M|$ of any n-by-n matrix M is as follows:

Pick any row of M, find the cofactor of each element in the row, and take the dot product of the row and the n-tuple of cofactors. Alternatively, pick a column of M and do the same thing. (Does this rule hold for a two-by-two matrix as well?)

Following are some useful properties of determinants:

- $|M| = |M^T|$.
- If two rows (or two columns) of M are identical, then $|M| = 0$.
- If M and B are both square, then $|MB| = |M||B|$.
- If B is formed from M by interchanging two rows (or columns) of M, then $|B| = -|M|$.
- If B is formed from M by multiplying one row (or column) of M by a constant k, then $|B| = k|M|$.
- If B is formed from M by adding a multiple of one row (or column) of M to another, then $|B| = |M|$.

A2.1.5 The Inverse of a Matrix

An n-by-n matrix M is said to be **nonsingular** whenever $|M|$ is not equal to 0. In this case, M has an **inverse**, denoted M^{-1}, that has the property

$$MM^{-1} = M^{-1}M = I$$

where I is the n-by-n identity matrix. Also, the inverse of a product of square matrices is

$$(AB)^{-1} = B^{-1}A^{-1}$$

It is simple to specify the elements of M^{-1} in terms of cofactors of M. Let A be the inverse of M. Then A has ijth element

$$a_{ij} = \frac{M_{ji}}{|M|}$$

That is, we find the cofactor of the term m_{ji} and divide it by the determinant of the whole matrix. Carefully note the subscripts here: the cofactor of m_{ji} is used when determining a_{ij}. An equivalent procedure for computing the determinant of M is as follows:

1. Build an intermediate matrix C of cofactors $c_{ij} = M_{ij}$.
2. Find $|M|$ as the dot product of any row of C with the corresponding row of M.
3. Transpose C to get C^T.
4. Scale each element of C^T by $|M|^1$ to form M^{-1}.

■ **EXAMPLE Find the inverse of**

$$M = \begin{pmatrix} 2 & 0 & 6 \\ 8 & 1 & -4 \\ 0 & 5 & 7 \end{pmatrix}$$

SOLUTION:

Build the matrix C of cofactors of M:

$$\begin{pmatrix} 27 & -56 & 40 \\ 30 & 14 & -10 \\ -6 & 56 & 2 \end{pmatrix}.$$

Next, find $|M|$ as $(2, 0, 6) \cdot (27, -56, 40) = 294$. Then transpose C and scale each element by $1/|M|$ to obtain

$$M^{-1} = \frac{1}{294} \begin{pmatrix} 27 & 30 & -6 \\ -56 & 14 & 56 \\ 40 & -10 & 2 \end{pmatrix}$$

Check this answer by multiplying out MM^{-1} and $M^{-1}M$ to obtain the unit matrix.

Orthogonal Matrices

For some transformations, such as rotations (see Chapter 5), the associated matrix has an inverse that is particularly easy to find. A matrix M said to be **orthogonal** if simply transposing it produces its inverse—that is, if $M^T = M^{-1}$. Therefore, $MM^T = I$.

If M is orthogonal, $MM^T = I$ implies that each row of M is a unit-length vector and that the rows are mutually orthogonal. The same is true for the columns of M. (Why?) For instance, if M is three-by-three, partition it into three rows as follows:

$$M = \begin{pmatrix} \dfrac{\mathbf{a}}{} \\ \dfrac{\mathbf{b}}{} \\ \mathbf{c} \end{pmatrix}$$

Then the triples $\mathbf{a}, \mathbf{b}$, and $\mathbf{c}$ are each of unit length and $\mathbf{a} \cdot \mathbf{b} = \mathbf{a} \cdot \mathbf{c} = \mathbf{b} \cdot \mathbf{c} = 0$.

A2.2 SOME PROPERTIES OF VECTORS AND THEIR OPERATIONS

A2.2.1 The Perp of a Vector; the Perp Dot Product

The perp and perp dot product apply only to two-dimensional vectors. As we saw in Chapter 4, the perp of a vector and the perp dot product provide useful tools for solving two equations in two unknowns.

The Perp of a Vector

Let vector $\mathbf{a} = (ax, ay)$. Then the **counterclockwise** perpendicular, or "perp", of $\mathbf{a}$, denoted by $\mathbf{a}^{\perp}$, is given by $\mathbf{a}^{\perp} = (-ay, ax)$, and the following properties hold:

a. Vector $\mathbf{a}$ and $\mathbf{a}^{\perp}$ have the same length: $|\mathbf{a}| = |\mathbf{a}^{\perp}|$.
b. Linearity:$(\mathbf{a} + \mathbf{b})^{\perp} = |\mathbf{a}^{\perp}| + |\mathbf{b}^{\perp}|$ and $(A\mathbf{a})^{\perp} = A\mathbf{a}^{\perp}$ for any scalar A.
c. Two perps make a negation: $\mathbf{a}^{\perp \perp} = (\mathbf{a}^{\perp})^{\perp} = -\mathbf{a}$.

The Perp Dot Product $\mathbf{a}^{\perp} \cdot \mathbf{b}$

a. The perp dot product $\mathbf{a}^{\perp} \cdot b = a_x b_y - a_y b_x$ with any two dimensional vector $\mathbf{b} = (b_x, b_y) = a_x b_y - a_y b_x$
b. $\mathbf{a}^{\perp} \cdot \mathbf{a} = 0$. ($\mathbf{a}^{\perp}$ is perpendicular to $\mathbf{a}$.)
c. $|\mathbf{a}^{\perp}|^2 = |\mathbf{a}|^2$. ($\mathbf{a}^{\perp}$ and $\mathbf{a}$ have the same length.)
d. $\mathbf{a}^{\perp} \cdot \mathbf{b} = -\mathbf{b}^{\perp} \cdot \mathbf{a}$. (The perp dot product is antisymmetric.)
e. $\mathbf{a}^{\perp} \cdot \mathbf{b}$ can be written as the determinant

$$\mathbf{a}^{\perp} \cdot \mathbf{b} = \begin{vmatrix} a_x & a_y \\ b_x & b_y \end{vmatrix}$$

f. If $\mathbf{a} + \mathbf{b} + \mathbf{c} = \mathbf{0}$, then $\mathbf{a}^{\perp} \cdot \mathbf{b} = \mathbf{b}^{\perp} \cdot \mathbf{c} = \mathbf{c}^{\perp} \cdot \mathbf{a}$.
g. $\mathbf{a}^{\perp} \cdot \mathbf{b} > 0$ if and only if there is a CCW turn from $\mathbf{a}$ to $\mathbf{b}$.
h. $\mathbf{a}^{\perp} \cdot \mathbf{b} = 0$ if $\mathbf{b}$ is parallel or antiparallel to $\mathbf{a}$.
i. $|\mathbf{a}^{\perp} \cdot \mathbf{b}|$ is the area of the parallelogram determined by vectors $\mathbf{a}$ and $\mathbf{b}$.

A2.3 SPHERICAL COORDINATES AND DIRECTION COSINES

In this section, we review the notion of spherical coordinates and summarize how to convert back and forth from spherical coordinates to Cartesian coordinates. Figure A2.3 shows how a point U is defined in spherical coordinates. R is

FIGURE A2.3 Definition of spherical coordinates.

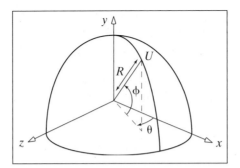

the radial distance of U from the origin, and ϕ is the angle that U makes with the xy-plane, known as the **latitude** of point U. θ is the **azimuth** of U, the angle between the xz-plane and the plane through U and the z-axis. ϕ lies in the interval $-\pi/2 \le \phi < \pi/2$, and θ lies in the range $0 \le \theta < 2\pi$.

With the use of simple trigonometry, it is straightforward to work out the relationships between these quantities and the Cartesian coordinates (u_x, u_y, u_z) for U. The equations are

$$u_x = R\cos(\phi)\cos(\phi)$$
$$u_y = R\sin(\phi)$$

[handwritten: $x = \rho \sin\phi \cos\theta$]
[handwritten: $y = \rho \sin\phi \sin\theta$]

(A2.3)

and

$$u_z = R\cos(\phi)\sin(\phi)$$

[handwritten: $z = \rho \cos\phi$]

One can also invert these relations to express (R, ϕ, θ) in terms of u_x, u_y, u_z:

$$R = \sqrt{u_x^2 + u_y^2 + u_z^2}$$

[handwritten: cartesian to spherical]

$$\phi = \sin^{-1}\left(\frac{u_y}{R}\right)$$

(A2.4)

$$\theta = \arctan(u_z, u_x)$$

The function $\arctan(\,,\,)$ is the two-argument form of the arctangent, defined as

$$
\arctan(y, x) =
\begin{cases}
\tan^{-1}(y/x) & \text{if } x > 0 \\
\pi + \tan^{-1}(y/x) & \text{if } x < 0 \\
\pi/2 & \text{if } x = 0 \text{ and } y > 0 \\
-\pi/2 & \text{if } x = 0 \text{ and } y < 0
\end{cases}
$$

(A2.5)

This function can distinguish between the case where both x and y are positive and the case where both of them are negative, unlike the usual form $\tan^{-1}(x/y)$, which always produces angles between $-\pi/2$ and $\pi/2$. Notice that the case where x is zero yet y is not zero, which leads to a catastrophic division by zero, is carefully avoided.

■ **EXAMPLE A2.4.1**

Suppose that point U is at a distance 2 from the origin, is $60°$ up from the xy-plane, and is along the negative x-axis. Hence, U is in the xy-plane. Then U is expressed in spherical coordinates as $(60°, 180°)$. Using Equation (A2.4) to compute U in Cartesian coordinates, we obtain $U = (-1, 1.732, 0)$.

Direction Cosines

The direction of point U in the preceding example is given in terms of two angles: the azimuth and the latitude. Directions are often specified in an alternative useful way through direction cosines. The direction cosines of a line through the origin are the cosines of the three angles it makes with the x-, y-, and z-axes, respectively. Recall that the cosine of the angle between two unit vectors is given by their dot product. Using the given point U, we form the position vector (u_x, u_y, u_z). From the preceding discussion, we see that the length of this vector is R, so it must be normalized to the unit-length vector $\mathbf{m} = (u_x/R, u_y/R, u_z/R)$. Then the cosine of the angle it makes with the x-axis is given by the dot product $\mathbf{m} \cdot \mathbf{i} = u_x/R$, which is simply the first component of $\mathbf{m}$. Similarly, the second and third components of $\mathbf{m}$ are the second and third direction cosines, respectively. Calling the angles made with the x-, y-, and z-axes α, β, and γ, respectively, we have, for the three direction cosines for the line from 0 to U,

$$\cos(\alpha) = \frac{u_x}{R}$$

$$\cos(\beta) = \frac{u_y}{R}$$

and

$$\cos(\gamma) = \frac{u_z}{R}$$

cartesian to spherical:

$$r = \sqrt{x^2 + y^2 + z^2}$$

$$\tan\theta = y/x$$

$$\tan\varphi = \frac{z}{\sqrt{x^2+y^2}}$$

$$x = r\cos\theta \sin\varphi$$

$$y = r\sin\theta \sin\varphi$$

$$z = r\cos\varphi$$

Note that the three direction cosines are related, since the sum of their squares is always unity.

Find the direction cosines of the vector $\mathbf{n}$, where

1. $\mathbf{n} = (1, 1, 1)$.
2. $\mathbf{n} = (2, 3, 4)$.

$$(0, 0, -5)$$

$$x_2 = r\cos\phi_2$$

$$y_2 = r\sin\phi_2$$

$$\phi_1 =$$

$$10° \mid \frac{2\pi}{360}$$

$(0, 0, -5)$

$(0, 0, 0)$

VRP

$(0, 0, 5)$

Appendix 3

Useful Class and Routines & SDL

This appendix defines some data types and algorithms that may prove useful in developing graphics applications. The basic types are set forth through various classes, some of which are fully defined and others of which have a number of methods declared, but are not defined. It is up to the reader to flesh latter out. Some classes are given only in a skeletal form, to suggest what might be developed in an actual application. With most classes, a relaxed approach to encapsulation is taken: Most data fields are declared public rather than private, as a matter of brevity and to avoid the need to define a large number of accessor and mutator functions. Another excellent source of classes and utilities may be found in the "Graphics Gems" series, whose on-line repository is http://www.acm.org/tog/GraphicsGems/index.html.

The classes defined in this appendix are collected in various header (.h) and source (.cpp) files, which are also available on the book's Internet site. (See the preface.) Please refer to the companion web site as some of the code fragments may have been improved and adjusted over time. The companion web site may have additional codes that programmers may find useful.

The Collections of Classes Described Here

1. Classes for 2D Graphics. These classes provide some support for drawing 2D figures and include IntPoint, Point2, Polyline, IntRect, Vector2, and Canvas.
2. RGBpixmap. This class provides support for creating and drawing pixmaps, including reading an image stored in the BMP format.
3. SDL. These classes support the manipulation and drawing of 3D scenes, including scenes described in the SDL. The supporting classes include Point3, Vector3, Color3, Light, Affine4, AffineStack, Material, GeomObj, Boolean, UnionBool, IntersectionBool, DifferenceBool, Shape, Cube, Sphere, TaperedCylinder, Square, Plane, Face, Mesh, Torus, Teapot, and Scene.
4. Noise. Among these classes are the Noise class for creating 3D noise and turbulence for solid texturing.
5. Ray-tracing classes. Includes: PointCluster, SphereInfo, Cuboid, Ray, HitInfo, and Intersection.

CLASSES FOR 2D GRAPHICS

```
// graphics2d.h // A collection of classes to support 2D
classes
#ifndef _GRAPHICS2D
#define _GRAPHICS2D
#include <string>
#include <iostream>
#include <fstream>
```

```
#include <strstream>
using namespace std;
#include <windows.h> //change if using xWindows or other platform
#include <assert.h>
#include <math.h>
#include <stdlib.h>
#include <gl/Gl.h>
#include <gl/Glu.h>
#include <gl/glut.h>
//@@@@@@@@@@@@@@@@@@@@ IntPoint class @@@@@@@@@@@@@@@@@@@
class IntPoint{ // for 2D points with integer coordinates
public:
int x,y;
void set(int dx, int dy){x = dx; y = dy;}
void set(IntPoint& p){ x = p.x; y = p.y;}
IntPoint(int xx, int yy){x = xx; y = yy;}
IntPoint(){ x = y = 0;}
};
//@@@@@@@@@@@@@@@@@@@@ Point2 class @@@@@@@@@@@@@@@@@@@
class Point2{ // for 2D points with real coordinates
public:
float x,y;
void set(float dx, float dy){x = dx; y = dy;}
void set(Point2& p){ x = p.x; y = p.y;}
Point2(float xx, float yy){x = xx; y = yy;}
Point2(){x = y = 0;}
};
//<<<<<<<<<<<<<<<<<<<<< PolyLine >>>>>>>>>>>>>>>>>>>>>>>>
class PolyLine{ // a polyline is a num plus an array of points
public:
int num;
Point2 pt[80]; // may need larger arrays in some circumstances
PolyLine(){num = 0;}
};
// @@@@@@@@@@@@@@@@@@@@@@@@@@@ IntRect class @@@@@@@@@@@@@@@@@@@@@@@@@@@@
class IntRect{ // a rectangle with integer border values
public:
int left, top, right, bott;
IntRect(){left = top = right = bott = 0;}
IntRect(int l, int t, int r, int b)
{left = l; top = t; right = r; bott = b;}
void set(int l, int t, int r, int b)
{left = l; top = t; right = r; bott = b;}
void set(IntRect& r)
{left = r.left; top = r.top; right = r.right; bott = r.bott;}
};
//@@@@@@@@@@@@@@@@@@@@ Vector2 class @@@@@@@@@@@@@@@@@@@
class Vector2{
public:
float x,y;
void set(float dx, float dy){ x = dx; y = dy; }
void set(Vector2& v){ x = v.x; y = v.y;}
void setDiff(Point2& a, Point2& b) // set to difference a - b
{x = a.x - b.x; y = a.y - b.y;}
void normalize() //adjust this vector to unit length
```

```
{ double sizeSq = x * x + y * y;
if(sizeSq < 0.0000001)
{
cerr << "\nnormalize() sees vector (0,0)!";
return; // does nothing to zero vectors;
}
float scaleFactor = 1.0/(float)sqrt(sizeSq);
x *= scaleFactor; y *= scaleFactor;
}
Vector2(float xx, float yy){x = xx; y = yy; }
Vector2(Vector2& v){x = v.x; y = v.y; }
Vector2(){x = y = 0;} //default constructor
float dot(Vector2 b) // return this dotted with b
{return x * b.x + y * b.y;}
void perp() // perp this vector
{float tmp = x; x = -y; y = tmp;}
float perpDot(Vector2& v) // return perp of this dotted with v
{return x *v.x - y * v.y;}
};
// a global Canvas object (described in Chapter 3) knows how
// to draw lines in world coordinates
// beginning of graphics2d.h
private:
Point2 CP; // current position in world
public:
float windowAspect;
Canvas (int width, int height, char* title);
void setWindow(float l, float r, float b, float t);
void setViewport(int l, int r, int b, int t);
float getWindowAspect(void) { return windowAspect;}
void lineTo(float x, float y);
void moveTo(float x, float y){CP.x = x; CP.y = y;}
void forward(float dist, int vis);
void initCT() // initialize the CT (model view matrix)
{
glMatrixMode(GL_MODELVIEW); glLoadIdentity();
}
void rotate2D(double angle)
{
glMatrixMode(GL_MODELVIEW); glRotated(angle, 0.0, 0.0, 1.0);
}
void translate2D(double dx, double dy)
{
glMatrixMode(GL_MODELVIEW); glTranslated(dx, dy, 0.0);
}
void scale2D(double sx, double sy)
{
glMatrixMode(GL_MODELVIEW); glScaled(sx, sy, 1.0);
}
void pushCT(void)
{
glMatrixMode(GL_MODELVIEW); glPushMatrix();
}
```

```cpp
void popCT(void)
{
setWindow(float l, float r, float b, float t)
{
glMatrixMode(GL_PROJECTION);
glLoadIdentity();
gluOrtho2D((GLdouble)l, (GLdouble)r, (GLdouble)b, (GLdouble)t);
if(t == b) return;
windowAspect = (r - l)/(t - b);
}
setViewport(int l, int r, int b, int t)
{glViewport((GLint)l, (GLint)b, (GLint)(r-l), (GLint)(t-b));}
void Canvas :: lineTo(float x, float y)
{
glBegin(GL_LINES);
glVertex2f((GLfloat)CP.x, (GLfloat)CP.y);
CP.x = x; CP.y = y;
glVertex2f((GLfloat)CP.x, (GLfloat)CP.y);
glEnd(); glFlush();
}
forward(float dist, int vis)
{
#define RadPerDeg 0.017453393 //radians per degree
float x = CP.x + dist * cos(RadPerDeg * CD);
float y = CP.y + dist * sin(RadPerDeg * CD);
if(vis) lineTo(x, y);
else moveTo(x, y);
CP.x = x; CP.y = y;
}
ngon(int n,float cx, float cy, float radius)
{
#define RadPerDeg 0.017453393 //radians per degree
if(n < 3) return; // bad number of sides
double angle = 0, angleInc = 2 * 3.14159265 /n; //angle
increment
moveTo(cx + radius, cy);
for(int k = 1; k <= n; k++)
{
angle += angleInc;
lineTo(radius * cos(angle) + cx, radius * sin(angle) + cy);
}
}
// end of graphics2d.cpp
```

RGBPixmap CLASS

```cpp
// RGBpixmap.h: a class to support working with RGB pix maps.
#ifndef _RGBPIXMAP
#define _RGBPIXMAP
#include <fstream>
// Needs the IntPoint and IntRect classes to be defined
typedef unsigned char uchar;
class mRGB{ // the name RGB is already used by Windows
public: uchar r,g,b;
mRGB(){r = g = b = 0;}
```

```
mRGB(mRGB& p){r = p.r; g = p.g; b = p.b;}
mRGB(uchar rr, uchar gg, uchar bb){r = rr; g = gg; b = bb;}
void set(uchar rr, uchar gg, uchar bb){r = rr; g = gg; b = bb;}
};
//$$$$$$$$$$$$$$$$$$ RGBPixmap class $$$$$$$$$$$$$$$$
class RGBpixmap{
private:
mRGB* pixel; // array of pixels
public:
int nRows, nCols; // dimensions of the pix map
RGBpixmap() {nRows = nCols = 0; pixel = 0;}
RGBpixmap(int rows, int cols) //constructor
{
nRows = rows;
nCols = cols;
pixel = new mRGB[rows*cols];
}
int readBMPFile(string fname); // read BMP file into this pix map
void freeIt() // give back memory for this pix map
{
delete []pixel; nRows = nCols = 0;
}
//<<<<<<<<<<<<<<<<< copy >>>>>>>>>>>>>>>>>>
void copy(IntPoint from, IntPoint to, int x, int y, int width,
int height)
{ // copy a region of the display back onto the display
if(nRows == 0 || nCols == 0) return;
glCopyPixels(x, y, width, height,GL_COLOR);
}
//<<<<<<<<<<<<<<<<< draw >>>>>>>>>>>>>>>>>>
void draw()
{ // draw this pix map at current raster position
if(nRows == 0 || nCols == 0) return;
//tell OpenGL: don't align pixels with 4-byte boundaries in
memory
glPixelStorei(GL_UNPACK_ALIGNMENT,1);
glDrawPixels(nCols, nRows,GL_RGB, GL_UNSIGNED_BYTE,pixel);
}
//<<<<<<<<<<<<<<<<< read >>>>>>>>>>>>>>>>>>
int read(int x, int y, int wid, int ht)
{ // read a rectangle of pixels into this pixmap
nRows = ht;
nCols = wid;
pixel = new mRGB[nRows *nCols]; if(!pixel) return -1;
//tell OpenGL: don't align pixels with 4-byte boundaries in
memory
glPixelStorei(GL_PACK_ALIGNMENT,1);
glReadPixels(x, y, nCols, nRows,
GL_RGB,GL_UNSIGNED_BYTE,pixel);
return 0;
}
//<<<<<<<<<<<<<<<<< read from IntRect >>>>>>>>>>>>>>>>>>
int read(IntRect r)
{ // read a rectangle of pixels into this pix map
nRows = r.top - r.bott;
```

```cpp
nCols = r.right - r.left;
pixel = new mRGB[nRows *nCols]; if(!pixel) return -1;
//tell OpenGL: don't align pixels with 4-byte boundaries in
memory
glPixelStorei(GL_PACK_ALIGNMENT,1);
glReadPixels(r.left,r.bott, nCols, nRows, GL_RGB,
GL_UNSIGNED_BYTE, pixel);
return 0;
}
//<<<<<<<<<<<<<<< setPixel >>>>>>>>>>>>>
void setPixel(int x, int y, mRGB color)
{
if(x>=0 && x <nCols && y >=0 && y < nRows)
pixel[nCols * y + x] = color;
}
//<<<<<<<<<<<<<<<< getPixel >>>>>>>>>>>
mRGB getPixel(int x, int y)
{
mRGB bad(255,255,255);
assert(x >= 0 && x < nCols);
assert(y >= 0 && y < nRows);
return pixel[nCols * y + x];
}
}; //end of class RGBpixmap
#endif
// RGBpixmap.cpp - routines to read a BMP file
#include "RGBpixmap.h"
typedef unsigned short ushort;
typedef unsigned long ulong;
fstream inf; // global in this file for convenience
//<<<<<<<<<<<<<<<<<<<<< getShort >>>>>>>>>>>>>>>>>>>>>>
ushort getShort() //helper function
{ //BMP format uses little-endian integer types
// get and construct in memory a 2-byte integer stored in
little-endian form
char ic;
ushort ip;
inf.get(ic); ip = ic; //first byte is little one
inf.get(ic); ip |= ((ushort)ic << 8); // or in high order
byte
return ip;
}
//<<<<<<<<<<<<<<<<<<<<< getLong >>>>>>>>>>>>>>>>>>>>>>
ulong getLong() //helper function
{ //BMP format uses little-endian integer types
// get and construct in memory a 4-byte integer stored in
little-endian form
ulong ip = 0;
char ic = 0;
unsigned char uc = ic;
inf.get(ic); uc = ic; ip = uc;
inf.get(ic); uc = ic; ip |=((ulong)uc << 8);
inf.get(ic); uc = ic; ip |=((ulong)uc << 16);
inf.get(ic); uc = ic; ip |=((ulong)uc << 24);
return ip;
}
```

```
//<<<<<<<<<<<<<<<<<< RGBPixmap:: readBmpFile>>>>>>>>>>>>
int RGBpixmap:: readBMPFile(string fname)
{ // Read into memory an mRGB image from an uncompressed BMP file.
// return 0 on failure, 1 on success
inf.open(fname.c_str(), ios::in|ios::binary); //read binary
char's
if(!inf){ cout 66 " can't open file: " << fname << endl;
return 0;}
int k, row, col, numPadBytes, nBytesInRow;
// read the file header information
char ch1, ch2;
inf.get(ch1); inf.get(ch2); //type: always 'BM'
ulong fileSize = getLong();
ushort reserved1 = getShort(); // always 0
ushort reserved2= getShort(); // always 0
ulong offBits = getLong(); // offset to image -
unreliable
ulong headerSize = getLong(); // always 40
ulong numCols = getLong(); // number of columns in image
ulong numRows = getLong(); // number of rows in image
ushort planes= getShort(); // always 1
ushort bitsPerPixel=getShort(); //8 or 24; allow only 24 here
ulong compression = getLong(); // must be 0 for uncompressed
ulong imageSize = getLong(); // total bytes in image
ulong xPels = getLong(); // always 0
ulong yPels = getLong(); // always 0
ulong numLUTentries =getLong(); // 256 for 8 bit, otherwise 0
ulong impColors = getLong(); // always 0
if(bitsPerPixel != 24)
{ // error - must be a 24-bit uncompressed image
cout << "not a 24-bit pixel image, or is compressed!\n";
inf.close(); return 0;
}
//add bytes at end of each row so total # is a multiple of 4
// round up 3*numCols to next mult. of 4
nBytesInRow = ((3 * numCols + 3)/4) * 4;
numPadBytes = nBytesInRow - 3 * numCols; // need this many
nRows = numRows; // set class's data members
nCols = numCols;
pixel = new mRGB[nRows * nCols]; //make space for array
if(!pixel) return 0; // out of memory!
long count = 0;
char dum;
for(row = 0; row < nRows; row++) // read pixel values
{
for(col = 0; col < nCols; col++)
{
char r,g,b;
inf.get(b); inf.get(g); inf.get(r); //read bytes
pixel[count].r = r; //place them in colors
pixel[count].g = g;
pixel[count++].b = b;
}
for(k = 0; k < numPadBytes ; k++) //skip pad bytes at row's end
```

```
inf >> dum;
}
inf.close(); return 1; // success
}
```

THE SCENE AND SUPPORTING CLASSES

```
// SDL.h
//definition of simple support classes:
#ifndef _SDL
#define _SDL
#include <string>
#include <iostream>
#include <fstream>
#include <strstream>
using namespace std;
#include <windows.h>
#include <assert.h>
#include <math.h>
#include <gl/Gl.h>
#include <gl/Glu.h>
#include <gl/glut.h>
// include RGBpixmap if you wish to add a pix map field to
Scene:
//#include "RGBpixmap.h"
//@@@@@@@@@@@@@@@@@@@@@ Point3 class @@@@@@@@@@@@@@@@@@@
class Point3{
public:
float x,y,z;
void set(float dx, float dy, float dz){x = dx; y = dy; z = dz;}
void set(Point3& p){x = p.x; y = p.y; z = p.z;}
Point3(float xx, float yy, float zz){x = xx; y = yy; z
= zz;}
Point3(){x = y = z = 0;}
void build4tuple(float v[])
{// load 4-tuple with this color: v[3] = 1 for homogeneous
v[0] = x; v[1] = y; v[2] = z; v[3] = 1.0f;
}
};
//@@@@@@@@@@@@@@@@@@@@@ Vector3 class @@@@@@@@@@@@@@@@@@@
class Vector3{
public:
float x,y,z;
void set(float dx, float dy, float dz){ x = dx; y = dy; z =
dz;}
void set(Vector3& v){ x = v.x; y = v.y; z = v.z;}
void flip(){x = -x; y = -y; z = -z;} // reverse this vector
void setDiff(Point3& a, Point3& b)//set to difference a - b
{ x = a.x - b.x; y = a.y - b.y; z = a.z - b.z;}
void normalize();//adjust this vector to unit length
Vector3(float xx, float yy, float zz){x = xx; y = yy; z = zz;}
Vector3(Vector3& v){x = v.x; y = v.y; z = v.z;}
```

```
Vector3(){x = y = z = 0;} //default constructor
Vector3 cross(Vector3 b); //return this cross b
float dot(Vector3 b); // return this dotted with b
};
// @@@@@@@@@@@@@@@@@@@@@ Color3 class @@@@@@@@@@@@@@@@@
class Color3 { // holds a red, green, blue 3-tuple
public:
float red, green, blue;
Color3(){red = green = blue = 0;}
Color3(float r, float g, float b){red = r; green = g; blue = b;}
Color3(Color3& c){red = c.red; green = c.green; blue = c.blue;}
void set(float r, float g, float b){red = r; green = g; blue = b;}
void set(Color3& c)
{red = c.red; green = c.green; blue = c.blue;}
void add(float r, float g, float b)
{red += r; green += g; blue += b;}
void add(Color3& src, Color3& refl);
void add(Color3& colr);
void build4tuple(float v[]);
};
//@@@@@@@@@@@@@@@@@@@@@@ light class @@@@@@@@@@@@@@@@@@@@@@
class Light{ // for a linked list of light sources' color and
position
public:
Point3 pos;
Color3 color;
Light* next;
void setPosition(Point3 p){pos.set(p);}
void setColor(Color3 c){color.set(c);}
Light(){next = NULL;}
};
// @@@@@@@@@@@@@@@@@@@@@@@@ Affine4 class @@@@@@@@@@@@@@@@@
class Affine4{// manages homogeneous affine transformations
// including inverse transformations
// and a stack to put them on
// used by Scene class to read SDL files
public:
float m[16]; // hold a 4-by-4 matrix
Affine4();
void setIdentityMatrix();
void set(Affine4 a);
void preMult(Affine4 n);
void postMult(Affine4 n);
}; // end of Affine4 class
//@@@@@@@@@@ AffineNode class @@@@@@@@@@@
class AffineNode{
// used by Scene class to read SDL files
public:
Affine4 * affn;
Affine4 * invAffn;
AffineNode * next;
AffineNode()
{
next = NULL;
```

```
affn = new Affine4; // new affine with identity in it
invAffn = new Affine4; // and for the inverse
}
~AffineNode() //destructor
{
delete affn;
delete invAffn;
}
};
//@@@@@@@@@@@@@@@@ AffineStack class @@@@@@@@@@@@@
class AffineStack{
// used by Scene class to read SDL files
public:
AffineNode * tos;
AffineStack()//default constructor;puts identity on top
{
tos = new AffineNode; // node with identity in it
tos->next = NULL;
}
void dup();
void setIdentity();// make top item the identity matrix
void popAndDrop();
void releaseAffines(); // pop and drop all remaining items
void rotate(float angle, Vector3 u);
void scale(float sx, float sy, float sz);
void translate(Vector3 d);
}; // end of AffineStack class
//this was Shapes.h
//Shapes class and Supporting classes
//@@@@@@@@@@@@@@@@@@@ Material class @@@@@@@@@@@@@@@
class Material{
public:
Color3 ambient, diffuse, specular, emissive;
int numParams; // for textures
float params[10]; // for textures
int textureType; // 0 for none, neg for solids, pos for images
float specularExponent, reflectivity, transparency, speed-
OfLight;
float specularFraction, surfaceRoughness;
void setDefault();
void set(Material& m);
}; // end of Material
//@@@@@@@@@@@@@@@@@@@@@@@ GeomObj class @@@@@@@@@@@@@@@@@@@
class GeomObj{
public:
//IntRect scrnExtnt;
GeomObj * next;
GeomObj(): next(NULL){}
virtual void loadStuff(){}
virtual void drawOpenGL(){}
virtual void tellMaterialsGL(){}
};
//@@@@@@@@@@@@@@@@@@@@@@@ Boolean @@@@@@@@@@@@@@@@@@@@@@@
class Boolean: public GeomObj{
public:
GeomObj *left, *right;
```

```
Boolean():left(NULL),right(NULL){}
virtual void drawOpenGL()
{ // just draw its children
if(left)left-[greater]drawOpenGL();
if(right)right-[greater]drawOpenGL();
}
};
//@@@@@@@@@@@@@@@@@@@@ UnionBool @@@@@@@@@@@@@@@@@
class UnionBool : public Boolean{
public:
UnionBool(){Boolean();} //constructor
};
//@@@@@@@@@@@@@@@@@@@@ IntersectionBool @@@@@@@@@@@@@@@@@@
class IntersectionBool : public Boolean{
public:
IntersectionBool(){Boolean();}
};
//@@@@@@@@@@@@@@@@@@@@ DifferenceBool @@@@@@@@@@@@@@@@@@
class DifferenceBool : public Boolean{
public:
DifferenceBool(){Boolean();}
};
//@@@@@@@@@@@@@@@@@@@ Shape @@@@@@@@@@@@@@@@@@@@@@@@@
class Shape: public GeomObj{
public:
Material mtrl;
Affine4 transf,invTransf;
//virtual Color3 texture(HitInfo& h, int whichTexture);
Shape(){mtrl.textureType = 0; mtrl.numParams = 0;}
void setMaterial(Material& mt){mtrl.set(mt);}
void tellMaterialsGL();
virtual void drawOpenGL(){}
}; //end: Shape class
//@$@$@$@$@$@$@$@$@$@ Cube class $@$@$@$@$@$@$@$@$@$@
class Cube: public Shape{
public:
Cube(){}
void drawOpenGL()
{
tellMaterialsGL(); glPushMatrix();
glMultMatrixf(transf.m); //load affine
glEnable(GL_NORMALIZE);
glutSolidCube(2.0); // a cube with vertices -1 to +1
glPopMatrix();
}
};
//@$@$@$@$@$@$@$@$ Sphere class @$@$@$@$@$@$@$@$@$@$@
class Sphere: public Shape{
public:
void drawOpenGL()
{
tellMaterialsGL(); glPushMatrix();
glMultMatrixf(transf.m);
glutSolidSphere(1.0,20,20);
glPopMatrix();
```

```
}
Sphere() { }
};
//@$@$@$@$@$@$@$@$@$@$@ TaperedCylinder class @$@$@$@$@$@$@$@$@$
class TaperedCylinder: public Shape{
public:
float smallRadius;
TaperedCylinder(){}
void drawOpenGL(){ /* to be implemented */}
};
//@$@$@$@$@$@$@$@$@$@ Square class @$@$@$@$@$@$@$@$@$
class Square: public Shape{
public:
Square(){}
void drawOpenGL(){ /* to be implemented */}
};
//@$@$@$@$@$@$@$@$@$@ Plane class @$@$@$@$@$@$@$@$@$
class Plane: public Shape{
public:
Plane() {}
void drawOpenGL(){ /* to be implemented */}
};
//################ class VertexID ##############
//used to define a Mesh
class VertexID{public: int vertIndex, normIndex;};
//############### class FACE ############
//used to define a Mesh
class Face{
public:
int nVerts;
VertexID * vert; // array of vertex and normal indices
Face(){ nVerts = 0; vert = NULL;}
~Face(){delete[] vert; nVerts = 0;}
};
//@$@$@$@$@$@$@$@$@$@ Mesh class @$@$@$@$@$@$@$@$@$
class Mesh : public Shape{
private:
int numVerts, numNorms, numFaces;
Point3 *pt; // array of points
Vector3 *norm; // array of normals
Face *face; // array of faces
int lastVertUsed;
int lastNormUsed;
int lastFaceUsed;
public:
void readMesh(string fname);
void writeMesh(char* fname);
void printMesh();
void drawMesh();
void drawEdges();
void freeMesh();
int isEmpty();
void makeEmpty();
Mesh();
virtual void drawOpenGL();
```

```
Mesh(string fname);
Vector3 newell4(int indx[]);
string meshFileName; // holds file name for this Mesh
}; // end of Mesh class
//@$@$@$@$@$@$@$@$@$@ Torus class @$@$@$@$@$@$@$@$@$
class Torus: public Shape{
public:
void drawOpenGL(){
tellMaterialsGL(); glPushMatrix();
glMultMatrixf(transf.m);
glutSolidTorus(0.2,1.0,10,12);
//if(doEdges) glutWireTorus(0.2,1.0,10,12);
glPopMatrix();}
};
//@$@$@$@$@$@$@$@$@$@ Teapot class @$@$@$@$@$@$@$@$@$
class Teapot: public Shape{
public:
void drawOpenGL(){ tellMaterialsGL(); glPushMatrix();
glMultMatrixf(transf.m);
glutSolidTeapot(1.0); glPopMatrix();}
};
//@@@@@@@@@@@@@@@@@ DefUnit & DefUnitStack classes @@@@@@@@@@@@@@
//used in Scene to read SDL files
class DefUnit{
// developed by Steve Morin
public:
string name, stuff;
DefUnit(string n, string s) {stuff = s;name = n;}
};
class DefUnitStack {
public:
DefUnitStack() {stack = NULL;}
void push(string n, string s);
void print();
int search(string s);
string contents(string s);
void release();
private:
struct D4S {
DefUnit *current;
struct D4S *next;
} d4s;
D4S *stack;
}; // end of DefUnitStack class
//+++++++++++++ TokenType +++++++++++++
enum mTokenType {IDENT, LIGHT, ROTATE, TRANSLATE, SCALE, PUSH,
POP, IDENTITYAFFINE, GLOBALAMBIENT, BACKGROUND, MINREFLECTIVITY,
MINTRANSPARENCY, MAXRECURSIONDEPTH, CUBE, SPHERE, TORUS, PLANE,
SQUARE, CYLINDER, CONE, TAPEREDCYLINDER, TETRAHEDRON, OCTAHE-
DRON, DODECAHEDRON, ICOSAHEDRON, BUCKYBALL, TEAPOT, DIAMOND,
UNION, INTERSECTION, DIFFERENCEa, MAKEPIXMAP, MESH, DEFAULTMATE-
RIALS, AMBIENT, DIFFUSE, SPECULAR, SPECULARFRACTION, URFACER-
OUGHNESS, EMISSIVE, SPECULAREXPONENT, SPEEDOFLIGHT,
TRANSPARENCY,REFLECTIVITY, PARAMETERS, TEXTURE, FTCURLY,
RGHTCURLY, DEF, USE, T_NULL, F_EOF, UNKNOWN };
//@@@@@@@@@@@@@@ Scene class @@@@@@@@@@@@@@@@@@@@@@@@
```

```cpp
class Scene{
public:
Light *light; // attach linked list of lights here
GeomObj * obj; // attach the object list here
Color3 background, ambient;
int maxRecursionDepth;
//must #include RGBpixmap.h to have following texture fields
//RGBpixmap pixmap[8]; //list of attached pixmaps
float minReflectivity, minTransparency;
//bool isInShadow(Ray& f); // for ray tracing: implementation
left to the reader
Scene():light(NULL),obj(NULL),tail(NULL) //default constructor
{
currMtrl.setDefault();
background.set(0,0,0.6f);
ambient.set(0.1f,0.1f,0.1f);
minReflectivity = 0.5;
minTransparency = 0.5;
maxRecursionDepth = 3;
}
Scene(string fname){Scene(); read(fname);}
void freeScene();
void makeLightsOpenGL(){/* to be implemented */}
void drawSceneOpenGL();
bool read(string fname);
GeomObj* getObject();
private:
// private stuff used only for reading a scene
int line;
int nextline;
ifstream *file_in;
strstream *f_in;
strstream temp_fin;
DefUnitStack *def_stack;
GeomObj * tail; // tail of object list
AffineStack affStk; // affine stack
Material currMtrl;
string nexttoken(void);
float getFloat();
bool isidentifier(string keyword);
void cleanUp();
mTokenType whichtoken(string keyword);
}; // end of Scene.h
#endif
//SDL.cpp
// support code for the classes in SDL.h
#include "SDL.h"
// Vector3 methods
Vector3 Vector3 :: cross(Vector3 b) //return this cross b
{
Vector3 c(y*b.z - z*b.y, z*b.x - x*b.z, x*b.y - y*b.x);
return c;
}
float Vector3 :: dot(Vector3 b) // return this dotted with b
{return x * b.x + y * b.y + z * b.z;}
void Vector3 :: normalize()//adjust this vector to unit length
```

```
{
double sizeSq = x * x + y * y + z * z;
if(sizeSq < 0.0000001)
{
cerr << "\nnormalize() sees vector (0,0,0)!";
return; // does nothing to zero vectors;
}
float scaleFactor = 1.0/(float)sqrt(sizeSq);
x *= scaleFactor; y *= scaleFactor; z *= scaleFactor;
}
// Color3 methods
void Color3 ::add(Color3& src, Color3& refl)
{ // add the product of source color and reflection coefficient
red += src.red * refl.red;
green += src.green * refl.green;
blue += src.blue * refl.blue;
}
void Color3:: add(Color3* colr)
{ // add colr to this color
red += colr.red ; green += colr.green; blue += colr.blue;}
void Color3 :: build4tuple(float v[])
{// load 4-tuple with this color: v[3] = 1 for homogeneous
v[0] = red; v[1] = green; v[2] = blue; v[3] = 1.0f;
}
//Affine4 methods
Affine4::Affine4(){ // make identity transform
m[0] = m[5] = m[10] = m[15] = 1.0;
m[1] = m[2] = m[3] = m[4] = 0.0;
m[6] = m[7] = m[8] = m[9] = 0.0;
m[11]= m[12] = m[13] = m[14] = 0.0;
}
void Affine4 :: setIdentityMatrix(){ // make identity transform
m[0] = m[5] = m[10] = m[15] = 1.0;
m[1] = m[2] = m[3] = m[4] = 0.0;
m[6] = m[7] = m[8] = m[9] = 0.0;
m[11]= m[12] = m[13] = m[14] = 0.0;
}
void Affine4 ::set(Affine4 a)// set this matrix to a
{
for(int i = 0; i 6 16; i++)
m[i]=a.m[i];
}
//<<<<<<<<<<<<<< preMult >>>>>>>>>>>
void Affine4 ::preMult(Affine4 n)
{// postmultiplies this with n
float sum;
Affine4 tmp;
tmp.set(*this); // tmp copy
// following mult's : this = tmp * n
for(int c = 0; c < 4; c++)
for(int r = 0; r <4 ; r++)
{
sum = 0;
for(int k = 0; k < 4; k++)
sum += n.m[4 * k + r]* tmp.m[4 * c + k];
m[4 * c + r] = sum;
```

```
}// end of for loops
}// end of preMult()
//<<<<<<<<<<<< postMult >>>>>>>>>>
void Affine4 ::postMult(Affine4 n){// postmultiplies this with n
float sum;
Affine4 tmp;
tmp.set(*this); // tmp copy
for(int c = 0; c < 4; c++)// form this = tmp * n
for(int r = 0; r <4 ; r++)
{
sum = 0;
for(int k = 0; k 6 4; k++)
sum += tmp.m[4 * k + r]* n.m[4 * c + k];
m[4 * c + r] = sum;
}// end of for loops
}
// AffineStack methods
void AffineStack :: dup()
{
AffineNode* tmp = new AffineNode;
tmp->affn = new Affine4(*(tos->affn));
tmp->invAffn = new Affine4(*(tos->invAffn));
tmp-[greater]next = tos;
tos = tmp;
}
void AffineStack :: setIdentity() // make top item the identity
matrix
{
assert(tos != NULL);
tos->affn->setIdentityMatrix();
tos->invAffn->setIdentityMatrix();
}
void AffineStack :: popAndDrop()
{
if(tos == NULL) return; // do nothing
AffineNode *tmp = tos;
tos = tos-[greater]next;
delete tmp; // should call destructor, which deletes matrices
}
void AffineStack :: releaseAffines()
{ // pop and drop all remaining items
while(tos) popAndDrop();
}
void AffineStack :: rotate(float angle, Vector3 u)
{
Affine4 rm; // make identity matrix
Affine4 invRm;
u.normalize(); // make the rotation axis unit length
float ang = angle * 3.14159265/ 180; // deg to
float c = cos(ang), s = sin(ang);
float mc = 1.0 - c;
//fill the 3x3 upper left matrix -
rm.m[0] = c + mc * u.x * u.x;
rm.m[1] = mc * u.x * u.y + s * u.z;
rm.m[2] = mc * u.x * u.z - s * u.y;
rm.m[4] = mc * u.y * u.x - s * u.z;
```

```
rm.m[5]  = c + mc * u.y * u.y;
rm.m[6]  = mc * u.y * u.z + s * u.x;
rm.m[8]  = mc * u.z * u.x + s * u.y;
rm.m[9]  = mc * u.z * u.y - s * u.x;
rm.m[10] = c + mc * u.z * u.z;
// same for inverse: just sign of s is changed
invRm.m[0]  = c + mc * u.x * u.x;
invRm.m[1]  = mc * u.x * u.y - s * u.z;
invRm.m[2]  = mc * u.x * u.z + s * u.y;
invRm.m[4]  = mc * u.y * u.x + s * u.z;
invRm.m[5]  = c + mc * u.y * u.y;
invRm.m[6]  = mc * u.y * u.z - s * u.x;
invRm.m[8]  = mc * u.z * u.x - s * u.y;
invRm.m[9]  = mc * u.z * u.y + s * u.x;
invRm.m[10] = c + mc * u.z * u.z;
tos->affn->postMult(rm);
tos->invAffn->preMult(invRm);
}
void AffineStack :: scale(float sx, float sy, float sz)
{ // post multiply top item by scaling
#define sEps 0.00001
Affine4 scl;// make an identity
Affine4 invScl;
scl.m[0] = sx;
scl.m[5] = sy;
scl.m[10] = sz;// adjust it to a scaling matrix
if(fabs(sx) < sEps || fabs(sy) < sEps || fabs(sz) < sEps)
{
cerr << "degenerate scaling transformation!\n";
}
invScl.m[0] = 1/sx; invScl.m[5] = 1/sy; invScl.m[10] = 1/sz;
tos->affn->postMult(scl); //
tos->invAffn->preMult(invScl);
}
void AffineStack :: translate(Vector3 d)
{
Affine4 tr; // make identity matrix
Affine4 invTr;
tr.m[12] = d.x; tr.m[13] = d.y; tr.m[14] = d.z;
invTr.m[12] = -d.x; invTr.m[13] = -d.y; invTr.m[14] = -d.z;
tos->affn->postMult(tr);
tos->invAffn->preMult(invTr);
}
// Material methods
void Material :: setDefault(){
textureType = 0; // for none
numParams = 0;
reflectivity = transparency = 0.0;
speedOfLight = specularExponent = 1.0;
specularFraction = 0.0;
surfaceRoughness = 1.0;
ambient.set(0.1f,0.1f,0.1f);
diffuse.set(0.8f,0.8f,0.8f);
specular.set(0,0,0);
emissive.set(0,0,0);
}
```

```
void Material :: set(Material& m)
{
textureType = m.textureType;
numParams = m.numParams;
for(int i = 0; i < numParams; i++) params[i] = m.params[i];
transparency = m.transparency;
speedOfLight = m.speedOfLight;
reflectivity = m.reflectivity;
specularExponent = m.specularExponent;
specularFraction = m.specularFraction;
surfaceRoughness = m.surfaceRoughness;
ambient.set(m.ambient);
diffuse.set(m.diffuse);
specular.set(m.specular);
emissive.set(m.emissive);
}
// Shape methods
void Shape :: tellMaterialsGL()
{
float amb[4],diff[4],spec[4], emiss[4];
float zero[] = {0,0,0,1};
mtrl.ambient.build4tuple(amb); // fill the array
mtrl.diffuse.build4tuple(diff);
mtrl.specular.build4tuple(spec);
mtrl.emissive.build4tuple(emiss);
glMaterialfv(GL_FRONT/*_AND_BACK*/,GL_AMBIENT,amb);
glMaterialfv(GL_FRONT/*_AND_BACK*/,GL_DIFFUSE,diff);
glMaterialfv(GL_FRONT/*_AND_BACK*/,GL_SPECULAR,spec);
glMaterialfv(GL_FRONT/*_AND_BACK*/,GL_EMISSION,emiss);
glMaterialf(GL_FRONT/*_AND_BACK*/,GL_SHININESS,mtrl.specularExpo
nent);
}
//Mesh methods
Mesh :: Mesh(){
numVerts = numFaces = numNorms = 0;
pt = NULL; norm = NULL; face = NULL;
lastVertUsed = lastNormUsed = lastFaceUsed = -1;
}
void Mesh :: freeMesh()
{ // free up memory used by this mesh.
delete [] pt; // release whole vertex list
delete [] norm;
for(int f = 0; f < numFaces; f++)
delete[] face[f].vert; // delete the vert[] array of
this face
delete [] face;
}
int Mesh :: isEmpty()
{
return (numVerts == 0) || (numFaces == 0) || (numNorms == 0);
}
void Mesh :: makeEmpty()
{
numVerts = numFaces = numNorms = 0;
}
void Mesh :: drawOpenGL()
```

```
{
tellMaterialsGL(); glPushMatrix();
glMultMatrixf(transf.m);
drawMesh();
//if(doEdges) drawEdges();
glPopMatrix();
}
Mesh :: Mesh(string fname){ // read this file to build mesh
numVerts = numFaces = numNorms = 0;
pt = NULL; norm = NULL; face = NULL;
lastVertUsed = lastNormUsed = lastFaceUsed = -1;
readMesh(fname);
}
Vector3 Mesh :: newell4(int indx[])
{ /* return the normalized normal to face with vertices
pt[indx[0]],...,pt[indx[3]]. i.e. indx[] contains the four
indices
into the vertex list to be used in the Newell calculation */
Vector3 m;
for(int i = 0; i < 4 ; i++)
{
int next = (i== 3) ? 0 : i + 1; // which index is next?
int f = indx[i], n = indx[next]; // names for the
indices in the
pair
m.x += (pt[f].y - pt[n].y) * (pt[f].z + pt[n].z);
m.y += (pt[f].z - pt[n].z) * (pt[f].x + pt[n].x);
m.z += (pt[f].x - pt[n].x) * (pt[f].y + pt[n].y);
}
m.normalize();
return m;
}
//<<<<<<<<<<<<<<<<<<<<<<<<<<<< readMesh >>>>>>>>>>>>>>>>>>>>>>>>>
void Mesh:: readMesh(string fname)
{
fstream inStream;
inStream.open(fname.c_str(), ios ::in); //open needs a c-like
string
if(inStream.fail() || inStream.eof())
{
cout << "can't open file or eof: " << fname << endl;
makeEmpty();return;
}
inStream >> numVerts >> numNorms >> numFaces;
// make arrays for vertices, normals, and faces
pt = new Point3[numVerts]; assert(pt != NULL);
norm = new Vector3[numNorms]; assert(norm != NULL);
face = new Face[numFaces]; assert(face != NULL);
for(int i = 0; i < numVerts; i++) // read in the vertices
inStream >> pt[i].x >> pt[i].y >> pt[i].z;
for(int ii = 0; ii < numNorms; ii++) // read in the normals
inStream >> norm[ii].x >> norm[ii].y >> norm[ii].z;
for(int f = 0; f < numFaces; f++) // read in face data
{
inStream >> face[f].nVerts;
```

```
int n = face[f].nVerts;
face[f].vert = new VertexID[n]; assert(face[f].vert !=
NULL);
for(int k = 0; k < n; k++) // read vertex indices for
this face
inStream >> face[f].vert[k].vertIndex;
for(int kk = 0; kk < n; kk++) // read normal
indices for this face
inStream >> face[f].vert[kk].normIndex;
}
inStream.close();
} // end of readMesh
//<<<<<<<<<<<<<<<<<<<<< drawMesh >>>>>>>>>>>>>>>>>>>>>>
void Mesh :: drawMesh()
{ // draw each face of this mesh using OpenGL: draw each
polygon.
if(isEmpty()) return; // mesh is empty
for(int f = 0; f < numFaces; f++)
{
int n = face[f].nVerts;
glBegin(GL_POLYGON);
for(int v = 0; v < n; v++)
{
int in = face[f].vert[v].normIndex;
assert(in >= 0 && in < numNorms);
glNormal3f(norm[in].x, norm[in].y, norm[in].z);
int iv = face[f].vert[v].vertIndex; assert(iv >= 0 && iv
< numVerts);
glVertex3f(pt[iv].x, pt[iv].y, pt[iv].z);
}
glEnd();
}
glFlush();
}
//<<<<<<<<<<<<<<<<<<<<< writeMesh >>>>>>>>>>>>>>>>>>>>>>
void Mesh:: writeMesh(char * fname)
{ // write this mesh object into a new Chapter 6 format file.
if(numVerts == 0 || numNorms == 0 || numFaces == 0) return;
//empty
fstream outStream(fname, ios ::out); // open the output stream
if(outStream.fail()) {cout << "can't make new file: " << fname
<< endl;
return;}
outStream << numVerts << " " << numNorms << " " << numFaces <<
"\n";
// write the vertex and vertex normal list
for(int i = 0; i < numVerts; i++)
outStream << pt[i].x << " " << pt[i].y << " " <<
pt[i].z << "\n";
for(int ii = 0; ii < numNorms; ii++)
outStream << norm[ii].x << " " << norm[ii].y << " " <<
norm[ii].z <<
"\n";
// write the face data
for(int f = 0; f < numFaces; f++)
```

```
{
int n = face[f].nVerts;
outStream << n << "\n";
for(int v = 0; v < n; v++)// write vertex indices for this
face
outStream << face[f].vert[v].vertIndex << " "; outStream
<< "\n";
for(int k = 0; k < n; k++) // write normal indices for
this face
outStream << face[f].vert[k].normIndex << " "; outStream
<< "\n";
}
outStream.close();
}
// Scene methods
//<<<<<<<<< methods >>>>>>>>>>
string Scene :: nexttoken(void) //########## nexttoken()
{
char c;
string token;
int lastchar = 1;
if (!f_in) {return(token); }
if (f_in->eof()) {return(token);}
while (f_in->get(c))
{
if (f_in->eof()) {
return(token);
}
switch (c) {
case '\n': nextline += 1;
case ' ' :
case '\t':
case '\a':
case '\b':
case '\v':
case '\f':
case '\r': {
if ( lastchar == 0 ) {return(token);}break; }
case '{': {
token = c; return(token); break;}
case '}': {
token = c;
return(token);
break; }
case '!': {
while ( c != '\n' && f_in->get(c)) {
}
nextline++; break;}
default: {
token = token + c;
lastchar = 0;
if ((f_in->peek() == '{') ||
(f_in->peek() == '}') ) {
if ( lastchar == 0 ) {
return(token);
} else {
```

```
f_in->get(c);
token = c;
return(token);
}
}
line = nextline;
}
}
}
return(" ");
}
//<<<<<<<<<<<<<< getFloat >>>>>>>>>>>>>>>
float Scene :: getFloat() //############ getFloat()
{
strstream tmp;
float number;
string str = nexttoken();
tmp << str;
if(!(tmp >> number))
{
cerr << "Line " << line << ": error getting float" << endl;
exit(-1);
}
else
{
char t;
if ( (tmp >> t ) )
{
cerr << "Line " << line << ": bum chars in number" <<
endl;
exit(-1);
}
}
return number;
}
//<<<<<<<<<<<<<<<< isidentifier >>>>>>>>>>>>>>>>
bool Scene :: isidentifier(string keyword) { //########
isidentifier
string temp = keyword;
if (!isalpha(temp[0])) return(false);
for (int count = 1; count < temp.length(); count++) {
if ((!isalnum(temp[count]))&& (temp[count]!='.'))
return(false);
}
return(true);
}
//<<<<<<<<<<<<<<< cleanUp >>>>>>>>>>>>>>>>
void Scene :: cleanUp() //######### cleanUp
{ // release stuff after parsing file
affStk.releaseAffines(); //delete affine stack
def_stack->release();
delete def_stack; // release the DefUnitStack memory
}
//<<<<<<<<<<<<<<<< freeScene >>>>>>>>>>>>>>
void Scene :: freeScene()
{ // release the object and light lists
```

```
                    GeomObj *p = obj;
                    while(p)
                    {
                    GeomObj* q = p;
                    p = p->next;
                    delete q;
                    }
                    Light * q = light;
                    while(q)
                    {
                    Light* r = q;
                    q = q->next;
                    delete r;
                    }
                    }
                    //<<<<<<<<<<<<<<<<< whichToken >>>>>>>>>>>>>>>>
                    mTokenType Scene :: whichtoken(string keyword)
                    {
                    string temp = keyword;
                    if ( temp == "light" ) return LIGHT;
                    if ( temp == "rotate" ) return ROTATE;
                    if ( temp == "translate" ) return TRANSLATE;
                    if ( temp == "scale") return (SCALE);
                    if ( temp == "push") return (PUSH);
                    if ( temp == "pop") return (POP);
                    if ( temp == "identityAffine") return (IDENTITYAFFINE);
                    if ( temp == "cube") return (CUBE);
                    if ( temp == "sphere") return (SPHERE);
                    if ( temp == "torus") return (TORUS);
                    if ( temp == "plane") return (PLANE);
                    if ( temp == "square") return (SQUARE);
                    if ( temp == "cylinder") return (CYLINDER);
                    if ( temp == "taperedCylinder") return (TAPEREDCYLINDER);
                    if ( temp == "cone") return (CONE);
                    if ( temp == "tetrahedron") return (TETRAHEDRON);
                    if ( temp == "octahedron") return (OCTAHEDRON);
                    if ( temp == "dodecahedron") return (DODECAHEDRON);
                    if ( temp == "icosahedron") return (ICOSAHEDRON);
                    if ( temp == "buckyball") return (BUCKYBALL);
                    if ( temp == "diamond") return (DIAMOND);
                    if ( temp == "teapot") return (TEAPOT);
                    if ( temp == "union") return (UNION);
                    if ( temp == "intersection") return (INTERSECTION);
                    if ( temp == "difference") return (DIFFERENCEa);
                    if ( temp == "mesh") return (MESH);
                    if ( temp == "makePixmap") return (MAKEPIXMAP);
                    if ( temp == "defaultMaterials") return (DEFAULTMATERIALS);
                    if ( temp == "ambient") return (AMBIENT);
                    if ( temp == "diffuse") return (DIFFUSE);
                    if ( temp == "specular" return (SPECULAR);
                    if ( temp == "specularFraction") return (SPECULARFRACTION);
                    if ( temp == "surfaceRoughness") return (SURFACEROUGHNESS);
                    if ( temp == "emissive") return (EMISSIVE);
                    if ( temp == "specularExponent") return (SPECULAREXPONENT);
                    if ( temp == "speedOfLight") return (SPEEDOFLIGHT);
                    if ( temp == "transparency") return (TRANSPARENCY);
```

```
if ( temp == "reflectivity") return (REFLECTIVITY);
if ( temp == "parameters") return (PARAMETERS);
if ( temp == "texture") return (TEXTURE);
if ( temp == "globalAmbient") return (GLOBALAMBIENT);
if ( temp == "minReflectivity") return (MINREFLECTIVITY);
if ( temp == "minTransparency") return (MINTRANSPARENCY);
if ( temp == "maxRecursionDepth") return (MAXRECURSIONDEPTH);
if ( temp == "background") return (BACKGROUND);
if ( temp == "{") return (LFTCURLY);
if ( temp == "}") return (RGHTCURLY);
if ( temp == "def") return (DEF);
if ( temp == "use") return (USE);
if ( temp == " " ) return (T_NULL);
if ( isidentifier(temp) ) return (IDENT);
cout << temp << ":" << temp.length() << endl;
return(UNKNOWN);
} // end of whichtoken
//<<<<<<<<<< drawSceneOpenGL >>>>>>>>>>>>>>>>>.
void Scene :: drawSceneOpenGL()
{ //draw each object on object list
for(GeomObj* p = obj; p ; p = p->next)
p->drawOpenGL(); //draw it
}
//<<<<<<<<<<<<<<< Scene :: read >>>>>>>>>>>>>>>>
bool Scene:: read(string fname)// return true if ok; else false
{
file_in = new ifstream(fname.c_str());
if(!(*file_in))
{
cout << "I can't find or open file: " << fname << endl;
return false;
}
f_in = new strstream();
line = nextline = 1;
def_stack = new DefUnitStack();
char ch;
freeScene(); //delete any previous scene
// initialize all for reading:
obj = tail = NULL;
light = NULL;
affStk.tos = new AffineNode;
affStk.tos->next = NULL;
while (file_in->get(ch)) {*f_in << ch;} // read whole file
while(1) //read file, collecting objects, until EOF or an error
{
GeomObj * shp = getObject(); // get the next shape
if(!shp) break; // no object: either error or EOF
shp->next = NULL; // to be safe
if(obj == NULL){ obj = tail = shp;} // empty list so far
else{tail->next = shp; tail = shp;} // add new object to queue
}
file_in->close();
cleanUp(); // delete temp lists, etc.
return true;
} // end of read()
//<<<<<<<<<<<<<< Scene :: getObject >>>>>>>>>>>>>>>
```

```
GeomObj* Scene :: getObject()
{ //reads tokens from stream f_in (a data member of Scene),
// building lights, getting materials, doing transformations,
// until it finds a new object
// returns NULL if any error occurs, or end of file
string s;
GeomObj * newShape;
mTokenType typ;
while ((typ = (whichtoken( s = nexttoken() ))) != T_NULL)
{
if(typ == UNION || typ == INTERSECTION || typ == DIFFERENCEa)
{
switch(typ)
{
case UNION: newShape = new UnionBool(); break;
case INTERSECTION: newShape = new IntersectionBool(); break;
case DIFFERENCEa: newShape = new DifferenceBool();break;
} // end of little switch
GeomObj* p = newShape;
p = getObject(); // get left child
if(!p) return NULL; // Error! should always get an object
((Boolean*)newShape)->left = p; // hook it up
p = getObject();// get right child
if(!p) return NULL;
((Boolean*)newShape)->right = p; // hook it up
return newShape;
}// end of if(typ == UNION etc....
switch(typ)
{
case LIGHT: {
Point3 p;
Color3 c;
p.x = getFloat(); p.y = getFloat(); p.z = getFloat();
c.red = getFloat(); c.green = getFloat(); c.blue =
getFloat();
Light *l = new Light;
l->setPosition(p);
l->setColor(c);
l->next = light; //put it on the list
light = l; break;}
case ROTATE: {
float angle;
Vector3 u;
angle = getFloat(); u.x = getFloat();
u.y = getFloat(); u.z = getFloat();
affStk.rotate(angle,u);break;}
case TRANSLATE: {
Vector3 d;
d.x = getFloat(); d.y = getFloat(); d.z = getFloat();
affStk.translate(d);break;}
case SCALE: {
float sx, sy, sz;
sx = getFloat(); sy = getFloat(); sz = getFloat();
affStk.scale(sx, sy, sz);break;}
case PUSH: affStk.dup(); break;
case POP: affStk.popAndDrop(); break;
```

```
case IDENTITYAFFINE: affStk.setIdentity();break;
case AMBIENT: {
float dr, dg, db;
dr = getFloat(); dg = getFloat(); db = getFloat();
currMtrl.ambient.set(dr,dg,db); break;}
case DIFFUSE: {
float dr,dg,db;
dr = getFloat(); dg = getFloat(); db = getFloat();
currMtrl.diffuse.set(dr,dg,db); break;}
case SPECULAR:{
float dr,dg,db;
dr = getFloat(); dg = getFloat(); db = getFloat();
currMtrl.specular.set(dr,dg,db); break;}
case EMISSIVE: {
float dr,dg,db;
dr = getFloat(); dg = getFloat(); db = getFloat();
currMtrl.emissive.set(dr,dg,db); break;}
case PARAMETERS: { // get a list of numParams parameters
currMtrl.numParams = (int)getFloat();
for(int i = 0; i < currMtrl.numParams; i++)
currMtrl.params[i] = getFloat();
break;}
case SPECULARFRACTION: currMtrl.specularFraction =
getFloat(); break;
case SURFACEROUGHNESS: currMtrl.surfaceRoughness =
getFloat(); break;
case TEXTURE: { // get type, 0 for none
currMtrl.textureType = getFloat();}
break;
case DEFAULTMATERIALS: currMtrl.setDefault();break;
case SPEEDOFLIGHT: currMtrl.speedOfLight = getFloat(); break;
case SPECULAREXPONENT: currMtrl.specularExponent =
getFloat(); break;
case TRANSPARENCY:currMtrl.transparency = getFloat(); break;
case REFLECTIVITY: currMtrl.reflectivity = getFloat(); break;
case GLOBALAMBIENT:
ambient.red = getFloat(); ambient.green = getFloat();
ambient.blue = getFloat(); break;
case BACKGROUND:
background.red = getFloat();
background.green = getFloat();
background.blue = getFloat();break;
case MINREFLECTIVITY: minReflectivity = getFloat(); break;
case MINTRANSPARENCY:minTransparency = getFloat(); break;
case MAXRECURSIONDEPTH: maxRecursionDepth = getFloat();
break;
case MAKEPIXMAP: { // get BMP file name for a pix map
/* to be implemented, along the lines:
int which = getFloat();// index of this pix map in pix
map array
if(which < 0 || which > 7){cout << "\nbad index of
RGBpixmap!\n";}
string fname = nexttoken(); // get file name for mesh
cout << "I got fname = " << fname << endl;
if(!pixmap[which].readBMPFile(fname))
{// read BMP file into this pix map
```

```
cout << " \ncan't read that RGBpixmap file!\n";
return NULL; } */
break;}// end of case: MAKEPIXMAP
case T_NULL: break; // The null token represents end-of-file
case DEF: {
string name, temp, lb, rb;
int l = line;
string inp;
name = nexttoken();
if ( whichtoken(name) != IDENT ) {
cout << "Error: Identifier expected." << endl;
return NULL;
}
if ( def_stack->search(name) ) {
cout << line << ": " << name;
cout << ": attempt to redefine. " << endl;
return NULL;
}
lb = nexttoken();
if ( whichtoken(lb) != LFTCURLY ) {
cout << "Error: { expected." << endl;
return NULL;
}
while ( whichtoken( temp = nexttoken()) != RGHTCURLY ) {
cout << temp << endl;
inp = inp + temp + " ";
if (!f_in) {
cout << "Error: end of file detected." << endl;
return NULL;
}
}
// Push the contents of the string onto the stack.
def_stack->push(name, inp);
break;} // end of case: DEF
case USE: {
string name;
name = nexttoken();
if ( whichtoken(name) != IDENT ) {
cout << line << ": " << name;
cout << ": identifier expected.";
return NULL;
}
if (! def_stack->search(name) ) {
cout << line << ": " << name;
cout << ": not defined.";
return NULL;
}
cout << def_stack->contents(name) << endl;
strstream *temp_fin = new strstream;
*temp_fin << def_stack->contents(name) << " ";
*temp_fin << f_in->rdbuf();
delete (f_in);
f_in = temp_fin;
break; } // end of case: USE
default: { // inner switch for Shapes
switch(typ)
```

```
{
case CUBE: newShape = new Cube;break;
case SPHERE: newShape = new Sphere;break;
case TETRAHEDRON: newShape = new Mesh("tetra.3vn");break;
case TORUS: newShape = new Torus;break;
case PLANE: newShape = new Plane;break;
case SQUARE: newShape = new Square;break;
case TAPEREDCYLINDER: newShape = new TaperedCylinder;
((TaperedCylinder*)newShape)->smallRadius =
getFloat(); break;
case CONE: newShape = new TaperedCylinder;
((TaperedCylinder*)newShape)->smallRadius = 0; break;
case CYLINDER: newShape = new TaperedCylinder;
((TaperedCylinder*)newShape)->smallRadius = 1; break;
case OCTAHEDRON: newShape = new Mesh("octa.3vn");break;
case DODECAHEDRON:newShape = new Mesh("dodeca.3vn");
break;
case ICOSAHEDRON:newShape = new Mesh("icosa.3vn"); break;
case BUCKYBALL: newShape = new Mesh("bucky.3vn"); break;
case DIAMOND: newShape = new Mesh("diamond.3vn"); break;
case TEAPOT: newShape = new Teapot; break;
case MESH: {// get a filename (with extension) for this
mesh
string fname = nexttoken(); // get file name for mesh
newShape = new Mesh(fname); break;
}// end of case: MESH
default: {
cerr << "Line " << nextline << ": unknown keyword "
<< s << endl;
return NULL;
}
} // end of inner switch
// common things to do to all Shape's
((Shape*)newShape)->mtrl.set(currMtrl);
// load transform and its inverse
((Shape*)newShape)->transf.set(*(affStk.tos->affn));
((Shape*)newShape)->invTransf.set(*(affStk.tos-
>invAffn));
return newShape;
}// end of default: block
} // end of outer switch
} // end of while
return NULL;
} // end of getObject
// DefUnitStack methods
void DefUnitStack :: push(string n, string s) {
D4S *temp_d4s = new D4S;
temp_d4s->current = new DefUnit(n, s);
temp_d4s->next = stack;
stack = temp_d4s;
}
void DefUnitStack :: print() {
D4S *temp = stack;
string t;
while (temp) {
cout << temp->current->name << ":" ;
```

```cpp
cout << temp->current->stuff << endl;
temp = temp->next;
}
}
int DefUnitStack :: search(string s) {
D4S *temp = stack;
while (temp) {
if ( temp->current->name == s ) {
return(1);
}
temp = temp->next;
}
return(0);
}
string DefUnitStack :: contents(string s) {
D4S *temp = stack;
while (temp) {
if (temp->current->name == s ) {
return(temp->current->stuff);
}
temp = temp->next;
}
return(NULL);
}
void DefUnitStack :: release()
{
while(stack)
{
D4S* tmp = stack; // grab it
//cerr << "releasing def_stack item: "<< tmp->current-
>name<< endl;
stack = stack->next; // advance p
delete tmp->current; // release 2 strings
delete tmp; // release node
}
stack = NULL;
}
// end of SDL.cpp
NOISE CLASS
//Noise.h
// Noise class for generating pseudorandom noise fields
//based on noise lattice a la Peachey/Perlin
#include <assert.h>
class Noise{
public:
Noise()//construct a noise object
{
int i;
index = new unsigned char[256]; assert(index);
for(i = 0; i < 256; i++) index[i] = i;//fill array with
indices
for(i = 0; i < 256; i++) // shuffle it
{
int which = rand() % 256; // choose random place in array
unsigned char tmp = index[which]; // swap them
index[which] = index[i];
```

```
index[i] = tmp;
}
noiseTable = new float[256]; assert(noiseTable);
for(i = 0; i < 256; i++) noiseTable[i] = rand()/32767.99;
} // end of constructor
float noise(float scale, Point3& p)
{ // linearly interpolated lattice noise
#define lerp(f, A, B) A + f * (B - A)
float d[2][2][2];
Point3 pp;
pp.x = p.x * scale + 10000; //offset avoids negative values
pp.y = p.y * scale + 10000;
pp.z = p.z * scale + 10000;
long ix = (long)pp.x; long iy = (long)pp.y; long iz =
(long)pp.z;
float tx,ty,tz, x0,x1,x2,x3, y0,y1;
tx = pp.x - ix; ty = pp.y - iy; tz = pp.z - iz; //
fractional parts
float mtx = 1.0 - tx, mty = 1.0 - ty, mtz = 1.0 - tz;
for(int k = 0; k <= 1; k++) // get noise at 8 lattice points
for(int j = 0; j <= 1; j++)
for(int i = 0; i <= 1; i++)
d[k][j][i] = latticeNoise(ix + i, iy + j,iz + k);
x0 = lerp(tx, d[0][0][0],d[0][0][1]);
x1 = lerp(tx, d[0][1][0],d[0][1][1]);
x2 = lerp(tx, d[1][0][0],d[1][0][1]);
x3 = lerp(tx, d[1][1][0],d[1][1][1]);
y0 = lerp(ty, x0, x1);
y1 = lerp(ty, x2, x3);
return lerp(tz, y0, y1);
}
float turbulence(float s, Point3& p)
{
float val = noise(s , p) / 2 +
noise(s * 2, p) / 4 +
noise(s * 4, p) / 8 +
noise(s * 8, p) / 16;
return val;
}
float marble(float strength,Point3& p)
{
float turbul = turbulence(10, p);
float val = sin(6 * p.z + strength * turbul);
return mySpline(val);
}
float gauss()
{ // Add up 12 independent noise samples. Sum is Gaussian
// with mean zero and variance 1.0.
float sum = 0;
for(int i = 0; i < 12; i++)
sum += noise();
return sum - 6.0;
}
private:
float* noiseTable; // array of noise values
unsigned char * index; //Pseudorandom indices
```

```
float mySpline(float x) // used for marble
{
if(x <-0.4) return 0.15 + 2.857 * SQR(x + 0.75);
else if(x < 0.4) return 0.95 - 2.8125 * SQR(x);
else return 0.26 + 2.666 * SQR(x - 0.7);
}
float latticeNoise(int i, int j, int k)
{ // return PR noise value on an integer lattice
#define PERM(x) index[(x) & 255]
#define INDEX(ix, iy, iz) PERM( (ix) + PERM((iy) + PERM(iz))
)
return noiseTable[INDEX(i,j,k)];
}
}; // end of Noise class
```

SOME CLASSES THAT ARE USEFUL IN RAY TRACING

```
//@@@@@@@@@@@@@@@@@@ PointCluster class @@@@@@@@@@@@@@@@@@@@@@
class PointCluster{
public: // holds array of points for the bounding hull of a
shape
int num;
Point3* pt;
PointCluster() {num = 0; pt = NULL;}
PointCluster(int n)// make a cluster of n points
{
pt = new Point3[n]; assert(pt);
num = n;
}
};
//@@@@@@@@@@@@@@@@@@@@@@@@@@ SphereInfo @@@@@@@@@@@@@@@@@@@@@@
class SphereInfo{// holds the center and radius of a sphere
public:
Point3 center;
float radSq;
void set(float x, float y, float z, float rsq)
{
center.set(x,y,z);
radSq = rsq;
}
};
//@@@@@@@@@@@@@@@@@@@@@@@@@@ Cuboid @@@@@@@@@@@@@@@@@@@@@@@@@@
class Cuboid{ // holds six border values of a cuboid
public:
float left, top, right, bott, front, back;
void set(float l, float t, float r, float b, float f, float bk)
{
left = l; top = t; right = r; bott = b; front = f; back =
bk;}
void set(Cuboid& c)
{
left = c.left;top = c.top; right = c.right; bott = c.bott;
front = c.front; back = c.back;
}
};
```

```cpp
//@@@@@@@@@@@@@@@@@@@@ Ray @@@@@@@@@@@@@@@@@@@@@@@@@@
class Ray{
public:
Point3 start;
Vector3 dir;
int recurseLevel;
int row, col; // for screen extents
int numInside; // number of objects on list
GeomObj* inside[10]; // array of object pointers
Ray(){start.set(0,0,0); dir.set(0,0,0); numInside = 0;}
Ray(Point3 origin); //constructor: set start point of ray
Ray(Point3& origin, Vector3& direction)
{ start.set(origin); dir.set(direction); numInside = 0;}
void setStart(Point3& p){start.set(p);}
void setDir(float x, float y, float z)
{dir.x = x; dir.y = y; dir.z = z;}
void setRayDirection(Light *L); //for shadow feelers
void setRayDirection(Vector3& dir); //for spawned rays
int isInShadow();
void makeGenericRay(GeomObj* p, Ray& gr);
};
//@@@@@@@@@@@@@@@@@@@@ HitInfo @@@@@@@@@@@@@@@@@@@@@@@@
class HitInfo { // data for each hit with a surface
public:
double hitTime; // the hit time
GeomObj* hitObject; // the object hit
int surface; // which surface is hit?
int isEntering; // is ray entering the object?
Point3 hitPoint; // hit point
Vector3 hitNormal;// normal at hit point
HitInfo()
{
hitObject = NULL; hitTime = -1000; surface = 0; isEntering =
0;
} void set(HitInfo& h)
{
hitTime = h.hitTime; hitObject = h.hitObject;
surface = h.surface; isEntering = h.isEntering;
hitPoint.set(h.hitPoint); hitNormal.set(h.hitNormal);
}
};
//@@@@@@@@@@@@@@@@@@@@ Intersection @@@@@@@@@@@@@@@@@@@@@@@@@@
class Intersection{ // hold the hit list
public:
#define maxNumHits 8
int numHits; // the number of hits
HitInfo hit[maxNumHits]; // list of hits;
Intersection(){numHits = 0;} // default constructor
void set(Intersection& intr)
{ // copy intersection info
numHits = intr.numHits;
for(int i = 0; i < maxNumHits; i++)
hit[i].set(intr.hit[i]);
}
};
```

SDL: SCENE DESCRIPTION LANGUAGE

Scene Description Language (SDL) is a very simple language for describing geometric objects and light sources in a clear, human-readable fashion. It is understood by the read() method of the Scene class. We first look briefly at the basics of the Scene class and then describe SDL and discuss how it is used.

To read a scene file, say, myScene.dat, written in SDL, we first define a global Scene object, say, scn, and call the read() method for it, giving it the name of some SDL file to process:

```
Scene scn; // create a Scene object
scn.read("myScene.dat"); // read the SDL file; make the scene
```

The file myScene.dat is read and interpreted, and a list of objects is built. A list of light sources is also built. These lists are available through the fields scn.obj and scn.light, respectively. The lists are used by the drawOpenGL() method described in Chapter 5 to render the scene using OpenGL's facilities or, alternatively, by shade() described in Chapter 12, to render the scene using ray tracing.

THE Scene CLASS

An object of the Scene class has several fields that describe the nature of a scene. The principal ingredient is a list of the geometric shapes that reside in the scene. The field obj is a pointer to the first shape in the list. To draw all of the objects on the list, we simply move through the list, telling each object to draw itself:

```
for(GeomObj* p = scn.obj; p != NULL; p = p->next)
    p->drawOpenGL();
```

Objects listed are of one type of Shape or another (Sphere, Cube, Icosahedron, and so on), and each type of Shape knows how to draw itself. Polymorphism is used here: all Shape types are derived from the base type GeomObj (short for "geometric object"), so any Shape type can reside on a list of pointers to GeomObj.

The following four fields are also in the Scene class:

```
Light* light;              // the light-source list
GeomObj* obj;              // the object list
Color3 background;         // the background color
Color3 ambient; // the global ambient color
```

In addition, three fields are used for ray tracing (see Chapter 12): maxRecursion-Depth, minShinyness, and minTransparency.

A3.1 SYNTAX OF SDL

SDL is case sensitive, but free form: multiple white-space characters (space, tab, newline, form feed, and so on) are equivalent to a single space. Comments begin with a '!' and continue to the end of the line. Keywords in SDL are used to specify different affine transformations, geometric objects, light sources, and attributes of the scene, such as the background color.

Creating Geometric Objects

An object is created and placed in the object list simply by stating its type. For instance, cube adds a cube object to the object list and sphere adds a sphere object.

Other geometric objects include (see sdl.h for a complete list) torus, plane, square, cylinder, cone, tetrahedron, octahedron, dodecahedron, icosahedron, buckyball, diamond, and teapot. When any of these object types is specified in the file, the corresponding object is added to the (end of the) object list.

There are additional geometric object types that require one or more parameters, which are either floating-point values or file names. The parameter is placed directly after the name of the object, as in

taperedCylinder.312 ! make a tapered cylinder with small radius .312

mesh pawn.3vn ! make a mesh

The first example creates a tapered cylinder object that uses the parameter to define its exact shape; the second creates a mesh object whose vertex and face lists are described in the file pawn.3vn. (A number of sample files in the 3vn format, including those for the icosahedron, diamond, and buckyball, are available on the book's web site.)

Managing Affine Transformations

An affine transformation is stored with each object as it is created. (The inverse of this transformation is also stored; it is used when ray tracing.) The specific transformation that is installed with the object is the current transformation (CT) that is in effect at that moment. Various keywords in the SDL file alter the CT. For example,

identityAffine

places the identity transformation (given by a unit four-by-four matrix) in the CT. This is the initial transformation when read() begins to interpret an SDL file.

SDL uses the words scale, rotate, and translate, each followed by suitable parameters, to alter the CT, in a manner similar to how OpenGL uses glScalef(), glRotatef(), and glTranslatef() to alter the modelview or projection matrices.

Specifically, each word postmultiplies the CT by the corresponding transformation and places the product back into the CT, as in:

CT=CT* Trans

where Trans is the four-by-four matrix that represents the new transformation.

The three verbs are as follows:

scale <sx> <sy> <sz>
rotate <ang> <ux> <uy> <uz>
translate <dx> <dy> <dz>

scale takes three floating-point parameters that are the scale factors in the x-, y-, and z-directions, respectively. rotate takes four parameters: the angle (in degrees) of the rotation and the x-, y-, and z-components of the axis about which the rotation is to be made. (Positive values of ang produce CCW rotations about the u-axis, as seen looking from point u toward the origin.) translate takes three parameters: the x-, y-, and z-components of the vector through which the translation is to be made.

For example, the commands

```
scale 2 1.3 -5.33
translate 4 -5 6
rotate 45 0 1 0
```

respectively create the matrices

$$
\text{Sc} = \begin{pmatrix} 2 & 0 & 0 & 0 \\ 0 & 1.3 & 0 & 0 \\ 0 & 0 & -5.33 & 0 \\ 0 & 0 & 0 & 1 \end{pmatrix}, \quad \text{Tr} = \begin{pmatrix} 1 & 0 & 0 & 4 \\ 0 & 1 & 0 & -5 \\ 0 & 0 & 1 & 6 \\ 0 & 0 & 0 & 1 \end{pmatrix}, \quad \text{and} \quad \text{Rot} = \begin{pmatrix} 0.707 & 0 & 0.707 & 0 \\ 0 & 1 & 0 & 0 \\ -0.707 & 0 & 0.707 & 0 \\ 0 & 0 & 0 & 1 \end{pmatrix},
$$

and each command postmultiplies the *CT* by its matrix and places the result back into the *CT*. A complete example is available below.

Stack of Affine Transformations

The *CT* is actually the top matrix in a stack of matrices. The words push and pop manipulate this stack:

- push makes a copy of the *CT* and pushes it onto the stack (making the top two items identical).
- pop pops the *CT* off the stack and discards it. The matrix that was just below the top item becomes the *CT*. If there is no item below the top item, pop does nothing.

Managing Material Properties

Installed in each object as it is created is a record of material properties, called the current materials (*CM*). This record consists of the following fields:

- four color fields, each an (r, g, b) triple: ambient, diffuse, specular, and emissive;
- six scalar fields (used by a ray tracer): specularExponent, specular Fraction, surfaceRoughness, speedOfLight, transparency, and reflectivity;
- three fields to describe texture properties of the object: textureType designates which texture is applied to the object, numParams is the number of parameters defined for the object, and params[] is an array of 10 parameter values. textureTypes are encoded as 0 for none, −1 for a checkerboard, −2 for a wood, and −3 for marble. The code makePixmap 2 filename.bmp reads a BMP file and assigns that to texture 2. textureType of 2 followed by the name of an image file creates a pixmap of the image.

Changes to the *CM* are managed by the following SDL words, each followed by one or more float's:

```
ambient <r> <g> <b>
diffuse <r> <g> <b>
specular <r> <g> <b>
emissive <r> <g> <b>
specularExponent <value>
specularFraction <value>
surfaceRoughness <value>
speedOfLight <value>
transparency <value>
```

```
reflectivity <value>
textureType <value>
parameters <value> <value> <value> p
```

The parameters keyword is followed by the number of parameters being specified and the list of parameter values. For example, to place the three values 4.5, 6, and −12 in the params[] array of subsequently defined objects, you would use

```
parameters 3 4.5 6 -12
```

The *CM* initially contains the following default values:

```
ambient = ( 0.1, 0.1, 0.1)
diffuse = (0.8, 0.8, 0.8)
specular = (0, 0, 0)
emissive = (0, 0, 0)
specularExponent 1
specularFraction 0
surfaceRoughness 1.0
speedOfLight = 1
transparency = 0
reflectivity = 0
textureType 0
```

The word defaultMaterials can be used to return the *CM* to these default values. The following are keywords having to do with light sources, global attributes, boolean objects, and pixmaps:

Light Sources

```
light <x> <y> <z> <r> <g> <b> !place a light at (x,y,z)having
color (r,g,b)
```

Specifying Global Scene Attributes

```
globalAmbient <r> <g> <b> !give the global ambient source the
color (r,g,b)
minReflectivity <value>
minTransparency <value>
maxRecursionDepth <value>
background <r> <g> <b>
```

The following is a simple SDL file:

```
! myScene1.dat - f.s.hill
! has several simple glowing objects
global Ambient .4 .2 .3
light 0 10 0 1 1 1 ! white light at (0,10,0)
background 0 0 .5
ambient .2 .2 .2
diffuse .8 .7 .6
emissive .8 0 0 !objects emit red
cube ! put a generic cube at the origin
emissive 0 1 0
! put a glowing ellipsoid at (2, 0, 0)
push translate 2 0 0 rotate 45 0 0 1 scale .5 .5 2 sphere pop
push translate -2 0 0 cone pop !and a cone at (-2, 0 0)
```

Boolean Objects

SDL also supports the specification of boolean objects, using the keywords

```
union
intersection
difference
```

Each of these verbs creates a boolean object of its specified type and places it in the object list. Each such object must be followed in the SDL file by two objects (each of which may be a geometric or a boolean object), which are placed as the left and right children of the boolean object that was originally created.

Boolean objects are defined (*infix* notation) by specifying the left child followed by the right child followed by the boolean operation. The following SDL code describes a scene that contains two boolean objects. The first is an intersection of a cube and the union of a tetrahedron and a Buckyball. The second is a difference of a tetrahedron and the intersection of a plane with the union of a torus and a dodecahedron.

```
light 1 2 3 0.2 0.3 0.4
intersection
cube ! left child of intersection
union ! right child of intersection
diffuse .2 .5 .7 tetrahedron !left child of union
rotate 180 3 4 5 buckyball !right child of union
difference !another boolean object
tetrahedron intersection !left child of difference
plane union !right child of intersection
dodecahedron torus !left child of union
```

The verb

```
makePixmap <value> <fname>
```

defines a pixmap to be used for texturing. The first argument is an integer used to identify the pixmap; the second is the name of a BMP file that contains the texture image. For example, the following SDL code

```
makePixmap 5 clouds.bmp
makePixmap 2 stone.bmp
texture 5
parameters 4 0 1 1 0
push scale 3 4 2 cube pop
texture 2
parameters 3 .2 .8 2
sphere
```

creates two textures. It then associates number 5 (along with four parameters) with a scaled cube, and number 2 (along with three parameters) with a sphere. (The issue of how the texture is actually applied to an object is, of course, left up to the programmer.)

A3.2 MACROS IN SDL

As a convenience, the keyword def allows you to combine any number of SDL commands into a macro and give them a single name. The SDL commands that form the body of the macro are enclosed in braces. For example,

```
def red {ambient 1 0 0 diffuse 1 0 0 }
```

associates the macro named red with the words shown. If, later in the SDL file, the command

```
use red
```

is encountered, the phrase ambient 1 0 0 diffuse 1 0 0 is placed at that point as if you had typed it there in the file. Macros can save typing and allow definitions to be reused. For instance, an "L"-shaped stack of four cubes can be defined with the code

```
def Lstack
{
push cube translate 2 0 0 cube
translate -2 2 0 cube
translate 0 2 0 cube pop
}
```

This macro can be used later to place several differently shaped L's in a scene. Code to do this might look like

```
use Lstack
push translate 3 2 4 scale .5 .5 .5 use Lstack pop
push translate -3 -2 -4 scale .5 .5 .5 use Lstack pop
```

A3.3 EXTENDING SDL

It is straightforward to add keywords to SDL. We describe how to do this through two examples.

■ EXAMPLE A3.3.1 Adding an attribute to the Scene class

Suppose you wish to add to the Scene class a new field, fogThickness, that describes the thickness of fog in the scene. To control the value to be placed in this field, you add a keyword, say fogginess, to the SDL language. The phrase fogginess 0.5 in an SDL file will change the value of fogThickness to 0.5. To accomplish this, you would make the following changes.

Changes Made in the File sdl.h

1. Add the field float fogThickness to the Scene class.
2. Add the item FOGTHICKNESS anywhere in the TokenType enumeration list.

Changes Made in the File sdl.cpp

1. In function whichtoken(), add the line if (temp == "fogginess") return (FOGTHICKNESS);
2. In the function getObject(), add the line case FOGTHICKNESS: fogThickness = getFloat(); break;

The issue of how to *use* this new field is, of course, up to the programmer. For instance, while developing a ray tracer, the programmer may add some code to the Scene::shade() method, such as: if(fogThickness > 0)*do something..;*

■ EXAMPLE A3.3.2 Defining a new type of object

Suppose you want to add a *pie slice* to the collection of possible objects appearing in scenes. This will be a portion of a thin circular disc lying in the *xy*-plane. The slice starts at angle 0 (directed along the *x*-axis) and continues CCW (as seen looking from (0, 0, 1) toward the origin) to angle *sweep*, measured in degrees.

Thus, if *sweep* is 180, the pie slice is half a pie in the positive *y*-quadrant, and if *sweep* is 360, the pie slice is a complete pie. We extend SDL so that the keyword `pieSlice` followed by a parameter for the `sweep` angle is recognized, as in

```
pieSlice 90
```

Changes Made in the File `sdl.h`

1. Define the `PieSlice` class with a field to hold the `sweep` angle, by means of the following code:

```
class PieSlice : public Shape {
public:
float sweep;
etc.
};
```

2. Code the appropriate methods, such as `drawOpenGL()`, for this class.
3. Add the item PIESLICE anywhere in the TokenType enumeration list.

Changes Made in the File `sdl.cpp`:

1. To the function `whichtoken()`, add the line

```
if (temp == "pieSlice") return (PIESLICE);
```

2. To the function getObject(), add the line

```
case PIESLICE:
newShape = new PieSlice;
((PieSlice*)newShape) ->angle = getFloat(); break;
```

Appendix 4

Fractals and the Mandelbrot Set

A4.1 INTRODUCTION

Computers are particularly good at repetition: they will do something again and again without complaint. In addition, the high precision with which modern computers can do calculations allows an algorithm to take closer and closer views at an object, effectively zooming in to ever greater levels of detail.

In this appendix we move toward infinity in various ways and exploit the power of computer graphics to reveal what is encountered along the way. We examine three approaches to the infinite: to the infinitely small, zooming in on ever greater detail or adding ever finer levels of detail to a figure; to the infinitely large, examining patterns that can be reproduced in certain ways into larger patterns; and to the infinitely often, studying what happens when a process is repeated again and again, conceptually forever.

We have seen in previous chapters how computer graphics can produce pictures of things that don't yet exist in nature, or could perhaps never exist. This is certainly true of the objects we study here, and computer graphics provides a powerful tool for investigating them. But here we are going further, and we will bump up against the inherent finiteness of any computer-generated picture: it has finite resolution and finite size and must be made in a finite amount of time. Thus the pictures we make can only be approximations to the creatures being studied: the observer of such a picture uses it as a hint of what the underlying true object really looks like.

A4.2 FRACTALS AND SELF-SIMILARITY

Where the world ceases to be the stage for personal hopes and desires, where we, as free beings, behold it in wonder, to question and to contemplate, there we enter the realm of art and of science. If we trace out what we behold and experience through the language of logic, we are doing science; if we show it in forms whose interrelationships are not accessible to our conscious thought but are intuitively recognized as meaningful, we are doing art. Common to both is the devotion to something beyond the personal, removed from the arbitrary.

Albert Einstein
(1879–1955)

We want methods that allow us to approach infinity—more precisely the infinitesimal—in an organized way. The methods will feature recursion, which modern computer languages manage very effectively. Recursion often makes a difficult geometric task extremely simple. Among other things, it lets one decompose or refine shapes into ever smaller ones, conceptually ad infinitum. Recursive algorithms can give rise to shapes that are both lovely and intriguing, or that have useful applications in science and engineering.

Many of the curves and pictures we describe here have a particularly important property: they are **self-similar**. Intuitively this means that they appear the same at every scale: no matter how much one enlarges a picture of the curve, it has the same level of detail. Some curves are **exactly self-similar**, whereby if a region is enlarged, the enlargement looks exactly like the original (except for a possible rotation and shift). Others are only **statistically self-similar**, such that the wiggles and irregularities in the curve are the same on the average no matter how many times the picture is enlarged.

Nature provides examples that mimic statistical self-similarity. The classic example is a coastline. Seen from a satellite it has a certain level of ruggedness, caused by bays, inlets, and peninsulas. As one flies in for a closer look, more details emerge. A bay takes on a certain ruggedness of its own that was not visible before. Zooming further, individual boulders and undulations in a beach give a similar roughness to the view. When one zooms in still further, smaller rocks and pebbles seem to produce about the same level of ruggedness. This process continues as one looks at individual grains of sand, as through a microscope. Other natural phenomena appear self-similar as well, such as the branches of a tree, the surface of a sponge, cracks in a pavement, and blood vessel systems in animals. Clouds are also roughly self-similar, and provide an interesting example. While flying in an airplane, it is difficult to judge how large a cloud is: is it small and close by, or large and distant?

During the 1970s Benoit Mandelbrot of Yale University (then at the IBM Research Center) brought together and popularized investigations into the nature of self-similarity (e.g., [Mandelbrot83]). He called various forms of self-similar curves **fractals**.[1] A line is one dimensional and a plane is two dimensional, but there are creatures in between. For instance, we shall define curves that are infinite in length yet lie inside a finite rectangle: their dimension lies somewhere between 1 and 2.

The work of Mandelbrot and others has spawned an enormous amount of investigation into both the mathematical and computer-graphics nature of fractal-like objects, and the excitement still continues in many centers around the world.

A4.3 THE MANDELBROT SET

In principle . . . [the Mandelbrot Set] could have been discovered as soon as men learned to count. But even if they never grew tired, and never made a mistake, all the human beings who have ever existed would not have sufficed to do the elementary arithmetic required to produce a Mandelbrot Set of quite modest magnification.

> *The Ghost from the Grand Banks*
> *Arthur C. Clarke*
> *(1917)*

Graphics provides a powerful tool for studying a fascinating collection of sets. The Mandelbrot set is thought by some to be the most complicated object seen in mathematics. It is based on a few surprisingly simple definitions yet is astonishingly rich in its structure, and when displayed with the help of computer graphics can yield awe-inspiring pictures of great beauty.

The Mandelbrot set arises from a branch of analysis known as **iteration theory**, which asks what happens when one iterates a function endlessly. Many key results of a related set, the Julia set, were developed early in the century (without the assistance of computers, of course) by Gaston Julia (1893–1978) and Pierre Fatou (1878–1929). Their ideas lay fallow for many years, until they were revived and

---

[1]   Mandelbrot coined this term from the Latin *fractus* meaning "fragmented" or "irregular" [Mandelbrot83], but it also suggests "fractional dimensional."

extended by Benoit Mandelbrot in the 1970s. As part of his research he used computer graphics to perform essential experiments, which stimulated conjectures along very fruitful lines, leading to further analysis and discoveries.

Several excellent accounts of the story behind these discoveries are available [Mandelbrot83, Peitgen88], along with beautiful images generated by techniques we shall describe below.

A4.3.1 Mandelbrot Sets and Iterated Function Systems

A view of the **Mandelbrot set** is shown in Figure A4.1. A color version is available in Plate 37. It is the black inner portion, which appears to consist of a cardioids along with a number of wartlike circles glued to it. In actuality its border is astonishingly complicated, and this complexity can be explored by zooming in on a portion of the border and computing a close-up view.

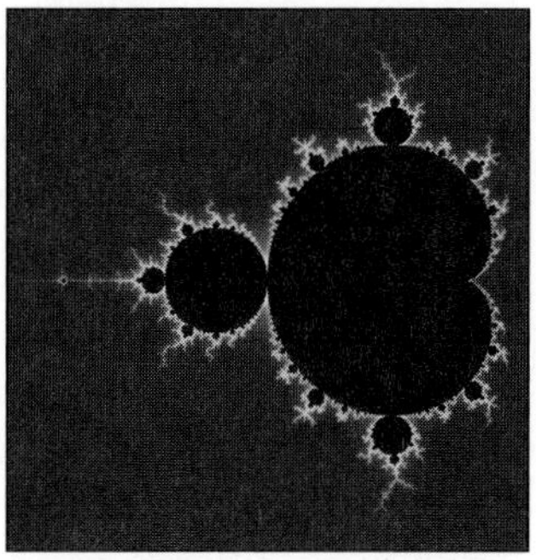

FIGURE A4.1 The Mandelbrot set

In theory this zooming can be repeated forever—the border is infinitely complex, in fact it is a fractal curve! Each point in the figure is shaded or colored according to the outcome of an experiment run on an iterated function system. The iterated function system of interest is shown in Figure A4.2. It uses the particularly simple function given in Equation (A4.1), where c is some constant.

$$f(z) = z^2 + c \tag{A4.1}$$

The system produces each output by squaring its input and adding c. We assume that the process begins with the **starting value** 0, so the system generates the sequence of values, or **orbit** (recall Chapter 2) shown in Equation (A4.2). (Check this

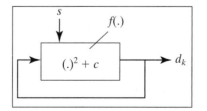

FIGURE A4.2 The iterated function system for the Mandelbrot set.

carefully.) Note that the orbit depends on only one ingredient: the given value of c.

$$d_1 = c$$
$$d_2 = (c)^2 + c$$
$$d_3 = ((c)^2 + c)^2 + c$$
$$d_4 = (((c)^2 + c)^2 + c)^2 + c \tag{A4.2}$$
$$\cdots$$

Note that for a given value of c, the orbit of 0 becomes the orbit of c after one iteration, so we get the same orbit behavior starting either at 0 or c. Orbits of c are the principal objects of interest for the Mandelbrot set. The basic question is: given the value of c, how do points d_k along the orbit behave as k gets larger and larger? Specifically, does the orbit remain **finite** (wherein *all* points on it are a finite distance from 0) or does it **explode** (shoot off to infinity)? As we define more precisely below, orbits that remain finite **lie in** their corresponding Mandelbrot set, whereas those that explode lie outside.

■ **EXAMPLE A4.1 Orbits of 0 for different c values**

Here we consider orbits with based on different values of c.

- Let $c = -1$. The orbit is $0, 0, 0, 0, 0, 0, 0, 0 \ldots$, which repeats endlessly. Thus, the orbit is finite and the value based on $c = -1$ is in the Mandelbrot set.
- Let $c = 1$. The orbit is: $0, 1, 2, 5, 26, 677, 458330, \ldots$, which explodes, and so the value associated $c = 1$ lies outside the Mandelbrot set.
- Let $c = -1.3$. The orbit of $s = 0$ is: $0, -1.3, \ldots$, which after 50 steps or so gets caught in a **periodic** sequence of the four values: $-1.148665, .019430, -1.299622, .389018, \ldots$, forever.

We can try to map out these results to see what range of values for c leads to finite orbits. Figure A4.3 shows a first attempt. It is very illuminating to experiment with other c's. For instance, as we increase c from 0, what's the largest value having a finite orbit?

FIGURE A4.3 What does the orbit of 0 do for each value of c?

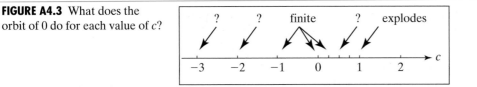

This system already exhibits intriguing dynamics. But things get incredibly richer when c is chosen to be a *complex number*, and complex arithmetic is used each time the function is applied. Moving the arithmetic to the complex plane was one of Mandelbrot's important contributions to the theory of the Mandelbrot set. The Mandelbrot set lives in the complex plane, the plane of complex numbers. Recall that in graphics we display complex numbers using a diagram where each complex number $z = x + yi$ is displayed at position (x, y).[2]

The system of Figure A4.2 works just as well with complex numbers as with real numbers. The value c is now complex, and at each iteration we square the previous result and add c. Recall that squaring a complex number $z = x + yi$ yields the new complex number as in Equation (A4.3):

$$(x + yi)^2 = (x^2 - y^2) + (2xy)i \qquad \text{(A4.3)}$$

---

[2] The reader unfamiliar with complex arithmetic can still use computer graphics to create pictures of the Mandelbrot set. Read the following material lightly and proceed to the discussion of the algorithms, which work entirely with points (x, y) having real coordinates.

Some Notes on the Fixed Points of the System

It will be useful when studying the Mandelbrot set to examine the fixed points of the system $f(.) = (.)^2 + c$. The behavior of orbits depends strongly on these fixed points—that is, those complex numbers z that map into themselves, so that $z^2 + c = z$. This gives us the quadratic equation $z^2 - z + c = 0$, and the **fixed points** of the system are its two solutions, given by:

$$p_+, p_- = \frac{1}{2} \pm \sqrt{\frac{1}{4} - c} \qquad\qquad (A4.4)$$

Note that because we are dealing with complex numbers there is no problem with taking the square root of $1/4 - c$, even if it is negative or complex. Appendix 2 shows how to take such square roots in a program. These are the two fixed points of the system. For the preceding example we obtain the two fixed points: $p_+ = 1.249323 - 0.333677i$ and $p_- = -0.249227 + 0.333677i$. If an orbit ever reaches a fixed point p, it gets trapped there forever. The two fixed points are positioned symmetrically at the same distance from the point $1/2 + 0i$.

We can gain further insight by characterizing a fixed point as **attracting** or **repelling**. Roughly speaking, if an orbit flies close to a fixed point p, the next point along the orbit will be forced as follows:

- closer to p if p is an attracting fixed point;
- farther away from p if p is a repelling fixed point.

If an orbit gets close enough to an attracting fixed point, it is sucked into it, but it is kept away by a repelling fixed point. It is not hard to show that a fixed point is attractive only if it lies within a distance of $1/2$ from the origin—that is, inside a circle of radius $1/2$ centered at the origin.

Figure A4.4 shows some example orbits for different values of c, superimposed on a crude rendition of the Mandelbrot set to help orient the eye. Each orbit is

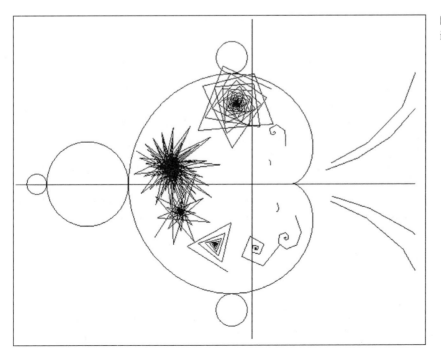

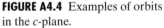

FIGURE A4.4 Examples of orbits in the c-plane.

shown as a polyline, beginning at its private value of c, which is shown as a dot. (We could have drawn each orbit beginning at 0, but this would clutter the picture.)

Note carefully that each dot shows the relevant value of c used in the system $f(.) = (.)^2 + c$ that is being iterated, as well as the starting point for the orbit.

If c is chosen *outside* of our Mandelbrot set, M, the resulting orbit explodes. Two exploding orbits are shown in the figure. If c is chosen just beyond the border of M, the orbit usually thrashes wildly around the plane and finally blasts off to infinity. Such orbits would confuse the picture beyond recognition and are not shown.

If the value of c is chosen *inside* M, the corresponding orbit can do a variety of things. For some c's it plunges immediately to a fixed point, or spirals into it (quite slowly if c is near the boundary of M). On the other hand, if neither fixed point is attractive, the orbit does not converge to a fixed value at all. Instead it gets caught in a cyclic sequence (almost at periodic sequence) of values that orbits about one of the repelling fixed points. For instance, orbits for c-values lying in the small circles at the top and bottom of M happen to have period 3.

A4.3.2 How to Compute Whether Point c Is in the Mandelbrot Set

Now we turn to an application that can be used for two purposes.

1. To study the nature of the Mandelbrot set in some detail.
2. To create dazzling full-color images of the Mandelbrot set.

Given that complex number c lies in M. The routine must examine the size of the numbers d_k of Equation (A4.2) along the orbit. As k increases, the value of $|d_k|$ either explodes (so c is not in M) or it doesn't (so c is in M). A theorem from complex analysis states that if $|d_k|$ ever exceeds the value 2, then the orbit will *definitely* explode at some point. The number of iterations $|d_k|$ takes to exceed 2 is called the **dwell** of the orbit, perhaps arising from how long the orbit dwells in a region.

But if c lies in M, the orbit has an infinite dwell, and we can't know this without iterating forever. The best we can do is to set some upper limit Num on the maximum number of iterations we are willing to wait for. A typical value is $Num = 100$. If $|d_k|$ hasn't exceeded 2 after Num iterations, we assume it never will, and we conclude c is in M. It turns out that orbits for values of c just outside the boundary of M often have an extremely large dwell, and if their dwell exceeds Num we wrongly decide they lie inside M. (Are values of c inside M ever wrongly interpreted?) A drawing based on too small a value of Num, therefore, will show a Mandelbrot set that is slightly too large.

We encapsulate these calculations in the routine dwell() shown in Figure A4.5. For a given value of $c = c_x + c_y i$ it returns the number of iterations required for $|d_k|$ to exceed 2, or it returns Num if 2 has not been exceeded after Num iterations. For convenience it defines a data type for the parameter to dwell().

At each iteration the current d_k resides in the pair (dx, dy), which is squared and then added to (cx, cy) to form the next d-value. The value $|d_k|^2$ is kept in *fsq* and compared with 4. This is equivalent to comparing $|d_k|$ with 2, yet saves having to take a square root. The function dwell() plays a key role in drawing the Mandelbrot set.

A4.3.3 Draw the Mandelbrot Set

We want to display M on a raster graphics device. To do this a correspondence is set up between each pixel on the display and a value of c, and the dwell for that c-value is found. A color is assigned to the pixel depending on whether the dwell is finite or has reached its limit.

```
int dwell(double cx, double cy)
  { // return true dwell or Num, whichever is smaller
   #define Num 100    // increase this for better pictures

   double tmp, dx = cx, dy = cy, fsq = cx * cx + cy * cy;
   // begin to calculate the orbit
   for(int count = 0; count <= Num && fsq <= 4; count++)
   {
       tmp = dx;                          // save old real part
       dx = dx * dx - dy * dy + cx;       // new real part
       dy = 2.0 * tmp * dy + cy;          // new image part
       fsq = dx * dx + dy* dy;
   }
   return count;                          // number of iterations used
  }
};
```

FIGURE A4.5 Estimating the dwell.

The simplest pictures of the Mandelbrot set just assign black to points inside M (where dwell has reached its maximum) and white to those outside (where dwell is smaller than its maximum). But pictures are much more appealing to the eye if a range of colors is associated with points outside M. Such points all have dwells less than the maximum, and we can assign different colors depending on the dwell size. Low values of dwell indicate "hot" points whose orbits exploded quickly, so they might be colored a fiery red or yellow. Higher values of dwell show the orbit's escape was more leisurely, so these points could be colored a cooler green or blue. Figure A4.6 shows one possible color assignment that uses five colors. The most beautiful pictures use many more colors, and these colors are chosen very carefully to maximize the esthetic appeal of the final picture. See the companion web site for stunning color versions.

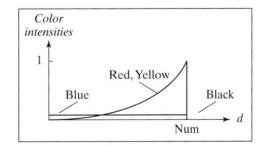

FIGURE A4.6 Assigning colors according to the orbit's dwell.

It only remains to see how to associate a pixel with a specific complex value of c. A simple approach is suggested in Figure A4.7. The user specifies how large the desired image is to be on the screen, using numbers such as:

- the number of rows, rows   (example: rows = 80)
- the number of columns, cols   (example: cols = 120)

This determines the aspect ratio of the image: $R =$ rows / cols. The user also chooses a portion of the complex plane to be displayed: a rectangular region having the same aspect ratio as the image. To do this the user simply specifies its upper

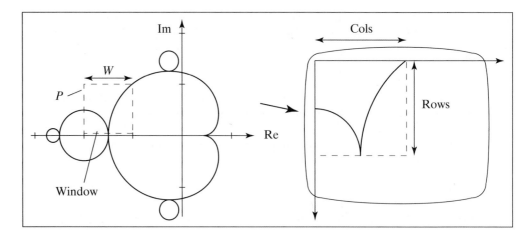

FIGURE A4.7 Establishing a window on M, and a correspondence between points and pixels.

left-hand corner, P, and its width, W. [For example: $P = -1 + .5i$, or $P = (-1, .5)$ and $W = 0.5$.]

The computer does the rest. The rectangle's height is set by the required aspect ratio. We decide to display the image in the upper left corner of the display, as suggested in the figure.

Now, to what complex value $c = c_x + c_y i$ does the center of the i,j-th pixel correspond? Combining the ingredients, it must be as given in Equation (A4.5):

$$c_{ij} = \left(P_x + \frac{i + \frac{1}{2}}{cols} W, P_y - \frac{j + \frac{1}{2}}{cols} W \right) \tag{A4.5}$$

for $i = 0, \dots,$ cols -1 and $j = 0, \dots,$ rows -1. (Check this out.)

The chosen region of the Mandelbrot set is drawn pixel by pixel. For each pixel the corresponding value of c is passed to dwell(), and the appropriate color that is associated with the dwell is found. The pixel is then set to this color. Figure A4.8 gives the algorithm in pseudocode.

FIGURE A4.8 Pseudocode for drawing a region of the Mandelbrot set.

```
for(j = 0; j < rows; j++)
    for(i = 0; i < cols; i++)
    {
        <find the corresponding c-value in Equation A5.5>
        <estimate the dwell of the orbit>
        <find Color determined by estimated dwell>
        setPixel(j, k, Color);
    }
```

A practical problem is that to study close-up views of the Mandelbrot set, numbers must be stored and manipulated with great precision. Double- (or higher-) precision arithmetic should be employed. Also, when working close to the boundary of the set, a larger value of *Num* should be used, as discussed above. Therefore, the calculation times for each image will increase as you zoom in on a region of the boundary of M. But images of modest size can easily be created on a microcomputer in a reasonable amount of time, and the results are well worth the wait.

A4.3.4 Some Notes on the Mandelbrot Set

What are the properties of the Mandelbrot set and its fiery extensions? It has been studied by a number of mathematicians, and many fascinating facts are known about it (see [Mandelbrot83], [Peitgen and Richter86], [Peitgen and Saupe88] for a wealth of ideas). These books contain many stunning pictures that were computed as described above.

1. The points $c = -1$ and $c = -2$ are in M, and as mentioned above, M is symmetrical about the real axis.
2. The largest "blobs" of the Mandelbrot set have been carefully scrutinized [Peitgen and Richter86]:

   - The boundary of the center blob of M is a cardioid having the parametric representation:

     $$c.x = .25 + .5(1 - \cos(t)) \cos(t) \qquad\qquad \text{(A4.6)}$$
     $$c.y = .5(1 - \cos(t)) \sin(t)$$

     Orbits inside this cardioid are attracted to a fixed point, given by one of the two solutions to $z^2 + c = z$.
   - The circle to the left of the cardioid has radius $1/4$ and center at $c = -1$. Orbits inside this circle become periodic with period 2.
   - The smaller circle to its left has radius 0.0607 and center at $c = -1.3107$. Orbits inside this circle become periodic with period 4.
   - The circles above and below the cardioid have radius 0.0954 and centers at $c = -0.1226 \pm 0.7449i$. Orbits inside this circle become periodic with period 3.

3. The boundary of the set is the most interesting place to look, and in fact turns out to be a fractal curve. As one zooms in ever closer on a region of interest—by using smaller and smaller windows—new details continually emerge. Figure A4.9 shows three successive zooms into the region centered at $c = -0.7469 + 0.1073i$.

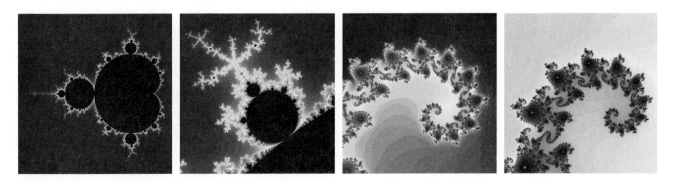

FIGURE A4.9 Zooming in on a region. (Courtesy of *Anton Feenstra*)

The last picture in the sequence uses the window with the lower left corner at $(-0.74758, 0.10671)$ and the top right corner at $(-0.74624, 0.10779)$. At each zoom a new world of detail becomes visible. For example, what was a single black dot at one zoom becomes an entire new wart figure at the next zoom (" ... a flea hath smaller fleas that on him prey; ... and so proceed ad infinitum."). It turns out that no two of the miniature warts are exactly alike. Another astonishing fact, proved by John H. Hubbard of Cornell University, is that the Mandelbrot set is connected [Dewdney88]: even though the tiny warts seem to float freely in the plane, there is always a wispy tendril of points that connects them to the parent set.

Appendix 5

Relative and Turtle Drawing

Drawing on my fine command of the English language, I said nothing.

Robert Benchley
(1889–1945)

INTRODUCTION

Significant advantage will be attained by adding one or two further drawing tools to our tool bag; certain drawing tasks become much simpler. It is often convenient to have drawing take place at the *current position* (currPos), and to describe positions relative to the current position. We develop functions, therefore, whose parameters specify *changes* in position: the programmer specifies how far the drawing point must go along each coordinate to the next desired point.

A5.1 TO DEVELOP moveRel() AND lineRel()

Two new routines are moveRel() and lineRel(). The function moveRel() is easy: it just moves the *current position* through the displacement (dx, dy). The function lineRel(float dx, float dy) does this, too, but it first draws a line from the old currPos to the new one and finally updates the currPos. Both functions are shown in Figure A5.1.

```
moveRel( float dx, float dy ) {
      currPos.set( currPos.x + dx, currPos.y + dy );
}
lineRel( float dx, float dy ) {
             lineTo( currPos.x + dx, currPos.y + dy );
    }
}
```

FIGURE A5.1 The two functions moveRel() and lineRel().

■ **EXAMPLE A5.1 An arrow marker**

Markers of different shapes can be placed at various points in a drawing to add emphasis. Figure A5.2 shows pentagram (as described in Figure A5.19) markers used to highlight the data points in a line graph.

Because the same figure is drawn at several different points, it is convenient to be able to say simply drawMarker() and have it be drawn at the currPos. Then

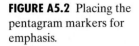

FIGURE A5.2 Placing the pentagram markers for emphasis.

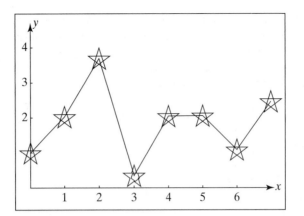

the line graph of Figure A5.2 can be drawn along with the markers using the following pseudocode:

```
moveTo(first data point);
drawMarker();                        // draw a marker there
for(each remaining data point)
{
        lineTo(the next point); // draw the next line segment
        drawMarker();                // draws it at the CP
}
```

Figure A5.3 shows an arrow-shaped marker, drawn using the routine in Figure A5.4. The arrow is positioned with its uppermost point at the currPos. For flexibility the

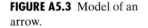

FIGURE A5.3 Model of an arrow.

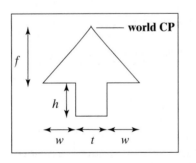

```
void arrow(float f, float h, float t, float w)
{
        lineRel(-w - t / 2, -f);            // down the left side
        lineRel(w, 0);                      // top of left side
        lineRel(0, -h);                     // across the arrow head
        lineRel(t, 0);                      // down the shaft of the arrow
        lineRel(0, h);                      // back up arrow shaft
        lineRel(w, 0);                      // across arrow head to the right
        lineRel(-w - t / 2, f);                  // back to original position
}
```

FIGURE A5.4 Drawing an arrow using relative moves and draws.

arrow shape is parameterized using four size parameters *f*, *h*, *t*, and *w*, as shown. Function `arrow()` uses only `lineRel()`, and no reference is made to absolute positions. Also note that although the `currPos` is altered while drawing is going on, at the end of drawing the `currPos` has been set back to its initial position. Hence the routine produces no side effects (beyond the drawing itself).

A5.2 TURTLE GRAPHICS

> The turtle lives 'twixt plated decks
> Which practically conceal its sex.
> I think it clever of the turtle
> In such a fix to be so fertile.

The Turtle
Ogden Nash
(1902–1971)

Another tool that we add is surprisingly convenient. The notion is that a turtle, which is conceptually similar to the pen in a pen plotter, migrates over the page, leaving a trail behind itself which appears as a line segment. It keeps track not only of where it is with the `currPos` but also of the direction in which it is headed. This is a form of **turtle graphics**, which has been found to be a natural way to program in graphics.[1] The turtle is positioned at `currPos`, headed in a certain direction called the **current direction**, `currDir` which is the number of degrees measured counterclockwise (CCW) from the positive *x*-axis.

It is easy to add functionality to control the turtle. First, we add three functions:

1. `turnTo( double angle )`. This function turns the turtle to the given angle and is implemented as

   ```
   turnTo( double angle ) {
         currDir = angle;   // turn to a specific angle
   }
   ```

2. `turn (float angle)`. This routine turns the turtle through `angle` degrees CCW; it is implemented as

   ```
   turn ( double angle ) {
         currDir += angle;
   }
   ```

   We use a negative argument to make a right turn. Note that a turn is a *relative* change in direction; we do not specify a direction, only a change in direction. This simple distinction provides enormous power in drawing complex figures with the turtle.

3. `forward (float dist, int isVisible)`, Finally, the function `forward()` is only a little more complex: the turtle moves forward in a straight line from the `currPos` through a distance, `dist`, in the current direction, `currDir`, and updates the `currPos`. Note here that `currDir` acts like a state variable, similar to background color and drawing color. If `isVisible` is nonzero, a visible line is drawn; otherwise nothing is drawn.

Figure A5.5 shows that in going forward in direction `currDir`, the turtle just moves in *x* through the amount $dist * \cos(\pi * currDir/180)$ and in *y* through the amount

---

[1] Introduced by Seymour Papert at MIT as part of the LOGO language for teaching children how to program. See, e.g., [Abel81]

FIGURE A5.5 Effect of the forward() routine.

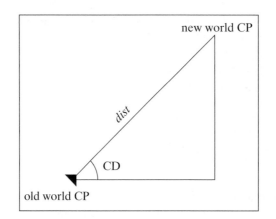

```
forward( float dist, bool visible ) {

        const double radPerDeg = 0.017453393f;

        double x = currPos.x + ( dist * cos( currDir * radPerDeg ) );
        double y = currPos.y + ( dist * sin( currDir * radPerDeg ) );

        if( visible )
                lineTo(x, y);
        else
                moveTo(x, y);
}
```

FIGURE A5.6 Implementation of the function forward().

$dist*$ sin($\pi *$ currDir /180), so the implementation of forward() is immediate (Figure A5.6).

Turtle graphics makes it easy to build complex figures out of simpler ones, as we see in the following examples.

■ EXAMPLE A5.2 To draw a unit square

To traverse a unit square using the turtle you need only draw its four straight edges with a 90-degree turn in between (Figure A5.7), as in the following

FIGURE A5.7 Drawing a unit square.

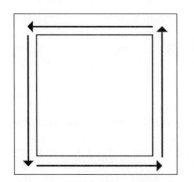

pseudocode. If you wish to have the turtle end up in the same direction in which it started, place a final `turn (90);` as the last instruction.

```
forward (1,1);        // draw one edge
turn (90);            // turn first corner
forward (1,1);        // draw the next edge
turn (90);            // turn second corner
forward (1,1);        // draw the next edge
turn (90);            // turn third corner
forward (1,1);        // draw final edge
turn (90);            // turn to initial direction
```

■ **EXAMPLE A5.3 Building a figure upon a hook motif**

The three-segment hook motif shown in Figure A5.8a can be drawn using the commands:

```
forward(3 * L, 1);  // L is the length of the long sides
turn(90);
forward(L, 1);
turn(90);
forward(L, 1);
turn(90);
```

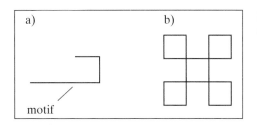

FIGURE A5.8 Building a figure out of several turtle motions.

for some choice of *L*. Suppose that procedure hook() encapsulates these instructions. Then the shape in Figure A5.8b is drawn using four repetitions of hook(). The figure can be positioned and oriented as desired by choices of the initial `currPos` and `currDir`.

■ **EXAMPLE A5.4 Polyspirals**

A large family of pleasing figures called *polyspirals* can be generated easily using turtle graphics. A **polyspiral** is a polyline where each successive segment is larger (or smaller) than its predecessor by a fixed amount, and oriented at some fixed angle to it. Its skeleton looks like:

```
for(<some number of iterations>)
{
  forward(length,1);    // draw a line in the current direction
  turn(angle);          // turn through angle degrees
  length += increment;  // increment the line length
}
```

Each time a line is drawn, both its length and direction are incremented. If `increment` is 0, the figure neither grows nor shrinks. Figure A5.9 shows several polyspirals.

FIGURE A5.9 Examples of polyspirals. Angles are: a) 60, b) 89.5, c) −144, d) 170.

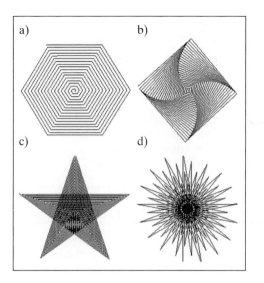

PRACTICE EXERCISES

A5.2.1 Drawing turtle figures

Provide routines that use turtle motions to draw the three figures shown in Figure A5.10.

FIGURE A5.10 Other simple turtle figures.

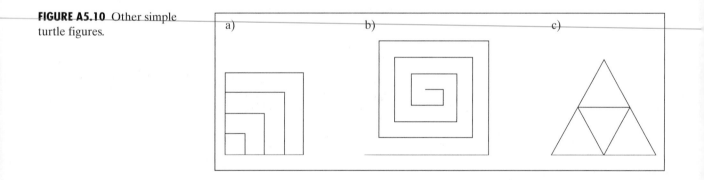

A5.2.2 Drawing a well-known logo

Write a routine that makes a turtle draw the outline of the logo shown in Figure A5.11. (It need not fill the polygons.)

FIGURE A5.11 A famous logo.

A5.2.3 Drawing meanders

A **meander**[2] is a pattern like that in Figure A5.12a, often made up of a continuous line meandering along some path. One frequently sees meanders on Greek vases, Chinese plates, or floor tilings from various countries. The motif for the meander here is shown in Figure A5.12b. After each motif is drawn, the turtle is turned to prepare it for drawing the next motif.

FIGURE A5.12 Example of a meander.

Write a routine that draws this motif, and a routine that draws this meander. (Meanders are most attractive if the graphics package at hand supports the control of line thickness—as OpenGL does—so that forward() draws thick lines.) A dazzling variety of more complex meanders can be designed, as suggested in later exercises.

A5.2.4 Other types of meanders

Figure A5.13 shows two additional types of meanders. Write routines that employ turtle graphics to draw them.

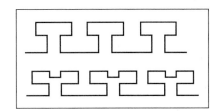

FIGURE A5.13 Additional figures for meanders.

A5.3 FIGURES BASED ON REGULAR POLYGONS

> "Bees ... by virtue of certain geometrical forethought ... know that the hexagon is greater than the square and triangle, and will hold more honey for the same expenditure of material.
>
> *Pappus of Alexandria*
> *(290–350)*

The regular polygons form a large and important family of shapes, often encountered in computer graphics. We need efficient ways to draw them. In this section we examine how to do this, and how to create a number of figures that are variations of the regular polygon.

---

[2] Based on the name Maeander (which has modern name Menderes), a winding river in Turkey [Janson 86].

A5.3.1 The Regular Polygons.

First recall the definition of a regular polygon:

> **DEFINITION:** A polygon is **regular** if it is *simple*, if all its sides have equal lengths, and if adjacent sides meet at equal interior angles.

As discussed in Chapter 1, a polygon is **simple** if no two of its edges cross each other (more precisely: only adjacent edges can touch, and only at their shared endpoint). We give the name **n-gon** to a regular polygon having n sides. Familiar examples are the 3-gon (an equilateral triangle), 4-gon (a square), 5-gon (a regular pentagon), 8-gon (a regular octagon), and so on. Figure A5.14 shows various examples. If the number of sides of an n-gon is large, the polygon approximates a circle in appearance. In fact this is used later as one way to implement the drawing of a circle.

FIGURE A5.14 Examples of n-gons.

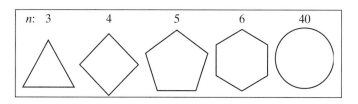

The vertices of an n-gon lie on a circle, the so-called *parent circle* of the n-gon, and their locations are easily calculated. The case of the hexagon is shown in Figure A5.15, where the vertices lie equispaced every 60° around the circle. The parent circle of radius R (not shown) is centered at the origin, and the first vertex P_0 has been placed on the positive x-axis. The other vertices follow accordingly, as $P_i = (R \cos (i - a), R \sin (i - a))$, for $i=1,\ldots 5$, where a is $2\pi/6$ radians. Similarly, the vertices of the general n-gon lie at:

$$P_i = (R \cos (2\pi i/n), R \sin(2\pi i/n)), \text{ for } i = 0, \ldots, n - 1$$

FIGURE A5.15 Finding the vertices of a 6-gon.

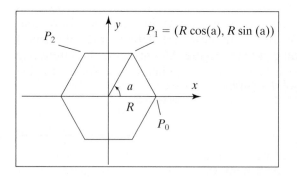

It's easy to modify this n-gon. To center it at position (cx, cy) we need only add cx and cy to the x- and y-coordinates, respectively. To scale it by factor S we need only multiply R by S. To rotate through angle A we need only add A to the arguments of cos() and sin(). More general methods for performing geometrical transformations are discussed in Chapter 6. The implementation to draw an *n*-gon is straightforward as we have seen at a number of times throughout the book.

■ **EXAMPLE A5.3.1 A Turtle-Driven *n*-gon**

It is also simple to draw an *n*-gon using turtle graphics. Figure A5.16 shows how to draw a regular hexagon. The initial position and direction of the turtle are indicated by the small triangle. The turtle simply goes forward six times, making a CCW turn of 60 degrees between each move:

```
for (i = 0; i < 6; i++)
{
    forward(L, 1);
    turn(60);
}
```

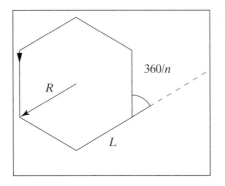

FIGURE A5.16 Drawing a hexagon.

One vertex is situated at the initial `currPos`, and both `currPos` and `currDir` are left unchanged by the process. Drawing the general *n*-gon, and some variations of it, is discussed in the exercises.

A5.3.2 Variations on *n*-gons

Interesting variations based on the vertices of an *n*-gon can also be drawn. The *n*-gon vertices may be connected in various ways to produce a variety of figures, as suggested in Figure A5.17. The standard *n*-gon is drawn in Figure A5.17a by connecting adjacent vertices, but as Figure A5.17b shows, a **stellation** (or starlike figure) is formed by connecting every other vertex. Figure A5.17c shows the interesting **rosette**, formed by connecting each vertex to every other vertex. We discuss the rosette next. Other figures are described in the exercises.

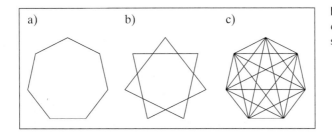

FIGURE A5.17 A 7-gon and its offspring: a) the 7-gon, b) a stellation, c) a 7-rosette.

■ **EXAMPLE A5.3.2 The Rosette and the Golden 5-Rosette**

The **rosette** is an *n*-gon with each vertex joined to every other vertex. Figure A5.18 shows 5-, 11-, and 17-rosettes. A rosette is sometimes used as a test pattern for computer graphics devices. Its orderly shape readily reveals any distortions, and the resolution of the device can be determined by noting the amount of crowding and blurring exhibited by the bundle of lines that meet at each vertex.

FIGURE A5.18 The 5-, 11-, and 17- rosettes.

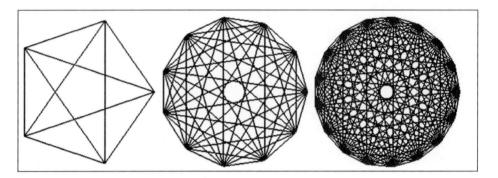

Rosettes are easy to draw: simply connect every vertex to every other. In pseudocode this looks like

```
void Rosette(int N, float radius)
{
        Point2 pt[<big enough value for largest rosette>];
        <generate the vertices pt[0],. . .,pt[N-1], as in
        Figure 3.43>
        for(int i = 0; i < N - 1; i++)
            for(int j = i + 1; j < N ; j++)
            {
        <forward(the right distance, 1>
        turn(the correct angle);      // where the correct dis-
                                         tance is the same for
                                         all steps as is the
                                         correct angle

            }
}
```

The 5-rosette is particularly interesting because it embodies many instances of the golden ratio φ (recall Chapter 2). Figure A5.19a shows a 5-rosette, which is made up of an outer pentagon and an inner pentagram. The Greeks saw a mystical significance in this figure. Its segments have an interesting relationship: each segment is φ times longer than the next smaller one (see the exercises). Also, because the edges of the star pentagram form an inner pentagon, an infinite regression of pentagrams is possible, as shown in Figure A5.19b.

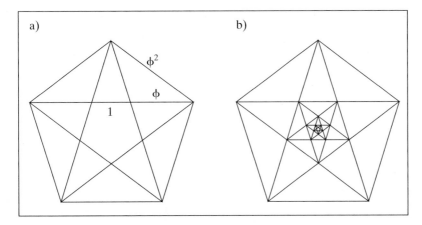

FIGURE A5.19 5-rosette and Infinite regressions—pentagons and pentagrams.

■ **EXAMPLE A5.3.3 Figures based on two concentric *n*-gons**

Figure A5.20 shows some shapes built upon two concentric parent circles, the outer of radius R and the inner of radius fR for some fraction f. Each figure uses a variation of an *n*-gon whose radius alternates between the inner and outer radii. Parts a and b show familiar company logos based on 6-gons and 10-gons. Part c is based on the 14-gon, and part d shows the inner circle explicitly.

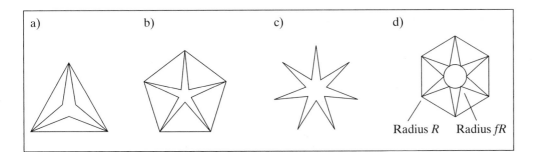

FIGURE A5.20 Familiar *n*-grams and *n*-gons.

PRACTICE EXERCISES

A5.3.1 Stellations and rosettes

The pentagram is drawn by connecting every other point as one traverses around a 5-gon. Extend this to an arbitrary odd-valued *n*-gon and develop a routine that draws this so-called stellated polygon. Can it be done with a single initial `moveTo()` followed only by `lineTo()`'s (that is, without lifting the pen)? What happens if *n* is even?

A5.3.2 How many edges in an N-rosette?

Show that a rosette based on an N-gon, an N-rosette, has $N(N-1)/2$ edges. This is the same as the number of clinks one hears when N people are seated around a table and everybody clinks glasses with everyone else.

A5.3.3 The geometry of the star pentagram

Show that the length of each segment in the 5-rosette stands in the golden ratio to that of the next smaller one. One way to tackle this is to show that the triangles of the star pentagram are golden triangles with an inner angle of $\pi/5$ radians. Show that $2*\cos(\pi/5) = \phi$ and $2*\cos(2\pi/5) = 1/\phi$. Another approach uses only two families of similar triangles in the pentagram and the relation $\phi^3 = 2\phi + 1$ satisfied by ϕ.

A5.3.4 Drawing the star with relative moves and draws

Write a routine to draw a pentagram that uses only relative moves and draws, centering the star at the `currPos`.

A5.3.5 Turtle drawings of the n-gon

Write `turtleNgon(int numSides, float length)` that uses turtle graphics to draw an n-gon with `numSides` sides and a side of length `length`.

A5.3.6 Drawing a potential logo

The logo shown in Figure A5.21 consists of three instances of a motif, rotated a certain amount with respect to each other. Show a routine that draws this shape using turtle graphics.   ■

FIGURE A5.21 A logo design.

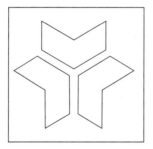

INDEX

We present here a complete and tested application in C++ that uses OpenGL to draw the IFS known as the 'Sierpinski Gasket' discussed in Chapter 2. The C++ code will be discussed thoroughly at the appropriate time. The Sierpinski Gasket figure generated by the code given here is also shown in Figure 2.47.

```cpp
//necessary includes

// types make a structure that holds a point //
struct GLintPoint {
  GLint x, y;
};

// random func //
int random(int m) {
  return rand()%m;
}

// drawDot - draws the next dot on screen //
void drawDot( GLint x, GLint y ) {
  glBegin( GL_POINTS );
    glVertex2i( x, y );
  glEnd();
}

// myInit - initialize various values //
void myInit(){
  glClearColor(1.0, 1.0, 1.0, 0.0);//choose background color
  glColor3f(0.0f, 0.0f, 0.0f);   //set the drawing color
  glPointSize(2.0);          //set point size
  glMatrixMode(GL_PROJECTION);   //load matrix mode
  glLoadIdentity();        //load identity matrix
  gluOrtho2D(0.0, 800.0, 0.0, 600.0); //defines a 2D orthographic projection
matrix
}

// sierpinski_render - display function //
void sierpinski_render() {
  glClear(GL_COLOR_BUFFER_BIT);     //clear the screen
  GLintPoint T[3] = {{10,10},{600,10},{300,600}};
  //defines the vertices of the triangle
  int index = random (3);       //choose the initial vertex randomly
  GLintPoint point = T[index];   //creates an array of 3 vertices
  drawDot(point.x, point.y);
  for (int i = 0; i < 55000; i++)  //draw 55000 dots of the Sierpinski Gasket
  {
    index = random(3);
    point.x = (point.x + T[index].x) / 2;
    point.y = (point.y + T[index].y) / 2;
    drawDot(point.x, point.y);
  }
  glFlush();          //flushes all unfinished drawing commands
}

// main //
void main( int argc, char **argv ) {
  glutInit(&argc, argv);        // initialize toolkit
  glutInitDisplayMode(GLUT_SINGLE | GLUT_RGB);// set display mode
  glutInitWindowSize(800,600);     // set window size
  glutInitWindowPosition(100,150);    // set window position
  glutCreateWindow("Sierpinski Window");   // set window title
  glutDisplayFunc(sierpinski_render);    // register display callback
  myInit();          // initialize
  glutMainLoop();        // go into a perpetual loop
}
```